1001 WALKS

YOU MUST TAKE BEFORE YOU DIE

1001 WALKS

YOU MUST TAKE BEFORE YOU DIE

COUNTRY HIKES, HERITAGE TRAILS, COASTAL STROLLS, MOUNTAIN PATHS, CITY WALKS

GENERAL EDITOR **BARRY STONE**

FOREWORD BY **JULIA BRADBURY**

UNIVERSE

A Quintessence Book

First published in the United States of America in 2015 by
UNIVERSE PUBLISHING
A Division of Rizzoli International Publications, Inc.
300 Park Avenue South
New York, NY 10010
www.rizzoliusa.com

2015 2016 2017 2018 / 10 9 8 7 6 5 4 3 2 1

ISBN: 978-0-7893-2915-8
QSS.WALK
LB1
Library of Congress Control Number: 2014949579

This book was designed and produced by
Quintessence Editions Ltd.
6 Blundell Street
London N7 9BH
www.1001beforeyoudie.com

Senior Editor	Ruth Patrick
Editors	Ruth Patrick, Fiona Plowman, Henry Russell
Designer	Damian Jaques
Cartographer	Martin Lubikowski
Production Manager	Anna Pauletti
Editorial Director	Jane Laing
Publisher	Mark Fletcher

Color reproduction by Colourscan Print Co Pte Ltd, Singapore
Printed in China by Midas Printing International Ltd.

Contents

Foreword | Julia Bradbury

My first outdoor adventures were with my dad Michael roving across the ragged White and Dark Peaks of the Peak District National Park in northern England. I was but a wee one and he would walk me so hard I thought my little legs were going to drop off, but our shared exploits were the beginning of a lifelong love affair for me, and from then on the world was my lobster. This amazing selection of 1001 world walks is potentially daunting, but don't be intimidated—they are here as inspiration to help you choose some escapades of a lifetime, from the extreme to the serene.

Friedrich Nietzsche said "All truly great thoughts are conceived by walking," but walking is about so much more than thinking. It is one of the world's most popular pastimes, a ubiquitous hobby enjoyed by millions. The opportunity to absorb your surroundings, share your adventures, and consume the complexion of a landscape or vista is one of life's greatest pleasures.

I was told years ago when I was on a walking trail through the heart of South Africa's Kruger National Park, that "you feel the soul of a country through the soles of your feet." Walking connects you to your surroundings in a distinctive way—you soak up your backdrop at a profoundly personal speed. You even feel things that you wouldn't necessarily detect in a car or on a bike. Like a gust of wind or a shake in the ground beneath you, perhaps caused by the movement of a herd of buffalo in Botswana or a dazzle of zebra in Zimbabwe. The relatively easy walking trails found in this book in both of these countries offer an opportunity to get close to wildlife in a unique way; you could find everything from crocodiles to hippos, cheetahs to wild dogs, quite literally at your feet.

The Bigfoot Trail in northern California starts in the fabulously named Yolla Bolly–Middle Eel Wilderness area and crosses through six other wilderness spots, one national park, and a state park, covering 400 miles (643 km) in all. The promised wildlife on the trail includes everything from bears, coyotes, and mountain lions to flying squirrels, hawks, and eagles; and the scenery will blow your mind. There's an abundance of flora and this region is said have the largest concentration of conifer trees anywhere in the world (more than thirty-two species). You will need top navigational skills, though, as well as a satellite phone and a lot of time to attempt this trail—perhaps more than a month. Be prepared to walk eight to ten days without being able to stock up on food and up to 30 miles (48 km) without the opportunity to fill up your water bottles. Parts of this trail don't even exist anymore. It's a big adventure for the very adventurous and there won't be any forest rangers to hold your hand, but if you're ever going to bump into Bigfoot, this is where it will happen!

If you want picturesque and handsome scenery with flawlessly precise trail signage, I thoroughly recommend walking in Germany. The easy 5-mile (8-km) hike through the stunning Berchtesgaden National Park is an alpine meadow dream straight out of a scene from *The Sound of Music*. For a more rugged and strenuous experience, walking in the state of Saxony on the border with the Czech Republic can keep you busy for weeks. The only problem I experienced hiking in Germany was finding anywhere to serve us post-8 p.m. schnitzels!

Rudyard Kipling wrote that Burma is "quite unlike any place you know about" and Myanmar is now an emerging destination that will take your breath away; at the eastern end of the Himalayas you can explore the Kachin Hills along a tough hiking route moving from village to village, taking in the remote and peaceful life of some of the most diverse ethnic groups in Asia.

The possibilities in this book are endless. Witness the extraordinary and surreal sight of the Banaue Rice Terraces in the Ifugao Mountains of the Philippines; test your map and compass skills in the rare beauty of Newfoundland, following ridges and valleys along Canada's stunning backcountry routes; discover Mayan relics in Mexico; or take your family for an "adventure above the clouds" along the Kepler Track in New Zealand. Wherever you end up, I wish you good luck with your adventures and remember: too much of a good thing can be wonderful.

Introduction | Barry Stone

My first experience of a serious trail was in Nepal in 1993. My wife, Yvonne, and I, while on our honeymoon, thought it might be fun to do a nine-day trek on the famed Tea House Trail following the Kali Gandaki Gorge south of Jomsom. Despite having a porter to carry our backpacks, by day three I had stretched the ligaments in my left knee almost to breaking point and every step was a new experience in pain. Our porter offered to carry me, an offer I stoically refused, although I acquiesced to a passing horseman who insisted I keep his bamboo walking stick. I struggled on. On day nine we walked for seven hours to catch one of only two buses a week that went deep into the mountains to the end of a sealed road, and that night collapsed onto a bed in a Pokhara hotel. We were spent and sore, but exhilarated, too. The next day Yvonne would begin to feel the first symptoms of typhoid, but on that Pokhara night we felt like conquerors. We had completed our first trek. We were hooked.

Walking is the most commonplace, most ubiquitous of human activities, and although we have been doing it as a species for about one and a half million years, walking as a leisure activity, as an end in itself, seems to be a comparatively recent phenomenon. To simply walk—to walk for pleasure—as distinct from having to migrate to find food or fresh pastures or round up the first domesticated animals only began to be referenced as a recreational pursuit in Western literature in the mid-eighteenth century. Now, in our postindustrialized age, the need to shed our urban confines (and create new green spaces within them) is more important than ever. We need to walk if only to shift our attention away from screens and switches, to pull ourselves out of our self-made technological cells and concentrate, instead, on that shifting shale slope or unstable scree field.

Walking takes us to places that no other modes of transport can access, into communities and environments where roads simply do not go. If you want to experience the Headhunter's Trail in the Malaysian state of Sarawak, for example, be prepared for a series of plank walks over alluvial swamps and a return trip in a dugout canoe. If you want to trek through the broad horizons of Sweden's Sarek National Park, which does not possess a single road within its 760 square miles (1,970 sq km), my advice is you'd better be able to read a map. Even in our urban environments there can be a wealth of wilderness. In Vancouver in British Columbia, the presence of the city below will offer little comfort as you climb the punishing 2,830 steps of Grouse Grind on its 30-degree incline to the summit of Grouse Mountain. So if you're wanting to narrow your focus, if you'd like to put all those stresses, distractions, and so-called "worries" into a healthier perspective for a month, a week, a day, or even an hour, this book is the only resource you'll ever need for a lifetime of finding the walk that puts the vagaries of everyday life back in their collective boxes.

There are countless examples in philosophy and literature of how walking clears and invigorates the mind—walking as "contemplative exercise." Oscar Wilde, George Orwell, Virginia Woolf, and Henry David Thoreau all loved to walk. In the 1750s, the Geneva-born philosopher Jean-Jacques Rousseau likened walking in The Alps to "being lifted above human society," and when in the midst of its peaks, he felt he had left behind "all base and terrestrial sentiments." Friedrich Nietzsche achieved his profligacy with words only after abandoning university and becoming a compulsive rambler. William Wordsworth would walk long hours through his beloved Lake District, while C. S. Lewis wanted not merely to walk, but to do so in silence and disliked walking with others. Emmanuel Kant walked around his home town of Königsberg every day at 5:00 p.m., regardless of the weather. In December 1933, at the age of eighteen, the great British travel writer Sir Patrick Leigh Fermor took more than a year to walk the length of Europe, beginning at the Hook of Holland and ending in Constantinople (now Istanbul). Walking with little more than the clothes on his back and a handful of letters of introduction, Fermor spent his nights wherever he could find shelter, from farmer's sheds and monasteries to castles and aristocratic estates. His account of this epic walk was conveyed to us, in stages, decades later in *A Time of Gifts* (1977), *Between the Woods and the Water* (1986), and finally *The Broken Road* (2013), published two years after his death.

Walking, however, is still seen by some as an annoying obstacle, a cumbersome way of getting from A to B. Unstructured time in the twenty-first century is often considered to be unproductive, and if something is seen as boring or uninteresting, it is referred to as "pedestrian." But the connotations inherent in "pedestrian" are hard to justify. Disregarding the obvious benefits to health, recent studies make much of the connection between walking and positive thinking. Walking has the capacity to sharpen our senses. It helps us to solve problems. It sets the mind free to the rhythms of its reveries. It is life stripped bare. In 1930, while on his famous Salt March to protest the British salt monopoly, Gandhi likened walking to an act of humility, an affirmation of the simple life. "There remains something proud in walking," Gandhi said. "We are upright."

The popularity of recreational walking, however, has long been on the rise, and is given fresh impetus with the declaration of each new national park and wilderness area, the construction of every new yard of boardwalk, and the clearing of every fresh, never-before-trodden trail. More than nine million adults in England alone now walk recreationally at least once a month—three times the number that go cycling—a trend that is being mirrored in every Western country. In Australia, walking remains the nation's most popular physical activity.

Marked trails may eliminate the need for a map and compass, but who says there must even be a trail? There are some walks here that, if you are not proficient with a compass or are unable to comprehend a topographical map, you probably should consider leaving to someone else. Alternatively you can walk all day over the sagebrush-covered, trail-less hills that surround the ghost town of Bodie high on the eastern, barren slopes of California's Sierra Nevada mountains. Just follow your nose.

Even within the jumbled, interrupted, and uneven landscapes of our urban environments, there remains the joy of "observational" walking, and not just on sidewalks. In New York City, the High Line through Chelsea neighborhood in Manhattan has been reinvented and transformed from a disused railroad into an elevated walkway, while the old pipeline from Westchester County that opened in 1842 and brought New York its first supplies of fresh water is now the Old Croton Aqueduct Trail. London has its marvelous Thames Path, and the Sydney Harbour Bridge cannot now merely be crossed, it can also be climbed. Restored towpaths alongside canals the world over can now be walked, such as the Canal du Midi in southern France and the Rideau Canal in Canada, and "rails-to-trails" projects—old railway lines converted to mixed-use paths—are proving hugely popular wherever they are established. No substantial piece of infrastructure, it seems, is immune from being either adapted or reimagined to provide us with unprecedented levels of access to our urban environments and engineering heritage. And this exponential growth of paths and trails is not limited to the Western world. In China, the Pearl River Delta Greenway, when finished, will have more than 1,000 miles (1,600 km) of mixed-use paths. But despite this growth in paths and trails, studies into the walking habits of people in the Western world suggest a mere 17 percent of all walking is done simply for the sake of it. Mostly we walk because we have to, and still need to get better at finding the time to walk for fun. Which is where this book comes in.

All the great mountain and overland trails are here, including the heavily trampled Tour du Mont Blanc, the W Circuit in Chile, the much-loved Pennine Way, and the Appalachian Trail. But there is also the barely visited splendor of the Alichur Valley in Central Asia's Pamir Mountains and the Valley of Castles in Kazakhstan's Charyn Canyon, a landscape that wouldn't be out of place in the American southwest. The great time-worn pilgrimage trails are here too, including the Camino de Santiago, the Via Francigena, and Japan's restored, remarkable Nakasendo Way.

Even if you don't fancy yourself a hardcore trailblazer, there are walks that will have enormous appeal. The Heritage section will take you on a stroll through Havana's Art Deco district, and down the streets of Brasília past the monuments to modernism of Oscar Niemeyer. If you have a weakness for wine and cheese, then you'll love the Bregenzerwald Cheese Road through the rolling hills of the Austrian Tyrol. Fans of literature will enjoy walking through the forests so beloved by Walt Whitman and Robert Frost. The Overland section has loop walks that return you conveniently to your starting point that require nothing in the way of navigational skills. Even lengthy overland trails are often segmented with numerous trailheads along the way, meaning you don't need to walk an entire trail to get a feel for it and to gain a real sense of accomplishment. Mountain routes may sometimes require ropes or cable-assists along precipitous trails with steep drop-offs, but many are along the base of mountains where elevation gains are kept to a minimum as you walk in the very shadows of the world's greatest mountains, such as Switzerland's awe-inspiring Eiger Trail, which takes you along the base of the Eiger's legendary North Face, rising 5,900 feet (1,800 m) above you.

There are no walks featured here that are not accessible and eminently doable (although some involve technical climbing and the appropriate cautions are mentioned), and some require the services of an accredited guide. There are short urban walks, riverside strolls, coastal trails, and walks under rainforest canopies in Costa Rica or over baking Middle Eastern deserts. There are trails through national parks, state parks, municipal parks, and through designated wilderness areas along trails both marked and unmarked. There are trails to the rims of volcanic calderas, easy trails with zero elevation gains along wadis and canyon floors, and overland trails that will take months to complete with accumulated gains in the tens of thousands of feet.

Whatever your passion, whatever your pace, this book features the walks you've been looking for, and is an affirmation of the simple joys that can only come from being an unabashed wanderer.

Note: The walks within the five chapters—Overland, Urban, Mountain, Heritage, and Coastal and Shoreline—are organized geographically by continent, country, and state or region, from west to east and north to south across the globe for easy reference. You will also find an index by country on page 12 and an index by distance on page 948. Technical information such as start and end points, terrain, and grade is given for all walks, and routes more than 1 mile (1.6 km) and less than 100 miles (161 km) feature links to specially commissioned digital route maps that enable you to view each trail plotted on Google Maps. Routes less than 1 mile (1.6 km), more than 100 miles (161 km), or with no specified trail feature an information link instead. Please note that the digital maps are intended to act as quick-reference locator guides rather than detailed route maps.

Index of Walks by Country

Overland trails can vary in length from a few hours' rambling through England's Cumbrian hills to several months on the Trans-Canada Trail. Depending on the degree of isolation and whether or not you intend to camp, the trails often require eight to ten hours of walking each day just to reach the next town.

OVERLAND

◄ Amble through a moss- and fern-draped wonderland on the Hoh River Trail in Washington State, USA.

Perseverance National Recreation Trail Alaska, USA

Start/End Perseverance trailhead, Juneau **Distance** 4.5 miles (7.2 km) **Time** 2 hours **Grade** Easy
Type Well-maintained gravel path **Map** goo.gl/ErpLPX

Ask your average Juneau resident and they'll tell you the Perseverence Trail was the first road of any note laid down anywhere in the state. Although nothing like the length of the Chilkoot and Iditarod trails (at 3.5 miles/ 5.6 km), it is still the trail that completes the Triple Crown of historic Alaskan trails.

Built over an old native hunting and "berry picking" track in the 1880s after Joe Juneau and Richard Harris discovered gold in the nearby Silver Bow Basin, the new trail provided access to the various gold mines of the Gold Creek Valley, including the famous Perseverance Mine, 4 miles (6.4 km) to the east of Juneau, which was once the richest gold mine in the world, with more than 20 miles (32.1 km) of tunnels and crosscuts. Now only a short stroll from downtown Juneau, the Perseverance trailhead attracts more than 30,000 walkers a year who are keen to head

up into the Silver Bow Basin and experience a little of the heady days of the Alaskan gold rush. The gravel path is wide and well maintained, and provides access to other local trails, including the Red Mill Trail and the beautiful Granite Creek Trail, which takes you past some spectacular waterfalls and alpine lakes during its own worthwhile three-hour return walk.

The Perseverance Trail, however, continues on, past old stamp mills, the remnants of old mining sites, and the 1,000-foot-deep (304.8 m) "hole" out of which much of its gold was taken. It is rare that so much scenery is packed into such a short walk. Streams tumble down the 3,000-foot (914-m) slopes of Mounts Juneau and Roberts, and black bears can be seen foraging contentedly in the valleys below. **BDS**

⬆ Walk the trail along what was Alaska's first road.

Beaver Lake to Herring Cove Loop Trail Alaska, USA

Start/End Herring Cove trailhead, Sawmill Creek Road, Sitka   **Distance** 3.5 miles (5.6 km)   **Time** 2 hours
Grade Easy   **Type** Forest trails   **Map** goo.gl/8RwpJG

What is there not to like about the fabulous, compact Beaver Lake to Herring Cove loop trail? It follows the foaming waters of a typically mossy-green, gushing Sitka creek through heavily wooded spruce forests; it passes within splashing distance of multiple waterfalls (one of which is more than 100 feet/30.4 m high); its switchbacks are barely noticeable; there are several fine views over nearby rugged mountains and there is even a tight squeeze through a rock passageway. It has a series of rock steps that take you up past a rushing cascade that deposits you on a ridge where the trail levels out, allows you to catch your breath, then passes through a scenic gorge with views up to a nearby avalanche chute, more waterfalls tumbling down the face of Bear Mountain, and on to the shoreline of Beaver Lake: a lovely lake surrounded by old growth forests and muskegs (bogs of sphagnum

mosses and sedge). The lake also has a quintessential piece of "Sitka hospitality" awaiting you—an aluminum boat tied up at the small dock at the western end of the lake, complete with oars and even a bailing jug, free to use for any who make it here.

On the banks of the lake there are abundant flowers, including yellow water lilies and masses of purple shooting stars. When returning to the trailhead, take time to look up through the underside of the broad, flat leaves of the Devil's Club—a plant with a stem covered in sharp, yellow spines that can grow up to 7 feet (2.1 m) high in these ravines. The translucent leaves of the plant grow in clusters and are a fabulous sight when looked through from below, diffusing the pure light of the Alaskan sun. **BDS**

⬆ The start of a walk through wonderful Sitka scenery.

Trans-Canada Trail
Canada

Start Railway Coastal Museum, St. Johns, Newfoundland
End Victoria, British Columbia; Tuktoyaktuk, Northwest
Territories **Distance** 14,000 miles (23,000 km) **Time** 2–3
years **Grade** Varied **Type** Multiple **Info** goo.gl/pMOUCF

When the world's largest network of recreational trails are finally linked together, which if all goes well will happen in 2017 on Canada's 150th birthday, the Trans-Canada Trail will become the world's longest trail, stretching for 14,000 miles (23,000 km) from the Atlantic to the Pacific and north to the Arctic Ocean.

How does one even begin to describe the sort of herculean effort that goes into the creation of such a trail, or of the myriad of trail types from pavement to scree to glaciers to forests—and all the environments through which it passes? It began in 1992 as an initiative to celebrate Canada's 125th year and when completed will pass through every province and territory in the nation, a network of almost 500 individual trails, connecting almost a thousand separate communities. If you were to walk its entire length you would pass over the dizzying Kinsol Trestle Bridge above the Koksilah River on Vancouver Island; hike through the 3,430 acres (1,388 ha) of the Glenbow Ranch Provincial Park between Calgary and Cochrane; and in Nova Scotia you'd walk the abandoned Musquodoboit railway line on the Salt Marsh Trail.

Thousands of Canadians have given their time to help make the trail a reality, and regardless of where you go you will never be far from a pavilion that will provide you with shelter, drinking water, and a little courage to keep going through Brigus Junction and Gambo, Rattling Brook and Foxtrap, Howley and Badger, Osmond and Corner Brook, and a thousand other places you've never heard of as you press ever forward along a trail that, as much as any trail anywhere, defines the nation through which it so gloriously passes. **BDS**

"The trail is made up of close to 400 individual trails, each with unique and varied features."

trailsbc.ca/trans-canada-trail

◄ The 613-foot-long (187 m) Kinsol Trestle over the Koksilah River was completed in 1920.

▲ The TCT is the world's longest network of recreational trails.

Walcott Quarry—Burgess Shale British Columbia, Canada

Start/End Takakkaw Falls, Yoho Valley   **Distance** 12 miles (19.3 km)   **Time** 10 hours   **Grade** Moderate
Type Rocky mountain trails   **Map** goo.gl/Uu7gQX

The Walcott Quarry is by far the most significant of all the Middle Cambrian deposits found in Canada's Burgess Shale Fossil Beds, one of the world's most celebrated fossil fields. Discovered in 1909 by the U.S. invertebrate paleontologist Charles Walcott, while hiking the Burgess Path above Emerald Lake, the 505-million-year-old fossils he found as he split open slabs of layered shale were astonishingly detailed, clearly showing muscles, organ tissues, and other soft-body parts that would otherwise have remained unknown to science. The fossils of what were once undersea creatures give us glimpses into the origins of multi-cellular life, as well as discoveries of early crabs, sponges, and other species that still refuse to fit with contemporary classifications.

Once you have hiked all of the forest trails that you came to the Rocky Mountains to hike and have seen enough of its grand granite peaks, you ought to spend a day doing one of the hikes organized every summer by the Burgess Shale Geoscience Foundation and Parks Canada. To walk through these hills with a knowledgeable guide is a rich and rewarding experience that opens a window on how the scenery around you has been formed, and how its landscape has altered over millions of years.

There is a full-day, ten-hour hike that begins in the Yoho Valley at Takakkaw Falls and takes you to Walcott Quarry, high above Emerald Lake, and a shorter seven-hour hike to the Mount Stephen Fossil Beds above the town of Field. Your guide's knowledge of earth sciences will provide you with one of the best days hiking that the Rocky Mountains can provide. **BDS**

⊞ An intricately detailed fossil found at Burgess Shale.

Stanley Glacier Trail Alberta, Canada

Start/End Stanley Glacier parking area, Banff–Radium Highway   **Distance** 6.5 miles (10.5 km)
Time 3 hours   **Grade** Moderate   **Type** Forest and mountain trails   **Map** goo.gl/4rERFp

The Stanley Glacier Trail takes you into a true "fire and ice" environment. In 1998, and again in 2003, the ecological clock of this area was wound back when the lower trail was burned down to its roots by fierce forest fires that scorched the earth and are responsible for the regrowth you see reclaiming the valley today, a young forest in which lodgepoles, willows, fireweed, liverworts, blueberries, and an abundance of wildflowers now grow prolifically in regenerated soils.

Stanley Glacier lies within the boundaries of Kootenay National Park, which was established in 1920 on the western slopes of the Rocky Mountains just off the Continental Divide. From the moment you pull up at the parking area trailhead on the Banff–Radium Highway, there's never any doubt which direction you'll be heading, with the snowcapped beacon of Stanley Peak clearly visible. You begin by crossing the

Vermilion River before a series of switchbacks takes you up 700 feet (213 m) in the first mile and a half through the regrowth area. The views hit you almost from the moment you get going on this terrific hike, and when you reach your first overlook you get an uninterrupted view up the length of the Stanley Basin, with a sea of boulders in its foreground and in the distance a wall of snow-covered summits.

How far you walk on this trail is up to you. The trail officially ends around two-thirds of the way up the valley, but for those who like a challenge you can carry on—the trail continues to the very end of the valley and up to the snow couloirs on Stanley's north face, while the trail to the glacier's bivy site affords great views of the toe of the glacier. **BDS**

⏏ Walk the Stanley Basin . . . and then on to its glacier.

Karst Spring Hiking Trail

Alberta, Canada

Start/End Mount Shark trailhead
Distance 6 miles (9.6 km)   **Time** 4–5 hours
Grade Easy   **Type** Logging road and forest trails
Map goo.gl/JAgmWq

Although the first 2.5 miles (4 km) of the Karst Spring Hiking Trail is along a typical and fairly pedestrian old logging road, plenty of interest lies beyond the trailhead. Your goal once you arrive at a T-fork on the logging road is Watridge Lake, reached only after negotiating a series of tricky turns through aromatic, dense evergreen forests. It is therefore best to bring a detailed hiking guide with you even though the walk is a relatively short one. At the lake follow a boardwalk and climb the trail above the creek to the source of Karst Spring, which gushes from a rock wall at the

---

"This area has been described as one of the most scenic in North America."

hikealberta.com

---

base of Shark Mountain, spewing its warm waters out of the conduits, fractures, joints, and bedding plains of the mountain's subterranean rocks. The source of the spring has never been precisely pinpointed, but its warm waters spawn a picture-perfect carpet of vivid green moss over the rocks and driftwood in its creek.

The trail can be hiked year-round and should certainly be considered as a winter hike, when you can marvel at the breathtaking mountain views as you cross the wooden boardwalk past frozen Watridge Lake. At that time of year you will see a myriad of ice crystal sculptures that drip off the logs lying across Karst Spring and form on the glistening surface of its gently flowing current. **BDS**

Voyageur Hiking Trail

Ontario, Canada

Start Sudbury, Lake Superior   **End** Thunder Bay,
Lake Superior   **Distance** 372 miles (599 km)
Time 6–8 weeks   **Grade** Moderate   **Type** Mixed:
asphalt, grass, soil   **Info** goo.gl/9BU5CN

The Voyageur Hiking Trail is a public wilderness-style hiking trail that runs from Sudbury to Thunder Bay at the head of Lake Superior in Ontario, Canada, and is planned to go farther still. The idea for the trail was first hatched by a group of volunteers and walking enthusiasts at a meeting in Sault Ste. Marie in March 1973, held for "persons interested in establishing a hiking trail along the precipice of the Cambrian shield" from Gros Cap on the shoreline of Lake Superior to Hiawatha Park north of Sault Ste. Marie. In the years since that meeting more than twenty different walking clubs, with the help of the Ontario government, have been adding new segments to the trail, including south across Manitoulin Island. The trail is now composed of more than nineteen distinct walks and stretches over 372 miles (599 km) through the lake-encrusted shorelines of Lake Superior and Lake Huron, paralleling the trade routes taken by the early French-speaking fur traders—the Voyageurs—who risked their lives opening up this part of the New World in the eighteenth century.

In keeping with those early traders the trail is a true wilderness experience, passing through some of the least populated regions of Ontario, and is strictly pedestrian only—hiking, backpacking, snowshoeing, and cross-country skiing. Its surface is a mixture of asphalt, grass, rock, compacted soil, and boardwalk, and some segments are part of the Trans-Canada Trail. It passes through private and publicly owned forests, and when it is not on the lakeshore it crosses over promontories and lookouts that afford sweeping views of the Great Lakes, much the same view that would have greeted the early fur traders. **BDS**

Grasslands National Park
Saskatchewan, Canada

Start/End The Crossing Resort, Highway 4, 3 miles (4.8 km) south of Val Marie **Distance** Various **Time** Various **Grade** Easy **Type** Grassy trail **Info** goo.gl/BhqESc

Grasslands National Park in the Canadian province of Saskatchewan, just north of the U.S. state of Montana, protects a true prairie wilderness. It is an area in which seventy species of mixed grasses are interlaced with fifty species of wildflowers in soils that have never felt the cold touch of the plow—the sort of environment that once covered vast swathes of the North American continent, 80 percent of which has been lost in Canada over the past two centuries of European settlement.

Today this beautiful park, separated into its east and west blocks, is covered by an impressive variety of trails, each with its own unique character: wildflowers on the Eagle Butte Trail; the remoteness of the North Gillespie Trail; 360-degree views on the Rock Creek Trail; rolling hills along the Frenchman River Valley on the Two Trees Trail; and 60,000 years of eroded strata visible in the Killdeer Badlands.

To the north of the 347 square miles (898 sq km) of the park can be found the most disturbed topography in the country: a land of wheat fields early settlers were encouraged to plant, and in so doing tore up the grama, fescue, spear, and other wild grasses that made up the prairies and sustained the animals that fed on it—the bison, prairie wolves, elk, wolverine, the black-footed ferret, and the plains grizzly bear. But here in the national park, the natural grasses are being added to and replenished all the time; the swift fox, coyote, and the plains bison have been reintroduced; and pronghorn antelope numbers are on the rise. Grasslands may not have the status of other, higher profile parks, but make no mistake, there are few more valuable pieces of real estate than these wonderful oceans of grass. **BDS**

"The park preserves a rich and complex ecosystem supporting an incredible diversity of plants."

www.greatcanadianparks.com

⊞ The trails are endless across Saskatchewan's oceans of grass that have never felt the plow.

Laurentian Trail Quebec, Canada

Start Rivière-à-la-Pêche Service Center   **End** Kilometre 35, The Parkway   **Distance** 45 miles (72.4 km)
Time 5–7 days   **Grade** Strenuous   **Type** Forest trails, timber boardwalks   **Info** goo.gl/ze8dmM

Located one hour's drive north of Trois-Rivières in La Mauricie National Park in the Canadian province of Quebec, the Laurentian Trail—established in 1998 and still not widely known—provides a fascinating walk through the mixed forest of the transitional zone that separates the boreal and deciduous forests of southern Canada.

It begins with a 4.5-mile (7.2-km) walk through mixed forest and beneath fern-draped rocky overhangs before you reach the first campsite at Hamel Creek, which itself is close to a lake that can make for a nice swim in summer. You then make your way through gently rolling terrain and stands of hemlock along the Saint Maurice River toward the fork for Omand Lake. This is one of the many bodies of water you'll encounter on this wetland-rich trail that bisects a region with which few Canadians are familiar—the

Laurentian Highlands—a region that is home to the largest exposure of Precambrian rocks on earth.

The trail is well designed, and its campgrounds, which all come with covered cooking shelters and good, flat sites, are always located close to a river or by a lake (although the abundance of water can make mosquitoes a real nuisance). It is well marked and because there are no real elevation gains or any exposed ridges it is easy to travel light. The other thing to remember is that it can only be done from east to west. There is also a temptation for inexperienced hikers to think the trail an easier challenge than it is. But hiking 15 miles (24 km) a day over five days isn't easy, so make a week of it and take the time to enjoy the solitude this less-traveled trail provides. **BDS**

⬆ Explore a transitional forest on a wetland-rich trail.

Long Range Traverse Newfoundland, Canada

Start Western Brook Pond **End** James Callaghan trailhead **Distance** 25.5 miles (41 km) **Time** 5 days
Grade Moderate **Type** Unmarked **Info** goo.gl/MOTM7V

If you are a Canadian and you love to hike, then you are likely familiar with the Long Range Traverse in Newfoundland's Gros Morne National Park. This trail, known throughout Canada for its navigational challenges and rare beauty, is not marked or even well maintained. It is a trail-less hike and completing it is a real "map and compass" job. This only adds to its reputation as one of North America's premier backcountry routes, a reputation that grows steadily with each passing season.

Following the ridges and valleys along the western coastline of the Great Northern Peninsula past some of Newfoundland's tallest peaks and overlooking the Gulf of St. Lawrence, the sublime views are quick to reveal themselves. Ascending the gorge after being dropped off by boat at your starting point at Western Brook Pond will take around four hours, but once you emerge from the granite and the handholds onto the top, Western Brook Pond fjord below and the backcountry beyond open out into what seems like infinity, a fact that keeps hiker numbers down and ensures that you'll have much of this pristine walk all to yourself.

There is a lot of water here—Little Island Pond, Marks Pond, Hardings Pond—so expect wet boots and socks. You will likely stray off course, so prepare for some bushwhacking through tuckamore (a Newfoundland term for stunted balsam firs and spruce trees), fording streams, and scrambling down small cliffs. Always follow your instruments—don't rely on game trails or caribou runs and bring a whistle to clear your way of the occasional bull moose. **BDS**

⬆ Bushwhack through tuckamore on a classic hike.

Chilkoot Trail
USA/Canada

Start Dyea, Alaska **End** Bennett Lake,
British Columbia **Distance** 33 miles (53 km)
Time 2 days **Grade** Moderate **Type** Mountain
trails **Map** goo.gl/ztnf69

Before Chilkoot Trail was ever a trail it was a well-trodden path, used by generations of local Tlingit people to trade seaweed, fish, and seal oil with other First Nation peoples in return for hides of moose and caribou. White settlement, the arrival of the Hudson's Bay Company, and the growth of the fur trade saw the demise of the Tlingit's trading system and the trail used by early settlers, explorers, and prospectors. Then came the discovery of gold in the Klondike in 1896, and the route over the Chilkoot Pass became one of only two primary routes into the region.

> *"Few trails of similar length offer more dramatic changes in climate, terrain, and vegetation."*

www.pc.gc.ca

A difficult trail that takes between three and five days to complete, what was once called "the meanest 33 miles in history" with steps cut into the ice approaching Chilkoot Pass to stop prospectors falling backward down its 42-degree incline, is now a more sedate affair that begins in the Coast Mountains outside the ghost town of Dyea, Alaska, and continues to Bennett in British Columbia. The pioneering sense of adventure is recaptured easily as you make your way out of Dyea along the Taiya River on the climb to Chilkoot Pass, including a 1,600-foot (488-m) ascent in only 2.5 miles (4 km) between Sheep Camp and The Scales. A series of lakes follows before your descent to Bennett Lake, the end of a great and historic trail. **BDS**

Enchantment Lakes
Washington, USA

Start/End Snow Lake trailhead
Distance 18 miles (29 km) **Time** 4–5 days
Grade Difficult **Type** Forest trails
Map goo.gl/ujTBHY

If you want to hike through a landscape that feels otherworldly, then try Enchantment Lakes in the state of Washington, USA. They lie in two alpine basins (an upper and lower) that are filled with post-glacial lakes and tarns, and are hemmed in by the towering Stuart Range. Although it was first mapped out in the early twentieth century, climbers didn't venture here en masse until the 1940s. The key landmarks have suitably mythological names, such as Gnome Tarn, Aasgard Pass, and Crystal Lake, and there are two main routes. The Snow Lake route (listed here) runs from a parking lot next to Icicle Creek and climbs 4,100 feet (1,250 m) in 6.5 miles (10.4 km), then another 1,900 feet (580 m) over the remaining 2.5 miles (4 km) to the Lower Enchantments. The going can be very tough in places, with sloping granite underfoot, and some sections involve scrambling over rocks. The other route into the basins, via Colchuck Lake, is shorter but even steeper, and bordering on dangerous.

Permits are needed before you're allowed into the Enchantments and the U.S. Forest Service controls who goes where and in what numbers, in order to protect the environment. There are campsites and toilets along the route—a full list is available from the ranger station at Leavenworth, where you obtain permits. In terrain like this you need to be prepared both physically and in terms of clothing and equipment. If you're carrying food with you, make sure it's kept in sealed containers to avoid attracting animals. You need to be a confident hiker to consider reaching Enchantment Lakes. **JI**

➔ Conquer the enchanting tarns, lakes, and passes.

Hoh River Trail
Washington, USA

Start/End Hoh Rain Forest Visitor Center/Glacier
Meadows   **Distance** 31.2 miles (50.2 km)
Time 3 days   **Grade** Easy to moderate
Type Footpath   **Map** goo.gl/mXkOfB

If you choose to take a walk along the Hoh River Trail, you'll be heading into one of the quietest spots in the continental United States, an area dubbed "One Square Inch of Silence" by groups dedicated to preserving the tranquillity of this part of Washington State in the damp, forested Pacific northwest.

The Hoh River Trail is an out-and-back path accessible from April until October. It follows the Hoh River eastward and is mostly flat for the initial 13 miles (21 km) before climbing sharply up to Glacier Meadows at 4,300 feet (1,310 m). The path, which is maintained by the U.S. National Park Service to a high standard, traverses subalpine meadows. There are a handful of stream crossings and one river crossing en route, with the quietest section just a few miles out from the visitor center, marked by a pile of stones. The rest of the trail is just as breathtaking, passing through a truly great wilderness that measures its annual rainfall in feet rather than inches, ending in a meadow by the side of a glacier at the foot of Mount Olympus.

There are plenty of campsites dotted along the trail so you can break your journey as you see fit. You do need to be careful of bears, however, particularly when it comes to storing any food that you carry with you. You don't, needless to say, want to keep it alongside you in your tent overnight—but staff at the Rain Forest Visitor Center can offer advice on what to do to limit the odds of becoming bear fodder.

Just remember, no matter how stunning the views, try not to gasp too loudly and break the precious silence. **JI**

◄ Amble through a moss- and fern-draped wonderland.

John Wayne Pioneer Trail
Washington, USA

Start Iron Horse State Park   **End** Idaho border
at Tekoa   **Distance** 300 miles (483 km)
Time 15–20 days   **Grade** Easy to moderate
Type Long-distance rail trail   **Info** goo.gl/5xJaOb

The John Wayne Pioneer Trail, which runs east to west across two-thirds of the state of Washington, was the result of the efforts of the John Wayne Pioneer Wagons and Riders Association and the personal vision of the organization's founder, Chic Hollenbeck, an unabashed fan of the iconic U.S. actor. The trail runs over 300 miles (482 km) along the old Chicago, Milwaukee, St. Paul, and Pacific Railroad route, also known as the Milwaukee Road. It begins near North Bend west of the Cascades at Rattlesnake Lake and runs all the way to the border with Idaho. The railroad,

"The Columbia River serves as a natural dividing line with a different trail experience on each side."

www.traillink.com

built between 1906 and 1909, and electrified in 1915, saw its last train in 1980. When the Milwaukee Railroad gave up its ownership of the line it was acquired by the state of Washington. Shortly after that Chic Hollenbeck began to champion its conversion.

The trail is family friendly with a light gravel surface, easy gradients, and plenty of places to camp. It has good signage and marked trailheads, and is popular with horseback riders, mountain bikers, teamsters, and even cross-country skiers. Its characteristics include trestle bridges, high desert, irrigated farmlands, wetlands, and cattle ranches. The farther east it goes the more primitive it becomes, passing over open rangelands and isolated ranching communities. **BDS**

Horsetail Falls Trail Oregon, USA

Start/End Horsetail Falls trailhead on the Historic Columbia River Highway   Distance 4.4 miles (7 km)
Time 2 hours   Grade Moderate   Type Woodland track   Map goo.gl/NOiEqT

Numerous rivers plunge down narrow valleys into the mighty Columbia River in Oregon and Washington states, but none are finer than the six falls visible on this fascinating hike. The elevation gain is not immense, but the effort is worthwhile for the experience of getting up close and personal with an impressive waterfall. The trail is approached along the Historic Columbia River Highway, begun in the spring of 1913 by chief engineer Samuel C. Lancaster, who put great store on providing easy access to sights such as these falls, although not at the cost of destroying "what God had put there."

The trail begins next to the 176-foot-high (53 m) Horsetail Falls, a single fall of water cascading down a narrow crack in the rock face. You then walk gently up Horsetail Creek to experience your second waterfall, the 80-foot-high (24 m) Ponytail Falls. Not quite so impressive, but you do get the chance to walk behind it and feel its spray on your face! Beneath the falls is a large cavern, created as the soft rock beneath the layer of basalt lava has eroded over the years. The trail then turns back toward the Columbia before heading west and then south up Oneonta Creek for the first of the three Oneonta Falls, the first and Lower Falls a middling 60 feet (18 m) high. The track then moves up the side of the Creek passing the smallest Middle and larger Upper Oneonta Falls, both of which can be scrambled down to view, before reaching the final waterfall, the impressive three-angled Triple Falls, a sizable 132 feet (40 m) high. Take a break, take some more photographs, and then head back down the trail to the trailhead. **SA**

⬆ **Six stunning waterfalls on a 100-year-old trail.**

Timberline Trail Oregon, USA

Start/End Timberline Lodge parking lot   **Distance** 39.8 miles (64 km)   **Time** 4 days   **Grade** Strenuous
Type Mountain trail   **Map** goo.gl/SEhfhB

The Timberline Trail begins and ends in the parking lot of the iconic Timberline Lodge: one of the United States' most recognizable hotels built on the slopes of Mount Hood, Oregon's highest mountain, and opened in the late 1930s by President Franklin Roosevelt. Most people opt for the clockwise route around the mountain, but regardless of direction, you take you can be assured a smorgasbord of superb views of Mount Hood's 11,249-foot (3,429-m) summit and its surrounding wilderness, not to mention some of the dominant volcanic peaks in the Cascade Range, including Mount St. Helens, Mount Rainer, and Mount Jefferson.

Presuming you head off in a clockwise direction, after a mile or so you begin a short descent into Little Zigzag Canyon, and from there through forest and open meadows to Zigzag overlook with its view across to Mississippi Head, a small but impressive mesa at the canyon's entrance. You then climb along a series of switchbacks to the expansive alpine meadows of Paradise Park and its campsites beneath the shade of its majestic hemlocks followed by the occasional rocky bluff and always the fabulous summit of Mount Hood towering above. Remember this is not a route to the mountain's summit, but instead it affords a rare appreciation of its geology, getting you up onto its ridges and rocky slopes. There is the fan-like Ramona Falls, and the lovely trail leading to Cloud Cap Saddle campground. The trail's highest point, Lamberson Spur (7,230 feet/2,203 m), is crossed, and you can look forward to camping in the flower-encrusted meadows of Elk Cove with an inspiring view of Coe Glacier. **BDS**

⬆ Circle one of North America's most beautiful mountains.

Jefferson Park

Oregon, USA

Start/End Various
Distance Various   Time Various
Grade Moderate   Type Multiple
Info goo.gl/8x3ocN

If you are in Oregon and looking for some exceptional backcountry hiking, look no further than Jefferson Park, a flat alpine plateau in the Willamette National Forest. This is exceptional wilderness, with a sea of wildflowers usually at their best in the second half of July in a stark alpine setting, and reflections of Mount Jefferson's sharp pinnacle reflected in the area's many lakes and ponds.

There are three approaches to choose from. The shortest and most popular, although also the least spectacular because it is mostly in the trees, is the Whitewater Trail. A more scenic option is the South Breitenbush Trail, but it is the most difficult and has the greatest elevation gain. The best option is to take an old friend—the Pacific Crest Trail. The approach here is on a well-maintained, excellent trail through huckleberry and heather-encrusted meadows fringed with Douglas fir and hemlock as you make your way toward 6,920-foot (2,109-m) Park Ridge which has, until now, kept Mount Jefferson all but hidden. Once you are on Park Ridge, one of Oregon's finest view points, the mountain reveals itself in all its glory, and the way to Jefferson Park 900 feet (274 m) below is easily navigated.

Once in Jefferson Park, you will be greeted with an abundance of trails through avalanche lilies and bear grass that take you onto various lakes, ponds, and campsites. The views from Russell Lake are quite possibly the best. With all the water here be sure to bring mosquito repellent, and if you come in August be prepared to encounter snow as well and, if you're lucky, the migrating California Tortoiseshell butterfly. Also bring a spare battery for your camera. You're going to need it. **BDS**

"Cool alpine lakes, surrounded by patches of trees and nice wildflower meadows …"

www.portlandhikersfieldguide.org

⬆ One of Oregon's finest backcountry trails will take you through some exceptional wilderness.

Sarah Zigler Interpretive Trail Oregon, USA

Start/End Peter Britt Gardens, Jacksonville
Distance 2.5 miles (4 km)   Time 2 hours
Grade Easy   Type Soil and gravel track
Map goo.gl/XTa1Uf

Swiss-born Peter Britt became a pioneer photographer of people and places during the fifty years he lived in Jacksonville, Oregon. He established Oregon's first winery and planted extensive orchards and gardens. After his death in 1905, his gardens became a public park and include an interpretive trail named after Sarah Zigler, an early settler whose original gold claim along Jackson Creek was donated by her granddaughter for the trail.

The trail begins in the Peter Britt Gardens and passes by the famous Britt Sequoia, planted in 1862 and which many people believe to be the oldest sequoia in Oregon. The trail then climbs up through the lush beauty of Jackson Creek and the Zigler Woods to the Britt Water Ditch. It was here that gold was first discovered in 1851, prompting a massive gold rush to Jacksonville the following year. Interestingly, the town became the site of the first Chinatown in Oregon, as Chinese immigrants arrived in the new town to seek their fortunes in the gold rush. For the next mile, the trail ambles through the trees alongside old mine workings. Once across Jackson Creek, the trail climbs through a forest of ponderosa pine, bigleaf maple, Douglas fir, and madrone to the top of a dry ridge planted mostly with chaparrals and the small Oregon White Oak. From here you get splendid views of the Siskiyou and Cascade Mountains to the southwest and east, respectively.

Walkers on the ridgeline can explore many side trails to old gold workings. As the trail loops back down the hill, the forest gets richer. Finally, the trail re-enters the lush gardens and passes by the Britt Pavilion, site of the famous Britt Music Festival. **SA**

John Day Fossil Beds National Monument Oregon, USA

Start/End John Day Fossil Beds Visitor Center
Distance Various   Time Various   Grade Easy to moderate   Type Pathways, boardwalks
Info goo.gl/MSuYpK

The John Day Fossil Beds National Monument in east-central Oregon, named after an early fur trader who never visited the area or found a single fossil, covers more than 13,837 acres (5,600 ha) of Badlands, riparian zones, and vast areas of semidesert shrubland. About 150,000 people a year come here to marvel at its fossil deposits spanning more than 40 million years, the Pacific northwest's only continuous record of the region's evolutionary history and the world's greatest trove of fossil beds from the Cenozoic era (66 million years ago to the present), the "Age of Mammals."

"Hikes at all three units allow visitors to explore the prehistoric past of Oregon and see science in action."

www.nps.gov

The monument is divided into three regions or units—Painted Hills, Clarno, and Sheep Rock—each with its own network of walking trails, open year-round during daylight hours. There are eight trails at Sheep Rock Unit, the longest being the 3-mile (4.8-km) Blue Basin Overlook Trail, the best for appreciating the monument's overall geology and scenery. The Clarno Unit has the wonderful Trail of Fossils, a 0.25-mile (0.4-km) loop and the only place where fossils still embedded in rock can be seen. The stunning mineral-stained slopes of Painted Hills Unit, with its deposits of plant, seed, and flower fossils, has Leaf Hill Trail and the Carroll Rim Trail, which climbs 300 feet (91.5 m) for a bird's-eye view of these mineral-rich hills. **BDS**

Bigfoot Trail
California, USA

> *"There have been more Bigfoot sightings here than anywhere in the world."*

bigfootsightings.org

⬆ The Bigfoot Trail has quail, mountain lions, owls, and flying squirrels—and is that Sasquatch among the trees?

Start Yolla Bolly–Middle Eel Wilderness **End** Redwood National Park **Distance** 400 miles (643 km)
Time 30–40 days **Grade** Moderate to strenuous
Type Long-distance trail **Info** goo.gl/rKpIBE

This long-distance hiking trail is the brainchild of writer Michael Kauffmann, who in 2009 proposed a route to showcase the biodiversity of the Klamath Mountain range. Thanks to him, walkers can observe no fewer than thirty-two different species of conifer, as great a concentration of such trees as exists anywhere on earth.

There is also an abundance of wildlife. Among the mammals are bears, bobcats, coyote, deer, gray foxes, mountain lions, and northern flying squirrels. Birds appear in all shapes and sizes: the largest are eagles, turkey vultures, hawks, and northern spotted owls; some of the smallest are grouse, band-tailed pigeons, and quail. The walk's most prominent watercourses—notably the South Fork of Cottonwood Creek and Black Rock Lake—teem with rainbow trout; the Middle Fork Eel River has Chinook salmon (where, sadly, fishing is forbidden).

Comparably fascinating is the wayside flora—the trail passes many of Northern California's 3,500 plant species—and the general scenery, particularly the first 27 miles (43 km) and the last 16 miles (26 km), as the Bigfoot Trail crosses and re-crosses the North California Coast Range. Also remarkable is the topography of the Red Buttes Wilderness, which is named for the color it derives from the high iron and magnesium content of its component rocks.

The Bigfoot Trail is not easy. Indeed, at the time of publication, there was no officially confirmed record of anyone ever having completed it. The best time to attempt it is October. There is snow in winter, and the California summer kicks in early, with high temperatures from the start of May. **GL**

Joshua Tree National Park Trails
California, USA

Start/End Oasis visitor center, Joshua Tree
National Park   **Distance** Various   **Time** 1 day
Grade Easy to moderate   **Type** Rock, dirt trails
Info goo.gl/gUBdO8

Although its habitat includes Arizona, Nevada, and Utah, the Joshua Tree—*Yucca brevifolia*—can be found in its greatest concentrations in California's Mojave Desert at elevations between 1,300 feet (400 m) and 5,900 feet (1,800 m). Named the Joshua Tree by Mormon settlers who crossed into the Mojave Desert in the mid 1800s, it grows rapidly for a desert plant, helped along by its deep and extensive root system, and its distinctive top-heavy network of branches gives it its unmistakable appearance. It has evergreen leaves, flowers from February to late April, and is one of four major "indicator species," meaning that when the Joshua Trees are healthy, so is their environment.

Joshua Tree National Park encompasses more than 1,200 square miles (463 sq km) of desert northeast of Palm Springs, a transitory zone between the Mojave and Colorado deserts that has resulted in a diverse mix of flora. And a diverse mix of trails, too. The Forty-nine Palms Oasis walk is a 3-mile (4.8-km) out-and-back trail that accesses a palm-tree oasis on the park's northern boundary. Warren Peak (1,000 feet/305 m) is another out-and-back hike with impressive views over the park's western region. The Wall Street Mill Walk takes you on a short 2-mile (3.2-km) return to an old gold mine, and the Cholla Cactus Garden loop trail winds through a dense and fascinating concentration of cholla cacti, a shrubby cacti with cylindrical stems comprised of segmented joints. For an unparalleled view of the park, you should head to the top of Ryan Mountain, a three-hour round-trip hike and a 1,075-foot (328-m) ascent on a dirt trail with stone steps that will reward with wonderful panoramas over Pinto Basin and a landscape of gnarled, twisted rocks. **BDS**

"The Joshua trees themselves are a strange and beautiful tree that enhance any desert landscape."

www.hikespeak.com

⤒ The strikingly eerie silhouettes of Joshua Trees pepper the desert landscape of the national park.

Craigs Creek Trail, Smith River
California, USA

Start/End South Fork Smith River
Distance 6.4 miles (10.3 km)   **Time** 3 hours
Grade Various   **Type** Old mining trail
Map goo.gl/5uoGmM

When Californian miners used to trudge along the route of northern California's Craigs Creek in the late 1800s, how could they have imagined it would one day become a popular trail for leisure hikers? Yet the same paths along which they used to lead pack animals are now used by hikers, horseback riders, and those heading for a refreshing dip in the crystal waters of Craigs Creek.

The trail runs alongside part of the undammed Smith River, then rises up the slopes of Craigs Creek Mountain before dropping back down into the Craigs Creek basin, where the creek and the Smith River meet, through a dense Californian forest full of ancient redwood trees, oaks, and Douglas firs. And all the time, the sound of the river's white water is never far away. Part of the walking route involves some climbing, so you need to be pretty fit. Even without the climbs, there is plenty of up and down along the trail, coupled with steep switchbacks on the final descent. In summer there's also plenty of poison oak lining the route that can be easily avoided but it does mean it's best not to take children with you. It's also worth remembering you can get poison oak from the fur of dogs, so maybe leave Fido at home, too.

There is a reward for all the hard work, however, including relics from the region's old mining days along the route, such as derelict machinery. At the end of the trail is a deep water hole, where Smith River and Craigs Creek converge, a perfect place to take a cooling, cleansing dip after your trek. This woodland oasis is surrounded with large rocks to lie on and bask in the golden Californian sunshine, while you ponder the return trek back through the forest. **JI**

"As you climb to vista points above the … Smith River, notice the … changes in vegetation."

www.fs.usda.gov

⊼   The trail runs for a while alongside the Smith River, before plunging into a dense and beautiful forest.

Palm Canyon Trail, Anza–Borrego Desert State Park
California, USA

Start/End Park Visitor Center
Distance 3.25 miles (5.2 km)
Time 1–3 hours   **Grade** Easy to moderate
Type Desert trails   **Map** goo.gl/yVPSxQ

Borrego Palm Canyon is an oasis of palm trees in southeastern California. It is part of the Anza–Borrego Desert State Park, which was founded in the 1920s and is a two-hour drive from San Diego. The V-shaped gorge that runs from west to east through the San Ysidro Mountains to the west of Borrego Springs is Borrego Palm Canyon, and when you reach the grove of palms that the Palm Canyon Trail is named after, it's hard to imagine a more vivid green could exist anywhere, let alone in the midst of an arid desert.

The easy-going, signposted trail runs up from the park visitor center to what is one of the largest palm oases to be found anywhere in California. Along the way you will pass smaller palm stands that offer shade from the intense desert sun and legions of cacti and even a waterfall, which is a popular rest stop and picnic area. You also cross over a stream bed, but barring any flash flood events the water level will be low and the stream is easily forded. Look out for grinding holes worn in the rocky canyon floor by the Native American peoples who once inhabited the region, and also be on the lookout for the occasional bighorn sheep.

It is important that you dress appropriately and be prepared for the desert conditions, with suitable shoes and headwear. You also need to make sure you have enough drinking water with you for several hours of walking. The climate is fairly mild in winter and spring, but you are still walking through an unshaded environment for most of the route. Around the waterfall and at times when the conditions are damp, be careful of the slippery stone surface under foot. **JI**

"It's a beautiful well-watered oasis, tucked away in a rocky, V-shaped gorge."

www.parks.ca.gov

⬆ The green oasis of Palm Canyon looks out of place in this stark, desert wilderness.

Humboldt Redwoods State Park Trails
California, USA

Start/End Various **Distance** Various
Time Various **Grade** Easy to strenuous
Type Well-maintained woodland trails
Info goo.gl/jg9HPo

The Humboldt Redwoods State Park in California covers more than 50,000 acres (20,000 ha) and contains the Bull Creek watershed and the Rockefeller Forest. It is also home to some of the largest and oldest trees in the country, such as the Founders Tree, nearly 350 feet (105 m) tall with a circumference around its base of 40 feet (12 m).

There are more than 100 miles (161 km) of hiking trails within the park, trails that range from short, half-mile ambles with an elevation rise too minimal to mention, to much longer treks through the heart of the mighty forest. Favorites include the Founders Grove Nature Trail, a short guided hike that exercises the mind as much as the legs. (Did you know, for example, that a giant redwood can release up to 500 gallons of water into the air everyday?) You're also taken past key points, such as the Dyerville Giant, a 1,600-year-old redwood that fell in 1991, and the sound as it crashed to earth was heard a mile away.

The park receives up to 80 inches (203 cm) of rain a year, mostly between October and May, so you need to be prepared for changes in the weather. It can be foggy on summer mornings but this usually burns off by lunchtime, and within the park there can be extreme differences in temperature.

Camping is not a problem at Humboldt Redwoods, with several family friendly campsites throughout the park, including some designated sites for horseback riders and their animals. Overall Humboldt Redwoods State Park offers a vast range of hiking and walking options for all ages and all abilities, and all under the cool canopy of the giant wooden arches of this cathedral of nature. JI

"This is the third largest California State Park and protects an environment unique to anywhere else on earth."

www.parks.ca.gov

⬅ Coast redwoods can be up to 1,800 years old.

⬆ When in the park, give your feet a rest and drive the 32-mile (51-km) Avenue of the Giants.

Trans-Catalina Trail
California, USA

"Though Catalina is a short ninety-minute boat ride away, it feels like another world."

www.everytrail.com

↑ Take your hiking poles on a trail that goes from sea to summit—and past herds of bison.

Start Avalon   End Starlight Beach
Distance 37 miles (59.5 km)   Time 4–6 days
Grade Easy to strenuous   Type Mix of existing roads and newer trails   Map goo.gl/qonmw3

Twenty-two miles (35.5 km) off the coast of southern California is the island of Santa Catalina, which is reachable via a short boat ride. The island is home to a 43,000-acre (17,400-ha) nature reserve and some stunning scenery, as well as an excellent hiking trail that opened to the public in 2009, parts of which follow established routes while others have been purpose-built.

The Trans-Catalina Trail crosses the island from Avalon in the southeast corner to Starlight Beach in the west. Along the way you'll pass herds of bison and field after field of wildflowers (don't worry, the bison will leave you alone if you give them a wide berth), but remember once you get to Starlight Beach you still have to get back to Two Harbors for the boat back to mainland California.

The scenery changes immensely along the 37-mile (59.5-km) route. In places the going is steep enough to warrant the use of hiking poles, while in others you're walking your way through lush forest. Also, don't think that because this is an island you're going to be cooled by any sea breezes. The center of Catalina is like a desert.

There are campsites along the route and you have to use these because free-range camping is not allowed on the island. All accommodation on Santa Catalina must be booked in advance, along with any transportation and food. Hiking permits are also required. The route takes you up around eight peaks on the island and you'll reach sea level four times. The hike is hard work and has to be spread over four or five days, but the rewards are enormous on this challenging island trek. **JI**

Snake River National Recreation Trail
Idaho, USA

Start Dug Bar   **End** Saddle Creek Trail junction
Distance 21 miles (34 km)   **Time** 7–10 hours
Grade Moderate   **Type** Rocky and dirt mountain trails
Info goo.gl/B1fvMH

Created eons ago by a volcanic hotspot that now lies beneath Yellowstone National Park, the Snake River's drainage basin extends into six states, its canyons the product of glacial-retreat flooding during the last ice age. The Snake River National Recreation Trail in the Wallowa–Whitman National Forest follows the course of this impressive, wild river, which marks the boundary between Idaho and Oregon on its Idaho side.

The trail has an immense variety of wildflowers and is also a prime destination for fly-fishing and river rafting—the river's infamous Rush Creek and Waterspout rapids can be easily spotted from the trail. Hikers have the thrill of walking through the Eagles Nest, a section of trail cut through a cliff face that is like walking through a tunnel only with one side remaining open, and the not-so-thrilling 3,000-foot (917-m) ascent of Englishman Hill. Several sections of the trail have also been blasted into the rocky overhangs and bluffs above the river.

Once at the Saddle Creek Trail junction you have the option of taking a side trail into the Hells Canyon Wilderness, home to the deepest river gorge in North America. This is a world of high canyons, mountain peaks, and steep slopes that break over into the Snake River Canyon, and some great views of the peaks of the Seven Devils Mountain Range—the She Devil, He Devil, Ogre, Goblin, Devil's Throne, Mount Belial, and Twin Imps. This trail is just one of many choices in an area with more than 2,900 miles (4,667 km) of hiking trails, including the Western Rim National Recreation Trail along the rim of Hells Canyon in an area the U.S. Congress has officially declared a "special place." **BDS**

"The trail goes across rocky slopes, under cliffs, and along grassy canyons."

www.fs.usda.gov

⊞ The grassy plains of wildflowers and views of the Seven Devils are two outstanding features of this walk.

Iron Creek to Sawtooth Lake
Idaho, USA

Start/End Iron Creek trailhead, outside Stanley
Distance 10 miles (16 km)   Time 6 hours
Grade Moderate   Type Rocky path
Map goo.gl/Dtt4k1

The granite Sawtooth range of the Rocky Mountains in southern Idaho get its name from its distinctive ragged-edged tops. The mountains abound in lakes, none finer than Sawtooth Lake itself, a small expanse of water 0.9 miles (1.4 km) long and 0.4 miles (0.6 km) wide. As the lake is 8,435 feet (2,571 m) above sea level, it remains frozen until early summer. At its southern end is Mount Regan, 10,190 feet (3,106 m), an impressively jagged peak named after a local pioneer, Timothy Regan.

The steep trail leads up to Sawtooth Lake from its trailhead at Iron Creek, outside Stanley, and back again, a round trip that takes up to one day to complete. As you are in the Sawtooth National Recreation Area, a trailhead pass is required. After a gentle climb up from the trailhead alongside Iron Creek, the trail veers sharply to the right around a grassy hillock and then sharp left as it begins to climb up the steep gradient on your right. A series of zigzag ascents alongside Alpine Lake finally brings you up to the north side of Sawtooth Lake itself. As you ascend, the views become more and more magnificent, the Sawtooth Mountains stretching all around you. It takes about four hours to get to the top of the trail and a couple of hours to descend, but allow lots more time for the many photographs you will want to take.

There are several places to camp, although beware of leaving campfires unattended, and dogs must remain on a leash at all times. The high altitude means that the area is often snowbound, so the best time to go is in July or August when most of the snow should have melted. **SA**

> *"With its forested route and views of a stunning lake … [this] is a first-rate snapshot of the gorgeous Sawtooth Wilderness."*

www.backpacker.com

⬆ Sawtooth Lake rests in an amphitheater ringed by the jagged peaks of the Sawtooth Mountains.

Boulder Chain Lakes Trail
Idaho, USA

Start/End Livingston Mill trailhead, Forest Road 667, nr Challis   **Distance** 20 miles (32 km)   **Time** 1 day   **Grade** Moderate to strenuous   **Type** Rocky path   **Info** goo.gl/Y1KEEw

The Boulder Chain Lakes are a stunning series of thirteen alpine and glacial lakes along Little Boulder Creek. They are located in the White Cloud Mountains of southern Idaho, themselves part of the Rocky Mountains, inside the Sawtooth National Recreation Area. The thirteen lakes each measure up to 1,600 feet (488 m) in length and are all about 9,000 feet (2,743 m) above sea level. These lakes are beautiful beyond belief—little oceans of blue surrounded by forests of pine and towering, rocky, mountains covered in the winter by snow.

The Boulder Chain Lakes Trail is a 10-mile (16-km) hike up to Red Ridge Pass and along the Boulder Chain Lakes to Windy Devil Pass, where you turn around and head back down again to the trailhead. The path rises steeply from 7,200 feet (2,195 m) at the trailhead to 10,000 feet (3,048 m) at Windy Devil Pass. The altitude and speed of ascent can be problematic, as can snow, so it is best to tackle this walk in July or August. However, the difficulties are easily forgotten by the pleasures this walk will bring.

Along the route you will walk through forests of pine and spruce, flats of willow, and expanses of sagebrush. Once alongside the lakes, though, you are in open country, with the landscape becoming increasingly alpine in appearance. The lakes are jumping with trout, but by now your attention should be focused on the final ascent to Windy Devil Pass, a boulder slope that looks more difficult than it actually is. Once on top of the pass, you can survey Merriam and Castle peaks to your south, two majestic mountains often topped with snow. You've earned this view, so make the most of it. **SA**

"This hike ... has just about every lure for the outdoorsperson: deep cool forests, mountain springs, lakes to fish or swim."

www.trails.com

⬆ Thirteen alpine, trout-filled lakes in southern Idaho will give you a day to remember.

Ice Box Canyon

Nevada, USA

Start/End Ice Box Canyon trailhead
Distance 2.5 miles (4 km)   **Time** 2–3 hours
Grade Strenuous   **Type** Rock, gravel, and dirt
trails   **Map** goo.gl/sUjfVf

Ice Box Canyon runs through Red Rock Canyon outside Las Vegas and gets its name from the drop in ambient temperature compared to the surrounding environment. This makes it a great way to escape the desert heat, but it's no easy trek. It may be less than 3 miles (4.8 km) long, but the going's pretty tough in places, with some rock scrambling and a trail that is loose and rough. The first section is fairly straightforward, taking you past desert willow trees and rocks worn smooth by wind and water. There are plenty of interesting rock formations, although the

---

"A good hike for a hot day … with seasonal waterfalls in the heart of Red Rock Canyon."

www.redrockcanyonlv.org

---

bottom of the canyon is strewn with boulders and this is where the scrambling comes in: climbing, heaving, and navigating up, over, and around the giant stones.

Once through this section you reach the actual Ice Box. Here you'll find a pool of crystal-clear canyon water with a small waterfall running into it. If you're feeling brave and agile you can climb higher into the final section, home to two more natural pools. Be careful here as the smooth rocks can be dangerously slippery. Even though this is a fairly cool spot you're still in the Nevada desert and on a very exposed trail. Temperatures can soar, so bring plenty of water. It's recommended to wear layers of clothing so you can adjust to the changes in heat. **JI**

Buckskin Gulch

Utah, USA

Start Wire Pass trailhead   **End** Lee's Ferry trailhead
Distance 13 miles (21 km)   **Time** 2 days   **Grade** Easy
to moderate   **Type** Sand and rock canyon bed
Map goo.gl/Vwifsk

You are at the entrance to Buckskin Gulch, a beautiful 13-mile (21-km) corridor of fluted sandstone rock that is thought to be the longest slot canyon in the world. The walk begins with an impossible-looking 2-foot-wide gap (0.6 m) through the aptly named Wire Pass that will have you taking off your backpack before you've even broken a sweat. You squeeze your way through to the streaked canyon walls beyond, where the walls of rock are so high that sunlight rarely ever reaches the bottom. You navigate your way through the remote Vermilion Cliffs Wilderness Area of southern Utah, south of the Grand Staircase-Escalante, west of Lake Powell and east of Zion National Park. And it's as remote as it sounds.

Buckskin Gulch is a tributary of the Paria River, itself a tributary of the Colorado River, and is the southwest's deepest slot canyon. Hiking it is a demanding challenge that will require a few things not common to the average hike, including a 20-foot (6-m) rope for the raising and lowering of packs (rappelling equipment is generally not needed). Be prepared for some scrambling over loose rock and wading in waist-deep rock pools—an occasional swim is not unheard of. Don't forget to pack your dry bags with warm clothing as campfires are not permitted. The persistent lack of sunlight also makes the canyon colder even than its surrounding desert environment. These are just a few things to keep in mind while scanning for the canyon's resident midget rattlesnakes on a trail once named in a list of the ten most dangerous hikes in the United States. **BDS**

⇨ Buckskin Gulch is an impressive slot canyon.

Queen's Garden Trail, Bryce Canyon Utah, USA

Start/End Sunrise Point
Distance 1.8 miles (2.9 km)
Time 2–2.5 hours   **Grade** Moderate
Type Mountain trails   **Map** goo.gl/DgOn5Z

The Queen's Garden Trail in Utah's Bryce Canyon takes you 320 feet (98 m) down into the canyon to a set of rock formations said to resemble Queen Victoria in her garden. There are two ways you can go, both starting and finishing at Sunrise Point. First you descend the side of canyon, then you can either turn around and go back the way you've just come, or you can carry on past a point on the canyon floor called Wall Street and climb up to Sunset Point on the other side. From here you can follow the trail around the rim of the canyon back to where you started.

"The trail is snowy in the early spring. The snow catches the morning light and reflects golden light."

www.everytrail.com

It's a short hike, but you'll need to be in decent physical shape before you start due to the steepness of the descent/ascent. One of the great and beguiling attractions of this trail are the changing perspectives of the canyon that confront you with virtually every step you take as you make your way toward the canyon floor. The rock formations you see around you are the hoodoos: tall stony spires that rise up from the sides and floor of the canyon. A good time to make the descent into the canyon is just before sunrise, with the help of a flashlight or headlamp. That way you'll be among the hoodoos as the sun comes up, adding an eerie element to the geological stage show that only Bryce Canyon can conjur. **JI**

Fisher Towers Trail Utah, USA

Start/End Trailhead parking lot
Distance 2.2 miles (3.5 km)
Time 4 hours   **Grade** Easy to moderate
Type Mountain trail   **Map** goo.gl/OU4aWc

Fisher Towers are a group of weathered pillars of mud-caked sandstone that stand 16 miles (25.5 km) from the town of Moab in Utah. The tallest of them, Titan, stands 900 feet (274 m) high. The pillars contain layers of sedimentary rock in different shades of red, brown, and even purple, and the lower sections are some 290 million years old with some of the towers still capped by huge rock slabs that fell from the cliffs above.

Fisher Towers Trail takes you on a 2.2-mile (3.5-km) trek past these stunning rock formations. It's not a difficult walk and it takes you along a well-kept trail,

"Moab is well known for bizarre geologic formations and Fisher Towers are some of the strangest."

climb-utah.com

but this is Utah and in summer the temperatures can soar around midday, so make an early start and be sure to carry enough water with you for the four-hour journey. There is a campsite and a picnic spot at the recreation area, but no drinking water. The Towers are popular with climbers so expect to see plucky souls scaling the rock walls. If they're directly above you, be wary of any falling stones or rocks. Also, take care during or after rain as rocks may have come loose. The Towers are stunning, with sheer vertical walls rising hundreds of feet above you. At some points of the walk you are quite high up, so you need a head for heights. This is a unique part of Utah that has been used as a film and TV location since the 1950s. **JI**

The Narrows, Zion National Park
Utah, USA

Start Temple of Sinawava, Zion Canyon Scenic Drive
End Chamberlain's Ranch   Distance 16 miles (25.7 km)
Time 2 days   Grade Easy to strenuous   Type Rock trail
Map goo.gl/OOXQ3Z

One of the must-do hikes on Utah's Colorado Plateau, The Narrows is the term given both to the thru-hike and to the section of vertical sandstone walls so beloved by walkers and photographers alike that tower up to 1,300 feet (400 m) above the confluence of the gorge and Deep Creek. In its top 100 list of the United States' greatest adventures, *National Geographic* magazine rated The Narrows number five.

Some two-thirds of the walking is done while immersed in the waters of the Virgin River, which lap from one side of the canyon to the other as it winds its way through 16 miles (25.7 km) of serpentine bends along its self-made gorge, past grottos and natural springs, and beneath hanging gardens of vibrant green. You may even have to swim some sections depending upon the weather, so be aware of flash-flooding and hypothermia. The current is a swift one; the rocks beneath the surface are as slippery as rocks can get, and the water can be chillingly cold. First walked in 1872 by the geologist Grove Gilbert, The Narrows of the North Fork of the Virgin River, to give it its full title, can be walked "top down" from the upper plateau starting at Chamberlain's Ranch, "down up," or "straight through." There are plenty of great little campsites along the way. Just remember to bring water-friendly, breathable footwear with toe protection.

For hikers the world over The Narrows has legendary status. Look out for bobcat, gray fox, ringtails, skunks, and eastern fence lizards. Swifts and woodpeckers can be seen in spring and sometimes in summer in a canyon guaranteed to cool you off even on the hottest Utah day. **BDS**

"... Unforgettable wilderness experience. However, it is not a hike to be underestimated."

www.nps.gov

⬆ Few U.S. trails are as "must-do" as this classic walk through the waters of the Virgin River.

Coyote Gulch Utah, USA

Start/End Water tanks on Fortymile Ridge Road   **Distance** 17 miles (27.3 km)   **Time** 8–10 hours, or overnight   **Grade** Moderate   **Type** Exposed sandstone, sand, creek bed   **Map** goo.gl/Rf5PPl

In a region that boasts many of the finest hikes to be found anywhere in the U.S. southwest, it is no mean feat when a hike is considered one of the region's favorites, but that is the mantle that Coyote Gulch, a tributary of the Escalante River in the midst of Utah's vast Grand Staircase-Escalante desert, proudly wears. The canyon's sandy stream bed, usually with a few inches of water that makes for some contented wading, also provides a favorable habitat for the many trees and plants that grow along the floor of the canyon, which most hikers prefer to access via the Crack-in-the-Wall, a narrow gap in the rocks near the trailhead on Fortymile Ridge Road.

It has everything—natural arches and bridges, narrow slot canyons, domes, and towering red rock walls up to 900 feet (274 m) high along a pretty strenuous route that requires overland navigation and rock scrambling, and is best done as an overnight hike. One of the first points of interest is the Jacob Hamblin Arch over Hamblin Wash, one of the loveliest spans in the country, and from there you'll want your waterproof shoes on as you wade through the stream's calf-deep waters, or just walk along its sandy banks until you reach Coyote Natural Bridge. There is also a must-do detour to Stephen's Arch, one of the largest in the nation with a span of 225 feet (68 m) and 160 feet (49 m) high and a great example of the spanning ability of Navajo sandstone. There are some lovely nooks on this hike, such as Dry Fork Narrows and Jug Handle Arch, and it is this very human scale, together with its stream and its often-shaded canyon floor, that make it such a memorable experience. **BDS**

⬆ A green oasis in the Grand Staircase-Escalante desert.

Delicate Arch Trail Utah, USA

Start/End Wolfe Ranch parking lot, Arches National Park **Distance** 3 miles (4.8 km) **Time** 2.5 hours
Grade Easy to moderate **Type** Desert trail, bare rock **Map** goo.gl/ba4RQW

Of all the sandstone arches that still stand against the march of "geologic deep time" across Arches National Park in Utah, none is more emblematic of these eroded symbols of the U.S. southwest than Delicate Arch. A geological "shrine" and one of the most photographed vistas on the Colorado Plateau this arch, once hidden in a sandstone fin, is a miracle of erosion. It even has its own postage stamp.

Although the trail is short and relatively straightforward, try and avoid doing it in the midday sun as there is no shade. It starts as a gravel path before beginning a steep climb along slickrock with great views of a striated mesa before leveling off onto a saddle sprinkled with pinyon pine and juniper. Cairns are now marking the route, and the final approach traverses a narrow rock ledge (that sounds worse than it actually is) and takes you by the rather unspectacular Frame Arch. There is more slickrock as you make your way to the viewpoint, which can make it a bit treacherous underfoot if it has been raining. With a little extra effort you can continue past the viewpoint and stand beneath the arch. Climbing it is not allowed, although marks that are consistent with the climbing technique known as "top roping" suggest that some have. Composed of Entrada Sandstone, Delicate Arch is a freestanding piece of natural sculpture without any of the flanking sandstone fins that help protect other arches here. With the background dominated by the symmetrical peaks of the La Sal Mountains, and the Cache Valley far below, there are few places in the southwest that are so easy to access, and yet so difficult to leave. **BDS**

⊡ Walk under North America's most famous natural arch.

The Maze
Utah, USA

Start/End North Point Road junction, or jet boat shuttle from Moab **Distance/Time** Various **Grade** Moderate to strenuous **Type** Bare rock **Info** goo.gl/QUPEUY

"Rarely do visitors spend less than three days in The Maze, and the area can easily absorb a week-long trip."

www.nps.gov

It is not unusual to find the labyrinth of this red rock jungle on a hiker's list of the "Ten Most Dangerous American Hikes." Located deep in Utah's Canyonlands National Park, it is a world of sandstone fins and interlaced dead-end canyons, with those that aren't dead ends looking the same as those that are. The fact that most of the hiking takes you down washes below ridgelines and cliff tops, denying you any visual vantage points that can help to determine where you are, does not help, either. Many of its canyons are so like the ones next to them that a topographic map is needed to tell them apart. Routes from mesa tops into canyons are cairned, but washes are often unmarked. In fact The Maze is virtually devoid of trails, has no real beginning or end once you are within it, and if you run out of water, what little water there is here frequently lies on the other side of all-but impassable topography.

Just getting to The Maze requires determination, being 50 miles (80 km) from the nearest paved road and only accessible by four-wheel drive down axel-busting roads. Permits are needed for an overnight stay and you will need one because it is simply too remote to do as a day trip. It was not until 1995 that a book detailing the fourteen natural arches The Maze was known to possess was published. Dozens more have since been catalogued.

For those who are not explorers at heart there are a few marked trails, including from the Doll's House to an overlook above the Colorado River, and the mile-long Maze Trail from the maze Overlook to the South Fork of Horse Canyon. These are lures tempting enough to bring out the canyon hopper in us all. **BDS**

⊼ This mesmerizing labyrinth of dead ends and mirror images is not for the inexperienced hiker.

Stewart Falls Trail
Utah, USA

Start/End Ranger Station (loop)
Distance 3.6 miles (5.8 km)
Time 1.5–3 hours **Grade** Easy to moderate
Type Dirt, gravel, and rock trail **Map** goo.gl/hZafvI

Stewart Falls is a 200-foot high (61 m) waterfall in northern Utah that drops down over two levels on the side of Mount Timpanogos. Even on a hot summer's day, the water is likely to be chilled and, if you want to, you can stand under the cascade and wash away the dust and grime you accumulated getting there. First however, you have to reach it, which involves a fairly short hike through fields and meadows, and then across the side of the mountain. As you get close to the falls, the trail drops to a rocky ridge that gives great views, not only of the waterfall but also of the valley beneath you.

There is another way to get there and that involves taking the chair lift from the Sundance Ski Area up to Ray's Summit before hiking down to Stewart Falls. The lift (used as a ski lift in winter) does give stunning views of Timpanogos. The going is pretty easy but you should wear appropriate clothing and check on the weather before you head out—it can get pretty hot in summer. Once you get to the falls you can allow yourself to get a soaking under the water. Beware though—this is melted snow from further up the mountain so it's going to be icy cold. Even the air down by the falls can be a lot colder than higher up on the trail. Once you've dried off, it's time to make the return hike.

The area around Stewart Falls is home to the Sundance Ski Resort, which has its own chalets. You are also well provided for on the camping front, and there are toilet facilities at the trailhead. This is one of the most beautiful spots in Utah, and the relatively relaxed walk combined with the stunning waterfall make it a popular destination for walkers. **JI**

"Stewart Falls is one of the most scenic and photogenic waterfalls in northern Utah. It falls in two tiers and is over 200 feet tall."

www.utah.com

⬆ If you like cold showers, you can stand in the glacial waters of Stewart Falls.

Albion Meadows Trail Utah, USA

Start/End Little Cottonwood Canyon Road   **Distance** 2 miles (3.2 km)   **Time** 3 hours
Grade Easy to moderate   **Type** Dirt track   **Map** goo.gl/ZDpXfT

An hour outside Salt Lake City in Utah is the mountain town of Alta, in Little Cottonwood Canyon. It's a great place to base yourself for walking and hiking in the area, which is a popular skiing spot in the winter. With the snow gone, the trails are surrounded by wildflower meadows and mountain streams.

The Albion Meadows Trail is one of the most popular in the Alta area. You have to share the dirt and gravel road with vehicles during summer but it's an easy enough hike. The trail itself is broken into Upper and Lower sections; the Lower trail has signs along the route explaining the history and wildlife in the area. The Upper Trail leads you to a campsite and to the Cecret Lake trailhead.

People come to Albion Meadows particularly to enjoy the spectacular wildflowers—an amazing 120 different species burst forth from mid-July to mid-August. There's also the Wasatch Wildflower Festival in late July. Even in summer you can still see snow glinting from the mountain tops. You can also see deer, mountain goats, and moose. The last are best observed from a distance as they can charge you if they feel threatened.

Utah is known for its thunderstorms so you need to be ready for changes in the weather. Thunder in this part of the world can be extreme and even deadly. The town of Alta itself is fairly quiet in the summer but there is a campsite at Albion Basin, although there's no power or running water. When you're out on the trail you'll be walking at high altitude so don't be surprised if you feel a little out of breath. Just take it steady though, and you will be fine. **JI**

⤒ The Albion Meadows Trail is a wildflower haven.

Devil's Garden Loop Utah, USA

Start/End Devil's Garden trailhead   **Distance** 8 miles (12.8 km)   **Time** 3–5 hours   **Grade** Easy
Type Dirt and rocky track   **Map** goo.gl/TjYLJZ

The Devil's Garden is part of the Arches National Park, near Moab in Utah. Erosion has worn away the ground to reveal large rocky projections that jut out of the earth. Some of these have been weathered to form arches and the Devil's Garden Loop takes in seven of these stony monoliths, with names such as Double O and Landscape Arch. There are shortened versions of the loop that take detours, but the full trail leads you to Dark Angel and Private Arch, which are as dramatic as they sound.

The trail itself is well maintained by the park authorities, but the going can be rocky and there's a bit of scrambling in places, along with a few narrow ledges to navigate. This is not the best hike to take when conditions are wet or snowy or hot. Remember this is Utah and you'll need to take extra water as there's nowhere along the route to refill your bottle,

although there are facilities at the trailhead. Devil's Garden is a popular spot for walkers. Arches National Park attracts a million visitors a year and Devil's Garden is one of its most popular hikes. It's best seen when it's not full of human traffic and you can fully appreciate the stunning landscape. There's a mixture of desert, canyons, and jaw-dropping stone formations. The trail isn't marked along its entire length, so you will need to keep your eyes peeled and watch out for the stone cairns that line the route.

On the accommodation front, Moab has plenty of hotels that cater for those planning a trek into Arches National Park. There are also campsites near Landscape Arch, but it is best to book these in advance as they fill up fast. **JI**

⊼ Loop around one of Arches NP's most popular trails.

Hayduke Trail
Utah/Arizona, USA

Start Arches National Park, Utah   **End** Kolob Canyon, Zion National Park, Utah   **Distance** 825 miles (1,328 km)
Time Up to 4 months   **Grade** Strenuous   **Type** Desert, sealed and unsealed roads   **Info** goo.gl/EC1Jxe

The Hayduke Trail should not be called a trail; to hike it is a feat of endurance on a wilderness route few have attempted and even fewer have finished. It begins in Utah, in Arches National Park near Moab, and twists a tortuous path through some of the most beautiful and rugged U.S. national parks—Canyonlands, Capitol Reef, Bryce Canyon, the Grand Canyon, and Zion—as well as many national forests. It was pieced together by hikers Joe Mitchell and Mike Coronella, who had completed a ninety-four-day trek in 1998 and a 101-day trek two years later, and was named in honor of George Washington Hayduke III, a character in Edward Abbey's novel *The Monkey Wrench Gang* (1975).

A mix of trail-less open desert and sealed roads, the Hayduke Trail has a water source, on average, just once every 20 miles (32 km), with one 38-mile (61-km) section from Yellowstone Mesa near Colorado City in Arizona to the East Fork of the Virgin River near Zion National Park in Utah completely dry. So make sure you have enough water. Appalled by the damage being done on those first pioneering treks as a result of oil exploration, damming, and overgrazing, Mitchell and Coronella now offer (expensive) hikes along the trail with a good percentage of the proceeds going to various environmental groups and a new foundation that promotes trail conservation.

The Hayduke Trail is a checklist of all the "must-see" sites on the Colorado Plateau, but conquering it requires resourcefulness and planning. It makes the Pacific Crest Trail and other signature trails look easy, it pays tribute to Abbey's own attempts at wilderness preservation, and it remains North America's most demanding walk. **BDS**

Wildcat Trail
Arizona, USA

Start/End Parking lot of Monument Valley's primitive campsite   **Distance** 3.1 miles (5 km)
Time 1.5–2 hours   **Grade** Easy to moderate
Type Rocky, desert trail   **Info** goo.gl/tFmRTi

The Wildcat Trail in the Navajo Tribal Park in Monument Valley is a 3.2-mile (5-km) loop around the magnificent Left Mitten, one of the valley's most iconic sandstone buttes and an symbol of the U.S. southwest. The left and right mittens are aptly named, every bit the shape that a mitten, eroded by wind and rain, could be. They are even properly oriented.

The trail enables visitors to get up close and personal to the edifice, which rises out of the desert in a region where much of the land is owned by the Navajo tribe, and where opportunities to walk on your own without a guide are highly restricted. Outside the boundaries of the Tribal Park you can walk unguided through areas that are not fenced, and the opportunities here are mind-boggling: Saddleback, King on his Throne, Castle Rock, Bear, Rabbit, and Stagecoach buttes form a 9 mile-long loop (14.5 km) over fairly level ground interrupted only by the occasional ravine and small cliff.

Your walk on the Wildcat Trail begins with a small descent from the trailhead to where you enter a wash and follow it before a sign points you onto the trail proper. A series of washes then takes you around the mitten and back to the beginning of the loop. You will pass through an interesting array of desert flora, including rabbitbrush, Russian thistle, prickly pear cactus, and narrowleaf yucca.

Remember it is hot and there is no shelter (and you are at 5,400 feet/1,646 m) so take plenty of water, but the good news is you may well find you are one of very few, if any, walking this lovely trail—most visitors prefer to do what Americans do best and drive the 17-mile (27.3-km) scenic route. **BDS**

Horseshoe Bend Trail
Arizona, USA

Start/End Horseshoe Bend trailhead off U.S. Hwy 89
Distance 1.5 miles (2.4 km)   **Time** 1.5 hours
Grade Easy   **Type** Sandstone and sandy paths
Map goo.gl/sEFuDg

Horseshoe Bend is the name given to this spectacular and much photographed bend in the Colorado River. The bend was created some five million years ago as the Colorado Plateau was in the midst of being uplifted, an event that resulted in the region's rivers becoming trapped in their own riverbeds and being forced into finding new, natural courses. Cutting its way through layer after layer of sandstone, the Colorado River carved the spectacularly unusual 270-degree bend seen today.

To reach the ridgeline where you can view this classic panorama, you start at the Horseshoe Bend trailhead just outside the town of Page, Arizona, and begin a small ascent up a sandy hill, which 200 million years ago was part of the largest system of sand dunes in North America, dunes that later hardened and went on to form the region's prolific deposits of Navajo sandstone that now stretch from Arizona all the way to Wyoming. When you reach the end of this very short trail not only will you be looking down from a height of 1,000 feet (305 m) off a cliff with no guardrails over a seriously dizzying layer of rock, but you will also have arrived at a fairly impressive juncture—a unique meeting place of culture and natural history with the vast Navajo Nation to your left, and to your right the mighty Colorado River, which flows on for 5 miles (8 km) toward Lake Powell in the Glen Canyon National Recreation Area.

The sand trail can make the going a little hard but as you approach the overlook the sand gives way to welcome bare rock. Remember to take water and sunscreen—although it is only a short walk, you'll be up there all day long. **BDS**

"Another of Mother Nature's little tricks ... that result in some of the weirdest, and neatest, formations."

www.travelsw.com

⬆ At Horseshoe Bend you can take your very own picture of the Colorado River's most famous curve.

Grand Canyon Rim Trail Arizona, USA

Start Pipe Creek Vista, East Rim Drive   **End** Hermits Rest   **Distance** 12 miles (19.3 km)   **Time** 6 hours
Grade Easy   **Type** Mostly paved road and gravel track   **Map** goo.gl/CriqsE

No matter how many times you have looked at photographs of the Grand Canyon, nothing prepares you for its awe-inspiring grandeur. This is nature on the broadest and most aged of scales, an epic slash in the ground carved out by the silver thread of the Colorado River far below you. You can walk into the canyon itself, but a far more leisurely approach is to walk along its southern rim and admire it from above.

Starting at Pipe Creek Vista, head west to Mather Point, the closest viewpoint from the park entrance and for many people their first sighting of the canyon itself. From here you walk on to Yavapai Point, where the glass observation platform lets you look straight down beneath your feet into the canyon. Not for the fainthearted, as the canyon is more than a mile deep here. On past Grandeur Point, from where you can see the entire Bright Angel Trail leading down to the canyon floor, to Maricopa, Powell, and Hopi Points. At Hopi Point you get some great views down to Salt Creek on one side and Monument Creek on the other. As the most northerly point jutting out into the canyon, this is where you get a great westerly view 20 miles (32 km) down the canyon. Mohave Point will also give you great views west, while the penultimate stop, at Pima Point, has panoramic views on all sides.

The Grand Canyon is best seen during those golden moments an hour after sunrise and an hour before sunset, when the light is low and the canyon walls present magnificent colors of red and orange. Hopi Point is the best spot for looking at the sunset, or Mohave or Powell Points if the former is too crowded. In truth, any view of the canyon is breathtaking. **SA**

⬆ Savor each moment on this mile-high rim trail.

White House Ruins Trail Arizona, USA

Start/End Trailhead of White House Ruins overlook   **Distance** 3 miles (4.8 km)   **Time** 2 hours
Grade Easy   **Type** Dirt trail   **Map** goo.gl/b9KpR3

The White House Ruins Trail is the only trail that takes you to the bottom of Canyon de Chelly National Monument on the edge of Arizona's Painted Desert without the need of a resident Navajo guide. And what a trail it is, starting at a trailhead on the canyon's rim before beginning its 600-foot (183-m) descent to the canyon floor along the edge of some steep drop-offs that provide plenty of inspiring views but are not for the fainthearted. In twenty minutes you are on the canyon floor and walking along the banks of an ankle-deep wash under the cool shade of abundant cottonwood trees until the sight of the 900-year-old ruins of the White House—a relic of the Anasazi (the "ancient ones")—in its spectacular setting under a sandstone overhang, stops you in your tracks. Begun in the late eleventh century, it spreads over two levels; the lower level containing forty-five to sixty rooms and four kivas (ritual rooms), and the upper level some 35 feet (10.6 m) above the canyon floor an additional twenty rooms. White plaster on the exterior of two of its rooms gives the ruin its name. Owned by the forty families of the Navajo Tribal Trust who live within its boundaries, Canyon de Chelly was called the "best unknown park in America" by *The New York Times*. You can feel almost alone here, or if you want a very real experience with the resident Navajo that is also possible. The monument encompasses 84,000 acres (34,000 ha) of Navajo land, the canyon is one of the southwest's most beautiful, and the trail and the White House—majestic as they are—are dwarfed by the soaring, streaked sandstone walls of this magnificent canyon. **BDS**

⬆ Majestic Anasazi ruins on the canyon floor.

Devil's Canyon Arizona, USA

Start/End Hackberry Creek   **Distance** 13 miles (21 km)   **Time** 6–8 hours   **Grade** Strenuous
Type Canyon trail   **Map** goo.gl/aA7BdH

The Devil's Canyon is an out-and-back trail involving constant scrambling to reach a downward swerve of layered swimming holes. It requires climbing equipment and at least one short swim. It starts to the east of the town of Superior, Arizona, at Hackberry Creek and proceeds along a streambed in the middle of a broad canyon. There is a precipice at one point where you can descend the 25 feet (7.6 m) drop by rope; alternatively, there is a way down on foot that involves only a 10-foot-drop (3 m) and a stepped series of rocks to the bottom.

Shortly afterward turn right into Devil's Canyon itself and follow the river downstream along an overgrown track. After 1.5 miles (2.5 km) you reach the highlight of the trip—the Five Pools—so named for the number of cascades that fall in sequence down to the lowest level. By the side of the first drop is a moored hand line on which you can lower yourself 10 feet (3 m) to the side of the first pool. From there, you will need to swim a short distance to the top of the second fall, which you can either slide down or descend to on foot by the path at the side. The second pool is the smallest, and the third is a 15-foot (4.5-m) drop from the second. The next drop is the biggest—60 feet (18 m)—and this needs to be abseiled. The effort is well rewarded by the fourth pool, the most picturesque of them all, and great for swimming, although the water can be chilly.

The fifth pool is not far below the fourth; it can be reached on foot along a path at the side. The return can be either the way you came or via a partial bypass back to the top of the biggest rappel. **GL**

⬆ Rock formations above the pools of Devil's Canyon.

Beamer Trail Arizona, USA

Start Little Colorado River/Colorado River confluence   **End** Tanner Rapids   **Distance** 9 miles (14.5 km)
Time 4 hours   **Grade** Easy to moderate   **Type** Sandy trails, rock ledges   **Map** goo.gl/2UPfZN

Tucked into a sandstone cliff overhang above Arizona's Little Colorado River is Beamer's Cabin, a tiny piece of man-made Grand Canyon history. Built long ago by Pueblo Indians, its rear wall and part of its ceiling are pure rock, but much of the rest of what was little more than a ruin was remodeled, stone by stone, by one of the pioneering Grand Canyon miners, Ben Beamer, who came to the canyon in the 1890s looking for gold and silver. Like many he had to content himself with asbestos and copper, and selling horses to early Mormon pioneers. He may not have become a wealthy miner, but he helped to create the basis for a lasting network of trails, including the Tanner Trail, a coarse grained path he hammered out of the earth connecting his old Pueblo cliff home to Palisades Creek, and the beginnings of what became known as Horsethief Trail, used by some of the canyon's more nefarious residents for less than honorable pursuits.

The trail is named in honor of Beamer and is located near where the Little Colorado joins the main branch of the Colorado at the threshold of the "Great Unknown." The scenery is stupendous—4,000 feet (1,219 m) straight up to the surrounding rims at the confluence of two great canyon systems, and the section of trail between Palisades Creek and the Tanner Trail passes some of the oldest sedimentary rocks in the region—the Grand Canyon Supergroup. The little-used trail varies from an easy walk along sandy slopes to a nerve-racking, step-by-step shuffle along the narrow, exposed edges of very high cliffs, a walk Beamer surely would have relished. **BDS**

⬆ Rocky sandstone slopes on the way to Palisades Creek.

Black Canyon of the Yellowstone Trail Montana/Wyoming, USA

Start/End Hellroaring/Blacktail trailheads   Distance 16.5 miles (26.5 km)   Time 1 day
Grade Moderate to strenuous   Type Woodland path   Map goo.gl/HNYpHq

The Black Canyon is the second largest canyon along the Yellowstone River, a remote stretch of the river that can be accessed only by backpackers. Predictably, the scenery is wild, the wildlife even more so, making this one-day trek in the north of the Yellowstone National Park a substantial adventure.

Leaving the evocatively named Hellroaring trailhead, the track drops steeply in a series of switchbacks to the Yellowstone River below. As you descend you look out across the long, sloping hillside of the Buffalo Plateau as it climbs toward the northern border of the national park and Hellroaring Mountain. A large steel footbridge takes you over the turbulent Yellowstone toward the base of the plateau. Our trail is now on the other side of Hellroaring Creek, which can be crossed when its waters are low. Otherwise, you have to make a 3.7-mile (5.9-km) diversion up the creek to the

northeast to cross via a wooden bridge and return on the opposite bank.

Once on Yellowstone Trail, you head west along the river, catching glimpses of it from rocky outcrops. Pronghorn antelope and elk amble around the plateau. At one point a pair of elk antlers has become completely embedded in the trunk of a tree, which now totally envelops it. At this point, the trail runs through stands of pine trees and open meadows, slowly moving downhill toward the river itself. Near the end of the trail you cross the Yellowstone over the Blacktail Suspension Bridge and climb south up Blacktail Deer Creek to the trailhead. While this trail can be done in one day, there are many campsites en route, making it ideal for a two-day expedition. **SA**

⬆ **Hike the Yellowstone River beneath Buffalo Plateau.**

Lee Metcalf National Wildlife Refuge Trail Montana, USA

Start Lee Metcalf National Wildlife Refuge   **Distance** 2.5 miles (4 km)   **Time** 1 hour   **Grade** Easy
Type Wooden boardwalk and paths   **Map** goo.gl/XsX2lg

Lee Metcalf was a U.S. representative and senator for Montana with a lifelong commitment to conservation, and the 2,800-acre (1,100-ha) wildlife refuge in Stevenson, Montana, established in 1963 was later named in his honor. It provides a habitat for migratory birds along the meandering Bitterroot River with its numerous ponds, marshes, streams, and water meadows. Around 2.5 miles (4 km) of nature trails give bird-lovers a great view of their feathered friends, and the trail includes a 0.5-mile (0.8-km) wheelchair-accessible section.

Despite the vast amount of water in the refuge, the area receives only 12 inches (30 cm) of rainfall a year. Luckily, the runoff from the Sapphire Mountains to the east and the Bitterroots to the west—both of which are clearly visible from the refuge—keep the area well irrigated. Birds present will depend on the season you visit, though year-round residents are seasonally joined by summer breeders and spring and fall migrants. To date, 238 species of migratory birds have been documented visiting the refuge. Resident trumpeter swans lurk in the ponds, along with gadwalls, hooded mergansers, and western grebes. Sharp-skinned hawks and northern harriers live in the meadows, with warbles, kinglets, owls, and woodpeckers in the woods. Wood ducks, ospreys, and bald eagles make their nest here, while flocks of Canada geese soar overhead. One lucky visitor once saw a great horned owl glide past with a snake dangling from its beak. Muskrats, white-tailed deer, and other animals live happily alongside the birds in this haven for the United States' wild fauna. **SA**

⬆ **Walk the Bitterroot River's refuge for migratory birds.**

Cascade and Grebe Lakes Trail Wyoming, USA

Start/End Cascade Lake Trail picnic area
Distance 5 miles (8 km)   **Time** 2 hours
Grade Easy   **Type** Meadows
Map goo.gl/Kw3YiH

Yellowstone National Park in Wyoming has more than 1,100 miles (1,770 km) of hiking trails, everything from hour-long loops to mountain traverses, and deciding which one or how many to attempt when visiting the jewel in the crown of the U.S. National Parks system can be a daunting experience. If a short walk is what's needed, then why not head for the peaceful meadows and lakeshores that surround Cascade and Grebe lakes. You connect to the path proper about a mile after leaving the picnic area. It takes you through expansive open spaces to the shores of this pretty

---

"Grebe Lake is a popular destination for day hikers, backpackers, and fishermen."

www.trailguidesyellowstone.com

---

lake, ringed on three sides by trees and full of cutthroat trout and grayling. It is a perfect spot for fly casting into its 36 acres (14.5 ha), and it is quite deep. The trail to Grebe Lake is on the Howard Eaton Trail, and it too has a reputation as a premier fly casting spot, chock-full of rainbow trout and grayling. The preponderance of fish also attracts birds, in particular ospreys, pelicans, and grebes, hence the lake's name. Circumnavigating Grebe Lake can be awkward because of its extensive marshes along its western shoreline, but once you've found yourself a comfortable spot for casting, you can sit back and marvel at Yellowstone from an uncommonly tranquil and wonderfully tourist-free perspective. **BDS**

Colorado Front Range Trail Colorado, USA

Start Wyoming border   **End** New Mexico border
Distance 876 miles (1,410 km)   **Time** 8–10 weeks
Grade Moderate   **Type** Paved, soft surface pathway
Info goo.gl/dPIwcC

The Colorado Front Range is a range of the Southern Rocky Mountains that runs north to south from central Colorado, north into Wyoming, and rises up to 10,000 feet (3,048 m) above the Great Plains to the east. It includes some of the state's famous mountains, such as Pikes Peak and Mount Evans. The Colorado Front Range Trail is a vision-in-progress, a collaboration between Colorado State Parks, the Colorado Front Range Trail project, and communities across Colorado to create what will become an 876-mile (1,410-km) trail across fourteen counties along the Front Range from Wyoming to New Mexico.

When finished, two-thirds of the trail will be paved, making it ideal for cycling, inline skating, and wheelchairs, and the terrain it crosses will vary from ranches, mining sites, state parks, farms, and swathes of mountainous landscape, all the way from its more populated northern sections around Denver and Fort Collins to the open spaces in the south, including the San Isabel National Forest and small rural towns, such as Lathrop and Trinidad.

Occasionally the trail will diverge along two or more separate routes to provide various recreational pursuits. It will follow creeks where possible, such as Fountain, Monument, Plum, and Cherry creeks, in its middle section from the town of Pueblo to Colorado Springs, and will offer various loop trails into the adjacent plains. Conceptual trails are still being worked out and much needs to be done, but with the support the trail has already generated throughout Colorado's disparate communities this ambitious trail is destined to be a stunning testament to the state's ongoing love affair with the great outdoors. **BDS**

Grizzly Creek Trail
Colorado, USA

Start/End Grizzly Creek, off Interstate 70
Distance 6.8 miles (10.9 km)   **Time** 5 hours
Grade Moderate   **Type** Track, rock scree, and bush
Map goo.gl/6LW7kI

Glenwood Canyon is a 12.5-mile-long (20.1 km) canyon on the upper Colorado River—the largest such canyon on the upper river with walls up to 1,300 feet (396 m) high. Five miles (8 km) along the canyon from the town of Glenwood Springs on the north side is the aptly titled Grizzly Creek Canyon, named for George P. Ryan who, in the 1880s, killed the largest grizzly bear ever seen in Colorado, somewhere up the canyon. The creek is still full of wildlife, although you will mostly hear songbirds and see butterflies and the odd mule deer or squirrel rather than hear the threatening sounds of a grizzly on the prowl.

The trail starts easily enough, gently rising up alongside the creek. It gets steeper around the 1.8-mile (2.9-km) point and then at 2 miles (3.2 km) rises at its steepest for the next mile and a half. The creek, which had disappeared from view for a time, now reappears close to the trail in a series of medium-sized waterfalls, one of which crosses the trail itself. Look out for cairns on the other side to guide you across. Up ahead you will see the diversion intake for Glenwood Springs's water supply.

Once you can see the pipe, the trail is almost at its finish; a few turns later and it has all but gone. To hike up to the diversion dam, you need to cross a lengthy scree field. The easiest route across actually climbs up the hill away from the creek. Look out for more cairns to guide you across the scree. Once across, there is a small clearing that leads up to the dam. If you get the season right, you can enjoy the splendid views and the wild raspberries, a much needed refreshment before you turn back down the trail again. **SA**

"The rims of Glenwood Canyon are capped by Mississippi and Pennsylvanian limestone."

www.gjsentinel.com

⊡ Hike a former grizzly habitat, now home to mule deer and songbirds, in Colorado's canyonlands.

South Rim Trail, Roxborough State Park Colorado, USA

Start/End South Rim parking lot   **Distance** 3 miles (4.8 km)   **Time** 1 hour 40 minutes   **Grade** Easy
Type Mountain trail   **Map** goo.gl/kP6h2b

One of the best things about living in Denver is its backyard. Just 25 miles (40 km) from the city is Roxborough State Park, a 3,000-acre (1,214-ha) area of sandstone spires, monoliths, and hogbacks rising from a green valley floor in the foothills of the Rocky Mountains. Several trails cross the park, linking particularly quirky rock formations and the haunts of bear, elk, and mule deer. The South Rim Trail, an easy hike looping the southern end of the park, presents a grandstand view of the whole. Come on a summer morning, when the intense red of the rock is set off by deep-blue skies, or in the late afternoon when the rock positively glows, though winter snow, spring flowers, and fall color also show off the rocks beautifully. You can admire the show from the benches dotted along the trail. Look up and you may see a golden eagle riding the thermals.

A day pass (no overnight stays are allowed) is obtained at the entrance to the park, where signs point the way to the trailheads. From the South Rim parking lot, the trail doubles up with Willow Creek Trail, crossing a grassy valley for the first 0.25 mile (0.4 km) and then climbing up to the ridge. Here, a geological sculpture park unfolds, with the red crests of 300-million-year-old sandstone tilting at a 60-degree angle.

For a more challenging hike, climb to Carpenter Peak, the highest point in the park at 7,160 feet (2,182 m), with the possibility of extending into the Douglas County Trail System via the Elk Valley Link. From Carpenter's summit, you can see the Dakota Hogback and the smudgy outline of Denver's downtown high-rises ranged along the horizon. **DS**

⬆ The views on the trail are beautiful in winter.

Bandelier National Monument Trail New Mexico, USA

Start/End Various, visitor center is one option   Distance Various   Time Various
Grade Easy to strenuous   Type Mountain trail   Info goo.gl/DiWUE7

Carved by the Rio de los Frijoles (Bean Creek) and sculpted by wind, this canyon leading to the Rio Grande has unusual rock formations and impressive views, but it's the human impact on the landscape that draws visitors—cliff palaces scooped out of the tufa cliffs more than 900 years ago by ancestral Pueblo peoples known to the Navajo as Anasazi. Elaborate cave dwellings, some multiple stories high and intended for several hundred people, riddle the 50-square-mile (129-sq-km) national park. In addition to these large man-made holes, the rock is pitted by "bubbles" caused by pockets of gas trapped in the volcanic tufa a million years ago, which gives the whole canyon a vaguely lunar feel.

Some 70 miles (113 km) of trails twist through the canyon. They range from the paved 1-mile (1.6-km) Main Loop Trail from the visitor center, a popular but evocative taster that takes in a variety of structures and petroglyphs in Frijoles Canyon (look out for images of turkeys, which the Anasazi raised) to very strenuous trails lasting several days and starting from different points around the rim. Heavy flooding over recent years has reconfigured some trails, so check on their status before setting out. Permits must be obtained for overnight stays.

Among Bandelier's more immersive backcountry trails are the 13-mile (20.9-km) Yapashi loop trail and the two-day, 22-mile (35.4-km) Painted Cave Trail, named for its cave art. Climbing in and out of canyons and crossing flat mesas, they take in wide views and ancient structures, and offer the possibility of spotting coyotes, mule deer, and elk (winter only). **DS**

⬆ Discover ancient caves in this New Mexico canyon.

Tent Rocks Trail
New Mexico, USA

Start/End Bureau of Land Management parking lot, off FR266   **Distance** 2 miles (3.2 km)
Time 1–2 hours   **Grade** Easy   **Type** Gravel paths
Map goo.gl/pv7g1t

Set within the Kasha-Katuwe Tent Rocks National Monument in north-central New Mexico, the Tent Rocks Trail takes you into the midst of a giant, open-air laboratory filled with remarkable cone-shaped rock formations, canyons, arroyos, and cliff faces streaked with lines of link and beige-colored rock, all the product of volcanic activity from the Jemez volcanic field seven million years ago, when vast amounts of pumice, ash, and tuff were deposited over the Pajarito Plateau. Even now when walking this fascinating trail you can see the telltale signs of this ancient event— tiny fragments of translucent obsidian (volcanic glass) still glistening in the soil.

The monument, located 40 miles (64.3 km) southwest of the state capital of Santa Fe, ranges in height from 5,570 feet (1,698 m) to 6,760 feet (2,060 m), and it has long been a sacred place for the Pueblo de Cochiti tribe, who named the area Kasha-Katuwe, which means "white cliffs." Archaeological surveys have traced human habitation here back almost 4,000 years, and to this day descendants of the Pueblo de Cochiti tribe still live in the surrounding area.

There are two trails within the monument, one that takes you into the canyon and another that takes you along an adjacent ridge so you can gaze down and marvel at the sheer complexity of it all. If you walk to the viewpoint first, you can then backtrack into the mouth of the canyon and its broad amphitheater, where the distinctive tent-shaped rocks rise up all about you. Some of the tent rocks reach as high as 90 feet (27 m). Eventually the caprock will be undermined and the rocks will topple, but that won't happen any time soon. **BDS**

"The complex landscape and spectacular geologic scenery … have been a focal point for visitors for centuries."

www.blm.gov

⬅ The white cliffs of Tent Rocks are the remnants of a seven-million-year-old eruption.

⬆ Tent Rocks' porous tufa is pockmarked with caves.

Catwalk National Scenic Trail
New Mexico, USA

Start/End Whitewater picnic area, 5 miles (8 km) northeast of Glenwood **Distance** 1 mile (1.6 km) **Time** 45 minutes **Grade** Easy **Type** Steel walkway **Info** goo.gl/9Z9BII

"The ruins of the mill still cling to the canyon walls overlooking the picnic area."

www.americantrails.org

On June 3, 1924, the world's first officially designated wilderness area was created—the Gila Wilderness in southwestern New Mexico. Its 872 square miles (2,258 sq km) encompass the East, West, and Middle Forks of the Gila River, as well as forests of ponderosa pine, aspen, and spruce-fir and pinyon-juniper woodlands. It has its predators (cougars and bobcats), its mammals (gray fox and black bears), and its reptiles (Gila monsters and Arizona coral snakes). It also has a seemingly endless choice of recreational pursuits, including horseback riding, fishing, and hundreds of miles of trails that you can access from any of its fifty-plus trailheads. One of the wilderness's most popular trails is also one of its oldest—the Catwalk Trail.

Built in 1930 by the Civilian Conservation Corps (CCC), a public relief program established to give work to unemployed, unmarried men in the wake of the Great Depression, the Catwalk Trail is a hanging walkway trail that follows the path of an old gravity-fed water pipeline that was laid down in 1893 through Whitewater Canyon, 20 feet (6 m) above the canyon floor to bring water to a long-since abandoned ore processing plant. The pipeline originally had plank boards over it and the men who built it dubbed it the "catwalk," and the name stuck. The hanging walkway made by the CCC was rebuilt in 1961, and today this impressive piece of engineering remains ideally placed, allowing access to a number of trails that spread out across the Gila Wilderness.

The town of Whitewater no longer exists, but the walls of Whitewater Canyon are just as high now as they were in 1893. And the Catwalk Trail can still take you there. **BDS**

⬆ A catwalk built to maintain a 100-year-old water pipeline is now a unique scenic trail.

Capulin Volcano Rim Trail
New Mexico, USA

Start/End Parking lot at the top of the crater
Distance 1 mile (1.6 km)   **Time** 30 minutes
Grade Easy   **Type** Mountain trail
Map goo.gl/ieotAh

As government inspector H. D. Harlan of the General Land Office said in 1890, Capulin Volcano is a "natural curiosity"—a solitary cinder cone in the flat, desert scrub of northeastern New Mexico. In fact, the volcano lies in the Rayton–Clayton volcanic field, and there are numerous, though less obvious, volcanic features in the landscape. The other volcanoes in the area have lost their cones and now look like flat-topped mesas. Harlan also described Capulin as "the most perfect specimen of extinct volcanoes in North America," helping to prevent it from passing into private hands and thus saving it from mining and drilling. U.S. president Woodrow Wilson declared it a National Monument in 1916, paving the way for tourism, and over the next fifty years the extinct volcano acquired an access road to its rim, a visitor center, and trails.

The near symmetrical cone rises 1,000 feet (304 m) from the plain. The 1-mile (1.6-km) trail, a paved but undulating path with some sharp climbs and dips, circles the crater. Signs along the way point out other volcanic features in the surrounding landscape, as well as views of five states—New Mexico, Colorado, Oklahoma, Texas, and Kansas—and the snowcapped peaks of the Sangre de Cristo Mountains in the distance. An additional 0.2-mile (300-m) vent trail descends inside the crater, which is now filled with shrubs and trees. Solid magma plugs the volcano's central vent, dating from the eruption that created the cinder cone 56,000 to 62,000 years ago. Mule deer, named for their tall ears, wild turkeys, and occasional pronghorn graze the crater's slopes, while a startling number of ladybugs swarm here in their millions in summer, at times turning whole shrubs red. **DS**

"Whichever way you look from the Crater Rim Trail, you'll enjoy stunning views."

trailsnet.com

⬆ A volcanic cinder cone rises out of the pancake-flat landscape of northeast New Mexico.

Pueblo Alto Trail Loop over Chaco Canyon New Mexico, USA

Start/End Pueblo del Arroyo parking lot   Distance 5.4 miles (8.7 km)   Time 4 hours   Grade Easy
Type Rock, gravel path   Map goo.gl/2UZ25f

The Hopi call it Yupkoyvi ("place beyond the horizon") and there is nothing like it anywhere in North America—the ruins of a series of pueblos surrounded by traditional villages belonging to the Chaco Anasazi, a culture that blossomed in the Chaco Plateau of northwestern New Mexico in the tenth century and grew to as many as 400 settlements with a population as high as 5,000. They used new approaches to masonry, with walls of rubble cores and exteriors of smooth, shaped stones that allowed them to construct four-story buildings. The Chaco culture was sophisticated and highly organized, the hub of an economic system that traded over a vast area of the southwest and then, coinciding with a prolonged drought in the mid-twelfth century, disappeared. The Chaco Anasazi left behind North America's largest group of pre-Columbian ruins, including Pueblo

Bonito, the largest Great House (built 828–1126) that once contained over 650 rooms more than two sections with massive masonry walls.

To obtain an inspiring view over Pueblo Bonito and the surrounding canyon, you can climb the Pueblo Alto Trail, a loop that takes you to the top of the mesa overlooking the ruins, a relatively straightforward climb that involves only the occasional necessity to squeeze your way between boulders and cliff. Once at the top and after having your senses blown away by the scale of the place, which is only fully appreciated by gazing down on it, continue along the trail to the prehistoric ruins of Pueblo Alto: another Great House, although tiny compared to the unique grandeur of Pueblo Bonito. **BDS**

⊤ Get a bird's-eye view of North America's greatest ruins.

North Country National Scenic Trail New York to North Dakota, USA

Start Crown Point, New York   **End** Lake Sakawkawea State Park, North Dakota   **Distance** 4,600 miles (7,403 km)
Time 6–8 mths   **Grade** Strenuous   **Type** Variable   **Info** goo.gl/VI7jKR

The North Country National Scenic Trail (NCT) is designed for dipping into rather than hiking end-to-end, though a small number of backpackers have done just that and some regular users spend their vacations completing consecutive sections. The longest of the country's eleven national scenic trails, the NCT passes through seven states—New York, Pennsylvania, Ohio, Michigan, Wisconsin, Minnesota, and North Dakota. It links state parks and national forests, and crosses private land. Optional detours to historic/cultural sites add interest. Volunteers have helped clear, build, and maintain the trail, parts of which are still being created. It's said that 40 percent of Americans live within a day's drive of the trail.

Kicking off in the lakes and peaks of the Adirondacks, the trail leads onto the wine country of Finger Lakes, taking in canals and beauty spots, as well as sites connected with the Revolutionary War. Pennsylvania brings bear-populated Allegheny National Forest and Moraine State Park, while Ohio focuses on Beaver Creek State Park and the Buckeye Trail. In Michigan, the route takes the Manistee River Trail and hugs the shoreline of Lake Michigan, and in Wisconsin it passes through the Chequamegon Forest and the Penokee Mountains. Minnesota takes the trail through designated wilderness to the Canadian border and then down to the Mississippi headwater, from where it heads into North Dakota's prairies, forests, and ghost towns. The scenic highlights are many, but the NCT is as much about experiencing festivals, local food, and different ways of life as it is about capturing exhilarating views. **DS**

⊡ **Dip your toes in North America's longest scenic trail.**

Cathedral Spires Trail
South Dakota, USA

Start/End Trailhead east of Sylvan Lake on Needles Hwy (SD 87/89) **Distance** 3 miles (4.8 km) **Time** 2 hours **Grade** Moderate **Type** Rocky path **Map** goo.gl/vUSuHM

Over millions of years, some of the granite Black Hills of South Dakota became eroded into the pillars, towers, and spires of rock known as the Needles. The group of nine needles at the far east of the region is known as Cathedral Spires, an obvious name for anyone who has ever seen a Gothic cathedral. Interestingly, the Needles were once proposed as the original site for the Mount Rushmore carvings, but were rejected by sculptor Gutzon Borglum because their granite was too poor and thin. Their escape from a dynamite and chiseled fate has spared them for

> "This moderately strenuous spur trail is a great natural history trek."

www.trails.com

enjoyment by walkers and climbers. Once you've paid the entrance fee to enter Custer State Park, where the Spires are located, and parked at the trailhead, the trail leads you uphill at quite a pace through forests of ponderosa pines and wildflower meadows. Once across Iron Creek you head up to circle the Spires themselves. At the end of the trail there are no magnificent views over countryside, as you are standing at the base of the Spires looking up at their great height. Many of the pine trees have been cut down because of pine beetle, allowing you wonderful views of the Spires and the intrepid mountaineers scaling their heights. Once you've had your fill, turn around and head down to trailhead base. **SA**

Buffalo Gap National Grassland South Dakota, USA

Start/End No official trails **Distance** Various **Time** Various **Grade** Easy **Type** Dirt roads, grassland **Info** goo.gl/TzNcsg

Buffalo Gap National Grassland is a huge area of classic prairie wilderness where buffalo once roamed in enormous herds. The buffalo have long gone but the grasslands are still there, forming an unspoiled, natural environment. This 925-square-mile (2,395-sq-km) corner of South Dakota is now a protected national resource.

It is mostly flat, open land, with big skies and distant horizons, and a few streams with scatterings of trees. At first it seems windswept and bleak, but the closer you look, the more hidden variety you discover. Wildlife includes coyotes and prairie dogs, hundreds of wildflowers and, of course, around fifty species of grasses. It is popular for all sorts of outdoor activities, from fossil hunting to fishing.

Hikers have free range to wander anywhere across the grasslands and over the more rugged surrounding areas, the "badlands." There are no established walking trails. There are no settlements either, and it is an area that few travelers pass through. Today's hikers either follow one of the few old two-track dirt roads or simply set off across the open prairie. Wherever you go, there are no particularly challenging conditions or dangers. Unrestricted camping is permitted, but you'll have to carry everything you need with you as there are no facilities. Remember to take your own water supply, and campfires must be treated carefully to avoid starting a grass fire that could spread rapidly because of the park's constant winds. The Indian Creek area near the heart of Buffalo Gap National Grassland is the favored area for wild walking. This is a trackless 24,000 acres (9,712 ha) of emptiness—a true wilderness experience waiting to be discovered. **SH**

George S. Mickelson Trail
South Dakota, USA

Start Edgemont   End Deadwood
Distance 110 miles (177 km)   Time 8 days
Grade Moderate   Type Stone and gravel trails
Info goo.gl/NDKfyN

Championed by South Dakota's two-term governor George S. Mickelson during his successful 1986 political campaign, the stone and gravel trail that bears his name weaves its way through the state's Black Hills. Sadly, he died in 1993 before he could see his vision fully realized. It showcases, almost at every turn, everything that the thick pine forests of this impressive range of mountains is known for—gold-panned creeks, prairie grass, evergreen forests, pinnacle rocky canyons, spruce forests, high desert, and mining towns. Virtually the entire trail follows an abandoned railway branch line built in 1890–91 by the Chicago, Burlington and Quincy Railroad, which abandoned its Black Hills line in 1983.

From the northern beginnings of the Black Hills through until it spills out upon the southern prairies, South Dakota's first rails-to-trails project's fifteen trailheads provide access to a rollercoaster ride along steepsided granite valleys, through four old railroad tunnels that were restored by the U.S. Forest Service, and more than 100 converted trestle bridges along a "civilized" grade that never exceeds 4 percent, although if you choose to walk south to north the segment from Dumont to Deadwood is considered strenuous, climbing some 1,600 feet (487 m) in 15 miles (24.1 km). Wildlife along the way includes bighorn sheep and pronghorn antelope, and even mountain lions have been sighted in increasing numbers in recent years along a trail that climbs its way from south to north. If you want to take it a little easier you can always start at Deadwood and from there it's all downhill until you reach the vast bison herds of Custer State Park. **BDS**

"Imagine a path where the ghosts of Wild Bill Hickok and Calamity Jane still roam … "

gfp.sd.gov

⬆ No trail shows off the beauty of the Black Hills quite like this one.

Castle Trail South Dakota, USA

Start Door and Window Trails parking area (eastern terminus)   **End** Fossil Exhibit Trail (western terminus)
Distance 10 miles (16 km)   **Time** 5 hours   **Grade** Moderate   **Type** Rock and soil trails   **Map** goo.gl/uYP2Gw

The longest-maintained trail in South Dakota's Badlands National Park, the Castle Trail traces a line along the northern edge of the Badland Wall weaving its way through a world of precipitous spires, sod tables, fins, and buttes—a world that may appear rock-like but is, in fact, little more than a fragile composition of soil, clay, and ash, susceptible to the erosive whims of wind and water.

Starting east at the Door and Windows trailhead and heading west, you cross open prairie before entering a series of rugged gullies cut by the forces that give the Badlands their ethereal quality. After a mile and a half you reach Medicine Root Trail at which point you bear left onto Castle Trail, which takes you along the Badland Wall, the rugged ridgeline on top of which Native Americans once stood and scanned the horizon for bison herds and approaching white men. It is a trail with very few if any difficult segments, although it is a steep and strenuous (but short) climb up to Saddle Pass and its wonderful views out over the White River Valley and a veritable sea of mixed-grass prairies.

The final section passes through a landscape of carved buttes and a series of dry washes that will bring you out along a not-too-well marked area of rolling mud hills where a little intuition won't be out of place in helping you find your way to the end of the trail at the Fossil Exhibit trailhead. There a final walk along the Fossil Exhibit Loop Trail, with its interpretive signs shedding light on the area's natural history and the ancient peoples who once lived here, is the perfect end to a dramatic, compact walk. **BDS**

⬆ **Walk an easy trail along the Badland Wall.**

Flint Hills Nature Trail Kansas, USA

Start Herington   End Osawatomie trailhead   Distance 120 miles (193 km)   Time 10 days
Grade Easy   Type Crushed limestone rail trail   Info goo.gl/plOuKM

The Flint Hills Nature Trail is the result of a "rails-to-trails" program in northeast Kansas that takes hikers through one of the few intact regions of tallgrass prairie remaining in the United States. The trail follows the old Missouri–Pacific rail line built by the Council Grove, Osage City, and Ottawa Railway in 1886. It passes through seven counties and a host of rural Midwest communities, and crosses over the fabulous Flint Hills, named after the deposits of residual flint laid down 250 million years ago, when much of Kansas was at the bottom of a shallow inland sea. The tall grass is at its most extensive near the trail's start at Herington and becomes more wooded the closer it gets to the town of Osawatomie.

The trail is the seventh longest rail-to-trail project in the country and is a segment of the American Discovery Trail, the nation's first coast to coast trail. The trail, which also bisects long tracts of woodland, is home not only to the tallgrass that once covered the western United States in a vast unbroken ocean of green, but also to an array of prairie plant life and wildlife, including bobcats, wild turkeys, and bobwhite quails. The trail is a quiet one, with several segments more than 6 miles (9.6 km) from the nearest public road, and it is wide as well, with the right of way often 300 to 600 feet (91–182 m) either side of what is an easy underfoot surface of fine, crushed limestone that has also been laid over all of the trail's old railroad bridges. Managed by the Kanza Rails-Trails Conservancy since 1995, when it acquired the land and began its transformation, the trail is the longest privately managed rail trail in the United States. **BDS**

⊼ Immerse yourself in this tallgrass prairie.

Lost Maples State Park
Texas, USA

Start/End Various   **Distance** Various
Time Various   **Grade** Easy to strenuous
Type Well-maintained forest trails
Info goo.gl/rfPUfa

"When conditions are right, the maple leaves put on a dazzling show of fall colors."

wildtexas.com

Lost Maples State Park is 5 miles (8 km) north of Vanderpool in Texas and opened to the public in 1979. Covering an area of more than 2,000 acres (800 ha) it received its name from the Bigtooth maple trees that were discovered here a long way from the nearest maple forests—hence "lost maples." There are also American sycamore, Texas red oak, black willow, and many more tree varieties within the park. These trees (specifically their leaves) form one of the main attractions for Lost Maples State Park. In fall the color change in the leafy canopy is so striking that people come from miles around to bask in the golden and red glow, so be prepared for crowds and consider pre-booking a camping spot. The peak foliage color is during the last two weeks of October and first two weeks of November. But all year-round the park is a popular spot with hikers, walkers, campers, and anglers, as are the 11 miles (18 km) of trails within its boundaries some of which are quite deliberately primitive (by U.S. standards at least) as development within the park is strictly controlled and limited. There are also two small lakes at the heart of the park where you can take a cooling swim. One of the more popular hiking routes is the 4-mile (6.4-km) Maple Trail that runs alongside the Sabinal River. This is pretty easy going while other routes, such as the East Trail and West Trail, are steep and rocky. Wherever you go, stick to the designated trails as footfall damages the shallow roots of the trees. There is plenty of wildlife to admire as you walk, including raccoon, bobcats, and armadillos.

Whether you come for the fall leaves or at any other time of the year, Lost Maples State Park offers great hiking, Texas style. JI

⬆ Aptly named, Lost Maples is far removed from the great maple forests of the Appalachians.

Outer Mountain Loop, Big Bend Texas, USA

Start/End Chisos Basin   **Distance** 30 miles
(48 km)   **Time** 5 days   **Grade** Strenuous
Type Rock, dirt, and stone trails
Map goo.gl/qmcwCB

You know you're in for a challenge when signs at the start of a trail warn you that previous walkers have died of dehydration along the route. Then again, the Outer Mountain Loop in Big Bend National Park is no ordinary jaunt. The "bend" in question is a wide, sweeping curve taken by the Rio Grande River, the border between Texas and Mexico, while the mountain refers to the Chisos Mountains around which the trail runs.

Speak to anyone who's done this multi-day challenge and the first thing they'll mention is water. There are few places along this route to refill water bottles; the Rio Grande is too polluted to be of much use and many of the streams and springs around the mountains are dry for much of the year. The only thing to do is carry your own supply and it's recommended that each hiker carries a minimum of one gallon per day. The key is caching: planning ahead and storing supplies of water at key points on the loop. At the end of Juniper Canyon Road and at the Blue Creek Ranch there are storage boxes where you can place your bottles (marked with name and date of collection).

The walk itself takes you into the heart of the Chisos Mountains and provides some staggering views, although it is recommended that you wear long sleeves and trousers to protect you against thorns and prickly undergrowth. There are plenty of camping spots along the route, however, you must camp at least half a mile from the path.

The Outer Mountain Loop is hard work. The going can be challenging and there's the constant concern about water, but the reward is to have taken on the Big Bend, and won. **JI**

Cedar Valley Nature Trail Iowa, USA

Start Waterloo   **End** Hiawatha Cedar Rapids
Distance 52 miles (83.6 km)
Time 3–4 days   **Grade** Easy
Type Rail trail   **Map** goo.gl/NwkzfX

The Cedar Valley Nature Trail runs along the former course of the Waterloo, Cedar Falls, and Northern (WCF&N) Railway, which was completed at the start of the twentieth century and dismantled in the 1980s. Consequently the path has no gradient steeper than 2 percent. The northern end of the walk is in Hiawatha, a suburb of Cedar Falls that holds a popular farmers' market every Sunday between the end of April and the start of November. Moving south, the first 10 miles (16 km) and the last 4 miles (6.4 km) of the trail are paved with asphalt; the remainder of the path is

---

"The Cedar Valley Nature Trail is one of the pioneer ' linear parks' in Iowa."

www.mycountyparks.com

---

covered with crushed limestone, the preferred surface for so many rails-to-trails conversions.

The route runs parallel to, and crosses once, the Cedar River, a major tributary of the Iowa River, which flows into the Mississippi. The surrounding scenery, which varies between forests, wetlands, farmland, and open countryside, has abundant wildlife, including badgers, deer, wild turkey, and a variety of songbirds. The six small townships along the way—Lafayette, Center Point, Urbana, Brandon, La Porte City, and Gilbertville—still retain vestiges of their previous lives as stops on the WCF&N line. The trail is often impassable on foot in winter, but is popular with snowboarders who love its gentle gradient. **GL**

Yellow River State Forest Iowa, USA

Start/End 729 State Forest Road **Distance** 13 miles (21 km) **Time** 4–6 hours **Grade** Easy to moderate
Type Various **Map** goo.gl/QkmR4R

Anyone who says that Iowa is all cornfields has evidently never hiked the Yellow River State Forest loop. Best begun 3 miles (4.8 km) west of Harpers Ferry the circuit starts with a gentle climb through beds of maidenhair fern to the top of a ravine, the descent into which is beneath an umbrella of hickory, cherry, and pine branches. Between the trees you can see walls of limestone and sandstone that have been patiently eroded over millennia by water to create a series of striking geographic features.

A mile (1.6 km) farther on and a right turn onto a gravel road soon leads to another path that passes through groves of ash, cottonwood, and elm. Four miles (6.4 km) from the start, a short steep hill must be climbed before hikers begin a gradual descent through tall grass and between rows of Scotch pine trees. In fall birdwatchers should take a short detour from here to Cedar Point Overlook, where hawks may be seen preparing for their migration. Also possible are sightings of the rare and endangered red-shouldered hawk. Some 8 miles (12.8 km) beyond the marshes of Paint Creek comes Heffern's Hill Camp, where leisurely or exhausted hikers can pitch their tents in its wide, grassy clearing.

The penultimate section of the walk involves a 300-foot (91.4-m) ascent in just over a mile (1.6 km), followed by a downhill stretch into a narrow creek where the limpid water is a temptation to begin some trout fishing by hikers and by the river's resident population of beavers. From this point on the going is easy through fields of horsetail then back to the starting point. **GL**

↑ Tallgrass, gorges, forests, and hills. Is this Iowa?

Stone State Park Trails Iowa, USA

Start/End Dorothy Pecaut Nature Center **Distance** 8 miles (12.8 km) **Time** 3 hrs **Grade** Easy
Type Parkland trail **Map** goo.gl/33vDrF

Every one of Stone State Park's trails has a particular designated purpose. Some are for horseback riding, others are for mountain biking and snowmobiling, and one of the paths is dedicated to cross-country skiing in the winter and hiking in the summer. At least there is no risk of one mode of transportation running into—or being hit by—someone getting around by another method. It's just as well there are such strict rules of separation, because Stone State Park draws vast numbers of visitors year-round every year, not only from nearby Sioux City but also from most other parts of the United States. Its attractions are certainly impressive, including its proximity to the untamed Big Sioux River and the geological formations along this transitional area between flat prairie lands and hills of sedimentary rock, the latter of which are rich in marine fossils deposited during the Cretaceous period.

The area is renowned for its wide range of flora, including silky aster, pasque flower, penstemon, blazing star, and yucca. There are numerous interesting and unusual species of birds, such as the ovenbird, the barred owl, and the turkey vulture. Also in evidence are coyote, white-tailed deer, and red fox. In addition to these natural beauties, the Dorothy Pecaut Nature Center—the start and finish point of this route—has a magnificent butterfly garden that houses rare species of the region, including the Pawnee skipper and the Olympia white. The walk suggested here is merely an entry-level sampler that will serve as an introduction to a magnificent park that rewards deeper exploration, and has an intricate network of other paths on which to do so. **GL**

⬆ Stone State Park's geology is typical of Iowa's Loess Hills.

Katy Trail
Missouri, USA

Start Machens **End** Clinton
Distance 238 miles (383 km) **Time** 24–28 days
Grade Easy **Type** Rails-to-trails
Info goo.gl/MGXGTS

The longest rails-to-trails conversion so far undertaken in the United States, Missouri's Katy Trail follows for most of its length the northern shoreline of the Missouri River over the line taken by the old Missouri–Kansas–Texas Railroad (KATY), created in 1865 and the first railway to cross into Texas across its northern boundary. The trail begins at Machens on the Missouri River and heads west, passing through Jefferson City, the state capital, and then into the suburbs of Columbia where it leaves the old railway line to cross the river at Boonville over the Missouri–Kansas–Texas Bridge, built in 1931–32 and incorporated into the trail in 2010. From there the trail continues to its terminus at Clinton, Missouri, from which the old KATY Railroad still runs into neighboring Nevada.

The trail has helped revitalize many of Missouri's old towns that flourished when the railway first came through but began to flounder when it ceased operating in 1986. It follows the Lewis and Clark National Historic Trail between Boonville and St. Charles, passes through several rural areas with a built environment that predates the Civil War, and has riotous fall views thanks to forests full of maple and sumac, as well as wetlands, valleys, and abundant wildlife, including deer, waterfowl, red-tailed hawks, and woodpeckers. The trail is almost entirely flat, ideal for strolling through "Boonslick Country," a fascinating old cultural enclave of pioneering towns, such as Arrow Rock and Fayette whose residents once played a key role in the development of Missouri's statehood and whose period homes will have you wondering how it must have been here when everything you saw around you was as far west as one could get. **BDS**

"The trail meanders through peaceful farmland and small-town Americana."

www.bikekatytrail.com

⬆ The Katy Trail has revived isolated communities that predate North America's Civil War.

Caroline Dormon Trail
Louisiana, USA

Start 1.5 miles east of Longleaf Vista   End Kisatchie
Bayou Campground   Distance 10.5 miles (16.8 km)
Time 5–6 hours   Grade Easy   Type Forest trails
Map goo.gl/hEgA2l

Caroline Dormon was born in northern Louisiana on July 19, 1888, to parents of modest means, and from her early childhood demonstrated an uncommon interest in plants, wildlife, and the world around her. As a schoolteacher in her late twenties she began to collect and preserve a collection of native flora, and in the years that followed her interests flourished to the point where it seemed there was nothing this gifted woman couldn't do: botanist, historian, prolific author, archaeologist, ornithologist, and horticulturalist. In 1930 she persuaded the U.S. Forest Service to establish Louisiana's first national forest—the Kisatchie National Forest—and became the first woman in the United States to be employed by that male-dominated organization. There are few trails in the United States—and few in the world—that come with the prestige and pedigree attached to them that the name Caroline Dormon provides.

The trail named in her honor passes through her beloved Kisatchie National Forest, which contains the state's most rugged landscapes and is the largest of Louisiana's three designated wilderness areas. It is a wild walk with rocky elevations in excess of 200 feet (61 m) along its 10.5-mile (16.8-km) out-and-back length and involves squeezing your way through large pieces of dislodged rock. There are occasional pools of muddy water, the product of springs finding their way through the fractured rocks along the way. The trail isn't particularly technical or challenging, but is the sort of walk that Caroline would have loved, showcasing mixed pine and hardwood forests with white oaks, grassy understory, and dense shrubbery, everything she fought so hard to protect. **BDS**

Sandstone Loop Trail
Louisiana, USA

Start/End Forest Highway 59 trailhead
Distance 36 miles (57.9 km)   Time 7 days
Grade Moderate   Type Rocky, mixed-use trail
Info goo.gl/6lNoHq

The Kisatchie National Forest is a 600,000-acre (240,000-ha) world of bayous, old growth pines, and bald cypress groves in central and northern Louisiana. It is Louisiana's only National Forest and is one of the largest intact tracts of natural landscape remaining in the state, which makes it an ideal environment for walking along its more than 100 miles (160 km) of dedicated trails that connect more than forty recreational areas. The popular Sandstone Loop Trail is a multi-use trail, which is closed every year for repairs from early January to late April (check prior to arriving),

---

"If you want to try a larger dose of true wilderness, take on a piece of the sandstone trail."

www.trails.com

---

is open to motorcycles, horseback riding, mountain biking, OHVs (off-highway vehicles), and hiking. Part of the Cenozoic uplands—an area that contains some of the state's oldest rocks, as well as seepage bogs, calcareous prairies, and flatwoods vegetation—the trail is a difficult one. In Kisatchie National Forest there is a 13-mile (21-km) water trail that has been established along Saline Bayou, a tributary of the Red River. The first Blackwater river in the U.S. south to be designated part of the National Wild and Scenic River system in 1986, the bayou winds its way through cypress hardwood bottomlands and provides a relaxing change of pace after scrambling over sandstone-encrusted, shoe-crunching surfaces. **BDS**

Elroy–Sparta Trail
Wisconsin, USA

Start Elroy   End Sparta
Distance 32 miles (51.4 km)
Time 10–12 hours   Grade Easy to moderate
Type Rail trail   Map goo.gl/JrNYtV

One of the first rails-to-trails to be opened in the United States, this walk is just as exciting a destination for train enthusiasts as it is for hikers thanks to the three original tunnels through which it passes and that have been preserved almost exactly as they were when the route was first operated as part of the Chicago and North Western (C&NW) Railway. They still have their original doors, which the railroad used to close in winter between trains in order to preserve a constant inside temperature of 45°F (7°C), and at both ends of each tunnel were huts for watchmen who opened and closed the doors as required.

On the journey from Elroy in west central Wisconsin you come first to the Kendall Tunnel and then the Wilton Tunnel, both of which are 1,320 feet (402 m) long, and lastly the Norwalk Tunnel, which is 0.75 miles (1.2 km) long. The state of Wisconsin purchased the rail line from the C&NW in 1965. It then lifted the track, laid the path with crushed limestone and the walkways over the numerous bridges with wooden planks, and installed railings along the parapets of each span for safety reasons. The line reopened in its current form two years later. The trail remains one of the most popular in the country.

The tunnels are unlit, so a flashlight may be required on all but the brightest days. They may also be a little damp thanks to spring water permeating their limestone walls. The trail is multi-purpose, so walkers need to be aware of cyclists, and there are camping, lodging, and bike rental facilities along the route, which is easily negotiated with gradients of no more than 3 percent. And if you don't like ascents, don't worry—the trail is all downhill. **GL**

"Traveling between Sparta and Elroy, the trail stretches through … wetlands, prairies, farmland, and unglaciated areas."

dnr.wi.gov

⤒ This pioneering rails-to-trails conversion in Wisconsin still passes through its three original tunnels.

Ice Age National Scenic Trail
Wisconsin, USA

Start Interstate State Park, St. Croix Falls   End Potawatomi State Park, Sturgeon Bay   Distance 1,200 miles (1,930 km)   Time Several months   Grade Easy to moderate   Type Various   Info goo.gl/zPgoUw

As recently as 12,000 years ago the landscape of much of North America was being formed by the retreat of colossal glaciers up to 2 miles (3.2 km) thick and hundreds of miles wide, and nowhere can the landforms that this era of glaciation left behind be better seen and appreciated than in Wisconsin. The Wisconsin Glaciation was the result of the advance and subsequent retreat of the Laurentide Ice Sheet, which scoured a series of high ridges 120 miles (193 km) long in the state's southeast and left behind a myriad of new landforms including a series of craters known as the Kettle Moraine, formed by melting ice water. The land was the preserve of cave lions, sabre-toothed cats, and mammoths, and while they may no longer be with us, the topography that was slowly being revealed prior to their extinction is. Two-thirds of Wisconsin today is still defined by this period of glacial activity, and the best way to experience the echoes of this ancient world is to walk the still-evolving Ice Age National Scenic Trail.

To walk the trail is to walk over layers of an often violent geologic past. It traces the outermost reaches of the Laurentide's terminal moraine, a circuitous route that follows the various glacial lobes that extended independently of one another as the ice sheet edged slowly southward. The segmented trail encompasses thirty of the state's seventy-two counties and remains a work in progress, crossing wetlands, rural communities, farms, prairies, and even the suburbs of Madison—the state's capital—and when finished will stretch from the border with Minnesota in the west to Lake Michigan in the east. And that's one mammoth walk. **BDS**

"More than 12,000 years ago, an immense flow of glacial ice sculpted a landscape of remarkable beauty across Wisconsin."

www.iceagetrail.org

⊞   The Ice Age trail passes through landscapes shaped 12,000 years ago by the Laurentide Ice Sheet.

Glacial Drumlin State Trail

Wisconsin, USA

Start/End Cottage Grove/Fox River Sanctuary
Distance 52 miles (83.6 km)   Time Various
Grade Easy to moderate   Type Asphalt and crushed
limestone   Map goo.gl/Et6QeR

The Glacial Drumlin State Trail follows the route of the old Chicago and North Western Railway through the Midwestern state of Wisconsin. It was developed in 1986 and for the first 13 miles (21 km) of the road it's paved with asphalt, then switches to crushed limestone for the remainder of the route. There is one short section, on Junction Road and County Highway Y near Jefferson, where you need to use a public road to connect between two halves of the trail. At all points it is suitable for walkers, cyclists, and joggers and on the asphalt section it's also used by inline

> *"Wood-planked bridges provide great viewpoints for the wetlands, where a host of wildlife thrives."*

www.traillink.com

skaters, although cyclists and skaters over the age of sixteen need to buy a pass before they go on the trail.

The trail is fairly level along its whole length and conditions are generally good, due to the nature of the man-made track. There are also sixteen wooden bridges, so you've no reason to get your feet wet. The Glacial Drumlin goes through several Wisconsin cities, from Cottage Grove to Waukesha, and in the city of Lake Mills it crosses Rock Lake on an old iron railroad bridge. There are plenty of rest stops along the trail and a number of parks with bathroom facilities. The Glacial Drumlin is an easy-going, well-maintained rail-trail that offers great scenery. In winter it's also open to skiers and snowmobilers. **JI**

Illinois Prairie Path

Illinois, USA

Start Interstate 88, Forest Park   End Elgin, Bennet Park, or Aurora   Distance 62 miles (100 km)   Time 3 days
Grade Easy   Type Bed of former rail track
Map goo.gl/nMjMtB

The problem of what to do with disused railway tracks has exercised the finest planners of our day. One retired naturalist, May Theilgaard Watts, came up with a solution having walked the footpaths of England and hiked the Appalachian Trail. Both of these were in open countryside, but she wondered why a successful trail could not be created near her home in the western suburbs of Chicago. The Chicago, Aurora, and Elgin Electric Railroad had abandoned its tracks, making them ripe for conversion into a suburban trail. In 1963 Watts wrote to the *Chicago Tribune* outlining her dream. From such simple beginnings came the Illinois Prairie Path, the first successful "rail-to-trail" conversion in the United States.

The new path slowly grew over the years to its present 62-mile (99.7-km) length. It follows the old rail tracks west of Chicago to a junction in Wheaton, DuPage County. Here the path splits into the southern Aurora and northern Elgin branches, with the Geneva Spur off the Elgin Branch heading due west to Bennet Park and the shorter Batavia Spur heading northwest off the Aurora Branch. The various paths run through suburban lands, although patches of the original prairie that give the path its name remind us of a long-forgotten rural past.

Walkers, cyclists, joggers, and horseback riders make use of its long straight routes, with plenty of comfort stations, drinking fountains, and benches along the way to revive jaded spirits. Concrete mile markers give out the distance from the central point of Wheaton, but in reality, walkers on this path are more content to enjoy the unusual ambience of a suburban walk rather than reel in the miles. **SA**

Grand Illinois Trail
Illinois, USA

Start/End Wes Block Trail Access, 2636 W. Fairview Road   **Distance** 575 miles (925 km)
Time 60 days   **Grade** Moderate
Type Various   **Info** goo.gl/dgDeaW

The Grand Illinois Trail (GIT) is the longest pathway in the state, created in the 1990s by filling in the gaps between some of the numerous detached walkways that previously crisscrossed the region. Anyone who completes the GIT and can produce a card with local stamps to substantiate his or her claim is eligible for the State Department of Natural Resources' official "Trailblazer" diploma.

The GIT is a circular route that is tangential to both Lake Michigan and the Mississippi River. Within its ring is a radial network that enables walkers to make easy detours to many other places of interest off the beaten track despite there being more than enough to take in on the main line, which passes through the city of Chicago as well as numerous small towns of the Midwest. For hikers with limited time or energy, the best arc is generally agreed to be in the southern section along the state canal trails between Joliet and the so-called Quad Cities—Bettendorf, Davenport, East Moline, Moline, and Rock Island—that straddle the Illinois–Iowa state line. An attractive alternative itinerary is the Jane Addams Trail, a 13-mile (20.9-km) segment of the route bordered by the Pecatonica River, Richland Creek, and Cedar Creek that takes travelers past natural wetlands and exposed rock embankments and links with Badger State Trail to the north in Wisconsin.

Although a complete circuit of the GIT is a big ask for even the fittest hikers, Illinois terrain is for the most part gently undulating and seldom steep, and nowhere on the route is far from hotels and hostels in which to rest up before resuming the quest for the coveted certificate. **GL**

"*It hugs historic canals, crosses unglaciated hills . . . and includes one of America's first rail-trails.*"
www.dnr.illinois.gov

↑ Illinois' longest pathway connects small mid-western towns on the Illinois–Iowa border.

Tunnel Hill State Trail
Illinois, USA

Start Harrisburg   **End** Karnak
Distance 45 miles (72.4 km)
Time 3–4 days   **Grade** Easy to moderate
Type Rail trail   **Map** goo.gl/fw7hoo

"At one time the rumble of freight cars reverberated through the narrow tunnel."

www.dnr.state.il.us

⊼ An 1870s tunnel and twenty-three trestle bridges can be found on this old Civil War-era railway.

The Tunnel Hill State Trail runs along what was formerly a section of the Cairo and Vincennes (C&V) Railroad, partly built by Civil War Union General Ambrose Burnside. The line opened in 1872 for the transportation of passengers and local produce, especially coal, salt, wood, peaches, and apples. The C&V struggled almost from its first day of operation, and was later taken over by a succession of bigger operators until ultimately it came under the control of the Norfolk and Southern (N&S) Railroad. In 1991, the N&S gave up the unequal struggle against road transportation and handed the C&V over to the state of Illinois, which set about changing the line into a trail for hikers, joggers, and cyclists. After the track had been lifted and replaced with crushed limestone and gravel, and toilets and water fountains had been installed at key points along the way, it was reopened in its present form in 2001.

The tunnel—the only one on the route—is about halfway between Harrisburg and Karnak. It was originally 800 feet (244 m) long but after a part of it collapsed in 1929, its length was reduced to its current 500 feet (152 m). Other marvelous feats of engineering along the line include twenty-three trestle bridges, the longest and highest of which at Breedon is 450 feet (137 m) long and 90 feet (27 m) high.

The trail starts out in flat farmland, passes through the Shawnee National Forest, emerges from the trees into an area of bluffs, and ends in a lush wetland and swamp. Two and a half miles (4 km) beyond Karnak, a spur that was formerly part of the Chicago and Eastern Illinois Railroad leads on to a fascinating wetlands center. **GL**

Pictured Rocks
Michigan, USA

Start Sand Point   End Grand Marais
Distance 34 miles (54.7 km)   Time 3–4 days
Grade Moderate   Type Mountain trail
Map goo.gl/8oHshX

For 42 miles (67.5 km) along Lake Superior's southern shore, Pictured Rocks National Lakeshore presents a geological spectacle, with unusual rock formations at every turn. Sea arches pierce headlands, turrets crown promontories, and striated cliffs rise tall and sheer. At the eastern end great rock buttresses give way to billowing sand dunes topped by marram grass.

The rock formations can only be fully appreciated from the water or on foot (road access is limited). Trails range from 1-mile (1.6-km) scenic treks from inland parking lots, to a 34-mile (54.7-km) section of the North Country National Scenic Trail, which cleaves to the shore from Munising in the west to Grand Marais in the east and doesn't miss a geological trick. The Pictured Rocks themselves, named for their colors— green, white, orange, and black—derived from minerals, stretch for 15 miles (24 km) from Sand Point to Spray Falls; Miners Castle, a sandstone turret, provides a postcard view of the rocks. From Miners Castle, the coastal trail enters Chapel Basin, an area with several campgrounds and short loops to waterfalls and inland lakes. Also here are Chapel Rock, the stranded pillar of a collapsed archway, with natural windows and a lone white pine perched on top, and Grand Portal Point, a stunning rock arch. At Spray Point, Twelvemile Beach unfurls.

The variety of things to see, from beaches and waterfalls to grouse and chipmunks (black bears, gray wolves, and white-tailed deer being much shier inhabitants of Pictured Rocks), makes the trail one of the most interesting in the northern part of the United States. Should it get too hot and tiring, you can always kick off the boots and wade into the lake for a dip. **DS**

"Sandstone cliffs, beaches, sand dunes, waterfalls, lakes, forest, and shoreline beckon ..."

www.nps.gov

⬆ A myriad of geological oddities await you on this great walk along the shoreline of Lake Superior.

Greenstone Ridge Trail
Michigan, USA

Start Lookout Louise, Rock Harbor
End Windigo   **Distance** 40 miles (64 km)
Time 4–5 days   **Grade** Strenuous
Type Mountain trail   **Map** goo.gl/kRIUVW

On the very edge of the Canadian border, in the upper reaches of Lake Superior, more than 400 rocky islands and islets comprise the Isle Royale National Park, a designated wilderness populated by moose, waterfowl, eagles, and wolves. Chief among the islands is the Isle Royale itself, a finger of land 50 miles (80.4 km) long and 9 miles (14.4 km) wide, with deep forests, lakes, and fjords. Although there are no paved roads, the island has a long history of human contact. There is prehistoric evidence of copper mining, as well as the remains of nineteenth-century mines. Disused lighthouses stand at points east, west, and south.

Canoeists and kayakers flock here to paddle the indented coastline, but hikers are also well served by the 165 miles (265 km) of trails. Greenstone Ridge Trail, an end-to-end route along the thin backbone of the island and up and over its highest peaks, is the finest of these. Jaw-dropping views of the island and archipelago fall away on either side, with the coastline of Ontario visible from the summits. Along the way are remnants of long-disused copper mines, an old fire tower atop Mount Ojibway, and pristine lakes. High campgrounds accessed along spur trails allow hikers to break for the night—often the time to spot a moose wading in a glacial tarn or hear the howl of wolves, and to see the pale-green giant lunar moth, which will almost certainly settle on your tent.

The last leg of this roller-coaster trail heads up Mount Desor, the island's highest point at 1,394 feet (425 m), and then Sugar Mountain, named after the sugar maples on its slopes. From the terminus at Windigo, you can hop on a boat for a fast track back to the start. **DS**

> *"This is the trail where many hikers … become backpackers for the rest of their lives."*
>
> www.michigantrail.maps

⊓ A trail through Lake Superior's Isle Royale includes abandoned lighthouses and disused copper mines.

17 Mile Trail

Ohio, USA

Start/End Springbrook Lake Area trailhead
Distance 17 miles (27.3 km)   **Time** 8 hours
Grade Easy   **Type** Forest trails
Map goo.gl/xqZL41

Regarded as one of Ohio's finest walking trails, the 17 Mile Trail takes you through forests of oak and pine, beneath the sun-dappled openings in its canopy, along creek beds and sandy trails, and over open prairie. It can be done in a day, but it makes much more sense to linger and do it in two, an easy task thanks to the trail's rest stops, campsites, and amenities. Known by various names, including the Oak Openings Trail and the Scout's Trail, having been maintained by local scout groups for several years, it is long enough to be considered a challenge by the avid hiker and offers a solitary day in the woods, particularly on weekdays when you are likely to be the only one on this stunning species-laden trail.

The trail does what all good trails should—it gets you into the heart of the environment through which it passes, in this case the 3,700 acres (1,497 ha) of the Oak Openings Preserve, the largest of the Toledo area Metroparks located between the towns of Whitehorse and Swanton. Described by the Nature Conservancy as "One of America's Last Great Places" this is a rare ecosystem. One-third of all Ohio's rare plants are found here, left alone to flourish in the preserve's 20-foot-deep (6 m) sandy soil set over a bed of blue clay, the waterproof foundation for all that lies above it and the remnant of a long-forgotten ice age lake. The trail takes you into the heart of this preserved, almost primeval landscape with its wetland swamps and vegetated dunes, its blueberry fields, tall grass prairies, hardwood forests, oak savannah, and even the recently reintroduced Karner blue butterfly—a treasure trove of nature in the environs of Toledo. **BDS**

"Tackle it in a day, or take two days to explore this long and winding path."

www.trails.com

⬆ Walk through thick forests and past a third of Ohio's plant species in "One of America's Last Great Places."

Courthouse Rock and Double Arch Trail Kentucky, USA

Start/End Auxier Ridge parking lot   **Distance** 6 miles (9.6 km)   **Time** 3 hours   **Grade** Easy
Type Mountain trail   **Map** goo.gl/flso3y

Red River Gorge in Kentucky's Daniel Boone Forest is one of the best places in the eastern United States to see natural rock arches—the fortuitous result of fracturing and weathering. There are more than 150 sandstone arches in and around the gorge, sculpted by wind and water over millions of years. Caves, cliffs, waterfalls, and rock shelters set off by thick woods and threaded by creeks add to the thrill of the gorge for climbers as well as hikers. The river itself at this point is a calmer, sleeker version of the one that whitewater canoeists paddle a few miles upstream, though impenetrable hemlock forest makes it hard to reach.

A maze of trails covers the area, and with a map you can combine different trails to extend and trim distances as necessary. For more ambitious hikes, Daniel Boone Forest offers trails that could easily take a month or more to explore.

From the parking lot on Tunnel Bridge Road, Auxier Ridge Trail—an easy but satisfying hike linking two of the most distinctive rock features in the area—heads north through woodland. After about 2 miles (3.2 km) it climbs to a sheer overlook with views of Haystack Rock, Double Arch, Long Wall, Raven's Rock, and, in the distance, the hemisphere of Courthouse Rock, all aptly named. The trail continues to the base of Courthouse Rock itself. On the return, the Auxier Branch Trail leads to the photogenic Double Arch. The rocky platform under the arch has outstanding views of Courthouse and Haystack, which are all the more grand in fall. The rock-hewn steps to the top of the arch lead to more views and a walk along the ridge. **DS**

⬆ Natural arches abound in Kentucky's Red River Gorge.

Bernheim Forest Millennium Trail Kentucky, USA

Start/End Guerilla Hollow Rd, Bernheim Arboretum   **Distance** 13.6 miles (21.8 km)   **Time** 7 hours
Grade Moderate   **Type** Wooded path   **Map** goo.gl/OsOVgU

After he had made a fortune selling the I. W. Harper brand of bourbon whiskey, U.S. businessman Isaac Wolfe Bernheim turned his attention to his legacy. In 1929 he founded an arboretum and research forest in Bullitt County, Kentucky. The 14,000-acre (5,600-ha) facility consists of a beech-maple forest with an arboretum containing more than 1,900 species of trees, shrubs, and other plants. Among its many claims to fame is its unrivaled collection of holly trees. Prickles aside, the forest contains several fine trails, of which the lengthy Millennium Trail is the best. However, given that this is a maintained area, access is limited from 7 a.m. to sunset with total closure on Christmas and New Year days and when temperatures are too high. Personal registration is also required for safety.

Described as a half marathon with hills, the well-signed Millennium Trail winds in a loop through glorious forests and along the exposed tops of ridges. The occasional steep climb can come as shock: walking in an anti-clockwise direction, the tracks runs straight up a steep hill at mile nine, but once at the top, the views are always fantastic. For a trail founded on whiskey, it is suitable that you can look down on the famous Jim Beam and Evan Williams' distilleries, but in reality it is the flora and wildlife you have come to see. The trees are magnificent, but so too are the deer and skunks, as well as the turkeys, hawks, and numerous other birds on display. Those who regularly walk the trail recommend that you take water, and be prepared for the mosquitoes and ticks. They also warn that it is easy to wander off trail. Keep looking for the triangular yellow blazes to keep you on track. **SA**

⤒ Walk or jog Kentucky's "half-marathon with hills."

Mammoth Cave Park Long Loop Trail
Kentucky, USA

Start/End First Creek trailhead, off Ollie Rd and Kentucky 728 **Distance** 15.1 miles (24.3 km) **Time** 8 hours **Grade** Moderate **Type** Wooded paths **Info** goo.gl/7Jb9ZT

Over the millennia, rainwater has worked its way under the limestone hills of central Kentucky to create at Mammoth Cave the world's most extensive network of caves and underground passages, with more than 350 miles (563 km) discovered so far and no doubt many more miles still to be mapped. Stalactites, stalagmites, and white crystal formations decorate the many tunnels and caves. The area is rightly a national park, but less well known are the natural wonders above the surface explored by this lovely loop.

The Mammoth Cave Park Long Loop Trail wanders in a lazy circle to the north side of the Green River and east of the Nolan River, the undeveloped side of the park. The Loop makes use of three different trails along its length. The usual circuit is anti-clockwise, first taking you south down the Wet Prong Trail and then east along the McCoy Hollow Trail and then north and finally home east along the First Creek Trail. When it is flowing, the Wet Prong stream needs to be crossed, but then fools you by soon disappearing into the caverns beneath the ground. Be prepared to clamber down into ravines and up a few climbs, but in reality, this is a largely level trail that is suitable for most hikers.

Attempt this walk in spring when the valleys are alive with waterfalls and covered with wildflowers, but it might be best to avoid the hot, humid summer months. Do be prepared for crowds. It is possible to camp out in one of twelve designated campsites, for which permits are required, but these sites can fill up during the holiday periods. Be advised also that the trail is often used by horses and the ground can get very muddy. **SA**

"Its vast chambers and complex labyrinths have earned its name—Mammoth."

www.nps.gov

⤒ Walk a loop trail along the Green and Nolan rivers above the world's largest network of underground caves.

Sheltowee Trace National Recreation Trail
Kentucky/Tennessee, USA

Start Morehead, Kentucky   **End** Big South Fork
National River and Recreation Authority, Tennessee
Distance 268 miles (431 km)   **Time** 14 days   **Grade**
Moderate   **Type** Rugged paths   **Info** goo.gl/xN5H5Q

A word of explanation: Sheltowee was the name given to the eighteenth-century pioneer and frontiersman Daniel Boone by Chief Blackfish of the Shawnee Tribe. It means "Big Turtle," and it is to Boone that this trail is dedicated, suitably marked along its length with white diamonds bearing the image of a turtle.

This glorious trail heads southwest through the Daniel Boone National Forest from the Knobs region of central Kentucky—so-called because its hills are conical and some have capstones that form cliffs underneath—onto the Cumberland Plateau and then down over the border to finish not far from Oneida in the Big South Fork National River and Recreation Authority in Tennessee. It passes along the narrow ridges and crosses the deep ravines that characterize eastern Kentucky, a rugged trail that can be tackled in short stages or conquered in a lengthy slog. The views are wonderful, but beware of the bears that live in the woods. Black bears are always hungry therefore all food must be suspended at least 10 feet (3 m) above the ground and 4 feet (1.2 m) away from any tree or pole. Better still, lock your food away in a vehicle or hard trailer.

As you head south, the trail crosses the Licking, Red, Kentucky, Cumberland, and Big Fork rivers and passes Cave Run, Wood Creek, and Laurel River lakes. A particular highlight is the Cumberland Falls, also known as Little Niagara or the Niagara of the South on account of its tumultuous flow of 3,600 cubic feet (100 cubic m) of water per second, which—under a full moon during a clear night—can set off a lunar rainbow (or moonbow) formed by the mist emanating from the water. **SA**

"Old homesteads, oil and gas wells, and logging tracts ... can be seen along the trail."

www.fs.usda.gov

⊡ The Daniel Boone National Forest and Cumberland Falls are just two of this trail's many highlights.

Natchez Trace National Scenic Trail
Mississippi, USA

Start/End Various   Distance 60 miles (96.5 km)
Time 4 days   Grade Easy   Type Trail
Map goo.gl/ySDF80 (red lines denote the five segments of the trail and orange denote the original Natchez Trace)

"[The] trail that became known as the Natchez Trace was the lifeline through the Old Southwest."

www.nps.gov

The Natchez Trace National Scenic Trail in Mississippi follows as best it can the old Natchez Trace, that ancient 450-mile-long (724 km) Native American pathway that was first trampled through the undergrowth by bison, deer, and other large game as they made their way from the nutrient-rich soils—the so-called "salt licks"—of central Tennessee, south to the grazing lands along the Mississippi River. It was then modified by Native Americans—who altered it to follow ridge lines and so minimize runoff after heavy rains—to avoid swamps and cross rivers at their easiest fording points. It was a path trampled deep into the earth by generations of hoofs and moccasin-clad feet, and a link to other pathways that stretched all the way from the Great Lakes of Canada to the Gulf of Mexico.

Rather than one continuous path, today's Natchez Trace Trail, which was designated a national scenic trail in 1983, consists of five segments amounting to some 60 miles (96.5 km) of mixed-use pathways—Potkopinu, Rocky Springs Trail, Yockanookany Trail (the longest section of which parallels the Ross Barnett Reservoir), Blackland Prairie Trail, and the Highland Rim. The Rocky Springs Trail section passes by the ghost town of Rocky Springs in Claiborne county, Mississippi. Once a popular watering place for travelers on the trail, it was first devastated by an outbreak of yellow fever in 1878 and then a weevil blight decimated its cotton crops. Finally, the natural spring that gave the town its name dried up. The last store closed its doors in 1930, but walkers can visit the remains of this historic site as they retrace the footsteps of the first Americans. **BDS**

Trace the path of generations of Native Americans on the Natchez Trace National Scenic Trail.

Tanglefoot Trail
Mississippi, USA

Start West Church Street, Houston
End Carter Avenue, New Albany
Distance 43.6 miles (70.1 km)   Time 3 days
Grade Easy   Type Asphalt   Map goo.gl/h4QZ92

The Tanglefoot Trail is the longest rails-to-trails project so far undertaken in Mississippi, on an old rail corridor built in the 1870s for the Gulf and Ship Island Railroad. It follows a natural trail used for centuries by Native Americans and later walked by some of the New World's most famous early explorers, including Hernando de Soto and Meriwether Lewis. It winds its way almost 44 miles (71 km) through the state's Appalachian foothills, through mature hardwood forests, Kudzu–draped trees and shrubs, wetlands, and the cotton and soybean fields of the Mississippi Hills National Heritage Area. Deep in the state's northeast corner, it is a region rich in the history of the struggle for civil rights, the site of various Civil War battlefields, and the birthplace of Elvis Presley.

Towns passed along the way include Houston; New Houlka, Chickasaw county's oldest town, founded in 1812; Algoma, settled in the 1830s on an old Native American trail; Pontotoc, whose name is a Chickasaw word meaning "land of the hanging grapes"; and the tiny communities of Ecru and Ingomar. It also passes the Ingomar Mounds complex, a 2,000-year-old burial mound included on the National Register of Historic Places.

The trail was opened on September 21, 2013, and caters to cyclists, inline skaters, wheelchairs, and horseback riding. It is the result of a grass-roots effort that began in 2005 and is a dream come true for many northern Mississippians, who are rejoicing that their communities are once again linked together by this vehicle-free route. The trail is named after "old Tanglefoot," the narrow-gauge steam train that once hissed its way through these idyllic landscapes. **BDS**

Cane Creek Canyon Trail
Alabama, USA

Start/End 251 Loop Road, Tuscumbia
Distance 9.1 miles (14.6 km)   Time 7 hours
Grade Moderate   Type Rock, dirt trails
Map goo.gl/2TUhjy

The Cane Creek Canyon Trail is a lovingly preserved slice of nature in the heart of farmland and suburban residential housing. It was saved from development by Jim and Faye Lacefield, retired educators who bought a 40-acre (16-ha) slice of it in 1979 and then gradually acquired adjoining parcels of land until they owned the whole canyon. Now maintained by them, with the help of the state of Alabama, it is open to the public year-round free of charge and is best visited between March and June and in winter—in high summer horseflies can be a bother.

" . . . an area of incredible Alabama wilderness. The diversity of the preserve is astounding . . ."

blog.al.com/keeping-alabama-forever-wild

Within this steep canyon run the clear waters of Cane Creek. In between lie streams, waterfalls, hardwood forests, and huge freestanding boulders. A highlight is Devil's Hollow, a semicircular rock shelter inhabited 10,000 years ago by Paleo-Indian hunters. Many parts of the canyon have their own individual microclimates that support more than 100 tree species and numerous plants. One of the rarest is French's shooting star, a fern that grows only beneath rocky sandstone overhangs and is found nowhere else in Alabama. The canyon reaches a dead end at the beautiful Karen's Falls. On the return hike, keep one eye out for deer flitting between the trees and the other on the sky for bald eagles. **GL**

Oak Mountain State Park Alabama, USA

Start/End North trailhead, Oak Mountain State Park **Distance** 13 miles (21 km) **Time** 4 hours
Grade Easy to moderate **Type** Forest and mountain trails **Map** goo.gl/rl3h2A

Most recommended tours of the spectacular fall colors of Alabama are by automobile, but there are many other options for those who prefer to walk. The pick of them are those that make up the 51-mile (82.1-km) network that runs in all directions around the 10,000-acre (40,500-ha) Oak Mountain State Park.

Of these, the best one to begin with is generally thought to be the South Rim Trail, which climbs steeply from near the park entrance and onto a high ridge. On reaching the summit at Peavine Falls—a beautiful cascade with a 65-foot (20-m) drop and surprisingly chilly water—walkers can either return the way they came or branch off onto the Peavine Falls Trail, which adds another 2 miles (3.2 km) to the total distance traveled and provides further opportunities to marvel at the magnificent reds and browns of the September and October foliage.

Oak Mountain State Park is impressively well organized, and all its routes are clearly color-coded. Among them are several loops, the longest of which, the Shackleford, is 6.5 miles (10.5 km) long and takes in part of the South Rim Trail. The shortest, the 1-mile (1.6-km) Wildlife Loop, starts and finishes at the Alabama Wildlife Rehabilitation Center.

Before or after this moderately strenuous hike, you can enjoy swimming, fishing, or boating on the surrounding lakes, or maybe a leisurely round of the park's eighteen-hole golf course. For younger visitors, there is a petting farm with goats, sheep, donkeys, ducks, and turkeys, and for anyone who feels that a day here is not long enough, there are cabins to rent and a camping area. **GL**

⬆ Fall colors abound on Alabama's Oak Mountain.

Allegheny River and Samuel Justus Trails Pennsylvania, USA

Start Emlenton   End Oil City   Distance 38 miles (61 km)   Time 2–3 days   Grade Easy
Type Rail trails   Map goo.gl/t704QD

These two contiguous trails combine to make a single relaxing walk, much of which is along the banks of the Allegheny River. The clearly marked path, which is paved throughout, follows the old Allegheny Valley Railroad, which closed in 1984. The gradients were easy enough for steam locomotives to ascend with heavy loads and so should be no problem for walkers.

As you leave the small township of Emlenton, heading generally northward upstream, the river stays on the left for a few miles before pulling away into a tight bend while the path continues straight on across the base of the U. Here you encounter the first of two reminders of the path's original purpose: the Rockland Tunnel, which extends for 2,868 feet (874 m). Although both this and the 3,350-foot (1,021-m) Kennerdale Tunnel, which is reached farther along the trail, have reflector posts along their whole lengths, neither is lit,

so it is advisable for anyone attempting this walk to take a flashlight.

After crossing a footbridge over Sandy Creek at its confluence with the Allegheny, you reach Franklin, a small town celebrated for its tree-lined streets and nineteenth-century architecture in British Victorian style. A noted landmark is the mansion of Senator Joseph Sibley, who made his fortune as an oil refiner.

Beyond Franklin, the Allegheny River Trail becomes the Samuel Justus Trail for the final 6 miles (9.6 km) of the journey. On both sides of the river the woodlands are punctuated by iron furnaces and operating oil wells, the twin sources of the region's wealth since the 1850s. This sets the tone for arrival at your destination, the aptly named Oil City. **GL**

⇧ Stroll the Allegheny River's graceful gradients.

Laurel Highlands Hiking Trail Pennsylvania, USA

Start Ohiopyle State Park   End Conemaugh Gorge,
near Johnstown   Distance 70 miles (112 km)
Time 5–7 days   Grade Moderate   Type Wooded
paths, rocky stretches   Map goo.gl/xusqas

In the west of Pennsylvania, just beyond the Allegheny Mountains, lies the string-like Laurel Ridge, a thin sliver of high ground that was made a state park in 1967. Along its length is a highland hiking trail celebrated for its varied terrain and staggering beauty.

Starting at the southern end of the trail in the Ohiopyle State Park, the track bumps up and down until leveling out on a ridge at around 2,700 to 3,000 feet (823–915 m) above sea level. At this height, the temperature is considerably cooler than the humid valley floor. From then on the trail gently undulates its way northeast until descending steeply down 1,500 feet (457 m) into the beautiful Conemaugh Gorge.

The trail is marked roughly every 100 feet (30 m) with small, yellow blazes. These are necessary to find your way, but in truth your attention will be focused on the spectacular scenery on either side of the ridge. Near the start, the twisting Youghiogheny River flows along to your right. Soon you are forced to ascend a 1,100-foot (335-m) stone staircase, the mushrooms and mosses of the lower slopes giving way to wildflowers and then towering hardwoods and groves of ferns. Mountain laurels—the state flower of Pennsylvania—line the route. The Seven Springs Mountain Resort is the highest point of the trail, at 2,950 feet (900 m), after which you hike down snowless ski slopes and pass through swathes of cherry, maple, and beech trees and clumps of giant cinnamon ferns before making your final descent. Six overnight trailheads make it easy to break this walk up into seven stages, but it is possible to cover the ground in five days. **SA**

◁ Frank Lloyd Wright's Fallingwater in the Laurel Highlands.

Buzzard Swamp Trails Pennsylvania, USA

Start/End Forest Road, east of Marienville
Distance 3.7 miles (6 km)   Time 1.5–3 hours
Grade Easy   Type Circular route
Map goo.gl/WnuY4c

The Buzzard Swamp Trails comprise an 11.2-mile (18-km) network of pathways, any of which may be explored as add-ons to this basic itinerary. The short circular walk suggested here passes through some of the best spots in Pennsylvania for viewing migratory birds, as well as several interesting species of fauna.

It begins and ends at the parking lot on Forest Road, 2.5 miles (4 km) east of Marienville along Lamonaville Road. From there, proceed south along a wide, grassy path through a hardwood forest and past several of the area's fifteen artificial lakes. About 1 mile

> *"Don't forget your binoculars or spotting scope for great views of the native fauna."*
>
> www.fs.usda.gov

(1.6 km) into the journey, there is a rocky outcrop around 100 feet (30 m) off to the left, a favorite spot for day hikers to take their first break. After just under 2 miles (3 km), turn right, and then after 1,200 feet, (366 m) right again along a dirt path that leads back through the forest to the starting point.

During the spring migration season, listen for the call of the Eastern meadowlark and keep an eye out for waterfowl, twenty-five species of which may be sighted around the ponds, as well as American coot, hooded merganser, and blue-and-green-winged teals. Later in the season, it is possible to see Eastern bluebirds, tree swallows, and American kestrels. One may be lucky enough to see osprey and bald eagles overhead. **GL**

Susquehannock Trail System
Pennsylvania, USA

Start/End Various **Distance** 85 miles (137 km)
Time 7–10 days **Grade** Easy to strenuous
Type Well-maintained forest trails
Map goo.gl/8wwiBn

The Susquehannock Trail System (STS) is a loop trail through the Susquehannock State Forest in Potter and Clinton counties in north-central Pennsylvania. It passes through three state parks as well as the Hammersley Wild Area, Pennsylvania's largest area without a road. Called a system due to the fact that it makes use of several different trails along its route, its origins can be traced to 1967, when it was the brainchild of William Fish, the publisher of Potter county's weekly newspaper *The Potter Enterprise* and a tireless advocate of outdoor recreation in the counties he often described as "God's country."

The Susquehannock Trail Club was formed at a Fish-inspired meeting in the suburban home of Delmar and Lois Kerr, where it was decided to make use of existing trails built in the 1930s by the Civilian Conservation Corps (CCC) and to make the new trail a loop, so people could return to their various starting points. A few years of scouting and clearing followed, and control points that the new trail must pass through were chosen, including Ole Bull and Patterson Parks and the Cherry Springs Fire Tower. Old fire trails built by the CCC that had deteriorated through lack of use were revitalized.

The loop now links sixty-three separate trails, any one of which would stand on its own as a slice of true Pennsylvania wilderness—the Fanton Hollow Trail; the Wild Boy Trail; the Seed-Study Trail; the Cherry Springs Trail; the Scheibner Trail, which descends 618 feet (188 m) on a 24 percent gradient; and the Hogback Trail down through Hogback Hollow—all happily giving up their individuality for the greater good of that triumph of local knowledge and passion that is the STS. **BDS**

"The STS is one of Pennsylvania's oldest and most venerable backpacking trails."

www.trails.com

⬆ The Susquehannock Trail System is a triumphant amalgam of local trails.

McDade Trail
Pennsylvania, USA

Start Hialeah   **End** Milford Beach
Distance 32 miles (51.4 km)   **Time** 2 days
Grade Easy to moderate   **Type** Rugged foot trail,
gravel path   **Map** goo.gl/mfJHrC

Named after a local, ecologically aware congressman, the McDade Trail passes through varied terrain from forests and farmland to rock piles and cliffs, interspersed with historic landmarks. For the first 5 miles (8 km), from the Hialeah picnic area to Turn Farm, the path runs along the western bank of the Delaware River, one of the nineteen designated Great Waters of North America. It is here that some of the first Europeans settled, although the area was inhabited by Native Americans long before they arrived, and it is possible you may find an ancient arrowhead or similar artifact on the ground (if you do, hand it in—it's U.S. government property). En route, you pass Smithfield Beach, where swimming is permitted in a roped-off area, and there are changing rooms and restrooms. On reaching Turn Farm, look out for the old smokehouse and a disused lime kiln. Moving north, the route becomes considerably steeper between the Owens trailhead and Bushkill, with one gradient an exhausting 35 percent, before the next 10-mile (16-km) section between the Eshback and White Pines trailheads flattens out. In winter, this section turns from a hiking trail to a ski trail, and a lure for cross-country skiers.

While the McDade Trail has thus far been mixed use, the final 2.75 miles (4.4 km), from Pittman Orchard to Milford Beach, is for hikers only. This part of the walk is through rolling hills and is predominantly rural, with the old silo at Snyder Farm one of the few human-made features. Much more likely are glimpses of the abundant wildlife: deer and foxes are common here, but there have also been sightings of bears and even the elusive bobcat. **GL**

"The perfect place to enjoy the scenic beauty of the Delaware Water Gap National Park."

www.poconosbest.com

⤒ The McDade Trail is a hiking trail in summer and a ski trail in winter.

Black Mountain Loop
New York, USA

Start/End Pike Brook Road
Distance 5.5 miles (8.8 km)
Time 4 hours   **Grade** Moderate
Type Mountain trail   **Map** goo.gl/80tMLI

The Adirondack Park in Upstate New York is huge; it's bigger than Yellowstone, Yosemite, the Grand Canyon, Great Smoky, and the Everglades put together. Two thousand miles (3,200 km) of hiking trails cross 6 million acres (2.5 million ha), which are dotted with 3,000 lakes. One of these is Lake George, an elongated body of water strewn with 400 islands and islets. Dubbed the "Queen of American Lakes," it is a wondrous sight that is best appreciated from the summit of Black Mountain on the lake's western shore.

The hike to the top of Black Mountain follows a streambed through woods and is, for the most part, fairly easy, apart from a strenuous stretch near the 2,646-foot (807-m) summit. An old fire tower stands at the top, and various trails head off to the mountain's small lakes, but the main reason for coming is the view. Before descending the southern edge of the summit toward Black Mountain Point, which eventually rejoins the ascent trail, take time to stand and stare. A host of other peaks—rounded Elephant and Sugarloaf, the jagged ridge of Tongue Mountain, and Sleeping Beauty—spread north and east, while below lies glittering Lake George, remnant of the glacier that squeezed through the mountains 12,000 years ago. The British fought the French here in the Battle of Lake George during the French and Indian War (replacing the Native American name for the lake with George, after their king), and during the 1920s, industrial magnates built extravagant homes on the western shore, which became known as Millionaires' Row. Those days are over, but Lake George and its mountains remain a place where hardworking New Yorkers come to escape and recharge. **DS**

Taughannock Falls Gorge Trail
New York, USA

Start/End Taughannock Falls Road parking lot
Distance 1.5 miles (2.4 km)   **Time** 1 hour
Grade Easy   **Type** Wheelchair accessible trail
Map goo.gl/kTzuTt

Occasionally, for whatever reasons, a great natural feature can slip below our radar and has a hard time getting noticed. The Taughannock Falls, a waterfall northwest of the town of Ithaca in New York, is one of those places. It is the highest single-drop waterfall east of the Rocky Mountains. Its primary cataract is a colossal 215-foot (66-m) drop, 33 feet (10 m) higher than Niagara Falls, and its waters flow down a gorge with cliffs that tower more than 400 feet (120 m) above it. Why there aren't parking lots, vending machines, turnstiles, and lines here is difficult to understand.

"[Taughannock] Waterfall is one of the outstanding natural attractions of the northeast."

www.reserveamerica.com

Nonetheless, there is a fabulous trail that will get you here, and if you arrive early enough, you may even have it all to yourself.

The Taughannock Falls Gorge Trail is located in Taughannock Falls State Park in the Finger Lakes region of central New York, and it is a short 0.75-mile (1.2-km) trail that is open year-round. There are 4 miles (6.4 km) of rim trails, too, which provide views of the upper gorge, but they are closed in winter. The Gorge Trail leads to an excellent viewing area at the base of the falls, which are set in a spectacular amphitheater-like canyon that makes for a great foliage walk in fall and even in winter, as mist combines with an ethereal background of ice-encrusted limestone cliffs. **BDS**

Long Trail
Vermont, USA

Start Williamstown **End** North Troy
Distance 272 miles (438 km)
Time 22 days **Grade** Moderate
Type Mainly gravel **Info** goo.gl/a8HF6F

Started in 1929 and completed two years later, this is the oldest long-distance hiking trail in the United States, created by the local Green Mountain Club, which still runs it today. The pathway extends north from the Massachusetts state line, across the whole of Vermont, to the Canadian border. It shares 100 miles (161 km) of its course with the Appalachian Trail. This is the section that runs along the main ridge of the Green Mountains and crosses most of that range's main summits; in order, from south to north: Glastenbury Mountain, Stratton Mountain, Killington Peak, Mount Abraham, Mount Ellen, Camel's Hump, Mount Mansfield—at 4,393 feet (1,339 m), the highest point in Vermont—and Jay Peak. In total, the Long Trail traverses six peaks of more than 4,000 feet (1,200 m) and twenty-one peaks of more than 3,000 feet (900 m).

The hiking season starts in June, but that month is often blighted by the troublesome blackfly. Thunderstorms are common in July and August, so the best time to make the trip is in September, the last month of the year in which the trail is open. Animals that you are most likely to see along the way are bears, beavers, chipmunks, deer, moose, porcupine, and rabbits. At rest stops, be sure to sample Long Trail Ale, a beer produced by the Long Trail Brewing Company, a microbrewery on the banks of the Ottauquechee River in Bridgewater Corners.

As this publication went to press, the Green Mountain Club had begun building a footbridge over the Winooski River at Bolton, which has, until now, been traversed by a variety of less than satisfactory methods, including a wooden railroad trestle and straightforward fording. **GL**

"One of Vermont's most enduring icons, a symbol of the high value Vermonters put on enjoying their natural environment."

www.nasw.org

⬆ North America's oldest long-distance trail runs along the ridges of Vermont's Green Mountains.

The Carriage Trails of Acadia National Park
Maine, USA

Start/End Various   Distance 45 miles (72.4 km)
Time Various   Grade Easy
Type Crushed local granite
Info goo.gl/9KmUbf

"The result of Rockefeller's vision ... is an integrated system of carriage roads that blends harmoniously with the landscape."

www.nps.gov

⊕ John D. Rockefeller Jr.'s bridges and carriage roads add beauty to an already stunning landscape.

The network of carriage roads that wind their way through the splendor of Maine's Acadia National Park on Mount Desert Island were a gift to the nation from the philanthropist John D. Rockefeller Jr. A skilled horseman, Rockefeller wanted to be able to ride on vehicle-free byways when staying at the Rockefeller Estate at nearby Seal Harbor. Construction began in 1913 and continued for twenty-seven years, resulting in a vast masterpiece of engineering: 45 miles (72.4 km) of working roads, 16 feet (4.9 m) wide and built to survive Maine's inclement weather with generous crowns and stone culverts to keep the paths drained. Determined to minimize impact on the environment, Rockefeller had the roads lined with retaining walls to prevent slippage and to maintain the integrity of the hillsides. Their guardrails of granite coping stones, affectionately called "Rockefeller's teeth," were quarried from the island, and that same granite was also used to grand effect on the seventeen steel and reinforced-concrete bridges that cross over its roads and streams. Even the cedar signposts, installed at intersections to help carriage drivers find their way, are still there to guide walkers, and roadsides are landscaped with blueberries and sweet fern.

The carriage roads that bisect the 11,000 acres (4,452 ha) of park donated by the Rockefellers can now be used by anyone for strolling, cycling, and, of course, coach rides. In winter, you can snowshoe and cross-country ski on them. Two ornamental gatehouses—at Jordan Pond and near Northeast Harbor—welcome visitors into this Alice in Wonderland-like space. "It's what God Himself would have done here," somebody once said, "if only he'd had the money." **BDS**

The Mianus Maze
Connecticut, USA

Start/End Parking lot, Merriebrook Lane,
Stamford   Distance 2–4 miles (3.2–6.4 km)
Time 45 minutes–1.5 hours   Grade Easy
Type Forest trail   Map goo.gl/jWCgJs

Mianus River Park is a woodland utopia straight out of
a fairy tale. Trout run through the tumbling river, frogs
and salamanders inhabit dark pools, toadstools spring
from tree roots, and woodpeckers hammer overhead.
You might even see a white-tailed deer peeping
through the foliage. In spring, violets, celandines, and
wood anemones fleck the forest floor.

For a first-class nature ramble within striking
distance of a major metropolis, Mianus is hard to beat.
Straddling the boundary between Greenwich and
Stamford, it lies just 40 miles (64.3 km) north of New
York City. A maze of trails totaling some 14 miles
(22.5 km) cross the wooded valley, many of them
named after their distinguishing features, such as Oak
Trail, Drop Off Trail, Deer Trail, and Fisherman's Trail
Loop. The 4.5-mile (7.2-km) Perimeter Loop is one of
the longer trails, with nice stretches alongside the river.

The name Mianus, after Chief Sachem Myn
Myano, is the only trace of the long Native American
presence in the river valley. White farmers colonized
the area in the 1600s, pushing out the Native
Americans. Chief Myano himself was shot and killed
by Colonel Daniel Patrick, who had already bought
much of Greenwich for twenty-five coats. Remnants
of stone walls and wells in the park date from these
times, though the early settlers tended not to farm the
land near the river, as it was uneven and difficult to
clear. The southern section of the park incorporates
Treetops State Park, which formed part of Hollywood
actress Libby Holman's country estate. In the 1940s
and 1950s, Holman entertained many well-known
stars and writers at Treetops, including Elizabeth
Taylor, Truman Capote, and Tennessee Williams. **DS**

*"The Mianus Maze is a 14-mile
loop trail that offers beautiful
river views and is perfect
for beginners."*

www.movoto.com

⊞ Walk a labyrinth of wooded Connecticut trails located
only 40 miles (64 km) from the bustle of New York.

Metacomet Trail Connecticut, USA

Start Hanging Hills **End** Rising Corner, Suffield **Distance** 63 miles (101 km) **Time** 5 days
Grade Easy to moderate **Type** Ridgeway path **Map** goo.gl/x2enGG

Part of the New England National Scenic Trail, this walk takes in a wide range of sights and sites, running for the greater part of its length along the Metacomet Ridge. A tilted basalt and fossil-rich sedimentary rock formation along cliff tops, the ridge affords extensive views over the surrounding countryside.

The first piece of built history encountered is Old Newgate Prison at East Granby. Originally a copper mine, it became a penitentiary and is now a museum. Next is the 165-foot-tall (50-m) Heublein Tower, formerly the home of the founder of Smirnoff, the vodka manufacturer. On the west side of Rattlesnake Mountain is a boulder cave in which, according to legend, an arsonist took refuge after trying to burn down the town of Farmington. In Farmington, the Hill-Stead Museum is worth a stop for its Impressionist paintings and ornamental gardens. Farther on you

cross the Hanging Hills of Meridien, where Hubbard Park was laid out by the landscape designer Frederick Law Olmsted. Take a few minutes here to climb to the observation deck at the top of Castle Craig Tower.

The path passes through several microclimates, which support a number of species that struggle to survive elsewhere, including Eastern red cedars, hemlock, and prickly pears. The trail is well marked with blue triangles, and the going is generally easy, although the rugged nature of some sections raises the degree of difficulty to moderate. The main potential hazards are lightning storms, parasitic deer ticks that may carry Lyme disease, poison ivy, and northern copperheads. In winter, extra care should be taken on icy surfaces near the numerous precipices. **GL**

⭱ A fossil-rich walk on New England's scenic trail.

Long Path New Jersey/New York, USA

Start George Washington Bridge, New Jersey   **End** New York Route 146, New York   **Distance** 347 miles (558 km)
Time 3 weeks   **Grade** Easy to moderate   **Type** Mountain, forest trail   **Info** goo.gl/eOp25F

When it was first conceived back in the 1930s, what is now the Long Path was never meant to be a continuous path but rather a collection of attractions that hikers were encouraged to find their own way to and from. It was the vision of Vincent Schaefer, a scientist for General Electric, who wanted to create a hiking path from the north of New York City, into the wilderness of the Adirondacks, but he was strongly opposed to it being marked. Rather, it would be "a route that a person having good 'woods' sense could use to move across a region using a compass and 'topo map,' and that in a meandering way would lead such persons to most of the interesting scenic viewpoints, rock formations, choice or unique vegetation, historical sites, and similar items."

As committed as Schaefer and others were to the idea, however, the intervention of World War II put

construction of the trail on hold until it was revived in the 1960s. The first section, from the George Washington Bridge to south of the Catskill Mountains, was completed in 1987. In 1991, at the age of eighty-five, Schaefer produced his own guide to the northern Long Path, complete with eighty sites he felt worthy of inclusion.

Today the Long Path remains a hybrid trail, but one with an enviable pedigree. It still retains its "wild" character, a true "bushwhack" through the peaks of the Adirondacks along roads that barely see a car and are being continually bypassed in a never-ending effort to create what Schaefer saw reflected in the words of the poet Walt Whitman: "a long brown path that leads wherever I choose." **BDS**

⬆ **Find your way along Walt Whitman's "long brown path."**

Batona Trail New Jersey, USA

Start Bass River State Forest   **End** Ong's Hat, Brendan T. Byrne State Forest   **Distance** 49.5 miles (79.7 km)
Time 3 days   **Grade** Easy   **Type** Dirt, sandy trails   **Map** goo.gl/PVYihg

New Jersey's Pine Barrens is one of North America's most interesting landscapes—a vast forested coastal plain. Its sandy acidic soil is low in nutrients, a fact that has helped keep settlers at bay and its population low—around twenty people per square kilometer compared to more than 1,000 people per square kilometer in the areas immediately bordering it. There are ghost towns in the Pine Barrens: abandoned villages that once provided the scant manpower for sawmills, grist mills, and paper mills that are long since gone.

Built by the Philadelphia-based Batona Hiking Club in 1961, the Batona Trail is an intrinsic part of this ethereal landscape and one of New Jersey's longest trails. It begins in the Bass River State Forest, passing through the Wharton State Forest before ending at the ghost town of Ong's Hat on New Jersey Route 72.

Although the trail for the most part avoids the Barrens's preponderance of sandy roads, about a fifth of it is in soft sand, which can make for slow going. The trail is not difficult, though, crossing a pancake-flat landscape alongside the country's largest cranberry bogs just an hour's drive from Philadelphia.

The Barrens's Pygmy Pitch pines live in a mutually beneficial relationship with their neighboring oaks, which grow so tall that they block out the sunlight the pines need to thrive. Blueberries and huckleberries are in abundance, as well as sassafras and sweet gum. And let's not forget the rare Pine Barrens tree frog. In all there are 850 plant species, 39 species of mammals, 300 species of birds, and 59 types of reptiles and amphibians here. Hardly "barren" at all, really. **BDS**

⬆ Discover the beauty of the Pine Barrens.

Beaver Brook Trail New Jersey, USA

Start Berkshire Valley Road trailhead, Jefferson Township   End Mahlon Dickerson Reservation
Distance 6.2 miles (10 km)   Time 5 hours   Grade Moderate   Type Dirt trail   Info goo.gl/bsCCEw

You need to work hard to get the most out of New Jersey's Beaver Brook Trail. This is a white-blazed trail that begins with a rather long and exhausting ascent, has precarious footholds and loose rocks, and at times becomes extremely narrow, with the occasional level hilltop of typical New Jersey bedrock. After the initial climb the trail is mostly a mix of short, level walks and descents through forests with thickish undergrowth.

After crossing a streambed that is simple to ford, even after heavy rains, the trail then climbs again and comes out at an overlook, where you will be able to catch glimpses of the Rockaway River. A final descent brings you down into an open area of forest, from where it is a short hike to Beaver Brook. Here the trail breaks to the left and follows the stream into a swampy area, where you will be able to view a series of impressive beaver lodges built of branches

plastered with mud, although probably not the nocturnal beavers themselves.

Black bears have been seen in the area, so stay aware, but generally all you will encounter along this tranquil trail are wooded ridges, the occasional hawk, and maybe some frogs. The trail is simplicity itself. It passes through a large rock called Split Rock, then instead of a nice wooden bridge to carry you across Beaver Brook, there is a well-positioned assemblage of planks. Even if you see a beaver, the real show is above you, in the impressive canopy of red maple, yellow birch, red oak, red cedar, white pine, and black birch—a kaleidoscope of fall colors that surely makes October the best time to walk one of New Jersey's least-trodden fall trails. **BDS**

⬆ Solitude is guaranteed on this seldom-trampled trail.

Gunpowder Falls, North and South Loops
Maryland, USA

Start/End Masemore Road, off Mount Carmel Road (Hwy 137) Distance 9.6 miles (15.4 km) Time 4 hours Grade Moderate Type Woodland, dirt paths, some rocky areas Info goo.gl/pJwM4y

Big Gunpowder Falls and Little Gunpowder Falls are two short freshwater rivers that join to form the Gunpowder River, a 6.8-mile-long (10.9 km) tidal inlet on the western side of Chesapeake Bay, just north of Baltimore. The rivers flow through the Gunpowder Falls State Park, the largest park in the small state of Maryland. The park is much enjoyed for its varied scenery of tidal marshes and inland hills, but it is only the latter that are experienced on this walk.

The two Gunpowder Falls trails form a figure eight. They offer a pleasurable ramble through mixed hardwood and conifer forests, alongside and above the scenic Big Gunpowder Falls. The South Trail follows the Big Gunpowder down its narrow, steep-sided valley. The path here is rugged, and progress can be slow over the many boulders and roots that line the way. Where the Mingo Branch joins the main river, prepare to cross the 12-foot-wide (3.7 m) creek on stepping-stones—this may involve a shin-deep wade outside the dry season. The trees are mainly river birches, oaks, mountain laurels, black walnuts, and white pines, with plenty of spring and summer flowers in season. Along the way you may spot red foxes, beavers, white-tailed deer, and wild turkeys. But please do not fish for trout: Big Gunpowder Falls is a stocked trout stream for which licenses are required.

Once under Interstate 83 and the York Road, the trail crosses over itself and becomes the North Loop. Evidence of earlier settlements can be seen on the north bank, where the mature forest has been replaced by quick-growing walnut and other recovery species of tree. Remains of a kiln and stone foundations are clearly visible. **SA**

"If you're craving beauty and shade at the same time, check out both the Gunpowder North Trail and Gunpowder South Trail."

baltimore.cbslocal.com

⬆ Two trails combine for a scenic loop over boulders, tree roots, and rushing creeks.

Sugarloaf Mountain

Maryland, USA

Start/End Various   **Distance** Various
Time Various   **Grade** Easy to moderate
Type Mixed trails in good condition
Map goo.gl/8aOUEU

Sugarloaf Mountain rises nearly 800 feet (244 m) from the farming landscape of Maryland, in the mid-Atlantic United States. In geological terms it's a monadnock, a mountain that sits in relative isolation, left behind after the erosion of the surrounding landmass. It is owned and managed by a private company, but is open to the public and used by hikers, horseback riders, and picnickers.

The mountain is home to a number of trails of varying lengths, from 2 miles (3.2 km) to around 10 miles (16 km). A number of them are marked and signposted, and one takes you on a loop of the mountain. The Saddleback Horse Trail runs for 7 miles (11.3 km) around the base of Sugarloaf and is open to hikers and horses year-round. Alternatively, the Mountain Loop Trail, marked with white signposts, takes you around the summit for 2.5 miles (4 km).

There are plenty of other routes on offer, which take in some stunning views from the lush woodland and rocky outcrops of the mountain's flanks. If you can't face the thought of ascending the whole thing, it is possible to drive partway up Sugarloaf Mountain, park, and then walk the final stretch to the summit.

Wildlife species habiting the mountain include white-tailed deer, flying squirrels, and red-shouldered hawks. At one point President Franklin D. Roosevelt considered building a presidential retreat here, but opted for Camp David instead.

There are picnic spots dotted around the mountain, and at the West View parking area, there's a snack bar run by a local family. There's no camping on the mountain itself, but the surrounding foothills host plenty of choice in accommodation. **JI**

"… there are lots of hiking opportunities available on the mountain for all levels of skill and stamina."

www.patc.us

⤒ Trails aplenty greet you on the summit of Maryland's isolated Sugarloaf Mountain.

Mount Vernon Trail Virginia, USA

Start Parking lot, Theodore Roosevelt Island wilderness preserve **End** Mount Vernon Estate **Distance** 18 miles (29 km) **Time** 7–8 hours **Grade** Easy **Type** Mixed-use pathway **Map** goo.gl/akQq7m

The Mount Vernon Trail runs parallel to the western shoreline of the Potomac River, overlooking the nation's capital. It begins near the Arlington Memorial Bridge and Theodore Roosevelt Island wilderness preserve—which itself has 2.5 miles (4 km) of walking trails—and runs south past the Navy Marine Memorial statue and Gravelly Point, with its sweeping panorama of the Washington, D.C. skyline. The old tobacco trading and shipbuilding town of Alexandria is bisected, then it's on past the nineteenth-century fortifications of Fort Washington and the Jones Point Lighthouse to the Mount Vernon Estate, the home of George Washington, the United States' first president. Along the 18-mile (29-km) mixed-use pathway, there are connections with a number of regional trails, including the Potomac Heritage National Scenic Trail and the Woodrow Wilson Bridge Trail.

It would be difficult to find a trail in the United States that ends at a more historic venue and provides a more idyllic spot to unwind and recuperate. The Mount Vernon Estate includes the main house, built in a somewhat "loose" Palladian style by an unknown architect and extended in stages over a forty-five-year period beginning in 1757, and an impressive collection of outbuildings. Once here, the walking need not stop. You can go on a tour of the mansion that includes the basement and the third floor, where Martha Washington retired after the death of George in 1799, or you could spend hours exploring its extensive gardens, visiting Washington's tomb, walking among the slave quarters, and just soaking up the atmosphere of this legacy to the nation's founder. **BDS**

⊤ Stroll the Potomac River to Mount Vernon.

New River Trail Virginia, USA

Start Pulaski **End** Galax or Fries **Distance** 57 miles (91.7 km) **Time** Variable **Grade** Easy
Type Rail trail **Map** goo.gl/RN6THh

The New River Trail is a 57-mile-long (91.7 km) path that follows along an old railway line in the state of Virginia, an 80-foot-wide (24.4 m) trail that runs through the heart of a 765-acre (310-ha) state park.

The trail starts in the town of Pulaski and runs to Fries Junction, where it splits, with branches going to both Fries and Galax. For 39 miles (62.8 km) the trail follows the line of the New River, and along its length are three major bridges, including one at Fries Junction that is more than 1,000 feet (305 m) long and provides a great view of the river. There are also thirty smaller bridges and wooden trestles, as well as two old railway tunnels more than 100 feet (30.5 m) in length.

The park is a popular place with walkers, joggers, cyclists, and horseback riders, as well as anglers and even canoeists. The trail is relatively flat and runs mostly through Virginian woodland, with the bed of the old railway line as its surface. The bridges are similarly well maintained and safe, and there is a respectable sprinkling of campsites along the route, as well as picnic areas and towns with shops and other amenities.

Landmarks you'll see along the route include the Shot Tower, which was built more than 200 years ago to make ammunition for local settlers. And, of course, there is the New River itself, the banks of which are right alongside you for much of the hike. There are several places in the park where it is possible to rent a kayak or canoe if you feel like going out on the water, and you're never too far from a site that reminds you that this was, for many years, part of the Norfolk Southern Railway. **JI**

⬆ **Experience the serenity of the New River.**

Old Rag Mountain, Shenandoah National Park
Virginia, USA

Start/End Trailhead at parking area
Distance 8 miles (12.8 km)   Time 7–8 hours
Grade Strenuous   Type Mountain trek
Map goo.gl/23rxSB

There aren't too many occasions when you're advised to watch a safety video before you head out on a trail, but Old Rag Mountain is not your average hike. Each year there are incidents on the mountain where walkers have to be rescued by park rangers, hence the need to make potential visitors aware of the challenges that Old Rag might throw at them.

There are approximately 500 miles (800 km) of trails around the mountain, which lies in the state of Virginia. Most of the trails are straightforward, but some are much tougher—the 8-mile (12.8-km) Old Rag circuit features a 3-mile (4.8-km) section that involves ascending 2,200 feet (670 m), equivalent to taking the stairs to the top of a 220-story building. There's also a lot of rock scrambling, squeezing through uncomfortably tight crevices, and even a section through a cave.

You need to carry your water supplies (at least a liter per person), have the right clothing and footwear, and wear layers, so you're prepared for changes in the weather. Given how long it can take to complete the circuit, it's also worth taking a headlamp, as it may be dark before you finish—another reason to start early in the morning (before 7 a.m.) and so benefit from missing the big crowds that Old Rag attracts. There are toilet facilities along the trail, and the National Park authorities would prefer you to use these rather than take a detour into the bushes.

Old Rag is an epic hike, but the reward for all that effort is plainly evident when you reach the top—the views over the Shenandoah National Park are truly breathtaking. Providing, of course, you have any breath left to be taken. JI

"A day on Old Rag is one of Shenandoah's premier experiences."

www.nps.gov

Old Rag is an epic mix of rock scrambling, crevice squeezing, and exhausting climbs.

Crabtree Falls

Virginia, USA

Start/End Trailhead at parking area
Distance 4.4 miles (7 km)   **Time** 3.5 hours
Grade Easy to moderate   **Type** Man-made,
forest trails   **Map** goo.gl/ltke9Y

In Virginia's George Washington National Forest there stands one of the highest sets of waterfalls east of the Mississippi. Crabtree Falls is more than 1,000 feet (305 m) high and is made up of five major drops, the tallest of which is 400 feet (121.9 m). It is thought to be named after William Crabtree, a settler who came to this part of the state in the late 1700s.

The hike starts out on a paved trail from the parking area, but don't miss walking down to the distinctive wooden footbridge that spans the Tye River in an impressive single arch and was built off-site and delivered in 1978 in one piece. The trail soon switches to dirt, but this path is kept in a good state of preservation, and there are handrails at its trickier points. There are numerous spots along the trail where you can get a good view of the mighty falls from behind the safety of railings and barriers. Don't think about scaling any rock walls or the stone walls higher up the path—the rocks around the falls are covered in a transparent algae that renders them as slippery as ice, and more than twenty people have died after falling from here in recent years. Just stick to the designated path and you'll be fine. All the cascades are impressive, and throughout your walk you'll be surrounded by the sound of thundering water. Although the trail is well maintained; it can get muddy and slippery, so you need decent footwear. There's a bulletin board at the start of the trail, which provides daily updates on conditions.

The view from the very top is of the Tye Valley—you can't actually see the falls from here, just the forest canopy. But the best views are on the way up, where you can gasp in awe at the giant cascades. **JI**

"Crabtree Falls is arguably the most beautiful set of waterfalls in Virginia."

www.hikingupward.com

⬆ Try not to slip on transparent algae while walking Virginia's trail of thundering waters.

Dolly Sods Wilderness West Virginia, USA

Start/End Various   **Distance** Various   **Time** Various   **Grade** Easy to moderate
Type Well-maintained footpath   **Info** goo.gl/gFddai

When Johann Dahle, known as John Dolly, came to the United States in the late eighteenth century to fight for the British in the Revolutionary War, little did he know he would one day be lending his name to an area of great U.S. wilderness. The Dolly Sods Wilderness covers more than 17,000 acres (6,880 ha) within the Monongahela National Forest in West Virginia. Its typical elevation is around 3,700 feet (1,130 m), and it forms a high plateau with bogs and heath more commonly found in parts of Canada.

It is also home to nearly 47 miles (75 km) of trails, many of which follow old logging roads and railroad lines. These vary in length from 6 to 15 miles (9.7–24.1 km) and cover terrain ranging from forests to riverbeds and swamps. The area used to be home to elk and mountain lion, but both species are now long gone. Fauna still present includes red and gray foxes, wild turkeys, bobcats, and bears. There are campsites, picnic sites, and cabins across the Dolly Sods, but visitors are told to "leave no trace," and all off-road vehicles are banned.

Parts of the Dolly Sods Wilderness were used for military training during World War II, and the area is known to be littered with old, live shells. Thankfully, the National Forest authorities give advice on how to stay safe, including keeping to designated trails and camping only in properly marked sites. The weather can change suddenly here, going from sun to snow to fog within an hour, and the temperature can drop to freezing at any time of the year. Snow can be expected from October to April, and the forest roads are not maintained through winter. **JI**

⊼ A high plateau filled with bogs and heaths.

High Meadows/Seneca Creek Loop West Virginia, USA

Start/End Seneca Creek parking area **Distance** 13.5 miles (21.7 km) **Time** 1–2 days **Grade** Moderate to strenuous **Type** Well-maintained footpath but possibly boggy **Map** goo.gl/aqyw9G

Seneca Creek in West Virginia's Monongahela National Forest is a 10-mile-long (16 km) stream named after nearby Seneca Rock. The creek is home to wild trout and is rated one of the best trout fishing spots in the United States. The area also offers exceptional hiking, particularly along the side of Spruce Mountain, one of the top trekking destinations in the eastern United States. The High Meadows/Seneca Creek loop is a great example of the quality of the local trails.

It begins on a short section of road but it's not long before you peel off onto the Lumberjack Trail (marked with blue diamonds), which, even on a dry day, can be boggy and is particularly hard going after rainfall. Once you've made it onto the High Meadows Trail proper, you'll come out into one of the many meadows that provide for some fabulous views of the Monongahela National Forest, with

Seneca Creek Valley stretching away from you to the north and south.

There are a number of waterfalls along the route, including Seneca Falls, which is accessible from an overlook. There are also crossing points over the stream in several places. Camping spots are plentiful and of a high standard, including one with its very own waterfall, and the whole area is crisscrossed with dozens of trails, so you could easily take a few diversions if the mood prevails.

High Meadows/Seneca Creek is a popular hiking route and offers a great experience for those able to cope with the muddy and damp conditions. At times the terrain can be challenging, but the great views and stunning waterfalls are ample compensation. **JI**

⌂ Waterfalls and bogs aplenty on a popular, muddy trail.

Greenbrier River Trail
West Virginia, USA

Start North Caldwell   **End** Cass
Distance 77 miles (124 km)   **Time** 7 days
Grade Easy to moderate   **Type** Rail trail, crushed sandstone   **Map** goo.gl/7EobWK

The Greenbrier River Trail follows the line of an old railroad that winds for 77 miles (124 km) through the state of West Virginia. Despite its length, it is not an arduous journey, as the track is made of crushed sandstone and is kept in good order by the West Virginia State Park authorities. It's also gently sloping (around a 1 percent gradient), which makes it popular not only with walkers, but also with cyclists and horseback riders.

For most of its length, the trail parallels the Greenbrier River, which offers plenty of opportunities for swimming and fishing (the river is home to small-mouth bass). There are plenty of campsites along the route, as well as B&Bs, hotels, and lodges, and there are toilet facilities every 10 miles (16 km) or so.

Despite the great facilities, the trail takes you through some of the most remote landscapes in West Virginia, passing old railroad workings and remnants of a once thriving logging industry. There are a few towns along the way, including Clover Lick and Marlinton, but for the most part the trail avoids bringing you into contact with civilization.

The trail crosses the Greenbrier River several times, but there's no need to get your feet wet as this is a rails-to-trails path, and there are numerous bridges to carry you over the water. There are also old railroad tunnels to take you through the hillsides—though you may need to take a flashlight with you.

The Greenbrier River Trail is an easily walked path, with good facilities, stunning scenery, and plenty to see and do along the way. No wonder, then, that it has been rated as one of the top ten hiking trails in the United States. **JI**

"It has achieved accessibility without compromising its remote character."

www.railstotrails.org

⊼ A rail trail takes you through some of West Virginia's most pristine, untouched landscapes.

Hatfield–McCoy Trail System West Virginia, USA

Start/End Various **Distance** Various
Time Various **Grade** Easy to strenuous
Type Maintained forest paths
Info goo.gl/F75IPC

There can't be many hiking routes in the world named after a bloody and violent feud between two rival families. The Hatfield and McCoy clans, living on the borders of West Virginia and Kentucky, slugged it out during the late nineteenth century. The reason for their mutual loathing ranged from ownership of a hog to who-sided-with-whom during the Civil War and even the occasional illicit relationship.

The barroom brawls and lynchings may be long gone, but now this part of West Virginia is home to a sprawling, complex system of off-road trails that are

---

"The trail system complements the natural beauty of the Appalachian Mountains."

www.americantrails.org

---

used not only by walkers but by riders of ATVs, bikes, and buggies. Horseback riders and mountain bikers also flock to them. Overcrowding isn't a problem, however, since there are more than 600 miles (965 km) of trails, covering six of nine West Virginia counties.

There are more than 100 separate hiking trails here, all color graded for difficulty from green to black. Although many of the tracks are old logging and mine access roads, it's a good idea to check on conditions beforehand. There are plenty of campsites in the area, along with hotels, B&Bs, and lodges.

The concept behind the trail system was to help reinvigorate the state. Its success is something not even the feuding families could argue about. **JI**

Cranberry Wilderness West Virginia, USA

Start/End Various **Distance** Various
Time Various **Grade** Easy to moderate
Type Wilderness paths
Info goo.gl/Etz3LF

The Cranberry Wilderness is seen by many as the crown jewel of the Monongahela National Forest. It covers almost 48,000 acres (19,425 ha), and in many ways is a true wilderness—dense overhead canopy, unmarked trails, and mountainous terrain. It lies in the Yew Mountains, part of the Allegheny range. The highest point, on Black Mountain, is 4,556 feet (1,389 m) high, while down at Williams River, it's a mere 2,400 feet (730 m) above sea level. The wilderness is crisscrossed by numerous trails of various lengths and difficulties, ranging from short 1-mile (1.6-km) treks to longer loops. Some are fairly flat and steady while others, such as the County Line Trail, drop 1,600 feet (488 m) in less than 10 miles (16 km).

The region was once part of the logging industry, but is now an officially designated wilderness area, and hikers should behave accordingly. Campfires are frowned upon and visitors are encouraged to camp more than 200 feet (61 m) from roads. Trails are unmarked, there are no bridges over the main river crossing points, and the ground underfoot will often be muddy and wet. The ability to use a map and compass is considered essential here, and the weather can change suddenly, so be prepared. In places you will need to be careful of bears, so any food will need to be properly packed and secured.

You will be rewarded, however, with stunning scenery: dense forests, waterfalls, and mountain peaks. Worth a mention is the Cranberry Glades Botanical area, 750 acres (304 ha) of bog, found at the southern tip of the wilderness. There's a 0.5-mile (0.8-km) boardwalk that leads into this area, and you can take a guided tour. **JI**

Craggy Gardens Trail North Carolina, USA

Start/End South end of the visitor center, at milepost 364   **Distance** 1.4 miles (2.25 km)
Time 30 minutes   **Grade** Easy   **Type** Mountain trail   **Map** goo.gl/xoepi9

The name of this trail is apt. In early summer, the rhododendrons, flame azalea, and mountain laurel that cover the caps (known as balds) of the Blue Ridge Mountains burst into bloom, covering them in nets of pink and purple flowers. The Craggy Gardens Trail showcases this annual display, as well as the defining image of the Blue Ridge Mountains—tier upon tier of gently rounded peaks stretching to a blue horizon.

The trail lies between mileposts 364 and 367 on the Blue Ridge Parkway, a scenic road built to connect North Carolina's Great Smoky Mountains National Park and Virginia's Shenandoah National Park. The road was one of President Franklin D. Roosevelt's many job creation projects during the Great Depression. From the visitor center it is a gentle uphill amble with steps cut into the rocks and strategically placed benches overlooking Craggy Flats and Craggy Knob, ending at

a picnic area with grills and tables. For more things craggy, on the other side of the visitor center, hikers can go the extra 1 mile (1.6 km) or so to Craggy Pinnacle, with its head-spinning view, dropping by Craggy Dome Overlook on the way, or take the more demanding 4.2-mile (6.8-km) trail (one way) to Douglas Falls, a 70-foot (21-m) sheer cascade. For a much more challenging hike, away from the many visitors who converge on Craggy Gardens in their thousands each year, keen hikers can take in a section of the long-distance Appalachian or Mountains-to-Sea trails, both of which pass through here. While early summer may be the best time to visit Craggy Gardens, September, with its fall colors, blackberries, and blueberries, comes a close second. **DS**

⬆ A trail of craggy flats, knobs, and pinnacles.

Mountains-to-Sea Trail North Carolina, USA

Start Clingman's Dome   **End** Jockey's Ridge   **Distance** 530 miles (853 km)   **Time** 40 days
Grade Moderate to strenuous   **Type** Long-distance trail   **Info** goo.gl/BLHbJo

This trail takes its name from the Great Smoky range at its western end and its eastern terminus on the sandy shores of the Atlantic Ocean. Commonly known as the MST, it reaches a height of 6,684 feet (2,037 m) as it crosses Mount Mitchell, the highest peak in the United States, east of the Mississippi.

Only the toughest walkers would contemplate the westbound MST: the gradients are too steep and unrelenting. Starting wisely from the western trailhead, near the border with Tennessee, hikers follow the Blue Ridge Parkway through the Appalachian Mountains. The track then proceeds through two great forests—the Nantahala and the Pisgah—between which lies the Middle Prong Wilderness, an area of steep bluffs and ridges around the headwaters of the Pigeon River. Next is Mount Mitchell and then a succession of parks in the Piedmont, the plateau that separates the

mountains from the eastern seaboard. On reaching the coast, the MST passes Cape Hatteras, the easternmost point of North Carolina's Outer Banks—if you are there on a clear day between April and October, when the lighthouse is open to the public, don't miss the view from the top. The route then passes through a chain of islands, some of which are reached by ferry, before its eastern terminus in Jockey's Ridge State Park, the site of a vast expanse of active sand dunes and a wind turbine farm. At the time of this book's publication, not all sections of the MST had been completed. However, the missing links can be extrapolated by reference to maps and the definitive guide *The Mountains-to-Sea Trail Across North Carolina* (2013) by Danny Bernstein. **GL**

⬆ Save your legs and walk this trail east to west.

Foothills Trail
South Carolina, USA

"This is truly some of the best backcountry wilderness that the southeast has to offer."

hikingthecarolinas.com

⬆ It may be a foothills trail, but it still takes you to South Carolina's highest point.

Start Table Rock State Park   **End** Oconee State Park
Distance 76 miles (122 km)   **Time** 6 days
Grade Moderate   **Type** Wooded paths, rocky surfaces
Info goo.gl/8F8SKm

To the east of the Appalachian Mountains, and separated from them by the Great Appalachian Valley, lie the fabled Blue Ridge Mountains. These mountains—noted for their bluish color when seen from a distance, which is caused by the isoprene released into the hazy atmosphere by its trees—run from Georgia to Pennsylvania. As they pass through the Carolinas, a lengthy trail clambers up and down their sides.

The Foothills Trail begins in Table Rock State Park and passes Pinnacle Mountain before it climbs Sassafras Mountain, at 3,553 feet (1,083 m)—the highest point in South Carolina. The trail then drops to Chimneytop Gap and Laurel Valley before rising and falling again to Lower Fork Falls. From there a series of steep ascents and descents carries the trail over the state border into North Carolina before recrossing the border to the Bad Creek Access.

The trail now runs alongside the Whitewater River before briefly crossing back into and out of North Carolina and on to Sloan Bridge. The trail eventually descends into the Chattooga River Gorge and runs parallel to the river before climbing back up to SC Highway 107 and on to its end at the Oconee State Park. If you've followed the above route carefully, you will by now be aware that this trail is no flat-footed ramble, but a sharp series of climbs and descents that will provide a testing time for your quad muscles.

If you are in pain, just remember to look at the views, and it will all be worthwhile. They are truly magnificent, especially down to the depths of the gorges and out over the canopy to the Blue Mountains that surround you. **SA**

Francis Beidler Forest Trail
South Carolina, USA

Start/End Visitor center, Francis Beidler Forest, Four Holes Swamp   Distance 1.75 miles (2.8 km)
Time 2 hours   Grade Easy   Type Wooden boardwalk
Map goo.gl/jnusnK

The National Audubon Society is the United States' premier environmental and conservation organization. Founded in 1905 and named in honor of John James Audubon, famed for his beautifully illustrated *Birds of America* (1827), the society runs wildlife refuges and parks in many states, including the Francis Beidler Forest in South Carolina. Beidler was a Chicagoan timber merchant who, in the early 1900s, turned his South Carolina timber forests in the Congaree Swamp into a nature reserve. The forest named after him is 40 miles (64.3 km) northwest of Charleston, a separate blackwater creek system covering more than 16,000 acres (6,475 ha) of mainly bald cypress and tupelo gum swamp, the largest such stand of this type of forest left anywhere in the world.

The forest trail consists of a loop of boardwalk that is wheelchair accessible and easy to stroll around in an hour or two. As you amble along, you pass trees that are more than 1,000 years old, listen to the sounds of birds and bugs, and soak up the atmosphere of this pristine sanctuary. There are 50 different species of reptile; 40 species of amphibians; 140 species of birds; and numerous mammals, arachnids, fish, and insects. Among the many mammals are nine-banded armadillos, opossums, bats, beavers, raccoons, coyotes, and squirrels of all descriptions. As for the reptiles, look out for turtles, lizards, snakes, and the daddy of them all, the American alligator.

As this trail is in a nature park, it is closed on Mondays and major public holidays and open the rest of the week from 9 a.m. to 5 p.m. There is no "best" season to visit, and canoe trips and naturalist-guided walks are also available. **SA**

Bartram Trail
Georgia to North Carolina, USA

Start Russell Bridge, near Satolah, Georgia
End Cheoah Bald, North Carolina   Distance 115 miles
(186 km)   Time 6 days   Grade Moderate   Type Forest, mountain   Info goo.gl/AjUUly

In 1773, the naturalist William Bartram began a four-year journey through what were then the eight southern colonies of Britain's North American empire, observing the native flora and fauna and surviving encounters along the way with hostile peoples and angry alligators. This nature trail closely follows his route through two southern states, and was created using references to landmarks in his journal.

The trail starts in the North Georgia Mountains and heads up the Appalachian Mountains into North Carolina. In Georgia, the 37-mile-long (59.5 km) trail at

> *"The Bartram Trail offers the consummate southern Appalachian experience."*
>
> www.gorp.com

first heads south along the Chattooga River before turning west and then sharply northeast along the Tennessee Valley Divide, rising up to Rabun Bald. Still in a seminatural state, the top of this mountain affords wonderful views across more than 100 miles (160 km) of the southern Appalachians.

Once over the border and into North Carolina, the trail heads northwest for a further 78 miles (126 km), twice joining the Appalachian Trail. It reaches its highest point at Wayah Bald, 5,385 feet (1,640 m) of mountainous magnificence topped with a stone observation tower. "Wa-ya" is a Cherokee word for "wolf," but those beasts decamped long ago. Go in spring when the rhododendrons and azaleas are in bloom. **SA**

Benton MacKaye Trail
Georgia to North Carolina, USA

Start Springer Mountain, Georgia **End** Big Creek, North Carolina **Distance** 300 miles (483 km) **Time** 21–28 days **Grade** Easy to moderate **Type** Long-distance trail **Info** goo.gl/UKtjSt

Benton MacKaye was the Massachusetts forester and regional planner who, in the 1920s, founded the Appalachian Trail. The route named in his memory was conceived as an alternative to the original path.

Both routes start from Springer Mountain, in the Chattahoochee National Forest. They share a common path for a short distance, but then the Benton MacKaye Trail peels off through Tennessee and ends in North Carolina. Its lowest point is 765 feet (233 m), at the Hiwassee River crossing; its summit is the 5,843-foot (1,781-m) peak of Mount Sterling.

"So, if a new wilderness experience is what you are out to find, the Benton MacKaye is waiting for you."

bmtguide.com

Scenic highlights include both natural and man-made wonders. The pick of the former are two cascades—Long Creek Falls in Georgia and Fall Branch Falls in Tennessee. Among the latter are Fontana Lake, a reservoir behind the Fontana Dam on the Little Tennessee River, and the swinging footbridge over the Toccoa River. Between these landmarks, the track regularly changes its character: long stretches beneath canopies of laurel and rhododendron are interspersed with open timberland and ridgetop tracks with stunning panoramic views.

The Benton MacKaye Trail is glorious when the weather is good, but in extreme conditions, it can morph from tame to wild. **GL**

Appalachian Trail
Georgia to Maine, USA

Start Springer Mountain, Georgia **End** Mount Katahdin, Maine **Distance** 2,160 miles (3,476 km) **Time** 5–7 months **Grade** Easy to strenuous **Type** Even forest trails to rock scrambling **Info** goo.gl/XfKlbL

Somebody once calculated that it would take the average person around five million steps to complete a thru-hike of the Appalachian Trail, possibly the world's most well-known trail. For those who achieve this remarkable feat, the reasons for doing so are as varied as the vagaries of life: a personal tragedy, a redundancy, a need to be challenged, or just a love of walking and wilderness. Even one of its approach trails, from Amicalola Falls to its official start at Georgia's Springer Mountain, is 8 miles (12.9 km) long. It is Mount Everest without the altitude, and together with the Continental Divide Trail and Pacific Crest Trail makes up the Triple Crown of U.S. long-distance hiking.

Given its impetus with the publication in 1921 of Benton MacKaye's article "An Appalachian Trail: A Project in Regional Planning," it winds its way between Springer Mountain in Georgia and Mount Katahdin in Maine. Half of its length is spent on the crests of the Blue Ridge Mountains, while other segments take you through nameless Pennsylvania gullies so rocky that walkers call them "Rocksylvanias." It is often referred to as "the long, green tunnel," because of its path through thick, mostly deciduous forests. But what it lacks in vistas it more than makes up for in biological diversity—only South America's rain forests contain more plant species per acre than can be found here.

The trail ranges from flat and smooth to lengthy graded climbs and rock scrambling. From rugged hiking above the tree lines of New England to the glacial hills of the Hudson Highlands in New York, the Appalachian Trail has something for everyone. **BDS**

⬌ Viewing the "long green tunnel" from above.

Mountain Creek Nature Trail Georgia, USA

Start/End Trading post off Interstate 27, west end of F. D. Roosevelt State Park   **Distance** 3.2 miles (5.1 km)   **Time** 2 hours   **Grade** Easy   **Type** Woodland paths   **Map** goo.gl/Lt1XyQ

The Franklin D. Roosevelt State Park—Georgia's largest—is a 9,049-acre (3,662-ha) expanse of trees and scrub on Pine Mountain Ridge. It contains many trails, including the delightful Mountain Creek Nature Trail.

The trail loops through a little more than 3 miles (5 km) of mixed forest, with creeks running through it and rocky outcrops poking above the trees. A high canopy of oaks, hickory, and loblolly pines form a roof over the midstory of smaller trees, such as red maples and sweet gums, and a dark forest floor of sparse shrubs. Oak leaf hydrangeas, rhododendrons, and

> *"This 3.2-mile-long loop trail introduces you to the plants and animals in a mixed oak-pine forest."*
>
> gastateparks.org

southern magnolias line the banks of the creeks, while chestnut and black leaf oaks stick to the dryer ridges. The creeks are full of small aquatic creatures and damselflies and dragonflies; other wildlife includes snakes, lizards, and chipmunks. Beware the venomous copperhead snake, which should be left well alone.

The best time to venture into this slice of paradise is early in the morning or just before sunset, when you can hear the red-bellied or Downey woodpeckers in noisy action and see the deer grazing in the forest glades. Walk around the loop in either direction, the frequent red markers helping you find your way. For the more adventurous, longer, and more arduous trails ramble around the rest of the park. **SA**

Okefenokee National Wildlife Refuge Georgia, USA

Start/End Richard S. Bolt Visitor Center   **Distance** Various   **Time** Various   **Grade** Easy   **Type** Elevated walkways and graded trails   **Map** goo.gl/Odxls2

The Okefenokee National Wildlife Refuge preserves a great swathe of Georgia swampland, the name of which comes from a Native American word for "trembling earth." The whole area was exploited as a major commercial source of timber from the start of the Columbian period to 1937, when its fauna and flora were first brought under protection. The trails are comprised of eight short routes that can be covered comfortably in a day from the starting point at the Richard S. Bolt Visitor Center. The Okefenokee is of particular interest to naturalists—the area has deer, squirrels, box turtles, gopher tortoises, and numerous species of snakes and birds. It is also of interest to anyone wanting to know more about the sustainable wood cultivation methods now practiced here.

The longest walk is the 4-mile (6.4-km) Longleaf Pine Interpretive Trail, which passes through pine forest and crosses the Suwannee Canal before merging into the Canal Diggers Trail, a 0.75-mile (1.2-km) loop around land that has been dedicated to riparian animals and plants. The Phernetton Trail is another loop, 1.25 miles (2 km) long, through the refuge's upland habitats; the Ridley Island Trail extends for a similar distance through wetlands to Chesser Island, a small outcrop of dry land near the edge of the swamp. The other optional routes are no more than 1 mile (1.6 km) long. The Upland Discovery Trail leads to a colony of endangered red-cockaded woodpeckers; the Chesser Island Homestead Trail takes visitors around the exterior of an historic residential property surrounded by native and exotic flora. The Cane Pole Trail returns to an observation platform overlooking the Suwannee Canal. **GL**

Kissimmee River National Scenic Trail
Florida, USA

Start Okee-Tantie, Lake Okeechobee   **Start** S65E
Lock Access Road, off junction of SR 70 and CR 599
Distance 23 miles (37 km)   **Time** 1–2 days   **Grade** Easy
Type Duckboard, towpath   **Map** goo.gl/3ZNJoJ

The Kissimmee River in south-central Florida is one of those remarkable rivers that never generates enough energy to wash out into the sea. Instead it flows south down a leisurely 134-mile (216-km) route out of East Lake Tohopekaliga and on through Lake Kissimmee into Lake Okeechobee, where it joins the headwaters of the vast, swamp-laden Everglades. For much of its route, the river is canalized, although oxbows are currently being reintroduced to slow the river down and rehydrate its flood plain.

The Kissimmee River National Scenic Trail runs parallel to the river, which is natural in some places and canalized in others. This trail is a flat amble on duckboards and towpaths through swamplands, pine flatlands, wild scrublands, and hammocks of oak trees. Let's be honest here. You don't go on this trail for its exciting or strenuous walking or for vistas of far-distant hills and deep valleys. Rather, you go for the abundant wildlife, as well as for the surprise that a state as crowded as Florida can still manage to have such an empty interior. Across the acres of empty water meadow it is possible to spot white-tailed deer, turkeys, wild hogs, sandhill cranes, and numerous water birds. Eagles and hawks soar overhead, while alligators lurk in the watery shallows. Along the way you will pass the remains of settler homesteads and small towns that flourished in the 1800s and then vanished as railroads took the place of steamboats.

The Kissimmee River National Scenic Trail is part of the much longer network of national scenic trails that stretches for roughly 1,300 miles (2,090 km) along the length of Florida, a worthy project to get the state of Florida, and its visitors, walking. **SA**

"The Kissimmee River National Scenic Trail … offers some of the best remote hiking in Florida."

www.secretfalls.com

⬆ Swamp cypress trees provide habitat for the abundant wildlife on the trail.

Everglades Trail Florida, USA

Start Various **End** Various **Distance** Various **Time** Various **Grade** Easy **Type** Paved walkway, boardwalk, trail **Info** goo.gl/1z2lPM

The Everglades Trail has no specified route, but for most it begins at Shingle Creek in urban Orlando, at the headwaters of the Everglades ecosystem, before heading southwest through the 12,000-acre (4,856-ha) Disney Wilderness Preserve and into Lake Kissimmee State Park and the dry prairie habitat of the Prairie Lakes Unit. Continuing south, it passes through dense stands of hickory before merging with the Lake Okeechobee Scenic Trail. Farther south, you enter the Biscayne and Everglades national parks, pass through a section of the 729,000-acre (295,016-ha) Big Cypress National Park with its mix of tropical and temperate plant life, and along a self-guided boardwalk through the old-growth cypress trees of Fakahatchee Strand Preserve State Park and its own 60 miles (97 km) of trails.

The history of the local Seminole people is told at the Collier–Seminole State Park before a walking trail takes you through the Florida Panther National Wildlife Refuge and finally to trail's end at the Seminole Ah-Tah-Thi-Ki Museum, a living replica of a Seminole village with more than 30,000 artifacts depicting Seminole life at the turn of the twentieth century.

Each Everglades Trail site is marked by its own green-roofed kiosk, and the best way to cover the trail in a reasonable time is to drive to each marker and walk from there. You can also canoe various segments. A nice detour is the Anhinga Trail, a self-guided 0.5-mile (0.80-km) paved walkway and boardwalk over a freshwater sawgrass marsh near the Royal Palm Visitor Center at the entrance to Everglades National Park. Sightings of turtles, herons, and egrets are common on this introduction to life in the Everglades. **BDS**

⬆ **The sun sets over the Everglades Trail.**

Florida National Scenic Trail Florida, USA

Start Big Cypress National Preserve   End Fort Pickens   Distance 1,400 miles (2,253 km)   Time 100 days
Grade Hard   Type Long-distance trail   Info goo.gl/8HVAJs

This long and demanding walk passes through tropical habitats and forests, travels along seashores, skirts the edge of the largest lake in the United States, and even crosses a time zone. For much of its length, walkers must beware of alligators, poisonous snakes, wild dogs, and bears. But don't let any of this put you off—this is one of the greatest foot journeys in the world, and one that amply rewards the time and effort required to make it.

It starts at Big Cypress National Preserve, between Miami and Naples, in the middle of an inspiring great swamp—a damp environment where wet feet are inevitable—before reaching the Seminole Reservation through a stretch of drained, open farmland. Next you reach Lake Okeechobee and an eastward deviation to Hobe Sound Beach on the Atlantic coast. Heading back inland, the path follows the Kissimmee River for

more than 100 miles (160 km) to Orlando, which, in spite of its proximity to one of Florida's main cities, is one of the most rugged and remote-feeling stretches of the whole route.

The Ocala section features pine scrub forest and some of the region's largest natural springs. A short detour takes in Hopkins Prairie, a great beauty spot that should not be missed. Beyond Palatka and the Osceola National Forest lies the legendary Suwannee River, with its steep sides and white water. Remember to put your watches back an hour from Eastern to Central time as you cross the Apalachicola River. In its penultimate stage the trail passes through the ancient forests and ravines of Eglin before its end at Fort Pickens, a former military fort on Pensacola Bay. **GL**

⊤ The trail begins at Big Cypress National Preserve.

Pipiwai Trail Maui, Hawaii, USA

Start/End Kipahulu Visitor Center   **Distance** 4 miles (6.4 km)   **Time** 3 hours   **Grade** Easy to moderate
Type Mountain trail   **Map** goo.gl/x0RwNM

Everybody enjoys a waterfall, particularly one as spectacular, and accessible, as the double waterfall in Hawaii's Haleakala National Park. Set in Kipahulu Valley, in the southeast corner of Maui, the two falls drop 600 feet (180 m) through a deep fern-filled ravine framed by rain forest. The 2-mile (3.2-km) Pipiwai Trail to the falls has plenty of interest for such a short trail. A vast banyan tree, with a root system worthy of a *Lord of the Rings* movie, spreads over the path at one point, while an extraordinary hall of giant bamboo might make hikers think they've fallen down a rabbit hole. Just before the bamboo forest, an overlook provides a view of the Makahiku Falls, a 200-foot (60-m) taste of what is still to come on the other side of the forest. On the far side of Palikea Stream—a transition watercourse between the two falls—the Waimoku Falls come into view, a stunning water chute plunging

400 feet (122 m) below. During periods of heavy rain, when the spectacle is even more dramatic, mini waterfalls spring from other areas of the cliff face.

This trail doesn't provide the opportunity to be alone with primeval nature—crowds can build up at bottlenecks on the trail and there is plenty of man-made infrastructure, such as bridges and non-slip stairs to dispel any such illusions—but the exhilaration of experiencing these falls trumps any misgivings about commercialization. Their power and beauty lift the spirits, and clouds of fine spray give hot, tired hikers a refreshing facial. However, there is a slight sting in the tail of this walk: the large number of mosquitoes. Come prepared, with plenty of repellent, and reapply as necessary. **DS**

⬆ **The giant bamboo forest on the Pipiwai Trail.**

Maunahui Forest Reserve Road Molokai, Hawaii, USA

Start/End Maunahui Forest Reserve access road, Hwy 46   **Distance** 19.6 miles (31.5 km)   **Time** 9 hours
Grade Moderate   **Type** Unsealed forest road   **Map** goo.gl/UtQ4LZ

Of the five main islands in the Hawaiian archipelago, Molokai is the smallest. Measuring only 10 by 38 miles (16 x 61 km), it lies 25 miles (40.2 km) to the east of the tourist magnet of O'ahu and its capital Honolulu. Yet, by contrast, Molokai receives only a fraction of the attention given its glitzy neighbor. Resisting attempts at development, it pursues an active policy of environmental protection that saw it ranked 10th out of 111 selected islands around the world in a *National Geographic* survey of sustainable destinations. Molokai is proud of the status quo it has achieved in balancing development with stewardship of its pristine beaches and mountainous landscapes. Nowhere is this better seen than on the Maunahui Forest Reserve Road through the Molokai Forest Reserve. It was created in 1912 to preserve the natural watercourses—waterfalls, ponds, and streams—that flow through here.

The first half of this climb is at a deceptively energetic 4 to 5 percent gradient, which is why you end up gaining an impressive 3,600 feet (1,097 m) by the time you're done. On the way, you pass by the historic Sandalwood Measuring Pit—a boat-shaped pit about 75 feet long (22.8 m)—which was dug during the early 1800s at the height of the sandalwood boom. Not long after the pit, you reach a lookout area over the southern rim of Waikolu Canyon, where camping is allowed with permits for periods up to one week. Although it is a forest road, it is rarely used by vehicles, leaving you free to enjoy being in the midst of eucalyptus, Norfolk pine, silky oak, and verdant fernery, on an island where nature rules supreme. **BDS**

⬆ The trail passes by Sandalwood Measuring Pit.

Bermuda Railway Trail
Bermuda

Start St. George's   **End** Somerset
Distance 18 miles (29 km)   **Time** 1–2 days
Grade Easy   **Type** Coastal path with paved sections
Map goo.gl/Qeopw8

"Probably the most scenic trail … offers a wonderful way of exploring the island from one end to the other."

www.bermuda-attractions.com

📷 The Bermuda railway once spanned the archipelago, from St. George in the east to Somerset in the west.

The Bermuda railroad was an ambitious single-track line built to link the full 22-mile (35.4-km) length of this island, from Somerset in the west to St. George's in the east. Construction was complicated by the choice of route close to the coast, which necessitated linking the various islands and headlands that form Bermuda with a series of bridges and causeways. It seemed like a good idea in the days before automobiles, but the moment they arrived in 1948, the railway was doomed. The result was that this expensive stretch of engineering operated only for seventeen years, and Bermuda now has one of the highest concentrations of car ownership in the world.

In 1984 the authorities converted the disused and largely forgotten rail track into a walking trail. Most of the original route could be used, creating a new walking path 18 miles (29 km) long. Some of the portions are paved, which encourages cyclists to use it, too. With its exposed coastal routing, the Bermuda Railway Trail has become one of the island's highest rated attractions. It is, of course, mainly flat and, unusual for Bermuda, well away from the noise of traffic. Walkers can enjoy great views of the sea, plus all the exotic flora and fauna the island offers. In many places the trail runs through steep rail cuttings, the sides now covered in heavy vegetation. There are also remains of stations and bridges along the route.

The geography of Bermuda means that there are gaps along the trail. For example, there are long interruptions when walkers reach towns such as St. George's or Hamilton, and some of the longer bridges have disappeared, leaving just a row of pillars protruding from the sea. **SH**

Mastic Trail
Grand Cayman, Cayman Islands

Start North Side   **End** Bodden
Distance 4.5 miles (7.2 km)   **Time** 2 hours
Grade Easy   **Type** Boardwalks, forest paths
Map goo.gl/HOHtxy

The highest point on Grand Cayman Island may be only 60 feet (18.2 m) above sea level, and the island itself only 76 square miles (197 sq km) in size, but that is no reason for it not to have a wilderness trail. For a small island, Grand Cayman has a wild and largely impenetrable interior, which has been left to evolve with little or no interference from humankind for the past two million years. The Mastic Trail takes full advantage of this untouched topography as it passes through Black mangrove wetlands, long-abandoned farmlands, ancient dry forests, all-too-rare West Indian cedars, impressive stands of royal and silver thatch palms, mahogany, flowering vines and wild orchids, all the while the air alive with birdsong. Part of the Mastic Reserve, the walk has garnered worldwide attention: In 1995, *Islands* magazine selected the trail as a finalist in their annual Eco-tourism Awards, and much of the land the trail is on has been declared "inalienable" and never to be developed by the island's National Trust.

Literally hacked out of the island's woodlands more than a hundred years ago to provide a trading route between the community of North Side and Bodden Town in the south, this canopied, tree-covered trail was once used to transport farm produce and thatch rope on donkeys and oxen led by men and women who walked it barefoot to preserve their footwear. With the construction of coastal roads, the trail fell into disrepair and stayed that way until 1994, when a series of grants enabled the National Trust to reopen this historic path and make it available to all those walkers who know that when it comes to walking trails, longer isn't always better. **BDS**

"The Mastic Reserve … protects part of the largest contiguous area of untouched, old-growth dry forest remaining on the island."

www.nationaltrust.org.ky

⬆ The Mastic Trail takes you through the island's many ecosystems and reveals its inner beauty.

Waitukubuli Trail
Dominica

Start Scott's Head   **End** Cabrits National Park   **Distance** 114 miles (183 km)
Time 12 days   **Grade** Strenuous   **Type** Jungle trails
Info goo.gl/YQd45M

The Caribbean's very first and only long-distance walking trail, the Waitukubuli Trail on the island of Dominica, the "Nature Island," showcases everything that this sun-drenched nation is known for: wild terrain—including gorges, rivers, the Glasse, Sari Sari, and Victoria waterfalls—and dense rain forests with leaves that turn emerald green in the Caribbean sun. There are dizzying coastal cliffs, a boiling volcanic lake, and Dominica's rich colonial heritage and cultural legacy as you pass through small villages and centuries-old plantations. Once you've walked the Waitukubuli Trail, you have earned the right to say you've ticked the Dominican box.

Leaving the town of Scott's Head in the country's far south and heading north, the route follows trails that were once taken by runaway slaves—the Maroons—who fled into the mountains to flee the country's coastal plantations. The trail takes you into the mountains, all the way to the Boiling Lake—a 328-foot-wide (100 m) expanse of frothing, steaming water, which should come as no surprise on an actively volcanic island. Walking the trail's entire length is a serious test of endurance, but its fourteen segments mean anyone can come here regardless of their level of fitness and walk as little or as much of it as they like.

Dominica has a history of resisting the sort of development common to many of its neighboring Caribbean islands, which is why the Waitukubuli Trail is such a must-do walk in the region, allowing hikers to see Dominica as it is before its forbidding topography starts to be conquered and the Eden-like environment through which the trail passes starts getting a little hemmed in. **BDS**

"Opens up and showcases the best of Dominica—culture/heritage, local lifestyles, and our island's rugged terrain."

www.waitukubulitrail.com

⌖ A trail that proudly demonstrates Dominica's traditional resistance to excessive development.

Morne Trois Pitons Summit Trail

Dominica

Start/End Parking area northeast of Pont Casse
Distance 4 miles (6.4 km)   **Time** 6 hours
Grade Strenuous   **Type** Mountain trail
Map goo.gl/gwhryC

The first few miles to the summit of Morne Trois Pitons in the south-central highlands of the Caribbean island of Dominica make for a pretty easy walk, but don't be fooled. The basalt remains of this former volcano and its surrounds created a land of precipitous inclines, hot springs, mud pots, lava tubes, sulfur vents, the world's second-largest boiling lake, and a fumerole—the Valley of Desolation. There are numerous lakes, including Boeri Lake, the country's second largest and set in the crater of an extinct volcano, and heavily incised valleys with no fewer than five vegetation zones, including montane thicket, mature rain forests below 1,509 feet (459 m), and montane rain forests above 2,000 feet (610 m), which are almost continually covered in cloud and fog and filled with ferns, mosses, epiphytes, stunted trees, and steps of slippery logs—so don't come here wearing sneakers.

The trailhead begins near Pont Casse, and the straightforward, well-marked trail soon begins its relentless ascent of the mountain along a seemingly endless series of log steps, which peter out about a third of the way up the mountain, where some serious rock scrambling with very few handholds becomes necessary. The closer you get to the summit, the more difficult the climb becomes, but the more fascinating, too, as you pass from mature rain forest into the elfin/cloud forest environment of the higher montane rain forest, not to mention the views that open up around you should you be lucky enough to be given a break in the clouds. Try to stay on the trail, which is well marked with ribbons, as some of the plants here are sharp and will inflict lacerations on bare legs. The views from the summit are stunning. **BDS**

"More than likely you will be enshrouded in mist while on the summit, but the rain forest on the mountain is very pristine."

www.summitpost.org

⤒ An undemanding trail that takes you through Dominica's rain forest into mist-shrouded cloud forests.

La Soufrière Cross-Country Trail St. Vincent

Start Rabacca   **End** Richmond   **Distance** 7 miles (11.2 km)   **Time** 8 hours   **Grade** Strenuous
Type Farm track, mountain path, and unmarked rock   **Map** goo.gl/GWCpc7

St. Vincent is the largest of the Grenadine Islands in the southern Caribbean Sea. The island is dominated by the country's highest peak, La Soufrière (or "the sulfurer"). This 4,048-foot-high (1,234 m) mountain is an active volcano that last erupted, harmlessly, in 1979. An eruption in 1902, however, killed more than 1,600 people. The climb to the top has become one of the attractions of the island. The hardiest visitors can walk across St. Vincent from one coast to the other, taking in the summit of La Soufrière. The island authorities recommend that you take an approved guide. The route is not easy to follow, and there are plenty of hidden crevices, steep cliffs, and sudden drops.

Most approach the volcano via the easiest path to the top, from the "windward side," or the east coast of the island facing the Atlantic. A farm track leads inland from the village of Rabacca through banana, coconut, and bamboo plantations. The trail becomes smaller and climbs steadily through rain forest, crossing dried lava streams, hot springs, and volcanic debris. The summit is marked by several craters dating back to previous eruptions. Toward the top of the main crater the path becomes a much steeper unmarked scramble. Finally, it reaches the rim of this 1-mile-wide (1.6 km) caldera. The views are exceptional, taking in the whole island and the massive crater with its green lake and active smoldering dome of lava in its center. The path circles the rim and descends on a difficult route to Richmond on the west coast. Another path leads down into the crater with the assistance of fixed ropes. Many visitors simply turn around at the crater and descend the 2 miles (3.2 km) back to Rabacca. **SH**

⬆ Scramble your way to a smoldering lava dome.

Welchman Hall Gully Barbados

Start/End Welchman Hall   **Distance** 1.5 miles (2.4 km)   **Time** 40 minutes   **Grade** Easy
Type Well-maintained paved footpath   **Map** goo.gl/tasjc5

The name of Welchman Hall Gully alludes to Welshman General William Williams—the gully used to be a part of a plantation owned by him. A small rocky gorge, 0.75 miles (1.2 km) long, near the center of Barbados, this sheltered strip of land between dramatic rock formations was cultivated by Williams more than 200 years ago. Formed when the roofs of caves collapsed in on themselves, today it is filled with a lush tropical forest with 150 different types of exotic plants and trees, including bamboo, coconut, ferns, and vines, although you can still see stalagmites and stalactites amid the rampant vegetation.

The Gully was bought by the Barbados National Trust in 1962 and was the trust's first property. Since then it has been successfully marketed as a "tropical forest cave" and has become a major attraction on the island, a rare surviving example of lush greenery on an island where much of the indigenous flora was cleared by colonial settlers to create sugar plantations. Welchman Hall Gully is also a rare, cool, and shady place for a leisurely stroll away from the glare of the harsh Caribbean sun. The path is easy and well maintained, and information boards along the route explain some of the area's important historical and botanical points. Some of the vegetation is natural to Barbados, although the Gully was also planted with spices, such as ginger, nutmeg, and cloves, plus an array of various palms and even cacao trees. A colony of green monkeys also lives in the Gully, and visitors often gather to watch them at feeding time. The site is run as a conservation and education project, too, with residential camps available for children. **SH**

⌅ A tiny gorge contains a wealth of geology.

Arbib Nature and Heritage Trail Barbados

Start/End Speightstown   **Distance** Various
Time 2–3.5 hours   **Grade** Moderate
Type Paved roads, country tracks, and rocky gullies
Info goo.gl/ii5vGS

The Arbib Nature and Heritage Trail is actually two different walks: one a moderately strenuous hike through rough countryside; the other a shorter easy stroll around Speightstown. Both are recent creations of the Barbados National Trust and are available as guided group walks that are normally booked in advance and start in the center of the island's second largest settlement, Speightstown. The shorter route is down Speightstown's side streets, hearing interesting snippets of the history of Barbados and spotting old buildings, such as the grand two-story church and the

"Interactive guided trail through rolling hills and cane fields, and dark and mysterious Whim Gully."

www.barbadosnationaltrust.org

movable "chattel houses" of plantation workers. Walkers often get a chance to see a game of *warri* in action, a traditional Barbados pit-and-pebble strategy game played in the shade of a tree that originated in Sudan 4,000 years ago. This more relaxed walking route takes around two hours.

The more adventurous three-and-a-half-hour route leads from Speightstown into more remote countryside to visit an old ruined fort, traditional plantations, and a spectacular natural gully. Whim Gully is an opportunity to discover unusual coralstone boulders and bearded fig trees. There's a bit of scrambling involved in the dark recesses of the gorge, so it's not for everyone. **SH**

Cumaca Caves Trinidad, Trinidad and Tobago

Start/End Cumaca
Distance 2.5 miles (4 km)   **Time** 1 hour
Grade Easy   **Type** Path through cocoa estate, forest trails   **Info** goo.gl/fNh98G

To access the Cumaca Caves on the Caribbean island of Trinidad, you first have to pass through a cocoa estate on a marked trail near Valencia Road that runs by a quarry outside the town of St. Albans. It is a trail that will never be blessed with a well-known trailhead, it will never be a well-maintained path, and it won't be making anyone's list of "world's greatest trails." Nor is it the most breathtaking of walks in terms of scenery or coastline views. It is, however, a walk that any serious birder would gladly detour to take, because it ends in the Cumaca Caves, and in those caves there lives the world's only nocturnal, fruit-eating bird—the Steatornis caripensis, or oilbird.

The Cumaca Caves were discovered by two travelers, Adam Richards and Victor Abraham, about whom little was known when they stumbled upon them while searching for a water source. Although it is generally agreed that they were the caves' founders, they were never heard of again after that. In 1911, the U.S. President Theodore Roosevelt came here, so intrigued was he by the oilbird story. Once inside the horizontal cave—an exit cave and the source of the North Oropouche River—there are three separate chambers, so be prepared to get wet at least to waist level.

Oilbirds are found throughout the northern regions of South America and navigate the same way bats do—using echolocation. Adults weigh as much as 17 ounces (482 g) and are mostly reddish-brown with white spots on their napes and exceptionally long wings, which help them to hover and change direction quickly, enabling them to navigate the little-known caves they call home. **BDS**

Pitch Lake
Trinidad, Trinidad and Tobago

Start/End Any point along the lake's edge
Distance 2 miles (3.2 km)   **Time** 1 hour
Grade Easy   **Type** Solidified asphalt
Map goo.gl/R7YjJL

The Pitch Lake in southwest Trinidad is unlike anything you have ever seen, a massive deposit of bitumen thought to be the result of the natural breaching of a nearby oil field, where rising oil has combined with water and local clays. The level of the lake has fallen gradually over time as locals have extracted the bitumen for commercial purposes, but it is still the world's largest natural deposit of emulsified asphalt. Some 100 acres (40.4 ha) in size and 250 feet (76.2 m) deep, its surface can form a shallow lake after heavy rain, and when the pitch is really flowing, it can create some gorgeous polygonal patterns that allow for a barefoot walk over its hot, smooth surface, which will live long in the memory. Beware, however: A full circuit of the pitch lake should only be considered under the watchful eye of a local guide, as there are some sections that can be soft, deep, and sticky.

Pitch Lake is not a recent phenomenon. For generations, local Amerindians believed it to have been created by the gods to bury a wayward tribe who offended them by eating sacred hummingbirds. In 1595, Sir Walter Raleigh visited the site and used its pitch to caulk his ships. The lake has been commercially mined since 1867 and will continue to be so, it is estimated, for another 400 years.

It is a rare sight—one of only three naturally occurring asphalt lakes in the world—and attracts thousands of tourists every year who walk over its fractured surface. It can be an inferno in summer, but in winter you can bathe in pools of sulfur-rich waters that form over it, some as deep as 10 feet (3 m), which provide a habitat for water lilies and an odd assortment of microbial, sulfur-loving plants. **BDS**

"You could well imagine the Pitch Lake is alive. It burps. It hisses. It consumes, eventually, all that is placed on it."

gotrinidadandtobago.com

⬆ A bitumen lake provides for a fascinating barefoot walk over polygonal-shaped stepping stones.

El Pauji–Wonken Trek Bolivar, Venezuela

Start El Pauji **End** Wonken **Distance** 45 miles (72.4 km) **Time** 6 days **Grade** Strenuous
Type Guided route through forest, savannah, river crossings, plus canoes **Info** goo.gl/RiUHap

At 11,500 square miles (30,000 sq km), Canaima National Park, which is roughly the size of Belgium, is one of the largest protected spaces in South America and the sixth largest in the world. A World Heritage Site, it is known locally as La Grand Sabana—the "Great Savannah." The geography of this part of southeast Venezuela is certainly distinctive, with much of the land being taken up by tabletop mountains known as *tepuis*, from one of which flows the Angel Falls, the world's highest waterfall. This route across a remote part of Canaima is a guided walk offered by commercial trekking operators who provide flights and overland transfers to the start and finish points. It is a serious expedition for experienced hikers, and you'll be carrying all you need for six days.

The trek starts in the bohemian honey-making village of El Pauji. The route leads through plantations and thick forest, crosses ravines and rivers, and visits villages of indigenous Indian tribes. Trekkers even use dugouts to travel on some stretches of river. The trail offers memorable views of waterfalls, towering *tepuis*, and vast expanses of savannah. After six days, it ends at the missionary village of Wonken in the heart of the National Park, surrounded by awe-inspiring *tepuis*. The discovery of the *tepuis* originally inspired Sir Arthur Conan Doyle to write the novel *The Lost World* (1912), which featured a time capsule of cavemen and prehistoric creatures isolated on top of an inaccessible flat mountain. Scientists have since found many unique species that have developed in isolation on top of *tepuis*—about a third of the plant species are found nowhere else on Earth. **SH**

⊡ Angel Falls is the world's highest waterfall.

Cotopaxi Circuit Cotopaxi, Ecuador

Start Pansaleo, Lasso entrance to national park   **End** Mulalo   **Distance** 49 miles (78.8 km)   **Time** 5–7 days
Grade Easy to moderate   **Type** Dirt roads, alpine tracks   **Info** goo.gl/6Y3Oa3

Only 17 miles (27.3 km) south of the Ecuadorian capital of Quito, and clearly visible from the city, the brooding grandeur of Cotopaxi seems to beckon all who gaze upon it. A graceful stratovolcano, it has erupted more than eighty times throughout its history, but it has been ten years since any significant seismic activity has been recorded. Hiking your way to its 19,347-foot (5,897-m) summit is now a popular guided round trip that no shortage of outfitters in Quito is prepared to offer. If after scaling its summit you're still wanting more, or if crampons, ice axes, and rope aren't your thing, the good news is that walking around the base of this majestic mountain also provides a very rewarding trek of its own.

It is by no means difficult or complex. The volcano is almost always within sight, and the trails are, for the most part, little-used dirt roads with barely a vehicle in sight. Much of the walk is through the Páramo, the high Andean grasslands, and water is generally plentiful (but make sure you purify it), with the exception of the final leg from Cerro El Morro to Mulalo. Along the way the chances of seeing Andean condors are good, and also eagles, owls, and high altitude hummingbirds. Nor is the environment as sparse as you might think. Rivers fed by snowmelt, grasslands carpeted with wildflowers, and primary woodlands are traversed, and no matter where you find yourself at the end of the day, there will be no problem finding a place to pitch your tent. Then you can sit and ponder the mountain's perfect conical shape and the classic image of what we all think a volcano should look be. **BDS**

⬆ Circle Cotopaxi on Equador's green Andean grasslands.

Nazca Plains Ica, Peru

Start/End Various   **Distance** Various   **Time** Various   **Grade** Easy   **Type** Rock and sandy desert topsoil
Info goo.gl/Qm2kIo

Created between 100 BCE and 700 CE by the very simplest of methods—scraping away the desert plateau's red dust to reveal the bare white rock beneath—the hundreds of geometric shapes on Peru's Nazca Plains have confounded archaeologists ever since the markings were rediscovered by the West in the 1920s. The shapes represent humans, birds, fish, and monkeys that, because of their enormity (some are as large as 660 feet/201 m across), have always been interpreted from the air, which only adds to the many theories as to why they were made, with traditional theories suggesting that they were meant to be seen by the gods, or maybe even by aliens. Recently, however, researchers have turned these theories on their heads and now claim the Nazca Lines were not meant to be seen from the air at all. They were meant to be walked.

Researchers at Leicester and Bristol universities in the United Kingdom believe the shapes were made to be seen "from within" and were important aids to ancient rituals. During a five-year period, about 3 miles (5 km) of lines were traced (walked) and studied. Research published in the journal *Antiquity* argues that the lines were made for walking and that the shapes are designed to be disorienting, and reveal unexpected features with each new direction taken. The experience one gets walking the Nazca Lines today is much the same as what would have been experienced 1,000 years ago. These subjective experiences are being added to scientific data, which is helping us toward an anthropological understanding of why these beautiful lines exist. **BDS**

⬆ The famous Nazca Lines were made to be walked.

Lençóis to Vale do Capão Bahia, Brazil

Start Lençóis   **End** Vale do Capão   **Distance** 16 miles (25.7 km)   **Time** 8 hours   **Grade** Moderate
Type Hills   **Map** goo.gl/7kFkxX

The Chapada Diamantina National Park in Bahia is named both for the diamonds that were mined here in the nineteenth century and for the steep cliffs (*chapada*) that provide one of its most striking topographical features. This popular day hike from Lençóis to the Vale do Capão is a reasonably easy way to see some of the cliffs and other outstanding scenery here. The walk is in the same region as the Vale do Paty, which is very much a separate, though equally fascinating, trail.

It is sometimes known as the Diamond Plateau or the Diamond Trail—when you walk from Lençóis to the Vale do Capão, you will be taking the old trails the nineteenth-century diamond prospectors followed to get from the main town, Lençóis, out into the valley on their hunt for treasure. Although the trails are fairly easy to walk, it's still advisable to book a local guide, as

the network of paths can sometimes be confusing, and it is easy to get lost. Guides can also take you off the trails to show you interesting features, such as caves and waterfalls, which also dot the landscape. You might still come across the occasional modern diamond prospector chancing his luck, although the business has been banned on a commercial scale to help protect the park.

If you have time in this magical landscape, then when you reach the village of Vale do Capão, an essential walk is to the Cachoeira da Fumaça—only about 2 miles (3.2 km). This is the highest waterfall in Brazil, a magnificent 1,247 feet (380 m) in height. It's so high, in fact, that the water never reaches the ground, vaporizing in the warm air as it falls. **MG**

⬆ Hike through a land of diamonds and steep cliffs.

Vale do Paty
Bahia, Brazil

Start/End Guine   **Distance** 50 miles (80 km)
Time 3–6 days   **Grade** Strenuous
Type Unmarked jungle trails
Map goo.gl/aYFwZO

No matter how tempting it may be or how much money you think you might save, do not even think of venturing into the Vale do Paty without a guide. The trails are rough and often unmarked, and legion are the stories of people who have gone out on their own and lived to regret the time they ventured into Brazil's most beautiful valley—the place "where the sky kisses the Earth."

Located within the boundaries of the Chapada Diamantina National Park in the state of Bahia, the Vale do Paty is a landscape of spectacular open plateaus, tumbling waterfalls, and majestic flat-topped mountains. It has been described as the finest wilderness trek in Brazil and one of the four most beautiful valleys in the world. There are three access villages to the trek: Guine, Andarai, and Vale do Capão, but most start from Guine, where it's a long 8-mile (12.8-km) walk through open terrain on the first day. As there are no marked trails, routes are optional, but all include a walk to the top of the 885-foot-high (270 m) Cachoeirao waterfall for lunch and stunning views over the valley. More memorable views up the valley can be had from the top of Morro do Castelo (Castle Mountain).

Vale do Paty is still home to a small group of local people who live simple lives and have great affection for the land, and it is possible to organize to stay overnight in their homes. There are few mosquitoes thanks to the high levels of tannins in the valley creeks and streams, which leaves you free to concentrate on the beauty around you as you explore its caves and swim in the water holes of this ancient valley, as close as you'll get to the "land that time forgot." **BDS**

"Still home to a handful of families living off the land as they have done for the past 150 years."

www.h2otraveladventures.com

⬆ It is plain to see why Vale do Paty has been named one of the most beautiful valleys in the word.

Pantanal
Mato Grosso do Sul, Brazil

Start/End Various **Distance** Various
Time Various **Grade** Easy to moderate
Type Wetland, forest, and grassland trails
Info goo.gl/w8Kbs2

A wetland twice the size of Portugal, the Pantanal is the largest freshwater wetland in the world, and at more than 81,082 square miles (210,000 sq km) it is one of the world's most important, sprawling across Bolivia and Paraguay but mostly lying within the boundaries of Brazil's Mato Grosso region. The Pantanal is said to be the highest concentration of large mammals on Earth, and because of the more open nature of the wetlands compared to, say, the Amazon, the wildlife is more easily seen. It's one of the best places in the world to see and photograph wildlife, with photo safaris on offer. Here live jaguars, pumas, wolves, caiman, tapirs, giant otters, anteaters, armadillos, capybara, and macaws galore, as well as a few species you'd hope not to encounter when out hiking, such as the anaconda. Bird species include flightless greater rheas (or emas), harpy eagles, egrets, herons, vultures, kingfishers, and hummingbirds.

There are no towns in the heart of the Pantanal and few live here, so a hiking trip has to be well planned and is usually done in organized groups that leave from either Cuiaba in the southern Pantanal or Campo Grande in the north. Planes and boats are the main means of exploration, although there is one dirt road. Tour companies work with the local *pantaneiros* in this area where trails change constantly. It isn't somewhere for the average hiker to head off alone. During the wet season (October to March) the water can rise by anything up to 16 feet (4.8 m), submerging some trails and producing a changed landscape when it subsides. However, the important thing is to go to this vast land and experience some of the magic that Mother Earth can still offer us. **MG**

Lençóis Maranhenses
National Park Maranhão, Brazil

Start/End Various
Distance/Time Various
Grade Moderate **Type** Sand dunes
Info goo.gl/5wCZu2

The Lençóis Maranhenses National Park is one of the most unusual places on the planet. It manages to have both awe-inspiring sand dunes and regular floods. Despite the heavy rainy seasons, it supports almost no vegetation. Even though there are sand dunes and a lack of vegetation, it is not technically a desert, and the lagoons formed here by the rains manage to give a home to many fish. It is an astonishing place. Established in 1981 the park covers an area of 598 square miles (1,548 sq km) on the northeast coast of Brazil just south of the equator. The nearest main town

"Mangroves, deserted beaches, buritis, a graceful kind of palm tree compose the park's diversity."

gobrazil.about.com

is Barreirinhas, which acts as the gateway to the park. You can only enter the park in a four-wheel-drive vehicle, and there are no direct access roads. No start point, no end point. No marked trails.

It is definitely worth hiring a local guide or booking an organized hike with a small group. Hiking alone in this vast area, where one sand dune soon starts to look like another, is a risky business. Besides, local guides will take you to the best blue-water lagoons, such as Lagoa Azul (Blue Lagoon) and Lagoa Bonita (Beautiful Lagoon). "Lençóis" is the Portuguese word for a bedsheet, because the white sand dunes resemble an almost endless series of white sheets billowing away into the distance. **MG**

Apolo Trail, Pelechuco to Apolo La Paz, Bolivia

Start Pelechuco   **End** Apolo   **Distance** 70 miles (112 km)   **Time** 7–8 days   **Grade** Strenuous
Type Ancient Incan track through jungle   **Map** goo.gl/EAkzV1

The trek through the jungle from Pelechuco to Apolo in the La Paz district of Bolivia is one of the most exhilarating in the country. It isn't one to be undertaken lightly, however. The normal trekking time of seven to eight days can be longer, depending on the weather, and as most people tackle the trek by starting from La Paz, which is a fourteen-hour drive away from Apolo, it can take anything up to two weeks to complete the hike. You are also advised to take a local guide rather than attempt the trek by yourself, and this can add another day or two to your time as you find one who's free, and organize the pack animals you'll also need. If fit, you will have a hiking experience through the Bolivian jungles of the Apolobamba Mountains that you will never forget.

Most of the hike is within the boundaries of the Madidi National Park, which covers huge swathes of tropical rain forest as well as the pristine peaks of the High Andes Mountains. You'll be trekking through jungle where by day you'll hear the shrieks of monkeys in the trees, and at night perhaps the howl of a jaguar. There are an astonishing 1,000 species of birds in the national park—that's 11 percent of the known species on the planet. You'll also see huge multicolored butterflies, llamas, and maybe even spectacled bears, South America's only bear.

The trek will make demands of you. You may need to wield a machete, and will need to fight off bugs and mosquitoes. You'll be hiking up to about 15,400 feet (4,694 m), with steep climbs and descents day after day. However, this trek, in the footsteps of the Incas, is sure to be filled with unforgettable moments. **MG**

⬆ Clouds cover the peaks of the Apolobamba Mountains.

Noel Kempff Mercado National Park Santa Cruz, Bolivia

Start/End Florida village on park boundary **Distance** Various **Time** Various **Grade** Moderate to strenuous
Type Mountain and dense forest trails **Info** goo.gl/qKxyxx

On the Bolivian border with Brazil stands one of the largest and most important national parks in the Amazon Basin. The Noel Kempff Mercado National Park covers a massive 5,880 square miles (15,230 sq km) and is home to more than 130 species of mammals, 620 species of birds, and the most diverse collection of amphibians and reptiles in the whole of North and South America. It is, naturally, a dream place for anyone who loves the natural world.

The park was founded in 1979 as the Parque Nacional Huanchaca, but its name was later changed to honor one of its greatest supporters and research scientists, Dr. Noel Kempff Mercado. In 1986, Dr. Mercado and two men with him were murdered by drug traffickers when they flew into the park and accidentally landed at a hidden cocaine laboratory. The park is about 375 miles (603 km) northeast of Santa Cruz City, which is the main jumping off point for visiting it. It's not the kind of place you can easily get to on your own, as there are only two entrances, both very remote. The usual way is to join an organized group and fly the two and a half hours from Santa Cruz City to the park for a mix of hiking, canoeing, and driving, while staying overnight in cheap lodges or camping. One thing you'll see is the Caparú Plateau, a massive table mountain that was unknown till it was discovered in 1910 by explorer Percy Fawcett. It's said that his descriptions of this new land inspired Sir Arthur Conan Doyle when he was writing his novel, *The Lost World* (1912). Hiking here, you'll feel that you, too, have discovered a lost world where visitors are few but the marvels are many. **MG**

⬆ Waterfalls tumble from the Huanchaca Plateau.

Valley of the Moon
Antofagasta, Chile

Start/End Various
Distance Various   **Time** Various
Grade Easy to moderate   **Type** Desert hiking
Info goo.gl/Sq7uWq

The Atacama Desert runs for about 600 miles (965 km) through Chile, between the staggering peaks of the Andes Mountains and the Pacific Coast. It covers a vast area of 40,541 square miles (105,000 sq km) and is renowned as the driest place in the world. There are parts of the Atacama that have never had any recorded rainfall.

One of the places in the desert that has, over the years, received some rain is the Valley of the Moon (Valle de la Luna). That rain has, along with past floods and the steady action of strong winds, helped produce the otherworldly landscape that gives the place its name. For here there are strangely shaped rocks and a range of hues almost like a rainbow made of stone. There are salt lakes, too, as if the valley in places has had a bizarre dusting of snow.

At the end of the day, as the sun sinks slow and low, the colors of the landscape transform yet again, gradually fading to black. If you are lucky enough to be here on or near a full moon, yet another special experience awaits you—the Valley of the Moon bathed in moonlight. You will also experience the extreme chill of nighttime in the desert, where temperatures regularly fall below freezing for most of the year.

The Valley of the Moon is situated 8 miles (12.8 km) west of San Pedro de Atacama, the closest town and main jumping-off point for visiting the valley. There are numerous organized tours on offer, which do allow you time to wander on foot, or you can hire a local guide. If you have your own transport, you can head into the valley on good roads and explore for yourself this surreal and haunting place. **MG**

"A valley of unique erosion patterns lends to a view like nothing on earth."

www.atlasobscura.com

← The setting sun enlivens the desolate expanses of the Atacama landscape.

↑ Wind erosion has resulted in fantastic formations in the rocks that rise above Atacama's dry sands.

Rano Raraku to Hanga Roa Easter Island, Chile

Start Rano Raraku   **End** Hanga Roa   **Distance** 12.5 miles (20 km)   **Time** 5 hours   **Grade** Easy
Type Coastal hike   **Map** goo.gl/7xz4tY

When you visit Easter Island, you will want to see its famous statues, and this gentle hike allows you to do so at an unhurried pace. It also allows you to appreciate the landscape of this beautiful place, alone in the middle of the South Pacific Ocean. The trail starts in Rano Raraku, the quarry where the stone for the statues came from, and it is an exhilarating place to begin any walk. An incredible 887 statues were carved on the island from the thirteenth to the early sixteenth centuries, the biggest is a remarkable 33 feet (10 m) high, and 397 of the statues are still here. Those that don't remain at Rano Raraku were transported around the island, which was another astonishing feat beyond the actual carving of them.

The quarry is inevitably the focal point of every person's visit to Easter Island, but if you can arrange to get there early in the morning before the tour buses arrive, you will have a much more magical experience. Spending time quietly with these strange figures is unforgettable.

From here you simply follow the path that runs along the south coast before cutting across the island to the capital. This part won't always be peaceful as the main road also runs this way, but you will have the pleasure of going by Ahu Tongariki, where fifteen huge statues were put up in a row in 1994. In other places you'll see lone statues, or fallen statues, which are poignant reminders of the passage of time. The whole hike, with the Pacific Ocean on one side and the vivid greenery of Easter Island on the other, is an exhilarating experience, and the walk ends in Easter Island's main town of Hanga Roa. **MG**

⬆ Easter Island's green hills tower over its famous statues.

Devil's Throat Boardwalk Misiones, Argentina

Start Iguazu Falls visitor center   **End** The Devil's Throat   **Distance** 0.6 mile (1 km)   **Time** 1 hour
Grade Easy   **Type** Boardwalk   **Info** goo.gl/P52jVz

One of the most spectacular waterfalls in the world straddles the border of Argentina and Brazil, and from both sides there are boardwalks through the rain forest to the top of their respective falls. On the Brazilian side, the views are panoramic, as the water tumbles from Argentina into Brazil. On the Argentine side, the falls are called Iguazu, and only here can you walk up to them and feel immersed in their raw, pulsating power. The Brazilian boardwalk is accessed from the colonial-style Hotel das Cataratas. A smooth concrete path zigzags down to the river through overhanging rain forest and once in the canyon, a walkway gives an overall view toward the central portion of the waterfalls known as the Devil's Throat.

The path on the Argentine side, however, is far more eventful. From the Iguazu Falls visitor center, a small tourist train carries you to the start of another raised boardwalk that leads walkers over islands and tributaries right to the top of the falls. The Argentine boardwalk is built on sturdy stilts across the water and is smooth enough for strollers, with strong handrails on each side. Due to the geography of the borders here, the Argentine boardwalk is able to lead to the very edge of the Devil's Throat, right above the thundering water. Whichever side you approach from, there are two constants—noise and water, generated by more than 275 waterfalls cascading down the sides of this deep U-shaped canyon and filling the air with spray and mist. Other longer paths lead through the rain forest, crossing islands and rivers. Look for guided night walks to the falls during a full moon, when you might see a "lunar rainbow." **SH**

⬆ A boardwalk on the edge of a thundering abyss.

Perito Moreno Glacier Walk Santa Cruz, Argentina

Start/End Bajo de las Sombras (boat embarkation)   **Distance** Various   **Time** Up to half a day
Grade Moderate   **Type** Glacier walk   **Info** goo.gl/jL7jRd

The enormous Perito Moreno Glacier is one of Patagonia's biggest visitor attractions. This solid river of ice—19 miles (30 km) long, 3 miles (4.8 km) wide at its mouth—is the world's third largest reserve of freshwater, and one of the few glaciers in the world that is still advancing. For most visitors the experience of the glacier simply involves staring at the 200-foot-high (60 m) ice face across the milky green water of Lake Argentina from viewing points or boat trips. There are, however, guided hikes available on the glacier itself.

First, you have to get to the glacier, usually from El Calafate, which is 48 miles (77 km) away. Tourist buses take visitors to a viewing walkway that gives good views of the spectacular face of the glacier. To get any closer, you have to join one of the group trekking tours with local operators. These vary from short one-

hour walks to half-day expeditions. From Bajo de las Sombras, these walkers are taken to the base of the glacier by boat, then through the forest and the rocky shoreline to reach the access points for the ice trail. The operators will supply you with crampon spikes to fit to the soles of your boots.

Once on the glacier, you'll see deep patches of blue ice, crevices big enough to walk into, sink holes down to the water beneath, and panoramas of spiky ice formations with snow-covered mountains behind. Thunderous sounds signal huge chunks cracking from the main glacier and floating off into the water. Rest assured that the guides are multilingual and experienced in leading a party on a safe route through the ever-changing ice landscape. **SH**

⬆ Walk before a towering wall of moving ice.

Cerro del Medio Trail Tierra del Fuego, Argentina

Start/End Ushuaia   **Distance** 8 miles (12.8 km)   **Time** 6 hours   **Grade** Moderate to strenuous
Type Mountain path   **Map** goo.gl/6ttBr4

Ushuaia is the southernmost city in the world and the capital of Argentina's Tierra del Fuego region at the foot of the country near the border with Chile. It is a bleak, windswept port, with mountains rising up behind it, that is home to a true frontier mentality in a remote settlement that is often the starting point for adventurous expeditions into Patagonia's wilderness, or south to Antarctica. Regular shoppers arrive in mud-splattered SUVs, and everyone is wearing the latest in outdoor hiking clothes.

This Cerro del Medio Trail gets you out of the city and into the foothills of the Andes. Starting at the Plaza de Mayo by the city center waterfront, it leads up the busy Calle Lasserre, past the Ushuaia Hotel, through the suburbs, and eventually joins an old logging track into the forested mountains beyond. As the path heads up the slopes, the views between the trees become more impressive. It's a good excuse to take a rest, stopping to look back to Ushuaia below and out across the Beagle Channel, the sheltered passage that most shipping takes to avoid the wild seas of Cape Horn farther south.

Gradually, the going gets steeper as the trail follows a stream beyond the tree line. After passing a small lake called Laguna Margot, things get strenuous as it climbs to the rocky summit of the Cerro del Medio ridge at 3,035 feet (925 m). From June to September expect these final stages to be snowy, and equip yourself accordingly. The final breathtaking panorama across the mountains, islands, and waterways of Tierra del Fuego is the reward for walkers. Plus, of course, the fact that it's downhill all the way back to Ushuaia. **SH**

⬆ Walking above Ushuaia on the Cerro del Medio ridge.

The Arctic Circle Trail
North Greenland, Greenland

"Ordinary trekkers can enjoy the wild and desolate tundra simply by following stone-built cairns."

www.cicerone.co.uk

⊼ Above 66° North, walkers can watch glaciers calving icebergs into the sea.

Start Kangerlussuaq **End** Sisimiut
Distance 103 miles (165 km) **Time** 8–10 days
Grade Moderate to strenuous **Type** Overland tundra trails **Info** goo.gl/ATYShl

The Arctic Circle Trail ends in Sisimiut, Greenland's second most populous city on the coast of Davis Strait in central-west Greenland, and begins close by the international airport at Kangerlussuaq near the town of Sondrestrom, which lies at the head of the Kangerlussuaq Fjord and was created by the United States armed forces in October 1941. What lies between these two remote outposts of civilization is a stunning open landscape of rolling tundra. This is a sea-level route, through valleys sprinkled with mirrorlike lakes and occasional herds of surprisingly approachable reindeer.

There is no food on the route so you have to bring absolutely everything with you, which means carrying a 44-pound (20-kg) knapsack, thus elevating the trek from moderate to strenuous. This, however, only acts as a lure to walkers from all over the world, who come here to experience true wilderness in a place where many of the rivers and mountains haven't even been named yet. There are a number of rather basic huts along the trail, but almost everyone here has their own tent and sleeping bag because you don't do this trail so you can hear others snoring. August is the best time to come. In June, swarms of mosquitoes can make life a misery.

The trail is free, the huts are free, and there's an option (also at no cost) of crossing one of the larger lakes along the way in a canoe. Many who have walked the route consider it to be one of the world's premier trails. The weather is generally good, there are wild berries along the way, and you are greeted by the lovely colonial-era houses of Sisimiut at the trail's end. **BDS**

The Inuit Trail

East Greenland, Greenland

Start/End Kulusuk   **Distance** 62 miles (100 km)
Time 10–12 days   **Grade** Easy to moderate
Type Open terrain, rocks, gravel, scree, snow
Map goo.gl/18mjqe

It is the monster of all Greenland backpacking options: an expedition that takes you along old Inuit trails to places that can be accessed only by foot after overnighting in true wilderness campsites. There are towering granite peaks reflected in the cool icy waters of Greenland's untouched inlets, and coastlines made rugged by the retreating ice of 10,000 years ago— places such as the 4.5-mile-long (7 km) Sermilik Fjord, where icebergs have been calving off in their hundreds for years now.

The trail is over challenging terrain. There are iceberg-laden beaches, rocky paths along cliffs and ridges, slippery granite rocks that require clambering over, and even occasional fog banks. Mosquitoes can be a nuisance, and the wind, too, but when the sun begins to go down each night and the horizon turns a bright array of orangey-red pastels, it's hard to think of anywhere better in the world you could possibly be.

The first settlement you reach after leaving your starting point of Kulusuk is Tiniteqilaaq, a jumping-off point for tours of the Sermilik glacier and the only place now, several days out, where you can buy fresh provisions—including Danish chocolates! Farther on there is a feast of natural wonders awaiting you, including the Qorlotoq lakes and the Valley of Flowers. They are followed by Tasiilaq, the capital of East Greenland, and the 1,968-foot-high (600 m) peak of Somandsfjell behind it, with scree slopes that make it a hard climb but with views that are worth the effort. Then you're back in Kulusuk, a beneficiary of generations of Inuit knowledge and experience of trails that are not permanent features and can disappear after a blizzard so are simply "remembered." **BDS**

"Greenlandic nature provides magnificent hiking experiences in an almost untouched landscape."

www.greenland.com

⊼ Hikers on the Inuit Trail descend toward the Sermilik Glacier.

Tasermiut
South Greenland, Greenland

Start/End Nanortalik   Distance 56 miles (90 km)
Time 6–7 days   Grade Easy to moderate
Type Open grasslands, meadows
Map goo.gl/tN2a4R

Listed by *National Geographic* magazine as one of the ten most spectacular places on Earth, Tasermiut in southern Greenland is a vast land of vertical mountains, lush green valleys, glaciers, and the fabulous Tasermiut Fjord. Your starting point is Nanortalik, "the place of polar bears" on Nanortalik Island, on the shores of the Labrador Sea, and your adventure begins with a boat transfer to the Kloster Valley on the mainland, past the first of many breathtaking views such as the massive Sermeg Glacier, which is responsible for one in ten of the icebergs that Greenland produces.

The next three days are spent hiking up the Tupaassat Valley, past glaciers and the Kangikitsoq Fjord, where there are views toward Cape Farewell, Greenland's southernmost point. If you're with a local Inuit guide (it is possible to do this trek independently), it won't be long until you get a lesson in how to fish for Arctic char, a large cold-water fish similar to salmon and lake trout. The rivers are also perfect for fly-fishing.

The next day is a real treat, even by southern Greenland standards, as you enter the Qinngua Valley, Greenland's only natural forest—a land of downy birch and gray-leaf willows that reach heights of up to 26 feet (8 m). More than 300 species of flora can be found here, and the valley also contains the remnants of an old Norse farm, perhaps the remainder of the mysterious Brattahlid, a Viking colony established by Erik the Red in the tenth century. The walk ends at the Saputit inlet, where a boat is waiting to return you to Nanortalik and a traditional meal of musk-ox washed down by some good Greenlandic beer. **BDS**

◁ The spectacular 44-mile-long (70 km) Tasermiut Fjord.

Laki to Skaftafell National Park East Iceland, Iceland

Start Laki **End** Skaftafell National Park **Distance** 47 miles (75.6 km) **Time** 8–9 days **Grade** Moderate
Type Exposed rock, open ground **Map** goo.gl/12KAPN

The trek from Laki to Skaftafell begins only after a five-hour drive from the capital of Reykjavík; wonderfully scenic as it is, you'll need a good night's sleep beforehand. The next day, as you begin your walk from the Laki lava fields along the roaring Hverfisfljot River, you have seven hours of hiking ahead of you. Not quite as long as the average eight hours you will have every single day over the next week, ending with a 15-mile (25-km) slog on Day 9, but still enough to make sure you'll be getting plenty of exhaustive, deep sleeps as you make your way along this fabulous Icelandic adventure trek.

The wild landscapes and challenges of hiking in Iceland await you, beginning with the landscape around Laki itself. It is the product of an eruption in 1783 that released an astonishing 30 billion tons of lava, the largest recorded flow from a single eruption.

This is followed by glacial river crossings, camping on moraines, skirting the rims of ancient craters, passing tumbling waterfalls, and traveling along the shoreline of the ice lake Graenalon. This is not a marked trail; it is a wild and extreme adventure best done in a group.

There are stunning far-off views to the Sulutindar Mountains—the pinnacle-like summit of Sula is a trail highlight—and the Nupsa River is followed as it makes its way through heavily incised canyons. The end of the trail is in the European Alps–like setting of Skaftafell National Park, a land of glacial tongues and jagged mountains renowned for its temperate climate and one of the first areas of Iceland to be settled. And home, too, to Grimsvotn, Iceland's most active subglacial volcano. **BDS**

⊼ **Walk an unforgettable trail over a wild landscape.**

Fimmvörðuháls South Iceland, Iceland

Start Skógafoss waterfall   **End** Thorsmork Nature Reserve   **Distance** 14 miles (22.5 km)   **Time** 5–6 hours
Grade Moderate   **Type** Mountain and glacial trails   **Map** goo.gl/bE8qtz

The Fimmvörðuháls, or Five Cairns Pass, was recently chosen by *National Geographic* magazine as one of the top twenty hiking trails in the world. It goes between two glaciers in the south of Iceland, Eyjafjallajökull and Mýrdalsjökull, beginning at a waterfall and ending in a nature reserve. It was made all the more dramatic in 2010, when the Eyjafjallajökull volcano erupted twice—you can now walk on the lava from that eruption, which is still warm. The trail was rerouted in the wake of the eruption, and, despite the likelihood of further eruptions, it remains the most popular hike in Iceland. Another part of its appeal is the lovely two-hour drive along the south coast from Reykjavík to reach the starting point.

The trail begins at the Skógafoss waterfall, which, at 82 feet (25 m) wide and 200 feet (61 m) high, is one of the biggest in Iceland. The constant spray produced by the fall means that on sunny days you can often see a rainbow. As you hike, there are views of the Atlantic and of glaciers and volcanoes as the trail slowly ascends with an overall height gain of about 3,300 feet (1,006 m). You pass over the ground of the Eyjafjallajökull eruption, and there are views of the two new craters that were created as a result, named Magni and Módi, after the sons of Thor, the Norse god of thunder.

There is something magical to see and think about on every step of the trail, which ends at one of the country's finest nature reserves, Thorsmork. Surrounded by three glaciers and with awe-inspiring views of the mountains, it's a place to rest and enjoy this remarkable Icelandic scenery. **MG**

⬆ A "top ten" hike in a land of fire and ice.

Hardanger Fruit Trail
Hordaland, Norway

Start/End Lofthus
Distance 3.7 miles (6 km)   Time 2 hours
Grade Easy   Type Local roads, paths, gardens
Map goo.gl/29B6FE

"Hardanger Fruit Trail takes you on a journey through the heart of Norwegian fruit production."

www.norwaves.com

Norwegian farmers have been growing fruit in Hardanger since monks first introduced fruit farming to the area in the late 1200s. Cherries, pears, apples, plums—almost half of the fruit consumed by Norwegians comes from the orchards around Lofthus. These fields can be walked in a delightful amble along the Hardanger Fruit Trail, through what locals affectionately refer to as "Norway's Orchard."

The Hardanger apple, Hardanger pear, Hardanger morello cherry, and Hardanger plum are now all "protected geographic names," such is the regard in which they are held. Throughout Europe these fruits are known for their fresh, tangy flavors, flavors that you can taste for yourself by shopping at the various small stalls set up along the quaint rural roads.

The trail takes you through the orchards of local Hardanger farmers, and it is a particularly lovely stroll in May when the cherry blossoms are in full bloom, or in August just prior to the apple harvest. A mix of sealed and unsealed roads punctuated with large information boards takes you to the farms around Opedal. There, you can stroll among some of the 600,000 fruit trees that make up the orchards of Ullensvang, and meet some of the local growers who are only too happy to talk you through the science of fruit growing and help you to appreciate the art of growing fruit above 60 degrees of latitude.

If you want to extend the walk, you can take a side trail to the nearby Skredhaugen Folk Museum, with its collection of preserved-timber farm buildings, or return to Lofthus and talk to the experts at the Norwegian Institute for Agriculture on how to grow the perfect fruit. **BDS**

⬆ The Norwegian summer is short, but local farmers make the most of it with their outstanding produce.

St. Olav's Way
Oslo to Trondheim, Norway

Start Oslo   End Nidaros Cathedral, Trondheim
Distance 401 miles (645 km)   Time 32 days
Grade Strenuous   Type Overland trails
Info goo.gl/S3YslM

In 1030 the exiled king of Norway, Olav II Haraldsson, was killed at the Battle of Stiklestad after returning to his beloved country from near Kiev in present-day Ukraine. He had fought in more than twenty battles and was just thirty-five years old when he died, a legend in his own time and a martyr in the making. The day after he was slain, his body was laid to rest in a simple wooden coffin and taken to the town of Nidaros (present-day Trondheim) and buried on the banks of the Nidelven River. When "signs and miracles" began to be reported there, he was made the country's patron saint, and a small chapel was erected on the site. In 1070, construction of a new church, Nidaros Cathedral, commenced—by that time the so-called Cult of St. Olav had spread throughout the Nordic countries and into Europe, and so it became one of the most popular pilgrimage destinations in the Western world.

Today a variety of pilgrimage routes that trace various aspects of King Olav's life can still be walked across the length and breadth of Norway, one of which is the demanding St. Olav's Way. Mostly flat but quite strenuous, it begins in one of the oldest neighborhoods of Oslo. From there, the route passes by Lake Mjosa and up the Gudbrandsdalen Valley, across the Dovrefjell Mountains and through the Oppdal and Gauldalen valleys into Trondheim and to the steps of its magnificent Nidaros Cathedral. Running mostly over old tracks and pathways, it is a trail that has been followed with little variation for more than 500 years. Today it continues to raise awareness of Norway's origins and helps to ensure that the legacy of St. Olav never dies. **BDS**

Hardangervidda Plateau Traverse Telemark, Norway

Start Eidfjord   End Uvdal
Distance 71.4 miles (115 km)
Time 7 days   Grade Easy   Type Open heathland, moors   Map goo.gl/6WYc2d

The Hardangervidda Plateau in the fjordland region of Norway is a 3,861-square-mile (10,000 sq km) swathe of pure Norwegian wilderness. It has northern Europe's largest stock of reindeer, is wonderfully rugged, and, although the weather can change as quickly as you can blink, it is without question one of the best off-the-beaten-path regions you'll find anywhere.

A good introductory walk can be made to the top of the plateau from the Sorfjord, followed by a descent to the town of Lofthus, with its stunning views of nearby Folgefonna glacier. You can also make

> *"The Hardangervidda Plateau is one of Norway's and Europe's most wondrous open spaces."*
>
> www.switchbacktravel.com

a three-day loop around the Hardangerjøkulen glacier along a steep and heavily exposed trail. Or if you are feeling intrepid, then why not attempt the "Across the Plateau" route, a seven-day traverse that takes you into the truly remote areas of the plateau, an often mist-shrouded world of wet and muddy paths through a carpeted realm of moorlands, mosses, lichens, and coarse high-altitude grasses; past ponds, lakes, and more than 250 excavated Stone Age sites.

The best time to hike here is from June to October. The plateau sits entirely above the tree line and is home to twenty-six Norwegian Trekking Association huts that are a pleasure to stay in, as well as fifteen private huts. **BDS**

Kjerag Summit Rogaland, Norway

Start/End Oygardsstolen visitor center   **Distance** 7.5 miles (12 km)   **Time** 5–6 hours   **Grade** Moderate
Type Mountain paths, bare rock   **Map** goo.gl/ysjd5C

The trail up Kjerag Mountain in Norway's southern region of Rogaland provides an option that very few trails in the world are in a position to offer. If you get to the top and are feeling out of breath, the good news is that you don't have to walk back down—you can base jump instead. Granted, it will require a parachute, which is something you should have thought of on the way up, not to mention some serious preparation, but the fact you can even contemplate base jumping from the summit down to the beautiful, 26-mile-long (42 km) Lysefjorden below should tell you something: the views you're going to get from atop this near-vertical cliff mean you'll be content to sit there catching your breath all day long if necessary.

Kjerag lures all sorts of people to its wonderful precipices. Base jumpers come here to plunge off its 3,556-foot-high (1,084 m) summit; climbers arrive to tackle one of the many routes to the top; tourists visit because the flat expanse of nearby Preikestolen (Pulpit Rock) is simply too crowded, while walkers come for the beauty of its approaches, the inspiring scenery that greets them from its peak, and to see the enormous 177-cubic-foot (5-cu-m) boulder, the Kjeragbolten, wedged into a crevice on the side of the mountain.

For decades people have admired its granite mountain face from below, but how much more thrilling it is to traverse its various ridges, to climb its fully exposed 60-plus degree pitch, and to grab hold of its chains to help you up its steepest sections. While a somewhat technical climb, it is by no means out of the realm of the fit, adventure-seeking hiker. **BDS**

⬆ Balance on Kjeragbolten—if you dare.

Padjelanta Trail Norrbotten, Sweden

Start Kvikkjokk Mountain Station   **End** Vaisaluokta or Áhkká   **Distance** 99 miles (160 km)   **Time** 8–14 days
Grade Moderate   **Type** Open fields, forest trails   **Map** goo.gl/Z8hOt1

Padjelanta, which takes its name from an indigenous Sami word that roughly translated means "the higher ground," is located in northern Sweden and is the country's largest national park. A vast plateau that encircles two huge lakes, Vastenjaure and Virihaure, it is where the traditional Sami people graze their reindeer during the summer. Traversing a flat, open, greenish-blue landscape made up of small, undulating hills, the Padjelanta Trail is ideal for less experienced hikers, despite its formidable length.

The trail begins in the south at the Kvikkjokk Mountain Station, taking you along the southern boundary of Sarek National Park and through the meadows, and pine- and birch-filled forests of the Tarradalen Valley. Expect to see elk here, before you enter the park at Tarraluoppal and are greeted by the soft gentle landscapes of Padjelanta. A series of government-run mountain huts in the Tarradalen Valley makes for excellent overnight stops, but once inside the park itself, all campsites are managed by the Sami.

The Sami settlement of Staloluokta is your first stop, and as you continue north you will pass through luxuriant flowering meadows and heathlands that take you into the heart of welcoming Sami camps situated alongside rivers and lake shores. It is an area with abundant water stores and softly rounded hills, and it is almost entirely above the tree line. More than 400 plant species have been recorded here—an impressive array for a Nordic alpine region—and there is a year-round scattering of animals, including arctic foxes, snowy owls, and wolverines. **BDS**

⬆ Walk in the footsteps of the indigenous Sami.

Sarek National Park
Norrbotten, Sweden

Start Sitoalvsbron (suggested)   **End** Kvikkjokk
(suggested)   **Distance** 60 miles (96.5 km)
Time 10 days   **Grade** Easy to moderate
Type No trails, open ground   **Map** goo.gl/jtpmX0

It is a feather in the cap to have completed a serious hike in Sweden's Sarek National Park—to have completed one successfully, that is, with no mishaps, no getting lost (or at least admitting to it), no getting injured, and having been able to look after and feed yourself in a true wilderness. The word "wilderness" is often overused (some designated wilderness areas have roads!). But not here. In Sarek there are no roads. Have an accident here if you're on your own, and you're in trouble. Its center, its heart, is a long way from the nearest habitation. If you come here, then you better be able to read a map. There are no trails or cabins, no facilities, and no information boards or signs that say "Wrong Way, Go Back." What the park does have are 200 peaks more than 5,900 feet (1,800 m) high and 100 glaciers, with massifs separated by deeply incised valleys and fast-flowing streams. There are equally beautiful mountains in Sweden, such as the Kebnekaise Mountains, but they are on a human scale—you get a feeling you can "conquer" them. There is no scale in Sarek, human or otherwise. Its horizons are too broad for scale. And there is certainly no conquering it.

The fauna is better and more diverse in the Vindel Mountains; your chances of seeing any large predatory animals here are slim (though there are moose, lynxes and wolverines, and sightings of predatory birds are assured), and the flora would disappoint a botanist, who would probably be happier hiking the Padjelanta. But if it's wilderness you're wanting, where a camp stove is a must because open campfires are encouraged only to dry sodden clothes, then Sarek is the park for you. **BDS**

"Nowhere else in Europe is there such a vast expanse of monumental, uninterrupted wilderness."

www.naturvardsverket.se

← Sarek National Park's Rapa Valley and Lake Laitaure.

↑ Scores of moose call Europe's last true wilderness home.

Kungsleden
Norrbotten to Västerbotten, Sweden

Start Abisko **End** Hemavan
Distance 280 miles (450 km)   **Time** 4–5 weeks
Grade Moderate   **Type** Open ground, tundra
Info goo.gl/wJZEhu

"The hiker's stuff of dreams …
bubbling brooks, foaming rivers,
and high mountain plateaus."

www.visitsweden.com

⬆ Midnight sun and a mountain stream on this
Scandinavian classic.

The Kungsleden (King's Trail) between Abisko and Hemavan in Swedish Lapland is an adventure-filled 280-mile (450-km) journey through one of Europe's great wilderness regions. Begun by the Swedish Tourist Association in 1906 with the construction of the mountain station at Abisko, the trail passes through birch forests and hidden glaciers; over moors and high mountain plateaus; across deep precipices, creeks, and rushing rivers; along U-shaped valleys, and through four national parks. It is an overwhelming landscape.

Taking a month or more out of one's life to hike its entire length is easier said than done, but if you are keen to experience it at least in part, then take a week to walk its northernmost segment from Abisko to the Sami settlement camp at Nikkaluokta. The walk will take you through the Tjaktjavagge valley, the most majestic valley in Swedish Lapland, as well as the Kebnekaise Mountains beneath Sweden's highest peak, Mount Kebne (6,926 feet/2,111 m), and up to the highest point on the entire route, the 3,750-foot-high (1,143 m) mountain pass, the Tjaktjapasset. There is also the comfort in knowing that this is a nice "civilized" trail in the best traditions of Swedish precision—rivers are crossed by suspension bridges, and huts are comfortable and well maintained.

The Abisko–Nikkaluokta section provides an uplifting mountain experience without the need for an exceptional level of fitness. The well-provisioned huts mean you need to carry only a 22- to 26-pound (10–12-kg) pack. Most people do the walk from north to south, so the warming sun is on their face for the journey—no small consideration when walking above the Arctic Circle. **BDS**

Uppland Trail
Stockholm/Uppsala, Sweden

Start Outskirts of Stockholm   **End** Uppsala
Distance 249 miles (400 km)   **Time** 3 weeks
Grade Easy   **Type** Forest and meadow trails
Info goo.gl/KZ1ONx

Hiking over Sweden's vast interior is a trail without boundaries. The right of public access to private lands has long been acknowledged here, and providing you act with consideration and responsibility and do not walk too near to private houses, you are free to walk on private land, spend hours in bogs collecting black grouse and cloudberries, pick flowers (provided they are not on Sweden's "Do Not Pick" list), explore the region's woodlands and meadows, and pitch a tent wherever and whenever your mood takes you.

One of the ultimate ways to experience this unfettered wilderness is on the Upland Trail, which extends for 249 miles (400 km) through the Uppland province north of Stockholm. It makes an easy day out for the city's residents and is also an accessible trail for visitors. The route is relatively flat with no difficult ascents—all you need to experience the rivers, ponds, bogs, marshes, and woodlands, with their resident woodpeckers, owls, and butterflies, is a sturdy pair of walking shoes.

The trail bisects heavily scented pine forests and passes through traditional farming communities that still use windmills. The trekking season for the Uppland is a couple of months longer than it is for the great wilderness trails in the colder north—the Padjelanta and the Kungsleden—and the trail's many bogs and marshes, as well as its creeks and streams, are easily crossed thanks to a series of well-placed footbridges (but bring a pair of rubber boots if hiking in the springtime). The placid waters and wooded promontories of Lake Mälaren in the south and the archipelago of the Dalälven River are also highlights on this excellent and popular trail. **BDS**

Skåneleden Trail
Skåne, Sweden

Start/End Various   **Distance** Various
Time Various   **Grade** Easy   **Type** Forest paths, riverbanks, sealed pathways, boardwalks
Info goo.gl/u5VjNO

Once a major Viking stronghold, Skåne is now a productive farming area, a land of open fields and flat horizons, forests and lakes, castles and manor houses. The Skåneleden Trail is a 625-mile-long (1,006 km) footpath through the charming landscapes and cultural highlights of this historic region. A series of interlocking figure-eights rather than a linear pathway, it can be traversed in segments as a series of loops.

The various routes cover an area in excess of 24,711 acres (10,000 ha), one-fifth of which is within protected reserves. There are the dense woodlands of

> *"A thrilling adventure with a fantastic variety of natural and cultural experiences."*

venturesweden.com

Vedema and Lake Immeln, viewing platforms over Lake Arriesjön outside Malmö, the wetlands and ravines along the southern slopes of the Hallandsåsen ridge, the long sandy beaches of Friseboda, the country estate of Fulltofta, and the Möllers woodlands.

There are eighty-nine sections in the trail network, many of which stand on their own merit, such as the 8.7-mile-long (14 km) Josefinelust to Strandbaden section: a mix of coastal villages, heathlands, and caves. Stone Age and Iron Age artifacts have been found in the seaside caves, and in the 1560s a wooden lighthouse stood on the cliffs above with flames that reached a height of 33 feet (10 m)—one of many intriguing facts you'll encounter along the way. **BDS**

Karhunkierros Trail Lapland/Northern Ostrobothnia, Finland

Start Hautajärvi visitor center   **End** Ruka Village   **Distance** 50 miles (80 km)   **Time** 3–7 days
Grade Easy   **Type** Forest trails   **Map** goo.gl/CmYp5y

In Finnish the word "Karhunkierros" means "Bear's Trail," despite bears not being a clear and present danger here. The trail lies within the boundaries of Oulanka National Park in northern Finland and was first marked out in 1955, a year before the park itself was established. The trail is Finland's most popular, with more than 15,000 hikers completing it each year—hardly surprising when you consider the scenic landscape it bisects, a world of primeval forests, Arctic fells, steep ravines, and shallow, rushing rivers.

The trail starts in Lapland and is a delight to walk: a mix of forest paths, riverbanks, suspension bridges, and *pitkospuut*, the ubiquitous Finnish wooden duckboards that will take you over some of the trail's rougher terrain. There are lean-to shelters and a series of excellent, spacious wilderness huts that have slow-combustion wood-burning fireplaces, timber bunk beds, tables inside and benches outside, kitchen facilities, and room to sleep up to fifteen people. Several timber and wire-mesh suspension bridges are so well maintained they look like they were built yesterday, and there are plenty of gorgeous views down to ponds and rivers from the many cliff tops along which the trail takes you.

There is also some impressive white water, including a demanding 1,967-foot (600-m) stretch from the Kiutaköngäs waterfall, one of Finland's most impressive falls. And at the old Mill of Myllykoski, you can sit on a wooden deck that extends over the rushing waters of the Jyrävä River in the midst of a forest of beech and pine as you experience "wilderness Finland" in all its pristine brilliance. **BDS**

⊡ Ravines, forests, and rushing rivers on the Bear's Trail.

Antrim Hills Way Antrim, Northern Ireland

Start Glenarm **End** Slemish Mountain **Distance** 22 miles (35 km) **Time** 2 days **Grade** Moderate
Type Meadows, open moorland **Map** goo.gl/VX3hqG

Established with the permission of local landowners, the Antrim Hills Way in Northern Ireland is a short trail—just 22 miles (35 km)—but it is not one for the fainthearted. It can be very wet underfoot and is completely exposed to whatever weather is thrown at it. However, this is all amply compensated for by the views you will have from this high coastal plateau over the mountains of Antrim all the way to Scotland.

The route is almost entirely off-road once you leave Glenarm village, weaving its way through farmland with robust populations of sheep and cows and over heather-laden fields and swathes of tussock grass. Your first hill is Black Hill (1,250 feet/381 m), then comes Scawt Hill (1,240 feet/378 m), one of Northern Ireland's numerous volcanic plugs. The spectacular basalt amphitheater of Sallagh Breas provides some of the route's best walking, before you cross an often

boggy approach to Antrim's fifth highest peak, Agnew's Hill (1,555 feet/474 m), a broad, flat summit that drops dramatically over a series of rocky bluffs to the seaport of Larne. On top of Agnew's Hill it becomes plain how the walk got its name: Carnearny, Big Collin, Slemish, Carncormick, Slievenanee, and Trostan, even the distinctive glaciated landscape of the distant Sperrins—the hills of Antrim surround you.

From Agnew's Hill you descend to a stony track over a wooden bridge and follow it to Greenmount Hill Farm, a traditional uplands hill farm home to more than 250 purebred Scottish Blackface sheep. More open fields then take you to the trail's end at Slemish Mountain (1,434 feet/437 m), where, according to tradition, Saint Patrick tended to his sheep. **BDS**

⬆ Slemish Mountain is the end point of the walk.

Wicklow Way
Dublin to Carlow, Ireland

Start Marlay Park, Dublin   End Clonegal, Carlow
Distance 80 miles (129 km)   Time 8–10 days
Grade Strenuous   Type Forest trails, narrow country
lanes, moorland   Map goo.gl/T5D2bk

"Ireland's first long-distance trek is as much cultural immersion as wilderness experience."

www.backpacker.com

⬆ One of Ireland's most beloved walks is a balance of wide green valleys and long, tiring climbs.

Opened in 1980 and Ireland's first waymarked trail, the Wicklow Way combines accessibility with wilderness. It begins in the suburbs of Dublin (thus guaranteeing its status as one of the country's most popular walks) and in no time brings you to the east–west ridges and valleys of the Wicklow Mountains, the largest granite surface field in Ireland, before eventually leading you into their tranquil foothills as you near the trail's end at the village of Clonegal in County Carlow.

Now the most westerly section of the E8 footpath that spans most of Europe, the Wicklow Way takes you by mountain lakes, past the extensive remains of monastic communities in the Glendalough valley, and through conifer-covered hillsides. Shortly after leaving Dublin, you are in a world of granite hills, heather-clad meadows, and streams that are the color of peat. Just don't be lulled into thinking the trail is easy. You need to be fit for this one. There are days spent on isolated stretches where a six- or seven-hour hike of 12 miles (19 km) is the only way to get to your next set of cotton sheets, and much of the way involves long and demanding ascents, despite the highest elevation being a reasonable 2,067 feet (630 m). Climbing out of the Glenmalure valley provides scenery that will take your breath away, and the Ow valley below Lugnaquilla (3,035 feet/925 m) is a highlight worthy of the world's best hikes. Be sure to linger in the seventeenth-century village of Shillelagh, and at Tinahely's historic market building.

If you have the reserves for it, a nice side spur is the 12-mile (19-km) return walk to Powerscourt Estate, an eighteenth-century Palladian mansion with gardens that are considered to be the finest in Ireland. **BDS**

Great Southern Trail

Limerick/Kerry, Ireland

Start Limerick   End Tralee
Distance 53 miles (85 km)   Time 4–5 days
Grade Easy   Type Rail trail, asphalt
Map goo.gl/UpeMbU

Not so very long ago, in the last days of steam, the locomotives of Ireland's Great Southern and Western Railway (GS&W) would struggle their way for more than 2 miles (3.2 km) up toward the Barnagh Tunnel in Limerick, between Newcastle West and Abbeyfeale. The gradient, which began as a difficult enough 1 in 80, lost little time in angling its way up to an even steeper 1 in 60, a ratio that would hardly be noticed if one were on foot but that borders on the ridiculous for a hissing, growling steam engine trying to pull a couple of hundred tons of carriages and coal in its wake. For ninety-five years, between 1880 and 1975, trains of the GS&W ran along these demanding rails, but now the railroad is at peace. Trains no longer belch their way along it, and today the only sound you hear in the rather spooky Barnagh Tunnel, apart from your own footsteps, is the plopping of water as it seeps its way out through the mortar that borders its beautifully dressed stones.

The mixed-use (walking and cycling) Great Southern Trail is a 53-mile (85-km) asphalt ribbon that runs through the quiet, untouched farmlands of west Limerick and north Kerry along the route taken by the Limerick to Tralee railway. In 2011 the trail's volunteers won a European Greenway Association's Special Jury Prize for their efforts in not only breathing life into the disused trail but also for managing, so far, to keep it all in public ownership.

And just try finding a "softer" trail in terms of the flora: mosses, lichens, shaggy-looking ferns, and liverworts abound throughout. At times it seems like the whole thing is dressed in green velvet, a secret garden where once there were sleepers. **BDS**

"A grand open-air trail through the gorgeous back country of west Limerick and north Kerry."

www.independent.ie

⬆ An abandoned rail line in County Kerry is now a ribbon of green.

Keenagh Loop Walk Mayo, Ireland

Start/End Bellanaderg Bridge **Distance** 7.5 miles (12 km) **Time** 4 hours **Grade** Moderate to strenuous
Type Mountain and river trails, laneways, green roadways **Map** goo.gl/29V20i

Remote wilderness, stunning scenery, a spectacular valley, waterfalls, and clear running streams: if you were free to design from scratch the perfect compact loop walk, you couldn't do much better than the Keenagh Loop Walk in north Mayo, Ireland.

This trail begins at the Bellanaderg Bridge—about 12.5 miles (20 km) outside Castlebar on Boghadoon River—and heads through the village of Derreen and over the shoulder of Letterkeeghaun. After almost 2 miles (3 km) of boggy ground, you should spot a concrete water tower. Turn right there and follow a small tributary of the Boghadoon, which gives you your first encounter with one of several waterfalls, before walking around 1 mile (1.6 km) to the beautiful and remote Glendorragha Valley. Following the river, you reach a line of old wooden fence posts, where you take a right turn and begin your ascent and traverse of

the eastern slope of Knockaffertagh Pass. Continue to follow the fence posts until you come upon the right bank of another small tributary, which you follow to the summit of Knockaffertagh. Keep to your left here, and after reaching the summit, look for an old sheep track as you descend and pass through an old farm gate and path that will take you past a series of derelict farmhouses and onto a sealed road for the final walk back to your starting point. The Keenagh Loop is a great introductory walk to Mayo's Atlantic blanket bog landscape. It provides fine views to Glenhest and Newport on the shores of Clew Bay on the outward journey to the south, while on the return north, there are panoramic views of north Mayo stretching all the way to the Atlantic Ocean. **BDS**

⤒ Walk the boggy landscapes of County Mayo.

Grand Canal Way Dublin to Offaly, Ireland

Start Lucan Road Bridge, Lucan   **End** Shannon Harbour   **Distance** 73 miles (117 km)   **Time** 5 days   **Grade** Easy
Type Grassy towpaths, gravel, asphalt canal-side roads and paths   **Map** goo.gl/U1srC9

The Grand Canal Way is one of two canals (the other is the Royal Canal Way) that connect Dublin, west through the midlands, to the River Shannon, Ireland's longest river. Work on the Grand Canal, originally conceived by the Commissioners of Inland Navigation, began in 1757 and reached Shannon in 1804. By 1837 it was carrying in excess of 100,000 people a year, and was a monumental project for its time. Typical produce seen on the canal during the nineteenth century included barrels of Guinness heading out of Dublin and tons of turf coming into it, to be burned in the city's fireplaces. Its forty-three locks remained open to commercial traffic until the last barge passed through in 1960.

The trail, which never leaves the canal's side, takes you through landscapes that have been all but ignored by modern agriculture thanks to an Act of Union in the late eighteenth century that set limits on the scale of industrial development and so helped the midlands remain a viable habitat for flora and fauna. Birds that have adapted to canal life include mute swans, waterhens, and mallards, while along its banks grow alder trees and willows, several species of grasses, various free-floating plants, some Canadian pondweed, and emergent vegetation such as horsetails and sedges.

Towns visited on the trail include Tullamore, home to Tullamore Dew of Irish whiskey fame, and the remains of the eleventh- and twelfth-century buildings of Rahan, before going on to join the Shannon at Shannon Harbour, past the tumbled-down remnants of tower houses and castles. **BDS**

⊤ It took five years to construct the canal.

Speyside Way
Highland, Scotland

Start Buckie **End** Aviemore **Distance** 65 miles (105 km) **Time** 8 days (not including Tomintoul Spur) **Grade** Easy to strenuous **Type** Woodland paths, sealed roads, forestry tracks **Map** goo.gl/CMs4ZU

Opened in 1981 and one of only a handful of Scottish long-distance routes, the Speyside Way in northeast Scotland offers reasonably straightforward walking along well-graded tracks and paths with a minimum of demanding ascents and descents. It originally ran only from Ballindalloch to Spey Bay, but today the trail connects the Moray coast with the foothills of the Grampian Mountains, following as closely as it can the valley of the River Spey.

Beginning at Buckie, the well-maintained trail provides an easy walk through woodlands and the

"Passing through the heart of whisky country, this trail is a must for those seeking the taste of the Highlands."

cairngorms.co.uk

heart of malt whisky country, past the distilleries at Glenlivet and Glenfiddich. You can also include a visit to Ballindalloch Castle, the "Pearl of the North" and home to the Macpherson-Grants since 1546. The section that follows, from Ballindalloch to Grantown, is the most demanding, with several steep gradients and two streams to ford that could prove awkward after heavy rains. The trail also takes you along the foothills of the Cairngorm Mountains in Cairngorms National Park, along paths that ring the largest area of ground more than 3,000 feet (900 m) to be found anywhere in Britain. The walk also has two spurs, one from Ballindalloch to Tomintoul and the other to Dufftown, a total of almost 20 extra miles (30 km). **BDS**

Great Glen Way
Highland, Scotland

Start Fort William **End** Inverness **Distance** 79 miles (127 km) **Time** 5–6 days **Grade** Moderate **Type** Forest trails, towpaths **Map** goo.gl/VWZiAe

Officially opened on April 30, 2002, by His Royal Highness Prince Andrew, the Great Glen Way is an excellent introduction to long-distance walking. A low-level journey along towpaths and woodland tracks, it follows Scotland's longest glen and rambles over its most significant geological fault line.

It can be walked in either direction, but most people choose to begin it beneath the shadows of Ben Nevis in Fort William. From there you skirt the shoreline of Loch Linnhe before linking up with the Caledonian Canal, built in 1822 to connect nearby Corpach to Inverness via lochs Dochfour, Ness, Oich, and Lochy. Ahead is Gairlochy, where you leave the canal to walk through tranquil forest trails along the western shoreline of Loch Lochy. After crossing the A82 you have the choice of either traversing the eastern shore of Loch Oich along an old rail line or continuing along its western side on the 8.4-mile-long (13.5 km) Invergarry Link, a steeper climb with great views. You then rejoin the canal path to Fort Augustus and begin your first real climb through the crofting community of Grotaig, where you will get your first glimpse of Loch Ness.

Continue along a secondary road above the loch before descending through verdant woodlands to the River Coiltie and on to Drumnadrochit at the foot of Glen Urquhart. Either pause here or hurry through the heart of "Nessie Country" before climbing through farmlands that provide exceptional views of the loch and, on a clear day, Scotland's east coast. Then comes Abriachan, another crofting community, and Craig Leach Forest, and finally the suburbs of Inverness, where canal and riverside paths take you to Inverness Castle on its cliff over the glistening River Ness. **BDS**

Cape Wrath Trail
Highland, Scotland

Start Fort William End Cape Wrath Lighthouse
Distance 194 miles (312 km) Time 12–14 days
Grade Strenuous Type Unmarked trail
Info goo.gl/vYzir7

The Cape Wrath Trail, pioneered by photographer and author David Paterson, is often called Britain's most challenging walk, and it is little wonder. A completely unmarked trail along traditional drover and funeral routes, some of which are hundreds of years old, it requires considerable skill to navigate. And if that isn't enough, there is a variety of side routes that can also be taken, all equally unmarked and often ambiguous. Mostly the trail is far removed from any type of services or facilities, and there is a number of streams that are unbridged and can be difficult to cross after heavy rains.

It's not the sort of walk you are gradually eased into. Shortly after leaving its starting point at Fort William, you find yourself in some of Scotland's most remote and difficult terrain. But here, remote means beautiful as you find yourself in the middle of the Great Glen, Glen Garry, and Glen Shiel, before the real wilderness hits you in the seriously big glens of Affric and Mullardoch. From Strathcarron to Inverlael is relatively short and easy, but the best still awaits you as you close in on Cape Wrath itself with its 922-foot-high (281 m) sea cliffs, the most northwesterly tip of the British mainland.

There are some seriously long days of walking on this trail, and while you can do it without a tent, it isn't advised, as you might just run out of daylight before hitting any real form of shelter. The West Highland Way is tame by comparison. Come here by all means if you know your own abilities, and maybe do it soon, before Scottish Natural Heritage decide to recognize it, signpost it, and perhaps rob this stunning walk of a little of its hard, crusty edge. **BDS**

"The expedition of a lifetime, traversing 200 miles of Scotland's wildest and most beautiful country."

capewrathtrailguide.org

⤒ Cape Wrath lighthouse at the most northwesterly point of the British mainland.

Trotternish Ridge
Isle of Skye, Scotland

Start Flodigarry   End Portree
Distance 23 miles (37 km)   Time 2 days
Grade Moderate   Type Sheep-cropped turf trails
Map goo.gl/xb8nXg

The Trotternish Ridge on the Isle of Skye's Trotternish Peninsula has sequences of Jurassic sedimentary rock overlaid by twenty-four Paleogene lava flows that are 1,000 feet (305 m) thick, intruded by dolerite sills and dikes. It has north–south trending faults, and its rock layers dip almost uniformly to the west, bowing to the setting sun. It has steep scarp slopes along its eastern fringes, the products of Europe's largest-ever landslides. There are stacks and pinnacles, all compressed and gouged out by the last ice age. There are rare plants and birds, and landforms with names such as the Old Man of Storr and Quiraing, the latter an old Norse word meaning "our massive rock face." It's also the longest inland cliff in Britain. Honestly, if you were a geologist, you would probably want to live here.

One of the most impressive ridge traverses anywhere, the Trotternish Ridge walk weaves its way along near-vertical cliffs and slippery inclines of volcanic rock, and offers those who go prepared with a map and a guidebook (it's easy to get lost as there isn't a designated path for the majority of the route) an experience to last a lifetime. It begins near Loch Langaig to the north of the peninsula, and continues past the Needle and the Prison rock formations. The route runs south over more summits and passes across mostly open terrain—the sight of the next ascent always challenges you to conquer it—toward The Storr, the ridge's highest point at 2,358 feet (719 m), with an eastern face that overlooks the Sound of Raasay. You will be hugging the cliffs along the ridge's eastern edge and always marveling at just where you are. **BDS**

◄ A world of faults, dikes, and uplifted sediments.

Formartine and Buchan Way
Aberdeenshire, Scotland

Start Dyce   End Peterhead
Distance 53 miles (85 km)   Time 4 days
Grade Easy   Type Rail trail
Map goo.gl/bHLv5w

One of Scotland's great little trails, the Formartine and Buchan Way utilizes the old railroad from Dyce on the outskirts of Aberdeen to the village of Maud, which ceased to carry passengers in 1965. From Maud, the line splits in two: north to Fraserburgh and east to Peterhead. The Peterhead section opened in 1862 and the Fraserburgh extension in 1865, both built by the Formartine and Buchan Railway Company. Local landowners were invited to invest in its construction, and so unusually had a say in where it would be laid. Some wanted it out of sight of their land, while others

"It passes through such a varied and interesting landscape that the outlook is constantly changing."

www.aberdeenshire.gov.uk

wanted it to pass by roads leading to their mansions. Trains could be stopped by landowners upon their request. Level crossings were installed where demanded, and farmers had the right to sack the signalmen if they felt they were doing a poor job. It was an oddity, a virtual "custom-built" line.

The Formartine and Buchan Way continues this unique tradition. Built for people who like to walk, cycle, and even ride horses, it is a safe, relatively flat path that is entirely off-road. It provides a relaxing stroll through fertile farmlands, past the stone township of Strichen (on the Fraserburgh route), and also takes you on woodland rambles under old rail bridges and past abandoned mills. **BDS**

Three Lochs Way
Argyll & Bute, Scotland

Start Balloch   **End** Inveruglas
Distance 34 miles (54.7 km)   **Time** 3–4 days
Grade Easy to moderate   **Type** Long-distance footpath
Map goo.gl/gOJc8B

Three Lochs Way connects the freshwater Loch Lomond on Scotland's High Boundary Fault, where the lowlands of central Scotland begin their transition into its famous Highlands, to the saltwater lochs of Gare Loch and Loch Long. The route opens into the Firth of Clyde, and along its way crosses glaciated glens and fjords and provides not only a link to the region's many towns and villages, but also a host of unexpected perspectives on well-known landmarks.

It begins in the town of Balloch, an enchanting village on Loch Lomond's southern shoreline and in no time you're looking at a view of this most famous of lochs from Stoneymollan Road, an old "coffin road" along which locals once carried their dead to be buried in the grounds of churches in nearby Cardross. Another coffin road—and for centuries before that it was a packhorse track—is the Highlandman's Road, used by the residents of Glen Fruin to get to their parish church at Rhu, near Helensburgh. The two ancient routes are now official Heritage Paths. The trail also passes through the Glen Loin Woodlands, a Site of Special Scientific Interest and notable for its red squirrels and views over the Arrochar Alps, and by an assemblage of military buildings from World War II near Glen Fruin that conducted the research into the famous "Bouncing Bomb" of inventor Barnes Wallis.

This mostly low-level trail may lack the sort of adrenalin-filled challenge that comes with steep ascents, and it might not have the wealth of panoramic views common to other Highland trails, but its gently ambling nature will get it onto the shortlist of the more genteel rambler, who appreciates the beauty inherent in all of nature's moods. **BDS**

"Gentle landscapes are gradually replaced by the scenic drama of mountain, crag, and loch."

www.threelochsway.co.uk

⬆ Moorlands and three lovely lochs—including Loch Lomond seen here—make this a walk to remember.

Rob Roy Way
Stirling/Perth & Kinross, Scotland

Start Drymen **End** Pitlochry **Distance** 79 miles
(127 km) **Time** 6–7 days **Grade** Moderate
Type Forest and shoreline trails
Map goo.gl/FErz4H

Anyone with even a nip of Scottish blood in their veins knows the story of Robert Roy MacGregor. Baptized on March 7, 1671 at Glengyle at the head of Loch Katrine, he joined the Jacobite rising with his father, Donald MacGregor, under the leadership of Viscount "Bonnie" Dundee. When Dundee was killed in 1689 the spirit went out of the rebellion, and Rob Roy became first a cattleman and then, after defaulting on a loan, was branded an outlaw. His house was burned down and his lands seized, although another version says his possessions were forfeited for his part in the rebellion. Whatever the truth, the life and legacy of Rob Roy remains a potent and heady mix of past glories in the Scottish struggle for independence.

The Rob Roy Way traces the footsteps of Robert MacGregor as it passes by the waters of Lochs Lubnaig, Earn, and Tay and through the forests of the Trossachs and a series of lovely glens and villages, such as Killin. The majority of the walk is along secondary roads, cycle ways, and forest trails, and it meanders its unhurried way through the very landscapes where Rob Roy and his fellow clansmen were active, all the while passing some of the finest Highland scenery Scotland has to offer. It also follows a trail above Loch Tay, frequented by Queen Victoria, who enjoyed the views it gave her over Ben Lawers. Avoiding summits, the trail traces its way around crannogs, abandoned crofts, and prehistoric stone circles left behind by the land's ancient inhabitants. Everywhere you walk here, the local stories—some of them appropriately embellished to be sure—will provide added layers of myth and legend to this charming walk. **BDS**

"Sense the history of Scotland as you travel through glens, along rivers and burns."

www.robroyway.com

⊡ Rob Roy Way mixes reality and myth in a heady mix of history, villages, and the glens Rob Roy called home.

Cateran Trail
Perth & Kinross/Angus, Scotland

Start/End Blairgowrie   **Distance** 64 miles (103 km)
Time 5 days   **Grade** Easy to moderate
Type Forest trails, meadows
Map goo.gl/733ZqR

"The trail takes its name from the feared cattle thieves who raided the rich lands of Strathardle, Glenshee, and Glen Isla."

www.caterantrail.org

⬆ Walkers on the Cateran Trail approaching the breathtaking scenery of the Spittal of Glenshee.

They were known as the Caterans, marauding thieves and rustlers who prowled and plundered their way through the lawless hills and valleys of the Scottish Highlands from the Middle Ages to the 1600s. The rich farmlands around Glen Isla, Glenshee, and Strathardle were often the target of their raids, and they would ride back into the night as quickly as they appeared using ancient drove roads running through isolated glens. The Caterans were more feared than wolves, and their raiding parties often numbered in the hundreds. Now, you can trace their footsteps on the Cateran Trail, a 64-mile (103-km) waymarked trail through the very heart of Scotland, an hour and a half north of Edinburgh. The trail passes through what *The Great Outdoors* magazine has called "the sort of Scotland walkers dream of" in a little-visited corner of Perthshire largely unknown to the wider walking community.

The route traces some of the old tracks and drove roads that the Caterans would surely have used. It starts in the market town of Blairgowrie, near the Ericht River, home to wild Atlantic salmon that spawn in its waters before passing through the Blackcraig Forest and into Strathardle, a glen farmed since the Bronze Age, before ascending to 2,100 feet (640 m) at Lairig Gate to the spectacular Spittal of Glenshee. Mount Blair at the southern end of Glenshee (the "Fairy Glen") can be climbed as an option, and then you enter Glen Isla, with its persistent links to Arthurian legends (Queen Guinevere was held captive here on Barry Hill by Mordred). After a traverse over the hills by Alyth, you pass the massive standing stones at Heatheryhaugh, where you can rest and ponder, before returning to Blairgowrie. **BDS**

West Highland Way
East Dumbartonshire to Highland, Scotland

Start Milngavie   **End** Fort William
Distance 95 miles (153 km)   **Time** 8 days
Grade Easy   **Type** Long-distance footpath
Map goo.gl/HOHcbS

The idea that a pathway should be made across the Scottish Highlands from Glasgow to the north, using old drove and military roads, was first mooted way back in the 1930s. It was only after the successful completion of the Pennine Way in 1965, however, that the first real steps to establish the West Highland Way were taken. What makes this easily navigable trail so memorable is how its appearance alters as you pass through its varying topography and geology, as lowlands gradually become highlands. It begins—if you go from south to north as most do—with farmlands and pastures characteristic of the region around Milngavie, then past the stunning but heavily peopled Loch Lomond on Scotland's High Boundary Fault. The relative solitude and otherworldly beauty of Rannoch Moor is a highlight: a land of peat bogs and lochans that can make for some arduous walking until an easy climb over the moorlands' highest point. A steep descent follows, revealing what many consider to be Scotland's most iconic mountain—Buachaille Etive Mór—and the whitewashed Black Rock cottage awaiting you in the foreground, probably the most photographed cottage in Scotland. After carefully crossing the A82, you come upon the Kings House Hotel, Scotland's well-known coaching inn built in 1746 and a true oasis, particularly in bad weather.

Leaving the Kings House, you climb to the summit of Buachaille Etive Mór—an ascent of 1,000 feet (305 m), with views of the Glencoe Mountains and more rough terrain to come. There is an almost vertigo-inducing view down to a small village at the head of Loch Leven before the final approach to Fort William and the end of every Briton's must-do journey. **BDS**

"Follows ancient and historic routes of communication and makes use of drove roads, military roads, and disused railway tracks."

www.west-highland-way.co.uk

⊞ Lowland moors, dense woodlands, Loch Lomond, and the Devil's Staircase await you on this classic hike.

Southern Upland Way Dumfries & Galloway to Borders, Scotland

Start Portpatrick   **End** Cockburnspath   **Distance** 212 miles (341 km)   **Time** 12–16 days   **Grade** Strenuous
Type Moorlands, field trails, secondary roads   **Info** goo.gl/FRaiXw

Weaving its way through a landscape of gently rounded, undulating hills, with only occasional rock outcrops, this landscape has been sculpted and hewn by the relentless process of glaciation. Bisected by Britain's first coast-to-coast, long-distance footpath running from the Atlantic Ocean to the North Sea, it has something for everyone. There are short sections that are ideal for a family day out, as well as long and arduous segments that only the experienced walker will complete in a single day. The route passes through sparsely populated landscapes, and although it avoids the high tops, it still manages an overall elevation gain in excess of 28,600 feet (8,717 m). From the west at Portpatrick, you pass over rugged cliffs, through sheep pastures, over low moorland and forest tracts, and to the hills around Glentrool. The route hugs the lowlands through the Galloway Hills

before crossing open moorlands again and through St. John's Town of Dalry. Sanquhar. St. Mary's Loch, the largest natural loch on the Scottish borders and reputed to be the deepest loch in Scotland, is skirted, followed by a series of heather-clad meadows and a final cliff top stroll that takes you into Cockburnspath.

Although the trail is marked, it is not easy navigating your way across mist-filled moorlands, of which there are many. The long distances between many of its stages need to be calculated accurately and planned for (it is no fun running out of daylight when you don't have a tent), and there is the issue of a lack of facilities. Yet properly managed and prepared for this is a wonderful walk through a living landscape. **BDS**

⬆ Walk through misty moors on a low-elevation classic.

River Ayr Way East Ayrshire/South Ayrshire, Scotland

Start Glenbuck Loch **End** Ayr **Distance** 41 miles (66 km) **Time** 3 days **Grade** Easy to moderate
Type Forest trails **Map** goo.gl/P68fFs

There is nothing quite like the satisfaction one gets from tracing a river along its entire length. The River Ayr Way opened in 2006 and already attracts more than 100,000 people a year. The longest river in Ayrshire flows from Glenbuck Loch, an artificial loch created in 1802 to power a series of large water turbines, and zigzags its way westward through the moorlands, sandstone gorges, and farmlands of south and east Ayrshire to the township of Ayr on the Firth of Clyde.

An inspiration for the poet Robert Burns and a hiding place for national hero William Wallace, the valley along which the river flows is rich in industrial history and is the site of the Catrine Mill (burned down in 1963) and its associated cotton works, sluices, and lades designed and built between 1787 and 1789 by the man responsible for the mills at New Lanark, David Dale. The mill transformed Catrine from a sleepy village into a thriving industrial center, and in 1827 two waterwheels were added with a capacity of 120 buckets each. The village of Sorn had at least four mills of its own, built to provide power for nearby Sorn Castle, and they were converted into church buildings when the mill closed in 1913. When the 169-foot-high- (51.5 m) Ballochmyle Viaduct was completed in 1848 to bring a railway into the valley, it was the largest masonry-spanned arch anywhere in the world.

The walk along Scotland's first "source to sea" path takes you past these sites and much more besides, including one of Britain's most significant Neolithic "cup and ring" sites, and lovely Ayr Gorge, where Robert Burns bade farewell to his sweetheart, Highland Mary, in 1786. **BDS**

⊡ A river walk highlights Britain's industrial beginnings.

Seathwaite to Sty Head and Grains Gill Cumbria, England

Start/End Seathwaite farmyard parking lot **Distance** 5.5 miles (8.8 km) **Time** 4 hours **Grade** Moderate
Type Gravel trails, old pack horse route **Map** goo.gl/twCayP

The first record of anyone complaining that the quality of a Lake District path was not what it used to be was in 1819, when a traveler along the path through Stake Pass out of Borrowdale remarked that the path was in a far worse state of repair than it was when he last walked it in 1809. The problem was erosion, and remarkably, even as recently as the 1990s, there was no legal requirement upon any organization to combat it. Then along came Fix the Fells, an amalgam of government, volunteers, and concerned locals that has since repaired and maintained more than 200 path sections. One path that benefited from this is the Seathwaite to Sty Head and Grains Gill trail.

The path begins in the Borrowdale Valley at the Seathwaite farmyard parking lot, and no sooner have you gotten into your stride on this old pack horse trail

then you reach Stockley Bridge, the beautiful and ancient stone footbridge built in 1540 (and widened in 1887). A gravel track leads to another bridge over Sty Head Gill, and as you climb to Sty Head Tarn, the view of Great Gable—one of the lake region's favorite mountains—rises up before you. Stop at Sprinkling Tarn for a bite to eat, skirt the sheer rock face of Great End, turn left at Ruddy Gill, and head back via a lovely drystone wall to Seathwaite farmyard.

It is thanks to the dedicated people of Fix the Fells that the words of the great Lakeland walker Alfred Wainwright still ring true: "Seathwaite, once in a little world of its own with few visitors, has become a pedestrian metropolis. Great days on the fells begin and end here." **BDS**

⬆ Fix the Fells has built a Lake District favorite.

Coast to Coast Walk Cumbria/North Yorkshire, England

Start St. Bees, Cumbria   **End** Robin Hood's Bay, North Yorkshire   **Distance** 192 miles (309 km)   **Time** 12–14 days
Grade Moderate to strenuous   **Type** Moorland, forest, and meadow trails   **Info** goo.gl/wIagGT

When you look at the start and end points of the Coast to Coast Walk, devised by the noted walker Arthur Wainwright in 1973, it is impossible to imagine linking St. Bees on the Cumbrian coast with the idyllic village of Robin Hood's Bay on the shores of the North Sea in North Yorkshire by a more pleasing, or more direct, route. It can, of course, be undertaken either way, but presuming you begin at St. Bees, the walk loses no time in indelibly impressing itself upon your consciousness as you walk through the beautiful Lake District valleys of Borrowdale, Grasmere, and Patterdale before passing by the peculiarly named mountain of High Street, which once had a Roman road over its 2,716-foot (828-m) summit.

You emerge from the Lake District into the gentler landscape of the Yorkshire Dales with its hills, rivers, and cliffs of carboniferous limestone, past the drystone walls and traditional villages of the Swaledale valley and the farmlands of the Vale of York. The vistas increase further still when you enter the North York Moors, and after traversing the valley of Eskdale, you reach the great cliffs of the North Sea coast, along which you walk the final miles until you glimpse the red roofs that line the maze of cobblestoned streets that is Robin Hood's Bay, the former haunt of seventeenth-century smugglers, tucked into one of Yorkshire's most raw, elemental stretches of coastline. The walk combines lofty scampers with knee-buckling ascents, and the agreeable surprise is, perhaps, that not all of the beauty on this walk is confined to the Lake District. The Vale of Mowbray, the Cleveland Hills—the surprises keep coming. **BDS**

⭡ Robin Hood's Bay marks the end of a modern classic.

Dales Way
West Yorkshire/Cumbria, England

Start Ilkley, West Yorkshire **End** Bowness-on-Windermere, Cumbria **Distance** 84 miles (135 km) **Time** 7–10 days **Grade** Moderate **Type** Country and moorland paths **Map** goo.gl/2wWlnM

"Offers a scenically attractive route from urban West Yorkshire to the Lake District."

www.dalesway.org

⬆ The Dales Way follows naturally occurring ancient routes of communication through welcoming villages.

When all the pubs along a route offer bed and breakfast, you know it's a popular trail, and the Dales Way crosses some of the best-known walking territory in Britain. Whichever direction you tackle it, the path leads up through some of England's most scenic landscapes. It reaches the watershed of northern England, then passes down the other side through yet more memorable scenery.

On the east side of the mountain ridge are the Dales; on the west are the Lakes. Both are classic fell country, with a patchwork of moorland and rough pasture divided by old drystone walls and weathered outcrops. Trees are found in groups around old stone farms or in sheltered valleys. The trail leads up the Wharfe Valley, or Dale, which is considered the most picturesque of Yorkshire's valleys. From the Yorkshire Dales National Park, the route crosses the Pennines, the "backbone of England," then drops down into the Lake District National Park to end with another scenic highlight at the shores of Lake Windermere.

There are steep sections, but the abundance of accommodation means that days can be split into short manageable chunks. This makes the Dales Way a good introduction to multiday hiking on officially designated long-distance trails. If you want to walk farther, it joins other trails to large cities, such as Leeds and Bradford. The walk can be seen as leading from England's largest urban conurbation (West Yorkshire) to its largest lake (Windermere). At one end of the trail is the old Victorian spa town of Ilkley. It stands beneath its moor, which is the subject of Yorkshire's unofficial dialect anthem: "On Ilkla Moor Baht 'At" (On Ilkley Moor Without a Hat). **SH**

Cleveland Way
North Yorkshire, England

Start Helmsley   End Filey
Distance 110 miles (177 km)
Time 9 days   Grade Moderate
Type Meadows   Info goo.gl/sjDQNG

Opened in 1969 and only the second in the national trail program of long-distance bridleways and walking paths, the Cleveland Way in North Yorkshire is a perfect mix of stunning coastal paths and typically stark and atmospheric Yorkshire moors.

Most people prefer to start inland in the market town of Helmsley, and head first north and then east around the boundary of the North York Moors National Park, a 60-mile (96.5-km) amble alongside the United Kingdom's largest tract of heather moorland, before reaching Saltburn on the coast and turning southward to follow the coast down to Filey. This features one of England's most dramatic cliff top walks, including Rock Cliff, east England's highest point, on a horseshoe-shaped national trail that takes you over one of the most untouched regions of northern England and past some of the north's finest listed buildings, including Helmsley Castle, Rievaulx Abbey, Whitby Abbey, and the Captain Cook monument. There are a few strenuous sections to negotiate on this "gentle amble," specifically the Cleveland Hills on the way to Kildale from the quaint village of Osmotherley that take you over Clay Bank Top to Round Hill and on up to Urra Moor, the walk's high point. One cannot really pass by North York Moors National Park, however, without venturing on one of its many wonderful trails. One of the best is the White Horse Walk spur at Sutton Bank, which takes you to the turf-cut White Horse of Kilburn after walking along an escarpment and down through woodlands beneath impressive cliffs, then back up to the horse—a series of views that author James Herriot once described as the finest in all England. **BDS**

Herriot Way
North Yorkshire, England

Start/End Aysgarth   Distance 55 miles
(88.5 km)   Time 4–5 days   Grade Easy
Type Circular long-distance walk
Map goo.gl/F5OQgA

North Yorkshire's Herriot Way is named after the veterinary surgeon and author James Alfred Wight Herriot. On the way you can visit the places where he lived and worked, and those made famous in the pages of his book *All Creatures Great and Small* (1972).

The walk is a circular long-distance path and can be done in either direction. If you choose a clockwise path, you leave Aysgarth in Wensleydale and head down to the Ure River, which you follow into Askrigg, a village that was the location for the James Herriot TV series (1978–90). From there you head to the hamlet of

"[The walk is] named after James Herriot who began his veterinary practice … in the late 1930s."

www.hfholidays.co.uk

Hardraw and England's highest single-drop waterfall. Hawes, Yorkshire's highest market town, precedes a climb up the county's third-highest mountain, Great Shunner Fell, utilizing the Pennine Way before a series of typical dales villages gives way to the bleakness of Gunnerside Moor and the relics of its once-thriving lead industry. From there it's on to the beautiful River Swale and then Grinton Lodge, a former nineteenth-century shooting lodge and now a youth hostel. Walking the Apedale Road will then take you into Dent, one of Yorkshire's prettiest villages. The fourteenth-century Castle Bolton, where Mary Queen of Scots stayed after the Battle of Langside in 1568 is next, and finally you return, contented, to Aysgarth. **BDS**

Pennine Way National Trail
England/Scotland

Start Old Nag's Head, Edale, Derbyshire **End** Border Hotel, Kirk Yetholm, Scottish Borders **Distance** 268 miles (431 km) **Time** 14–16 days **Grade** Strenuous **Type** Country paths **Info** goo.gl/2XNqbE

It was Tom Stephenson—journalist, champion of walkers' rights, and from 1948 the secretary of the Rambler's Association—who wrote in an article published in the *Daily Herald* on June 22, 1935 titled "Wanted: A Long, Green Trail" that it was about time England had a national trail of the type the United States had been introducing. What he proposed eventually became, thirty years later at its official opening in 1965, the Pennine Way, a 256-mile-long (412 km) route across the backbone of the Pennines, separating northeast and northwest England, running from the Peak District in Derbyshire to Kirk Yetholm in Scotland. It is not a walk for novices. Covering its entire length will see you walk across more than 200 bridges and through almost 300 gates, and pass by more than 450 waymarkers. Of course, you are also free to do as little or as much of it as you like by joining the trail at one of its more than 530 access points.

Most walk it from south to north because the guide books are oriented that way, but from whichever end you begin, walking it will be a life-changing experience: Yorkshire Dales National Park, Hadrian's Wall, and Northumberland National Park, from the South Pennines' gritstone moors to the remoteness of the North Pennines and the glorious bleakness of the Cheviot Hills. There are many highlights. For some it is the clints and grikes of the carboniferous limestone pavements above Malham Cove; for others it is the descent from Auchope Cairn to the mountain hut above Hen Hole. Whatever it is, wherever it is, be sure to come here and find it. And have something awe-inspiring about which to tell your grandchildren. **BDS**

"Offers some of the finest upland walking in England. A once in a lifetime experience."

www.nationaltrail.co.uk

◄ The Pennine Way crossing Hadrian's Wall near Roman defensive structure Turret 37a in Northumberland.

⬆ Outcrops of carboniferous limestone paving above Malham Cove in North Yorkshire.

Yorkshire Wolds Way East Yorkshire/North Yorkshire, England

Start Hessle   **End** Filey Brigg   **Distance** 78 miles (125 km)   **Time** 5–6 days   **Grade** Easy
Type Country footpaths   **Map** goo.gl/GcnIWz

The Yorkshire Wolds is a little-known, picturesque corner of northeastern England—wide expanses of rolling chalk landscapes dotted with small market towns and quiet villages. The Yorkshire Wolds Way curves right across the heart of these rural downs, from the north shore of the Humber Estuary to reach the North Sea at the small seaside resort of Filey.

Many locals still use the old name for this region—the East Riding of Yorkshire—and it is an area characterized by big skies, sweeping panoramas, and secluded hidden valleys. The main attraction is the relaxed landscape with open farmland rising and falling into dry valleys and neat patches of woodland. There could be wildflowers in the hedges, red kites in the sky, and sheep grazing in a field, with a view of the sea behind or perhaps a traditional country pub with a beer garden. Trail highlights include the deserted village

of Wharram Percy, rows of pretty estate cottages in Londesbrough village, and an inspiring sequence of publicly funded sculptures.

The route is easygoing and well marked, with no steep climbs despite the rolling terrain. Small sections follow roads or bridleways shared with cyclists and horses, but the majority of the walk is on country footpaths designated only for walkers. One end the path offers a close-up view of the Humber Bridge, passing right under what was once the longest single-span bridge in the world. Farther north, walkers can stop off at Staxton's Wolds Gallery, which showcases local art. Descending the final escarpment from the Wolds down to the sea, the route winds down to the wild headland at the end of Filey's long, sandy beach. **SH**

⊕ **Yorkshire's crescent of chalk hills and green valleys.**

Viking Way Lincolnshire to Rutland, England

Start Barton-upon-Humber   **End** Oakham   **Distance** 147 miles (236 km)   **Time** 2 weeks   **Grade** Easy
Type Footpaths, towpaths   **Info** goo.gl/z3NFwO

For centuries, the rich, flat farmland of England's east coast was easy prey for Viking raiders, who later became settlers. The Viking Way's trailhead at Barton-upon-Humber must have been an easy landing point for them. It stands on the south bank of the sheltered broad estuary. Barton now stands in the shadow of the impressive modern suspension bridge across the Humber. The path runs roughly north to south across this region of gentle countryside dotted with historic towns and villages. This area was once known as "the Danelaw," because it was ruled by newcomers from Scandinavia, but walkers soon discover that the Viking Way is not completely about Vikings.

The first stretch crosses the rolling countryside known as the Lincolnshire Wolds, to the old Roman stronghold of Caistor, then runs along the Bain Valley to another Roman settlement, Horncastle. Stretches of the Roman wall are still visible here. The route continues along a former railway track and across typical Lincolnshire fenland. Sections of the route pass along the towpath of the Grantham Canal. From Horncastle, the Viking Way follows the Witham Valley into the historic county town of Lincoln. Here it leads to the eleventh-century cathedral and down the High Street, lined with half-timbered buildings. From Lincoln, walkers follow the route of two old Roman roads, Ermine Street and Sewstern Lane, and along the escarpment known as "Lincolnshire Edge." The path briefly enters Leicestershire before crossing into Rutland. The Viking Way passes one of Europe's largest man-made lakes, Rutland Water, and ends in England's smallest county, Oakham. **SH**

⛰ A Viking path ending in England's smallest county.

Dart Valley Trail
Devon, England

Start Totnes **End** Dartmouth
Distance 17 miles (27.3 km) **Time** 1–2 days
Grade Easy **Type** Marked riverside footpath
Map goo.gl/iw4qc9

The Dart estuary twists and turns between steep wooded banks and lush rolling farmland and is known as one of England's most beautiful valleys. The river flows south from the bohemian market town of Totnes to the English Channel at the historic maritime town of Dartmouth. The area is a tourist magnet, with attractions such as the Dart Valley steam railway, the Royal Naval College of Dartmouth, and Agatha Christie's house and gardens at Greenway.

As an alternative to riding on the old steam railway or taking one of the guided boat trips, Devon

> *"Ancient woodland, a steam railway line, and one of the most beautiful rivers to be found."*
>
> www.bbc.co.uk

County Council has created this easy riverside ramble. The path starts in Totnes and heads down the west bank to Greenway. Ferries here mean walkers can continue to the sea on either the west or east bank.

This holiday area of South Devon is known as the South Hams. Gentle hills slope down to the river, with protected stretches of ancient oak woodland along the riverbanks. Well-marked paths cross fields and pass through the woods with plenty of small ups and downs, but nothing too strenuous. Highlights along the route include the pastel-painted, thatched cottages in Dittisham, Tuckenhay, and Ashprington villages, and views of exclusive yachts moored along the estuary. **SH**

Bath Skyline
Somerset, England

Start/End University of Bath
Distance 6 miles (9.6 km) **Time** 3 hours
Grade Easy to moderate **Type** Fields, forest trails, pathways **Map** goo.gl/XwL6G8

Few cities or towns in England provide the panorama of architectural purity to be seen in the World Heritage city of Bath, founded by the Romans around 60 CE at the bottom of the Avon Valley. Nowhere can the beauty of its Georgian terraces, the Gothic Bath Abbey, and the lush green hills that envelop it be better appreciated than by walking the Bath Skyline, the most downloaded walk of more than 170 walks on the National Trust's website.

The walk encircles the city, so it can be started anywhere, constantly dipping in and out of meadows and tranquil woodlands, and through a series of kissing gates. There are a number of historical must-sees along the way, including the eighteenth-century Sham Castle folly—designed in the 1750s by Sanderson Miller, pioneer of Gothic Revival architecture—and the site of an old quarry once used by the Romans to build their new settlement. There is the landscape of exposed rocks and tree roots that is Bathampton Wood, "key" stones that were once used as markers for a long-since overgrown racetrack at Bushey Norwood, and an Iron Age fort on Little Solsbury Hill. You even cross a Palladian-style bridge in Prior Park Landscape Garden, one of only four in the world.

Researchers at the University of Bath recently constructed an energy map for Bath Skyline walkers and calculated that completing the walk burned an average of 735 calories, which is equivalent to playing ninety minutes of football or forty-five minutes of squash, and almost the exact amount of calories consumed in a typical Sunday roast, making the Bath Skyline the perfect antidote for an afternoon of self-indulgence. **BDS**

Cotswold Way
Gloucestershire/Somerset, England

Start Chipping Campden, Gloucestershire
End Bath, Somerset **Distance** 102 miles
(164 km) **Time** 8–10 days **Grade** Moderate
Type Long-distance walking trail **Info** goo.gl/1CtkLk

It was two Gloucestershire resident ramblers, Tony Drake and Cyril Trenfield, who first proposed a route along the Cotswold Edge escarpment through the Cotswold Hills. They certainly knew what they were doing. This much-loved long-distance walk has since become one of England's quintessential rambles, giving those who tread it unrivaled views of idyllic villages and jaw-droppingly beautiful landscapes, such as the limestone grasslands of the Cleeve Hill Ring and the Leckhampton Loop. Even if it rains, your spirits are almost guaranteed not to be dampened.

It starts in the Gloucestershire market town of Chipping Campden, and what follows from there is a heady assortment of beech-crowned ridgelines and escarpment spurs that look over distant farms and villages. There are deep valleys and endless drystone walls that bisect meadows of wild garlic and bluebells. It offers breathtaking views over the Severn Valley, and goes through the high streets of numerous Cotswold villages with their cottages of locally quarried limestone before coming to an end in Somerset's World Heritage city of Bath. Not only do you pass through some of England's most eye-catching natural environments, but you also walk by a wealth of built history, such as the Neolithic burial chamber at Belas Knap; fifteenth-century Sudeley Castle, which was the birthplace and burial site of King Henry VIII's sixth wife, Catherine Parr; and Broadway Tower, a Saxon tower built in the form of a castle in 1799.

The Cotswold Way is also run once a year north to south as a ten-stage relay race, the Cotswold Way Relay. The record is held by Darryl Carter of Middlesex: 20 hours and 36 minutes. Imagine what he missed. **BDS**

"It explores one glorious village after another—each with some memorable feature."

www.contours.co.uk

⬆ A walk on the Cotswold Edge provides panoramic views over limestone grasslands and Neolithic burial sites.

White Horse Trail Wiltshire, England

Start/End Westbury White Horse   **Distance** 90 miles (145 km)   **Time** 6–10 days   **Grade** Easy to moderate
Type Chalk paths   **Map** goo.gl/NkfOn3

The Wiltshire White Horses are a series of mostly 300-year-old chalk carvings etched into the Wiltshire hills, the turf cut away in the shape of giant horses to reveal the white stone underneath. Some date back thousands of years; others are more recent, but all are distinctive landmarks in a quintessentially English rustic setting. This walk was created by Wiltshire County Council to promote the white horses as a tourist attraction. It loops in a circuit over the rolling downland of the north of the county, passing through market towns such as Marlborough, Pewsey, and Devizes, and was designed to approach each of the horses from the best vantage points.

The horses are all impressive sights amid dramatic scenery, but the route also passes other Wiltshire attractions, such as the Ridgeway (England's oldest road) and the Kennet and Avon Canal. It's a circular route, so

walkers can start anywhere, although all official publications start at one of the most prominent horses, at Westbury. This looks out across the Vale of Pewsey and stands alongside an ancient hill fort.

The trail is hilly and some gradients are steep, but none are very high. The highest point on the trail is at Milk Hill, next to the Alton Barnes white horse, which is just under 1,000 feet (305 m) high. This horse was cut in 1812 and can be seen from up to 22 miles (35 km) away. Each horse has a story: Marlborough's horse was designed by a local schoolboy in 1804, the Hackpen horse appeared in 1834 to commemorate Queen Victoria's coronation, and Cherhill's horse was cut in 1780 by workmen following instructions shouted through a megaphone from below. **SH**

⬆ The Alton Barnes white horse can be seen for miles around.

The Ridgeway Wiltshire to Buckinghamshire, England

Start Avebury, Wiltshire   **End** Ivinghoe Beacon, Buckinghamshire   **Distance** 85 miles (137 km)   **Time** 4–7 days
Grade Moderate   **Type** Stony path, tarmac   **Map** goo.gl/2YHTes

They call the Ridgeway England's oldest road, and for at least 6,000 years it was the preferred route used by soldiers, traders, drovers, livestock, horses, and carts. Originally, it was part of a trail from the English Channel in Dorset to the North Sea at the Wash in Norfolk. Known as the Greater Ridgeway, it is now covered by four different long-distance paths. The Ridgeway itself is the best-known section, and runs from Salisbury Plain to the Chilterns. It was originally built across the ridges of the chalk downs of southern England to allow safe and dry progress above the untamed woods and wild muddy countryside below.

It crosses five counties: Wiltshire, Oxfordshire, Berkshire, Hertfordshire, and Buckinghamshire. The path starts at the Avebury World Heritage Site, which also includes Europe's biggest stone circle and the mysterious man-made Silbury Hill. The marked route leads past a sequence of ancient monuments, such as hill forts, tombs, and earthworks. Other sights along the way include the British Prime Minister's country residence at Chequers. There are stretches along the banks of the Thames and through leafy Wendover Woods. The Ridgeway ends at Ivinghoe Beacon, a prominent landmark in the Chiltern Hills, where signaling bonfires have been lit throughout history.

In practical terms the route passes some distance from most towns and can feel surprisingly remote. Walking west to east is preferable because of the prevailing wind direction. Wild camping is not allowed officially, however, clean, careful campers are rarely challenged. The path is mostly chalky stone, but it can get pretty rutted and muddy in winter. **SH**

⬆ Uffington white horse and hill fort is a worthwhile side trip.

Nickey Line
Hertfordshire, England

Start Hollybush Lane, Harpenden   End Midland Hotel, Hemel Hempstead   Distance 7 miles (11.2 km)
Time 3–4 hours   Grade Easy   Type Rail trail
Map goo.gl/KMGTkc

The Nickey Line is an old rail line in Hertfordshire that once linked Harpenden to Hemel Hempstead. The last passenger train ran the line in 1947, and in the years that followed, much of the train bed was left to suffer the ravages of time until the Dacorum and St. Albans councils purchased the land in the early 1980s and began transforming it into the green walking and cycling corridor that exists today.

The line opened to the public in 1985, and it now forms part of the Sustrans National Cycle Network. It continues to fulfill its original purpose by linking the towns of Harpenden, Redbourn, and Hemel Hempstead. Of particular interest to railway enthusiasts, from Harpenden this wooded trail takes you through deep ravines that were once railway cuttings and past the relics of stations long past, complete with overgrown platforms, the occasional railway sleeper left in place after the rails conversion, and even signal posts—all eerie reminders of a simpler, bygone time.

It also takes you down Redbourn village High Street, once an old Roman road, and centuries later a halfway house for coaches, and there is even an alternate trail to nearby Rothampsted Estate, once the home of Sir John Lawes, the inventor of superphosphate, which heralded the era of chemical fertilizers. The trail continues through long stretches of converted rail cuttings and even goes under the M1 before emerging near the Midland Hotel in Hemel Hempstead. Who cares if Hemel Hempstead was voted the ugliest town in the United Kingdom in 2013? What better reason, then, to get on the Nickey Line at Hemel Hempstead and start walking. **BDS**

"The Nickey was expensive to build and, most agreed, too steep for a railway."

www.hertsmemories.org.uk

⬆ An old railway-turned-trail still links the high streets of small Hertfordshire towns.

Essex Way

Essex, England

Start Epping Station   **End** The Old Lighthouse, Harwich
Distance 82 miles (132 km)   **Time** 5 days
Grade Easy   **Type** Way-marked country footpaths
Map goo.gl/Rr4kmO

On the Essex Way you get to walk to the oldest wooden church in the world, to visit the home of the man suspected of regicide, and to cross a 2,000-year-old Roman road along an easy flat path from London to the sea. This National Trail runs west to east (or vice versa) in the eastern county of Essex. Most prefer to begin at the western end and walk toward the North Sea. The starting point is in Epping, once known as the haunt of notorious highwayman Dick Turpin. Now it is the last station on the Central Line of London's Underground system.

Walkers cross the old Roman road to Colchester on the way to Greenstead, site of the world's oldest wooden church, dating back to the ninth century. The trail passes through classic English country villages, such as the old lace-making settlement of Coggeshall where the little Blackwater River meanders through a picturesque low-lying landscape. It continues through leafy green lanes, past Langham Hall, home of Sir Walter Tyrrell who fled to France after being suspected of killing King William II while they hunted together with bows and arrows in 1100.

The council's waymarking involves white signs featuring two poppies. This is attached to gateposts, stiles, and footbridges along the path as it passes through open farmland, ancient woods, and river valleys lined with trees. Toward the end, the trail leads along the Seawalls, a defensive system against erosion by the waves of the North Sea. It ends at the 200-year-old Harwich lighthouses. These high and low lights are 500 feet (152 m) apart, but if a boat is on the correct course to enter Harwich Harbour, they appear to sit one right above the other. **SH**

Saffron Trail

Essex, England

Start Southend   **End** Saffron Walden
Distance 71 miles (114 km)   **Time** 4 days
Grade Easy   **Type** Coastal path, country trail
Map goo.gl/6oYsOJ

This gentle long-distance trail crosses England's eastern county of Essex, from the popular seaside resort of Southend to the historic town of Saffron Walden. The trail's starting point overlooks Southend's sandy beach and the longest pleasure pier in the world, then travels through the grounds of Hadleigh Castle, where the romantic ruins still dominate the Essex Marshes below and walkers can enjoy spectacular views across the wide mouth of the Thames Estuary. The Saffron Trail is a mix of interesting urban walking and varied countryside rambles.

"Miles and miles of walking in the wilds of the Essex countryside."

www.essexwalks.com

For once, the recommended direction is from the coast heading inland. The landscape becomes hillier as the trail heads north, away from the flatlands and rivers around the estuary. These hills never reach more than 350 feet (91 m) in height, and the walk is categorized as easy. Heading through Great Dunmow and past sixteenth-century Leez Priory, walkers will note how the villages become more rural and isolated away from the coast. At the village of Newport, the path passes rows of half-timbered houses and ends at the medieval market town of Saffron Walden. The picturesque town's name comes from the saffron that was extracted from crocuses once grown there and thought to be a potent remedy for the plague. **SH**

South Downs Way
Hampshire to East Sussex, England

Start Winchester, Hampshire   End Eastbourne, East Sussex   Distance 100 miles (160 km) Time 10–12 days   Grade Easy   Type Long-distance footpath   Map goo.gl/Q5l9tg

"Experience some of our finest countryside between Winchester, the first capital of England, and the white chalk cliffs of Eastbourne."

www.nationaltrail.co.uk

⬆ The beautiful views of the South Downs and the Jill windmill as seen from inside the Jack windmill.

For around 5,000 years humans have been walking where Cheesefoot Head, Arundel, Devil's Dyke, Ditchling Beacon, and the chalk cliffs of the Seven Sisters leading to Beachy Head now stand. They walked it because it was a safer and more comfortable route to take than the much wetter lowlands. Later, Iron Age settlers cleared its forests for agriculture, giving the South Downs the open spaces we see today. The Romans farmed the downland, too, and the population of humans and animals swelled under the Normans. Centuries passed and little changed until World War II, when huge acreages went under the plow. All these phases gift walkers on the South Downs Way with the views from the northern crest of the South Downs escarpment: arable fields, dense woodlands, pastures, meadows, wheat dancing golden in the summer, birchwood, beech, and gorse. And the windmills of Jack and Jill.

The South Downs Way connects Winchester in Hampshire with Eastbourne in East Sussex, only descending from its lofty escarpment when a river valley intrudes upon its line. It opened in 1972 and was the first National Trail to be given dual use as a bridleway along its entire length. You have the English Channel as a wayward companion along its easternmost reaches, but it is the history forged by those early inhabitants that really is your constant companion. There are Iron Age dikes, mounds, and lynchets, and faint reminders of hundreds of Bronze Age burial barrows as you stroll by on old Roman trails along which legionnaires once marched to Londinium, on a walk that knows how to provide an unmatched sense of one's place in history. **BDS**

Greensand Way
Surrey/Kent, England

Start Haslemere, Surrey   **Start** Hamstreet, Kent
Distance 108 miles (174 km)   **Time** 7–8 days
Grade Moderate   **Type** Linear footpath
Info goo.gl/6zPxE2

Acknowledged by the Saturday Walkers' Club to be southeast England's finest long-distance walk, Greensand Way is a hilly route that passes through some of the lesser traveled nooks of the Surrey Hills before entering Kent and tracing a line through the Chart Hills, Sevenoaks Weald, and the Medway Valley, all the way to the edges of Romney Marsh, a stone's throw away from the Kent coast. It follows the Greensand Ridge, a horseshoe-shaped escarpment of sandstone and a green mineral called glauconite, that runs roughly parallel and to the south of the North Downs ridge, and takes you to the highest point in southeast England, Leith Hill in Surrey.

Much of the walk passes through ancient and maturing woodlands, with bluebells in the spring and a rainbow of ankle-high colors in autumn. Mansions and their obligatory parklands also dot the Surrey Hills, providing an architectural tour de force and adding interest to an already impressive landscape with their specimen plantings of trees and shrubs. Villages and farms along the way provide not only respite for wearied legs, but also a veritable timeline of England's social and economic development as you pass by medieval granaries, lime kilns, catslide roofs, kissing gates, canals, Surrey's highest windmill, various priories, and the traces of a possible Roman road at Jelley's Hollow. You also walk through the "twin" communities of Little Chart and Great Chart in Kent, the former of which began making paper in 1770. There are also a number of National Trust lands and buildings to be found along this quintessential slice of England, such as Chartwell, Winston Churchill's home from 1924 to 1965. **BDS**

"The [Greensand] Way takes its name from the layers of sandstone in each of which is found the green-colored mineral glauconite."
www.ldwa.org.uk

⬆ The Greensand Way is a walk through ancient forests and ankle-deep swathes of flowering meadows.

Via Francigena
England/France/Italy

Start Canterbury Cathedral, England   End Rome,
Italy   Distance 1,180 miles (1,899 km)   Time
3 months   Grade Moderate to strenuous   Type Farm
trails, sealed roads   Info goo.gl/n7KKxh

The Via Francigena, the "way through France," is an
ancient pilgrimage road that ran from Canterbury in
England all the way to Rome. In the fourth century,
when pilgrimages to Rome went from a trickle to a
torrent after the Roman Empire adopted Christianity
as its official religion, the route for Britons took many
through Canterbury and down through northeastern
France, along the Rhine Valley, and over the Alps at the
Great St. Bernard Pass, and on to Rome. The route is
essentially the same now as it was then.

Unlike most contemporary long-distance footpaths,
however, which generally do their best to avoid towns
and villages, the Via Francigena, being a pilgrimage
route with people requiring lodging, determinedly
seeks them out. Where once it was a two-way street
with everyone returning home the same way they
came, now it is a thru-hike, and companies such as
UTracks will take your baggage on to the next town
and arrange your bed for the night, leaving you free
to just walk.

Decades ago the only people with an interest in
the Via Francigena were scholars. Then pilgrims who'd
walked other pilgrim trails began taking an interest in
recovering its original route. In 2007 a group of cyclists
completed it, as best they could, from Canterbury to
Rome in just sixteen days. In 2009 the Italian
government launched an initiative to reclaim their
sections, and now the Via Francigena is again being
walked more or less as it once was. Some might say it
lacks the pilgrim-friendly accommodation and sense
of camaraderie found along the Way of St. James, but
these nuances take time to develop—and the Via
Francigena is in no hurry. **BDS**

*"Many thousands of pilgrims
have followed this stunning trail
to Rome since medieval times."*

www.macsadventures.com

← The famous medieval towers of San Gimignano
dominate this hill town in the province of Siena.

↑ A typical medieval alleyway in a hill town on
the Via Francigena.

Offa's Dyke Path
Wales/England/Wales

Start Chepstow, Monmouthshire   End Prestatyn, Denbighshire   Distance 177 miles (285 km)
Time 2 weeks   Grade Moderate to strenuous
Type Path, mountain trail, towpath   Info goo.gl/2QxIIL

The landscape keeps changing on this ancient trail along the border between England and Wales because it follows a man-made structure rather than the contours of the landscape. The route of the path dates back to the eighth century, when King Offa ordered a bank and ditch to be dug in the Welsh March lands. The plan was probably to create a barrier between his Saxon kingdom of Mercia and the untamed Welsh tribes to the west. Ancient texts describe the "great dyke" as running "from sea to sea." The ridge of the dike is visible in many places and often still forms the national border today.

The coastal resort of Prestatyn, on the Irish Sea in north Wales, is 177 miles (285 km) from the trail's start at the cliffs near the mouth of the Wye River at Chepstow. The path passes through eight counties, crosses the border more than twenty times, and traverses three different Areas of Outstanding Natural Beauty. The dike crosses gentle rolling farmland, heather-clad hills, and bleak rocky moorland. Look out for Norman strongholds, prehistoric hill forts, and medieval abbeys and churches. Highlights along the way include the secondhand-book town of Hay-on-Wye, the Offa's Dyke Centre in Knighton, and a romantic castle on a bend in the river at Chepstow. The path includes challenging sections in the Shropshire Hills and Black Mountains, where you'll need experience, good boots, and navigation skills in bad weather. There are very gentle stretches along the towpath of the Montgomeryshire Canal and meadows of the Wye Valley. Most of the ups and downs are mild, but note that the total height climbed completing the route is equivalent to scaling Mount Everest. **SH**

"Along the way it visits a succession of historic border towns and attractive villages."

www.contours.co.uk

⏏ The path traverses the undulating Clwydian Range, which features a dramatic series of hill forts.

Celtic Way
Wales/England

Start Strumble Head, Pembrokeshire
End St. Michael's Mount, Cornwall   **Distance** 699 miles
(1,125 km)   **Time** 8–10 weeks   **Grade** Moderate to
strenuous   **Type** Path   **Info** goo.gl/8XrRQA

Historic sites such as Stonehenge, Tintagel Castle, Avebury stone circle, Cadbury Camp, and Glastonbury Abbey form an ancient thread to this long-distance walk. These sites are not all necessarily Celtic in origin, but the Celtic Way is a path through areas where the Celtic influence was strong, long after the rest of the United Kingdom became Roman, Saxon, and Norman.

The path starts on a rocky headland at the extreme southwestern corner of Wales. The cliffs of Strumble Head overlook a small rocky island called Michael's Isle. From Pembrokeshire, the route twists around the coast of south Wales and back through southwest England to Cornwall. The path ends on the sands of Marazion, looking out to the castle on another "Michael's island"—St. Michael's Mount.

These southwestern areas are dotted with sites connected with mysticism and prehistory. The Celtic Way passes by more than 100 ancient monuments, tombs, and hill forts. Some are linked to druids, legends, and early Christian stories. Highlights include the Iron Age and Roman remains at Caerleon in south Wales, Glastonbury Tor in Somerset, and Silbury Hill in Wiltshire. Guide books on the route also point out dozens of stone circles, holy wells, burial chambers, waterfalls, and hermits' cells. The landscapes that walkers see today are memorable, too. The scenery of the coastal sections is particularly dramatic, but other memorable stretches include crossing the wilds of Dartmoor, Bodmin Moor, and the Brecon Beacons. Alternative routes across Exmoor and through Dorset are offered, giving a choice of visiting sites such as the hill fort at Maiden Castle and even a cross-channel journey to St. Michael's Mount in Brittany, France. **SH**

Wye Valley Walk
Wales/England/Wales

Start Chepstow   **End** Plynlimon
Distance 136 miles (219 km)   **Time** 12–14 days
Grade Easy to moderate   **Type** Long-distance trail
Info goo.gl/feXPik

One of the truly iconic river walks of Britain, the Wye Valley Walk meanders its way beneath the cliffs and through the meadows, ruins, and glades of the Wye Valley, following the country's fifth longest river on its journey from the limestone gorges around Chepstow to the river's source, the mountains around Plynlimon. It zigzags its way back and forth along the English–Welsh border, and along the way you pass a veritable tome of English and Welsh history, which begins with Chepstow Castle, one of the first stone-built Norman castles in Britain. Then comes the Angidy Ironworks,

> *"Follow the Wye through the battle-scarred Anglo-Welsh borders to where it pours in rocky cascades."*
>
> www.wyevalleywalk.org

the first blast furnace in Britain; Monmouth Castle, the birthplace of Henry V; the Mappa Mundi at Hereford Castle; and a restored sixteenth-century Welsh longhouse at Gilfach Farm Nature Reserve, with its 400 species of lichen. Iron Age hill forts dot the landscape. Woodlands abound, too, including Merrivale Wood, with its ash, oak, and wild cherry trees, and the limestone grasslands of Common Hill, with its orchid reserve, glowworm beetles, and herd of Dexter cattle.

In 1798, poet William Wordsworth wrote "Lines Composed a Few Miles above Tintern Abbey" here, and over the centuries many artists and writers have sought inspiration in the valley's wooded glens and from the precipices of its sublime outlooks. **BDS**

Waterfalls and Ridges of Brecon Beacons Powys, Wales

Start/End Blaen-y-glyn parking lot   Distance 9 miles (14.5 km)   Time 6 hours   Grade Moderate
Type Rock and grassy paths   Map goo.gl/Wp3VMO

Wales's Brecon Beacons National Park is home to a series of waterfalls and ridges, an exploration of either of which would make a fabulous stand-alone walk. Here, however, you can do both in a loop walk, which is probably best done in an counterclockwise direction as this gets the bulk of the climbing out of the way early as you ascend to your first goal—the peak of Craig y Fan Ddu.

The climb to Craig y Fan Ddu is a 1,640-foot (500-m) slog and a hard scramble, but the views across the surrounding valleys once on the summit are inspiring, with a glacial valley clearly discernible to the right and the town of Port Talbot and the sea beyond it to the left. And it is on Craig y Fan Ddu that you begin to appreciate the wealth of the bird life here, which includes peregrines, kestrels, ravens, and red kites being lifted high on the constant thermals.

Continue along the escarpment you now have before you and follow the eastern rim until you reach a cleft where a waterfall cascades into the valley below. From there it's about 1 mile (1.6 km) to the main Brecons escarpment at Bwlch y Ddwyallt, past an old quarry before a climb to Fan y Big (2,360 feet/ 719 m) for a memorable panorama over the park. Descend on a stony path from there to the Gap Road, cross an old Roman road, and continue south, turning left at a cairn before reaching the Upper Neuadd reservoir. There you will make your way through stands of Scots pines to the Taff Trail. Then it's 1 mile (1.6 km) to the Talybont-on-Usk road and the end of one of the United Kingdom's great ridge/escarpment circumnavigations. **BDS**

⬆ The Brecon Beacons ridges offer spectacular views.

Glyndwr's Way National Trail Powys, Wales

Start Town clock, Knighton   **End** Montgomery Canal parking lot, Welshpool   **Distance** 135 miles (217 km)
Time 9 days   **Grade** Strenuous   **Type** Footpath   **Info** goo.gl/48qjmV

Named in honor of Owain Glyndwr—a fourteenth-century folk hero, self-proclaimed prince, and son of a wealthy local landowner—Glyndwr's Way is a multi-purpose path in mid-Wales that begins at the base of the clock tower in the half-timbered town of Knighton on the River Teme, and winds its way through moorland, farmland, forests, and woodlands, ending in a public park by the Montgomery Canal in Welshpool. The walk was granted National Trust status in 2000 to honor the 600-year-old Welsh Revolt (also called the Glyndwr Rising) led by Glyndwr against King Henry IV.

Along the way you'll walk through some of the loveliest corners in Wales. After leaving Knighton you pass through Llangunllo, an unspoiled town on the edge of the Radnor Forest in the Lugg Valley, and a series of idyllic villages including Llanbadarn Fynydd (a "UK Village of the Year" recipient), Abbeycwmhir, in the midst of a labyrinth of hanging oak forests and a community of red kites, then through the Cambrian Mountains to Machynlleth, ancient capital of Wales and seat of the rebel Glyndwr's parliament.

The village of Llanbrynmair is an historic departure point for the New World, where ninety-nine people once left in a day for a fresh start in the United States. You skirt Lake Vyrnwy, with its ninety bird species, including the peregrine falcon, on the way through the moors, valleys, and waterfalls of the Cownwy Valley. On a clear day, from the walk's highest point of 1,650 feet (510 m) at Foel Fadian you can see across the beautiful Dulas Valley back to the Irish Sea as you skirt the lower slopes of Mount Snowdon and make your way at last to the delights of Welshpool's produce markets. **BDS**

⬆ The beautiful Ithon Valley south of Llanbadarn Fynydd.

GR3 Loire Valley Trail

Pays de la Loire, France

Start Mont Gerbier de Jonc   **End** La Baule
Distance 773 miles (1,244 km)   **Time** 17–20
weeks   **Grade** Easy to moderate   **Type** Meadows,
riverbanks, roads   **Info** goo.gl/yydrzv

The walking trail that extends the length of the Loire Valley in central France, the GR3, begins at the source of France's longest river at Mont Gerbier de Jonc—a volcanic mountain in the Massif Central, the innocuous three springs of which mark the river's humble beginnings—and ends at the river's mouth at La Baule, a one-hundred-year-old coastal resort on the Atlantic coast in southern Brittany. The Loire is France's only remaining untamed river, and the long-distance GR3 trail takes you through its forests and past its vineyards and grand châteaux.

Following the natural course of the river, the trail is a long one, and it is a matter of deciding which sections to walk in order to maximize your experience. Just remember that there is a lot more to this valley than the châteaux of Chinon, Azay-le-Rideau, Amboise, and Clos-Luce, where Leonardo da Vinci spent the final years of his life. Along this aristocratic-embossed river, there are also countless slate-roofed villages, farms, and big, beautiful cities, such as Tours, with its quaint medieval streets and half-timbered houses.

However, the GR3 trail does not always, it has to be said, follow the most scenic of routes. The section from Sache to Azay, for example, can be missed in favor of a minor road on the north bank of the Indre River, a tributary of the Loire that runs between them, because this makes for a far lovelier walk. For the most part, though, the GR3 will take you to all the places you have in your mind's eye when you think of coming to the historic heartland of France—to the vineyards of the Touraine, to its very own Valley of the Kings. **BDS**

"The GR3 is one of the first, if not the first, GRs that was marked all the way [in 1947]."

www.traildino.com

◁ Walking the GR3 will take you through vineyards, farms, and slate-roofed villages, as well as past châteaux.

△ Sunflower fields in the Loire Valley.

Les Hauts de Veyrignac
Aquitaine, France

"Located on the left bank of the Dordogne in the heart of Black Perigord."

www.veyrignac.com

⊞ The beautiful Cathédrale Saint-Sacerdos in medieval Sarlat, near the beginning of the walk.

Start/End Parking lot, Veyrignac
Distance 8 miles (12.8 km)   **Time** 4 hours
Grade Easy   **Type** Sandy, forest paths
Map goo.gl/2HQccY

If you're looking for a walk that passes through one of the loveliest regions of France that pretty much guarantees you won't be jostling with other walkers; that takes you along stony tracks and through woodlands and past cottages; that gives you the up-close perspectives that can make you feel like you are trespassing, then this delightful walk in the fields of the Dordogne is for you.

The walk begins in the tiny village of Veyrignac, population 300, on the left bank of the Dordogne River in the heart of Black Perigord, just a few miles from Sarlat. It continues past rows of chestnut trees and along the edge of a shallow valley to the mostly sixteenth-century former Cathar stronghold of Château de Fenelon. Open every day except Tuesdays for tours, the château was used as a location in the U.S. film *Ever After* (1998), which starred Drew Barrymore. A small descent then takes you into the dark and forbidding-looking Font Marine valley, past the beautifully restored mill of Moulin Haut and a forest of stunted oaks and isolated houses with moss-draped stone walls and ponds.

You then enter the hamlet of Rocanadel, where you can pass by the ruins of its fifteenth-century castle, then continue through more woodlands, vineyards, and a small shallow valley with decaying drystone walls. The small flower-filled hamlet of Valeille is next, and then the even smaller hamlet of Rechou. More woodlands follow; you pass some more barns, then a cemetery, another assortment of old stone walls, a fig tree, and finally Veyrignac, with its decaying Romanesque church, comes into view once more, at the end of a very French afternoon. **BDS**

Fontainebleau Forest Trails
Ile-de-France, France

Start/End Château de Fountainebleau
Distance Various   **Time** Various   **Grade** Easy
Type Well-maintained forest trails, rock paths, bare rock
Info goo.gl/twPEZx

When people think of Fontainebleau, they invariably think of the magnificent Château de Fontainebleau, the sixteenth-century royal residences that were the creation of Francis I and his architect Gilles le Breton and were later significantly extended by Catherine de Medici. Yet Fontainebleau is equally known for the 61,776 acres (25,000 ha) that make up its fabulous forest and the former royal hunting grounds that surround it, as well as the town of Fontainebleau itself. Now home to many of Europe's most endangered species, the forest is also criss-crossed by more than 990 miles (1,593 km) of trails.

Parts of both the GR1 and GR11 pass through the forest, which is blessed with a myriad of sandstone cliffs and overhangs graded from beginner to expert. There are also two demanding and serious gorges— the Gorges de Franchard and Gorges d'Apremont— both of which have brought rock climbers here for decades, a sort of proving ground for Parisians and other northern urbanites to hone their skills before setting off for the greater challenge of the Alps.

Parisians began coming here by train in 1849, and before that by horse-drawn coaches to escape increasingly busy streets. Writer Robert Louis Stevenson moved to Barbizon, close to Fontainebleau, in 1875 and wrote of his love for its forest in *Treasure Island* (1883). Pierre-Auguste Renoir painted here, as did Claude Monet, who painted the Bodmer Oak, one of the forest's best-known trees. This was an "augmented" forest—hand planted with chestnuts, birches, junipers, maples, beeches, and great oaks—and it still makes up the landscape today as you meander through the many dappled shades of French history. **BDS**

"Fontainebleau remains a pure pleasure for nature lovers, due to its dense and varied flora and fauna."

www.fontainbleau-tourisme.com

⊡ Walk for days without seeing another soul in one of France's most picturesque, mist-shrouded corners.

Tour du Lot Midi-Pyrenees, France

Start/End Rocamadour   **Distance** 319 miles (513 km)   **Time** 30 days   **Grade** Easy
Type Forest trails, graded paths   **Info** goo.gl/NJkCeN

The Tour du Lot is a 319-mile-long (514 km) mix of footpaths, bridleways, GR routes, rural roads, and farmers' tracks that follows—as best it can—the periphery of the Lot Department in southwestern France. This is a walk that seduces on so many levels—the food and wine, the Foie gras, the castles of the Cathars, the mist-shrouded valleys, the old mills and skeletal wooden footbridges over placid, blue-green rivers. Just pick a route, such as the section from Carrenac to Bretenoux. Here the trail meanders along the Dordogne River and passes under the huge cliff top Château Castelnaud, a Middle Age fortress with a fabulous armory museum and views over the medieval village of La Roque-Gageac, built to rival the Château de Beynac. Two châteaux, one of them a fortress; a medieval town; and the Dordogne River make an average day's sights on the Tour du Lot.

The circuit was designed and created in the 1990s by volunteer walkers, cyclists, and equestrian riders, all of whom dreamed of a nonmotorized trail tracing the boundaries of the department. The Tour was officially opened in April 1997, and most people begin it in the village of Rocamadour, a popular pilgrimage site dramatically situated on a mountainside promontory above a tributary of the Dordogne River.

Walkers who have completed the entire circuit speak of how they walked for days without seeing another tourist—hard to understand when pit stops include Spanish *jambon*, pan-fried calamari, and venison with blue cheese sauce, all washed down with one of the local red wines. It is more enticing, still, if you walk it in truffle season ... **BDS**

⊡ Lot rooftops of terra-cotta and hand-hewn schist tiles.

Martel Trail, Verdon Gorge Provence-Alpes-Côte d'Azur, France

Start Chalet de la Maline **End** Point Sublime **Distance** 8.5 miles (13.6 km) **Time** 5–6 hours
Grade Moderate **Type** Forest trails **Map** goo.gl/8oowsf

The Verdon Gorge is the largest canyon in Europe, and over the last two million years its mammoth cliffs of calcareous rock and Jurassic limestone have been eroded by the Verdon River as it cut through the plateau between Avignon and Nice. As late as the nineteenth century, these precipitous gorges were considered impenetrable, having been ventured into only by local woodcutters who lowered themselves below its rim on ropes in search of boxwood stumps, the perfect wood for making the balls for the French game of boules.

Up to 2,296 feet (700 m) deep, the gorge has a multitude of hiking options, probably the finest of which is the Martel Trail, named after the great French speleologist Edouard-Alfred Martel, who in 1905 became the first man to make a successful descent from the rim to the canyon floor. Created by the Touring Club of France, the Martel Trail has over time become recognized as the classic Verdon Gorge hike. It follows the Verdon River as best it can, sometimes via overhangs and occasionally along its riverbanks. If you begin at Chalet de la Maline, you will have an easier time, as its steepest sections will be descents, not ascents. Remember to bring a flashlight because two tunnels (328 feet/100 m and 2,198 feet/670 m long) await you with no powered lighting. The trail is a thrilling one, with long stone staircases carved into the rock face with attached cables for extra safety, endless twists and turns that give tantalizing glimpses of the river below, and always above you those magnificent cliffs, until you emerge into open sunshine on the approach to Point Sublime. **BDS**

⊼ Walk down to the floor of Europe's largest canyon

Pieterpad
Groningen to Limburg, Netherlands

"It is an easy trail to walk straight, [or] ramble around the countryside or... along the well-laid roads."

www.indodutchconnect.com

⬆ Walking the Pieterpad is always easy through a mix of woods, heathlands, and charming Dutch villages.

Start Pieterburen **End** St. Pietersberg
Distance 306 miles (493 km) **Time** 27–30 days
Grade Easy **Type** Long-distance footpath
Info goo.gl/S24wJU

The Pieterpad (Peter Path) began when two friends, Catharina Elisabeth (Toos) Goorhuis-Tjalsma from Tilburg in the southern province of Noord-Brabant in the Netherlands and her friend Bertje Jens from Groningen in the north, decided to plan a walking route to link their respective hometowns. The Pieterpad now runs from Pieterburen, north of Groningen, to just outside Maastricht in the south. Here it connects to the GR5, which runs southward into Belgium. The path is frequently used by pilgrims en route to Santiago de Compostela in Spain.

The Pieterpad was inaugurated in 1983 and has become the country's most popular long-distance walking path. It parallels, in a rough approximation, the border with Germany and can be walked year-round and in either direction. It is well serviced by public transport and it is well signposted. The walking may always be easy, but it is never dull, taking you through numerous traditional Dutch villages and rolling farmlands. Several castles and châteaux are visible from the trail, too, including Castle Vorden, where a small plaque honors the ladies mentioned above, and Castle Slangenburg, the moated guesthouse belonging to the Benedictine Abbey of St. Willibrord in Gelderland. Yet it is the quaintness of the path that is so endearing. There are the working windmills of De Hoop in Sleen and De Wachter in Zuidlaren, the historic village of Winsum, the Viking and Roman archaeological sites around Doetinchem, and the town of Hellendoorn, where scenes for the war movie *A Bridge Too Far* (1977) were filmed. The walk requires more than the usual amount of research so it can be appreciated for the great trek it is. **BDS**

Saar–Hunsrück Trail

North Rhine-Westphalia, Germany

Start Perl   End Trimmelter Hof
Distance 135 miles (217 km)
Time 15 days   Grade Moderate   Type Natural paths
Info goo.gl/1j7Zh5

Opened in 2007, it took just two years for the Saar–Hunsrück Trail to be voted Germany's most beautiful hiking trail in 2009. Certified by the German Hiking Institute as a Premium Hiking Trail, more than 70 percent of the trail is natural tracks over meadows and hills, and it offers a diversity of landscape and man-made history that is hard to match. It begins in Perl with the Quirinus Chapel, the Baroque garden of the Von Nell Chateau (1733), and an ancient Roman archaeological park with a contemporary tavern that serves meals based on Roman recipes. Built history,

"Discover romantically situated lakes, enchanted valleys, and fantastic panoramas."

www.saar-hunsrueck-steig.de/en/

however, soon gives way to nature on the second day as you make your way to the "Saar Bend" and the view from atop the Cloef, and the day after that the Saarholzbach Valley, with its old stone markers that once set the border between France and Germany.

History is still all around you, of course. There is the rail museum at Losheim am See; the Museum for Mechanical Music and Curiosities at Weiskirchen, with its old barrel organs; and the Dugstuhl Palace and Münchweiler Palace at Wadern. There are water mills, copper mines, Celtic fortresses, and even an old nail forge. Don't lose sight of the fact that it is the constant meshing of built history with nature that made this trail number one. **BDS**

Ith–Hils Loop Trail

Lower Saxony, Germany

Start Hannover   End Hamelin   Distance 50 miles
(80 km)   Time 2 days   Grade Moderate
Type Forest and rock trails, farm tracks
Map goo.gl/DyUuNZ

The Ith–Hils Loop Trail, inaugurated in January 2013, connects the Ith and Hils mountain ridges in Lower Saxony's Weserbergland hills. Split into seven stages, it begins in Hannover and ends in Hamelin, and on the way it takes walkers through the spectacular rock formations of the Ith Ridge: at 14 miles (22.5 km), the longest line of crags to be found in northern Europe.

The Ith Ridge runs in a northwest–southeast line through the Leine Uplands, from Coppenbrügge to Holzen, and has been a magnet for walkers and climbers for generations. And glider pilots, too. The updrafts around the Holzen Gap saw the Luftwaffe build a glider school here during World War II—the Ith Reichs Glider School. Stands of wood anemone, a pretty spring flower with musky-smelling leaves, are everywhere, and lovely mauve clusters of Corydalis—a native of the high mountains in tropical east Africa and a food source for the larvae of butterflies—are in abundance. Streams move across the ridge flow west into the Weser River or east to the Leine.

The highest point on the Ith Ridge is the Lauensteiner Kopf (1,440 feet/439 m), where there is an observation tower, and the entire ridge is lined with outcrops of striking rock formations that draw an endless line of hikers and climbers. All the crags are named (Adam and Eve, Devil's Kitchen, Frog Head), and there are caves, too. Rothesteinhöhle cave was rediscovered in 1853 by Alfred Wollemann, surrendering artifacts dating to the Bronze Age. Cultural highlights along the way include a pottery museum at Duingen and the Erich Mäder Glass Museum in Grünenplan, on a trail that truly has something for everyone. **BDS**

Weserbergland Trail

Lower Saxony, Germany

Start Hannoversch Münden   End Porta Westfalica
Distance 140 miles (225 km)   Time 12 days
Grade Easy to moderate   Type Forest trails
Info goo.gl/ozVTNn

The ever-present tranquillity of the Weser River as it flows northward to the North German Plain; the translucent foliage of endless swathes of beech and oak; historic half-timbered towns and palaces; Hamelin, home of the mythic Pied Piper; as well as Sababurg Castle, the fourteenth-century fortress once encircled by its defensive thorn hedge and where Sleeping Beauty awaited the arrival of her prince are just some of the delights that await you on this demanding trail through the shadows of the Weserbergland hills.

The trail begins at the Weser River in Hannoversch Münden and includes a crossing of the Mecklenburgh wetlands with its extensive grasslands, over the craggy Hohenstein Cliffs, and through the town of Bodenwerder, upstream from Hamelin. Bodenwerder is famous as the birthplace of Baron Münchhausen, the nobleman known throughout Germany as the "teller of tall tales"—stories that were effectively folk tales, some of which had been around for hundreds of years before Münchhausen appropriated them.

The trail also passes Germany's second-oldest porcelain factory at Fürstenburg, and in the small town of Hoxter, first settled during the reign of Charlemagne, you will find the Imperial Abbey of Corvey, founded by Charlemagne's son in 814 and still in possession of its priceless library of 67,000 books. Yet, it is the rolling landscapes of the Solling Hills that are most likely to captivate, with their freely roaming population of wild boar, deer, sheep, and stags, most of which you'll see if you scramble up the Bunter sandstone ridge and cast your eyes over this fairy tale land. **BDS**

Schlaube Valley Trail

Brandenburg, Germany

Start/End Eastern shore, Grosser Müllroser Lake
Distance 15.5 miles (25 km)   Time 1 day
Grade Easy   Type Forest and valley trails
Map goo.gl/dzPvzv

Often described as the most picturesque valley in Brandenburg, the Schlaube Valley in the Oder-Spree Lakeland region, only 50 miles (80.4 km) east of Berlin, is a tunnel valley and a remnant of the last ice age. The Schlaube Valley Trail begins in the spa resort town of Müllrose as a lakeside walk along the shoreline of Grosser Müllroser Lake and from there enters the canopied woodlands along the Schlaube River, continuing along narrow paths and woodland trails to the Kupferhammer, an old copper mill that has reinvented itself as a restaurant. Schulzenwasser and

"The River Schlaube meanders idyllically through wild and romantic valleys."

www.germany.travel

Hammersee lakes follow, then a moderate ascent to the hilltop Siehdichum Lodge.

The Bremsdorfer Mühle, a half-timbered mill where the Schlaube River flows into the Grosser Treppelsee Lake, still has its water wheel, and a walk through an untouched valley brings you to the Kieselwitz mill in the town of the same name. The trail ends at the final mill of Schlaube Mühle on the southernmost shore of Wirchensee Lake, where you should look for the Waldsee Hotel and its sun terrace that has wonderful views out over the lake. If you want to take a side trip, you can walk to Ragowar mill, which was built in the 1670s. It's the only mill in the valley that still has its original machinery intact. **BDS**

Eselsweg
Hesse/Bavaria, Germany

Start Schlüchtern rail station, Hesse
End Grossheubach, Bavaria **Distance** 79 miles (127 km)
Time 6 days **Grade** Easy **Type** Forest trails
Map goo.gl/3TKaL9

Maintaining a constant elevation between 1,300 (396 m) and 1,640 feet (500 m) and studiously avoiding anything resembling a town or village, the Eselsweg (Donkey Path) is a long-distance path that winds beneath the ancient beeches and oaks of the wonderful Spessart (derived from the word "woodpecker") forest, a fairy-tale world of ancient trees and crab orchards, which long ago was the private hunting grounds of German nobility. The path takes you through the largest continuous stretch of forest remaining in Germany along the same route once used by donkey caravans to transport salt from the region's medieval salt caves to the port cities on the Main River.

The trail begins in Schlüchtern and climbs past the old monastic center of Bergwinkel. The rest of the path is a series of gentle, undulating inclines that keep you close to 1,600 feet (487 m), with enough small towns a half a mile or so away to provide a bed for the night, places such as Wiesen and Jakobsthal. From Heigenbrücken to Weibersbrunn, there is a detour to an overlook with views to the Geiersberg, the Spessart's highest point at 1,922 feet (586 m). The final stage, from Wildensee to Grossheubach, traverses a 7.5-mile-long (12 km) ridgeline and continues to Kloster Engleberg, high above the Main River. You can make one last detour up to the town of Miltenberg, or take the 612 steps down into Grossheubach, and the journey's end. The Donkey Path isn't the only trail through the Spessart. The Snow White Trail takes you into the old mirror-producing town of Lohr, and the nearby Frammersbach hills attract mountain bikers from across Europe to its network of challenging trails. **BDS**

"[The woods] have a long history of forestry, since Spessart oak is highly valued and traded all over the world."

www.walk-in-europe.com

⤒ Germany's largest remaining swathe of forest is home to an undulating trail through the Spessart.

Rennsteig Trail
Thuringia, Germany

Start Horschel   End Blankenstein
Distance 104 miles (167 km)   Time 9 days
Grade Moderate   Type Forest roads
Info goo.gl/YqdXkR

The Rennsteig Trail wasn't always a recreational walking trail. It began its life in the thirteenth century out of necessity as a boundary path through the Thuringian Forest in the very heart of Germany, separating the Duchy of Franconia, one of the great tribal duchies of medieval Germany, from the Landgraviate of Thuringia, the largest state in the region. It was also a language border, keeping apart the dialects of Upper Franconia from those of central Thuringia. It would be many centuries before this trail would begin to be considered purely for its ability to provide a good day out.

The Rennsteig Trail has arguably become the nation's most popular and well-known route and it has lost none of its considerable charm as it winds its way along a series of wide, forested ridges from Horschel, outside the town of Eisenach, to Blankenstein, on the Saale River, near the Czech border. It is a quiet walk, far from main roads through largely uninterrupted spruce forest, and it is surprisingly level considering the mountainous terrain through which it passes, varying in height from 2,300 feet (701 m) to 2,950 feet (899 m). There are steep inclines at either end, however, and the first four days from Horschel involve a steady rise to the trail's high point of Plänckners Aussicht (3,182 feet/970 m). During the Cold War, the Russians had a listening post on the summit of Schneekopf, and near Frauenwald you can visit a fallout shelter built for the old East German military—one of many points of historical interest on a trail that has seen more history than most. **BDS**

◁ This popular trail is an 800-year-old boundary path.

Frankenweg
Thuringia/Bavaria, Germany

Start Untereichenstein   End Harburg
Distance 321 miles (516 km)   Time 21 days
Grade Easy to moderate   Type Forest, mountain trails   Info goo.gl/pbyFOD

The Thuringian–Franconian Highlands extend through the forests of central Germany, southwest through Upper Franconia, along the Upper Main Valley and the hills of the Franconian Alb, and southeast in the direction of the Czech Republic's Bohemian Massif. It is through this forested, mountainous world that the Frankenweg (Franconia Walk) weaves its considerable magic. It begins where the Rennsteig, Thuringia's much-loved high-altitude trail, ends, and for the next 321 miles (516 km) it bisects the finest of Franconian scenery. It takes you down the slopes of the Höllental

"A long-distance trail of unusual excellence ... it passes a great variety of Franconian scenery."

www.walk-in-europe.com

valley, along the banks of the Wilde Rodach River to the fortified castle of Festung Rosenberg, near the historic town of Kronach. The Kirchleuser Platte, a vast limestone plateau, is crossed, and the walk also takes you deep into Franconia Switzerland, a region so-named by nineteenth-century artists and poets who thought its hills comparable to those in Switzerland. From Pottenstein, ensconced at the confluence of the Weihersbach, Haselbrunn, and Puttlach valleys, a series of historic towns and valleys follows—Hersbruck and Altdorf and day-long sections along the edge of the Franconian Alb—and the walk ends in a Franconian landscape of meadows and open plateaus at Harburg. **BDS**

Gorges Trail
Baden-Württemberg, Germany

Start Stühlingen   End Wehr
Distance 74 miles (119 km)   Time 6 days
Grade Moderate   Type Rock and dirt trails
Map goo.gl/sNBcID

"A succession of narrow paths, dramatic climbs, and tranquil forest trails."

www.schluchtensteig.de

Opened in 2008, the Gorges Trail, better known to Germans as the Schluchtensteig, is aptly named. The Wutach, Gutach, Rötenbach, Wehra, and Haslach gorges are all traversed as you make your way through this secluded and heavily wooded region of the southern Black Forest. The trail may officially be tagged moderate, but be sure you come prepared with a quality pair of Gortex-lined hiking boots. This is no "forest path," but a mix of rough and often damp trails. It can be torturously narrow and have steep inclines, and even requires the climbing of the occasional ladder.

The Wutach Gorge was created when a river that once flowed into the Danube was diverted at the close of the last ice age and now flows to the Rhine. It is around 18.5 miles (29.7 km) long and up to 200 feet (61 m) deep, a depth achieved with the help of the rushing meltwaters from the long-gone Feldberg Glacier. Now a conservation area, there are a number of trailheads and paths here, and the Wutach is typical of the heavily incised gorges you will discover that come complete with tiny covered bridges, rubble slopes, and waterfalls too numerous to mention. On the leg from Sankt Blasien to Todtmoos, there is a vantage point with views out to the Swiss Alps.

While the walk is renowned for its spectacular gorges, it also passes through an extremely diverse topography that includes the gentle uplands of Dachsberg and the Wehra Valley, and along the shoreline of the Schluchsee, the Black Forest's largest lake. It also regularly ascends to rocky promontories that provide some sizable views over the many summits of the Black Forest's endless wooded peaks. **BDS**

⬆ This narrow Black Forest trail takes you through some of Germany's most interesting, and slippery, gorges.

Westweg
Germany/Switzerland

Start Pforzheim, Germany   End Basel, Switzerland
Distance 173 miles (279 km)   Time 12–14 days
Grade Moderate   Type Long-distance hiking trail
Info goo.gl/JPZ7x5

Started in 1900 by the Baden section of the Black Forest Society, what became known as the Westweg (West Trail) was completed three years later and has been the model for every long-distance walk in Germany ever since. It has remained one of the country's most renowned trails. It is not difficult to understand why. Despite its impressive length, it passes through only twelve towns or villages, preferring instead to weave through the moorlands, valleys, uplands, and lakes of this wonderfully wooded mountain range. There is simply no better way to see it; however, keep in mind that 173 miles (279 km) is a long way. You need to be fit for this one, especially as its quite long segments lend themselves to walks of some 15 miles (24 km) per day, and there are segments where the distance between hotels is lengthy. If you don't have a sleeping bag, you might have to walk an extra hour to find a bed.

The walk begins in Pforzheim, known for its cuckoo clocks and jewelry; then comes the relative bustle of the spa town of Baden-Baden, before the path's much-touted solitude hits you as you make a steep descent into the Kinzig Valley on the border of the northern and middle Black Forest, where the streams are so pure you can fill your water bottles from them. An equally steep climb on the trail's western variant takes you to the summits of Feldberg (4,898 feet/1,493 m) and Belchen (4,639 feet/1,414 m), the Black Forest's highest and third highest peaks, respectively. The last two days are spent at altitude (around 2,788 feet/850 m) before you descend past the extensive ruins of the twelfth-century Röttein Castle and on to Basel and the end of your journey. **BDS**

Romantic Road Hiking Trail
Bavaria, Germany

Start Würzburg   End Füssen
Distance 249 miles (400 km)   Time 4 weeks
Grade Moderate   Type Meadows and forest trails
Info goo.gl/5Wevj4

Germany's nostalgic Romantic Road, which winds its way from the Bavarian town of Füssen in the south to Würzburg in the north, is either driven or walked by more than two million tourists every year and is the country's oldest tourist route. It is most associated with asphalt and being behind a wheel, but the long-distance hiking route provides a slower alternative, avoiding roads as it takes you through fields, forests, and meadows, and into ancient imperial cities such as Schillingsfürst and Donauwörth, places you would likely miss in the rush of traffic, in which slowing

> *"Visit the local museums and enjoy the landscape as you make your way from the Main to the Alps."*
>
> www.toytowngermany.com

down is far from easy. Walking the Romantic Road ensures that you slow down and linger in Gothic parishes and squares.

The walk is a ramble in the best sense of the word, beginning in the north with a stroll through vineyards outside Würzburg followed by the enchantment of the Tauber Valley. You'll see magnificent Rothenburg and Weikersheim, as well as Creglingen, with its renowned Church of the Lord, but you'll also cross the unique landform of the Ries, Germany's only circular meteoric crater, and the thrill of descending into stunning medieval Nördlingen, one of the few remaining towns in Germany where it is still possible to walk around the entirety of it on its preserved ramparts. **BDS**

Wimbachklamm Waterfall Trail Bavaria, Germany

Start/End Ramsau trailhead
Distance 0.5 mile (0.8 km)   Time 1 hour
Grade Easy   Type Wide gravel path, boardwalk
Info goo.gl/tKPirW

You will not find the Wimbachklamm Waterfall at the forefront of any Berchtesgaden-organized travel expo—not with everyone so intent on driving up to the Eagle's Nest where Hitler and his generals planned their invasions of Poland and Russia. Other attractions are the many fine walks in the area around the Obersalzberg, or driving the fabulous Alpenstrasse, Germany's breathtaking Alpine Road that brings people here in their cars from all around Europe, where they zoom past the Wimbachklamm turnoff without even realizing it.

"A safe wooden path … allows walkers to be captivated by this unique work of nature."

ramsau.de

The waterfalls and gorge at Wimbachklamm can be easily missed, and that is a travesty. The gorge almost qualifies as a slot canyon it is so narrow, and it doesn't reveal itself until you are almost on top of it. The river is only 3 feet (1 m) wide, but the cliffs that empty into it are 100 feet (30 m) high or more. The noise is constant—a hundred tiny waterfalls all cascading into a small gorge. Mosses, ferns, and greenery are everywhere, emerging from every crack and crevice in the gorge's permanently glistening rock faces. A wooden boardwalk takes you through the heart of this fairy tale gorge, and such is its utter beauty that a walk that can be done non-stop in ten minutes takes two hours. Do not miss it. **BDS**

King Ludwig Way Bavaria, Germany

Start Near Lake Starnberg   End Near Füssen
Distance 60 miles (96.5 km)   Time 8 days
Grade Moderate   Type Meadows, forest trails,
rock paths   Map goo.gl/ExTccp

A walk that was particularly loved by the monarch whose name it now bears, King Ludwig Way was named in honor of Ludwig II of Bavaria, who reigned over an independent mountain kingdom from 1864 until his death in 1886. The walk, one of Germany's most popular, begins close to Lake Starnberg where Ludwig's lifeless body was found in mysterious circumstances, and ends at his fairy-tale castle, Neuschwanstein, not far from Füssen. Along the way the scenery is breathtaking, from the deep lush green of the Bavarian lowlands to the beginning of the Alps and the path's highest point at Hohenpeissenberg (3,241 feet/988 m), known across Germany for having the finest panoramic view of any Bavarian mountain and for being the highest point north of the alps.

There is also some impressive man-made scenery. In addition to Neuschwanstein itself, the most popular tourist attraction in Germany, there is Andechs Monastery (with its excellent brewery); Diessen Cathedral on the shores of Lake Ammersee, which you approach through a beautifully thick and heavily wooded gorge; the church at Wies; and Rottenbuch Monastery. After Rottenbuch, a walk through its surrounding meadows brings you to Wieskirche, the oval Rococo pilgrimage church built in the 1740s and now a UNESCO World Heritage Site. The walk continues through Steingaden to a magnificent abbey, founded in 1147, and the final day is spent walking through Pöllatschlucht Gorge, with the reward of Neuschwanstein waiting to greet you when you emerge. **BDS**

➡ The fantastical castle of Bavaria's King Ludwig.

Sultans Trail
Austria to Turkey

Start Vienna   **End** Istanbul
Distance 1,375 miles (2,212 km)   **Time** 15 weeks
Grade Strenuous   **Type** Long-distance hiking trail
Info goo.gl/OsZdaZ

When Süleyman Kanuni, better known to history as Suleiman the Magnificent, conquered great swathes of Europe at the head of his Ottoman army, he was stopped at the gates to Vienna. He tried to conquer the city again three years later, in 1532, but failed. Sultans Trail was built to trace his progress from his base in Istanbul to the city of Vienna, but today it is a path of peace, not war. It is a hugely ambitious attempt to link and celebrate the diverse nations that this multiuse hiking and cycling trail passes through: Austria, Slovakia, Hungary, Croatia, Serbia, Romania, Bulgaria, Greece, and Turkey.

The trail can be hiked at any time of year, although it would make sense to avoid the Turkish section in mid-summer and the mountainous Bulgarian section in mid-winter. In many places it is possible to find hotels, guesthouses, or basic accommodation. In more rural places, you may have to ask around to see if you can stay in a private house. Note, for certain sections you will need to be self-sufficient and carry a tent.

The trailheads are St. Stephen's Cathedral in Vienna, whose bells were cast out of captured Ottoman cannons, and the tomb of Suleiman the Magnificent himself in Istanbul. The route passes through major cities, including Bratislava, Budapest, Timişoara, and Sofia and showcases not only some of the best scenery of this part of Europe, but its culture and history too. It also takes the visitor through rural areas that don't normally get too many visitors, in an attempt to regenerate the local economies and give them a financial boost, which also gives the long-distance hiker a chance to go to places that are definitely off the beaten path. **MG**

"A new historic long-distance hiking trail from Vienna to Istanbul."

www.sultanstrail.com

◄ St. Stephen's Cathedral in Vienna with its striking tiled roof marks the beginning of this epic trail.

⬆ Walking through morning mountain fog in Bulgaria.

Lechweg Austria/Germany

Start Lake Formarinsee, Austria   **End** Füssen, Germany   **Distance** 78 miles (125 km)   **Time** 6–7 days
Grade Easy   **Type** Long-distance path   **Map** goo.gl/FpW7Wc

The Lechweg (Lech River Trail), which opened in 2012, mirrors the character of the river that lends it its name. At times wild, gentle, and natural (a rare thing in alpine Europe), it's an easy, long-distance route that takes you through one of the continent's last remaining wild river landscapes. It's the first cross-border, long-distance path certified by the European Ramblers' Association. It begins on the shores of Lake Formarinsee in the midst of the northern Limestone Alps of Austria's Vorarlberg province and takes you through Lech am Arlberg, a past recipient of Europe's most beautiful village award, before continuing on to the highest dairy and butcher in Austria—the Wälder Metzger in the village of Warth. It winds its way through the Lech Valley to the town of Holzgau and past Baroque-era houses that still have their original painted facades before crossing a 656-foot-high (200 m)

suspension bridge over Hoehenbachschlucht gorge (or an alternative path past Simms waterfall for those who don't like to be 110 feet (33.5 m) above the ground). You then pass a fabulous waterfall in Doser, known throughout Austria for its myriad of butterflies and orchids, before continuing through floodplains and along the valley on the gravel banks of the Lech, crossing into Germany at Pinswang.

Now in the heart of German Bavaria, it isn't long until views of King Ludwig II's childhood residence, Hohenschwangau, and the castle at Neuschwanstein greet you. The walk ends at the Lech Falls in Füssen, once the center of German lute- and violin-making and the town that provided many of the exterior facades for the classic movie *The Great Escape* (1963). **BDS**

⯅ Discover the stunning valleys of the Lech River Trail.

La Senda del Oso Asturias, Spain

Start Tunon **End** Entrago (more popular choice of two possible endings) **Distance** 13 miles (21 km)
Time 2 days **Grade** Easy **Type** Mountain, forest trails **Map** goo.gl/YOqH1m

This walk in Asturias in northwestern Spain is not called La Senda del Oso (The Path of the Bear) because there's any chance of coming across brown bears, although you are most certainly passing through one of the country's last remaining brown bear habitats. The name more probably arose because of the proximity of a brown bear conservation project. So although there are bears here, you most likely won't encounter one.

The path follows an old rail line that was in more or less constant use by miners until 1963 and is shaped something like an inverted Y, joining together the valleys of Santo Adriano, Teverga, Quirós, and Proaza. It isn't long after you head off along the Trubia River that you meet the first of many tunnels, then a covering of beech and ash filtering dappled light onto the loose gravel trail. Next the hamlet of Villaneuva with its stilt

houses appears, followed by a medieval bridge, and then the trail's high point, La Montana del Oso—Bear Mountain—home to the Paca and Tola reserve with its handful of bears. It is their only home, their environment now depleted.

Back along the Trubia River there are yet more tunnels—poorly lit and a hundred years old. You then reach the fork in the Y path. To the right is the way to Entrago, through the magnificent Entrepenes and Valdecerezales gorges—twenty more tunnels and nine bridges. To the left is the quaint town of Caranga de Abajo, which you can reach via dense coverings of oak, beech, and holly. The question is whether to go left or right? It's the only tough choice you'll need to make on the Path of the Bear. **BDS**

⊞ An old rail line through tunnels in a Y-shaped valley.

Cares Gorge
Asturias, Spain

Start Poncebos   **End** Caín   **Distance** 9 miles
(14.5 km)   **Time** 4–5 hours   **Grade** Easy
Type Rocky mountain trail
Map goo.gl/7lQEP7

It's not easy trying to describe adequately the dramatic setting of the trail that winds its way above the Picos de Europa (Peaks of Europe) on the northern coast of Spain. Almost the entirety of its three enormous massifs is composed of limestone that some suggest is the largest single limestone outcrop in all Europe. Cave art attests to human habitation dating to the Paleolithic era, and its soils have been tilled for more than five millennium. The place is still so isolated that agriculture continues by hand and the valleys are home to the endangered Cantabrian

---

"Deservedly the most popular walk in the Picos takes hikers into the heart of the central massif."

www.roughguides.com

---

brown bear, wolves, and an impressive array of butterflies. The central and western massifs of Spain's first national park are separated from one another by the majestic Cares Gorge, a 1-mile-deep (1.5 km) gash created by the Cares River, the path above which is the park's most popular hiking trail. This trail, one of the most spectacular in Europe, follows the gorge that splits the Picos de Europe in two for 7.5 miles (12 km), clinging to the mountains that rise up around it. Most of the path has been carved straight into the cliff, with occasional arches hewn out of its more exposed overhangs. You need to be wary; while the path is flat, it is also narrow, with hundreds of feet between you and the river. **BDS**

Via Verde de la Sierra
Andalusia, Spain

Start Puerto Serrano   **End** Olvera
Distance 22 miles (35 km)   **Time** 2–3 days
Grade Easy   **Type** Asphalt and compacted earth
Map goo.gl/48uMOY

The development of vias verdes or "greenways"—disused rail lines converted into trails for non-motorized transport—began in Spain in 1993 and has come a long way since, in a country that, by the mid-1990s, had more than 4,722 miles (7,600 km) of abandoned rail lines. Spain now has more than a hundred such trails, with a total length in excess of 1,242 miles (2,000 km); one of these is the Via Verde de la Sierra—the Greenway of the Sierra Mountains.

The Sierra railroad was a project conceived in the early twentieth century that, when completed, would run from Jerez de la Frontera to Almargen in the Guadalete basin and would link military bases in Cartagena and Cádiz. However, the arrival of the Spanish Civil War (1936–39) put an end to the project, and the resultant austerity of the postwar years saw the line officially abandoned in the 1960s after its stations, tunnels, and viaducts had already been constructed (its tracks were laid but ripped up to make weapons, save for a 13-mile (21-km) section from Jerez to the sugar mill at Jédula).

The Sierra Greenway runs from Puerto Serrano to Olvera and follows the base of the southernmost mountain range on the Iberian Peninsula, along the banks of a series of rivers and through some seriously grand scenery, such as the Rock of Zaframagón, a 1,916-foot-high (584 m) limestone escarpment, which is home to Europe's largest colony of Griffon vultures. Add to that four viaducts, thirty tunnels (most with automatic lighting), and five railroad stations through Andalusia's beautiful, untouched countryside, and you have the trail that was voted Best Greenway in Europe in 2009. **BDS**

Beas de Granada to Granada
Andalusia, Spain

Start Beas de Granada   **End** Granada
Distance 10 miles (16 km)   **Time** 1 day
Grade Easy   **Type** Exposed ridge trail
Map goo.gl/LUVKMv

If you ever find yourself in Spain's Sierra Nevada mountains or visiting the culturally rich and beautiful historic city of Granada and are wanting spectacular mountain views without having to expend a whole lot of effort, then the ridge walk from Beas de Granada—a small town to the city's northeast—back to Granada along an old shepherd's trail is the walk you have been looking for.

The trail follows the Vereda del Barranco del Abogado, a track used by shepherds and farmers for generations and established as an ancient right of way. It is wide enough to be safely negotiated and straightforward enough to easily navigate. All you have to do is get yourself to Beas, a feat any of Granada's taxi drivers will be happy to help you achieve, and the trail will then take you back all the way into the heart of the city.

You can walk this route throughout the year, but do what you can to avoid it in summer, as its complete lack of shade makes it tough going on a hot day. However, from May to June, the views can be especially pretty when the mountains have been given a coating of snow.

The trail may be a short one, but it provides some of the most expansive views of the Sierra Nevada to be had anywhere. While in Beas de Granada you might like to first check out some of the many hiking options available. This small town is a well-known hub for hiking, particularly the many trails that wind through the Sierra de Huetor, a small mountain range with deep springs that were once used to provide Granada with its water. The name "beas," incidentally, is supposed to mean "path." **BDS**

"As it takes you right back into the heart of Granada, it's the perfect walk if you're staying in the city."

www.treksierranevada.com

⊞ A ridgeline above Granada provides expansive views of the Sierra Nevada without any exhaustive ascents.

Chillar River
Andalusia, Spain

> "A walking stick is very useful, as the riverbed is stony. In places the canyon is so narrow that you can touch both sides at the same time."

www.walkingeurope.info

⬆ Walking in the shady canyon of the Chillar riverbed is the perfect antidote to a brutally hot Andalusian day.

Start/End Municipal sports center, Nerja
Distance Various **Time** 1 day **Grade** Easy
Type Riverbank, pebbly river bottom
Info goo.gl/TFZryS

Southern Spain can be a stifling environment through which to walk if you do it in June, July, or August during a hot Andalusian summer. This walk along the Chillar River on the Costa del Sol, however, is a cool, pleasant exception to the region's many exposed overland tracks and ridge walks. The river (more of a swift-flowing stream than a river, but flowing nonetheless courtesy of the *fabrica de luz*, a small hydroelectric station upriver) is endlessly refreshing. Come prepared to get your feet joyously wet, and don't forget to take a towel with you, because as you ascend into the narrowing, shade-filled canyon, there are pools of deep water in which it's possible to swim. It is impossible to lose your bearings on this short walk—just follow the river upstream and turn around whenever you want to and retrace your footsteps. Although the walk is an easy one, take care, however, to keep your footing when you cross over the river's pebbly bottom.

The track is, of course, unsurfaced, and traces the banks of the river until you reach the confluence of the Higueron River, which enters from your left. Keep to the right and soon you will come to a small cement works. The canyon narrows just beyond here, and the walk continues for a few miles, then it becomes increasingly interesting as the canyon walls rise to heights of around 1,000 feet (305 m). If you keep going, you will pass the La Presa dam, where the river begins to widen. For a different perspective you can return via a series of irrigation canals that provide lovely views over the entire Chillar Valley—a good return for a 10-mile (16-km) return walk and a delightful way to occupy a hot Spanish day. **BDS**

Montesinho Natural Park Trails

Bragança, Portugal

Start/End Franca   **Distance** Various
Time 1 day–1 week   **Grade** Various
Type Forest trails, dirt paths, unmaintained trails
Info goo.gl/Cz6IsO

The Montesinho Natural Park in northeast Portugal, close to the Spanish border, covers an area of 290 square miles (751 sq km) and has been described as one of the wildest areas in Europe. Called Tras-os-Montes ("behind the mountains") because of its unspoiled and remote nature, wolves and wild boar are found here, in a region noted for the diversity and abundance of its wildlife. In all, there are almost a hundred villages and hamlets within the park's boundaries, with a population of about 8,000 people. Ancient villages, such as França and Montesinho, make good bases for hikes out into the rugged landscape, and there are numerous options available, from easy to slogging it. You can choose to walk through pastures, scramble along streambeds and gorges, hike over heather-covered hills, stumble across hidden archaeological sites, and stride through thick forests of oak and chestnut trees. Good maps and navigation skills are essential as you could go all day and only encounter the occasional shepherd. Other wildlife that lives in the park includes deer, foxes, and rarely seen Iberian lynxes. Count yourself lucky if you get even the briefest glimpse of this critically endangered creature. You're more likely to see the Iberian eagle and other raptors soaring in the skies.

Maps and brochures with suggested walks are available at the two main park information offices, located in Bragança and Vinhais. Signs direct you to some of the old villages, where people still cling to a harsh, rural lifestyle, baking their own bread, making wine, and tilling the fields. It's the kind of place where visitors are made hugely welcome, and you may well find yourself invited into homes as you pass by. **MG**

"There are still a few places in Portugal that truly feel like the middle of nowhere, and the [Montesinho Park] is one of them."

www.roughguides.com

⬆ Montesinho Natural Park has beautiful forests of chestnut and oak, and over eighty medieval villages.

Serra de Sintra Lisbon, Portugal

Start/End Various **Distance** Various **Time** Various **Grade** Moderate
Type Mountain trails **Info** goo.gl/15zN7P

Visitors to Lisbon often take in a day trip to the pretty and historic town of Sintra, about half an hour away and now a UNESCO World Heritage Site. Few, however, have the time to explore the Serra de Sintra (Sintra Mountains) to the west of the town, between Sintra and the Atlantic Ocean, which is a shame because they offer a glimpse into an attractive part of the Portuguese landscape. People in Portugal have long known it as a place of mystery and superstition.

By most people's standards these are not really mountains at all, with the highest point only 1,736 feet (529 m) above sea level, but they have been known since antiquity as the Lunae Mons (Mountains of the Moon), which illustrates for how long they have been regarded as a strange and foreign place. Today, Moon Hill is the site of a nature reserve, while another attraction within the region is the Capuchin Convent,

which was dug out of the surrounding rocks in 1560 and is still inhabited today.

The mountains are filled with a wide variety of trails, which take the curious hiker to megalithic monuments, through quiet farming villages with tempting taverns, and to the highest point, Peninha. Here, where the Virgin Mary is said to have made a miraculous appearance, you'll find a chapel and a cluster of other buildings. You will also enjoy breathtaking views down to the coast. From here you can see Cabo da Roca, the most westerly point of mainland Europe. It was described by one Portuguese poet as "where the land ends and the sea begins," adding one more layer of mystery to the Mountains of the Moon. **MG**

⊤ Meander through Portugal's Mountains of the Moon.

Algarve Way Faro, Portugal

Start Alcoutim **End** Cape St. Vincent **Distance** 160 miles (257 km) **Time** 10–14 days **Grade** Strenuous
Type Long-distance hiking trail **Info** goo.gl/oOXVTB

Most people associate Portugal's Algarve with beaches and golf courses, but inland there is some spectacular scenery, and the Algarve Way threads its way through much of it. It starts at the Spanish border and ends at the point where Portugal's southern and western coasts meet at the 246-foot-high (75 m) cliffs of Cape St. Vincent, Europe's most southwesterly point. This long-distance path is also the westernmost section of the Grand European walking route E4/GR13. A world away from the beach resorts of the coast, the Algarve Way goes through rustic towns and quiet villages, where you'll find cobbled streets rather than sand underfoot, and instead of souvenir shops you'll find people selling honey and local handicrafts.

The route is divided into fourteen sections, each starting and ending where accommodation is available. It's well planned for recreational walkers,

although to attempt the whole distance is a strenuous challenge as the trail passes over some of the highest points in the Algarve. Needless to say the views are stunning, and in places you will be looking down on the coast. You'll pass through pine forests and cork forests, where wild boar roam. You'll see fields filled with colorful wildflowers, and in the skies will probably spot eagles and hawks. Spring and fall are the best times to tackle the walk. The route was first established in 1997, thanks to a group known as the Wednesday Walkers, who had worked with the Portuguese government and local environmentalists. They managed the hike in eleven days. It was later properly waymarked so that today anyone can enjoy some of Portugal's most beautiful scenery. **MG**

⊡ Algarve Way is a challenging walk above a famous coast.

Ponte sa Barva to Gorropu Gorge Sardinia, Italy

Start Ponte sa Barva   End Gorropu Gorge
Distance 3.5 miles (5.6 km)   Time 2.5 hours
Grade Easy   Type Rocky paths, gravel, riverbank, and
bare rock   Map goo.gl/WcLT7U

It is one of Europe's deepest gorges, an inverted S with rock walls as high as 983 feet (300 m), carved out of the surrounding Supramonte karst plateau by Sardinia's Flumineddu River, which is still eroding and deepening the limestone rocks over which it flows. Starting at Ponte sa Barva, in no time you pass a series of small springs after which the path begins to narrow. A grove of oak trees comes and goes, then a small descent takes you down to the riverbank of the Flumineddu, where you get your first sight of the gorge's characteristic snow-white boulders—and then

> "A natural spectacle with . . . sheer rock walls so close together they almost touch."

Brendan Sainsbury, *Hiking in Italy* (2010)

you look up, and up—at the walls of the spectacular Gorropu Gorge.

If you're a hardened climber, you might like to tackle Hotel Supramonte, a near-vertical, 1,312-foot-high (400 m) limestone cliff (there are three climbing routes in the canyon of varying degrees of difficulty). If you choose to continue up the gorge, the route is spectacular, with lots of clear pools of water filtered clean by the rock-filled river. Carry on to where the canyon begins to narrow seriously into a small niche of overhanging rock walls only feet apart. You can continue along the bottom of the gorge, but the rocks get bigger, and this is only really recommended for experienced boulder-hoppers. **BDS**

Val d'Orcia Tuscany, Italy

Start/End Montalcino   Distance Various
Time Various   Grade Moderate
Type Paths through vineyards, olive groves
Info goo.gl/Ku95wz

South of Siena is a part of Tuscany that stands out, even by Tuscan standards. The Val d'Orcia (also written as "Valdorcia") is a region of gently undulating hills, wheat fields, vineyards, and olive groves, so special and picturesque that it has been made a UNESCO World Heritage Site. Atop some of the hills stand medieval castles, in the valleys are hamlets and villages, and tucked away you will find peaceful abbeys. A network of paths takes the hiker from one to the other, and you could spend a day, a week, or a month here.

The area is to the west of Montepulciano, so not surprisingly paths will often lead you to the vineyards where some of Italy's finest wines are produced. In fall the lush green vineyards are a fine sight, although in truth there is no bad time to visit the Val d'Orcia. As well as the wine, you're sure to find yourself indulging in other local produce to fortify you for the delightful hiking. Truffles, cheeses, chestnuts, wild boar—all these and more will be found on the menu.

This region also inspired Renaissance artists to capture its splendor and serenity. Monasteries, such as the twelfth-century Abbey of Sant'Antimo close to Montalcino, are set apart in serene, peaceful places. Montalcino is a walled medieval city, and while towns such as Pienza are tiny, they contain glorious palaces and lively piazzas where you can unwind at the end of what is sure to have been a rewarding day's walking. You might want to enjoy a glass of the local Brunello wine and a plate of pecorino cheese made in Pienza to help you savor the moment. **MG**

➡ **Val d'Orcia is the Tuscan landscape of popular culture.**

Florence to Siena "Chianti" Trail Tuscany, Italy

Start Piazza della Signoria, Florence   **End** Piazza del Campo, Siena   **Distance** 47 miles (75.6 km)
Time 4–5 days   **Grade** Easy   **Type** Rural lanes and pathways   **Map** goo.gl/GK7nVF

Traditionally associated with squat-like bottles enclosed within ubiquitous straw baskets, the wines of the Chianti region in Tuscany first began to evolve their distinctive characteristics in the early 1700s. They developed, south of Florence, in the vicinity of the villages of Gaiole, Radda, and Castellina, with their histories of habitation dating back to the Etruscans. To walk along the backbone of the Chianti Hills, along paths used by generations of farmers, through undisturbed tracts of woodlands, and to be able to look down upon valleys where the famous grape has been grown for more than 300 years is not only a feast for the feet, but also a feast for the senses.

Beginning in Florence's Piazza della Signoria, you will pass by everything that signifies you are in Italy: small churches overlooking village piazzas, tiny hamlets, abbeys, castles, lines of cypress trees, olive groves, and vineyards. The walk also provides an unaccustomed degree of solitude in a region steeped in tourism, so expect a day or two when the only people you meet are disinterested locals and maybe the occasional mushroom hunter. The wildlife, however, is another story. Don't be surprised if a wild boar crosses your path, though more likely encounters will be with partridges and pheasants. Don't think it too pleasant a stroll either. Stages can be long and tiring with constant ups and downs, which compete with fabulous landmarks to take your breath away, such as the Abbey of Fattoria di Monte Scalari near San Polo. Finally, you come off the ridges for the walk into Siena, through the vineyards of Castello di Brolio, and into the historic Piazza del Campo. **BDS**

⊡ **The enchanting greenery of the Chianti Hills.**

Siena to Orvieto Tuscany/Umbria, Italy

Start Siena   **End** Orvieto   **Distance** 50 miles (80 km)   **Time** 7 days   **Grade** Easy
Type Rural roads and farm trails   **Map** goo.gl/D5kpZg

In Italy, the thirteenth century was the era of the city-state—independent autonomous entities that controlled their own affairs and those of the surrounding villages. Siena and Orvieto were two such entities that once joined forces and managed to conquer most of southern Tuscany. When disputes over territory arose in the 1250s, Orvieto switched its allegiance to Florence, but by the mid-1300s, Orvieto's elite had alienated so many people that its status as a city-state came to an end, and by the end of the fourteenth century, it had been overrun and its wealth plundered by Breton mercenaries. Siena, which in the meantime had gained control of the prosperous region of Chianti, couldn't have been happier.

There is much beauty to be seen on a week-long walk south, from Siena to Orvieto, over the rolling hills of Tuscany, but there is a lot here that you cannot see,

too. The more you learn of the politics and struggles that characterized this idyllic corner of Italy for hundreds of years, the more you will see.

Companies such as UTracks will take your bags to the next hotel, leaving you free to amble your way through fortified towns such as Buonconvento, sleepy and relaxing hamlets like Castelnuovo, along the beautiful Val'Orcia, and to the medieval thermal springs in Bagno Vignoni. When you arrive in Orvieto, don't forget to book a tour of the ancient Etruscan caves beneath the town, and to seek out the labyrinth of escape tunnels that led from the houses of nobles through the tufa (limestone), in the event their enemies should strike in the night in the era of state versus state. **BDS**

⬆ **The exterior walls of the town of Buonconvento.**

Taormina to Castelmola
Sicily, Italy

Start Porta Messina, Taormina
Distance 2.6 miles (4.2 km)   **Time** 2 hours
Grade Easy   **Type** Paved pathway
Map goo.gl/zezs2M

There are a few walks in Sicily in which a smorgasbord of beautiful views on the scale of this one become available to anyone who is prepared to do a relatively short hike—but not many. First, you will need to tear yourself away from the Ionian beaches of Taormina, itself not an easy task, leaving the home of Goethe and D. H. Lawrence, and then find the old mule path out of town that now goes by the name Salita Branco. From there it is all up, past profuse splashes of bougainvillea and the extant remains of an old Roman aqueduct that will confirm what your calf muscles are telling you—that you are engaging on a fairly decent, though short-lived, climb. You continue along the side of Monte Tauro, accompanied with thoughts of what lies just a couple of miles ahead of you—the mountain-top village of Castelmola—which draws you ever onward.

When you reach a main road, you need to cross it and then look for a lane, which takes you to a small cluster of homes and a pedestrian sign that will point you the rest of the way. Soon you pass beneath a series of crags above which Castelmola sits, and over your shoulder there is the sight of an old necropolis, which you will actually have a much better view of on the way back down, after you have spent a few hours in the shady cafés of this medieval town's hub, the Piazza San Antonio.

An added bonus on this short walk, with its fantastic views down over Taormina, is a surprisingly impressive view of the sloping flanks of distant Mount Etna, with its scars cut by ancient lava flows that can still be seen, all the way down to the warm waters of the Catania coast. **BDS**

> *"Some steep sections, so it's a good way to work off all the fine Sicilian meals."*

www.italyheaven.co.uk

⬆ A mule path takes you above the terra-cotta roofs of Taormina to the medieval marvel of Castelmona.

Plitvice Lakes National Park
Lika-Senj/Karlovac, Croatia

Start/End Entrance #1   Distance 12 miles
(19.3 km)   Time 8 hours   Grade Easy
Type Boardwalks and forest paths
Map goo.gl/2ddI99

Plitvice Lakes National Park, southeastern Europe's oldest national park, was granted UNESCO World Heritage status in 1979 and is Croatia's number one tourist attraction with more than 1.2 million visitors a year. It isn't hard to see why. Though mostly known for its string of sixteen terraced, trout-filled lakes extending over 5 miles (8 km) and connected by a series of gorgeous waterfalls, the lakes in fact comprise just a small fraction of the park's tufa-filled 116 square miles (300 sq km)—a vast swathe of deep woodlands populated by brown bears, wolves, boars, and deer, with the blue waters of its lakes and waterfalls the jewel in its crown.

Although they are surrounded by mountains, the paths around the lakes and through its woodlands hold little in the way of elevation gains and are essentially a series of overland trails. Within the park there are numerous walks of varying lengths that take you to the Upper Lakes area—twelve lakes set over a bed of Upper Triassic dolomite—and the Lower Lakes area, set in a porous limestone canyon with walls of up to 130 feet (40 m) high. The beautiful blue hues of the waters of the lakes are a result of being saturated with dissolved calcium carbonate, and the lakes are fed by numerous underground springs and streams. Several miles of well-maintained boardwalks take you across the lakes for close-up views of waterfalls in the midst of a karst landscape of exceptional beauty.

The park is also one of Europe's biodiversity hotspots, with an exceptionally high level of endemic and rare plants including Europe's most beautiful orchid, the Lady's Slipper, and an interesting array of carnivorous plants. **BDS**

Oder–Neisse Cycle Route
Germany/Czech Republic/Poland

Start Zittau   End Usedom Island
Distance 335 miles (539 km)   Time 20–25 days
Grade Moderate   Type Cycle path
Info goo.gl/RruCgA

Although developed as a cycling trail, the Oder–Neisse Cycle Route also offers hikers the chance to share the tracks and take on a long-distance challenge through some of the most diverse scenery in Central and Eastern Europe. As well as following the rivers from which it gets its name, the route runs almost the entire length of the German–Polish border, providing a mix of natural and man-made beauty through unspoiled landscapes and medieval towns. It starts in the historic mountain city of Zittau, close to where Poland, Germany, and the Czech Republic meet. After

"The wet meadows along the Order River are a paradise for storks … and ground-nesting birds."

www.oderneisse-radweg.de

hiking for three or four weeks you will reach the shores of the Baltic Sea. Although it's a lengthy hike, and one that needs planning in advance, it is mostly easygoing and well signposted. Another overnight stop could be in the German town of Görlitz, from where a stroll across the river bridge takes you into the Polish town of Zgorzelec. This route is an indication of how easily international boundaries break down when you are walking through these borderlands. A similar experience happens in the German town of Guben, a stone's throw across the river from Gubin in Poland. The hike ends fittingly on the Baltic island of Usedom, which sums up the spirit of the hike as part of it is in Germany and part in Poland. **MG**

National Blue Trail

West to East Hungary

Start Irrott-kő Mountain   End Hollóháza
Distance 701 miles (1,128 km)   Time 10–12 weeks
Grade Easy to moderate   Type Forest, mountain paths
Info goo.gl/S65Gg6

Created in 1938, this claims to be Europe's oldest long-distance path in a country known for its large, flat plains and with a history of rural peasantry that meant walking was often the only way to travel. Hungary is proud of its rural traditions, so it should come as no surprise that this tiny country has more than 13,000 miles (21,000 km) of walking trails, of which the National Blue Trail is justifiably its most famous.

If you want to begin at the official starting point you first have to climb (or drive to) a mountain—Irrott-kő (2,900 feet/884 m) on the Hungarian–Austrian

---

"The National Blue Trail is a very old trail … and is the pride of the country."

www.traildino.com

---

border. From there you descend to the 700-year-old town of Kőszeg before crossing the Little Hungarian Plain, a 3,088-square-mile (8,000 sq km) tectonic basin and part of the giant Pannonian plain, which encompasses most of the country and makes for easy, flat walking. There are ascents on this trail, mostly through the Northern Hungarian Mountains (Börzsöny, Mátra, Bükk), but this is not the Alps. Hollókő is a village nestled in a valley in the Cserhát Mountains, whose ethnographic history is so intact, it has World Heritage status. You also pass the stalactite caverns at Aggtelek, another World Heritage Site. The trail ends in Hollóháza in northeastern Hungary, the last of its hundred-plus villages and rural hamlets. **BDS**

Bükk Plateau

Heves, Hungary

Start/End Szilavásvárad
Distance 4.5 miles (7.2 km)   Time 3 hours
Grade Easy   Type Forest and grassy trails
Map goo.gl/RsEVmF

Bükk National Park in northeastern Hungary was established in 1976 and protects an area rich in karst formations, including caves, ravines, and numerous "swallow-holes," depressions in the ground formed when natural processes of erosion remove the bedrock above to create large holes that are often connected to subterranean passages. This is Hungary's most biodiverse mountain region. The country's longest (2.5 mile/4 km) and deepest (800 feet/244 m) cave, István Lápa, is here along with upward of 800 others, and the park contains an enormous trove of plant and animal life, including several extremely rare species of iris and the globally threatened clouded apollo butterfly, as well as the barometers of any truly unspoiled wilderness: the imperial, the golden, the short-toed, and the lesser spotted eagle.

The plateau, which has been inhabited since Paleolithic times, rises 2,625 feet (800 m) to 3,280 feet (1,000 m) above the surrounding plains and offers a range of truly exquisite walks through a protected and largely untrammeled landscape. The felling of trees here has been banned for more than a century, and one of the interesting options is to walk from the village of Szilavásvárad to a forest of giant old-growth trees, the Oserdő. To walk through the Oserdő is an experience to remember; giant trees have been left to grow old gracefully and to fall to the forest floor when their time has come, returning nutrients to the soils that encourage saplings to grow up alongside their fallen ancestors. The cycle of nature is plainly revealed here, and it is easy to see as you walk through this pristine wilderness why the Hungarians have named it Oserdő—their haunting, primeval forest. **BDS**

Delphi to the Corycian Cave

Thessalia, Greece

Start Delphi   **End** Corycian Cave   **Distance** 11.3 miles (18 km)   **Time** 2–3 hours   **Grade** Easy to moderate
Type Dirt and gravel paths, sealed road
Map goo.gl/nsUAMv

Excavated by a team of French archaeologists in 1969, the Corycian Cave in the Parnassos Mountains near the Sanctuary of Apollo at Delphi produced a wealth of artifacts, including bone flutes, Mycenaean shards, and more than 50,000 terra-cotta figurines. It was a cave of refuge, providing sanctuary from every invader who ever passed through northern Greece, from the Persians in the fifth century to the Germans in the 1940s. It is steeped in legend, too, from being a place of worship dedicated to the god Pan to being used by the Delphi gods, who performed orgiastic rites with local nymphs.

Visitors to the Sanctuary of Apollo who feel like spending some time away from the hordes of tourists who flock to that ancient site, can reward themselves with a leisurely walk into the Parnassos Mountains, where they can visit the Corycian Cave that still has so much to reveal about life in the period of Classical Greece. It is an undemanding trail that begins outside Delphi at an E4 marker and climbs up the so-called "evil steps" through rock and scrub to a cobbled pathway, which takes you into the hills and to views over the Gulf of Corinth, then on to the mountains of the Peloponnese.

Leaving the E4, you follow a set of red square markers the rest of the way through forests of fir and cypresses, and along the banks of the very streams that fed ancient Delphi below. The path emerges onto a sealed road that takes you through the grounds of a small church in the village of Panaghia, and from there you can almost see the cave in the hills above. And the best part of all? You will likely have its 196-foot (60-m) cavern all to yourself. **BDS**

"[The cave] plays a significant part in Delphi mythology, since it was sacred to Pan."

www.roughguides.com

⬆ A seldom-trod path takes you high into the Parnassos Mountains and into an historic sanctuary.

Richtis Gorge

Crete, Greece

Start/End Exo Mouliana   **Distance** 3 miles (4.8 km)
Time 5 hours   **Grade** Easy to moderate
Type Rocky paths, streams
Map goo.gl/fFThZJ

There are a few options to hiking the Richtis Gorge, but the best (if you have two cars) is to drive both to secluded Richtis beach, the trail's end, then drive one back to your starting point at an old stone bridge at Lachanas, walk the gorge, then get in the car you parked at the beach and drive back. That takes about three and a half hours. Or you can hike the gorge down to the beach and straight back up again, which takes a little over five hours. Whichever route you choose (try returning via the gorge; the road is a bit monotonous), you are guaranteed a fabulous walking

"Go for a relaxing hike in this bit of unspoiled nature that feels a little bit like a jungle."

www.tripomatic.com

day on one of Crete's prettiest trails. The gorge itself is about 3 miles (4.8 km) long, and the trail is marked with colored arrows that guide you down through a dense forest of oak, chestnut, and plane trees with ivy-draped limbs, and the deeper you go into the dark recesses of this fairylike wonderland, the more surprises await you: wild berries, mushrooms, herby scents, and numerous pools of clear, refreshing water. There are palm trees, old stone bridges, water mills, and a large stone oven. After about an hour you get your first glimpses of the open sea as you make your way toward the gorge's best kept secret—the 49-foot-high (15 m) Richtis Waterfall—just a twenty-minute walk from Richtis beach. **BDS**

Samaria Gorge Walk

Crete, Greece

Start Xyloskalo guesthouse   **End** Agia Roumeli
Distance 10 miles (16 km)   **Time** 6 hours
Grade Easy to moderate   **Type** Rock trails
Map goo.gl/ZtQJXE

Even in the midst of a typically crowded, hot Cretan summer, a hike through the Samaria Gorge, a designated World Biosphere Reserve, on the island's remote south coast can be—if you time it right and leave early enough—a blissfully solitary experience that begins with a 24-mile (38.6-km) bus ride from the city of Hania to the small guesthouse of Xyloskalo. From there this dramatic trail will take you on a downhill trek descending 5,000 feet (1,524 m) through some of Greece's most stunning scenery before coming to a conclusion on a black sand beach on the Libyan Sea.

Descending to the gorge's floor and emerging by its meandering stream will take about an hour along a series of sharp and steep switchbacks. Then follows 8 miles (12.8 km) of gentle downhill trails along the creek's banks, which takes you past deserted farmhouses and occasional sightings of agrimi—wild Cretan mountain goats. At the trail's halfway point, you come to the gorge's narrowest point—the "Iron Gates"—where only 10 feet (3 m) separate the 1,000-foot-high (305 m) cliffs that rise up around you.

Signs of civilization gradually begin to appear as you walk the trail's final stages. Small communities start revealing themselves, including the town of Agia Roumeli, the end of the walk. It is the point of departure via ferry for the hour-long trip past some of Crete's finest beaches and the picturesque fishing village of Loutro to Chora Sfakion, where buses will take you back through undisturbed Cretan villages to your starting point at Hania. **BDS**

➡ Inspiring scenery awaits on this spectacular gorge walk.

Gauja National Park Pārgauja, Latvia

Start/End Sigulda   **Distance** Various   **Time** Various   **Grade** Easy   **Type** Forest trails
Info goo.gl/VgYFis

Gauja National Park was established in 1973 and is only 30 miles (48 km) from the Latvian capital of Riga. It was Latvia's first national park and remains its largest and most diverse. At its heart is the Gauja River valley, a 59-mile-long (95 km) glaciated valley with plenty of tributaries and deep, heavily incised ravines that are shadowed by massive sandstone cliffs, relics of the Devonian period. There are more than 900 plant species in Gauja, 148 species of birds, and almost 50 species of mammal. The variety in its landscapes is no less impressive, with a diversity in terrain shapes that would be the envy of any national park. These include the Gauja Formation—layers of fine-grained sandstone up to 260 feet (79 m) deep from the Middle Devonian—that has yielded impressive quantities of fossilized fish and that is exposed and easily visible along the banks of the Gauja River.

If you're in Latvia, there is no finer network of walking routes anywhere in the country than those that spread out over this fascinating park. People have been bringing their walking poles here since the mid-1800s to delight in its rocky outcrops, hidden caves, and dense forests. The Līgatne Nature Trails are a series of walks that fan out over the left bank of the Gauja River, outside the town of Līgatne, which is itself worthy of a stroll if only to see the impressive row of thirty nineteenth-century timber residences, built for its paper mill workers. While in Līgatne you should also make time for a walk to the top of Zvārtes Rock— it's only 60 feet (18 m) high, but it is 350 million years old and, tradition says, was once the meeting point for local witches. **BDS**

⊼ Gauja has stunning geologic and biological complexity.

Dancing Forest Trail and Epha's Height Trail Lithuania/Russia

Start Klaipeda **End** Sambia Peninsula **Distance** Various **Time** Various **Grade** Easy
Type Forest and sand dune trails **Info** goo.gl/lfu3rq

The Curonian Spit is one of Europe's most unusual yet little-known features: a slender and gracefully curving set of sand dunes that stretches for 61 miles (98 km) between Lithuania in the northeast and the Russian territory of Kaliningrad to the southwest. It divides the Curonian Lagoon from the Baltic Sea and is a UNESCO World Heritage Site. This strange topography was created by glacial action millions of years ago. Man has also had his impact here, as the spit was once covered in forest, but the cutting down of trees allowed the sand dunes to take over. In some cases the land took its revenge on humankind by eventually burying entire villages under encroaching sand dunes.

One road runs the length of the spit, and from it are various short but stunning trails that allow you to see and explore this remarkable landscape. One of the most popular is the Dancing Forest Trail, also known locally as the Drunken Forest Trail. It's clear how it got its name, as it weaves through a whole series of strangely shaped pine trees that do, in fact, look as though they are dancing. The real reason for their shape remains a mystery, but it's thought that it is due to a combination of winds and the unstable sandy soil.

The Epha's Height Trail is another enjoyable walk that allows you to enjoy views of and from one of Europe's highest sand dunes. Petsh's Dune varies in height (200–210 feet/61–64 m) and is named for the German Franz Epha, who had the unusual job of being a dune supervisor. Epha pioneered new techniques for stabilizing the dunes and was the first to implement the planting of new trees to reduce erosion and help preserve this unique landscape. **MG**

⤴ See the dancing trees of Lithuania's Curonian Spit.

Neman River Trail
Minsk Oblast, Belarus

Start/End Dokudovo
Distance 6.2 miles (10 km)   **Time** 2 hours
Grade Easy to moderate   **Type** Forest tracks and
country lanes   **Map** goo.gl/CE8W5T

Several countries in Central and Eastern Europe have recently joined together in an environmental push to create new tourist routes called "greenways," heritage trails for hikers and cyclists, developed along natural corridors, former rail lines, riverbanks, or historic trade routes. They usually link tourist attractions and are maintained by the communities along their length, a trail type long popular in the United States.

The former Soviet satellite of Belarus has created four greenways, the best known of which is the Neman River Trail. The Neman River is a major waterway in the region, running for 568 miles (914 km) from its source in Belarus to the sea in Kaliningrad, a broad, deep river that is navigable for most of its length. This short walking route passes through riverside landscapes that are often celebrated in Belarusian poetry and art. This picturesque part of the Neman River has a special significance in local culture, and the trail starts and finishes in the pretty medieval village Dokudovo, looping down through scenic water meadows and forests to the Neman River, and then back to the village.

The trail is well marked with green signs, and highlights along the route include a 150-year-old Russian church, a local folklore museum, fortifications from World War I, and archaeological sites dating back to the ninth century. Near the river itself, look out for beaver dams and a new protected marshland nature reserve. An additional path (signed in blue) allows walkers to reach the city of Lida, with its trapezium-shaped fortress, 16 miles (25.7 km) away. Accommodation close to the trail is available at agro-tourism farms. **SH**

"Provides access to many interesting natural and historical sites in the Lida region."

greenways.by

⬆ An ambitious trail along the Neman River helps to spread the greenway concept through Belarus.

The Horse Paths of Igumeny
Minsk Oblast, Belarus

Start Smilavichy   End Ivanichi   Distance 12.5 miles
(20 km)   Time 4 hours   Grade Easy   Type Forest
tracks, country lanes, and quiet asphalt roads
Map goo.gl/yWnYfL

There are walks that severely test the physical stamina of their participants, and there are walks that take you to remote natural wonders. The Horse Paths of Igumeny, however, is in a category all its own—a walk that immerses you in an unfamiliar rural culture. In fact, the walking of it seems almost secondary. It involves an agreeable combination of local forest tracks and paved country roads that normally would take about half a day to traverse, but there's more to this trail than meets the eye. This route has been established as one of the greenways of Central and Eastern Europe.

The Horse Paths of Igumeny, which are located about 19 miles (30.5 km) east of Minsk, are intended for nonmechanized transport, which includes walking, of course, but here in the Republic of Belarus they are also dedicated to horse-drawn carriages. The logo for the trail is a simple image of a traditional Belarusian village house, drawn in the style of Jewish modernist artist Marc Chagall, who was born in Belarus in 1887. The name "Igumeny" is the ancient name for the town of Charven, which stands to the east of the trail and is an historic center for the region.

The route itself passes through forests, lakes, and old farms across gentle, unspoiled countryside. There's an old Orthodox monastery, a state-run carp farm, and a museum dedicated to the life of locally born nineteenth-century composer Stanisław Moniuszko. Probably of more interest to visitors, however, are the various traditional activities available along the path, which include handicraft courses, folk music demonstrations, and tastings of the local specialty—honey. **SH**

Mineral Water Trail
Harghita, Romania

Start Miercurea Ciu   End Baile Tusnad
Distance 16 miles (25.7 km)   Time 6–7 hours
Grade Easy   Type Forest tracks and unpaved roads
Map goo.gl/fx54dS

The Mineral Water Trail was opened in 2004 and was one of the first of the greenway trails in Romania. It opens up a delightful part of the country, taking visitors on an easy hike through a series of medicinal mineral water springs along the Olt River in the Eastern Carpathian Mountains. The trail begins in Miercurea Ciuc, the small main city of Harghita County in eastern Transylvania. It's in the center of Romania and surrounded by an estimated 2,000 or so sparkling mineral water springs. Six of these have been reconstructed as part of the creation of the trail, while

> *"The culture of mineral water bathing has been a tradition for hundreds of years."*

www.epce.ro

others feature swimming pools. Miercurea Ciuc itself has two spas, as well as indoor and outdoor pools, where you can bathe in the health-giving thermal water from the springs.

In one of the villages that the trail passes through, Tusnad Sat, you can visit the Mineral Springs Museum and learn the history of what has been a thriving local business for centuries. Another village, Lazaresti, has more than fifty springs, and the trail ends in the spa town of Baile Tusnad. As well as its spa, this features St. Ann's Lake, the only crater lake in Central and Eastern Europe. There are also several loop trails leading off the main one, between 5 to 25 miles (12–40 km) long, in this charming, little-known rural part of Europe. **MG**

Lycian Way
Muğla/Antalya, Turkey

Start Fethiye   **End** Antalya
Distance 316 miles (508 km)   **Time** 28 days
Grade Medium to strenuous   **Type** Stony footpaths
and old mule trails   **Info** goo.gl/zXVkqC

The Lycian Way, officially opened in 1999, was the first of Turkey's five long-distance trekking routes, and avoids all of the tourist hot spots. It weaves its way for more than 300 miles (482 km) along the southern Mediterranean coastline, often along steep gradients on rocky limestone-encrusted paths and old mule trails that once linked the villages of ancient Lycia on the mountainous Tekke Peninsula.

The coastal views and the gorges, peaks, and ridges that rise above the Mediterranean in this once-remote region are never dull. Even the Ottomans called it the "frontier" and it was known as the "pirate coast" by others because of its many hidden coves and small offshore islands. The independent-minded Lycians who lived here were an ancient people and they had an advanced culture, having absorbed many influences from their Greek neighbors and later their Roman conquerors. Historic sites passed along the way include the amphitheater at Patara, the sunken ruins at Uçağiz, and dozens of tombs and sarcophagi.

The trail is waymarked with white and red splashes, and access to public transport is available along its entire length. Spring and fall are the ideal times to hike it, and at the end of every day, you'll have no trouble finding a pension, hotel, or village house to lay down your head. Summer should be avoided; it is just too hot, and although winter temperatures can be quite mild, it can also be pretty wet and dreary. Whatever the weather, the chance to walk through cedar forests, the Butterfly Valley near Faralya, or the ridgeline at Finike, not to mention the fascinating experience of walking through contemporary rural Turkey, is one that should not be missed. **BDS**

"Take a blind man to Lycia and he'll immediately know from the smell of the air exactly where he is."

Cevat Şakir, Turkish author

⬆ Hiking in the hills above Patara Beach on the Turkish Riviera.

Carian Trail
Muğla/Aydin, Turkey

Start Alinda   **End** Bay of Marmaris
Distance 512 miles (824 km)   **Time** 5–6 weeks
Grade Strenuous   **Type** Long-distance hiking trail
Info goo.gl/ZUWomP

The Carian Trail is the latest in an excellent series of long-distance walks that have been created over recent years in Turkey. It was inaugurated in February 2013, and winds its way through the provinces of Aydin and Muğla in southwest Turkey. This was the land of the Carian people, and the walk is a delightful mix of mountain, shoreline, thick forest, and colorful flowers, and it passes through a host of interesting archaeological sites. It starts at the remains of the old Carian city of Alinda, and ends in the bustling modern tourist resort and port of Marmaris, a nice blend of ancient trails and modern metropolis.

From Alinda the trail goes westward through the Beşparmak Mountains to the Lake Bafa Nature Park and another ancient Carian city, Herakleia, under Latmus. The trail then passes through dramatic hill and mountain scenery to Labraunda, which was one of the holiest sites of the Carian civilization. It reaches the sea on the Gulf of Gökova, where there is an additional, optional loop trail to extend the walk around the popular but heavily trampled Bodrum Peninsula.

The main trail heads east through the dazzling beauty of the Turkish coastline, past a host of impressive archaeological sites, including Keramos and Knidos. Here, the spectacular coast is full of jagged peninsulas, secluded beaches, busy little tourist towns, and plenty of places to spend a relaxing evening with fine food to fortify you for the next day's hiking. The whole trail is a tough effort, but even to do short stretches through this area will remind you that Turkey has some of the best coastline to be found anywhere on the Mediterranean's ancient shores. **MG**

Ihlara Gorge/Goreme Trails
Aksaray, Turkey

Start Ihlara village   **End** Selime   **Distance** 10 miles
(16 km)   **Time** 4 hours   **Grade** Easy
Type Gorge walk by a shady stream
Map goo.gl/mjzgRD

The Ihlara Gorge is about 10 miles (16 km) long and is one of the most impressive natural features near the village of Ihlara. It is a well-watered valley, with lush greenery and unusually formed slopes, where the rock formations look like a series of witches' hats buried beneath the ground.

In addition to the many natural features, there are man-made attractions, too: Hundreds of underground houses have been carved out of the rocks and churches have been built into the rock faces. The gorge was an important monastic center during the

---

"It is believed that the valley housed more than 4,000 dwellings and 100 cave churches."

www.goreme.com

Byzantine period, and many of the original frescoes painted at the time still remain.

This blend of features attracts many people to come and walk along the gorge, following the stream that runs through it and enjoying the shade of the trees along its banks. The valley was carved out thousands of years ago by the Melendiz River, and although the sides aren't hugely impressive—only averaging about 330 feet (100 m) deep—it is still one of the most enjoyable hikes in this part of Turkey. The easygoing terrain provides plenty of opportunity to think about the history of this place, which at one time was home to more than 80,000 people, including the monks of its monastic communities. **MG**

Valley of Roses Ouarzazate, Morocco

Start/End Kelaat M'Gouna or Ouarzazate **Distance** 20 miles (32 km) **Time** 2 days **Grade** Easy
Type Desert trail **Info** goo.gl/tGLTOS

People don't usually think of roses as desert plants, but, in fact, they thrive in that type of arid climate. Morocco's Valley of the Roses, north of the small fortified village of Kelaat M'Gouna near Ouarzazate, is perfect evidence of that. The Mgoun River flows through the valley and turns the barren land into a verdant oasis, a magical green carpet of sweet-scented roses. The area is Morocco's "rose capital," where the flowers flourish, where they produce rose water, and where they have an annual Rose Festival.

The Rose Festival involves music concerts, street parades, displays of local arts and crafts, lots of food, and Berber dancing, and it takes place each May, if you want to time your hiking to coincide with it. You can visit the village distilleries all year round to see how they make the rose water and discover in the process that it takes 7.7 tons (7 tonnes) of flowers to produce just 2 pints (1 l) of rose water. Visiting the valley takes up several hours if you start from Kelaat M'Gouna, and most of the day if you book an organized excursion from Ouarzazate. The trip is best done in springtime when the roses are at their best. This is why the Rose Festival is held in May, to celebrate the new crop.

Two days allows enough time to walk the valley properly. Begin at the village of Kelaat M'Gouna and follow the riverbed for about 10 miles (16 km), past abandoned *ksours* (fortified adobe villages) to Hadida in the heart of the valley. From Hadida you continue to follow the river past striking ocher cliffs to the village of Tourbist and ending at Bou Tharar, one of Morocco's quaintest villages, before retracing your steps back to Kelaat M'Gouna. **MG**

⬆ Breathe in the scents of Morocco's Rose Capital.

Grand Erg Oriental Algeria/Tunisia

Start/End Tataouine   **Distance** Various   **Time** Various   **Grade** Various
Type Desert trails   **Info** goo.gl/eSEpLO

An *erg* is a field of sand dunes, a veritable sea of sand, and the Grand Erg Oriental is the second largest continuous expanse of sand in the Sahara Desert, exceeded only by the Libyan Desert. It stretches between Algeria and Tunisia, and for practical and political reasons it is most easily accessed from Tunisia.

The Grand Erg Oriental extends roughly 125 miles (200 km) north to south and 375 miles (600 km) east to west. While not quite as vast as a real sea, it is still one of the most astonishingly beautiful sights on Earth. Those who have traveled in deserts know that they are far more interesting and diverse places than many people who have not been to them imagine. In parts they are bleak and desolate, but the *erg*, with its endless billowing dunes of golden sand, is the desert of everyone's dreams. However, because of the extent of it, the changing nature of the lands, and the constant risk of sandstorms, it is not a hiking expedition to undertake on your own.

The safest and best way to do it is in an organized group from one of the Berber towns and villages in southern Tunisia, with Tataouine being one of the most popular and readily accessible. From there you can arrange trips onto the Grand Erg Oriental, accessing it via the single main road that goes there. Trips can be anything from short visits using 4 x 4 vehicles to longer stays that include trekking and camping. There are oases in the *erg* where you can camp or stop for refreshments and cool off. Seeing any desert on foot is life-enhancing, and the Grand Erg Oriental is surely one of the most beautiful and accessible desert experiences available. **MG**

⊓ The Grand Erg is one of the Sahara's great sand seas.

Pays Dogon Trek

Mopti, Mali

Start/End Mopti **Distance** 1–7 days
Time Various **Grade** All types
Type Village trails
Info goo.gl/R2EH8y

The region in central Mali where the Dogon people live is one of the most fascinating parts of the country and draws many curious travelers. There are various ways of exploring here, including organized excursions, but one of the best options is on foot, by walking between villages. The Dogon have retained their traditions and are noted for many characteristics, such as their animalistic religious beliefs, striking carvings—including the masks that they wear to perform their traditional dances—and the unique architecture of their villages, which includes granaries with pointed roofs. Men and women have separate granaries, with only the male granary used to store grain, an indication of wealth. The villages themselves are strikingly unusual, with their houses set on cliff faces that can extend up to 1,600 feet (488 m) high.

If you want to book a guide or join a tour, then you can do so in Mali's capital, Bamako. There are also three main towns in the Dogon region where this can be arranged: Bandiagara, Bankass, and Douentza. Surrounding these are hundreds of villages that are quite used to visitors. Hikes between them can be strenuous in places, due to the hilly terrain, and you can often camp overnight in the villages if you're prepared.

This is one part of the world where you should consider joining an organized tour by a reputable tour company. In some towns there seem to be more "genuine" Dogon guides than there are Dogon people, and though there are plenty of reputable guides, there is a risk of a poor experience. But a well-organized tour will be one of the most fascinating experiences of your life, meeting this intriguing people and hiking in their country. **MG**

"Here, hiking offers more than a glimpse of beautiful central Mali.... Walking becomes a cultural experience."

www.chron.com

← The Dogon live along the 120-mile-long (200 km) Bandiagara Escarpment.

↑ A typical adobe exterior wall of a Dogon home.

Ounianga Lakes Trails Ennedi Ouest, Chad

Start/End Shoreline of Lake Teli **Distance** Various **Time** Various
Grade Easy **Type** Sand **Info** goo.gl/1siZMC

No, they aren't mirages, but you could be forgiven for mistaking them. The Ounianga Lakes are a collection of eighteen, mostly freshwater though occasionally brackish and saline, interconnected lakes in the Sahara Desert of northern Chad. They are the country's first UNESCO World Heritage Site, and by any measure you care to use, they are remarkable. Located in the hyperarid Ennedi region of the world's largest desert, they cover an area of almost 155,676 acres (63,000 ha) and are found in two concentrations almost 25 miles (40 km) apart, the relics of a single, giant lake that occupied the basin here more than 10,000 years ago.

One of the secrets of the lakes' longevity is the vast expanse of floating reeds that cover almost half of their surface area and so greatly reduce the rate of evaporation. Lake Teli, the largest of the lakes, is less than 30 feet (9 m) in depth, despite covering an impressive 1,077 acres (436 ha). The lakes are a unique hydrological system, able to sustain large amounts of water in one of the world's driest environments.

Getting to the Ounianga Lakes isn't easy, but tourism is slowly growing here. Contact the French tour company Point Afrique, which can provide you with information regarding safety and accessibility. Be sure you register in N'Djamena before setting out and that you have your Autorisation de Circuler, which gives you permission to travel outside the capital, with you at all times. Point Afrique takes groups to the lakes almost every day during the tourist season, and once there, you are free to walk as far as you'd like along lakeshores surrounded by a sea of golden sand dunes, and green lines of palms fringing their banks. **BDS**

⬆ **The eighteen shimmering lakes are no mirage.**

Kyalavula Loop Bundibugyo, Uganda

Start/End Kyanjiki **Distance** 15.5 miles (25 km) **Time** 3 days **Grade** Strenuous
Type Forest and mountain trails **Map** goo.gl/ptt1gJ

The Rwenzori Mountains National Park is a UNESCO World Heritage Site and one of the most diverse national parks in Uganda. Its terrain ranges from lakes and glaciers to the third, fourth, and fifth highest mountains in Africa. The third highest, Margherita Peak, is 16,795 feet (5,119 m) high. There are numerous hiking trails within the park's 386 square miles (1,000 sq km), especially in the mountains. The Kyalavula Loop is a challenging hike that takes you through forest to mountaintops with views that make you feel you're on top of the world. From here you can see Lake George, beyond which is the equator.

The park is noted for its plants and trees, which include endemic and endangered species, but there is also a very healthy wildlife population with various monkeys and apes, including chimpanzees, as well as forest elephants, antelope, and more than 200 bird species. These range from tiny rainbow-colored bee-eaters to the vast silhouettes in the sky of black eagles and bearded vultures. You're sure to see and hear some of the apes and monkeys as you climb through the forests on the first part of this trek, which finally leads you above the trees and bamboo to spectacular views of valleys and lakes.

The path continues to test hikers as it climbs even higher, eventually reaching Kalalama Camp at a height of 10,354 feet (3,156 m). Just as the park is well served with trails, it is also well provided with camps for hikers to rest overnight. From Kalalama the trail goes back down through the bamboo forests and on into the thick mountain forests before returning to its starting point at Kyanjiki. **MG**

⬆ From forests to mountaintops on a Ugandan jungle trail.

Rift Valley
Rift Valley, Kenya

Start/End Various   Distance Various
Time Various   Grade All grades
Type Trails of all kinds
Info goo.gl/7r6BnX

"In Kenya much of the Rift remains an expanse of raw Africa that dazzles the eye with its haunting grandeur."

africanadrenalin.co.za

⬆ The Rift Valley was given its name by the nineteenth-century British explorer John Gregory.

One of the great natural wonders of the world, the Rift Valley runs from the Middle East to Central Africa and in total is about 3,700 miles (5,760 km) long, although exact estimates vary depending on where you regard the start and end points to be. Formed over the course of some 30 million years, it runs the entire length of Kenya from north to south. At its narrowest it is 19 miles (30 km) across, and at its widest, some 63 miles (101 km).

In Kenya the valley is noted for its lakes and its volcanoes, some of which are still active. It is also home to abundant wildlife, and hiking here is a remarkably rich experience in a plethora of ways. To walk in what can occasionally be a cauldron, and to know you are in a valley yet not be able to see the sides, is a very strange feeling. To be on foot and to share the valley floor with antelopes, giraffes, zebras, and other animals brings nature so much closer. However, the landscape is also shared with creatures that are not so benign, which is why you should always be sure to walk with a guide who knows the area. To startle a lion slumbering in the shade of a large bush is a hiking experience that you will definitely want to avoid.

You can hike in the valley without following specific trails, but there are also numerous designated routes of varying lengths that range from an easy few miles to a strenuous few days. You can join organized hiking tours in Nairobi and in many of Kenya's other major towns, or simply hire guides locally when you venture out into the bush areas. The choices are limitless, and the pleasures of hiking in the Rift Valley of Kenya enormous. **MG**

Walk with the Maasai
Mara/Mwanza/Shinyanga, Tanzania

Start/End Various **Distance** Various
Time Various **Grade** All grades
Type Safari-like trails, rough hiking
Info goo.gl/s9dMOg

The annual migration of more than one million wildebeest in the Serengeti is the largest mammal migration in the world and one of the seven natural wonders of Africa. It takes place from January to March, but even if you are not able visit then, hiking in the Serengeti in the company of the native Maasai is one of the great walking experiences—indeed, privileges—that you can have.

The Serengeti Plain is also home to one of the largest concentrations of lions in Africa, making it one of the best places to visit to have a chance of seeing them in the wild, and also not a place to go wandering around on your own. The native Maasai come armed both with rifles and with knowledge. The rifles are usually a precautionary measure, in case any lions get a little too close for comfort—a warning shot in the air lets them know to keep their distance. The Maasai's knowledge will help you understand the plants and animals of the Serengeti better, and they will teach you about the ways of their people. What greater thrill is there than to sit around a campfire in the African bush and listen to stories such as how a Maasai boy must kill a lion with his bare hands before he can be regarded as a man.

There are numerous ways of organizing walks with the Maasai, with many international tour companies offering the option. You can also make arrangements locally in various towns and cities in Tanzania. You can choose how long and how demanding you want the hiking to be, depending on your fitness and the time you have at your disposal. Needless to say, the longer, the better for what will be one of the highlights of your life. **MG**

"Experience the wild wonders of Tanzania from the unique perspective of the people who call it home."

www.nationalgeographicexpeditions.com

⬆ This walk gives you the chance to see the Serengeti through the eyes of the Maasai people.

Lake Eyasi and Empakai Crater
Arusha, Tanzania

Start/End Ngorongoro Crater
Distance 37 miles (59.5 km) **Time** 4–5 days
Grade Easy **Type** Forest and open trails
Map goo.gl/v8iRR3

Southwest of Tanzania's famous Ngorongoro Crater is Lake Eyasi, an elongated salt lake on the floor of the Great Rift Valley, and from the accounts of the few who have been there, it is a fascinating "must do" walk. Maasai guides are happy to take small walking groups through the high grasslands from Ngorongoro Crater to the lake, and donkeys are used to carry water and your supplies. The return walk takes around four to five days, during which time you have the chance to meet the lake's inhabitants, an ancient race of hunter-gatherers called the Hadzabe, distant relatives of the Bushmen of the Kalahari who also speak the unique "click" language. There are several tour companies that organize one- to two-day walks with the Hadzabe hunters.

In the other direction, about 30 miles (48 km) north of Ngorongoro, along the Arusha–Serengeti road, lies the steep rim of Empakai Crater. A hidden gem seldom visited by tourists, until just a few years ago the preserve was populated with only rangers and researchers. It is possible to descend the crater to the soda lake and forest below and return to the crater rim in half a day. It is also possible to walk on to Naiyobi village and camp overnight.

Walking tours called "Crater Highlands Treks" are also becoming increasingly popular, with many groups walking on from Empakai to the foot of Ol Donyo Lengai and Lake Natron in the scorching floor of the Rift Valley. A nighttime ascent of Ol Donyo Lengai is also possible from the Natron campsite. This is a region that offers adventurous walkers a lot of fascinating options once you have exhausted the splendor of Ngorongoro. **BDS**

"A journey through the heart of Tanzania not unlike the romantic accounts of Ernest Hemingway."

www.tropicaltrails.com

⊼ Two "paths less traveled" show that the Ngorongoro Crater is just the beginning of an African adventure.

Luangwa Valley Walking Safari
Lusaka, Zambia

Start/End Luangwa River Camp, Luangwa
River **Distance** Various **Time** Various
Grade Easy **Type** Safari hiking trails
Info goo.gl/ulc8ro

The Luangwa River is one of the main tributaries of the mighty Zambezi River, and the Luangwa Valley that it runs through covers an area of about 20,000 square miles (51,800 sq km). The area is so big that it contains within it four separate national parks: North Luangwa, South Luangwa (which allows night safaris), Luambe, and Lukusuzi. The sheer size of the place, its unspoiled nature, the lack of human habitation, and the huge amount of freshwater naturally make it a real draw for wildlife. It's one of the best places in Zambia to go on a wildlife walking safari, and has been described as one of the greatest wildlife sanctuaries in the world.

You have a very good chance of seeing some of Africa's most exciting creatures here, including lions, leopards, cheetahs, buffalos, crocodiles, hippos, giraffes, wildebeest, antelopes, jackals, hyenas, wild dogs, and zebras. Bird species are too numerous to mention but include several species of bee-eaters, weaver birds, woodpeckers, vultures, harriers, hawks, falcons, herons, kingfishers, and owls, as well as eighteen different types of eagle.

Most walking safaris are organized by the many wildlife lodges in the valley, so before booking somewhere to stay, check what they have to offer. Night safaris in the South Luangwa National Park, for example, are quite special, while some lodges arrange very good safaris for families. To boost your chances of seeing wildlife, travel in the dry season (May to November), because that's when the animals congregate around the freshwater supplies and are easier for your guides to find. If you only ever take one walking safari in your life, then Luangwa Valley would be an excellent choice. **MG**

"Walking in the Luangwa ... is one of the best ways to get a taste of wild Africa."

www.naturalhighsafaris.com

⬆ A walking safari is a chance to get up close and personal with a huge variety of wildlife.

Fish River Canyon Trails
Karas, Namibia

Start Hobas   **End** Ai-Ais
Distance 53 miles (85 km)   **Time** 5 days
Grade Strenuous   **Type** Tough canyon trek
Map goo.gl/MbRFds

"The gods were in a generous mood when they devised a hiking trail through Namibia's Fish River Canyon."

www.theguardian.com

⤒ On this walk you will be treated to unusual sights, such as this communal birds' nest.

⤷ Once you are in the canyon, the trail is not fixed.

If you want a reason for hiking the Fish River Canyon, you only need to know that it is the biggest canyon in Africa and the second largest in the world after the Grand Canyon in the United States. In all it is some 100 miles (160 km) long, up to 17 miles (27 km) wide in places, with sides that soar up to 1,800 feet (549 m) high. Large parts of the canyon are privately owned, but you can hike about half of it on the trail that runs from Hobas, a popular site for looking out over the canyon, to Ai-Ais, where a relaxing hot-water spa resort awaits the weary hiker. For part of the way you'll be hiking close to the border between Namibia and South Africa.

In geological terms the canyon was formed 650 million years ago, but according to local legends it was actually made by a dragon's tail whipping the earth. From the viewpoint at Hobas you can certainly see why the legend arose, as the canyon snakes away in front of you, just like a curving tail. This is a hike that needs some planning and that can be done only between May and September. At other times of the year, either the desert temperatures get too hot or the rainy season comes in and the trail is simply not safe to attempt.

One of the hardest parts of the route is the initial steep descent from the viewing point to the canyon floor. After this the trail straightens out and you can enjoy cooling dips in natural pools, as well as the truly awe-inspiring scenery. The pools attract wildlife, and you might see antelope or possibly the rare Hartmann's mountain zebra. What you are sure to experience is one of the most exhilarating walks in the whole of Namibia. **MG**

Waterberg Wilderness Trails Otjozondjupa, Namibia

Start/End Waterberg Camp **Distance** Various **Time** Various **Grade** Easy to moderate
Type Open rocky trails **Info** goo.gl/shP3Oc

The Waterberg Wilderness area of central Namibia is one of the country's most diverse hiking destinations. It stands on the slopes of the striking Waterberg Plateau, on top of which lies the Waterberg Plateau National Park. The remote and relatively inaccessible nature of the plateau, which stands some 500 feet (152 m) above the surrounding plains, has resulted in endangered species being moved there to enable them to recover their numbers.

It is an astonishing landscape, with limestone rocks carved into strange shapes by the elements, and numerous springs that bring freshwater and a lush look. The freshwater springs feed thick wooded areas, which together with the grasslands and ravines that also exist on the plateau provide a wonderful variety of walks. One of the most popular is the Waterberg Wilderness Trail, which leaves from the Waterberg Camp on the plateau. It's a four-day hike led by armed rangers, which sets off every Thursday from April to November. You sleep in huts and must carry your own food and sleeping bag.

There are many other great walks in the area. You can do an unguided hike from the rest camp of 31 miles (50 km), once the rangers are happy that you're capable of taking it. In all there are nine different trails around the rest camp, of varying lengths and degrees of difficulty. One of the best is the Mountain View hike, which takes you to the rim of the plateau for some remarkable views. Wildlife to watch out for—apart from snakes—include black and white rhinos, buffalos, giraffes, various antelopes, hyenas, jackals, leopards, and cheetahs. **MG**

⬆ The view from the Waterberg Plateau.

Namib Naukluft Hiking Trail Erongo, Namibia

Start/End Naukluft campsite or old farmhouse at Naukluft   **Distance** 75 miles (120 km)   **Time** 8 days
Grade Strenuous   **Type** Long-distance hiking trail   **Map** goo.gl/uLs7Jt

The Namib Naukluft Hiking Trail is a demanding hike in the Namib Naukluft National Park, a park that ranges in habitat from the ancient Namib Desert to the peaks of the Naukluft Mountains. This trail takes in both desert and mountains and can be done only between March and October as the rest of the year is too hot for safe trekking. Even in the "cool" season, temperatures can still top 86°F (30°C).

The trail is such a challenge that when booking your place in advance—which is necessary—you will also be sent a medical form confirming your fitness to hike it. You must travel in a group of three to twelve people. You'll need to take plenty of water for each day as there are few chances to top up along the way.

The first day's trek is deceptive because the trail is fairly straightforward, apart from a couple of steep ascents. You are hiking on a zebra trail, and you may

well encounter one of these animals on your way. Leopards live in this area, too, but sightings are much less common.

Refuges are available along the trail for overnight shelter, and the first will be welcome as the second day begins with some serious descents. In one place there are chains anchored to provide a little help. Over the following days the pattern of tough climbs and steep descents repeats, with another use of chains in one spot to climb down a waterfall.

This is clearly a hike for only the fit and well-prepared walker, but the incentive for taking the test is the chance to hike in the world's oldest desert, see magical desert sunsets, and cool off at the end with a plunge into the Naukluft River. **MG**

⬆ The Naukluft Trail is a grand desert odyssey.

Okavango Delta Walking Safari
Ngamiland East, Botswana

Start/End Nxabega Safari Camp
Distance Various   **Time** Various
Grade All kinds   **Type** Safari trails
Info goo.gl/xmueOM

The Okavango Delta covers an area of 6,500 square miles (16,835 sq km) and is one of Africa's top spots for seeing wildlife on a walking safari. The waters of the delta draw all kinds of creatures, and depending where you go and at what time of year, you might see elephants, rhinos, hippos, lions, leopards, cheetahs, giraffes, crocodiles, hyenas, and more. It's estimated that about 200,000 animals make their way to the delta at different times of the year.

Choosing the best time to go is the most important decision, as the animals are migratory and their movements change with the seasons. Midwinter, from about June to August, is when the waters are at their highest and boating safaris are the most popular. A better time for hiking is September to October, which is the dry season, when the waters recede and animals are drawn to the edges of the delta because of the availability of water. An unusual feature of the delta is that the waters from the Okavango River do not actually flow into the ocean. They evaporate or are absorbed by the plant life there. If you're more interested in birds than in seeing the big five (lions, elephants, rhinos, leopards, and buffalos) then the rainy season from November to April is the best time.

Walking safaris can be booked through the various lodges that are set up in the delta, or there are hiking companies that will take you in there for a few days, camping at basic campsites overnight. Walking for several hours a day and observing the wildlife on foot is a memorable experience. To stand under the African sun in silence and watch animals such as giraffes or elephants feeding or otherwise interacting with one another is unforgettable. **MG**

"With every step you will become more aware of nature and notice fascinating details."

okavango-delta.botswana.co.za

⬆ The delta's waters begin in far-off Angola and finally disappear into the sands of the Kalahari Desert.

Kruger National Park

Limpopo, South Africa

Start/End Berg-en-Dahl
Distance Various   **Time** Various
Grade All grades   **Type** All types
Info goo.gl/Z3C9pf

If you want to spend more than just a few days hiking in Africa, then head for Kruger National Park, one of the biggest game reserves on the continent, covering an area of about 7,580 square miles (19,632 sq km) and home to more species of large mammals than any other game reserve. You stand a good chance of seeing the big five mammals here.

There are now seven official wilderness trails in the park, and to enjoy one of these you must join an official trail group led by a ranger. Overnight accommodation is in wilderness camps, and you will spend several hours a day out in the bush, trekking from one camp to the next. On the way you should experience some memorable close-up encounters with the wildlife. In addition to the big five, other animals you are certain to see include giraffes, zebras, hippos, crocodiles, hyenas, and numerous antelopes. There are also more than 500 species of bird found in the park, though not all are present at the same time.

The Bushmans Trail is also a good option if you are interested in seeing elephants and rhinos, while rhinos, cheetahs, and lions are all prevalent on the Metsi-Metsi Trail. The Nyalaland Trail is rich in both fauna and flora, and the Wolhuter Trail includes a visit to a rocky outcrop with outstanding views as far as the eye can see. Some of the other trails pass close to the rivers in the park, which naturally draw the wildlife. Note that different trails leave from different camps within the park and need to be booked in advance. Whichever trail you choose, whether it is one or several, you are guaranteed wonderful and memorable wildlife encounters. **MG**

Num-Num Trail

Mpumalanga, South Africa

Start/End Pongola Express Camp
Distance 23 miles (37 km)   **Time** 5 days
Grade Strenuous   **Type** Looped mountain trail
Map goo.gl/Onb1hf

The Num-Num Trail loops through the impressive scenery around the Skurweberg mountain pass. It is named after the Num-Num tree, one of 109 native species of tree that have been identified in the area. The trail isn't long, but the demanding terrain makes it slow going. You can recuperate in the five campsites that have been set up along the way, to divide the trail into five manageable sections.

The trail begins and ends at the Pongola Express Camp, which is actually two railway carriages turned into dorms. You can book to hike with a group but can

---

"A five-day hike … that winds over, across, and through some of Mpumalanga's loveliest landscapes."

www.southafrica.net

---

also follow the trail alone. You can also pay for what they call "slackpacking"—leaving your main bags behind for onward transportation to the next overnight camp while you carry only a day pack.

On the first day, you pass strange rock formations on the way to the next camp, God's Window, where the views over the Komati Valley are heavenly. The next day is the longest, at 5.9 miles (9.5 km), up mountains and across gorges. On the following day the trail mostly follows streams, with plenty of chances to cool off with a swim, and ends with the stunning sight of a waterfall plunging over a cliff. The trail then continues over grassland, through more gorges, and past waterfalls, before returning full circle. **MG**

Klipspringer Hiking Trail Northern Cape, South Africa

Start/End Klipspringer Hiking Trail reception area   **Distance** 25 miles (40 km)   **Time** 3 days   **Grade** Strenuous
Type Looped trail   **Map** goo.gl/zklJBP

The Augrabies Falls National Park covers an area of 317 square miles (820 sq km). It is named for the 197-foot-high (60 m) waterfalls that you will see as you start this short but tough hiking trail through some of the park's finest scenery. This is also a diamond-mining area, and you might be driven on by the thought that the biggest horde of diamonds in the world is said to be concealed beneath the swirling waters at the foot of the cascade.

However, the real jewel of this hike is a gorge that runs for 11.25 miles (18 km). The hike starts by clinging to the sides of the gorge, which are up to 787 feet (240 m) deep. You'll need sturdy walking boots for this rugged terrain. From a practical point of view, note that the trail is closed from mid-October to the end of March, as conditions then are simply too hot for safe hiking. You will also need to be sure to

book your camping spot at the campsite at the start and end of the trail in advance. For the rest of the trail, overnight accommodation is in simple huts with bunk beds.

The trail eventually descends to the floor of the gorge and changes from rocky terrain to strength-sapping sandy stretches of hiking. One of the notable natural features you'll see will be the so-called quiver trees (actually giant aloes), which get their name because the local Bushmen used the branches to make quivers for their arrows. Their prey would have included the monkeys and baboons that you may encounter along the way, with perhaps a glimpse of one of the smaller wild cats. This is one of the best hikes in this part of South Africa. **MG**

⊼ Descend into one of Africa's most impressive gorges.

Rim of Africa Western Cape, South Africa

Start Pakhuis Pass **End** Outeniqua **Distance** 404 miles (650 km) **Time** 54 days **Grade** Strenuous
Type Long-distance mountain trek **Info** goo.gl/bS3gZi

The Rim of Africa is the best mountain trail in South Africa and one of the most exciting and exhilarating long-distance hikes in the world. It starts at Pakhuis Pass in the Cederberg Wilderness Area, known for its startling rock formations and a popular place for adventure activities. It is also home to forests of the endemic and endangered Clanwilliam cedar trees, which give the Cederberg Mountains their name.

The trail then passes through several more of South Africa's mountain ranges: Cape Fold, Hex River, and Outeniqua. These mountains form the heart of the Cape Floral Region, one of only six recognized floral kingdoms in the world. There are more than 9,000 species of plants here, two-thirds of which occur nowhere else.

Because it is such a physical test, the hike has been broken up into eight sections, each of which can be done in six to eight days. The first section through the Cederberg mountain range would be enough on its own to make it into any list of classic hikes. You'll see strange rock formations, the rock art of the local San Bushmen, cool pools to swim in, and views, as if from the roof of the world, not just the rim of Africa.

Subsequent sections of the trek feature more rock formations, ridge walks, more pools for swimming in, and a chance to hike through South Africa's unique version of Mediterranean heathland known as fynbos. Much of the trail passes through private land, so it's important to keep to the official route. The whole trail was developed only recently as a private initiative to help protect the natural beauty of the mountains and to preserve their delicate ecosystems. **MG**

⊕ Traverse the mountain passes of the Western Cape.

Ankarana National Park
Antsiranana, Madagascar

Start/End Mahamasina   **Distance** Various
Time Various   **Grade** Moderate to strenuous
Type Forest trails, exposed rock
Info goo.gl/mtDRaK

"Ankarana is well known for its extensive caves systems, formed by slightly acidic rivers running through limestone formations."

www.wildmadagascar.org

⊼ Ankarana's razor-sharp karst badlands are known in Madagascar as *tsingy*.

It is worth traveling a long way for the privilege of walking through the 70 square miles (182 sq km) of Madagascar's Ankarana National Park. This region of deeply eroded limestone in the far north of the country is a veritable fortress of limestone caves, ridges, and pinnacles called *tsingy*. They were shaped over time with the help of more than 6.5 feet (2 m) of annual rainfall, creating Africa's largest network of underground caves (inhabited by the world's only cave-dwelling crocodiles), which lie below one of the planet's most extraordinary rock landscapes, a 900-foot-high (274 m) karst plateau of deciduous forests, lakes, and canyons surrounded by tree-studded, grass-filled savannah.

The walking here is memorable but difficult. The terrain requires patience and sure-footing, it can be horribly hot in summer, and there are scorpions. You cannot walk through here without a guide. But the lure of this park is strong—day walks range from two to more than nine hours, while multiday hikes leave nothing out, taking you into bat-filled caves, through lemur-filled forests, along delicate *tsingy* ridgelines, and over impressive cable suspension bridges. Best visited in the dry season from April to November, Ankarana contains one of the world's densest populations of primates, including dwarf lemurs, and one of the island's most undisturbed communities of crowned lemurs. It is also home to the local Islamic Antankarana people—the "people of the limestone rocks"—who farm vegetables, chicken, and cattle.

Tsingy means "where one cannot walk barefoot," and when you come here and see it for yourself, you'll understand why. **BDS**

Tsingy de Bemaraha National Park
Mahajanga, Madagascar

Start/End Various
Distance Various **Time** Various
Grade All grades **Type** All types
Info goo.gl/8irUUW

Tsingy is a Malagasy word describing a place where you cannot walk barefoot. One look at the limestone needles that are the park's most notable feature shows you how appropriate the name is. These surreal creations have been produced by groundwater undermining parts of the earth and leaving behind needle-like protrusions. Fortunately for the hiker, there are no trails on top of the *tsingies*, but plenty of trekking opportunities at ground level in this otherworldly landscape.

The areas that now comprise the Tsingy de Bemaraha National Park and the Tsingy de Bemaraha Strict Nature Reserve next to it were designated a UNESCO World Heritage Site in 1990. At first they were off-limits to visitors. It was only in 1998, with the creation of the 279-square-mile (723-sq-km) national park, that visitors were permitted to go trekking in the region. The larger 329 square miles (852 sq km) of the nature reserve can also now be visited.

Hiking in the national park is the best way to see the wonders of this part of Madagascar's west coast. It has been described as being to Madagascar what Madagascar is to the rest of the world—a unique paradise full of unusual and endemic species. New creatures are still being discovered here. Its relative inaccessibility helps to keep it special and pristine, and you will need to either join an organized tour or hire a local guide if you wish to get to and from the park and not get lost in its bewildering mix of forests, caverns, canyons, rivers, and waterfalls. You will see lemurs and numerous brightly-colored birds: there are more than 100 bird species recorded here. It's one of the world's most extraordinary places. **MG**

Mare-aux-Cochon
Seychelles

Start/End Le Niol or Port Glaud
Distance 0.5–6 mile (0.8–1 km) **Time** 3 hours
Grade Easy to moderate **Type** Looped mountain trail **Map** goo.gl/RzcEAw

---

The Seychelles is all about the ocean—luminous seas, palm-fringed beaches, and diving—and from the perspective of a chaise longue on Mahé's white sands, the interior of the island looks daunting: a jungle-covered hulk of granite crossed by few roads. The thought of exploring the island on foot is probably not at the top of most visitors' to-do list.

Yet the Morne Seychellois National Park in the northwest of the main island of Mahé beats even the beaches when it comes to scenery, and is the place to come for an overview of the island and the nearer

---

"The freshwater marshes of the upper lands … are an ecologist's dream come true."

en.seyvillas.com

---

islands of the Seychelles archipelago. The Department of Environment has cut six official national trails of between 0.5 miles (0.8 km) and 6 miles (9.6 km) in length into the rain forest, centering on the valley of Mare-aux-Cochon, a high altitude wetland of international importance. The trails interconnect and can be combined to create longer or shorter hikes. A good circular option leads through Port Glaud and the Mare-aux-Cochon marsh, an area rich in tropical plants and bird life that also has caves and waterfalls. Although the trails are short, a degree of planning is advisable, as the tropical heat becomes unbearable after midday, even during the cooler and drier period between June and September. **DS**

Qadisha Valley Liban-Nord, Lebanon

Start/End Bsharri   **Distance** Various   **Time** 1–4 days   **Grade** Easy   **Type** Mountain trails
Info goo.gl/YdAvOk

The Qadisha Valley (*qadisha* is Aramaic for "holy"), often Anglicized as "Kadisha Valley," is one of the most extraordinary and beautiful spots in Lebanon, a heavily incised gorge with lush vegetation that looks more like Switzerland or Austria than the typical desert image of the Middle East. Here you'll find Lebanon's highest mountain, Qurnat as-Sawda, at an impressive 10,131 feet (3,088 m).

Inhabited since at least the third millennium BCE, it was once a place for hermits and monks seeking undisturbed peace, with monasteries hewn out of the many rock faces. You will find the monasteries still in place, and also the caves that were turned into churches by their resident monks. Some of these cave churches still contain original paintings dating back to the thirteenth century, which is one of the reasons the valley was declared a UNESCO World Heritage Site in 1998. You will find a choice of excellent trails, one following the valley floor and others leading off on spurs to some of the more interesting sites up the sides of the valley. Other paths lead along the top, and from there you can find different trails that take you down again to the valley floor.

Whichever route you follow, sooner or later you'll find yourself in one of the little villages that are set dizzily on top of the valley or cling precariously to the slopes; for example, Bqaa Kafra, the highest village in the country at 5,741 feet (1,750 m). You just need to spend a few hours in the "Holy Valley" (although you may want to make it more than that) to know that you have discovered one of the world's most special places. **MG**

⬆ Discover Lebanon's ancient "Valley of Monasteries."

Israel National Trail Northern to Southern, Israel

Start Dan   **End** Eilat   **Distance** 625 miles (1,000 km)   **Time** 40–60 days   **Grade** Strenuous
Type Long-distance hiking trail   **Info** goo.gl/ztCHr1

From the Lebanese border to the Red Sea shores of the Gulf of Aqaba at Eilat, the Israel National Trail zigzags its way through the entire country, linking some of its most significant spots. *National Geographic* magazine has listed it as one of the best hikes in the world, but it is certainly not a trail to be undertaken lightly, as only forty percent of hikers actually manage to complete it. One of its challenges is that for long stretches of the southern sector, which goes through the testing Negev Desert, you have to be self-sufficient and carry all your food and supplies with you. Some hikers stash supplies in places along the route in advance, rather than carry them through the heat, but it is also possible to complete it in separate sections.

The trail was opened in 1995. Starting at Dan, it leads south, skirting the Sea of Galilee, then turns abruptly west past Nazareth and on to the shores of the Mediterranean. This makes for a pleasant hike along the coast, but also avoids the West Bank area. In Tel Aviv it jumps back inland again toward Jerusalem before curving south through the Negev and running parallel to the border with Jordan, down to Eilat on the Gulf of Aqaba.

Hikers will be able to see the wonderfully contrasting landscapes of Israel, from desert to lush valleys, forests, and lakes, and from the Mediterranean shores to the hilly landscape around Jerusalem. Due to the tough nature of the hike, it is recommended that you start in February or October to avoid the worst heat of the summer. In spring the land is green and carpeted with flowers, and you will experience Israel in a unique, unforgettable way. **MG**

⬆ The trail traverses both lush and barren landscapes.

Wadi Qelt
West Bank

> "The biblical events which likely occurred on this route include ... the story of the Good Samaritan and Jesus's travels from Jericho."

www.bibleplaces.com

⤒ The wadi saw its first monastic communities establish themselves here in the fourth century.

Start Jerusalem–Dead Sea Highway trailhead
End St. George Monastery   Distance 4.3 miles (6.9 km)
Time 4–5 hours   Grade Easy   Type Dirt paths, bare rock   Map goo.gl/HkvCQt

Wadi Qelt (also known as Nahal Prat) receives in excess of 60,000 visitors a year, making it one of the most popular hiking spots in Israel. Its parking lot is woefully too small to cater for all visitors, so expect to park your car somewhere along the road that winds its way down to the trailhead from the Jerusalem–Dead Sea Highway.

The wadi, which runs east to west and crosses a significant slice of the northern Judean wilderness, is reached via a series of shimmering water holes, including Ein Prat Spring, Wadi Qelt's uppermost spring, before ascending east in the direction of Jericho. The trail to the wadi is color-coded green and blue, so there is no chance of getting lost: the green trail guides you along the top of the riverbed before meeting up with the blue trail, which takes you on a steep descent down to the spring.

This is a magical walk through a deep, water-filled desert gorge with plenty of water deep enough for swimming, and high canyon walls that provide a wonderful respite from the desert heat. There are also some quite extensive remains of ancient aqueducts, built to channel water from the wadi's springs, that are worth exploring.

At the end of the trail you arrive at the Greek Orthodox monastery of St. George, a monastic community that can trace its origins back to the early fifth century. It fell into disuse after the Crusades, but was restored in the late 1800s. Once there, you have a choice: you can double back the way you came or take the shorter, though far less scenic, road that follows the top of the canyon back to your car. **BDS**

Ein Gedi Nature Reserve
Southern, Israel

Start/End Wadi David ticket office
Distance Various **Time** 30 minutes–1 day
Grade Easy to strenuous
Type Desert trails **Info** goo.gl/WjmMM9

The area around the Dead Sea is alive with diverse wildlife, and the Ein Gedi Nature Reserve, created in 1971, is one of the most important nature reserves in Israel, sitting between the Judaean Desert and the waters of the Dead Sea. Within the reserve you can find four freshwater springs, various waterfalls, and two streams that flow year-round. All of these naturally make the area appealing for animals: foxes, wolves, hyenas, and a few spotted leopards live here, although they're not always easy to make out. What you will probably see are hyraxes (small mammals) and ibex—the wild goats from which the name En Gedi comes (it means "kid spring" and has been in use since biblical times).

The reserve is also very attractive to hikers, with several trails ranging in difficulty from easy to strenuous and lasting from half an hour to a full day. Some of the shorter ones are popular with families since children can easily cope with them, and the reserve is only about an hour's drive from Jerusalem, making for an enjoyable day trip that is usually combined with a dip in the Dead Sea to cool off. The lower section of the David Stream Trail is one of the busiest since it is one of the easier hikes and ends at the impressive David Waterfall.

More intrepid hikers will find plenty of trails to suit them, too, and some of them even involve a little rock climbing. The Upper David Trail takes you to the top of the David Waterfall and to a couple of the springs, including the Ein Gedi Spring, and past some of the archaeological remains that have been found in the area, including a temple from the Chalcolithic period dating back 5,000 years. **MG**

"Not too far from Jerusalem, yet it feels worlds away. Ein Gedi is one of the most popular escape spots for Israelis...."

www.touristisrael.com

⤒ Ein Gedi offers a variety of hiking trails in a spectacular setting in the stark Judean Desert.

Wadi Mujib Gorge

Balqa, Jordan

Start Wadi Mujib vistor center   End Various
Distance Various   Time Various   Grade Moderate
to strenuous   Type Desert and mountain trails
Map goo.gl/Ak3E8d

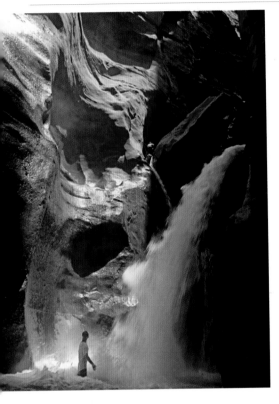

"Over 420 species of plants [and] 102 species of birds have been recorded to date. It is a safe haven for mountain animals."

www.visitjordan.com

⊞ Wadi Mujib Gorge contains more than 400 plant species and hundreds of species of birds and animals.

The Mujib Nature Reserve was created on the shores of the Dead Sea to help protect some of the area's wonderful wildlife, such as leopards, wolves, jackals, and foxes, but it also provides people with wonderful walking opportunities. There are some easy trails here into Wadi Mujib and Wadi Hidan, but hiking in this protected area is strictly controlled, and you must arrange everything through an official guide; you will need one with you in order to get into the Mujib Nature Reserve.

But it is worth it—Wadi Mujib in particular is recognized as one of the country's great hikes, and the gorge is known as "Jordan's Grand Canyon." While not quite on that same scale, Wadi Mujib does offer some strenuous hikes, and parts of the gorge are wild and remote, which offers protection for the animals. It's possible to do a two-day trek, camping overnight. The birdlife is particularly rich, featuring the humble Dead Sea sparrow and the giant Lammergeier.

The Mujib Siq Trek is another spectacular hike through this dramatic desert landscape. It is actually part of the bigger Wadi Mujib gorge, constituting the end section where the walls of the gorge narrow to create dramatically high sides. Given that it is a desert, you might not be prepared for the conditions—you will get very wet indeed. If you start the hike in the hills, you abseil down a 66-foot-high (20 m) waterfall as you make your way to the Dead Sea. For a shorter option, you can also simply splash your way upstream, between high sandstone walls, until you reach the waterfalls. Either way, and whichever hike you choose, you will likely be overwhelmed by this awe-inspiring natural landscape. **MG**

Wadi Himara

Madaba, Jordan

Start/End Dead Sea Highway 1 hour south of Amman
Distance 2 miles (3.2 km) **Time** 6 hours
Grade Easy **Type** Mountain and
desert trails **Map** goo.gl/MK1PTO

For most visitors the Dead Sea—at 1,401 feet (427 m) below sea level, the lowest point on the planet—means an opportunity to float on the water and have your photograph taken while reading a newspaper. Or covering yourself in the sea's healing mud, which is said to have therapeutic qualities. But that is only scratching the surface. In the hills and deserts of the Jordan Rift Valley, to the east you will find some of Jordan's most exhilarating and rewarding walks.

The Dead Sea got its name because its high salt level prevents anything but microscopic organisms from living in it. The nearby hills, however, are anything but dead: the wildlife includes camels, jackals, foxes, hares, hyenas, wolves, and mountain goats. There are even a few leopards, but you would have to be extremely lucky to see one of those. You're more likely to spot a smaller wild cat in the rocky terrain of the wadis, the caracal, which can be identified by its black and white ear tufts. Eagles, vultures, and various hawks are also common.

The Mujib Nature Reserve offers easily accessible hikes, but there are many more options in the hills around here. One impressive option is the upper trail at Wadi Himara, which not only affords spectacular views down toward the Dead Sea, but also ends at Jordan's longest waterfall at 262 feet (80 m). A challenging choice is the hike along Wadi Numeira, which starts in the hills and takes you back down to the Dead Sea. Because it is a good nine or ten hours of hiking, you will need to be well-equipped and plan ahead. A good guide is also useful in the hills to take you to places you would never be able to find by yourself. **MG**

"*The lowest point on Earth, the Dead Sea is as steeped in religious heritage as it is salty. . . . [It is] undeniably beautiful.*"

Time Out

⊡ The hills around Wadi Himara concel Jordan's two tallest waterfalls and crystal-clear streams.

Wadi Rum
Aqaba, Jordan

Start/End Wadi Rum village **Distance** Various
Time 5 days, or a series of day hikes
Grade Moderate **Type** Desert Trails
Info goo.gl/ienmjL

Wadi Rum is the biggest wadi (valley) in Jordan and one of the most dramatic places in the Middle East. It is a big draw for visitors to the country and driving safaris are popular, but the best way to experience the place is to get out and see it on foot. It's such a vast area, though, that you must have a guide with you. There have been instances of visitors wandering off alone and getting lost, then needing to be rescued by helicopter, so don't take any chances.

Some of the best guides here are the local Zalabia Bedouin people, who not only know the wadi area intimately, but also will add to the experience by sharing stories with you. You will also learn so much more about life in the desert and increase your chances of spotting and identifying the wildlife here. This includes wolves, foxes, hyenas, jackals, gazelles, and several species of wild cats, including the Arabian leopard. Birds of prey are common, with 19 species recorded here and 119 different bird species in all. The Bedouin also know the plants of the desert and can identify which are edible, which are poisonous, and which have medicinal properties.

You will already know what's so special about the landscape here if you have seen the film *Lawrence of Arabia* (1962), because much of it was filmed in Wadi Rum. The red sandstone and granite rocks seem to swirl and change color as the light changes. There are several rock bridges, linking different formations, and you will see petroglyphs made by the Nabataeans, one of the ancient peoples who lived here. There is a feeling of immensity and grandeur; the light seems more intense and the silence can be overwhelming. This is not just a hike, it's an experience. **MG**

"Wadi Rum is a protected area [of] dramatic desert wilderness in the south of Jordan.... You can stay overnight in a Bedouin tent."

www.wadirum.jo

← Now home to the Zalabia Bedouin, Wadi Rum has been inhabited since prehistoric times.

↑ A Purple Um Sahn sandstone formation at Wadi Rum.

Manakhah to Al Hajjarah Trek Sana'a, Yemen

Start Manakhah **End** Al Hajjarah **Distance** 3 miles (4.8 km) **Time** 1 hour **Grade** Easy
Type Rough roads, stone paths **Info** goo.gl/RS5yOa

In the beautiful Haraz Mountains of Yemen, ancient villages cling to rock faces as they have done for a thousand years and more—this is the abiding image of Yemen that is most familiar to the world. It's hard to single out the most beautiful, but two that have become especially popular with hikers and trekkers are Manakhah and Al Hajjarah. Just a few rugged miles separate the two; the walk between them is short but packs more drama than you'll find on longer walks elsewhere.

Manakhah is the main town in the region and it is used as a base by hikers who want to explore the area, be it on a trekking expedition of several days or for only a few hours. Unfortunately, due to security concerns, the numbers of visitors have dwindled and many of the hotels had to close down, but the rewards are certainly there for the brave traveler, and in Al Hajjarah you might find one or two guesthouses offering basic accommodation to visitors.

A short walk to the west from Manakhah, a rough road leads up the mountain and takes you to an even more spectacular place, Al Hajjarah. Another good base for hikers, the village was founded by the Sulayhid dynasty in the eleventh century and was once a bustling market town because it lay on the main road between the Red Sea port of Al Hudaydah and the Yemeni capital Sana'a. Prosperity meant that many grand houses were built into the cliff faces, some of them up to eight floors high. It's an almost surreal sight, like a painting by M. C. Escher, and it is as dramatic a setting today as it has ever been, and one you will see nowhere else in the world. **MG**

⬆ **Yemen has an architecture all of its own.**

Valley of Castles, Charyn Canyon Almaty, Kazakhstan

Start/End Canyon rim **Distance** 6.2 miles (10 km) **Time** 2 hours **Grade** Easy
Type Rock paths, bare rock **Map** goo.gl/8DGUO7

When you come to Kazakhstan and somebody tells you they have the world's second largest canyon there, but that hardly anyone outside of Kazakhstan knows about it, don't go spoiling their day by saying that actually you've researched it, and it turns out that the canyon is really only the world's seventeenth largest. It is, after all, still pretty big. And beautiful far beyond its ranking.

Located about 93 miles (150 km) east of the city of Almaty and with the magnificent Tian Shan Mountains on the distant horizon, Charyn Canyon's heavily fissured walls of red clay follow the Charyn River for 50 miles (80 km). The canyon is desolate, and in summer can be extremely hot. Almost on the same latitude as Nevada's I-80, the topography is strangely familiar. But here there are no facilities, no marked trails, and no handrails to help you negotiate the tricky descent to the valley floor. And it is really remote—the border with China is only 74 miles (120 km) away.

The canyon's most striking section—and without hiking it, no amount of alternate trail walking here will be enough—is the so-called Valley of Castles, a series of odd-shaped rock formations that resemble battlements or keeps. With a little planning it is possible to hike in and camp overnight in the valley's only designated campsite, where locals will organize a river crossing for you in locally woven baskets. Fossils have been found here, too, in the strata of the exposed, wind-eroded cliffs that reveal millions of years of history, and you can even raft the Class VI rapids of the Charyn River. Arizona and Kazakhstan never looked so much alike. **BDS**

⊥ Descend into Kazakhstan's Arizona-like canyons.

Bayanaul National Park
Pavlodar, Kazakhstan

Start/ End Zhayau Musa Monument, Zhasybai Lake
Distance Various   **Time** Various
Grade Easy   **Type** Mountain trails
Info goo.gl/R3UFDF

One of the most scenic parks in Kazakhstan, the Bayanaul National Park is extremely popular, boasting numerous tourist facilities: there are holiday cottages for rent, campsites, hotels, and several lakes for watersports within the park's boundaries. Mountain biking and rock climbing are other draws—and, of course, hiking. The park features three large freshwater lakes: Sabyndykol, Jasybay, and Toraigyr, with Jasybay in particular being renowned for the purity of its water. This was the country's first national park in 1985, and several places within the park are considered

> *"Bayanaul is a picturesque corner of nature. . . . [It] attracts visitors with its beautiful lakes and caves."*
>
> www.visitkazakhstan.kz

sacred. Guided tours to see the highlights are available, but it is best to head off on one of the hiking trails within the park's 169,151 acres (68,453 ha).

Trails lead through meadows and forests, and you'll almost certainly see deer and squirrels. Also present in good numbers is the endangered argali, or mountain sheep, the largest wild sheep in the world, and you will get to see eagles and hawks, which are among the fifty bird species found here. Another unusual feature of the park is the Bayanaul pine, which grows out of the rocks. A collection of strangely shaped rocks is part of the unusual landscape; the larger rocks have been given names according to their shapes. **MG**

Fairy Meadow Trail
Gilgit-Baltistan, Pakistan

Start/End Jhel trailhead
Distance 18 miles (29 km)   **Time** 2 days
Grade Strenuous   **Type** Mountain trails
Map goo.gl/uzt27w

The pine and fir forests at the foot of Nanga Parbat, the ninth highest mountain in the world, are so enchanting that they have been given the name Fairy Meadow. There are numerous hiking options here: you can hike to Fairy Meadow, on trails around Fairy Meadow, or you can trek from Fairy Meadow to the base camp on Nanga Parbat. Tackling Nanga Parbat itself is something for serious mountaineers only: the second highest mountain in Pakistan after K2, it is one of the most dangerous climbs in the world and has earned the nickname "Killer Mountain." It still has never been climbed in winter.

Nanga Parbat is a towering 26,660 feet (8,126 m) at the western end of the Himalayas, an immense peak that dominates the landscape, and the Indus River flows around it through one of the deepest gorges in the world. The peak was first climbed in 1953 and not conquered again until 1962. If you limit yourself to hiking in the area, you will be walking in one of the world's greatest landscapes.

To get to Fairy Meadow is an adventure in itself as you leave the Karakoram Highway and travel along the Fairy Meadow Road, described as one of the most dangerous in the world. Parts of it are so narrow they can only be passed on foot or by bicycle, but eventually the stark and rugged road will take you to the lush pastures at Fairy Meadow. From here, one of the most exhilarating walks you can take is to the base camp for Nanga Parbat, scrambling over glaciers and strolling through grassy meadows in one of the most dramatic settings on the planet. **MG**

➔ A great introduction to the Karakoram Range.

Valley of Flowers
Uttarakhand, India

Start Govindghat **End** Valley of Flowers
Distance 10.6 miles (17 km) **Time** 5 hours
Grade Strenuous **Type** Mountain trail
Map goo.gl/whBQuj

When you initially see the Valley of Flowers in Uttarakhand, you wonder if someone has somehow managed to artificially alter the landscape. But no, the flower-filled valley really does have that intensity of color—blues, yellows, purples, reds, oranges, whites, and violets. For once, the cliché "carpeted with flowers" is true, as the whole valley floor and slopes are covered by more blooms than you will ever have seen before in one place. There are almost 500 species of flowering plants to be found here, including poppies, daisies, and orchids.

The area became the Valley of Flowers National Park in 1982 and it is also a UNESCO World Heritage Site. In addition to its array of flowers, the area provides refuge for wildlife, including bears, deer, snow leopards, and the unusual Himalayan blue sheep. The beautiful vision comes at a price, however: it is best seen during monsoon season, which isn't the best time for hiking this fairly tough trail. If you want to see the flowers in their prime, allow for a stay of a few days to give yourself plenty of time.

The trail starts in the town of Govindghat at an elevation of 5,997 feet (1,828 m), where the Alaknanda and Lakshman Ganga rivers meet. To get to the Valley of Flowers you take a steep uphill hike as the valley ranges in elevation from 10,500 feet (3,200 m) to 21,900 feet (6,675 m). It is this huge variation and the associated mix of climates that allow for the proliferation of flowers growing here and, while it may not be true that some people actually faint due to the pungent aromas they encounter here, the sight of the Valley of Flowers in full bloom is certainly intoxicating. **MG**

"Still pristine and enchanting … legends are associated with the park, and locals believe it is the playground of fairies."

www.travel.india.com

⬆ The valley has a distinct microclimate, heavy with mists and low cloud that help keep its soils moist.

Gorakhgad Trek
Maharashtra, India

Start/End Dehri village
Distance 10 miles (16 km)   **Time** 4–5 hours
Grade Strenuous   **Type** Dense forest trails
Map goo.gl/o5K5KK

The peak of Gorakhgad juts out of the surrounding jungle like a green pyramid alongside its slightly smaller twin peak of Machhindragad. It looks like an imposing challenge to hike to the top, and, indeed, the last stretches involve some rock climbing and scrambling, but many local people tackle the hike, and it is perfectly attainable if you are reasonably fit. For once here is a hike that is popular during monsoon season when the jungle bursts into life with the arrival of the rains, although it does make climbing, and holding on to the slippery rock surfaces in particular, more difficult.

At the top of 2,135-foot-high (651 m) Gorakhgad, you'll find a small fort and a temple, as well as several large caves. The main draw, though, is the truly breathtaking 360-degree view of the surrounding countryside, with imposing mountain ranges visible in every direction.

The trek starts from the village of Dehri, near the Gorakhshanath temple. Before long, you reach a small plateau where you can take a breather and enjoy good views of the surrounding plains. After an hour or so of fairly tough climbing and scrambling across some scree, another plateau offers a second welcome resting place. From here you can also see the fort and temple on top of Gorakhgad.

The final stretch up to the summit involves some precipitous climbing, using hand- and footholds carved into the rock, and this is not a climb that anyone who suffers from vertigo would look forward to. But it does give you a great sense of satisfaction to arrive at the top and marvel at the views of the mountains and plains that surround you. **MG**

"The hike goes through one of the lushest jungles in the region. Hiking in the monsoon season is the outstanding feature of the trek."

www.indiahikes.in

⊡ Gorakhgad attracts climbers from around the world to its verdant, green pinnacles.

Brahmagiri Trek Karnataka, India

Start/End Iruppu Falls   Distance 11.3 miles (18 km)   Time 8 hours   Grade Moderate
Type Mountain trail   Map goo.gl/kOu86Y

Brahmagiri Hill is a holy peak in the Brahmagiri Mountains on the border between the states of Karnataka and Kerala in southern India, measuring 5,276 feet (1,608 m) high. The Brahmagiri trek passes through dense mountain forests, which make it slow going, but it isn't overly strenuous for anyone who is reasonably fit, although there is a very steep uphill climb as you approach the peak. The hike combines the shadowy beauty of the forest with fabulous mountain views and also takes you into the Brahmagiri Wildlife Sanctuary, where you will almost certainly see wild elephants and other animals.

Iruppu Falls is the usual starting point for the round trip up to Brahmagiri Hill. These scenic falls can get very busy with pilgrims coming to visit the nearby Rameshwara Temple, a well-known temple to the god Shiva only 1.25 miles (2 km) away and connected to the falls via an easy path. Most people visit the falls and return; far fewer take the mountain and forest trails to climb to the top of Brahmagiri.

Parts of the trail lead through thick grasslands, and here, as well as in the forest, you need to be prepared for leeches—they are the less attractive aspect of the local wildlife, but they will soon be forgotten when you get your first thrilling sight of the herds of elephants that live in the sanctuary. There is a lesser chance of seeing tigers, although they do live here; other creatures to watch out for include deer, macaques, wild dogs, otter, giant squirrels, and beautiful green-winged emerald doves. There are snakes, too, including king cobras, so take care when setting out on this short but remarkable trek. **MG**

⊡ This is one of Karnataka's most popular trails.

Chitwan National Park Walking Safari Narayani, Nepal

Start/End Jungle Safari Lodge   **Distance** Various   **Time** Various   **Grade** Easy to moderate
Type Open grasslands, forest trails   **Info** goo.gl/B64pw4

The Chitwan National Park was the first national park in Nepal and was almost immediately designated a UNESCO World Heritage Site. It is one of the major attractions of the country, which, given how stunning Nepal is, is quite an accolade. It is home to tigers and leopards, as well as bears, rhinos, crocodiles, and an astonishing variety of birds and butterflies. A walking wildlife safari here is very different from (but every bit as appealing as) a safari in Africa, the difference being that here you are in a subtropical monsoon climate. Mid-June to around mid-September is when most of the annual rainfall happens, so this is definitely the period to avoid.

The varying terrain means that hikes here can be anything from easy strolls on level ground to tougher climbs with numerous ascents and descents. The park ranges in height from 330 feet (100 m) to 2,674 feet (815 m) above sea level and covers an area of 360 square miles (932 sq km), a landscape of mixed grasslands, forests, marshlands, and mountains.

An essential stop should be the elephant breeding center, where you can get close-up views of the gentle giants that are bred here to provide animals for the popular elephant safaris, which you can easily combine with hikes in the park. There is also a crocodile breeding center. The park is renowned for its programs to protect three of its star attractions: the one-horned rhinoceros, the royal Bengal tiger, and the gharial crocodile. Tiger sightings are rare, but glimpses of wild rhino, which often venture close to the park's villages, will be one of the highlights of a visit to this special part of Nepal. **MG**

⬆ One of the rope bridges in Chitwan National Park.

Shilin Stone Forest

Yunnan, China

Start/End Main entrance, Stone Forest scenic area **Distance** Various **Time** Various **Grade** Easy **Type** Open and wooded trails **Info** goo.gl/AlSn15

China is full of remarkable landscapes and striking features that you find nowhere else on Earth. One of these is definitely the Stone Forest, or Shilin, about 75 miles (120 km) from Kunming, the capital of Yunnan province. Being so close to a major city, it is a popular day-trip destination, as well as a fascinating area for hiking.

Although most visitors don't venture too far from the well-trodden paths, the Stone Forest is made up of several different areas covering 140 square miles (363 sq km) altogether, so there are plenty of places to explore well away from other visitors. Within the area you will find caves, lakes, and waterfalls, as well as the different sections of stone forest. There are also hotels nearby so you can stay locally and go out hiking at any time rather than be dependent on a tour bus.

The limestone formations of the stone forest seem to jut out of the earth like a series of needles or stalagmites, and they do indeed form forests of stone in an array of shapes and sizes. Wandering the trails that wind through the various stone formations, the landscape seems at times like the surface of a distant planet; at others you are reminded of Stonehenge in England. But even Stonehenge is "modern" by comparison, since these formations are thought to have been created more than 270 million years ago, when the sea retreated and left limestone rocks behind for the wind and rain to carve into natural sculptures. The unusual formations of the stone forest have been regarded as one of the world's great wonders, ever since they were discovered at the time of the Ming Dynasty—and they remain just as wondrous today. **MG**

"Walking through the Stone Forest, visitors marvel at the natural stone masterpieces and are bewitched by the intricate formations."

www.china.org.cn

← Some of the stone formations are 100 feet (30 m) tall.

↑ The Stone Forest is part of the South China Karst, a UNESCO World Heritage Site.

Li River Guangxi, China

Start Yandi Dock **End** Xingping **Distance** Various **Time** 1 day–1 week **Grade** Easy
Type Riverside trails **Info** goo.gl/AS1OOD

The Li River has been called the most beautiful river in China, and the remarkably shaped karst hills that frame it are among the most unique landscapes in the country. Weathering has sculpted the limestone rocks into all manner of strange shapes, and a cruise between the city of Guilin and the small town of Yangshuo is a hugely popular trip. Even better, though, is to hike the riverside trails, which will bring you into more direct contact with this achingly lovely landscape and constitutes a far more serene way of enjoying this laid-back rural area than simply passing through it all cocooned on a boat.

There are plenty of walking options to choose from, depending on how much time you have available and where you want to start and end the hike. You can hire local guides, join an organized hiking excursion, or simply do it by yourself. One of the best stretches is between Yandi Dock, near Guilin, and the town of Xingping, which takes five to six hours and passes some of the river's most impressive scenery. From Xingping it's easy to get back to Guilin or to go on to Yangshuo.

Hiking here isn't just about seeing the unusual hills, though. Stretches of the walk will take you through bamboo forests, past orchards and rice fields, and through little rural villages—and you will have a chance to meet local cormorant fishermen. This traditional way of fishing, from small boats and using a cormorant, is one of the most distinctive sights on the Li River, and to watch the men at work, against the backdrop of the haunting hills, is a truly memorable experience. **MG**

⬆ A cormorant fisherman on the Li River.

Dragon's Backbone Rice Terraces Guangxi, China

Start/End Longsheng   **Distance** Various   **Time** Various   **Grade** Moderate   **Type** Rice terrace trails and roads   **Map** goo.gl/8hiujh

One look at the Dragon's Backbone Rice Terraces and you won't need to ask how they got their name. These remarkable terraces curve away into the distance as far as the eye can see, rippling around the hilly slopes like the back of a dragon or a mythical giant green snake. It is nigh-on impossible not to take photograph after photograph of the astonishing views that this trail provides, where man met with nature and produced something both useful and extraordinary.

The terraces were begun in the thirteenth century and new ones were constantly added, serving the villagers well through the centuries. For some years now, in addition to providing the annual crop of rice, they have also brought visitors to the area. Also known as the Longsheng Rice Terraces, or the Longi Rice Terraces, they are found near the town of Longsheng, about 56 miles (90 km) northwest of Guilin. This makes them an easy day-trip destination for visitors from the city, and that is how most people visit them, but staying in or near Longsheng itself is a much better option for enjoying the terraces on foot. They are attractive all year round, whether covered by the frosts and snow of winter, the green shoots of spring and summer, or the golden look of the rice in the fall, so walking is enjoyable in all seasons.

Another reason to stay locally and explore the terraces at leisure on foot is the opportunity it gives you to spend some time with the local people. Mostly of the Zhuang ethnic group, they have a great folk tradition, wear colorful clothing, and are noted for their wine making. Staying with a local family, too, can turn a visit here a very personal experience. **MG**

⊡ The terraces were built from the thirteenth century.

Pearl River Delta Greenway
Guangdong, China

Start/End Guangzhou   Distance 1,000 miles
(1,600 km) over six routes   Time Various
Grade Easy   Type Sealed pedestrian and cycleways
Info goo.gl/8MOS84

The concept of "greenways"—long, narrow ribbons of greenery that pass through an urban environment, providing recreational space for a city's inhabitants—have long been popular in the United States, which now has in excess of 1,000 greenways in more than 30 cities and 140 rural communities. It is an idea that is still relatively new to China, but the city of Guangzhou in Guangdong province is working to change that, building hundreds of miles of greenways to help connect the people of the Pearl River Delta, the low-lying region surrounding the estuary where the Pearl

"The greenways provide an ideal place for outdoor activities. . . . They play a vital role in connecting cities."

www.szdaily.com

River, the country's second largest river by volume, flows into the South China Sea.

The greenways, designed with the assistance of New York City's Institute for Transportation and Development, are not merely functional but also aesthetic, lined with trees, flower beds, fountains, and even waterfalls. It is a proactive response by the Chinese authorities to the problems of urban fragmentation and high building density, and it serves as a blueprint for greenways across the country. The Pearl River greenways will eventually stretch over more than 1,000 miles (1,600 km) and link 200 forests, parks, and conservation areas on pedestrian and bicycle paths, connecting people to nature. **BDS**

MacLehose Trail
Hong Kong, China

Start Pak Tam Chung   End Tuen Mun
Distance 62.5 miles (101 km)   Time 5 days
Grade Strenuous   Type Long-distance trail from
beaches to mountain peaks   Map goo.gl/vRgTYe

Hong Kong is so firmly associated with high-rise buildings, city buzz, and population density that it can come as a surprise to find that it also encompasses mountain peaks, deserted coastlines, and peaceful green valleys. The MacLehose Trail was opened in 1979 to help people enjoy this other Hong Kong, taking them on a long-distance hike through the New Territories, which, in fact, make up 83 percent of Hong Kong. The city is but a small part of it.

Because of the undulating nature of the terrain, it is a tough hike, but definitely a rewarding one. The landscape is varied, and the trail passes several of Hong Kong's highest peaks: the highest point is Tai Mo Shan (Big Hat Mountain), at 3,140 feet (957 m). It stands in Tai Mo Shan Country Park, just one of the eight country parks that the trail passes through. Mostly, the hike takes you on relatively quiet paths, although there are a few stretches on paved highways, a necessary evil in order to join all the points of interest together.

In all, there are ten separate stages of the trail, ranging from easy to strenuous and from about two to five hours of walking. Unless you can organize transport at certain points, it is best to try to tackle the whole trail in one go as there are sections where it is a long way to the nearest road.

Along the way you will hike over beaches, along mountain passes, down into valleys, and through quiet villages, some of them almost deserted—and all of these a long way from the busy, densely packed city and its landscape of towering skyscrapers. The MacLehose Trail is an experience of Hong Kong that few people ever get. **MG**

Hong Kong Trail
Hong Kong, China

Start Victoria Peak   **End** Big Wave Bay
Distance 31 miles (49.8 km)   **Time** 2 days
Grade Strenuous   **Type** Long-distance footpath
Map goo.gl/5vzOpa

Hiking the Hong Kong Trail is the best way to see the most attractive parts of Hong Kong Island, as it has been designed to take you through all five of the island's country parks. The trail meanders around and makes what is actually quite a small island seem much larger.

It is divided into eight separate sections, so you can tackle them individually if you don't have the time or the energy to do the whole trail in one challenging walk. It takes a little planning, as there are no campsites or other places to stay along the way, so you'll need to think about transport and overnight accommodation in advance. No section will take longer than three hours to walk, and some are naturally easier than others, but to do the whole trail will take at least two full days.

The trail's first section begins at iconic Victoria Peak, which rises to 1,811 feet (552 m) on the west of the island, so before you even begin the walk, you get some fabulous views from the slopes of the highest peak on the island (the summit is closed to the public and has a telecommunications tower on it). The peak is also easily accessible by public transport and about seven million people visit each year. By setting off on the first part of the trail, though, you will soon leave the crowds behind as you circle around the peak and enjoy more fabulous views and finally reach Pok Fu Lam Reservoir.

The trail then takes you to the slopes of the island's second highest mountain, 1,745-foot (532-m) Mount Parker, and around several other peaks, finally depositing you on the eastern side of the island, at Big Wave Bay for a welcome dip in the sea. **MG**

"There's a beautiful rural world within a hiking boot's throw of Hong Kong's downtown."

www.discoverhongkong.com

⊡ From Victoria Peak to Big Wave Bay through five parks, the Hong Kong Trail leaves nothing to chance.

Stone Dream Valley Trail
Chiayi, Taiwan

Start/End Immortals Dream Garden, Fengshan
Distance 3 miles (4.8 km)   Time 3 hours
Grade Strenuous   Type Mountain trail
Info goo.gl/ZMuzKt

> *"Fengshan remains a very out-of-way kind of place, sitting at the foot of the breathtaking cliffs of Tashan."*

Richard Foster, travel writer

⬆ In Stone Dream Valley ancient trees grow out of vertical rock walls.

You will find the towering cliffs of Tashan in the geographical center of Taiwan, a little to the north of Alishan—indeed, the name means "Tower Mountain" and on its slopes is a hanging valley known as the Stone Dream Valley. It is a dream-like landscape, a hidden paradise of palm trees and tea plantations, of caverns and waterfalls, mist-shrouded mountains and tropical forests sticky with heat and humidity.

To get to Stone Dream Valley you must first hike to the evocatively named Immortals Dream Garden from the village of Fengshan, clambering over rock slides and wobbling across suspension bridges. Here you can spend the night and enjoy beautiful valley views, before embarking on the short but tough hike into Stone Dream Valley. This allows you an early start and the chance to get back to Fengshan later the same day, rather than trying to tackle the lengthy challenge in one go.

There are two trails into the valley, and it is best to go in on the upper trail and save the easier lower trail for coming back out. The path will take you through woods and by streams, over rocks and along sheer cliffs until you get into Stone Dream Valley itself. Here, a stream runs over the stones that give the valley its name and gathers together in numerous still rock pools. The water creates an abundance of plant life in this strange, ethereal place, which has an aura of otherworldly mysticism that recalls the imaginary world conjured up by J.R.R. Tolkien in his novel, *The Lord of the Rings* (1954).

Returning on the lower trail you'll see more streams, caves, sheer cliff faces, and trees of gigantic size—a dream of a valley. **MG**

Piagol Valley
Jeollanam-do, South Korea

Start Yeongok Hiking Information Center
End Piagol Samgeori Distance 5.5 miles
(8.8 km) Time 5 hours Grade Moderate
Type Forest paths Map goo.gl/dLkiYW

The Piagol Valley provides one of South Korea's premier autumn trails and is one of the best places in Asia for visitors to see the fall colors in full splendor. The valley is a fabulous sight at any time of year, with streams flowing gently through thick woods, but it is best to go in late October, if you can, to see the display, when the leaves are likely to be at their most spectacular. The annual Piagol Autumn Foliage Festival celebrates this remarkable transformation from green into a palette of rich hues. The Piagol Valley is renowned for the way in which the leaves turn a truly vivid red, with gentler tones of orange and gold adding to the visual kaleidoscope.

The valley lies between the peaks of Nogodan and Banya, on the slopes of 6,283-foot-tall (1,915 m) Jirisan Mountain, home to several Buddhist temples and the source of many local legends. The path that leads up the valley is easy enough to hike, but you need to allow plenty of time as there will be numerous photographic opportunities along the way. The name of the valley can be translated as "Millet Field Valley": pi-bat-gol is the name of the predominant crop that used to be farmed here in the past, and the word became slightly corrupted along the way, changing to "Piagol."

It is a 5.5-mile (8.8-km) walk from the information center through Jikjeon village, Pyogomakteo, and the Piagol shelter to Piagol Samgeori (or you can drive to Jikjeon and save an hour's walk, if you prefer). The trail is a flattish one that takes you past ponds and springs, with the final segment to Piagol Samgeori a steep ascent that deposits you on the main ridge of Jirisan Mountain. **MG**

"Jirisan is perhaps Korea's most famous (and beloved) mountain. For hikers it also boasts spectacular views."

www.discoveringkorea.com

⤒ It is said there are three things that are red in Piagol—the leaves, the ponds, and the people.

Nakasendo Way
Tokyo to Kyoto, Japan

Start Tokyo   **End** Kyoto   **Distance** 334 miles (538 km)   **Time** 7–8 weeks
Grade Strenuous   **Type** Long-distance trail
Info goo.gl/A3ykzD

During the Japanese Edo period, between the seventeenth and the nineteenth centuries, there were two routes that connected the main cities of Tokyo and Kyoto: one was the Tokaido, or Eastern Sea Route; the other was the Nakasendo, the "road through the mountains," the better and far more popular route, which continues today and has been transformed into one of Japan's most popular long-distance trails.

Over time, parts of the original route fell into disrepair, and other parts were replaced by modern highways that strayed from the original path. Some sections have now been restored, and it is once again possible to take the ancient road through the mountains, hiking from village to village and getting a taste of the traditional, more rural Japanese way of life, away from the neon lights of its urban centers. The route passes through almost seventy towns and villages between Tokyo and Kyoto and, while walking its entire length is certainly an option if you have eight weeks to spare, experiencing selected segments with a guide from Walk Japan, who can bring the history alive, is an ideal compromise.

You will be rewarded with hikes through the Kiso Valley—one of the most scenic sections of the trail, with its rugged mountainous landscapes—and you can stay at traditional inns, pass beautiful lakes, and, when in season, see woods filled with cherry blossoms. But you will also hike through sections of the modern cities. As well as connecting the cities of Kyoto and Tokyo, the Nakasendo Way seamlessly joins Japan's past with its present. This is not only an exceptional hike, but also a remarkable cultural experience. **MG**

"The Nakasendo Way follows the most enjoyable, scenic, and best-preserved parts of the old road."

www.walkjapan.com

⬅ The route passes through a fascinating granite bed of rocks in the Kiso River valley.

⬆ Sections of the original trail are continuing to be unearthed and restored.

Kyushu Olle Trails Kumamoto, Japan

Start/End Various   **Distance** Various   **Time** Various   **Grade** Easy to moderate
Type Forest and mountain paths, beaches   **Info** goo.gl/POope7

The concept of the *olle*—a hike that is not only about being on a trail but is designed to immerse the individual in the culture and history of the land and to encourage interaction with the people who live there—originated in South Korea, on its southern island of Jeju, in 2007. Kyushu, the closest of Japan's four main islands to South Korea, has always relied on tourism from that country to bolster its economy and to help make up for the fact that of the 100 most famous mountains in Japan, which the Japanese walk so obsessively, only six are in Kyushu. So the *olle* concept was introduced to Kyushu in 2009, and its success since then has been nothing less than staggering.

More than 800,000 people walked on one of the twenty-four *olle* trails in Kyushu in 2012, and Kyushu Olle, the organization responsible for the establishment and growth of Kyushu's *olle* trails, is now in partnership with South Korea's Jeju Olle, sharing its logo and distinctive guidepost ribbons.

Kyushu *olle* routes include the Takeo course—a town with hot springs an hour from Fukuoka—which is renowned for its 3,000-year-old camphor trees and its 400-year-old ceramics industry; the Kirishima-Myoken course, through dense cedar forests on a path first walked by Sakamoto Ryoma and his bride, Oryo, in the late 1800s (Japan's first modern "honeymoon path"); and the Ibusuki course, which begins at Japan's southernmost railway station and takes you through farmland and along the black sand beach of Nagasakibana to the conical Mount Kaimon, breathing fresh life into Kyushu's proud past. **BDS**

⬆ Kyushu's *olle* trails bring the island's past to life.

Khongoryn Els Gobi Desert, Mongolia

Start/End Ger camps near Ongii Khiid   Distance Various   Time Various   Grade Moderate
Type Sand dunes   Info goo.gl/TVkr5A

As far as adventure experiences go, it is hard to top hiking in the Gobi Desert. The biggest desert in Asia covers an estimated area of about 500,000 square miles (1,295,000 sq km) in Mongolia and China, and just to walk in even one tiny corner of it is a remarkable experience that will give you a feel for the immensity of the desert.

The Gobi Desert, like other deserts, is home to several different ecosystems, and only certain parts feature the characteristic sweeping sand dunes that seem to roll on into infinity. One such dune area can be found at Khongoryn Els, which is part of the Gobi Gurvansaikhan National Park, the largest national park in Mongolia at the northern edge of this immense desert. Khongoryn Els is a popular and easy access spot for the most dramatic portion of the desert's dune system, yet most people who come here make only a brief visit, perhaps walking for an hour or so. The best experience is to arrange to spend two or three days hiking away from the busiest areas and getting a true feel for the majesty and power of the desert.

Another reason for spending longer is that the best times to experience the desert are at sunrise and sunset, when the drama of the dunes is emphasized by the angled intensity of the light. A longer visit also gives you more time to discover the flora and fauna of the desert, but you are unlikely to see the elusive snow leopard that can be found here. The name Khongoryn Els means "Singing Sand," and once you have heard the desert "sing," the experience will stay with you forever. **MG**

⊤ The dunes here rise to 1,000 feet (305 m) high.

Valley of Geysers
Kamchatka, Russia

Start/End Petropavlovsk
Distance 3.7 miles (6 km)   **Time** 2 hours
Grade Easy   **Type** Open, volcanic terrain
Info goo.gl/aHb3nf

If you're walking through the Valley of Geysers on Russia's Kamchatka Peninsula, one of the world's last true wildernesses—with an area larger than that of Germany and Austria combined—let no one question your determination. This is not an easy place to get to. Firstly, it's a flight to Tokyo or Vladivostok, depending upon which direction you're coming from, then a flight to the peninsula's capital of Petropavlovsk. Once you've done walking the backstreets of this charming city on Avacha Bay—with its hills dotted with pre-Communist–era timber houses—it's a final bone-shaking flight on an old Soviet MI-8 cargo helicopter—likely to be the ride of your life—north to the remote Valley of Geysers, a UNESCO World Heritage Site, for a walk that will probably seem to be a rather sedate affair in comparison to the journey. But thinking that would be a mistake as big as the landscape that surrounds you.

After shoehorning your way out of the helicopter's cargo area, you step out into the world's second largest area of geysers, discovered by Russian scientist Tatyana Ustinova in 1941. In 2007, a massive mudflow buried two-thirds of the valley's ninety geysers, although Velikan Geyser, the valley's largest, was spared and is still active, as are many others. You can walk as you please here, geysers and time being your only considerations. Well, those and the Kamchatkan brown bear. Best guess is there are 16,000 of them on the peninsula, but nobody really knows. There are hardly any roads to go out on and count them. Don't bother looking for cairns or waymarkers either. Just try not to step into a geyser or come between a mother and her cub. This is Russia, after all. **BDS**

> *"Kamchatka's protected territories, its reserves, parks, and sanctuaries, hold some of the Earth's most exquisite natural wonders."*
>
> Julia Phillips, *Moscow Times*

⊡ Russia's spectacular Valley of Geysers, famed for its steaming hot springs, is a natural wonder of the world.

Kachin Tribal Village Trek
Kachin, Myanmar

Start/End Upper Shangaung village
Distance 32 miles (51.4 km)   Time 10 days
Grade Strenuous   Type Mountain trails
Map goo.gl/BVklrd

At the foot of the eastern end of the Himalayas, in northern Myanmar, the Kachin Hills house some of the most diverse ethnic groups in Asia. The Kachin people have adapted to life in an area split by mountain ranges and ravaged by war. The steep hills and deep valleys cover an area of 19,177 square miles (49,670 sq km), and the highest point is Bumhpa Bum in the Kumon Bum Mountains, at 11,191 feet (3,411 m).

Although the region is remote and the villages are peaceful, the inhabitants are accustomed to welcoming adventurous travelers and greet them with the traditional hospitality that Myanmar is famous for. Spending some time in the area allows you to hike from village to village, enjoying the simple guesthouse accommodation and discovering the differences between the various Kachin people. While some of the hikes can be strenuous, others are more moderate, and along the way you'll get to see mountain streams and waterfalls, crystal-clear lakes, fast-flowing rivers, and whitewater rapids.

But the main appeal is to meet and learn about the Kachin people. It is important to remember that there are various different ethnic groups covered by the name Kachin, and you should try to find out which group people fall into. Hiring a guide who can translate for you as well as lead you on hikes is the best approach. The people wear colorful costumes, and although some are Buddhists, the majority are actually Christian, which is just one of the many surprises in this area full of delights, with its natural mountainous landscape of snowcapped peaks and unique communities who have lived here for thousands of years. **MG**

Kalaw to Inle Lake Trek
Shan, Myanmar

Start Kalaw   End Inle Lake
Distance 24 miles (38.6 km)   Time 2–3 days
Grade Moderate   Type Hill trails
Map goo.gl/N5CPvN

To walk among the tribal hill villages of Myanmar is an experience in itself, but this particular trek is scenically very special, ending at the country's second largest lake. Inle Lake, surrounded by mountains, and one of the highest lakes in Myanmar. The sight and gentle sounds of the fishermen on its waters create a rare sense of serenity. Another reason for the walk's popularity is that there are two main routes, and some other options, too, so you can make the trek last for two or three days, depending on your fitness level and how much time you have. You will need to take a local

"The air is cool, the atmosphere calm, … [and] the hills offer some of the best trekking in Myanmar."

Lonely Planet

guide, but these can be found easily in the charming old colonial hill station of Kalaw—actually they will probably find you first. You can also arrange to have your bags transported to Inle Lake, if you don't wish to return to Kalaw.

Whichever route you take, you will have the chance to stay overnight in one or more of the tribal villages; you will see people going about their daily lives in fairly primitive conditions, so be prepared. There are several different ethnic groups in the area, including the Taung Yo, the Danu, the Palaung, and the Pa'O (distinguishable by their orange turbans). There is also the chance to visit and stay at a monastery—an opportunity not to be missed. **MG**

Son Doong Cave Quang Binh, Vietnam

Start/End Cave entrance **Distance** 10 miles (16 km) **Time** 1 day **Grade** Moderate
Type Cave trails **Info** goo.gl/aXZUCm

Can you really hike in a cave? Well, the answer is yes if it is the world's largest cave, measuring more than 5.5 miles (8.9 km) long, high enough to house a 40-floor skyscraper, and big enough to contain a section of jungle with trees up to 100 feet (30 m) tall, complete with a river running through it.

The Son Doong Cave was discovered in 1991 but was kept secret by the local farmers who found it. Its existence was revealed only in 2009, and in 2013 it received its first visitors. It provides a truly unique hiking opportunity below the Earth's surface for anyone strong enough and willing to make the 260-foot (79-m) rope descent into the cave. The single rope currently offers the only way to get in.

The cave is located in the Phong Nha-Ke Bang National Park, which is about 300 miles (490 km) south of Hanoi. You should also allow time to explore the rest of the park, which contains more than 300 other caves and is noted for its lush limestone landscape featuring wooded hills, forests, and slow-flowing rivers. One of the other caves, the Phong Nha, was previously the biggest cave in Vietnam—but only until the Son Doong Cave, which is five times as large, was discovered.

Son Doong is now Phong Nha-Ke Bang's star attraction. The name literally means "mountain river cave," and it is estimated that it was formed two to five million years ago. A partial collapse of the roof lets in the light, which is how the jungle began to grow inside, and monkeys, flying foxes, and hornbills can now be found in the cave. Take a hike deep into this remarkable lost world. **MG**

⬆ Enter the dark world of Vietnam's "mountain river cave."

Banaue Rice Terraces Ifugao, Philippines

Start/End Banaue   **Distance** Various   **Time** Various   **Grade** All grades   **Type** Dirt paths, rice terraces
Info goo.gl/z9cRen

The Banaue Rice Terraces in the mountains of Ifugao in the Philippines are both ordinary and extraordinary. For 2,000 years the people who live in the Ifugao Mountains have grown rice on these terraces that are carved out of the precipitous slopes. For them, they are practical and essential for survival, but to the rest of the world these terraces are uniquely beautiful, attracting people from all over the globe to admire them.

The rows of green rice plants, separated by the billowing lines of the access paths, are a wonderful, surreal sight. For the most complete experience, arrange to stay in one of the many villages that dot the area, such as Batad or Bangaan, so you can see the terraces in the misty early morning light and again in the evening when the sun goes down, casting shadows that emphasize the terraces' haunting beauty.

The terraces rise to an average height of about 5,000 feet (1,524 m) and were built mostly by hand—a monumental achievement that is hard to appreciate until you actually see them. They help to channel rainwater from the rain forests farther up the mountainside and to irrigate the rice. An almost infinite number of trails weaves through them and the mountain forests that separate one terrace from the next.

There are easy trails if you stick to level ground or more strenuous ones if you prefer to challenge yourself and hike up and down the mountainsides. Whichever route you choose, the experience of being in this magical landscape is something that will stay with you forever. **MG**

⬆ The rice terraces are a national cultural treasure.

Bukit Tabur
Selangor, Malaysia

Start/End Kampung Klang Gates   Distance 3 miles
(4.8 km)   Time Half a day   Grade Moderate to
strenuous   Type Forest and mountain path, steps, fixed
ropes   Map goo.gl/Qjz2VF

*"The sheer size of the ridge
provides a dramatic backdrop
to Kuala Lumpur."*

www.naturemalaysia.com

⬆ The Bukit Tabur trail runs over the world's longest
quartz ridge.

A series of recent accidents has seen a shadow fall
over the hiking trails at Bukit Tabur. Hikers have died
falling from the ridge, and others have been seriously
injured in a string of incidents, and as a consequence
the authorities have imposed a strict permit system.
Anyone found on the trail without a permit is now
threatened with prosecution. No climbing is currently
allowed during the week—only at weekends—and
going with an experienced guide is recommended.

So why are people still determined to visit the
place and walk its trails? Bukit Tabur, a prominent
semicircle of quartz cliffs rising out of thick forest at
the edge of the city, is a well-known spot among
locals and visitors to the capital, Kuala Lumpur. It is
claimed to be the longest and oldest ridge of quartz-
rich rock in the world. Its highest point is less than
1,640 feet (500 m) and the hard-to-find trailhead is
only 12 miles (19 km) away from the city center, so it
has become a popular day-trip destination. The path
winds between exposed clusters of crystalline rock
and dense vegetation. It can be very narrow at times,
and occasionally there are serious exposed drops on
both sides. Some steep sections have fixed ropes to
help climbers, and there are a few areas near the
summit where you will need to scramble.

Walkers are attracted by the views over the
city, the reservoirs in the rain forest below, and the
flora and fauna, which include a colony of wild
mountain goats, thirty different species of frogs, and
some plants that grow nowhere else in the world.
But with the recent record of accidents, it's clearly also
a walk to be taken seriously and tackled with the
utmost care. **SH**

Headhunter's Trail
Sarawak, Malaysia

Start Kuala Medawai park ranger office   End Limbang
Distance 16 miles (25.7 km)   Time 4 days   Grade Easy
to moderate   Type Forest trails and narrow wooden
boardwalks   Map goo.gl/4h1dsh

It isn't nearly as scary as it sounds, but 100 years ago this trail was no place for hiking. The local Kayan people, fierce warriors of the Orang Ulu ethnic group, have lived in longhouses along the banks of the Baram, Reiang, and Tabau rivers in the interior of the modern Malaysian state of Sarawak for countless generations—and they were headhunters. Now on the Headhunter's Trail you can walk along some of the old tracks that they used in their near-constant clashes with other indigenous groups.

The only real sense you get now of this violent past is if one of the older Kayans shows you a tattoo depicting the heads they once regularly took as part of the spoils of war, or when you see the skulls still displayed as you pass through the villages located in the UNESCO World Heritage–listed Gunung Mulu National Park. This is a fascinating region of karst formations and mountainous equatorial rain forests, as well as a wondrous system of limestone caves, including Lang Cave and the phenomenal 1.2-mile-long (2 km) Deer Cave, which you access via a 1.9-mile (3-km) plank walk through primary rain forest over peat and alluvial swamps.

A challenging walk of four to five hours up Gunung Api leads to its sea of famously jagged limestone pinnacles—a forest of stone—and the following day a 7-mile (11.3-km) slog takes you through the jungle along the infamous Headhunter's Trail, used by the Kayan people to raid the longhouses of the Murut people along the Limbang River. From there, you take a boat and go up the river to the town of Limbang, thirty minutes from the Brunei capital of Bandar Seri Begawan. **BDS**

Gunung Leuser National Park   Sumatra, Indonesia

Start/End Bukit Lawang
Distance Various   Time 1–3 days
Grade Easy to moderate   Type Jungle trails
Info goo.gl/hw8nTA

Gunung Leuser National Park in northern Sumatra is best known for the Bukit Lawang Orangutan Sanctuary where you can see orangutans being fed and trained for release or returned to the wild. You can go on jungle hikes in the national park that enable you to spot these remarkable creatures in the wild.

Bukit Lawang is a good base from which you can organize jungle treks of varying lengths, usually one to three days with overnight camping and using a local guide (highly recommended; unless you know the trails you can easily get lost). You also need a permit to

---

"This biosphere reserve covers a vast area of tropical rain forest … with a range of ecosystems."

www.unesco.org

---

enter the national park. Other places where you can hire guides include Ketembe, Kedah, and Tangkahan.

The park covers an area of 3,061 square miles (7,928 sq km), and its highest point is Mount Leuser, rising to 11,093 feet (3,381 m)—one of only two places where you can still find orangutans, since much of their habitat has been lost due to logging. The park also acts as a refuge for other rare animals, including the Sumatran elephant, Sumatran rhino, and Sumatran tiger. However, you are most likely to see orangutans, although they are wary of humans. Spending a night in the jungle is a memorable experience, and trekking through it will give you a chance to see a remote and extraordinary part of the world. **MG**

Waterfall Trail

Lombok, Indonesia

Start/End Senaru **Distance** 2 miles
(3.2 km) **Time** 1.5 hours **Grade** Easy
Type Stairs, mountain paths, river crossing
Map goo.gl/CvcsRk

Just getting to the beginning of the Waterfall Trail on the north coast of the Indonesian island of Lombok is an adventure in itself, even more so if you hire a scooter and go there yourself instead of paying for a driver and car. The coastal road is virtually the only sealed road available, so getting lost is almost impossible, even in the absence of anything resembling an accurate map of the area. Just continue along the road until you arrive at Senaru village, where you can park your scooter, cross the road, and begin the walk to the two jungle waterfalls that tumble down the flanks of the foothills of Mount Rinjani, Indonesia's second highest mountain at 12,224 feet (3,726 m).

You will be told that you need to take a guide, but, in fact, the path to the waterfalls is well worn, and there should be enough tourists on the way with their own guides to provide you with an unpaid escort. The first waterfall, Sendang Gile, with its 100-foot-high (30.5 m) drop is at the end of a ten-minute walk down a concrete staircase that takes you deep into the rainforest. While beautiful, it is only a teaser for what follows.

The second waterfall, Tiu Kelep, is spectacularly set deep within a shaded gully, reached after a half-hour walk from the first on an easy-to-follow trail. On the way, you twice have to cross a shallow but swift-flowing, boulder-strewn river before the final approach to the waterfall's base, where you can strip down to your swimsuit and take a plunge in the thundering, swimming pool–sized water hole, your senses assaulted by the pounding water and the tropical spray that envelops you. **BDS**

> *"It is said locally that every time you swim behind the main waterfall of Tiu Kelep you become a year younger."*

www.lomboklinks.com

⤴ The general editor's son, Jackson Stone, admiring a waterfall on the lower flanks of Mount Rinjani.

Komodo National Park
Komodo Island, Indonesia

Start/End Entrance, Komodo Game Reserve
Distance Various **Time** Various
Grade Easy **Type** Island trails
Info goo.gl/tJssCh

For anyone who loves both wildlife and walking, there are certain places that are sure to be on the bucket list. These include seeing the Galapagos Islands and the plains of Africa—and visiting Komodo Island in Indonesia to see the world's largest lizards, the fearsome Komodo dragons.

Komodo National Park was created in 1980 to help protect these creatures, which, although they look as if they need no protection, are, in fact, threatened. There are only 4,000 or 5,000 of them remaining, and they died out on nearby Padar Island in 1975. The concern is that out of the dragon's entire population, only about 350 are breeding females. While the dragons have been turned into something of a tourist attraction, with organized feedings attracting huge crowds, increased research and the maintenance of a controlled habitat help these remarkable reptiles to survive.

If you want to hike in the national park, it takes a little planning, as accommodation is limited to staying in rangers' huts, which must be booked in advance. An easier option is to rent a boat locally, since the boats are allowed to anchor offshore and thereby provide a primitive floating guesthouse if you don't mind sleeping on the deck. This allows you to hike on Komodo, Rinca, and Padar, the islands that make up the national park, and to enjoy them at dawn and dusk, away from the crowds of visitors. With a knowledgeable local guide, you should be able to watch the Komodo dragon undisturbed. To see this throwback to the age of the dinosaurs in its natural habitat is one of the finest wildlife experiences in the world. **MG**

"On the equator but very arid and hilly, Komodo has amazing scenery and the largest lizards in the world."

www.komodo.travel

⬆ A guide should accompany you at all times in the rugged volcanic terrain of Komodo National Park.

Bibbulmun Track Western Australia, Australia

Start Kalamunda   **End** Albany   **Distance** 623 miles (1,003 km)   **Time** 7–9 weeks   **Grade** Moderate
Type Open terrain, rock, and dirt trails   **Info** goo.gl/XTv75a

First suggested as a possibility by walking groups the Perth Bushwalkers and the Western Walking Club in 1972, the Bibbulmun Track has since become one of the world's great long-distance walks, beginning in the Perth suburb of Kalamunda and winding its way through the Wandoo woodlands and the mixed jarrah and dense forests of the north, all the way to the white karri forests of Albany's sweeping and largely undeveloped southern coastline around Walpole and Denmark. There, the forest transitions into the giant canopies of the Red Tingles, the world's oldest living eucalypts.

Passing through some of the finest scenery in the southwest, the track is named after the Aboriginal Bibbulmun tribe, the region's original inhabitants, and was officially opened in 1979. It passes through twelve Western Australian towns and is sprinkled with

no fewer than forty-eight campsites. Along the way you will see vast areas of granite outcrops, wetlands, and swamps with their white-flowered paperbarks, banksias, tea trees, and the rare Warren River cedar.

A major upgrade to the track in the 1990s not only significantly altered its original route, but also gave it a distinctly "Appalachian" feel with the construction of a series of three-sided lean-tos, each one spaced within a day's walk of the next, with rainwater tanks, picnic tables, and fire pits. The walk is a mostly level one with only a few climbs on forgiving gradients, such as the approach to Mount Dale and the summit of Mount Cuthbert, Perth's premier slab climbing venue, as well as nearby Mount Vincent with its views to distant and very flat horizons. **BDS**

⤒ Western Australia's classic, from the woods to the sea.

Larapinta Trail Northern Territory, Australia

Start Telegraph Station   **End** Mount Sonder   **Distance** 138 miles (222 km)   **Time** 12–14 days
Grade Easy to moderate   **Type** Quartzite, rock   **Info** goo.gl/e2OuBv

Now recognized as one of Australia's most spectacular inland trails, the Larapinta Trail was opened in stages from 1989, and today you can walk along the entirety of its twelve sections, starting at the old Telegraph Station just north of Alice Springs, in the heart of the country's "Red Center." It continues along the backbone of the MacDonnell Ranges in the West MacDonnell National Park, ending with a comfortable six-hour ascent up the eastern flank of Mount Sonder, the trail's high point at 4,527 feet (1,380 m).

The entire trail is accessible by 4x4, making it easy to traverse as little or as much of it as you like in a shortish walking season that begins in June and ends in August. On the way you'll pass through many of the sort of features that give inland Australia so much of its allure: arid mountains, steep red-rock gorges, dry creek beds, and the occasional water hole, always

making the most of the terrain and its raft of spectacular viewpoints. Most of your time is spent walking on quartzite, the product of what geologists call the Alice Springs Orogeny, a rare mountain-building episode in the continental plate, raising the land here when the surrounding Amadeus Basin contained a vast inland sea.

It has taken a long time to "trail build" the Larapinta Trail in the heart of the world's oldest continent. Every landform you see is ancient, its fractured, angled rock formations straight out of prehistory. And the campfire tales told by the local Arrernte people, the land's traditional custodians, make sure the evenings are as memorable as the walk itself. **BDS**

⤒ Sift through ancient sediments on the oldest continent.

Valley of the Winds Northern Territory, Australia

Start/End Kata Tjuta parking lot   **Distance** 4.5 miles (7.2 km)   **Time** 3–4 hours   **Grade** Moderate
Type Rocky desert path   **Map** goo.gl/c4eCxD

Kata Tjuta (many heads) is the traditional Aboriginal name for the grouping of a large, panoramic swathe of domed rock formations more commonly known as the Olgas, formed from sediments similar to granite that were generated from the coarse-grained Mount Currie Conglomerate some 550 million years ago.

Aborigines believe the great snake king Wanambi once lived on the summit of Mount Olga, itself 98 feet (30 m) higher than Uluru (Ayers Rock), which is only 25 miles (40 km) to the west. Wanambi only came down from it in search of water during the dry season. There are many myths associated with this dream-like place, but the Anangu people, who have lived here for the past 22,000 years, rarely share them with outsiders, a reluctance that only increases the air of mystery you begin to feel the moment you first see the outline of the thirty-six beguiling summits.

The Valley of the Winds is a full circuit walk that takes you through the middle of the Olga Gorge and around a selection of domed monoliths. Although this can be done easily in two hours, it often takes three or more because the wondrous scenery and towering rocks of up to 1,771 feet (540 m) may distract you. The path is rocky and requires a reasonable degree of fitness to negotiate, but there are various water holes to be found along the way—and some welcome distractions, including finches qand even budgies. If you do this walk in the summer, make sure you've finished it by noon. It is best to start early regardless of the season in order to witness the early morning light strike the rocks and turn them into walls of flame. **BDS**

⬆ See red rocks under blue skies at Kata Tjuta.

Tabletop Track Northern Territory, Australia

Start/End Litchfield National Park, link walk at Florence Falls **Distance** 24 miles (38.6 km) **Time** 3–5 days
Grade Moderate to strenuous **Type** Rock and dirt trails **Map** goo.gl/3OWCQD

Tabletop Track is a circular track in Litchfield National Park in Australia's Top End, an excellent long-distance bushwalk for the experienced, fit, and well-prepared bushwalker. Take a satellite phone, if you have one, or at the very least a personal locator beacon and a topographic map, and always tell someone when you are going, precisely what route you are taking, and when you plan to get back. This isn't the sort of place where you want to take a wrong turn.

The park begins some 60 miles (96 km) southwest of Darwin and is one of the jewels in Australia's national park network. The track encircles the park's central sandstone plateau, the most prominent feature, and some of the Top End's most beautiful swimming holes. It is accessible from various link walks, which means you end up walking farther than the official length of 24 miles (39 km). There are spring-fed waterfalls—such as Florence Falls and Wangi Falls—and numerous rock pools; the natural reservoirs of water in this arid land will astound you. Litchfield may be less well known that its cousin Kakadu, but it is equally spectacular with lily pads, dragonflies, orange-flowered trees, skies of the deepest blue, and, perhaps the most important thing in this part of the world, crocodile-free swimming holes. There are also several shorter walks you should do, such as the Florence Creek Walk between Florence Falls and Buley Rockhole, the Green Ant Creek Walk to the top of Tjaetaba Falls, and the Sandy Creek Walk that takes you past cycad-filled hillsides. They all take about ninety minutes each, get you out of the sun, and allow you to immerse yourself in refreshing waters. **BDS**

⬆ Discover Litchfield's magnificent Wangi Falls.

Kings Canyon Rim Walk
Northern Territory, Australia

Start/End Kings Canyon trailhead parking lot
Distance 3.5 miles (5.6 km)   Time 3–4 hours
Grade Moderate to strenuous   Type Exposed
rock and soil paths   Map goo.gl/XFB77Y

"The walk skirts the edge of Kings Canyon, allowing you to peer over sheer sandstone cliffs into the shadowy depths of the gorge."

www.australiangeographic.com.au

⇧ Kings Canyon reveals Australia's outback beauty from vantage points both high and low.

Ernest Giles, the English-born explorer and veteran of three expeditions into the heart of Australia in the 1870s, was the first European to set eyes on the magnificent Kings Canyon, which he named after the sponsor of his expedition, Fieldon King. Of the canyon he said, "Could it be transported to any civilized land, its springs, glens, gorges, ferns, zamias [cacti], and flowers would charm the eyes and hearts of toil-worn men."

The canyon was first opened to tourism in 1961 by the Cotterill family, who owned a homestead 62 miles (100 km) away—close by Australian standards. Back then, they received just a few hundred visitors a year and drove them to the canyon in a 1940s Dodge weapons carrier. Nowadays that same number of tourists arrives here every day to walk one of Australia's most spectacular rim walks. You can spend days walking its myriad of chasms, rock pools, striped rock domes, and 400-year-old cycads. The Garden of Eden—an oasis of miniature bonsai-like trees, eucalyptuses, and prehistoric ferns—rings a permanent water hole 885 feet (270 m) below the rim, which stands almost as high above the canyon floor as Melbourne's tallest skyscraper, a lookout over the canyon's red and white sandstone cliffs.

The walk begins with a strenuous ascent to the rim known locally as "Heartbreak Hill." At the halfway point it descends to the Garden of Eden, and the final stage takes you through a maze of sandstone domes. If you start early, you might glimpse hill kangaroos, spinifex pigeons, or even a white-plumed honeyeater, all among 600 plant species that make this area the most diverse of any in Australia's arid heart. **BDS**

Lost City
Northern Territory, Australia

Start/End Heartbreak Hotel, Cape Crawford (helicopter)   **Distance** 3–5 miles (4.8–8 km)
Time 2 hours   **Grade** Easy   **Type** Unmarked, bare rock, silica encrusted paths   **Info** goo.gl/ndAEbx

Ask one hundred Australians and ninety-nine will tell you they've never heard of the Abner Range—not a surprising statistic when you consider the remoteness of the place, which is the reason there was no tourism here before 1992. The range in Australia's arid Northern Territory is home to one of the most spectacular areas of karst formations on the continent, a north–west elongated ovaloid plateau measuring 12.5 miles (20 km) by 25 miles (40 km), which rises above the plains of the McArthur River system. The "Lost City" is the name given to its forest of sandstone rock pinnacles, which is best accessed via helicopter and provides a veritable labyrinth of passageways and tunnels in a quintessential Australian outback setting.

The pinnacles are 97 percent silica sand, what geologists call Abner Sandstone, held together with an outer crust of iron (hence the lovely red tinge), calcite, lichens, silica, and manganese. They are 1.4 billion years old, dating back to the pre-Cambrian period—twice as old as Uluru (Ayers Rock), the distinctive monolith in the nation's "Red Centre." You won't find any fossils here: these rocks were formed before life on Earth even began.

There is, however, evidence of past Aboriginal habitation, including caves and rock faces with hand stencils and various other ritualistic markings. The silica's porous nature has resulted in lovely walking trails that capture snake trails and wallaby paw prints, and there is a nice mix of flora that includes grevilleas and green plums. Rangers are working to develop a trail system that accesses various rock art sites and rock formations in a part of the world that remains in a continual state of discovery. **BDS**

"The 'Lost City' is dotted with towering sandstone formations. These natural pillars remind many observers of skyscrapers."

www.about-australia.com

⊡ In a time before there were even fossils, the Lost City was already taking shape.

Standley Chasm
Northern Territory, Australia

Start/End Standley Chasm
Distance 0.3 mile (0.5 km)   Time 40 minutes
Grade Easy   Type Exposed rock, sand, gravel
Info goo.gl/ItkebY

"Surging floodwaters over thousands of years are responsible for this beautiful site … it is at its most impressive on a sunny day."

www.nt.gov.au

⬆ Bisect one of the MacDonnell Ranges' most famous "gaps" on one of Australia's best-known outback trails.

Standley Chasm is one of the many "gaps" in the MacDonnell Ranges, a spectacular series of parallel ridgelines that runs east to west for 400 miles (644 km) through the heart of Australia either side of the town of Alice Springs. The gorges and canyons that characterize this ancient, weather-beaten range were created between 300 and 350 million years ago in a continuous process of folding, faulting, and erosion. Standley Chasm, the result of thousands of years of erosive floodwaters, is among them. The best time to walk the chasm (it is a short walk that should take only some twenty minutes one way) is midday, when the overhead sun lights up both sides of the chasm's walls at the same time. However, while an early morning or late afternoon walk will likely bring you into contact with the wildlife, including the long-nosed dragon, and an impressive array of birdlife.

Only 31 miles (50 km) west of Alice Springs on Larapinta Drive, Standley Chasm, part of the Larapinta Trail, is one of the real standout geological features of the MacDonnell Range. Most noticeably, it offers a vivid palette of colors—the red and ocher of the canyon walls, the green of the tenacious flora, and the white of the ghost gum eucalypts on the canyon walls. These walls reach heights of 262 feet (80 m) and remain mostly hidden from view until you are virtually in the midst of them—a fabulous surprise.

Like so much of the surrounding landscape, it is Aboriginal land but named in honor of Mrs. Ida Standley, a schoolteacher who moved to Alice Springs from Adelaide in 1914 after an advertisement for a teacher for the school, located behind the local jail, went unanswered. **BDS**

Sunshine Coast Hinterland Great Walk
Queensland, Australia

Start Lake Baroon   **End** Mapleton Falls
National Park   **Distance** 36 miles (57.9 km)
Time 3 days   **Grade** Moderate   **Type** Forest
trails   **Map** goo.gl/nQpD9A

An hour's drive north of the Queensland capital of Brisbane is the Blackall Range, one of the state's most dramatic terrains, with spectacular escarpments and views that stretch inland over rolling mountains and valleys east to the Pacific Ocean. You can access this dense green world on the Sunshine Coast Hinterland Great Walk, which begins at an old Aboriginal fighting ground at Lake Baroon, crosses the Maleny-Mapleton plateau, and continues along the Blackall Range past the tumbling Kondalilla Falls, where you can cool off in rain forest rock pools or rock-hop down creeks that flow into the Obi Obi Gorge.

The trail rambles over numerous peaks and ravines, linking several parks and reserves, including Kondalilla National Park, Mapleton Falls National Park, and Mapleton Forest Reserve, and leads through eucalyptus woodlands, rain forest ravines, palm-filled gullies, and forest creeks. There are some steep ascents, but nothing extreme, and the track is peppered with inviting, mountain-fresh water holes for a cooling dip, usually backed by a beautiful waterfall and spectacular lookouts across the ranges or to the coastal fringe. The signage is excellent, and so is the camping.

The sound of the cicadas is regularly broken by the call of the whipbird—an unmistakable sign that you are deep in the Australian bush—and the forest canopy is dominated by the imposing bunya pine, with cones the size of bowling balls. There are four primary access points—Baroon Pocket, Kondalilla Falls, Mapleton Falls National Park, and Mapleton Forest Reserve—and segments vary from fifteen-minute strolls to seven-hour slogs through a boulder-laden, waterfall-draped, tropical forest. **BDS**

"Winding through the spectacular Blackall Range ... the Great Walk traverses some of Queensland's most scenic natural areas."

www.queenslandholidays.com.au

⊤ Enjoy a beguiling mix of subtropical rain forest, waterfalls, and tall, open forests of eucalyptus.

Heysen Trail South Australia, Australia

Start Cape Jervis   **End** Parachilna Gorge   **Distance** 746 miles (1,200 km)
Time 60 days   **Grade** Easy   **Type** Rock, gravel, and dirt trails   **Info** goo.gl/A8kETq

To walk the length of the Heysen Trail—named in honor of the great German-born Australian artist Hans Heysen, who achieved fame for his watercolors depicting the Australian bush and in particular its towering gum trees—is to walk through virtually every landscape the state of South Australia can offer.

The trail begins on the coastal fringes of the Fleurieu Peninsula and passes through various state and national parks and historic townships, over the famous Adelaide Hills, and through the award-winning vineyards of the Barossa and Clare valleys, 90 miles (145 km) north of Adelaide. It continues through the lush Gilbert Valley and on to the imposing grandeur of Wilpena Pound, a wonderful amphitheater of rock in the Flinders Ranges and one of Australia's most impressive natural environments, often visited by Heysen. First proposed by Warren Bonython,

a long-distance walker who spent years walking the South Australian outback, the trail opened in 1992 after beginning as a track through the Mount Lofty Ranges in the late 1970s.

Mostly built for walking, cycling and horseback riding are permitted on some sections. The trail is not regularly cleared (some maintenance is carried out by the Friends of the Heysen Trail), and there can be some steep gradients. However, overall it is easy walking, despite a lack of campsites, and a trail to be completed in stages rather than a straight walk-through—which makes sense considering it is the longest walking trail on the continent. There is talk of extending it by 310 miles (500 km) to Mount Babbage, a remote place—even by Australian standards. **BDS**

⤴ See territory that inspired a great landscape artist.

Paperbark Camp Trails New South Wales, Australia

Start/End Paperbark Camp   **Distance** 0.5 mile (0.8 km)   **Time** 1 hour   **Grade** Easy
Type Forest path   **Info** goo.gl/jZxon8

As any ornithologist will tell you, you can gauge the health of an ecosystem by the number and variety of birds that inhabit it. This is how you know, when you come to Paperbark Camp in Jervis Bay, on the south coast of New South Wales, and walk its wetland and river trails, that you are in a special environment. Red wattlebirds, Eastern spinebills, red-browed firetails, the endangered Eastern bristlebird, and the Laughing Kookaburra, which marks its territory with a raucous laugh, and a dozen more on a veritable "who's who" list of exotic Australian birds can be found here.

The paperbark trees, with their distinctive paper-like bark, surround and permeate Paperbark Camp, an ecofriendly tented retreat. The forest is equally diverse and has a lovely trail that takes you through a preserved area of estuary wetland that parallels Currambene Creek, which runs alongside the camp

and continues for 5 miles (8 km) to the coastal town of Huskisson, where it empties into the ocean at Jervis Bay. An important roosting and feeding area for wading birds, Currambene Creek is an important wintering ground for northern hemisphere migratory waders. But birds are not all you will see here. There are gray kangaroos among a parade of forty-two native mammal species, fifteen types of lizards, seventeen frog species, numerous bats, and a rare tortoise species. It is a colorful walk. Punctuating the white and gray shades of the paperbarks are rainbow lorikeets, Australian king parrots, crimson rosellas, and even magnificent yellow-tailed black cockatoos—just another of the "in-camp residents" that make this place such an unmissable treat. **BDS**

⬆ The paperbark trees surround the camp.

Beechworth Gorge Scenic Walk Victoria, Australia

Start/End Freeman on Ford B&B, Beechworth   **Distance** 7 miles (11.2 km)   **Time** 3 hours   **Grade** Easy
Type Ravine trails, sealed road   **Map** goo.gl/pp9lmG

The historic town of Beechworth in the northwest corner of rural Victoria was once awash with gold. In 1852, the precious metal was discovered here, and the town became known for its extensive use of hydraulic sluicing, a process of washing and removing dirt. So much gold was found in central and northeastern Victoria in the 1850s that it was enough to pay off the national debt. Today, Beechworth has thirty-two buildings listed by the National Trust and it remains the best-preserved gold rush town in Victoria.

But there is more to do here than stroll down its idyllic streets. Surrounding the town, on the edge of its tiny urban heart, is an impressive mix of walking trails, from a circumnavigation of delightful Lake Sambell (once the site of the Rocky Mountains Mining Company open-cut sluice operation) in less than an hour to the more than 7 miles (11 km) of walking trails

that wind through Beechworth Gorge. Recreational access to the gorge was greatly improved in 1926 when a 3-mile-long (4.8 km) road was laid down, and today an additional wealth of well-maintained trails take walkers onto paths through the dry environment to appreciate the resident flora of stringy barks, cypresses, red gums, and lilies, as well as fauna that include kangaroos, koalas, and possums.

Historic markers harking back to the golden era include Newton Bridge, built by Scottish stonemasons in 1875, and the remains of Chevalier's Mill, built in 1855 to supply the town with flour and sawn timber. You can also see the Cascades waterfall and Fiddles Quarry, one of the many quarries that gave the town the beautiful cut granite you can still admire today. **BDS**

⊼ **Stroll through the remains of an Australian gold rush.**

Two Bays Trail Victoria, Australia

Start Dromana, Port Phillip Bay   **End** Westernport Bay, Mornington Peninsula National Park   **Distance** 16 miles (25.7 km)   **Time** 2 days   **Grade** Easy   **Type** Gravel paths, grass tracks   **Map** goo.gl/LxjFpb

First proposed in 1984 by Stefanie Rennick, a physical education and arts teacher at Bentleigh High School in the eastern suburbs of Melbourne, the Two Bays Trail links Victoria's two great bays, Port Phillip Bay and Westernport Bay, via the Mornington Peninsula's longest continuous track. The result of years of planning by volunteer groups and Parks Victoria, the trail is best walked over two or more visits (no camping is allowed, and there are no towns on the trail)—ample time to appreciate the trail's diversity.

The trail begins on the beach at Dromana, a popular seaside town with sweeping views over Port Phillip Bay. The climb up from the beach to the 997-foot-high (304 m) granite summit of Arthurs Seat gets the hard stuff out of the way at the outset, and after stopping to admire the panoramic views and—on a good day—the skyline of Melbourne in the distance, you continue through Seawinds Gardens, a popular picnic spot with landscaped gardens, and on through Arthurs Seat State Park with an optional walk on the T. M. McKellar Circuit, a sloping 0.6 mile (1 km) walk over undulating bushland.

Perhaps you'll encounter Eastern gray kangaroos, blue tongue lizards, koalas, and echidnas before emerging onto Waterfall Gully Road and Gardens Road. But the asphalt here does not last, and you are soon in Mornington Peninsula National Park, where the walking is exceptional, the park being home to the largest swathe of vegetation on the peninsula. Then head in the direction of Cape Schanck, the peninsula's southernmost tip that separates Bass Strait from the calm waters of Westernport Bay. **BDS**

⊥ Take in two bays and Melbourne's favorite peninsula.

Overland Track
Tasmania, Australia

Start Ronny Creek   End Lake St. Clair
Distance 40.5 miles (65 km)   Time 6 days
Grade Moderate to strenuous   Type Overland trails
and split log boardwalks   Map goo.gl/Lsk17N

One of the many Tasmanian tracks that can be relied upon to provide a sensory overload is the Overland Track in the shadows of the world-renowned Cradle Mountain. Countless paddocks, villages, luscious rain forests, and lakes, including Australia's deepest, Lake St. Clair, are just some of the scenic delights that await. And that isn't even accounting for the side trips.

On this trail there are plenty of alternative routes you can take, including an ascent of 5,305-foot-tall (1,617 m) Mount Ossa, Tasmania's highest peak in the very heart of Cradle Mountain-Lake St. Clair National Park. You can also veer off to numerous pristine waterfalls and rivers. The trail lives up to its status of "Australia's must-do track." It is one of the best walks you can do if you want a do-it-yourself wilderness experience. You can select how and when to tackle this trail and which side trips to take, and whether to catch the ferry from Narcissus Hut at the head of Lake St. Clair to Lake St. Clair Visitors' Centre or to continue for another 10.9 miles (17.5 km) around the lake.

A demanding walk like this takes time, and an average traverse will last around six days. Having some degree of physical fitness is necessary to tackle this track, but there are plenty of areas to stop and enjoy the serene Tasmanian landscape. When you reach Lake St. Clair, the view is phenomenal. Here you can see just how far you have walked, and there is Cradle Mountain, with its familiar ridge and countless shades of green, yellow, and brown so famously embedded into Australia's landscape. You can finish at Narcissus Hut or continue for an extra day through untouched rain forest. **AS**

"As well as a physical challenge, this walk is a true communion with nature. You'll see lakes, forests, gorges … and steep, stony peaks."

www.australia.com

⬆ The Overland Track is Australia's premier alpine walk.

➡ The track bisects a landscape of glacial valleys, buttongrass moors, rain forests, and eucalyptus forests.

Te Araroa Trail North Island to South Island, New Zealand

Start Cape Reinga, North Island **End** Bluff, South Island
Distance 1,863 miles (2,999 km) **Time** 4 months
Grade Strenuous **Type** Beaches, mountain and forest trails, sealed pathways **Info** goo.gl/YLaONA

New Zealanders call it simply the "Long Pathway," and on it you can be anywhere from one or two days between towns to a week or more in total wilderness. Accommodation will range in style from typically welcoming campgrounds to isolated mountain and backcountry huts. You will be walking an average of 15 miles (24 km) a day and "tramping it"—what the locals here call hiking—for four months, walking 994 miles (1,600 km) across the North Island and almost 869 miles (1,399 km) through the South Island. Beaches, volcanoes, forests, cities, rivers, and fields—by the time you are done walking the Te Araroa Trail, you will feel like there isn't a peak, valley, or farmer's field left that you haven't been a part of.

Most decide to walk the route from north to south, starting in early spring at Cape Reinga on the Aupouri Peninsula and ending at Bluff, New Zealand's southern-most town (if you don't count Oban on Stewart Island), negotiating the South Island's Southern Alps after the winter snows have melted.

It all began as an idea in 1975 to create a Pennine Way–type scenic trail. By 2003, segments had been opened, but the trail was far from complete, a fact that didn't stop a few people from walking it, anyway. The trail was officially opened in 2011, and it has proven one of the greatest adventures you can have in a country that prides itself on providing memorable outdoor experiences. New exciting side-trails have also been opened, such as the three-day Motatapu Alpine Trek, just one of hundreds of options on this tramp of a lifetime. **BDS**

⇐ The "Long Pathway" is a New Zealand odyssey.

Lake Waikaremoana Great Walk Hawke's Bay, New Zealand

Start Onepoto **End** Hopuruahine
Distance 27 miles (43.4 km) **Time** 4 days
Grade Easy to moderate **Type** Mountain, forest, and lakeside trails **Map** goo.gl/br96U3

The landscape surrounding Lake Waikaremoana, New Zealand's deepest lake at 839 feet (256 m), is often talked about as resembling how everything "used to be"—that is, before the arrival of white settlers. Primitive rain forests, remote lakeside beaches, giant trees—the home of the Ngai Tuhoe Maori tribe must look today much as it always has, except for the beautiful lake, which was created by a mass landslide of rock and debris brought down the mountainsides by an earthquake more than 2,000 years ago. Well, they don't call New Zealand "the shaky isles" for nothing.

"A refuge among prehistoric rain forest with access to some of New Zealand's most iconic birds . . . ."

www.greatwalks.co.nz

You start this designated "Great Walk" at an old armed constabulary redoubt, making your first serious climb to the top of Panekire Bluff: a tough initiation, although the trail is generally well marked and all rivers are bridged. Follow a ridgeline to 3,871-foot-high (1,180 m) Puketapu Trig and stay at Panekire Hut.

The next day descend through podocarp and beech forests to campsites on the lake's shoreline. Take the thirty-minute detour to the lovely Korokoro Falls before traversing a series of small ridges to another campsite, Maraunui. On your final day cross the bridge into Marauiti Bay, over the neck of the Puketukutuku Peninsula, and on to the Hopuruahine suspension bridge, ending a memorable few days. **BDS**

Heaphy Track Tasman, New Zealand

Start Brown and Aorere rivers   **End** Kohaihai   **Distance** 50 miles (80 km)   **Time** 4–5 days
Grade Easy to moderate   **Type** Mountain and forest trails   **Map** goo.gl/5aEBGA

Located deep in the northwest of New Zealand's South Island, the Heaphy Track in the Kahurangi National Park traverses more than 48 miles (77 km) of one of the country's newest parks. Beginning at the confluence of the Brown and Aorere rivers, it continues across vast expanses of tussock downs and through enveloping forests and groves of nikau palms. It is a wide path and generously "benched"— so it is popular with people of all ages and represents an excellent introduction to long-distance walking for the novice, as well as a genuinely exhilarating experience for the hardened tramper.

The track is named after the pioneering explorer Charles Heaphy who, together with fellow explorer Thomas Brunner and two Maori guides, set off from Nelson for the West Coast in 1846 on an arduous five-month trek along an old Maori trail through the "unexplored world." The Heaphy Track now runs through much of this land and is one of New Zealand's most diverse walks, with views over alpine downs, passing through subalpine landscapes, and emerging onto the wild West Coast.

The first day, if going from east to west, takes some effort with a 3,000-foot-high (914 m) ascent to Perry Saddle, but a dip in the cold waters of Gorge River will make you forget all that. Then it's a descent to Gouland Downs and a memorable walk along the Heaphy River through a rain forest of *kowhai* and cabbage trees and past orchids, mosses, and flax bushes, which give the track its nickname "flora walk." There are camping options aplenty as well as well-equipped Department of Conservation huts. **BDS**

⬆ One of the rope bridges on the Heaphy Track.

Hollyford Track Southland, New Zealand

Start Te Anau **End** Martins Bay **Distance** 34 miles (54.7 km) **Time** 3 days **Grade** Easy
Type Muddy forest trails **Map** goo.gl/eII89a

If you feel a little tired after your first day on the Hollyford Track, consider the old pioneering days and men such as Davey Gunn. Gunn was a bushman who lived in the Hollyford Valley in the 1930s and once covered three days' worth of hiking in twenty hours to raise the alarm about a plane crash in Big Bay. Against a fierce headwind on Lake McKerrow, he rowed with oars that didn't match and with broken ribs, and ran the last few miles after the horse he was riding couldn't go on.

Or think of the unlucky Frederick Fitt, who was stranded by a flooded river for a week. When they found him, he had no shirt, shoes, or socks on, and had been driven mad by sandflies. Or the Maori chief Tutoko, who liked to greet white settlers by wearing an American Civil War uniform. What is often called New Zealand's most beautiful valley may not provide the longest trek you can do on the South Island, nor may it be the steepest or the most remote, but this much is guaranteed: nowhere else will you hear stories so tall or encounter so many people willing to tell them.

The Hollyford Track is a three-day valley walk through a labyrinth of greenery so dense that it seems to hem you in. But never fear—the trek is so inspiring that you will be too distracted by the beauty around you to worry about catching your breath after a tough climb, the steepest of which is a 551-foot (168-m) scramble, a genteel upward hike that seems to sum up what the Hollyford Track is all about. It's a little bit like the nursery rhyme—not too easy, not too hard, a track that is "just right." **BDS**

⊞ The track follows the Hollyford River to the west coast.

Walking through the world's greatest cities and towns in the twenty-first century is an exciting possibility— renovated elevated railroads, scenic greenways, tranquil riverside paths, revitalized historic town centers, and an increasing international network of trails provide a dazzling array of walking choices.

URBAN

← Stroll along the High Line, New York City's reborn elevated railroad that *National Geographic* called the "miracle above Manhattan."

Irishtown Nature Park New Brunswick, Canada

Start/End Elmwood Drive parking lot   **Distance** Various   **Time** 2 hours–1 day   **Grade** Easy
Type Sealed and chipped pathways   **Info** goo.gl/8HIcJf

Entirely contained within the boundaries of the city of Moncton, New Brunswick, the Irishtown Nature Park is a rarity—a triumphant amalgam of wetlands and forest in a well-planned mix of land and aquatic environments that provides a tranquil setting for a variety of outdoor and environmental pursuits. Comprising 250 acres (101 ha) of lakes and streams set among 2,200 acres (890 ha) of forest, the park offers a variety of outdoor pursuits, including kayaking, mountain biking, cross-country skiing, and walking. Moncton is fortunate to have a gem like this on its doorstep. Every city should be so lucky.

Interpretive signs explain the park's long association with the town, which began when it was chosen as Moncton's first water source in the mid-1800s. There's even a small museum—the one-room Tankville schoolhouse—that is the beginning and end of a small loop trail running through a maturing hemlock forest. Longer trails include the red trail (2.9 miles/4.6 km), which begins in the parking lot on Elmwood Drive and follows the park's outer boundary; and the yellow trail (3.6 miles/5.7 km), which is groomed for year-round walking and runs along the park's main lake.

Irishtown Nature Park is also a gathering point for birds, courtesy of the park's many feeding stations, and for the growing number of Moncton's avid birdwatchers, too. Yellow and purple finches, hairy and downey woodpeckers, nuthatches and doves are just some of the birds you'll spot here when you come to see for yourself just how compatible man and nature can be. **BDS**

⬆ Irishtown achieves harmony between man and nature.

Kay Gardner Beltline Trail Ontario, Canada

Start Allen Road **End** Mount Pleasant Road **Distance** 6 miles (9.6 km) **Time** 2 hours **Grade** Easy
Type Maintained pathways and footpaths **Map** goo.gl/1VinQY

The Toronto Belt Line Railway opened for the first time in 1892 and was built to service the burgeoning outer suburbs to the north of the city. However, the line never turned a profit, and after two years the passenger trains stopped running and the line lay abandoned. Parts of the line were later used for freight services, but by the 1970s even these had ceased, and the stage was set for a fight over whether or not it should be converted into a cycle path. It was one of the first such battles to be fought in Canada.

Today, the Kay Gardner Beltline Trail is a mixed cycling and walking trail and is a much-loved part of the City of Toronto Discovery Walks program, which helps to link up the city's ravines, parklands, and wealth of outdoor spaces. It begins close to Eglinton West subway station near the Allen expressway and runs to Mount Pleasant Cemetery. It is an ideal trail for families, with wide paths that accommodate children who might want to cycle and still leave plenty of width for cyclists and walkers to pass without having to take a deep breath.

One ravine that is easily accessible from the trail is Cedarvale, a natural ravine with heavily inclined sides and a footpath that runs along its floor. It contains some sizable wetlands to the east of Bathurst Street, and also has some impressive areas of natural regrowth forest. The path is heavily used even in winter, and joins up with the Nordheimer Ravine to form a single trail throughout midtown Toronto—a testament to the vision those early supporters of the Beltline Trail had for a city accessible by greenery and not just by sidewalk. **BDS**

⊡ An abandoned railway is now a Toronto drawcard.

Sellwood Riverfront to Johnson Creek Loop Oregon, USA

Start/End Sellwood Riverfront Park   **Distance** 3.7 miles (6 km)   **Time** 2–3 hours   **Grade** Easy
Type Riverfront and sidewalk   **Map** goo.gl/epIz3O

Portland, perhaps more than any other U.S. city, was made for walking. There are the long, steep ridgelines on the city's west with their views over Portland and beyond to the beauty of the Cascade Mountains; there are walks that take you down along a scenic, ravine-encrusted valley floor, and others that deposit you alongside the picturesque Willamette River. There are also walks that take you through sought-after neighborhoods past houses built in the Arts and Crafts style of the early twentieth century, and through lesser-known districts such as Linnton. This was once home to heavy industry and shipping terminals, but now provides access to a network of wooded urban hills and valleys that would almost certainly have been lost had Linnton become the big city of its dreams.

If you want to pick a walk offering fine views over the city, which will help you decide where to go next,

take the Sellwood Riverfront to Johnson Creek Loop. Beginning at Sellwood Riverfront Park, walk north through the largely untouched river frontage past cottonwood trees and over a pebbly beach. You then turn east away from the river and toward Oak Park with its native Oregon white oak trees and the Oaks Amusement Park, one of the ten oldest amusement parks in the United States. Walk through the 160-acre (64.75-ha) Oaks Bottom Wildlife Refuge, the city's only wetland, and scale an 80-foot (24-m) bluff to Sellwood Park, with its thickly planted firs and masses of rhododendrons.

And from there the walk takes you onto Sellwood Boulevard with its expansive city views and the always funky public art on display at Share-It Square. **BDS**

⬆ The pretty riverfront at Sellwood is perfect for a stroll.

Golden Gate National Recreation Area California, USA

Start/End Presidio visitor center   **Distance** Various   **Time** 1 hour to a full day
Grade Easy   **Type** Forest trails   **Info** goo.gl/yROjIe

The Golden Gate National Recreation Area (GGNRA) covers the hills and bluffs immediately to the north and south of San Francisco's famous Golden Gate Bridge, and its 75,000 acres (30,350 ha) make it one of the largest urban parklands in the world. More than twice the size of San Francisco itself, the GGNRA embraces federal, public, and private lands and chronicles thousands of years of history, including the legacy of the indigenous Miwok and Ohlone tribes. There are sites related to the Spanish Empire and to the Mexican Republic, to California's extensive maritime history, and even to the Gold Rush. There are almost 740 historic buildings within the GGNRA, nine cultural landscapes, and more than sixty archaeological sites. This labyrinth of history is mixed with a region of high biological diversity, and half of the bird species in the United States, as well as bobcats, quails, and black-tailed deer, can be found here among windswept beaches, coastal chaparral, woodlands, salt marshes, redwood groves, and wetlands. The question is deciding which walk to choose.

There is the 11-mile (18-km) Land's End Coastal Trail to the northwest corner of San Francisco Bay, which takes you through hillsides of cypresses and wildflowers, and rewards you with views of the Marin Headlands and the bridge. Or why not try whale spotting on Muir Beach, hiking to the Point Bonita Lighthouse, or scaling Hawk Hill on the Marin Headlands and look for migratory birds of prey? Or if you have more time, why not take a tour of Alcatraz or stroll through the redwoods in Muir Woods. Deciding to come to GGNRA is easy. Good luck with the rest. **BDS**

⬆ Leave the city behind for havens such as Muir Beach.

Nob Hill California, USA

Start Washington Street **End** Pine Street **Distance** 0.5 mile (0.8 km) **Time** 45 minutes **Grade** Easy
Type Sidewalk **Info** goo.gl/hqTqBB

San Francisco is built over more than forty hills, but none have the pedigree and the stature of Nob Hill, the neighborhood of choice for the city's elite. It was once little more than a ridgeline of gnarly oak trees, and its first residents built shacks and raised goats and chickens. By the 1850s, Stockton and Powell streets on Nob Hill's lower slopes began to be developed, but the higher ground around what is now Jones Street remained untouched. The invention of the cable car in the 1870s brought the mansions of the city's wealthy merchants and railroad barons, all of which were destroyed in the earthquake and fire of 1906.

Nob Hill grew from its ashes and provides an outstanding walk that is begun at the cable car museum on the corner of Mason and Washington streets. From there you ascend Mason Street for two blocks, past Brocklebank Apartments, where Alfred Hitchcock filmed James Stewart stalking Kim Novak in *Vertigo* (1958), then cross to the Fairmont Hotel, which was nearing completion in 1906 when the quake tore it down. (Tony Bennett sung "I Left My Heart (in San Francisco)" in its lounge.) Across the street is the Flood Mansion, damaged in 1906 but later restored in marble. California Street is next, and maybe a visit to the Top-of-the Mark bar at the Mark Hopkins (now Intercontinental) Hotel, followed by a walk through Huntington Park, the Masonic Temple at the corner of Taylor and California streets, Grace Cathedral, then left onto Sacramento Street and ending with the rounded, Gaudí-like balconies of the exquisite Chambord Apartments, all blissfully set above the city's "bawdy" waterfront. **BDS**

⊡ Coit Tower and San Francisco, as seen from Nob Hill.

Cameron Park Trails Texas, USA

Start/End Bosque River Trail **Distance** Various **Time** Various **Grade** Easy to moderate
Type Natural trails **Info** goo.gl/z9rHO1

Cameron Park in the city of Waco in Texas is spread over 416 acres (168 ha) along the Brazos and Bosque Rivers. It was built in 1904 and is named after a local philanthropist, William Cameron. It not only has its own road system, but also a network of well-maintained trails and paths suitable for walkers and mountain bikers. Horses are allowed in some areas but are restricted from some of the trails. The system is graded with the paths color coded for level of difficulty, from green for beginners, through blue for intermediate, to black and red for advanced and expert, respectively. There's a fair amount of elevation change—one reason the trail system is so popular with mountain bikers. It even hosts an annual bike race.

Cameron Park Trails appeal to walkers of all ages and abilities. If you want a gentle stroll beside the water, you can take the River Trail or if you want

something more challenging, you could head for the Outback or Powder Monkey. Or you can combine the shorter sections to make your own route around the park, which has facilities ranging from picnic spots and restrooms to shelters and even a baseball diamond. There are a number of parking areas available, so you can drive into the heart of the park and set off from there. The landscape varies, from woodland and forestry to the grassy riverside. There are also 100-foot-high (30.5 m) cliffs and even some stands of bamboo forest. Although it can get hot, you're kept in the shade of one of its many trees most of the time. The surface itself is compacted soil, and there are numerous wooden bridges to carry you across the ravines and gullies. JI

⊡ Cameron Park—a woodland grows out of an urban park.

Gateway State Trail
Minnesota, USA

Start Cayuga Street, St. Paul   **End** Pine Point County Park   **Distance** 18 miles (29 km)   **Time** 6 hours   **Grade** Easy   **Type** Converted rail trail, paved pathways   **Map** goo.gl/utCKkR

A trail system that runs through the urban heart of the city of St. Paul in Minnesota, through the cities of Maplewood and North St. Paul, and through Washington county to Pine Point Regional Park, northwest of Stillwater, the Gateway State Trail follows a portion of the old Soo Line Railroad that once connected St. Paul to Duluth. The conversion of the rail line into a trail system was made possible in 1980 when an order was given by the Interstate Commerce Commission to abandon the line on the condition that it would be converted into a recreational, multiuse trail. And multiuse it certainly is: walkers, cyclists, inline skaters, horseback riders (on a 10-mile-long (16 km) adjacent path east of Interstate 694), and roller skaters. It is wheelchair accessible, and in winter, snowshoers and even cross-country skiers all make use of this well-trodden, almost entirely flat, and popular trail that links up the city's wetlands, parks, and farmlands in a triumph of far-sighted urban renewal. The people of greater St. Paul have taken the path to their hearts, too—the trail is the most popular nonmotorized trail in the state of Minnesota.

It begins on Cayuga Street just to the north of the state capital, and takes you into the 248-acre (100-ha) Phalen–Keller Regional Park, which contains the city's only swimming lake. It also offers a connection to the Bruce Vento Regional Trail, and the trail ends at Pine Point Country Park, a nature reserve of pine forests, lakes, and marshes that itself has 5 miles (8 km) of multiuse trails. Additional land has also been purchased that will see the Gateway State Trail extended to Taylors Falls, an area of stunning forested bluffs and impressive cliffs, and from there into neighboring Wisconsin. **BDS**

> *"Located on a converted rail trail, the Gateway State Trail offers eighteen miles of paved trail."*
>
> www.dnr.state.mn.us/state_trails/gateway

↑ Minnesota links a series of wetlands and green spaces, and creates a triumph in urban renewal.

Charles C. Jacobus Park Nature Trail
Wisconsin, USA

Start/End Hillside Lane
Distance 0.9 mile (1.4 km) **Time** 1 hour
Grade Easy **Type** Park trails
Info goo.gl/Niazwh

It isn't easy to find an example of a well-preserved woodland set deep in a genuine urban environment, but the Charles C. Jacobus Park Nature Trail in the town of Wauwatosa, Wisconsin, is an outstanding example of just that. Designated a National Recreation Trail in 2006, the trail, which by the late 1990s had fallen into a state of disrepair after first being laid out in the mid 1960s, received some much-needed funds from the Charles Jacobus Park Neighborhood Association, the city of Wauwatosa, and the state of Wisconsin. This funding saw the replacement of signage, the restoration of walkways, the addition of stone steps, the renewal of aging railings, and even the construction of a new wooden bridge. This concentrated effort breathed new life into a trail that showcases more than 160 species of native flora and fauna, which are inscribed on Wisconsin's threatened and endangered species list.

The new signage, one of the perks of receiving a National Recreation Trail designation, tells the story of the trail and its surroundings on a series of stainless steel, acid-etched signs that educate all those who come here about the fragile nature of the park and the role they can play to preserve it. The park also has a playground, athletic fields, and extensive picnic areas. In addition, this "woodland island in metropolitan Milwaukee" has one of the city's finest displays of spring wildflowers. The park provides an invaluable resource to local schools that conduct interpretive walks for children, to teach them about environmental awareness and conservation, and also provides everyone with an undisturbed landscape in the midst of their city. **BDS**

"It is a unique natural outdoor classroom for schoolchildren and area citizens."

www.americantrails.org

⤒ One of the United States' finest slices of urban woodland is now a stunning National Recreation Trail.

Chicago Lakefront Trail
Illinois, USA

Start Hollywood Avenue **End** 71st Street
Distance 18 miles (29 km) **Time** 8–10 hours
Grade Easy **Type** Mixed-use pathway
Map goo.gl/FjnkEC

The Chicago Lakefront Trail is one of the most heavily trafficked open spaces in North America, and it is not difficult to understand why. Soccer fields, playgrounds, beaches, volleyball fields, and baseball diamonds can all be accessed by walking it, and it provides unrivaled views of the great Chicago skyline. It is a mixed-use shoreline path used by thousands of walkers and cyclists every day along the edge of Lake Michigan.

The inevitable and all-too-frequent crossing of various intersections certainly does little to enhance the maintaining of the "zone" that one would otherwise be well settled into here, but on the plus side there are the welcome diversions of Lincoln Park's 1,208 acres (488 ha), the largest public park in the city; Grant Park, which dates back to the city's founding and is home to the Art Institute of Chicago and is a must-visit diversion; Burnham Park; and Jackson Park, which still has some of the buildings created for the 1893 World's Fair, including the Japanese Osaka Garden, the Palace of Fine Arts (now the Museum of Science and Industry), and the Norway Pavilion.

More than just a lakefront trail, it is a stroll through the city's rich history and diversity of its built environment. There is the South Shore Cultural Center, with its Mediterranean Revival–style architecture and private Lake Michigan Beach, and the magnificent Navy Pier, the city's 3,000-foot-long (914 m) landmark in Streeterville, built in 1916. Today the pier is the city's top tourist attraction, with its gardens, public sculptures, and embarkation point for boat tours of Lake Michigan; it is also home to the tall ship *Windy*. More than a walk, this is one impressive trail of urban discovery. **BDS**

"Chicago's Lakefront Trail is an active and eco-friendly way to see Chicago."

www.choosechicago.com

← The trail is the boundary between the famous Chicago skyline and the chilly waters of Lake Michigan.

↑ Chicago's Lakefront Trail is a mixed-use triumph in urban planning.

Wolf River Greenway Trail Tennessee, USA

Start Walnut Grove   **End** Humphrey's Boulevard   **Distance** 2 miles (3.2 km)   **Time** 1 hour   **Grade** Easy
Type Man-made path   **Map** goo.gl/VSQSJi

The Wolf River Greenway runs for a little less than 2 miles (3.2 km) along the southern side of the Wolf River in Tennessee. Work on the Greenway, a narrow stretch of protected land with a 10-foot-wide (3 m) paved trail for walkers and cyclists to share, began in 2010, and the eventual aim is for it to connect Memphis with the neighboring cities of Germantown and Collierville—a distance of 30 miles (48 km).

The trail begins in downtown Memphis and then heads out of the city. Along this corridor there are rest areas, butterfly gardens, wildflower meadows, and picnic spots. This section is used by local schools, which bring classes here to learn about the environment. The area is also used by walkers, joggers, cyclists, and rollerbladers. There is even an annual Dinner on the Greenway event, to which hundreds of people come out on a fall evening to enjoy music and food.

The path itself is easily navigated, level, well maintained, and accessible to those with disabilities. There is also an impressively long bridge that connects the Greenway with other trails in nearby Shelby Farms Park. This steel-and-wood construction straddles the Wolf River and is open to pedestrians and cyclists. The aim of the Greenway is to provide a safe environment for locals and visitors to get close to the Wolf River. There's an alcohol and firearms ban along its length, and pedestrians have the right of way at all times. The walk is a great way of blurring the edges between the urban world of Memphis and the lush Tennessee countryside. While the conveniences of the city are never far away, it's easy to lose yourself in the slow pace of the trail's natural setting. **JI**

⬆ **The Wolf River Harbor in Memphis.**

Wissahickon Green Ribbon Trail Pennsylvania, USA

Start Schuylkill River trail   **End** Upper Gwynedd township   **Distance** 20 miles (32 km)   **Time** 6 hours
Grade Easy   **Type** Riverside and forest trails   **Map** goo.gl/YbnQH3

What a disorienting trail this is. It just doesn't feel like you're in Philadelphia when you're on it. A dozen or so steps into the Wissahickon Green Ribbon Trail in the parks network that is Fairmount Park, and you already feel a world away from urban concerns. In 1854 the city's first water fountain was built into its ancient rocks for travelers coming to the city on the old Forbidden Drive. Sometimes there are so many praying mantises on it, you have to be careful not to step on them. There are also gorgeous stone bridges and even a covered bridge—the only one still standing within the boundaries of a U.S. city. People walk the Wissahickon Gorge at night with headlamps, and sit under its waterfalls. One local even says she prefers it to New York's Central Park.

The Wissahickon Valley was carved out by the creek of the same name more than 125 million years ago, and the hyperactive nature of the geology here means that the rocks you are passing were once more than 10 miles (16 km) beneath you, a process that so heated them that they changed their very nature, from granite bedrock into a blistered schist. This is good news for the walker with a keen eye and maybe a geo-hammer—there are crystals everywhere here, tiny little fragments of garnet (red and burned orange), mica (black and translucent), kyanite (a light, sky blue), and tourmaline, a semiprecious gem filled with iron, magnesium, lithium, and potassium. So remember to bring a bucket (and some protective eyewear) and come wander some of the prettiest, mineral-studded trails to be found anywhere east of the Mississippi. **BDS**

⬆ This trail brings the wilderness to the city.

High Line
New York, USA

Start Gansevoort Street   End West 34th
Street   Distance 1.5 miles (2.4 km)
Time 1 hour   Grade Easy   Type Sidewalk, original
tracks   Map goo.gl/Hy217m

Elevated railways—railways where the tracks are set on platforms high above street level—first appeared in U.S. cities in the 1860s. New York City's first experiment with the notion of rapid transit was the West Side and Yonkers Patent Railway, which opened in 1868, and within twelve years, most New Yorkers lived just a ten-minute walk from their local station. The trains were dirty, noisy, steam-powered, and they blocked sunlight, but they were also able to move people about at an unprecedented rate, and helped transform the city into a bustling, thriving metropolis.

In 1934, the West Side Improvement Project opened with 13 miles (21 km) of track that eliminated 105 street-level crossings, and it is a section of that ambitious project, from Gansevoort Street in the Meatpacking District through Chelsea to West 34th Street, that has been preserved and redesigned as an "aerial greenway."

It was the 'Friends of the High Line' who, in 1999, proposed the transformation of what had become an urban relic into a new urban park for the city. Now accessed via stairways and elevators, the High Line has been a key ingredient in the revitalization of the Chelsea district. Plantings of wildflowers and various grasses have augmented the self-seeding process that had already been occurring naturally along its long-abandoned tracks, and lounges provide relaxing views over the Hudson River. Parts of the original track have been left in place, too, inlaid into new sections of pavement encircled by fields of wildflowers to create an elevated island of green that National Geographic called "The Miracle above Manhattan." **BDS**

◧ Walkers enjoying the sunshine on the High Line.

Central Park
New York, USA

Start/End Various
Distance Various   Time Easy
Grade Easy   Type Paved and unpaved paths,
grass   Info goo.gl/Ihsqwm

Central Park, the lungs of New York, was designed by Frederick Law Olmsted and Calvert Vaux. More than 1,500 residents were forcibly removed from the area when work began in 1858, and construction continued with few interruptions until the park was officially opened in 1878. Today more than 25 million people walk its 853 acres (345 ha) and over its Great Lawn and woodlands every year, and its network of pathways, open spaces, and hidden nooks still remain faithful to Olmsted and Vaux's original vision of providing New Yorkers with a green, tranquil retreat.

"No matter the season … this national historic landmark is a setting for enjoying many pursuits."

www.centralpark.com

There is a surprising 58 miles (93 km) of walking trails within Central Park. The Great Lawn, Cedar Hill, the Ramble, Sheep Meadow, Harlem Meer, Wildflower Meadow, the Loch—the list of sites and experiences is endless, and you can walk more than 6 miles (9.6 km) on marked trails over steep inclines and rugged paths that are often unpaved without passing over the same part twice. The Ramble alone, between 73rd and 78th streets, has 38 acres (15 ha) of woodland and a maze of trails that Olmsted liked to call his "wild garden." Central Park remains a peaceful and refreshing counterpoint to the city's rigid grid of right-angled streets, the only place left where you can still get lost, and for all the right reasons. **BDS**

Greenwich Village Walking Tour
New York, USA

Start Bleecker Street   End Washington Square
Distance 3 miles (4.8 km)   Time 2 hours
Grade Easy   Type Sidewalk
Map goo.gl/2SqGMH

Greenwich Village—that tiny slice of Lower West Side Manhattan bordered by Broadway, the Hudson River, and Houston Street—achieved its contemporary and well-deserved reputation as a magnet for bohemians, intellectuals, and artists in the 1960s. Long before then, however, it was already home to writers such as Henry James and Edgar Allen Poe, and it has always been the sort of place where people with artistic flair feel free to express themselves.

These days, struggling artists might find Greenwich Village rents a little difficult to afford, but nothing can take away from the fact that it remains one of New York's most appealing neighborhoods, with its leafy avenues, Federal-style buildings, and ivy-clad brownstones. You can start the walk at Bleecker Street, and stroll past a line of antique dealers between Bank and Charles streets before veering off down Christopher Street, the birthplace of the Gay Liberation Movement and the site of the famous Stonewall Rebellion in 1969.

At 75 ½ Bedford Street is what is regarded to be the Village's narrowest house at just 9.5 feet (2.9 m) wide, and at 86 Bedford Street is the simple door to Chumleys, a former speakeasy in the days of Prohibition. Barrow Street is another wonderful walk past period homes and Italianate brownstones, as is postcard-perfect Morton Street. On Macdougal Street you can still see the historic Provincetown Playhouse, which was managed by playwright Eugene O'Neill in the 1920s and was the venue for many of his plays. Walk the perfection of Washington Mews and end at Washington Square, the Village's "town square," with its triumphal arch designed by Stanford White. **BDS**

"The Village . . . was once the incubating ground of artistic, social, and political movements that have shaped U.S. history."

www.freetoursbyfoot.com

⤒ The Village's bohemian streets are a walker's haven of alleyways and leafy avenues.

Coney Island Boardwalk
New York, USA

Start/End Nathan's Famous
Distance 2.5 miles (4 km)   **Time** 1 hour
Grade Easy   **Type** Boardwalk
Map goo.gl/UoHJdE

The Riegelmann Boardwalk, named in honor of New York politician Edward J. Riegelmann but better known to the world as the Coney Island Boardwalk, was built in 1923 along the southern shore of Coney Island in the New York borough of Brooklyn. It was built at a time when the island—which had long been a "people's playground" for an emergent working class, or as nineteenth-century Cuban writer José Marti described it an "immense valve of pleasure opened to an immense nation"—was beginning to lose its allure.

When the boardwalk was added, Coney Island was still a cacophony of cafés, concert halls, dance halls, and honky-tonk bawdiness—the so-called "Sodom by the Sea"—and it was slow to acquire its eventual aura of respectability. When the New York subway reached Coney Island in 1920, a five-cent train ride brought a new wave of tourists, which crowded access to its famous beach and necessitated the construction of a promenade to reclaim the beach for the people.

The boardwalk helped make the beach truly democratic, leading to the demise of waterfront property held by bathhouse proprietors and of the barbed wire that then extended deep into the breaking waves. At 80 feet (24 m) wide and running for half the length of the beachside resort, it not only gave the beach back to the masses, but also the construction of accompanying groins and walls to fight erosion led to the reclaiming of more than 2.5 million square feet (232,250 sq m) of beach. Today, a walk along the Coney Island Boardwalk recalls the glorious days of yesteryear, and it is still a fabulous spot to catch those refreshing Atlantic breezes. **BDS**

"An ideal summer respite from the hectic and steamy city... sunny skies and rolling waves make for the perfect getaway."

www.nycgovparks.org

⬆ It may be showing its age, but Coney Island's boardwalk is still one of New York's finest strolls.

Brooklyn Bridge New York, USA

Start/End Bridge approach, Manhattan or Brooklyn   **Distance** 1 mile (1.6 km)   **Time** 1 hour
Grade Easy   **Type** Sidewalk   **Info** goo.gl/uSVO7j

When it comes to enjoying the best views of the New York skyline, few vantage points provide the panoramic view afforded by walking over the beautiful Brooklyn Bridge, which was built in 1883 and designed by engineer John Augustus Roebling. More than 5,980 feet (1,822 m) in length and 276.5 feet (84.2 m) high, it was the largest suspension bridge in the world at the time, built to connect the boroughs of Brooklyn and Manhattan over the East River.

Walking across it also provides intimate views of the bridge itself. There is something intoxicating about being immersed within its network of pylons and limestone and granite towers, and looking at the city through its web of suspension cables. There is the thrill of framing aspects of the city skyline through its soaring Gothic arches, an echo of the cathedral city of Alsace in France, the Roebling family's home

town. The arches form a triumphal gateway between Manhattan and Brooklyn.

The bridge's pedestrian walkway, which sits blissfully above the hum of the traffic below, can be accessed on the Brooklyn side at the intersection of Tillary Street and Boerum Place, and on the Manhattan side at City Hall. In the 1990s, *TIME* magazine's then-art critic Robert Hughes said that the beauty of the United States is in its bridges, and nowhere is that more true than in Roebling's masterpiece. It can be an insanely busy place, especially on weekends, with walkers, joggers, strollers, and wheelchairs vying for position. The views are best walking from Brooklyn to Manhattan, but you can walk toward Brooklyn—just don't forget, every now and then, to look over your shoulder. **BDS**

⬆ The bridge was dubbed the "eighth wonder of the world."

Newport Cliff Walk Rhode Island, USA

Start Easton's Beach   **End** Bailey's Beach   **Distance** 3.5 miles (5.6 km)   **Time** 2 hours   **Grade** Easy
Type Paved walkway   **Map** goo.gl/bPbiip

This is a heavenly variant on Scylla and Charybdis: on one side of the route is the unrivaled beauty of the Atlantic seaboard; on the other, some of the most opulent and beautiful private dwellings in the United States. Go slowly, lest every time you look right, you miss something on your left, and vice versa.

The mansions to your right as you walk southward from Easton's Beach are all products of the Gilded Age of the last quarter of the nineteenth century. Rosecliff was built by the heiress to the riches of the Comstock Lode silver deposit in Nevada. Marble House looks like the White House in Washington, D.C., and is not much smaller. The Breakers was built for the Vanderbilt family. Ochre Court resembles a French château. Rough Point, formerly another Vanderbilt property, is in the style of an English manor house; it is now a museum.

Just beyond Rough Point, the path crosses a bridge over a yawning chasm that marks the start of the wilder section of the trail, through winding pathways that occasionally run along the tops of 70-foot-high (21 m) cliff tops that may disconcert the timid, but afford breathtaking ocean views. Elsewhere, precipices may be hidden by dense undergrowth, and the thickets may contain poison ivy. The National Recreation Trail maintains a public right of way over private property, and as a landlord you need to be a "people person," because more than a quarter of a million people make the Newport Cliff Walk every year. The journey ends at Bailey's Beach, a sandy shore that is mainly private, but at one end of which is a public section known locally as Rejects' Beach. **GL**

⬆ Walk by the mansions of the United States' Gilded Age.

Atlantic City Boardwalk
New Jersey, USA

Start Absecon Inlet   End Ventnor City
Distance 4.5 miles (7.2 km)   Time 2–3 hours
Grade Easy   Type Boardwalk
Map goo.gl/lXEM4v

"Sun, sand, towering resort hotels, the bustling boardwalk, the awe-inspiring Atlantic ..."

www.atlanticcitynj.com

⬆ Honed in the turbulence of Atlantic hurricanes, Atlantic City's boardwalk has stood the test of time.

National Geographic once called the Atlantic City Boardwalk "the grandfather of all boardwalks." Built to keep the sand out of ritzy oceanfront hotels, it went on to become the most popular walkway on the eastern seaboard of the United States, providing the inspiration for many that would follow. The country's first boardwalk began humbly enough in 1870: only 10 feet (3 m) wide and laid in 12 feet (3.6 m) sections. It was small enough to be taken up every year and stored away from the ravages of winter. By the end of its first decade, however, it had become so splintered from being walked on that the city council ordered a new one be built, this time a little wider and much, much longer. What began as a commerce-free zone, with no businesses allowed closer than 30 feet (9 m), by 1883 had 100 merchants and traders with an Atlantic City Boardwalk address.

Atlantic storms came and went, and with each one the boardwalk grew, becoming stronger. It was given supportive pilings so tides could wash beneath it, and railings, too. By the early 1900s, it was the city's greatest attraction, surpassing the ocean it was built to showcase. Songs were written about it and movies were filmed there. "It is an iridescent bubble on the surface of our fabulous prosperity," wrote *The New York Times* in 1929, just months before a stockmarket crash took down the U.S. economy. Yet even in the depths of the depression, hundreds of thousands still crammed its aging boards. "It was Disneyland," wrote author and historian Bryant Simon, "before there was a Disneyland." The feet of Marilyn Monroe, Frank Sinatra, Bing Crosby, Ed Sullivan, and countless more have trodden it. Maybe yours should, too. **BDS**

Ocean City Boardwalk

Maryland, USA

Start South 2nd Street   End 27th Street
Distance 3 miles (4.8 km)   Time 1 hour
Grade Easy   Type Boardwalk
Map goo.gl/qm4Kym

Ocean City in Maryland, which calls itself without flinching "America's Greatest Family Resort," was founded in 1879, and since then has banned the sale of alcohol within its city boundaries. That, and the community's approach to ensuring families have a relaxing and comforting time from the moment they arrive here, is a welcoming thought if you have children. Once you're here, the chances of them heading off in all directions the moment they see the city's fabulous 3-mile-long (4.8 km) boardwalk are better than even.

Ocean City is built on a barrier island that was once nothing more than a vast area of sand dunes and swamps until four Methodist ministers arrived there in 1879 and decided to build a Christian camp and retreat that they called Ocean City. The rest, as they say, is history. The boardwalk, which runs from South 2nd Street to 27th Street, was built in 1880 and extended five years later. Two fires followed, in 1893 and 1927, and after the second fire the boardwalk was rebuilt on concrete piers closer to the ocean. The Wonderland Amusement Park opened on the boardwalk in 1965 and a second, Playland's Castaway Cove, would follow.

The classic wooden boardwalk still has some of those early amusement rides, including the timeless Herschel–Spellman carousel (since 1902), which is still worth lining up for, or you could try the newer and scarier Runaway Train roller coaster. Mostly, however, the boardwalk is a place for walking—well, strolling, in fact—as you walk off the calories after indulging in a portion of its renowned Thrasher's french fries. **BDS**

Historic Annapolis Ramble

Maryland, USA

Start/End Various
Distance Various   Time Various
Grade Easy   Type Sidewalk
Info goo.gl/14sLoK

Annapolis is a city steeped in history that stretches back to the time of Queen Anne, the eighteenth-century British monarch after whom it was named. It is called the "Athens of America," a Maryland seaport on Chesapeake Bay that was once the U.S. capital, and has witnessed the Revolutionary War, the slave trade, and the Civil War. Its boatyards built minesweepers and patrol boats during World War II, and today they construct world-leading racing yachts. Annapolis is also home to the U.S. Naval Academy and to St. John's College, one of the oldest universities in the country.

"If you're a history buff, Annapolis and Chesapeake Bay belong on your bucket list."

www.visitannapolis.org

The Historic Annapolis Ramble passes through the narrow streets of the city, past stunning Georgian architecture and buildings that were once home to the country's Founding Fathers, including some of the signatories to the Declaration of Independence. The ramble takes you down to the waterfront, with its marina of giant yachts, which itself offers an hour of pleasant pier-strolling, and also takes you past alehouses, coffee shops, and restaurants. Buildings worth noting include the Paca House, the Brice House, and waterfront warehouses once used for drying tobacco. There are plenty of guided tours available, or you can take your own route in one of the most historic and beautiful small cities in the United States. **JI**

Myrtle Beach Boardwalk South Carolina, USA

Start 14th Avenue pier   End 2nd Avenue pier   Distance 1.2 miles (1.9 km)
Time 1 hour   Grade Easy   Type Boardwalk   Map goo.gl/AoiiLZ

Beginning at 14th Avenue and extending for more than a mile along Myrtle Beach's pristine, golden sands to 2nd Avenue, this is not a boardwalk with the sort of history common to its counterparts at Coney Island or Atlantic City. Yet its statistics are no less impressive. Completed in May 2010, it took just nine months to build, consumed more than 800,000 lineal feet (243,840 m) of timber, is held together by 300,000 nails, more than 500,000 screws, and 10,000 bolts, and the city planted 600 palmetto trees to help give it its finishing touch. The result is one of the finest boardwalks in the country, ranked number two by *Travel & Leisure* magazine, which is quite a feat: from not existing at all to second best in just two years.

Like other popular seaside communities in the United States, Myrtle Beach had its own boardwalk for twenty years until a hurricane destroyed it in 1954. The city then went without a boardwalk for more than fifty years, settling instead for a less grandiose seaside pavilion. When the pavilion closed in 1999, the push was on in earnest to replace it with a new, hurricane-proof boardwalk. Now, the boardwalk is in three segments: the North Dunes section with its 8-foot-wide (2.4 m) raised wooden walkway over a sand dune landscape; the busier Central Wooden Boardwalk, with the more traditional boardwalk environment of shops and carnival atmosphere; and the South Promenade section, with its oceanfront park and benches set in a more natural landscape and with various secondary paths. It is a boardwalk built to withstand nature and meet modern needs, and old-fashioned enough to deliver a sense of nostalgia. **BDS**

⬆ Myrtle Beach's new boardwalk has an old-fashioned feel.

Fort Jefferson National Monument Florida, USA

Start/End Garden Key beach **Distance** Various **Time** Various **Grade** Easy
Type Masonry, sand **Info** goo.gl/VOC4l5

Key West is generally thought to be as far west as you can go in the Florida Keys. Mile Marker One is there, and all you see as you look toward the setting sun are the waters of the Gulf of Mexico. However, the geologic footprint of the Keys continues unseen beneath the water, surfacing for one last gasp 68 miles (109 km) farther west at the Tortugas Atoll, a collection of seven small islands and islets, home to some of the healthiest coral reefs remaining off the North American coast, and the site of one enormous fort.

Dry Tortugas National Park is the smallest national park in the United States—just 93 acres (37. 6 ha)—so if you forget to bring your walking shoes, it isn't really going to matter. It's also the park to visit if you've always wanted to conquer a U.S. park but never had the time. This is one of the best beach walks you can have anywhere in the country, not only because of its

unmatched isolation or location in the midst of one of the most pristine bird and marine sanctuaries in the United States, but also because of the presence on Garden Key of the monolithic Fort Jefferson, an unfinished coastal fortress begun in 1846 and the largest masonry construction in the Western hemisphere.

You can come here on the daily ferry, but it is more exciting by seaplane, as nothing can beat the thrill of landing on water and stepping off the seaplane onto sand so fine it squeaks when walked on. The fort (with guided tours available) provides a fabulous walking experience as you circle the ramparts above its 2,000 brick archways and look out onto the calm, turquoise waters of the stunning gulf that envelops you. **BDS**

⬆ Walk the beaches around the smallest U.S. national park.

Santo Domingo City Walk Dominican Republic

Start El Altar de la Patria   **End** Alcázar de Colón   **Distance** 1.5 miles (2.4 km)
Time 2 hours   **Grade** Easy   **Type** Sidewalk   **Map** goo.gl/gIsnDY

The Dominican Republic belonged to Spain from the time of its discovery by Christopher Columbus in 1492 to its independence in 1844, and this short trip through the Zona Colonial of the capital city offers a history of all those mostly colonial five centuries.

The walk begins in Parque Independencia at El Altar de la Patria, a white marble mausoleum that contains the remains of Los Trinitarios, the three founders of the Dominican Republic. Leaving the park through the gate named La Puerta del Conde, part of the fortress that surrounded the original Spanish settlement, you then come to San Nicolás de Bari Hospital, a sixteenth-century building with a ground plan in the shape of a cross. With its upright sections for worship and its lateral arms for the sick, it was the first of many hospitals in Latin America to adopt this ecclesiastically inspired design.

The next landmark is the Consistorial Palace, the former town hall of a Baroque design with a tall white clock tower, and nearby is Santa María la Menor, the oldest cathedral in the Americas, consecrated by Pope Julius II in 1504. At the adjacent Amber Museum, there are fine examples of the mineral on display, and a souvenir shop. Then comes the Pantéon Nacional, which houses the tombs of the Dominican Republic's most distinguished public figures.

The Museo de las Casas Reales was built by the Spanish from 1511 to house its government. It now displays a fascinating collection of relics of the colonial era. The walk ends at the Alcázar de Colón, formerly the governor's residence and now an art gallery that is the most visited museum in Santo Domingo. **GL**

⬆ A city walk spanning five centuries of colonial history.

Christiansted City Walk St. Croix, U.S. Virgin Islands

Start/End Fort Christiansvaern **Distance** 3 miles (4.8 km) **Time** 3 hours **Grade** Easy
Type Sidewalk **Map** goo.gl/mQecEq

The Christiansted National Historic Site on the northern shores of St. Croix in the U.S. Virgin Islands is the island's historic center and primary tourist destination. It was laid out in 1734 by the island's first Danish governor, Frederik Moth, and no time was lost in instituting a raft of strict building codes that, together with the decline in the sugarcane industry in the early nineteenth century, led to the preservation of the town's imposing public buildings. The approximately 30 acres (12 ha) of this compact old town, bordered by Queen Street to the southeast, Kings Cross Street to the west, and the harbor to the north—with its narrow alleyways, shaded sidewalks, and old brick paths—makes for an ideal walking tour. As good a place as any to start it is at Fort Christiansvaern, the city's four-pointed citadel built to defend the town in the age of pirates.

Built largely out of the ubiquitous yellow bricks that were brought to St. Croix as ballast from Europe in the holds of Danish sailing ships, Fort Christiansvaern began its life in 1749 as a fort, and in the late 1800s became the island's police station and courthouse. The boardwalk from the seaplane terminal to the old wharf makes for a pleasant diversion, while other must-see buildings include the Steeple Building, the city's first Lutheran church; the Old Danish Scale House, with its huge scales that were used to weigh everything from bags of sugar to hogs' heads; the Customs House, where taxes on the island's imported goods were determined; and the Danish West India and Guinea Company Warehouse, the headquarters of the all-powerful Danish West India Company. **BDS**

⬆ Fort Christiansvaern is a highlight of this walk.

Bridgetown City Walk
Barbados

Start National Heroes Square **End** Bridge House
Distance 3.5 miles (5.6 km) **Time** 4 hours
Grade Easy **Type** City walk
Map goo.gl/U5I1oi

"[Bridgetown's] many sights and old colonial buildings can easily occupy a day of wandering."

www.lonelyplanet.com

⬆ National Heroes Square is the obvious start point for a perfect day's strolling under the Caribbean sun.

From the mid-seventeenth century to 1966, Barbados belonged to Britain. Though now independent, this small island in the West Indies retains the appearance of an English county that has been miraculously transported to the Caribbean, and in some ways its capital Bridgetown is more British than London.

Start any walking tour in National Heroes Square (formerly Trafalgar Square), where the highlights are its fountain and the statue of British naval hero Lord Nelson. From there stroll along the waterfront down Princess Alice Highway until reaching the Pelican Village Craft Centre, where a right turn takes you past the public market to Kensington Oval, the home of Barbados cricket. The Oval ground was substantially modernized for the 2007 World Cup but still retains much of its original atmosphere, and everywhere are reminders of the great West Indies players who were Bajan born and bred: the three "W"s, Clyde Walcott, Everton Weekes, and Frank Worrell; the legendary opening partnership of Desmond Haynes and Gordon Greenidge; the fast bowlers Wes Hall and Malcolm Marshall; and, in the view of many, the greatest of them all, Sir Garfield Sobers.

On the way back toward the city center, you'll pass St. Mary's Church; the Jubilee Gardens—opened in 1888 to celebrate Queen Victoria's fifty years on the throne—the Cenotaph, which honors the fallen in World Wars I and II; and the Nidhe Israel Synagogue. Divert slightly into Queen's Park to see one of the island's largest trees, a gigantic baobab, and after finishing the walk outside Parliament Buildings back in National Heroes Square, head down through Independence Arch for a drink at the waterfront café at Bridge House. **GL**

Parque Metropolitano Guanguiltagua Trails
Pichincha, Ecuador

Start/End Avenida Eloy Alfaro
Distance 3.7 miles (6 km)   **Time** 3 hours
Grade Easy   **Type** Park walk
Map goo.gl/ddpCis

Parque Metropolitano Guanguiltagua in Quito, Ecuador, is the largest urban green space in South America. With an area of 1,376 acres (557 ha), it is more than one and a half times larger than Central Park, New York, and more than twice the size of London's Hyde Park and Kensington Gardens combined. And it is a lot wilder, too. The world's highest capital city, Quito is 9,350 feet (2,850 m) above sea level, so even after acclimatizing (there is a special room for this purpose in the airport arrivals hall), one can struggle for breath. No prolonged walk at an altitude this high is easy, not even one as short as this: the fastest recorded time for running it is thirty minutes.

The best place to begin to walk its many trails is on Avenida Eloy Alfaro, named after the man who was twice president of Ecuador in the late nineteenth and early twentieth centuries. It stands in the north of the city on the steep sides of Bellavista Hill behind the Estadio Olímpico Atahualpa, Ecuador's national soccer stadium. Most of the trails run through dense eucalyptus forest, interspersed with modern sculptures and herds of grazing alpacas. At breaks in the trees you can see a reservoir, which is within reach via a short detour. In the distance, three great landmarks are visible: the vast stratovolcanoes Cotopaxi (19,347 feet/5,897 m) and Antisana (18,714 feet/5,704 m), and the outstretched basin of the Guayllabamba River. By Ecuadorean standards this circuit is undemanding, a short entry-level excursion. Parque Metropolitano has literally hundreds of other trails, very few of which are clearly marked, so it's easy to get lost. But don't let that put you off: the place is breathtaking in more ways than one. **GL**

"Take a stroll through the fragrant eucalyptus forests in the Parque Metropolitano, which has splendid views of Quito."

www.insightguides.com

⬆ Basilica Del Voto Nacional and other landmarks can be seen from Quito's Parque Metropolitano.

Olinda City Walk Pernambuco, Brazil

Start Igreja do Carmo (Church of Carmo)   **End** Igreja de São Pedro (Church of St. Peter)   **Distance** 3 miles (4.8 km)
Time 3 hours   **Grade** Easy   **Type** City walk   **Map** goo.gl/KXGtgX

This walk through historic Olinda on Brazil's northeast coast abounds with religious buildings. It best begins at the sixteenth-century Igreja do Carmo (Church of Carmo) and leads to the Convento de São Francisco, a Franciscan monastery of similar age. Next is the Museum of Sacred Art and the Observatory, a center of astronomical research until the 1970s. Igreja da Conceiçao (Church of Conception) is the retreat of the reclusive Sisters of Dorothy, who reject the outside world, even for medical assistance. From there a steep slope leads to Santa Casa de Misericórdia (Holy House of Mercy), the first hospital in Brazil. Igreja do Amparo (Church of the Protector) was founded in the sixteenth century by musicians and contains an altar dedicated to their patron saint, Cecilia. Igreja do Nossa Senhora do Rosário dos Homens Pretos (Church of Our Lady of the Rosary of Black Men) was built by African slaves in

the seventeenth century. The morning ends beneath the tower of Igreja de São João (Church of St. John).

After lunch you can visit the Regional Museum, set in an eighteenth-century colonial home, and Casa dos Bonecos Gigante (House of Carnival Dolls). The next stop, Mercado da Ribeira, was a slave market but now sells craft products. The walk continues via the Museu do Mamulengo (a puppet museum with more than 1,500 exhibits), the governor's palace, and Igreja e Mosteiro de São Bento (the Church and Monastery of St. Benedict) to the nineteenth-century neo-colonial Casarão Vermelho. The walk ends at Igreja de São Pedro (Church of St. Peter), in the same square as the house reputed to be Olinda's oldest dwelling, access to which is through an upstairs window. **GL**

⊡ Olinda's churches offer a reflective day's walk.

Brasília Modernist Architecture Walking Tour Brasilia, Brazil

Start National Library   End Esplanada dos Ministerios   Distance 5 miles (8 km)   Time 4 hours
Grade Easy   Type City walk   Map goo.gl/CzjGk4

Brasília is the purpose-built capital of Brazil. Work began in the 1950s, and the city formally took over from Rio de Janeiro as the seat of government in 1960. This is not really a city built for walking—its designer, Lúcio Costa, predicted everyone would soon travel everywhere by car or bus. But he failed to foresee soaring oil prices or the rise in concern about the environment, and while Brasília is much friendlier to automobiles than pedestrians, this walk remains a good introduction to the work of Oscar Niemeyer, the architect who designed most of its official buildings.

Starting at the National Library, head east to the Museu Nacional Honestino Guimarães and then past Niemeyer's masterpiece, the Catedral Metropolitana. This magnificent place of worship—most of which is underground—has sixteen curved columns, a stained-glass interior, and three aluminum angels suspended from the ceiling. Farther along the road is the building Niemeyer created for the Brazilian Foreign Ministry, the Palácio de Itamaraty. Entering Praça dos Tres Poderes (Plaza of the Three Towers), you can see the legislative, judicial, and executive seats of government.

Four other Niemeyer creations should not be missed. The Memorial J.K. houses the remains of Juscelino Kubitschek de Oliveira, the president who opened the new capital, and the Memorial dos Povos Indígenas is a museum of indigenous Indian culture. The Cláudio Santoro National Theater is naturally lit on the inside and has three auditoria. The Esplanada dos Ministerios—a row of identical office buildings—demonstrates that Niemeyer could produce edifices that were utilitarian as well as triumphalist. **GL**

⌂ Brasília Cathedral is Niemeyer's modernist masterpiece.

Tijuca Forest Rio de Janeiro, Brazil

Start Alto da Boa Vista   **End** Pico da Tijuca   **Distance** 3 miles (4.8 km)   **Time** 3–5 hours   **Grade** Moderate
Type Forest climb   **Map** goo.gl/COjHoY

Tijuca National Park is the world's largest urban forest. It almost disappeared during the colonial period, but it was redeveloped from 1861 by order of Dom Pedro II, Emperor of Brazil, whose concern for the environment was more than a century ahead of its time.

The trail in this hand-planted rain forest begins at the entrance to the park at Alto da Boa Vista. Walk for around an hour and a half, past the 97-foot-high (30 m) Cascatinha Taunay waterfall, the Mayrink Chapel with its beautiful painted interior panels, and Os Esquilos restaurant, until you arrive at Bom Retiro, a picnic spot where the road ends. From here the path to the right of the drinking fountain is a steep ascent that culminates in a flight of steps carved into the rock face. On the way up, there are great views over Rio de Janeiro at the Paulo e Virginia Grotto, the Vista do Almirante, the Mesa do Imperador, and the Vista

Chinesa. Not guaranteed, but highly likely, are sightings of ocelots, howler monkeys, and numerous varieties of exotic birds. At the top is Pico da Tijuca, 3,353 feet (1,022 m) above sea level, from where there are magnificent views of the city center, the statue of Christ the Redeemer, and the famous beaches at Ipanema and Leblon.

This is a challenging walk, with an average uphill gradient of 14 percent over rocky terrain. There are often fallen trees along the way that need to be clambered over or detoured around. Although much of the route is shaded by the forest canopy, dehydration is a hazard, especially in summer, and walkers need to beware of precipices with big drops that are often disconcertingly close to the path. **GL**

⊞   A hand-planted forest is the world's largest urban jungle.

Bellavista District Santiago, Chile

Start Montecarmelo   **End** Terraza Bellavista   **Distance** 5 miles (8 km)   **Time** 3 hours   **Grade** Easy to moderate
Type Sidewalk   **Map** goo.gl/53mB7w

The bohemian quarter of Chile's capital has been a magnet for arty, alternative types since at least the 1950s, when Pablo Neruda, the future Nobel laureate, made his home there. It's full of bars, restaurants, and music venues, and has its share of seedy dives, too.

To walk it, start at Montecarmelo, formerly a monastery and now a cultural entertainment center. Then head down Avenida Bellavista and check out the lapis lazuli artifacts and listen to sales assistants tell you that their gemstones are the bluest in the world. Now leave Avenida Bellavista behind and walk into Calle Dardignac, the heart of the Bellavista neighborhood. Among the best of the tapas bars in this street are Azul Profundo and Kilomètre 11680.

On Calle Constitución, there is Plazoleta Mori, dominated by a red house that combines a variety of architectural styles, and Neruda's house, named La Chascona (the woman with scruffy hair) for one of his wives, Matilde Urrutia, which is now a museum of his life and work. Nearby, in Calle Fernando Márquez de La Plata, is a small amphitheater in which there are weekend performances and poetry readings.

Calle Pio Nono is on the outer edge of the sophisticated part of Bellavista. The area to the north is scruffier, but retains its charm. At Plaza Caupolicán is the entrance to Parque Metropolitano, one of the world's largest urban green spaces. Also in the square is the lower terminus of a funicular that runs via Santiago Zoo to Terraza Bellavista. From here a cable car goes up a hill topped by a huge statue of the Virgin Mary, and on the summit you have great views over the city and, on clear days, the Andes. **GL**

⬆ Take the cable car up San Cristóbal Hill after your stroll.

Arthur's Seat and Holyrood Park
Edinburgh, Scotland

"... the perfect antidote to the streets of Edinburgh, a climb on to Arthur's Seat grants a breathtaking view."

The Guardian

⊡ Is it Camelot or merely what Robert Louis Stevenson described as a mountain of "bold design"?

Start Scottish Parliament on Queen's Drive, parking lot
End Arthur's Seat summit **Distance** 2.75 miles
(4.4 km) **Time** 1–2 hours **Grade** Easy
Type Pathways, grassy trails **Map** goo.gl/R79LTb

At only 823 feet (250 m), Arthur's Seat—the highest point in the grouping of tiny, extinct volcanic peaks that form the greater part of Edinburgh's Holyrood Park—may indeed be just a hill, but to the writer Robert Louis Stevenson it had a grandeur that many a higher peak may have lacked. Although its size made it a "hill for magnitude," he wrote, it was nevertheless "a mountain in virtue of its bold design."

One of the contenders for the site of mythical Camelot, and the spot where Edinburgh girls once bathed their faces to make themselves more beautiful in crystal springs that ran down its slopes, Arthur's Seat sits at the center of Edinburgh, about a mile to the east of Edinburgh Castle. There are two ways to the summit: one on a rocky diagonal path up its long escarpment of Salisbury Crags; the other on the main walking path to the back of the crags that bears right onto a grassy path, which takes you on an easier alternate route to the top of the crags. Already the panoramas are stupendous, with views down to Holyrood Palace and the Scottish Parliament, and as far as Leith and the Firth of Forth.

Following the escarpment, there are views to the Arthur's Seat summit and a set of stairs that zigzags up its heavily inclined flank before curving around it like a contour and taking you on a final, rather rocky, ascent to the summit. There you can contemplate its many references in literature, from Mary Shelley's *Frankenstein* (1818) to Jules Verne's *The Underground City* (1877). Coming down you pass over patches of grassy, lumpy ground and over gorse with great views toward St. Margaret's Loch before emerging—not too worn out—back onto Queen's Drive. **BDS**

Thames Path
London, England

Start Stone marker near Kemble   End Thames Barrier, Woolwich   Distance 184 miles (296 km)   Time 12–14 days   Grade Easy   Type Long-distance walking trail   Info goo.gl/tOXtWf

Alongside the river that was once the lifeblood of medieval England, and that prior to the Ice Age was a tributary of the Rhine (when the English Channel was just a dry, shallow valley), runs the Thames Path— the only long-distance walking trail in England that follows a river along the entirety of its course, from its source to its tidal waters.

The Thames Path begins in the Cotswolds, so you are relaxed even before you start. This wonderful trail was first mooted in the 1880s, when it was thought that the Thames towpath, having fallen into disrepair as Britain's expanding railways took over from its rivers as the preferred means of transport, might be preserved and transformed into a long-distance trail. However, it was only in the 1970s that the Ramblers Association and the River Thames Society persuaded the government to undertake a study, and the plan was approved in 1989. New footbridges were erected, 1,200 signposts put in place, the towpath was rejuvenated, and the route officially opened in 1996.

Starting from Kemble, the path takes you through farmlands until you reach the charming market town of Lechlade, where the river becomes navigable; this is also the location of St. John's Lock, the river's first lock. From there it is a series of easy crossings as you go from bank to bank, from north of Oxford to Henley-on-Thames, over the oldest bridge at Newbridge and a climb over the symmetrical domes of the Wittenham Clumps and its remnants of an Iron Age fort. After passing Hurley and Marlow, two of the river's oldest settlements, as well as Windsor Castle and Eton, London finally beckons, with the trail ending at the Thames Barrier. **BDS**

"This is a world-class walk along the enchanted River Thames … [and] London never seems so alive as it does on the South Bank."

Rowan Pelling, *Telegraph*

⊡ The Thames Path offers views of historic landmarks, such as Windsor Castle with its distinctive Round Tower.

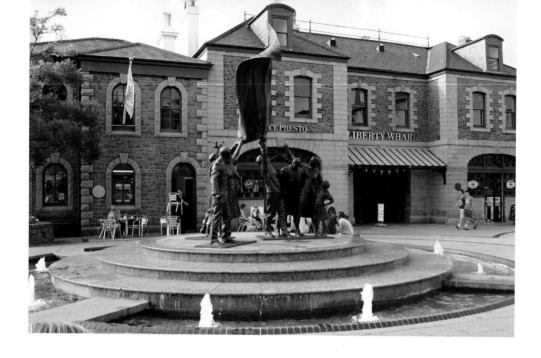

St. Helier Walking Tour Jersey, Channel Islands

Start/End Liberation Square   **Distance** Various   **Time** 1 hour–1 day   **Grade** Easy
Type Roads, sidewalk, parkland   **Info** goo.gl/JB1OAj

Victor Hugo once described the Channel Islands, a stone's throw away from the Normandy coastline, as "pieces of France fallen into the sea and picked up by England." Now British to the core, they were once a part of the Duchy of Normandy, but regardless of who holds the title deed, the archipelago's collection of churches, castles, fortifications, cliff top paths, and wooded interiors makes them a walkers' paradise—and nowhere is it more walker-friendly than in St. Helier, Jersey's tiny capital.

You can get a map for a walking tour of the city from almost anywhere once you arrive, but the fact is, there is so much to see—so many interesting historic nooks and crannies—that even the very best-intentioned of organized walks soon descends into a myriad of detours and tangents as you discover one unexpected site after another. A good point to begin, at least, is Liberation Square, and from there either Mulcaster or Conway streets takes you straight into the town center where the options suddenly seem to overwhelm you. There is Bond Street, with the wonderful sash windows of its old merchant houses; Royal Square, which was the town's market place until 1802; the tiled roofs of the seventeenth-century houses on Vine Street; and the 1930s Art Deco influences of Halkett Place.

You can walk down to the slipway at Le Dicq, where a promenade path will take you to La Collette Gardens on the slopes of Mount Bingham, or just ramble through town where you might seek out St. Helier's first prison at Charing Cross, with its "debtor dungeon" beneath the road. **BDS**

⬆ A statue recalls Jersey's liberation from Nazi occupation.

Mont Saint Michel Basse-Normandie, France

Start Pré Salé   **End** L'Abbaye du Mont Saint Michel   **Distance** 5 miles (8 km)   **Time** 2–3 hours
Grade Easy   **Type** Various   **Map** goo.gl/psK1oo

The world-famous monastery of Mont Saint Michel sits atop an island around 0.5 mile (0.8 km) off the coast of Normandy, at the mouth of the Couesnon River. There are several easy ways of reaching it, but walking is the best, not least because it avoids all but one percent of the 3.2 million visitors who throng the place every year. Start anywhere on the mainland (Pré Salé is a recommended departure point) and set off across the sand dunes that appear at low tide.

But think before doing this unescorted. The sea retreats 9 miles (14 km) along this coastline and returns quickly, and there is a mean tidal range of 36 feet (11 m), meaning the water may rise as much as 50 feet (15 m). Even when the tide is out, there are still pools of water that may be suitable for paddling, but may also be deep enough to drown in. There are also quicksands, so use the services of a local guide

who really knows the terrain. While it may be tempting to take waterproof footwear and clothing, the recommended rig is bare feet and shorts: the former so that you can better feel the "give" in the sand; the latter because they afford greater freedom of movement, and you're pretty sure to get wet, anyway.

On reaching the island of Mont Saint Michel, you can begin the steep climb to its peak. On the way you pass numerous watering holes and retail souvenir outlets, but finally you will reach the marvelous eleventh-century Romanesque abbey and church, with its underground chapels and crypts, and can admire the fortifications added by the French King Charles VI—a real treat. **GL**

⌂ A tidal flat walk, with a beacon you can't miss.

Left Bank, Seine Ile-De-France, France

Start Chaillot Palace   **End** Notre-Dame   **Distance** 4 miles (6.4 km)   **Time** 3 hours   **Grade** Easy
Type Sidewalk   **Map** goo.gl/aq60Qu

This walk stakes no claim to encompass the whole of the French capital, but it does give the visitor a fabulous introduction to the city. Naturally, the total distance may be covered in less than the time suggested, but there is much to take in en route.

The starting point at the Chaillot Palace has been chosen partly because it is a beautiful building housing the historic Naval Museum, the Museum of Mankind, and the Cinema Museum—but mainly because it provides a wonderful view of the next stop along the way, the Eiffel Tower, which you reach by crossing the Pont d'Iéna.

You might like to climb to the viewing platform near the top of the 1,056-foot (322-m) landmark, then proceed across the Champ-de-Mars to the Place Joffre, turn left, and walk straight on past L'Ecole Militaire on Avenue de la Motte-Picquet into Les

Invalides, a garden full of museums and monuments detailing French military history.

Eventually, you return to the riverbank, turn right, and walk along the Quai Voltaire past the entrance to the magnificent Musée d'Orsay art gallery in a former railway station that now houses important works by a range of artists, including many leading Impressionists and Post-Impressionists.

On reaching the sixteenth-century Pont Neuf—the oldest bridge in Paris—you cross onto the Ile de la Cité and into the shadows of Notre-Dame, the great Gothic cathedral, which was begun in 1163 and largely completed by the middle of the fourteenth century, concluding a walk that is guaranteed to whet the appetite for exploring Paris in detail. **GL**

⊞ Open-air stalls line the elegant quays of the River Seine.

Ile Saint-Louis Ile-De-France, France

Start/End Rue Saint-Louis-en-l'Ile   **Distance** Various   **Time** Various   **Grade** Easy
Type Pavement   **Info** goo.gl/5F6XH9

The Ile Saint-Louis on the Seine is one of two natural islands on the river, connected to the surrounding city by five bridges. Once used for grazing cattle and to stockpile wood for winter, the island is now often full to overflowing with tourists, particularly in summer. And for good reason: this is one of the city's prettiest neighborhoods, with row after row of gorgeous seventeenth-century townhouses. Without question, if you're here at just the right time in the late afternoon, when the sun strikes the Quai de Bourbon and the Pont Marie, the beauty of Paris will take your breath away.

The guidebooks say that an hour and a half is all you need to explore the streets here, but in truth you can spend far longer if you have the luxury of time. The island's two bookstores alone, the Librairie Ulysses and the Librairie de Paris et son Patrimoine,

will consume an hour each. The residents love the sense of "separateness from the city" and refer to walking over the Pont de la Tournelle as being "on the way to the Continent." Take your time to walk along the romantic riverbanks and soak up the village atmosphere as you look over the water at the Latin Quarter to one side and Le Marais on the other. Ile Saint-Louis is the very heart of the French capital.

The monumental buildings on the island include the baroque seventeenth-century church Saint-Louis-en-l'Ile, but it is the streets with their small shops, fromageries, and groceries that really enchant—not to forget the legendary establishment of Berthillon on rue Saint-Louis-en-l'Ile, arguably home to the finest ice cream in France and a destination in itself. **BDS**

⊡ Admire the historic buildings on this island enclave.

Bruges Historic Center

West Flanders, Belgium

Start/End Markt (Market Square)
Distance 3 miles (4.8 km)   Time 3 hours
Grade Easy   Type Cobbled streets
Info goo.gl/1UWINO

The city of Bruges derives its name from the Old Dutch word for "bridge," a suitable description for a city built on water. Canals run through the city, which was once connected to the North Sea by the Zwin channel. During the Middle Ages, Bruges was one of the main trading centers in Europe. Merchant ships used its canals and wharfs to export woolen textiles across Europe and to import spices from the Levant, grain from Normandy, and wine from Gascony. The city was renowned for its textile and later lace production and became a major financial center—the world's first stock exchange opened here in 1309.

The town's prosperity did not last, however, as the Zwin channel silted up in the 1500s and the city lost its markets to nearby Antwerp. Yet that decline has been a blessing in disguise, for the city was never industrialized or modernized: the medieval core has remained unaltered to this day, escaping both twentieth-century redevelopment and high-rises and damage during the two world wars.

The historic center of Bruges is a delight to walk around, its quiet cobbled streets and open squares showcasing a wealth of beautiful buildings. Start and finish at the Markt (market square), with its medieval gabled houses. The Heritage Walk signposted on information boards on the back of the city map boards will take you to some of the most treasured buildings, but in reality, any organized or informal tour will satisfy. Worth visiting are the Stadhuis, the Gothic city hall, and the Belfort, an octagonal belfry rising 272 feet (83 m) above the square below. **SA**

⬅ The Markt is located in the heart of the city center.

Western Canal Ring

Noord Holland, Netherlands

Start Prinsengracht 191   End Keizersgracht 401
Distance 2 miles (3.2 km)   Time 2 hours
Grade Easy   Type Sidewalk
Map goo.gl/WRHkpH

This is not a walk for fitness fanatics, in fact you are more likely to gain weight than lose it with the starting point at Amsterdam's famous Pancake Bakery where you can eat the great Dutch specialty with almost every imaginable topping or filling. Appropriately fueled you now turn left into Prinsengracht and walk past lookalike terraced buildings that line the canal with ascending door numbers until you see one particular entrance that has a long line of people outside at all times—the Anne Frank House, former home of the famous teenage diarist.

> *"This is one of Amsterdam's most gorgeous areas, with grand old mansions and speciality shops."*
>
> Lonely Planet

Next comes Westerkerk, a seventeenth-century Protestant church and one of the most prominent sights on the Amsterdam skyline. A short distance farther south are the Nine Streets, a warren of quirky boutiques, galleries, and cafés. Continue down Prinsengracht to the junction with Wolvenstraat, turn left, and examine the embroidered linen clothes for sale at Laura Dols. At the next junction turn right onto Herengracht and right again into Huidenstraat. Be sure to try the fruit tarts at the Pompadour patisserie.

Continue west for a few paces, then turn left onto Keizersgracht and finish the walk at Huis Marseille, a photography museum in a restored seventeenth-century canal house with a garden at the back. **GL**

Lübeck Historic Center Schleswig-Holstein, Germany

Start/End Holstentor (Holsten Gate)   Distance 5 miles (8 km)   Time 2 hours   Grade Easy
Type Sidewalk, cobblestones   Map goo.gl/WkmgT8

If the Royal Air Force had known on the night of March 28, 1942, before it dropped 25,000 bombs on the historic center of Lübeck, that the town once had a reputation as "the place that said 'no' to Hitler," when in 1932 the then-independent city forbade him to campaign here, would it have gone a little easier on it?

However, in wartime, sentiment counts for little, particularly when a town is uncomfortably close to a strategic seaport. The firestorm that followed was so fierce it melted the bells in St. Mary's Church, and three years after the war was over, they were still removing the rubble. All this makes the restoration of the city (which was rebuilt from 1949) and the subsequent bestowing of World Heritage Site status in 1987 all the more remarkable.

Originally founded in 1143 as the western world's first Baltic city, the historic center of Lübeck, home of writer Thomas Mann, has been meticulously restored to its former medieval, mercantile glory, complete with all the architectural quirks and features common to towns and communities through northern Holland and all the way to Gdansk: tiny brick homes with ornate, stepped gables, big masonry and brick churches, and cobbled alleyways.

Walking tours are big business in Lübeck but it is also possible to devise your own route to take in the major sights. The town hall, the castle monastery, the Koberg quarter with its fifteenth- and sixteenth-century Patrician houses between the cathedral and St. Peter's Church are among more than a thousand reborn buildings in a city that knows all about the art of meticulous preservation. **BDS**

⊤ St. Mary's remains the tallest building in old Lübeck.

Barefoot Path North Rhine-Westphalia, Germany

Start/End Bad Sobernheim   **Distance** 2.2 miles (3.5 km)   **Time** 1 hour   **Grade** Easy
Type Mud, grass, sand, gravel   **Map** goo.gl/KfMSkO

In the town of Bad Sobernheim, in Germany's Nahe Valley, there is a path that is open every summer, no matter the weather. Rain, flooding, unseasonal snow—in fact, the muddier and messier it gets, the more this short trail seems to be in vogue. Called the Barefoot Path, it is one of a growing number of trails throughout Europe where the quality of your footwear is of no consequence. All you need is, well, a pair of feet and maybe a sense of humor.

Open from May to October, from 9 a.m. to 8 p.m., the Barefoot Path runs along the scenic Nahe River and is a merciful respite for feet that are normally encased in tight walking shoes. Sand, bark, soft gravel, mud, and grass—the surfaces are kind to the feet in a region that knows something about the rejuvenating capacity of mud baths, and it is commonly accepted that feeling various elements on the soles of your feet

can have beneficial effects on your heart, can improve muscles involved in strengthening the spinal cord, and can increase metabolism. Vascular problems, hip ailments, or leg cramps—an increasing amount of research is suggesting that going without shoes can improve all these problems, and more.

The Nahe River is in the Saarland district, a land of ravines, forests, floodplains, and the town of Bad Sobernheim itself, which was first chartered in 1292 but only began to grow in the mid 1800s. The town is the only one in Germany with a Felke bath, a series of body treatments pioneered by the nineteenth-century naturopath and Protestant pastor Emanuel Felke. What better recommendation, then, for a muddied pathway? **BDS**

⬆ Discover the Nahe River, one of the Rhine's tributaries.

Cologne Cathedral, South Tower
North Rhine-Westphalia, Germany

Start/End Roncalliplatz
Distance 311 feet (95 m)
Time 10 minutes   Grade Easy
Type Stairs   Info goo.gl/Pme6uD

Is it a walk or is it a climb? However you choose to define it, ascending the stairway inside the South Tower of Cologne Cathedral, the Gothic masterpiece begun in 1248 on the site of seven previous structures and completed only in 1880, offers substantial visual rewards with views over the city and the broad, languid Rhine River below.

The tower's entrance can be found at the cathedral's southern side, on the square of Roncalliplatz, and it takes you down a flight of stairs below street level and through the cathedral's mighty foundations to the first step of the spiral staircase at the base of the South Tower, which is narrow enough for two people to walk side by side and long enough to accommodate hundreds. Your first stop is the belfry, 291 stairs up. Here, at 173 feet (53 m), is the magnificent Bell of St. Peter, or, as the locals say, the "Dicker Pitter" (thick Peter). Cast in 1923, it weighs 24 tons and, with a diameter of more than 10 feet (3 m), was once the world's largest free-swinging church bell.

From there it's up to the tower's observation deck at 319 feet (97 m), now completely fenced in to prevent suicides. The views are appropriately panoramic, beginning with the facing side of the North Tower, which is 3 inches (7 cm) taller than the South Tower, all the way to the hills of the Siebengebirge when the weather is good. The church remains the city's second tallest structure, and its spires are Europe's second tallest after Ulm Minster. These spires were, in fact, a navigational aid for allied airmen during World War II, and the church suffered fourteen hits from Allied bombers. Yet it failed to collapse, and is now a UNESCO World Heritage Site. **BDS**

"The cathedral can be seen from nearly every point in the center … it is the pride of the people."

www.cologne.de

⬆ The city's first Christians met on this site in Roman times, and the first church was erected in the ninth century.

Tiergarten
Berlin, Germany

Start/End Schloss Bellevue   **Distance** Various
Time Various   **Grade** Easy
Type Gravel paths, sidewalk
Info goo.gl/uKwceu

The woodlands of Berlin's Tiergarten (literally "animal garden," because wild animals were once kept there for hunting), designed in the 1830s by Prussian gardener and landscape architect Peter Lenne, may seem to the untrained eye like a mature old forest. But it is not. By the end of World War II, the residents of Berlin had plundered every piece of wood they could scavenge here, burning it to stay warm through the winter of 1944, and for several years afterward in a city that was little more than a bombed-out shell with no electricity and little running water. The beautiful urban forest that is found here now, bisected by the boulevard Unter den Linden and various other thoroughfares, is a mere seventy years old.

The Tiergarten is wonderfully situated just across the road from the Reichstag and stretches from within a stone's throw of the Brandenburg Gate all the way to the Berlin Zoo, so it can easily be combined with a walking tour of the greatest sights of the city. It boasts romantic bridges, ponds and waterways, and lush open lawns as well as public buildings, including the Bellevue Palace built in 1876 and now home to the German president, all connected by a 14-mile (23-km) network of pathways and trails.

Just step a few feet past the thick greenery, and the noise of the city seems to evaporate. Once amid the flowerbeds and rhododendrons, there is a temptation to stop walking and simply sit on one of the many benches and marvel at the English-style gardens; its quiet, hidden nooks and the sheer diversity of the landscapes can easily turn an hour-long stroll into a day of contented bliss. **BDS**

Nördlingen Rampart Walk
Bavaria, Germany

Start/End Any of the rampart towers
Distance 1.5 miles (2.4 km)   **Time** 45 minutes
Grade Easy   **Type** City walls, ramparts
Map goo.gl/2OMTfS

You almost feel like a voyeur, peering down into the courtyards, backyards, and private spaces of Nördlingen's unsuspecting residents as you stroll along the battlements that encircle this wonderfully preserved medieval town. A woodpile here, a vegetable patch there, a bedroom, a study, a quiet nook... it's enough to make you want to circle it twice. Walk it once to look inward, then again to look out over the new city that has grown up all around it.

Nördlingen is one of the few fifteenth-century communities left in Europe with its ramparts still fully

> *"The top of the 'Daniel' is just perfect for enjoying panoramic views of the medieval town."*
>
> www.bavaria.travel

intact. Stop anywhere and simply look down into the medieval streets to easily get your bearings. There are no crowds here: walking the ramparts is an unhurried and serene experience. You can do a circuit inside an hour, and then explore the town. The ramparts are covered, too, so you can walk here in comfort whatever the weather.

Nördlingen lies at the base of the Ries Crater, a 15 million year-old, 16-mile (25-km) wide meteoric crater, the rim of which can be seen from the top of the Daniel Tower of the town's fifteenth-century Gothic St. Georg's Church. The tower was made from the very stones that long ago were made available by the meteor's impact. **BDS**

Graz Historic Center Styria, Austria

Start Burg (castle)   **End** Uhrturm   **Distance** 1.05 miles (1.7 km)   **Time** 1 hour   **Grade** Easy
Type Cobbled streets, sidewalks   **Map** goo.gl/ZYl6F5

The name Graz comes from the Slovene word *gradec*, meaning "small castle," as some ancient Slovenes once built a small castle on the main crag that dominates the city. The Slovenes have always considered this Austrian city to be politically and culturally more important than their own capital, Ljubljana, across the Slovenian border to the south, and they are still an important presence today. Graz is a city of more than 300,000 people, with several universities—and the Old Town is one of the best-preserved city centers in central Europe.

The historic center is a real architectural delight. Since the city sits at a point where central Europe, Italy, and the Balkan states converge, it has absorbed influences from all three. The old buildings are constructed in many styles, forming a townscape well deserving of its UNESCO World Heritage Site status.

There are many good walks to take around the old town. One starts at the Burg (castle), built for Austrian emperor Maximilian I, then moves on to the Gothic Dom (cathedral), built by Emperor Frederick III. Walk past the mausoleum of Emperor Ferdinand II to the Glockenspiel, a musical clock that plays different melodies three times a day as wooden statues of a dancing couple cavort in its gabled windows.

A quick sprint past the Gemaltes Haus (painted house) brings you to the Landhaus, a sixteenth-century structure housing the Styrian state parliament to this today. Next up are the Rathaus (city hall) and finally the Uhrturm, the thirteenth-century clock tower on top of the Schlossberg (castle mountain) that dominates the skyline of this fabulous city. **SA**

⊡ There have been settlements here since the Copper Age.

Madrid Walking Tour Madrid, Spain

Start Real Academia de Bellas Artes de San Fernando   **End** La Botillería   **Distance** 4 miles (6.4 km)
Time 4 hours   **Grade** Easy   **Type** Sidewalk   **Map** goo.gl/p5exrS

What better place to begin a walk in Madrid than at the spot where Pablo Picasso and Salvador Dalí began their careers, the Real Academia de Bellas Artes de San Fernando. From here head west through the Puerta de Sol, the geographical center of Spain, along Calle de Postas to Plaza Mayor, the great square that has at various times been a rallying point, a place of public execution, and a bullring.

Leave the square to go down a stairway beneath Arco de Cuchilleros and past Botín, reputedly the world's oldest restaurant, which has been serving roast suckling pig since 1725. After twisting back through narrow streets, you reach the Convento del Corpus Christi; ring the doorbell to buy *yemas* (candied egg yolks) from the nuns.

Beyond this cloistered retreat lies Plaza de la Villa, a square surrounded by buildings of three different periods: the fourteenth-century Plateresque Casa de Cisneros, the fifteenth-century Mudéjar-style tower Torre de los Lujanes, and the seventeenth-century Habsburg Casa de la Villa. On Calle Mayor you pass a monument to the victims of a bomb in 1906 that killed many but not its intended victim, King Alfonso XIII.

Turning right onto Calle Bailén, you pass the Catedral del la Almudena and continue to the Palacio Real, the largest palace in Western Europe. Farther north you enter the statue-lined gardens of Plaza Oriente, on the far side of which is the Teatro Real opera house. Next door you find La Botillería, a Belle Epoque café where you may end the tour with a drink on the terrace that is overlooked by the house in which Diego Velázquez painted *Las Meninas* (1656). **GL**

⌂ Religion and art will slow your Madrid walk to a crawl.

Ronda Walking Tour Andalusia, Spain

Start/End Plaza de Toros bullring **Distance** 2 miles (3.2 km) **Time** 3 hours **Grade** Easy
Type Sidewalks and paths **Map** goo.gl/CfOhr3

Prehistoric remains, including rock paintings, are found near Ronda, which was first settled by the Celts in the sixth century BCE. They called it Arunda, while the later Phoenicians settlers called it Acinipo. The current city, however, is Roman in origin, set up as a fortified post by Scipio Africanus during the long Second Punic War (218–201 BCE) between Rome and Carthage. Since then the city has passed under Suebi, Byzantine, Visigoth, and Arab control until, after a brief siege, it finally came under Spanish control in 1485. Its large Muslim and Jewish populations were either forcibly converted or expelled. In 1936, Fascist sympathizers were thrown off a cliff, an event fictionally chronicled by Ernest Hemingway in his novel *For Whom The Bell Tolls* (1940).

The city is perched high up on steep hills and is bisected by the El Tajo Canyon, which was carved out by the Guadalevín River below. Ronda is something of a tourist trap, which makes it very busy during the peak summer season. But come in the winter, and the place is nearly deserted.

An ideal city stroll starts at the Plaza de Toros bullring and crosses the misnamed New Bridge (completed in 1793), heading into the old town. From there, follow a counterclockwise direction, taking in the Mondragon Palace, the city hall, and a few of the many old churches and shady squares. At the end of the old city lies the principal gateway and much of the walls that date back to the 1200s. From here, head back through the old city and across the Arab or Old Bridge into the main town and follow the streets adjacent to the canyon back to the bullring. **SA**

⤒ **Puente Romano spans the canyon at Ronda.**

Mantua and Sabbioneta City Tour Lombardy, Italy

Start Mantua   End Sabbioneta   Distance 20 miles (32 km)   Time 5–6 hours   Grade Easy
Type Sidewalk   Map goo.gl/54xvcf

Mantua, the birthplace of the poet Virgil, is the starting point for this walk. Marvel at the Palazzo Ducale, the centuries-old residence of the Gonzaga family, rulers of the city until the eighteenth century and patrons of Claudio Monteverdi, who used to play in the magnificent Sala dello Specchio every Friday evening. The palace buildings are the work of Giulio Romano, and the grounds feature hanging gardens and the Church of Santa Barbara, which contains a priceless sixteenth-century organ.

You can spend half a day here before you even begin to explore the city's old squares and other cultural highlights, which include Antonio Bibiena's Teatro Scientifico in the Accademia Virgiliana, where Mozart played on his first tour of Italy, while for Verdi fans there is the House of Rigoletto. Mantua's numerous churches include the Rotonda of San Lorenzo, San Francesco, and San Sebastiano. Another highlight is the Castello di San Giorgio with frescoes by Andrea Mantegna.

Exploration of Sabbioneta is best begun on the city walls, where you can see the neat results of Renaissance urban planning outstretched before you. Next visit the Palazzo Giardino with its Ancient Gallery and the Teatro all'Antica, an architectural wonder designed by Vincenzo Scamòzzi, a pupil of Palladio.

Although the journey between these great musical centers may be undertaken on foot without difficulty, the route crosses a flat section of the Po Valley but remains out of sight of the river itself. Consequently, many visitors plan each city as a separate walk and drive between the two. **GL**

⊡ **Looking down on Mantua's Piazza Sordello.**

Grand Canal
Veneto, Italy

Start/End Hotel Gritti Palace
Distance 5 miles (8 km)
Time 4 hours–1 day   **Grade** Easy
Type Promenades, sidewalks   **Map** goo.gl/OdTeXx

The Grand Canal used to be the site of an ancient river that flowed into this now-famous lagoon. People had been living here since long before the rise of the Roman Empire, because to live on a lagoon was to be safe from attack. They lived in houses propped up on stilts that were driven into the lagoon's mud floor and traded fish and salt. When the Romans arrived, the site was populated on a larger scale, but it wasn't until the ninth century that the city's 117 mud islands began to take shape and an interconnected city built on a foundation of wood pilings began to emerge. Today, the Grand Canal is at the epicenter of the engineering marvel that is Venice, and the pleasure of walking along it increases proportionally with one's understanding of how it came about.

This marvelous city built on wood, which over time becomes petrified in its oxygen-free, mineral-rich sunken environment, is a true walker's paradise. There is no such thing as a wrong turn here, no getting lost, and definitely no getting bored. Of course, it is terribly crowded all day, but if you are staying on the island, you can wait for the tourist crowds to dwindle as afternoon turns to night and the city reveals its unique nighttime charm.

A word of caution: the canal waters may look beautiful, but have been used for trash disposal for centuries. When Katharine Hepburn fell into one during a scene in the film *Summertime* (1955), she contracted conjunctivitis, which bedeviled her for the rest of her life. So walk the Grand Canal by all means, and well into the night—just don't fall in. **BDS**

◁ The canal is a showcase of four centuries of architecture.

Old Bridge Trail
Santa Brigida Liguria, Italy

Start/End Chapel of Santa Brigida
Distance 4 miles (6.4 km)
Time 2–2.5 hours   **Grade** Easy
Type Rural trails   **Map** goo.gl/jm9Gwv

Liguria is simultaneously attractive and challenging. Its beauty is legendary—providing inspiration for poets and painters, particularly during the Romantic period. But its location, hemmed in between the Mediterranean Sea and the Maritime Apennine mountain range, means there are only two coastal roads leading to it, and progress can be painfully slow. Furthermore, away from the historic Cinque Terre, some of the coastal development is dispiriting.

For walkers prepared to struggle their way through jostling crowds, this short circular route offers

> *"The Ligurian coast … is crisscrossed with ancient trails that predate Christianity."*
>
> www.active-traveller.com

rewards off the beaten track. It starts near the fifteenth-century chapel of Santa Brigida in the coastal town of Celle Ligure, then descends steeply into the wooded valley of the Merea River. The next landmarks are a ninth-century stone bridge and the home of a hermit named Luigi with clairvoyant powers. After a series of rock pools and a waterfall, you get to an old rectangular drystone herdsman's shelter. Moving on through fields of lavender you reach another stone bridge between the villages of Pietrabruna and Dolcedo—the latter is worth a detour for the medieval streets and a snack at one of the bars. The final quadrant is a climb back up the hillside through olive groves, past a sheep shelter, to the starting point. **GL**

Herculean Addition Emilia-Romagna, Italy

Start/End Este Castle   **Distance** 5 miles (8 km)   **Time** 3 hours   **Grade** Easy   **Type** Sidewalk
Map goo.gl/1EOSOe

In the 1400s, the medieval city of Ferrara—on the banks of the Po di Volano River, in the plains of Emilia-Romagna—was one of Europe's wealthiest cities, and being wealthy meant wanting to grow. The first addition to the city was built in 1451, but still the city grew. Consequently, an ambitious urban plan, the Herculean Addition, was initiated by the Duke of Ferrara, Ercole d'Este, and designed by his favorite architect, Biagio Rossetti. The addition redefined Ferrara, more than doubling its size, and in the process turned it from a medieval fortress into a Renaissance masterpiece.

The expansion also transformed the city into a walker's paradise, with more than 5.5 miles (9 km) of "new" city walls still remaining that have been tweaked to take not only walkers but also cyclists around the ramparts of this lovely city. And while a walk through Florence, that other great Renaissance city,

can be an obstacle course of buses, cars, and tourists, in sleepier Ferrara, all you need to be mindful of is keeping clear of the thousands of bicycles—the preferred mode of transport for most—that glide through its streets.

A glorious boulevard, on top of which sits the impressive Este Castle, separates medieval Ferrara, with its bricks, cloisters, and jumble of roads and alleyways, from the open spaces, parks, and palazzi of Renaissance Ferrara, and both are equally worthy areas for hours of strolling. If you visit the convent of Sant'Antonio during the allotted hours and ring the bell, the nuns will let you in and you can sit in the outer church and hear their cracked, aging voices singing the public vespers. Now *that's* Italy. **BDS**

⬆ Explore an inspired early example of urban expansion.

Florence City Tour Tuscany, Italy

Start Hotel Lungarno   **End** Westin Excelsior Hotel   **Distance** 6 miles (9.6 km)   **Time** 1 day
Grade Easy   **Type** Sidewalk   **Map** goo.gl/9xssMQ

There is arguably only one way to see Florence—with a Leica camera hanging around your neck, loaned to you for the day as a guest of the Hotel Lungarno on the south bank of the Arno River, just a dice roll from the famous Ponte Vecchio.

Start the walk by wandering down the Via de Bardi to Piazzale Michelangelo, with its bronze copy of *David* (1501–04; the original is across town in the Galleria dell'Accademia), and from there to the small church of Santa Felicita, the city's second oldest church and home to Jacopo da Pontormo's masterpiece *The Deposition* (1528). Thirty minutes into your walk and already you will have probably taken more pictures than you can count.

Just a few streets, and fifty more pictures west, is the Basilica di Santo Spirito, the well-known fifteenth-century church with a facade of smooth stone by the famed former goldsmith turned innovative architect, Filippo Brunelleschi.

Crossing the Arno, you get to the plain-looking church Santa Trinità, where the ceiling frescoes still have the capacity to excite even the most hardened Florentine. They are truly staggering, and include *The Adoration of the Shepherds* (1485), as well as scenes from the life of St. Francis. More pictures.

Walk along the Arno to the Piazza Ognissanti, which began life as a picturesque village in the twelfth century and is now overlooked by the Westin Excelsior Hotel, which has grown considerably from when it was a sixteenth-century private residence, a grand sanctuary in which to end a memorable day of pavement pounding over a glass of red. **BDS**

⬆ Brunelleschi's dome defines the Florentine skyline.

Villa Borghese
Lazio, Italy

Start/End Piazza del Popolo
Distance Various   **Time** 1 day   **Grade** Easy
Type Sealed pathways, well-maintained trails
Info goo.gl/sJzvJL

"Some of the finest sights are tucked away next to green lawns. ... You'll walk through the ages of Rome."

New York Times

⬆ An aristocratic vineyard transformed into an open space for all Romans—and visitors—to enjoy.

With an area of around 200 acres (80 ha), the gardens of Villa Borghese are the largest public gardens in Rome. This beautiful park, with its villas, fountains, sculptures, centuries-old trees, and seamless mix of Italian- and English-style landscaped gardens was built on land once owned by the seventeenth-century Italian cardinal and avid art collector Scipione Borghese, who in 1605 decided to transform one of his family's old vineyards into the largest gardens constructed in Rome since antiquity.

Villa Borghese stretches from the Piazza del Popolo to the Via Veneto, and in between you can find miles of bush-lined pathways, statuaries, an artificial lake (home to the nineteenth-century Temple of Aesculapius), the century-old Bioparco Zoological Gardens, and tranquil "secret gardens" that beckon you to enter, such as the Giardino dei melangoli (Garden of Bitter Oranges). And, as the name suggests, there are villas here aplenty, among them Villa Giulia, built as a summer home for Pope Julius III (now the Etruscan Museum), and Villa Medici, completed in 1544 for Cardinal Marcello Crescenzi.

And yet it is the gardens, not the buildings, that make Villa Borghese so beloved a spot, covering the city in a glorious canopy of green, with idyllic spaces such as the Gardens of Muro Torto. The Romans have been accustomed to walking the gardens of Villa Borghese ever since the Borghese family began opening its beautiful outdoor realm to the public on Sundays and public holidays—and the Italian poet Giuseppe Gioachino Belli captured the sentiments of every Roman when he wrote "Long live the heart of Prince Borghese." **BDS**

Rome Underground Tour

Lazio, Italy

Start Basilica of San Clemente
End San Nicola in Carcere   Distance 4 miles
(6.4 km)   Time 3.5 hours   Grade Easy
Type City walk   Map goo.gl/TjOl7k

Everyone knows Rome, the Eternal City, either from personal experience or from images in art, film, and photography. Until quite recently, however, few had ever seen it from below. However, excavations in the late twentieth century opened up passageways beneath the city's streets that have provided a whole new way of seeing this ancient metropolis.

This route, one of many possible ones, starts in the twelfth-century Basilica of San Clemente under mosaics of the crucified Christ amid trees and doves and frescoes by Masaccio and Masolino in the Cappella di Santa Caterina. From there you take a narrow flight of stairs to the fourth-century lower basilica. Another staircase takes you even farther down to a level that was used from the sixth century BCE by worshippers of Mithras and in the first century CE was the site of apartments and the Roman mint.

Returning to street level, you can walk to the Basilica of Santi Giovanni e Paolo, with its monastery and bell tower on the site of a temple dedicated to the emperor Claudius. The tower has been excavated, and visitors may now admire its pagan frescoes and garden with outdoor pool. You can also see a house that is believed to have been where the two apostles of Christ, after whom the current foundation is named, were held before their martyrdom.

After the Circo Massimo, where horse races were held during the Roman Republic, you reach San Nicola in Carcere (St. Nicholas in Prison). This church has, uniquely, grown on three pagan temples of the third and second centuries BCE, the columns of six of which can still be seen within the modern church. Then return underground to examine the foundations. **GL**

Naples by Night Tour

Campania, Italy

Start Porta Nolana railway station
End Hotel Excelsior   Distance 3 miles (4.8 km)
Time 1.5 hours   Grade Easy   Type Sidewalk
Info goo.gl/qjqGWw

Don't let the doomsayers put you off. Yes, Naples has a garbage problem, and it is probably connected to organized crime. The city is full of unspecified dangers. Never walk the streets at night, they will tell you. The traffic is a blight, its scooters can kill, and the alleyways are much too dark.

But impressions require perspective. Any city where café owners stand about chatting animatedly on the sidewalk, and inside serve such excellent lasagne, must be good. And the dark gives it all such a wonderful edge.

> *"The centro storico [is] dense, dark, and intoxicating; its ancient Greek streets teem with hidden treasures."*
>
> Lonely Planet

Begin at Pompeii, stay there all day, and catch the train back to Naples. When you emerge from the Porta Nolana railway station in the fading light, slowly navigate your way back toward your hotel (ideally the Hotel Excelsior, overlooking the Castel dell' Ovo, the city's oldest standing fortification), but take your time.

Which route to take? It's up to you, but do not miss the Caffetteria Depretis on the Via Depretis and the Caffè Del Professore on the Piazza Trieste with its *caffè nocciolato* (with hazelnut cream). Stroll along the well-lit harbor or past the San Carlo Opera House and into the Galleria Umberto I; then into the Via Partenope, and the harbor-facing balconies of the Hotel Excelsior, Naples' finest hotel. **BDS**

Acropolis to Agora Tour
Athens, Greece

Start Acropolis Metro Station
End Agora   **Distance** 2 miles (3.2 km)
Time 3–4 hours   **Grade** Easy
Type Gravel paths   **Map** goo.gl/I3dYqF

"The Athenian Acropolis is the supreme expression of the adaptation of architecture to a natural site."

whc.unesco.org

If there is one modern city you can go to and find history on every single street corner, then surely it has to be Athens—the birthplace of democracy, the cradle of philosophical thinking, and the center of one of the first great empires.

The walk from the Acropolis to the Agora links two of the most significant sites in the city. You start at the Acropolis metro station, an easy-to-find spot and home to an interesting display of artifacts of ancient Greek history, including casts of the Parthenon Marbles (most metro stations in Athens have similar displays). Head up to street level and walk through the city streets toward the modern Acropolis Museum. You can either go inside or carry on toward the Acropolis itself. Here, you pay for a ticket to enter the archaeological site, which is also valid for the Agora later on.

There is a huge amount to see at the Acropolis, including a footpath that takes you to the very top of the site, looking down over the city, and also the Theater of Dionysus and the Odeon of Herodes Atticus. Then it is time to move on toward the Agora, the heart of ancient Athens and the "gathering place" of the city-state, which also served as a bustling market place. To get there from the Acropolis you head northwest along Theonas Road, where another museum awaits with exhibits dating back to the seventh century BCE.

There are some organized tours you can take that will guide you step by step along the way, which is useful, not so much because you might get lost, but because they describe the layers of history that surround you in fascinating detail. **JI**

⬆ Begin at Athens' great citadel, on its rocky plateau, and end at the city's ancient "gathering place."

Kalamaja District

Tallinn, Estonia

Start/End Kalamaja railway station
Distance 3 miles (4.8 km)
Time 1 hour–1 day **Grade** Easy
Type Sidewalk **Info** goo.gl/N4Zfsd

If you like the idea of walking through an historic Baltic neighborhood where entire blocks of buildings still sit on their centuries-old, unaltered grid pattern of streets and remain today as faithful representations of a simple, working-class architectural style that survived decades of Soviet occupation, then you need to come to the Estonian capital of Tallinn. But not to the cobblestone streets of the Old Town, as wonderful as those streets are. Walk them, to be sure, but when you're done, exit the city gates and walk ten minutes to the neighborhood of Kalamaja.

> *"Kalamaja . . . is home to some of Tallinn's most interesting cafés and restaurants."*

www.balticguide.ee

Kalamaja has become popular, especially among students. It is still relatively inexpensive to live in and it has more character in a single lane than entire districts elsewhere. It was the city's primary fishing harbor for centuries (the name Kalamaja means "fish house"). In 1870, when the fledgling suburb was connected by train to the city of St. Petersburg, it was the dawn of a new era. Factories began to appear everywhere, and the workers all needed somewhere to live. Today, the legacy of working-class values is cherished by Kalamaja's new residents who realize the importance of the timbered treasures they now call their own. Development is regulated too, to preserve this unique symphony of wood. **BDS**

Riga Historic Walk

Riga, Latvia

Start Freedom Monument **End** Kaku Maja
Distance 4 miles (6.4 km) **Time** 4 hours
Grade Easy **Type** Sidewalk, cobblestones
Info goo.gl/hpiLnb

This tour of the Latvian capital begins at the Freedom Monument, a statue of a woman erected during the nation's first period of independence (1919–40). Then make your way to the top of Bastion Hill, with its fourteenth-century Powder Tower, which was reduced to rubble by Swedish invaders in 1621, then rebuilt in 1650 with 8-foot-thick (2.5 m) walls.

Walk back into town to Torna, a shopping street that runs parallel to the Old City Walls. Here the highlight is the Swedish Gate, one of several fortifications that is no more recent than the seventeenth century, but appears younger after being "improved" when Latvia was part of the Soviet Union (1940–91). Troksnu, a narrow street, leads to St. James Church (Lutheran until the Swedish occupation; since then Roman Catholic) and the Saeima (parliament). Next is Tris Brali (Three Brothers), Riga's oldest stone residential buildings, one of which now houses the Museum of Architecture, and Riga Castle, built in the fourteenth century by Livonian knights and later the official residence of the head of state.

After Riga Cathedral is Melngalvju Nams (House of the Blackheads), a grand civic structure built in 1344, demolished in 1948, and reconstructed in the 1990s. Nearby is the Latvian Riflemen Monument, originally intended to honor Lenin's personal bodyguard, but now commemorating all Latvian soldiers. The last leg takes in the Mentzendorff House, the home of an eighteenth-century merchant, the Great and Small Guildhalls, and Kaku Maja (Cat House), so named because of the two feline statues on the roof that were positioned with their backsides showing by the original owner as an insult to his next door neighbor. **GL**

Mir Castle
Grondo, Belarus

Start/End Mir Castle
Distance 0.5 mile (0.8 km)
Time 1 hour   **Grade** Easy
Type Sealed pathways   **Info** goo.gl/jbxTQk

Belarus may not be on top of everyone's list of countries for walking, and the Stalinist architecture of its rebuilt capital, Minsk, is not to everyone's liking. But an exception should be made for Mir Castle, an extraordinary concoction southwest of the capital that has UNESCO World Heritage status. A local duke, Yuri Ilyinich, began to construct the Gothic-style castle in the late 1400s. It consists of five towers surrounding a large courtyard, the whole building measuring roughly 246 feet (75 m). When the Ilyinich dynasty died out in 1568, the castle passed into the hands of

---

"This collection of wooden houses is spread over a hillside with good views."

Lonely Planet

Mikolaj Krzysztof "the Orphan" Radziwill, a major Polish-Lithuanian noble who added a two-wing, three-story palace in a vaguely Renaissance style inside the eastern and northern walls. After some Baroque retouching, the castle was abandoned for nearly a century and damaged in the Napoleonic Wars.

Sold in 1817, Mir Castle changed hands a few times until, in 1895, it was sold to the Russian prince Nikolaj Sviatopolk-Mirski, who rebuilt and restored the castle. But the building's new good fortune only lasted until German forces occupied it in 1941, using it as temporary ghetto for local Jews. After the war, the castle was used for housing and suffered damage before it was once again rescued and restored. **SA**

Svan Tower and Museum of Ethnography Tbilisi, Georgia

Start/End Vake Park
Distance 11 miles (17.7 km)
Time 3 hours   **Grade** Easy
Type Park walk   **Map** goo.gl/c8dW1I

This walk gives visitors to Georgia an opportunity to get away from the center of Tbilisi to a popular local recreation area on the outskirts of the city. It starts and ends at the entrance to Vake Park on Chachavadze Avenue, and although it involves a steep ascent, the zigzag pathways are at a steady gradient.

Approaching from the roadside, descend the steps and head for the biggest landmark you can see, the Svan Tower (Svan refers to Svaneti, the northernmost province of Georgia and the ethnic subgroup that lives there), passing the statue of Lady Victory, erected during the Soviet era to celebrate the end of what many Russians and the people of the Caucasus still call "the Great Patriotic War" (World War II).

The final approach to the tower is the trickiest section: the best way up is as close as possible to the overhead lines of the cable car (anyone who doesn't fancy this section may take the cable car instead, if it is working). As you near the tower, the precise purpose of which is now lost to history, you can see down its wooded northern slopes to Turtle Lake, a popular recreation spot for local Tbilisians. Around 2 miles (3 km) farther on is the Open Air Museum of Ethnography, a collection of seventy mostly wooden houses spread over a hillside with views across Tbilisi. Nearly all the dwellings contain traditional furnishings, rugs, and utensils. In the archaeological section is a sixth-century basilica.

On the return journey, retrace your steps to the tower and then head west along a different zigzag path that will bring you right back to the entrance on Chachavadze Avenue. **GL**

Peter and Paul Fortress
St. Petersburg, Russia

Start Ioannovskiy Ravelin   **End** Peter the
Great statue   **Distance** 4 miles (6.4 km)
Time 4 hours   **Grade** Easy   **Type** Sealed paths,
sidewalk   **Map** goo.gl/Ens7xU

This castle, built on an island in the Neva River to defend Russia against a Swedish invasion that never came, became the core of the new city constructed by Tsar Peter the Great to give his nation "a window to the West." You walk onto the island through the Ioannovskiy Ravelin on the eastern side, one of a pair of structures built to protect the flanks of the fortress, and toward the ticket office, an eighteenth-century pavilion originally erected to display a sailing boat built by Peter the Great.

Start the tour in the Peter and Paul Cathedral, with its 400-foot-high (122 m) bell tower topped off with a gilded cupola and attendant angels. The interior contains the tombs of most of the Russian tsars, including the last one, Nicholas II, who was murdered during the Revolution of 1917. Also see the Grand Ducal Burial Vault, where some members of the Russian royal family are interred: those who were deemed insufficiently eminent to lie under the same roof as the rulers.

Next to the cathedral is the mint (it is still in operation), and beyond it the Trubetskoy Bastion, which is now a city museum but was once a prison complete with a torture chamber—on one of the cell walls you can read the graffito "Tonight I am to be shot because I had an education." Also worth a look is the arsenal, a plain neoclassical building that has served a variety of purposes over the years in addition to its original intended use as an armory.

In front of the guardhouse you can see a modern statue of Peter the Great that gives a reminder of the tsar's imposing physique—he was an impressive 7 feet (2.1 m) tall. **GL**

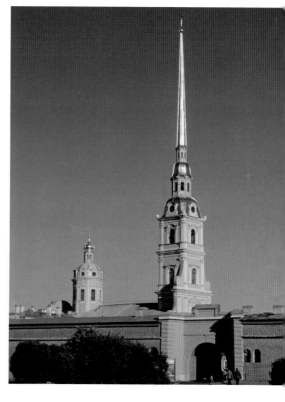

"You can see it from far off, with its impressive bell tower, topped by a gilded angel and chimes that play the hymn of the tsars."

www.travel.michelin.com

⬆ The fortress later became a prison for "dissidents" that included Tolstoy and Dostoyevsky.

Arbat Walking Tour Moscow, Russia

Start Arbatskaya Ploshchad **End** Tinkoff Brewery **Distance** 4 miles (6.4 km) **Time** 4 hours
Grade Easy **Type** Sidewalk **Map** goo.gl/B9POAj

Arbat is without a doubt Moscow's trendiest street and one of the few that is traffic-free. The pavement is full of portrait painters, musicians, and performance artists and is lined by souvenir shops with often incredible markups on *matryoshka* dolls that are painted with the faces of celebrities.

The walk starts on the corner of Arbatskaya Ploshchad (Arbat Square), outside Praga Restaurant, which is worth a look for its opulent decor. Heading west, note the Wall of Peace with its hand-painted tiles. Turn left off Arbat and take the next right onto Krivoarbatsky Pereulok, a narrow street full of Constructivist architecture, including Melnikov House, which consists of two linked cylinders and features hexagonal windows. Turn right back onto Arbat for a look at the bronze statue of songwriter Bulat Okudzhava who lived nearby and often performed on this spot.

On the left is a turning onto Spasopeskovsky Pereulok, where you can see the eighteenth-century Church of the Savior of the Sands, and Spaso House, the residence of the U.S. ambassador to Russia.

Returning to the main drag you pass a statue of Alexander Pushkin and his wife, Natalia Goncharova, outside their home, now a museum. At the western end of Arbat is the Ministry of Foreign Affairs, one of the so-called Seven Sisters—almost identical wedding cake–like buildings at key points in Moscow that were opened by Stalin in 1947 for the thirtieth anniversary of the Russian Revolution and the 800th of the foundation of the city. Turn right here onto Novinskiy Bulvar, then left onto Protochny Pereulok to finish the walk at the Tinkoff Brewery and restaurant. **GL**

⤒ Arbat Street runs through Moscow's historic heart.

Sokolniki District and Park Moscow, Russia

Start/End Sokolniki metro station   **Distance** 2 miles (3.2 km)   **Time** 2 hours   **Grade** Easy
Type Sidewalk and park trails   **Map** goo.gl/xO7oeE

Sokolniki is one of Moscow's oldest suburbs and its park, Sokolniki Park, is four times the size of London's Hyde Park and is named after the famous tsarist falcon hunts that used to take place here (*sokol* means "falcon"). The suburb is also one of Moscow's most architecturally interesting, and the good news is that the Moscow metro can deliver you to its very center, where you emerge from one of the oldest metro stations on the network and into a district that proves that there is a lot more to Moscow than the traditional routes around the city center.

Head first for architect Pavel Tolstykh's triumphal Church of the Resurrection on Sokolnicheskaya Square, one of the few churches that was never forced to close its doors during the Soviet era; then look for 3rd Rybinskaya Ulitsa and walk by the Extra M pasta factory that has been making pasta here since 1883. It is here that the district's architecture really hits you. Next door to Extra M is the Art Nouveau mansion of the factory's first owner, German merchant Johan Ding, and looking over the road you can see the Burevestnik Workers' Club, designed and built by the great avant-garde architect Konstantin Melnikov.

Turn right onto Ulitsa Sokolnichesky Val and into Sokolniki Park and walk to the Big Rosaria: a rose garden with fountains and geometric garden beds, benches beneath vine-covered pergolas, and acres of woodlands. Make sure you exit on First Polevoi Pereulok and walk by another Melnikov masterpiece, the futuristic-looking Rusakov Workers' Club, with its striking cantilevered concrete seating. Then walk down Ulitsa Stromynka and back to Sokolniki metro. **BDS**

⬆ Sokolniki Park is a forest enclave in Moscow's suburbs.

M'Zab Valley Ksour
Ghardaïa, Algeria

Start/End Ghardaïa
Distance 6 miles (9.6 km) **Time** 1 day
Grade Easy **Type** Earthen paths
Info goo.gl/A9WDi3

The Mozabites are a branch of the large Berber Iznaten tribe, who live in isolation 370 miles (595 km) south of Algiers in the northern Sahara. Followers of the minority Muslim Ibadi movement, and speaking Mozabite (a Berber language) rather than Arabic, they have always valued their independence. The Mozabites were only colonized by the French some fifty-two years after the latter took over the rest of the country in 1830, and they remained distinct from the rest of Algeria when it gained independence in 1962.

Their five walled cities (*ksour*), built during the tenth century, are unique. Ghardaïa is the capital and the only one to have admitted Europeans, Jews, Arabs, and other foreigners. El-Atteuf is the oldest settlement in the entire region, Melika is populated by Black Africans, while Beni-Isguen is the sacred center, which prohibits all non-Mozabites from parts of the town and all foreigners from spending a night within its walls. Bounoura completes the five, known as the Pentapolis.

The five cities are located on rocky limestone outcrops along the Wad M'Zab Valley. The Ibadi beliefs of the people have created a strict organization of space and land. A central citadel in each has a fortified mosque with a minaret that is also a watchtower. Around the mosque lie houses of standard size and cubic construction in concentric circles. UNESCO has added the villages to their list of World Heritage Sites.

It is best to walk the Pentapolis with a guide who will check streets and alleyways, often no wider than a cart, to make sure photographs are allowed. The villages are connected by time-worn trails that make for easy hiking, providing you take care to avoid the valley's frequent sandstorms. **SA**

"Designed for community living, while respecting the structure of the family."

whc.unesco.org

⬆ The five walled cities of the Wad M'Zab Valley still offer inspiration for modern town planners.

Casbah at Algiers

Algiers, Algeria

Start/End Hilltop citadel
Distance 8 miles (12.8 km)   Time 1 day
Grade Easy   Type Walkways and stairs
Info goo.gl/FGiOn9

A walk through the Islamic Casbah of Algiers—a city within a city—will take you up and down flights of stairs and through alleyways that wind between homes, walled gardens, mosques, palaces featuring Ottoman-period architecture, and the ruins of the old citadel. The buildings themselves offer an interesting urban landscape of clotheslines and views out over the bay.

There really is no point in trying to plot your way with a map—it's simpler to just enter and follow your nose. However, for those determined not to spend hours wandering the same maze-like streets over and over again, the recommended route is to start at the top at the sixteenth-century hilltop citadel and make your way down. If you do take a wrong turn, don't fret, because as the Casbah sprawls its way down the hillside to the Mediterranean, you need only keep your eye on the coastline to get your bearings again.

A riotous display of period patterned tile work, vibrant window and door dressings, whitewashed architecture, and colorful produce stalls and restaurants are all part of a confusing labyrinth of lanes—some dark and encroached upon by buildings, others offering impressive vistas of Algiers—and winding alleyways that, very often, lead to dead ends. The Casbah's 350 streets and alleyways make up 9.3 miles (14.9 km) of walkways, and while elsewhere in Algiers traffic is mostly always at a chaotic gridlock, the narrow streets within the Casbah mean the area is car-free, making it an urban walker's dream. The Casbah is steeped in history, but combined with that are the very present, everyday rituals and routines of those who call it home, which make for an unforgettable experience. **NE**

Avenue Habib Bourguiba

Tunis, Tunisia

Start Lake Tunis   End Place de l'Indépendence
Distance 2 miles (3.2 km)   Time 2 hours
Grade Easy   Type Pavement
Map goo.gl/10Uziz

Habib Bourguiba was the leader of the Neo Destour movement that led Tunisia to independence from France in 1956. He became the country's first prime minister and then in 1957 its president until he resigned in 1987. Every town in the country has a road named after him, but none is grander than the Avenue Habib Bourguiba that runs from east to west through the center of Tunis. The avenue began life as the Promenade de la Marine, which the French colonial authorities designed as the Tunis version of the Champs-Elysées in Paris. The Cathédrale Saint-

"The central thoroughfare of Tunis, and the historical, political, and economic heart of Tunisia."

www.mygola.com

Vincent-de-Paul de Tunis followed in 1897. Renamed the Avenue Jules-Ferry in 1914, after the French politician, the avenue became the entertainment center of the city. The Art Nouveau municipal theater had opened in 1902 and was joined by hotels, shops, and restaurants.

The obvious point to begin a stroll down this most European of avenues is in the city's heart at the base of its famous obelisk-shaped Monumental Clock. From there, head for the Cathédrale Saint-Vincent-de-Paul, and after that, the Place de l'Indépendance and the Bab El Bahr, the great triumphal arch of Tunis. Removed by the French in 1848, it is now one of the symbols of a proud and independent Tunisia. **SA**

Ghadames Old Town Walk
Ghadames, Libya

Start/End Ghadames Old Town
Distance 2 miles (3.2 km)   Time 2 hours
Grade Easy   Type Roads and alleys
Info goo.gl/7TJVYX

Tucked up in the north of Libya, on the border with Algeria and just below the southern tip of Tunisia, lies the oasis and town of Ghadames. It is commonly understood that its name derives from the ancient Berber tribe of Tidamensi and was corrupted by the Romans into Cydamus, which eventually evolved into Ghadames. More interesting, however, is the belief of some of the local populace that the name derives from the Arabic words for "lunch" (*ghada*) and "yesterday" (*ams*). Allegedly, some people who had camped in the area left behind some food from the previous day's cooking. When one of their number returned to collect the items, the hoof of his horse broke through into the waters of the oasis. Around such a legend, the town was born.

Ghadames is known as the "pearl of the desert" and it is one of the oldest walled towns in the Sahara. Its houses are mainly divided vertically, with a ground floor to store supplies, a single story for the family, and an open-air terrace on the roof for the women. All are made of mud mixed with straw, and lime and palm tree trunks. Uniquely, the entire town is under cover, as the narrow alleyways between the houses are roofed in, providing much-needed protection from the fierce sun. Tourist numbers have been down since the overthrow of Muammar Gaddafi, but local tour guides wait for the day when they return and again ask to walk through the labyrinth of streets and alleyways. Walks usually begin at the museum in the town's Turkish fort, going on to include the Old Town Spring Water Pool and the town's groves of fruit trees. **SA**

⬅ Ghadames is an impressive pre-Saharan settlement.

City of the Dead
Cairo, Egypt

Start/End Salah Salem Highway
Distance 4 miles (6.4 km)   Time 3 hours
Grade Easy   Type Earthen paths
Info goo.gl/eOQtQH

There are few walks that take you around a housing estate, and none that visit a housing estate quite like this one. For the City of the Dead, below the Mokattam Hills in southeast Cairo, is an estate of the dead that now also houses the living. The Cairo Necropolis, as it is also called, was established soon after the Islamic conquest of Egypt in 642. Arab commander 'Amr ibn al'As founded the first Islamic capital of Egypt at Al-Fustat, now absorbed by Cairo, and built his family's graveyard at the foot of Mokattam Hills. Other leading families buried their

"I've lived here for 80 years and my family has lived here for 350. King Farouk is buried near my house."

Abdul Aziz Sahel, City of the Dead resident

dead nearby, and the graveyard grew to its present 4-mile (6.4-km) length. From the start, the custodians of noble families' graves lived in the cemetery, as did the people in charge of burial services and a group of Sufi mystics. As Cairo's population grew, the poorest took refuge in the graveyard, converting old graves and mausoleums into housing and workshops. After an earthquake in 1992, many thousands more took shelter here. Sanitation is limited, and electricity comes from a nearby mosque. Most of the graves lie along a warren of paths and alleys that make it ridiculous to suggest a route. It's best to wander at will, admiring the astonishing architecture, being respectful to the dead, and to the living, too. **SA**

Lamu Historic Town Walk
Coast, Kenya

Start/End Lamu waterfront
Distance 3 miles (4.8 km) **Time** 2 hours
Grade Easy **Type** Earthen road
Map goo.gl/d1OL37

The Swahili people of East Africa traded up and down the length of the Indian Ocean's west coast, setting up trading ports in the Lamu archipelago off the coast of what is now Kenya. Lamu was first established in 1370, making it Kenya's oldest continually inhabited town. Colonized by the Portuguese in 1505 and then taken over by the Omanis in 1652, it became part of the Sultanate of Zanzibar in the nineteenth century. In 1885 the Germans took an interest in the region, establishing East Africa's first post office in the town in 1888—an achievement marked by the German Post Office Museum. Lamu and the rest of Kenya then fell under British control in 1890, before the country became independent in 1963.

Among the many fine buildings in Lamu is the two-story stone fort, which the traveler Thomas Boteler observed in 1823 was "constructed so slightly that in all probability the discharge of the honeycombed ordnance would soon bring the whole fabric to the ground." More recently, the fort was used by the British to inter Mau Mau rebels during the uprising (1952–60). Other fine Swahili buildings line the waterfront, from where slaves—the slave trade was only abolished in 1907—ivory, turtle shells, rhinoceros horns, and other items were once exported. The old part of town is inscribed in the UNESCO World Heritage List as "the oldest and best-preserved Swahili settlement in East Africa." Walking around the town is a delight, as there are no cars on the island. All transport and heavy work is done by donkeys, which is why the island boasts a donkey population of more than 3,000 and a sanctuary that treats them all, free of charge. **SA**

"The fascinating buildings ... numerous mosques, the narrow streets, and no cars offer a charming experience."

www.kenyabook.com

⊡ Lamu's fort is more robust than it may appear.

Stone Town Heritage Walk
Zanzibar, Tanzania

Start/End Stone Town seafront
Distance 4 miles (6.4 km)   Time 4 hours
Grade Easy   Type Paved roads, earthen paths
Info goo.gl/kOLSID

Since the entire town of Stone Town is designated a UNESCO World Heritage Site, it follows that every walk here is a heritage walk. Stone Town is the ancient center of Zanzibar, which is now part of Tanzania, but in the 1840s it was the capital of an Omani-dominated trading empire that stretched along the east coast of Africa, via Oman, and into the Persian Gulf. The island traded spices, gold, ivory, and other luxury materials around the Indian Ocean, but, most profitably, it trafficked slaves from the mainland to plantations and households along the coast, the evidence of which is clear in the town.

The seafront of Stone Town is lined with impressive neocolonial buildings, many of them restored by the Aga Khan, leader of the island's dominant Ismaili Muslim community. The House of Wonders is well worth a visit—the tallest building in East Africa when it was completed in 1883, it was the first to have an electric elevator. Now a museum, its sparse collection includes a fabulously battered 1950s Ford Zephyr once owned by the first president of Zanzibar, Abeid Karume. The heart of the town, however, is in the narrow streets that are filled with shops selling food, fabric, and tourist goods. The wooden main doors of the buildings are frequently intricately carved and studded with brass.

A guided walking tour of Stone Town takes around four hours and includes the old Arab fort, the Old Customs House, and the Forodhani Gardens on the seafront, dating from the 1930s. It ends at the wonderful Darajani Market, Stone Town's vibrant heart, with its dawn fish auctions and nightly cacophony of touts, antiques dealers, and spice traders. **SA**

Fan Walk
Western Cape, South Africa

Start Cape Town Station   End Cape Town Stadium   Distance 1.6 miles (2.5 km)
Time 1 hour   Grade Easy   Type City walk
Map goo.gl/w63puK

Opened in time for the 2010 FIFA World Cup held in South Africa, the Fan Walk served a dual purpose. It was firstly an easy but interesting way to get soccer fans from the city's main railway station to the Cape Town Stadium for matches. More importantly, it was designed with longevity in mind so that visitors to the city could enjoy a fun and safe walk or cycle ride, whether they were going to a match or not.

The walk goes along Loop Street, which comes to life at night with its numerous bars and clubs. At night the Fan Walk is well lit and allows you to enjoy some of

> *"The new Cape Town Fan Walk is quite an experience … easy, safe, well signposted, and entertaining."*
>
> www.expatcapetown.com

the city's nightlife in a safe atmosphere. You cross the busy Buitengracht Street on a pedestrian foot bridge, giving you a good look down on the activities below. Close by is St. Andrew's Square, which is another lively place with colorful outdoor sculptures and views of Table Mountain in the distance. The walk also passes through the De Waterkant district, which dates back to the 1700s and boasts some of the finest historical houses in Cape Town. One of the pleasures of the walk is its mix of ancient and modern Cape Town. It ends at the Cape Town Stadium, an impressive structure that was purpose-built for the World Cup. It took almost three years to build and cost an incredible R4.4 billion (about US$600 million/£250 million). **MG**

Walled City of Baku

Absheron, Azerbaijan

Start/End Nizami Square/Salyan Gates
Distance 2 miles (3.2 km)   Time 3 hours
Grade Easy   Type Cobblestones
Info goo.gl/gr3lKK

"The walled city of Baku represents an outstanding and rare example of an historic urban ensemble and architecture."

whc.unesco.org

At 92 feet (28 m) below sea level, by the side of the Caspian Sea, Baku has the distinction of being both the lowest capital city in the world and also the largest city in the world below sea level. The capital of independent Azerbaijan since 1991, Baku dates to the first century CE and has, over time, been under Persian, Ottoman, and Russian control. Economically, the city made its money from oil. In the late 1200s, Marco Polo reported a stream of oil gushing "in such abundance that a hundred ships may load there at once," while a Turkish scientist in the early 1600s reported that Baku was surrounded by 500 wells. Large-scale oil production began in 1876, and by the early 1900s, Baku was producing a fifth of the world's oil.

The Old City was entered by two gates and was defended by dozens of cannons lining the walls. The fifteenth-century Shirvanshah's Palace is an outstanding example of Azerbaijan architecture. To walk through this ancient city today is to go back in time to a pre-industrial age of trade and commerce. Commercial guides are more than happy to show you around, but this is an atmospheric place that is easily explored by yourself.

You could walk Baku's streets for a week and never see the same thing twice. Old fortress walls, first erected in the twelfth century, surround the Inner City. Within is Meydan Square, the Caravansaray with its medieval courtyard, the Maiden's Tower, and the seventeenth-century Gasin-bey Bath House with its exit out to the Aliagha Vahid garden. The elegant, 100-year old Baku Boulevard follows the city's shoreline on the Caspian Sea. This compact and very walkable city offers delights for everyone. **SA**

⤒ Traditional Azerbaijani carpet sellers outside the Maiden Tower in the Old City of Baku.

Orange Routes
Tel Aviv, Israel

Start 5 Shalom Aleichem Street
End Suzanne Dellal Center   Distance 3 miles
(4.8 km)   Time 3 hours   Grade Easy
Type Sidewalk   Info goo.gl/SmnQp7

Tel Aviv is the de facto capital of Israel, home to the many foreign embassies that do not recognize Jerusalem as the national capital. It is the country's second city, famed for its laid-back atmosphere, lively nightlife, and Bauhaus architecture. Historically, this Jewish town grew up alongside the much older, Arab-inhabited port of Jaffa, which it absorbed in 1950. Jaffa became famous for the export of its sweet and almost seedless oranges, and it is this connection that has been used to set out four possible Orange Routes around modernist Tel Aviv. Each one is designed to highlight the city's wealth of avant-garde architecture, including its several fine museums.

Many Bauhaus architects fled to Israel after the Nazis came to power in Germany in 1933. They designed more than 5,000 modernist buildings, the greatest concentration of such architecture in the world, in an area now known as the White City. Construction continued until the 1950s, but for a time its future was threatened as tastes changed. Today, its importance is recognized, and the White City is a UNESCO World Heritage Site. The Orange Route is clearly marked with orange and green markers. Along the way it passes many famous buildings, most notably Independence Hall, the former home of Meir Dizengoff, the city's first mayor, and the place where Israel's independence was proclaimed in 1948. This route also passes the Haganah Museum, dedicated to the underground military organization; the former home of Haim Nahman Bialik, Israel's national poet, and Migdal Shalom tower, the city's first high school. The last has an observation deck, affording fine views of this most cosmopolitan of cities. **SA**

"[Bialik House] combines Eastern and Western styles and features beautiful tiles made at Bezalel."

www.gemsinisrael.com

⊡ The stark, white modernist architecture of Tel Aviv can be admired on the Orange Route.

Isfahan
Isfahan, Iran

Start Naqsh-e Jahan Square
End Hasht Behesht Gardens **Distance** 3 miles
(4.8 km) **Time** 3 hours **Grade** Easy
Type Roads, sidewalks **Info** goo.gl/mvYSq2

Like all big cities in Iran, modern Isfahan is congested, noisy, and clamorous. However, it is also one of the most beautiful cities in the world and a UNESCO World Heritage Site of wonder and magnificence. Once the capital of Persia (1598–1722), and at that time one of the largest cities in the world, Isfahan lies abut 210 miles (338 km) south of Tehran, the modern Iranian capital. A local proverb states that "Isfahan is half of the world," for its palaces, mosques, boulevards, and squares are among the finest on the planet.

An ancient town dating from the Elamite civilization (2700–1600 BCE), Isfahan came into its own under the Safavid dynasty, from 1501 to 1736. Shah Abbas the Great made the city his capital in 1598, combining religion, commerce, and imperial power in one place and endowing it with many striking buildings. New bridges crossed the Zayandeh Rud River, serving as aqueducts or linking the town together. New mosques and many fine houses were built. Most important, the city was remodeled around the Naqsh-e Jahan Square, an oblong measuring 525 feet (160 m) by 1,667 feet (508 m). Around this new garden square stand the Shah Mosque to the south, Ali Quapu Palace to the west, Sheikh Lotfallah Mosque to the east, and the Keisaria gate to the north, which opened into the Grand Bazaar.

The best way to appreciate Isfahan is to do what its residents love to do—walk its gardens, its bridges, its great public squares, its tree-lined boulevards, and its historic bazaar. Naqsh-e Jahan Square makes a great starting point for walks with an English-speaking guide to the Lotfallah Mosque, the Ali Quapu Palace, and the Hasht Behesht gardens. **SA**

> *"Four hundred years ago, Isfahan was larger than London and more cosmopolitan than Paris."*
>
> www.smithsonian.mag.com

⬆ The Shah Mosque is a masterpiece of Persian architecture, famed for its seven-color mosaic tiles.

Ittihad Park, Palm Jumeirah

Dubai, United Arab Emirates

Start Al Sufouh Road   End Aquaventure Beach
Distance 4.3 miles (6.9 km)   Time 4 hours
Grade Easy   Type Sidewalk
Info goo.gl/H9VdJn

When construction of the Palm Jumeirah, the extraordinary manmade archipelago off the Jumeirah coast of the United Arab Emirates (UAE), began in June 2001, even its architects might have struggled to appreciate the opportunities for walking offered by the development, with its multiple arms resembling the fronds of a gargantuan palm tree. But the Palm Jumeirah, now home to hundreds of enviable waterfront residences, was also designed with the visitor in mind. It has numerous hotels, resorts, and activities, and its very walkable stretch of parkland brings vivid shades of green to the artificial oasis.

Ittihad Park runs in a straight line along the Palm Jumeirah's "trunk," which connects the shoreline and the Golden Mile apartments. The park provides an eco-friendly focal point for the island's residents and visitors. With the monorail into Dubai gliding by overhead, it is a mix of meandering pathways and playgrounds covering an area in excess of 25 acres (10 ha). A jogging or walking track, 2 miles (3.2 km) long, traces its fringes.

What is especially interesting, though, is the use of indigenous plants, which enables visitors to see much of the region's primary flora without having to search out the plants in the extreme heat of their natural environment. There are Farfar trees, with their narrow, pale-green leaves, and medicinal plants such as *daya*, *halool*, *qsad*, and *arash*, a veritable flora pharmacy used to treat diabetes, constipation, sore eyes, and dermatitis respectively. In total there are more than sixty species of desert shrubs and plants here, bringing life and color to the borders of new urban trails on the edge of the Persian Gulf. **BDS**

Alleyways of Zabid

Al Hudaydah, Yemen

Start/End Zabid old town
Distance 6 miles (9.6 km)   Time 4 hours
Grade Easy   Type Earthen paths
Info goo.gl/AlhjQ2

One of the oldest towns in Yemen, Zabid sits on the western coastal plane near the Red Sea and was the capital of Yemen from the thirteenth to fifteenth centuries. Its university established it as a center of Islamic learning; it was also one of only two places in the Arabian Peninsula growing indigo, and it became a center of cotton production. Since 2000, the city's UNESCO World Heritage listing has been endangered, as its souk is falling down and many fine buildings have collapsed, with at least 40 percent of them replaced by concrete structures. Despite this, Zabid is

> *"Zabid is one of those sites where real history intermingles with myths and popular culture."*
>
> Omar Abdulaziz Hallaj, conservationist

still worth visiting. The old fortified city sits on a rise above a river junction and boasts four entrance gates. Inside, a network of narrow alleys runs between the burned brick houses, most of which have the plan of a reception room opening into an enclosed courtyard.

A good place to begin walking is the Asa'ir Mosque, the city's first mosque and its historic and religious heart, with the walk continuing on westward through the souk in the direction of the skyline-dominating Great Mosque. But be warned: the city is a labyrinth of serpentine alleyways, and the tangle of houses and buildings, made of baked and unbaked clay, reused wooden planks, and roofed with straw, will confound even the most determined attempts at route planning. **SA**

Sana'a Old City
Dhamar, Yemen

Start/End Bab al-Yaman (Yemen Gate)
Distance 6 miles (9.6 km)   **Time** 5 hours
Grade Easy   **Type** Paved and earthen paths
and alleys   **Info** goo.gl/UfiI9g

According to legend, the city of Sana'a was founded by Shem, son of Noah, making it one of the oldest populated cities in the world, although historically it only dates to around 500 BCE. Its current name is probably derived from a South Arabian word for "well-fortified." Today, Sana'a is the capital of Yemen and, at more than 7,500 feet (2,300 m) above sea level, one of the highest capital cities in the world.

Sana'a sits on the crossroad of two major trading routes linking the old city of Marib in the east to the Red Sea in the west. Trade, capital city status, its key role in the spread of Islam, and strategic importance have all contributed to the creation of one of the world's most outstanding cityscapes, well deserving of its UNESCO World Heritage Site status. The old city is surrounded by clay walls 30–46 feet (9–14 m) high. Within are more than 100 mosques, including the Great Mosque, built while Muhammad was still alive almost 1,400 years ago, twelve hammams (baths), and, most famously, 6,500 houses. These fortress-like towers, built of rammed earth and burned brick, stand several stories high above a stone ground floor, looking like medieval skyscrapers in their verticality.

A good path to take through the old town, one that truly exposes the visitor to the daily life of this ancient city, would begin at the fish market behind the Italian Embassy on Old Airport Road. From there the route continues to Cairo Street and the Al-Mankal Restaurant, a venue popular with foreigners and serving a great mix of local and foreign dishes. After that, continue along Cairo Street to lush Attan Park, just off 60 Meters Road. The challenge then is to discover the direction of the spice market. **SA**

"Sana'a must be seen, however long the journey, though the hardy camel droop, leg-worn on the way."

Traditional Yemeni Poem

◄ The city's dressed stones and handmade bricks are decorated in gypsum.

▲ The old spice market is full of the aromas of cinnamon, cumin, cloves, and incense.

Shibam Hadramaut, Yemen

Start/End Shibam main gate   **Distance** 3 miles (4.8 km)   **Time** 3 hours   **Grade** Easy
Type Earthen paths   **Info** goo.gl/BikdyO

Faced with attacks from Bedouin raiders out of the desert, and from the unwanted attentions of jealous local rivals, the citizens of Shibam in eastern Yemen thought tall. In order to better protect themselves from attack, they built tall tower houses, rising between five and eleven stories high above the valley floor. Although the city dates from the third century CE, when it was the capital of the local Hadramaut kingdom, most of the houses were built during the 1500s, and many of these have since been rebuilt many times.

The city of Shibam sits on a walled platform that stands on a rocky spur high above the Wadi Hadramaut. It was profitably located at an important caravan halt on the local spice and incense trade route, which provided the wealth that went into building the houses. The tower houses themselves are built entirely of sundried, mud bricks, with each floor having one or two rooms. In order to protect the building from rain and wind, the walls are routinely resurfaced with fresh layers of mud. The houses are densely arranged on a rectangular grid pattern of streets and squares, making it a confusing delight to wander around the narrow alleys and peer up at the mud-brick walls and small windows above.

Shibam is virtually a car-free environment, and is one of the world's earliest examples of urban planning using multi-storeyed buildings. A walk can begin at the old market in the main street of Al-Hawta, but really, in this astonishing labyrinth it hardly matters where it starts. A hillside twenty minutes outside the city makes a great vantage point for photographs. **SA**

⬆ Marvel at Yemen's "Manhattan of the desert."

Lower Peirce Trail Central, Singapore

Start Near #72 Old Upper Thomson Road   **End** Casuarina Road   **Distance** 2,952 feet (900 m)   **Time** 1 hour
Grade Easy   **Type** Boardwalk   **Info** goo.gl/pqNs6C

The Lower Peirce Trail through Singapore's Central Catchment Nature Reserve is a series of boardwalks that takes you on a short but memorable walk through one of the city's last remaining stands of mature secondary forest along the boundary of the Lower Peirce Reservoir, named in honor of Robert Peirce, the municipal engineer of Singapore from 1901 to 1916. The Lower Peirce Reservoir is Singapore's second reservoir, completed in 1910 after damming the upper reaches of the Kallang River.

This easy boardwalk trail is suitable for families and the elderly. The reservoir itself is home to a huge variety of flora and fauna. There are rubber trees and oil palms, remnants of a former rubber plantation, 100 species of ferns, and more than 900 flowering plants, many of which you can read about on the trail's numerous information boards. Animals include plantain and slender squirrels—both common throughout Singapore, Malaysia, and Thailand—clouded monitor lizards among the leaf litter on the forest floor; and Malayan water monitors that can grow up to 6 feet (1.8 m) in length and are sometimes mistaken for crocodiles. White-bellied fish eagles soar over the reservoir, and the trees are filled with monkeys, including long-tailed macaques and crab-eating macaques, large seed dispersers that make them both invaluable assets for a healthy forest. The Lower Peirce Trail is much underrated. It has more plant species than can be found in all of North America, and more animal species than live in Yellowstone National Park, which proves that there's a lot more to Singapore than skyscrapers and neon. **BDS**

⬆ Capture sunset at the Lower Peirce Reservoir.

Dulle-gil Trail, Bukhansan National Park
Seoul, South Korea

Start Uiryeong-gil entrance   End Gyohyeon
Uiryeong-gil entrance   Distance 43 miles (69 km)
Time 3 days   Grade Easy to moderate
Type Paved, earthen path   Map goo.gl/4QeBYm

"A walk along the trail leads hikers through lush forests to temples perched on mountain crags. . . ."

english.visitkorea.or.kr

⊓ A national park in the heart of Seoul is one of the world's most-visited urban parks.

There are few national parks inside cities, but Bukhansan in Seoul, South Korea, is one. The park comes as quite a surprise when the bustling metropolis sprawls into view through the mountains and trees. It is named after the three peaks of Bukhansan Mountain (the name of which means "mountains north of the Han River"), but it was originally called Samgaksan, the "three horned mountains"—a more apt name given the sharp granite peaks that stretch up to 2,744 feet (836 m). The park itself covers 31 square miles (80 sq km) and was set up in 1983. It contains heavily forested areas, with dozens of gorges, temples, the Bukhansanseong Fortress built in 1711 to protect Seoul from invasion, and numerous walking trails, of which the 43-mile-long (69.2 km) Dulle-gil Trail is probably the best.

The one disadvantage of having a national park inside a city is that the city's inhabitants inevitably walk all over it, weakening its ecosystem. As a result, access to the park is sometimes restricted, and walks can be closed. The circular Dulle-gil Trail connects the forests paths and villages along the foothills of the Bukhansan and Dobongsan Mountains. The trail consists of twenty-one sections, each named after its defining characteristic, such as "the path of meditation" or "pine tree forest trail." Most of the path meanders around the base of the two mountains, but the final section crosses between the two mountains in an area that was closed to the public until 2009 because of infiltration by North Korean armed forces. As a result, its ecosystem is in the best shape of all the sections, and access is thus limited to 1,000 walkers per day; reservations must be made in advance. **SA**

Petropavlovsk City Walk

Kamchatka, Russia

Start/End Teatralnaya Square
Distance 3 miles (4.8 km)   **Time** 1–2 hours
Grade Easy   **Type** Gravel roads
Info goo.gl/cEBf5z

Petropavlovsk is the only international gateway to the wilderness that is the Kamchatka Peninsula, and you need to pass through here to get to the many wonders that lay beyond. Once here, you should spend at least a day to experience the richness that this city, with its provincial feel, set around the shoreline of Avacha Bay, provides. Especially in its hills.

The city was founded by Dutch navigator Vitus Bering in 1740, though when you fly in and look out the window, the landscape seems so devoid of human habitation that you can be forgiven for thinking he never came here at all. The city is an outpost in a vast wilderness, home to 11 percent of the world's volcanoes and a bear population that is only estimated. When you walk its streets, you feel this isolation and its frontier spirit, a product of the city being closer to the west coast of the United States than it is to Moscow, eleven time zones to the west.

There is a wealth of enchanting pre-Soviet timber houses in the hills immediately above the town center, which are easily accessed by timber stairways that take you up from the city and immerse you in quiet residential streets filled with brightly colored, ordinary houses in varying states of disrepair. As you walk you catch occasional glimpses down to the city's central Teatralnaya Square, with its impressive statue of Lenin looking east toward North America, but it's hard to tear your eyes away from the houses that now surround you. Constructed in the vernacular style of the early 1900s, but with dormer windows, corrugated roofs, ornate lintels, and windows all tarnished with age, these houses are kept alive by a community of free spirits living in a challenging land. **BDS**

"At a corner of this huge country, at the very edge of the world, the Kamchatka Peninsula juts 1,500 kilometers into the Pacific."

www.themoscowtimes.com

⊼ The city tumbles down its surrounding hills to the main square, where the statue of Lenin stands sentinel.

Sydney Harbour Bridge
Climb New South Wales, Australia

Start/End Southern pylon **Distance** 0.6 mile (1 km)
Time 1.5 hours **Grade** Easy
Type Steel steps and walkways
Info goo.gl/5Bia28

Most people who visit Sydney, and many who live there, want to climb it. Bill Gates, Will Ferrell, Antonio Banderas, and Usain Bolt have all been suited up and put through the same safety drills, given the same radios, and hooked up to the same stainless-steel rope that never leaves your harness. The Sydney Harbour Bridge, completed in 1932 and years ahead of any other bridge of its period, is one of the world's great engineering feats and a symbol of a nation. It gives you the finest possible view of the world's largest harbor from the best vantage point. Walking through the lower sections of the bridge—through the midst of support beams and millions of rivets, past two of the four giant pylons that support it, and behind its meticulously quarried Australian granite blocks—for an Aussie it's like being introduced to a distant family member you always knew you had but never met.

Once you emerge from the interior of the bridge onto the upper arch, which you follow all the way to the top, you are treated to views over the harbor and city, out to the Tasman Sea to the east and the Blue Mountains to the west. Sydney Harbour Bridge Climb, the only company permitted to take you to its summit, employs talented guides who bring the experience alive with an entertaining commentary coupled with an obvious enthusiasm for their work.

During the period of its construction, only two men ever fell from the bridge to their deaths—an astonishingly small number for the time—and as many as 10,000 dropped rivets are still at the bottom of Sydney Harbour. **BDS**

◄ Immerse yourself in one of the world's great bridges.

Spit Bridge to Manly Walk New South Wales, Australia

Start Spit Bridge   End Manly Cove   Distance 6 miles (9.6 km)   Time 3 hours   Grade Easy
Type Well-graded dirt trail, sealed path   Map goo.gl/668qn9

The Spit Bridge to Manly Walk is a secluded trail through the heart of Sydney's northern suburbs. It connects a series of wonderfully scenic walks—the Dobroyd Walk, the North Harbour Walk, and the Fairlight Walk—that together take you along the cliffs and around the inlets and beaches of the harbor, east toward the heads, to beautiful Manly. Situated across the harbor from the din of the city, Manly is the bearer of a famous slogan created in 1940 by the Port Jackson and Manly Steamship Company: "Seven miles from Sydney, and a thousand miles from care."

The trail begins at Spit Bridge and runs along the harbor's northern beach above Crater Cove, a fascinating slice of Sydney's history now largely forgotten where, instead of mansions or a waterfront park, all you'll find is an eclectic collection of old corrugated iron shacks and huts on a rocky headland.

These ramshackle buildings started to appear during the 1920s and were squatted in, until their residents were forced to leave when the cove was made part of Sydney Harbour National Park in the 1980s. Few "Sydneysiders" are aware that it exists, and the walk down to it is on an unmarked trail that national parks prefer not to advertise.

The trail continues along the water's edge and affords the opportunity to learn of other forgotten aspects of the city's colonial past, such as Forty Baskets Beach, where fish were caught to feed Sudanese soldiers in the 1880s—just one more historical aside that reveals itself on a trail that offers more than simply lovely views over the finest natural harbor on Earth. **BDS**

⬆ See Sydney's beachside suburb of Manly Bay.

Dunedin Heritage Walks Otago, New Zealand

Start/End Moray Place, Dunedin   **Distance** 2.8 miles (4.5 km)   **Time** 2 hours   **Grade** Easy
Type Roads   **Map** goo.gl/WKg5kD

On May 20, 1861, Australian prospector Gabriel Read reported: "At a place where a kind of road crossed on a shallow bar, I shoveled away about two and a half feet of gravel, arrived at a beautiful soft slate, and saw the gold shining like the stars in Orion on a dark frosty night." That place was Gabriel's Gully, close to the banks of the Tuapeka River in Otago, New Zealand. The discovery led to a gold rush that brought in 14,000 prospectors by Christmas. The nearby coastal settlement of Dunedin fast grew into New Zealand's largest city, its many fine buildings a testament to the wealth the gold find brought.

Two Heritage Walks wind around Dunedin's streets, both starting from the circular Moray Place in the city center. The southern Heritage Walk 1 starts from the First Church and heads out along Princes Street to the Union Bank, before returning via Bond Street and the High Street past Dunedin Gaol to finish at the Law Courts in Castle Street. The northern Heritage Walk 2 starts at Trinity Church on the corner of Stuart Street and passes St. Joseph's Cathedral, Wain's Hotel, the Grand Hotel, and the public library, before returning along Princes Street to end at St. Paul's Cathedral on the Octagon, in the middle of the Moray Place circle. Each walk takes about an hour, and bronze plaques laid in the footpath identify the direction each route takes. Oval plaques attached to many of the buildings provide historical information about a cityscape that has in its churches, cathedrals, law courts, railway stations, libraries, hotels, and banks the finest collection of Victorian and Edwardian buildings in the southern hemisphere. **SA**

⊞ **Dunedin Railway Station on Anzac Square.**

Mountain ranges provide some of the world's most exhilarating walking experiences. Switchbacks, saddles, ridge lines, and the lofty summits they lead to create memories that last a lifetime. But if the Mount Hua Plank Walk or Machu Picchu's "Hike of Death" don't appeal to you, circuits around the base of mountains and massifs offer low-altitude thrills of their own.

MOUNTAIN

← A circuitous walk around the "fortress of stone." Mount Pelmo Circuit, Veneto, Italy.

Harding Icefield Trail

Alaska, USA

Start/End Seward Hwy parking area, Kenai Fjords
National Park   Distance 8.2 miles (13.2 km)
Time 6–8 hours   Grade Strenuous
Type Rocky, snowy   Map goo.gl/LZztKH

It's steep, it's snowy, and there is the real possibility of avalanches. Named for President Warren G. Harding—the maligned White House incumbent from 1921 to 1923—the Harding Icefield covers 300 square miles (777 sq km) of Alaska's remote Kenai Mountains, not counting the glaciers that descend from it, which increases the total area to nearly four times that figure. But though the Harding Icefield trail represents only a fraction of this frozen frontier, it provides an unforgettable glimpse into an icy otherworld.

The route begins on the valley floor, amid a forest of cottonwood and alder, the latter associated with cool, moist ground. This gives way to meadows of heather, through which the trail winds above the tree line. Vegetation includes salmonberries, the red-flowered raspberries that attract black bears. At approximately 1 mile (1.6 km) and 1,000 feet (305 m) of elevation unfold a spectacular view of the valley floor and the terminus of the Exit Glacier, so called because it marked the end of the first recorded crossing of the icefield in 1968. It's receding at a rate of about 1 mile (1.6 km) each century, although audibly cracking ice and rushing waters suggest the shrinkage is accelerating.

Make it past this faltering monument to the Pleistocene epoch, negotiating a trail that turns from invigoratingly rocky to strenuously snowy, and you'll claim your prize. The icefield is, as the National Park Service guide rhapsodizes, and with good reason, "a window to past ice ages. A horizon of ice and snow that stretches as far as the eye can see, broken only by an occasional nunatak." **BM**

◀ An icy-netherworld in the Alaskan wilderness.

Donoho Basin Trails

Alaska, USA

Start/End Kennecott Mill Town
Distance 14 miles (22.5 km) return trip to Donoho
Peak   Time 1–2 days   Grade Strenuous
Type Open, rocky terrain, ice   Map goo.gl/v57luN

A walk into the Donoho Basin in the Wrangell-St. Elias National Park & Preserve begins with an interesting morning of exploring in the former mining town of Kennecott, which sprang out of nothing in 1900 after two local prospectors, Clarence Warner and Jack Smith, decided to walk their horses to a green patch of hills that from a distance looked like good grazing land, but was actually a mountain of copper ore.

You begin the walk across the moulins and meltwater streams of the Root Glacier under Donoho Peak and into the Donoho Basin by walking north out

"The park is a rugged yet inviting place to experience your own adventure."

www.nps.gov

of Kennecott on an old wagon road alongside the Kennecott Glacier, built in the 1920s to supply a mine high up on Root Glacier. Emerging from the trees to a fabulous view of Mount Blackburn (16,390 feet/4,995 m) only 20 miles (32 km) away, you merge onto Root Glacier where you make your camp. The next day you attach your crampons and walk across the glacier's aerated surface, discovering ravines, sliding down natural water slides, or maybe practicing your rappelling skills. There is also the option of climbing Donoho Peak (6,696 feet/2,040 m), although the climb is a long one with substantial scrambling over loose rocks. The view of Mount Blackburn's stunning south face tops off this grand trek into an icy world. **BDS**

Kesugi Ridge Alaska, USA

Start Little Coal Creek trailhead   **End** Byers Lake campground   **Distance** 27.4 miles (44 km)   **Time** 2–3 days
Grade Strenuous (boulder hopping)   **Type** Open rocky terrain   **Map** goo.gl/X1Cusl

Kesugi, in the language of the local Tanaina people means "the ancient one," and the trail that runs along the Kesugi Ridge—in Alaska's Denali State Park, just outside the boundary of Denali National Park—provides everything that makes hiking in Alaska such an unforgettable experience. You can camp on comfortable, soft tundra ridges like the one on Ermine Hill or by the shores of Skinny Lake; lose yourself in forests of alder, birch, and spruce; find yourself waist-deep in a bone-chilling glacial-melt river; and pick blueberries (if you're there in August), all the while keeping an eye out for the ubiquitous grizzly and black bears.

A well-marked trail on mostly open terrain, the walk could be done over a long weekend, but this is not the sort of environment that lends itself to timetables. There is so much to see and so much

solitude to soak up that four days are better than three, and five better than four. And what you see every day is the spectacle of the 20,320-foot (6,193-m) Mount McKinley massif dominating the bright blue sky as you walk along the broad Kesugi Ridge.

To maximize your time on the trail, you need to start at the Little Coal Creek trailhead, which cuts out half of the overall elevation gain that would be confronting you if you were to begin at the alternate Byers Lake trailhead, although it is still a demanding 2.5-mile (4-km) ascent up to the ridge. In no time at all, though, you are above the tree line with Denali National Park visible in all its glory, before you return through a broad tundra landscape onto Troublesome Creek Trail for the walk back to your trailhead. **BDS**

⬆ **Kesugi Ridge in the summer months.**

Goat Trail, Wrangell-St Elias National Park Alaska, USA

Start Skolai Pass   **End** Glacier Creek   **Distance** 26 miles (42 km)   **Time** 6–8 days   **Grade** Strenuous
Type Wilderness, mountain trail   **Map** goo.gl/PfFpXd

Walking beneath towering faces of multicolored rocks, watching misty waterfalls tumble down a mountain, hiking alongside frothing rivers bouncing between boulders, and staring at thick forest climbing up the slopes of cloud-covered peaks—these are classic Alaskan wilderness experiences, and if you fancy tackling truly remote terrain in the United States' extreme northwest, this route is a great place to start.

The trail is known as an "introduction to Alaska" and indeed it is, with the main part of the route a 100-year-old prospectors' path that will have you gasping at the determination of these pioneering miners. You need to be pretty adept at wilderness hiking here, but even the hardiest of today's walkers need to reach the start of the route by hiring an airplane—a short bush flight that gets you from McCarthy to the high Wolverine landing strip.

Only then do you embark on some challenging wilderness, including unmarked tundra that will test your navigation skills, unbridged fast-moving rivers that require confidence and experience to cross, and having to traverse steep scree slopes with a level of exposure that will test all but the boldest.

This is a walk that guarantees memorable sights, whether it is white mountain goats foraging among brown mountain vegetation, clouds drifting halfway up a steep-sided mountain pass, or the area's glacial lakes viewed from rocky paths high above. And if the route sounds too daunting, note that there are commercial guided walks available and that some of them take an easier route avoiding those tricky river crossings. **SH**

⬆ Navigate old goat paths over Alaskan tundra.

Vancouver Island Spine Trail
British Columbia, Canada

Start Vancouver   End Cape Scott Provincial Park
Distance 435 miles (700 km)
Time 20 days   Grade Moderate
Type Trail   Info goo.gl/srhYrJ

Vancouver Island's topography is rugged and complex. While only a few of its summits rise to more than 7,000 feet (2100 m), its valleys are deep, often as low as 700 feet (225 m), which means if you want to walk from north to south or vice versa on the soon-to-be inaugurated Vancouver Island Spine Trail, you have a lot of very serious climbs ahead of you.

The trail is the work in progress of the Vancouver Island Spine Trail Association, which plans to create a continuous trail from "Mile Zero" in Vancouver, along the Trans-Canada Trail as far as Lake Cowichan, then west to Port Alberni using the Canadian Northern Pacific Railroad trail, before turning north and heading for the Beaufort Range with stunning views of Beaufort Lake, and the Forbidden Plateau of Strathcona Provincial Park. Trails at the island's northern end will either be new or will run along old logging routes, and everywhere roads will be avoided to preserve the trail's wilderness feel. The route will take hikers beneath Victoria and Schoen peaks, rather than over them, in order to avoid winter snowfalls and thus provide a longer walking season. The trail will finish at Cape Scott Provincial Park on the island's northernmost tip, and when completed will offer the first continuous, unified path along Vancouver's mountainous spine.

Throughout 2014 and 2015, major sections will have been completed and funds raised for its signage. Maps will be developed and a guidebook published. The official opening is scheduled for 2016, but much of the trail can be walked now for those who can't wait to experience Vancouver Island's wilderness as never before. **BDS**

"The time is now to ... join up the last of the ancient forests and rugged coastlines of the length of Vancouver Island."

www.vispine.ca

⬆ Hike and climb your way along Vancouver Island's first top-to-toe traverse.

Grouse Grind
British Columbia, Canada

Start Grouse Mountain Gondola   **End** Grouse
Mountain summit   **Distance** 1.8 miles (2.9 km)
Time 1.5–2 hours   **Grade** Strenuous
Type Trail, steps   **Map** goo.gl/WX2w51

The walk begins in North Vancouver, at the base of the
Grouse Mountain Gondola, and may only be 1.8 miles
(2.9 km) in length, but by the time you struggle your
way to the summit, it will have felt much longer.
Vancouver's most popular trail, which attracts more
than 100,000 hikers a year, ascends more than 2,800
feet (853 m) on a 30-degree slope and has been
tramped by so many people that maintenance crews
have had to install steps along its route to prevent
erosion. But steps do little to alleviate the pain.

The trail is marked at every "quarter," and if the
climb is proving a struggle by the first quarter mark,
you might seriously want to consider turning back.
There are warnings not to attempt it if you have high
blood pressure, or heart or respiratory issues. For
those of you who choose to continue, make sure you
carry plenty of water and warm clothing. Spring-like
conditions at the base can change to sleet and below-
zero temperatures at the summit. The trail is not
patrolled. You have been warned.

When you reach the top, having successfully
negotiated the 2,830 steps, you can take in the area's
flora before making your way to the Grouse Mountain
Chalet, where you can buy a ticket for the gondola
ride back down. Downhill hiking of the trail is not
permitted due to potential rock falls and congestion
on the narrower sections of what is affectionately
called "Mother Nature's Stairmaster," although an
alternate route along the parallel British Columbia
Mountaineering Club (BCMC) trail is possible. You can
also buy a Grouse Mountain Grind Timer Card if you
want to compare your performance against other
"Grouse Grinders." **BDS**

*"This trail is very challenging. Keep
in mind that there is a wide range
of mountaintop trails that might
better suit the average hiker."*

www.grousemountain.com

⊞ The woodland scenery makes the pain of climbing
just under 3,000 steps worthwhile.

The Rockwall Trail
British Columbia, Canada

Start Floe Lake trailhead   End Paint Pots
trailhead   Distance 34 miles (54.7 km)
Time 5 days   Grade Moderate   Type Rocky
Map goo.gl/dOl8OY

A wealth of rocky riches awaits visitors to Kootenay National Park, from its hot springs to its marble canyons. The pinnacle, however, is the Rockwall Trail. It has hanging glaciers, vast meadows of wildflowers, larch forests, one of Canada's highest waterfalls—the 1,148-foot-high (350 m) Helmet Falls—and three high alpine passes. But what makes it extra special is the feature after which the Rockwall is named: an 18-mile (29-km) nearly unbroken wall of limestone cliffs that, at its peak, towers 2,952 feet (900 m) above its base.

Beneath the wall, the trail rises and falls as it traverses a trio of alpine passes—Rockwall Pass, Tumbling Pass, and Numa Pass (the last is the route's highest point). Other attractions include the Tumbling Glacier—which, if you're lucky, you may see calving—and Wolverine Pass. The pass is where the wall gives way to the west, affording splendid views of other peaks in the Vermilion Range, of which the Rockwall is the easternmost escarpment. The Wolverine is flanked by the appropriately forbidding Mount Drysdale to the north and Mount Gray to the south.

The Rockwall itself can be accessed from several points. Each of the alpine passes boasts a trail from the Kootenay Parkway, meaning you can sample sections of it on a day's hike rather than committing to five days. Routes to Numa Pass wind from the Floe Lake and Numa Creek trails, the former focused on a lake into which a small glacier above calves its ice.

Ravaged by fire in 2003, Kootenay National Park's flora has been spectacularly regenerated, yet its main attraction remains the Rockwall Trail. **BM**

◁ The beautiful Tumbling Pass on the Rockwall Trail.

Iceline Trail
British Columbia, Canada

Start/End Whiskey Jack Wilderness Hostel
Distance 13 miles (21 km)   Time 8 hours
Grade Moderate to strenuous   Type Trail
Map goo.gl/2PpYt1

If you want a comfortable place from which to begin a challenging trek, you could do a lot worse than the Whiskey Jack Wilderness Hostel, located on a lakeshore within sight of one of the highest waterfalls in Canada, the 738-foot-high (225 m) Takkakaw Falls in British Columbia, 16 miles (26 km) from Lake Louise. Whiskey Jacks has hot showers and cold beers, and an expansive outdoor deck from which to ponder your upcoming hike through Yoho National Park on its great Iceline Trail.

The official elevation gain of 2,250 feet (686 m) is a little misleading, since the trail involves a lot of ups

> ## *"Possibly one of the most spectacular hikes in the Rockies."*
> www.trailpeak.com

and downs over lateral moraines, but it's unlikely you'll be worrying too much about the status of your legs; Yoho is an old Cree word for "awe and wonder," and the views on this wonderful hike will fill your senses. The Iceline Trail is one of Canada's signature hikes, and if glaciers and glacial geomorphology excite you, then you'll be in hiking heaven. There's the President Range, with its fringe of hanging glaciers; views to the Wapta Icefield; and easy walking past glacial lakes and ponds.

Remnants of the retreating Emerald Glacier are so close that if you do a bit of scrambling above the trail, you can reach out and touch it, and the sound of the glacier moving and scraping over rock will stay with you long after the hike is done. **BDS**

Helm Creek Trail to Cheakamus Lake
British Columbia, Canada

Start/End Helm Creek campground
Distance 8.5 miles (13.6 km)
Time 4 hours **Grade** Easy **Type** Forest trail
Map goo.gl/TVDxyl

"Beautiful, climbable mountains all around. Amazing fields of snow that run all the way to the base of Black Tusk well into July."

whistlerhiatus.com

⬆ Cheakamus Lake is a real treat to view in all its glacial glory.

In the famously rugged region of the Coast Mountains that extends inland from coastal Vancouver to Whistler Mountain in the Fitzsimmons Range, there aren't a lot of hikes that are flat and could be categorized "easy." This is why the Helm Creek Trail to Cheakamus Lake is such a refreshing standout. The lake, located to the south of Whistler Mountain in Garibaldi Provincial Park, is set within a classic wilderness that was officially awarded its "wild" status way back in 1927. And while the walk might not have any gradient to speak of, this charming trail still boasts plenty of views of the surrounding rugged, glacier-capped peaks of an alpine world composed of dormant stratovolcanoes belonging to the age-old Garibaldi Volcanic Belt.

The trail is a meandering one that begins at the Helm Creek campground (with nine tent sites if you prefer an early start) and follows the twists and turns of Helm Creek until a side trail branches off along the lakeshore. It is an invigorating walk, through lush forests on an undefined trail typical of the area. It weaves its way past creeks and meadows and under towering cedar trees that give the trail a lovely aroma and the occasional obstacle, too, when old trees fall across the trail, including one giant that fell in 2012, necessitating a 66-foot (20-m) detour!

The trail passes campgrounds and tiny beaches to Singing Creek, and is ideal for families. An alternative trail leads to Helm Lake with its fabulous views to Whistler's famous volcanic pinnacle, Black Tusk. But it is the memory of emerging onto the view of the lake's turquoise waters and the aroma of its ancient cedars that will linger most in the memory. **BDS**

Lions Binkert Trail
British Columbia, Canada

Start/End Lion's Bay trailhead
Distance 10 miles (16 km)   Time 8 hours
Grade Strenuous   Type Forest trails, exposed rocks,
gravel   Map goo.gl/3YlOiz

If you have been a resident or visitor in the city of Vancouver for more than a day or two, chances are you are familiar with the East and West Lion peaks that poke their summits up above the line of the nearby North Shore Mountains. They were first climbed in 1899 almost by accident, when hunters chased a small herd of goats up a steep, rocky incline, and suddenly found they had nowhere else to go but down. The indigenous Squamish people call them Ch'ich'iyuy Elxwikn, meaning "Twin Sisters," and together they represent one of the most recognizable features on the Vancouver skyline.

The trail to West Lion summit begins at the trailhead at Lion's Bay, an hour north of Vancouver on the Sea to Sky Highway, and immediately plunges you into dense stands of typical North Shore forest before climbing steadily on an old logging road with occasional glimpses of Howe Sound to your right. The next few hours will be spent negotiating a series of switchbacks and clambering your way over fallen trees before you emerge onto Howe Sound Crest with its spectacular view to the now tantalizingly close summit of West Lion, and it is a great spot to stop for lunch.

This is where it can get tricky. People have died attempting to scale the summit of West Lion because the path goes along some seriously exposed sections where slipping is most definitely not an option—it really is best left to expert climbers. But for those who continue, hang on tightly to roots and branches and to whatever handholds you can get as you look forward to the coming views of Black Tusk, Needles, Cathedral, and other peaks while helicopters bring tourists in for a closer view of you, "the mad climber." **BDS**

Wapta Icefield Hike Alberta/
British Columbia, Canada

Start Num-ti-Jah Lodge parking lot, Bow Lake, Alberta
End Peyto Lake, British Columbia   Distance 8 miles
(12.8 km)   Time 3 days   Grade Moderate   Type Snow,
ice trail   Info goo.gl/cWIUf9

Centered on the Continental Divide, northwest of Mount Gordon and straddling Banff and Yoho national parks, the glaciers known as the Wapta Icefield feed many lakes and rivers in the area. First traversed in 1897 by the Rocky Mountains pioneer Jean Habel, you can now do a three-day traverse of this icy realm, beginning at Bow Lake, north of Banff, and ending at Peyto Lake.

The Wapta Icefield Hike begins on the shoreline of Bow Lake and ascends up the mountain trail, past aging moraines and through forest before emerging onto a vast alpine cirque surrounded by summits and

"Standing on an icefield is like being on the ocean where you'll get a sense of the vastness of the glacier."

canadianrockieshiking.com

glaciers. A final ascent gets you to Bow Hut at 7,709 feet (2,350 m), a large hut with cooking facilities and capacity for some thirty guests. From Bow Hut it's a spectacular day of ice walking toward Peyto Hut, ascending the slopes of Bow Glacier and onto the flat expanse of the Wapta Icefield. You can take a quick side trip to Polaris Peak for a panoramic view of dozens of ice-laden peaks before descending upon the Peyto Glacier and over the occasional smallish crevasse, which means ropes, harnesses, and crampons are required. After a well-earned night at Peyto Hut, you descend down Peyto Glacier—a rare opportunity to see a retreating glacier up close—and the traverse ends on the shores of beautiful Peyto Lake. **BDS**

Brewster Glacier Skywalk
Alberta, Canada

Start/End Columbia Icefield Glacier Discovery Centre **Distance** 1,640 feet (500 m) **Time** 1 hour **Grade** Easy **Type** Glass and wooden boardwalk **Info** goo.gl/SHHOQB

"It really provided a unique fit in terms of expanding the range of services and experiences for visitors to the park."

Greg Fenton, Parks Canada

⤒ "Float" on a glass cloud 918 feet (280 m) above Alberta's glorious Sunwapta Valley.

The vision was to do more than simply build another viewing platform. Here was an opportunity to raise awareness of the processes of glaciology and geology and the complexities of the vast Columbia Icefield, North America's largest subpolar icesheet.

The experience of the skywalk starts long before you arrive at its spectacular cantilevered overlook, with a series of interpretive stops along its approach providing insights into the Sunwapta Valley below and how the flora and fauna around and below you have adapted to their subalpine environment. You can learn how waterways created by melting glaciers have helped humans to discover newfound habitats, and of the evolutionary history of the Canadian Rocky Mountains around you. The skywalk achieves all this as you walk along its impressive 1,640-foot-long (500 m) boardwalk and then tops it all off with a view to remember.

The viewing platform extends 100 feet (30.5 m) over the Sunwapta Valley and is a dizzying 918 feet (280 m) above the valley floor. Cut straight into the native bedrock and built with weathering steel, glass, and wood, it offers a barrier-free wilderness experience to people of all abilities, taking visitors out above the valley to stand on the glass platform with very little between the land below them and the sky above.

The winning design in a competition that saw sixty entries from around the world vying for the contract, what was once just a roadside pullout on the highway at Tangle Ridge off the Icefield Parkway not far from the Athabasca Glacier is now an unmissable addition for visitors to the nearby jewel of Alberta, Jasper National Park. **BDS**

Parker Ridge Trail
Alberta, Canada

Start/End Parker Ridge trailhead
Distance 3.1 miles (5 km)   Time 2 hours
Grade Easy to moderate   Type Forest, alpine trail
Map goo.gl/F1jUhx

If you're a hiker and you're in the area of the Columbia Icefields in northern Banff National Park, then the Parker Ridge Trail is an absolute must. Try, however, to walk it either in the early morning or late in the afternoon, because the trailhead is off a large parking lot right on the Icefield Parkway and is guaranteed to be crowded in the middle of the day, particularly in summer. Do your bit to preserve the environment and avoid the temptation to "shortcut" the trail's series of switchbacks (the alpine vegetation here is delicate) and take your time to walk through its forest of subalpine fir and spruce. As you near the ridgeline, keep your eyes out for bighorn sheep, and if you're lucky maybe even a grizzly or two.

The trail is undemanding and straightforward, but don't forget to take a coat with you, as winds on the ridge can be cold, even on a warm day. The first third of the trail is over avalanche paths past several stands of stunted alpine fir and soil covered in wildflowers fed by the melting snowpack. Trees are then left behind as you enter the alpine zone, characterized by moss campion and forget-me-nots that thrive in this stunning wind-blown, tundra-like landscape. From here the trail climbs quickly, and the reward at trail's end seems out of proportion to the amount of effort expended—a magnificent view of the mighty 5.6-mile (9-km) Saskatchewan Glacier, the primary water source for the North Saskatchewan River. In good weather you can see all the way to the source of the glacier in the southern Columbia Icefield, and behind it towers the snow-clad peak of the sentinel-like Castleguard Mountain, standing at 10,965 feet (3,342 m). **BDS**

Redearth Creek to Shadow Lake
Alberta, Canada

Start Redearth Creek parking area   End Shadow Lake Lodge   Distance 9 miles (14.5 km)
Time 3.5–4.5 hours   Grade Easy   Type Old mining road, forest trails   Map goo.gl/xevoAi

Shadow Lake sits beneath the towering granite face of Mount Ball (10,863 feet/3,311 m) on the Continental Divide at the border of Banff and Kootenay national parks. Mount Ball is a relatively little-visited peak due to the fact that it cannot be seen by the thousands who pass close to it each day on the nearby Trans-Canada Highway. This also applies to the lake that sits beneath its summit, which is why a hike to Shadow Lake is one of the most rewarding and serene walks that can be enjoyed in this popular region of the Rocky Mountains.

"Shadow Lake is one of the more impressive lakes along the Great Divide."
Canadian Rockies Trail Guide, 2007

While it is possible to get to Shadow Lake and back in a day, it would be remiss not to spend a night at the fabulous Shadow Lake Lodge, an elaborate and spacious backcountry log cabin accessible only by hiking or cross-country skiing.

Three-quarters of the hike is made up of an old mining road that was laid down along Redearth and Pharaoh creeks in the 1920s, which makes for a gradual climb and a chance to take in the breathtaking scenery. After 6.5 miles (10.5 km), the trail to the lake branches off and takes you through thick forest for about 1.5 miles (2.4 km) to the campsite and the lodge. And once you have refueled, the lake and glacier-laden Mount Ball will just make you want to keep on hiking. **BDS**

Centennial Ridge Trail Alberta, Canada

Start/End Ribbon Creek trailhead   **Distance** 10 miles (16 km)   **Time** 10 hours   **Grade** Strenuous
Type Grassy, rocky paths   **Map** goo.gl/6Gt9Nb

Spare a thought for Samuel Evans Stokes Allen. The Philadelphia-born pioneer spent his late teens and early twenties mapping the mountains of Alberta. Sadly, Allen Sr. viewed his son's alpinism dimly. Depressed, the budding cartographer succumbed to dementia and spent his final four decades in unhappy confinement, never knowing that one of the mountains in the Canadian Rocky Mountain's Valley of the Ten Peaks had been renamed in his honor.

Mount Allen is home to an appropriate monument to his thwarted ambition: the Centennial Ridge Trail. The highest maintained hike in the Rockies, it rewards steadfast souls with panoramic views of this most iconic of regions (the Valley of the Ten Peaks appeared on Canadian twenty-dollar bills issued in 1969 and 1979). Yet to conquer it is to overcome frequently fearsome winds, a sudden steep ascent—1,969 feet

(600 m) in less than 1.25 miles (2 km)—no water or shade, and, in summer, swarms of annoying bugs. To add to the trail's heritage, Mount Allen housed the ski lodge and hill for the 1988 Winter Olympics, hence the outcrop known as Olympic Summit that forms part of the trail to the mountain.

The rewards for your efforts of walking the trail are spectacular scenery that, as one reviewer enthused, will have you reaching for your camera at every twist and turn of its rapid but short series of switchbacks. The views become more breathtaking with every passing hour—you may even be so busy marveling at the mountainous panorama and intriguing rock formations that you miss the occasional mountain lion sharing the scenery with you. **BM**

⊼ Walk the Rocky Mountains' highest maintained trail.

Pacific Crest Trail Canada/USA

Start Manning Park, British Columbia   **End** Campo, California   **Distance** 2,650 miles (4,265 km)
Time 4–6 months   **Grade** Strenuous   **Type** Rock, dirt trails   **Info** goo.gl/1QRCzY

The Pacific Crest Trail (PCT) is one of the world's great trails, and it passes through many of the finest landscapes that the North American continent has to offer. It begins at the Canadian border, crosses the Columbia Gorge, and weaves its way down through the northern Cascade Range. In Oregon, the inclines of the Cascades make way for relatively easy walking through lush, old-growth forests punctuated by volcanoes, ridgelines, and lakes. The southern Cascades see a turn in the trail as you enter the solitude of Northern California and enter into the famous Sierra Nevada Mountains with their iconic peaks and valleys, one of the world's great trail hotspots. Finally, you emerge from the mountains south of Mount Whitney and come to the beginning of the trail's final 700 miles (1,130 km) through the deserts of Southern California, having passed through six of North America's seven ecozones, almost sixty mountain passes, and seven national parks. Around 300 people attempt the thru-hike each year, and of those, less than two-thirds succeed. Spending between five and six months of your life conquering this acknowledged "beast" of a track is not to be taken lightly.

The trail began in the 1930s as a series of unconnected walks in various states, and even those humble beginnings may well not have happened for decades had it not been for the valiant petitioning for a continuous border-to-border trail by two indomitable backcountry pioneers Clinton Clarke and Warren Rogers. Now the PCT is known the world over, and while it will demand everything you have, the memories will last a lifetime. **BDS**

⊼ The PCT is one of America's "Triple Crown" traverses.

Emmons Moraine Trail Washington, USA

Start/End White River campground **Distance** 4 miles (6.4 km) **Time** 2 hours **Grade** Easy to moderate
Type Paved to rocky trail **Map** goo.gl/cOJlnz

The Emmons Moraine Trail is proof that you don't need a week and a backpack full of food and blister bandages to witness fabulous backcountry vistas. Located in Washington's Mount Rainier National Park, this great trail is open from July to October, and accessible from the White River campground or, for travelers with a sense of history, from the Paradise Inn, built in 1916 on Mount Rainier's southern slopes.

The trail begins beneath a canopy of trees at the foot of a valley. For a mile it shares a path with the Glacier Basin Trail (a strenuous six-hour walk), crossing creeks that cascade into the White River below. At an intersection, a sign points to the Emmons Moraine Trail, and a log bridge crosses the river (assuming it hasn't been destroyed by snowmelt) to the path on the moraine itself, an accumulation of earth and stones carried and deposited by glacial activity.

The moraine affords near-uninterrupted views of the volcano that gives the Mount Rainier National Park its name, the White River, and Goat Island Mountain, an elongated ridge on Mount Rainier's northeastern flank. And of course you have the view you came here for, the closest view possible of Emmons Glacier on Mount Rainier's northeastern flank, short of being on the glacier itself. With a surface area of more than 4 square miles (10.3 sq km) and an elevation of close to 14,000 feet (4,267 m), the glacier is a behemoth, descending nearly 9,000 feet (2,743 m) into the White River and creating, courtesy of displaced silt, some beautifully colored ponds of melted ice, and joining with the Ingraham Glacier to provide one of the most stunning mountain vistas in the Pacific Northwest. **BM**

↑ Crossing a river of glacial meltwater on the trail.

Hidden Lake Trail Washington, USA

Start/End Sibley Creek trailhead   **Distance** 9 miles (14.5 km)   **Time** 6 hours
Grade Moderate to strenuous   **Type** Mountain paths, rocky terrain   **Map** goo.gl/ftfRUI

People who have walked this trail high up in Washington's North Cascade Mountains say it is one of the finest two-day walks they have ever done and a continuous delight to the senses. You will find expansive meadows overflowing with wildflowers such as cow parsnip and fireweed, heather-clad granite boulders and outcrops, stream-laced snowfields, alpine nooks that provide refuge for the area's abundant wildlife, a mountain hut to sleep in, and best of all, a panorama of jaw-droppingly beautiful serrated peaks the equal of which would be hard to find anywhere in the lower forty-eight states.

Getting to this scenic wonderland starts with a steady climb through dense forest to where the switchbacks begin and a mudslide or trail slump would not be uncommon. Leaving the canopy behind, you enter an alder-filled avalanche chute and cross the East Fork of Sibley Creek. At 5,200 feet (1,585 m), you get a marvelous view of Mount Baker on the west horizon, and a little farther on, unhindered views of various Cascade peaks to the west and south. After 4.2 miles (6.8 km) of exhilarating climbing, you reach a saddle from where you can see the 7,088-foot (2,160-m) Hidden Lakes peak to your left, the Boston Basin beyond, and the path to the Hidden Lake overlook and mountain hut to your right. It's an 800-foot (244-m) rough-boulder scramble descent to reach Hidden Lake, but to do so you lose the views you have fought so hard to acquire. Instead, why not walk over to the mountain hut, built in 1931 and restored in the 1960s by Fred Darvill, one of the Cascade Mountains' early pioneers, relax, and just … look. **BDS**

⊞ A great walk into the North Cascade mountains.

Hall of Mosses Trail
Washington, USA

Start/End Hall of Mosses visitor center
Distance 0.8 mile (1.3 km) Time 1 hour
Grade Easy Type Forest paths
Info goo.gl/YCjf12

Drenched by between 12 feet (3.6 m) and 14 feet (4.2 m) of rainfall each year, the mountain areas above the Hoh, Quinault, and Queets river valleys on the western slopes and ranges of Washington's Olympic National Park contain in their mist-shrouded peaks the finest remaining examples of temperate rain forest to be found anywhere in North America. Here, isolation is a blessing. Explorers first came to the Olympic Peninsula in the mid-1800s, but the region—with its vast stands of Sitka spruce and hemlock and heavy inclines—proved so rugged that it wouldn't be until 1889, the year Washington achieved statehood, that the first organized expedition into its interior was mounted.

The Hall of Mosses Trail in the Hoh Rain Forest is a 0.8-mile (1.3-km) loop trail that takes you into the heart of a rare ecosystem that is undisturbed, thanks mostly to its forbidding remoteness. Entering it is like stepping into a storybook. Crossing a small bridge over a moss-filled stream, you walk up a small incline and onto the loop trail that is flat and easy to navigate, and once you're on it, you won't want to leave. Stunning moss-draped branches from coniferous and deciduous old-growth trees overhang this trail filled with dappled light and a hundred shades of green. Moss and lichen-encrusted rocks are all about you. There are a few open spaces here, but not many, and much of the rain forest is lined with nurse logs, ferns, mosses, and various species of temperate plants.

There is an excellent campground with eighty-eight sites that is open year-round, but if you come, be prepared to get wet. You couldn't put a trail in a better position to capture all the fog and rain that the Pacific Ocean is capable of providing. **BDS**

"This aptly named loop exhibits stunning, moss-draped branches and towering old growth with an educational twist."

trailpedia.org

⬆ A tiny loop trail through a moisture-laden rain forest proves that less can be more.

Wonderland Trail
Washington, USA

Start/End White River campground (and various other options) **Distance** 93 miles (150 km)
Time 10–14 days **Grade** Strenuous
Type Wilderness trail **Map** goo.gl/Wwjvco

Mount Rainier is one of the most visually prominent mountains in the world, standing clear of its foothills with few competing peaks nearby. This snowcapped mountain is an active volcano, and at 14,411 feet (4,392 m) high, it dominates the surrounding landscape.

In 1915, a trail was constructed around the base of the mountain, climbing and descending over its ridges in a circuit of 93 miles (150 km). The highest pass it crosses is at 6,750 feet (2,057 m), and the total ascent for the trail is a strenuous 22,000 feet (6,706 m).

A few hundred dedicated walkers complete the route each year, drawn by its spectacular trails that pass through conifer forests, glaciers, deep wooded valleys, snowfields, clear lakes, and alpine meadows, and over rivers on primitive bridges. There are swathes of wildflowers and the chance to spot wildlife such as elk and black bears.

The Wonderland Trail has twenty-one campsites, all equipped with "bear poles" to hang food supplies high out of the reach of prowling bears (and rodents). There are many trailheads on the route, so walkers can tackle shorter sections, all of which are within the Mount Rainier National Park. You will need a permit if you plan to stay for longer than a day. The complete circuit takes most walkers up to two weeks, but in 2006, superfit trail runner Kyle Skaggs raced around the trail in just 20 hours 53 minutes.

Most Wonderland Trail attempts are made in late summer, but the trail can have snow covering as late as July. For the rest of the year, the route is inaccessible; the snow is so deep, it completely covers the forests. In fact, Mount Rainier has suffered the deepest snow ever recorded: up to 90 feet (27.5 m) deep. **SH**

"Perhaps the biggest aspect in planning to hike the Wonderland Trail is you knowing your hiking skills, abilities, and habits."

www.nps.gov

⤒ This tough trail around Mount Rainier is two weeks of ups and downs on an active volcano.

Cleetwood Cove Trail
Oregon, USA

Start East Rim Drive   End Cleetwood Cove
Distance 1 mile (1.6 km)   Time 1 hour
Grade Strenuous   Type Mountain trail
Map goo.gl/kGrb6m

The only authorized access to the shoreline of Oregon's Crater Lake, the Cleetwood Cove Trail was opened in the summer of 1960 and has been taking hikers down its switchbacks to the edge of the lake ever since.

At 1,943 feet (592 m) deep, Crater Lake is the deepest lake in the United States, a remnant of what was once Mount Mazama, which erupted in a series of cataclysmic explosions 7,000 years ago to form the volcanic caldera we see today. Over time, the caldera filled with snowmelt and rainwater to create the lake.

Every day in summer, an average of more than 700 people walk this short but demanding trail to see for themselves the impossibly blue waters of the lake, one of the clearest bodies of water in the world, and to cast their eyes over the perfection of its glorious interior. Once you reach the rim, the trail meanders gently down the wall of the caldera to Cleetwood Cove, past rest stops that you'll want to take advantage of on the strenuous hike back up along its 11-degree gradient. Hiking or climbing off the trail within the caldera is prohibited, and if it's rainy or foggy at the base of the crater, chances are you'll see nothing when you reach the rim, so take note of the conditions. Fortunately, you have the option of walking some of the 90 miles (144 km) of trails in the surrounding Crater Lake National Park if the weather is less than favorable.

Once inside the caldera, if you're so inclined, you can continue your trail walking on Wizard Island, the volcanic cinder cone at the lake's western end. This excursion is itself a day trip that provides its own unique perspective onto one of North America's most unforgettable vistas. **BDS**

"The trail is recommended only for those in good physical condition."

www.craterlakeinstitute.com

⬆ A short though strenuous trail ends with views over one of North America's most beautiful lakes.

Backbone Trail

California, USA

Start Will Rogers State Historic Park   **End** Point Mugu State Park   **Distance** 68 miles (109 km)   **Time** 7 days   **Grade** Moderate   **Type** Long-distance mountain trail   **Map** goo.gl/4KiZ7M

The Backbone Trail is the result of the cooperation of various public and private organizations and individuals, including the National Park Service, who worked together to create not only the Backbone Trail, but also the Santa Monica Mountains National Recreation Area through which it runs. A ridgeline trail through the Santa Monica Mountains had been a dream of local hikers and walkers for fifty years, and construction of the trail, which is ideal for both walkers and mountain bikers, began in the early 1980s. It winds its way over the peaks and down into the canyons of the Santa Monica Mountains, from its high point on the summit of the 3,111-foot (948-m) Sandstone Peak to its lowest, Point Mugu State Park's Ray Miller trailhead, just over the Pacific Coast Highway from Thornhill Broome Beach. On its way, the trail passes through oak woodlands and chaparral-covered hillsides, over a patchwork of public lands, fire roads, and old animal trails, with only the more recent sections built to conform to modern trail standards.

Because the trail has been "pieced together," not all sections are open to all users. Mountain bikers, for example, are permitted only on its fire roads unless otherwise specified. For walkers, however, it is a joy. Up to 150 species of blooming wildflowers can be seen on the trail, but there are patches of poison oak, too, so remember to bring protective clothing. Birdwatchers will be busy, with up to 380 bird species in the region, a third of which are non-migratory. And don't forget the TV series *M*A*S*H* (1972–1983) when you pass through the trail's midway point, Malibu Creek State Park—its 7,000 acres (2,833 ha) provided the outdoor setting for the series. **BDS**

High Sierra Trail

California, USA

Start Crescent Meadow trailhead   **End** Whitney Portal trailhead   **Distance** 65 miles (105 km)   **Time** 7 days   **Grade** Strenuous   **Type** Alpine trail   **Map** goo.gl/vznBfR

Between Sequoia National Park's Crescent Meadow to the west and the Sierra Nevada's Whitney Portal to the east, walkers can escape civilization and experience a world of panoramic peaks, mountain lakes, forests, and rivers on the High Sierra Trail.

The trail can be divided into seven segments: Crescent Meadow to Nine-Mile Creek; Nine-Mile Creek to Precipice Lake (the latter a snowy oasis immortalized by photographer Ansel Adams); Precipice Lake to Moraine Lake (including Big Arroyo bowl, a smorgasbord of switchbacks); Moraine Lake to Kern Hot Spring; Kern

> ## "The trail ... offers hikers spectacular views of the Great Western Divide."
>
> www.visitsequoia.com

Hot Spring to Upper Kern Canyon (where Junction Meadow offers campsites amid thick forest); Upper Kern Canyon to Guitar Lake (the latter is the trail's best place to watch a sunset); and Guitar Lake to Mount Whitney Summit (14,505 feet/4,421 m), and the descent to Whitney Portal. Much of this high-altitude trail is above 10,000 feet (3,048 m), so bring warm clothes.

Rightly proud of this fine trail, the National Park Service strictly regulates the trail. Permits are required, warnings are issued about floods that render creeks impassable, the use of soap is forbidden, food containers are required by law so as not to attract bears, and in the Mount Whitney region, all human waste must be taken out with you. **BM**

Yosemite Grand Traverse

California, USA

Start Ansel Adams Wilderness **End** Tuolumne Meadows
Distance 60 miles (96.5 km) **Time** 6–7 days
Grade Moderate to strenuous **Type** Long-distance
mountain trail **Info** goo.gl/PLdd2P

The Yosemite Grand Traverse is one of North America's classic hikes. It begins in southern Yosemite in the Ansel Adams Wilderness, and continues over Post Peak Pass with views to the Minarets and various other Sierra Nevada summits, before negotiating the switchbacks over Isberg Pass (10,750 feet/3,276 m) and entering Yosemite National Park proper. Then comes a welcome 2,500-foot (762-m) descent to the scenic Merced River, with views of the stunning Clarke Range before ending on the shoreline of Lake Washburn (7,200 feet/2,194 m). The following day is spent hiking toward your jumping-off point for the scaling of the world-famous granite monolith Half Dome, which rises 4,800 feet (1,463 m) above the Yosemite Valley. Once considered unscaleable, it is now a very manageable feat with cabling over the steepest sections, making it a day out for the serious walker.

After descending Half Dome, the trail joins briefly with the famous John Muir Trail along a segment that many regard as the trail's most beautiful—the Yosemite High Camp. From there you have the option of a small detour to Upper Cathedral Lake, and from the high camp it's just a few miles to the trail's end at Tuolumne Meadows and its surrounding high country, studded with a myriad of granite peaks and domes.

Some of the trailhead logistics are challenging, and going with an experienced guide is recommended. The hiking is mostly strenuous at elevations of more than 11,000 feet (3,352 m), and you'll have to carry all your own food in bear-resistant cans plus sleeping bags and tents—but the rewards will last a lifetime. **BDS**

◄ Yosemite Valley—El Capitan (left) and Half Dome (right).

Mist Trail

California, USA

Start/End Happy Isles, Yosemite Valley **Distance** 3 miles
(4.8 km) to Vernal Fall, 7 miles (11 km) to Nevada Fall
Time 2–5 hrs **Grade** Moderate to strenuous
Type Steep, slippery trails, granite **Map** goo.gl/du9vFm

Not for nothing did the Mist Trail get its name, with two wonderful waterfalls meaning you'll likely return damper than when you began. Sadly, some don't return at all: in the twenty-first century alone, the trail has claimed more than fourteen lives, giving it one of Yosemite's most dangerous reputations. Fortunately, visitors who stay out of the water should be safe, as the danger lies not on the trail itself but in the currents of the tempting waters that feed into the falls.

The trail begins at Happy Isles in the Merced River at the far eastern end of the Yosemite Valley. The

> *"You can get covered with spray close to two of Yosemite's rock-star waterfalls."*
>
> www.yosemitehikes.com

Vernal Fall comes into view by the end of the first mile, but to reach the top, more than 600 steep, slippery granite steps cut into the cliff will need to be negotiated. The risk of seasonal falling ice and rocks, coupled with the ever-present waterfall spray, means this part of the trail is closed in winter when the falls can be accessed only via the John Muir Trail, snow permitting. From the top of Vernal, the Mist Trail goes from moderate to strenuous as it continues to Nevada Fall.

The climax of the trail offers three splendid sights to determined visitors. There's the Nevada Fall itself, the 1,700-foot (518-m) granite dome known as Liberty Cap, and—returning along the John Muir Trail—the back of mighty Half Dome. **BM**

John Muir Trail California, USA

Start Happy Isles trailhead   **End** Mt. Whitney (Whitney Portal) trailhead   **Distance** 210 miles (338 km)
Time 10–22 days   **Grade** Moderate to strenuous   **Type** Long-distance mountain trail   **Info** goo.gl/WYuxJK

Although it was the explorer and early member of the Sierra Club Theodore Solomons who first thought of it, the John Muir Trail (JMT) was named after the Scottish-born naturalist and wilderness advocate who devoted his life to the preservation of the wilderness of the United States. Completed in 1938, it traverses through pristine Sierra Nevada backcountry following the Pacific Crest Trail, from Yosemite National Park south through the jagged spires of the Minarets and the volcanic landscape around Devil's Postpile National Monument to Mount Whitney (14,505 feet/4,421 m). It is a true wilderness trail, passing by canyons thousands of feet deep and coming into contact with civilization only by circumstance. One section, from Sherman Pass in the south to Tioga Pass in the north, goes for 140 miles (225 km) without crossing so much as a road. And if you're doing the trail from north to south,

climbing 6,000 feet (1,828 m) out of the Yosemite Valley in the middle of summer can be one heck of a slog.

But you don't tackle the JMT in its entirety if all you want is a mediocre challenge. On your trek, you'll cross seven mountain passes, all in excess of 11,000 feet (3,400 m), ascend Yosemite's Half Dome, and pass gorgeous alpine lakes such as Virginia Lake and Silver Pass Lake: both perfect places to pitch your tent at the end of a hard day. And speaking of down time, don't forget to pack a copy of Muir's *My First Summer in the Sierra*, the perfect companion to help you appreciate the beauty that surrounds you, for as Muir reminds us: "Everybody needs beauty as well as bread, places to pray and play in, where Nature may heal and cheer…" **BDS**

⛰ Walk in the footsteps of a pioneering naturalist.

Methuselah Trail California, USA

Start/End East of Schulman Grove visitor center, Ancient Bristlecone Pine Forest   Distance 4.2 miles (6.7 km)
Time 2–3 hours   Grade Moderate   Type Exposed rock, dirt trails   Map goo.gl/F7j5QJ

The bristlecone pine is the world's oldest living thing, and grows at altitudes just below the tree line in isolated groves in a select and often hard-to-access subalpine areas of the Western United States. Extraordinarily tolerant of drought, thanks in part to its extensive and shallow root system, the pine has thick, waxy needles that help it to retain what moisture it can find, and its wood is dense and resinous, helping it to fend off insects and parasites. Some trees have been dated to more than 5,000 years old, and their gnarled branches, with deeply fissured reddish-brown bark, make them a favorite of photographers. These ultimate survivors are among the most remarkable of all living things, and to be able to walk amid them in their remote locations, often with views of the Great Basin High Desert spreading out all around you, is to walk through living history. To pass by something—to

reach out and to touch something—that was alive when Ramesses II was building his pyramids at Giza and that is still alive today is a feeling worth going a long way out of your way to acquire.

One of the more accessible in a generally inaccessible sprinkling of bristlecone groves is the Schulman Grove in the Inyo National Forest high in California's White Mountains. The Methuselah Walk, named after the grove's oldest bristlecone, starts at the visitor center and weaves its way through the grove at an altitude of close to 9,200 feet (2,800m), a fact that quickly slows you down as you huff and puff your way through the thin atmosphere that hovers over these arid, dolomite-rich slopes. The Patriarch Grove is farther still … if you have the lungs for it. **BDS**

⬆ Touch the knarled beauty of Earth's oldest living things.

Telescope Peak Trail California, USA

Start/End Mahogany Flat campground   **Distance** 12.5 miles (20 km)   **Time** 7–9 hours   **Grade** Strenuous
Type Well-maintained trail   **Map** goo.gl/aeYwcd

It was named Telescope Peak because it was thought you couldn't see any farther from the summit than you could with the naked eye, not even if you had a telescope. Few who have stood here and marveled at its 360-degree wraparound panorama would argue. From its 11,049-foot (3,368-m) summit in California's Death Valley, you can see every sort of geological feature that makes this national park so unique: alluvial fans, canyons, mountain ranges, dry lake beds, salt flats, and the sand dunes of the Panamint Valley. Not only that, but when you arrive at the summit you'll have an enviable view: you can look down at Badwater, at -282 feet (-86 m), the *lowest* point in the western hemisphere, then across to the summit of Mount Whitney (14,505 feet/4,421 m), the *highest* point in the continental United States. And that is a view worth climbing for.

The hike is strenuous and the entire route is fully exposed to the elements, so take plenty of sunscreen and water, and remember that the temperature on the summit can be considerably cooler than on the valley floor. It begins to the east of Roger's Peak with a steeply graded ascent that is hard going until it levels off onto a saddle that takes you to Bennett Peak, which continues at a moderate grade. After three easy-going miles you reach a grove of rare, gnarled bristlecone pines, the world's oldest living trees. From there you negotiate thirteen irregular switchbacks on Telescope Peak's northeast face, and along the way, maybe see a chipmunk, a rock wren, or even a sagebrush lizard before the safe crest walk takes you to its small, rocky summit, and those unique views. **BDS**

⬆ Mount Whitney viewed from the salt flat of Badwater.

Grand Sawtooths Loop Idaho, USA

Start/End Grandjean trailhead   **Distance** 63 miles (101 km)   **Time** 5–9 days   **Grade** Moderate
Type Rocks and rivers   **Map** goo.gl/7kUNHX

Ravaged by fire in 2012, the Sawtooths—Idaho's contribution to the Rocky Mountains—continue to house some of the state's most stunning scenery. And the Grand Sawtooths Loop is the best way to see it. From its Grandjean trailhead, a 5-mile (8-km) uphill hike takes you to the Trail Creek Lakes. This quintet of glistening gems is among the many alpine water features to be enjoyed in the Sawtooths, and a legacy of its glacial ancestry.

A diversion of less than a mile takes you to Observation Peak (9151 feet/2789 m), the only Sawtooth to include a trail to the summit. Well-graded and maintained trails mean even the ascents with the greatest elevation gain should be within the capabilities of most hikers. However, the loop is accessible in its entirety only from July through August: for the rest of the year, the cold renders many of the passes—including

four above 9,000 feet (2,743 m)—impassable. It is also best hiked clockwise, as beginning from the east renders the trail formidably steep.

Points of interest include the McGown Lakes—ranging from a modest 157 feet (48 m) to an impressive 689 feet (210 m)—and Sawtooth Lake. The trail to the latter zigzags along fifteen switchbacks, but persevere and you'll be rewarded by a vast, sparkling oasis, flanked by Mount Regan and Alpine Peak.

Much of the Sawtooth range can be viewed satisfactorily by car, but hitting the trails is the best way to appreciate all it has to offer. And should you run short of supplies, you're not too far from Stanley in Custer County—although its city status belies its size: as of 2012, its estimated population was sixty-seven. **BM**

⤒ Hike the Sawtooth Mountains' only summit trail.

Kings Peak

Utah, USA

Start/End Henry's Fork trailhead
Distance 28 miles (45 km)   **Time** 3 days
Grade Strenuous   **Type** Mountain trail
Map goo.gl/jcaa9W

Not quite a hike and not quite mountaineering, Kings Peak, the highest point in Utah at 13,528 feet (4,123 m), is only for the tough. Everything about this glacial landscape in this designated state wilderness is outsize—a huge spread of mountains and broad valleys dotted with hundreds of lakes. The weather is fickle: A perfect summer's morning can turn to heavy rain, lightning, or hail (snow is present in considerable quantities between November and June).

Topping the list of essential equipment is a tent—there are multiple campsites along the trail. The first

---

"Even if Kings Peak wasn't the tallest mountain in Utah ... it would be an incredible hike anyway."

www.utahoutside.com

---

5 miles (8 km) are a gentle warm up for what lies ahead. From the trailhead, the path winds through pine woods, following the course of Henry's Fork River, then crosses an open valley, where the pyramidal Kings Peak comes into view At Elkhorn Crossing, the trail turns left to ford the river (there is a bridge a little farther upstream) to start a gradual climb above the tree line. After Gunsight Pass, the trail drops into a valley before zigzagging up to Anderson Pass at 12,700 feet (3,870 m). The final 0.8-mile (1.3-km) climb to the summit is a long, hard slog through boulders that can take several hours to complete. It defeats some hikers. Having come this far, however, it would be a shame not to bag that peak. **DS**

Brighton Lakes Trail

Utah, USA

Start/End Brighton Resort parking lot, Big
Cottonwood Canyon   **Distance** 4 miles (6.4 km)
Time 2.5 hours   **Grade** Easy   **Type** Mountain trail
Map goo.gl/DP7oKl

In late May, Brighton Lakes emerges from its winter guise as a popular ski resort serving locals from Salt Lake City, just 30 miles (48 km) away. Snowmelt reveals a classic alpine landscape formed by glaciers 10,000 to 30,000 years ago, with rugged peaks and grassy valleys reflected in three exquisite lakes—Mary, Martha, and Catherine. Add abundant wildflowers in July through August, and maybe an elk, and it's the kind of scene that used to be found on candy boxes.

A well-worn, well-signed trail with mainly gentle inclines links the three lakes. Catherine is named after the wife of William S. Brighton, who bought Big Cottonwood Canyon in the 1870s and opened a small hotel on the land, bringing tourism to the area for the first time. While Brighton improved and enlarged the hotel, and also opened a general store, his wife looked after the guests. She caught and cooked mountain trout, landing them in her apron. Sadly, their marital mountain idyll had a tragic ending. In 1894, Catherine died of a heart attack while serving lunch; her husband died of blood poisoning nine months later.

From the trailhead, the path passes under one of the ski lifts then sets off through a sprinkling of spruce trees to Lake Mary—the largest lake on the trail—crosses a bridge, and passes a cascade. From Mary it heads higher to Martha, with its picturesque islets of pine, and then to Catherine, where snow lingers into June. Extensions to Sunset Peak, Pioneer Peak, Mount Tuscarora, or Mount Wolverine make the experience more challenging and peaceful. Alternatively, there are other lakes to explore on the opposite side of Lake Mary, including Lake Silver, where Catherine caught trout, and Twin Lakes. **DS**

Estes Canyon–Bulls Pasture Loop
Arizona, USA

Start/End Estes Canyon picnic area, Ajo Mountain Drive   **Distance** 3 miles (4.8 km)   **Time** 3 hours   **Grade** Moderate   **Type** Mountain trail   **Map** goo.gl/DaFMNx

This walk in Arizona's Organ Pipe Cactus National Monument is perfect if you want to feel the Wild West beneath your feet. A three-hour walk (a day pass can be obtained from the visitor center on Highway 8) takes you into the rocky foothills of the Ajo Mountains and a magical landscape. Pink and ocher-colored rocks rear out of a valley floor bristling with candelabras of rare organ pipe cactus and huge stands of saguaro cactus, whose distinctive prongs symbolize the American Southwest. Some of the saguaros are 40 feet (12 m) tall and 200 years old.

From the parking lot, the trail crosses Estes Canyon, following the course of the dry wash to a junction. Here, Estes Canyon trail heads left and Bull Pasture trail right (the trails converge later, so you can set out on one and return on the other). On a spring morning, choose the cacti-peppered Estes Canyon trail to see the cacti in bloom before the flowers close late morning. Woodpeckers and finches nest in cavities in the taller saguaros—a desert take on the cuckoo clock.

After crossing the riverbed and climbing for 1.5 miles (2.5 km), the trail branches off to Bull Pasture, named for the bulls that grazed here until the area's ranches closed in the 1970s. If you are used to seeing herds of Herefords grazing in lush water meadows, you might wonder how ranching was possible in this hostile land. In fact, the cattle fed on grasses and small cacti over a vast area watered by hand-dug wells.

From Bull Pasture Overlook, views unfurl over the Sonoran Desert to Mexico. Back at the junction, the scenic switchbacks of the Bull Pasture trail lead back to your starting point. **DS**

"Everything about [Organ Pipe Cactus National Monument] is unique and [it is] quite unlike anywhere else in the world."

hikearizona.com

⬆ A trail featuring cactus flowers and stunning views to Mexico.

South Kaibab Trail Arizona, USA

Start South Kaibab trailhead **End** North Kaibab trailhead **Distance** 21 miles (34 km) **Time** 3–4 days
Grade Moderate to strenuous **Type** Mountain trail **Map** goo.gl/yqOp4r

There are many ways to see the Grand Canyon, from flying overhead in a helicopter to trekking through it on horseback, but the best way to experience this 1-mile-deep (1.6 km) fissure in the earth's crust is on foot. With a backpack and a pair of binoculars, you can stop to take in its features and its grandeur.

To do this, you need to leave the rim. Three maintained trails descend into the canyon: the North Kaibab from the north rim (closed in winter), the South Kaibab from the south rim, and a third trail—Bright Angel—offers an alternative descent from the south. In three to four days you can hike the canyon from rim to rim, descending via the scenic South Kaibab Trail, crossing the Colorado River at Kaibab Suspension Bridge, staying at the Bright Angel campground, and ascending via the longer and more solitary North Kaibab Trail, with stops at Cottonwood

campground or Pump House Residence. Developed from Native American mule tracks, the switchbacks descend through five ecosystems, passing from a lush topping of evergreens and ferns to desert scrub at the canyon's base. With each twist in the trail comes a brand new vision of splendor—a precipitous drop, a waterfall, or the sight of a condor wheeling far overhead. At Skeleton Point, on the South Kaibab Trail, the red ribbon of the great Colorado appears for the first time far below.

More than four million people visit the Grand Canyon each year, 95 percent of whom just peer over the top. You won't be alone on a walk below the rim, but you can easily walk for an hour or more immersed in the canyon's magic without seeing another soul. **DS**

⛰ Be one of the five percent who venture below the rim.

Iceberg Lake Trail Montana, USA

Start/End Iceberg Lake trailhead   **Distance** 9.6 miles (15.4 km)   **Time** 4 hours   **Grade** Strenuous
Type Rock, dirt trails   **Map** goo.gl/oB5FGa

The Iceberg Lake Trail in Montana's Glacier National Park is a prime habitat for grizzly bears, a true grizzly corridor. So if you come here, be sure to bring a can of bear spray with you, hike only in groups, make a lot of noise as you go, and don't be surprised if the trail is closed due to excessive bear activity. If you think that sounds inconvenient, spare a thought for how the bears must feel—this fabulous trail has become one of the most popular walks in the park, bringing thousands of hikers every year into the midst of their natural, increasingly encroached habitat.

The trail to the lake is one of the park's gems and one of Glacier National Park's easier hikes. The trail lies mostly on the windy eastern side of the park, so remember to bring a windproof, waterproof jacket as the winds, even on a warm day, can be chilly, and rain can be unexpected as approaching weather systems

are hidden from view. The walk is a short one, with much of its 1,275-foot (389-m) ascent done in its early stages after leaving Many Glacier Road, after which it's an easy walk over open terrain above Wilbur Creek, with Mount Henkel and Altyn Peak rising imposingly above you before an exciting detour through the 250-foot-long (76.2 m) Ptarmigan Tunnel, cut through the Ptarmigan Wall in 1930 using nothing but jackhammers. Go through it, come back to the trail, and continue through open terrain and the final approach to the lake. The lake itself is surrounded by 3,000 feet (914.4 m) of rock face that flank it like an amphitheater, keeping its waters in year-round shadow and providing the walker with an experience that will not easily be forgotten. **BDS**

⬆ Iceberg Lake is a Glacier National Park gem.

Highline Trail Montana, USA

Start/End The Loop, Going-to-the-Sun Road   **Distance** 12 miles (19.3 km)   **Time** 1–2 days   **Grade** Strenuous
Type Well-maintained mountain, forest trails   **Map** goo.gl/F1bjiT

This popular trail along Montana's Continental Divide is best done by parking at The Loop east of McDonald Lodge on the Going-to-the-Sun Road, taking a shuttle to Logan Pass, and hiking back. Although sometimes called the Highline "Loop" Trail, it really isn't a loop at all, the word referring only to a pronounced bend in the road near where the trail ends. Often described as one of the United States' most scenic trails, the path provides spectacular views at virtually every turn, including one "infamous" section that takes you along a precipitous ledge with 100-foot (30-m) drop-offs to the road below that may only be around a third of a mile in length, but to anyone with a fear of heights, it will seem much longer.

The trail hugs the cliffs along what is known locally as the Garden Wall. On the trail's early stages, there are views east to the peaks of Mount Oberlin and Mount Cannon, before an ascent takes you up to Haystack Pass (7,024 feet/2,140 m), the saddle between the Garden Wall and Haystack Butte.

After climbing to 7,280 feet (2,218 m), the trail begins its descent toward Granite Park, with views to Swiftcurrent Mountain (8,436 feet/2,571 m), and on to Fifty Mountain Backcountry campground. Or you could take the alternate Swiftcurrent Pass Trail to the Granite Park Chalet, now a National Historic Landmark built by the Great Northern Railway in 1915. This is a wonderful though simple lodge with no electricity and twelve guest rooms with a kitchen and a no-frills propane stove—a great spot to stop for afternoon tea, or to turn a one-day hike into a more gentle two-day ramble along two of the United States' finest trails. **BDS**

⬆ Breathtaking views of Montana's high ground.

Continental Divide Trail Montana to New Mexico, USA

Start Glacier National Park, Montana **End** U.S.–Mexico border, New Mexico **Distance** 3,100 miles (4,989 km)
Time 6 months **Grade** Moderate to strenuous **Type** Mountain trail **Info** goo.gl/q2HcGk

One of the Triple Crown of U.S. long-distance hikes (the others being the Appalachian Trail and the Pacific Crest Trail), the Continental Divide Trail is referred to as a "journey along the backbone of America." Tracing a line down the Continental Divide over the Rocky Mountains, it crosses five U.S. states: Wyoming, Idaho, Colorado, Montana, and New Mexico. In an average year, only a dozen or so people manage to thru-hike it, such is its forbidding length, and although the trail is open to horseback riding, nobody has so far managed to ride it within a calendar year.

The trail stretches from the Canadian border in the north to the Mexican border in the south and was established by an Act of Congress in 1978. It represents one of the largest U.S. conservation efforts ever undertaken—and the landscape it passes through makes it a living museum of the American West. From the glacial valleys of Montana to the deserts of New Mexico, it is the highest trail in the United States, ranging in heights from 4,000 feet (1,219 m) to 14,000 feet (4,267 m). The trail has opportunities for hunting, sightseeing, fishing, snowshoeing, cross-country skiing, horseback riding, and hiking. Follow in the footsteps of explorers Meriwether Lewis and William Clark, discover abandoned mining sites, become gloriously "lost" in Colorado's 780-square mile (2,020-sq km) Weminuche Wilderness, walk the Monarch Crest up into the Collegiate Peaks (home to many of Colorado's finest summits), or wander for hundreds of miles through Wyoming's open plains and steaming thermals. No other trail offers such a wealth of wilderness or better defines the phrase "getting away from it all." **BDS**

⬆ Traverse the peaks of North America's backbone.

Grand Teton Loop
Wyoming, USA

Start/End Jenny Lake   **Distance** 33 miles (53 km)
Time 4 days   **Grade** Moderate to strenuous
Type Long-distance mountain trail
Map goo.gl/sdLRKu

"Starting in Hurricane Pass, every view for several miles frames the three Tetons in all their glory."

national.geographic.com

⬆ A journey into the Tetons' backcountry will bring you face to face with towering walls of rock.

The Grand Teton Loop is a classic circuit of Wyoming's Teton Range. It immerses you in the shadows of its highest peaks, and a minimum of four days is required to let its grand vistas creep into your subconscious and also to allow time for all those must-do side trips. If you start at Jenny Lake, the trip begins with a gentle boat ride across the lake, followed by a short walk to your starting point, the mouth of Cascade Canyon. From there, you make your way through the multitude of day-trippers to Hidden Falls and Inspiration Point. After that, the human traffic begins to thin out, and the farther you go into the canyon, the more the backcountry beyond starts to open up. Pretty soon, you will be on your own.

The loop takes you 33 miles (53 km) through the heart of the Teton Range, over Hurricane Pass with its stunning views of the back of the main range, and down into the Alaska Basin, a subalpine, pond-encrusted expanse on the range's western slopes and occasional moose habitat. It is also the perfect place to pitch a tent for a night or even two, and savor the surrounding views.

From the Alaska Basin you continue to hike up Buck Mountain Pass to Static Peak Divide (11,000 feet/ 3,353 m), and from there down into Death Canyon (bring insect repellent!) with its campsites and bear bins. Campsites at Phelps and Bradley lakes can fill up fast, so make sure you get your permits in early. The Tetons is a compact range, only 40 miles (64.3 km) in length, but while it may be relatively easy to get your feet around it, getting your mind around these towering walls of rock that can blot out the horizon is something else entirely. **BDS**

Cloud Peak Trail
Wyoming, USA

Start/End Misty Moon Lake
Distance 23 miles (37 km)   Time 2–3 days
Grade Strenuous   Type Unmarked mountain trail
Map goo.gl/nBph1t

This is a route for those excited by bouldering and scrambling along an unmarked route to the summit of a serious mountain. Cloud Peak is the highest point in the Bighorn Mountains, reaching a snowcapped 13,167 feet (4,013 m). Tackling the southwest ridge is the easiest way to the summit. Most hike in from trailheads, camp near the foot of the mountain, and tackle the ascent/descent in a day. One popular route is via Misty Moon Lake, leading above the tree line through rocky valleys to Paint Rock Creek. This includes some easy, rock-hopping river crossings.

> *"[This] is the ultimate alpine adventure, taking you below the majestic peaks of the Southern Alps."*
>
> Routeburn Track brochure

Hazards you may face on the trail include biting insects, sudden mountain storms, and lingering patches of snow and ice, deep into summer. Whatever approach you take, you meet the Summit Trail at the foot of the mountain. This leads to 3 miles (4.8 km) of hopping from one huge gray boulder to the next, following an indistinct line of cairns. The route leads up a steep, jagged ridgeline with exposed drops on either side, but doesn't require ropes or specialist equipment. It offers inspiring views, but is aimed at experienced mountain walkers. The summit will reward you with a spectacular wilderness panorama of foothills, forests, and lakes in all directions. **SH**

Teton Crest Trail
Wyoming, USA

Start Phillips Pass trailhead, Hwy 22, Teton Pass
End String Lake trailhead   Distance 37 miles (59.5 km)
Time 3–5 days   Grade Moderate to strenuous
Type Mountain trail   Map goo.gl/iBF4j7

The Teton Crest Trail is the signature hike of Wyoming's Grand Teton National Park, linking the range's summits, divides and passes, its alpine lakes, and its spectacular overlooks. You can start at the Phillips Pass trailhead, but the options are many, and whether you stick to the official trail or take various linkages in a daisy-chain approach is really up to you. The majority of the path rarely falls below 8,000 feet (2,438) as it threads its way through the Grand Teton National Park and the adjacent Jedediah Smith Wilderness, all the way affording views of what is arguably the most photogenic mountain range in the continental United States.

The eastern side of the range is the most photographed, thanks to an absence of foothills that provides an uninterrupted view of its towering peaks. The western side of the range is hidden by a series of prominent foothills and is not so quick to reveal itself. But some things are better appreciated only when strived for, and the rugged beauty of the western range is there for all who walk the Teton Crest Trail.

Pioneered by the great American mountaineer Paul Petzoldt, who made his first ascent of the Grand Teton at the age of sixteen in 1924, the trail officially begins at Granite Creek trailhead, but if you want to cheat a little, you can take a tram to 10,450-foot-high (3,185 m) Rendezvous Peak and traverse down to Marion Lake. From there it's on to Death Canyon, Sheep Steps, and Indian Paintbrushes, and up to Hurricane Pass, where Grand Teton, Middle Teton, and South Teton will all be staring you in the face, the greatest "peak view" you can have in the United States. **BDS**

Red Beds Trail, Devil's Tower
Wyoming, USA

Start Devil's Tower visitor center   End Tuolumne Meadows   Distance 3 miles (4.8 km)   Time 2–3 hours   Grade Easy   Type Well-maintained and signed footpath   Map goo.gl/VOyPwd

Devil's Tower is a geological feature rising eerily out of the Wyoming prairie like a giant volcanic thimble. The cliffs of this ancient volcano are vertical but mysteriously grooved, and its flat rock summit is 5,114 feet (1,559 m) above sea level. The tower is such an extraordinary sight that it was chosen as the first U.S. National Monument in 1906—and featured in the film *Close Encounters of the Third Kind* (1977). Geologists believe the hard volcanic rock of the tower was left standing as the rest of the softer rock in the surrounding land eroded away. It is a sacred area for Native American tribes, who call the tower "Bear Lodge," and is almost as sacred for today's climbers, who line up to scale its vertical walls.

Various walks circle this bizarre monolith. There is a short 1.2-mile (2-km) paved trail close to the base of the tower, a popular tourist route that has negligible elevation and plenty of information boards along its route. It starts and finishes at the Devil's Tower Trading Post, a general store and café at the entrance to the grounds of the National Monument. You need to pay the entry fee before taking this path through the boulders at the base. It has sections of ponderosa forest, with chipmunks, squirrels, and deer. The views are better, however, from the more distant Red Beds Trail. A U.S. outdoor association once voted its route one of the top ten walks in the country. This path also starts at the tower's visitor center and, as well as offering views of the tower, it passes distinctive cliffs of red sandstone and white gypsum, wildflower grasslands, sparse "badlands," and even a prairie dog "town." **SH**

◁ Watch for bright lights on the Red Beds Trail.

Peaks Trail
Colorado, USA

Start/End Frisco or Breckenridge   Distance 8 miles (12.8 km)   Time 1–3 hours   Grade Moderate   Type Signed trail   Map goo.gl/6pmcG9

Whether you walk, jog, or cycle it, Peaks Trail is a well-signed path that is easy for anybody to navigate. The dirt, stone, and pine needle paths—made obvious due to the popularity and regular use of the trail—allow people to reach points of interest, including Rainbow Lake, one of Colorado's more serene places. With numerous trails such as the Gold Hill Trail leading off the main path, the hike can be anything from a short leisurely walk to a half- or full-day expedition.

The best times to hike are from early June through to late September, but bear in mind that this is a high

> *"A classic out-and-back trail that you can start from either Frisco or Breckenridge."*
>
> www.everytrail.com

altitude trail that is subject to sudden, potentially severe weather changes. With the highest elevation point at 10,200 feet (3,109 m), there is a possibility of altitude sickness, but the fresh air combined with abundant scents from the surrounding pine forest are utterly captivating. With openings showing views of a spectacular outback, it is easy to see why Colorado is nicknamed "Summit Country."

There is a choice of starting points, either at Breckenridge or at Frisco. If you select the more popular Breckenridge route, you will be descending for most of your journey. For the more adventurous who prefer an uphill route, there is the challenging Frisco start. **AS**

Switzerland Trail
Colorado, USA

Start/End Sugar Mountain Road
Distance 14 miles (22.5 km)   **Time** 1 day
Grade Easy   **Type** Dirt track, gravel trail
Map goo.gl/CtdLjy

The Switzerland Trail is based on the route of a narrow gauge mountain railway that was built in 1883 to service the remote mining area in the Front Range Hills, about 30 miles (48.2 km) west of Denver. When mining declined soon afterward, the rail company switched to attracting tourists to the dramatic scenery in this rugged part of Colorado and renamed the line "The Switzerland Trail." Adventurous Boulder and Denver residents would take the train into the mountains for summer walks and picnics.

By 1919, however, rail traffic began to decline as motorcars increased in popularity. The line was closed, but while the track was pulled up and sold, the flattened rail bed remained, and has now been converted to a trail for walkers and mountain bikers. Off-road vehicles are allowed on some sections, although most walkers report that it's rare to encounter a vehicle. The route is officially listed on the country's National Register of Historic Places.

With spectacular views around every corner, the Switzerland Trail makes an ideal day hike. Being designed as a railway route means that the gradients are gentle—between 2 and 5 percent, despite crossing terrain at between 7,000 and 9,000 feet (2,133–2,743 m) above sea level. The trail passes historic sites, such as the restored Blue Bird Mine and the ghost town of Caribou, once a busy silver mining settlement. Walkers find plenty of reasons to enjoy the former rail route: The path curves around the sides of mountains on rock embankments, winding through sparse pine and aspen woods, thick conifer forests, and Alpine-style meadows. Between the trees are inspiring glimpses of the snowcapped peaks to the north. **SH**

"Named for the spectacular mountain scenery along this remote and former railroad route."

www.traillink.com

⬆ The views are certainly reminiscent of Switzerland on this Front Range rails-to-trails amble.

Bull-of-the-Woods Trail, Wheeler Mountain
New Mexico, USA

Start/End RV parking area, Taos Ski Valley
Distance 15 miles (24.1 km)　**Time** 8 hours
Grade Strenuous　**Type** Mountain paths, rocky ground
Map goo.gl/2vYhQ9

Named in honor of U.S. Army Major George Montague Wheeler, who led a party of surveyors and naturalists throughout New Mexico and the U.S. southwest collecting data for ten years, Wheeler Peak (13,161 feet/4,011 m) in the Sangre de Cristo (Blood of Christ) Range is New Mexico's highest mountain. Likely to have been scaled first by Native Americans from the nearby Taos Pueblo, this mountain at the southernmost end of the Rockies is a spectacular year-round climbing and wilderness experience; and walking it in summer requires no special equipment.

There are two trails to the summit: the Bull-of-the-Woods Trail, which is the safest to take in winter because it has virtually no avalanche danger, and the Williams Lake Trail—built in 2011 in just fourteen days by an eight-member U.S. Forest Service team—which offers a quicker route to the summit, but is less scenic. Bull-of-the-Woods climbs steadily from its trailhead in the Taos Ski Valley, with the good path you started on becoming a dirt road as you gain altitude. Crossing the shoulder of Bull-of-the-Woods Mountain, you leave the forest and are met with stunning views of Grant Peak before passing over the eastern slope of Frazer Mountain and its resident population of bighorn sheep. At 12,000 feet (3,657 m), there is a small descent of 300 feet (91 m) into La Cal Basin, a verdant little spot and a great place to consider pitching your tent if overnighting. From there it's a moderate climb involving more switchbacks onto a rocky but easily navigable ridge. Then it's quickly down a saddle, and in a few minutes you approach the highest point in New Mexico, a feat that should have you smiling. Providing you've dodged the afternoon thunderstorm. **BDS**

"Whether backpacking or day hiking, Wheeler Peak offers a spectacular outdoor experience."

www.summitpost.org

⏏ Hike up New Mexico's highest mountain on one of two trails over saddles and switchbacks.

Harney Peak South Dakota, USA

Start/End Sylvan Lake   **Distance** 7 miles (11.2 km)   **Time** 4 hours   **Grade** Moderate
Type Mountain trail   **Map** goo.gl/9Y7aqO

Harney Peak rises out of the Black Elk Wilderness in the Black Hills of South Dakota, a craggy gray hulk jutting out of a sea of ponderosa pine. Sacred to the Lakota Sioux—Black Elk was a Lakota medicine man who had a vision on Harney Peak—the hills were a battleground in the U.S. Indian Wars. In 1874, Colonel Custer, charged with finding a suitable place for a fort, led a U.S. Army expedition into the Black Hills, then part of the Great Sioux Reservation. On discovering gold, Custer triggered a gold rush. The encroachment led to the Black Hills War of 1876. At their most famous encounter, the Battle of the Little Bighorn, Native American forces (including a twelve-year-old Black Elk) annihilated the U.S. Army, and Custer was killed. The Sioux won the battle, but not, of course, the war.

This is great walking country, crisscrossed with interconnecting trails. Mount Rushmore lies to the north; Custer State Park spreads south. From Sylvan Lake, a blue jewel in a granite crown, the path climbs steadily, rolling over mini peaks and troughs and constantly moving between dappled shade, sunlit glades, and spirit-soaring views. As the path nears the summit, the going gets more strenuous, but generally it is a very manageable climb.

Four states are visible from Harney Peak—Wyoming, Nebraska, Montana, and South Dakota itself. Steps hewn into the rock lead up to a former watchtower for forest fires, disused since the 1970s. At 7,244 feet (2,208 m), this is the highest point in the United States, east of the Rockies. You would have to travel to Mount Toubkal in Morocco's Atlas Mountains before getting any higher. **DS**

⊼ See into four states from Harney Peak's summit.

Mount Rushmore to Horsethief Lake South Dakota, USA

Start Mount Rushmore parking lot   **End** Horsethief Lake   **Distance** 9 miles (14.5 km)   **Time** 6 hours
Grade Easy to moderate   **Type** Dirt trail   **Info** goo.gl/5Kmyu4

In the 1920s, state historian Doane Robinson hit upon an ambitious but inspired idea to attract tourists to South Dakota—a giant sculpture of the most admired U.S. presidents carved into the rock face of the Black Hills. The idea received federal backing, and sculptor Gutzon Borglum set to work on Mount Rushmore, helped by a team of 400 miners who blew out the rock with dynamite while hanging off the cliff in cradles. The sculpture took fourteen years to complete, a feat made more difficult by spiraling costs. When Borglum died just months before completing the project, his son Lincoln, who was also a sculptor, stepped in to add the finishing touches.

Robinson's initiative succeeded. More than two million visitors a year converge on Mount Rushmore to see presidents Washington, Jefferson, Theodore Roosevelt, and Lincoln gazing to the horizon in all their granite splendor. Most of these visitors do not venture beyond the 1-mile (1.6-km) Presidential Trail, even though Mount Rushmore connects with a network of Black Hills trails and serves as a neat cultural appetizer to a half-day hike to Horsethief Lake.

The trail to Horsethief Lake passes through the very essence of the Black Hills—there are granite needles, boulder-strewn slopes, and magnificent stands of pine, culminating in a lake that sits like an opal in a green velvet box. The going is reasonably straightforward, save for a stiff ascent at the start, and leaves time for an hour or two of lakeside lounging on the wooden piers. You can watch the dragonflies, listen to the plop of trout, or join the kids jumping off the lava rocks and into the crystal-clear water. **DS**

⬆ Immerse yourself in the granite of the Black Hills.

Guadalupe Peak Texas, USA

Start/End RV parking area, Pine Springs campground   **Distance** 8.4 miles (13.5 km)   **Time** 6–10 hours
Grade Moderate to strenuous   **Type** Mountain   **Map** goo.gl/kRxtw3

At 8,749 feet (2,667 m), Guadalupe Peak in Guadalupe National Park is the highest point in Texas, and together with its neighbor, El Capitan, forms the kind of platform from which Native American warriors would ride and do battle in movies of the Wild West. The sight of this limestone wall from the highway is startling. What geological wizardry fashioned it? In fact, the range is part of an ancient coral reef formed in a tropical inland ocean 250 million years ago and was later lifted by tectonic activity.

All hikers must register at Pine Springs' visitor center before setting off, which is 0.5 miles (0.8 km) from the trailhead. At the start, 4 miles (6.5 km) of switchbacks wrap around the mountainside, falling away to sheer drops in places. As the path climbs and temperatures grow cooler, the prickly pear and agaves of the desert floor grow sparser and pockets of pinion pine and Douglas fir appear. Marine fossils litter the park, their skeletal frames immured within the rocks.

A bridge across a crevice marks the final ascent. At the summit, huge views stretch in every direction. To the south, below El Capitan, salt lakes glint on a desert plain that extends to the Earth's curvature; to the north, the Guadalupe National Park unfurls, a lush landscape of green peaks and wooded canyons. Hikers can record their impressions in a visitors' book kept in a metal box next to a monument commemorating the Butterfield Overland Mail service, the mail coaches that first linked eastern and western United States. The ruins of a Butterfield stagecoach station can be inspected back at the visitor center. It was the highest station on the 2,800-mile (4,500-km) route. **DS**

⊤ The towering summit of Guadalupe Peak.

Boquillas Canyon Trail Texas, USA

Start/End Boquillas Canyon Spur Road   Distance 1.4 miles (2.25 km)   Time 2 hours   Grade Moderate
Type Sand, rock, and footpath   Map goo.gl/8opAuv

The Rio Grande River curves through Big Bend National Park after having spent a millennia carving its distinctive rocky gorges and canyons. At the eastern edge of the park is this short trail along the U.S. side of the river, and it is a great introduction to the terrain of this dry, hot border region.

The path climbs steeply from the parking lot, up through the rocks and vegetation to a cliff overlooking the river, where you can see over the border and into Mexico. The path descends to the riverbank via a big sloping sand dune that is as easy to slide down as it is to walk. It then leads into the mouth of the canyon along grassy banks, over pebbles and sandy river beaches, with sheer rock faces towering above you on either side. The route continues until the walls of the canyon meet the river, which can be at different points at different times of the year. The Rio Grande can be very shallow here in the summer and becomes wider and faster with the rains of winter. Walkers can explore farther into the canyon along the slow shallow summer river using a combination of wading and walking exposed sandy beaches. Whatever the river is like, however, there comes a point when it is time to stop and retrace your steps to the parking lot.

The Mexican shore is part of the Maderas del Carmen protected area. Inhabitants of the village of Bouquillas often defy border restrictions to row boats or ride horses across the river to sell souvenirs, such as walking sticks and carvings, to visitors. Beware that at the height of summer it can get extremely hot for walkers in the canyon. Wear sunscreen and head coverings, and bring plenty of drinking water. **SH**

⬆ Hike a less-traversed trail of the Rio Grande.

South Rim Loop
Texas, USA

Start/End Chisos Mountain Lodge parking lot
Distance 12.6 miles (20.2 km)   **Time** 1–2 days
Grade Moderate to strenuous   **Type** Way-marked trail
Map goo.gl/Fm4pkE

This route through the Big Bend National Park in Texas bridges the gap between a simple day hike and an overnight backpacking trail, and while there is a stretch of long, hard ascents, it is possible for most walkers to complete it in a day. It will be a very tiring session, however. There are campsites available on the route if you prefer to break the hike with an overnight stop, but then you will have to carry a lot more equipment on the two-day walk. The trail comprises a loop that rises onto a towering escarpment—known as the South Rim—and back, offering what are claimed to be the best views in the park, which explains why many call it "the best hike in Texas."

The South Rim Loop is a high rock cliff that overlooks the southern part of the Big Bend National Park. As the path rises from the Chisos Basin, it zigzags to reduce the gradient. It's still hard going, though, particularly in summer. The reward, however, is a sequence of viewing points at the edge of the South Rim, featuring views down canyons cutting through the mountains, across stretches of desert, mountain creeks, and hazy hills more than 20 miles (32 km) in the distance. The wildlife can be shy and elusive, but walkers have spotted black bears, mountain lions, deer, jackrabbits, and foxes near the trail.

The path leads past a series of weathered rock pinnacles, along a creek bed, and through sparse woodland. A short offshoot continues up to the summit of Emory Peak, the highest point in Big Bend National Park. The 2-mile (3.2-km) round trip is worth contemplating for the additional views, but only if you have the stamina for the additional 1,000 feet (305 m) of ascent. **SH**

"Big Bend is a hiker's paradise, containing the largest expanse of roadless public lands in Texas."

www.nps.gov

⬆ Canyon and river views abound in this adventurous Big Bend National Park cliff walk.

Ozark Trail
Missouri, USA

Start St. Louis   End Arkansas border and beyond
Distance 400–700 miles (643–1,126.5 km)
Time 3–4 weeks   Grade Easy to moderate
Type Long-distance trail   Info goo.gl/PPtjo8

Essentially, the Ozarks aren't mountains. According to geologists, the region that covers most of the southern half of Missouri is actually an elevated and heavily dissected plateau, a broad dome full of anticlines, a remnant of a long-past era of volcanism. The problem is that most geologic domes are so large that they can only be recognized as such from above, in satellite imaging for example. Geologists might prefer more scientific terms, but for the vast majority of us, the Ozarks remain simply this: 47,000 square miles (121,729 sq km) of "mountains" and forests, the largest mountainous region in the United States between the Appalachians in the east and the Rocky Mountains in the west. And it is one grand wilderness through which to put a trail.

The Ozark Trail began in 1977 at a meeting of local landowners and trail users who met to discuss the pros and cons of building a trail that would begin in suburban St. Louis and go all the way to Arkansas, traversing the Missouri Ozarks on the way. It was good timing. Missouri at that time had a "trail deficit," and it was agreed that another 500 miles (805 km) or so of new trails wouldn't go amiss.

The trail is divided into 20 to 30-mile (32–48-km) segments, each one named for a local natural or historical feature. In 2013 the Ozark Trail Association celebrated its tenth year of operation, and there was much to celebrate: 50 miles (80.5 km) of new trails in 2012, and 280 more miles (450.6 km) adopted—the product of more than 91,000 hours of volunteers' time. If a trail can be measured by the amount of work its supporters put into its maintenance, the Ozark Trail is one of the healthiest you will ever walk. **BDS**

Clingmans Dome
Tennessee, USA

Start Parking lot, Clingmans Dome Road   End Observation tower, Clingmans Dome   Distance 0.5 mile (0.8 km)   Time 15–20 minutes   Grade Easy
Type Paved   Info goo.gl/TGk8BU

As the highest point in the Great Smoky Mountains National Park, Clingmans Dome is hard to resist. It's a chance to step away from the scenic details of the park and survey the magnificent whole—a succession of forested peaks tumbling 100 miles (161 km) toward the horizon. Fall color, winter snow, and new spring growth bring their particular drama to the 360-degree vista, as does the changing nature of the mountain's "smoke"—the steamy breath of the lush vegetation—that can either be a fine veil or a churning maelstrom, depending on the weather. Dawn and sunset add rich

> *"As the most accessible peak in the Smoky Mountains, it is a popular destination for the panoramic view."*
> www.clingmansdomerevealed.com

hues, from pale pink to deep purple. One of the names given to the mountain by the Cherokee is said to be "shaconage"—blue.

From the parking lot, a broad 0.5-mile (0.8-km) paved path, suitable for strollers and wheelchairs with a strong person to push, spirals to the top of the observation tower, taking the many visitors above the canopy of Fraser fir trees—a relic from the last ice age—and adding another 54 feet (16.4 m) to Clingmans 6,642-foot (2,024-m) height. In 1858, surveyor Thomas Lanier Clingman, a state senator and Confederate general before he explored and measured mountains, pulled out his barometer and accurately calculated the mountain's height. **DS**

Alum Cave Bluff Trail
Tennessee, USA

Start/End Parking lot, U.S. Hwy 441
Distance 4.4 miles (7 km)   **Time** 3–4 hours
Grade Moderate   **Type** Forest, mountain trail
Map goo.gl/Jaq6Ur

"Hike through a rock arch on this scenic trail through old-growth forest and enjoy spectacular views."

www.nps.gov

⬆ Hike to an alum mine for a glimpse into the past before climbing to some great Smokies overlooks.

Deciduous woodland, boulder-strewn streams, and steps cut into rocks leading to romantic overlooks make the Alum Cave Bluff Trail one of the most scenic hikes in the Smokies, especially in spring and fall. It also offers the possibility of seeing bears. There are around 1,600 bears in the Smokies, and they sometimes wander onto this trail. Whether you think bears are pesky panhandlers or the main reason for coming to the Smoky Mountains, stringent park rules (backed up by large fines) apply. The most important thing is to keep your distance and move on—bears can run 30 miles per hour (48 kph) when inclined.

The trail follows Alum Cave Creek for the first 1.3 miles (2 km), then climbs a stone-hewn staircase to duck under Arch Rock, a giant slab of rock overhanging the trail. Shortly afterward, Inspiration Point is a good spot to draw breath before pushing up to the overhang known as Alum Cave, once mined for alum by the Epsom Salts Manufacturing Company and a reminder of life in the Smokies before it became a national park in the 1930s. Forced to move outside the newly created park, hundreds of mountain families left their culture behind. Before they went, a sound recordist named Joseph S. Hall traveled around the Smokies recording the music of the hills—folk, gospel, country, and blues. To extend the hike, follow signs for Mount Le Conte. The trail climbs steeply, passing a succession of overlooks. The names are evocative: Little Duck Hawk Ridge, Eye of the Needle, Gracie's Pulpit. At Le Conte Lodge, a rustic inn with cabins (reserve a year in advance), short trails continue to Clifftop (0.2 miles/0.3 km) and Myrtle Point (0.75 miles/ 1.2 km) on Mount Le Conte, for panoramic views. **DS**

Chimney Tops Trail
Tennessee, USA

Start/End Chimney Tops Trail parking lot,
Newfound Gap Road   Distance 4 miles (6.4 km)
Time 3–4 hours   Grade Moderate to strenuous
Type Mountain trail   Map goo.gl/cVSD8q

In the Cherokee language, "chimney tops" means "forked antler" (*Duniskwalgunyi*). Both names paint the picture—twin pinnacles of exposed rock rising out of the tree-covered hills. Technically a double-cap rock knob, the Chimneys is one of the most popular trails in the Great Smoky Mountains National Park. The last leg is a scramble on hands and knees, and any other protuberance that gives you purchase. It isn't too difficult—you often see families tackling the trail—but you will need a head for heights.

The reward is a botanical extravaganza for much of the trail's length, and from the top, at 4,724 feet (1,440 m), outstanding views over the Sugarland Massif, the dark-green foliage around Little Pigeon River, and two of the highest peaks in the Smokies: Mount Le Conte (6,593 feet/2,010 m) and Mount Kephart (6,217 feet/1,895 m).

From the trailhead the path follows Road Prong Trail, a riverside corridor that traces an old Cherokee trail. From February through April, iris, violet, columbine, bleeding heart, and orchids cover the forest floor; in May and June the showy rhododendrons, flame azalea, and pink-and-white mountain laurel take over, heralding summer sunflowers, gentian, asters, black-eyed Susans, Sweet Joe Pye, and more. Come fall it's all about the trees as maple, oak, beech, and buckeye form a burnished canopy. The river also demands attention, as it crashes through boulders and tumbles into quiet pools.

At 0.9 miles (1.5 km), the trail for Chimney Tops peels off to the right to reach flower-filled Beech Flats. From there, it's a stiff mile (1.6 km) of switchbacks to reach the top of the ridge and the final tricky ascent. **DS**

Whispering Spruce Trail
West Virginia, USA

Start/End Spruce Knob parking lot
Distance 0.5 mile (0.8 km)   Time 30 minutes
Grade Easy   Type Gravel path
Info goo.gl/CUxgU8

A stone-and-steel observation tower crowns the summit of Spruce Knob, the highest point in West Virginia. Its 360-degree views are a must for summit baggers, and visitors have an array of options for reaching the top of this peak. As there are easy forest roads leading to the summit, the vast majority of visitors simply drive there, but for the more adventurous there is the 0.5-mile (0.8-km) Whispering Spruce Trail. In addition, Spruce Knob can also be reached via the 6-mile (9.6-km) Huckleberry Trail, which extends north along the ridgeline. This is a demanding route, involving

> *"Easily in the top five backpacking routes in the mid-Atlantic . . . and the best camping to be found."*
>
> www.hikingupward.com

some rock scrambling along exposed mountain ridges. It links to other trails, and the Spruce Knob–Seneca Rocks National Recreation Area surrounding the mountain offers a network of 75 miles (121 km) of hiking routes and campsites.

The higher reaches of Spruce Knob have an alpine feel. Among huge gray boulders and grassy meadows, the pine trees are misshapen by the wind. On clear days there are wide views from the summit, but in winter, snow may make the upper reaches inaccessible. The Whispering Spruce Trail encircles the observation tower. The views are great, but it's primarily a nature trail around the summit plateau. It's an easy, wide, well-graveled path with a gentle gradient. **SH**

West Rim Trail Pennsylvania, USA

Start Rattlesnake Rocks parking lot   **End** Colton Road   **Distance** 30.5 miles (49 km)   **Time** 3 days
Grade Moderate   **Type** Forest trail   **Map** goo.gl/gA7nxd

Outside magazine once called this trail "the best hike in Pennsylvania," and few who have ever walked it would argue the point The West Rim Trail runs along the 1,000-foot-high (305 m) walls of Pine Creek Gorge, a product of the last ice age and a gash in the earth, which native Pennsylvanians like to refer to as the "Grand Canyon of the East," carved out by Pine Creek ever since the Laurentide Glacier dammed its northeasterly flow 20,000 years ago and sent it on the course that it maintains to this day.

The trail is characterized by a steep ascent regardless of which of its two trailheads you begin at, though once either initial climb is out of the way, the "in-between" segments are far more forgiving. If you begin at Rattlesnake Rocks, you pass immediately into a thick canopy of hemlock, oak, and maple before beginning a pretty arduous 950-foot (289-m) climb in

just 2 miles (3.2 km) to the flat open spaces of the Allegheny Plateau. A mile farther along the trail, keep an eye out for Gillespie Point—at 1,800 feet (549 m), the so-called "Matterhorn of the Alleghenies"—and continue past various basic campsites until you reach an overview of the river making a dramatic S-turn below and then pitch your tent in anticipation of the vistas still to come. The next day will bring bird's-eye views of the river, and peregrine falcons above. The final day is spent walking through more forests of white birch, maple, and red oak and along the very edges of the escarpment over rocky outcrops with views of the valley and surrounding farms before descending 675 feet (205 m) to the northern trailhead on the Colton Road near Ansonia. **BDS**

⬆ Hike the West Rim above Pennsylvania's "Grand Canyon."

Plateau Mountain via Warner Creek Loop Trail New York, USA

Start/End Notch Inn Road trailhead   **Distance** 8 miles (12.8 km)   **Time** 8 hours   **Grade** Strenuous
Type Rocky paths, mountain trails   **Map** goo.gl/mvvUWo

Located in the southeast region of New York state, the Catskill Mountains are more akin to a dissected plateau than a mountain range, an area created by swift flowing rivers, water deposits, and glacial action that shaped the landscape we see today. Only 100 miles (160 km) northwest of New York City, the many resorts that are nestled among the thirty 3,500-foot (1,066-m) summits of the Catskills have long made it a favorite getaway for New Yorkers, and one of the countless trails that plunges you deep into its wooded, stream-filled forests is the Warner Creek Loop Trail, recently blazed through by the volunteers of the Catskill Mountain Club.

This well-designed route with mostly moderate uphill climbs includes a couple of early switchbacks with views of Edgewood Mountain and a series of overlooks as you approach the crest of Daley Ridge, a 1,300-foot (396-m) ascent from the trailhead. From Daley Ridge you climb up through spruce and fir trees and past more overlooks to the highest point on the trail with views back over Daley Ridge and down to Stony Clove Notch.

The trail narrows on its final approach to the summit ridge of Plateau Mountain (3,840 feet/1,170 m) and passes through the "Dark Woods," a heavily wooded spruce–fir wonderland. Here the Warner Creek Trail ends as it merges with the red-blazed Devil's Path, which takes you along Plateau Mountain's flat summit ridge, the Catskills' longest near-level ridge traversed by a marked trail. But beware, the descent is a serious one: 1,600 feet (487 m) in only 1.5 miles (2.4 km) on a 20 percent gradient over a rocky and uneven surface, back to trailhead. **BDS**

⬆ This trail is an oasis of calm in the Catskills.

Killington Peak, Bucklin Trail Vermont, USA

Start/End Bucklin trailhead, Wheelerville Road   Distance 7.2 miles (11.5 km)   Time 5 hours
Grade Moderate   Type Mountain trail   Map goo.gl/OjX3ee

Killington Peak, Vermont's second highest point at 4,235 feet (1,290 m), lies in the Coolidge Range of the Green Mountains, which in turn are part of the Appalachians, the north–south arc of mountains that makes up the Rockies' shorter East Coast twin. The Bucklin Trail ascends the western side of the peak. It combines three satisfying ingredients of a good hike: a picturesque warm-up along a wooded river valley, a strenuous heart-pumping climb, and the reward of staggeringly far-reaching views.

Killington is snowy between November and May, even when it hasn't been snowing (as the state's principal ski area, Killington has snow-making facilities that are second to none), so come in summer or, better still, fall, when the Green Mountains that gave Vermont its name are every shade of red, gold, orange, and brown.

From the trailhead, the first 1.4 miles (2.25 km) of the trail tracks back and forth across Brewers Brook, shaded by birch and beech trees, which produce a plump cushion of fallen leaves in fall. After 3.3 miles (5.3 km), the increasingly steep path intersects with the Appalachian Trail and Long Trail at Cooper Lodge, a basic bunkhouse for hikers. From here, the last leg is considerably tougher, with a 1,000-foot (305-m) hand-over-hand scramble up Killington Spur to emerge on the rocky summit. Five states are visible from here: Vermont, New Hampshire, New York, Maine, and Massachusetts. A gondola brings non-hikers to the top of Killington (along with mountain bikers), and after a wander around, you can join them at the ski lodge, just below the ridge. **DS**

⬆ Look into five states over a canopy of green.

Camel's Hump Vermont, USA

Start/End Trailhead parking lot, Duxbury Road **Distance** 12.5 miles (20 km) **Time** 10 hours
Grade Strenuous **Type** Mountain trail **Map** goo.gl/H4QNvM

Camel's Hump State Park in the Green Mountains of Vermont is one of the best places in the country to see fall foliage. The sugar maples turn first, vermilion torchbearers in a month-long parade. By October, a subtler but no less stunning palette spreads across the park, as the hues of beech, oak, aspen, and birch turn richer and darker.

The park is a 20,000-acre (8,093-ha) remnant of a larger tract of woodland bequeathed to the state by nineteenth-century publisher and philanthropist Joseph Battell, who had bought the woodland in order to preserve the view from his windows. At the park's center is Camel's Hump itself, a double-crowned 4,083-foot (1,244-m) peak, which is featured on the back of the state quarter. Its web of trails range from 1-mile (1.6-km) saunters to demanding ascents of the summit. Myriad permutations take in overlooks, beaver ponds,

and even the remains of a B-24 Liberator bomber that crashed on the mountain in 1944. Recommended for serious hikers is the section of the Long Trail from Massachusetts to Canada that crosses the top of Camel's Hump on a north–south axis. Taking the Long Trail from Winooski River to the peak, you can either continue down the other side to the parking lot on Route 17 (another 12.5 miles/20.1 km), or return to the start via the Alpine Trail, transporting hikers from a sylvan understory of mossy boulders, fern-filled hollows, and bubbling brooks to alpine tundra above the timberline. When it comes to views, Camel's Peak doesn't disappoint. On a fine day they stretch to Mount Marcy in New York and Mount Washington in New Hampshire. **DS**

⬆ Camel's Hump is a hub for foliage lovers.

Hut to Hut Presidential Traverse

New Hampshire, USA

Start Valley Way trailhead   End Elephant
Head marker, Crawford Notch   Distance 22 miles
(35 km)   Time 2–3 days   Grade Strenuous
Type Mountainous, rocky terrain   Map goo.gl/YrQAhr

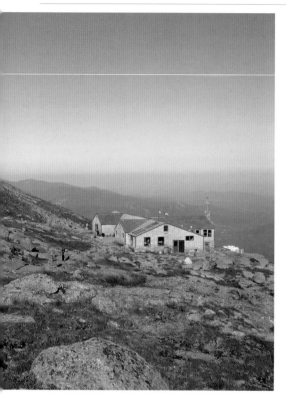

"This is a popular trip, and in good weather it is spectacular, with about one and half days above tree line."

home.earthlink.net

How much one enjoys a walk, wherever it may be, will always depend to some extent upon the weather, and nowhere can that truism be more keenly felt than on the Hut to Hut Presidential Traverse through the White Mountains of New Hampshire. Typical of the eleven summits you pass on this walk is Mount Washington (6,288 feet/1916 m), whose buttressed ridges rise up below the confluence of two jet streams capable of plunging temperatures to 60 degrees below zero and that once saw wind speeds of more than 230 miles per hour (370 kph). Here you are very exposed to the elements, so don't forget warm clothing.

The traverse takes you over or just below the summits of eleven very presidential New Hampshire mountains: Mount Webster, Mount Jefferson, Mount Jackson (named after a state geologist, not a president), Mount Clay, Mount Adams, Mount Eisenhower, Mount Clinton, Mount Franklin, Mount Madison, Mount Monroe, and, of course, Mount Washington. All the peaks are above the timberline, and the views along the trail are superb. May to August is best, though May can be pretty muddy after spring rains.

Most begin at the northern end of the range and head south, past huts owned and maintained by the Appalachian Mountain Club, such as the Lakes of the Clouds Hut on Mount Washington, the trail's highest hut at 5,012 feet (1,527 m), which offers six spots in the "dungeon," or the country's very first mountain hut at Madison Springs, which opened in 1888. However, a more prescient concern than where to lay one's head is the altitude gain: almost 9,000 feet (2,743 m) in two days, past the huts that are usually full of weary, though very contented, strangers. **BDS**

⬆ A potentially chilly but immensely rewarding trek amid jet streams and Presidential peaks.

Ammonoosuc Ravine Trail

New Hampshire, USA

Start/End Base Road parking lot
Distance 6.2 miles (10 km) **Time** 6 hours
Grade Easy to moderate **Type** Hike with some scrambles **Map** goo.gl/S7GQrL

The Ammonoosuc is one of only two New Hampshire rivers to be designated "wild and scenic," meaning that it must be "preserved in free-flowing condition ... for the benefit and enjoyment of present and future generations." Appropriately, the trail to which it gives its name is a rocky oasis replete with stunning waterfalls and overlooks.

Straightforward to begin with, the trail from the Base Road parking lot grows steeper after forty-five-minutes. Past pretty Gem Pool it ascends the highest cliffs along the Ammonoosuc Ravine, so prepare for rough, rocky, sometimes slippery terrain and stream crossings. But persevere, and you'll soon rise above the tree line and arrive at the Lakes of the Clouds Hut, which is open throughout the summer, though you'll need to check precise dates and book well in advance. This popular lodge takes its name from the set of small lakes that form the source of the Ammonoosuc River, which was named by the Native American Abenaki tribe; Ammonoosuc means "small, narrow fishing place." Once full of trout and salmon, the water can still yield catches for adventurous anglers.

The ravine trail officially concludes at the hut, and even allowing for a late-morning departure and time to cool your heels in the lakes (swimming is not permitted), you can still get there and back by sunset. But should you have a penchant for peak bagging, other opportunities present themselves. Ascend 300 feet (91 m) from the hut, and you'll be able to cross Mount Monroe off your list. Or follow the Crawford Path northward for 1.5 miles (2.4 km), passing junctions with other trails, and you'll summit breezy Mount Washington. **BM**

"[The overlook is] a nice place to break out the ol' stove and cook up some food and relax."

www.summitpost.org

⬆ The waterfalls encountered on the Ammonoosuc Ravine Trail are a tonic to the ascents on the path.

Crawford Path New Hampshire, USA

Start/End Mt. Clinton Road parking lot   End Mt. Washington summit   Distance 8.5 miles (13.6 km)
Time 1–2 days   Grade Moderate   Type Rocky but well maintained   Map goo.gl/EYvLcw

The Crawford Path is the oldest continuously maintained footpath in the United States. It originated in 1819 with settler Abel Crawford and his son Ethan, who blazed a trail to Mount Pierce, a path that subsequently extended across the southern peaks in the Presidential Range—the highest of New Hampshire's White Mountains—to the summit of Mount Washington and was later transformed into a bridle path by Abel's grandson, Thomas. In the past two centuries its route has been changed just once, redirecting travelers to the Lakes of the Clouds Hut, and in the late 1800s, guidebook author M. F. Sweetser observed that it "can be followed without a guide by anyone of ordinary intelligence."

The mountains remain the path's main attractions, with Mount Pierce being the more manageable of the two. Turning right at the Crawford Path's junction with the Webster Cliff Trail takes you to a gradual incline, with good footing, and within minutes you'll have bagged one of the 4,000 footers (1,219 m) for which this range is famous. Mount Washington—more than 2,000 feet (610 m) higher—is more imposing, and the trail is rockier, but the climb is particularly enjoyable if approached from the Crawford, leading on from the Ammonoosuc trail.

"Despite nearly 200 years of wear by boots and horses' hooves," writes the Museum of the White Mountains' Adam Jared Apt, "it is still only a narrow scuffed line on the mountains' surface, and when few other hikers are within view, it continues to leave the impression of wildness and remoteness that it did when Abel Crawford and his son blazed it." **BM**

⊺ This rewarding hike reveals a wild landscape.

Humu'ula Trail to Mauna Kea Summit Hawaii, USA

Start/End Mauna Kea visitor center **Distance** 7 miles (11.2 km) **Time** 8 hours **Grade** Strenuous
Type Cinder cones, gravel, rock **Map** goo.gl/po6K91

If you were to measure the dormant volcano Mauna Kea on the Big Island of Hawaii from its oceanic base 19,000 feet (5,791 m) below sea level to its above sea level summit of 13,796 feet (4,205 m), it would be the world's tallest mountain. It is 100 million years old, and there is a permanent layer of permafrost 35 feet (10.6 m) deep at its summit, and the dry environment there, combined with a stable airflow, makes it an ideal location for two high-altitude pursuits: astronomical observation and summit walking.

Hikers come here lured by the possibility of walking through alpine tundra, U-shaped valleys, and cirques, and over extinct rock glaciers, striated bedrock, and glacial tills. Be prepared for a very long and exhausting day—the average return time is eight hours, so be sure you leave early enough to be back by 6 p.m., because this is one mountain you don't

want to be coming back down in the dark. Also be sure to pack sunscreen, a broad-brimmed hat, plenty of water, lip balm, long pants, a long-sleeved shirt, and maybe even a dust mask to reduce "lung-burn" from breathing in all that cold, dry air.

The Humu'ula Trail is 7 miles (11.2 km) of "straight up," with an elevation gain of 4,600 feet (1,402 m) from the visitor center. That's a five-hour ascent at a pace of about a mile-and-a-half per hour, a reasonable speed unless you run marathons. The first mile has an exhausting grade of 40 percent over loose cinders, but it soon eases to 13 percent, with more secure footing. After passing Lake Waiau, you will see your goal—the largest assemblage of astronomical observatories in the world on the summit of Mauna Kea. **BDS**

⬆ From start to finish its up, up, and up.

Copper Canyon

Chihuahua, Mexico

Start/End Recohuata Hot Springs, Pamachi
Distance 43 miles (69 km)   **Time** 5–7 days
Grade Strenuous   **Type** Rocky, exposed trails
Map goo.gl/P5fRpV

"[Expect] plunging vistas, soaring stone spires, and a menagerie of parrots and jaguars."

www.backpacker.com

⬆ Copper Canyon is deeper than the Grand Canyon and has mostly unmarked trails.

If venturing into the Grand Canyon seems too predictable, why not try northwest Mexico's network of six canyons, collectively known as Copper Canyon (Barranca del Cobre), after the seam of green minerals found there. The option given here is to hike from Pamachi to Tararecua Canyon and back. Day trips and sunrise to sunset excursions are also available from the town of Creel. A guide is imperative, whether you're walking for a day or camping for a week. With many trails unmarked, canyon guides come across lost hikers almost every day.

These, however, need to be seen as minor concerns, all surmountable with a good dose of common sense and the acquiring of a little local knowledge. The reward is interaction with genuine natural wonders: rocks that rise to the heavens, valleys that plunge more than 5,500 feet (1,676 m), wildlife that ranges from wild cats to marijuana plants, hot springs and waterfalls, and more than 20,000 square miles (51,800 sq km) of terrain. So deep is the canyon that in winter it can be freezing on its rims and upper reaches, yet a subtropical 104°F (40°C) on the floor. Encampments of the Tarahumara people who are indigenous to Chihuahua provide opportunities to experience local culture and replenish supplies on native ranch lands that give the sort of Wild West feel of which the Copper Canyon's larger Arizona counterpart can only dream.

Should the terrain appeal but the tribulations daunt, the Chihuahua al Pacífico railroad, also known as "Chepe," cuts through Copper Canyon. Those made of sterner stuff, however, should drink in this marvel at a walking pace rather than within the confines of a moving, cloistered carriage. **BM**

Pico Turquino Summit
Cuba

Start Alto del Naranjo   **End** Pico Turquino summit
Distance 6.3 miles (10.1 km)   **Time** 2 days
Grade Strenuous   **Type** Mountain paths, wooden stairs
Map goo.gl/wxrtwN

Turquino is believed to be a corruption of the Spanish word *turqui*, meaning "turquoise," for the mountain does appear deep blue in certain lights. The peak is Cuba's highest, at 6,476 feet (1,974 m), and is part of the Sierra Maestra range in the southeast of the country. Its summit is easily accessible, with two routes to choose from. One begins on the southern coast at Las Cuevas, where it is easier to arrange transport but has the disadvantage of a sharp ascent and descent on the same day, which can be knee-shattering. The easier and more preferable route starts inside the national park at Alto del Naranjo.

From here, one trail leads off to La Comandancia, the headquarters of the revolutionary army of Fidel Castro during his fight against the Batista regime in the late 1950s, but a visit there will eat into the time you have to attack the main mountain. The other well-marked trail leads you up after five hours to Aguada de Joaquin, your lodge for the night. The tropical mountain vegetation and abundant wildlife along the way make the effort worthwhile. The next morning, you face a steep one-hour climb up to the Joaquin peak, a slog that is the most arduous part of the trek. From there it is another three-hour up-and-down trek to Pico Turquino, the highlight of which is the Pass of the Monkeys, a chasm crossed by climbing wooden ladders. Once on top of the mountain, you are greeted with a bust of José Marti, the hero of the Cuban independence movement in the late nineteenth century. Irritatingly, trees restrict the views from the top, but there is a viewpoint a little way down the mountain to the south that affords fantastic views over the Caribbean. **SA**

Old Vinegar Hill
Trail Jamaica

Start Maya Lodge and Hiking Centre, Jacks Hill, Kingston   **End** Crystal Springs
Distance 25 miles (40 km)   **Time** 2–3 days
Grade Easy   **Type** Trail   **Map** goo.gl/PrX8Ec

Centuries ago on the Caribbean island of Jamaica, the most efficient way to get from above the town of Port Antonio on the island's northern coastline to the island's capital, Kingston, in the south was to walk or ride by donkey, mule, or horse along the Old Vinegar Hill Trail. It is a path hundreds of years old, eked out and worn into the landscape through necessity, and it has continued to be a necessity for small communities of highland Jamaicans ever since.

The trail begins at the Maya Lodge and Hiking Centre and winds up through the hills along what locals

> *"Perhaps only a handful of people (local farmers) use this route each month."*

www.guidetocaribbeanvacations.com

call the Fairy Glades Trail, then through Silver Hill and Morris gaps before traveling along the Grand Ridge of the Blue Mountains, where you'll ascend to 5,700 feet (1,737 m). You'll pass through cloud forests—pristine montane environments of vegetation populated by trees dripping with epiphytes—and over jagged limestone rocks awash with lichens, mosses, and orchids before descending to trail's end at the 156-acre (63-ha) Crystal Springs, a wellness retreat first built by English settlers as a sugarcane plantation in 1655.

The trail is a "working" path as much as a walking one, so you're likely to come across more locals than you will people with headlamps and walking poles—which has to be a good thing. **BDS**

Gros Piton Nature Trail St. Lucia

Start/End Interpretation Center, Fond Gens Libre   Distance 4 miles (6.4 km)
Time 4–5 hours   Grade Moderate   Type Mountain trails   Map goo.gl/NhNvmC

When you approach the volcanic island of St. Lucia in the eastern Caribbean, not far from the currents of the Atlantic Ocean, you could be forgiven for allowing your eyes to stray to the island's highest point, Mount Gimie, at 3,117 feet (950 m) above sea level. Forgiven, because although Mount Gimie may be the island's high point, it is the spectacle of the Pitons—located between the towns of Soufrière and Choiseul on the island's western side—that are St. Lucia's most recognized and prized landmarks.

Gros Piton (2,529 feet/771 m) and its little brother, Petit Piton (2,437 feet/743 m) are volcanic plugs, linked by the Piton Mitan ridge, and they are the most spectacular formations in a complex piece of geology that includes sulfurous fumeroles and hot springs. Some 150 plant species are found on Gros Piton, and almost 100 species on its smaller neighbor.

Getting to the summit of Gros Piton is a relatively straightforward exercise that does not present any dangers, nor require any special skills. The trail snakes its way around the mountain on a gradual ascent that leads to views of Anse L'Ivrogne and takes you past caves, rock shelters, and overlooks that were once used as hideouts by freedom fighters during the slave rebellion of 1748. As you ascend, deciduous woodlands give way to middle-zone rain forests and upper mountain dwarf forests. Once on the summit there are two viewpoints, one looking south and the other north toward Petit Piton. Birds you may see on the way include the St. Lucien wren and the red neck pigeon. Two hours later you're again at sea level—a half-day mountain ascent to savor. **BDS**

⬆ Ascend a mountain summit in just half a day.

Volcán Maderas/Concepción Ometepe Island, Rivas, Nicaragua

Start/End La Flor (Concepción)/Balgüe (Maderas)   **Distance** 5.5 miles (8.8 km), Maderas; 6 miles (9.6 km), Concepción
Time 8 hours, Maderas; 10 hours, Concepción   **Grade** Moderate to strenuous   **Type** Dirt trails   **Map** goo.gl/mA9X5d

When they came here in the early 1500s, the Spanish conquistadors called Lake Nicaragua the "freshwater sea"—its sheer size causing them to consider it more of an ocean than a lake. Ometepe Island, which means "two hills," rises from its waters and, at 106.5 square miles (276 sq km), it is as large as the lake that surrounds it. It's also large enough to be home to the two "hills" that dominate it—the stratovolcanoes Concepción and Maderas.

It's possible to summit Concepción (5,282 feet/ 1,610 m) and Maderas (4,573 feet/1,394 m), and both offer contrasting experiences. Maderas has its own cloud forest on its upper slopes, and a lagoon fills its inactive crater, which has laid dormant for more than 3,000 years. Once at its peak, you can descend to the lagoon, a tough but rewarding walk into a mist- and howler monkey-filled environment. Concepción is a little more restless, having last erupted in 1986. Smoke still wafts up from its crater, and there are numerous fumeroles on its slopes. Concepción is a tougher climb than Maderas and a longer one, too—steeper and with more rocks and boulders near its summit.

Both will likely have dense cloud waiting for you when you reach their peaks, and their trails will get wetter and muddier the higher you go. Your clothes will be soaked by humidity and sweat, it will be cold, and any wind will only add to your discomfort. So savor the soaring views that will greet you, because your stay on their summits will be a short one, though Maderas has its sheltered lagoon and Concepción the option of standing as close as you dare to the warming smoke of its smoldering crater. **BDS**

⬆ The beautiful cloud forests of Volcán Maderas.

Monteverde Cloud Forest Reserve Trail
Puntarenas, Costa Rica

Start Forest entrance **End** La Ventana observation deck **Distance** 1.2 miles (1.9 km) **Time** 1.5 hours **Grade** Easy **Type** Forest paths **Map** goo.gl/WPdHQz

"Immerse yourself in the exotic cloud forest and experience a world full of biodiversity."

www.reservamonteverde.com

⬆ Orchids such as the *Psychopsis krameriana* can be found on the trail in the Monteverde Cloud Forest.

Under certain atmospheric conditions in tropical or subtropical mountainous environments, the forests are smothered in a dense layer of clouds. These clouds often form as fog, which condenses onto the leaves of the trees and then drips down to the plants and forest floor below. In such conditions, the sun has a hard time shining through the clouds. The rate of evaporation is therefore slow, providing the plants with moisture that supports a wide biodiversity. The most common form of plants are epiphytes, nonparasitical plants such as lichens, bromeliads, and orchids, which grow on trees and collect their nutrients from the air, moisture, and debris that surround them.

Clouds forests are rare, making up only 1 percent of global woodland. One of the finest cloud forests is Monteverde in Costa Rica. Set up in 1972 and now covering some 810 acres (328 ha), the forest is home to more than 100 species of mammal, 400 birds, and 1,200 amphibians and reptiles. It is also one of the few remaining habitats that supports six species of the wild cat family—jaguar, ocelot, puma, oncilla, margay, and jaguarundi—as well as the endangered three-wattled bellbird and the fabulous quetzal. Among the many trails through the forest is the Sendero Bosque Nuboso, or Cloud Forest Reserve Trail. Pick up a self-guided tour booklet from the entrance shop, in either Spanish or English, and enjoy the lush scenery and varied wildlife that greets you on your way (look out in particular for the strangler fig plant). Another fine trail is El Camino (The Road), a 1.2-mile-long (2 km) trail that is more open than the others, letting in more sunlight and thus more butterflies. The bird-watching is particularly good on this trail. **SA**

Ciudad Perdida Trek
Sucre/Magdalena, Colombia

Start El Mamey   **End** Ciudad Perdida
Distance 14.5 miles (23.3 km)   **Time** 3 days
Grade Moderate to strenuous   **Type** Stone steps,
muddy paths   **Info** goo.gl/TdPOPY

In 1972 a group of local treasure hunters stumbled on a series of stone steps rising up the mountainside in the Sierra Nevada de Santa Marta range in Colombia. As they rose to the top of the steps, they discovered an entire abandoned city. When artifacts from the city began to appear on the black market, archaeologists quickly became involved, and between 1976 and 1982, they painstakingly restored the site. It is now known that this lost city—originally called Teyuna after the Tairona peoples who built it—was created around 800 CE. Needless to say, the local descendants of the original builders were scathing about the discovery, rightly pointing out that they had always known about the site but kept quiet to avoid publicity.

The city consists of 169 circular stone terraces carved into the steep mountainside, linked by cobbled roads and stairs. These once supported the wooden huts, markets, meeting places, and other buildings that were home to up to 10,000 inhabitants. Only a quarter of this vast city has been uncovered from the jungle. Access to the site is up a bone-crunching set of 1,200 slippery stone steps. Unaccompanied tours are prohibited, forcing you to use one of four expensive tour operators. The whole trek takes three days to get there, although it is possible to do it in two if you really push yourself. Most of the trekking is done in the morning before the afternoon rains, and numerous perils are present along the way, from wildlife to the terrain. The journey, however, is more than worthwhile, for you pass through dense jungle accompanied by wildlife of all descriptions. The city itself is truly awe-inspiring, created by an advanced civilization few people are familiar with. **SA**

"Though the ruins themselves are impressive, the tiring but gorgeous five-day trek is what sticks in most travelers' minds."

www.gadling.com

⬆ Trek to a terraced lost city more than 1,000 years old, deep in the Colombian jungle.

El Cocuy National Park Circuit Boyaca, Colombia

Start Guican   **End** El Cocuy   **Distance** 43 miles (69 km)   **Time** 7 days   **Grade** Strenuous
Type Rocky paths   **Map** goo.gl/RjZJsM

As the Andes stride north into Colombia, they split into two ranges. The eastern one, known as Cordillera Oriental, heads northeast up to the border with Venezuela. Almost on the border lies the El Cocuy National Park, a high-altitude region carved out by glaciers to form a landscape of gouged-out lakes, steep mountain slopes, and swathes of glacial debris known as moraine. Predictably, the park is favored by climbers anxious to tackle its twenty-one peaks, but the area also has a number of challenging walks.

The most popular walk begins in the village of Guican and heads around the park in a clockwise direction to end a week later in El Cocuy. This walk is strenuous, for there are no people living along the route, so you will be sleeping in a tent and carrying all your own food and cooking equipment. At this high altitude—mostly above 9,000 feet (2,750 m)—bad weather is always a problem and temperatures can drop sharply at night. Be prepared for snow on the higher passes. The trek is well marked with cairns, but unless you are an experienced hiker, it is advisable to hire a guide at Guican, or obtain one in advance. Hiring a horse to carry your luggage can also help. Given these issues, the best time of year to do this adventurous trek is between December and mid-March. But be warned: the Colombian government has closed the circuit at times, citing environmental damage, so do check before committing yourself to this epic trek. But if you get there, enjoy seven days of the most glorious walking, over eight epic passes and alongside numerous lakes in some of the most beautiful scenery imaginable. **SA**

⬆ El Cocuy has moraines, lakes, passes, and peaks.

Roraima Trek Bolivar, Venezuela

Start/End Paraitepui   Distance 36 miles (57.9 km)   Time 5 days   Grade Strenuous
Type Mountain and forest trails   Map goo.gl/JtT4BU

Mount Roraima (9,219 feet/2,810 m) is the highest of Venezuela's flat-topped Auyán-tepuí mountains. Their "Lost World" landscape was beloved of author Sir Arthur Conan Doyle, who immortalized the vast, inaccessible mesas as evolutionary outposts where dinosaurs and other creatures defied extinction, isolated from the perils of nature and man.

It is difficult not to picture these images as you leave civilization behind and begin your trek into the midst of the forbidding monoliths. Yet despite their inaccessibility and size, the *tepuís* are surprisingly straightforward, nontechnical climbs, although whether you categorize an ascent of Mount Roraima as "moderate" or "strenuous" will depend to a large extent on whether or not you avail yourself of porters to carry your gear. Taking a porter certainly will spare your back, and help out the local Pemon villagers, too.

From your start point in the village of Paraitepui it is a four-hour hike to your camp at Rio Tek, with another four- hour hike the day after, uphill all the way to your 6,233-foot-high (1,900 m) base camp at the foot of Mount Roraima. The next day, day 3, it is up—straight up—2,624 feet (800 m) to the summit. On the way the jungle begins to thin and the views appear, none more daunting than the sheer 1,312-foot-high (400 m) quartzite face above you—climbers call it "the Wall." Fortunately, though, what you are looking for is "the Ramp," a gradual slope that eventually deposits you on the plateau—a world of heavily fissured and eroded rock formations, and trails to places with otherworldly names like the Valley of the Crystals. But alas, no dinosaurs. **BDS**

⬆ Hike the summit of Arthur Conan Doyle's Lost World.

Kaieteur Falls
Potaro-Siparuni, Guyana

Start/End Pamela Landing, Potaro River
Distance 26 miles (42 km)   **Time** 16 days
Grade Moderate to strenuous   **Type** Unmarked jungle
trails   **Map** goo.gl/29crvJ

Four times higher than Niagara Falls and twice as high as Victoria Falls on the Zambia/Zimbabwe border, the 822-foot-high (251 m) Kaieteur Falls was first seen by foreigners when the British geologists James Sawkins and Charles Brown came to Guyana in 1870 to map the country's interior on behalf of the British government. It's one of the world's most beautiful waterfalls, as well as the world's largest single-drop waterfall, with 23,400 cubic feet (663 cu m) of water per second, plunging over a sandstone and conglomerate precipice before continuing over a series of cascades and tumbling down into the Potaro River.

Part of the Kaieteur National Park is in the epicenter of Guyana's rain forests, and the trek is a challenging and exciting experience that begins with a boat ride up the Potaro River and an overnight stay beneath Amatuk Falls. The next day, if the weather is good, you can scramble your way along rocks and boulders to Big Stone Waterfall, with the night before the ascent spent in hammocks at Waratuk Falls. The following day has an eight-hour hike through the forest that brings you to Tukeit Hill below the falls, where there is chance for a refreshing swim in the Potaro River.

The climb to the top of the falls the following day is arduous, and can be downright horrible if it happens to be raining—a reasonable expectation considering you are in a rain forest. The climb takes about four hours and ends with stunning views over one of the world's great waterfalls, and the promise of a comfortable night's sleep in the government-built and -maintained Kaieteur Guest House. **BDS**

➡ Trek to the world's largest single-drop waterfall.

El Altar Crater
Chimborazo, Ecuador

Start/End Hacienda Releche, Candelaria
Distance 16 miles (25.7 km)   **Time** 2 days
Grade Moderate   **Type** Mountain tracks
Map goo.gl/QLYchD

When, in the 1500s, the Spanish first saw this mountain, they thought it resembled two nuns and four friars listening to a bishop around a church altar and so named it El Altar. The local Inca called it Kapak Urku—"sublime mountain"—for it is truly magnificent. Situated 105 miles (170 km) south of Ecuador's capital, Quito, this extinct volcano is in the western end of the Sangay National Park and reaches up to 17,451 feet (5,320 m) above sea level. Its nine mountain peaks form a horseshoe-shaped ridge that surrounds a caldera (a collapsed magma chamber that has filled up with water), a lake known as Laguna Collantes or Laguna Amarilla. The Inca reported that the top of the mountain had collapsed in about 1460 after seven years of volcanic activity, but in reality the caldera long predates that event.

The nine peaks are an arduous climb best left to trained mountaineers. Much more accessible, however, is the hike up to the rim of the caldera overlooking the lake. The trek starts at around 10,500 feet (3,200 m) and climbs steeply, eventually reaching the Collantes night shelter. The trek then continues the next day across the Collantes Plain to the plateau beside the turquoise-green crater's lake. Here you can get excellent views of the lake below and the nine snowcapped peaks around you. If you are lucky, you may also see the awesome Andean condor in full-winged flight. Be warned: this is a muddy hike up tracks regularly mangled by horses' hooves, although you might be tempted to add to the mess by riding some of the trek on horseback. Rubber boots are recommended. Also be warned that the refuge is cold and damp, so come prepared. **SA**

"A breathtaking crater set within an amphitheater of jagged, ice-capped peaks."

www.roughguides.com

⬆ A turquoise lake, set below nine snow-laden summits, awaits at the end of an often muddy slog.

Alpamayo Circuit

Ancash, Peru

Start Hualcayán   End Cashapampa
Distance 48 miles (77 km)   Time 11–12 days
Grade Strenuous   Type Mountain tracks
Map goo.gl/rskASI

In 1966, an international survey of mountain climbers tried to answer a difficult and deeply subjective question: Which mountain, of all the mountains on Earth, was the most beautiful? The consensus, it turned out, was that Alpamayo in the Peruvian Cordillera Blanca—the "White Range"—was the mountain most deserving of such a prestigious title. A photograph, sent to the German magazine *Alpinismus* by U.S. photographer and climber Leigh Ortenburger, of the mountain's perfect pyramid of ice that is its southwest face accompanied an article that was written in the wake of the survey. In the July 1966 issue of *Alpinismus*, the 19,511-foot-high (5,947 m) Alpamayo was officially given the title: "The World's Most Beautiful Mountain." Few that have seen this mountain up close have since disagreed.

To walk the circuit around Alpamayo is to embark on a stunning visual extravaganza through the heart of the Peruvian Andes. High passes are crossed, 19,000 foot-high (6,000 m) fluted peaks surround you, glaciers beckon, and vertical walls of ice inspire. You walk alongside alpine lakes and pass through local Quechua farming communities in the Los Cedros valley who are eager to welcome you into their villages. The Cordillera Blanca is one of the world's great mountain ranges, with fifty summits exceeding 18,700 feet (5,700 m), and it is home to the largest number of tropical-zone glaciers on Earth. You cross the Continental Divide, and eventually join the Santa Cruz trail for the home stretch into Cashapampa. There is just no punch that this memorable trek does not pack. Alpamayo is also one of the Andes most-climbed mountains. But that is a whole other story. **BDS**

"The Cordillera Blanca range provides some of the most spectacular and varied trekking."

www.lonelyplanet.com

⊞ Breathtaking views will reward the hikers brave enough to tackle the Alpamayo Circuit.

Santa Cruz Trek Ancash, Peru

Start Vaquería **End** Cashapampa **Distance** 31 miles (49.8 km) **Time** 4 days
Grade Moderate **Type** Rocky, gravel trails **Map** goo.gl/vG8CJn

The Santa Cruz Trek is a high alpine route through Peru's Cordillera Blanca. Although often thought of as a "busy" trail, it is nowhere near as busy as the Inca Trail; in fact, you can spend days here and see very few people. Even though it is not a difficult trail in terms of elevation gain or rates of ascent, it can be a challenge when you consider its overall elevation. The good news is that it can be done without a guide, without a donkey, and even without a map. Really.

The trail begins with a jolting four-wheel-drive transfer from the town of Huaraz to the village of Vaquería, and from there it's a three-hour hike to Paria, where you can rest up before the next day's assault on the trail's high point—a crossing of the Punta Union pass at 15,583 feet (4,750 m). The hike to the pass is along an old pre-Columbian trail, which was used for centuries to transport goods from the eastern Andes to the populated valleys in the west. Along the way, views over the Santa Cruz and Huaripampa valleys and some of the Peruvian Andes grandest peaks—Artesonraju, Tawllirahu, and the majestic Alpamayo—will make this a day to remember.

The following day is spent encountering yet more towering peaks, which shouldn't come as a surprise in a region that has one of the highest concentrations of big peaks in the Western Hemisphere with 33 18,000 foot-high (5,486 m) summits in a narrow corridor just 112 miles (180 km) long. You'll eventually descend into the Santa Cruz Valley, past spectacular Lake Arhuaycocha, with its turquoise waters and its glacier, and next day you'll come to this dizzying journey's end. **BDS**

⬆ The Huaraz Cordillera is typical of this trek's horizons.

Huayhuash Circuit Ancash, Peru

Start/End Chiquián   **Distance** 101 miles (162 km)   **Time** 12 days   **Grade** Strenuous
Type Rock, gravel, dirt mountain trails   **Info** goo.gl/sOJGCe

It is a bold claim—the single most rewarding hike anywhere in South America. Really? Well, before deciding, you should maybe test that claim for yourself, but keep in mind the following: This is a serious, high-altitude trek all of which takes place above the tree line. It is isolated, with extremely limited access to roads, and set in a landscape where few people live. Almost every day, you're crossing a 15,748-foot-high (4,800 m) pass. As if that weren't enough, there's even the option of climbing the 17,552-foot-high (5,350 m) Mount Diablo Mudo—the "Mute Devil"—which is considered a "moderate" mountaineering challenge, but is a highly exposed climb, with ice slopes up to 45 degrees. So unless you have crampons, best to stick to the track.

The challenges, of course, are matched by the rewards. Being above the tree line means that the views are panoramic and never-ending. At around the halfway point, near Lake Viconga, there are some hot springs, which, despite being a long way off the best hot spring experience you can have in Peru, are certainly welcome after six nights camping at this altitude. Four hours after leaving Lake Viconga comes the highest point on the trail—the pass of Punta Cuyoc at 16,404 feet (5,000 m).

The sights on this circuit are too numerous to mention. The best scenery is on the cordillera's eastern side, where there are also a number of trout-filled lakes. Just remember that 101 miles (162 km) is a very long way in these conditions, and the many tempting side trails lead to awesome scenery but are unmarked, so don't attempt them without a guide. **BDS**

⬆ The book *Touching the Void* (1988) popularized this trek.

Huayna Picchu "Hike of Death"

Cusco, Peru

Start/End Machu Picchu
Distance 1.3 miles (2.1 km)   **Time** 2 hours
Grade Easy   **Type** Stone stairs, mountain trails
Map goo.gl/wLinsO

The much-trodden trail to Machu Picchu, the ancient city of the Incas, appears elsewhere in this book, but if you want to see Machu Picchu as the condors see it, from above, then that involves climbing another trail altogether, and it's not one for the fainthearted. To get to your destination, which is the summit of that lovely green spike of a peak you see looming above the monument in every second postcard, you have to—that's right—do some more climbing. You'll have to walk from Machu Picchu to Huayna Picchu on the so-called "Hike of Death."

Thousands of people walk the trail up to Machu Picchu every day, but only the first 400 people who line up outside the bus depot in Aguas Calientes are allowed to climb Huayna Picchu (also known as Wayna Picchu). And, as if the climb to the viewpoint isn't enough, with its stone stairs devoid of handrails, there is a hair-raising walk to the Templo de la Luna, the otherworldly and much-overlooked Temple of the Moon on the other side of the peak, which is exquisitely carved into a network of caves. The temple, which is probably a burial site, features some of the finest craftsmanship to be seen at Machu Picchu, including double-jamb entryways and some classic trapezoidal stonework.

Whether the "lost city" of Machu Picchu was ever truly lost is debatable. When explorer Hiram Bingham arrived here in 1911 there were three farming families living in its ruins and cultivating its terraces. However, with so few surrounding peaks other than Huayna Picchu, and with paths able to provide views of this astonishing site, maybe it was more a case of forgotten, rather than lost. **BDS**

"For many people climbing Huayna Picchu is one of the highlights when visiting Machu Picchu."

www.howtotraveltomachupicchu.com

⬆ Carved into the mountain's granite, the Hike of Death staircase climbs a staggering 1,000 feet (305 m).

Colca Canyon to Oasis Sangalle
Arequipa, Peru

Start/End Cabanaconde
Distance 5 miles (8 km)   **Time** 6.5 hours
Grade Moderate   **Type** Narrow, pebble-strewn path
Map goo.gl/KUV5zR

If only it were in the United States, then everyone would know about it. But it has had so many names in the past that maybe we've just confused ourselves—the Valley of Wonders, the Valley of Fire, the Lost Valley of the Incas. Colca Canyon would be the must-see destination in whatever country it found itself, but it is in Peru, and so must be content with living in the shadows of glorious Machu Picchu. Almost twice as deep as Arizona's Grand Canyon, this enormous gash in the Earth's surface in southern Peru, with its pre–Columbian terraced fields stacked up like pancakes on its precipitous slopes, should be on the itinerary of any Peruvian visit.

People come here not only to see the canyon, but also to get up close to its healthy population of condors, which sadly are in decline most everywhere else in South America. Here they can be seen in numbers riding the canyon's thermals in search of food. One of the best spots to watch them is Cabanaconde, the start point for a hike to the Oasis Sangalle resort on the canyon floor.

You can hike here with or without a guide. If your goal is to get to the bottom, you should know that you'll be starting at around 11,000 feet (3,352 m) above sea level and descending to 6,500 feet (1,981 m), only to turn around after resting to go back up again. It can be completed in a day, but most people prefer to spend at least a night amid the palms at Oasis Sangalle on the canyon floor (where there are thatched adobe huts for overnight stays), to gird themselves for the coming ascent. You can also take a dip in the pool that is set between two huge rocks; a final act of indulgence before the punishing climb back up. **BDS**

"The oasis itself is really lovely and a huge contrast to the dry dusty and rocky landscape of the surrounding valley."

www.backpackerben.co.uk

⬆ The Colca River flows through the world's second deepest canyon, a favorite haunt of the Andean condor.

Choquequirao Trail
Arequipa, Peru

Start/End Cachora   Distance 40 miles (64 km)
Time 5 days   Grade Strenuous
Type Mountain trails, stone paths
Map goo.gl/SZqnvv

The Incas were good at hiding their cities. There is Machu Picchu, of course, which wasn't rediscovered until 1911, and the legendary lost city of Paititi, described by sixteenth-century Jesuits but never found, thanks to (if you believe the conspiracy theorists) a four centuries-long Vatican cover-up. And then there is Choquequirao. Similar in design and structure to Machu Picchu, it sprawls over more than 4,400 acres (1,800 ha) along a glaciated peak 9,842 feet (3,000 m) above the Apurimac River, the source of the Amazon, no less, in southern Peru's Arequipa Province.

Choquequirao is less traveled, though more grueling than the Classic Inca Trail, but when you get there, it's all wonderfully familiar. There are the same huge ridgelines, the same snowy peaks and panoramas, the same terraces that resemble giant staircases, and the same level of craftsmanship, with stones cut and put together with such precision that you can't even slip a credit card in their joints.

The Choquequirao Trail starts at Cachora, a small farming village three hours' drive from Cusco. Hugging the cliffs above the Apurimac River, it first takes you to a viewpoint at Capuliyoc, from where you can almost see your goal. A 3,937-foot (1,200-m) descent back to the river leads to a campground, and the next day you have a brutish 4,921-foot-high (1,500 m) climb along switchbacks to the village of Marampata, beyond which the dirt trail turns to a stone path and suddenly you are on Choquequirao plaza. Only 1 percent of visitors to Machu Picchu come here; reason enough to go climb that little bit higher. **BDS**

← The Apurimac River below is lost among the peaks.

Classic Inca Trail to Machu Picchu
Arequipa, Peru

Start Piscacucho   End Machu Picchu
Distance 28 miles (45 km)   Time 4 days
Grade Moderate   Type Mountain trails, stone and granite paths   Map goo.gl/J8b52n

Everybody has a favorite trail, a favorite destination, the single greatest adventure they ever had. And more people have placed the ancient Inca city of Machu Picchu at the top of their "greatest destination" list than any other single destination on Earth.

There are hundreds of Inca trails in Peru—around 24,854 miles (40,000 km) of them—all of them worth doing, but only one seems to matter, even though your lungs, knees, and feet will take a beating over the four days you traverse the Sacred Valley, as you struggle toward that sunrise on the fourth day. The

> *"That first unforgettable sunrise view from Intipunku is just the start …"*
> www.roughguides.com

trail follows the Urubamba canyon and soon after that the climbing starts: up the steep Llullucha valley, through polylepis woodlands, and into the treeless grasslands of the puna. Crossing the Warmiwañusqa pass (13,776 feet/4,200 m), you suddenly have views of the trail ahead and the Huayanay massif at your rear. Day 3 and you're on your first genuine Inca stairway, as you pass the ancient site of Runkuracay. The trail is now a giant's causeway, a massive stone-buttressed pathway that takes you through cloud forest, a world of mosses, orchids, and ferns, which on day 4 at last deposits you on the threshold of Intipunku—the Sun Gate. And suddenly, after years spent dreaming, it is all around you. **BDS**

Volcan Misti Arequipa, Peru

Start/End Chiguata   Distance 15.5 miles (25 km) via Aguada Blanca   Time 3–4 days
Grade Moderate   Type Loose sandy trails, scree   Map goo.gl/09wQ48

If you want to gain a mental picture of the sweeping breadth and sheer bulk of Peru's Volcan Misti, consider this: The base camp on one of the two routes to its summit was named Monte Blanco, in honor of Mont Blanc. The base camp got its name because it is situated at about the same height as the summit of western Europe's highest mountain and yet, from the Monte Blanco camp, there is still more than 3,200 feet (1,000 m) to ascend until you arrive at its summit. Where Mont Blanc ends, Volcan Misti begins.

At 19,101 feet (5,822 m) this behemoth, which towers over the Peruvian city of Arequipa 10 miles (16 km) to the southwest, is an impressive site, and scaling it requires serious preparation. Two days up and two days down (you can pitch a tent anywhere on the mountain) helps you avoid any acclimatization issues, although if you're a fit and experienced climber it is

possible to summit it in one long day. Just remember to take plenty of water.

There is a choice of two trails—the Aguada Blanca route, which is considered the easier option despite its trailhead at 12,139 feet (3,700 m) being a little more difficult to reach (and a permit is needed); and the southern Pastores route, with its 11,154 feet (3,400 m) trailhead. Once at the top, after a steep and exhausting though far from technical climb, you can marvel not only at its two concentric summit craters—the larger measuring 2,723 feet (830 m) in diameter—but also from the summit you will see Peru's very own "Ring of Fire," a line of volcanoes comprising Chachani, Ubinas, Sabancaya, Coropuna, and the snowcapped peaks of Ampato and Hualcahuaic. **BDS**

⊡ Misti is a classic, conical stratovolcano.

Christ the Redeemer Trail Rio de Janeiro, Brazil

Start Parque Lage, Jardim Botânico   **End** Christ the Redeemer   **Distance** 1 mile (1.6 km)   **Time** 2 hours
Grade Easy   **Type** Stone paths, rocks, concrete road   **Map** goo.gl/Qzc9e2

The idea to build a gigantic religious statue on top of the Corcovado Mountain in Rio de Janeiro, then the capital of Brazil, was first mooted in the 1850s. The idea was revived in 1920, when the city's Roman Catholics proposed a large statue of Christ. Work started in 1922 and finished in 1931. When completed, the 700-ton (635-tonne) statue stood 98 feet (30 m) tall on its 26-foot-high (8 m) pedestal, with an arm span of 92 feet (28 m). A stunning piece of Art Deco design, Christ the Redeemer remained the tallest statue of Christ in the world until a rival appeared in Poland in 2010.

Ever since the statue was built, it has been an icon for the city. The views from the statue over the city and its bays and beaches below, out to the ocean beyond, are superb, which is why so many people want to visit the statue. As a result, the crowds at the top can be intense. Therefore, it is best to avoid visiting on weekends and public holidays. The trail itself starts from Parque Lage in the Jardim Botânico and, despite the steep ascent, is relatively easy. There is a path most of the way up, except for about 30 feet (9 m) of rocks, where there is a chain for support. The last stage is up a concrete road. On the way, you pass through a rain forest with tropical plants and capuchin monkeys.

Once at the top, you need to buy a ticket in order to gain access to the base of the statue, and the lines can be long. Incidentally, for those who can't manage the walk, there is also a train service going up the mountain—hence the crowds of unfit tourists who greet you at the top. **SA**

⊼ Walk to the base of Rio's Art Deco masterpiece.

Estrada da Graciosa
Paraná, Brazil

Start Quatro Barras
End Sâo Joâo da Graciosa   **Distance** 23 miles (37 km)
Time 2 day   **Grade** Easy   **Type** Cobbled
and paved roads   **Map** goo.gl/Jx7bgI

"A spectacular cobbled road that runs … through the mountains and the Marumbi National Park."

www.footprinttravelguides.com

⊼ Marumbi National Park has evolved to become one of Brazil's most popular eco-tourism locations.

When the Portuguese first colonized this southern coastal part of Brazil in the mid-1500s, they were presented with what looked like the impenetrable barrier of the Serra da Graciosa that sealed off the continent from the coast. There appeared to be no way through its thickly forested woods and steep crags. However, the Portuguese soon discovered the native trails that led inland, forcing their African slaves to pave them with river stones for easier access. The mule trade in slaves, gold, silver, textiles, and other items soon prospered, creating the flourishing inland city of Curitiba and an equally flourishing port at Paranaguá. By the 1880s, the trade route was busy enough to deserve its own specially built roads and a railway that wound its way around the mountain slopes, across rivers, and through forests, down to the sea.

It is the cobbled section of one of those roads that forms the heart of the Estrada da Graciosa trail. Starting at Quatro Barras, to the east of the bustling city of Curitiba, the route winds its way through the Serra da Graciosa inside the Marumbi National Park. Along the way are fire grills to prepare lunch, and shelters and campsites for rest. The original mule trail runs alongside the road. Although the route is along a road, your progress is far from quick, for the road is narrow, windy, and sometimes collapses after heavy rainfall. If you have enough stamina, extend your walk for another 13 miles (20 km) south to Morretes, founded in 1721 and considered to be one of the prettiest colonial towns in southern Brazil. Its whitewashed buildings with painted window frames straddle a rock-strewn river, the entire town surrounded by hills of the deepest green. **SA**

Illampu Circuit, Cordillera Real La Paz, Bolivia

Start Sorata **End** Millipaya
Distance 47 miles (75.6 km)
Time 8–10 days **Grade** Strenuous
Type Mountain paths **Map** goo.gl/Iw08qB

Situated in the far west of Bolivia and running to the southeast of Lake Titicaca, the Cordillera Real mountain range is only 17 degrees south of the equator. That ought to make the mountains hot, but, in fact, they are quite heavily glaciated, thanks to the moist air masses from the nearby Amazon lowlands that keep them cool. The range is not that big, measuring only 78 miles (125 km) in length and a bare 12 miles (20 km) in width. Yet it packs in seven peaks higher than 19,700 feet (6,000 m), including Illampu at 20,892 feet (6,368 m), and many more above 16,410 feet (5,000 m).

Illampu is the fourth highest mountain in Bolivia and is known to be the hardest of the high peaks in the country to climb. The circuit course around its circumference and that of the neighboring Ancohuma peak is a different matter, and it is a popular hike for fit walkers. Starting at the village of Sorata at the foot of the mountain, the trek heads up for a long day's haul to Lacatiya. The next day is spent crossing the 15,584-foot-high (4,750 m) Paso Illampu, which affords great views of the mountain's northern peak, and then past some still-worked gold mines. The next three days are spent climbing up to passes at high altitudes and then dropping down into the valleys below. Finally, the trail goes around the southwest side of the cordillera and descends via the Carizal and Chojna Kota lakes to Millipaya. The scenery along the way is magnificent, with the snowcapped Illampu and Ancohuma to one side and green fertile valleys to the other. Some of the tours that operate along the route will provide mules for your luggage, which will be most welcome in this environment. **SA**

Central Chilean Inca Trail Libertador, Chile

Start North of Rancagua **End** Temple of the Sun **Distance** 8 miles (12.8 km) **Time** 6 hours
Grade Easy **Type** Mountain tracks
Map goo.gl/QV6F13

In around 1220, Manco Capac founded the Inca state at Cuzco in what is now Peru. For the next 200 years, the Incas controlled little more than the surrounding valley, but after 1438, they began a huge territorial expansion that brought them the largest empire in the pre–Columbian Americas. It stretched from Ecuador in the north to central Chile in the south, a long, thin territory held together by a series of well-built roads. Much of this Qhapaq Nan, or road system, still survives today, making it ideal for long-distance walks or short strolls.

"The only sounds you will hear are the melody of songbirds and the bleating of the goats."

www.rent-a-guide.net

Predictably, the most popular Inca trails are in Peru, particularly leading up to Machu Picchu. The lesser-known Chilean trails are much quieter but equally enjoyable and impressive. A good trail starts to the north of Rancagua, almost at the southern tip of the Inca lands. It leads first to an Inca hillside fort on La Compania, a hill in the foothills of the Andes. It is more an archaeological site than a tourist magnet, and so you often have it to yourself. The trail then leads on to an Incan Temple of the Sun, the southernmost one in the empire, where Incan priests practiced complex rituals and ceremonies that involved both astronomy and religion, including some human sacrifices. Both sites recall the full majesty of Incan power. **SA**

Villarrica Traverse Araucanía, Chile

Start Villarrica Ski Center   **End** Puesco   **Distance** 52 miles (83.6 km)   **Time** 5–6 days   **Grade** Strenuous
Type Mountain tracks   **Map** goo.gl/IzyZB7

The Villarrica National Park lies in southern Chile, not far from the town of Pucón. Its centerpiece is a line of three volcanoes—Villarrica, Quetrupillán, and Lanín—that perversely stretch from west to east against the general north–south direction of the Andes of which they form a part. The park is also home to such wildlife as pumas, coypus, Harris' hawks, and the wonderfully named Molina's hog-nosed skunk, which unusually has a resistance to the venom of the local pit vipers. Most people, however, will probably go to the park for its stunning scenery of mountains and lakes, and its great treks.

The Villarrica Traverse crosses the park around the south of the Villarrica volcano to Puesco, almost at the border with Argentina. The trek can be done in a hardy four or a more leisurely five to six days, with camping overnight. The path is marked with yellow-painted iron stakes, wooden signs, and, in barren areas, cairns. The route itself begins at the last curve of the road before the ski center, where there is a big, informative map and notice board. From then on, you are in a natural wilderness, following the circumference of the Villarrica volcano across lava flows and through highland grass, wooded forests, and steep river valleys. The trek then heads southeast across the high-level volcanic ridge and on past the second volcano, Quetrupillán, its exploded crater a majestic sight. On past the milky Lake Blanca, you take a quick skip across the border into Argentina, toward the final volcano, Lanín, before heading down through increasingly greener and wetter vegetation at the southern end of the park to Puesco. **SA**

⊡ A traverse through lava flows, valleys, and woodlands.

Dientes Circuit Isla Navarino, Magallanes, Chile

Start/End Puerto Williams   **Distance** 33 miles (53 km)   **Time** 5 days   **Grade** Strenuous
Type Grassy and rocky paths   **Map** goo.gl/gF5m7y

Quite rightly, the Dientes Circuit on Isla Navarino has been described as the most southerly trek in the world. To give you an idea of where it is, the views of the Cape Horn straits are superb. Navarino lies below the Argentinian half of Tierra del Fuego, the "Land of Fire," although it forms part of Chile. Just getting there is an adventure, requiring a flight south from Punta Arenas, Chile's southernmost city, to Puerto Williams. You can also make the trip by boat, either direct from Punta Arenas, along the Strait of Magellan and the Beagle Channel, or from Ushuaia to Puerto Navarino and then by road.

The Dientes Circuit was first developed in the early 1990s, but, while marked out, the route is still far from clear. Any potential trekker needs to be self-reliant and good at route finding. Because of its location, the circuit is largely free of fellow walkers. It

also has no refuges along the way, so come prepared. Start the trek outside the tiny village of Puerto Williams and follow the thirty-eight red signage markers on the cairns in a clockwise direction. These are hard to spot as the markers are only painted on one side and the cairns are difficult to distinguish from their rocky surroundings. The route involves crossing four significant passes, as well as a mass of beaver ponds and dams in the valleys below. The winds that sweep up from Antarctica can knock you off your feet, so beware. The route is broken up into five stages, each one taking around five hours to complete, although the long daylight hours of the southern hemisphere give you plenty of time to rest along the way. And also to enjoy this fabulous walk. **SA**

⊞ The world's southernmost trek is not for novices.

W Circuit
Magallanes, Chile

Start Refugio Torre Central   **End** Torres del Paine
Distance 36 miles (57.9 km)   **Time** 4–5 days
Grade Moderate   **Type** Well-trodden mountain trails
Map goo.gl/LWBpHb

One of the most popular walks in Chilean Patagonia, the W Circuit brings the wilderness of this untamed region to the everyday hiker and gets you face to face with glaciers, icebergs, soaring mountains, and the vertical grandeur of the Torres del Paine, the Towers of Pain, so beloved of hardcore mountaineers.

The trail, which is best walked during the small window that the Patagonian summer provides from December to February, begins at Refugio Torre Central, goes past a lodge at Los Cuernos, and continues into the French Valley before heading into the Chileno Valley to the Torres del Paine, a complex geological mix of mountains and glacial lakes with a profusion of wildlife that, when all combined, provides some of the best sensory-laden landscapes the world of hiking can offer.

The W Circuit winds its way along a W-shaped route that ends at the base of the Torres del Paine. It is a generally accessible walk, with only minimal ascents and descents, and its highlights are many—the Grey Glacier, the various *refugios* (mountain huts), the snow-covered mountainsides of the French Valley, and the Chileno Valley. How long it takes you to complete will depend on how much ground you plan to conquer each day. But why hurry? Six days here is better than five, and seven days better than six. You need no excuses to linger here. But if you plan to stay in the region's excellent *refugios*, make sure you book them far in advance. They are well maintained and their staff provide truly delicious meals. Or just bring a tent and treat the *refugios* as wayside restaurants as you walk your way through the majestic Chilean wilderness. **BDS**

"A challenging, rewarding, and unforgettable trip through forests, mountains, and glaciers."

www.cascada.travel

⬅ The blue waters of Nordenskjold Lake set below the jagged pinnacles of the Torres del Paine summits.

⬆ Llamas are a common sight on the W Circuit.

Rano Kau Summit
Easter Island, Chile

Start Hanga Roa   **End** Rano Kau summit
Distance 3 miles (4.8 km)   **Time** 1 day
Grade Easy   **Type** Earth paths, gravel road
Map goo.gl/rgLrtp

Easter Island in the Pacific Ocean is one of the most remote inhabited islands in the world, its population of 5,800 living 1,289 miles (2,075 km) away from their nearest neighbors on Pitcairn Island and 2,182 miles (3,512 km) from the coast of Chile. Famously, the island is also home to 887 monumental statues, called moai, carved and erected by the Rapa Nui people from 1100 to 1680. Standing in lines on stone platforms or by themselves on the hillsides, these heads and torsos are up to 32 feet (9.8 m) high, an eerie relic of a once-thriving Polynesian culture.

As the triangular Easter Island is only 15.3 miles (24.6 km) long and 7.6 miles (12.2 km) wide, it is easy to ramble around it in a few days. A more structured walk is up to the summit of Rano Kau on the southwest tip of the island. This mountain is an extinct volcano formed between 210,000 and 150,000 years ago. Its crater, which measures almost 1 mile (1.6 km) across, contains a large lake. Sheltered from the wind and rain by the mountain walls that surround it, the crater has its own microclimate, allowing figs and vines to flourish. It once contained the last toromiro-flowering tree in the wild, which unfortunately was cut down for firewood in 1960. The species is gradually being reintroduced to the island using seeds collected from a single tree by the explorer Thor Heyerdahl.

The trail to the Rano Kau summit starts at Hanga Roa and heads south to the mountain, climbing up through a eucalyptus forest to the crater rim, where it joins a gravel road. It then winds along the rim to the ranger station and climbs up to the summit at Orongo. The views of Easter Island are, without doubt, sensational. **SA**

"Rano Kau has a crater lake which is one of the island's only three natural bodies of fresh water."

www.easterislandtourism.com

⤒ After viewing the famous statues, why not climb up to the crater of an extinct volcano?

Llama Trekking

Jujuy, Argentina

Start/End Tilcara **Distance** 3 miles (4.8 km)
Time 4 hours **Grade** Moderate
Type Rocky mountain paths
Info goo.gl/YdTRta

It is very disconcerting to research "Llama trekking," in the hope of finding some wonderful trek in the Andes, only to come up with large numbers of treks specific to your own country. Llama trekking in the hills south of London is not what we are after. But such treks are a testament to the versatility of these domesticated and highly intelligent, friendly camelids, once indigenous to the Andes but now used around the world as guard and pack animals. Their wool is very soft and lanolin-free, while their meat is apparently very edible. All that said, it is best to see llamas in the land from which they came.

There are many llama treks advertised in Argentina, all using the animals to carry your luggage and provisions while you walk, as, of course, llamas cannot be ridden. A llama can carry about a quarter of its body weight for 5 to 8 miles (8–13 km), so they are excellent for a half-day trek. One such trek is in the narrow Quebrada de Humahuaca valley, in the province of Jujuy in the far north of Argentina. This beautiful valley is multicolored in its rocky striations, studded with cactus plants and adobe villages along the way. The llamas are happy to oblige you, but are interested in anything green to eat and have a tendency to stop for no apparent reason and look around them.

The trek itself climbs up from Tilcara to the Garganta del Diablo (Devil's Gorge) before returning along a little-known trail back to the village. This trek is ideal for families, although those with younger children might prefer to take another trek along the valley floor. All treks in this region can be done at any time of the year. **SA**

Nahuel Huapi Traverse

Neuquén/Rio Negro, Argentina

Start Cerro Catedral, Neuquén **End** Arroyo Lopez,
Rio Negro **Distance** 25 miles (40 km)
Time 5 days **Grade** Strenuous
Type Mountain tracks **Map** goo.gl/bbT7dF

The Nahuel Huapi National Park in the foothills of the Patagonian Andes is the oldest national park in Argentina. Established in 1934, it covers an area of 2,722 square miles (7,050 sq km) of high-altitude snow peaks, lower hill slopes, and grassy steppes, with some limited rain forests. The park gets its name from the vast lake in its center, Nahuel Huapi, which in the local Mapuche language means "jaguar island." Much like Loch Ness in Scotland, the lake has its own monster, the Nahuelito, which apparently looks like a giant water snake with humps and fishlike fins.

> *"Beautiful wildflowers, numerous bird species, pumas, and deer can be seen in the forests."*
>
> walkopedia.net

The park offers many treks, the best of which is the five-day, clockwise traverse of the entire park that connects the main overnight *refugios* of Frey, Jakob, Laguna Negra (Italia), and Lopez. Camping is free at the *refugios*, which provide basic accommodation, meals, and use of the kitchen. Take your own sleeping bag. Charges vary, and you don't need to book in advance. This traverse is strenuous due to its steep, descending scree slopes and abrupt ascents, as well as the poor quality of its markings. The section of the trek between the Jakob and Laguna Negra *refugios* is rocky and can be dangerous in bad weather. The park office advises that it is done with a guide, but they do allow experienced trekkers to walk it unattended. **SA**

Cerro Campanario Rio Negro, Argentina

Start Cable car station   **End** Campanario summit   **Distance** 3 miles (4.8 km)   **Time** 1 hour   **Grade** Easy
Type Dirt path   **Map** goo.gl/m3hkDu

San Carlos de Bariloche is a scenic but tourist-filled city in the Rio Negro province of western Argentina, not far from the border with Chile. The city sits by the side of Nahuel Huapi Lake and has the feel of an alpine town, the result of a deliberate attempt by the city's planners in the 1930s to emulate in wood and stone a typical alpine settlement. To add to this European picture, the shops sell handmade chocolates and men loiter in the streets with St. Bernards waiting to have their photographs taken. The city is also known as the "Honeymoon Capital" of Argentina. Up close, this is all a bit twee, but the city does take on a different perspective when viewed from the top of the nearby Cerro Campanario, which provides a 360-degree panorama of the surrounding lakes and mountains that *National Geographic* has selected as one of the ten best vistas in the world.

There is a chairlift up to the top, but the walk is just as easy, although the trail is not that well marked. Take the number 10, 20, or 21 bus from the Centro Civico and in about 11 miles (17 km), or twenty minutes, when the driver shouts out the name of the stop, join the crowd and get off the bus. The path up the hill is located by the side of the cable car station. The dirt path is steep and there are no stairs or sidewalk, so it is best to avoid attempting the walk on a rainy day when it will be slippery. There are some forks at which you will need to make a decision about which way to go, but this shouldn't cause any problems as most of the trails generally meet up farther up the hill. Once at the top, the views are fantastic, and the coffee shop is most welcome. **SA**

⬆ Walk a trail above Argentina's honeymoon capital.

Llao Llao Circuit Rio Negro, Argentina

Start/End Llao Llao Hotel   **Distance** 9 miles (14.5 km)   **Time** 4 hours   **Grade** Easy
Type Woody paths, paved roads   **Map** goo.gl/IrTnBJ

One of the most acclaimed hotels in the world is found 15.5 miles (25 km) west of San Carlos de Bariloche, the tourist resort in the Rio Negro province of southern Argentina. Nestled in the foothills of the Andes on a hill between the Moreno and Nahuel Huapi lakes, the Llao Llao Hotel was built entirely of wood by the Argentinian architect Alejandro Bustillo in 1939. Unfortunately, it burned down within a few months, but it was replaced two years later with a sturdier version in reinforced concrete and stone. The hotel closed in 1976 due to funding problems, but it was eventually restored and reopened in 1993. Since then, it has won numerous awards as one of the leading and most beautiful hotels in the world.

The circuit around the park in which the hotel sits combines three trails to make a satisfying three- to four-hour loop. As you come into the park from the hotel, a statue of a green Jesus on the cross marks the first trail on your left. The track passes through a grove of elegant Arrayanes trees, notable for their cinnamon-colored bark, and along Lake Moreno.

It then joins the road until, just past the park rangers' information building, you join the Lake Escondido trail and walk back toward the rangers' office. The third trail—at first gradually and then more steeply—heads up through the forest to Cerro Llao Llao, a small hill that, at the top, affords far-reaching views over this beautiful landscape of lakes and wooded hills, with the Andes Mountains in the distance. Most of the circuit follows wooded forest paths, but about twenty minutes is spent walking along a paved road. **SA**

⬆ Stroll the lakeside trails of the Llao Llao Circuit.

Fitz Roy Loop
Santa Cruz, Argentina

Start/End El Chalten
Distance 11.5 miles (18.5 km)   **Time** 6 days
Grade Moderate   **Type** Mountain trail
Map goo.gl/OhscHf

A trek to the towering granite spires of the Fitz Roy massif, the crown jewel of Argentina's Los Glaciares National Park, is one of the world's greatest and most spectacular hikes. It carries you through a vast and largely empty landscape inhabited by guanacos (a close relative of the llama), a few local gauchos, and the ever-present condors soaring overhead. The weather is unpredictable at best, so come prepared, but also be ready to have your senses assaulted by the grandeur and beauty of the massif's soaring pinnacles that rise up to 6,000 feet (1,828 m) above the glaciers at their base. The 8,500-square-mile (22,015-sq-km) Los Glaciares National Park is a land of almost vertical granite spikes, of which Fitz Roy, named in 1877 after Robert Fitzroy, captain of HMS *Beagle*, has become its most iconic image.

The classic route along Fitz Roy's barren, unforgiving slopes involves a 6.5-mile (10.5-km) hike to the base of the mighty Cerro Torre (10,262 feet/3,128 m), part of a four-mountain chain and one of the most coveted peaks in the world of mountaineering. A path takes you from there to a high plateau and an overnight at Camp Poincenot. The next day you set off early and cross a moraine and boulder-strewn field for a fabulous Fitz Roy sunrise beneath the Rio Blanco glacier at Laguna Sucia, followed by a 5.5-mile (9-km) walk along the valley of the Rio Blanco and an ascent up the Rio Electrico Valley. Hard work, but spare a thought for those wanting to get to Fitz Roy's summit. As many as 100 people can ascend Mount Everest in a single day, but here? Maybe one successful ascent a year. **BDS**

⬅ Circle Argentina's most famous mountain peak.

Shackleton Crossing
South Georgia Island

Start King Haakon Bay   **End** Stromness Bay
Distance 26 miles (42 km)   **Time** 4 days
Grade Moderate to strenuous   **Type** Snow, ice,
exposed rock   **Map** goo.gl/Wx32Tu

Having been beaten to the South Pole in 1911 by Roald Amundsen, Ernest Shackleton decided he would cross the Antarctic continent from sea to sea via the South Pole—the last, great feat of Antarctic exploration. It all ended in disaster, however. When his ship, the *Endurance*, sank in pack ice, he and five members of his crew made an 800-mile (1,287-km) journey north to South Georgia Island in an open boat, but when they arrived in May 1916 they were forced by a terrible storm to land on its unpopulated southern coastline. Not wanting to risk a voyage to the

"With its boundless opportunities to observe wildlife ... South Georgia is a true Antarctic oasis."

www.polarexplorers.com

whaling stations on the island's northern coast, Shackleton and two of the five men, Tom Crean and Frank Worsley, instead chose an overland route never before attempted, and, over the next 36 hours, traveled 32 miles (51 km) to the whaling station at Stromness. This famous walk can now be done again, thanks to Polar Explorers. Your traverse begins at King Haakon Bay, where Shackleton made landfall, and over the next four days by ski, foot, and by *pulk* (low-slung toboggan) you retrace the steps of the famous man— the initial 2,500-foot (762-m) ascent to the Murray Snowfield, along the Trident Ridge to Crean Glacier, the descent down Fortuna Glacier, and all the way to Stromness Bay. Extraordinary. **BDS**

Laugavegurinn Hiking Trail
Capital Region, Iceland

Start Skógar   **End** Landmannalaugar
Distance 34 miles (54.7 km)   **Time** 3–5 days
Grade Easy   **Type** Exposed rock, tundra trails
Map goo.gl/l6Xgg5

"Laugavegurinn" means "hot springs route," and as you are stepping carefully over the Laugahraun lava field, or approaching the Storihver hot spring, it isn't hard to see why. But there is a lot more than hot springs in this varied and spectacular landscape. If you begin at Skógar and head north, you pass around twenty waterfalls in the first two hours as well as the Eyjafjallajökull volcano, which released so much ash in April 2010 that it closed airports throughout Europe.

The Laugavegurinn Hiking Trail is Iceland's most popular, and one of the reasons for its popularity is its wealth of landscapes. There are four glacial rivers that need crossing, which can be easy in good weather but a little tricky after heavy rain. Just remember to avoid the temptation to cross them at their narrowest point—that's usually where they are at their deepest. And the highest point on the climb may seem like a mild 3,608 feet (1,100m), but remember that 3,500 feet (1,000 m) in Iceland can carry the same environmental "punch" as 10,000 feet (3,000 m) in mainland Europe, so come prepared and always check for weather warnings before setting out. The trekking season is a short one and is weather dependent—huts on the trail usually open in the last week of June and close early September.

Trifling concerns, though, all of them, when compared to the broad spectrum of colored hills that surround you as you walk across the vast plateau of Brennisteinsalda, or touch the warm volcanic rocks from the lava wall near Thórsmörk. Glaciers, terrain that varies from sand to birchwood, ice caves, and more—no wonder this trail regularly makes lists of the world's best walks. **BDS**

"This 3 to 5-day hike goes through the most amazing landscape on Earth."

icelandinpictures.com

◁ Hike the "hot springs" route along Iceland's popular trail.

⬆ Walking past lava holes near Thorsmork.

Jotunheimen Traverse Oppland, Norway

Start Gjendesheim **End** Turtagro **Distance** 58.5 miles (94 km) **Time** 4 days **Grade** Strenuous
Type Exposed mountain trails **Map** goo.gl/4Z5v7N

The Jotunheimen Traverse is one of Norway's grand walks, and when you understand the kind of terrain through which it passes, it's easy to understand why it has been held in such high esteem by generations of Norwegian hikers. The Jotunheimen mountain range has the highest concentration of summits more than 6,561 feet (2,000 m) in northern Europe. There are alpine lakes and glaciers, everything you would expect from the best mountain scenery Norway can offer, and once you get past the popular Besseggen Ridge (30,000 people a year walk this ridge and have seriously eroded its trails), the crowds are quick to disappear, leaving you virtually alone in the wilderness that stretches out before you.

There are views along this grand traverse of mountain summits that you will long remember, not the least of which is the sight of the gloriously angular peak of Kyrkja (6,666 feet/2,032 m), and the panorama you get ascending the summit of Glitterind (bring your crampons) from the Gletterheim lodge. In Norse mythology, this place was known as the "Land of the Giants," and an attempt at the summit of Galdhopiggen (8,100 feet/2,469 m) should be on your "give it a go" list of challenges here. An excellent network of huts is maintained by the Norwegian Hiking Association, and camping is also allowed throughout the park. But it is not all about summits. The valleys here are as broad and as deep as your eyesight allows you to see, and, when combined with waterfalls and a hike across the Svellnosbrean Glacier, it isn't hard to see why this walk is one of the finest alpine experiences Norway can provide. **BDS**

⬆ This traverse is Norway's ultimate mountain hike.

Dublin Mountains Way Dublin, Ireland

Start Shankill **End** Tallaght (Sean Walsh Memorial Park) **Distance** 26.7 miles (43 km) **Time** 9 hours
Grade Strenuous **Type** Mountain trails, country paths, rural roads **Map** goo.gl/XycWY3

Where the Wicklow Mountains extend into County Dublin, they are known locally as the Dublin Mountains. In 2008 the Dublin Mountains Partnership was established with the purpose of improving the recreational experiences of the thousands of Dubliners who regularly sought sanctuary in "their" mountains, and had been calling for a proper network of trails to be established since the 1980s. Work on the trail began in 2008, and the first section opened in June 2009. The official opening was October 2010. The Dublin Mountains Way went from being a government-sanctioned idea to a fully fledged trail in only two years. That's what passion can do.

It starts, perhaps unsurprisingly for Ireland, at Brady's Pub in Shankill. From there it heads up into Rathmichael Wood and along the Lead Mines Way, through Barnaslingan Wood to a breathtaking view over Dublin from the Scalp. There is much to admire on this well-thought-out trail. It passes quarries where much of the stone that still constitutes Dublin's great public buildings came from, and takes you through the spruce and larch-filled Ticknock Forest to the summit of Three Rock at 1,457 feet (444 m). It even makes sure you go by the door of the highest pub in Ireland—Johnnie Fox's, established in 1798 in the town of Glencullen. A dangerous pit stop, you might say, considering what is to come: the forests of Ballyedmonduff, the 1,532-foot-high (467 m) summit of Tibradden with its granite-strewn slopes, and the slender gorge of the Glenasmole Valley. Still, there should be plenty of walkers behind you, willing to pick you up and tell you where you are. **BDS**

⬆ Hike the forested slopes of the Dublin Mountains.

Old Man of Hoy
Isle of Hoy, Orkney, Scotland

Start/End Moaness **Distance** 15 miles (24.1 km) **Time** 4–6 hours
Grade Moderate **Type** Footpath, moorland
Map goo.gl/BEOiUO

The sparsely populated Orkney Islands lie off the north coast of Scotland and mostly offer low-lying gentle landscapes—apart from the Isle of Hoy. "Hoy" means "high" in Norse, and this is a spectacularly mountainous island. Its famous landmark is high, too: a 450-foot (137-m) pinnacle of red sandstone standing alone in the wild Atlantic off the west coast. This iconic sea stack was first climbed live on BBC TV in 1966, the conquering team led by British Everest climber Sir Chris Bonington.

There is, however, an easier way to see the Old Man of Hoy up close, and that's to walk this circular route around the top of Hoy. It starts and finishes at the pier, where the Stromness ferry arrives, and follows a trail down through the glen via rare patches of woodland to the tiny remote hamlet of Rackwick, where a few ancient stone cottages with turf roofs huddle next to a rugged pebble and sand beach facing the North Atlantic.

Follow the footpath up the heather moor and grassy cliffs to a spot known as Tuaks of the Boy, a convenient and natural viewing platform jutting out right next to the Old Man of Hoy. The path then heads north across uneven moorland, via a picturesque spot named Goo of the Sow. At St. John's Head, peer over the edge as closely as you dare—these are the highest vertical sea cliffs in the United Kingdom.

Turn east here across unmarked wilderness. You are heading for the top of Cuilags, a small mountain of 1,427 feet (435 m). From here you can look out across the whole of the island, the historic harbor of Scapa Flow, and the rest of the Orkneys. Then it's downhill all the way back to the ferry. **SH**

"High sea cliffs offer excellent walking and the west coast in particular abounds natural beauty."

www.visitscotland.com

⤴ Walking around the Old Man of Hoy is an easier proposition than climbing it.

Aonach Eagach Ridge Walk
Highland, Scotland

Start/End Parking lot west of Allt-na-reigh
Distance 5.75 miles (9.5 km)   **Time** 6–9 hours
Grade Strenuous   **Type** Rock trails, exposed ledges
Map goo.gl/hPzfSh

One of the great challenges in the rich realm of Scottish walks, the Aonach Eagach ridge walk is the sort of experience you either are easily talked out of or boast about when you have done it. The walk, though it is more of a climb, follows the linear ridge along the side of Glen Coe in the Lochaber region of the Scottish Highlands, from Sron Gharbh to Sgorr nam Fiannaidh. It is dangerous, it can be frightful, and it certainly isn't without its technical difficulties. The ridge is extremely narrow at certain points, and you will be roped up to other climbers. But if you aren't lacking in confidence and don't have a problem with heights, then traversing this epic slice of Scottish topography will live forever in your memory.

It is a route for scramblers, really, rather than ramblers, along what is generally considered to be the narrowest ridge found anywhere on the British mainland. There are slab-encrusted cliffs to negotiate after Sron Gharbh at Am Bodach, followed by a scrambling descent to a narrow ridge and on to Meall Dearg and its excellent view of the other Glen Coe peaks. But the ridge ahead is where it gets scary—especially the section known affectionately as the "Crazy Pinnacles." And once past the Munro top of Stob Coire Leith, there is no easy way down from Aonach Eagach.

Fortunately, for those of us with vertigo issues, all is not lost. There is an alternative route to the ridge's summit of Meall Dearg from the north, over a rock-strewn and often boggy path with some steep ground as you near the ridge, but it is not a particularly difficult walk and certainly nothing like the above rope-assisted approach. **BDS**

Goatfell Summit Isle of
Arran, Argyll & Bute, Scotland

Start Brodick   **End** Goatfell summit
Distance 10.5 miles (16.8 km)   **Time** 3 hours
Grade Strenuous   **Type** Roads, forest paths, moorland
Map goo.gl/ZeCHd7

A Corbett, in Scottish Highland speak, is any peak with a height of between 2,500 feet (762 m) and 3,000 feet (914 m), with a minimum 500-foot (152-m) prominence. The first list of 221 Corbetts was compiled in 1921 by the British climber John Rooke Corbett. Today, the total stands at 449, one of which is Goatfell summit on the northern end of the Isle of Arran.

If you only have a day to spare, it's possible to catch the CalMac ferry from the Scottish mainland, make a reasonably strenuous three-hour ascent from Brodick to the summit, and then head back down

"A spectacular example of an open, rugged, upland landscape formed during the last ice age."

www.nts.org.uk

again in time to board the afternoon ferry home. An alternative route begins in the exquisite seaside village of Corrie, 6 miles (9.7 km) to the north of Brodick.

The quicker route follows the coastal road through Brodick, while the climb proper begins at Cladach. Waymarked paths at Cnocan tempt you to the left or right of the main path, but keep your eyes straight and continue until you pass through a gateway in an old drystone wall. As you gain altitude, the stands of birch begin to thin out, and you cross a heathery, grassy moorland before a steep gradient takes you to the shoulder of Meall Brac. From there it's a steep climb through boulders and granite outcrops to the summit, with the entire Isle of Arran squarely at your feet. **BDS**

Three Peaks Challenge
Scotland/England/Wales

Start/End Fort William, Scotland   **End** Snowdonia, Wales
Distance 24 miles (38.6 km)   **Time** 24 hours   **Grade**
Strenuous   **Type** Various   **Map** Ben Nevis: goo.gl/etUW2I ;
Scafell Pike: goo.gl/Qc1uOa ; Snowdon: goo.gl/c1zz1B

Stepping from your car at 2 a.m. in unappealing darkness at the foot of Scafell Pike, the Three Peaks Challenge suddenly doesn't seem such a good idea. By lunchtime, however, hopefully staggering down from the summit of Snowdon, your aching limbs are rewarded by a great sense of achievement. The concept is simple enough: walk up the three highest mountains in Scotland, Wales, and England often within twenty-four hours. The details are trickier. You need a driver willing to rush you between the Scottish Highlands, English Lake District, and Snowdonia in North Wales, a total distance of 450 miles (724 km). So most attempts are made in teams, often for charity, with a designated driver resting during the climbs.

The accepted starting point is the foot of Ben Nevis, Britain's highest peak. The "tourist path" doesn't involve any scrambling but is a serious mountain walk with the hazards that implies: it often involves navigation to the summit in snow and whiteout conditions. Ideally, you survive and descend at sunset, to be driven through the night to England's Scafell Pike. The lowest of the three peaks is nevertheless the hardest, with a boulder-strewn route and a rocky scramble to the summit made more demanding by the darkness and bleariness of the early hours.

Most Three Peak attempts happen in midsummer and, if all goes according to plan, the sun is rising as you descend, compensating weary walkers with a glorious view of the valley below. Another long drive then takes you to Snowdon in Wales. This midday walk has the greatest chance of good views, but care is needed on the initial descent down the Miners' Track, where exhausted muscles can lead to mistakes. **SH**

> *"It will be one of the most memorable experiences you will have."*

www.ukchallenges.co.uk

⬆ When you reach the Wasdale approach to Scafell Pike during the challenge, it will be shrouded in darkness.

Pony Path to Cadair Idris

Gwynedd, Wales

Start/End Ty Nant   Distance 3.1 miles (5 km)
Time 1.5 hours one way
Grade Easy   Type Forest trails, open fields
Map goo.gl/fMwR2m

Cadair Idris (2,927 feet/892 m) is located at the southern end of Snowdonia National Park and is the second most popular mountain in Wales after Snowdon, despite only being Wales's seventeenth highest mountain. But despite failing to attain the 3,000-foot (914-m) mark, which seems to be a kind of barometer among Welsh mountains when it comes to grandeur, the views from its ridge are no less impressive, especially when looking down upon the craterlike lake of Llyn y Gadair and across to the Mawddach Estuary. But before you can do that, you have to get up there, and that's where the much-trodden Pony Path comes in.

The Pony Path begins at the end of the footpath near the parking lot at Ty Nant and continues through a forest of birch, sycamore, and ash. Turn right when you reach a small grove of chestnut trees, and soon you're climbing steadily up a grassy hillside. The trees fall away all except for dwarflike, twisted hawthorns, and the views begin to open up. Markers help you on your way past frost-shattered rocks, and in no time you're on top of cliffs looking over Llyn y Gadair. Then comes a view of Goat Lake, and minutes later you're on the summit.

Being in Wales means Cadair Idris is not without its myths and legends. If you fall asleep on the summit, it is said you'll wake up as either a poet or a madman, and the lakes surrounding it are supposed to be bottomless. It has also been called Arthur's Seat, a reference to King Arthur, though this is the result of a mistranslation. But as anyone who has climbed up the Pony Path will tell you, there's a lot more to Cadair Idris than meets the eye. **BDS**

Glaciers of the Vanoise Circuit Rhône-Alpes, France

Start/End Pralognan-la-Vanoise
Distance 37 miles (59.5 km)   Time 6–7 days
Grade Moderate   Type Various
Map goo.gl/Xku9Th

The trail that takes you on a circuit of the great Glaciers of the Vanoise, in Vanoise National Park in the French Alps, begins in Pralognan-la-Vanoise before passing through the villages of Barioz and Bieux and joining the GR55. Views of the Grande Casse follow, and you end your day at the Refuge du Col de la Vanoise (8,257 feet/2,517 m), built in 1902.

The days that follow are no less dramatic, with plenty of scree walking over the Col de la Masse and a veritable who's-who of Vanoise alpine lakes, including Lac de Plan d'Amont and the twin lakes of Aussois.

"On foot, you can get to understand and really feel part of the mountain environment."

english.parcnational-vanoise.fr

From the Refuge de l'Arpont you can make a steep climb to Lac de l'Arpont on an unmarked trail that requires a little route finding for views of the Glacier de l'Arpont, with the added advantage that you can overnight at the Refuge du Plan Sec (thus gaining more than an hour on the traditional route that involves overnighting in the Refuge du Fond d'Aussois).

There are panoramic views aplenty on this route through the heart of the Vanoise, particularly over to Mont Blanc and the Glacier de la Vanoise, the massif's primary glacier. The circuit ends with a steep descent to the Cirque de l'Arcelin, where you meet up with a cairn-marked path that will take you back to your start point at Pralognan. **BDS**

Aiguilles Rouges Rhône-Alpes, France

Start/End Le Buet   **Distance** 31 miles (49.8 km)   **Time** 4–6 days   **Grade** Moderate
Type Mountain trails   **Map** goo.gl/TmcfnW

If you are looking for a vantage point that gives you views over the glaciers of Mont Blanc, the summits of Chamonix, and the very roof of Europe itself, you can do no better than hike the magnificent Aiguilles Rouges, the Red Rocks of the French Prealps. A crystalline mountainous massif of granite spires encrusted with iron-rich gneiss that glows red in the morning light, the Aiguilles Rouges runs to the north of the Mont Blanc massif and draws multitudes of hikers every summer, lured by its colors, compact ruggedness, abundant flora, and endless views.

The highest point is Belvedere (9,728 feet/2,965 m) in the eastern part of the range. Its name means "beautiful viewpoint," no doubt referring to the 360-degree panorama it gives you of the surrounding peaks, with gorgeous Lac Blanc at its base. There are no glaciers in the Aiguilles Rouges, but some of its faces abound in vegetation that includes sundews, a multitude of orchids, and surprisingly curious ibex. Walks vary from crowded shorter hikes in the southern-facing slopes above Chamonix to more isolated treks for the more adventurous, or you can combine the two experiences into one walk, the splendid "Tour of the Aiguilles Rouges."

Beginning in the tiny village of Le Buet, you cross the Col des Montets pass, and then to Lac Blanc before plunging into the isolated Col de Brevent, leaving the crowds behind. A couple of days of remote walking and staying in mountain refuges follows before a tough two-day climb up Mont Buet, from Vieux Emosson to the summit, a walk that Cicerone guides have lauded as the most beautiful ascent in the world. **BDS**

⊕ Mont Blanc's best vantage point is the Aiguilles Rouges.

Walkers Haute Route France/Switzerland

Start Chamonix, France **End** Zermatt, Switzerland **Distance** 112 miles (180 km) **Time** 13–15 days
Grade Strenuous **Type** Mountain trails **Info** goo.gl/dYypG1

In only two weeks you will have walked in the shadows of ten of the twelve highest peaks in the Swiss and French Alps and through some of their most spectacular valleys. You'll walk through picture-book hamlets and discover meadows, fragrant forests, icy streams, and mighty glaciers. The Walkers Haute Route from Chamonix, France, to Zermatt, Switzerland, is the trek that every mountain lover needs to tackle—providing the prospect of almost 50,000 feet (15,240 m) of ascents along the way doesn't put you off. The route compares well with its famous cousin, the Tour du Mont Blanc; it is longer and higher, and its walking is more arduous. What could be better than trekking from Mont Blanc, western Europe's highest mountain, to the Matterhorn, the continent's most elegant? And don't forget the in-between: eleven mountain passes, each one a vista over an impossibly sublime landscape.

The original route was first laid out toward the end of the nineteenth century, but that was a "truer" example of mountaineering, following the Pennine Alps out of necessity via a series of glacier passes and high enough to come with the very real option of bagging a few 13,000-foot (4,000-m) or higher summits along the way. Today's route never reaches above 9,850 feet (3,000 m), nor does it require the skills of a trained mountaineer or any specialized equipment. It crosses no glacier passes. But you don't need to be on a peak to feel on top of the world. The Grand Combin de la Tsessette, Pigne d'Arolla—they will all tower over you as you weave your way through a complex mass of mountains, cols, and connecting valleys on the walk you always knew you had to do. **BDS**

⬆ Walk in the shadows of Europe's highest peaks.

Tour du Mont Blanc
France/Italy/Switzerland

Start/End Various **Distance** 105 miles (169 km)
Time 10–12 days **Grade** Strenuous
Type Graded mountain trails
Info goo.gl/MqAhoz

First explored on an organized "pedestrian tour" in 1767 and climbed for the first time in 1786, Mont Blanc is where modern-day mountaineering all began. With its 15,780-foot (4,810-m) bulk making it Europe's tallest mountain, Mont Blanc's summit and upper slopes are forever covered in snow and ice. The Italians call her Il Bianco (the White One); the French, La Dame Blanche (the White Lady), though its literal translation is, of course, White Mountain. And while plenty of far-off, panoramic views of the massif are easily had at a dozen viewpoints and resort towns, most notably Chamonix in France, in order to gain a true appreciation of just what the roof of Europe is made of you need to walk through the midst of it. The most famous trail you can walk is the great circumnavigation of the mountain, the Tour du Mont Blanc, the most popular long walk in Europe.

The massif is surrounded and intersected by seven valleys that spread across three countries. Most tours start in Les Houches in France, about 4 miles (7 km) from Chamonix, and most head off in a counterclockwise direction, up to the Col de Voza before descending to Le Champel in the Val Montjoie, along the range's western extremity (though there is also a tougher option up to the Bionnassay glacier). There are a lot of alternative routes on the Tour du Mont Blanc (there are two routes down into the Vallée des Glaciers, for instance), and other peaks that would be magnets themselves anywhere else in the world—Grandes Jorasses, Aiguille du Midi, Mont Dolent—are all mere courtiers among the 400 summits and 40 glaciers that make up the gleaming realm of the White Mountain. **BDS**

"A 105-mile wilderness hike set to make the heart soar and the adrenaline rush."

www.walkingthetmb.com

◩ Walkers take in the scenery of the Col de Voza.

◩ Hike around the Mont Blanc massif where modern-day mountaineering began in the 1700s.

Mont Sainte-Victoire Provence-Alpes-Côte d'Azur, France

Start/End Vauvenargues **Distance** 2 miles (3.2 km) to 40 miles (64 km) **Time** 4 hours to 2 days
Grade Easy to moderate **Type** Well-maintained mountain trails **Map** goo.gl/HvdF3o

Mont Sainte-Victoire fascinated the great artist and Post Impressionist Paul Cézanne almost to the point of obsession. This stunning 3,317-foot-high (1,011 m) limestone peak near the town of Aix-en-Provence is a commanding presence in the surrounding landscape, and for Cézanne it was an endless source of artistic inspiration. It features in paintings such as *Bathers at Rest* (1876–77), *Mont Sainte-Victoire Seen From Bellevue* (1892–95), *Mont Sainte-Victoire* (1902–04), and *Mont Sainte-Victoire Seen From Les Lauves* (1904–1906). In total, the mountain has a presence in more than eighty of his works—oils on canvas, watercolors, and sketches—over more than twenty years. It is fair to say that he loved it, as did Pablo Picasso and Wassily Kandinsky, and once you have walked along some of the 155 miles (250 km) of trails that thread their way over and around it, you may well fall in love, too.

The area surrounding Mont Sainte-Victoire is a designated "Grand Site"—one of three dozen such sites across France recognized for their outstanding natural beauty—with the 11 x 3-mile (18 x 4.8-km) massif of Mont Sainte-Victoire at its center. The most popular routes are those across the top of the massif, all of which involve an hour-long ascent and which vary in length from a four-hour circumnavigation of its perimeter and walking a section of the GR9—which runs along its entire length—to two-day routes around its base. From its summit you can see over the rolling patchwork of Provence's farmlands as far as the southern Alps. And if you have a keen eye—a painter's, perhaps—you'll also see that a mountain doesn't have to blot out the sky to get one's attention. **BDS**

⬆ Climb the mountain that inspired Cézanne.

Lac du Distroit Provence-Alpes-Côte d'Azur, France

Start/End Rabioux Valley trailhead   **Distance** 10 miles (16 km)   **Time** 8 hours
Grade Easy   **Type** Meadows, scree   **Map** goo.gl/0xqOkR

The Lac du Distroit is an infrequently visited lake 8,264 feet (2,519 m) high in Ecrins National Park in a mountainous region in the Dauphiné Alps to the south of Grenoble, above Châteauroux-les-Alpes. It is a land of glaciers, alpine pastures, and subalpine forests. The trail to the lake begins at the trailhead in the Rabioux Valley and ascends from the valley floor along the south-facing slopes beneath the Chabreyret ridgeline, providing great views across the valley to the conifer, pine, and larch-covered slopes of the northern side of this narrow valley. The trail then merges with the expansive alpine pastures of Le Distroit, with almost guaranteed sightings of marmots in the mornings. Golden eagles appear in the afternoons, rising up on the valley's thermals, which makes the sighting of marmots far less likely later in the day. The path continues to gain altitude, and passes a series of shepherd huts at Clot Egout before ascending up the steep slopes of Les Gourpes in the shadows of the Croix de Razinette (8,058 feet/2,456 m), a good spot to stop for lunch.

After lunch descend to a little-used path that winds, beneath the high pastures of the Barre du Distroit and the scree slopes above, to the lake itself. While it may not possess the grandeur of other alpine lakes, what it lacks in size it more than makes up for in solitude. Very few hikers come here, or even know of its existence, and on most days it is possible to sit on its shoreline and not see another living soul. From the lake the trail drops down past an empty cabin in the midst of some abandoned pastures and eventually takes you back toward the parking lot through ancient woodlands filled with 700-year-old larch trees. **BDS**

⬆ A spectacular view of the Rabioux Valley.

Mont Bego Loop
Provence-Alpes-Côte d'Azur, France

Start/End Casterino **Distance** 15.5 miles (25 km)
Time 3 days **Grade** Easy to moderate
Type Mountain trails, open terrain
Map goo.gl/WeHHoO

Mont Bego, at 9,423 feet (2,872 m), is a bulky-looking mountain, but it is by no means the highest peak in the French Maritime Alps. However, what it lacks in elevation it more than makes up for in its wonderfully exposed geology—layers of flat, exposed schist and sandstone, which are covered in thousands of petroglyphs up to 5,000 years old that tell in abundant detail of what life was like for Europe's Bronze Age inhabitants. Mont Bego's slopes are an outdoor gallery, a treasure trove of figures and scenes etched, often deeply, into its rocky canvasses. The quantity of images here is mind-boggling—around 15,000 depictions on more than 1,600 surfaces in the Val Fontanalba sector, in excess of 17,000 figures on almost 2,000 surfaces in the Vallée des Merveilles (Valley of Marvels) in the southern and western sectors, and hundreds more scattered in other outcrops.

Located at an elevation of between 6,562 feet (2,000 m) and 8,858 feet (2,700 m), in what was Italian territory until 1947, access to the various sectors is straightforward, and don't be put off by the place names you have to pass to get there, such as Devil's Peak and Hell Valley. It would all be worth walking through the most uninteresting landscape to visit, but instead the appetizer is almost as mouthwatering as the main course—a land of high cols, glacially shaped valleys, gorgeous lakes, and jagged mountains.

It is thought that Mont Bego was once a sacred mountain, and there is some correlation between the placement of the engravings and the position of the sun during the solstice and equinox. Whatever their initial purpose, the engravings of Mont Bego are worth walking a long way to see. **BDS**

"To understand the remoteness of the Valley of Marvels you must go on foot."

www.completefrance.com

⬆ Bronze-Age rock carvings and designs on the slopes of Mont Bego.

Via Alpina
Monaco to Italy

Start Palace Square, Monaco **End** Trieste, Italy
Distance 3,100 miles (4,989 km)
Time 4–5 months **Grade** Moderate to strenuous
Type Various **Info** goo.gl/pT26jG

It is easy to be daunted by the statistics that accompany the Via Alpina, Europe's first trans-Alps route: eight countries, 342 stages, and more than 3,100 miles (4,989 km), made up of five color-coded sections (red, yellow, purple, green, and blue), one of which— the Red Trail—crosses a national border forty-four times. But the good news about this trail is that, providing you have the time, it is not beyond the means of any reasonably fit person to conquer.

The Purple Trail winds its way through Slovenia, Austria, and Germany, through the Eastern Limestone Alps, and crosses nine of the ten long-distance trails that traverse the Austrian Alps. The Yellow Trail takes you from Trieste, Italy, on the Adriatic Coast, up into the pastures of the Allgäu, through the heart of the Dolomites. The Green Trail, the shortest of the five, begins in Lichtenstein and crosses into the Rhine Valley and the eastern shoreline of Lake Geneva. The Blue Trail follows the Italian/Swiss border, from the glaciers surrounding Monte Rosa and down into the tranquil villages of the Piedmontese and Maritime Alps. The Red Trail, by far the longest with 161 stages, crosses the Julian Alps and Bernese Alps, passes Mont Blanc, and travels through the Aosta Valley and the Ligurian Alps.

The Via Alpina is more than just another long-distance trail. It was created to help preserve the history and cultural heritage of the Alps in a rapidly changing world. Slovenian villages, patron saint festivals in Italy, small farms in rural France, and alpine cheese makers—hundreds of communities benefit from this visionary route, designed to help keep the character of the Alps forever unique. **BDS**

"One of the longest and most spectacular hiking trails in all of Europe and perhaps the entire world."

viaalpina.com

⬆ Europe's first trans-Alpine route will likely be the greatest test of endurance you will ever tackle.

Felsenweg Bürgenstock
Lucerne, Switzerland

Start/End Hammetschwand elevator
Distance 5 miles (8 km)   **Time** 2 hours
Grade Easy   **Type** Well-maintained cliff path,
dirt trails   **Map** goo.gl/ZlRngH

"Mount Bürgenstock is more than a mountain— it's a legend."

www.wanderland.ch

⊡ Hike a mountain beloved by Sophia Loren and Audrey Hepburn—then take this elevator back down.

Some mountains, by virtue of their enviable location, seem to get all the attention. Take Mount Bürgenstock, for example, overlooking Switzerland's Lake Lucerne. The almost mythological hold this mountain has on the Swiss people began with the so-called rock face path, the Felsenweg. In 1900, engineers created a 1.5-mile (2.5-km) panoramic path around the mountain, accessed via the Bürgenstock Bahn, built in 1888 and the oldest electric funicular railway in the country. The path was described at the time as the "most beautiful mountain promenade in the world." Maybe it still is. Audrey Hepburn married Mel Ferrer in the Bürgenstock Chapel in 1954. Sophia Loren had a private villa here. Charlie Chaplin and Yul Brynner vacationed here. Everyone falls in love with the Bürgenstock.

A popular vacation destination since the 1870s, hotels and taverns were built near its summit. The Felsenweg was made predominantly for hotel guests to walk, so they could better admire the lake that was 1,500 feet (457m) below them, and the mountains beyond. Then came that audacious metallic wonder, the Hammetschwand elevator. The highest outdoor elevator in Europe, it still looks as cutting edge in its design as it did when it was completed in 1905. The Hammetschwand took its first passengers' breath away as they soared up through the midst of its 498-foot (152-m) vertical exoskeleton, and still does today.

Once you are up here, the Felsenweg is only the beginning. In two hours you can walk the sloping Bürgenstock summit and venture further, over meadows and through forests—a seductive landscape that has been luring visitors for almost 150 star-studded years. **BDS**

Swiss Path
Lucerne, Switzerland

Start Rütli   End Brunnen   Distance 22 miles
(35 km)   Time 8 hours   Grade Easy to moderate
Type Pathway (partly wheelchair accessible)
Map goo.gl/BMB85e

It is not common in Switzerland for a pathway to be given a name, but an exception was made in 1991 with the Swiss Path. It begins in the mountain meadow of Rütli, on the shoreline of Lake Uri, and continues in a loop to the resort town of Brunnen. It was created to celebrate the 700th anniversary of the Old Swiss Confederacy in 1291, and every Swiss citizen is represented by a 0.25-inch (5-mm) segment of the path.

The path can be walked in either direction and be picked up at several piers along the shore of the lake, as well as by bus and train at each of the towns through which it passes. Starting at Rütli, you climb a gentle 1,148 feet (350 m) to Seelisberg, with its panoramic lake views, before a steep 4-mile (6.5-km) descent to stroller-friendly Bauen. At this point you can opt for an additional two-hour loop between Bauen and Isleten with beautiful vantage points. From there, the path runs for approximately two hours along the lake shore and through a nature reserve on the Reuss delta to Flüelen, the halfway point. The Axenstrasse, one of the most beautiful roads in central Switzerland, is then followed above the steep eastern shore of the lake until you reach the carillon at Tellskapelle at the foot of the Axenberg Cliffs. There, according to legend, William Tell escaped his captors before beginning the rebellion that led to the establishment of the Old Swiss Confederacy.

From Tellskapelle it's a little more than 2 miles (3 km) to Sisikon, and from there it's a 1,300-foot (400-m) ascent to the overlook at Morschach, with its stunning view of the Alps. You then pass through the picturesque village of Stoos before the final walk down into Brunnen and journey's end. **BDS**

Schynige Platte to First
Bern, Switzerland

Start Schynige Platte station   End Upper gondola
station, First   Distance 9 miles (14.5 km)
Time 6–7 hours   Grade Strenuous
Type Mountain trails   Map goo.gl/NaW2rF

If only every trail could begin like this. You're sitting in the open carriages of the Schynige Platte cog railway, first opened in 1893, from Wilderswil via Interlaken over the Lütschine River and through alpine pastures up into the valley of the Bernese Oberland. As you ascend, the three white giants of Eiger, Mönch, and Jungfrau appear, before the line ends at Schynige Platte station at 6,520 feet (1,987 m), after a journey of only 4.5 miles (7.25 km) and an elevation gain of 4,659 feet (1,420 m). Some might say the "fun part" is done with. Others would say it has hardly begun.

"This one-day hike is in a class of its own . . . . The panoramic views you will find here are unrivaled."

www.jungfrau.ch

The trail from Schynige Platte to First is a great Swiss panoramic trail. It begins just below the station platform, where a sign points you to the Faulhornweg, which you take for a short distance until a fork leads you onto a ridge overlooking the Brienzersee, followed by a descent on a metal ladder that deposits you on the Oberberg path. By now, the great views this path is renowned for have opened up as you press on across sloping limestone pavements along the southern flank of the Faulhorn to the Berghotel Faulhorn, Switzerland's oldest mountain hotel. From the hotel, descend to the Gassenboden saddle and down to Lake Bachalpsee. Follow the path past a second lake, until you reach First's upper gondola station. **BDS**

Trift Glacier Suspension Bridge Bern, Switzerland

Start/End Triftbahn tram station
Distance 4 miles (6.4 km)   Time 3–4 hours
Grade Easy to moderate   Type Wooden planks
Map goo.gl/mA8dOQ

As the twentieth century drew to a close, it was still possible to reach the Trift Hut in the mountains beyond the Trift Glacier by crossing the glacier itself. The glacier, however, was retreating, and by 2003 the hut and the trails beyond could no longer be accessed on foot. The toe of the glacier had moved, and where there was once ice, there was now a glacial lake. Something had to be done.

The Trift Glacier is located in the Uri Alps in central Switzerland. It is 3.1 miles (5 km) in length, and has an area of almost 6.5 square miles (17 sq km), dimensions

> *"There aren't many hikes in the Alps that can pack as much adventure into a half-day outing."*
>
> www.alpenwild.com

that aren't particularly noteworthy. But what makes this glacier something of a novelty is what now spans it— the solution to accessing the Trift Hut beyond—the world's longest pedestrian-only suspension bridge.

This beautiful bridge spans 560 feet (170 m) and is 330 feet (100 m) high. It was completed in 2009 and replaced an earlier bridge built in 2004. To get to the bridge you take the Trift cable car across the Trift gorge and on to the Trift valley, and from there it is about an hour's walk to the bridge, a lightweight piece of engineering made of steel, aluminum, and natural wood. It provides a view that is hard to take your eyes off in a gorge where the wind can be funneled at speeds of up to 124 miles per hour (200 kph). **BDS**

Eiger Trail Bern, Switzerland

Start Eigergletscher alpine station   End Alpiglen alpine station   Distance 3.7 miles (6 km)   Time 2 hours
Grade Easy to moderate   Type Rock and gravel paths, scree fields   Map goo.gl/xAQGY5

The Eiger, the Mönch, and the Jungfrau in the Bernese Oberland represent the Triple Crown of Swiss mountains. There are few sights in the world of mountaineering that compare to the overwhelming spectacle of standing at the base of the 5,900-foot (1,800-m) vertical north face of the limestone buttress that is the Eiger, and although the Panorama Trail might provide you with a better overall view of this towering monolith, no trail gets you physically closer to it than the aptly named Eiger Trail.

The Eiger Trail is a superb high-alpine adventure that takes you through the lake-filled landscape of the Grindelwald—which can have snow even in summer— and past a glorious waterfall; it also brings you to within touching distance of the mountain's legendary north face. The trail is straightforward and not technical—just follow the yellow markers that say "Eiger trail—Alpiglen 2h" through a large scree field, followed by a descent through another scree field and alpine pastures and past a number of small cairns erected as a memorial to those whose lives have been taken while trying to complete one of mountaineering's greatest challenges. A number of narrow gullies follow, as well as waterfalls of varying sizes, before the trail turns left toward Alpiglen. The path is not wide; however, there is no exposure and it is well maintained.

The Eiger was first conquered in 1858, and first referred to as "mons Egere" in documents dating to the mid-1200s. So you are walking in the shadows of not only one of the world's greatest mountains, but also the first high peak in the Swiss Alps to be given a traceable name. **BDS**

Titlis Cliff Walk
Bern/Obwalden, Switzerland

Start/End Ice Flyer chairlift station
Distance 328 feet (100 m) **Time** 10 minutes–1 hour
Grade Easy **Type** Stainless steel, stretch metal
Info goo.gl/8gaNHD

Familiarizing yourself with the numbers only does so much in preparing you for what is to come. You will be 1,640 feet (500 m) above the ground and 9,977 feet (3,041 m) above sea level. You will take roughly 150 steps from when you first step onto the bridge to when you step off it 328 feet (100 m) later. The whole structure is just 3.3 feet (1 m) wide, and it sways when the wind blows.

The Titlis Cliff Walk suspension bridge in Switzerland's Urner Alps is the highest suspension bridge in Europe. It was built to celebrate the 100th anniversary of the first cable car to connect the nearby towns of Gerschnialp and Engelberg, which opened in January 1913. The bridge took engineers five months to build and is designed to withstand wind speeds of up to 120 miles per hour (190 kph), and to walk across it costs you nothing.

The views are, of course, spectacular. Mount Titlis (10,623 feet/3,238 m) is the highest peak in this section of the Alps and provides stunning vistas of endless snow-clad peaks and the valley of Engelberg. The bridge spans from the south face of the mountain's summit across to the Ice Flyer chairlift via an underground tunnel and viewing platform, and represents a daunting site—it is on the list of the world's "ten scariest bridges." Although it takes only a few minutes to cross, this is an impossible walk to make without wanting to stop at almost every step to appreciate the Alps from a perspective that has only been possible to enjoy since this beautiful piece of engineering was first unveiled to the world in December 2012. The bridge is closed in bad weather, so check the forecast before planning your trip. **BDS**

"To cross the bridge, you'll need nerves as strong as the steel cables from which it hangs."

www.titlis.ch

⊓ The pulse-racing, heart-stopping, vertigo-inducing Titlis Cliff Walk.

Aletsch Glacier
Valais, Switzerland

Start Jungfraujoch railway station   **End** Fiescheralp
cable station   **Distance** 6–9 miles (9.6–14.5 km)
Time 10 hours   **Grade** Easy to moderate   **Type** Ice,
alpine trails   **Map** goo.gl/MMVLIV

A hike across Switzerland's Aletsch Glacier in the
eastern Bernese Alps—at 14 miles (23 km), Europe's
longest glacier—does not have to be daunting. If
walked with a certified tour group, it is, in fact, a safe
and spectacular experience.

It begins with an ascent to the Jungfraujoch, the
Top of Europe, on its famous railway. At Europe's
highest railway station, you organize yourself into a
roped group and begin your descent down into the
continent's largest glaciated area. In no time at all you
are walking over a vast glacial plain and are on your
way to your first stop, the Swiss Alpine Club's
immaculate Konkordia Hut (9,350 feet/2,850 m).
Located on a rocky outcrop above the glacier, this is
where you stay overnight before embarking on the
great day's walking ahead.

The next day starts with breakfast at 5:30 a.m. and
an early departure at 6:00 a.m. Heading south, a track
takes you back onto the glacier and along a middle
moraine, where the view of the glacier sloping away
to your right fills your field of vision. Its sheer
immensity is overwhelming, despite it being only a
fraction of the glacier's length. Looking back over your
shoulder, it is possible to reconstruct your entire
journey as you cross the glacier to Märjelensee, a lake
on its eastern side, before leaving the ice to follow
easy alpine paths to the cable station at Fiescheralp.

There are plenty of simpler options for viewing
the glacier that don't include actually walking on it,
but why miss an opportunity to cross such a mighty
natural feature? Just contact Grindelwald Sports in
Grindelwald, and let them take you on the glacial ride
of your life. **BDS**

*"The jewel of UNESCO's Jungfrau–
Aletsch World Heritage Site where
… an endless stream of ice makes
its way toward the majestic peaks."*

www.myswitzerland.com

◄ Edging toward Konkordia Hut, which overlooks
the glacier.

▲ The Aletsch Glacier is Europe's longest—a good
reason to walk across, not along, it.

Matterhorn Circuit Valais, Switzerland

Start Jungen (via lift from St. Niklaus) **End** Zermatt **Distance** 70 miles (112 km) **Time** 8–12 days
Grade Strenuous **Type** Rocky paths, glacier crossings, scree fields **Map** goo.gl/o2L8OE

The first three days are easy, but don't be fooled. A circuit of the fabled Matterhorn is a seriously strenuous trek best suited for those with previous mountaineering experience. Most of the second half of the circuit takes place in a high alpine environment that requires strength of body and mind along trails that have linked communities in the surrounding Swiss and Italian valleys for centuries.

It begins gently enough, with a crossing of the Augstbord Pass (9,465 feet/2,885 m), followed by a descent on a well-groomed path to the village of Gruben. From Gruben you cross the Forcletta Pass before a serious 4,265-foot (1,300-m) descent to the rapidly developing alpine resort of Zinal and a cable car assist up into the high pastures of the Col de Sorebois. The Matterhorn has yet to reveal itself as more descents into valleys follow, as well as a thrilling

crossing of the Haute Glacier d'Armor on your way to the Col Collon (10,112 feet/3,082 m) and the lovely turquoise waters of the Lago di Place Moulin. It isn't until a high-level traverse on the way down to Cervinia that the mountain comes into view, its south face towering above the small alpine village. The walk into Cervinia is a ten-hour slog, but also ten hours of magnificent Matterhorn views. From Cervinia, chairlifts take you to Testa Grigia (11,414 feet/3,479 m), a rocky outlook on the Italian–Swiss border, followed by a descent down glacier slopes to Trockener Steg (9,642 feet/2,939 m). And then the circuit is complete. From Trockener Steg, all that's left is a ride via the Furgg and Furi stations down to Zermatt and the promise of mattresses and filtered coffee. **BDS**

⊞ **The Matterhorn mesmerizes with its classic form.**

Monte Rosa Circuit Switzerland/Italy

Start Mattmark   **End** Zermatt   **Distance** 80 miles (129 km)   **Time** 10–13 days   **Grade** Strenuous
Type Mountain trails, snow   **Map** goo.gl/CdMG7a

Make no mistake, this is one tough walk. It is high altitude, you need to be self-sufficient, the snow can be deep, and there are crevasses, too. It may not possess the singular grandness of Mont Blanc, but there are ten summits in excess of 13,100 feet (4,000 m). When Leonardo da Vinci came here to see it for himself, he remarked that the mountains seemed to dominate even the clouds above them. Located in the Pennine Alps on the Swiss–Italian border, Monte Rosa is Switzerland's highest mountain and the second highest in the alps at 15,203 feet (4,634 m). It is the "Pink Mountain"—a paradise of cascading glaciers, the Matterhorn, the Weisshorn, and the Dom—a massif of Himalayan proportions.

After a day spent acclimatizing in the Saas Valley outside the alpine town of Mattmark, it's up to Monte Moro Pass and into Italy's Piedmont region to see for the first time the grand 6,000-foot (1,828-m) eastern face of Monte Rosa at the head of the Anzasca Valley, the first of many a jaw-dropping panorama. There is the old military mule path that you take up to Passo del Turlo, and the tantalizing faraway view you get of the highest mountain hut in all of Europe—the Capanna Margherita, on Punta Gnifetti. A gondola-assisted ride gets you past the Sasso del Diavolo (Devil's Stone) and on to the Colle del Pinter (9,247 feet/2,818 m) for lunch and stunning views to Mont Blanc and the Grand Combin. Finally, after a gondola ride to Plateau Rosa (11,588 feet/3,532 m) in the midst of the Monte Rosa massif, it's one last, wild walk down the Theodul Glacier to the Trockner Stegg station, and then down to Zermatt. **BDS**

⛶ Monte Rosa and the Gorner Glacier.

Piz Lunghin
Ticino, Switzerland

Start/End Maloja   **Distance** 6 miles (9.6 km)
Time 1 day   **Grade** Moderate to strenuous
Type Scree, mountain paths, open rocky terrain
Map goo.gl/bqz7AO

When you stand on the grassy slopes outside the town of Maloja in Switzerland's Upper Engadin and look across at the pyramid-shaped summit of Piz Lunghin, you could be forgiven for thinking you've bitten off more than you can chew. The summit of Piz Lunghin certainly looks challenging enough—a typical alpine peak, sculpted and steep and only welcoming to those familiar with rope work and with an immunity to vertigo. And therein lies the attraction. The reality is, however, that it isn't all that difficult a climb. As you approach the summit, the trail takes a circuitous route, and the final way to the top is on a footpath that traverses a snowfield, and in no time the summit is tantalizingly close above scree-covered slopes. If you want to feel like a mountaineer and get that alpine "high" without the physical, technical stuff, then 9,120-foot-high (2,780 m) Piz Lunghin is for you.

Approaching Piz Lunghin from Maloja means you need to be self-sufficient: there are no chairlifts or mountain cafés. But man-made diversions are the last thing on your mind as you pass by beautiful 8,149-foot (2,484-m) Lake Lunghin, the source of the Inn River, which you will have followed briefly after leaving Maloja. The path from the lake leads to a flat and rocky, lunarlike landscape, and then a ridge follows with an intimidatingly steep 2,952-foot (900-m) drop to the valley below, although the ridge is sufficiently wide to make it a pretty straightforward traverse.

Once you get to the end of this ridge the dome-shaped summit is just a few minutes' walk away, and from the top you can retrace your ascent from Lake Lunghin all the way to your starting point of Maloja—far, far below. **BDS**

"Magnificent distant views of mountain peaks … and a lake with crystal-clear waters."

www.walkingswitzerland.com

⬆ Don't be fooled by its forbidding appearance—this is an easy, climbable peak via a circuitous route.

Val Roseg

Ticino, Switzerland

Start/End Pontresina
Distance 8.7 miles (14 km)   **Time** 2–3 hours
Grade Moderate   **Type** Unsealed road
Map goo.gl/o2pS57

This walk may not take you to any grand Swiss summits, along saddles, or over mountain passes—if you want that, then there is a mind-boggling choice of options available in Switzerland's Upper Engadin. What this walk down the beautiful Val Roseg will do, however, is get you into the very heart of the mountains on trails that will have you looking mostly up, rather than down, as you pass waterfalls, coniferous forests, a swift-flowing glacial river, majestic rocky outcrops, a gorgeous glacial lake at the head of the valley, and the summit of Piz Bernina (13,284 feet/4,049 m), the highest mountain in the Eastern Alps and the most easterly peak higher than 13,100 feet (4,000 m). And the best place to stay for any forays into the Val Roseg is Pontresina, an historic mountain village full of traditional Engadine houses and grand belle époque hotels. Why? Because here the valley trail begins at your doorstep—no need to arrange cars or drop-offs or annoying pickups. You just start walking. Or, if you like, you can take a horse-drawn carriage.

Carriages have been taking visitors from Pontresina into the Val Roseg to the Hotel Restaurant Roseg Glacier (6,562 feet/2,000 m) for decades, in summer and winter. A popular choice for many who do this is to then walk the 4.5 miles (7.2 km) back to Pontresina along an unsurfaced road, through forests of fragrant stone pine and larch, to admire the views and walk off a hearty meal. At the hotel there is a 1.2-mile (2-km) glacier trail that leads to the base of the Roseg Glacier, and, if you've a few days to spare, a series of valley trails can take you deep into the Bernina massif, for that "peak" Swiss experience. **BDS**

Fürstensteig Trail

Liechtenstein

Start Gaflei   **End** Planken   **Distance** 7.5 miles (12 km)   **Time** 5 hours   **Grade** Moderate to strenuous   **Type** Well-maintained unpaved stone and rock paths   **Map** goo.gl/DWk5bp

For a civilized, quaint little place that can make even Switzerland seem noisy, Liechtenstein's Fürstensteig Trail is really out there. It has been called "treacherous" and the views "dizzying"; certainly no place for anyone who suffers vertigo. It clings to the edge of the mountainside on paths that have been virtually sculpted into the rock face and are little more than goat tracks on occasions, while being well graded and quite safe. The trail is almost a rite of passage for every Liechtensteiner and the most famous hike you can do in this 62-square-mile (160-sq-km) principality.

"The Fürstensteig trail wends its way through the clouds above the Rhine valley at 2,000 meters . . ."

The Independent

Also known as the "Prince's Path," it first began to be chiseled out in 1898 to provide a precipitous pathway to Austria, and it begins gently enough at an altitude of 4,593 feet (1,400 m), passing through Alpine meadows. Soon, however, it starts its climb up and along the ridgelines of the Rhaetian Alps, including the walk's spectacular high point of Kuhgrat Ridge (6,965 feet/2,123 m). The more exposed sections have steel wire cables and balustrades to grab onto; however, it certainly pays to be a sure-footed hiker. There's no doubt though that this would be a premier hike in whatever country it happened to traverse; the fact Liechtenstein can claim it is an adrenalin-filled coup for this tiny Alpine nation. **BDS**

Princess Gina Trail
Liechtenstein

Start/End Malbun   **Distance** 7.5 miles (12 km)
Time 5 hours   **Grade** Moderate
Type Narrow mountain paths, open terrain
Map goo.gl/XYUvcd

"Hikers who have the time should not miss out on climbing the Naafkopf peak."

www.tourismus.li

⬆ Steel ropes over ridgelines and along craggy paths help you keep your footing on this panoramic hike.

Named in honor of the much-loved Princess Gina of Liechtenstein, the wife of Prince Franz Josef II and mother of ruling Prince Hans-Adam II, this fabulous circular hike begins in the town of Malbun where you are presented immediately with a choice that separates the real hikers from, well, the rest of us. You can either take the chairlift to the station at Sareis (a 1,312-foot/400-m ascent that saves an hour), or just crack on. If you do decide to take the lift you cannot be judged—anything that gets you up onto the higher elevations of this beautiful trail any sooner has to be worth considering.

The high point of the trail is the summit of Augstenberg mountain (7,739 feet/2,359 m), which is actually on the border of Switzerland and Austria. From the top of this peak you have an unforgettable panorama of Swiss and Tyrolean peaks stretching to the horizon. The summit of Augstenberg is difficult to leave behind until you realize that the path down to the Pfälzerhütte (6,916 feet/2,108 m) has excitement of its own—a steep, tortuous trail secured by wire ropes on its more exposed sections that keeps your mind focused on the next step. The Pfälzerhütte is everything a mountain hut should be: wonderfully situated high in the Naaftal Valley with eleven beds, fifty-one dormitory bunks, and a cavernous group room. It is also a perfect starting point for climbing Naafkopf (8,432 feet/2,570 m), Liechtenstein's third-highest peak, if the urge should grab you.

From the Pfälzerhütte, the path takes you down to Alp Gritsch and into pine forests to the village of Tälihöhi, and the final descent back through meadows and pastures to Malbun. **BDS**

Rappenstein Hike

Liechtenstein

Start/End Steg   **Distance** 8.7 miles (14 km)
Time 5 hours **Grade** Strenuous
Type Mountain paths, open terrain
Map goo.gl/RWTyUh

The initial sight of the Rappenstein from the Rhine Valley below—part of an assemblage of peaks that rises nearly 6,000 feet (1,828 m) above the surrounding meadows—can intimidating, with its west-facing slopes, all craggy and steep, daring you to scale them. Its eastern face, however, is more benign: a mix of grassy slopes with manageable gradients; the sort of approach that almost anyone can do along an extraordinary carpet of high Alpine greenery. And the same rewards await you at the top.

The trail begins in the mountain resort town of Steg and goes to the Sücka mountain hut before branching off to the left at Kulm to follow the primary ridge of the Liechtenstein Alps, an undulating walk that takes you to the Rappenstein Saddle via the Goldlochspitz (6,923 feet/2,110 m). From there you descend onto the saddle and make your way forward, with magnificent views over the Falknis Range to the south to spur you on. Once you reach the summit of Rappenstein (7,290 feet/2,222 m), the views are truly breathtaking—over the Rhine Valley to Switzerland's Glarus and Appenzell Alps. To return, just head back down the saddle and take the right branch of the trail down to Alp Gapfahl, and follow the Valuna Valley back to Steg.

The Rappenstein Trail is the most practical way to reach the summit, but is by no means the only way. You can also drive from Kulm through Triesenberg towards the ridge. Follow the Kulstrasse to a narrow tunnel, get out of your car, walk through the tunnel, and you'll see a sign to Rappenstein that will soon lead you to the main ridge trail in a well-signed country that always provides plenty of options. **BDS**

Grüschaweg

Liechtenstein

Start/End Vaduz   **Distance** 6.8 miles
(10.9 km)   **Time** 3.5 hours   **Grade** Easy
Type Mountain and forest trails
Map goo.gl/VxbOi2

There can't be many more agreeable and wholly civilized places from which to start any walk than in the quiet, traffic-free, and pedestrian-friendly Market Square of Liechtenstein's capital Vaduz. The Grüschaweg (Grüscha Way) begins on the Schlossstrasse pathway, which leaves Vaduz and heads up through steep forested slopes to the Kanzile, a small overlook that gives fine views back over the town and its surrounds. The Schlossstrasse continues to Vaduz Castle, the palace and official residence of the Prince of Liechtenstein, which sits majestically on its cliff-side promontory.

> *"At intervals, information boards along the route relate stories from the huge wealth of sagas."*
>
> www.wanderland.ch

The route then runs through the Princely Forest, along a nicely graded mountain path toward the village of Triesenberg where you can visit the Walser Museum, see a 400-year-old traditional Walser house that is still standing near the town cemetery, and learn the history of the Walser people—speakers of a German dialect who migrated through the Alps in the twelfth and thirteenth centuries. There are also reminders of Walser folklore in the form of wooden sculptures created by local artist Rudolf Schädler.

Upon reaching the tranquil hamlet of Rotaboda the signposts begin to point back in the direction of Vaduz Castle, and back down the hill to the Market Square in Vaduz. **BDS**

Hermann's Walk North Rhine-Westphalia/Lower Saxony, Germany

Start Rheine End Velmerstot
Distance 106 miles (170 km) Time 8 days
Grade Easy Type Forest trails
Info goo.gl/iYMN8E

Hermann's Walk in the Teutoburg Forest, a range of forested hills in the northern Central Uplands of Lower Saxony and North Rhine-Westphalia, was named after the first century CE Germanic chieftain Arminius (or Hermann), who led an alliance of German tribes to overwhelming victory against three Roman legions at the Battle of Teutoburg Forest in 9 CE, killing an estimated 15,000 Romans. Hermann has been a symbol of German national unity ever since, and a monumental statue of him can be seen in the town of Detmold, close to the reputed battle site.

"The trail passes many sights of historical interest [and] is dotted with dramatic natural features."

www.germany.travel

There is much to like about this walk that leads from the lowlands of Münsterland to the historic centers of Detmold and Tecklenburg. It follows a series of ridgelines that provide panoramic views, and it is easily navigable with no significant ascents or descents. It passes by the Hermann Monument; Bad Iburg Castle; and the Externsteine, five extraordinary rock pillars that were a sacred site for centuries before paganism was outlawed by Charlemagne in 782 and it became a home for hermit monks.

The winding, narrow paths are never more than a few miles from the nearest town. Ravines, heaths, meadows, and spruce—this scenery is, as Arminius himself might have said, worth fighting for. **BDS**

Harz Witches' Trail Lower Saxony/Saxony-Anhalt, Germany

Start Osterode, Lower Saxony End Thale, Bode Valley, Saxony-Anhalt Distance 58 miles (93 km)
Time 3.5–4 days Grade Easy Type Footpath
Map goo.gl/nFhl27

The Harz Witches' Trail is part of the broader Harzer Wandernadel, a trail system that threads its way through the highest mountain range in northern Germany and encompasses three federal states. It begins in the medieval town of Osterode in Lower Saxony, passes through the Harz and Upper Harz national parks, crosses the old Iron Curtain, and ends in the Bode Valley, near Thale in Saxony-Anhalt, one of the most geologically diverse rock canyons north of the Alps.

The network of trails throughout the Harz has gained an enthusiastic following, but few are as beloved as the enchanting Witches' walk that mixes culture with history and more than 1,000 years of iron-ore mining. It takes walkers through picturesque villages full of half-timbered houses, along ancient trade routes over the Clausthal-Zellerfeld plateau, and across moorlands to the optional ascent of Brocken Mountain—at 3,746 feet (1,142 m), the Harz's highest peak—where legend has it that witches gathered on Walpurgis Night (the traditional spring festival when April turns into May). You can give the summit a miss, though, walk through a series of unspoiled brooks and meadows, and reconnect with the trail farther on. There are ditches and tunnels to navigate, including the Dyke Ditch, the longest artificial ditch in the Upper Harz and a vestige of a complex irrigation system dating back to the sixteenth century, and a dripstone cave, the result of geological processes deep within the Harz's layers of gypsum, dolomite, and limestone. The Witches' Trail is a rare example of nature harnessed successfully for the common good. **BDS**

➔ The sylvan charms of Germany's Harz Witches' Trail.

Southern Harz Karst Trail

Lower Saxony to Saxony-Anhalt, Germany

Start Pölsfeld   **End** Förste   **Distance** 145 miles (233 km)   **Time** 2 weeks   **Grade** Moderate
Type Rock and dirt paths, some asphalt
Info goo.gl/gNCeig

If you love to walk but also have an abiding interest in geology, then the Southern Harz Karst Trail is for you. The trail passes through the largest deposits of gypsum rock cover in Central Europe and displays a wealth of karst phenomena, including creeks that disappear and reappear where water levels change drastically, disappearing into the ground and carried down subterranean passageways of limestone and dolomite rock, only to reemerge elsewhere.

This is a landscape rich in biological diversity that has been eroded over eons into a land of 20,000 sinkholes, as well as dolines, hollows, and vast underground caves, including the Heimkehle show cave. But the trail isn't without its dangers: the fractious nature of karst rock sees more than 5 tons (4.5 tonnes) of debris every year break free from the interiors of its many caves and overhangs, and crash to the cave floor or valley below. If you see signs warning against entering a cave or scrambling over a rocky outcrop, take note.

Few hiking routes can rival this trail when it comes to demonstrating the pervasive power of water. At the Rhume Spring, a confluence of limestone and karst layers, water is forced to the surface at the rate of 88 cubic feet (2.5 cu m) of water per second—528,000 gallons (200,000 L) a day. Two hundred and forty million years ago, the karst cliffs at Westersteine were covered by a shallow inland sea, and as with most seas, there was once a reef. Looking closely, it is still possible to see which side of the formation faced the open water and which side was open to the calmer lagoon. A "trail of secrets" indeed, but secrets that are happily shared with those with a keen eye and an enquiring mind. **BDS**

"The walking trail snakes its way through a fascinating region of high biodiversity, [with] rare and heavily protected flora and fauna."

www.germany.travel

⭱ Outcrops of gypsum and a wealth of karst formations provide much to keep both mind and body busy.

Erzgebirge–Vogtland Ridge Trail
Saxony, Germany

Start Altenberg-Geising   **End** Blankenstein
Distance 180 miles (290 km)   **Time** 2–3 weeks
Grade Moderate   **Type** Mountain trail
Info goo.gl/ASpSS9

Marking the border between Germany and the Czech Republic, the Erzgebirge (the name means Ore Mountains) drop abruptly to Czech Bohemia on the southern side and melt gently into Saxony to the north. The trail along the ridge, a 2011 revival of an old hiking trail dating from 1904, lies just inside the German border. It links a string of modest peaks, topped by Mount Fichtelberg at 3,986 feet (1,215 m), and also medieval villages and towns accessed by short spur trails. Two-thirds of the way along the trail, the ski resort of Oberwiesenthal is the highest town in Germany at around 3,000 feet (914 m).

The complete trail takes between two and three weeks, depending on the time given to the numerous distractions along the way. These range from Seiffen Toy Village, whose woodworking studios supply toys and nutcrackers to Christmas markets all over Germany, to narrow-gauge steam trains at Pressnitz. There are also lakes and rivers to see, as well as the basalt columns at Hirtstein, ruined castles, and romantic lookouts.

This region formed part of East Germany before German reunification. As the name suggests, the Ore Mountains are laden with metals and minerals, and old tin mines and silver mines dot the trail, some of which are open to the public. During the Cold War, the mountains were mined for uranium in a secret operation to supply the Soviet Union's nuclear industry. A relic from World War II is the Lehesten Wall at Sparnberg, where long-range ballistic missiles were tested by the Nazis and later the Soviets. Less sinisterly, topaz, also known as the "Saxony diamond," is also found in the mountains, most visibly at Topaz Cliff, the glittering outcrop of Schneckenstein. **DS**

"The uphill climb is worth the effort as the Erzgebirge rewards you with stunning panoramic views over idyllic landscapes."

www.erzgebirge-tourismus.de

⬆ An almost forgotten 100-year-old hiking trail is revived along the German–Czech Republic border.

Berchtesgaden National Park
Bavaria, Germany

"*Here, you can leave the noise and stress of everyday life far behind and draw new energy from the untouched landscapes.*"

www.koenigssee.com

⤒ Berchtesgaden National Park has hundreds of miles of trails through the gorges and meadows of the Eastern Alps.

Start/End Kugelmühle parking lot
Distance 5 miles (8 km)   **Time** 2–3 hours
Grade Easy   **Type** Well-maintained gorge trail, open fields, forest paths   **Info** goo.gl/Eb6TrE

The beginnings of today's Berchtesgaden National Park—an area of 21,000 acres (8,500 ha) in the southeast of the park—came under the protection of the state in 1910 and was organized after the national park model that had been pioneered in the United States with the creation of Yellowstone National Park in 1872. Today, it has grown to 51,890 acres (21,000 ha), stretching from Lake Königssee to Grosser Watzmann (8,900 feet/2,713 m), the highest mountain located within German territory and the superstar of the Berchtesgadener Land. The only national park in the German Alps, it has a simple motto: "to leave nature to its own devices"—stewardship with minimal human interference.

Berchtesgaden National Park now has in excess of 142 miles (229 km) of walking trails, everything from light trails through alpine meadows to alpine slogs up to mountain summits. There is a 2-mile (3.2-km) round trip to the viewpoint of Malerwinkl over Lake Königssee, a 3.8-mile (6-km) return walk to the base of Grosser Watzmann peak's east face, an 8-mile (13-km) round trip along the alpine pastures of the Bindalm to the Austrian border and back, and an 11-mile (18-km) return hike to the top of Gotzenalm, an area of high pasture on the western end of the Hagen Mountains with fabulous views over the Watzmann massif.

One popular hike is on the trail along Almbach Gorge, one of the most beautiful gorges in the Eastern Alps with waterfalls and crystal-clear pools of mountain-fresh water. The hike, too, is full of options, including a spur to Maria Gern, Berchtesgaden's most beautiful church, and various trails to typically green, serene Bavarian high alpine pastures. **BDS**

Höllental Loop, Zugspitze
Bavaria, Germany

Start/End Kreuzeckbahn Talstation **Distance**
11 miles (17.7 km) **Time** 8 hours **Grade** Moderate
to strenuous **Type** Well-maintained stone paths
Map goo.gl/BxVO9e

The Höllental (Hell Valley) Loop around the base of
the Zugspitze, Germany's highest mountain, has been
described as "a hike through hell to see heaven." This
moderate to strenuous trail begins and ends at
the lower Kreuzeckbahn Talstation and takes around
eight hours to complete. It can be divided into
the following segments: from the Kreuzeckbahn
Talstation through the Höllental Gorge to the cottage
at the Höllentalangerhütte; from the cottage to the
Kreuzeckbahn Bergstation (at the summit); and from
there back to the starting point at the Talstation. The
best time to complete the circuit is from late May to
mid-October when the Höllentalangerhütte is open.

Though the word "Zugspitze" has been mentioned,
there is no need to feel daunted at the prospect of
circling this beautiful, imposing mountain that is
home to the country's only glacier. Elevation gains are
minimal, and there is the fabulous Höllental Gorge to
negotiate—enough of a reason to come here in itself.
In the gorge there are lit tunnels hewn into the cliffs,
small bridges to cross, and steps to climb, and all the
while the turquoise glacial waters of the Hammersbach
stream thunder away below you. Of course, it is also
possible to climb to the summit of the Zugspitze,
which was first conquered in 1920, but if you have no
energy left after eight hours of serious hiking, there
are three motorized options to the top: the Bavarian
Zugspitze railway, the Tyrolean Zugspitze cable car,
and the Eibsee cable car, the last departing from near
the shoreline of Eibsee Lake with an elevation gain
along the way of 6,398 feet (1,950 m). However, if you
feel like you've cheated upon reaching the summit,
well, you can always walk down. **BDS**

*"The route through the Höllental
counts as one of the classic
hiking trails and is among the
most beautiful and exciting."*

www.real-adventure.eu

⬆ Circling Germany's highest mountain still leaves
open the option of getting to the top—via cable car.

E5, Oberstdorf to Merano

Germany/Austria/Italy

Start Oberstdorf   **End** Merano
Distance 101 miles (162 km)
Time 7–10 days   **Grade** Strenuous
Type Mountain trail   **Map** goo.gl/BHokjh

The Alpine chunk of the E5 long-distance trail that stretches from the Atlantic coast to Verona, Italy, is one of the great routes through the Alps. Carved out by pilgrims and traders centuries ago, it wriggles along soaring ridges and plunges down valleys. This natural roller coaster takes in Germany, Austria, and Italy and can be completed over the course of a week. The trail breaks down into manageable day-long hikes, with overnight stops in alpine *hütten*—wooden chalets with flower-decked balconies and restaurants lined with hunting trophies. Backpacks can be placed on freight cable cars on some sections of the trail.

From the ski resort of Oberstdorf in Bavaria, the route passes through meadows straight out of *The Sound of Music* (1965) to rocky chasms with icy waterfalls fed by snowmelt, and dark and silent forests. Magnificently horned ibex and the resonant sound of cowbells flesh out the alpine idyll, and there are plenty of cozy inns where weary hikers can refuel with coffee and a slice of apple strudel.

The highest point on the hike is the Pitztaler Joch (9,826 feet/2,995 m high), then the trail passes the Rettenbacher and Tiefenbacher glaciers and crosses into Italy at Timmelsjoch, a high pass connecting the Otztal and Passeier valleys. Do not be surprised to find signs saying "Wilkommen"—the overwhelming flavor in this autonomous region of northern Italy is more Austrian than Italian, reflecting the fact that it was part of the Austro-Hungarian Empire until the end of World War I. You will see men in lederhosen and will quite likely be greeted by a cheery "Grüss Gott!" rather than "Buon giorno!" even when you get to sophisticated Merano, the final stop. **DS**

> *"Fresh mountain air, wonderful landscapes, and diverse fauna invite you to tie your hiking boots."*

www.oberstdorf.de

⬆ From Bavaria through Austria to Italy, this segment of the E5 is one of the great routes through the Alps.

Stubai Rucksack Route
Tyrol, Austria

Start Neder   End Neustift
Distance 50 miles (80 km)   Time 9 days
Grade Strenuous   Type Various
Map goo.gl/tJOC8p

Drivers heading south at great speed through southern Austria and the Brenner Pass into Italy will probably ignore the Stubai Alps to their west, a range of mountains named after the Stubaital Valley on their eastern side. It is a remote area, but also a hiker's paradise, crisscrossed with numerous paths and more adventurous trails. One of the best is the Rucksack Route, a hardy nine-day trail through some stunning alpine scenery.

The Stubai Rucksack Route starts in the village of Neder and heads in a southerly clockwise direction toward the Italian border before heading back north to almost complete the circuit at the village of Neustift. Both villages are easily accessible from Innsbruck. Each night of the trek is spent in a hut, a misnomer for what is actually more like a guesthouse or mountain inn, complete with a restaurant, shop, and other amenities. Reservations are not required unless you are with a large party.

The trail itself—which can be completed in a shorter time if you really push yourself—follows grassy or rocky mountain paths, although there is quite a lot of scrambling over rock scree and sometimes snow. Some of the sections are steep, the trail itself rising 6,315 feet (1,924 m) up to the highest point—the 9,480-foot-high (2,890 m) Grawagrubennieder pass—at around the halfway stage. Along the way, longer alternative routes can be taken between huts, and short excursions can be added to climb nearby mountains or to visit photogenic lakes. Given the high altitude, it is advisable to do the walk between July and mid-September, when the weather is warm and almost all the snow has melted. **SA**

Pinzgau Ridgeway
Salzburg, Austria

Start Schmittenhöhe   End Stuhlfelden
Distance 15.5 miles (25 km)   Time 1–2 days
Grade Easy   Type Mountain trails
Map goo.gl/iet1hW

Located in the Kitzbühel Alps and part of Route 02 A, the Austrian long-distance path, Pinzgau Ridgeway, runs along gentle, slate-encrusted crests and peaks for 16 miles (26 km), at an average height of 6,561 feet (2,000 m). The ridgeway is 3,280 feet (1,000 m) above, and parallel to, the lovely Salzach Valley below, with constant and spectacular views over the peaks of the High Tauern and the Zillertal Alps. And it also affords fine views of some of Austria's mightiest peaks— Grossglockner, Kitzsteinhorn, Granatspitze, Sonnblick, and Grossvenediger.

"Schmittenhöhe is popular for skiing, but when the snow melts, it boasts luscious green meadows ..."

www.kaprunerhof.at

You can take a cable car to Schmittenhöhe (6,446 feet/1,965 m) above the town of Zell am See, then start walking westward over the Kettingtörl (5,839 feet/1,780 m) and the Kettingkopf (6,118 feet/1,865 m) to the Pinzgau Hut (5,577 feet/1,700 m). The trail does at times follow the crest of the ridge, but most of the time runs just below it. Refuge huts are never far away, and variations to the official route abound with peaks such as Maurerkogel (6,804 feet/2,074 m) and Leitenkogel (6,610 feet/2,015 m) within easy reach. The final climb is to Bürgl Hut (5,574 feet/1,700 m) and then down to the Mühlbach Valley and to the town of Stuhlfelden in the Salzach Valley. Experienced hikers can do it all in one long, immensely rewarding day. **BDS**

Hallstatt Trail Upper Austria, Austria

Start/End Catholic church cemetery, Hallstatt   **Distance** 1.5 miles (2.4 km)   **Time** 1 hour   **Grade** Easy
Type Forest trail, paved road   **Map** goo.gl/vZLKEp

The village of Hallstatt, a UNESCO World Heritage town on the shores of Lake Hallstatt in the Dachstein region of Austria, is a gorgeous sight even at street level, wedged in between the lake and the mountains that rise up a stone's throw from the waterfront. A market town since the early fourteenth century, Hallstatt used to be somewhat difficult to reach—the only way to get here until well into the 1890s was either by boat or by walking along one of many serpentine trails that surround it. It still has just under 1,000 permanent residents.

Nowadays, of course, a highway brings people here in their hundreds every day to marvel at the town's timeless appearance, strung out along the shoreline of the Hallstatter See. But although times have changed, the trails that were once the town's access to the outside world are still there—they have

even been improved—and it is possible to rise above the throngs of visitors below and climb up above the town on the panoramic trail.

To begin with, look for the Catholic church on the road to Marienruhe (the trail starts in its cemetery) and in no time you will see the views that the trail is named for as you look down upon Hallstatt's signature church spire, the market district, and the ferry docks. A gravel forest road takes you higher still as you pass information boards that tell you the history of the village. The trail winds its way along Mühlbach canyon, one of the prettiest trail segments in the entire Salzkammergut, and provides stunning views over Lake Hallstatt and the vast Dachstein beyond. **BDS**

⬆ Hallstatt is best when seen from above.

Dachstein Ice Cave Upper Austria, Austria

Start/End Dachstein/Krippenstein cable car station **Distance** 2,624 feet (800 m) **Time** 1.25 hours
Grade Easy **Type** Sealed pathway outside, metal boardwalks, and stairs inside **Info** goo.gl/DJrN2q

The Ice Sounds concert series is performed every year by international musicians, many of whom play for some of the world's most prestigious orchestras. Yet you won't hear an Ice Sounds concerto in a concert hall, city park, or anywhere on the streets of Salzburg, Leipzig, or Prague. To hear this performance, you will have to drive into the mountains—up into the big mountains of Upper Austria's Dachstein region, where you park your car, take the Dachstein Krippenstein cable car to its intermediate station, walk up a sealed pathway to a door cut into the side of a mountain, and enter the world of the Dachstein Ice Cave.

Attending an Ice Sounds concert here is a bonus, however. Most visitors come here to marvel at the interiors of these giant caverns of ice and rock. These are extraordinary enough. The caves have been open to visitors since 1913, and the complex contains the Gigantic Ice Cave, one of the world's largest ice caves. Each year it attracts more than 150,000 people, who come to wander its subterranean netherworld of passageways on a one-hour guided walk past Percival Dome and Tristan Dome. Also in the cave complex are Mammoth Cave with its ice formations, Realm of the Shadows, and Midnight Dome, all of which are fed by icy waters that continually seep through the mountain of rock under which they sit. The giant icicles and ice sculptures in this magical environment are sure to enthrall everyone.

Allow a couple of hours to walk the steep path to the entrance and do the tour, and remember to wear something warm—the temperature inside is a constant 35.6°F (-2° C). **BDS**

⊞ The cave lies high above Austria's Trauntal Valley.

Mount Katrin

Upper Austria, Austria

"*The Salzkammergut is a paradise for easy hiking … the Katrin in addition offers fantastic views over the valleys.*"

www.eurothermen.at

⤒ Mount Katrin in western Austria has three peaks and a myriad of possible hiking trails.

Start/End Katrin cable car station, Bad Ischl
Distance 3 miles (4.8 km)   Time 4 hours
Grade Moderate   Type Mountain paths
Map goo.gl/e923Hi

The Salzkammergut region of western Austria is magnificent even by Austria's standards. High snow-topped peaks, wooded mountain slopes, green fertile valleys, and ice-blue lakes make for an impressive sight on any day of the year. One of the more approachable mountains is the 5,060-foot-high (1,542 m) Mount Katrin outside the town of Bad Ischl. There are two ways up and down this mountain, so depending on your fitness levels and stamina, you can either walk or take a cable car. Walking up is perfectly possible, but no one will blame you if you take the cable car back down again to save your weary legs (it runs from May 1 to November 2).

The walk up Mount Katrin is slow, obviously—the cable car races past you in twelve minutes—but the view as you rise up the mountain is breathtaking, with views to the Dachstein Glacier and across the surrounding countryside to seven lakes and three valleys, as well as to the nearby peaks. At the top, you are only a few feet away from the Emperor Franz Joseph summit cross, commemorating the last but one Habsburg emperor, whose nephew was shot at Sarajevo in June 1914, thus prompting the outbreak of World War I a few weeks later.

Different nature and "breathing" trails lead off in various directions. One of the best walks takes you in a circle over the three highest peaks of this mountain: the Katrin itself, the Elferkogel, and the Hainzen. The trail is well marked, and the views from each peak superb. After such an effort, you might find respite in the Katrin alpine chalet, with its range of reviving foods and a sun terrace to enjoy, or in the more upmarket mountain restaurant. **SA**

Heilbronn Circular Trail
Upper Austria, Austria

Start/End Dachstein Krippenstein cable car
station   Distance 3.7 miles (6 km)
Time 3 hours   Grade Easy   Type Gravel paths
Map goo.gl/GiRxXo

Krippenstein stands 6,890 feet (2,100 m) above sea level, commanding Lake Hallstatt and the wider Salzkammergut region of western Austria below. It would be a daunting climb were it not for the cable car that whisks you up the mountainside. Once at the top, the stroll around the summit is surprisingly easy. The Heilbronn Circular Trail starts at the Krippenstein Lodge at the cable car station and proceeds in a clockwise direction past the Ice Cave and steeply up over the Margschierf crest, the path taking you through a real lunar landscape of barren rocks and green meadows full of spring flowers. The next stop is the Heilbronn Cross and then on to the end of the trail, the Gjaidalm alpine center and restaurant.

From here it is but a short walk up to the highlight of the trail at the top of the mountain. The Five Fingers is probably the most spectacular viewing platform to be found in the Alps: the fingers are each about 13 feet (4 m) long and stick out over a chasm that is 1,310 feet (400 m) deep. The finger on the left has a metal frame for taking photographs; the second finger has a glass bottom through which you can look down into the abyss below; the middle finger is shorter than the others and has the feel of a springboard that seems to symbolize the freedom of the mountains; the fourth finger has a hole in the floor for looking straight down; and the fifth finger sports a free telescope for looking at the magnificent views. This may not be for the fainthearted, but if you have made the effort to get this far, a little more exertion will do no harm, and you will be rewarded with magnificent views. **SA**

"The family-friendly trail lends itself to comfortable walking .... And with a bit of luck, you may see some chamois grazing."

www.obertraun.net

⊡ The spectacular Five Fingers platform is just another reason to walk this rewarding circular trail.

Coma Pedrosa Summit La Massana, Andorra

Start/End Arinsal   **Distance** 10.6 miles (17 km)   **Time** 7 hours   **Grade** Strenuous   **Type** Well-defined rock and gravel trail, open rocky terrain   **Map** goo.gl/KS2iVX

The highest point in the landlocked eastern Pyrenees principality of Andorra, the pyramid-shaped Coma Pedrosa (9,656 feet/2,943 m)—surrounded on its lower elevations by glacial lakes, alpine meadows, and forests of fir, pine, and birch—provides a strenuous though straightforward ascent to its summit.

The walk begins at the ski resort of Arinsal at the base of the Ribal waterfall. After ten minutes, take the path to the confluence of the Coma Pedrosa River and the Pla de l'Estany River, cross over two log bridges, and walk through a pleasant narrow valley until you come to a spot that provides a view over the broadening of the upper combe—an impressive sight. Two and a half hours into the walk, you can stop for a drink and a meal at the Coma Pedrosa refuge (7,454 feet/2,272 m), the area's only manned hut, before pressing on for another hour to the Estany

Negre, the Black Lake, given its name because of its dark, frigid waters that are often surrounded by snow, even in summer. From the lake, it is another hour's climb to Coma Pedrosa's summit. You can return by the same route; however, there is an alternative down through Malhiverns pass and back along the left shoreline of the Black Lake to the main path.

There are sixty-five peaks rising to more than 6,500 feet (1,981 m) in this tiny nation, and millions of people are drawn here every year to walk its hills and valleys (although mostly they come to ski). For those who might be wanting a longer time on the trail, the path passes close to the GR11, which runs through the Pyrenees and connects the Mediterranean and Cantabrian seas. **BDS**

⬆ The dark waters of Estany Negre—the Black Lake.

Haute Route Pyrenees France/Spain

Start Hendaye   **End** Banyuls-sur-Mer   **Distance** 559 miles (900 km)   **Time** 6–7 weeks   **Grade** Strenuous
Type Unmarked mountain traverse   **Info** goo.gl/z100MB

How much time you allow for the Haute Route Pyrenees (HRP) is dependent on the usual variables, such as your fitness level, determination, and climbing skills—but it also involves a little guesswork. The distances are hard to estimate, as trail markers only tell you how far you have to go to the next point in hours, not in miles or kilometers, and published distances can vary from as "little" as 497 miles (800 km) to more than 621 miles (1,000 km). Well, what's a couple of hundred kilometers for a hardened walker with some basic rock-scrambling skills and, perhaps, a gap year to fill?

Rock-scrambling skills you will most certainly require and, if there are snowfields, you will also need a trekking pole, crampons, and an ice ax. Naturally, the later in the season you travel, the less snow you will have to deal with—which is a good thing, because on this demanding traverse there are some snowfields, and if you happen to fall into a slide, you could injure yourself.

The HRP is an unmarked trail beginning on the Atlantic Coast at Hendaye, traveling the entire length of the mighty Pyrenees, and finishing in the Mediterranean town of Banyuls-sur-Mer. Unlike the GR10 and GR11, which generally follow a low-level route, the HRP runs on the high ground instead, and often crosses the border from France into Spain and back again, just to get you on the highest possible path. Despite this, it is not a technically difficult walk for the most part, although the constant gaining and losing of altitude can be a little taxing with an estimated total gain of some 30 miles (48 km)—more than enough to make a gap year memorable. **BDS**

⬆ The view from the summit of Pico de Aneto at dawn.

Gavarnie–Ordesa Circuit
France/Spain

Start/End Gavarnie   **Distance** Various
Time Various   **Grade** Moderate to strenuous
Type Snow, graded rock trails, open rocky terrain
Info goo.gl/oMxg92

"Probably the finest single walk in the Pyrenees for drama and variety".

www.walkopedia.net

⬆ There are several 9,840-foot (3,000-m) peaks bordering the cirque, all of which can be easily climbed.

Many who have walked the Gavarnie–Ordesa Circuit say there is no finer walk in the whole of the Pyrenees. Certainly no walk begins with the sort of "bang" this one does, with a walk through the Breche de Roland, the massive notch in the Cirque de Gavarnie cliff line, which is fascinating enough to have an entry all of its own elsewhere in this book.

The most popular starting point is on the French side, where the main valley is located, in the town of Gavarnie. From there, it is a two-hour hike to the base of the cirque, at either end of which are several peaks in excess of 9,840 feet (3,000 m). One of the finest walks in the cirque is a balcony walk that runs along the contours of the upper cirque to Port de Boucharo and the border with Spain, with views out over the grand expanse of cliffs that rise to the main ridge separating France from Spain.

A further series of balcony walks heads back in an easterly direction to the shelves and cliffs above the cirque. As you make your way to the Refuge des Sarradets, you will also be treated to views of Europe's highest single-drop waterfall.

Hiking options here are virtually limitless. The Ordesa Canyon is a 9-mile-long (15 km), beautifully proportioned glacial gauge, up to 3,280 feet/1,000 m deep, that can be walked in six to seven hours and that has Monte Perdido—the third highest peak in the Pyrenees—at its conclusion. Or if ice climbing is your preferred thing, the Cirque de Gavarnie provides the best climbs in Europe outside Norway, with the three natural tiers of the cirque offering a challenging series of tough ascents, particularly the first wall, which is more than 820 feet (250 m) high. **BDS**

Brèche de Roland
France/Spain

Start/End Col de Tentes   **Distance** 3.5 miles (5.6 km)
Time 2.5 hours   **Grade** Moderate to strenuous
Type Rocky, gravel paths, bare rock, scree
Map goo.gl/t162JV

When you first see it, you hardly believe it—a massive gash 131 feet (40 m) wide and 328 feet (100 m) high in a limestone ridge in the Pyrenees that looks as though it has been kicked out by the boot of an angry giant. Naturally, a legend was created to explain it. Count Roland, an eighth-century Frankish officer under the command of Charlemagne who, hundreds of years after his death, became a mythic figure in medieval Europe, sliced the rock open with his sword Durendal in an attempt to destroy the sword after losing the Battle of Roncesvaux Pass in 778. There are better explanations for La Brèche's existence, of course, but none are as interesting.

Geologists call it a "defile"—a notch or gap—a narrow gorge that restricts lateral movement. Part of the Gavarnie–Ordesa massif—the highest limestone massif in Europe—La Brèche de Roland (9,209 feet/2,807 m) sits on the border of France and Spain and can be reached after about an hour's walk from the Refuge des Sarradets (8,487 feet/2,587 m), around 656 feet (200 m) below it, over a steep slope covered in stones and scree. The notch is in the Cirque de Gavarnie, an amphitheater-like valley in the Haute-Pyrenees containing 16 summits in excess of 9,840 feet (3,000 m) and the highest waterfall in Europe, the Grande Cascade, with a drop of 1,417 feet (432 m).

Getting to Gavarnie's famous notch requires effort and stamina and should only be attempted from mid-June to mid-September, beginning at Col de Tentes. From there, it's five hours of hiking joy to a doorway between two countries. And if myths and legends still count for anything these days, maybe a window onto the past, as well. **BDS**

San Adrián Tunnel
Pais Vasco, Spain

Start Zegama (Gipuzkoa province side)   **End** Zalduondo
(Álava province side)   **Distance** 9.3 miles (15 km)
Time 3 hours   **Grade** Easy   **Type** Stone, rock path
Map goo.gl/2HY6K5

Occasionally, a small segment of a much longer walk is worth singling out, and nowhere more so than here. The San Adrián Tunnel is part of the famous pilgrims' walk, the Way of St. James. A natural trail carved out over a millennium by the erosive power of water, the tunnel linking the Basque provinces of Alava and Gipuzkoa has a natural opening at either end and a hermitage in its interior.

Recent archaeological digs have found evidence that a medieval castle of reasonable size once existed just beyond the tunnel entrance, and there are some

---

"The tunnel is perhaps the route that best reflects the Basque Country."

www.tourism.euskadi.net

---

indications that a cemetery and an inn were also built there. The road the Romans built on either side of the San Adrián Tunnel, high in the Montes de Urquilla, linked France to the medieval kingdom of Castile. In fact, the Romans were not the first ones here. A mere 6.5 feet (2 m) below the arch they had built, relics from the Bronze Age have been unearthed. It seems that humans have been walking through this natural hole in the Basque mountains for a very long time indeed. By the thirteenth century, with the constant threat of attacks from the Normans along the coast, the high trail via the San Adrián Tunnel had become a popular alternative route for French pilgrims on their way to the plains of Alava. **BDS**

Sierra de Aitana
Valenciana, Spain

Start Benimantell   End Sella   Distance 60 miles (96.5 km)   Time 4 days   Grade Moderate
Type Mountain and forest trails, mule tracks
Map goo.gl/XVhlTO

It's only thirty minutes' drive from the beaches of the Costa Blanca, yet the Sierra de Aitana massif—the most imposing massif on the Spanish Mediterranean—remains known only to the lucky few. This is a walk with the whole package: limestone amphitheaters; ruined Moorish castles perched on distant hill tops; verdant valleys complete with natural springs; Paleolithic rock paintings; iron ladders bolted to near-vertical rock faces; and mule tracks that take you along precipitous ridges. Olives grow on terraced hillsides, and you can still see the remnants of snow wells from

> *"Spectacular ridge walks amid limestone towers and rural landscapes of the Aitana massif."*
>
> www.exodus.co.uk

the old snow industry. You can walk its valleys and lower elevations through avocado and citrus orchards, and if that is all you want to do, you will have no regrets. Most people, however, come to climb the peaks—Seralla (4,465 feet/1,361 m), Aixorta (3,805 feet/1,160 m), Aitana (5,111 feet/1,558 m), and Puig Campana (4,625 feet/1,410 m). Climbing all four is usually done over four days, with 3,280 feet (1,000 m) of height gain each day, and each day will fascinate. There are no GR-like paths here—these are centuries-old trails used by hunters, merchants, and farmers and they go in straight lines over peaks rather than around them—another reason why you'll have them largely—and gloriously—all to yourself. **BDS**

El Caminito del Rey
Andalusia, Spain

Start/End Gaitanes Gorge   Distance 2.5 miles (4 km); wooden slat/glass panel central section, 0.9 mile (1.5 km)   Time 1 hour   Grade Easy   Type Wooden slats, glass panels   Map goo.gl/qlCKoN

This walk might have one rival for the title of world's scariest trail—but only one—in the Plank Walk along the vertical rock wall of Mount Hua in China. El Caminito del Rey, near Alora in southern Spain, is a concrete pathway that was built between 1901 and 1905 to provide construction workers more direct access between the two hydroelectric power plants at Gaitanejo Falls and Chorro Falls. Pinned into the wall with steel rods at a level of 330 feet (100 m) above the floor of the narrow Gaitanes Gorge in El Chorro canyon, and a scant 3.3 feet (1 m) wide, the King's Way—so named because King Alfonso XIII crossed it on his way to the inauguration of the nearby Conde del Guadalhorce dam in 1921—has gone through various stages of repair and disrepair ever since.

Closed at both ends in 2000 after a number of people tragically lost their lives attempting to cross what had become a very dilapidated structure, the path has only recently undergone a lengthy restoration process using wooden slats and the occasional glass floor panel. The new *caminito*, opened by Alfonso's great-grandson Felipe, will inspire a new generation of thrill seekers to cross it. There are a number of trails leading along the rims of Gaitanes Gorge, and many on the floor of the gorge, and all of them seem to end up at one end of the walkway or the other. El Caminito is simply impossible to ignore. Standing on the floor of the gorge by the Guadalhorce River and looking up, it seems as if there is not a more staggering-looking pathway anywhere in the world. And perhaps there isn't. **BDS**

▣ The newly restored path is a feat of engineering.

GR221 Drystone Route
Mallorca, Spain

Start Port d'Andratx **End** Port de Pollença
Distance 87 miles (140 km)
Time 8 days **Grade** Moderate
Type Long-distance path **Info** goo.gl/JT7IDL

"The path is lined with drystone terraces (hence the name), where olive trees have been grown for centuries."

www.seemallorca.com

The GR221—otherwise known as the Ruta de Pedra en Sec, or the Drystone Route—was created by the Mallorca government to give visitors a different experience of their island. It's designed for those who want to see rural Mallorca and do more than spend their days basking on its glorious beaches. It's much more, however, than just another mountain trail. Mallorca's limestone-encrusted interior has long been utilized by everyone, from ninth-century Arabs and tobacco smugglers to its latter-day residents and farmers, to provide for all kinds of structures, from pathways, huts, and buttresses to hold back cultivated terraces, to limestone snow pits for the storage of snow and ice (snow is extremely rare, but it can happen). Even ancient bread ovens made from limestone blocks and stone water channels can be found in its mountainous interior, all of which help to make this fascinating trail a walk through both the island's natural landscape and its built heritage.

The trail begins in the south at the fishing village of Port d'Andratx and continues for 87 miles (140 km) through typical Mediterranean scrub and the evergreen oaks and pines of the rugged Serra de Tramuntana Mountains, following old limestone paths, forest trails, and mule paths that pass through the interior's mountain towns, villages, and estates before emerging at Port de Pollença in the north.

The GR221 takes you close to the coast and up to the island's loftiest peak, the Coll de ses Cases de sa Neu, at more than 3,280 feet (1,000 m), but don't be surprised if it is the Tramuntana's wonderful stone terraces, declared a UNESCO World Heritage Site in 2011, that linger longest in the memory. **BDS**

⤴ The GR221 gets you away from Mallorca's beaches and up into its mountainous limestone interior.

Masca Gorge Trek
Tenerife, Spain

Start Masca   **End** Bay of Masca
Distance 5 miles (8 km)   **Time** 3 hours
Grade Moderate   **Type** Exposed rocks, mountain
trails   **Map** goo.gl/8BW6H7

Until around 1990 the tiny village of Masca—high in the Teno mountains of Tenerife, the largest of the Canary Islands off the northwest coast of Africa—was accessible only via a long, sandy track from the city of Santiago del Teide. Since then, a sealed road has snaked its way into these dramatic mountains and is reason enough to come here to this gorgeous village with its stone houses and views over ravine walls to the Atlantic Ocean even if you don't continue the journey into the forbidding Masca Gorge. But, of course, walk it you will. Outsiders don't come here just to walk Masca's streets.

The trail to the gorge begins just to the left of a ridge that runs through the center of town, a beginning easy enough for even casual hikers despite it being a steep initiation with a nice complement of loose rocks.

As you move into the gorge proper, the walls on either side of the ravine climb to 1,968 feet (600 m) above sea level and narrow to only 65 feet (20 m) apart. At this point you've entered the Masca world, an environment of twisting, heavily eroded rocks and endemic vegetation, a visually overwhelming place with striated volcanic walls in shades of ocher, brown, orange, and red, and all of the tints in between that dance above and about you whenever you look up, which is often, to gaze up at the gorge's serrated rim.

After three hours of gorge-traversing, you begin to hear and smell the ocean, and you eventually stumble out onto a rocky beach on the Bay of Masca where, providing you've done all of the proper groundwork, a boat should be waiting to take you to the harbor of Los Gigantes. **BDS**

"Those with vertigo should stay away ... there are various points ... where chains have been installed for your safety."

www.tripadvisor.co.uk

⊼ The deep and narrow Masca Gorge, with its walls of beautiful earth tones.

Igueste de San Andres to Chamorga Tenerife, Spain

Start Igueste de San Andres **End** Chamorga
Distance 8 miles (12.8 km) **Time** 4 hours
Grade Moderate **Type** Mountain path, stone steps, quiet road **Map** goo.gl/IaTxLW

While south Tenerife is hot, dry, and encrusted with back-to-back tourism, the mountainous north is wild, beautiful, and remote. The northeastern corner of this Spanish island is particularly unspoiled. Igueste de San Andres is a tiny seaside village near the northeastern tip. It's a picturesque settlement of whitewashed houses clinging to steep slopes leading up from the Atlantic. From here, there's a climb down to a beach occasionally used by nudists. The village is more popular, however, as the starting point of trails into the Agana Mountains.

> *"This route . . . around the Angana peninsula . . . stands on its own merit as a fine day's walk."*
>
> Paddy Dillon, *Walking on Tenerife*

Chamorga is another remote but pretty hamlet, this time high in the mountains at the end of a road that snakes through the Aganas. It's not far from the coast, but the fact that it stands at more than 1,800 feet (549 m) shows what this walk is like.

The path is usually clear and easy as it winds through woods and open rocky terrain but there's a bit of scrambling on rough slopes. Sometimes the trail seems to disappear and you must follow cairns. The route passes Playa de Antequerra, a beach of black volcanic sand.

The path becomes easier to follow as it approaches Chamorga. Many walkers continue to the northwestern coast beyond. **SH**

El Teide Caldera
Tenerife, Spain

Start/End The cable car station or Parador Hotel
Distance 6.5 miles (10.5 km) **Time** 2–3 hours
Grade Easy/moderate **Type** Rocky mountain path
Map goo.gl/UNsrHu

The remains of a massive volcanic eruption dominate Tenerife, one of the Spanish Canary Islands off the northwest coast of Africa. The island's peak, El Teide (12,198 feet/3,718 m), is higher than any mountain on mainland Spain and one of the world's largest volcanoes on a popular European holiday island just 30 miles (48 km) across.

The vast caldera surrounding El Teide suggests the mountain that was here before the last major eruption was far larger. What has been left from that massive explosion is a huge volcanic area that is now a UNESCO World Heritage Site and Spanish National Park covering 73 square miles (190 sq km) of the island's center.

It's a hot desert of strange red, yellow, and brown rock formations and ancient lava fields dotted with colorful plants found nowhere else in the world. Trekkers can climb El Teide, but the mountain is often shrouded in cloud, obscuring views. It's a hard and rather featureless slog to the top, although there is a government-run refuge for walkers to stay overnight near the summit. Better views and more interesting walking can come from tackling a loop around the caldera at the base of the mountain. There is a network of official trails in the Park, and the selected walk is a loop comprising two of the best.

Start at the car park for the El Teide cable car or the car park of the Spanish Government's *parador* hotel. The walk is a circuit of trails numbers 16 and 19 marked on a map available from the park office. The route follows an old dirt track within the remains of the ancient crater through some of the most spectacular parts of this unique moonscape. **SH**

GR20
Corsica, France

Start Calenzana **End** Conca **Distance** 112 miles (180 km) **Time** 15 days **Grade** Strenuous
Type Ill-defined mountain trail
Info goo.gl/A7VQpa

Established in 1972 and often described by hikers from around the world as one of the toughest treks of their lives, the GR20, from the northwest of Corsica through its mountainous interior to Conca, is a long-distance trek unlike any other. What it asks of you is often underestimated, and this has led to some undeserved criticisms from underprepared hikers. The route winds through the island's wild mountains, alpine pastures and lakes, and although it takes fifteen days without any distractions to walk it, there are also possible detours into the heart of traditional Corsican villages. Who wouldn't want to spend a night or two with a local family and sample the island's rich heritage of meats, cheeses, and homemade wines, if for no other reason than to give your shattered senses a chance to recover from the daily challenge of this demanding trail?

Actually, there is no real trail to speak of. Mostly, you'll be walking the "granite isle's" rugged terrain, strewn with rocks and stones of all shapes and sediments, and if you miss a marker, you'll be doubling back and muttering as you go, so stay aware. The huts are basic, with the exception of those at Haut Asco and Castel de Verghio, and bedbugs are common. Bring a tent, and avoid them and the snoring multitude of hikers who think they're being smart by traveling light.

Travel in June if you can, before the refuges fill up, and walking south to north rather than north to south provides more time to prepare for the difficulties that lay ahead. However, don't let the GR20's formidable reputation put you off experiencing one of Europe's most beautiful walks. **BDS**

"Considered to be the most difficult of all the GR routes and one of the most beautiful mountain trails in Europe."

www.corsica.forhikers.com

⊼ It's rugged, mountainous, and tortuous, and there isn't even a trail in the traditional sense.

Alta Via 1 Trentino Alto Adige, Italy

Start Toblach   **End** Rifugio Bianchet   **Distance** 74 miles (119 km)   **Time** 11 days   **Grade** Easy to moderate
Type Rocky, mountain paths, gravel forest roads   **Map** goo.gl/w7uJUo

As always with the Alta Via routes—medium-to-high altitude, north–south running mountain trails that bisect the Dolomites—there is the dilemma: which one to choose? There are six in total, varying from six to thirteen days, from easy rambles to rope-assisted ascents. All are well serviced by huts, which means you don't need to morph into a pack animal, and get you well off the beaten path.

Probably the best option for beginners is the Alta Via 1: it is a true "walk," with no glacier crossings or rock climbing involved. It will take you through much of what makes the Dolomites so unique—the Fanes of the South Tyrol, a selection of peaks around the lovely town of Cortina, the massive bulk of Mount Pelmo, and the Parco Nazionale Dolomiti Bellunesi, a land of grassy peaks, glacial cirques, and karst basins, and a wild heart filled with ravines, ridges, rock spikes, and crags. For World War I buffs, some of the most thrilling sections are around Passo Falzarego, with cable-assisted sections giving access to the tunnels dug by Italian soldiers through the Piccolo Lagazuoi. If you want to understand why these mountains glow so pink in the early morning and late afternoon light, you can thank French geologist Déodat de Dolomieu, after whom the Dolomites are named, who, in 1788, discovered the principal ingredient in their composition—calcium magnesium carbonate. Or forget what you just read and stay with the myth—that these Monti Pallidi, these Pale Mounts, were long ago covered in the finest gossamer, which grows in a myriad of pinkish-orange hues, a tapestry made by moonbeams for a beautiful princess bride. **BDS**

⬆ A classic north–south route through the Dolomites.

Friedrich-August Trail Trentino Alto Adige, Italy

Start Passo di Sella   **End** Compaccio   **Distance** 6.5 miles (10.5 km)   **Time** 5 hours   **Grade** Easy
Type Well-graded mountain trails   **Map** goo.gl/HwdKzO

In the early 1900s, Friedrich August III, newly crowned king of Saxony, visited the South Tyrol town of Alpe di Siusi near Compaccio—the largest mountain plateau in Europe and the undisputed king of mountain plateaus outside of the *tepuis* of Venezuela. When he saw the panorama of mountains that stretched before him, the king wanted more than anything to give his name to a local trail. Consequently, the Friedrich-August Trail, the trail with the impeccable pedigree, was born.

The walk begins at Passo di Sella, and from there it's a short climb to the Friedrich-August hut, where the actual trail starts. It is an easy path that allows you to circumnavigate the six major summits of the Dolomites' Sassolungo Group—a wonderful alpine wilderness full of huge rock faces, ice gullies, ledges, pinnacles, and even a small glacier—in around five

hours. On the way, you will be able to admire some of the finest Dolomite panoramas, including views over the Sassolungo/Langkofel and Sasso Piatto/Plattkofel Mountains, as well as of the Sella massif to the east and the Pale di San Martino to the south.

From the Friedrich-August hut, walk along a contour line to the Sasso Piatto hut (7,545 feet/2,300 m) and then onward over volcanic subsoils to the Passo Duron, a high mountain pass that connects the Zoldo and Cordevole valleys, before starting the descent to Saltria, from where a bus will take you back to your starting point.

If you are the sort of person who likes walks that provide maximum thrills for minimal effort, this is one walk that you really need to do before you die. **BDS**

⤒ The trail offers great views of the Sassolungo Group.

Pala Ronda Trails Trentino Alto Adige, Italy

Start/End San Martino   **Distance** 5 miles (8 km) "soft" trek; 8 miles (12.8 km) "hard" trek   **Time** 4 days (soft);
5 days (hard)   **Grade** Moderate to strenuous   **Type** Bare rock, gravel trails   **Map** goo.gl/8HY8vz

The Dolomites are universally acknowledged as one of the finest walking regions in the world, and the paths that crisscross them are as numerous as the strands in a spider's web. The Pala Group, in eastern Trentino, is characterized by three distinct geographical units—the northern section with more than 6,670 acres (2,700 ha) of protected spruce and fir woodlands; the western section, which is part of the 43-mile-long (69 km) Lagorai Range; and the southern section, which contains the Pale di San Martino, the peaks that provide the views and the thrills you will encounter on the Pala Ronda trek.

There are two options you can take: the "soft" trek or the "hard" trek, both of which start in the town of San Martino. The soft trek involves either a three- or four-hour hike, depending upon which path you take, and a 3,280-foot (1,000-m) ascent to Rosetta hut on

the eastern edge of the Pala plateau at a height of 8,467 feet (2,581 m). If you have any energy left after that rather torturous start, you can walk an extra twenty minutes to the peak of Cima Rosetta at 8,999 feet (2,743 m). The next day is exhilarating as you walk to the Fradusta Glacier, more of a glacier remnant really, and its tiny lake. You are now in the heart of the Pale di San Martino mountain group. After an overnight stay in the Pradidali hut, you traverse the Pradidali Valley to your final accommodation at Treviso hut before crossing the Canali Pass and onto the plateau itself and a three-hour return to Rosetta hut. The "hard" option takes you right across the Pala Group and involves climbing and using pegs and wooden crossbars (stemples). You have been warned. **BDS**

⤒ The hard trek is pictured above.

Mount Pelmo Circuit Veneto, Italy

Start Alleghe **End** San Vito di Cadore **Distance** 26 miles (42 km) **Time** 4 days **Grade** Easy
Type Well-maintained mountain trails, gravel paths **Map** goo.gl/7e5KlM

Ever since anyone can remember, the eastern face of Mount Pelmo, the mountain that separates the Val di Zoldo from the Boite Valley in northern Italy, has been known as Caregon del Padreterno—"the doge's seat"—because of its distinctive wide glacial cirque in the shape of a giant chair. It dominates what many consider to be the most beautiful mountain in the Dolomite range. There are two summits on Mount Pelmo—7,335 feet (2,236 m) and 10,393 feet (3,168 m)—and they rise majestically over its 1,000-foot-high (305 m) rock faces.

The circuit can be done in either direction, and there are three huts spaced evenly around it that can provide either a bed for the night or a refreshing meal to help you on your way. After completing a circuit of Pelmo, you can then consider doing the same with neighboring Mount Civetta (10,564 feet/3,220 m),

with its pinnacles and chiseled summits, beautifully reflected in the waters of Lago d'Alleghe, and complete a rough figure eight. If you begin in the west at Alleghe and head eastward to finish at the town of San Vito di Cadore, you will be guaranteed a smorgasbord of memorable views.

The English-born author and mountaineer John Ball was the first to summit Mount Pelmo in September 1857, and what he wrote in his travelogue, *A Guide to the Eastern Alps*, in 1868 is still true today: "From whichever side you look, but above all from east and south, a gigantic fortress of the most massive architecture appears, not broken up into minarets and pinnacles like most of its rivals, but defended purely by the highest of sheer bastions . . . ." **BDS**

↑ A circuitous walk around the "Fortress of Stone."

The Alpine Trail
Liguria, Italy

Start/End Colle Melosa   **Distance** 6 miles (9.6 km)
Time 5–6 hours   **Grade** Moderate to strenuous
Type Mountain trails, cabled routes
Map goo.gl/39IoE5

Liguria's Alpine Trail was hewn out of the rock by hand in between the two world wars. The walk begins high in the Ligurian Alps, 5,249 feet (1,600 m) above sea level at the Rifugio (refuge) F. Allavena in the town of Colle Melosa on the French border, and from there it's a short walk to the beginning of the trail proper. The limestone rocks that soon envelop you are Dolomite-like in appearance, and there are even a couple of *Via Ferrata* (iron road) options—alpine routes cut into the rock face by partisans to take ammunition and supplies in times of war—along the way if you're so inclined. There are some steep descents on this trail, and it's not for the squeamish, but all are accompanied by magnificent views. For some you will need the aid of cabling as you make your way down the eastern face of Mount Toraggio and into the Gola dell'Incisa (5,528 feet/1,685 m), a deep and impressive gully. From there it's a hard one-hour climb to the summit of Mount Toraggio (6,560 feet/2,000 m).

Leaving the summit you cross briefly into France as you walk along the eastern face of Mount Pietravecchia through forests of European larch, rhododendrons, and, in August and September, wild raspberries. From there it is a straightforward walk through meadows to the Valetta Pass at 5,528 feet (1,909 m), and from there, back to Colle Melosa.

The Ligurian Alps have been shaped over millennia by erosion and water into a fantastical range of high plateaus and mountain passes with sinkholes and karst formations. Their proximity to the Mediterranean has resulted in a large number of endemic plants that make any high-altitude hike in this diverse region an experience to remember. **BDS**

"By far the most beautiful trail in Liguria and one of the best in Europe."

www.walkingliguria.co.uk

⬆ Northern Italy's Ligurian Alps are home to one of Europe's finest mountain walks.

Monte Titano
San Marino

Start/End P3 parking lot
Distance 1 mile (1.6 km)   Time 1 hour
Grade Easy   Type Stone paths
Map goo.gl/PRdHVh

San Marino is considered to be the world's oldest surviving independent city-state and is able to trace its independence back to the thirteenth century. The San Marino Historic Center and the surrounding Monte Titano on which it is built continue to reflect what life was like in medieval Italy. The last in a line of some 200 Italian city-states, San Marino remains a testimony to the ideas and principles of what makes a free republic. Thanks to the isolation that came with being at the top of Monte Titano, the city's walls, bastions, gates, fourteenth-century convent and eighteenth-century

"Straddling the transition from land to sky, San Marino is protected by its old defensive walls."

www.italia.it

theater—even its institutional functions—have been spared all that is wrong with modern urban planning.

From the parking lot a little way down the mountain—a massive limestone outcrop that defines this tiny republic—a panoramic trail takes you up along the ridge of Monte Titano and past each of its three towers on a stone pathway that links them all in a dramatic cliff-top walk. The first tower, Montale, was built in the fourteenth century and is now privately owned, but the others are open to the public. The second tower, the Castello della Cesta (1253), is the highest, and provides the best views. The third tower, Guaita, was built in the eleventh century and is the largest and architecturally most impressive. **BDS**

Umbriano
Umbria, Italy

Start Colleponte   End Umbriano
Distance 2.3 miles (3.7 km)
Time 1.5 hours   Grade Easy
Type Undefined trail   Map goo.gl/d4ydXy

The Italian village of Umbriano, perched on a rocky outcrop in front of the Abbey of San Pietro in Valle, was constructed in the latter years of the ninth century and abandoned in 1950. Legend says it was the very first village of the Umbrian people, and it is accessible only on foot. It overlooks the Valnerina Valley and provides a lovely short walk, as long as you don't lose your way getting there.

Drive the SS209 through the Valnerina Valley to Macenano, and from there to the hamlet of Colleponte. Cross the Nera River, turn right, look for a cemetery, park your car, and walk across another bridge, past some houses, and look for a fork in the road. Go right at the fork, past a spring, and you come out once again at the Nera River. Now if you have come this far, you should give yourself a pat on the back, because this village was abandoned for a reason. A narrow path then takes you along a hillside on quite a steep gradient in the direction of the village, and when you reach yet another spring, after about 1,100 feet (360 m), you ought to have an excellent view of your destination. After passing a third spring, you'll reach yet another fork, at which point you take the left trail, and with some good fortune, you have reached Umbriano.

Another starting point, from the village of Precetto, should also get you there if you follow a dirt road paralleling the Black River, and you'll eventually see the Abbey of San Pietro on the right. Of course, if neither of these serpentine routes makes any sense, and you can't find a local to help you on your quest (unlikely), at the very least you've had a fun day of discovery in the Umbrian hills. **BDS**

Villetta Barrea to Civitella Alfedena
Abruzzo, Italy

Start Villetta Barrea **End** Civitella Alfedena
Distance 6 miles (9.6 km) **Time** 3 hours
Grade Easy **Type** Forest and rural trails
Map goo.gl/mvMu1V

Abruzzo National Park—at the back of Italy's knee—is remote. Its tiny stone-built villages, some almost invisible in the misty green hills, are strung together by single-track roads that see more sheep than vehicles. Wolves lope through its black pine forests, and chamoix climb high into its limestone peaks. It is wilder and more rugged than Umbria or Tuscany. If not another world, then certainly the Abruzzo is in another century.

The best way to experience its timelessness is to hike its network of 150 trails. One of the loveliest is the Villetta Barrea to Civitella Alfedena loop, a very manageable morning hike through the Sangro Valley. From Villetta Barrea, the trail climbs gently through pine and beech forest to emerge in front of a spectacular green-baized bowl. Gradually ascending to the Colle Jaccolo (3,894 feet/1,187 m), from where there is a sweeping view of the valley behind, the trail then rolls down to the small town of Civitella Alfedena, which sits like a pinkish pyramid stacked into the hills and crowned by a church tower. Look out for waymarkers—the park's logo of a seated bear—hand painted on rocks and trees. Civitella's cobbled streets conceal a wolf museum and a few little bars where you can stop for a beer and some pecorino cheese with bread, although you may do better to wait until you get back to Villetta Barrea, which has a choice of good restaurants.

From Civitella Alfedena the trail loops back to Villetta Barrea via the Barrea Reservoir and the Sangro River. The chances of seeing a wolf or a bear are small, but keep an eye on the sky above the higher ledges and ridges and you may spot a golden eagle. **DS**

"Civitella Alfedena lies in the Upper Sangro Valley at the foot of the Monti della Meta, on a small hill overlooking Lake Barrea."

www.virtualtourist.com

⊡ Abruzzo National Park's Sangro Valley offers a picturesque trail linking two historic villages.

Gran Sasso
Abruzzo, Italy

Start/End Santo Stefano   **Distance** Various
Time Various   **Grade** Easy to strenuous
Type Open fields, dirt paths, mountain trails
Info goo.gl/bZnuUo

Even if it hadn't been for Operation Eiche—the German raid on the Campo Imperatore Hotel on Gran Sasso in Italy's Apennine Mountains on September 12, 1943 to rescue Italian dictator Benito Mussolini—Gran Sasso would still be famous. The highest mountain in the Apennine Mountains has the southernmost glacier in Europe, the Calderone at the foot of Corno Grande, and its high-altitude prairies contain a rich variety of flora and fauna (2,000 plant species throughout the park), with beech, silver fir, and oaks on its lower elevations. Gran Sasso is now the centerpiece of the Gran Sasso and Monti della Laga National Park, established in 1991 and home to the highest mountains in continental Italy, south of its northern alps, and with Rome a convenient 82 miles (132 km) away. Better still, despite its proximity to the nation's capital, it remains remarkably free of tourists. Hiking possibilities within its 545 square miles (1,413 sq km)—the largest protected area in Europe—are endless, and the spectacle of Gran Sasso itself, rising up out of the pastures of the surrounding Campo Imperatore, is a sight not soon forgotten. There are 190 miles (305 km) of trails here that can be either walked, cycled, or traversed on horseback, as well as mountain climbing—it was here in 1573 that Francesco De Marchi scaled Corno Grande (9,553 feet/2,912 m) and gave birth to Italian mountaineering. Serious tourism started here with the construction of the Garibaldi Refuge in 1886; however, you don't need to go "up" to enjoy yourself here. Just walk across the pastoral landscapes of the Campo Imperatore Plateau—Europe's "Little Tibet"—and be inspired by what rises up around you. **BDS**

"A remote and unspoiled region. Beautiful villages perch on hilltops and are surrounded by the majestic peaks of the Appennine[s]."

www.hedonistichiking.com

⭡ The Gran Sasso has high alpine meadows, Europe's southernmost glacier, and remarkably few tourists.

Mount Stromboli Summit Walk Stromboli Island, Italy

Start/End Scari   **Distance** 2.8 miles (4.5 km)   **Time** 6 hours   **Grade** Strenuous
Type Concrete, ash, and cinder-covered paths   **Map** goo.gl/O1Sqc8

The ancient Romans called Stromboli, in Italy's Aeolian Islands off the north coast of Sicily, the Lighthouse of the Mediterranean. Some volcanologists believe this stratovolcano has been in various eruptive states for as long as 5,000 years, albeit mostly small explosions with associated lava fragments and ash. A violent eruption in 2003 closed it to hikers for two years, and since 2005 a reorganized trail network now allows free access to its many trails below 400 feet (122 m). Above this you must be accompanied by a guide, and the return journey back to Scari is usually done at night, to maximize the mesmerizing glow of its incandescent stones and fiery displays. It may look a straightforward ascent, but it is not without its complications. Once you leave the concrete path that takes you out of town, the brush vegetation can easily be set ablaze, and if climbing at night, the routes back down in the

volcano's soft, warm sands can be difficult to pinpoint. These are minor concerns compared to the prize view, however, and the walk should take around three hours as you zigzag your way toward Stromboli's rim and watch the surrounding ground turn from green to its lunar-like landscape of black and gray.

Once you are on the rim, it can be very difficult to drag yourself away, especially when you find a cozy spot above the crater and begin to gaze on its hellish interior. In 2007, two new craters opened on Stromboli's summit, but despite the mountain's restless nature, accidents and injuries over the years have been remarkably few considering how many people want to see the Sciara del Fuoco, Stromboli's "stream of fire." **BDS**

⬆ Conquer the lighthouse of the Mediterranean.

Mount Etna Summit Sicily, Italy

Start/End Rifugio Sapienza   **Distance** 7.9 miles (12.7 km)   **Time** 6 hours   **Grade** Moderate
Type Ash and cinder-covered paths   **Map** goo.gl/TYF5FZ

The mistake you can make when considering an ascent of Sicily's 10,991-foot (3,350-m) Mount Etna is thinking that walking to the summit and back is the only option you have. While an ascent to the craters of this beautiful stratovolcano is certainly a must-do experience, there is so much else to see and do as well. Why not take a speleological tour of Grotta del Gelo, the various other lava tunnels of the Piano dei Dammusi, or walk to the Mount Nero volcanic cone created by the eruption in 1646? You can also explore Etna's northern and southern slopes and hike to some of the eruptive vents made during the mountain's eruption in 2002. The mountain has so much more to reveal than just the craters on its summit. However, the summit must be conquered, and the best way to get there is to begin at the Rifugio Sapienza on Etna's southern face.

From Rifugio Sapienza (at 6,561 feet/2,000 m) the height gain is about 3,280 feet (1,000 m), but there are a couple of options to choose from: head to the cable car station and look for the jeep track that you can follow to Rifugio Alpino (it is illegal to go past this point without a guide) and beyond.

The more rewarding option, however, is to take a short walk down to the start of the Schiena dell'Asino route, which takes you up to the ridge La Montagnola, where you can walk through a field of ash cones around the east side of the crater. It is hard work, but this way you will have a real sense of accomplishment when you arrive, and it's a viewpoint favored by those in the know as a "safe" spot should things heat up. **BDS**

⬆ There is far more to Mount Etna than its fiery summit.

Główny Szlak Sudecki
Lower Silesia, Poland

Start Swieradów-Zdrój   **Start** Paczków
Distance 217 miles (350 km)   **Time** 2 weeks
Grade Moderate   **Type** Mountain and forest trails
Info goo.gl/j8bdvs

The Główny Szlak Sudecki follows the line of the Sudetes Mountains, stretching from southwestern Poland, along the border with the Czech Republic, and on into eastern Germany. Just what territory the Sudetes cover has changed with the centuries, and there was a massive dislocation of the region's population during and after World War II in the wake of Nazi Germany claiming the region as Germanic Sudetenland, only to have much of its German population expelled after the war. Czechs don't much like the word "Sudety" because of its associations, but the popularity of the name Główny Szlak Sudecki and the growing interest in this demanding trail is proof of how it has endeared itself to the Polish people.

The trail, which was begun in 1947, begins in Swieradów-Zdrój, a spa town in the Kwisa Valley of the Jizera Mountains. From there, it enters the Krkonoše Mountains, the birthplace of the Elbe River and a popular holiday destination in summer and winter, and one of the most traditional regions in Central Europe. The trail merges with the Polish–Czech Friendship Trail for 12 miles (19.3 km) as it ascends Snezka (5,256 feet/1,602 m), the highest point on the Silesian Ridge, before descending into the Rudawy Janowickie range in the Western Sudetes.

The trail then passes through the Owl Mountains, enough of a destination on its own with its labyrinth of trails; the late thirteenth-century Grodno Castle in Zagórze Sląskie, and the mountain's resident Eurasian eagle owl; and Stołowe Mountains National Park, Poland's only sandstone mountain range. There are mountain huts and hotels along the way, and the trail is open year-round. **BDS**

"The Stolowe Mountains make a fantastic impression, full of mushroom-shaped formation, bludgeon-like rocks . . . ."

www.poland.travel

⬆ This much-loved trail meanders through the beautiful Sudetes Mountains.

Rysy Summit
Lesser Poland, Poland

Start/End Popradske Pleso station
Distance 11 miles (17.7 km)   **Time** 8 hours
Grade Strenuous   **Type** Open rocky terrain
Map goo.gl/x794PG

Mount Rysy in Poland's central High Tatras, on the border with Slovakia, is a perfect mountain to climb for those who like a choice of peaks to conquer after a long ascent. It has three: its middle peak at 8,212 feet (2,503 m), a southeast peak at 8,114 feet (2,473 m)—both in Slovakia—and its northwest peak, which is Poland's highest point at 8,199 feet (2,499 m). Once climbed by Russian revolutionary Vladimir Lenin himself, there are two paths to its summit, one from the Polish side and the other beginning in Slovakia. Since the two countries joined the European Union in 2004, it is now possible to begin your climb in one country and finish it in the other, providing you climb between mid-June and the end of October, otherwise the Slovak route will be closed.

This is by no means a technical climb, but the time to do this walk needs to be between August and September when the weather is at its warmest. In July the mountain is bedevilled by thunderstorms, and there is a high risk of avalanches in winter. A good overnight stay, if you start in Poland and plan on camping, is the Polish Alpinism Association base camp on Szalasiska meadow; or if you prefer a mountain hut, the only choice, and a good one, is the Morskie Oko Chalet, which is located on a moraine by the post-glacial Lake Morskie Oko.

The Rysy summit can often be crowded, however, especially in summer, and don't be surprised if you're sitting shoulder to shoulder with strangers. After all, it is the highest point in the High Tatra Mountains that is accessible to lone hikers without having to be in the company of a guide. Just try and get there early, before the crowds arrive. **BDS**

"Offers one of the widest and richest summit panoramas in the Tatras ... one can admire all prominent High Tatra peaks."

www.summitpost.org

⊼ No peak can make you feel you have conquered the Tatra Mountains quite like Mount Rysy.

Polish–Czech Friendship Trail Poland/Czech Republic

Start Szrenica   End Okraj   Distance 18.5 miles (29.7 km)   Time 2 days   Grade Moderate
Type Mountain paths   Map goo.gl/qk7nT7

The Krkonoše Mountains are the high point of the broader Sudetes Mountains that stretch from eastern Germany to the border along the northern Czech Republic and into southwest Poland. This path runs along the main ridge of the mountains, crossing or traversing every one of its summits, and was inaugurated on June 16, 1961, at the height of the Cold War, when it was open only to Czech and Polish residents and was used as a clandestine meeting point for various Czech and Polish dissidents, including Václav Havel. It was officially named the Polish–Czech Friendship Trail only in 1993, after the dissolution of Czechoslovakia. Checkpoints were left unmanned, and inspections slowed to a trickle, but to this day, anyone crossing it still needs to carry valid ID with them, despite all border controls being eliminated in 2007.

The trail mostly stays clear of the area's abundant hardwood forests, weaving instead through mountain meadows that have been used for pasture for almost 200 years, with occasional converted shepherd huts where you can stay overnight. It traverses the helmet-shaped, granite-encroached Wielki Szyszak, the Czech Republic's tenth highest mountain, passes areas of mountain pine shrub, and ends at Okraj, a former Cold War checkpoint. Open all year, it is maintained by the staff of its adjacent national parks, and its trails are always clearly marked, with distances on the Polish side shown in hours and on the Czech side in kilometers—a convenient piece of bureaucratic whimsy for anyone who likes to know just what country it is they're walking through. **BS**

⬆ Beautiful meadows and forests on the Friendship Trail.

Mount Triglav Summit Gorenjska, Slovenia

Start/End Bohinj Valley   **Distance** 21 miles (34 km)   **Time** 2–3 days   **Grade** Strenuous
Type Mountain trails, exposed rock   **Map** goo.gl/knD9kk

"Triglav is not just a mountain; Triglav is a kingdom." When Austrian–Italian botanist and author Julius Kugy, the pioneer of mountaineering in Slovenia's Julian Alps, wrote those words, no one knew better than he the intimate connection this famous mountain, which features on their national flag, had with the Slovenian people. Kugy roamed the mountainsides and valleys of the Julian Alps with local herdsmen, pioneered fifty new trails, and conquered previously unconquered and often unnamed peaks. No "outsider" knew the Julians quite like Kugy. Of all these mountains, Triglav was his favorite.

Its north face alone is 3,937 feet (1,200 m) high and an awe-inspiring 9,842 feet (3,000 m) wide, and the mountain that is "every Slovenian's duty to climb" is the highest in the country at 9,396 feet (2,864 m) and can be reached by more than twenty different routes,

all of which begin in its valleys below—the Vrata, the Kot, the Krma, and the Bohinj. The Vrata Valley is the most popular starting point for experienced hikers who revel in the challenge its north face presents, but for novices, the main approach is from Bohinj to the south. The summit is surprisingly scalable and can be done comfortably with two overnight stays in mountain huts. The Bohinj approach takes you past the Savica Waterfall, past glacial lakes, and over the Hribarov Plateau. Once you reach its summit, such is the mountain's dominance of the peaks below and its position at the confluence of the Alps, the Adriatic Sea, and the central European lowlands that it gives you a superlative panorama of green pastures, open ocean, and alpine summits. **BDS**

⊡ The summit of Triglav as seen from Dom Planika hut.

Slovenian Mountain Trail Podravska to Obalno-Kraska, Slovenia

Start Maribor   End Ankaran   Distance 310 miles (499 km)   Time 6–8 weeks   Grade Strenuous   Type Mountain and ridge trails, forest paths   Map goo.gl/6Lji6M

There are more than 6,000 miles (9,656 km) of trails weaving their way through Slovenia, and of those, more than 80 percent are mountain trails. The E7, which runs from the Black Sea to the Atlantic, enters Slovenia in the region of Primorska and runs through the south of the country before exiting into Croatia. The E6 runs from the Adriatic to the Baltic seas, enters Slovenian territory at Koroska in the northwest, and runs south to Notranjska. Slovenia can be proud of its mountain trails, and not only its segments of Europe's long-distance footpaths, either. Long before there was an E6 or an E7, or any other Es for that matter, there was the Slovenian Mountain Trail, Europe's very first long-distance trail.

Opened in 1953, this popular trail, so beloved of the Slovenian people, was initially meant to be a circular trail that began and ended in the northeast in the medieval town of Maribor on the Drava River. It was then changed to link up the country's wealth of mountainous hiking trails and now runs for 310 miles (499 km), from Maribor to Ankaran in the country's deep southwest near the Italian border overlooking the Gulf of Trieste. The trail traverses all of the country's primary Alpine ranges, including the volcanic Pohorje range, and the limestone-encrusted Julian, Kamnik, and Karawank Alps. If you hike through, you'll have ascended an astonishing 28 miles (45 km) on a direct route that includes the summit of Mount Triglav itself, which, at 9,396 feet (2,864 m), is Slovenia's highest point, as the trail makes its way south over a series of east–west alpine ridges on its final approaches into sunny Ankaran. **BDS**

⊤ Walk Europe's very first long-distance trail.

Risnjak National Park Primorsko Goranska, Croatia

Start/End Risnjak National Park entrance, Bijela Vodica   Distance Various   Time Various   Grade Easy
Type Grass and forest trails   Map goo.gl/1go5Gy

Located in the mountainous "great green heart of Croatia," Risnjak National Park is part of a lovely crescent-shaped range of mountains that begins to the north of Croatia in Slovenia and arcs its way south in a mesmerizing mix of limestone-riddled valleys and forests full of bare, rocky peaks and hidden dells. The area has been a magnet for scientists and botanists since the early 1800s because of its exceptional diversity of flora and fauna, and in 1949, botanist Ivo Horvat suggested the area be set aside as a national park. A small section was protected in 1956, and this was later enlarged and the park established in 1997. It is small, just 24.5 square miles (63.5 sq km), but it is nevertheless a key area of conservancy, a meeting point for coastal and continental vegetation zones and an overlapping region between the Dinaric and Alpine zones.

The park is characterized by karst features, such as dry meadows, underground streams, and deep caves. The Risnjak and Snjeznik massifs connecting the Alps and Dinaric mountains are an important biological corridor for plants and animals, including wolves and lynx, and its seldom-seen brown bears.

Naturally, there are numerous trails, but it would be negligent to single out any one trail and divert attention from the rest. Everywhere you walk, there is a trail, whether you're walking on a carpet of narrow-leaf bluegrass, carnation grass, or evergreen sedge, whether on the junegrass around dwarf pines or through meadows of tall oat grass. This was a palette of green, long before anyone thought to put down a trail. **BDS**

⤴ Risnjak is Croatia's beating heart of biodiversity.

Mount Maglić Summit Loop
Republika Srpska, Bosnia–Herzegovina

Start/End Trailhead 11 miles (17.7 km) from Tjentište   Distance 5 miles (8 km)
Time 4–5 hours   Grade Moderate
Type Mountain trail   Map goo.gl/48uCOk

Sutjeska National Park, established in 1962, is Bosnia–Herzegovina's oldest national park and home to one of continental Europe's last two remaining primeval forests, with towering 200-foot-high (61 m) beech trees and endemic black pines in its thick, coniferous forests. The Sutjeska River is responsible for having carved out the beautiful valley through which it flows, and the entire park is a showcase of European wilderness, a land where glacial lakes are lovingly called "mountain eyes." If all this isn't enough, there's a challenging summit as well. Rising up over the Sutjeska Valley is Bosnia–Herzegovina's highest mountain—Mount Maglić.

Maglić (7,828 feet/2,386 m) sits on the border of Bosnia and Montenegro and is part of a massif that consists of two primary peaks—Veliki Maglić itself, and Crnogorski Maglić in Montenegro, a tantalizing 6.5 feet (2 m) higher! An ascent of Maglić from the Bosnian side begins gently enough amid pastures, but it soon begins its rise over tricky and potentially hazardous terrain. It hugs the sides of the mountain, where you need to use hands as well as feet to scramble up, with cabling as handrails on the more exposed sections, which helps to dampen the creeping onset of vertigo. Maglić is often foggy (its name means "fog") and is a challenging climb even for experienced climbers. However, once on the summit, the views over Bosnia's other impressive peaks—Sujeska, Tara, and Piva—and the mountains over the border in Montenegro, as well as the beautiful heart-shape Lake Trnovačko, set within an ampitheater of mighty peaks, are memorable and well worth the effort in getting to the "roof of Bosnia." **BDS**

"The view from the summit is just marvelous—first of all to neighboring Volujak and Bioc and Trnovačko Lake."

www.mountaintour.ba

⬆ Its name means "fog," but once on this challenging summit hopefully the views will last a lifetime.

Subra Summit
Herceg Novi, Montenegro

Start Kameno   **End** Subra summit
Distance 12.5 miles (20 km)   **Time** 2 days
Grade Easy to moderate   **Type** Marked mountain
trails   **Map** goo.gl/BYpJgk

The Orjen massif on the border of Montenegro and Bosnia–Herzegovina is a desiccated, karst-strewn region of Cretaceous limestone, containing caves, canyons, and sinkholes, as well as all the erosive features you get wherever there is a lot of rainfall. The Orjen Mountains receive the highest rainfall in Europe—between 15 feet (4.5 m) and 17 feet (5.1 m) per year, which can lead to slippery and uncomfortable hiking if you go there from late fall through to late spring. However, if you come here in the summer, when the skies are often clear (and the temperatures blisteringly hot), this often overlooked region will provide you with great hiking through some fascinating and untrampled landscapes.

The trail will take you over lapiez (deeply fissured limestone paving), and along an old Austro–Hungarian pack horse route. There are two huts to break your journey, the Vratlo hut and the Orjen saddle hut, but you need to book them through the Subra Mountaineering Association in nearby Herceg Novi. There are also plenty of places where you can pitch a tent. Subra Mountain (5,509 feet/1,679 m) is by no means the highest point in the Orjen massif, but the walk there is interesting, and the views, once there, are exceptional. It begins at the town of Kameno on a 6-mile (9.6-km) road that leads to a series of switchbacks to Vratlo Pass (3,854 feet/1,175 m) and Vratlo hut. From here it takes four hours to return to Subra summit on a trail that winds its way through areas of polje, large elongated closed depressions that are flat and make for easy walking. From Subra's summit you will see the Subra amphitheater, and its plateaus contain some of the world's finest examples of microrelief karst. **BDS**

"Subra is an exceptional mosaic of speleological sites . . . . There is more empty space beneath you than rock to walk on."

www.montenegro.com

⬆ Desiccated limestone, sinkholes, and caves—the Subra summit trail is a karst-lover's dream.

Accursed Mountains

Shkodra, Albania

"The wild north of Albania is probably one of the last great European adventures."

www.walksworldwide.com

⊡ Walk the undiscovered beauty of Theth National Park, home to Europe's last unclimbed rock wall.

Start Shkodra   **End** Lake Koman
Distance 80 miles (129 km)   **Time** 8 days
Grade Moderate   **Type** Mountain and forest trails
Map goo.gl/422JSn

There's an old Albanian story about how the Accursed Mountains got their name. Long ago two brothers went out hunting, and as they were making their way through the forest, they discovered a beautiful fairy. They asked her to choose one of them, but she liked them both—one for his looks, the other for his bravery. When the brave one killed his brother and took the fairy home to meet his mother, she was so enraged that she placed a curse on the fairy and on the mountains where they found her.

In the past, things haven't always gone to plan in Albania, but one thing you can count on today when you walk the well-marked trails through the Accursed Mountains is a transforming experience of nature. It is a spectacular and almost impenetrable setting, with just a handful of high passes allowing access to small farms and communities in deeply incised valleys that seem almost cut off from the outside world. One of many trails begins in the historic town of Shkodra and passes down into the Bogra Valley (where the sealed roads come to an end) and over Diagonal Pass and into Theth National Park, an untouched world of waterfalls, caves, and canyons dominated by the vertical 3,280-foot (1,000-m) south face of Albania's version of the Matterhorn, Mount Arapit, which is that rarest of things—an as yet unclimbed vertical European rock wall.

Follow in the footsteps of shepherds over the Valbona Pass and then descend into the breathtaking beauty of the Valbona Valley as you make your way to the fjord-like Lake Koman, where a ferry—if all goes according to plan—will take you back to the Albanian capital, Tirana. **BDS**

Pindos Horseshoe Trail
Epirus, Greece

Start Vradeto   End Papingo
Distance 36 miles (57.9 km)   Time 3–4 days
Grade Moderate to strenuous   Type Mountain
Map goo.gl/C7cTWx

With its amazing necklace of islands, classical ruins, and turquoise seas, Greece is a European leader in the beauty stakes. Its head-turning mountains spread from the country's northern borders almost to its coast, in wave upon wave of precipitous peaks. Much of this landscape is impenetrable to hikers, but the Zagori region of the Pindos Mountains, bordering Albania and Macedonia, is more approachable. It is a land of ancient mule trails, tumbling streams, and dramatic gorges, with forty-eight perched villages that seem molded from the mountains themselves. Nimble-footed sheep and chamoix cross a scene that has barely altered in centuries.

At the center is Vikos Gorge, one of the deepest narrow canyons in the world at 3,000 feet (914 m). The Pindos Horseshoe Trail, a very manageable four-day, at most, hike, dips in and out of the gorge, crisscrossing rivers and streams via distinctive hump bridges built by itinerant Albanian workmen in the nineteenth century There are remote monasteries, stunning lookouts (Beloi offers a soaring view down the length of the gorge), and at Vradeto, the start of the hike, a dramatic, rock-cut staircase down to the village of Kapesovo—until the 1970s, these steps were the only route between the two villages. Little detours to Dragon's Lake, named for the newts that live there, and Astrak, one of the highest peaks in the Pindos (7,992 feet/2,436 m), add interest as well as mileage for a longer hike. The small villages around the rim of the gorge offer comfortable accommodations as well as simple inns and refuges, with shady terraces where hikers can take the weight off their feet for an hour or so and soak up the sheer tranquillity. **DS**

Bucegi Natural Park Trails
Dâmbovita, Romania

Start/End Various   Distance Various
Time Various   Grade Easy to strenuous
Type Mountain and forest trails, waymarked paths
Info goo.gl/MEBtNx

The Bucegi Mountains, part of the Southern Carpathians, are full of the ingredients that make Romanian history a delicious mix of fact and myth. The Bucegi were the home of the Dacians, an ancient race of Indo-Europeans who first settled present-day Romania, and also of their gods, who included Zamolxis, the supreme being who lived deep beneath its summits in a labyrinth of caves with a retinue of priests—the "Cloud Swallowers." There are still caves here that have never been explored, and twisted rock formations said to be of an old shepherd woman

---

"The Bucegi Mountains owe their fame to the spectacular landscapes and the accessibility of their routes."

transylvaniaoutdoor.com

---

named Dochia and her sheep, all turned to stone by a terrible, age-old curse.

All of which adds depth and mystery to a region replete with intriguing walking trails. The highest point—Omu Peak (8,218 feet/2,505 m)—dominates a landscape of nine post-glacial valleys, within which there are twenty-two mountain chalets that enable walkers to explore a web of routes. (Be sure to include the Morar Needles, breathtaking pinnacles of rock set in a natural ampitheater.)

Always stay in designated campsites. You may not encounter any Cloud Swallowers, but there are plenty of brown bears capable of some gnarly swallowing of their own. **BDS**

Kom–Emine Sofia to Burgas, Bulgaria

Start Mount Kom **End** Cape Emine **Distance** 434 miles (698 km) **Time** 20–25 days **Grade** Easy to moderate
Type Mountain trails, dirt tracks, grassy pathways **Info** goo.gl/NcZNSM

The Kom–Emine is Bulgaria's most famous mountain trail. It follows the crest of the Stara Planina (Old Mountain), the country's longest mountain range, and its name is derived from its start and end points: Mount Kom (6,614 feet/2,016 m), on the border with neighboring Serbia—about 50 miles (80 km) north of the Bulgarian capital, Sofia—and Cape Emine, Bulgaria's "stormiest cape," on the Black Sea coast.

It crosses a land of ancient trails eked out by generations of farmers and peasants. Along goat tracks, cart tracks and trails made by sheep and wild horses, the Kom–Emine (the final leg of the international route E3) follows a labyrinth of pathways as best as it is able, and this is by no means the only way across. Don't be too worried if you find that there is an acute lack of reliable maps, an odd thing considering the trail's unquestioned popularity with

Bulgarian hikers, or of signposts, which seem better oriented for those heading west to east.

The Kom–Emine has an average elevation of 2,411 feet (735 m), and if you walk its entire length through the Stara Planina, you will scale, if you have the stamina, more than 100 peaks (or you can go around them). The trail takes around three weeks to walk in summer, and add a week to that if you choose a winter crossing. The end of its segments all finish within sight of a chalet or some other form of guest accommodation, and the signage has been gradually improving. Anyway, it is the trail's grassy ridges, forests of beech and oak, and herds of free-roaming horses, not its markers, that you'll remember long after you are finished. **BDS**

⊡ **Walk the crest of Bulgaria's "Old Mountain."**

Mount Vihren Summit Blagoevgrad, Bulgaria

Start/End Vihren hut **Distance** Various **Time** 3 hours **Grade** Easy
Type Mountain trails, bare rock **Info** goo.gl/0fV5bJ

Considered by many to be Bulgaria's most beautiful mountain range, with more than sixty peaks in excess of 8,200 feet (2,500 m), the UNESCO World Heritage Pirin Mountains, with their marble and granite peaks and pristine glacier lakes, lure hikers from across Europe who want to experience exceptional walks without the crowds common to many of Western Europe's more trampled pathways.

The town of Bansko makes an ideal base for exploring the Pirins, whether it be the karst formations and soaring cliffs around Mount Vihren, or the centuries-old spruce forests in the Yulen Reserve, or a walk up to Vihren hut, from where you can hike the cirque of the Banderishki Lakes. You can take the chairlift to Bezbog hut for a richly rewarding walk to the summit of Polezhan Mountain (9,354 feet/2,851 m) and its jaw-dropping views over seventeen lakes, including glacial Popovo Lake, the Pirin mountain range's largest and deepest lake. However, no visit to the Pirin Mountains is complete without an ascent of its highest and most famous summit, Mount Vihren (9,560 feet/2,914 m). There are three approaches you can take—the southwest approach beginning at Vihren hut (6,397 feet/1,950 m) along open terrain; the Koncheto Shelter approach, which provides stunning views of the Pirin massif from the adjacent Koncheto Ridge; and the northern approach along the Golem Kazan (Giant Cauldron), beneath the breathtaking splendor of Vihren's 1,000-foot-high (305 m) northern face. The southwest approach is the most popular choice for tourists, and it takes about two and a half to three hours to the summit from Vihren hut. **BDS**

⬆ Explore sixty-plus peaks of the Pirin Mountains.

Borzhava Ridge
Zakarpats'ka, Ukraine

Start/End Pylypets **Distance** Various
Time Various **Grade** Easy
Type Well-maintained mountain trails
Info goo.gl/hDSEPu

"Curved like a dragon's tail turned to stone, the Borzhava Ridge rises over the rest of the mountains like an island over the sea."

www.ukrainianweek.com

⬆ Walk the peaks and valleys of Europe's second-longest mountain range.

Shaped, as the locals like to tell you, like the tail of a dragon that has been turned to stone, the Borzhava Ridge is a wide, level ridge located between the Vovcha and Rika rivers in Transcarpathia. It is dissected by valleys up to 3,280 feet (1,000 m) deep and rises above the peaks of Ukraine's central Carpathians, the second longest mountain range in Europe. On its slopes are the country's highest alpine pastures, and it is an area beloved by snowboarders in winter, while in summer it continues to draw hikers from all over Europe and beyond, who come to walk its steep but gradual slopes and its curvaceous trails. Old Soviet military bases that once prevented access here are long gone, and the hills are once again the domain of the hiker. Separated from the Alps by the Danube River, the mountains here may not have the glaciers, snow fields, and bold peaks found farther to the west, but they are certainly extensive—more than 70,359 square miles (182,228 sq km) in size and surrounded by plains, which from ground level provide stunning views of a mountain system that has much in common in terms of flora, fauna, and climate with the middle regions of the Alps.

Beginning in the village of Pylypets, which still has several intact seventeenth-century wooden churches and is quickly getting accustomed to its new status as a starting point for the ridge and surrounding mountains, you walk toward Borzhava Ridge through forests of beech until you reach the tree line at around 3,280 feet (1,000 m). Above it, the horizon opens up with views over the peaks of Mahura, Gemba, Verkh, and Velykyi. Blueberry and bilberry patches complete the charms of Ukraine's alpine mountains. **BDS**

Mount Ararat Trails
Iğdır, Turkey

Start/End Doğubayazit   **Distance** 41 miles
(66 km)   **Time** 5 days
Grade Moderate   **Type** Rock and sand trails
Map goo.gl/kAYMxG

At 16,853 feet (5,137 m), Mount Ararat is Turkey's highest mountain, with a permanently glacier-capped peak that can be climbed anywhere on its lower slopes without ropes during the summer, but if you want to reach the summit, then you'll be needing crampons. There are two camps on the way up: Camp #1 at 10,990 feet (3,350 m) and Camp #2 at 13,369 feet (4,075 m). Three hours separate the two camps, and the trail to Camp #2 is the steeper and rougher section. The idea is to reach the summit early enough on the third day of your ascent to witness the spectacular sunrise, which means getting up around 1:15 a.m. for a climb that should take a reasonably fit person around five and a half hours. The summit of Ararat is no walk in the park.

On your way to your departure point—the town of Doğubayazit, from where you get a 4x4 drive to the mountain—remember to make a stop at Van Castle on Lake Van, a vast fortress built by the little-known Urartu kingdom in the eighth century BCE, and take a boat ride across the lake to see the exquisitely carved stonework of a tenth-century church on Akdamar Island. You are, after all, at a rare crossroads—from Ararat's summit you will be looking into Iran, Azerbaijan, and Armenia. In other words, you are probably never going to be in this remote corner of the world again, so make the most of it. The easiest route is from the south, and the climb, while a long one, is straightforward and nontechnical. Permits are needed, and you cannot attempt the summit without a guide, but that doesn't stop thousands of people every year from climbing Ararat, a mountain of myth and legend at the top of Anatolia. **BDS**

"The highest mountain in Turkey is also the legendary mount described in the Bible where Noah landed his ark."

www.allaboutturkey.com

⤒ The climb is a long one with two base camps, but the view at the top into three countries is one to remember.

Jebel Toubkal Circuit Sous-Massa-Draa, Morocco

Start/End Imlil   **Distance** 37 miles (59.5 km)   **Time** 4 days   **Grade** Strenuous
Type Mountain hike   **Map** goo.gl/RuqXlR

The Jebel Toubkal Circuit is a trail around the base of Jebel Toubkal—at 13,671 feet (4,167 m), the highest mountain in the Atlas range. The ascent of the peak adds another 7.5 miles (12 km) but requires an extra day. The start and finish point, Imlil, is 37 miles (60 km) south of Marrakesh and easily reached from the capital by truck or taxi. The village is well equipped for hikers, with many hostelries and restaurants.

The circumambulation of the Toubkal massif runs along high passes between oasis valleys and high valleys. The former are the sites of traditional Berber villages—mud-brick, semifortified constructions. The latter offer great panoramas that extend from the white peaks of the mountain range to the brown expanses of the Sahara Desert.

Day one takes you uphill to the pass at Tizi Likemt and then down to the village of Azib Likemt, where you camp for the night. On day two you cross flat terrain to Amsouzert, the pick of the Berber settlements, with dormitory accommodation. The highlight of day three is the only lake in the region—Ifni, 164 feet (50 m) deep and 7,546 feet (2,300 m) above sea level. It is from here that anyone attempting the summit should start the final ascent. After a night nearby, it is all downhill on the final day through the villages of Sidi Chamharouch and Aremd, along the banks of the Mizane River, and back to Imlil.

The trail is best undertaken in late spring or early fall—winter is too cold; summer is too full of tourists and dehydration can be a problem. Although there are some springs, it is essential to bring adequate supplies of purified bottled water. **GL**

⊞ A tough trek around the Atlas Mountains' highest peak.

Jebel Tazekka Taza-Al Hoceima-Taounate, Morocco

Start/End National park road to the south of the mountain   Distance 10 miles (16 km)   Time 4–6 hours
Grade Easy to moderate   Type Mountain tracks   Map goo.gl/qvcKHm

The dusty, rutted track winds up through the scented cedars with regular hazy views of the woods below and the neighboring mountain ranges. You may be climbing a 6,496-foot-high (1,980 m) peak in the Atlas Mountains, but the walk up Jebel Tazekka is a surprisingly easy hike, and on a hot, dry summer's day it's hard to imagine that in the winter it is often topped with snow. Gradients are relaxed and the unpaved track is wide and easy to follow, on a route leading from the national park road below the mountain used by trucks working on the forests or driving up to maintain the telecommunication masts at the summit.

The walk could be completed in a long day's round trip from Fez, although stopping in one of the campsites would make it a more relaxing experience. The mountain forms the centerpiece of the Tazekka National Park in Morocco's Atlas Mountains, a mountainous area with gorges, caves, waterfalls, and protected forests of oak, cork, and cedar trees. Jebel Tazekka's conical summit is dominated by these protected trees, and the masts and their supporting buildings. Clambering onto rocky outcrops is a good way to see the views beyond the trees and buildings, and while many climb this gentle peak §to discover the ancient cedars near its summit, others are driven simply by a determination to tackle the mountain that dominates much of the surrounding park.

Whatever your motivation, it's a good trek through woods where you might spot red deer, wild boar, and jackals. The views can include snowy mountains to the south and the renowned Taza Gap, the mountain pass between the Rif and Atlas ranges. **SH**

↑ The higher reaches of Tazekka National Park.

Mount Sinai Summit
South Sinai, Egypt

Start/End St. Catherine's monastery
Distance 4.3 miles (6.9 km)   **Time** 3 hours
Grade Moderate   **Type** Desert trail, stone stairs
Map goo.gl/553cF6

Mount Sinai (7,497 feet/2,285 m) in the southern Sinai Peninsula is generally considered to be the biblical Mount Sinai, the place where Moses received the Ten Commandments from Jehovah, and so is revered by Christians, Jews, and Muslims alike. The Greek Orthodox monastery at the base of the mountain, St. Catherine's, was built in the sixth century and today is a UNESCO World Heritage Site.

The monastery marks the commonly accepted starting point for the one thing everybody comes here to do: hike to the summit of the mountain, bed down in whatever nook can be found in the shadows of the small Greek Orthodox chapel there, and walk back down in the morning after sufficient contemplation of a stunning sunrise. The hike doesn't require a guide, and it's impossible to get lost—just follow the person in front of you and trust they are doing the same thing.

There are two routes to the top: the shallower Siket El Bashait, about a 2.5-hour hike, or the shorter though steeper Siket Sayidna Musa, the daunting 3,750 "steps of penitence," which starts as a camel trail in a gully behind the monastery (you can take a camel partway if you wish). Be prepared for a lot of company on the way up and not a whole lot of privacy once you get there. The panorama of peaks, however, is an impressive one considering the relatively short ascent, and the sunset is one that will live long in the memory. There is also a palpable sense of camaraderie: not everyone's motivation for climbing it may be religious, but there is an undeniable bond between yourself and the collection of strangers that surround you—a rare thing indeed at any time. **BDS**

"A night camped out here under a star-filled sky allows you to wake up to one of the most beautiful sunrises imaginable."

www.roughguides.com

⤒ St. Catherine's is one of the world's oldest working monasteries.

➔ Fossilized riverbeds are common throughout southern Sinai.

Pico de Fogo Summit Walk
Fogo, Cape Verde Islands

Start/End Cha das Caldeiras   **Distance** 7.5 miles
(12 km)   **Time** 5–7 hours   **Grade** Strenuous
Type Bare rock, volcanic landscape
Map goo.gl/Oxm2Uz

The volcano Fogo rises out of the island of Fogo, a volcanic island like few others. The volcano is the island, and the island is the volcano, and its summit sits at 9,281 feet (2,829 m), a third of the height of Mount Everest. Located in the Cape Verde Islands, Fogo is an active stratovolcano whose main cone last erupted in 1675 but burst to life again via a subsidiary vent in 1995. The island is almost perfectly round and 16 miles (25 km) in diameter, with the northern, southern, and western sides of its large summit caldera virtually inaccessible due to near-vertical fault scarps. This means that if you want to walk through the clouds to its lofty summit, your final approach will be from the east, the only side open to the sea.

The walk to its summit and back takes around seven hours and begins at a track on its northern face, followed by a long climb up heavily sloping gullies through sand-like fragments of lava called lapilli. A small field of spatter cones marks the beginning of the main ascent, and it is truly a brute of a climb—a 3,000-foot (914-m) gain at an incline of between 30 and 40 degrees. Of course, there is the usual compensation that comes with the gaining of altitude. In this case, the opening up of the northern half of the crater with its vast lava flows and dozens of tiny volcanic craters called scoria. This is where the ancient cliffs of the original crater once stood, which rose still hundreds of meters more and were obliterated in one massive rock slide. Nowhere else in the world is the evidence of a lateral collapse on this scale so well preserved—a fitting reward for this strenuous hike. **BDS**

↩ The entire island is an active stratovolcano.

Elliot's Pass
Ascension Island

Start/End Old Marine Barracks
Distance 1.9 miles (3 km)   **Time** 1.5 hours
Grade Easy   **Type** Well-maintained mountain trails
Info goo.gl/XNVFa3

First cut into the forested slopes of Green Mountain in 1839, Elliot's Pass was intended as a 360-degree lookout for the British Royal Marines who were stationed there. It encircles the mountain at a height of 2,400 feet (732 m) and was widened in a precarious operation with a bulldozer during World War II to enable U.S. jeeps to access a new radar station on the mountain's southeastern flank.

In June 2005 Green Mountain became the island's first national park, a fitting development as its surrounds are home to various species of land crabs

---

"If you only have time for one walk on Ascension Island, let it be this one."

www.virtualtourist.com

---

and six of the seven plants that are endemic to the island, including the Ascension Island parsley fern that was listed as extinct in 2003 until its rediscovery in 2009. The path received a much-needed facelift in 2013, with new signage, picnic tables, restoration areas for its endemic plants, and a lot of clearing of invasive plants such as guava and ginger. New information boards have also been installed to highlight the endemic plants that can be found along the trail.

There are other paths here, too, including the walk to Dew Pond, which takes you to the highest point on the island at 2,817 feet (858 m), and perhaps a sighting of the rare African clawed toad, most probably introduced to the island during World War II. **BDS**

Meket to Lalibela Amhara, Ethiopia

Start Weldiya   **End** Lalibela   **Distance** 100 miles (160 km)   **Time** 1 week   **Grade** Easy to moderate
Type Mountain path   **Map** goo.gl/52RMOA

Discover the inspiring people and villages of Ethiopia's rural highlands by trekking this adventurous route along the ridge of the Meket escarpment from the hill town of Weldiya. This vast mountainous belt towers over the dusty farmland below, giving walkers constant views over the countryside while they explore the stunning basalt scenery above.

Ethiopia is a dry, mountainous country. This route crosses its northern region, which is dotted with ancient remains and treasures. Communities still farm with ox-drawn plows and simple hand tools. These are very poor but friendly, polite people, and walkers are warmly welcomed as they arrive in villages along the rim of the Meket plateau. The path leads to Lalibela, the former capital and one of Ethiopia's most sacred sites. An amazing labyrinth of eleven churches was hewn into the rock here in the twelfth century.

Some walkers include a trek to the summit of Abuna Yosef, (13,976 feet/4,260 m), high above Lalibela, which features a selection of churches built in caves and among the rocks. It is also one of the few remaining refuges of the endangered Ethiopian wolf.

Commercial ecotourism operators run guided hikes on the route across the Meket escarpment with accommodation in thatched village huts. Alternatively, independent walkers can hire local guides very cheaply. Much of the walking on this route is relatively easy. The altitude dilutes the equatorial heat, and the gradients on the escarpment are gentler than in the higher mountains. Few trekkers visit these parts, though, where it is common to meet wide-eyed children who have rarely seen an outsider. **SH**

⬆ Walk above traditional villages on the Meket escarpment.

Geech to Chenek Amhara, Ethiopia

Start Geech   End Chenek   Distance 10 miles (16 km)   Time 1 day   Grade Moderate to strenuous
Type Mountain paths   Map goo.gl/AmSMuy

It's a trek that confirms Ethiopia's status as one of the most mountainous countries in Africa. Starting at 11,745 feet (3,580 m) in the village of Geech, in the rugged Simien Mountains National Park, the path leads along the edge of a spectacular escarpment to the village of Chenek, 10 miles (16 km) away. Ethiopia is growing in popularity as an extreme trekking venue, thanks mostly to its central plateau, which is rarely lower than 6,562 feet (2,000 m), and twenty-five mountains whose peaks rise more than 13,123 feet (4,000 m) above some of the world's deepest canyons.

The trek between Geech and Chenek is often described as one of the finest walks in Africa, as one hikes over the summits of Intye (13,353 feet/4,070 m) and Immetgogo (12,881 feet/3,926 m), with the 360-degree view from the top of Immetgogo overlooking the entire mountain range and the vast simmering plains of the lowlands beyond. Simien Mountains National Park was declared a World Heritage Site in 1974 and coming here may well result in sightings of rare wolves, ibex, and even baboons.

The end of the trail at Chenek is in a wide, verdant high-altitude (12,073 feet/3,680 m) valley, the village framed by a semicircle of cliffs with the mountain of Bwahit looming above. Some walkers leave here on a track accessible by off-road trucks, but others use Chenek as a starting point for even more adventurous treks deeper into the mountains. They mostly begin in Bwahit and can end perhaps on Ras-Dashan, Ethiopia's highest mountain at 14,928 feet (4,550 m), which despite being only 10 miles (16 km) farther east, is separated by a 5,250-foot-deep (1,600 m) gorge. SH

⊡ The Simien Mountains have some of Africa's best hiking.

Erta Ale
Afar, Ethiopia

Start/End El Dom
Distance 6.2 miles (10 km)   Time 6 hours
Grade Moderate   Type Pebbled dunes
Map goo.gl/6Lwccd

Erta Ale is a geological phenomenon, a shield volcano in northeastern Ethiopia's Danakil Desert that is 18.6 miles (30 km) wide with a 0.4-square-mile (1-sq-km) caldera at its summit. Inside the crater are two pit craters, one in the north that is inactive but that held a lava lake in 1968 and again in 1973, and another to the south that contains one of the most astonishing natural features on the planet: a permanent lava lake with a surface temperature of almost 1,000 degrees Fahrenheit (535 degrees Celsius). The lake has been in existence for almost 100 years and is linked to a shallow magma chamber. Whereas other volcanic craters have fissures, steam vents and occasional incandescent displays of fiery rock, only here can you see a molten lake of lava, with magma swallowing up rocks and with the air so hot you can barely keep your eyes open. Yet it is impossible to close them.

Getting to Erta Ale is not easy. From Addis Ababa take a car to Mekele on the edge of the Danakil Desert. Continue from there first to the dusty hamlet of Hamed Ela, then to the makeshift community of El Dom—a final slog that can take anywhere from five hours to an entire day. The walking begins at El Dom. While little actual climbing is done, the trek is nonetheless a tough one owing to the harsh conditions underfoot and exposure to an often blistering heat for three to four hours. You'll also need to wear a scarf over your mouth to prevent sulfur inhalation. The view, however, makes you forget it all as you gaze down at the only window into our molten earth that our planet sees fit to show us. **BDS**

Stare into the heart of Ethiopia's "smoking mountain."

Kilembe Trails
Western Region, Uganda

Start UWA ranger's post   End Ranger's post near Kalalama Camp   Distance 33 miles (53 km)
Time 6–7 days   Grade Strenuous   Type Hiking
Map goo.gl/4cN5S7

This East African mountain range, known as the "Mountains of the Moon" and protected as a World Heritage Site, offers one of the most breathtaking treks in the world. Stretching for 74.5 miles (120 km), the Rwenzori range contains the third highest peak in Africa. The snowcapped mountains have a striking view from miles away, but only while hiking can you experience the range's true grandeur.

If walking the entire 33 miles (54 km) from ranger's post to ranger's post, you will need experience, great physical fitness, and a strong mindset. This track is

"These densely forested peaks ... offer an exploratory adventure of the purest kind."

www.simonseeks.com

known as the hardest track in Africa and therefore needs to be treated that way. There are, however, easier options for those unable to complete the full route. The trek provides an impressive variety of landscapes, from luscious rain forests with squawking monkeys and singing birds, to towering bamboo forests and enormous black rocks capped with snow. There are myriad species of flora and fauna, full of color, scents, and textures. The range of wildlife that can be found in this area is astounding, although the threat from poaching could mean that some species are harder to spot than others. The Rwenzori trek is an unmatched sensory experience, and the pure beauty of the natural landscape will be hard to forget. **AS**

Gorilla Walk
Western/Northern, Rwanda

Start/End Volcanoes National Park HQ
Distance Various   **Time** Various
Grade Moderate to strenuous
Type Mountain hike   **Info** goo.gl/is8VUD

Most of the 3,000 square miles (7,800 sq km) of national park around the Virunga Mountains is in the Democratic Republic of Congo. However, the section of it in Rwandan territory has the largest number of gorillas and is more practically accessible by tourists.

The route of this walk varies according to the location of the animals. Sightings are not guaranteed, but the local trackers who go out ahead of tour parties at first light are so experienced at finding the gorillas that the Rwandan authorities are justifiably proud of their success rate. Gorilla walks depart from the base

"Gorilla trekking safaris offer a magical encounter that transcends any other 'wildlife' experience."

www.expertafrica.com

daily at 7:30 a.m. Typically, they involve one and a half to three hours uphill through verdant forest; the often slippery downhill return predictably takes two-thirds of the climb time. Waterproof gear is essential.

Your time with the gorillas is strictly limited to one hour, and there are numerous rules attached. Do not go on the trip if you have an infectious illness, as colds and upset stomachs can be passed easily to the gorillas. Cancellations in such cases get full refunds. If a gorilla stares at you, politely avert your eyes. If a baby gorilla comes toward you, do not attempt to touch it, lest you arouse the parent's protective instincts. Do not eat in their presence, and leave no trace of yourself behind when you reluctantly leave. **GL**

Ol Doinyo Lengai
Arusha, Tanzania

Start/End Nainokanoka
Distance 1.8 miles (2.9 km)
Time 5–7 hours   **Grade** Strenuous
Type Grass and ash paths   **Map** goo.gl/52mYz9

Ol Doinyo Lengai in northern Tanzania is not like other volcanoes. The unusual carbonate-rich composition of the lava it ejects sees it solidify at much lower temperatures than volcanoes elsewhere. Although black or brown in color when ejected, within hours after settling, the lava turns a ghostly, pale white and creates a volcanic palette that seems to change after each event and is never the same experience twice. So when you come hiking here, you're walking over a landscape like no other—up a mountain from which the ash and dust of past eruptions helped create the fertile plains of the Serengeti.

This Maasai-named "Mountain of God," officially classified as "permanently erupting," towers 6,562 feet (2,000 m) above the Great Rift Valley and is the region's only active volcano. The trail to the summit is fully exposed to the sun and therefore a challenging one, both physically and mentally, but it is not especially technical. There are various approaches you can take, but the best is from the east and begins over steep grassy slopes between heavily incised gullies. The trail soon turns to a mix of grass and ash, and there is an uncomfortable transit along a narrow ridge that drops off sharply on either side, which will involve some scrambling on hands and knees.

The views from the crater of the Gregory's Rift escarpment and over the extinct line of the Avenue of the Volcanoes are unforgettable—when the weather cooperates—and this is without doubt one of the most thrilling and rewarding of the many rift valley treks. Consider climbing here at night to take in an early morning sunrise and avoid that energy-sapping east African sun. **BDS**

Ngorongoro Crater Rim
Arusha, Tanzania

Start/End Various
Distance 6 miles (9.6 km)
Time 2–3 hours **Grade** Easy **Type** Mountain and forest trails **Map** goo.gl/WOvD19

A guided walking safari along the rim of Tanzania's Ngorongoro Crater can be done in only two to three hours. Although short, it is guaranteed to be one of the transforming half-days of your life. The crater—the world's largest dormant, intact, and unfilled caldera—was created when this ancient volcano erupted and then fell in on itself two to three million years ago. It is 2,000 feet (610 m) deep and covers a vast 100 square miles (260 sq km); in it live around 25,000 large African animals, including black rhinos, hippos, wildebeests, zebras, impalas, and lions—a veritable who's who of Africa's great beasts.

There are multiple starting points for this walk, courtesy of the many lodges and observation posts that are sprinkled around the rim, any one of which makes an ideal base for a day's hiking. This means there is no official length, either. There is no better series of vantage points from which to take in the great immensity of the African landscape, and walking here makes a pleasant change from spending your days in the back of game-viewing 4x4s. The trail takes you through open woodlands and acacia forests in areas that are still inhabited by the local Maasai, and it is an easy one with no climbs of any real significance.

Although you won't be able to shake off the ubiquitous armed ranger who'll be accompanying you, any thoughts of charging lions will be far removed as you marvel at the views from the Oloirobi viewpoint out over the African savanna; views are so immense they obscure the hundreds of tourists walking and driving across the world's largest unbroken caldera. **BDS**

" … see tracks and signs and have the feeling of isolation that comes from trekking in the African Bush."

www.wildthingsafaris.com

⤒ Hike a portion of Ngorongoro's massive rim and get a feeling of isolation without spending days on the trail.

Mount Kilimanjaro, Marangu Route
Kilimanjaro, Tanzania

Start/End Marangu Gate
Distance 43 miles (69 km)   **Time** 5–7 days
Grade Strenuous   **Type** Mountain trails
Map goo.gl/P2NW6b

One of the most popular routes to the summit of Africa's tallest mountain Kilimanjaro (not least because it is also the most inexpensive), the Marangu Route takes a day less than other trails. This allows you a day to acclimatize before heading to the summit on the fifth day.

This walk is not for the squeamish. Each day involves five to six hours hiking on a 43-mile-long (69 km) trail, with the rest day on day three spent at Horombo hut at 12,155 feet (3,705 m), one of a number of huts strung out over a small plateau. From Horombo on day four, a choice of two trails continues on through an alpine desert habitat to the "saddle" between Kibo and Mawenzi peaks, the goal being the stone-built Kibo hut with its sixty bunk beds and platform toilets. Still another 3,920 feet (1,195 m) above you, Uhuru (Swahili for "freedom") Peak awaits you, at the pinnacle of the world's highest freestanding mountain. The final day involves a difficult ascent to the summit, and the beginning of your descent. Uhuru Peak is the goal—the highest point on the crater rim of Kibo—one of three volcanic cones that make up Kilimanjaro and the only one that is dormant (the other two are extinct).

Just a few tips: wrap your digital camera in your sleeping bag because batteries don't cope well with low temperatures (it can be -18°C/0.4°F at the summit); and remember to "walk high, sleep low"— always sleep as low as possible the night before the final ascent to lessen the effects of altitude. Most of all, though, revel in where you are: 30,000 people a year climb Kilimanjaro, and one in four don't make it. So climb slow. **BDS**

"The panoramic views from the top of Mount Kilimanjaro must be seen to be believed."

www.intrepidtravel.com

⬆ Some 1,200 types of vascular plants inhabit Kilimanjaro's approaches.

➡ The glaciers on Kilimanjaro's summit are predicted to be gone by 2060.

North Drakensberg Traverse Lesotho, South Africa

Start Sentinel Peak parking lot   **End** Bushman's Nek border post   **Distance** 142 miles (230 km)   **Time** 12–15 days
Grade Strenuous   **Type** Rough ground, animal trails, and chain ladders   **Info** goo.gl/TaZxXb

The North Drakensberg Traverse often makes the experienced walker's top ten list of the world's best walks, and it isn't hard to fathom why if you've ever seen the magnificent escarpment that gives the "Berg" its name. Its buttresses, basalt cliffs, sandstone outcrops, clear mountain streams, awesome precipices, and secret Little Berg gorges offer a true wilderness experience. Walking it is not about "how far" or "how much," it is about rewarding the senses. The Drakensberg stretches from the eastern Mpumalanga province all the way down to Cape Province in a continuous, massive escarpment that belongs to South Africa's great interior plateau. The 124-mile (200-km) long crescent-shaped section from Sentinel Peak to Bushman's Nek is a hiker's wonderland, and the wide, vertical walls of the amphitheater in Royal Natal National Park and the plateau behind it alone

make it worth coming here—to say nothing of the myriad smaller hikes that see many hikers return year after year, never walking the same trails twice.

The Grand Traverse is the mother of all possible Drakensberg hikes—142 miles (230 km) on an unmarked route over approximately two weeks, with views of the Eastern Buttress from Cleft Peak, a sunrise seen from Didima Cave, views over the Injisuthi Valley, and encounters with Basotho ponies on the High Berg that will stay with you forever. The Drakensberg also contains within its valleys and overhangs a deep array of rock paintings that tell of the legacy of the South African Bushman and the animistic beliefs of these hunter-gatherers, and so walking here is a cultural experience as well as a physical one. **BDS**

⬆ A demanding trail navigated via a series of checkpoints.

Table Mountain Summit Western Cape, South Africa

Start/End Parking area near lower cable car station **Distance** 5.3 miles (8.5 km) **Time** 5 hours
Grade Moderate **Type** Rocky trails, stone steps **Map** goo.gl/voJVTy

You can take a cable car to the summit of Table Mountain and walk back down, or you can walk up if you'd like and catch the cable car down. But really, unless you walk all the way up and back, you can never really say you've done it. And it isn't as easy as it looks. The mountain casts a kind of spell over you, with its beauty, proximity to the city, and lovely flat plateau somehow combining to suggest that climbing it will be, well, a bit of a walk in the park. Think again.

The most popular route to the summit is the Platteklip Gorge Trail (the only trail approved for people not wanting a guide), which begins close to the cable car station on the mountain's northwestern side. But whether or not you make it to the summit in the 2.5 hours that it should take will depend to a large degree on the unpredictable Cape Town weather, which can have high cloud obscuring the summit or else seriously strong ocean winds, either of which can close mountain and cable cars alike to all traffic, motorized or not.

Presuming, though, that the weather is good and you have your walking shoes on, then you are in for a treat. The Platteklip (meaning "flat rock") Trail runs right up the middle of the mountain and is the most obvious route up. Once through the zigzags, stepped paths, and the natural sandstone inclines of Platteklip Gorge, a right-hand path leads to the upper cable station, and from there to the summit beacon at 3,556 feet (1,084 m), with Cape Town and the Cape of Good Hope laid out before you—and the silvery reflections of one very tempting cable car. **BDS**

⬆ Hike a "flat-rock trail" up a flat-topped mountain.

Cirque de Mafate
Réunion Island

Start Cilaos   End Sans Souci
Distance 25 miles (40 km)   Time 2–3 days
Grade Moderate to strenuous   Type Mountain hike
Map goo.gl/6Gmn3A

The Cirque de Mafate is a caldera on Réunion Island. It is almost completely encircled by towering cliffs, formed by the partial collapse millions of years ago of Piton des Neiges, which at 10,069 feet (3,069 m) remains the tallest peak on this wonderfully rocky island.

The only break in the Cirque de Mafate is the outlet for the Rivière des Galets (Pebble River), and the remoteness and inaccessibility of the region made it a favored refuge in the eighteenth and early nineteenth centuries for slaves fleeing the island's sugar plantations. The runaways (known as maroons) settled on the flattish lands in the basin of the Cirque and built numerous small hamlets (known as *îlets*) that are still inhabited today.

The route starts at the Taïbit Pass and goes to Marla, the southernmost *îlet*. It takes around five hours at a brisk pace, but it is worth proceeding slowly in order to savor the beautiful tamarind forest en route, the perfect spot for an overnight camp. There are two other ways into the Cirque. The more demanding of them involves a short-distance elevation gain of 2,437 feet (743 m) through La Brèche Pass to the north of Le Maïdo, a 7,234 feet (2,205 m) peak. The views here are spectacular, but the 4,921-foot (1,500-m) drop at the edge of the trail is daunting. The other path is the GR2 heading south from Sans Souci.

On entering the Cirque, the next *îlet* after Marla is either Les Trois Roches or La Nouvelle, depending on which path you choose. Other places worth stopping at are Roche Plate, Ilet des Orangers, Ilet des Lataniers, Ilet à Malheur, Grande Place, Cayenne, and Aurère. The suggested walk leaves the Cirque along the banks of the Rivière des Galets and ends at Sans Souci. **GL**

"This rugged and wild cirque is the only one of the island's three natural amphitheaters that's accessible only on foot or by helicopter."

www.reunionisland.net

⬆ A remote caldera trail takes you into the midst of an island full of mountains.

Piton de la Fournaise
Réunion Island

Start Bourg-Murat **End** Enclos Fouqué
Distance 15.5 miles (25 km) **Time** 5 hours
Grade Moderate to strenuous **Type** Mountain hike
Map goo.gl/uyx1Lc

Piton de la Fournaise (Peak of the Furnace) is a volcano on Réunion Island in the Indian Ocean. The best approach begins at Bourg-Murat on the Route Forestière du Volcan, a forestry road that ends at Pas de Bellecombe, where a flight of stairs descends to the floor of the adjacent caldera.

On the way down there are two huge piles of lava slag that were deposited by earlier eruptions. One is named Formica Leo; the other, the Chapel Rosemont (for its shape, not because of any religious purpose). From the latter, there are two possible onward routes. The one to the right is shorter but steeper, and it will take you to Crater Bory in around forty-five minutes. The route to the left is easier but longer. It will take around one and a half hours to walk in spirals around Dolomieu, a crater that dropped more than 1,000 feet (305 m) during an eruption in 2007. Remnants of its original level are still visible above the current surface.

At the peak of Le Volcan is L'Enclos Fouqué, a caldera 5 miles (8 km) in diameter. It is almost surrounded by cliffs, but a breach on its southeastern side is open to the sea, which eventually will cause the whole mountain to collapse.

The steps are safe, but that is more than can be said for the surroundings. Not only is Le Volcan one of the world's most active volcanoes, but also the weather is hard to predict and may change rapidly from searing heat, with the attendant risk of sunstroke, to torrential rain or zero-visibility fog. The paths, though well marked, are narrow, and straying from them is dangerous. Hence, the crater is often closed to visitors, so check before heading out. **GL**

Le Morne
Mauritius

Start Trailhead at Le Morne's base **End** Metal perimeter fence **Distance** 1.5 miles (2.4 km) **Time** 4 hours
Grade Moderate to strenuous **Type** Hill climb
Map goo.gl/eoPjcq

Le Morne is a 1,824-foot-high (556 m) basalt outcrop that forms a spectacular promontory in southwestern Mauritius. During the eighteenth and early nineteenth centuries, it was a refuge for runaway slaves from the island's sugar plantations, thus becoming a symbol of liberty and later a UNESCO World Heritage Site.

Today, however, access to the 30-acre (12-ha) area is somewhat limited. One part of the summit remains private property, where only guided tours are permitted by prior arrangement, while all other areas are a wildlife sanctuary and hence off limits to walkers.

> *"Le Morne is the star of many postcards … [but] the view from the top is even more spectacular."*
>
> Lonely Planet

The route given here goes as far up as possible without any special arrangements. It begins near the seashore and ascends a dirt road that changes into a winding footpath. The course then becomes very steep and passes along streambeds—beware, as many of the rocks are loose and slippery. The gradient of the final section is so steep that you will have to use your hands to help you continue. Again, care is needed, because the rocks may come away or even crumble. You'll know when you've reached the private property because a metal fence bars your way. The beautiful tropical vegetation that lines the route includes mandrinette and boucle d'oreille; the former occurs only in Mauritius; the latter is the national flower. **GL**

Lebanon Mountain Trail
North to Nabatiye, Lebanon

Start Al-Qoubaiyat   End Marjaayoun
Distance 274 miles (442 km)   Time 26 days
Grade Moderate to strenuous   Type Long-distance
hiking trail   Info goo.gl/IqxntL

The Lebanon Mountain Trail is an adventurous 275-mile (442-km) track that explores more of Lebanon that any other trail in the country. It starts in the north at Al-Qoubaiyat and goes southwest, following the spine of the country as best it can, and finishes at Marjaayoun. The trail has altitude gains of up to 6,000 feet (1,828 m), which give sweeping views of ancient landscapes, and it passes through seventy-five towns and villages. Every season unveils varying aspects of the landscape, from snowcaps in the cooler months to luscious greenery in spring. The trail offers

> *"Offers charm, spirit, and beauty in a country that is still bearing the scars of its long civil war."*
>
> www.theguardian.com

something different along each segment of the trip, and it benefits from the conservation work of a number of local communities who work to preserve the trail and its impressive heritage. The scale of the track can be daunting and forbidding for some, but there are shorter options for less experienced hikers. There are twenty-six segments along the trail, most of which go through at least one village. The segments vary between 6 and 10 miles (10–16 km) in length, and there are rest stops at regular intervals, so weary hikers can rest and continue when they are ready. These sections take advantage of the trail's less strenuous grades, making it an achievable feat for anyone with determination and an adventurous spirit. **AS**

Hajar Mountain Trails
Fujairah, United Arab Emirates

Start/End Al Hala   Distance Various
Time Various   Grade Moderate to strenuous
Type Rock, stone tracks
Info goo.gl/6HhbeX

Walking along what is really nothing more than a centuries-old goat track that ascends high into the barren mountains of the Arabian Peninsula, clinging to a GPS that you only purchased the day before and are still getting used to, may not be everybody's idea of how to venture off into unfamiliar terrain. However, for visitors to the United Arab Emirates (UAE), who, after a day or two in its cities, with their often gaudy and unchecked development, are yearning to get away from it all, the promise of finding relief from the noise and the heat isn't hard to understand.

In the east, near the Omani border, lie the foothills of the Hajar Mountains, while to the north, the Ruús Al Jibal region contains peaks as high as 6,560 feet (2,000 m). The central Hajars, on the border with Oman, offer routes along ancient Bedouin trails, many of which are still used today. Needless to say, walking within this harsh environment is not easy. Countless millennia of relentless desert sun have heavily eroded the baked ground, with many sharp-edged rocks and boulders the result of being split and shattered by intense heat.

There are few paths (other than the previously mentioned goat track). Unlike in neighboring Oman, there seems to have been little thought given in the UAE to the provision of signage, and a lack of identifiable features in the terrain makes it difficult to orient yourself. Which takes us back to that GPS. Learn to use it, and you can go wherever you please in these mountains. It will encourage you to leave those weather-beaten tracks and discover hidden villages that will make any trek through these beautiful, stark mountains a walk to remember. **BDS**

Balcony Walk, Jabal Shams
Ad Dakhiliyah, Oman

Start/End Khateem village
Distance 10.5 miles (16.8 km) **Time** 4 hours
Grade Moderate **Type** Rock, gravel, and sand paths
Map goo.gl/uoqb9D

It is called the Balcony Walk, and it is aptly named—a well-marked trail that gets you as close to the edge of what is sometimes optimistically referred to as Oman's "Grand Canyon," without actually putting you over it. And it is one of Oman's most popular trails: a four-hour, out-and-back, rocky path and ancient donkey trail that begins near the summit of Jabal Shams (9,858 feet/3,005 m), Oman's highest mountain (the actual summit itself is home to a military installation and is off-limits). The Jabal Shams mountain range is in northeastern Oman, and in order to get to the trailhead at the village of Khateem you need to drive an hour from Nizwa, one of Oman's oldest cities at the base of the Western Hajar Mountains.

From Khateem, you walk beneath rock overhangs and above perpendicular walls of rock with the village of Nakhr a collection of dots on the canyon floor below you as you follow the familiar red, white, and yellow waymarkings and hiker's cairns. The trail traces a torturous line past massive sedimentary limestone formations along kilometer-high ridges and cliff edges. It passes by abandoned villages and even an occasional waterfall, all the while producing vertigo-inducing views. Although it's an exposed walk through an intensely arid-looking environment, it can be done in tennis shoes, if that's all you have, and doesn't require any nasty scrambling.

The final objective before turning back to Khateem is the deserted village of As Sab, a group of abandoned stone houses and impossibly narrow agricultural terraces that was once home to fifteen or so families who have since been relocated to the valley far, far below. **BDS**

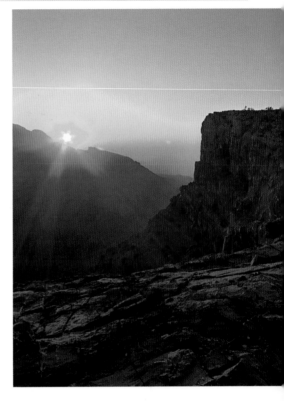

"A natural, rocky trek to the highest point in Oman [with] spectacular views into Wadi Nakhar."

www.omantourism.gov.om

⊡ Oman's "Grand Canyon" is an open-air museum displaying more than 500 million years of geologic history.

Alichur Valley Grono-Badakhshan, Tajikistan

Start/End Alichur village   **Distance** Various   **Time** Various   **Grade** Strenuous   **Type** Undeveloped mountain and valley trails   **Info** goo.gl/ub8Mf8

If you're planning to come to Tajikistan in Central Asia and walk through the Pamir Mountains' Alichur Valley, then the assumption needs to be made that you are a fully independent, hardy, adaptable, and experienced hiker. If you're not, then you shouldn't be coming here. Trekking in the Pamir Mountains, particularly here in the Murghab district, where no point is below 9,800 feet (2,987 m) elevation, is about as tough as overland trekking gets. There are endless waterless expanses and distances so vast they are deceptive. There is the risk of altitude sickness, and exposure to sun, cold, and snow glare are ever-present concerns. However, if you're properly prepared—and providing you satisfy all the requirements of the Tajik Ministry of Security (Vazorati Amniyat)—the breathtaking beauty of the world's least visited mountain range, coupled with the overwhelming hospitality of its nomadic Tajik and Kyrgyz inhabitants, means it will be one of the most enriching experiences you'll ever have.

The Alichur Valley is a good introduction for the first-time visitor. It runs from east to west for around 40 miles (64.3 km) and is up to 5 miles (8 km) wide. The main Khorog to Osh road runs through it, so you're never too far from bitumen, and in summer the valley is dotted with shepherd encampments. There are numerous side valleys worth exploring, such as the Bazar-Dara Valley in the shadows of Peak Alichur (19,038 feet/5,803 m), and from Alichur village, you can walk for 16 miles (25.7 km) to the eastern shoreline of Lake Yashilkul, and from there maybe to Lyangar River or Lake Sarez—all places in a landscape any Western tourism commission would love to call its own. **BDS**

⬆ This valley is one of Asia's least-visited regions.

Baltoro Glacier Gilgit-Baltistan, Pakistan

Start/End Askole   Distance 108 miles (174 km)   Time 2–3 weeks   Grade Moderate
Type Mountain path   Info goo.gl/48x1vn

It is one of the most fabled spots in mountain lore, referred to by most as "Concordia"—or, to the poetically inclined, "the throne room of the mountain gods." Concordia is the meeting point of two enormous glaciers in a natural bowl deep in the Karakoram Mountains. It is one of the most mountainous spots on Earth, surrounded by four peaks of more than 26,000 feet (7,925 m). It is where the Godwin–Austen Glacier flows down from the world's second-highest mountain, K2, which is 6 miles (10 km) away, and meets the Baltoro Glacier: one of the world's biggest glaciers, a 39-mile-long (62 km) river of ice feeding the mighty Indus River.

Getting there is far from easy; you start in a small, remote village of mud huts and enter one of the highest mountain wildernesses on the planet. Initial temperatures can top 86°F (30°C), but fall below freezing later in the trip. You'll need to be prepared for high altitudes: Concordia stands at 14,750 feet (4,500 m). If that isn't enough of a challenge, this northern area of Pakistan is sporadically engulfed in violence and terrorism. There are regular international warnings to avoid the region, and commercial expeditions are often canceled or postponed. Nevertheless, a few brave souls are always ready to tackle the route. From the village of Askole, most trekkers join a guided party with porters. Eventually, the route leads onto the Baltoro Glacier itself, its surface so rough that ordinary walking boots are sufficient to grip the ice. It takes about a week to reach Concordia, but some walkers still aren't satisfied and take an optional expedition to K2 base camp. **SH**

⬆ See the longest glacier outside the polar regions.

Markha Valley Trek Jammu and Kashmir, India

Start Chilling   **End** Martselang   **Distance** Various   **Time** 5–12 days   **Grade** Moderate to strenuous
Type Mountain path   **Info** goo.gl/UgjRsO

The Markha Valley Trek is considered the best route through the rugged mountainous region of Ladakh in northern India. It's a trail that passes ancient Buddhist monasteries, where red-robed monks greet you, and stops at remote mountain villages, where barefoot children stare at you with wide eyes. You'll discover high pastures where yaks graze and lonely barley fields on riverbanks far from the nearest roads.

There are other starting points for Markha Valley that make the trail harder and longer. Wherever it starts, however, the trail is almost always tackled in an eastward direction. This is because the approach to the mountain pass at Gongmaru La is so challenging if walked east to west. This windswept and barren valley, marked by cairns and Tibetan prayer flags, stands at 16,800 feet (5,130 m). It has all-around views across mountain peaks, but the wind and altitude ensure it is

not a place to linger for long. If you still want more climbing, trail walkers have the chance to ascend a major Himalayan peak nearby—the 20,997-foot-high (6,400 m) Kang Yatse.

It's possible to stay in village teahouses along the way, apart from the night before crossing Gongmaru La, an unpopulated approach that requires the pitching of a tent. The harsh weather at these altitudes means that the trek is best done between June and October. The rest of the valley is comparatively benign. There are spectacular jagged peaks and gorges to admire, but the trail itself is more gentle. The path passes a wide valley dotted with wildflowers, terraced pastures, and the camps of nomadic tribes, whose way of life hasn't changed for centuries. **SH**

⬆ Trek the Markha Valley through "Little Tibet."

Padum to Sarchu Jammu and Kashmir, India

Start Padum   **End** Sarchu   **Distance** 76 miles (122 km)   **Time** 9 days   **Grade** Strenuous
Type Mountain path with river crossings   **Map** goo.gl/xOnQ7C

Deep in a pristine valley, the milky white river curves around a jagged rocky outcrop, topped by an ancient whitewashed monastery. Not far away, shaggy yaks graze by the animal-skin tents of a tribe of nomads. Later, you follow the path as it winds far into the distance, across a high-altitude grassy plateau toward a daunting range of snowcapped peaks. You could drive from Sarchu to Padum in seven hours along the Leh–Manali Highway, but you'd miss so much if you did. Take this trail through the mountain valleys instead, and although it takes longer, you'll discover a series of memorable sights far from any road.

This trek in the northern Indian region of Ladakh starts slowly as walkers gradually acclimatize to the altitudes that dominate the route. It begins at 17,800 feet (4,500 m) in the Rupshu Valley, where the only inhabitants are Changpa Tibetan nomads tending their livestock. Days start early in order to cross rivers before the day's melting snow makes them too deep. You'll see the stone huts of friendly shepherds, and prayer walls and banners fluttering in the cold wind high on the deserted slopes of a mountain. You'll walk through hot, empty desert valleys and cross high mountain passes that make you feel as if you are on top of the world. At more than 16,400 feet (5,000m), you almost are. Highlights include the Zanskar Valley, with its ancient stone bridges and welcoming villages. Here you'll find Phuktal Monastery, one of the hidden sights of India. The twelfth-century structure is built into the face of a mighty cliff and leads into a cave in the rock and then to a spring that has delivered fresh water for centuries. **SH**

⊡ Conquer India's "land of high passes."

Shali Tibba Trek
Himachal Pradesh, India

Start/End Khatnol **Distance** 8.7 miles
(14 km) **Time** 6 hours
Grade Moderate **Type** Mountain path
Map goo.gl/PDjqJl

Start at the old summer capital of the British Raj at Shimla and from there it's a 30-mile (48-km) drive through the hills of Himachal Pradesh to the remote hamlet of Khatnol. The view from the terraced fields at Khatnol is inspiring: you overlook a steep-sided green valley, rising to the isolated mountain peak of Shali Tibba beyond. Walkers can stay at a small guesthouse in the village. Shali Tibba is one of the highest points in the Shimla region and is visible from the ridge above the capital on a clear day. The mountain's summit is topped by a temple to the Hindu goddess

"This isolated peak provides a magnificent vantage point for a panoramic ... view of Himachal."

www.indiahikes.in

Kali. From Khatnol, a rough mountain road leads up through the cedar and spruce trees. The track climbs sharply, but peters out amid the rocks. Walkers follow a well-defined ancient stone trail from here. This repeatedly zigzags to gain height on the steep south face. The fittest walkers head straight up the steep incline to save time. Flat clearings between the trees give you a chance to look out at the views. Eventually, the path reaches an arched gate to a temple with an old bell hanging from it. Beyond is a red stairway winding through the rocks. Two small concrete huts here provide overnight refuge for pilgrims and walkers. A further fifty red steps take you to the temple at the peak and the tremendous views. **SH**

Chembra Peak
Kerala, India

Start/End Meppadi
Distance 5.6 miles (9 km) **Time** 5–6 hours
Grade Easy to moderate **Type** Mountain path
Map goo.gl/qfIiEL

At 6,900 feet (2,103 m), Chembra Peak is the highest point in Kerala's Wayanad Hills, and its sharp, green summit points up into the skies of southern India. Yet, despite the mountain having an impressively vertical profile that suggests seriously steep inclines and an aching ascent, the fact is hikers soon find the path to be a relatively easy one, which any moderately fit person can conquer.

Before you start, however, call in at the Forest Range Office in Meppadi for a permit. Local guides are available here, and the range office also rents trekking equipment, including tents. Most walkers drive or catch a bus to the start of the trail, 3 miles (5 km) away where its start is marked by a white, three-story forest watchtower. Once above the initial forest, the path to Chembra is well-defined and crosses gentle slopes that are mostly open grassland.

Halfway up, you'll find a distinctive heart-shaped lake, sometimes called "Love Lake," which attracts lovesick locals. The fact that the spring-fed lake has never dried up, even in the scorching heat of summer, is taken as a kind of romantic symbol. Indian visitors sometimes camp alongside the lake. Rather less romantically, there are also the ruins of stables and a pavilion built by British colonial plantation owners, who would come here to escape the heat and play golf in the evening.

Beyond the lake a sequence of five false summits leads to the true peak, and if the top of the mountain is clear of cloud, there are rewarding views looking out over lush tea plantations, and the forests rolling away toward the distant Nilgiri Mountains, the dark greenery sliced by silver slithers of rivers and lakes. **SH**

Annapurna Circuit

Dhawalagiri, Nepal

Start Besisahar **End** Pokhara
Distance 128 miles (206 km) **Time** 3 weeks
Grade Strenuous **Type** Mountain path
Info goo.gl/xX1IM9

The Annapurna Circuit is often judged to be among the world's best long-distance trails, and it passes through an extraordinary range of environments— from hot subtropical jungle to high-altitude snow and glacier-clad mountains. This fascinating route circles the Annapurna range of mountains, which contains some of the world's highest summits, including six mountains more than 23,620 feet (7,200 m) high. The trail itself rises to a high point of 17,769 feet (5,416 m) when crossing the Thorong La Pass. It's a memorable spot, surrounded by a choppy sea of white-capped peaks. Yet the hike begins at just 2,490 feet (760 m), in the humid town of Besisahar, amid terraces of lush rice paddy fields. Swinging wood-and-rope bridges hang across river gorges as gradually the path climbs through dank canyons, pine forest, and tangled rhododendrons to grassy yak pastures and wild mountain panoramas.

The route rises so far that most schedules include several days of rest to acclimatize. Accommodation is usually in simple teahouses, and there are plenty of interesting side trips off the main route. Years ago the trail passed through a completely road-free area, but bitumen is now beginning to appear all around the Annapurna region. Roads make it easier to reach sections of the trail and improve trading for villagers, but purists bemoan the changes they are bringing. Walkers will still have memorable social encounters along the trail—it's an age-old route that's always busy and is a vital trade route between remote communities. You're sure to meet characters, from hospitable locals to fellow trekkers from all over the world and, of course, those inquisitive yaks. **SH**

"You will also pass many local people en route, providing a kaleidoscope of changing faces."

www.adventurecompany.co.uk

⯅ The Annapurna Circuit follows ancient pathways in the shadows of gigantic peaks.

Upper Mustang Dhawalagiri, Nepal

Start/End Jomsom   **Distance** 70 miles (112 km)   **Time** 8 days   **Grade** Moderate   **Type** Open rocky terrain
Map goo.gl/4gGl70

It is a world of reds, yellows, and browns, a landscape of eroded sandstone pillars and discontinuous moraine terraces: an almost treeless moonscape. The region of Upper Mustang, the former Kingdom of Lo, is in north-central Nepal, although its traditions and cultural emphasis are more Tibetan than Nepalese. It lies in the rain shadow of the mighty Himalayas, which accounts for its dry climate and barren appearance, and is surrounded by more than thirty mountains over 19,680 feet (6,000 m) high. The trails here are predictably high, too, ranging from 9,200 feet (2,804 m) to 12,400 feet (3,780 m). To walk through its semiarid deserts, over its deep ravine and rock shelves, and through its whitewashed settlements—with their fields of barley, wheat, and buckwheat, and their black, red, and white chortens and monasteries, which keep alive the spirit of Tibetan Buddhism—is truly a great experience.

The classic trail here is the Upper Mustang trek to the region's capital, Lo Manthang, a walled medieval town that is also home to the king of Mustang who, despite still being held in high regard by his people, has little real power. After flying to Jomsom from Kathmandu, you walk toward the boundary of Upper Mustang through the world's deepest gorge, the Kali Gandaki, until you reach Kagbeni, where you'll need to show your (expensive) permit. You will also know you've crossed into Mustang when you see the colored houses of Chele. From Chele, you cross a series of large spurs and pass through valleys of juniper trees. Finally, four days after leaving Jomsom, while standing on a ridge above the town of Charang Khola, you at last see Lo Manthang, the walled city of Mustang. **BDS**

⬆ **Nepal is the walker's nirvana.**

Langtang Valley Trail Bagmati, Nepal

Start/End Syabru Bensi   **Distance** 65 miles (105 km)   **Time** 6 days   **Grade** Moderate   **Type** Mountain path
Map goo.gl/ZDnO5r

Only 19 miles (31 km) north of Kathmandu, the Langtang Valley is the closest and easiest way of walking among massive Himalayan snowcapped mountains and glaciers. A winding mountain road leads from Kathmandu to Syabru Bensi, the start and finish of this trail, and it's a bumpy day's drive. Syabru Bensi is a remote little place, strung out along a dusty street in the shadows of mountain giants, an unlikely gateway to a region of acclaimed trails.

The Langtang Valley Trail was once an important trading route with Tibet. Today, it runs through part of a Nepalese national park, passing thick pine forests, lush grassy meadows, and classic mountain scenery. A trail that constantly ascends and descends, it is without any terribly challenging gradients. More of a problem may come from the thin air as the route climbs high into the central Himalayas. The climb from

Kathmandu is gradual though, and most walkers acclimatize as they proceed. The highest altitude on the trail is 12,697 feet (3,870 m).

The main trail heads east along the river from Syabru Bensi to reach the Langtang Valley, dominated by the snowy peak of Langtang Lirung (23,773 feet/7,246 m). You'll pass water mills, yak pastures, ancient shrines, and several pedestrian suspension bridges. Most walkers stay in a mix of simple local hotels, village teahouses, and tents. Before returning to Syabru Bensi, walkers have the option of a two-hour round trip to the rocky summit of Kyangjin Ri (14,272 feet/4,350 m), which is festooned with prayer flags and offers a wraparound panoramic view of this mountain kingdom. **BDS**

⬆ Retrace the footsteps of ancient merchants.

Everest Base Camp
Sagarmatha, Nepal

Start/End Lukla   **Distance** 78 miles (125 km)
Time 2 weeks   **Grade** Strenuous
Type Mountain path
Map goo.gl/zCeAI4

You might not quite be up to an ascent of the world's highest mountain, but trekking to Everest Base Camp could be the next best thing. This trail into the high Himalayas takes you to the plateau beneath the renowned icefall at the foot of Everest, a small flat rocky shelf at the center of an amphitheater of towering snowy peaks. Most climbers are based in this desolate spot during their attempts on the summit.

Base Camp is 11,500 feet (3,500 m) below the summit of Everest, but reaching it still presents quite a challenge: it sits at a dizzy 17,590 feet (5,361 m) above sea level. Trekkers usually fly from Kathmandu into the start point at Lukla, though it is possible to trek independently to Lukla; most hikers hire Sherpa guides and porters, or join commercial hiking groups. From here the route ascends and descends, following the Dudh Koshi River into the Sagarmatha (Everest) National Park. The path crosses glaciers, traverses steep valleys, and climbs high-altitude passes, and the trail includes side trips to ascend smaller peaks that offer views of some of the highest mountains in the world.

Increasingly, you'll catch glimpses of Everest in the distance. As the altitude rises, trekkers need to allow for rest days to acclimatize, which is why the journey up to Base Camp takes twice as long as the trek back down. Hikers also have a chance to experience local culture while staying in small teahouses each night. You'll pass towns, villages, and monasteries en route, including a school founded by Everest pioneer Sir Edmund Hillary in the village of Kumjung. **SH**

➡ Trek to the greatest base camp of them all.

Mera Peak Summit Sagarmatha, Nepal

Start/End Lukla   **Distance** 113 miles (182 km) via Amphu Laptsa Pass   **Time** 27 days   **Grade** Strenuous
Type Mountain path   **Info** goo.gl/MSRixT

Mera Peak is one of Nepal's highest mountains that you can scale without specialist mountaineering skills. At 21,247 feet (6,476 m), this is a seriously high mountain, yet most fit hill walkers can manage it in the company of a commercial trekking party. Getting there isn't quite so straightforward, however. Most fly in from Kathmandu to the high mountain airstrip at Lukla. Then it's a long hike, through forests and pastures, that leads up into a wilder alpine environment. The path crosses a high pass at Zatrwa La, then dips steeply down and up again at the Hinku Valley.

Mera Peak stands at the watershed of the Hinku and Honga valleys in the heart of the Himalayas, and the route there is designed to gain height gradually, allowing walkers to acclimatize to the altitude over a period of about a week. The climb up the north face of Mera isn't hard, and for hikers it represents an ideal

introduction to a true Himalayan experience up a glacier and snow slopes, with no more than thirty-degree gradients. The final ascent to the summit is a little steeper, but there are fixed ropes in place to help. Hikers wear crampons and carry ice axes, and trekking parties are roped together. More problems occur because of the high altitude and cold than the terrain. It can drop to minus 4°F (20°C) on the mountain at night and can get very windy. The journey involves camping for a night on a rocky outcrop on the mountain's north ridge at 19,028 feet (5,800 m), and the reward is one of the most famous views in the Himalayas. From the summit of Mera Peak, you can see five of the world's six highest mountains, including Mount Everest. **SH**

⊡ The Mera Peak trail is Nepal's highest "walk-up" trail.

Snowman Trek Paro to Wangdue Phodrang, Bhutan

Start Paro village **End** Sephu village **Distance** 211 miles (340 km) **Time** 3 weeks **Grade** Strenuous
Type Often muddy gravel and dirt mountain trails **Info** goo.gl/7byOzy

Universally regarded as the most difficult trek in a country replete with challenging trails, the Snowman Trek follows a spine of the Himalayas from Paro in the west to Trongsa in the east. After an initial detour to Taktsang, Bhutan's famous "Tiger Monastery," the trail is joined, and by the time you're done you will have crossed eleven high mountain passes, threaded your way through dense cedar and bamboo forests, passed by waterfalls, skirted the edge of glaciers (no glacier walking involved), and explored the gorgeous mountain villages of Goyok and Lingshi on a slender sliver of a path that has been used for centuries by Bhutanese traders and farmers.

Black bears can be glimpsed on the approaches to this high-altitude path on which you'll be camping for as many as sixteen consecutive nights above 13,123 feet (4,000 m). You're likely to see Himalayan blue sheep and if you're really lucky a snow leopard. However, if it's been raining, it's the mud you'll notice first, then maybe the leeches. This is a strenuous and demanding traverse. Trekking companies won't take you unless you can demonstrate that you have the fitness to complete it. So don't leave it to chance—get fit. Don't miss the thrill of climbing Sinche La Pass (15,977 feet/4,869 m) or inching your way to Tsemo La Pass (16,090 feet/4,904 m) for its view across to mighty Chomolhari—providing the weather cooperates, that is. The failure rate for this trek because of the region's remoteness and unpredictable weather verges on 50 percent. More people have stood on Mount Everest's summit than have finished the demanding Snowman Trek. **BDS**

⊡ The trek passes through many beautiful villages.

Chomolhari Trek Paro/Thimphu, Bhutan

Start/End Paro Valley   **Distance** 33 miles (53 km)   **Time** 6–7 days   **Grade** Moderate
Type Mountain, gravel paths   **Map** goo.gl/l7KpDv

Chomolhari (or Jomolhari)—the sacred source of Bhutan's Paro River that straddles the border between Bhutan and Tibet—is a great Himalayan mountain with a north face that towers 8,900 feet (2,710 m) above the Tibetan plains. The mountain lacks the sort of mountaineering legacy common to other Himalayan peaks, due to the difficulty of access from the Tibetan side and trekking restrictions in Bhutan, and so far has seen only six successful ascents. However, there are no restrictions on walking to its base camp, which is only a three-day trek from Paro Valley.

At 23,997 feet (7,314 m), Chomolhari is the country's second highest peak. The path to its base camp—which forms part of the Snowman Trek—might be rock strewn, muddy, and shared with pack animals, but it is not difficult. Your first glimpse of the mountain comes on the second day, from the camp at Thangkthanka

(11,545 feet/3,520 m) inside Jigme Dorji National Park. It is here that the terrain becomes more challenging, and if you're going with a tour operator, you will switch from horses to yaks at this point. The following day is an easy walk to Jangothang, Chomolhari base camp at 13,340 feet (4,066 m), which you should arrive at with enough energy to spare to walk thirty minutes to a viewpoint out to Jichu Drake (22,290 feet/6,794 m), Chomolhari's neighboring and lesser known peak. You can pitch your tent in the shadows below Lingshi Dzong, a fortress monastery that was built in 1668 to commemorate the victory over an invading Tibetan army. European climbers call Chomolhari the "Matterhorn of the Himalayas"—an apt description for one of the Himalaya's most beautiful mountains. **BDS**

⬆ Chomolhari is the "Matterhorn of the Himalayas."

Druk Path Paro/Thimphu, Bhutan

Start Paro Valley   **End** Thimphu   **Distance** 33 miles (53 km)   **Time** 6 days   **Grade** Moderate to strenuous
Type Mountain trails, shale, exposed rock   **Map** goo.gl/TgxUmi

The six-day Druk (Dragon) Path follows an ancient trading route through blue pine forests, past alpine lakes, along heart-stoppingly narrow high ridges, and past *dzongs* (monasteries) and villages. It is Bhutan's most popular trail, thanks mostly to its proximity to the capital, Thimphu, but also because it gives access to so much in such a short time, including spectacular views of the world's highest, still-unscaled peak, Gangkar Puensum (24,835 feet/7,570 m).

It begins with a tough 3,280-foot (1,000-m) ascent on the first day after leaving the National Museum in Paro Valley, and a ninety-minute ascent on the second day puts you in the midst of alpine forests and groves of dwarf rhododendrons, a land of herders and yaks. The next two days, providing you haven't succumbed to altitude sickness, are happily spent camping by the alpine lakes Jimgelang Tsho, Janetso, and Simkotra Tsho. Day five should bring your first views of Gangkar Puensum and several other mighty Himalayan peaks.

The final day on the Druk Path involves a 4,265-foot (1,300-m) descent past Phadjoding Monastery, once one of Bhutan's richest monasteries, but after years of neglect, it found itself listed by the World Monuments Fund as one of the world's five most endangered cultural monuments. It is still an impressive sight, however, and remains one of the country's most important meditation sites. As well as being home to more than forty monks, it is now also a refuge for underprivileged boys. The final descent into the Thimphu Valley is through forests of blue pines, offering great views of the city and the promise of some much-needed rest for aching knees. **BDS**

⊡ The Tiger's Nest Monastery in Paro Valley.

Mount Kailash
Tibet, China

Start/End Lake Manasarovar
Distance 32 miles (51.4 km)   Time 3 days
Grade Moderate   Type Rocky, open terrain
Map goo.gl/FclrqO

Every year thousands of pilgrims come to Mount Kailash, a remote peak in the equally remote Kailas Range in southwestern Tibet, as they continue a tradition that says good luck will come to all those who complete a circuit of this revered mountain. Hindus and Buddhists walk it in a clockwise direction, while Jains and followers of Bonpo (a non-Buddhist Tibetan sect) take a counterclockwise route. Either way, it is a 32-mile (51.4-km) circuit, a feat of endurance that includes crossing an 18,372-foot-long (5,600 m) pass on a route some pilgrims manage to complete in one day. It's possible to walk around Mount Kailash in a day, despite its terrain and high altitude, but unless you have a higher purpose for being here, allow three days to admire the perfection of each of the four faces of this 22,112-foot-high (6,740 m) mountain.

Mount Kailash is believed to be a stairway to heaven, but as it's considered sinful to walk on the mountain itself, you have to circumambulate it. The only person ever recorded to have climbed it was an eleventh-century Buddhist yogi named Milarepa. When the Chinese government gave permission for a Spanish team to climb it in 2001, the international outrage was so strong that the Chinese revoked their permit. "I would suggest they go and climb something a little harder," said mountaineer Reinhold Messner. "Kailash is not so high, and not so hard."

"Precious Snow Mountain," as Tibetans call it, is situated alongside Lake Manasarovar, and it is the loop around Kailash, combined with a wash in the lake's waters, that is believed to bring salvation. **BDS**

← The pyramid-like summit of Mount Kailash.

Ganden Monastery to Samye Monastery Tibet, China

Start Ganden Monastery   End Samye Monastery
Distance 50 miles (80 km)   Time 5–6 days
Grade Moderate to strenuous   Type Open rocky trails   Map goo.gl/O2bMio

Widely regarded as one of the finest walks anywhere in the world, this trail is at high altitude. It begins, after a 43-mile (69-km) drive from the Tibetan capital of Lhasa, at Ganden Monastery, situated at 13,940 feet (4,249 m) and one of Tibet's monastic universities.

After ninety minutes, you'll arrive at a saddle on an ascending trail with views over the Kyichu Valley; pass through the village of Hepu (where yaks will be rented for the rest of the trek) and an old nunnery, Ani Pangong; before camping in the Yama Do Valley at the end of the first day. The trail continues with a demanding

> *"Unforgettable trekking in one of the most beautiful areas of Tibet. A pilgrimage between two holy sites."*
> besthike.com

ascent over the Shogu-La Pass (17,224 feet/5,250 m) before descending to Samye Monastery at 11,600 feet (3,535 m), Tibet's first Buddhist monastery founded in 779 on the north bank of the Yarlung Tsangpo River.

There is a lot of climbing on this trek, including at Chitu-La Pass (16,732 feet/5,100 m), with its vast rock field. There are also meadows and lovely alpine forests, but be prepared for some serious ups and downs. Once past Chitu-La Pass, however—and its basin containing three small lakes—the trail widens and becomes easy to negotiate as you enter a forest of rhododendrons. Soon after, Yamalung Hermitage and a final four-hour walk, you reach the spires of Samye Monastery. **BDS**

Shalu–Ngor–Narthang Trek Tibet, China

Start Shigatse–Gyangtse road **End** Narthang Monastery **Distance** 25 miles (40 km)
Time 2 days **Grade** Easy **Type** Rocky terrain, dirt paths, meadows **Map** goo.gl/Yu5V3Z

If you're the sort of person who'd like to experience a Tibetan trek, but cannot spare the time or don't have the inclination for a week or more of huffing and puffing your way along high-altitude trails, then a walk from Shalu Monastery to Narthang Monastery via the monastery at Ngor is a near-perfect compromise. There are two passes you need to cross along the way, but neither are at the sort of altitudes you generally have to negotiate here. Although two days is all the walking time you need, there is always the option of extending the trip to four or five by spending a day at each monastery, discovering their individual delights and staying overnight in local villages.

A minibus from the town of Shigatse will get you to your start point on the Shigatse–Gyangtse road, and from there you walk for about an hour along a sealed road. After about forty minutes, you reach a

tenth-century shrine, and Shalu Monastery (12,775 feet/ 3,894 m) is in the hills to the shrine's west. Nestled in a small valley near the Niyang River, Shalu was founded in 1040 and restored after a bad earthquake in 1333. From Shalu to Ngor Monastery (14,025 feet/4,275 m) takes around ten hours, but you can hire a horse at Shalu and overnight in the Chaklung Valley. Remember to take your own water on this pleasant stretch through eroded hills and gullies, valleys of wildflowers, and past fields of barley and canola. It's a six-hour walk past whitewashed houses and along a broad gravel plain to Narthang Monastery (13,700 feet/ 4,175 m), which presents a ruined spectacle with its massive mud walls. However, its resident monks will give you a warm Tibetan welcome. **BDS**

⬆ Reddish-gray mountains of the Showa La pass.

Mount Emei Sichuan, China

Start/End Wannian Temple   **Distance** 38 miles (61 km)   **Time** 2–3 days   **Grade** Moderate to strenuous
Type Mountain paths, stone steps   **Map** goo.gl/TVsCXZ

In a country that for thousands of years has revered its mountains as places of solitude and reflection, and as the preferred locations of monasteries and hermit's huts, there are few that are written of so poetically and with as much unabashed fondness as Mount Emei. It has been described as "a huge green screen in the southwest of the Chengdu Plain," with a shape that resembles the "eyebrow of a girl" and a summit that "reaches to the sky."

From its 10,103-foot (3,079-m) summit, you can look east over the plains or west to the Daxinganling Mountains. Its waterfalls and streams have names such as Flying Waterfall Hanging over Dragon Gate and Listen to the Spring beside the Tiger Brook. Some 5,000 years ago Emperor Xuanyuan came here to receive Taoist teachings; 3,000 years later the first monastery was built, and ever since Mount Emei has been a place of pilgrimage and worship, the highest of the four sacred Buddhist mountains of China.

Buddhist temples, grottoes, and artwork can now be found all over this sacred mountain, linked by a vast network of trails that are busy at the base with hawkers and street vendors, but once you start climbing, you soon leave the crowds behind. After four hours of ascending, you can overnight at the Elephant Bathing Pool Temple, and from there the final climb to the Golden Summit and its giant Buddha statue will take you about two hours. On the summit, unless you arrive early, you will be immersed in people again, thanks to buses and cable cars that bring those not willing to make the climb. The walk back down takes around seven, largely solitary, hours. **BDS**

⊞ Emei is home to more than seventy monasteries.

Mount Hua Plank Walk
Shaanxi, China

Start/End Base of Mount Hua
Distance Various **Time** Various
Grade Moderate **Type** Rock paths, stairs,
plank walkway **Info** goo.gl/Df7HGh

It has been described as the world's most dangerous walk, and if you look at the photograph of the plank walkway sticking out optimistically from the vertical rock face of Mount Hua's south peak in China's Shaanxi province shown at right, you probably wouldn't argue. If you have anything approaching a fear of heights, though, don't do it. If you suspect you might *develop* a fear of heights while on it, or plan on wearing an old pair of tennis shoes, or if you've just lost your job or recently broken up, don't do it. Better still, come to think of it, better to just not do it.

Some would say that to malign what is a perfectly wonderful and unique walk, just because people have fallen off and died while attempting it, is unfair. After all, there are chains and handholds chiseled into the rock for you to grip, and even a harness can be worn if you're so inclined. If you are properly prepared and use common sense, however, there really is no reason why the ascent of one of China's five sacred mountains—there is a Taoist temple on the summit and a number of other temples and shrines dotted across its slopes and peaks—cannot be the greatest adrenaline rush you've ever had with your shoes on.

Even without the plank walk, the towering granite spire that is Mount Hua would be one of China's premier hiking destinations. The mountain has five distinct peaks—north, south, east, west, and a central peak—all of which are of a similar height. The south peak with the terrifying plank walkway is the highest at 7,070 feet (2,155 m), but there are a myriad of trails to choose from, and the views, all the way down to the Yellow River, are incomparable. Just remember to hang on. **BDS**

"[Involves] steep staircases, vertical ascents, and a plank trail consisting of wooden platforms bolted onto the mountainside."

www.huffingtonpost.com

← Fortunately, there are many other hiking options over and around Mount Hua's five distinct peaks.

↑ The plank walk is every bit as terrifying as it looks.

Upper Trail, Tiger Leaping Gorge Yunnan, China

Start Qiaotou End Walnut Grove Distance 14 miles (22.5 km) Time 2–3 days Grade Easy to moderate
Type Mountain trail Map goo.gl/jI8egF

There is a lot to recommend on the hike along the Upper Trail of China's Tiger Leaping Gorge (there is a lower trail, but it's a poor option): it is yet to become commercialized; you don't require a guide to do it; and the views as you head out from your starting point, the village of Qiaotou, will last you a lifetime. Just be sure to politely refuse the many offers from the local Naxi people of a pony to help you on your way. This is one fabulous hike, and you don't want to be doing it in a saddle.

Tiger Leaping Gorge is a canyon on the Jinsha River—a tributary of the upper Yangtze River and a contender for the world's deepest river canyon, thanks to the twin peaks of Haba Snow Mountain at 17,703 feet (5,396 m) and Jade Dragon Snow Mountain at 18,360 feet (5,596 m), between which the Jinsha flows. According to legend, in order to escape from a

pursuing hunter a tiger leaped 80 feet (25 m) across the gorge to freedom.

The trail is marked and well-maintained. It passes waterfalls and heated guesthouses reminiscent of the teahouse trails of Nepal, which can provide you with a refreshing, sweet rosebud tea and a hot shower. The precipitous trail is Nepal-like, too, taking you through forests of pine and bamboo and coming precariously close to cliffs that fall away to the distant river below. If tempted, when you reach the trail's end at Walnut Grove by the river's edge after descending from the clouds, you can continue with a guide into the mountains beyond. These are inhabited by Tibetan and Yi tribes and you can discover why Yunnan is China's most ethnically diverse province. **BDS**

⬆ The Yangtze River has carved out a breathtaking gorge.

Baiyang Waterfall Trail Hualien, Taiwan

Start/End Tiangxiang   **Distance** 1.5 miles (2.4 km)   **Time** 2 hours one way   **Grade** Easy
Type Stone, forest trail   **Map** goo.gl/TfwpOu

The Baiyang Waterfall Trail that winds its way down Taroko Gorge in Taiwan's Taroko National Park is about as tranquil as a walk in the woods can get. It is cut into a beautiful valley and threads its way along a winding, rocky cliff, with every step accompanied by the sound of the rushing water below. There is a wide array of flora and fauna, some quite wonderful cool tunnels to walk through if you're doing the trail in summer, and at the end there's the reward of a two-tiered waterfall that cascades over a 656-foot-high (200 m) cliff, complete with a suspension bridge and observation deck. But that's not the end of it. If you walk another 980 feet (300 m), you'll reach what locals call the "water curtain"—a ribbon-thin wall of water that emerges from a tunnel roof—behind which you can walk between the water and the tunnel wall or just stand in and have a shower to refresh you for the walk back, which, considering your surroundings, won't be anytime soon.

There are seven tunnels on the way to the Baiyang Waterfall, some of which are lit and some of which are not—a nod to their resident bat populations. The magnificence of the waterfall only reveals itself as you emerge from the seventh and final tunnel, and rarely has a destination had such a sense of the dramatic. Long before you see it, you can hear it.

The trail and its tunnels were built by the Taiwan Power Company in the 1980s, when it was thought that the valley could be utilized for a hydroelectric scheme. Thankfully, that never came to pass, and the Baiyang Waterfall Trail remains one of Taiwan's most peaceful and lovely walks. **BDS**

⬆ The trail loops its way down to the waterfall.

Tunnel of the Nine Turns Trail Hualien, Taiwan

Start/End Entrance to Jiuqudong tunnel
Distance 2.4 miles (3.8 km)   Time 2 hours
Grade Easy   Type Smooth, wide pathways;
tunnels   Map goo.gl/a93TTy

Taroko National Park, in the northwest of Taiwan, is famous for its 12-mile (19.3-km), steep-sided marble gorge. The park covers an extensive area either side of the river totaling about 355 square miles (919 sq km). In this wild expanse, there are plenty of opportunities for walkers to explore the mountains, rivers, bridges, tunnels, waterfalls, and thick forest of the area. The Chongde Trail, for example, leads from the park down to the cliffs and pebble beach of the Pacific seashore. The Huitouwan to Lianhua Pond route takes walkers up a beautiful ravine, over a delicate suspension bridge, and then to a small lake in the mountains.

The walk we have chosen to highlight here is the Tunnel of the Nine Turns Trail, one of the major sights of the Taroko National Park. This route starts from the central cross-island highway that leads through the middle of the park. The walk is only 1.2 miles (1.9 km) long, but many walkers do it, then come back the same way. It passes through the most popular part of the park, where sheer blue-gray rock faces are no more than a few feet apart, with the Kelan River rushing between them. The lush vegetation clings to the sides of the ravine, and the walkway passes through tunnels in the faces of the gorge and under overhanging marble rocks along the side of the river, which is sometimes far below. The path is wide and smooth and has sturdy safety barriers at potentially dangerous spots. Watch out for unusual air currents here. The wind blows down the wider valley beyond and squeezes into the narrow gorge, forcing the air up to create strange vertical winds. **SH**

◁ The Kelan River slices through the Taroko Gorge.

Mount Yushan Summit Nantou, Taiwan

Start/End Upper Dongpu parking lot, Express
Way 21   Distance 14 miles (22.5 km)
Time 2 days   Grade Moderate to strenuous
Type Mountain path   Map goo.gl/vFcSrb

Perched at the top of one of the highest mountains in the western Pacific, watching the sun rising above the ocean horizon, is a memorable experience. It can be the reward for a relatively simple hike to the top of Mount Yushan. Taiwan's highest peak is 12,966 feet (3,952 m) above sea level, making it the fourth-highest mountain on any island in the world. The path to the top is straightforward but tiring; it can be done in one day, but two is better. For the one-day permit, however, you must prove your experience of high-altitude walking by providing a photograph of

> *"In late spring . . . the mountain flowers are in full bloom on Batongguan meadow."*
>
> www.go2taiwan.net

yourself at the summit of another 10,000-foot (3,048-m) peak. Everyone else must settle for a two-day permit. This means hiking to the Paiyun Lodge, a mountain cabin at 11,161 feet (3,402 m). It takes six hours of walking up moderate gradients to reach the lodge. The well-maintained trail is clear to follow, and there are even toilets. Paiyun has catering and around 100 beds, but it has to be booked in advance. The normal timetable is to leave Paiyun at 3 a.m. for the summit climb. This two-hour trek is steeper and harder. Walkers must tackle scree slopes in the dark and endure noticeably thinner air. It's worth it for the sunrise from the peak, though, which, on a clear day, includes seas visible on both sides of the island. **SH**

Mount Beichatian
Taoyuan, Taiwan

Start/End Xiao Wulai   **Distance** 10 miles (16 km)
Time 1 day   **Grade** Strenuous   **Type** Boardwalk,
stairways, ladders, ropes, mountain path
Map goo.gl/bT2J6V

"Given that Beichatian can be done in a day from Tapei, it is incredibly remote and feels very much like a high mountain trek."

hikingtaiwan.wordpress.com

⬆ Wooden boardwalks and rope ladders assist hikers onto the peak of this muddy mountain.

Not all mountains are bare chunks of dry rock. Taiwan's Mount Beichatian is a hefty peak of 5,666 feet (1,727 m), but its slopes are covered with forest. Far from dusty stone pathways, walking up Mount Beichatian is all about conquering muddy slopes through the trees.

Thankfully, some of the steepest sections are ascended by makeshift wooden ladders and dangling ropes, but it's not unusual for walkers to end up covered in mud by the time they reach the summit. It's worth the effort, however, as the trail winds through spectacular towering forests of ancient redwoods. Some of these are so huge, you can walk underneath the roots. In fact, one climber, who got lost on the mountain in 2010, spent the night sleeping in a hollow under a tree while rescuers scoured the mountain in vain. He was discovered walking into the parking lot at the base of the mountain in the morning. The path passes streams gushing down between the trees, occasionally cascading as misty waterfalls. These often have romantic names, such as White Veil or Full Moon. Some streams can be crossed on wooden bridges or by walking on top of a naturally fallen tree.

The Mount Beichatian climb is a popular hike in Taiwan because it can be done in a day from the island's capital, Taipei. Hikers generally approach from two directions. The shortest route is through the southern trailhead at Xiao Wulai, a five-hour trek to the summit. The second is via Manyueyuan, a longer trek of about eight hours to the top. Some walkers camp in the woods halfway up. Note that the muddy slopes lead to frequent landslides, and the routes often change or are closed because of this. **SH**

Jiangziliao Cliff Trail
New Taipei, Taiwan

Start/End Parking area by the Earth God Temple on County Route 31   Distance 5 miles (8 km)
Time 2 hours   Grade Easy to moderate
Type Forest track   Map goo.gl/rCHozN

From a parking lot on the bend of a little-used country road a short drive from the busy port city of Keelung, the Jiangziliao Cliff Trail winds high above a swift-flowing stream. The path is reached via stone steps that are cut into the steeply rising hillside, and occasionally, there are stretches of rope that can be used as handrails to assist walkers along its steeper gradients. This rough trail climbs up through the Jiangziliao hills until, eventually, a huge boulder protrudes above the stream giving walkers a bird's-eye view of the water flowing over the rocks below. The trail then continues a little way upstream to a secluded waterfall.

Jiangziliao may not rank among the biggest waterfalls in Taiwan's lush hills and mountains, but it is certainly one of the prettiest. Located in a tranquil setting in a clearing in the forest, its stream plunges 50 feet (15 m) into a clear circular pool eroded from the sandstone. The stream then tumbles down a series of steps in the rock, each one a small circular pool worn into the smooth stone, before flowing away through the forest.

Follow the path a little farther above this waterfall and you will see the stream trickling across an intricate web of tiny gullies eroded into a flat bed of rock, forming more appealing little shallow round pools. On the opposite bank, looming overhead, is the overhanging face of Jiangziliao Cliff. This 100-foot-high (30 m) rock face is festooned with green climbing plants and trees precariously hanging from crevices. The impressive cliff and the cold pools of mountain water create a perfect sheltered spot to relax on a hot Taiwan summer's day. **SH**

Youkeng Old Trail and 1,000 Step Path
New Taipei, Taiwan

Start Sandiaoling railway station   End Shifen
Distance 15 miles (24.1 km)   Time 8 hours   Grade Strenuous   Type Steep forest and mountain path
Map goo.gl/Ljlltu

This route starts at Sandiaoling in the mountainous Keelung Valley, less than an hour's train journey southeast of Taipei. From there, take a short walk along the rail tracks to the village of Yuliao, where the trail proper leads up into the woods by a stream. You'll need a local map, as the forest is crisscrossed with paths. Youkeng Old Trail is just one of them and can be hard to follow in the thick vegetation. The way-marking signs on the trails are only in Chinese. The Old Trail leads through the lush ferns, creepers, and trees parallel to the railway, all the way to Dahua station. On

> *"The 1,000 Step Ridge ... is a lot more attractive and worthwhile than the name might suggest!"*
>
> www.taiwandiscovery.wordpress.com

the way, it passes waterfalls, ruined miners' houses, and remote farms. Some sections follow the narrow concrete path alongside the rail tracks. This scenic stroll takes around three hours, and you could finish at the station and take the train home. However, this route continues more adventurously on a path over Mount Youkeng to join Mount Neipinglin ridge. Some of it is arduous, with steep muddy slopes to be tackled, often while clinging to tree branches for support. The Neipinglin ridge path leads into the Pinghu Forest's recreation area. The descent to Shifen is via the 1,000 Step Ridge Path, a sequence of log steps down through the woods. Finally, the path reaches the village after passing underneath a highway flyover. **SH**

Teapot Mountain
New Taipei, Taiwan

Start/End Jinguashi Gold Ecological Park
Distance 7 miles (11.2 km) **Time** 5 hours **Grade**
Moderate to strenuous **Type** Steps and surfaced paths,
some fixed ropes and scrambling **Map** goo.gl/nT6hvz

The trail starts in the Jinguashi Gold Ecological Park, a free attraction celebrating the north coast's gold mining heritage from the Japanese colonial era. Follow the tracks of the former railway past the mine and find the start of the real path, which leads steeply up under a wooden arch. The distances aren't great, but there are a lot of wood and stone steps as the path climbs rapidly up into the green Keelung Mountains. Occasional shady pavilions are provided for a rest from the sun, and halfway up you'll find the romantic stone ruins of an ancient Shinto temple.

Teapot Mountain's strange rock formations look somewhat like a teapot and, strangely, the rocky summit is hollow, and the path leads up inside the "teapot." Walkers scramble out of the vertical rock tunnel to encounter breathtaking views of Taiwan's northeast coast.

From the summit of Teapot Mountain most people continue along a grassy ridge to Banpingshan, another small rocky peak with even more spectacular panoramic coastal views. The route then descends back to Jinguashi via the pretty tourist town of Jiufen, with plenty of classic Taiwanese teahouses for refreshment. Note that the grasses along this route can be taller than you are. The Silver Grass variety in particular has sharp leaves, so long trousers and long sleeves are advisable. Clambering up the final parts of Teapot Mountain and Banpingshan involves using fixed ropes, but it's not as hard as it sounds. Most fit walkers tackle these sections easily. More importantly, there are very few trees along the whole route, so shade is at a premium during the hot months. A hat, water, and sunscreen are vital. **SH**

> *"Jinguashi is a magic place, built onto steep, grassy slopes beneath the ... extraordinary rocky flourish of Teapot Mountain."*

www.taiwandiscovery.wordpress.com

⬆ Teapot Mountain's summit provides great views over Taiwan's northeast coastline.

Baekdu-daegan Trail
Seoul, South Korea

Start Jinbu-ryeong   **End** Cheonwang-bong
Distance 456 miles (734 km)   **Time** 7–8 weeks
Grade Strenuous   **Type** Mountain trails
Info goo.gl/IJvXID

The Baekdu-daegan mountain ridge runs for 1,056 miles (1,700 km) down almost the entire length of the Korean Peninsula, from Baekdu Mountain—high in North Korea and on the border with China—south to Cheonwang-bong Mountain (6,282 feet/1,915 m), South Korea's highest peak. Considered the "spine" of the nation, this impressive mountain range features prominently in Korean thought, philosophy, and practice, although sadly the prospect of walking the entire length of its crest—the long-held dream of every Korean hiker—remains elusive as long as the demilitarized zone (DMZ) through which it crosses still exists and the Korean Peninsula remains divided.

For South Koreans, the trail begins at Jinbu-ryeong, a pass just south of the DMZ, and if you were to walk the entire 456 miles (734 km) south to Cheonwang-bong, you would bisect no fewer than seven national parks—Jiri-san, Deogyu-san, Songni-san, Worak-san, Sobaek-san, Odae-san, and Seorak-san—as well as two provincial parks, Mungyeong-saejae and Taebaek-san, on a trail that will take you either over or close to hundreds of peaks. It can be a very tough trail, and it offers a true sense of isolation despite never being too far from civilization, whether it be hikers out for a day's walk, numerous Buddhist temples and hermit's refuges, or farmers in the mountains' foothills who grow everything from wild vegetables to ginseng. The trail is being walked by increasing numbers of foreigners who want to experience what it's like to pass through the heartland of this ancient country, along a mountain range infused with what Koreans call *gi*, a divine energy that infuses the entire peninsula with its protective power. **BDS**

"*Baekdu-daegan . . . is a strong symbol of identity and nationalism for the people of both Koreas.*"

www.hikekorea.com

⤒ Baegundae Peak is the highest summit in this South Korean trail that passes through seven national parks.

Gajisan Ridge Loop Gangwon, South Korea

Start/End Seongnamsa Temple   **Distance** 5 miles (8 km)   **Time** 4–5 hours
Grade Moderate   **Type** Mountain, forest trails   **Map** goo.gl/E5Bw5w

Gajisan Provincial Park in South Korea's Baekdu-daegan Mountains is a ninety-minute drive north of the city of Busan. Known locally as the Yeongnam Alps, they possess, if you believe the local hype, a "balance of beauty and heroic features" that is "greater than the Alps in Europe." While that claim may be hyperbole, these mountains are still beautiful, and, while they do not provide for any extended trekking, they do offer a fabulous choice of half-day and full-day hikes among some truly gorgeous landscapes. The park's highest peak is Gajisan at 4,068 feet (1,240 m), from the summit of which you can look north over a crenellated jumble of summits that stretch to the horizon, including Unmunsan (3,667 feet/1,118 m) Ssalbawi (3,638 feet/1,109 m), and Gwibawi (3,664 feet/1,117 m). However, it is the Gajisan Ridge Loop, not the other peaks, that everyone comes here to conquer.

The trail begins at Seongnamsa Temple and initially is not marked. Later, a series of colorful ribbons tied to trees serve as markers. The trail ascends steeply for about an hour through foothills, west past Ssalbawi and on toward Gajisan itself. You emerge onto an unsealed road near Gwibawi and a half hour later are passing Ssalbawi's rock outcrops with more stunning views out over the Eonyang Valley, followed by an easily negotiated forty-five-minute climb along Gajisan's ridgeline that takes you straight to its summit. On the way back, the trail descends to a paved road that comes out just above a parking lot and the Seongnamsa bus stop. The route is well marked (in Korean only), and the entire loop can be completed in four to five hours. **BDS**

⤒ A great loop with views over the Eonyang Valley.

Daedunsan Mountain Trails Jeonbuk, South Korea

Start/End Daedunsan Mountain cable car   **Distance** 4.5 miles (7.2 km)   **Time** 5 hours   **Grade** Moderate
Type Rock trails, suspension bridges, stairways   **Map** goo.gl/VVDlgQ

The mountain that is high on every climber's list of Korea's most beautiful peaks—Daedunsan in northern Jeollabuk-do, halfway between Jeonju and Daejeon—is set within a large provincial park and has a labyrinth of trails and staircases that hug its many crenellated, craggy summits. Climbers come here to test their climbing prowess on peaks such as Daedunsan, while thousands more come simply to walk the park's impressive network of trails, to climb staircases bolted onto near-vertical mountainsides, and to cross the most famous suspension bridge in Korea.

The suspension bridge spans a deep ravine and is reached after walking along a steep red staircase. The return hike from the base of the mountain takes five hours, and if you do the walk in fall, a kaleidoscope of colors accompanies you all the way. The trail is steep, so wear appropriate footwear, but overall it is a moderate hike that any reasonably fit person can do. Largely unknown to foreigners, Daedunsan Mountain is a collection of random, jagged, granite summits—Chilseongbong and Janggunbong—and other formations, including Samseonbawi Rock and Yonmungul Cave. There are also the historic temples of Taegosa, Ansimsa, and Sinsounsa. Newly installed cable cars get you above the valley and shorten many of the hikes that would otherwise take hours. After a day of traversing stairways and suspension bridges, you can finish off with a walk to the northern ridge that extends from Macheondae Peak to Nakjodae Peak. If you're there in October, you can marvel at the hues that come alight around you in the midst of one of South Korea's most unforgettable landscapes. **BDS**

⤒ Daedunsan's 164-foot-long (50 m) suspension bridge.

Land's End Trail
Jeonnam, South Korea

Start Wolchul-san National Park   End Ddang Ggut
Distance 60 miles (96.5 km)   Time 6–7 days
Grade Moderate   Type Ridgelines, forest trails
Map goo.gl/qcy8oJ

Land's End Trail crosses South Korea's southernmost range of mountains, beginning in the Wolchul-san National Park and continuing south along the long, open ridges of Deokryung-san before entering Duryun-san Provincial Park, with its wealth of ancient Buddhist hermitages scattered through its hills. Leaving Duryun-san, the trail's halfway point, the path passes through the Ilji-am tea hermitage and by a monolithic eighth-century Buddhist carving of Maitreya, who it is believed will be a future Buddha. The final three days of the trail follow the crusty

> *"Passes through fantastic rocky landscape in the rural heartland of Korea's … Jeolla-do district."*

www.hikekorea.com

ridgeline of the Dalma and Dosol-bong mountains, heavily incised pinnacles of stone that have given the region the nickname "Spiny Dragon." South Korea is a land of myths and legends, and hiking through its interior brings you face to face with the beliefs that have helped shape it into the country it is today.

On the final two days of the trail, the mind becomes focused more on the mountains themselves as you walk on the ridge of Ddang Ggut Ji-maek past old fire towers and more hermitages chiseled into walls of near-vertical rock. There are a few rope-assisted climbs on this leg, but nothing too difficult, and the trail eventually descends through forest to the seaside community of Ddang Ggut. **BDS**

Mount Mashu Summit
Hokkaido, Japan

Start/End Lake Mashu trailhead
Distance 4 miles (6.4 km)   Time 4–5 hours
Grade Easy   Type Well-maintained mountain trail
Map goo.gl/QbPgbs

You might think Akan National Park is a little off the beaten track, tucked away in the eastern regions of the northernmost Japanese island of Hokkaido. And tucked away it is, but, when word gets out about something, the world can suddenly become a very small place. The large caldera lakes, volcanic peaks, and thick forests of Akan receive more than 6.5 million visitors a year, and that's no accident. Not even the very real possibility of sighting a Japanese brown bear keeps people away. The opportunities for walks and longer hikes in this pristine environment are endless, and one of the best—a walk that gives an appreciation of the Hokkaido backcountry and a summit climb without an arduous ascent—is the trail to the rim of Mount Mashu.

Mount Mashu, also known as "Kamuinupuri" (God's Mountain) is located on the southeast side of Lake Mashu, a freshwater caldera lake that was once a stratovolcano and is now filled with some of the clearest water on the planet. A hike to Mashu's 2,814-foot-high (858 m) volcanic summit can be made from Observatory #1 overlooking Lake Mashu, in about two and a half hours along a well-maintained and signposted trail, which begins gradually enough, but becomes steeper the closer you get to the crater rim. On the summit, you get your reward: a panoramic view of Lake Mashu and neighboring Mount Nishibetsu, and if the air is clear you can see all the way to the peaks of Shiretoko National Park.

When you descend, be sure to have a walk around Lake Mashu, which is entirely protected, with not so much as a single building on its shoreline. Japan's neon cities have never seemed so far removed. **BDS**

Mount Meakan
Hokkaido, Japan

Start/End Nonaka Onsen parking lot or Lake Onneto
Distance 7.5 miles (12 km)   Time 5 hours
Grade Moderate   Type Forest, mountain trail
Map goo.gl/sk1gOi

Mount Meakan is an active volcano in Akan National Park near the center of Japan's northern Hokkaido Island. The mountain rises to a relatively humble height of 4,918 feet (1,499 m), but its top features a complex layout of overlapping cones and craters marking previous eruptions. The relatively easy hike to the summit gives walkers a rare chance to stare down into the smoldering mouth of an active volcano.

There are several walking routes up the mountain, but two of the main ones rise from the west side. One starts at a small parking lot a short drive down a gravel track from the Nonaka Onsen spa hotel; the other is a similar track leading from the south side of Lake Onneto. The trailheads are both about 2,500 feet (760 m) above sea level already, so you've only got about half the ascent to go. Note, however, signs warning walkers about the dangers of fumes from the volcano: "Turn around if you start to feel ill."

The marked paths are gradual inclines up through a thick forest, with occasional steeper sections. About halfway up the slopes, the forest clears and there are views back to the lake and across other nearby mountains. Signs of volcanic activity start to appear, such as patches of yellow deposits and sudden areas of bare white ash devoid of vegetation. Toward the summit, the path crosses barren volcanic mounds. Stone cairns have been built to guide walkers across these featureless dunes of volcanic material, and at the very peak a bright yellow rope has been erected to mark the path. Once at the summit marker, dare yourself to peer into the depths of the crater, although volcanic fumes frequently obscure the turquoise pond below. **SH**

"An active volcano offers a unique opportunity to stare into the mouth of a hissing volcanic crater."

www.japanhike.wordpress.com

⊕ Mount Meakan is a complex mix of nine overlapping cones, with a triple crater at its summit.

Mount Takao

Tokyo, Japan

Start/End Kiyotaki cable car station
Distance 1.9 miles (3 km)   Time 3 hours
Grade Moderate   Type Paved pathways
Map goo.gl/8C9uPG

It's no surprise that a small mountain less than an hour's journey from the center of Tokyo is a very popular spot for day trippers. Mount Takao is only 1,965 feet (599 m) high, but it offers many walking routes and attracts more than 2.5 million visitors a year. The mountain is part of Meiji no Mori Takao Quasi-National Park, and the attractions around its base include an arboretum with 1,000 different types of trees. The slopes of the mountain, however, are covered with far fewer species: it's a pristine forest of native cedars, fir, pines, and beeches. The thriving wildlife here includes wild boars and monkeys.

Mount Takao is renowned as the site of a medieval samurai battle, which ended with the ritual suicide of the defeated leader. It is also known for the twin tunnels that were dug right under the heart of the mountain that house the Ken-O Expressway, a Tokyo outer ring road.

Visitors can choose to walk up the mountain or take a chairlift halfway up. There are also six nature study trails, with information boards about flora and fauna at regular intervals along the way. There is a temple among the trees on the way up as well. The pick of the routes is the unpaved Inariyama Trail, which avoids the cable car and funicular stations and follows the more dramatic ridge up the side of the mountain. As it's such a popular day trip, only 30 miles (48 km) from one of the world's biggest cities, facilities are numerous and civilized. Toilets are provided along the routes, and there are noodle bars at the summit. The rewarding views from the top include the cityscape of Tokyo and the distant snowy summit of Mount Fuji. **SH**

"Mount Takao is one of the closest natural recreation areas to central Tokyo, offering ... attractive hiking opportunities."

www.japan-guide.com

⤒ Mount Takao is a mountain wilderness within the boundaries of the Tokyo metropolitan area.

Mount Fuji

Shizuoka, Japan

Start/End Fifth Station (Go-Gome)
Distance 8.5 miles (13.6 km)   **Time** 1–2 days
Grade Easy   **Type** Rocky, gravel paths
Map goo.gl/GqaH5j

At 12,388 feet (3,776 m), Mount Fuji is Japan's tallest mountain and one of the world's highest standalone peaks. It is also the world's most-climbed mountain, due to its relative lack of difficulty and its proximity to the almost 40 million people that live in nearby Tokyo. Although it might be a disappointing fact that the mountain looks far more beautiful from a distance than it does up close, it is nonetheless an exhilarating experience to climb, thanks to its iconic status as the nation's most revered mountain and the views from its mighty summit.

There are four possible routes to the top, with most walkers choosing to get as far as they can on the first day, then continuing on to the summit the following morning. You can also choose to hike through the night and reach the summit in time for the sunrise, although this is a more challenging option, which carries an increased risk of altitude sickness. Once on the summit, a walk around the crater takes about an hour.

Eight out of every ten climbers—which equates to a staggering 300,000 people a year—choose the Yoshida Trail as their preferred route to the summit. It is not a technical climb, but it is not easy, either, with much of it over loose gravel and volcanic debris that occasionally requires handholds. The Yoshida Trail has the highest number of huts of any of the routes (more than a dozen), but can be horribly crowded during the peak climbing season from mid-July to the end of August, with as many as 8,000 people per day, a positive aspect if you're sociable. If you're not, however, then you should probably be on a different mountain. **BDS**

"The most crowded trail to the summit . . . On the positive side, there are . . . separate uphill and downhill tracks."

www.japan-guide.com

⊼ Ascend the graceful symmetry of Japan's holiest mountain, set above the junction of three tectonic plates.

Mount Aso Kumamoto, Japan

Start/End Asosan Ropeway   **Distance** 6 miles (9.6 km)   **Time** 4 hours   **Grade** Easy to moderate
Type Ash and cinder trails   **Map** goo.gl/9RTdOS

The world's largest active caldera measures in excess of 70 miles (112 km) in circumference and belongs to a composite volcano 30 miles (48 km) north of Kumamoto City on the Japanese island of Kyushu. Mount Aso is Japan's largest active volcano, yet curiously only a very few take the trouble to venture beyond its phalanx of souvenir stalls and walk to its summit, Taka-dake, at 5,223 feet (1,592 m). More curious still is the fact that a gondola makes the ascent pretty straightforward, and you can even drive to a parking lot a minute's walk away. If you prefer to earn your views, however, then a gondola isn't going to entice you on the ascent to the summit. What awaits you at the top is enticement enough.

The most direct route to the summit of Mount Aso involves a gentle teaser of a climb to begin with, then a steep ascent along an exposed spine that takes you straight to Taka-dake itself. A good boulder-hopper will reach the ridge of Tengu-no-butai in a little over an hour, and the summit just ten minutes later, but allow ninety minutes if you need a little conditioning. Either way, it's not a physically demanding feat. Once you get there, you'll be met with fantastic views right down into the smoking heart of the caldera, and, if there isn't any cloud, your view will include close-ups of nearby Mount Kuju and Mount Sobo—a big reward considering the effort made. A short walk along the crater then presents you with a choice: turn right and descend along Sensuikyou Ridge, or turn left and walk right on down into the caldera itself, a lunar-like landscape devoid of vegetation—and of people, too. **BDS**

⬆ A moderate climb up Japan's most active volcano.

Gorely Volcano Summit Kamchatka, Russia

Start/End Campsite at Gorely base   **Distance** 8 miles (12.8 km)   **Time** 8 hours   **Grade** Easy to moderate
Type Open volcanic terrain, ice, scree slopes   **Map** goo.gl/9OfzJU

The Kamchatka Peninsula is the sort of place that everyone is searching for. Larger than Germany and Austria combined, this giant peninsula—which extends below Siberia southward toward Japan like a fish-shaped pendulum—is one of the world's last true wildernesses, home to 11 percent of the entire world's volcanoes and thousands of Kamchatkan brown bears. A quarter of all the salmon in the Pacific Ocean spawn here in the swift-flowing and unfettered rivers, and the only way to get anywhere beyond the capital, Petropavlovsk–Kamchatsky, is in Soviet-era MI-8 cargo helicopters flown by daredevil, chain-smoking Russian pilots. Could anywhere on Earth possibly be more exciting?

If you go there, it has to be assumed that you already possess an uncommon zest for life, which means climbing in the back of an MI-8 and flying to a campsite at an elevation of 3,280 feet (1,000 m), a few miles from Gorely volcano with a view to walking on its rim the following day, circling its hissing caldera, and then returning to camp. All this is weather permitting, for the elements here can ruin even the best-laid plans faster than a Bolshevik revolt. But you have to try, and if the weather is kind, it will be a day you will never forget.

Gorely volcano (6,000 feet/1,829 m) is a geological jigsaw, a massive complex of five overlapping stratovolcanoes with eleven summit craters and another thirty on its flanks. The climb itself is relatively straightforward, but trying to understand why you can't get it out of your head after you've left? Well, that can take years. **BDS**

⬆ A remote volcano in the land that time forgot.

Taung Kalat

Mandalay, Myanmar

Start/End Base of Taung Kalat stairway
Distance 836 feet (255 m)   **Time** 2 hours
Grade Easy   **Type** Stairs
Info goo.gl/vi1FRG

Taung Kalat (Pedestal Hill) is a sheer-walled volcanic plug in central Myanmar, on the summit of which is a Buddhist monastery that you access via a 777-step, monkey-lined stairway. The summit is 2,417 feet (737 m) above sea level and this fascinating volcanic remnant—which stands alone in a mostly flat surrounding landscape—would be eye-catching enough even if it were not crowned with a monastery. The plug is the product of the same seismic forces that created Mount Popa (4,981 feet/1,518 m), the dormant volcano to the northeast with its mile-wide caldera that those

---

"Its golden spires encrust the top of the rock, and … can be seen gleaming like a mirage."

amazingstuff.co.uk

---

who live around the base of Taung Kalat like to call "Mother Hill."

The walk—or, rather, the climb—to the top of Taung Kalat is steep, and you will need to be on guard against the stairway's resident and very mischievous monkeys, which are plentiful and have a keen eye for anything shiny or edible.

Taung Kalat is an hour's drive from the city of Bagan. There is no shortage of locals who will volunteer to take you to the summit, but a guide is not needed. Both Taung Kalat and Mount Popa are popular pilgrimage sites, particularly during festival season on the Nayon Full Moon in May/June. The views extend all the way to the Irrawaddy River. **BDS**

Fair Trek

Luang Prabang, Laos

Start/End Luang Prabang
Distance 16 miles (25.7 km)   **Time** 2 days
Grade Moderate   **Type** Jungle, hill trails
Map goo.gl/yROzc9

More than a third of the population of Laos lives well below the international poverty line, and Fair Trek, a multinational tourism initiative, aims to help the poorest Laotian communities by combining adventurous walking holidays with assistance for some of the most remote areas. This promising initiative, which offers a chance for hikers to stay in poorer communities while at the same time generating sustainable income, seeks to avoid commercial influences, such as new hotels, and also organizes working holidays for volunteers to help build schools in isolated places.

This trip to Luang Prabang is typical of the Fair Trek offerings. It involves a spectacular two days of guided trekking through little-visited countryside in the north of the country, where, for around six hours a day, you will be hiking past paddy fields, through lush rain forests, up jagged mountain ridges, and along jungle rivers. The visit also includes a boat ride to an "elephant village" and some dramatic waterfalls.

There are no Holiday Inns at the end of each day, though. Instead, meals and overnight stays are in simple villages along the route, which usually means sleeping in basic bamboo huts just as the locals do, with shared outside facilities. It does, however, offer a unique chance to get to know these friendly village people and experience how they live. The villagers themselves benefit from hosting the paid guests at a fair price and also have a chance to sell their traditional handicrafts. The Fair Trek system also helps preserve their traditional rural cultures through performances of dances and music, and guests are even encouraged to sample the local whiskey. **SH**

Ho Chi Minh Trail

Hanoi to Ho Chi Minh City, Vietnam

Start Hanoi   **End** Ho Chi Minh City
Distance 1,000 miles (1,600 km)
Time 3–4 months   **Grade** Easy to moderate
Type Paved road   **Info** goo.gl/FA5iug

The Ho Chi Minh Trail was the network of supply routes that enabled the North Vietnamese to reinforce and supply its troops fighting in the south of the country during the Vietnam War. It's an intrepid web of jungle roads, hidden paths, supply dumps, tunnels, bunkers, and bridges through the jungles of Laos, Cambodia, and Vietnam. The total network covered 12,500 miles (20,100 km) and was considered one of history's major feats of military engineering. Trucks could drive for hundreds of miles hidden under tree canopies; even bridges were submerged under the water to be invisible to U.S. planes.

Much of the original trail has been reclaimed by the jungle, especially the most secret parts through Laos and Cambodia, and even the known stretches are littered with unexploded armaments. The Vietnamese government has therefore created a route to serve as the tourist version of the Ho Chi Minh Trail. The Ho Chi Minh National Highway runs the length of Vietnam, from Hanoi to Ho Chi Minh City (formerly Saigon). It doesn't loop into Laos and Cambodia like the original trail, but it does include many sections that were used to move men and supplies during the war. The paved road gives walkers (bikers, cyclists, and drivers) the opportunity to travel in the steps of the communist guerillas. Its route passes close to famous sites, including the battlefield of Khe Sanh and the ancient royal city of Hue. This marathon trail down the backbone of South East Asia also allows access to fabulous mountain scenery, simple rural communities, and historic sites, including military cemeteries reminding visitors that around 30,000 North Vietnamese died on the Ho Chi Minh Trail. **SH**

"The mountain paths ... offer visitors to Vietnam an adventurous alternative to the well-worn coastal route."

www.theguardian.com

⊞ The Ho Chi Minh Trail offers spectacular views of the surrounding jungle tree canopies.

Chocolate Hills Bohol, Philippines

Start/End Chocolate Hills complex, Carmen   **Distance** 3–5 miles (4.8–8 km)   **Time** 1–1.5 hours
Grade Easy to moderate   **Type** Hard-surfaced paths, steps   **Map** goo.gl/LmfQSy

The most popular tourist attraction on the island of Bohol in the Philippines is a bizarre geological formation. The Chocolate Hills are hundreds of grass-covered domes of limestone between 100 and 150 feet high (30–45 m). There are more than 1,700 of these tiny mountains in an area of about 20 square miles (50 sq km), with the flat land between them generally paddy fields or forest. The hills are normally green, but they can turn brown in the hottest, driest spells of summer, hence the name Chocolate Hills.

For serious hikers, the options are somewhat limited. There are some unofficial paths that can be walked between the hills, but you risk straying into private property unless you hire a local guide. Others simply walk along the roads through the hills, such as the road from Sagbayan to Sierra Bullones, or the quieter road from Balilihan to Hanopol. Visitors mostly travel to the town of Sagbayan to see the hills, one of which has been developed with a pathway to the top, where there is a viewing platform, café, and children's playground. The Chocolate Hills complex at Carmen is perhaps the best way of discovering these natural wonders. It includes two natural chocolate hills plus a range of man-made developments, including a hotel, restaurant, conference center, and swimming pool. Ignore these and tackle the long cement walkway to the top of one of the hills instead. This involves more than 200 steep stairs, covered decking rest stops along the way, and a sturdy handrail to aid your climb. At the top is a 360-degree panorama of the strange conical hills. For the descent, there's a longer but less steep, zigzagging trail to the foot of the mountain. **SH**

⊼ Marine limestone hills set over clay foundations.

Cameron Highlands Pahang, Malaysia

Start/End Near Brinchang police station   **Distance** 4 miles (6.4 km)   **Time** 2–3 hours   **Grade** Moderate to strenuous   **Type** Muddy jungle path   **Map** goo.gl/Opy5mZ

The Cameron Highlands is a mountainous region of northern Malaysia that has been popular as a retreat from the heat and humidity of the lowlands since colonial days. It's a landscape of green hills, tea plantations, golf courses, and lush mossy forests. Walkers are drawn to the area to explore a network of trails through the hills, ranging from sedate paved paths through tea estates to challenging steep and rugged paths through thick jungle.

Look for a trail map that is sold widely in the region's capital Tanah Rata. Many trekkers hire local guides as some of the paths are hard to find. Beware, however, because reports suggest that prospective guides have, in fact, been removing trailhead signs in order to drum up business. The main trails are numbered. Number One ascends one of the highest peaks in the highlands. At 6,666 feet (2,031 m) high,

Mount Brinchang can be spotted from most places in the highlands with its distinctive telecommunications tower at the top. The views from the top can be far-reaching on a clear day, but such days are rare.

The jungle trail that begins near Brinchang town is typically hard to find. The start involves climbing over a large drainage pipe and into the forest to find the 2-mile-long (3.2 km) path up to the peak. The track is steep and there are tangled roots and branches to negotiate. It becomes a wonderfully atmospheric damp mossy forest farther up, and the slopes are usually enveloped in cool mists. If the clouds clear, take advantage of the viewing tower at the top. Locals suggest early morning is the best time for views from the summit—before the mists have formed. **SH**

⬆ Misty, mossy trails through green hills and tea estates.

Timpohon Trail, Mount Kinabalu
Sabah, Malaysia

Start/End Kinabalu Park headquarters
Distance 10 miles (16 km) **Time** 1–2 days
Grade Strenuous **Type** Mountain path, stone steps
Map goo.gl/bWd8ZC

At an elevation of 13,435 feet (4,095 m), Mount Kinabalu is Borneo's highest peak and the tallest mountain between the Himalayas and Papua New Guinea. Its imposing granite slopes are the central focus of Kinabalu Park. The 291-square-mile (754-sq-km) park is a UNESCO World Heritage Site, protecting one of the world's richest collections of flora and fauna. At its center is a mountain so prominent that it has acquired spiritual importance to the largest local ethnic group, the Kadasan Dusun people. Its name translates as "revered place of the dead." Various mountain trails start at the headquarters on the park's southern boundary and itself at an altitude of 5,128 feet (1,563 m). Hikers have to pay a fee and register before tackling the mountain.

The Timpohon Trail starts a short walk away at a wooden archway called the Timpohon Gate. A clear path leads up the forested slopes, with sections of steps cut into the rock and occasional wooden pavilions as rest stops; about two-thirds of the way up, there's a guesthouse—Laban Rata.

By now the change of altitude will be affecting you, and most walkers arrange to stay the night to get their breaths back. Prebooked hikers can get food, showers, and a dormitory bed. Most set off early from Laban Rata to reach the summit for sunrise. The pre-dawn darkness makes the final steep push to the summit a challenging final assault over often-slippery wooden steps and smooth rock slabs with guide ropes. The summit plateau is a cold shock for climbers emerging from the tropical rain forest below. **SH**

← Kinabalu's summit is a vast plateau above the clouds.

Toraja Land Trails
Sulawesi, Indonesia

Start/End Tana Toraja **Distance** Various
Time Various **Grade** Easy to moderate
Type Forest and mountain trails
Info goo.gl/hvELjl

To walk through the valleys and villages of Toraja Land in the central highlands of the Indonesian island of Sulawesi is to be immersed in a world once inhabited by headhunters and animists, a land of ancient granaries built on stilts and strange boat-shaped wooden houses with swooping roof lines that look like sails. There are rituals that go on for days, featuring displays of fire and the slaughtering of pigs and water buffalo in honor of the dead. Rice is grown here on terraced hillsides—monuments to hundreds of years of endless toil—that lie amid valleys where the ghosts

"A journey into the strange world of the mysterious Toraja people is truly a rare adventure."

www.toraja-info.com

of ancestors look out from burial caves over verdant paddy fields. Women carry rice and vegetables in baskets tied to the end of heavy poles, there are cockfights in the village squares, and children play in the mud of the rain forest. Once you've walked through Toraja Land, these images never leave you.

The villages have maintained an unusually high degree of physical and traditional purity, a rare thing in this age of globalization. Several days are needed to take it all in—at least a day (preferably two) in the valleys, and two to three days in the uplands, where you can stay in an authentic local house. Just make sure you choose a reliable local guide because there is no signage to point you in the right direction. **BDS**

Mount Bromo East Java, Indonesia

Start/End Cemoro Lawang **Distance** 2 miles (3.2 km) **Time** 1 hour **Grade** Easy **Type** Mountain path, steps
Map goo.gl/rqOxGB

The Bromo Tengger Semeru National Park on the Indonesian island of Java covers 310 square miles (800 sq km) of otherworldly volcanic landscapes with the main attraction the active volcano Mount Bromo. At 7,641 feet (2,329 m), it isn't the highest or most dangerous of Indonesia's volcanoes, but it does have a picturesque cone that is easily accessible, and a savanna-like landscape inside that is astonishing.

A small tourist industry has grown up around the mountain, involving touts trying to push sunrise jeep tours and horseback rides at visitors. Thankfully, independent trekkers can simply ignore all these, for the reality is that Bromo is an easy one-hour walk from the nearest village. The trail to the volcano crosses what has been christened the "Sand Sea"—a barren ash-covered landscape. Most tourists pay for rides on roughly treated ponies across the sand, but it's easy to

walk across. The path then rises up the side of the crater on 250 concrete steps. From here, you can peer into the caldera, see the smoke emerging, and smell the sulfurous fumes.

Experiencing sunrise from a mountain is always memorable, but there's no need to pay to join a crowded jeep full of tourists. It takes around two hours to hike the 3 miles (4.8 km) to the neighboring mountain of Gunung Penanjakan to watch the sunrise across Bromo and its sister peaks, Kursi and Batok.

From the viewing platform on Penanjakan, you'll be able to make sense of the volcanic landscape. The three cones of Bromo, Kursi, and Batok have actually emerged within a vast outer crater that is 6 miles (10 km) across, of which Penanjakan is a part. **SH**

⬆ Craters within craters, Bromo is a sensation.

Mount Rinjani Summit Lombok, Indonesia

Start Senaru or Sembalun Lawang   **End** Rinjani   **Distance** 6.2 miles (10 km)   **Time** 7 hours
Grade Moderate to strenuous   **Type** Mountain trail   **Map** goo.gl/bTsuy0

By the time you step onto the rim of Mount Rinjani on the Indonesian island of Lombok, your senses have already been assaulted. You have passed through a primary rain forest, a dense monsoon rain forest, and dry savannas; and maybe seen, or at least heard, long-tailed gray macaques, silver leaf monkeys, deer, wild pigs, and maybe even a leopard cat.

Rinjani (12,224 feet/3,726 m) is Indonesia's second highest volcanic peak and the walk, although a straightforward one, is spectacular. You can begin at the village of Senaru on Rinjani's northern flank or at Sembalun Lawang on the eastern side, which is closer and not so much of a slog. You can't climb Rinjani without an authorized guide, and a porter will carry your provisions for you. You move out through farmland and into the forested lower slopes of the mountains for an arduous seven-hour ascent that should see you arrive at the crater rim with maybe an hour's worth of daylight to savor the views while your guide and porter make camp. Remember to bring warm clothes and a waterproof parka. Rinjani receives 78 inches (2 m) of rainfall a year, though going in the dry season from April to November will improve the odds of staying dry. The next morning, after what will be one of the more memorable sunrises you've ever seen, you can walk down to the lake for a swim or bathe in a series of hot springs while you consider whether or not to go one step further and climb from the rim to the volcano's actual summit. It's a five-hour return trek to a spur at the crater's far end, from the top of which, on a clear day, you can see the island paradise of Bali shimmering in the distance. **BDS**

⯅ A stunning crater, hot springs, and great sunsets.

Bluff Knoll Summit Western Australia, Australia

Start/End Bluff Knoll parking area **Distance** 3.7 miles (6 km) **Time** 3–4 hours **Grade** Moderate
Type Mountain paths, exposed rock **Map** goo.gl/uRhDUc

The Stirling Range in the great southern region of Western Australia is one of the continent's most isolated mountain ranges and the only range in the entire southern half of this vast state. Its peaks rise as high as 3,592 feet (1,095 m) above sea level, and the region's weather patterns often cause its peaks to be shrouded in mist, cloud, and even (surprisingly) sprinkled with an occasional snowfall. Its unique flora includes 1,500 plant species of which 80 are endemic, and no visit to Western Australia's southwest is complete without an excursion to these isolated, rugged mountains.

Routinely making the top ten list of Australia's greatest walks, hiking to the summit of Bluff Knoll gets you to the highest trail point in the Stirling Ranges at 3,520 feet (1,073 m). Gazing up at the face of Bluff Knoll from the parking lot below that marks the start of the ascent, it is a daunting sight. The track takes you around the western face of the bluff, with views over craggy, crenellated Coyanerup Peak and on to the peaks of the western Stirlings. Next is the saddle between the two mountains, where you take a turn first to the east and then to the north, past scattered dwarf grass trees as you ascend Bluff Knoll's sloping southern approach. Here the flora becomes almost bonsai-like, with tiny melaleucas set in small beds of mosses and an alpine-like assortment of wildflowers, shrubs, and mountain herbs. On the summit the views extend forever—to the east are the silhouettes of the Arrows; to the south, small lakes filled by mountain runoffs; and dry salt beds to the north. Find a rocky crevice to shelter from the wind, and enjoy. **BDS**

⬆ Hike the summit of the remote Stirling Ranges.

Mount Sorrow Ridge Trail Queensland, Australia

Start/End Trailhead, 500 feet (150 m) north of Kulki day-use area turnoff   **Distance** 9 miles (14.5 km)
Time 6–7 hours   **Grade** Strenuous   **Type** Mountain trails, mud   **Map** goo.gl/1dx60U

In order to walk the Mount Sorrow Ridge Trail first you have to get to the city of Cairns in far north Queensland. Then you hire a 4x4 and you continue north for about 65 miles (105 km) on the Captain Cook Highway until you reach the Daintree River, where "the mountains meet the sea." You then cross the river on its only ferry, which may or may not be running depending on whether or not heavy rains have swollen the river and/or if the ferry is down for maintenance. Once on the other side, you then drive another 23 miles (37 km) to the Kulki day-use area, get out, walk for ten minutes until you reach a gravel area, and there you will see the first official signpost for the Mount Sorrow Ridge Trail. You have made it to Cape Tribulation, and you are now about to ascend Mount Sorrow—you may wonder, "Are the place names trying to tell me something?"

The Daintree Rain Forest is 140 million years old, and the trail to Mount Sorrow begins in the depths of its lowland valleys and does nothing but ascend until you reach the summit. Leeches can be a problem, so remember to bring long pants, and, of course, lots of water. It is not a climb for the fainthearted, either. In addition to the heat and the insects, the humidity can be positively stifling. As it is a lengthy round trip, don't leave after 10 a.m. or you run the risk of coming back in darkness.

The panoramic views from the summit are stunning, although it's a pity that the Queensland government hasn't yet decided to build a shelter there so you can get out of the sun on this exposed overlook across the world's oldest rain forest. **BDS**

⬆ Climb from the coast to a rain forest–filled ridge.

Carnarvon Great Walk
Queensland, Australia

Start/End Carnarvon Gorge, Carnarvon
National Park   **Distance** 53 miles (85 km)
Time 6 days   **Grade** Moderate   **Type** Forest,
bush trail   **Map** goo.gl/dQ9COK

This well-marked, circular walk starts in Carnarvon Gorge, the main attraction of Carnarvon National Park in the heart of Queensland. The trail is designed to take six days, although this means short walking days between the only campsites along the route, which some walkers might find insufficiently challenging. Carnarvon Gorge is one of the highlights of day one. Among its white sandstone cliffs are rocks covered with Aboriginal stencil art dating back 20,000 years. The wooded gorge is 19 miles (30.5 km) long and 1,900 feet (600 m) wide at its mouth.

> *"Experience a remote and beautiful landscape of towering sandstone cliffs . . . and shaded side-gorges."*
>
> www.nprsr.qld.gov.au

The path winds through giant ferns, palms, and cycads, with birds chattering overhead. Side paths lead to waterfalls, rock formations, fixed-ladder climbs, and picturesque creek crossings on stepping-stones. From the bend in the Wagooroo River, the trail climbs out of the main gorge via the narrow Boowinda Gorge slot canyon and onto a basalt plateau above, known as the "Roof of Queensland." This higher path cuts through mixed bush and forests to the Mount Moffat area, where tourists go to see the sculpted sandstone outcrops. The walk then loops through forests thick with vines and flowers, punctuated by distinctive basalt rock formations, eventually leading back to the start point via the verdant river canyon. **SH**

St. Mary Peak Wilpena Pound South Australia, Australia

Start/End Rawnsley Park Station
Distance 13 miles (21 km)   **Time** 7–9 hours
Grade Moderate   **Type** Unmarked rock and gravel trails
Map goo.gl/qaDGij

The largest mountain range in South Australia and one of the most forbidding outback landscapes, the Flinders Ranges—366 square miles (95,000 ha) of folded, faulted, and heavily eroded sediments—contain some of Australia's great wilderness walking trails. They rise north of Port Pirie on the Spencer Gulf and continue for 270 miles (430 km) to Lake Callabonna, a dry salt lake an hour's drive from the meeting point of Queensland, New South Wales, and South Australia. They feature the Arkaroola wilderness in the north, Mount Remarkable National Park in the south, and the iconic Wilpena Pound, an ampitheater of mountains in the heart of Flinders Ranges National Park. People tried to farm Wilpena Pound in the early twentieth century, and failed. Today two properties—Wilpena Pound Resort and Rawnsley Park Station—welcome guests year-round to walk its trails and sample outback living. Rawnsley Park hasn't entirely given up on making a traditional living here, though: it has 3,000 sheep—one for every 6 acres (2.4 ha) of dry, waterless scrub.

Wilpena Pound is the jewel in this national park, a horseshoe-shaped syncline once thought to be an ancient volcano. Its highest point, St. Mary Peak—3,839 feet (1,171 m)—can be climbed in a day, and from its summit you have an uninterrupted view of the wall of mountains that almost completely encircles the Pound's gently sloping interior. Temperatures can climb to 113°F (45°C) in summer, so make sure you come in midwinter (July/August). On the way back to Rawnsley, take the Malloga Falls trail across the Pound's floor to a small waterfall at the base of Edeowie Gorge. **BDS**

Six Foot Track
New South Wales, Australia

Start Katoomba **End** Jenolan Caves
Distance 27.5 miles (44.2 km) **Time** 2–3 days
Grade Moderate **Type** Forest trails
Map goo.gl/a9fUDH

The Six Foot Track is located in the Blue Mountains National Park, which is a two-hour drive west of Sydney. Originally marked out as a bridle trail in 1884 and made 6 feet (1.8 m) wide so horseback riders could ride it three abreast, it was intended to be a shortcut to the Jenolan Caves, the world's oldest system of open limestone caves that now receives more than 250,000 visitors a year. The track begins 3 miles (4.8 km) west of the mountain town of Katoomba, at the Explorer's Tree, into which it is claimed the first Europeans to find a path through the Blue Mountains to the plains beyond—explorers Gregory Blaxland, William Lawson, and William Wentworth—carved their initials.

After falling into disrepair, the track was reopened in 1984 and does its best to follow the original route, although little of the original trail remains. It descends through Nellie's Glen, past Bonnie Doon Falls and a wonderland of fernery, and emerges into the broad openness of the Megalong Valley, where it follows the course of the Coxs River, used by local Aborigines for thousands of years as a crossing point through the mountains. The river is crossed once, at Bowtell's Swing Bridge—a suspension bridge built in 1991 by the Royal Australian Engineers.

The next day you begin your ascent—1,500 feet (457 m) in 1.5 miles (2.4 km)—up onto the Mini Mini Saddle and the highest point of the track on Black Range. Then, after a short walk along a paved roadside, it's back on the trail again for the last few miles through a forest of gray gums and stringy barks, amid cockatoos and bellbirds and all the magical sounds of the Australian bush. **BDS**

"A fantastic journey exploring the natural beauty and historic stories of this part of the Blue Mountains."

www.sixfoottrack.com

⊼ The first section of the Six Foot Trail runs alongside Megalong Creek.

Mount Gower Summit
Lord Howe Island, NSW, Australia

Start/End Parking lot trailhead **Distance** 8.5 miles
(13.6 km) **Time** 8 hours **Grade** Strenuous
Type Mountain trails and rope-assisted paths
Map goo.gl/vOz5Zl

A crescent-shaped volcanic remnant 372 miles (600 km) east of the New South Wales mainland, Lord Howe Island is dominated at its southern end by two mountains—Mount Lidgbird (2,549 feet/777 m) and Mount Gower (2,870 feet/875 m). Only Mount Gower has an authorized trail, although what passes for a trail here can at times be difficult to follow. The ascent is on a steep gradient and involves occasional rope-assisted climbs up near-vertical rock faces, as well as trails that hug the lower slopes of the mountain before the real climb begins. It's not the sort of thing you want to attempt on your own, and if you would like to go with a group and share the experience, the man to see is fifth-generation islander and veteran of more than 1,000 Mount Gower climbs, Jack Shick. For 70 percent of those who get to the top, he says, it's the most physical thing they have ever done.

Lord Howe Island is a UNESCO World Heritage Site, and for good reason. Its forest is uncontaminated by the outside world, and a large proportion of its flora and fauna is endemic. It has the world's southernmost coral reef in its lagoon; the woodhen, a flightless bird found nowhere else; and providence petrels so unafraid of humans, they fall out of the sky and land at your feet if you can master the correct birdcall. Naturalist David Attenborough described Lord Howe Island as "so extraordinary it is almost unbelievable." There is no better place to see it than on top of Mount Gower's plateau-like summit, sitting in the coolness of its moss forest and pitying all those who have not yet made the journey to see it. **BDS**

⬅ The island as seen from the summit of Mount Gower.

Australian Alps Track
Victoria to ACT, Australia

Start Walhalla **End** Canberra
Distance 404 miles (650 km)
Time 5–10 weeks **Grade** Strenuous
Type Forest track, wilderness **Info** goo.gl/ZFzzOr

Wading through rivers, crossing makeshift log bridges, and scrambling along mountain ridges characterize one of Australia's toughest trails. The path includes the highest peaks in each of the three states it passes through: Mount Kosciuszko (the continent's highest mountain), Mount Bogong, and Bimberi Peak. With more than 88,000 feet (27,000 m) of climbing and descending overall, on average it is the equivalent of climbing a small mountain every day. Not surprisingly, many tackle only segments, but those hardy enough to attempt the whole route start in the former gold-

"Pitch your tent in the wilderness, stay in campgrounds, historic huts, or alpine resorts."

www.australia.com

mining town of Walhalla, Victoria. From here it's more than 400 miles (648 km) northwest to Tharwa on the outskirts of Canberra. In between, the track crosses the highest mountains on the Australian mainland and long stretches of remote and rugged terrain.

Walkers need to be fit and self-reliant, with good navigation skills. The reward is the satisfaction of completing an adventure across Australia's finest alpine landscapes and experiencing beautiful forests, glacial lakes, and dramatic rocky ridges. The route passes through five "wilderness areas" and four national parks. The names of landmarks along the way reflect the nature of the environment—Mount Despair, Horrible Gap, and the Terrible Hollow. **SH**

East Sherbrooke Forest Lyrebird Trail Victoria, Australia

Start/End Grants Picnic Ground
Distance 4.4 miles (7 km)   Time 2 hours
Grade Easy   Type Broad, well-maintained
forest trails   Map goo.gl/IKBDke

If you want to see the Australian ground-dwelling lyrebird in its natural habitat, first book yourself into the sumptuous Tyneside Gatehouse in the lush Dandenong Ranges, an hour's drive east of Melbourne. Get up early the next morning and walk the trails of Sherbrooke Forest, a fern- and towering mountain ash-filled wonderland of greenery in a sea of pale, ghostly barks.

The East Sherbrooke Forest Lyrebird Trail is a loop route that begins and ends at Grants Picnic Ground. Setting off on Lyrebird Track, you veer right onto Neumann Track and into an open area of grassy

> *"Your rewards may include the thrilling song and perhaps a glimpse of the superb lyrebird."*
>
> parkweb.vic.gov.au

meadows, where lyrebirds like to gather and dig in the soft, moist soil for worms and insects. Paddy Track and then Welch Track take you along a steep incline where lyrebirds can always be seen engaging in early morning foraging. Unless you walk these trails at the right times, you can spend years living in the communities that dot the Dandenong Ranges and never see these elusive birds that are famous for their ability to mimic both the natural and artificial sounds in their environment, including the calls of other native birds, such as the kookaburra, and animals, such as koalas. During the breeding season from June to August, they sing, adding to the beauty of an already beautiful forest. **BDS**

Murray to the Mountains Rail Trail Victoria, Australia

Start Wangaratta   End Bright
Distance 60 miles (96.5 km)   Time 2 days
Grade Easy to moderate   Type Cycle and foot path
Map goo.gl/mOKHnP

Discover the pretty rolling landscape of Ned Kelly country on this former rail track through northeast Victoria. Since the notorious outlaw's day, the rails and sleepers have been removed and replaced with a well-surfaced, road-like path all the way from Wangaratta to Bright. Now it's a clearly signposted and well-maintained tourist route, and there are even public restrooms provided along the way.

The Murray to the Mountains route is considered one of Australia's best rail trails. The surrounding countryside is a popular region, and the path passes through scenic spots—such as the Ovens and King valleys, Everton Hills, and Alpine High Country—and charming villages and towns, including Wangaratta, Beechworth, Rutherglen, and Bright. There are plenty of distractions along the way, including cafés, bars, and ice cream shops, and many walkers stop for meals, sightseeing, and wine tastings. The North East Victorian countryside is a mix of natural bush, scrubby highland, and charming cultivated farmland, where sheep and cattle graze in lush grass dotted with wildflowers. Highlights along the way include historic old tobacco sheds, vineyards and wineries, and relics of a prosperous gold-mining era.

There are views of hills and picturesque valleys from the old rail track, but only one significant long slow gradient up to Beechworth. Walkers can admire the old rail engineers' work in the brick arches, embankments, and cuttings. The path is bitumen sealed, so that it is useable whatever the weather. Less manicured sidetracks lead off at several points for those who fancy more rugged adventures. Note that it's also popular with cyclists and horseback riders. **SH**

Western Arthurs Traverse
Tasmania, Australia

Start/End Scotts Peak Dam
Distance 43 miles (69 km)   **Time** 6 days
Grade Strenuous   **Type** Mountain paths and
scrambles, muddy trails   **Map** goo.gl/LzLJuy

This fierce and gnarled landscape is only 56 miles (90 km) from the Tasmanian capital of Hobart, but it feels a world away in the heart of this harsh World Heritage wilderness of unspoiled terrain. The Western Arthurs are known for their dazzling quartzite pillars, like rows of tall teeth rising from dense forest, as well as beautiful natural bowls of water perched among the peaks. The traverse involves a serious scrambling and mud-slogging trek across these impressively jagged rocky mountain pinnacles, ridges, and gullies. Plunging forests and thick, prickly scrub surround muddy moorland, tranquil lakes, and fast-moving mountain rivers. Open high ground is peppered with severely weathered gray rock outcrops. From the sudden discovery of a rare wildflower or unfamiliar bird, to the massive panoramas of completely undisturbed countryside, the traverse certainly promises walkers a memorable experience.

From one end to the other, the Western Arthur Range is only 9.5 miles (15.2 km) long, yet it comprises 22 major peaks. You'll have to carry everything you need for the trek, including tent, food, and sleeping bag. Needless to say, it's not a walk for beginners. A few hundred brave souls tackle this route every summer, although snow and heavy rain can occur suddenly at any time. February and March are reckoned to be the safest months, but serious wet-weather gear is essential whenever you attempt it. The route is marked with signs, orange triangles, stone cairns, and a simple path of flat slabs, so good navigation skills are needed. Campsites along the way range from dry wooden platforms raised above the lakeside to crude muddy clearings in the forest. **SH**

"Scales some of the most demanding and scenic terrain in Australia."

www.australiangeographic.com.au

⊤ Come prepared for mud-caked paths, slippery descents, and plenty of prickly *scoparia* scrub.

Mount Alava Loop American Samoa

Start/End Faleo'o   **Distance** 7 miles (11.2 km)   **Time** 2–4 hours   **Grade** Moderate to strenuous
Type Mountain trail, steps, rope ladders   **Map** goo.gl/YaI4q3

The Mount Alava loop has one of the most luxurious lookouts that American Samoa has on offer, although getting to the lookout is a different story. Leading to the 1,610 ft (491 m) summit, this track, totaling 783 steps and fifty-six ladders, will guarantee that if you want the views, you're going to have to work for them.

Throughout the trek you will see some of American Samoa's most spectacular landscapes, including Pola Island. With endless seas covering the horizons and luscious greenery surrounding you, this is more than a hike—it is an escape from modern daily life, allowing you to revel in the abundant scents of the flora that characterizes this lush trail.

As you ascend you will hear harmonizing songbirds beneath a canopy of native trees, which provide welcome shade for much of the route. Once at the summit you will find yourself in a verdant clearing overlooking Matafoa with the Pacific Ocean on one side and American Samoa's relaxed capital city of Pago Pago on the other.

Completing this rewarding trail can be hard on the hiker, but the picturesque lookout and pleasant landscape more than compensate for the exertion needed to overcome the often oppressive humidity and steep gradients. Although it is a short hike, effort is required to maintain a decent pace. However, the restoration of a cable car line, disused since the late 1980s, has been mooted, and there are plenty of spots along the way where walkers can stop. You must also allow a little time for your senses to be overwhelmed by the enchanting sights and sounds of American Samoa's tangled, tropical forests. **AS**

⬆ Mount Alava takes hikers into a verdant world.

Tongariro Northern Circuit Waikato, New Zealand

Start Whakapapa Village **End** Mount Ruapehu   **Distance** 26.7 miles (43 km)   **Time** 3–4 days
Grade Moderate   **Type** Rock, scree, boardwalk, gravel trail   **Map** goo.gl/764Dl3

One of a handful of designated New Zealand Great Walks, this moderately challenging hike varies from tracks to boardwalks to uneven rock-strewn surfaces as you circumnavigate the stark beauty of Mount Ngauruhoe, a classic stratovolcano and the youngest vent in the Tongariro volcanic field on the North Island's Central Plateau. The mountain first made its presence felt 2,500 years ago and has had more than forty-five eruptions in the past century alone, although a recent decline in seismic activity suggests another any time soon is unlikely.

The circuit takes you through the midst of a world of volcanic landforms. Vents and scoria cones are common sights as you walk the heavily eroded track to your first night's accommodation at Mangatepopo Hut. The next day you're scrambling over a succession of the mountain's old lava flows from its 1949 and

1954 eruptions and making the steep climb to Mangatepopo Saddle and across its adjacent drainage basin. There are the Emerald Lakes—old explosion pits turned turquoise by the minerals that flow into them from the craters above—and you also skirt a series of craters, including the large flat-topped North Crater. It's a lunar-like world of gravel fields, dry stream valleys, and jagged lava forms of the Oturere Valley.

You can also ascend to Ngauruhoe's summit along a trail that begins as a poled route, but soon ends at the foot of a broad ridge, taking you to the crater rim along a path of scree, gravel, and volcanic ash. Once there, beware of any fumaroles that may emit unpleasant and overpowering gases. However, the view is more than worth it. **BDS**

⬆ A world of volcanic landscapes and sulfuric vents.

Crucible Lake

Otago/West Coast, New Zealand

Start Makarora **End** Crucible Lake
Distance 40 miles (64 km) **Time** 3–4 days
Grade Strenuous **Type** Scree, ice, exposed
mountainside **Map** goo.gl/afb3Lg

The prospect of climbing up into the mountains on New Zealand's South Island so you can swim in a lake full of icebergs may not be to everyone's liking, but if you're a wilderness enthusiast, this place is heaven. Crucible Lake is not an easy place to get to. First, cross the Makarora River and follow the Young River to the twenty-bunk Young Hut. The next day, ascend to the tree line and follow the valley before climbing a grass spur for four hours to Gillespie Pass. Descend over snow grass plains to Siberia Stream, and another hour's walk to the comfort of Siberia Hut. From there, a

"This beautiful little iceberg-studded lake lies in the heart of Mount Aspiring National Park."

www.tourism.net.nz

narrow spur, a river crossing, and a snow grass flat are all that separate you from your goal. Crucible Lake is in Mount Aspiring National Park, a land of beech and podocarp rain forests below, and alpine lakes, waterfalls, and glaciers above. The hike there is very far off the beaten track and is best suited to those with previous backcountry experience. Set in a hanging valley beneath several glacier-laden summits, its waters are covered in both flat slabs of ice, which have formed over winter, and genuine icebergs that have calved off from the surrounding glaciers and plunged into the lake's frigid waters. Sadly, you cannot camp here, due to the fragile nature of the surrounding fields of alpine herbs. **BDS**

Cascade Saddle Route

Otago/West Coast, New Zealand

Start Raspberry Creek parking lot **End** Dart Hut
Distance 15.5 miles (25 km) **Time** 12 hours
Grade Moderate **Type** Rock, dirt trails
Map goo.gl/Xxem1A

A popular alpine pass in the South Island's Otago region, the Cascade Saddle Route in Mount Aspiring National Park doesn't actually take you over the Cascade Saddle itself because it is impassable. Instead it takes you along a spur behind Aspiring Hut and crosses back above the saddle before beginning its descent into the breathtaking Dart Valley, where a landslide in January 2014 blocked the Dart River and created a lake 1.9 miles (3 km) long.

Accessing the Cascade Saddle Route trailhead requires effort. From Wanaka, it is a 33-mile (54-km) drive, most of which is on unsealed roads, to the Raspberry Creek parking lot. From there, it's a short walk to the preferred starting point in the West Matukituki Valley. (The trail can also be done in reverse, from Queenstown starting at the Dart or Rees tracks, but this is substantially more challenging.) From Aspiring Hut, you make a steady ascent through mixed beech forests, and once above the tree line look for the easy-to-spot orange pole markers that will take you through a landscape of snow grass and tussock along a ridge and around the occasional easily navigable ledge. At the top of the ridge, after passing through a steep gully, you'll reach a pylon, and from there its downhill to Cascade Creek and an easy, flat approach to the saddle. Then it's down again, along unstable, exposed slopes to the base of the Dart Glacier. Keep to the river's left bank, cross the bridge over Snowy Creek, and go to Dart Hut, with its thirty-two bunk beds, comfy mattresses, flush toilets, and coal burner—the end of a long day's walk. **BDS**

➡ The Dart River lies beneath the glacier that is its source.

Kepler Track
Southland, New Zealand

Start/End Lake Te Anau control gates
Distance 37 miles (59.5 km)   **Time** 3–4 days
Grade Moderate   **Type** Gravel, rock, and dirt trails
Map goo.gl/7GFF70

They call it "the adventure above the clouds"—a track that begins in the beech forests of Lake Te Anau and Lake Manapouri and takes you to tussock-laden alpine landscapes on the slopes of Mount Luxmore. You access all this via a U-shaped glacial valley in Fiordland National Park—New Zealand's fjord, lake, rain forest, and mountain-encrusted wonderland where annual rainfall is measured in feet and beauty abounds.

The Kepler Track is a perfect choice for families, offering a mildly challenging three- to four-day hike over spectacular terrain. It is accessible and has excellent facilities: boardwalks have been laid over its boggy patches, its steeper sections have stairs, and its streams have bridges. The forests below the tree line are filled with ferns, mosses, and lichens, and between Lake Manapouri and Rainbow Reach is a wire-brush-dominated wetland.

The Luxmore Hut (3,560 feet/1,085 m) is the usual goal at the end of the first day, and the following day is the climb up to the route's highest point, the Luxmore Saddle (4,600 feet/1,400 m), which provides breathtaking views across the park, before a ridge walk to Iris Burn, a walk-in campsite in the Iris Burn Valley. Another low saddle follows to a gorge that brings you out on river flats and an overnight at Moturau Hut near Shallow Bay. You then cross several streams to arrive at the Waiau River (the Upper Waiau was the fictional river Anduin in the *Lord of the Rings* movies; 2001–03) before returning to the start point by the shores of Lake Te Anau. The first paths up here were cut by a local farmer, Jack Beer, who sought grazing pastures for his sheep, and the track officially opened in February 1988. **BDS**

"Your reward for the hill climb is a long section above bushline with marvelous panoramic views of the Kepler Mountains."

www.doc.govt.nz

⬅ The Kepler Track snakes along the hillside and into the clouds.

⬆ A suspension bridge crosses the Waiau River.

Dusky Track Southland, New Zealand

Start Hauroko Burn Hut   **End** West Arm, Lake Manapouri   **Distance** 52 miles (83.6 km)
Time 10 days   **Grade** Strenuous   **Type** Muddy trails, mountain paths   **Map** goo.gl/1Tw23P

The Dusky Track, a fabulous backcountry hike through a Jurassic-like environment over two mountain ranges and across three valleys deep in the Fiordland National Park, gets exciting before you've even reached the trailhead, which you access after a boat ride across New Zealand's deepest lake, Lake Hauroko. From there it's a six-hour slog to Halfway Hut, a misnomer if ever there was one because there are another nine days to go until you reach the end of this hike, which an increasing number of people are choosing to experience each year in preference to the higher-profile Milford Track. Established in 1952, it's one of New Zealand's longest and most isolated tracks. It weaves its way through a fern-draped wonderland of fallen trees, rotted moss-covered logs, and tree roots below canopies of silver beech, peppertrees, and fuchsias. Like its more famous cousin, this is an often wet and muddy route as most treks in Fiordland generally are, but the fact that its accessibility (only via air or sea) ensures there won't be any crowds more than compensates for soggy feet.

Highlights are many: traversing Pleasant Range with its views over the Kilcoy and Dingwall mountains and, to the south, the Dusky Sound itself; the climb to Lake Horizon, not to mention the warmth of the trail's succession of wonderful huts to shelter you from the abundant rain the region gets every year. Even if you don't take the two-day side trail down to Supper Cove in Dusky Sound, sloshing through the mud-filled Deadwood Flats and marveling at U-shaped valleys from the saddle at Centre Pass will ensure you never forget the time you conquered the Dusky Track. **BDS**

⬆ Dusky Track is one of the South Island's remote trails.

Routeburn Track Southland, New Zealand

Start Routeburn Shelter, Lake Wakatipu   **End** The Divide, Milford–Te Anau road   **Distance** 20 miles (32 km)
Time 2–4 days   **Grade** Easy to moderate   **Type** Gravel, dirt trails   **Map** goo.gl/ly7El2

There is a point in New Zealand's Southern Alps that should be signposted as a kind of Holy Grail of mountaineering, because it is on this spot that all of the reasons why people take to the mountains come together in one broad, dramatic sweep. At this spot, known as Key Summit, many of the peaks of Mount Aspiring National Park surround you. Not only that, but you can also see down three of the South Island's most beautiful valleys: the Greenstone, which drains into the Pacific Ocean; the Hollyford, which flows west into the Tasman Sea; and the Eglinton, which runs southward into the Southern Ocean.

As if all that weren't enough, you can also look across to the Darran Mountains rising up between the Hollyford and Cleddau valleys, and the sea beyond. These were the mountains where Sir Edmund Hillary prepared for his historic climb to the summit of Mount Everest in 1953. Needless to say, it's a good spot to stop for lunch.

Key Summit is a small side trip off the Routeburn Track, one of New Zealand's designated Nine Great Walks, an easily navigable and walkable route that connects Mount Aspiring National Park to Fiordland National Park via the Harris Saddle. The trail can be walked in either direction and takes you along the shoreline of Lake Harris, with its stunning views up Routeburn Valley, and to the magnificent Earland Falls (570 feet/174 m). You also walk through grasslands filled with ribbon wood trees, silver beech forests, and alpine wetlands, all the wonders you expect of a hike in one of the world's premier hiking regions through New Zealand's glacier-hewn landscape. **BDS**

⬆ Key Summit is a mountaineering holy grail.

HERITAGE

Heritage walks include petroglyphs, ancient burial mounds, battlefield parks, canalways, temple complexes, and monasteries. Everything from the crumbling remains of ancient Roman walls to sacred, well-worn pilgrimage trails and rediscovered indigenous trading routes are featured, bringing our history to life and illustrating what it means to be human.

← The Pont du Gard aqueduct in Provence, France, was built by the Romans to carry water and has been a footbridge since the Middle Ages.

Alexander Mackenzie Heritage Trail
British Columbia, Canada

Start Quesnel   End Bella Coola
Distance 280 miles (450 km)   Time 3 weeks
Grade Strenuous   Type Mountain trail
Info goo.gl/rGkx9b

"The awesome natural beauty of the area remains as it was and little has changed on the Central Coast."

www.bcgrizzlytours.com

⬆ The Alexander Mackenzie Heritage Trail runs near Hunlen Falls in Tweedsmuir Park.

For centuries before Europeans arrived on the North American continent, the indigenous tribes in what is now British Columbia had established a network of trails that extended from the interior of the continent westward to the Pacific Coast. These trails were a vital means of communication between groups separated by immense and often forbidding landscapes, and they were also used to transport food and other goods. One of the region's staple commodities transported on these remote tracks was a fish called the eulachon, which was rendered or dried into fat, which is why the tracks were called "grease trails."

In 1793, twelve years before Lewis and Clark's pioneering expedition to the Pacific Coast, a man named Alexander Mackenzie—a Scottish fur trader who worked for the North West Company—became the first European to reach the west coast. He was taken there along grease trails, led there by First Nations people. The trail that now bears his name follows in his extraordinary footsteps.

This ambitious trail is a patchwork quilt of old wagon roads, forest trails, horse trails, and riverbanks. In Tweedsmuir Park, it even becomes an alpine trail, and later a fjord, and you pass lakes too numerous to mention. The trail also educates you on the 6,000-year history of its indigenous founders, with more than 100 archaeological sites right on or by the trail, including another 250 miles (402 km) on either side of it. If you decide to hike its entire length, you need to be the experienced, self-reliant type. It tries to follow the original trail where it can, but mostly contents itself with getting as close as possible to one of North America's genuinely epic journeys. **BDS**

Rideau Canal National Historic Site
Ontario, Canada

Start Ottawa   **End** Kingston   **Distance** 124 miles (200 km); 240 miles (386 km) including side trails
Time 15–20 days   **Grade** Easy   **Type** Various
Info goo.gl/lqtBHr .

The Rideau Canal in Ottawa—a chain of lakes, rivers, and canal cuts that stretches from the head of Lake Ontario to Ottawa—was built under the supervision of Lieutenant Colonel John By of the Royal Engineers, and to this day it exerts a strong influence on its landscape and the lifestyle of Ottawa's inhabitants. Constructed along with various other forts and defensive canals to be a bulwark against a presumed U.S. attack on British colonies in upper Canada, it was designed to provide secure passage between Montreal and the British naval base at Kingston, an alternative to the St. Lawrence River. Work began in 1826, with a 5,000-strong labor force and more than 1,000 stonemasons working in cedar swamps, lakes, and backwaters that could be reached only by canoe.

The canal became a UNESCO World Heritage Site in 2007, and you can now walk much of its extensive network of locks, forts, and mills, including the eight Ottawa Locks around which the modern city of Ottawa grew, as well as a one-hour circuitous walk to the village of Burritt's Rapids, where the white water of the Rideau River was harnessed to operate a sawmill. There is also the Merrickville Blockhouse, the canal's largest fortification built to house troops in the event of an attack; a walk through the three interconnected locks around Jones Falls; and nearby Basin Trail, a short walk over irregular bedrock with its covering of thin, acidic soil in a woodland of red and white oak, hemlock, white pine, ferns, and lichens. The trail's end is at Kingston Mills, one of the canal's most impressive structures, with its four limestone locks with a lift of 12 feet (3.6 m), a fitting example of the canal's triumphal engineering. **BDS**

"Maintained by Canada's Parks service, it is arguably the most scenic and historic waterway in North America."

www.rideau-info.com

⊺ One of the great engineering feats of nineteenth-century Canada is now one of Ontario's finest ambles.

Bon Echo Provincial Park Ontario, Canada

Start/End Mazinaw Rock   **Distance** Various   **Time** 1 hour–1 day   **Grade** Easy to moderate
Type Forest trail   **Info** goo.gl/gcLWZ3

Bon Echo Provincial Park in south central Ontario has a lot going for it. It has the 328-foot (100-m) Mazinaw Rock escarpment, bejeweled with hundreds of ancient Aboriginal pictographs, which rises dramatically above Ontario's second deepest lake (476 feet/145 m). It also has a civilized mix of hiking trails ranging in length and difficulty from half a mile to more than 10 miles (16 km), interpretive boat tours on Mazinaw Lake for when your feet need a breather, and campsites to suit everyone.

Bon Echo Provincial Park got its name not long after the Bon Echo region was purchased by Dr. Weston Price and his wife in 1899, when the logging companies and those farmers the loggers helped sustain moved to greener pastures. Price named it Bon Echo because of the Mazinaw escarpment's acoustic ability to bounce sounds across Mazinaw Lake. Today the area has an enviable reputation for backwoods camping together with its plentiful trails. These include the Abes and Essens Lake Trail, which consists of three interconnecting loops that take from three and a half to seven hours to complete; the mile-long High Pines Trail to a series of eerily still ponds set among hemlocks, pines, and a maze of wetlands; and the fascinating Shield Trail, a two-hour walk of 3 miles (4.8 km) that takes you into the rugged beauty of the Canadian Shield, with its dense hardwood forests and cedar lowlands. Also, the Alpine Club of Canada is happy to kayak you around to the base of Mazinaw Rock itself for the Cliff Top Trail—straight up, no ropes, on stairs, and a pathway, and a great way to end a perfect day's walking. **BDS**

⊡ **Explore the hardwood forests of the Canadian Shield.**

Nez Perce National Historic Trail Oregon/Montana, USA

Start Wallowa Lake, Oregon   **End** Bear Paw Battlefield, Montana   **Distance** 1,170 miles (1,883 km)   **Time** Various (trail is not continuous)   **Grade** Moderate to strenuous   **Type** Open ground   **Info** goo.gl/oN895i

For generations the Nez Perce Native American tribe lived peacefully in scattered communities on the broad, flat plains west of the Rocky Mountains. A nomadic people, they roamed across a vast area encompassing present-day Idaho, Oregon, Washington, and Montana. They called themselves the Niimiipuu, simply, "the people," not Nez Perce, a name meaning "pierced nose," erroneously given to them by early French fur traders. In the mid-1800s the Nez Perce split into two factions; one agreed to move to a reservation in Idaho, while the other steadfastly refused, and on June 15, 1877, they began to walk east under the leadership of Chief Joseph, crossing the Rocky Mountains in the hope of finding refuge in Canada. Chief Joseph led 800 men, women, and children on what proved to be a doomed trek, and the course they took in trying to evade a pursuing U.S. cavalry

can now be traced on the Nez Perce National Historic Trail, only selected sections of which can be walked and with permission necessary for those sections that pass through privately owned land.

In 1986 the circuitous trail they took was made part of the Historic Trail network, and the history of the Nez Perce is commemorated at thirty-eight sites, managed by the USDA Forest Service, that begin at Wallowa Lake in Oregon and continue through north central Idaho, the northern tip of Yellowstone National Park, through the Clearwater basin and over the Bitterroot Mountains along centuries-old paths. The trail ends at Bear Paw Battlefield near Chinook in Montana, where, after a five-day battle, the Nez Perce surrendered in October 1877. **BDS**

⭱ Retrace the Nez Perce's own "Trail of Tears."

Bodie Ghost Town California, USA

Start/End Visitor parking lot **Distance** Various **Time** Various **Grade** Easy **Type** Dirt roads, timber boardwalks **Info** goo.gl/PpEQH4

There isn't a place like Bodie anywhere else in the United States. With more than 170 buildings in a state of "arrested decay," it is the largest ghost town west of the Mississippi River, an old mining town that, in the 1880s, had a population of more than 10,000 and a murder a day. It made Tombstone, Arizona, look civilized in comparison, and still trades on a quote by a little girl whose parents moved from San Francisco to Bodie in 1887: "Good-bye, God," she said. "I'm going to Bodie."

The town is located more than 8,000 feet (2,438 m) above sea level on the dry eastern flanks of the Sierra Nevada Mountains near the California–Nevada border and getting here requires some effort; the snow can drift to depths of 16 feet (5 m) in winter. Once here, however, you won't want to leave. An old bucket still hangs over a well on Green Street. There are hitching posts and boardwalks, as well as flat tin cans littering the ground and a peculiarly Bodie kind of roof shingle from more than 100 years ago. All that is missing is clumps of tumbleweed passing by—but the elevation is too great for that. Come here midweek near the end of the season, and even though 100,000 people visit every year, you just might have it all to yourself.

There are no defined trails or markers because that would be an encroachment, and while Bodie is a fully fledged California State Park, you wouldn't be aware of that if you miss the sign on the way in. There are no turnstiles, no neon, and no vending machines—just you, some high-range shrubs, such as rabbitbrush and sagebrush, the sound of your foosteps, and the ghostly echoes of an all-too-familiar wild Wild West. **BDS**

⬆ Bodie's eerie main street is frozen in time.

Sloan Canyon Petroglyphs Nevada, USA

Start/End Sloan Canyon trailhead   **Distance** 2 miles (3.2 km)   **Time** 1.5 hours   **Grade** Easy
Type Rocks, sandy wash   **Map** goo.gl/Ve7N1I

Often referred to as the "Sistine Chapel of Native American rock art," the 300-plus art panels and 1,700 individual elements and depictions that constitute the Sloan Canyon Petroglyphs are so precious and fragile that their location is not openly publicized. The canyon is also closed to camping, hunting, and off-road vehicles; cycling, horseback riding, and walking are encouraged only on certain designated trails.

To get to the site, which is on the southeast edge of the Las Vegas Valley south of Henderson, begin at the trailhead and continue along the Sloan Canyon Wash for about one mile (1.6 km), then press on through a series of increasingly rocky little canyons that require little more than a brief scramble. Then almost without warning you are there, most likely all alone, in the midst of a wonderland of ancient art with a volume and density that is virtually without precedent in North America. It is still a significant and sacred site to the many Native American tribes who contributed to it, a record of observations and reminiscences that spans almost two millennia.

Most of it is what experts call "basin and range tradition," with its abundance of abstract motifs and vertical lines almost nonexistent. Circular forms far outweigh rectilinear designs. Bighorn sheep are depicted most, which makes sense. Sinks in the rocks stored water; the sheep came for the water, and the people for the sheep. There's also an odd helmeted figure that is stunning in its complexity, which researchers here call the Space Alien. The hope is that these treasures can be preserved, as the drone of an expanding Las Vegas draws ever nearer. **BDS**

⊤ Sloan Canyon has a unique collection of ancient rock art.

Grimes Point Interpretive Trail Nevada, USA

Start/End Grimes Point Archaeological Site overlook   Distance 1 mile (1.6 km)   Time 1 hour   Grade Easy
Type Singletrack path   Map goo.gl/1lki85

One of the largest, most accessible of all petroglyph sites in the United States, Grimes Point Trail takes you into the midst of a vast expanse of rocks in an area that was first visited by Native Americans more than 8,000 years ago. Then the surrounding area was submerged under an expansive freshwater lake, part of a larger network of lakes and waterways that covered much of Nevada and western Utah, ringed by cottonwood trees and alive with birdlife and waterfowl. Now all that remains here are boulders the color of chocolate, a brown outer layer or patina that revealed the lighter surface beneath when etched by the artist. Designated a National Recreation Trail in 1978, the trail was built by the Youth Conservation Corps and is an easy walk that provides close-up views of its many petroglyphs, which scholars mostly agree are not a form of writing but rather depictions of everyday life.

Not far from Grimes Point Trail is Hidden Cave Trail, a 1-mile (1.6-km) loop that can be visited only on a guided tour. It features petroglyphs and several caves in which prehistoric hunter-gatherers once lived: caves that were formed by the wave action of ancient Lake Lahontan 13,000 years before the area was first inhabited and water levels began to fall. This loop features exceptional examples of rock art and has yielded many valuable artifacts, including stone scrapers used to butcher small animals. Perhaps more important still, the Grimes Point and Hidden Cave trails offer a stark reminder of the harsh reality of climate change. Guided educational programs for anyone wanting to know more about the prehistory of the Great Basin can also be arranged. **BDS**

⬆ Grimes Point pit-and-groove petroglyphs.

Union Pacific Rail Trail Utah, USA

Start Park City   **Start** Echo Reservoir   **Distance** 28 miles (45 km)   **Time** 1 day   **Grade** Easy
Type Paved and cinder trail   **Map** goo.gl/2vUvDv

In 1854, Utah's territorial government offered a $1,000 reward to anyone who could locate a coal seam within 40 miles (64 km) of Salt Lake City. Four years later a strike was made at Chalk Creek, later renamed Coalville. In the early 1870s, in response to a growing demand for coal to fuel pumps used in extracting water from mines, it was decided to create a new utility, the Summit County Railroad Company (SCRC), which set about building a narrow gauge rail line between Coalville and Park City. While it was doing that, the Union Pacific followed the route the SCRC was laying down and built its own broader gauge spur line alongside it, creating two parallel railway lines. Today's Union Pacific Rail Trail therefore has a majestic average width of 125 feet (38 m).

What is now the Historic Union Pacific Rail Trail State Park begins at Park City near Utah's Wasatch Mountains, crosses a series of wetland meadows around Silver Creek Canyon, passes through historic Coalville, and runs along the Weber River to Echo Reservoir, created with the completion of Echo Dam in 1931. The rail line remained in use until 1989, when plans were made to turn it into a nonmotorized recreational trail, the first such trail in Utah.

Part paved and part cinder trail, it is a technically simple trail to navigate, with a constant, steady downhill grade of between 2 and 3 percent if you start at Park City. It is great for mountain biking in the summer and Nordic skiing in winter, through a varied range of wildlife that includes deer, beavers, foxes, bald eagles, and—if the Rails-to-Trails Conservancy can be believed—moose. **BDS**

⬆ Salt Lake City's Union Pacific railroad station.

Petroglyph Point Trail Colorado, USA

Start/End Chapin Mesa Museum   **Distance** 3 miles (4.8 km)   **Time** 2.5 hours   **Grade** Strenuous
Type Rock and dirt trails   **Map** goo.gl/oKPB5C

Mesa Verde National Park is one of those rare places on Earth. Once you have immersed yourself in it, you cannot forget it. It lingers in the memory. It is many things: a sacred site for Native Americans, a climbing haven of ladders and kivas for children and child-like adults, and a bright, shining light for anyone with an interest in archaeology, anthropology, or history, or anyone who wants a better understanding of their place in the world.

It is most famous, of course, for its fabulous multistoried cliff dwellings, home to the ancient Pueblo communities we now call the Anasazi. They lived here among its canyons from the seventh century, first in pueblos and later, around the twelfth century, building in its cliff-side niches before abandoning it all for reasons we still do not fully know. It is also home to the pictorial record of their time

here—a remarkable panel of rock art that you can access via the Petroglyph Point Trail.

The trail is a narrow one as it loops around the west side of Chapin Mesa, past alcoves and overhangs, and it is a testimony to the skill of the trail builders, who cut steps into solid rock along essentially the very same trail the ancient Anasazi themselves would have taken. The trail is an interpretive one, but to get the most out of it you should go with a local guide. At Post #24 you reach a series of well-preserved geometric shapes and animal representations in an area 15 feet (4.5 m) wide by 6 feet (1.8 m) high set amid a forested area below the rim of Spruce Canyon on one of the best all-round hiking trails this wonderful park offers. **BDS**

⬆ Petroglyphs shed light on the lives of the Anasazi.

Flume Trail South Dakota, USA

Start Calumet trailhead, Sheridan Lake   **End** Coon Hollow trailhead   **Distance** 11 miles (17.7 km)   **Time** 4 hours
Grade Easy to moderate   **Type** Forest trail   **Map** goo.gl/Z2uFyp

For decades during the period of inexorable expansion westward across the Great Plains, there had been rumors of gold beneath the surface of the Black Hills of western South Dakota, but it wasn't until 1874 and General George Custer that the precious metal was found in the silt of French Creek. Within a year, the rush was on. Towns, villages, and gold and silver camps sprang up everywhere, bringing with them not only wealth, but also all the trappings associated with open-slather mining, such as flume trails.

The flume trail that begins near the Sheridan Lake campground southwest of Rapid City gives hikers easy access to terrain that is both beautiful and historic. This flume trail carried its gold-revealing water from Spring Creek, west of the campground, to the placer diggings on the outskirts of Rockerville. The flume only operated for five years, and in that time it

helped miners extract more than $20 million of gold from the traditional lands of the now-displaced Sioux and Cheyenne tribes.

The trail—now devoid of many of its timbers, sieves, and artifacts—still weaves a concave path through the Black Hills. Two tunnels built about 0.5 mile (0.8 km) into your walk kept the water flowing, both drilled and blasted through solid rock of metamorphic schist. The longest is only 100 feet (30 m) long, and their entrances were rebuilt in 1985. Walking through them is a treat, but you can take paths around them if you prefer. Inside is an atmospheric space that has not altered in more than 130 years. On the trail, watch out for original planks, still embedded with their square-head nails. **BDS**

⬆ A Gold Rush relic has become a Black Hills classic.

Effigy Mounds National Monument
Iowa, USA

Start/End Effigy Mounds National Monument visitor center   **Distance** 14 miles (22.5 km)   **Time** 1 day   **Grade** Easy   **Type** Grass, forest trails, boardwalks   **Map** goo.gl/gnG2Xg

The Late Woodland period (300–1000 CE) along the Mississippi River in North America was a time of great change. Population levels were increasing, communication between disparate groups was on the rise, and people began congregating into large, well-planned communities. Corn was introduced, bow and arrow technology improved, and the construction of conical-shape effigy mounds for the dead (although many are in the shape of bison, lynxes, bears, birds, and turtles) by the group we now call the Effigy Moundbuilders took place. These mounds extend from Dubuque in Iowa, north into Minnesota and Wisconsin, along Wisconsin's border with Illinois, and from Lake Michigan to the Mississippi River.

The mounds at Effigy Mounds National Monument cover an area of 2,526 acres (1,022 ha) of deciduous forests and remnants of tallgrass prairie, and the site preserves some 200 Native American mounds that were raised along the Mississippi River between 450 BCE and 1300 CE. The 2-mile (3.2-km) Fire Point Trail is a popular walk for people of all ages and it takes you along scenic overlooks on 300-foot (91.4-m) bluffs and past more than two dozen burial and ceremonial mounds. Some of the conical mounds along the bluffs date back almost 3,000 years.

It is possible to spend an entire day hiking through this delicately preserved ecosystem on 14 miles (22.5 km) of trails. They include the Yellow River Bridge Trail, a 0.5-mile-long (0.8 km) boardwalk accessible to the disabled, which offers access to the park's impressive wetlands, home to resident nesting birds, as well as muskrats, frogs, and turtles. All the trails are open from sunrise to sunset. **BDS**

"The 200-plus American Indian mounds are located in one of the most picturesque sections of the Upper Mississippi River Valley."

www.nps.gov

⊡ Sunlight filters through the deciduous forests that are home to 1,500-year-old burial mounds.

Sauk Trail

Illinois to Michigan, USA

Start/End Various
Distance Various
Time Various   **Grade** Easy
Type Forest trails   **Info** goo.gl/6qw2yn

Native American trails once crisscrossed the U.S. continent like a spider's web. The original inhabitants of the New World had, for centuries before the arrival of the pilgrims, already understood how to use the topography of the land to create networks of pathways to facilitate trade and communication and to help in the gathering and distribution of food. The Sauk Trail, a largely forgotten trail used by now forgotten nations—the Potawatomi, the Piankashaw, the Kaskaskia, and the Peoria—was just one of thousands of such trails.

The Sauk Trail once ran through the states of Michigan, Illinois, and Indiana. It followed the glaciated shoreline of Lake Michigan and the north bank of the Illinois River, but it was often hard to trace even in the early 1800s because of the number of side trails. Some identified sections do, however, still exist. One is in the Johnson-Sauk Trail State Recreation Area in Illinois; another remnant runs from Dyer, Indiana, to Frankfort, Illinois. Early settlers and fur traders used these well-worn paths, as did the military, and in 1835 the Chicago to Detroit stagecoach stuck largely to the Sauk Trail, which one newspaper described as a "huge serpent, lazily pursuing its onward course."

Today, after more than three centuries of white settlement, these ancient trails—the lucky ones—are either all but erased or have been bent so far out of shape, they are barely recognizable. This is why it is important to remember and treasure trails such as the Sauk Trail in the Midwest, the Mohawk Trail in New York, the Great Osage Trail over the Ozarks, and the Assunpink Trail in central and west New Jersey. Their like will never come again. **BDS**

"The park sits astride a trail that led Native Americans from Lake Michigan to the confluence of the Mississippi and Rock rivers."

dnr.state.il.us

⬆ The Sauk Trail is a powerful reminder that Native Americans built North America's first trail systems.

Towpath Trail
Ohio, USA

Start Harvard Road trailhead   End Canal Lands
Park trailhead   Distance 84 miles (135 km)
Time 7 days   Grade Easy   Type Crushed limestone
paths   Map goo.gl/AUaBJJ

"There are 84 miles to explore, both on foot and by bicycle, and in some places—by horseback."

www.ohioanderiecanalway.com

Ohio was a growing state of 580,000 people when construction on the Ohio and Erie canals began in the 1820s. Travel, however, was still difficult as there were few good roads. There had long been talk of cutting a canal that would run south from Lake Erie and through the state's most populous regions to the Ohio River as part of a wider network of canals that would span the nation. Work began in July 1825, and workers were paid 30 cents a day, plus a jigger of whiskey. Two years later, on July 3, 1827, the first boat left Akron and traveled through forty-one locks and over three aqueducts and reached Cleveland the next day.

From 1827 to 1913, teams of mules hauled barges and canal boats laden with produce and sightseers up and down this historic canal, and the trail today follows as closely as possible the course of the original towpath. Developed by the National Park Service, the path passes many of the canal's original locks and related infrastructure, providing walkers with an ideal perspective on the forests, farmlands, and wetlands of the Cuyahoga River Valley, part of the surrounding Cuyahoga National Park.

A total of forty-eight trailheads means that you can start and finish pretty much wherever you choose and see whatever most takes your fancy. Choices include Beaver Marsh, home to a community of beavers that moved in when the canal went into disrepair; the 65-foot-high (20 m) Brandywine Falls, and a hike to the Brandywine Gorge Trail; Fort Laurens, Ohio's only Revolutionary War–era fort; or the rural farms of the Wildcat Basin and Tuscarawas River Valley. There are plenty of delights to be enjoyed along this historic, tranquil pathway. **BDS**

⬆ Towpath trails follow canals that were once the highways of an expanding North America.

Ghost Town National Recreation Trail
Pennsylvania, USA

Start Saylor Park **End** 300 Prave Street
Distance 36 miles (57.9 km) **Time** 3 days
Grade Easy to moderate **Type** Limestone path
Map goo.gl/I45Hbb

They might not be the kind of ghost towns celebrated by popular culture, but the remnants of early 1900s coal mining communities on the Ghost Town National Recreation Trail in western Pennsylvania open a window on the past that is every bit as fascinating as the old timber towns of the Wild West. Mines in the Blacklick Creek Basin reached peak coal production during the 1940s, and although this had fallen by the mid-1990s, decades of acid discharge from underground mines, poorly reclaimed surface mines, and coal refuse piles had severely degraded the region's rivers and streams. The Ghost Town National Recreation Trail is just one part of the nonprofit Blacklick Creek Watershed Association's approach to revitalizing the region's natural environment.

The idea to build a trail began in 1991, when a salvage company donated a 16-mile (25.7-km) stretch of the Ebensburg and Blacklick Railroad. Further donations saw the trail extended, and once again a thread connected the now-abandoned coal mining towns of Webster, Armerford, Scott Glenn, Beulah, Claghorn (population 400, 150 of whom were miners), Lackawanna, Bracken, and, of course, Wehrum, the largest of the towns, which in its heyday had more than 230 houses, a bank, a hotel, a local store, and even its own jail. At the midpoint of the trail is the Eliza Furnace, a National Historic Landmark dating from 1846, which at its peak employed more than ninety men and produced almost 1,100 tons (998 t) of iron a year. Now, when you walk this tranquil and informative trail you are likely to see deer and chipmunks one minute, and mining slag the next; an ironic legacy in a rejuvenated valley. **BDS**

"A glimpse of the early 1900s as the rail trail passes through several abandoned coal mining towns."

www.americantrails.org

⬆ Once the site of heavy mining industry, Blacklick Creek is today transformed into a nature reserve.

Walt Whitman Trail
New York, USA

> "The cozy museum will give you ... just enough information to make you feel like you are walking along in Walt's footsteps."

voices.yahoo.com

⊼ Walk the trails that were once trodden by one of North America's great literary legends.

Start/End Walt Whitman homestead
Distance 4.25 miles (6.8 km)   Time 2 hours
Grade Easy   Type Forest trails
Map goo.gl/APTJxo

Walt Whitman, the great U.S. poet and essayist, was born in 1819 in West Hills, Long Island, and self-published his first landmark work, *Leaves of Grass*, in 1855. During the Civil War, he visited wounded Union soldiers in New York before traveling to Washington, D.C., to care for his own wounded brother. He stayed in the city for eleven years and took a job as a clerk, always struggling to make ends meet on a clerk's salary and helped along by an occasional royalty. He spent his declining years in Camden, New Jersey, in a two-story clapboard house, always writing and unknowingly building a legacy that would transform him into a giant of U.S. literature.

A nice way to reflect on the life of the great man is to take a book of his poems along with you as you set out on the Walt Whitman Trail. It begins at the Whitman homestead in West Hills, Long Island, and takes you along a walking and bridle path through the nearby woodlands where Whitman himself once walked. You can hike to the top of Jayne's Hill—at 400 feet (122 m), it is the highest point on Long Island—and continue through woodlands dominated by white pines, beech, oaks, hickories, and laurels.

The homestead is now a State Historic Site and it is listed on the National Register of Historic Places; it also has an interpretive center that houses a fine collection of Whitman's letters, portraits, and manuscripts. However, it is likely that simply walking the hills and paths that surround the site will bring you closest to the man who loved to immerse himself in the natural environment. "After you have exhausted what there is in business, politics, conviviality, and so on," he once wrote, "what remains? Nature remains." **BDS**

Old Croton Aqueduct Trail
New York, USA

Start Croton Dam **End** Van Cortlandt Park
Distance 26 miles (42 km) **Time** 2–3 days
Grade Moderate **Type** Earth and grass
Map goo.gl/QLxqQs

This 26-mile (42-km) trail atop the Old Croton Aqueduct passes through the farmland, towns, and villages of Westchester county and ends at Van Cortlandt Park in the Bronx. Much of it runs parallel to the Hudson River. Along the way are industrial heritage sites, such as weir buildings where the water's flow was regulated, brick ventilator towers, and bridges; literary associations, such as Sunnyside, the riverside home of author Washington Irving, and Sleepy Hollow, the town that inspired Irving's eponymous ghost story; and views, gardens, and wildlife. In the town of Ossining, hikers can sometimes join a guided tour into the aqueduct itself. It's a journey through time, from rural backwaters to metropolitan sophistication; above all, it's a jump-on jump-off neighborhood resource for dog walkers, joggers, cyclists, horseback riders, and birders. Even cross-country skiers use the linear park.

The aqueduct opened to great fanfare in 1842, when it was urgently needed. Manhattan may be surrounded by water, but it is brackish, and the fresh springs and wells of the island could not support the escalating population. The new aqueduct used gravity to bring water into the city from Westchester county, and it transformed lives.

The New York City Department of Parks and Recreation has picked up the trail's baton in Van Cortlandt Park and produced a map that tracks the aqueduct to Central Park, the site of the old Receiving Reservoir, remnants of which can still be seen. This isn't a trail as such, but if you are the sort of person who likes to finish what they begin, you can download the route from its website. **DS**

"One of New York City's best-kept secrets. Follow this 160-year-old route and keep a sharp eye out for the history at your feet."

www.nycgovparks.org

⬆ Trace the path taken by the first water pipeline to bring water to the people of New York City.

Hudson Valley Rail Trail
New York, USA

Start Intersection of New Paltz Road and Route 299
End Walkway Over the Hudson **Distance** 7.5 miles
(12 km) **Time** 4 hours **Grade** Easy **Type** Paved
Map goo.gl/G2v64s

"Offers thrilling river views and connects riverside parks, cultural attractions, and historic points of interest."

nyparks.com

When compared to many other successful rails-to-trails conversions across the United States, the Hudson Valley Rail Trail may seem a tad short—only 7.5 miles (12 km)—but what it lacks in distance it more than makes up for in sheer scenic delight. It passes through hardwood forests; underneath two gorgeous stone-arch bridges; over the popular kayaking and canoeing thoroughfare that is Black Creek; along a green corridor through the idyllic hamlet of Highland, with its cafés and delicatessens lining the trail; and finally onto and over the Walkway Over the Hudson—the reinvented, steel-cantilevered Poughkeepsie Bridge (1889), now the longest elevated pedestrian bridge in the world. The bridge, which ceased taking traffic in the 1970s, was the spur for the rails-to-trails birth in 2009, when it was given new life as a route-shortening option for the installation of a new generation of fiber-optic cables.

Once over the Hudson River, you can also connect with the Dutchess Rail Trail that, should you still have the legs for it, takes you a further 13 miles (20.9 km) to the town of Hopewell Junction, providing, of course, you can tear yourself away from the view that the 21-foot-high (65 m) Walkway Over the Hudson provides. The bridge, North America's longest when it was completed, is a designated National Historic Civil Engineering Landmark. Originally built to connect New York and New England to the growing national rail network, it fell into disrepair after being severely damaged by fire in 1974 and it has since been reinvented as a "pedestrian park," 1.25 miles (2 km) in length and providing public access to the Hudson River's scenic landscape and waterfront. **BDS**

⊡ Take a stroll over one of North America's famous rivers on the country's longest elevated pedestrian bridge.

Robert Frost Interpretive Trail
Vermont, USA

Start/End Route 125 parking area outside Ripton
Distance 1.2 miles (1.9 km)   **Time** 30–45 minutes
Grade Easy   **Type** Gravel path and boardwalk
Map goo.gl/unX1dl

The great U.S. poet Robert Frost moved to Vermont from New Hampshire because he wanted "a better place to farm and especially grow apples." He settled in a log cabin in Ripton, on the Homer Noble Farm in the Green Mountains. He was a farmer first and poet second, and the farm would become his summer home for the next twenty-three years. Much of the verse we are so familiar with today—poems that were rooted in the state's rock-strewn soil—was written on the farm and in the small log cabin that still stands there. The area surrounding Ripton was officially designated Robert Frost Country in 1983. There is a Robert Frost Memorial Drive; a Robert Frost Wayside Picnic Ground; the Bread Loaf School of English established in 1919 in Middlebury, which Frost first visited in 1921 and returned to regularly over the next forty-two years; and the Robert Frost Interpretive Trail.

The trail is a short walk through lovely woodlands and fields of blueberries and huckleberries, with occasional plaques annotating Frost's poetry mounted along the way. It was developed by the Green Mountain National Forest, with the assistance of some of Frost's old friends, including Reginald "Doc" Cook, who chose the poems and arranged the installation of the plaques. A writer himself, Cook has authored numerous books detailing Frost's life and legacy, and would often join the poet on long walks through the neighboring Bread Loaf Woods: "When we went outside in the fields and woods he proved as deliberately deviable a walker as a talker. We commonly started from his Ripton cabin, picked up two walking sticks and entered the woods with Gillie, a Border collie, hugging our heels." **BDS**

"His poems are more than rooted in the state's landscape, they are the landscape: its stony and frugal soil, its shimmering green glens."

www.nytimes.com

⤒ Walk through the fields and woodlands that helped to inspire one of North America's finest poets.

Delaware and Hudson Rail Trail Vermont, USA

Start/End Castleton trailhead
Distance 19.8 miles (31.8 km)
Time 5 hours   Grade Easy
Type Rail trail   Map goo.gl/sw1irt

The Delaware and Hudson Rail Trail runs on a converted railroad corridor in western Vermont, along the border with New York state. The firm that ran the line fell on hard times in 1980, and subsequently closed it down. The trail runs in two distinct sections between the settlements of Castleton and Poultney, and West Pawlet and West Rupert. The gap in between is centered around the town of Granville in New York state, a good spot to stop for a visit.

The route is mostly flat and is used by hikers, joggers, horseback riders, and mountain bikers. The

> *"Scenery includes a ... perspective of rural Vermont's dairy farms, meadows, woods, and small towns."*
>
> www.trails.com

surface is based on the railway's original cinder ballast, plus gravel and stone. There are seventeen wooden railway bridges along the route, some of them 100 feet (30.5 m) long, all of which are safe and easy to navigate.

The trail takes you past some of Vermont's many dairy farms, as well as rolling meadows, dense forests, small rural towns, and a slate quarry (the trains that used to rumble down this track were known as "slate pickers"). At the start of the southern section, it dips into New York state briefly but then runs back into Vermont, and there are plenty of places to stop along the way for food and drink on a route that is good for families and novices. There's plenty of wildlife to enjoy, too, including herons, ducks, and beavers. **JI**

Freedom Trail Massachusetts, USA

Start Boston Common visitor center   End Bunker Hill Monument   Distance 2.5 miles (4 km)   Time 1.5–2 hours   Grade Easy   Type Mostly brick pathway
Map goo.gl/g1gp8n

Boston's Freedom Trail, which connects a total of sixteen historic Revolutionary War sites throughout the city—all linked by the famous parallel red lines of the Freedom Trail marker—was the brainchild of local veteran newspaperman William Schofield, who loved the history of his hometown but would constantly lose his way whenever he went for a walk to its various historic sites. "Being a Swamp Yankee descendant," he once said, "I had always been interested in Yankee history. So here I am in the most historic city in the country. I used to go wandering all over the place and I found out that when I'd go looking for something it was never there." Frustrated, Schofield began to develop a prototype trail in his "Have You Heard" column in the *Evening Traveler*, and for two weeks he continued to embellish and refine it, adding Bunker Hill and the *USS Constitution*, until he received a telephone call from Boston's mayor John Hynes, who told him the city would implement his plan, which Schofield initially called "Freedom Way."

Now known as the Freedom Trail, the route is a fascinating walk through downtown Boston and U.S. history. Local silversmith and key revolutionary Paul Revere's house; the Old North Church, where two lanterns were lit on April 18, 1775, to signal that the British were coming by sea; the Old South Meeting House; the Old Corner Bookstore; and the Park Street Church are buildings that have all been saved from demolition or radical reinvention. They are all still alive with the spirit of independence in a city whose location always guaranteed it would be center stage in the colony's struggle toward self-expression and its inevitable rejection of British rule. **BDS**

Potomac Heritage National Scenic Trail

Pennsylvania to Virginia USA

Start Allegheny Highlands, Pennsylvania
End Chesapeake Bay **Distance** 830 miles
(1,336 km) **Time** 3 months **Grade** Easy to
moderate **Type** Gravel, asphalt **Info** goo.gl/IdS8r0

The Potomac Heritage National Scenic Trail (PHT) was created to showcase and provide greater access to the historical, cultural, and natural features of the Ohio and Rappahannock river watersheds. It's different to most other North American national trails that have a defined path in that the PHT is more of a suggested route, with a host of spurs, side trails, and alternatives that often see it split, with both alternatives running on either side of the Potomac River, after which it was named. Of course, a trail this long is never a standalone creation. The PHT made use of many existing pathways, such as the Chesapeake and Ohio Canal Towpath and the Laurel Highlands Hiking Trail. Nevertheless, it remains a fine example of what grass-roots organizations—in this case, the Potomac Heritage Trail Association—can achieve when it comes to the building and continued maintenance and improvement of trails.

The trail passes through no fewer than five distinct geographic regions. Beginning in the Allegheny Highlands it breaches the eastern Continental Divide, pierces the gaps of the Blue Ridge Mountains at Harpers Ferry, and ends at the mouth of the Potomac River. On the way it passes well-known places, such as the Great Allegheny Passage, and others that are barely known at all, such as Point of Rocks, an ancient Native American trading route. The trail takes you through old colonial settlements and the birthplaces of some of the nation's Founding Fathers, across Civil War battlefields, and into the finest Washington, D.C., museums, fulfilling an early vision—albeit a century or two later—to connect the interior territories with the bustling eastern seaboard. **BDS**

"Along the way, the scenery, history, and economic evolution of the nation come into focus."

www.npca.org

⬆ A large network of trails runs through the lands of North America's Founding Fathers.

Spotsylvania Court House Battlefield Hike
Virginia, USA

Start/End Exhibit shelter on Grant Drive
Distance 5.5 miles (8.8 km)   **Time** 3 hours
Grade Moderate   **Type** Dirt paths
Map goo.gl/WhqlLZ

The Battle of Spotsylvania Court House, fought between the army of the Potomac under the command of Lieutenant General Ulysses S. Grant, and the army of Northern Virginia, led by the hero of the Confederacy, General Robert E. Lee, was one of the five bloodiest battles of the U.S. Civil War. Fought from May 8 to 21, 1864, in Spotsylvania County, Virginia, it was a tactically inconclusive battle that saw Grant fail to dislodge Lee's entrenched positions at the crossroads of Spotsylvania Court House, which Lee's army had reached ahead of Grant's. Claiming more than 32,000 casualties, it was the costliest engagement of Grant's Overland Campaign in 1864.

There are four main battlefields in Fredericksburg and Spotsylvania National Military Park. Of all the individual trails, however, it is the Spotsylvania Court House Battlefield Hike that is the favorite of most seasoned Civil War walkers. Walking here is a somber experience. Head to Brock Road and find where Union Major General John Sedgwick, as he was directing the placement of his artillery onto the Confederate lines on May 9, boasted that the enemy "couldn't hit an elephant at this distance." Moments later he fell dead into a staff sergeant's arms, shot through the eye. Hike to Laurel Hill where the fighting started when the Maryland Brigade rushed the Confederate defenses. Walk over the open field where Robert E. Lee pitched his command tent, and see the foundations of the McCoull House where 1,492 Union soldiers were buried. Or visit the two chimneys—the remains of Landrum House field hospital, which survived the war only to burn down in 1905, tired, perhaps, of preserving the memories of the horrors it saw. **BDS**

> *"If viewed as one campaign, the Wilderness/Spotsylvania Campaign is the bloodiest in American history."*

www.nps.gov

⬆ Monument commemorating soldiers who fought in one of the bloodiest American Civil War battles.

High Bridge Trail
Virginia, USA

Start Rice   End Pamplin City
Distance 31 miles (49.8 km)   Time 2 days
Grade Easy   Type Rails-to-trails, hard-packed,
fine gravel   Map goo.gl/5R8w9s

The crowning glory of the High Bridge Trail is, not surprisingly, the High Bridge itself, a railway bridge built over the Appomattox River in 1854 to connect the towns of Petersburg and Lynchburg. The bridge is as impressively long as it is high—2,400 feet (731 m) long, in fact, and 125 feet (38 m) at its highest—and it was built with pedestrians in mind even then, with a footpath running alongside the tracks. We are lucky to still have it. A bone of contention during the last days of the Civil War, it was fought over on April 6 and 7, 1865, and the retreating Confederacy even set it alight. However, the fire burned itself out and the bridge survived. The war ended two days later.

The last train crossed the High Bridge on October 26, 2004. Two years later the Norfolk Southern Railway donated 31 miles (49.8 km) of track to the state of Virginia, making possible the creation of the linear High Bridge Trail State Park, with the bridge, appropriately renewed and strengthened, as its centerpiece. The bridge opened on April 6, 2012, after twelve months had been spent converting it from an abandoned rail bridge to a multiuse trail ideal for walking, cycling, and horseback riding. It is Virginia's longest recreational bridge and among the longest in the United States. Now on the National Register of Historic Places, this magnificent bridge is part of a trail that runs through the towns of Burkeville, Farmville, Pamplin City, Prospect, and Rice. Covered observation decks on the bridge encourage users to take a break and gaze out over the canopy of greenery growing in abundance along the riverbanks below and to marvel at the sheer scale and beauty of this triumph of engineering. **BDS**

"The trail's finely crushed limestone surface and dimensions make it easy for everyone to enjoy."

www.dcr.virginia.gov

⬆ The High Bridge Trail affords fabulous views over the surrounding forests.

Birmingham Civil Rights Heritage Trail

Alabama, USA

Start/End Kelly Ingram Park
Distance 5 miles (8 km)   **Time** 2–3 hours
Grade Easy   **Type** Paved interpretive trail
Map goo.gl/gN1PBF

In the early 1960s, Alabama was the anvil on which many of the struggles and victories of the Civil Rights Movement were hammered. There is the jail cell where Martin Luther King, Jr. penned his famous "Letter from Birmingham Jail" in which he wrote that "justice delayed is justice denied." It was to Birmingham that Fred Shuttlesworth, the pastor of the city's Bethel Baptist Church who once declared "I wasn't saved to run," invited King in April 1963 to lead a series of protest marches in which police brutally turned on the protestors in Kelly Ingram Park. Months later, on September 15, 1963, the church that had become a staging ground for civil rights activists was bombed, killing four young girls who were getting ready for Sunday School in the church's basement. No matter where you walk in the town of Birmingham, you are never far away from bitter memories.

The Birmingham Civil Rights Heritage Trail was established in an effort to preserve the lessons learned from the days of segregation. There are currently more than seventy sites along the trail, all of which are deemed of national merit, with highly innovative signage. You will also find photographs of the events that took place a matter of feet from where you are standing during the days of the Birmingham Movement, quotes from the participants, and even lesson assignments. They are designed to challenge the viewer both emotionally and spiritually.

So when visiting Birmingham, if you want to do a more challenging excursion on the tourist circuit, make your way over to Kelly Ingram Park, and get yourself ready to "walk the walk." Birmingham is no longer a "stigma city." **BDS**

"Graphic photographs and dramatic cut-outs in the … signs add to the rich experience."

birminghamal.org

⬆ The trail reminds walkers of the struggle faced by protesters to overturn the Jim Crow segregation laws.

Trail of Tears National Historic Trail
Georgia to Oklahoma, USA

Start/End Various
Distance Various   **Time** Various
Grade Easy   **Type** Various
Info goo.gl/lBYWYb

Every October the Cherokee Historical Association hosts the Annual Trail of Tears Memorial Walk, an event inaugurated in 2007 to honor those of the Cherokee, Chocktaw, Chickasaw, Seminole, and Muscogee Creek Native American Nations, who were removed from their traditional lands after the passage of the Indian Removal Act of 1830. Their forced marches westward to the "Indian Territories"—lands not yet settled or allotted to become the new state of Oklahoma—led to thousands perishing en route from exposure, starvation, and disease, and the policy remains one of the saddest episodes in U.S. history. The annual walk begins at the Cherokee Historical Association, in the town of Cherokee, North Carolina, and continues on the Cherokee River Loop Trail. It is one of many small walks that it is possible to do as a way of remembering the forced relocation and suffering the Indian nations east of the Mississippi River were made to endure before the United States began its "Manifest Destiny" of westward expansion.

In Georgia there are many sites you can visit to recall those dark days, including a 3-mile-long (4.8 km) paved walkway that connects the site of the farm of John Ross, a Cherokee elder who fought against relocation, to the site of Ridge farm, the home of a prominent white family who were signees to the 1835 Treaty of New Echota, which resulted in the Cherokee's removal from Georgia. The Chief Vann House Historic Site in Chatsworth, Georgia, is a 23-acre (9.3-ha) park and site of the house built by James Vann, a Cherokee leader and businessman who built a 1,000-acre (450-ha) plantation. The family lost its home when forced to relocate to Oklahoma. **BDS**

"This tragic chapter in American and Cherokee history became known as the Trail of Tears."

www.nationalparks.org

⊞ This walk is a reminder of how "Manifest Destiny" impacted upon the destiny of others.

Chattanooga Civil War Battlefields Georgia/Tennessee, USA

Start Chickamauga   **End** Chattanooga   **Distance** 16 miles (25.7 km)   **Time** 4–6 hours   **Grade** Moderate
Type Field and roadway   **Map** goo.gl/2Dkr9Z

During the U.S. Civil War, Chattanooga was a strategically vital railroad hub for the Confederacy, and this historic trail follows in the footsteps of Union General William S. Rosecrans as he advanced on the city from the camp he had pitched in Chickamauga. The ensuing two-day battle involved 120,000 troops, of whom 34,000 were killed or wounded in what was one of the war's bloodiest battles.

Starting at Chickamauga Battlefield, the walk passes through lush green fields and shady patches of forest, interspersed with monuments to the fallen of both sides. Approaching Chattanooga, you climb the slopes of Missionary Ridge, the natural southeast boundary of the city. The winding roads to the crest are again full of memorials. Foreign visitors express surprise at the strength of feeling that still remains about the "war that set brother against brother."

On the ridge, you pass the National Cemetery, the last resting place of thousands of Union soldiers. Also not to be missed here is a replica of The General, the locomotive that starred in *The Great Locomotive Chase* (1956), the Disney movie about a famous Civil War incident. Journey's end is Lookout Mountain, the summit of which, Point Park, has its own plaques explaining the events of 1863. The promontory gives sweeping views over the Chattanooga Valley. Of special interest is Signal Mountain, home to Signal Point, from which troop movements throughout the area were observed. It also overlooks the Tennessee River as it passes through the Tennessee Gorge, a reminder of the strategic importance of the high ground this trail takes you over. **GL**

⊡ A once-vital railroad hub is now a memorial to the fallen.

South Beach Art Deco District Florida, USA

Start/End Art Deco Welcome Center   Distance Various   Time Various   Grade Easy
Type Pavement   Info goo.gl/fChFQP

The Art Deco District in South Beach, Miami—the first urban district in the United States to be listed on the National Register of Historic Places—is an eclectic collection of mostly commercial buildings that triumphantly reflect that period in urban design characterized by the Art Deco movement of the 1920s and 1930s with its outrageous angles, vibrant pastels, exaggerated ornamentation, Art Deco reflected the flamboyance and exuberance of a nation in a period of prosperity, innovation, and promise—an architecture of confidence for a brassy, interwar United States.

The walk is a short one—only a few city blocks—but it can take you all day if you're an art lover. The Art Deco buildings first began to appear in the wake of the great Miami land boom of the 1920s (and the Great Miami Hurricane of 1926), and the city has more than 800 examples of the style. There is the perfect

symmetry of The Webster at 1220 Collins Avenue, and The Carlyle Hotel at 1250 Ocean Drive, which opened its doors in 1941. The latter remains the hotel of choice in the district, with its three distinctive vertical dividing protuberances on its exterior—the standard Art Deco "rule of thirds." There is also The Breakwater at 940 Ocean Drive, with its copious display of neon that lights up the night like some intergalactic lightsaber. However, the district's finest example of the sublime art style is probably the Bass Museum at 2100 Collins Avenue, with its exterior of fossilized paleolithic coral and a glorious series of bas-reliefs above its entrance.

A good place to start walking is the Art Deco Welcome Center at 1001 Ocean Drive. Just grab a map—and may the pastels be with you. **BDS**

⬆ The exuberant Art Deco style is alive and well in Miami.

Old San José del Cabo Art Trail Baja California Sur, Mexico

Start/End Plaza Central **Distance** 0.3 mile (0.5 km) **Time** 20 minutes to 2 hours **Grade** Easy
Type Sidewalks **Info** goo.gl/emfuE5

Every Thursday evening between November and June, a buzz builds in San José del Cabo as visitors and locals converge on the town's old quarter for Open Studios, when more than twenty art galleries and studios open their doors to the public. Drifting through the tight grid of streets, gallery hoppers browse the white walls and terra-cotta patios of the quarter's lovely old casas, looking at paintings, sculpture, ceramics, and photography, sipping on wine and nibbling *botanas* (Mexican tapas) as they go. Mariachi add to the sense of occasion.

The quality of the art is high, with new shows and artists-in-residence introduced over the season. A walking trail designed by the Art District Association, to promote the artists and gallery owners, links the top galleries and plots the best of the restaurants that have sprung up to cater to the trade. From the Plaza Central, the route heads west along Calle Obregon to Calle Guerrero, taking in side streets, and then returns to the square via Calle Comonfort. The best places for national and international artists are Patricia Mendoza (corner of Obregon and Hidalgo), Corsica (Obregon), and Frank Arnold (Comonfort); Casa Dahlia on Calle Morelos displays contemporary fine art by Bajan artists in one of the oldest buildings in the quarter.

The atmosphere and colonial architecture are as appealing as the art, and strolling the short route can take a surprisingly long time. The mellow vibe—which drew the artists in the first place—loosens the purse strings as well as the hesitation that some people feel when visiting art galleries, and many sales are made in spite of the barely perceptible pressure to buy. **DS**

⤒ An uplifting trail around an artistic neighborhood.

Campeche Historic City Walk Campeche, Mexico

Start Plaza Principal **End** Seafront boardwalk **Distance** 4 miles (6.4 km) **Time** 4 hours **Grade** Easy
Type Sidewalks **Map** goo.gl/xDUMzs

Campeche is a colonial seaside city built on the site of a preexistent Mayan settlement named Kimpech, the remains of which are still visible. Founded by the conquistadors in 1540, then razed to the ground in 1663 by buccaneers, it was rebuilt as a fortress city and became the focal point of maritime commerce along the Gulf of Mexico. Today, its major industry is tourism, and it trades heavily on its historical links with piracy.

Start at the Baroque Catedral de Nuestra Señora de la Soledad in the Plaza Principal and visit the adjacent Museo de la Architectura Maya in a former fortress, then proceed from there to the *malecón*, the seafront promenade. In between, be sure to take a look at the sixteenth-century Church of San Francisco and the San Francisco Monastery, the site of the first Christian mass on Mexican soil in 1517. And don't miss the two main gates either: Puerta del Mar (Sea Gate),

with a stone-carved galleon on its door, and Puerta de la Tierra (Land Gate). Also of interest are the remains of the city wall between them. Other must-sees include the Baluarte (Bastion) de Santiago, with its botanical garden; the Carvajal Mansión, a seventeenth-century house in Moorish style; and Casa de las Artesanías Tukulná, an old private residence that is now a handicraft museum and sales outlet.

Around 30 miles (48 km) to the southeast of Campeche is Edzná, the site of some magnificent Mayan ruins. Guided tours go there daily. Another popular excursion is a boat trip across the gulf to the nearby island of Jaina, where there is a vast Mayan necropolis from which hundreds of bodies have been recovered and are now displayed. **GL**

⬆ Enchanting architecture can be found in Campeche.

Mayan Trails at Chichen Itza Yucatán, Mexico

Start Ball court **End** Akab Dzib **Distance** 4 miles (6.4 km) **Time** 4 hours **Grade** Moderate
Type Archaeological site **Map** goo.gl/emtu4S

The site of this long abandoned but marvelously preserved Mayan city occupies an area of only around 1.5 square miles (3.9 sq km), but because of the potential ferocity of the Mexican heat, this walk is best undertaken, if possible, in the early morning. It begins at one of Chichen Itza's thirteen ball courts, or *juego de pelota*. The rules of the ancient Mesoamerican game that was played here are lost, but they are thought to have been similar to those of modern racquetball. A little way to the east is the Temazcalli, a sweat bath divided into a waiting gallery, a water bath, and a chamber in which steam was produced by pouring water onto heated stones.

The next major sights are the Templo de los Guerreros (Temple of the Warriors), the Tzompantli (Platform of the Skulls), the Templo de los Tigres (Temple of the Jaguars), and the largest of the *juegos*

de pelota. Then comes the most famous Chichen Itza landmark—El Castillo, or the Pyramid of Kukulcan, the feathered serpent god. Unfortunately, it is no longer permissible to climb the huge stairway to the top.

Returning roughly in the direction in which you came, you will pass the Tomb of the High Priest, the Casa de los Metates (House of the Grinding Stones), and the Templo del Venado (Temple of the Hunt), while to your left is the sinister Cenote de Xtoloc (Well of Sacrifice). The route nears its end at the Edificio de las Monjas (Building of the Nuns), which in more recent times was a nunnery complex, but in the time of the Mayas, it was the city's ornate royal palace. The last stop is at Akab Dzib (House of Dark Writing), a palace with hieroglyphic inscriptions. **GL**

⊞ Chichen Itza's impressive Temple of the Warriors.

Tulum to Yaxuna Quintana Roo/Yucatán, Mexico

Start Tulum   **End** Yaxuna   **Distance** 70 miles (112 km)   **Time** 4 days   **Grade** Strenuous
Type Jungle trails   **Map** goo.gl/GM1Ysa

On a cliff top overlooking the Gulf of Mexico, the ancient trading city of Tulum is one of the richest treasuries of Mayan relics, with grand temples and public buildings containing numerous statues and stele (upright stone slabs or tablets), all set in lush, tropical surroundings. Along the coast is Xel-Ha, a port next to a lagoon of the same name. The surrounding area has numerous cenotes, deep water-filled holes in the limestone crust of the earth into which people were thrown to appease the Mayan gods.

Although there is a highway from here to Coba, 27 miles (43 km) away, it is busy and unsafe for pedestrians. Use it by all means, but take the bus. Alternatively, there are numerous walking routes that go across the country, but the best one varies from season to season, so it is advisable to hire a local guide. In fact, it's probably essential: the terrain is jungle.

Coba, thick in vegetation and surrounded by five lakes, is dominated by the Nohoch Mul pyramid, the largest structure of its type in the Yucatán Peninsula, at 136 feet (41.5 m) high. Around this focal point, stone and plaster roads radiate across 30 square miles (80 sq km) of palaces, temples, halls, plazas, and courts—a total of 6,500 buildings. The thoroughfares may seem clearly defined near the central precinct, but beware: the jungle is quick to reclaim territory, and many of the trails peter out quickly. Anyone contemplating the 43-mile (70-km) walk to Yaxuna should again hire the services of a local guide. Those who make it there will find another great city, albeit one in a much more advanced stage of decay than the two visited earlier. **GL**

⬆ Mayan columns defy the ravages of time in Coba.

Old Havana Walking Tour
Havana, Cuba

Start Casa de la Obrapia, Calle Obrapia
End Plaza de San Francisco   Distance 4 miles (6.4 km)
Time 3.5 hours   Grade Easy   Type Sidewalks
Map goo.gl/XfCToR

Havana, the Cuban capital, got off to a bad start when it was founded on the wrong—that is to say, the south—coast of the island in either 1514 or 1515. Two attempts were then made to reestablish it on the north coast before, in 1519, a suitable site was found in Puerto de Carenas (Careening Bay), a natural harbor around which the city soon grew. Havana served as a springboard for Spanish conquests of the Americas, as well as a stopping-off point for the gold-laden galleons on their way home to Spain. Gradually, the city grew into three distinct areas, the UNESCO–listed Havana Vieja (Old Havana), downtown Vedado, and the newer suburban districts. Over its 500 years, Havana has acquired some of the most diverse architecture in the world, from colonial and Baroque buildings to some fine Art Deco structures.

Art Deco came to the residential area of Miramar in 1927, and it soon spread to Marianao, Vedado, and other areas of wealth and prestige. Suitably, given its importance in the Cuban economy, the Bacardi white rum company built a stylish Art Deco headquarters on Avenida de Bélgica (Egido) in Havana Vieja in 1930, at the time the largest building in the city. The Hotel Nacional de Cuba and the Lopez Serrano soon followed, the latter inspired by the Rockefeller Center in New York City. Art Deco was soon supplanted by modernist buildings, but the lack of recent development in the city has meant that its few examples are well preserved and much loved. Walking tours around Havana take in these fine buildings, but it is up to you if you want to go with a guide or just stroll by yourself, soaking up the atmosphere of this beautiful city. **SA**

"A pleasant place to stroll around and get a sense of what life in Cuba used to be like 200 years ago."

www.planetware.com

⊤ Art Deco continues to flourish in Old Havana in the absence of excessive development.

San Agustín Archaeological Park Trails Huila, Colombia

Start/End San Agustín Archaeological Park
Distance 6 miles (9.6 km)   Time 1 day
Grade Easy   Type Dirt paths, tracks
Map goo.gl/MGEXm1

Well before Columbus first visited the Americas in 1492—and later had his name given to the country of Colombia—the peoples of what is now the southwest of the country developed an advanced mythology and set of beliefs allied to a highly visual sense. They were an advanced agricultural society that developed complex funerary rites linked to the spiritual power of the dead and the supernatural world. These beliefs were exhibited in a series of more than 500 monumental stone statues and watercourses in San Agustín. Among the extraordinary sculptures is a representation of a warrior with two bodies and two heads joined together, integrating masculine and feminine. Another shows a mother giving birth while the male midwife looks east to the rising sun, representing life. La Fuente de Lavapatas is a complex maze of canals and pools carved into the bedrock of the stream, with surrounding reliefs that show a wide range of different creatures. The canals through which the water flows form a maze from which no water can escape, evidence of the high levels of engineering that these people attained.

Quite what happened to these ancient masters we do not know, but at some time between 1300 and 1400 CE, they felt threatened by invaders and fled to take refuge in the Orinoco and Amazon river basins, leaving their stone world behind. Their entire complex is now a UNESCO World Heritage Site, open to the public, and which can be easily walked around. There are two main sites and four smaller sites, all within easy reach of each other via bus. Avoid the wet season from April to June, and watch out for the hard sell from tourist operators, but otherwise, marvel. **SA**

Colonial Coro Historic Walk Falcón, Venezuela

Start/End Plaza Bolívar
Distance 2 miles (3.2 km)   Time 3 hours
Grade Easy   Type Cobbled streets
Map goo.gl/7Ds8lb

Santa Ana de Coro—to give it its Spanish name—was established in 1527 by Juan Martin de Ampués. The city's first governor, General Ambrosius Ehinger, arrived in 1529. He made the city the capital of Venezuela province, and in 1531 set up the first bishopric in South America. The city served as a beachhead for expeditions into the interior, but its climate was harsh, and pirates raided constantly. In 1578, the capital was moved to Caracas, and in 1636 Coro lost its bishopric. Hurricanes destroyed much of the town in the 1700s. Fighting during the wars of

"You could happily spend a couple of days just wandering through the colonial streets."

www.hosteltrail.com

independence against Spain and then in civil wars during the 1800s left the place largely deserted. Only in the last century has the town recovered.

Coro stands out for its interesting mixture of Spanish colonial architecture and Dutch influences, acquired via its island possessions off the coast. The mud and wattle houses are laid out in a checkerboard pattern that breaks up abruptly, leaving straight streets with dead ends. Old churches and numerous houses line the cobbled streets. Of particular interest is the cathedral, begun in 1583, and the oldest Jewish cemetery in South America, founded in the 1800s by Jewish migrants from Dutch Curacao. Numerous walking tours wind around the city's streets. **SA**

Cusco Architecture Tour
Cusco, Peru

Start Plaza de Armas   End Sacsayhuaman
Distance 6 miles (9.6 km)   Time 4 hours
Grade Easy   Type Sidewalks and tracks
Map goo.gl/M6Zc8c

The Inca of Peru were nothing if not thorough when it came to town planning. When, in the 1400s, the Inca ruler Pachacuteq came to rebuild the 3,000-year-old pre-Inca city of Cusco, 11,160 feet (3,400 m) high in the Andes, he totally remodeled it according to rules of urban geography yet to be thought of in Europe. The religious and government buildings were grouped together and surrounded by royal palaces. Surrounding this compound, but clearly isolated from it, were separate areas for workers' housing and their agricultural, industrial, and artisan production. Never were the smells from the animals or industry to pollute the rarefied atmosphere enjoyed by the rulers. Cusco's sixteenth-century Spanish conquerors unusually respected the civilization they found, preserving the original street plan and urban divisions while imposing their own faith and design styles in the shape of Baroque churches, monasteries, and large houses built over and around the buildings of their predecessors.

Cusco is a delight to walk around, either by yourself or as part of a guided tour. Most routes start in the central Plaza de Armas and take in both Inca ruins and Spanish glories. The Inca buildings are well worth it just for their amazing stonework: gently inclined walls of vast blocks of stone and trapezoidal doorways, cut and fit to perfection. Equally impressive is the Cathedral of Santo Domingo, the first Christian church built in Cusco and now a major repository for archaeological artifacts and colonial art. Tours then leave the city and climb the steep hill to the fortress complex of Sacsayhuaman, where the closely spaced stones in the vast walls were fitted together without the aid of mortar. **SA**

"Cusco is a truly breathtaking experience, nestled in the mountains just begging to be explored."

theonlyperuguide.com

⬅ The interior of the Cathedral of Santo Domingo.

⬆ Many examples of precision Inca masonry can be seen in modern Cusco.

Petrópolis to Teresópolis

Rio de Janeiro, Brazil

Start Petrópolis   **End** Teresópolis
Distance 22 miles (35 km)   **Time** 2 days
Grade Strenuous   **Type** Grass paths, rock faces
Map goo.gl/OG8ueX

The Sierra dos Orgaos mountain chain runs along the back of Rio de Janeiro in Brazil. The mountains got their unusual name, which means "Range of the Organs," from the Portuguese, who thought their hilltops resembled organ pipes. The mountains are now a national park and a firm favorite for walkers escaping the city below. One of the best routes is the Travessia, a 22-mile (35-km) hike between the towns of Petrópolis and Teresópolis—sites of historical and cultural interest can be visited in both. A permit is required before starting the walk, available from the park's ticket office.

"The Imperial Museum, an ancient summer palace [at Petrópolis], is the most visited site of all."

www.trekking-andes.com

The first day of the two-day trek is a fairly grueling experience, a possible twelve-hour day that seems to be all uphill. It is best to start as early as possible. The route begins with a shallow ascent alongside a river. A steady climb then takes you through lush jungle and up into scrub and grass. The climbs up and down Castelos do Açu and Morro do Março are steep, but nothing compared to the 7,425 feet (2,263 m) Pedra do Sino, or Bell Rock, where the intrepid walker is required to scale what looks like an impassable overhang wedged in a fold of the sheer rock face. Once over, it is only thirty minutes to the night shelter at the halfway stage. The next day's walk is a downhill delight, a five-hour stroll down the mountain slopes to Teresópolis. **SA**

Sucre Historic Walk

Chuquisaca, Bolivia

Start Plaza 25 de Mayo   **End** La Recoleta
Distance 4 miles (6.4 km)   **Time** 3 hours
Grade Easy   **Type** Sidewalks
Map goo.gl/ZyVZ4o

Bolivia is one of those sensible countries that has more than one capital city. If it's political or administrative affairs you are after, then head for La Paz in the north, but if it is something judicial or constitutional, then Sucre in the south is your destination. Like most Bolivian cities, Sucre is high up in the Altiplano, or Andean Plateau, so the city's elevation of 9,222 feet (2,811 m) gives it a cool, temperate climate all year round. It's an old city, founded by the Spanish in 1538 with the unlikely name of Ciudad de la Plata de la Nueva Toledo (Silver's City of New Toledo). After Bolivia became independent from Spain in 1825, it acquired its new name in 1839, when it was renamed in honor of the revolutionary leader Antonio José de Sucre. The city is also nicknamed La Ciudad Blanca, as many of its fine colonial-style houses are painted white.

Sucre is packed with old and beautiful buildings, so it is not at all surprising that the city has been designated a UNESCO World Heritage Site. It also has a number of historic walks that show off the architecture to good effect. The main one begins at Plaza 25 de Mayo, at the center of the city, and takes in the fine Metropolitan Cathedral and the House of Liberty, where Simon Bolívar founded the Bolivian Republic and wrote its constitution.

After a stop at the Indigenous Art and Textiles Museum, the walk continues to La Recoleta, the historic site of the original city and also the city's highest point, which provides a great view of the red-tiled roofs and white plastered walls. **SA**

➦ A walk through Sucre is an architectural tour de force.

Valparaíso Historic Walk

Valparaíso, Chile

Start Prat Pier   End Reina Victoria Funicular
Distance 4 miles (6.4 km)   Time 4 hours
Grade Moderate   Type Stone paths and sidewalk
Map goo.gl/5J75SQ

The historic port of Valparaíso was engulfed by a major fire that broke out on April 12, 2014. Thousands were evacuated, at least twelve people were killed, and the old center of the city came under threat as strong Pacific coastal winds blew the flames in its direction. It was not the first time Valparaíso had been threatened by fire, but its beauty and historic importance have always meant that every effort is made to protect this lovely city from harm.

A Spanish expedition led by Juan de Saavedra first sailed into Valparaíso Bay in 1536, naming the new town after his native village of Valparaíso de Arriba in Cuenca, Spain. It remained an insignificant village until Chile gained its independence from Spain in 1818. As the base for the new Chilean navy and stopover point for ships rounding Cape Horn at the tip of South America, the city prospered, notably when the California Gold Rush of 1848 to 1849 brought in ships full of men on their way north to make their fortunes. And there's a reason the city is known as Little San Francisco and the Jewel of the Pacific. Its buildings are grand, with Latin America's oldest stock exchange, Chile's first public library, and the headquarters of the oldest Spanish language newspaper in continuous publication—*El Mercurio de Valparaíso*—among them. The city also has the continent's first volunteer fire department. All these sights and more can be seen on one of the many walking tours around this historic gem. The Fundacion Valparaíso has mapped out a good one that starts at Prat Pier on the waterfront and then loops through Pleasant Hill, once home to British immigrants, followed by the labyrinthine streets of Cerro Concepción. **SA**

"*Valparaíso is the most intriguing and distinctive city in Chile.*"

www.roughguides.com

⬆ A walk through Valparaíso will take you through its hillside districts.

Recoleta Architecture Tour
Buenos Aires, Argentina

Start Recoleta Cemetery   End Palais de Glace
Distance 0.6 mile (1 km)   Time 3 hours
Grade Easy   Type Sidewalks
Info goo.gl/YVv9ve

At the beginning of the eighteenth century, the Recollect Fathers, members of the Franciscan Order, established a monastery and a church, with an attached cemetery, in the north of Buenos Aires. In time, they gave their name to the neighborhood. During the 1870s, rich people fled the cholera and yellow fever epidemics that affected the packed city center and built their new mansions in Recoleta. Today, the district is the most stylish and expensive neighborhood in Buenos Aires: home to private mansions, foreign embassies, and luxury hotels, as well as being the cultural and artistic center of the city.

Numerous walking tours exist to guide tourists around the architectural and historical delights of Recoleta, but one of the best starts at the Recoleta Cemetery, final resting place of Evita, the former first lady Eva Peron. The tour then continues to the Nuestra Señora del Pilar Basilica, built in 1732 and still with many of its original fixtures, fittings, and paintings, and the Recoleta Cultural Center, which features numerous local and international exhibits. After a pause to shop in the upmarket Buenos Aires Design Mall, the tour continues to the Plaza Francia, a park where children play during the week but that comes to life at the weekend as dozens of artists attempt to sell their wares. On then to the Museo Nacional de Bellas Artes, then for a strong coffee and people watching at Café La Biela. From here, the tour passes a number of fine hotels, all of which provide a good lunch or an uplifting cocktail or two, and two good restaurants, before finishing with more culture at the Palais de Glace, a former ice-skating rink turned into a museum and exhibition hall. **SA**

Jesuit Missions of the Guaranis Argentina/Brazil

Start Santa Ignacio Mini, Argentina
End Sao Miguel das Missoes, Brazil   Distance Various
Time Various   Grade Easy   Type Earth and stone
paths   Map goo.gl/NPPSH6

During the seventeenth and eighteenth centuries, the Jesuit Order made determined efforts to convert the Guarani people of South America to Christianity. The Jesuits gathered the unfortunate natives into Indian Reductions (mission towns) in order to convert, tax, and govern them more effectively. A number of such settlements were built, each with a church, a residence for the Jesuit fathers, and regularly spaced houses for the natives, laid out around a large square. Five of these reductions—San Ignacio Mini, Santa Ana, Nuestra Señora de Loreto, and Santa Maria la Mayor in

"A visit of the vestiges makes for a fascinating glimpse into a page of history."

travel.michelin.com

Argentina, and Sao Miguel das Missoes in Brazil—are now protected as UNESCO World Heritage Sites.

The five sites lie in tropical jungle and are all in different states of repair. Sao Miguel das Missoes is in ruins, although the facade of the church is still standing. San Ignacio Mini, once the home to more than 4,000 Guarani, is probably the best preserved, while Santa Ana has a ruined church accessible by a monumental stairway. Nuestra Senora de Loreto once included a printing press, but is now ruined. Santa Maria la Mayor has important remains of the Jesuit residence. Although these five ruins are spaced out, they are easily accessible by public transport or car and are well worth a visit. **SA**

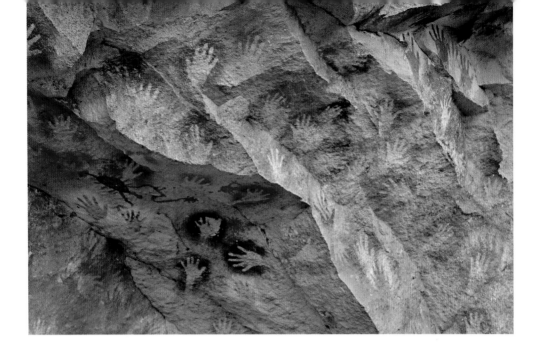

Cueva de las Manos Santa Cruz, Argentina

Start/End Cueva de las Manos visitor center   **Distance** 0.6 mile (1 km)   **Time** 10 minutes
Grade Easy   **Type** Compacted earth   **Info** goo.gl/zXJpa9

Deep in Patagonia, along a ledge in the canyon of the Pinturas River, a narrow trail leads to a UNESCO-recognized gallery of ancient rock art known as the Cueva de las Manos (Cave of the Hands), after its 5,000-year-old stencils of human hands. In neighboring rock shelters, stylized representations of hunters chase guanacos (a type of llama) and rheas, the large flightless birds that roam Patagonia to this day. These figures, dating from around 9,000 to 1,500 years ago, are shown using weapons and different hunting strategies, including entrapment and ambush. In one, the artist has incorporated a fissure in the rock to suggest a canyon into which the running guanacos will plunge to their death. But the hands composition, created by blowing yellow, red, white, and black mineral pigments around a splayed hand, is the most haunting—a powerful example of

the human impulse to make a mark, to say "I was here." Similar stencils have also been found in caves in France, Spain, and Australia.

The caves can only be visited on a guided walk from the visitor center. For a longer hike to the caves that explores the surrounding landscape, the Estancia Cuevas de las Manos, on Route 40—37 miles (59.5 km) from Perito Moreno—offer guests guided hikes of either 12 miles (19.3 km) from the estancia or of 4 miles (6.4 km) from the rim of the canyon to the caves. Archaeologists believe the deserted valley, sparsely covered in scrubby bushes, save for a riparian thread running along its base, is very much as it would have been when the hunter-gatherers who made the rock art lived in its caves. **DS**

⬆ Humans lost to history have left their mark in this cave.

Colonia Del Sacramento Historic Quarter Colonia, Uruguay

Start/End Posada Plaza Mayor   Distance 2 miles (3.2 km)   Time 3 hours   Grade Easy
Type Cobbled streets   Map goo.gl/8r51j3

The city of Colonia del Sacramento in southern Uruguay must have changed hands more times than almost any other town in the world. Founded by the Portuguese in 1680, the new town was immediately taken over by the Spanish, who had settled on the other side of the River Plate at Buenos Aires. Returned to the Portuguese in 1681, it was twice more taken over by the Spanish, each time reverting to Portuguese rule after a year or two. In 1777, Spanish forces retook the town and held it until they were evicted in 1811 by a local alliance seeking independence. It returned to Portuguese rule in 1817, until newly independent Brazil took it over in 1822. Finally, when Uruguay became independent in 1828, the city found its home. Surprisingly, given its history, this town is one of the most peaceful and beautiful in the region, its old quarter a UNESCO World Heritage Site.

Dotted around the tree-lined main square of Posada Plaza Mayor are a number of fine buildings, including the city gate and wooden drawbridge, the ruins of the seventeenth-century Convent of San Francisco, a number of eighteenth-century Portuguese houses, a lighthouse, and an old bullring. Its history is evident in its fusion of Portuguese, Spanish, and postcolonial styles, its single-story buildings washed in a variety of bright and pastel shades. Interestingly, this is one old South American town that does not sit rigidly on a grid pattern, adapting itself to the layout of the land with allowances made for military necessities. Numerous tours operate around the city, which is easily accessible on foot. Ferryboats operate out of Buenos Aires, making this a great day out across the Plate. **SA**

⌷ Colonia's timeless purity will mesmerize and seduce.

Akershus Festning Oslo, Norway

Start/End Main gate of the fortress   **Distance** 0.5 mile (0.8 km)   **Time** 2 hours   **Grade** Easy
Type Stone paths   **Info** goo.gl/8HnkuC

The "festning," or fortress, of Akershus was built in Oslo harbor to protect the Norwegian capital from attack from the sea. Part fortress and part prison, Akershus Festning is currently used for official events and shindigs for dignitaries and visiting heads of state; it is also a mausoleum for members of the Norwegian royal family. It houses an armed forces museum and a second museum commemorating the Norwegian Resistance during World War II.

The fortress itself was begun in 1299 during the reign of Håkon V, in response to an attack on Oslo by a Norwegian nobleman, Earl Alv Erlingsson. It first saw battle in 1308, when it was besieged by the Swedish Duke of Södermanland. The Swedes then consistently attacked it, most notably in 1716 during the Great Northern War between Sweden and its many enemies. But neither the Swedes nor anyone else took the fortress, which throughout its history had successfully evaded capture by all foreign forces. However, when the German forces invaded Norway in 1940, the fortress surrendered without a fight. The Germans executed several Norwegian resistance fighters in the fortress; the Norwegians in turn, on the country's liberation in May 1945, executed eight Norwegian collaborators tried for war crimes, most notably the wartime leader Vidkun Quisling. Despite this military past, the castle has also been a royal residence, refashioned during the reign of Christian IV in the early 1600s into a Renaissance palace. This makes it a joy to wander around or discover on a guided tour, the contrasting necessities of military strength and luxury living presenting many surprises. **SA**

⤒ The prison-fortress of Akershus sits in Oslo harbor.

Croagh Patrick Heritage Trail Mayo, Ireland

Start Balla   End Murrisk   Distance 38 miles (61 km)   Time 4 days   Grade Moderate   Type Woodland, bog, minor roads, mountain tracks   Map goo.gl/ESp1Ms

The huge array of historical and archaeological sites you pass while walking the iconic Croagh Patrick Heritage Trail are too numerous to mention in their entirety. There is the Round Tower and medieval altar of the seventh-century Christian monastic settlement at Balla (Balla Alainn, the "beautiful wall") and the ruined remains of Gweesdian Castle. There is the "Abbey that refused to die"—the twelfth-century Ballintubber Abbey, having survived the Reformation and a subsequent attempt by Oliver Cromwell to burn it down in 1653—and the ethereal Murrisk Friary on Clew Bay, with its gorgeous east window and its line of carved human heads on its external wall. Natural features include the 1-mile-long (1.6 km) Aille River cave, one of Ireland's longest river caves, the 183 acres (74 ha) of Brackloon Wood with its forest of Atlantic oaks that once covered much of Ireland and the wood of which was used to construct

the oak docks of Liverpool, as well as fields of rushes mixed with thistles, briars, and whitethorn.

And all along the trail, the bedazzling quartzite pyramidal mountain of Croagh Patrick (2,506 feet/ 764 m) is visible, the site where in the fifth century Saint Patrick fasted for forty days thus transforming it into a revered site for Christian pilgrims, which still sees 15,000 people a year climb its summit on the last Sunday of July—"Reek Sunday."

The trail follows this old pilgrim route through the fields of west Mayo and its many historical and religious sites, along quiet stone-walled country lanes, forest trails, and open moorland. And while Croagh Patrick may not officially be a part of the trail, good luck fighting the temptation to climb it. **BDS**

⬆ A trail rich with history, archaeology, and religion.

Miner's Way and Historical Trail
Leitrim to Roscommon, Ireland

Start/End Arigna, Co. Leitrim   **Distance** 73 miles (117 km)   **Time** 5–7 days   **Grade** Moderate to strenuous   **Type** Open roads, paths, forest trails, moorland   **Map** goo.gl/7GS7rm

In a region where the agricultural land was never better than poor, the iron and coal mining industry that could trace its beginnings back 400 years in and around the town of Arigna in the Irish county of Leitrim saw its inhabitants through their fair share of difficult times, including the famine of 1845 to 1852.

The Miner's Way and Historical Trail is a complex and demanding figure-eight circuit through the hills and valleys of the counties of Leitrim, Sligo, and Roscommon, linking many of the old mine sites and following the paths that the miners took to their

> *"The walking route is a moderate National Waymarked Trail taking on average six days to complete."*

www.activeme.ie

workplaces in the Arigna mines. Many of the mines remain accessible, and it is not recommended that you attempt to enter them. On the way, the terrain varies from field paths and old roads to moorland, and passes by the Boyd Cistercian Abbey and through the grounds of nineteenth-century Kilronan Castle.

The trail also leads you to Labby Rock—an impressive portal dolmen that is one of the largest monuments of its type in Ireland—and touches the shorelines of three lakes: Lough Allen, Lough Arrow, and Lough Key. It crosses the Corry, Curlew, and Bricklieve mountains and passes by the 5,300-year-old megalithic tombs at Carrowkeel, Ireland's largest concentration of passage tombs. **BDS**

Tipperary Heritage Way
Tipperary, Ireland

Start Vee Gap above Clogheen   **End** Cashel   **Distance** 35 miles (56 km)   **Time** 2 days   **Grade** Moderate   **Type** Forest trails, bitumen roads   **Map** goo.gl/3o4H4u

The Tipperary Heritage Way follows, as best it can, the course of the River Suir in Ireland's southern midlands, a river that flows through a valley rich in history, which was once home to some of Ireland's earliest settlers as well as to bands of marauding Norman and Viking conquerors. The history here is palpable; replete with ruined abbeys, medieval churches, and ancient paths. The 18-mile (29-km) segment from Cahir to Cashel is particularly pretty, as it takes you through verdant pastures paralleling the River Suir and past the impressive ruins of the Athassel Priory, built by the Augustinians in the thirteenth century. There is also the atmospheric ruin of Hore Abbey, the Cistercian monastery with its rare north-facing cloister, a nod perhaps to the significance of the nearby Rock of Cashel, one of the most visited tourist sites in Ireland.

It all begins at the Vee Gap in the Knockmealdown Mountains—which gets its name from the V-shape gap in the mountains—near the village of Clogheen on the Tipperary–Waterford border. The route then follows a millennium-old track that used to link Cashel with the port town of Ardmore, a route once walked by Saint Patrick and King Henry II. Riverside sections can sometimes be overgrown and boggy, but if dry, the banks of the Suir provide plenty of excellent campsites. The only real negative for this otherwise fabulous trail is that more than half of it is on local roads, a fact that will likely color the experience for many walkers who prefer if not a wilderness experience then one that is not interrupted by the sound of passing traffic. It is a drawback that undoubtedly robs the walk of some of its potential appeal, but it is still a worthwhile exercise. **BDS**

St. Finbarr's Pilgrim Walk
Cork, Ireland

Start Drimoleague   **End** Gougane Barra
Distance 23 miles (37 km)   **Time** 2 days
Grade Moderate to strenuous   **Type** Country
paths   **Map** goo.gl/Xw8DNk

Little is known for certain about the sixth-century Irish saint for whom this walk is named, but according to tradition, St. Finbarr spent his life warning local people to reaffirm their faith in Jesus, despite Ireland having been converted to Christianity by St. Patrick in the mid-fifth century. Finbarr is believed to have made his most inspirational speech from the Top of the Rock at Drimoleague.

Taking this promontory as their starting point, modern hikers (many of whom are Catholic pilgrims) follow in the legendary footsteps of the holy man who, having made his famous address, withdrew for quiet contemplation in an oratory (small church) on an island in the lake at Gougane Barra, where he became a hermit.

Ireland has a reputation as a verdant country with gently rolling hills, but walkers should not be deceived: this route is tough, especially as it crosses three hill and valley systems—the Ilen, the Mealagh, and the Ouvane—which have steep sides and frequently boggy floors. Along the trail are fine views of Bantry Bay and some of the region's major peaks including Sugar Loaf, Hungry Hill, Mullaghmesha, and Cnoc Baoi, the last of which, at 2,294 feet (699 m) above sea level, is the highest point in West Cork.

St. Finbarr's Pilgrim Walk (Irish: Slí Bharra) is too much to undertake in a single day, and people break their journey at the village of Kealkil, near which is a pair of neolithic standing stones, a radial stone cairn, and a stone circle. The most picturesque section of a consistently scenic route is the final descent to the shores of the lake from the boulder-strewn hills that encircle it to form a huge natural amphitheater. **GL**

"The entire walk is steeped in Celtic history and archaeological remains."

www.discoverireland.ie

⊓ Walk in the footsteps of an Irish saint, ending at St. Finbarr's Oratory in Gougane Barra.

Forth and Clyde Walkway W. Dunbartonshire to Edinburgh, Scotland

Start Bowling Basin **End** Edinburgh Quay **Distance** 35 miles (56 km)
Time 5 days **Grade** Easy **Type** Surfaced towpath **Map** goo.gl/lREAbl

Designed by civil engineer John Smeaton and completed in 1790, the Forth and Clyde Canal was the largest single engineering project undertaken in Scotland, and by the mid-1800s it was transporting more than three million tons of produce and ferrying in excess of 200,000 passengers annually through the scenic Clyde Valley and passing by the spectacular Falls of Clyde. Built to provide a link between the east and west coasts of Scotland, the canal and its forty locks remained in continuous use until 1963 when it was closed to through traffic to avoid the necessity of building a traffic bridge over it.

The walk begins at its westernmost point of Bowling Basin where the canal enters the Firth of Clyde, and continues eastward through Glasgow, Clydebank, Bishopbriggs, Kilsyth, and Falkirk, before ending at Edinburgh's Lochrin Basin. It can be completed in three roughly equal sections: from Bowling Basin to Auchinstarry Basin at Kilsyth; from Auchinstarry Basin to Linlithgow Canal Centre; and from Linlithgow to Lochrin Basin at Edinburgh Quay. Despite its occasional proximity to large towns, it still manages to achieve a distinctly rural feel with the help of urban backwaters such as the Possil Marsh Nature Reserve, a loch in the midst of Glasgow. Once in the countryside, most walking is along remodeled and very green embankments.

The canal has now been reopened and restored, thanks to the £78-million Millennium Link Project. The world's largest equine sculptures—two 100-foot-high (30.4 m) horse heads from Celtic mythology by artist Andy Scott—were unveiled in November 2013 near Falkirk, a gleaming addition to a reborn pathway. **BDS**

⬆ **Walk along the pretty towpath of an artificial waterway.**

Antonine Way Falkirk to W. Dunbartonshire, Scotland

Start Bo'ness   **End** Old Kilpatrick   **Distance** 37 miles (59.5 km)   **Time** 3 days   **Grade** Easy
Type Well-maintained grass paths, surfaced paths, forest trails   **Map** goo.gl/2evzJ1

The Antonine Wall, the construction of which began in 142 CE and took twelve years to complete, runs across what is now central Scotland between the Firth of Forth and the Firth of Clyde. It was built on the orders of Emperor Antoninus Pius, and while significant in its day as the northernmost boundary of the Roman Empire, its remnants are now hard to find. Certainly, it was nothing like the line of milecastles, turrets, and double portals begun farther south twenty years earlier by Emperor Hadrian. Constructed from ramparts of soil packed and faced with turf on a stone foundation, the wall was always going to erode, and much of what was the Antonine Wall has long since been lost to us, either built over or simply left to deteriorate.

If it wasn't for the efforts of William Roy, the famous Scottish surveyor and antiquarian who located and then mapped what he could of it in 1764, there might not even be an Antonine Way today. The rediscovery of the 37-mile-long (59.5 km) wall made possible the creation of the Antonine Way, which includes urban sections such as the Tamfourhill Walk to the south of Camelon; a lovely 300-foot-long (91-m) section in Polmont Wood; and the Seabegs Wood Walk, a 2-mile (3.2-km) hike through a fabulous oak wood to a section that parallels the Forth and Clyde Canal. One of the most intact forts of the Antonine Wall is Rough Castle, where the earthworks for the old ramparts and associated ditches are clearly visible; the Callendar Park section also has extensive visible remains; and a circular loop in the grounds of the Kinneil Estate leads past its Roman "fortlet," marked out by wooden posts. **BDS**

⬆ Roman defensive pits on the Antonine Way.

Clyde Walkway Glasgow/ South Lanarkshire, Scotland

Start Glasgow   End New Lanark
Distance 40 miles (64 km)   Time 5 days
Grade Easy   Type Long-distance pathway
Map goo.gl/AiNUW2

The Clyde Walkway is a fabulous cycling, mountain biking, and walking route that begins in Glasgow's west end at the confluence of the Clyde and Kelvin rivers. For anyone with an interest in industrial history, the walk is a treat, with many examples of Britain's industrial heritage showcased in its bridges, including Clydesholm Bridge (1695–99); Cartland Bridge (1822), one of Scotland's most elegant bridges; and the delicate triumph in iron that is Carfin Footbridge, an iron suspension bridge built as part of the Carfin Estate, which once occupied the land on the river's northern

> *"The walkway is ideal for wildlife enthusiasts or people that just enjoy the countryside."*
>
> www.northlanarkshire.gov.uk

embankments at Crossford. Linked pathways from the Cartland Bridge can take you to Cleghorn Glen Woodlands, part of the Clyde Valley Woodlands National Nature Reserve.

Closely following the Clyde for almost its length, the walk ends in the superb eighteenth-century village of New Lanark, a UNESCO World Heritage Site since 2001, thanks to the vision of its founder David Dale, who in 1786 built its cotton mills on one of only three Clyde River waterfalls and powered them with the newly invented cotton spinning machines of Richard Arkwright. Dale also saw to the construction and design of the mill's workers' cottages in one of the earliest examples of a planned community. **BDS**

Hadrian's Wall Path Tyne & Wear to Cumbria, England

Start Wallsend, Tyne & Wear   End Bowness-on-Solway, Cumbria   Distance 85 miles (137 km)
Time 5–8 days   Grade Easy   Type Footpath, road, sidewalks   Map goo.gl/dg29ub

The Roman emperor Hadrian built an extraordinary fortified wall right across the northern border of England almost 2,000 years ago, a defensive barrier against hostile Scottish tribes that was manned and maintained for 300 years. Today, the wall is a UNESCO World Heritage Site, and this coast-to-coast long-distance national trail follows its route from the North Sea to the Irish Sea.

The footpath is surprisingly easy to traverse, since the highest point is only 1,130 feet (344 m). The wall itself was originally up to 20 feet (6 m) high and 20 feet (6 m) wide, plus a ditch, and was mostly made of dressed blocks of stone. When the Romans left, locals pilfered stone for their own buildings, so today the highest parts are only about 10 feet (3 m) tall. In some places, the wall and its ditch have disappeared altogether. Walkers will find many other attractions along the route, such as the Segendum Roman Baths in Wallsend, the Roman Army Museum at Greenhead, and Chesters Roman Fort at Chollerford. In places you can still see some of the eighty milecastles that were built right along the wall as gateways and customs points. There were special forts on both sides of the wall, too; the best preserved of them is at Housesteads.

Both the wall and the path pass through attractive wild scenery that is mostly remote moorland and rough rolling pasture, and there are stretches through the cities of Carlisle and Newcastle at either end. In these urban areas there's often nothing left to see of the wall. If you're only going to walk part of the route, the central rural stretches are the best options. **SH**

▣ Milecastles and ditches on the "edge of empire."

Cheshire Ring Canal Walk
Cheshire to Staffordshire, England

Start/End Macclesfield Canal
Distance 97 miles (156 km)
Time 5–7 days   Grade Easy
Type Towpath   Map goo.gl/HlCHtd

"This walk offers the solitude of countryside, the hustle and bustle of city streets, and views of the Cheshire Plain and Peak District."

www.ldwa.org.uk

⬆ There are ninety-two locks over six canals on this popular cruising circuit.

Urban stretches can add interest and variety to a long-distance walk, and this circuit around England's northwest includes sections of both green countryside and big cities. It's a mix that works: the rich farmland and villages of Cheshire contrast with stretches of canal that flow right through the heart of Manchester.

You'll find yourself walking behind historic factory buildings, along trendy restored waterfronts, and past brick warehouses and wharves that were once thriving parts of the Industrial Revolution. The same path later weaves through rolling hills, deciduous woods, and leafy villages, before heading out into wilder country via the Peak District National Park.

The mix of environments is a result of the route, which involves a circuit linking six different canals (the Macclesfield, Peak Forest, Ashton, Rochdale, Bridgewater, and Trent and Mersey) through three counties. It's easier than it sounds. Simply follow the signs: a blue-and-white logo of a bridge and barge.

Historians will note that the 1761 Bridgewater Canal was the first of the Industrial Revolution, built to transport coal from the mines to the mills. The others that followed came amid a wave of enthusiasm for the new watery highways. Soon, however, the railways took over, and today these historic waterways are used by narrowboats and walkers. Highlights include canal tunnels, towering factory chimneys, busy swing bridges, and multiple flights of locks, as well as a deer park and beautiful views of the Pennine Hills. One unmissable example of industrial heritage is the Anderton Boat Lift near Northwich. This ingenious Victorian contraption lifts and lowers boats from the Trent and Mersey Canal into the Weaver River. **SH**

Derwent Valley Heritage Way
Derbyshire, England

Start Ladybower Reservoir   **End** Derwent Mouth
Distance 55 miles (88.5 km)   **Time** 4–9 days
Grade Easy to moderate   **Type** Riverside, field, and
woodland paths, roads, sidewalks   **Map** goo.gl/R5ihLK

On a map of England, the valley of the River Derwent appears to run right down the middle of the country. It had a central role in history, too, being at the heart of the Industrial Revolution that changed the world.

The section between Matlock Bath and Derby has been granted World Heritage status because this is where the factory system was first employed. In the Derwent Valley, water power was first successfully harnessed for textile manufacture. That historical accolade alone would be enough to make this an appealing walking trail, but there's another reason: the river cuts through swathes of fabulous countryside, including a memorable gorge at Matlock Bath, the wild and rocky hills of the Derbyshire Dales, and the picturesque spot where it joins the River Trent. The trail also passes the magnificent Chatsworth House, home of the duke and duchess of Devonshire.

It is a scenic way to view some important industrial archaeology, including historic mill complexes and the elaborate watercourses that powered them. The riverside route visits Cromford, home of industrial pioneer Sir Richard Arkwright; passes through the center of the city of Derby; and visits the canal village of Shardlow, known as "the Rural Rotterdam." Shardlow is Britain's most complete inland port from the golden age of canal traffic, with more than fifty protected historic buildings around its complex of waterways.

You'll see the settlements that were built especially for the mill workers, and all the railways, roads, and bridges that came with industrialization. Yet the walk, which is clearly waymarked with distinctive yellow and purple disks, is still within a beautiful landscape that has changed little over two centuries. **SH**

"Explore the Derwent Valley on foot and you will experience magnificent scenery, heritage, and wildlife."

www.nationalheritagecorridor.org.uk

⊡ The Derwent Valley is a living outdoor museum of England's industrial age archaeology.

Monarch's Way Worcestershire to West Sussex, England

Start Powick Bridge, Worcester   **End** Shoreham-By-Sea, West Sussex   **Distance** 615 miles (990 km)
Time 6–8 weeks   **Grade** Easy   **Type** Footpath, road, sidewalks   **Info** goo.gl/RPvmNe

When King Charles I was captured and executed by parliamentarians, his son, the twenty-one-year-old Charles II, tried to rally Royalists against Oliver Cromwell's Roundheads, but was heavily defeated at the final battle of the English Civil War at Worcester in 1651. The young king then spent six harrowing weeks dodging cavalry patrols with a huge price on his head, a life or death exercise that saw Charles dressing as a farm laborer and sleeping rough.

The exact route of his flight is known, as he later delighted in recounting the details to diarist Samuel Pepys. Monarch's Way follows in his footsteps, winding its haphazard way from Worcestershire to West Sussex, via counties as disparate as Devon, Gloucestershire, Staffordshire, and Shropshire. By virtue of its length, the trail is a major undertaking, but it is usually tackled in short sections.

Walkers are rewarded with numerous tales of seventeenth-century daring as they pass by Boscobel House, where Charles famously hid in an oak tree, and Moseley Hall, where he hid in a priest hole. Luckily, the king's route took him to places that have since become some of England's major tourist sights. For example, the king slept among the stones at Stonehenge, and visited Stratford-upon-Avon, Bath, and the Cotswolds.

His route touched the World Heritage Dorset coast, when he planned to escape by boat from Charmouth, only to have his plans thwarted at the last moment, and he ended up on the Sussex coast at Brighton. Charles finally bribed a ship's captain to sail him to the safety of France. He stayed there for nine years before being welcomed back as king in 1660. **SH**

⊞ Retrace the flight of the young Charles II.

Dartmouth Castle Walk Devon, England

Start/End Coronation Park, Dartmouth   **Distance** 3.4 miles (5.5 km)   **Time** 1 hour   **Grade** Moderate
Type Woodland path, tarmac path, streets   **Map** goo.gl/AU9v9E

This walk offers a slice of West Country nautical history. It is a short trail from the harbor of an ancient seafaring town to the castle built to defend it. Medieval castles stand on opposite shores at the narrow rocky mouth of the estuary here, and you can still see evidence on the rocks of the great iron chain that was pulled taut between the castles at night to deter pirates.

Dartmouth is in a narrow, steep-sided, deep-water estuary that was once a vital port. King Richard the Lionheart and the Crusaders sailed from here, the Pilgrim Fathers called in, and it saw action during the Hundred Years' War and the Spanish Armada. Today, it is an upmarket tourist destination, evidenced by a fleet of expensive yachts bobbing where the Royal Navy's galleons once moored.

The walk leads from beneath the Royal Naval College, along the Embankment, and across the bridge over the inner harbor, which is surrounded by timber-gabled houses. Wander through narrow streets of overhanging Tudor buildings or continue along the old waterfront. The path leads up into the woods on the cliffs beyond the town. In spring, these are full of wildflowers. Spot the matching castle on the opposite shore at the narrowest point of the estuary.

Walk over the hill where Roundheads and Royalists fought for control of the town in the English Civil War, then drop down to Dartmouth Castle itself, perched above the water. The towers, tunnels, and artillery positions cry out to be explored. Tired? Take the return journey by water taxi. Your excuse will be catching the memorable sight of the ancient waterfront from the best vantage point. **SH**

⬆ This castle has guarded the Dart Estuary for 600 years.

Basingstoke Canal
Hampshire/Surrey, England

Start Penny Bridge, Hampshire
End West Byfleet, Surrey   **Distance** 32 miles
(51.4 km)   **Time** 1–3 days   **Grade** Easy
Type Towpath   **Map** goo.gl/8wuZYS

Canals were created all over England in the Industrial Revolution, and the Basingstoke Canal was built in 1794 as a new commercial route between London and North Hampshire. The route wound through the home counties countryside before joining the River Thames at Weybridge.

The canal wasn't a great success, however, and the opening of a railway line almost parallel to it proved its death knell. It fell into disuse and became overgrown, and during World War II it was incorporated into a defensive line across southern England, in case of

---

"The canal not only serves as a recreational amenity but is also a notable wildlife habitat."

www.basingstoke-canal.org.uk

German invasion. The remains of old tank traps and pillboxes can still be seen.

From the 1960s, campaigners started calling for its restoration, and finally, Surrey and Hampshire councils took on the project. After eighteen years of work, 32 miles (51.5 km) of the original route was reopened. This stretch is navigable for boats but is more popular with walkers. Highlights along the route include a flight of thirteen locks through the woods at Deepcut in Surrey, the small tree-lined lakes along the canal near Mytchett, and the pretty canalside cottages in the village of Odiham. The trail is the original towpath—flat and easy—and it passes under and over many eighteenth-century bridges. **SH**

Jack the Ripper Walk
London, England

Start Durward Street, Whitechapel
End Ten Bells Pub, Spitalfields   **Distance** 8 miles
(12.8 km)   **Time** 3 hours   **Grade** Easy   **Type** Sidewalk
Map goo.gl/Lyx6n1

It was a killing spree that has had investigators puzzled for more than a century. How could a man, dressed in the attention-grabbing upper-class garb of a cloak and top hat manage to slit the throats of five young prostitutes in the streets and alleyways of Whitechapel and elude capture? Who could it have been? Was it Lewis Carroll, the author of *Alice's Adventures in Wonderland* (1865)? Was it Queen Victoria's grandson, the duke of Clarence? Or was the killer a German-born merchant seaman named Carl Feigenbaum, who worked on ships that docked regularly in Whitechapel, and who was caught in New York in 1896 fleeing a Ripper-style murder and later executed? Or, worse still for conspirators, were the five murders just part of a wider series of killings used by a drunken journalist named Thomas Bulling who wanted a story?

Let nothing, however, get in the way of a jolly good walk around London's streets, preferably at night, trying to figure it all out, despite the murder sites having been mostly redeveloped. Start at the site of murder #1, that of Mary Nichols in Bucks Row (now Durward Street) behind Whitechapel station. Then proceed to murder #2, that of Annie Chapman at 29 Hanbury Street; and murder #3, that of Elizabeth Stride at Dutfields Yard in Berner Street (now Henriques Street). A bench facing Mitre Square is where the body of Catherine Eddowes was found, murder victim #4, whose throat had been cut to the spine and abdomen cut open. Murder victim #5, Mary Kelly, was found in her residence at 13 Millers Court, Dorset Street, now a parking lot at Whites Row, although the Ten Bells Pub, where Mary drank her final drink, still stands as a testimony to her tragic life. **BDS**

Craig y Ddinas
Gwynedd, Wales

Start/End Parking lot near Cors y Gedol Hall
Distance 4 miles (6.4 km)   **Time** 2–3 hours
Grade Easy to moderate   **Type** Rural pathway
Map goo.gl/kBcasi

Craig y Ddinas is an Iron Age hill fort on an isolated rock 1,138 feet (347 m) above sea level that commands a wonderful view of Cardigan Bay and is itself overlooked by three mountain peaks: Moelfre, Diffwys, and Llawlech.

The fortifications are well preserved, with visible features, including some of the original stone ramparts and the remains of round houses of varying periods, from Neolithic to the time of the Roman occupation. The exact purpose of the fort is lost in the mists of antiquity, but many archaeologists and historians believe that it is more likely to have been a refuge and a meeting place than a primitive castle.

The path to the summit is no less interesting. Along it hikers pass a prehistoric burial cairn, Bronze Age mounds of burned stone, and the foundations of several buildings from the Middle Ages. Next come the remains of Cors Uchaf, a Viking settlement in a sheltered valley, a site that went undetected for almost 1,000 years until revealed by aerial photography. The final section of the ascent is dominated by the fort itself, which looms above the path. After pausing for a rest and the breathtaking views, the return journey is back along the same path.

The start of the trail is easily accessible by car, just off the A496 between Harlech and Barmouth. The walk is a well-maintained track and therefore easy to negotiate, but there are several stiles to be climbed, and the whole area is liable to become boggy in the rainy season, which the Welsh mostly say ends in May and starts again in June. This is largely self-deprecation, but they also say that there is many a true word spoken in jest. **GL**

"Craig y Ddinas … boasts a very dramatic location with wonderful views of the sea and the mountains."

www.eryri-npa.gov.uk

⊡ Craig y Ddinas is on Dinas Rock, a carboniferous limestone promontory in Brecon Beacons National Park.

Harlech Castle and Dunes Walk Gwynedd, Wales

Start Harlech Castle **End** Harlech town **Distance** 6.2 miles (10 km)
Time 3 hours **Grade** Easy **Type** Beach **Map** goo.gl/RWYQeO

This undemanding walk starts on the limestone cliff top that is surmounted by Harlech Castle. Construction of this great fortification—now partly ruined, but no less impressive—began in 1283 after English king Edward I defeated Welsh prince Llywelyn ap Gruffudd. The castle was largely successful in keeping the Welsh in check, although it was captured in 1404 and held for five years by rebel leader Owain Glyndŵr.

The route takes you down to sea level across Royal St. David's Golf Club. Here we turn right and advance northward across Morfa Harlech, one of Britain's finest sand dune systems, which currently covers an area of 4 square miles (10 sq km) and is still growing, around one quarter of which has been afforested with Corsican pine trees.

After around 3 miles (4.8 km), the shore curves right to form the south bank of Afon Glaslyn (Glaslyn River). Stop here a while and look straight ahead across the estuary at Porthmadog, the terminus of two preserved narrow-gauge railways, the Ffestiniog and the Welsh Highland. Then turn to your right for a distant glimpse of Portmeirion, the village designed and built in the early twentieth century by Sir Clough Williams-Ellis and based on Portofino, Italy, and the setting for the 1960s cult television series *The Prisoner*.

It is possible to walk farther up the Glaslyn, but beware of the advancing water. If you're thinking of extending the basic itinerary, be sure to consult the local tide charts before setting off. A perfect way to end this walk is by taking a chilly dip in Cardigan Bay and then a traditional English (and, indeed, Welsh) portion of fish and chips. **GL**

⭱ The Welsh hills on the right of northbound walkers.

Tomen y Mur Gwynedd, Wales

Start/End Trawsfynydd **Distance** 4 miles (6.4 km) **Time** 3 hours **Grade** Easy
Type Fields, generally rough terrain **Map** goo.gl/BCZuTG

One of the best-preserved Roman military complexes in Britain, the first-century CE ruins of Tomen y Mur is one of Wales's premier archaeological sites, spread over a considerable slope that offers superb views over a surrounding landscape of bleak though beautiful moorlands. Considerable sections of the fort's old stone walls are plain to see, as is its southeast entrance with its double-guard chambers, piers, and stone blocks. Other foundations include all of the associated buildings found in a Roman fort, including a military amphitheater, the only amphitheater at an auxiliary fort so far found in the British Isles, and a possible compensation for what was at the time a very remote posting in a largely lawless region.

There is also a parade ground, a bathhouse, a rest house, a winged tribunal mound, and, of course, the site's most prominent feature—the raised motte, or medieval castle mound adapted by the Normans in the eleventh century. There is an 8-foot-long (2.4-m) bridge abutment that is still intact, a number of well-preserved burial mounds, and in the hills above are the outlines of a series of Roman practice camps.

The fort had a short life: built around 78 CE under the reign of Governor Gnaeus Julius Agricola, the man responsible for overseeing the conquest of Britain, it was abandoned in 140 CE. Now under the management of Snowdonia National Park, the site is a circular walk along a series of well-trodden paths, and is at the crossroads of no fewer than four Roman roads. This fascinating glimpse into life on the frontiers of the Roman Empire will involve many hours of contented, trouble-free strolling. **BDS**

⊼ Explore one of Britain's most diverse Roman sites.

Huw Tom Upland Walk

Conwy, Wales

Start Penmaenmawr   **End** Rowen
Distance 6 miles (9.6 km)   **Time** 4.5 hours
Grade Easy   **Type** Sidewalk, grassy and rocky
paths   **Map** goo.gl/t7gwfV

A straight-through walk from Penmaenmawr on the coast through the mountains paralleling the Conwy Valley to the small town of Rowen, the Huw Tom Upland Walk is a walk through time, sprinkled with historical remnants and relics. The hike begins on Penmaenmawr's Bangor Road. From there you head east toward the limestone headland of the Great Orme, and from there over open fields, past a farmhouse, and through the first of many kissing gates to a steep ascent toward the Jubilee Pillars, erected in 1888 to celebrate Queen Victoria's Jubilee the previous year.

"…spectacular views of the Conwy Valley, the Great Orme, across the coast, and Liverpool Bay."

www.open-walks.co.uk

All along the route there are gates and stiles to pass through and over, including ancient stiles over high stone walls. There's also a Neolithic stone circle of five stones, about half of which have been excavated and which you get to after passing through the village of Bryn Dedwydd, following the tree-lined track, then diverging onto the North Wales Path and then through a farm gate. You will need a keen eye if you're going to find all the treasures these ancient fields hold. Don't miss the Maen Crwn, a glacially carved round stone that is thought to have been used 4,000 years ago to mark an ancient trail, or the Maen y Bardd, a Neolithic burial chamber near a Roman trail that will lead you down to the trail's end in Rowen. **BDS**

Llangollen Round

Denbighshire, Wales

Start/End Llangollen   **Distance** 33 miles
(53 km)   **Time** 1 day (challenge), 4 days (at leisure)
Grade Easy to moderate   **Type** Meadows, forest trails
Map goo.gl/3GI28D

One of Wales's most exhilarating high-level walks, the Llangollen Round in Denbighshire takes you on a circular route over each of the summits that surround the picturesque Vale of Llangollen in the country's northeast. The views on this walk are seriously good: Snowdon and the mountains of northern Wales; the limestone escarpment of Wenlock Edge, itself a fabulous walk; the Shropshire Hills; the Dee Valley; and an Iron Age hill fort on Llantysilio Mountain (Moel y Gaer—Welsh for "bald hill of the fortress"). And last but by no means least you get to cross the utterly spectacular Pontcysyllte Aqueduct over the River Dee, the 1,007-foot-long (307 m) so-called "stream in the sky," begun in 1795 with its eighteen piers and nineteen glorious arches. And while Britain's largest and longest aqueduct is part of the official trail, there is also a ground-level alternative.

Created to help raise funds for Cancer Research UK and inspired by the book *The Llangollen Round* (2011) by local author Judy Smith, the trail is fully waymarked and runs through a pleasant mix of limestone grasslands; open heather moorland, which is at its blooming best from August to September; and woodlands, both deciduous and coniferous. The trail also connects to some of the finest walks in Wales, including Offa's Dyke Path, the Clwydian Way, and Llangollen's own canal walk. The highest point is Moel Fferna (2,066 feet/630 m), but the ascent to it is a gentle one, and the entire trail is well within the capabilities of the average walker. And for those who have issues with navigation, fear not—you are almost always within sight of your starting point, the charming town of Llangollen in the valley below. **BDS**

Brecon and Monmouthshire Canals
Monmouthshire/Powys, Wales

Start Brecon   **End** Five Locks, Cwmbran
Distance 35 miles (56 km)   **Time** 2–3 days
Grade Easy   **Type** Sealed and gravel pathways,
bridge crossings   **Map** goo.gl/Y52oPg

Once an important corridor in southern Wales for the transportation of coal, ironstone, and processed lime, the Brecon and Monmouthshire Canals—the first stage of which opened in 1796 from Newport to Pontnewydd—would eventually connect the old market town of Brecon to the Severn Estuary. Today it is affectionately known as the "Mon & Brec" and is enjoying its retirement as one of Britain's most picturesque towpaths, though nowadays it is a landlocked canal with much of its length lying within the boundaries of Brecon Beacons National Park.

Restoration of the canal, which had suffered all of the ravages associated with more than a century of decline and neglect, began in the 1970s and has been a constant work in progress ever since. And there are days when it must seem as busy as ever, with in excess of 400 private boats plus rental boats for the growing numbers of tourists plying its waters every year.

Walking along its banks is a serene experience, through the verdant Usk Valley with its array of wildflowers; birdlife, including kingfishers, herons, and mallards; and some wonderful villages, such as Gilwern and Talybont-on-Usk. The latter is nestled beneath the Central Beacons and is an excellent base for the Henry Vaughan Walk, named after the seventeenth-century Breconshire-born author, poet, and physician known for, among other works, his collection of poems titled *The Swan of Usk* (1651).

There is much along this lovely path to admire, such as aqueducts, locks, lift bridges, and the canal itself. There is also a healthy smattering of local pubs to ensure you slow down and appreciate the natural and built beauty around you. **BDS**

"There is a fine four-arch masonry aqueduct ... at Brynich, many fine stone bridges, and a number of lift bridges along the route ..."

www.canaljunction.com

⊞ The Mon and Brec is an eclectic mix of birdlife, wildflowers, and eighteenth-century engineering.

Dinan Walled Town Walk
Brittany, France

Start/End Dinan Tourist Information Office
Distance 2 miles (3.2 km) **Time** 1.5 hours
Grade Easy **Type** Path, ramparts
Map goo.gl/Qy2Jlc

Dinan is a walled town in Brittany in northwest France, within the Côtes-d'Armor département. It straddles the River Rance, although most of the town lies up on the hill above the water. The area on the riverbank itself is known as Port Dinan.

What makes this pretty market town so striking is the medieval architecture. It dates from the thirteenth century (the town even features in the Bayeux Tapestry) and includes the Jacobins Theatre, St. Malo's Church, and St. Saviour's Basilica. There are also original city walls dating from the eleventh century, which you can walk around.

If you head to the Dinan Tourist Information Office, you'll be able to get a detailed map of the town, which includes the circular walk of the old ramparts. These offer a great view of the town and down to Port Dinan in the foot of valley. You can take a detour whenever you wish to explore the winding streets and quaint stores. You could also visit Dinan Castle, which is home to a museum.

There are plenty of places to stay within Dinan itself, which although it is located in a fairly quiet area of France is still popular as a tourist destination. And there are lots of places to eat and drink with cafés and crêperies around every corner. Many people come just for the architecture, with tightly packed timber-framed medieval houses stretching as far as the eye can see.

It takes around ninety minutes to complete the walk of the town walls (without stops), and if you have the time, why not stroll down to the port? You have to be ready for a rather steep return trip, but there's always the promise of a crêpe to will you on. **JI**

"Dinan's old town is a warren of narrow streets where it appears that time has stood still."

www.brittanytourism.com

⬆ If you make only one stop in Brittany, it must be Dinan, with its beautiful medieval architecture.

GR3 Loire Valley Châteaux Trail

Pays De La Loire/Centre, France

Start Blois   End Montrichard
Distance 60 miles (96.5 km)   Time 6 days
Grade Easy   Type Country lanes, gravel, forest
tracks   Map goo.gl/cVDdH8

The Loire Valley, between Sully-sur-Loire and Angers, conjures up the ancien régime more evocatively than anywhere else in France. Lush vineyards roll north and south of the river, and every bend seems to reveal a multiturreted château whose exquisite formal gardens spread out like an intricately embroidered gown. At any moment, you expect to see a royal hunting party returning from one of several ancient forests in the valley, triumphantly carrying a wild boar on a pole.

Awarded World Heritage status by UNESCO, this part of the Loire is ideal hiking territory. There are no great hills, distances between villages and towns are short, and there are opportunities for a degustation or two in the home of Sancerre, Pouilly Fumé, Chenin, and other great white wines. As well as the string of châteaux, there are the pretty towns of Amboise and Chinon, monasteries, and historic cities such as Orléans—liberated from the English by Joan of Arc in 1429—and Tours, the capital of France under Louis XI. Hikers need to plan their route carefully, combining sections of the Grand Randonnée 3 (GR3), the long-distance trail along the whole length of the Loire (though it frequently diverts from the river itself), with stretches of the Loire à Vélo cycle path, which hugs the river more closely, as well as on trails devised by the regional tourist boards. The route you follow will depend on the sights you wish to see. For example, a leisurely six-day hike of around 60 miles (96.5 km) from Blois to Montrichard could take in Blois itself, a designated town of art and culture; the châteaux of Chambord, Cheverny, Fougères, and Troussay; and the eleventh-century Abbaye de Cornilly, as well as vineyards and beauty spots. **DS**

Paris Modern Architecture Tour

Ile-De-France, France

Start/End Various
Distance Various   Time Various
Grade Easy   Type Sidewalk
Info goo.gl/bm2wZT

Paris is one of the most densely populated cities in Europe, with a dazzling array of architectural styles. No surprise then that a number of different organizations offer guided tours of the city's architecture.

There are several different walking tours available covering various themes, such as modernism. In the early twentieth century, Paris was home to some of the world's most experimental architecture, with designers such as Le Corbusier, Jean Prouvé, and Charlotte Perriand at work in the city. The 16th arrondissement is a particularly rich hunting ground

> *"For centuries Paris has been the laboratory where … architects … have come to test their ideas."*
>
> www.archdaily.com

for examples of modernism. There are buildings designed by Hector Guimard, famous for designing the Paris Metro signs. Then there is the Villa la Roche and Maison Jeanneret, designed by Le Corbusier, and structures designed by Robert Mallet-Stevens.

Other architecture walks here take you to the iconic public buildings—Le Louvre, Trocadero, Nôtre-Dame and many other venues—led by private guides who can give you the full history behind some of Paris's most outstanding architecture. Alternatively, you could do some research before you set off and plan out a route of your own, allowing you to take in the rich and varied architecture of one of the world's greatest cities. **JI**

Paris Catacombs
Ile-De-France, France

Start/End Various   Distance 1.2 miles
(1.9 km)   Time 1 hour   Grade Easy
Type Underground stone paths
Info goo.gl/bSU7Yp

It is not the grandest of ideas to attempt to explore the Paris Catacombs on your own as you may stay down there a lot longer than planned. In 1793, Philibert Aspairt went down on his own, thinking all would be well. His body was found eleven years later.

The catacombs contain the skeletal remains of around six million former residents of the French capital. They had been buried above ground, but by the nineteenth century, Paris's graveyards were overflowing. Bones were exhumed and taken down into existing tunnels beneath the city—remnants of limestone mining and quarrying. The bones weren't just arranged at random. They were stacked in a neat and orderly fashion, with entire walls being formed out of skulls and thigh bones. In the miles and miles of tunnels, you come face to face with mortality, in the form of a subterranean "empire of the dead."

Entering unauthorized sections of the catacombs is illegal and they are patrolled by their own police force. Some brave souls do risk going down into these areas—they call themselves "cataphiles"—but they know where they're going and operate in groups.

There is a tourist-friendly entrance to the catacombs at Place Denfert-Rochereau, and from here you can take a guided tour of the tunnels, or at least a small section of them. And there's more to be seen than just bones: there are monuments and engraved stone tablets, many reflecting the fragility of life above. The tours are extremely popular, and the lines for the catacombs can be as long as two hours. It is possible to book ahead, and some companies offer bespoke, personal tours, but these can be considerably more expensive. **JI**

"In the late 1800s, the larger underground crypt areas were . . . used as mini concert halls."

www.parislogue.com

⬆ The catacombs were first opened to tourism, albeit tentatively, in the nineteenth century.

Hemingway's Paris
Ile-De-France, France

Start Rue Cardinal-Lemoine 1
End River Seine **Distance** 3 miles (4.8 km)
Time 3 hours with stops **Grade** Easy
Type Sidewalk **Map** goo.gl/VTlT8c

Ernest Hemingway lived in Paris from 1921 until 1928. He arrived as a twenty-two-year-old with his new wife, Hadley Richardson, escaping the respectable but dull existence that lay in store for them in North America. They settled in lodgings in the Latin Quarter and quickly became protégés of Gertrude Stein and her lover Alice B. Toklas, and met Ezra Pound, James Joyce, and Pablo Picasso at the womens' weekly salons. By 1923, Hemingway's *Three Stories and Ten Poems* had been published, but it was *The Sun Also Rises* in 1926, based on a real journey he took to Spain with his Paris friends and written in Parisian cafés, that forged his trademark style.

To walk in Papa's footsteps, begin at Rue Cardinal-Lemoine 1, where a plaque marks the Hemingways' first apartment, and then cross Boulevard St.-Michel to the Jardin du Luxembourg, where Ernest caught pigeons for the cooking pot and Hadley came to escape their cramped living conditions. Les Closerie des Lilas, the café where Hemingway often wrote, lies south on Boulevard du Montparnasse (No. 171), from where the west side of Luxembourg leads to Rue Nôtre Dame-des-Champs, the location of the couple's second apartment (No. 13), and Stein's former home at Rue de Fleurus 27. From there it is a short walk to the atmospheric cafés of Les Deux Magots and Flore on Boulevard St.-Germain, and the secondhand bookstalls along the Seine, where Hemingway liked to browse. Pilgrims can even stay in the room where Hemingway and Hadley spent their first night in Paris—room 14 of Hotel d'Angleterre on Rue Jacob. Be sure to take a dog-eared copy of *A Moveable Feast* (1964), the posthumously published memoir of Hemingway's Paris years. **DS**

"This is the walk the way Hemingway liked it, no metro, no buses."

www.slowtrav.com

⊓ Walk the streets of the Latin quarter and you can still see Paris as Hemingway would have seen it.

Bellevue Loop
Champagne-Ardennes, France

Start/End Hautvillers   Distance 5 miles
(8 km)   Time 2.5 hours   Grade Easy
Type Vineyard trails, secondary roads,
forest trails   Map goo.gl/HNpUXT

A land of rugged, rolling terrain, ridgelines, and dense forests of steep valleys and fast-flowing rivers that traditionally have always limited the scope for large-scale agriculture, the Champagne-Ardennes region in northeastern France is today home to some of the country's finest vineyards. A good spot to start this short but rewarding walk is in the central square in the village of Hautvillers, the home of Dom Perignon himself, the seventeenth-century Benedictine monk who did so much to secure the prestige and longevity of the French champagne industry.

From Hautvillers's village square, follow the markers of the GR14 up into the hills and vineyards above the town, with its sweeping views over the springs and rivers of the Marne Valley. Continue on the Rinsillons Forest trail, then follow the yellow trail markers to Bellevue, where you can visit the Royal Champagne hotel and restaurant, located among lush vineyards in a former coach house that was once a favorite stopover point for Napoleon Bonaparte, and an excellent base for the exploration of some of the surrounding maisons.

After an extended stay in the Royal Champagne's cellar, with its 280 superb Brut and rose vintages, walk—as best you can—down the road into Champillon. After that, you climb up into the hills above Champillon and on to the Rinsillons Forest Road. Look for the Bellevue Forest track and follow it for about a kilometer, then take a vineyard path that should take you back to your starting point at Hautvillers. If you should take a wrong turn somewhere along the way, or lose focus and end the day a little lost, so much the better. **BDS**

"Overlooking the Marne Valley, the vineyards glide smoothly toward Epernay."

www.champagne-ardenne-tourism.co.uk

⬆ Vines planted on the gently sloping hills overlook the River Marne.

Alsace Wine Trails

Alsace, France

Start/End Riquewihr   **Distance** 11 miles
(17.7 km)   **Time** 5 hours   **Grade** Easy
Type Compacted earth and country lanes
Map goo.gl/Alh4ZW

Twisting between the foothills of the Vosges Mountains and the plain of the River Rhine, the Alsace Wine Trails link 100 winemaking towns and villages between Marlenheim, in the north, and Thann, 105 miles (169 km) south. Few of the villages are more than 1 mile (1.6 km) apart, and forty-seven of them have signposted wine trails (*sentiers viticoles*), which take hikers off the road and into the vineyards. Here they can chat with the vintners; unpack a rug, some cheese, and a *tarte a l'oignon*; and sample a vintage or two—Rieslings, Gewürztraminers, and Sylvaners, or the Alsatian Pinot Noir. Such trails offer a more relaxed wine-tasting experience than those among the grand appellations of Burgundy, Bordeaux, or the Rhône. Making way for tractors and seeing up close the art of growing the vines create an intimate sense of *le terroir*.

The trails are designed to showcase not only the wines but also half-timbered villages, medieval ramparts, and the many picture-postcard views. For all of these, head for Riquewihr and the start of the Grands Crus Wine Trail, linking six Hansel and Gretel villages and several top vineyards, including the tiny Clos-Ste-Hune, whose Riesling ranks among the world's top whites, and the Sporen vineyard, the source of a desirable Gewürztraminer. The tourist board organizes free guided tours, but the trail can be hiked independently.

Opportunities to refuel are everywhere, from *winstubs* (wine rooms) serving sausages and pork knuckle with *choucroute* (the local version of sauerkraut) to Michelin-starred restaurants. Many of the trails close in the month leading up to the harvest; but they reopen in late October, when the fiery patchwork of fall creates a splendid backdrop for harvest festivals. **DS**

Ode to the Neanderthal

Aquitaine, France

Start/End Eglise de Tayac
Distance 7.5 miles (12 km)   **Time** 6–12 hours
Grade Easy to strenuous   **Type** Rugged
Info goo.gl/b2NpPw

It may read like the title of an epic poem, but Ode to the Neanderthal is actually an organized hike through a breathtakingly beautiful part of France.

You begin in a rugged, wooded valley and head toward more than twenty caves that were inhabited by both Neanderthal and Cro-Magnons. This part of the Dordogne was where they lived, hunted, and roamed from 130,000 BCE to 30,000 BCE. Remnants of their existence have been found within the caves and rock shelters on this trail. There are also cave paintings and rock art.

> *"This hike offers everything prehistoric you could wish for, such as caves, caves, shelters, caves…"*
>
> www.slowtrav.com

This is a tough walk that lasts up to a full day. In some places, you have to crawl into tight spaces and onto rocky ledges. There are also narrow sections of the trail that have a drop on one side. You'll need a decent level of fitness and stamina and suitable clothing, a headlamp for walking after sundown and visibility in the caves, and your own water supply.

There is a shorter version of Ode to the Neanderthal called the Mammoth Trail. This still takes a few hours to complete but is slightly less arduous.

The Dordogne is a popular tourist destination, so there is no shortage of places to stay. If you want to go home with memories of something unique and challenging, Ode to the Neanderthal awaits. **JI**

Ring of Eyzies Trail Aquitaine, France

Start/End Les Eyzies de Tayac   **Distance** 3 miles (4.8 km)   **Time** 1.5 hours   **Grade** Easy
Type Track   **Map** goo.gl/arqX74

Caves and rock shelters riddle the Vézère Valley in the Dordogne first inhabited by Cro-Magnons some 35,000 years ago. This is a Palaeolithic Shangri-la, rich in fish and reindeer, where the people didn't only hunt and gather food, but also had time for art.

The valley's twenty-five decorated caves include two of southern Europe's great cave canvases—Grotte de Rouffignac and Lascaux, with their huge herds of running bulls, bison, and horses—but visits to these famous sites are restricted (and, in the case of Lascaux, confined to a replica cave called Lascaux II). For a more intimate experience of the Vézère Valley, get off the beaten track and follow the 3-mile (4.8-km) Ring of Eyzies Trail along the west bank of the river from Les Eyzies de Tayac, past prehistoric sites, through fern-filled hollows, and under overhangs, and with dramatic views of the gorge and its tributary canyons.

Beginning at Les Eyzies de Tayac's Musée National de Préhistoire, where flints and examples of prehistoric art carved into bone and antler tell the story of the valley, the trail crosses to the west bank of the river, hugging the cliff as it curves east. From here a succession of significant sites unfolds, beginning with the Abri de Cro Magnon, where a laborer discovered the first Cro-Magnon remains in 1868.

A little farther along is the Gorge d'Enfer (Hell's Gorge), a string of impressive caves and overhangs, the highlight of which is a 3-foot-long (1 m) relief of a salmon in the Abri du Poisson. Farther along the valley are a cave filled with stalagtites and stalagmites and the Laugerie Haute, one of the longest rock shelters in the region. **DS**

⬆ Dwellings carved into rock overhangs in the valley.

Canal du Midi Midi-Pyrenees/Languedoc-Roussillon, France

Start Toulouse, Haute-Garonne **End** Etang de Thau, Hérault **Distance** 150 miles (241 km)
Time 12–15 days **Grade** Easy **Type** Towpath **Info** goo.gl/NMyAze

The Canal du Midi is well known for its great corridor of plane trees, originally planted to stabilize the canal's banks and now a dappled canopy for hikers, following its course east from the Garonne River in Toulouse to Etang de Thau, near Sète on the Mediterranean, a stately progress through scenic southwestern France. Also known as Pays Cathare, for the medieval heretics of Languedoc—the inspiration for Kate Mosse's novel *Labyrinth* (2005)—the region is a land of abbeys and castles, including the magnificent citadel of Carcassone. It is also a bastion of classic French cooking, with duck and goose on every menu (cassoulet, confit, and foie gras) and food markets on every town square.

Commissioned by King Louis XIV in 1666, though first considered by Leonardo da Vinci, the canal is an extension of the Canal de Garonne between Toulouse and the Atlantic, effectively linking two oceans. Now a UNESCO World Heritage Site, it is considered a marvel of seventeenth-century engineering that overcame many hydraulic challenges. Some of the solutions are said to have come from the army of 1,000 Pyrenean laborers of both sexes who built the canal; unlike the military engineers in charge of the project, they had plenty of experience of getting water to go uphill. The canal's ninety-one *écluses* (locks) culminate in a spectacular staircase of nine locks at Béziers.

The towpath can be hiked over the course of twelve to fifteen days, with time for leisurely visits to local historical highlights. There are plenty of places to stay en route—every town and village seems to have a Hôtel de France—and there are lockkeepers' cottages for coffee and floating *épiceries* for picnics. **DS**

⊺ The canal was first envisaged by Leonardo da Vinci.

Regordane Way Auvergne/Langeudoc-Roussillon,France

Start Le Puy-en-Velay, Haut Loire   **End** Saint-Gilles, Gard   **Distance** 140 miles (225 km)   **Time** 12–14 days
Grade Moderate   **Type** Dirt and gravel tracks, forest paths, village streets   **Info** goo.gl/v2vcJP

In medieval Christendom's pilgrimage hierarchy, the Regordane Way, also known as the Chemin de Saint Gilles (Way of St. Giles), was the fourth most important pilgrimage route after Jerusalem, Rome, and Santiago de Compostela, and one of the busiest. Following the route of Caesar's army as it marched down to fight the Gallic tribes of the Auvergne in 52 BCE, and doubling as one of Europe's most important north–south trading routes, it eventually led pilgrims to Saint-Gilles, where the relics of St. Gilles still lie in the crypt of the Benedictine abbey church. St. Gilles, a seventh-century hermit, is one of the Fourteen Holy Helpers, whose intercession is thought to be effective against diseases.

Recently revitalized as the Grand Randonnée 700, the Regordane Way sets off from Le Puy-en-Velay. Climbing steadily, it then rolls over the Massif Central, a landscape of grassy plains, thick forest, and remote farms, where the country's size (France being the third largest country in Europe) is perhaps most apparent, and into the rugged Cévennes. The wide-open spaces belie the intermittent periods of industry along the route, such as nineteenth-century silk spinning and coal mining. Small towns and villages with hotels and auberges punctuate the trail, often reached by short spur trails, but careful planning with detailed maps is necessary to be sure of a meal and a bed each night.

At La Bastide Puylaurent, the trail begins its gradual descent through a softer landscape of lush vineyards and orchards toward the Mediterranean. The end point of Saint-Gilles lies on the edge of the Camargue, a magical wetland reserve famous for wild horses and wintering flamingos. **DS**

⊞ Retrace Caesar's march south to confront the Gauls.

GR70 Stevenson Trail Auvergne/Languedoc-Roussillon, France

Start Le Monastier-sur-Gazeille, Haute-Loire   **End** Saint-Jean-du-Gard, Gard   **Distance** 120 miles (193 km)
Time 12 days   **Grade** Easy   **Type** Bridleways, drove roads, rural, forest trails   **Info** goo.gl/6H2XoO

In September 1878, author Robert Louis Stevenson departed Le Monastier-sur-Gazeille in the Haute Loire with his donkey, Modestine, and 12 days and 120 miles (192 km) later, arrived in the village of Saint-Jean-du-Gard. Stevenson made the journey to help himself come to terms with the fact that his great love, Fanny Osbourne, whom he would later marry, had returned to the United States. He also wanted to discover the Cévennes, the impoverished and sparsely populated lands of the Protestant Camisards, who rebelled against the Catholic Louis XIV in 1702 after suffering years of repression. Stevenson, a Protestant by upbringing, kept a diary of his journey, and in 1879 it was published under the title *Travels with a Donkey in the Cévennes*, an account so precise that it is possible to retrace his route, which is known today as the GR70, the Stevenson Trail.

The GR70 is a public hiking trail through the Cévennes Mountains that allows walkers to follow in the footsteps of the great Scottish adventurer, who was in his late twenties when he made his journey. The Upper Loire Valley, majestic Arquejole Viaduct, granite city of Pradelles, Gardille Forest, volcanic uplands, and schist valleys are all still here, and much of it just as Stevenson would have seen it.

Before you begin, read Stevenson's book. The personality of Modestine, the stubborn and manipulative donkey whom he was never able to get the better of, makes for enjoyable reading and is still, even after more than 130 years, a good preparation for a walk that will take you through the barren, rock-encrusted, and heather-laden hillsides of the Cévennes. **BDS**

⬆ See the Cévennes as Robert Louis Stevenson saw them.

Ocher Trail

Languedoc-Roussillon, France

Start/End Parking lot on outskirts of Roussillon **Distance** 1.5 miles (2.4 km)
Time 30 minutes–1.5 hours **Grade** Easy
Type Sandy, dirt paths **Map** goo.gl/2yfHYO

In the hills and gullies just outside the Provençal village of Roussillon there is a small network of pathways that takes you through a fairy-tale landscape of vivid greens, browns, and reds. These human-made trails, quarried hillsides, and resurgent pine forests were once the heart of the vibrant French pigment trade. In the final decades of the eighteenth century through the 1930s, these hillsides were overflowing with quarries and ocher factories that employed thousands involved in the supply of ocher and various other pigments to the nation's burgeoning textile industries. The ocher pigments found in the clays around Roussillon and nearby villages—such as Gargas, Rustrel, and Villars—were among the finest anywhere, and business continued to thrive until the early decades of the twentieth century, when new mining techniques were developed. Thankfully, the pigment-rich hills around Roussillon can still be walked, and the tradition of separating ocher from clay still appreciated, on Roussillon's Ocher Trail.

There is a choice of two trails: one that takes thirty minutes and the other an hour through tiny valleys and cuttings showing the ocher deposits in the earth. The glory days of the ocher trade can be appreciated at Roussillon's Conservatory of Applied Ocher and Pigments, where the steps in extracting the ocher can still be seen, from the extraction of the sand to the drying of the purified ocher and the cutting of it into briquettes and its subsequent firing and crushing—an art almost lost to time but still alive in the reddish-brown hills of this beautiful village. **BDS**

◄ The hills of Roussillon are alive with pigments.

Van Gogh Walking Tour

Languedoc-Roussillon, France

Start Site of the Yellow House **End** Langlois Bridge, Canal d'Arles à Bouc **Distance** 12 miles (19.3 km)
Time 5 hours **Grade** Easy **Type** Cobblestones, sidewalk **Map** goo.gl/Hfiug7

Artist Vincent van Gogh came to live in Arles in 1888, and the two years that he spent there proved to be a period of great profligacy. More than 200 canvases, including *Starry Night Over the Rhône*, *Café Terrace at Night*, and *The Yellow House* (all 1888) were produced in an inspiring explosion of creativity that has drawn people to this beautiful town ever since. Today, the Van Gogh walking tour takes you through the town the artist loved so much, past a series of cement easels sited where the great man must have stood as he captured the buildings, parks, and people of 1880s Arles.

"He would rest his easel on the riverbank whenever the wind allowed him to."

www.arlestourisme.com

You can begin anywhere, but as good a place as any is the site of the Yellow House, just three minutes from the Arles railway station beyond the city walls. The house itself was sadly bombed during Allied raids in World War II, but the house behind it in the painting survives. Now walk to the Place du Forum by the banks of the Rhône, and the scene from *Café Terrace at Night* is before you (the cafe is called Café Van Gogh).

Walk along the Boulevard des Lices to see *A Lane In the Public Garden at Arles* (1888), the Espace Van Gogh to see the barely altered *Garden of the Hospital at Arles* (1889), and stroll along the lovely Canal d'Arles à Bouc to the Langlois Bridge, a drawbridge across the canal painted by the master in 1888. **BDS**

Carcassonne
Languedoc-Roussillon, France

Start/End Pont Vieux
Distance Various
Time Various   **Grade** Easy
Type Sidewalk   **Info** goo.gl/MXSVai

Located in the Aude plain—a crossroad of valleys that links the Mediterranean to the Atlantic and the Pyrenees to the Massif Central—Carcassonne has been an occupied site since Neolithic times. It began to be fortified before the Romans arrived and extended its walls in the first century BCE. The Visigoths and the Arabs traded it back and forth in battle in the eighth century, but it wasn't until the end of the thirteenth century that it achieved the appearance that is known to us today.

The citadel is nothing less than a marvel, and is best approached on foot across the Pont Vieux from where you see laid out before you its double line of turret-studded walls as you enter the city through the Narbonnaise Gate—and this is where the choice of where to walk becomes bewildering. There is the ramparts walk, which ideally should be undertaken late in the day so that you can admire those golden Pyrenean sunsets, but that is only one of the dozens of options on offer here. There is also the Church of Saint-Nazaire with its magnificent stained-glass windows, and the citadel's alleyways and streets make for a memorable stroll.

Hours later take your tired feet back over the Pont Vieux, and in the shadows of the citadel is the picturesque district of Trivalle with its two little streets—Rue de la Barbacane and Rue Trivalle. Or, alternatively, why not hire a bicycle and cycle along the towpath of the UNESCO–listed Canal du Midi, one of the oldest working canals in Europe. Just don't leave without tasting Carcassonne's signature dish— sausage, pork, and a duck leg in a pot of steaming haricot beans. Yum! **BDS**

"Within these fairy-tale fortifications sits a castle, a basilica, and a small town."

www.creme-de-languedoc.com

⬆ The fourteenth-century bridge over the River Aude leads to the fairy-tale citadel of Carcassonne.

Cathar Trail
Languedoc-Roussillon, France

Start Port-la-Nouvelle   End Foix
Distance 124 miles (200 km)   Time 2 weeks
Grade Moderate   Type Mountain paths
Info goo.gl/NWhwwV

In medieval times, the Languedoc region of southern France was home to a Christian sect called the Cathars, nonconformists with a simple, unmaterialistic belief system that put them at odds with the Catholic Church, which saw them as heretics. It also didn't help that there was a number of powerful Cathar noblemen. In the thirteenth century, Pope Innocent III launched a crusade against them.

The Cathar Trail takes walkers through a number of old Cathar towns and villages, including Foix, Durban, and Saint-Julia-de-Bec. It also passes many of the Cathar castles that still stand in the Languedoc, such as Peyrepetuse, Queribus, and Montségur. It was the fall of the last to the Catholic crusaders that marked the end of the Cathar reign.

Many of the places you pass are the sites of massacres, with Cathars who refused to renounce their faith burned to death on mass pyres. Marked with red and yellow signposts, the trail takes around two weeks to complete, and some of the paths were in use in Cathar times, often as ways to escape approaching inquisitors. Although the going is never extreme, some walkers pencil in rest days to give themselves a chance to recover. You'll also need to plan your trip and book accommodation in advance.

Even without the rich and bloodied history of the region, the landscape along the Cathar Trail would be worth the trip, ranging from mountainous paths to forests, vineyards, and lagoons. And there are legends of buried treasure in this part of the world, too. In Rennes le Chaute, a nineteenth-century priest was said to have uncovered a vast haul of Cathar wealth. Better pencil in another rest day. JI

"Put your foot on the Cathar Trail, and you'll be transported eight centuries [back in time]."

www.audetourisme.com

⬆ The lush, green vegetation on the Cathar Trail makes it a joy to hike.

Pont du Gard Trail Provence-Alpes Côte-d'Azur, France

Start/End Maison de la Pierre   **Distance** 4.8 miles (7.7 km)   **Time** Various
Grade Moderate   **Type** Man-made path   **Map** goo.gl/YFT21q

The Pont du Gard is a staggering construction by any measure: a three-tier aqueduct straddling the Gardon river valley to the west of Avignon in southern France. It was designed to carry water from Uzès to the city of Nîmes. But when you consider it was built by Roman engineers before the time of Christ, it's even more jaw dropping. No metal cranes, generators, or hydraulic machinery. Just ropes, pulleys, and muscle power. The aqueduct, built in 19 BCE by Roman Marcus Vipsanius, hasn't carried water for a long time, but it is in good condition and is a popular tourist attraction. It has been used as a footbridge since the Middle Ages, and today is visited by hikers who take advantage of a number of different trails that wind around the bridge.

The Pont du Gard Trail takes you through the site (there are two visitor centers—one on each bank of the river) and across the bridge itself. This gives you access to viewing points around the valley so you can take in the majesty of the Roman construction. The path winds through the forests that surround the bridge, forming a loop around the valley. There's also an official local hiking trail, marked with a yellow line, which takes you in a circuit around the bridge. The French authorities have also built a trail system that they hope will form a history lesson—two trails, one of which will take you along a Roman path to an historic quarry. The other runs to a modern quarry that feeds the construction industry.

The Pont du Gard is a UNESCO World Heritage Site. There are excellent visitor facilities and the area has seen heavy investment in recent years, including the multilingual visitor centers. **JI**

⬆ The aqueduct is a feat of Roman engineering.

Lavaux Vineyard Terraces Vaud, Switzerland

Start Lausanne   End Chillon Castle   Distance 20 miles (32 km)   Time 1–2 days   Grade Easy
Type Sealed pathways, dirt and grassy trails   Map goo.gl/1ZhIhm

When it comes to grapes, few in the world have the sort of pedigree enjoyed by the grapes that grow on the vines of the Lavaux Vineyard Terraces, which stretch for 4.5 miles (7.25 km) along the south-facing northern hills above Lake Geneva. Thought to have first been planted by the Romans, the terraces can be traced with certainty back to the eleventh century when these hills were the pride of early Cistercian and Benedictine monasteries, and the vineyards a major factor in the rise in influence of nearby Lausanne. Even after ten centuries, the hills here remain a prime example of a well-preserved human-made landscape, a rare productive embrace of man and nature.

There are 1,977 acres (800 ha) of terraced vineyards to cycle or walk through at Lavaux, and a 20-mile-long (32 km) path that begins in Lausanne and ends at Chillon Castle will get you here. Or, if you prefer, just drive out of the city and give yourself more time to meander along the myriad paths that make up no fewer than seven separate walking circuits interspersed with information boards that detail every step in the process of wine production. You can stay in the vineyards or, if you prefer, get above them. For stunning views, take the walk from Lutry to Cully and the viewpoint at Chemin-des-Echelettes, or if you are feeling especially fit, take the 2.5-hour walk up to the Tower of Gourze, before returning to the vines via Riex and Cully.

Whatever options you choose to take, one thing remains: the chance to sample locally produced wines in a mind-boggling array of cellars, and even participate in the daily work of viticulture with a half-day stint in one of Lavaux's ancient vineyards. **BDS**

⬆ Vines have been grown at Lavaux since Roman times.

Ramparts of Ypres
West Flanders, Belgium

Start Ammunition Dump   **End** Menin Gate
Distance 2 miles (3.2 km)   **Time** 2 hours
Grade Easy   **Type** Paths, sidewalks
Map goo.gl/cOGGLg

The ancient Flemish town of Ypres has long been contested by rival powers. Spanish, French, and Austrian rulers have all fought over the town, which changed hands many times before it finally became part of independent Belgium in 1830. The town was fortified to keep out invaders, its first earthen ramparts built in 1385. These were then strengthened and replaced by stone and earthen structures and a partial moat to cope with more powerful assault weapons. The Spanish added further fortifications in the 1600s, while at the end of that century, major fortifications were built by French military genius Sébastien Le Prestre de Vauban. The ramparts and fortifications still survive today and make an enjoyable walk.

The walk starts at the Ammunition Dump, built by the Dutch army on the foundations of an earlier French building in 1817. It then passes through the Lille Gate, an important entrance to the city, rebuilt by Vauban, and goes past the Ice Cellar, an insulated freezer once used to store meat and fish. The next stop is the Menin Gate, a reminder that the military history of Ypres is a recent event. The Ypres salient was one of the most fought-over stretches of land on the Western Front during World War I. Thousands lost their lives in battles fought near Ypres, many of them leaving the city to fight through the Menin Gate. In 1927, a new gate was unveiled, bearing the names of 54,896 British and Commonwealth soldiers who died in the salient before August 1917, but whose bodies were never found. Every night, at 8 p.m., a bugler from the local fire brigade sounds the Last Post in memory of those commemorated on the gate. It is one of the most mournful and moving experiences imaginable. **SA**

"The ramparts are now beautiful places of mature trees and quiet water and wildlife."

www.walkopedia.net

⬆ The Menin Gate commemorates the British and Commonwealth soldiers who were killed at Ypres.

Neolithic Flint Mines at Spiennes
Hainault, Belgium

Start Hyon   **End** Spiennes
Distance 2.5 miles (4 km)   **Time** 1 hour
Grade Easy   **Type** Grassy paths
Map goo.gl/zOjSYS

Six thousand years ago, Stone Age miners near the modern-day town of Mons, in the Borinage area of Belgium, burrowed underground in search of flint— the hard crystalline rock that defined Neolithic technology. When split, shaped, and polished, flint made effective weapons and tools.

Using stone axes and reindeer horn picks, the miners carved out one of the earliest examples of an underground mine, an advancement on the open-cast mining that had gone on previously. Today, this mine is a World Heritage Site, nestling modestly in the Belgian countryside. A ladder takes visitors down one of several 20-foot-deep (6 m) mine shafts to where the miners would have worked almost in darkness, with just the light filtering down from the entrance and reflecting off the chalk walls. Today, electric lighting reveals a warren of caverns, illuminating the miners' astonishing achievement and bringing to life the often rather dead experience of looking at Stone Age flints in museums. The marks left by the picks look startlingly fresh.

It is possible to get to the mines by car, but a marked trail through farmland from Hyon to Waudrez passes close to the site at Spiennes after about 2.5 miles (4 km). For an extended hike after visiting the mine, continue on the trail for 12 miles (19 km) to Waudrez near the medieval town of Binche. The area's history of mining lasted until well into the twentieth century, with coal mining dominating until the 1960s. Vincent van Gogh lived in two mining villages in the area as a young man, and the poverty he witnessed among the miners is said to have inspired *The Potato Eaters* (1885), his first successful painting. **DS**

"Spiennes is one of the best-known examples of prehistoric flint mining."

whc.unesco.org

⤒ Descend into a labyrinth of tunnels that supplied flint from Neolithic times through to the twentieth century.

Comic Strip Trail
Brussels, Belgium

"There is no such thing as going to Brussels without a good dose of fries, chocolate, and most importantly, comic strips."

www.eurotriptips.com

⤒ The buildings of Brussels are bringing the "Ninth Art" to all those who are still young at heart.

Start/End De Brouckere Metro Station
Distance Various   Time Various
Grade Easy   Type Sidewalk
Info goo.gl/XHapUU

When it comes to comic strips—the so-called "Ninth Art"—Belgium can hold its head up with the very best. Tintin, Spirou, the Smurfs, the Daltons, and Lucky Luke all sprang from the imaginations and pens of Belgian artists, and it is hard to walk around the streets of Brussels and not be pleasantly surprised by the "speech balloons" that confront and entertain you from underneath some fifty or more of the city's gables.

So in touch is the city with its comic strip tradition that it has even created a Comic Strip Trail, and a good place to start is the De Brouckere Metro Station. From there to rue de l'Ecuyer and your first stop, the Gaston Lagaffe Wall on the tall, narrow-sided wall of the commercial building at 7 rue de l'Ecuyer. Then on the rue du Marais, pop into the Marc Sleen Museum for a perspective on the life and work of the creator of Nero and Nibbs, and gaze at the walls of the Belgian Comic Strip Center.

Still on the rue du Marais, enter the Galeries Saint-Hubert, created in 1847. It is one of the oldest covered passageways in Europe and has connections to the comic *Les Témoins de Satan* (*Satan's Witnesses*) and *L'Opéra de la Mort* (*The Opera of Death*). After crossing rue des Bouchers you'll see the jewelry store Ciel, mes bijoux (Heavens, my jewels) from the famous Tintin book *Les Bijoux de la Castafiore* (*The Castafiore Jewelry*).

At Place St.-Géry there is the wonderful Nero's Wall, more Tintin on Hergé's Wall, the comic strip wall "Le Jeune Albert" (Young Albert), and everywhere comic book stores and stops such as the Comic Cafe, all of which mean that it's a good idea to allow a day for this wonderful stroll. **BDS**

Battlefield of Waterloo Trail

Walloon Brabant, Belgium

Start Q. G. de Napoleon museum **End** Visitor's center, N5 **Distance** 5.2 miles (8.4 km) **Time** 4 hours **Grade** Easy **Type** Gravel paths, dirt roads **Map** goo.gl/8wtZAH

The trail through the farmlands of Waterloo, where on June 18, 1815, forces of the Belle Alliance coalition under the command of the duke of Wellington defeated the French forces of Napoleon—who only three months earlier had returned to Paris from exile—are through fields that have not changed much over the past 200 years and give little hint of the slaughter that happened on that fateful Sunday.

The walk begins at the Q. G. de Napoleon Museum, where Napoleon spent the night prior to the battle. From there, follow the N5 along the route he took to the battlefield, past La Belle Alliance Inn, which became his headquarters on the day of the battle, then cross the N5 and walk down a dirt road to where the French cavalry and Imperial Garde thundered toward the British lines. Walk west from here, and you are on the battlefield itself. You can see the ridgeline to the northwest that concealed the British reserves lying in wait behind it and that fooled the French into assuming they had abandoned their positions. A dirt road takes you to the top of the ridge, and from there it's a short walk to the fortified Hougoumont farm, the southernmost point in the British lines defended by soldiers of the Scots and Coldstream guards.

It becomes obvious when walking down the Chemin des Vertes Bornes why Wellington chose to conceal his cavalry and reserves here to await the French advance. A 2-mile (3.2-km) walk then brings you to the Butte de Lion monument, an artificial hill completed in 1826 to commemorate the battle, and finally walk to Wellington's observation post, where he directed his troops on what proved to be the last day of the Napoleonic Wars. **BDS**

"There were no American soldiers fighting in this battle but our country today is still influenced by the events that occurred here."

Boy Scouts of America

⬆ A wonderful network of trails gets you into every corner of the last battle of the Napoleonic wars.

Bastogne Historic Walk Luxembourg, Belgium

Start/End Bastogne War Museum   **Distance** 14 miles (22.5 km)   **Time** 6 hours   **Grade**   Easy
Type Fields, forest paths, village streets   **Map** goo.gl/6YtSfg

Every December, the town of Bastogne in Belgium holds the Bastogne Historical Walk to commemorate the anniversary of the Battle of the Bulge, Germany's last major offensive on the western front in World War II. Tanks and other World War II–era vehicles fill the streets, participants in 1944 military uniforms lie in ambush, and women and children play the part of refugees wheeling carts.

The Battle of the Bulge took place between December 16, 1944 and January 16, 1945. In a last-ditch attempt to turn the tide of the war, Hitler planned to split the Allied lines and gain the port of Antwerp. The German offensive created a "bulge" in the Allied lines and all but encircled the town of Bastogne, a strategically important juncture of sealed roads along which tanks, men, and motortrucks could easily move. The defense of the besieged town by the

U.S. 101st Airborne Division and its contribution to the subsequent Allied victory are two of the proudest triumphs in U.S. military history. However, the wider Battle of the Bulge was also one of the costliest for the U.S. army. In all, there were an estimated 80,000 U.S. casualties and 160,000 German casualties.

The walk links key sites of the battle around the Bastogne area in three trails of 4, 8, and 14 miles (7, 13, and 22 km), and anyone is free to join in. During the rest of the year, visitors can do a 5-mile (8-km) loop to the villages of Bizory, Margaret, and Neffe, whose north–south ridges and clumps of forest provided clear sight lines and cover. Any walk should begin in the Bastogne War Museum, which opened in 2014 to mark the seventieth anniversary of the battle. **DS**

⬆ Bastogne witnessed Germany's last major offensive.

Jordaan Neighborhood Walking Tour Noord Holland, Netherlands

Start Westerkerk **End** Woonbootmuseum **Distance** 2.5 miles (4 km) **Time** 3 hours **Grade** Easy
Type Paved roads **Map** goo.gl/PKnoMu

In the early 1600s, new and fashionable merchants' houses sprung up in the Grachtengordel area west of the Singel in Amsterdam. To the west of this district, city planner Hendrick Staets laid out the marshy area for those workers whose dirty industries had been banned from the city center. Its network of narrow streets and canals followed the course of old drainage ditches. Immigrants fleeing religious persecution settled here, one group of which, the Protestant Huguenots from France, called the district a *jardin*, or garden, a name later corrupted to Jordaan. Historically, the area has always been poor but famous for its old alehouses, some of which still survive today. Now it has a more bohemian attitude, its old workers dwellings now housing interesting shops.

A good place to start your leisurely stroll around the Jordaan is at the Westerkerk, begun in 1621 and boasting both the tallest tower in the city at 272 feet (83 meters) and the longest nave of any Protestant church in the Netherlands. As you walk north up the Prinsengracht, you will pass the entrance to Anne Frank's house, the hiding place for the Frank and van Pels families until they were betrayed to the Nazis. The walk continues to the Noordekerk, a church for working-class parishioners, with a statue commemorating the 1934 Jordaan riots against cuts to unemployment benefit. The riots worked, as the cuts were themselves cut. The walk then continues through the beautiful Boomstraat and Karlhuizersstraat residential streets before heading back south to the Johnny Jordaanplein, named after a twentieth-century Dutch folk singer, and the Houseboat Museum opposite. **SA**

⊞ The Jordaan district has become bohemian.

German Fairy Tale Route
Bremen to Hesse, Germany

Die Lage Marburges und
umliegende Gegend
ist ne ulf sehr schön
Besonders wenn man
in der Nähe des
Schlosses steht und
da herunter sieht, die
Stadt selbst aber sehr
hässlich Ich glaube es
sind mehr Treppen
auf den Straßen als
n den Häusern. In ein
Haus geht man gar
m Dache hinein."
Brüder Grimm

"Your journey will lead you . . . through the narrow alleys between timber-framed houses way up to . . . fortified castles."

German Fairy Tale Route promotional material

⬆ The Brothers Grimm once complained that there were more stairs than streets in Marburg.

Start Hanau **End** Bremen **Distance** 370 miles (595 km) **Time** 4–6 weeks **Grade** Easy to moderate **Type** Forest and mountain trails, town roads **Info** goo.gl/VImxec

"There was once a poor man who lived with his wife and three daughters. He was happy with his lot but for one thing: he was afraid that his daughters, who were no longer as young as they once were, had lost their belief in fairy tales . . ."—the Grimm brothers. Wilhelm and Jacob Grimm are among the most famous Germans in history. Not only were they accomplished storytellers, with their collection of folk- and fairy tales translated into more than 160 languages, but they also made contributions to the fields of linguistics, history, and the development of the German legal system.

The trail created to honor them begins at the brothers' birthplace at Hanau, outside Frankfurt, and runs north to Bremen, past many of the locations made famous in stories such as *Hansel and Gretel*, *Little Red Riding Hood*, *Cinderella*, and *Rapunzel* published in 1812. Some of the links the castles, towns, and buildings have to the tales, however, are tenuous. Bremen, for example, was never actually reached on the journey the animals in *The Bremen Town Musicians* (1812) set out on, while the only link to Snow White in the Snow White House is a plaque in an upstairs bedroom telling of a local girl forced to live abroad by her horrible stepmother in 1554.

Mythology, by its nature, isn't easy to pin down, but in the end it doesn't really matter. It is the forests on this trail that are the real highlight: undisturbed swathes of European beech and towering 1,000-year-old oak trees in an environment so complex and complete it was given World Heritage status; a forest so thick you can imagine someone leaving behind them a trail of bread crumbs, so they could find their way home. **BDS**

Berlin Wall Trail
Berlin, Germany

Start/End Potsdamer Platz   **Distance** 100 miles (160 km)   **Time** 14 days   **Grade** Easy
Type Sidewalk and forest paths
Map goo.gl/LijrkJ

It was the embodiment of the Cold War era, a deadly 100-mile-long (160 km) wall that separated East and West Berlin. Now little more than a relic, it is possible to walk its fourteen signposted sections in their entirety, starting at Potsdamer Platz on a route that soon has you far from the well-known sections in the heart of Berlin and walking in fields and woodlands, along the banks of the Teltow Canal, and down the street of the once-divided rural community of Lübars.

If you only have a day, as most people do, you can start at the East Side Gallery on Muhlenstrasse on the eastern bank of the Spree River where the longest surviving single section still stands as an open-air museum. Another section of the inner wall is reached at Stralauer Platz, and if you continue over the Schillingbrucke Bridge, you reach the Peter Fechter Memorial. Fechter was only eighteen years old in 1962 when he became one of the first people to be killed trying to escape East Germany after running into the "death strip." More than 5,000 people attempted to escape over the wall from 1961 to its dismantling in 1989, and 100 died in the attempt.

From the site of the Fechter killing, make your way down the Zimmerstrasse to the touristy replica of the Checkpoint Charlie border crossing (the original is in the Allied Museum in Dahlam in southwest Berlin). There are twenty-two historical points of interest between the East Side Gallery and the Brandenburg Gate. An impressive section of the wall also remains between the Luftwaffe Headquarters building on Wilhelmstrasse and the preserved foundations of the Gestapo headquarters. On Bernauerstrasse, there is a memorial to the once-divided city. **BDS**

"Traveling along the Berlin Wall Trail, the traces of Cold War tensions are never too far away."

www.germany.travel

⬆ A partial remnant of one of the most infamous dividing lines in history.

Rhine Castle Trail Rheinland-Palatinate, Germany

Start Bingen **End** Koblenz **Distance** 65 miles (105 km) **Time** 6 days **Grade** Moderate
Type Pathways, forest trails **Map** goo.gl/rtzFcd

The Rhinesteig follows the eastern bank of the Rhine for 200 miles (320 km), sometimes tight to its banks; at other times wandering through woods and meadows, but usually up on its cliffs. But the famous stretch, awarded World Heritage status in 2002, is the castle-studded section between Bingen and Koblenz that poet Lord Byron, in *Childe Harold's Pilgrimage* (1812), called: "A blending of all beauties, streams and dells/ Fruit, foliage, crag, wood, cornfield, mountain vine/ And chiefless castles breathing stern farewells/From grey but leafy walls, where ruin greenly dwells."

The Rhine Gorge, as this section is known, also has its own trail called the Rhine Castle Trail, on the west bank of the river, and the best way to get the most out of the valley is to hop between the two banks and trails as you move downriver. There are no bridges between Bingen and Koblenz, but ferries cross back and forth between the towns and villages, making visits to vineyards and sightseeing easy. And there is plenty to see. Vineyards climb precipitous east bank slopes, and at every twist in the gorge, the sky-piercing turrets of castles make the rugged cliffs even craggier. Castellated watchtowers and toll stations also dot the banks, reminders of the days when the Rhine was a highway for trade and armies.

At the Lorelei, a 433-foot-high (131 m) cliff soaring above a bend, the gorge narrows. This is a magnificent but dangerous spot where, it is said, mariners have been pulled into the depths by a mythical siren. At Koblenz, the end of the gorge, the Mosel flows southwest to France—another scenic river, more wine, and more stories. **DS**

⬆ Discover the beauty of the Rhine valley's many castles.

West Palatinate Way Rheinland-Palatinate, Germany

Start/End Hohenecken Distance 254 miles (409 km) Time 20 days Grade Easy
Type Woodland paths Info goo.gl/lUvwSZ

This circular walk passes through undemanding terrain consisting mainly of alternating woodland and cultivated fields, but it is no longer an officially maintained trail. The regional tourist board and the local rambling club that formerly ran it cooperatively gave up in 2009 because they were failing to attract enough hikers who would spend money in local shops and hostels.

The route, however, is still well used with many casual walkers dipping in and out of short sections, while significant numbers still do half the loop and return to their starting point along a diametric cross link between Kaiserslautern and Landstuhl. A few hardcore hikers even attempt the whole circuit.

Most who use it set off from Hohenecken, a suburb of Kaiserslautern, which is the biggest town on the way. Among the highlights of the first section are the villages of Leimen (birthplace of tennis champion Boris Becker) and Eppenbrunn, with its 1-mile-long (1.6 km) colored sandstone cliff.

As the path nears the French border the forested landscape becomes dotted with fortifications: Sickinger Schloss at Landstuhl, two ruined castles at Wolfstein, and the walled town of Kirchheimbolanden. Just before the walk's end, a short detour from the village of Hochspeyer leads to the Cistercian Abbey at Otterberg.

The Palatinate in southwest Germany is one of the country's least visited areas. But there is much to interest geologists, especially students of loess formations, and historians, for whom there are numerous relics of a time when this now tranquil rural backwater was one of the world's most bitterly contested frontiers. And the food and drink are wonderful. **GL**

⊡ An unmaintained trail that still ticks all the boxes.

Ausonius Way
Rheinland-Palatinate, Germany

Start Bingen am Rhein   **End** Trier
Distance 67 miles (108 km)   **Time** 7 days
Grade Easy   **Type** Forest trails, meadows
Map goo.gl/41U8zn

Decimius Ausonius was a poet and a lecturer in rhetoric, the art of discourse designed to help writers and artists persuade and inform their audiences. He was born in Bordeaux, France, around 310 CE, and worked as a teacher for thirty years until 368 CE, when he was summoned by Roman emperor Valentinian I to accompany him on his German campaigns. In 375 CE Ausonius was made Praetorian Prefect of Gaul (Germany), and spent many days walking through the hills and valleys of the Rhine. This was a period of rapid Roman expansion in Gaul, with wide stone roads marked by milestones and watched over by guard towers punctuating the landscape. One such road that Ausonius would often travel led from the town of Bingen on the Rhine through the Hunsrück hills to Augusta Treverorum (now Trier) on the Mosel.

You can now retrace the steps of Ausonius on the Ausonius Way, beginning in Bingen and passing through the towns of Rheinböllen, Simmern, Kirchberg, and Belginum, and finishing in Trier. Traveling the route in 12-mile (20-km) stages will take you about a week, passing through the iron ore–rich hills of the Hunsrück and through the town of Kirchberg where Ausonius would often stop for the night on his regular coach journeys to Trier: "I arrived at the dry village Denzen (meaning Kirchberg)," he wrote in 370 CE, "where the surrounding fields thirsted for water." Not a lot has changed. The town is still high on its hill in an exposed position, making it vulnerable to drought.

There is a multitude of post-Roman sites on this trail that demand attention, too, such as the iron ore sites around Rheinbollen and Simmern's landmark Schinderhannes Tower. **BDS**

> *"[Ausonius] immortalized his impressions of the journey in his poem 'Mosella.'"*

www.maasberg.ch

⬆ Pass through a landscape between the Rhine and Mosel rivers once crisscrossed by Roman roads.

Limes Trail
Hesse, Germany

Start Observation post 4/49, Grüningen **End** Kleinkastell Holzheimer Unterwald **Distance** 478 miles (770 km) **Time** 12–14 days **Grade** Easy **Type** Forest trails, meadows **Info** goo.gl/qQokYE

The Upper Germanic and Rhaetian Limes once represented the northernmost boundary of the Roman Empire in Germany and stretched for more than 480 miles (772 km). It was the second longest human-made structure on Earth after China's Great Wall, ordered to be built by the Emperor Domitian in 83 CE to guard against incursions from the Germanic Chatti tribe. It consisted of more than 900 wooden defensive towers (later replaced by stone towers) as well as trenches and some 120 sentry posts. The wall was strengthened under succeeding emperors Hadrian and Antonius Pius, and remains today the longest cultural monument in Germany.

There are numerous points along what is essentially a driving route from which you can start: from the Rhine in the north to the Danube in the south. If you start at Grüningen, east of the upper Rhine at observation post 4/49, for example, you'll see one of the route's finest Roman towers, complete with ramparts, trenches, and a palisades fence. From there, trail signs take you to the excavated foundations of a second tower at Holzheimer Unterwald. Information boards along the way provide facts about the Limes Trail and where its other structures, now gone, would have been located.

Another reconstructed wooden tower can be seen outside Bettenberg, and after a steep climb, the foundations of a further tower can be observed at Schrenzerberg. The walk is a picturesque one, made memorable because of the Roman associations, towns such as fifteenth-century Butzbach with its buttressed houses, and the ruins of thirteenth-century Burg Grüningen. **BDS**

"A real walking vacation, passing through forests, green hills and streams of the Rhineland."

www.andantetravels.co.uk

⤴ The beautiful marketplace in Butzbach features well-preserved half-timbered houses.

Merchants' Bridge
Thuringia, Germany

Start/End Merchants' Bridge, Erfurt
Distance 394 feet (120 m)   **Time** 1 hour
Grade Easy   **Type** Cobblestones
Info goo.gl/S4kexV

It is estimated that 11 million people a year walk across the Merchants' Bridge in Erfurt, capital of the state of Thuringia. This equates to Australia's entire population every twelve months, and 100,000 of them do it in only three days during the annual Merchants' Bridge Festival.

The bridge, the Krämerbrücke, was built in the late twelfth century, and the six stone arches beneath it still prop up its 394-foot (120-m) length, the longest stretch of inhabited buildings of any bridge in Europe. Erfurt achieved city status in the eighth century and has history by the bucket load. The ancient Romans marched through here on their way to Britain when it was a Pagan backwater, and it has always been at the crossroads of important trading routes. Martin Luther spent ten years of his life here and was so influential that 90 percent of Erfurt's Catholic residents joined the Protestantant Church.

Although the bridge is Erfurt's most prominent historic landmark, it isn't the bridge itself that makes it so special. It is the people who live above its half-timbered shops and those who trade on it who give it its life. People such as Bettina, who came here in 1996 and sells local jams and wooden boxes; Gabriele and Joachim with their wooden toys and ornaments who came here in 1984 and never left; and Martin, the self-taught puppeteer who sketches and then creates magnificent puppets and marionettes for use by theater groups throughout Germany.

Strolling from shop to shop, it's easy to become a little envious of a community of people who act together to preserve and protect their common homes, and who open their doors to the millions who walk by them every year. **BDS**

"Craftsmen demonstrate the skills of the past, jesters supply fun and games, minstrels sing, and sword fighters do battle."

www.germany.travel

⊡ The Krämerbrücke, first mentioned in 1117, still stands on the six original barrel vaults.

Görlitz Historic Walk
Saxony, Germany

Start/End Untermarkt (lower market)
Distance Various   **Time** Various
Grade Easy   **Type** Sidewalk
Info goo.gl/eKaXsY

If city officials ever decided to organize an historic walking tour of Germany's easternmost town of Görlitz, complete with plaques and brochures, then you would have to feel for the poor bureaucrats whose job it would be to map out the route. Görlitz escaped being bombed in World War II, and there are more than 4,000 listed historic buildings there. Block after city block, any one of which would be quite at home in Paris or Prague, radiate out in all directions from its center. There is nothing out of place, nothing to jar the eye. No McDonald's. It's like the winning entry in a giant LEGO® competition to create the perfect period city. Yes, some of its buildings—maybe even many of its buildings—are gray and shabby and in need of a little care. But this merely adds to its realism, and oh how preferable they are to the manicured perfection of renovated historic designer-brand stores in those "sophisticated" European cities whose facades are ruined by gaudy signage and interiors filled with over-priced handbags.

First mentioned in a royal decree in 1071, Görlitz is custom-made for walking. It is flat, its streets are broad, and it is wonderfully compact. And the architectural time line that threatens to overwhelm you with its grandeur showcases everything from early Gothic to Baroque to the flamboyance of Art Nouveau. Renovations follow a strict set of guidelines, windows and doors cannot be altered, and original colors of the buildings have to be maintained.

So, where to start? Well, not that it matters, but why not the Untermarkt with its fourteenth-century town hall and its clock, added in 1584? And from there? That is where it starts to get tricky. **BDS**

Richard Wagner Walking Tour Saxony, Germany

Start/End Frauenkirche, Dresden
Distance Various   **Time** Various
Grade Easy   **Type** Sidewalk, cobblestones
Info goo.gl/2AGWYw

The composer Richard Wagner moved to Dresden from Leipzig in 1814, a year after his birth. He returned to Leipzig in 1828 after a period of moving from Würzburg to Magdeburg, Königsberg, Riga, and Paris, he returned to Dresden in 1842 and presided over the premier of three of his operas—*Rienzi* (1840), *The Flying Dutchman* (1841), and *Tannhäuser* (1845)—at the Saxon State Opera. He later fled the city after becoming embroiled in the 1848 revolution and having a warrant issued for his arrest. There are a lot of things you can see on Dresden's Richard Wagner walking tour,

> *"Richard Wagner changed the city's musical focus while drawing inspiration from the city itself."*

www.dresden.de

including the tower of the Kreuzkirche, built in the early twelfth century and burned down five times since. From its upper windows Wagner looked down upon the mayhem in the streets below and reported troop positions to his revolutionary compatriots.

Another highlight is the magnificent Frauenkirche, dating back to the eleventh century, with an interior large enough for the 1,300 musicians who gathered there to perform Wagner's *Love-feast of the Apostles* (1843). The farmhouse in the Dresden suburb of Graupa, where he wrote most of his three-act opera *Lohengrin* (1850), is open to the public. And various addresses where his family lived can all be visited in a walk that highlights the music and history of this great city. **BDS**

Painters' Way
Saxony, Germany

Start/End Bad Schandau **Distance** 70 miles
(112 km) **Time** 8 days **Grade** Moderate
Type Rocky inclines, crevices, gravel and dirt paths
Map goo.gl/grRVkS

The reason why part of Germany is named Saxon Switzerland involves a nineteenth-century Germanic tendency to romanticize its more beautiful "Swiss-like" landscapes, a trend that began here in 1766 when two obscure Swiss artists, Anton Graff and Adrian Zingg, were appointed to the faculty of Dresden's prestigious art academy. The two men, who fell in love with the craggy mountains along the Elbe River on Germany's border with then-Czechoslovakia, came up with the name Saxon Switzerland. It wasn't Swiss in the sense of snow-clad peaks and grand summits, but it was undeniably scenic, rocky, and otherworldly. Zingg's painting *The Cow Shed* (1786) is one of the best-known paintings from the period, and the inspiration behind the aptly named Painters' Way, a 70-mile (113-km) well-groomed and clearly marked trail through this beautiful corner of southeast Germany.

The trail takes you through forests of beech, fir, and pine, and there is a contemplative calm here that must have reminded Zingg of home. Arriving at the cow shed of Zingg's painting, the view opens up over an ocean of greenery and crenellated rock formations. A little farther up through a narrow crevice in a nearby cliff is the vantage point from which the Romantic artist Caspar Friedrich created his atmospheric oil painting *Wanderer above the Sea of Fog* (1818).

This beautiful trail through heavily incised and fissured sandstone rocks, canyon-like ravines, rock needles, labyrinthine caves, and last but not least the fabulous Schrammsteine cliffs is conveniently situated just a few miles outside the city of Dresden. **BDS**

→ The mountains along the Elbe River are an artist's delight.

Dessau-Wörlitz Garden Realm Saxony, Germany

Start/End Wörlitz Park
Distance Various   Time Various
Grade Easy   Type Grass, garden paths
Info goo.gl/wBBjzB

The Garden Realm of Dessau-Wörlitz is one of Europe's finest examples of eighteenth-century "Age of Enlightenment" English-style landscape design. More than just a garden, it spreads across its 55-square-mile (143-sq-km) floodplain near the confluence of the Elbe and Mulde rivers like a vast, green mosaic in the midst of the historic principality of Anhalt-Dessau. It is a naturalistic landscape deliberately at odds with the common Baroque formality of the time, created at the behest of Duke Leopold III who had recently returned from a Grand Tour of Europe.

"Palaces, gardens, and countless smaller structures are embedded in this unrivaled cultural landscape."

www.gartenreich.com

Declared a UNESCO World Heritage Site in 2000, the landscape comprises many parks, palaces, and gardens laid out between 1764 and 1800, and using the waters of the Elbe to give it life. It is the venue for a perfect day's walking, or even two. At its core are its historic gardens with their associated palaces, buildings, and sculptures, but add to that a playground of bridges, watchtowers, and statuary, complemented by ornamental plantings set around fields, meadows, and orchards. One of its most beautiful buildings is the Schloss Luisium, the neoclassical home of Princess Louise of Anhalt-Dessau, with its tiny but functional rooms, set in its own 35-acre (14-ha) garden filled with statues, gatehouses, and a ruined arch. **BDS**

Krakow–Moravia–Vienna Greenways Poland to Austria

Start Krakow, Poland   End Vienna, Austria
Distance 484 miles (780 km)   Time 48 days
Grade Moderate   Type Tarmac roads, dirt tracks
Info goo.gl/msxLRh

To describe a walk as passing through "the longest alley of fruit trees in Europe" is certainly enticing. And in the case of this lengthy greenway, it is an entirely accurate description, for this trail runs through some of the continent's most fertile and heavily planted lands. The greenway starts in Krakow and passes southwest through Moravia in the Czech Republic before heading south to Vienna in Austria. The trail runs along back roads and through fields and forests, as well as alongside lakes, rivers, and creeks and through nature reserves. Most of it is flat, but there are some hilly sections with the occasional steep climb. Unfortunately, it is necessary to use some busy roads, but these are necessary to connect once again with the off-road trails. The trail is well marked and signposted, and offers a number of diverting themed loops to interesting sites and expeditions. Information boards along the route direct walkers to attractions in the area, as well as to picnic, camping, and rest areas.

The greenway is packed with historic interest. Krakow was once Poland's capital and is alive with historic buildings. Just outside the city, the trail passes Oświęcim and the Nazi death camp at Auschwitz. Once in Moravia, it goes through the nature reserve of the Moravian Karst region, which has some of the best caves in Europe. As its crosses the Austrian border, it passes through some of the best vineyards and wine cellars in Europe. Along its route are many fine old towns, UNESCO World Heritage Sites, local breweries, monasteries, and churches, as well as a wealth of connections to the area's Hapsburg rulers. Its length will mean that most people will take it in stages, but this is a walk that repays dedication. **SA**

Bregenzerwald Cheese Road
Tyrol, Austria

Start/End Mountain Cheese Factory, Schoppernau
Distance Various   **Time** Various
Grade Easy   **Type** Meadows, mountain trails
Info goo.gl/au9yo8

In the farming communities spread across the lush, green alpine meadows of Bregenzerwald in western Austria, there are twelve cows on average for every farm owned by the region's 1,200 farming families. This is a region in which people still believe in the philosophy that "small is beautiful," where an interconnected network of families and communities with traditions that are still cherished can continue to farm and to prosper in an era of increasing globalization and big business. It was the desire to preserve this simple, ancient way of life, and this philosophy of working for yourself and perfecting a craft, that led to the creation of the Kasestrasse: the Cheese Road.

At the last count, there were 200 members of the Cheese Road route, and that number is growing. It isn't a marked route, though, so there are no conveniently signposted trails or pathways—this is the sort of walk that you have to "sniff out," literally. You can begin at the Mountain Cheese Factory in Schoppernau, if you like, but from there you are on your own. However, the farms of the region are not too far apart, and families are very welcoming to hikers who turn up unannounced. They are happy to take them on tours of their farms and show them the various aspects of cheese production. And at the many huts that dot the hillsides, you can buy a meal and sample the local cheeses—particularly kaseknopfle, a very cheesy pasta dish and a local specialty. Many hotels and restaurants are members of the Cheese Road, too, providing they have a minimum of five Bregenzerwald cheeses on their menus—a far from onerous requirement. **BDS**

"It isn't a street or a road in the usual sense, but rather a union of experts from various disciplines."

www.austria.info

⬆ Along this trail there are ample opportunities to sample the fine cheeses of the Bregenzerwald.

Brine Pipeline Trail
Upper Austria, Austria

Start Ebensee **End** Halstatt
Distance 25 miles (40 km) **Time** 3 days
Grade Easy **Type** Mountain trails, wooden
planks **Map** goo.gl/S2p9Y1

It is the oldest pipeline in the world. Construction began in 1595 and took ten years to complete. Built to run 25 miles (40 km) through the mountains and valleys of the Dachstein region of Upper Austria, from Lake Halstatt to Lake Traunsee, it took brine—water with approximately 26 percent salt content—from Halstatt, the most productive salt mine in the entire Salzkammergut, to a new salt processing works in Ebensee. It was the continuing development of a long tradition. Salt had been produced in Halstatt for 7,000 years, and to walk the Brine Pipeline Trail now not only

"The route covers many kilometers of stunning … scenery such as green woodland and rugged cliffs."

www.touristlink.com

gets you in touch with the beauty of the Dachstein, but it also is an education in the production of salt.

The Brine Pipeline Trail follows the course set by the astonishing 13,000 hollowed-out trees that made up its pipes. The first day's walking is from Ebensee to Bad Ischl—a demanding 12 miles (20 km). From Bad Ischl, you walk to the village of Lauffen, once a place of pilgrimage for local people who would come here to pray for deliverance from the wild, untamed waters of the flood-prone Traun River, and from there to the village of Bad Goisern—a total of 6 miles (9.6km). The final day is a 6-mile (9.6-km) walk along the western shoreline of Lake Halstatt to its historic salt mine, which continued to mine salt until the 1960s. **BDS**

Beethoven Trail
Vienna, Austria

Start Pasqualati House **End** Theater
and der Wien **Distance** 1.8 miles (2.9 km)
Time 2 hours **Grade** Easy **Type** Sidewalk
Map goo.gl/7WesQv

Beethoven may not be a son of Vienna—he was born in Bonn, Germany—but at the age of twenty-two he made his way to the European music capital to study under Haydn. It was 1792, the year after Mozart's death. Between his arrival in the city and his death in 1827, Beethoven moved homes more than seventy times.

A trail published by the local tourist board traces some of Beethoven's homes and haunts. A good place to begin is Pasqualati House, now a museum, at Mölker Bastei, where the composer wrote his Fourth, Fifth, and Seventh symphonies in the top-floor apartment. Among the scores, paintings, and clocks is the composer's death mask. From there, a fifteen-minute walk south past the Hofburg Palace, where Beethoven premiered his Eighth Symphony during the Congress of Vienna in 1814, is Lobkowitz Palace, where the private premier of his Third Symphony, *Eroica*, took place. Nearby, in the multimedia Haus der Musik, visitors can pretend to conduct the Vienna Philharmonic Orchestra playing *Eine Kleine Nachtmusik*. From here, a five-minute walk farther south leads to the Theater an der Wien.

In order to visit Eroica House in Oberdöbling, where Beethoven composed most of his Third Symphony, or Heiligenstadt, where he wrote the Heiligenstadt Testament—a famous letter to his brothers in which he despaired of his deafness and contemplated suicide—you will need to hop on tram No. 37. Both places, once pretty villages, lie in Vienna's northern suburbs. Tram No. 71 will take you to the Zentralfriedhof (Central Cemetery) in Simmering, where Beethoven's remains lie alongside those of other musical greats including Schubert, Johann Strauss (Sr. and Jr.), Brahms, Gluch, Salieri, and Schoenberg. **DS**

Camino de Santiago
Pyrenees, France/Northern Spain

Start Saint-Jean-Pied-de-Port   **End** Santiago
de Compostela   **Distance** 484 miles (780 km)
Time 28–30 days   **Grade** Easy to moderate
Type Medieval walkway   **Info** goo.gl/JuQRfq

There is no single Camino de Santiago (Way of St. James). The term may be applied to a route from anywhere in the world that ends at the shrine to the apostle in the Cathedral of Santiago de Compostela. The most popular path—the Camino Francés—extends from Saint-Jean-Pied-de-Port in southwest France, crosses the Pyrenees, enters Spain after Roncesvalles, and runs through Pamplona, Logroño, Burgos, and Léon.

Once on the trail it is hard to lose your way—it is signposted with concrete bollards every 0.3 miles (500 m) and there are thousands of other pilgrims making the same journey. Traffic is heaviest during Lent and around the Feast of St. James on July 25; the most crowded section year-round is to the west of Sarría. There are also numerous cheap pilgrim hostels (*albergues* or *refugios*) all along the route.

It is popularly said that the Camino de Santiago cannot see a mountain without crossing it, but this is largely unfounded. Much of the terrain is easy, but may be slippery in the rain for which northern Spain is justly notorious. The most challenging section is the final leg that traverses steep hills and valleys. At Lavacolla, 6 miles (10 km) east of Santiago, is Monte de Gozo (Mount of Joy), up which pilgrims are supposed to race and the winner declared king of the group. Also here is the river in which medieval pilgrims would wash themselves—often for the first time since leaving home—before completing the journey.

Beyond Santiago, some dedicated hikers carry on for another 47 miles (75 km) to Cape Finisterre, the westernmost point of mainland Europe. Those who make it this far traditionally burn their walking clothes on the beach. **GL**

"You learn more about your feet than you would ever have thought possible!"

www.santiago-compostela.net

⊡ The Camino de Santiago traverses the lush landscape of Spain's verdant northern regions.

Antonio Gaudí Walking Tour
Barcelona, Spain

Start Plaça Reial   **End** Park Güell
Distance 5 miles (8 km)   **Time** 2.5–3 hours
Grade Easy   **Type** City tour
Map goo.gl/b9kGLZ

This walk provides an introduction to the work of the architect and designer who did more than anyone to embellish a city that, even without his contribution, would still be one of the most beautiful in the world.

Start in the heart of the Barri Gòtic (Gothic Quarter), at the nineteenth-century Plaça Reial (Royal Plaza) with its Gaudí-designed ornate lanterns, and proceed onto La Rambla, the marvelous tree-lined street with two narrow lanes for motor vehicles separated by a broad walkway with a myriad of kiosks and buskers, a street filled with life that the poet Lorca described as the thoroughfare he wished would never end. Along the way you pass Palau Güell, a mansion built for industrialist Eusebi Güell that reveals the essence of Gaudí's style—facades that appear organic, and concrete that twists and curves like the branches of a tree.

When you arrive at the Passeig de Gràcia you can look upon one of his mature works, Casa Batlló, a grand midterrace structure from which straight lines appear to have been banished. Farther north, you encounter Casa Milà, which Gaudí, warming to his organic theme, made to resemble the rock face of a quarry. Next, you come to what is generally agreed to be the chef d'oeuvre, the unbelievably ornate Church of the Sagrada Família. Gaudí was commissioned to design it in 1883, but it took so long to construct, he did not live to see its completion: he was killed by a tram in 1926.

This physically undemanding but aesthetically stimulating itinerary ends on a hillside in the area of the city once known as El Carmel, until Gaudí turned it, between 1900 and 1914, into a garden complex with typically idiosyncratic architectural elements in what is today known as Parc Güell. **GL**

"[Gaudí's style] is intensely human, full of the imagery of nature and religion, and defiantly original."

www.barcelona-life.com

⬆ Gaudí's masterpieces impart a Renaissance feel to an already beautiful city.

Historic City of Toledo
Castilla La Mancha, Spain

Start Toledo Cathedral   End Alcázar
Distance 4 miles (6.4 km)   Time 4 hours
Grade Easy   Type City walk
Map goo.gl/aA7WkX

With expansion restricted by the Tajo River that surrounds it on three sides, the historic center of Toledo occupies little more than 1 square mile (2.6 sq km). Yet within that small area lie so many historic buildings and outstanding works of art that this tour merely scratches the surface of the city's bounty.

Start at the hilltop cathedral, an architectural masterpiece that was completed in the fifteenth century and synthesizes the Gothic, Renaissance, and Baroque styles. Note particularly the main altar, behind which is the wildly romantic *Transparente*, with a host of marble cherubs seated on white clouds. Don't miss the attached art gallery, which contains several masterworks by Raphael and Caravaggio, and El Greco's *The Disrobing of Christ* (1577–79).

From here, head west past the misleadingly named Casa del Greco (it was never the artist's home) to the Sinagoga del Tránsito. The latter was built in the fourteenth century, then forcibly converted into a church, but was recently restored to its original purpose as a place of Jewish worship. Farther along the Calle San Juan de Dios is the Museo de Victorio Macho, a repository of work of the great twentieth-century Spanish artist. From there, carry on east along the riverbank to the Alcázar. This great fortress was a Roman camp in the third century and later became a Muslim stronghold, only to be transformed after the Christian Reconquista by the Spanish kings Alfonso VI and Alfonso X. Built on the city's highest ground, the Alcázar affords great views of the surrounding region and is currently home to the Spanish Army Museum. The walk ends near its starting point: the Alcázar is only a five-minute walk from the cathedral. **GL**

Route of the Monasteries of Valencia   Valenciana, Spain

Start Gandía   End Alzira   Distance 56 miles
(90 km)   Time 3–4 days   Grade Easy
Type Marked paths, disused rail tracks
Map goo.gl/4KowJX

Although this route is primarily of interest to Roman Catholics, there is much to interest nonreligious visitors on a walkway that traverses bridle paths and disused roads and railway lines along Spain's Costa Blanca. The going is easy throughout, and the right way is clearly marked with red and white signs bearing the code GR-236.

The walk starts in Gandía, then heads south. The first stop after 5 miles (8 km) is at Alfauir, where the monastery of Sant Jeroni de Cotalba is a pleasing synthesis of Gothic, Renaissance, and neoclassical.

"The countryside between the monasteries is really quite special at times."

www.idealspain.com

Next is the convent of Corpus Christi, just north of Luchente (Llutxent) and Santa María monastery, shortly after the village of Simat de la Valldigna. The latter stands on land granted around 1300 by King James II of Aragón to the Cistercian order, so that its monks could withdraw inland to safety away from marauding Barbary pirates on the Mediterranean coast.

In Carcaixent, Aquas Vivas (Aigües Vives) was an Augustinian foundation until the twentieth century when it was converted into a hotel, and the last monastery, Santa María de la Murta, was granted to the Hieronymite order by Pope Gregory XI in 1376. The walk ends at the railroad station in Alzira, a small town on the banks of the Júcar River. **GL**

Valletta Heritage Trail
Valletta, Malta

Start City gate **End** St. John's
Cathedral **Distance** 2.2 miles (3.5 km)
Time 2 hours **Grade** Easy **Type** Paved roads
Map goo.gl/1Iu4TC

*"The grid of narrow streets boasts
some of Europe's finest artworks,
churches, and palaces."*

www.visitmalta.com

⬆ "Valletta is a city of palaces built by gentlemen
for gentlemen"—Benjamin Disraeli.

In 1565, the Order of St. John of Jerusalem, also known as the Knights Hospitaller, fought off a lengthy siege by an Ottoman Turkish fleet. When the siege was lifted, the grandmaster of the order, Jean de Vallette, decided to build a new capital city on the island of Malta. The foundation stone was laid on March 28, 1566, his Baroque city slowly emerging over the next decades. Laid out on a grid pattern and surrounded by walls, Valletta is one of the most planned cities in Europe and withstood a lengthy bombardment by Italian and German forces during World War II. The island came close to starvation, and its entire population was awarded a collective George Cross—Britain's highest civilian award for gallantry—by King George VI in 1942.

Valletta is a great city to stroll around and soak up the sights. Start at the main city gate and immediately head up the steep steps to your left to the Triq il-Papa Piju V. You will now be walking around the city walls in a clockwise direction. On your way you will pass St. John Cavalier, the embassy of the Order of St. John; the various bastions or fortifications that protect the city from attack from Marsmxett Harbor; and on to the war museum at the end of the island. On the east side of the town is the Siege Bell, which rings daily at noon to commemorate those who died during World War II. As you complete the lap around the city, you will come back to Triq ir-Repubblika, the main street. A short walk up the street brings you to St. John's Cathedral, a Baroque treasure house that contains two famous paintings by Caravaggio, who took refuge on the island in 1607 after murdering a man in Italy. **SA**

Mount Brione Forts
Trentino Alto Adige, Italy

Start/End Riva del Garda, Porto San Nicolò **Distance** 4 miles (6.4 km) **Time** 3 hours **Grade** Easy **Type** Dirt, asphalt tracks **Map** goo.gl/R4dQxA

In 1852, the military authorities of the Austrian Empire began to build a series of forts on the northern shore of Lake Garda to protect their northern Italian possessions. Italian nationalists were threatening Austrian rule over this region of Italy, and so the Austrians decided to invest in proper defenses. The site they chose was Mount Brione, an oblong mountain dominating the lake below. The Festung Abschnitt, or "fortified sector," was long in construction, only completed in 1907. In 1918, the entire area would become part of Italy, and the forts would become redundant.

The first fort, San Nicolò, was erected close to the lake in 1860 to 1862, followed by Forte San Alessandro on top of the mountain in 1881. Forte Batteria di Mezzo, on a ridge of the mountain, was completed in 1900, with the final fort, Forte Garda, on its lower slopes, finished in 1907. Along with the forts, the Austrians also built a series of communication and combat trenches, observation posts, military roads, and other installations, ready for the day when their mighty empire would come under attack from hostile Italians anxious to reunify their homeland under their own rule. The hike from the lakeside up to the forts and back down again is a three-hour walk on a steep hill. Once at the top, you can see why the Austrians chose this hill for their fortifications—its dominance over the lake is total. Starting at San Nicolò by the lake, you head up a section of the Path of Peace, through groves of olive trees, first to Forte Garda and then the Batteria di Mezzo. At the top, head for the northern peak and the remains of San Alessandro before returning back to the lake. **SA**

Path of Peace
Trentino Alto Adige, Italy

Start Tonale Pass **End** Marmolada **Distance** 336 miles (540 km) **Time** 28–30 days **Grade** Strenuous **Type** Forest and mountain trails, open terrain **Info** goo.gl/FhJ1TL

The Trentino Front was World War I's forgotten war, an offensive launched by the Austro-Hungarian Empire against Italy and fought in the northern Alps and Dolomites. The Path of Peace was created over five years (1986–1991) to commemorate this conflict, and to honor those of both sides who fought and died in it.

The Path of Peace begins at the Tonale Pass on the Trento/Brescia border, from where you can walk to the Paradiso Pass. The path is a perfect blend of mountain passes, refuges, and war-related sites. Walk the Sentierro delle Cascate (Path of the Waterfalls) and

> *"This path links the places where the Great War left its mark amid … a majestic and serene landscape."*
>
> www.visittrentino.it

visit the shelter of Trevina with its impressive collection of war relics. Then ascend the 7,391-foot (2,253 m) peak of Monte Cadria and pass by Austro-Hungarian army posts on the old military road to Pozza di Cadria.

At Rovereto, visit an ossuary that contains the remains of more than 20,000 soldiers, and in the hills above, the trenches. There were tunnels and "mine warfare," and one blast erased forever a part of the mountain known as *il dente Italiano* (the Italian tooth). There are also ruins of buildings—the Austro-Hungarian fort of Sommo Alto, and the remains of defensive stone walls. All the stuff of war, fought in the shadows of Italy's most beautiful peaks. **BDS**

Bologna Food Walk
Emilia-Romagna, Italy

Start/End Piazza Maggiore
Distance 5.6 miles (9 km)   Time 4 hours
Grade Easy   Type Sidewalk
Map goo.gl/knOV8U

Italians call Bologna *"la dotta, la grassa e la rossa"*—"the learned, the fat, and the red." Certainly it is the "learned," being the site of Italy's first university, and it has a proud association with the left side of politics, too, the "red" struggle of socialism. But it is the city's unrivaled reputation as the home of Italy's finest pasta that bestows upon Bologna the mantle of the "fat." And there is a trail of sorts, as coherent as a trail can be in a city with more than 29 miles (40 km) of arcades, that attempts to capture a little of the essence of Bologna's love affair with its food.

"Even the simplest dishes in cheap and cheerful trattoria can be gourmet delights."

www.everytrail.com

Start your pilgrimage at the city square, the Piazza Maggiore, dominated by the fourteenth-century Basilica di San Petronio. It was in the streets that radiate out from this very spot that tortellini and tagliatelle (the ribbon-like pasta that is supposed to go with bolognese sauce; not spaghetti) were invented, and what better place to start than the cobblestone streets of the city's medieval market—the Quadrilatero. From there, walk to Via Drapperie 6 and buy some tortellini from the Art of Bread; to Tamburini at Via Caprarie 1 for some mortadella, a culinary delicacy and one of the vital ingredients in tortellini; and for handmade pasta, stroll over to Dante Zanetti at Via Pescherie Vecchie 6/b. The options are endless. **BDS**

Etruscan Way: Sovana to Pitigliano Tuscany, Italy

Start Sovana   End Pitigliano
Distance 5 miles (8 km)   Time 4 hours
Grade Easy to moderate   Type Earthen and stone-cut paths   Map goo.gl/KNkqPC

The Etruscans are the hidden people of history, a mysterious tribe who may or may not have come from Asia Minor sometime during the 1200s BCE and settled in what is now Tuscany in Italy. They built mud-brick houses and cities, buried or cremated their dead— much of our evidence of them comes from funerary remains—and from around 616 BCE contributed the line of kings who ruled Rome until they were overthrown and a republic declared in 510 BCE. By 393 BCE, the Etruscans were no more, subsumed by the Romans, and left to history.

The Etruscans gave us two legacies: a series of hilltop towns and the extraordinary Vie Cave, the "excavated roads" for which the region is famous. The Etruscans cut these deep channels into the volcanic tufa rock, probably using them as a defense system but also as a network of roads and water channels to serve their hilltop settlements. Some of these almost vertical cuts are more than 32 feet (10 m) deep and were cut with great skill and ingenuity. The Vie Cave can be explored at the southern end of the Etruscan Way, which stretches north from Tuscany, across the Apennines to Emilia Romagna. It is possible to complete the whole route in about five or six days, and a popular section is at the southernmost end of the route, from the Etruscan necropolis of Sovana to the hilltop city of Pitigliano. Sovana was an Etruscan village developed by the Romans and later the Lombards, boasting a fine castle and a beautiful Romanesque cathedral, as well as many architectural remains. The route then heads along the Vie Cave to Pitigliano, a breathtakingly beautiful hilltop town packed with historic buildings, a great end to a fascinating expedition. **SA**

Ponte Vecchio
Tuscany, Italy

Start/End Ponte Vecchio, Florence
Distance 295 feet (90 m)
Time Various   **Grade** Easy
Type Stone paving   **Info** goo.gl/VFG2S9

The Ponte Vecchio in Florence is a medieval stone bridge that crosses the Arno River. It is lined with houses and shops, something that was commonplace in the past but now marks it as one of the world's most striking bridges. As a result it's a popular draw with tourists and is often teeming with people. It is thought that the first bridge built at this spot was constructed in Roman times, but the bridge that is there today dates from 1345, when it was constructed to replace one destroyed in a raging flood.

In the Middle Ages, houses were built on the Ponte Vecchio, and these were used by butchers, fishmongers, and tanners. In the sixteenth century, the first grand duke of Tuscany, Cosimo I de' Medici, wanted a way of crossing the bridge without having to fight the crowds—he had homes on either side of the river. So in 1564 he commissioned a raised, enclosed corridor— the *Corridoio Vasariano*—that runs above the shops. In 1593, Duke Ferdinand I replaced the functional shops with goldsmiths because, it is said, of the smell and the waste, and still today the bridge is home to a number of jewelers.

The bridge is an interesting place to explore, with crowds of people window-shopping among the jewelers. There are also musicians and street performers. But don't be tempted to follow the tradition that flourished for a while, of fixing a padlock to the railings. This was supposed to show your true love for someone (with the key tossed into the river below) but there's now a fine for anyone caught doing it. During World War II, Ponte Vecchio was the only bridge in Florence to survive the German withdrawal—allegedly on the orders of Hitler himself. JI

"The bridge is at its most beautiful at dusk, especially when seen from the Ponte Santa Trinita."

www.aviewoncities.com

⊤ The architectural style of the original bridge contrasts with that of the *Corridoio Vasariano* running above it.

Aventine District of Rome Lazio, Italy

Start Temples of the Forum Boarium   **End** Pyramid of Caius Cestius   **Distance** 1 mile (1.6 km)   **Time** 4 hours
Grade Easy   **Type** Paved road, sidewalk   **Map** goo.gl/ui1qTA

The Aventine Hill in the south of Rome is one of the seven historic hills on which the city was allegedly founded in 753 BCE. In this founding myth, Remus set himself up on the Aventine while his twin, Romulus, chose the Palatine Hill. Originally outside the city's initial boundaries, the hill was settled by the overspill population from the crowded city and was eventually bound within the new city walls, built after the Gauls sacked Rome in 390 BCE. Temples were built, and the site became a smart residential address.

A walk around this fascinating area starts in the north at the Temples of the Forum Boarium, two wonderfully preserved temples from the second century BCE. The Temple of Portunus is rectangular and that of Hercules, a perfect circle. From here, head south to Santa Maria in Cosmedin, a sixth-century church with later additions. Set into its wall is the Mouth of Truth, which is possibly a drain cover, dating back to before the fourth century BCE. Traditionally, its jaws snapped shut on those who told lies. From here, stroll into the Circus Maximus, a vast Roman racetrack used for chariot racing. Down at the end of the Via di Santa Sabina is the Orange Garden, which affords great views over the city. A short stroll away is the Cavalieri di Malta Square, a walled piazza designed by Piranesi in 1765 and named after the Knights of Malta. A bronze keyhole in the priory door at number three provides a miniature glimpse of St. Peter's Basilica in the distance, framed by a tree-lined avenue. The tour ends at the Protestant Cemetery, where poet John Keats is buried, and at Rome's only pyramid, the tomb of Caius Cestius, a Roman magistrate, can be found. **SA**

⊡ Palatine Hill and Circus Maximus as seen from Aventine Hill.

The Forum Lazio, Italy

Start/End Ticket office, Via dei Fori Imperiali   **Distance** 3 miles (4.8 km)   **Time** 4 hours   **Grade** Easy
Type Gravel paths, sidewalks   **Info** goo.gl/ZFqEnb

"When in Rome, do as the Romans do" is always good advice, especially where the Forum is concerned. Every ancient Roman went to the Forum, which was the center of Roman political, judicial, and commercial life. Here, the Senate met to decide new laws, existing laws were argued over by lawyers in the various basilica, the gods were worshipped in the many temples, and triumphal arches were erected by emperors to celebrate their military victories. The playwright Plautus remarked that the area was full of "lawyers and litigants, bankers and brokers, shopkeepers and strumpets, good-for-nothings waiting for a tip from the rich." And it can still feel a bit like that today.

The Forum is a delight to wander through, but there is no single route to follow. Large crowds in the summer months make some areas congested, so it is best to wander at will, searching out those quieter areas that still breathe the air of ancient Rome. But there are some things that must be seen. It doesn't look much today, but the stone plinth of the Rostra—close to the commanding, red-brick Curia building—was where members of the public addressed the nation. Mark Antony's famous address to "Friends, Romans, Countrymen," was delivered here. Among the many monuments is the Arch of Titus, erected in 81 CE to celebrate the achievements of Titus and Vespasian in suppressing the Jewish revolt. One stone relief shows Roman soldiers carrying off the contents of the Temple of Jerusalem. Up on the Palatine Hill, to the south of the main Forum, is the vast palace of Augustus (seen opposite). Just outside the main area is Trajan's market. **SA**

⬆ The Forum was a political gathering place.

Pompeii Walking Tour
Campania, Italy

Start Piazza dell'Anfiteatro **End** Porta Marina
Distance 2 miles (3.2 km) **Time** 3 hours
Grade Easy **Type** Stone roads and paths
Info goo.gl/nFcyjA

Pompeii is the ultimate horror story, a busy Roman town going about its daily business when, on either November 23 or August 29, in 79 CE—experts differ about the exact date—the town was buried beneath the hot gassy surges and clouds of volcanic ash that poured out of the erupting Mount Vesuvius. The event was recorded vividly at the time by Pliny the Younger, the lawyer whose admiral uncle died in the tragedy. But then Pompeii came back to life in 1748, when the first of its ruined buildings was discovered by a Spanish team of investigators. Since then, almost the entire town has come to light, its ruined streets, public buildings, temples, houses, and shops providing an unrivaled chance for us to understand what a Roman town looked like and how it worked. Most extraordinarily, the layers of volcanic ash preserved human bodies that have since disintegrated. Filled with plaster, these voids now show the citizens of Pompeii in their final anguished minutes of life.

There are numerous commercial, guided walking tours of Pompeii, many of which allow you to skip the lines that form each day at the entrance. But the general consensus is that it is best to do it yourself, helped perhaps by an audio guide rented from the tourist office and a good map of the city. Start at either of the two entrances and then wander at leisure along the stone-paved streets. The Temple of Apollo is the most important surviving temple, and the Forum is still impressive despite its ruined state. Look out for the many frescos that decorate the walls, some of which are wonderfully erotic, and the Latin graffiti carved on many walls. Above all, soak in the atmosphere of this highly evocative ruined town. **SA**

"No archaeological site in Italy has the drama or size of Pompeii."

www.walksofitaly.com

← The partial remnants of a magnificent colonnade.

↑ In all, the remains of some 1,150 Pompeii citizens have been unearthed since excavations began.

Piazza Armerina
Sicily, Italy

Start/End Piazza Garibaldi
Distance Various   Time Various
Grade Easy   Type Sidewalk
Info goo.gl/gqoElb

The town of Piazza Armerina is nestled deep in the Sicilian hinterland, sitting on a 2,296-foot-high (700 m) plateau about 21 miles (34 km) from the city of Enna. It is a well-trampled tourist destination, founded in the Norman era, and has a stunning historic quarter. This includes a magnificent Baroque cathedral on Piazza Garibaldi, which is the town's high point, and a wonderfully preserved fortress, Spinelli Castle. The town was made to be walked, with a labyrinth of streets that ascend and descend around its ancient, cultivated slopes. But it is not the churches, the fortress, or Piazza Armerina's network of alleyways that bring people here from across Europe. What draws people here is something that not a lot of towns, even in Italy, have enough of—beautifully preserved villas such as Romana del Casale.

Built as a hunting lodge by a Roman patrician in the fourth century CE, the villa is home to some of the finest and most extraordinarily vivid Roman mosaics to be found anywhere in Italy. Constructed in four main sections, the villa has a dining area, complete with elliptical courtyard, an entry comprising thermal baths, rooms that were the private residence of the owner, and a separate living area with guest rooms. The villa was rediscovered in the 1800s after being almost totally buried by a landslide seven centuries earlier. However, it wasn't until a series of excavations in the 1900s that the scale of the mosaic flooring was fully realized—more than 37,670 square feet (3,500 sq m) in total, as well as wall mosaics, columns, coins, and capitals—a treasure trove of ancient Rome that will have you walking until your feet hurt. **BDS**

"The mosaics which decorate almost every room . . . are the finest mosaics in situ anywhere in the Roman world."

whc.unesco.org

⊼ The mosaics, most likely by North Africans, depict ancient myths, Homeric adventures, and daily life.

Wooden Architecture Trail
Southern Poland, Poland

Start/End Haczów **Distance** 200 miles
(320 km) **Time** 2 weeks **Grade** Moderate
Type Paved roads, sidewalks
Info goo.gl/O3CNM9

Małopolska (Lesser or Southern Poland) is heavily
wooded and its trees provide the main construction
material for buildings in the area. Of particular note are
the wooden Roman Catholic churches, all built by
local and unknown craftsmen in the Gothic style. The
churches were built using a horizontal log technique
for the framework, which was then covered with
wooden slatted walls and a steeply sloping roof
covered with wooden tiles. All have short towers with
either a cupola dome or a pointed roof on top. These
beautiful churches were sponsored by local noble
families and became status symbols in the region.

The churches were built between the late 1300s
and the late 1700s. The earliest is the Church of the
Blessed Virgin Mary and Archangel Michael at Haczów,
which dates to 1388, although its many-colored
Gothic decorations date from the late 1400s. The first
mention of a wooden church at Debno is even earlier,
in 1335, although the current church was erected in
the late 1400s. Its decorations are very fine, the ceiling
and walls painted using stencils from the 1400s and
1500s. Other churches stand in Binarowa, Blizne,
Lachowice, Lipnica Murowana, Orawka, Sękowa, and
Szalowa; all are listed as UNESCO World Heritage Sites.

These churches, as well as hundreds of other
historic timber buildings in Lesser Poland, can be found
on the Wooden Architecture Trail, a 932-mile (1,500-km)
driving trail that is becoming increasingly popular with
hikers who like to walk the varying distances between
its churches, chapels, manor houses, museums, and
villas. The network of connecting trails is being
expanded every year by hikers and lovers of the tactile
beauty of wood. **SA**

*"Experience the living history of
the Małopolska Region (Southern
Poland) enshrined in the marvels
of its wooden architecture."*

www.poland.travel

⊡ The route takes in nine wooden churches that have
miraculously survived the centuries.

Churches of Peace in Jawor and Swidnica
Lower Silesia, Poland

Start Swidnica   **End** Jawor
Distance 24 miles (38.6 km)
Time 6 hours   **Grade** Easy
Type Road verge   **Map** goo.gl/aJqUca

In 1648, the Peace of Westphalia ended the religious and territorial wars that had raged throughout Europe for thirty years. The treaty ended religious divisions by stating that the faith of the ruler be obligatory for his subjects. In the case of Silesia—once governed by Austria, but now in southwest Poland—this meant its people were required to be Roman Catholics because they were part of the Catholic Hapsburg Empire of Austria. Protestants were persecuted. However, the Hapsburg emperor did allow the Lutherans in Silesia to build three churches to commemorate the end of the war. These churches were to be built in the temporary materials of wood, loam, and straw; be placed outside the city walls; have no steeples or church bells; and they had to be built within one year.

The Churches of Peace at Jawor and Swidnica are Europe's largest timber-framed religious buildings and both can involve hours of careful, observational walking. The Church of the Holy Ghost in Jawor is vast—143 feet (43.5 m) long, 46 feet (14 m) wide, and 52 feet (15.7 m) high. It seats more than 5,500 people, and is decorated with more than 200 paintings by the seventeenth-century painter Georg Flegel. The Church of the Holy Trinity in Swidnica is similarly impressive in scale and decoration. This is observation walking at its most painstaking and rewarding, with post-and-beam construction, half-joints, horizontal connecting rails, diagonal crossed struts, and shingle roofs waiting to catch the eye.

Visiting either church is more a shuffle than a walk, really, as you inch your way through the harmonious timbered world of Andreas Gamper, seventeeth-century master craftsman. **SA**

"The Churches of Peace bear testimony to the quest for religious freedom."

whc.unesco.org

⤒ The Church of Peace at Jawor is one of Europe's largest timber-framed religious buildings.

Kraków's Royal Way
Lesser Poland, Poland

Start/End The Barbican, Kraków
Distance 1 mile (1.6 km)
Time 2 hours   **Grade** Easy
Type Paved   **Map** goo.gl/Fm2ggw

The Old Town of Kraków is an elegant jigsaw of three of the great architectural movements of Europe—Gothic, Renaissance, and Baroque. At one end is the Barbican and St. Florian's Gate, a remnant of the thirteenth-century city walls, and at the other Wawel Castle, the seat of the kings of Poland from 1319 until the beginning of the seventeenth century. Between the two is the Royal Way, along which the royal family showed themselves to their subjects. Dead kings were laid in state in St. Florian's Church, near the relics of St. Florian, the patron saint of Poland, and then taken to Wawel Cathedral for burial.

Walking the Royal Way is the customary start to any stay in Kraków. The city's main sights and finest facades line the route, as do the smartest cafés, shops, and galleries. In summer, set off early to escape bottlenecks, although crowded narrow streets perhaps capture the spirit of Kraków's past better than solitary waiters sweeping deserted squares. From the Barbican, the route follows Florianska Street, passing the Pharmacy Museum—crammed with medieval pots and potions—and Mariaki Church, where a trumpeter sounds a bugle from the tower every hour. Rynek Główny, one of the largest market squares in Europe, forms a spectacular interruption to a string of historic churches. Take a chair at any of the cafés spilling from its arcade and gaze upon the Cloth Hall, a Renaissance rebuilding of the fourteenth-century original.

From the market square, Grodzka Street heads up to the twin peaks of the Royal Way—the cathedral and the castle perched over the Vistula River. In 1978, Karol Józef Wojtyła set off from here to the Vatican to become Pope John Paul II. **DS**

"The route is still used for religious and secular processions and these are always vibrant occasions."

www.local-life.com

⤒ Stroll Kraków's famous royal boulevard from Wawel Castle to the Barbican.

Prague Historic Walk
Stredocesky, Czech Republic

Start Prague Castle   **End** Old Town Square
Distance 0.6 mile (1 km)   **Time** 1 hour
Grade Easy   **Type** Sidewalk, cobblestones
Info goo.gl/rOZqWQ

Walking through Prague not only brings to life the history of the city itself, but also reveals its role in the evolution of European culture. As capital of the kingdom of Bohemia, Prague has been the seat of two Holy Roman Emperors, and in the fourteenth century it was the third largest city in Europe after Rome and Constantinople. In 1347, Holy Roman Emperor Charles IV founded Charles University, where the ideas of master and philosopher Jan Hus gave rise to the Hussites and planted the seeds of the Reformation. In the eighteenth and nineteenth centuries, Prague rivaled Vienna as a center for music, producing composers such as Dvořák and Janáček.

Straddling the banks and islands of the Vitava River, Prague has four historic centers—Hradčany, Mala Strana (Lower Town), Stare Mesto (Old Town), and Nove Mesto (New Town)—which form one of the loveliest architectural ensembles in Europe, topped by a sea of red-tiled roofs and gilded spires. Begin your walk in Hradčany, where Prague Castle—founded in the ninth century and now the modern seat of government—stands next to St. Vitus Cathedral, a fourteenth-century masterpiece. From here, roads lead down to Charles Bridge, built in 1357 and later capped by thirty stone saints, which links to the prairie-sized Old Town Square. This is the site of public gatherings and protests, from medieval executions to attacks on Soviet tanks in 1968. Around the edge are some of Prague's finest buildings, including the Gothic Týn church and the multifaced Astronomical Clock. Get here on the hour to see its parade of the twelve apostles and the personifications of Death, Avarice, Vanity, and Invasion come to life. **DS**

"St. Vitus Cathedral, distinctly visible from much of the historical center of Prague, houses many priceless works of art."

www.praguewelcome.cz

⊡ Prague Castle, Europe's largest castle complex, overlooks a fairy-tale city of domes and cupolas.

Cesky Krumlov Historic Walk
Jihocesky, Czech Republic

Start Hrádek   End Snornosti Square
Distance 6 miles (9.6 km)   Time 1 day with stops
Grade Easy   Type Sidewalk, cobblestones
Info goo.gl/bS69CT

The word "picturesque" does not do justice to the little town of Cesky Krumlov, built within a figure of eight in southern Bohemia's Vltava River. Built between the thirteenth and seventeenth centuries to an artistic level more usually found in larger places, the town reflects its prosperity as a stop on a major European trade route and its openness to influences from Austria and Italy. As trade routes shifted, Cesky Krumlov became a backwater, and new development ceased. When UNESCO awarded it World Heritage status in 1992, it said it was central Europe's "best-preserved and most representative surviving example of a small medieval town." It was a dusty but beautifully kept heirloom discovered in Europe's attic.

A walk through the town (vehicles are banned) should not be too concerned with ticking off sights, although a good portion of time is likely to be spent at the castle (Hrádek), with its high round tower, summer palace, gardens, riding school, and theater. The principal pleasure in Cesky Krumlov is to wander, absorbing the little details as well as the elegant whole—Gothic spires, Renaissance doorways, Baroque gables, and Rococo flourishes on pastel-colored facades. It is a town of two halves. On the north bank of the river, the castle rises above the Renaissance arsenal, Gothic convents, and Baroque belfries, really a town in itself with its own town hall; on the south bank, across a modest bridge, is the tight little knot of the town proper, centering on Snornosti Square, lined by handsome burghers' houses with ornamental gables and contrasting colored quoins. Push open the doors of some of the chic shops and cozy restaurants to look inside. **DS**

Moravia Wine Trails
Jihomoravsky, Czech Republic

Start/End Various   Distance 16–180 miles
(25.7–290 km)   Time 2 days–3 weeks
Grade Easy to moderate   Type Country lanes,
gravel tracks, bridleways   Info goo.gl/FDAecQ

Think of the Czech Republic and it is beer not wine that usually springs to mind. However, in Southern Moravia, on the border with Austria, rows of vines cover hill after hill. The Moravian wine industry is charmingly local in character, with many vineyards not much bigger than large backyards. Some vineyards are tended by part-time vintners, who drive down from Prague on the weekends to pick and crush the grapes or open their "cellars"—caves scooped out of hillsides that have acquired their own genre of architecture through the addition of grand doors and porticoes.

"Walk through the breathtaking landscapes of Southern Moravia along the newly opened wine trails".

www.pragueviennagreenways.org

The Czech tourist board has designated ten wine trails, ranging from Bzenec Wine Route, at only 16 miles (26 km), to the Moravian Wine Route the backbone of the network at 180 miles (290 km), which runs from Znojmo in the west to Uherské in the east. Znojmo is good for aromatic whites, and the Velké Pavlovicie Wine Route, which has the largest number of registered wine producers, is best for reds. The scenery is as attractive as the wine. Color-coded signs point the way along country lanes between fields of cereals and sunflowers as well as vines, with church towers nestling in the hollows. Sleepy villages, often radiating from elegant squares of Austro–Hungarian vintage, have inns for rest and refreshment. **DS**

Iron Curtain Trail

Norway to Bulgaria

Start Kirkenes, Norway   **End** Tsarevo, Bulgaria
Distance 4,750 miles (7,650 km)   **Time** 14–16 months
Grade Strenuous   **Type** Paths, paved roads, wooden
boardwalks   **Info** goo.gl/d6uyLc

In the chilling words of British wartime prime minister Winston Churchill, uttered in Fulton, Missouri, on March 5, 1946: "From Stettin in the Baltic to Trieste in the Adriatic an iron curtain has descended across the Continent." This fortified structure was built by the Soviet-led Communist regimes of Eastern Europe ostensibly to defend their borders against U.S. attack, but in reality to prevent their people from fleeing to freedom in the West. It remained one of the most heavily armed frontiers in the world until the curtain finally came down in 1991 at the end of the Cold War.

> *"For almost half a century, Europe was forcibly divided into East and West by the Iron Curtain."*

www.ironcurtaintrail.eu

After the Iron Curtain fell, a certain nostalgia for its existence, as well as a desire to remember it, arose in reunified Europe, in spite of the need to put behind it a particularly divisive part of its history. A trail was devised to follow the complete border, extending from the north of Norway and Finland south and then east to the Bulgarian–Turkish border on the Black Sea. It is the middle section, following the old frontier between East and West Germany down to the Slovenian border with Hungary that is the most atmospheric. The route passes many old border posts and fortifications. Much of the trail is still in development, awaiting funding. The parts that are open are best taken in easy stages. **SA**

Amber Trail

Hungary/Slovakia/Poland

Start Szentendre, Hungary   **End** Kraków, Poland
Distance 244 miles (392 km)   **Time** 10 days
Grade Strenuous   **Type** Cross-country, medieval
path   **Info** goo.gl/Jsfg2L

This demanding itinerary traverses part of the ancient trail along which merchants carried amber—"the gold of the North"—from the Baltic, where it was gathered, to the Mediterranean, where it was sold at great profit. The route starts in the lovely village of Szentendre, 6 miles (10 km) north of Budapest. From there it proceeds to Visegrád, 10 miles (16 km) distant, where the King Matthias Palace and the Solomon Tower dominate the landscape. The next leg takes you through a nature reserve along the banks of the Danube, which is crossed at the border with Slovakia and the entrance to Esztergom. From there, you pass via Brhlovce, a village with houses carved out of rock faces, to Banská Stiavnica, a UNESCO-protected village of outstanding natural beauty.

The section from here to Liptovský Mikuláš is the hardest on this trail, but the effort is amply rewarded by the glorious views over the Low Tatras hills, which, lovely as they are, struggle to compete with the Kvacianska Valley, with its waterfalls and limestone caves and the open-air folk museum in the village of Zuberec. Between Bobrov and Lipnica Wielka, cross the border into Poland and make your way to Lanckorona and its folk architecture, and from there to Kalwaria Zebrzydowska, with its thirty-two chapels representing the Stations of the Cross and its imposing Bernadine monastery. Journey's end is at Kraków, a city that cannot be seen in a single day. Among the essential sights here are Wawel Castle, the Old Market Square, and the Kazimierz Jewish quarter. Some hikers continue from here along the banks of the Vistula River to Niepołomice, where there is a fourteenth-century hunting castle. **GL**

Budapest Art Nouveau Trail
Budapest, Hungary

Start Kossuth tér **End** Muvész coffee house,
near the opera house **Distance** 4.5 miles (7.2 km)
Time 4–6 hours **Grade** Moderate **Type** Sidewalk
Map goo.gl/9BzYZT

Art Nouveau defines Budapest in much the same way as skyscrapers define New York, and this walk is a perfect introduction to this style of late-nineteenth and early twentieth-century art and architecture. It also provides glimpses of some of the other great attractions of the Hungarian capital.

Start on Kossuth tér (square), outside the national parliament, construction of which began in 1884, and do not be surprised if it reminds you of the Houses of Parliament in London. Both had the same architect, Imre Steindl. From here you pass near Magyar Szecesszió Háza, a gallery and café in a house built in 1903 by Emil Vidor, a leading light of the Art Nouveau style. Next comes the statue of Imre Nagy, the Hungarian leader who was tried in secret and executed two years after the Soviet invasion in 1956, and Szabadság tér (Freedom Square), before arriving outside Posta Takarékpénztár. This former Post Office Savings Bank was designed in 1900 by Odön Lechner in a fusion of Art Nouveau and Hungarian vernacular style. Note the bees crawling up toward the beehive, which symbolize the wisdom of saving money, and the winged dragons and serpents on the roof.

After walking through Belvárosi Vásárcsarnok (Inner City Market Hall), past the neoclassical Szent István tér (St. Stephen's Basilica) and across Roosevelt tér, you reach Gresham Palace, built in 1907. After years of neglect, it has now been restored to perfection by its current owners, the Four Seasons hotel chain. Walk by the Hungarian Academy of Sciences before ending the trail at the Muvész Coffee House near the neo-Renaissance opera house, both of which are well worth extended visits. **GL**

"Incorporating motifs from old Hungarian architecture, particularly that of Transylvania, folk art, and even oriental features."

visitbudapest.travel

⊡ The Gellért Baths is the most famous Art Nouveau-style thermal spa in Budapest.

Trogir City Walk Split-Dalmatia, Croatia

Start Riva **End** Kamerlengo Castle **Distance** 2.4 miles (3.8 km) **Time** 2 hours **Grade** Easy
Type Ancient stone sidewalks **Map** goo.gl/URTPEO

Here, the imprint of the Greek *cardo maximus* (main north–south street) incorporates a corner of Roman paving; there, a Renaissance balcony overlooks a Norman fountain; and over here, above a doorway, a winged lion of Venice raises a stone paw. A walk through the Croatian port of Trogir is a journey through the major epochs of European civilization. Since its founding by Hellenistic traders in the third century BCE, the city has passed through the hands of Roman, Byzantine, Norman, Hungarian, and Venetian invaders, all of whom left their stamp. Encased by Venetian fortifications and dangling from the mainland like a pendant, it is on a par with fellow World Heritage Site Dubrovnik when it comes to scenic settings.

It's not difficult to devise your own trail around Trogir, but professional guides read the honey-colored stone fluently, pointing out hidden features and relating snippets in the island's turbulent history. Any trail is likely to begin on the yacht-lined Riva and then head to John Paul II Square, where the main sights are clustered. These include the Cathedral of St. Lawrence, where master masons once carved an intricate microcosm. Among the stone putti, apostles, angels, plants, and beasts, God pokes his head out of the barrel-vaulted ceiling in the St. John of Trogir's chapel. After a look at the loggia and clocktower and Cipiko Palace, with its Venetian–Gothic triple window on the west side of the square, take any of the radiating streets to more palaces and churches. Alternatively, walk out of the Land Gate and follow the walls to St. Mark's Tower and Kamerlengo Castle, built in 1430 to guard the jewel-like city. **DS**

⬆ **Trogir is a heady mix of Greco-Roman and Venetian.**

Sanctuary of Olympia Peloponnese, Greece

Start Stadium **End** Villa of Nero **Distance** 2 miles (3.2 km) **Time** 4 hours **Grade** Easy
Type Rock paths **Map** goo.gl/cBTPYD

The site of the Olympic Games in the classical era, the Sanctuary of Olympia provides a fascinating day's walking through the monuments of an ancient empire. There are the remains of the gymnasium built in the third century BCE and originally lined with porticoes; the Palaestra, with its fabulous Doric columns; and the workshop in which Pheidias sculpted the great statue of Zeus—one of the Seven Wonders of the Ancient World.

Farther south is the Leonidaion, which was once a guest house, and from there on the right are the remains of the Bouleuterion, a set of ancient administrative buildings. And on the left to the north, at the heart of the Altis (central area), is the Temple of Zeus, built in the fifth century BCE in the Doric style and almost as big as the Parthenon in Athens. Beyond this great edifice is the Pelopion, a mound on which a black ram would be ritually sacrificed to the gods. Close by is the monument built by Alexander the Great in memory of his father, Philip II of Macedon, and the Temple of Hera—Hera was the wife of Zeus—built in the first century BCE when the Greeks first began to allow female participation in sport.

To the east, past the Metroon, a shrine to Rhea—mother of Zeus—and the treasuries at the foot of Mount Kronios, lies the vast rectangular paved area that was the site of the original Olympic Games. To the south, across an open stretch of land that used to accommodate the hippodrome, the villa of Nero remains intact. It was here that the Roman emperor would stay when he took part in the games, now yours to stroll through under the Peloponnese sun. **GL**

⬆ A glorious testament to contests, rather than conflicts.

Street of the Knights
Rhodes, Greece

Start/End Old Town of Rhodes
Distance 656 yards (600 m)   **Time** 1 hour
Grade Easy   **Type** Cobblestones
Info goo.gl/2Wr3mt

When you enter the Old Town of Rhodes, with a view to walking its medieval streets, and you look about you at its maze of alleyways and the 200 streets that aren't even named, it's easy to feel a bit overwhelmed. Fortunately, there is a starting point that is hard to miss—the famous Street of the Knights—an avenue constructed over an even more ancient pathway, which remains to this day as one of the best-preserved medieval thoroughfares in Europe.

In the sixteenth century this street—at the northern end of the city, in an area known as the Collachium—ran from the port in a straight line to the Acropolis of Rhodes. It was lined with inns belonging to all the nations of the world, and all built to house the knights, the so-called "soldier monks" of the Order of St. John. The inns were places for the knights to meet to discuss the issues of the day, as well as a place to pray and to eat. The pristine condition of the street today is mainly thanks to the Italians, who dismantled all the ungainly looking wooden balconies placed over it by the Turks and restored its late medieval character.

The street was an ancient meeting point of world cultures. There is the Inn of Spain, the Inn of Provence, and the Inn of France—the last still recognizable (despite being used as a mosque by the Turks) with its three lilies and royal crown of the French coat of arms and the Grand Master d'Aubusson's cardinal's hat. The date 1495 is still visible, carved into the door frame. Though now more a museum piece than a living, breathing street, it nonetheless has the power to captivate as you stroll along its cobblestones at the beginning of a deep blue, Rhodos day. **BDS**

"The Street of the Knights is the location of several inns dating back to the Middle Ages."

www.historymedren.about.com

⤴ The Street of the Knights is a fifteenth-century time capsule.

Pirin Wine Trail
Blagoevgrad, Bulgaria

Start Bankso   End Melnik
Distance 28 miles (45 km)   Time 3 days
Grade Moderate   Type Mountain trails
Map goo.gl/3AMCGj

The Pirin National Park of southwest Bulgaria is listed by UNESCO as a place of universal value for its beauty, geology, flora, and fauna. The gateway to the mountains is Bankso, a ski resort built around a kernel of traditional buildings with 3-foot-thick (1 m) stone walls, heavy timber eaves, and steep terra-cotta roofs. Designed to withstand the long snowy winters and also as attack, these fortified houses testify to a prosperous past long predating the modern enthusiasm for skiing. Historically, Bankso grew up to serve traders traveling through the Pirin Mountains from the south, in particular wine merchants transporting goatskins of red wine by packhorse from Melnik. The wine was popular in Austria and England.

Melnik still produces wine (a dry red, which can be sampled in local bars), but these days it is summer hikers who ply the old wine route through the Pirin. Leaving Bankso, the three-day signed trail to Melnik—with overnight stays in mountain refuges (hizha) that supply simple meals and clean bedding—climbs alongside streams and waterfalls to emerge in a landscape of hanging valleys, horns, and spurs dotted with clusters of clear blue lakes that the locals call "eyes." Descending via the Melnik Pyramids—serrated sandstone ridges—it is worth making a detour to Rozhen Monastery, 3 miles (5 km) southeast of Melnik, to see its collection of more than 100 rare icons. Like the fine old houses of Bankso and Melnik, the monastery is decorated with murals and carvings by members of the Bankso Art School, which sprang up in the eighteenth century as part of the Bulgarian National Revival, a political and cultural campaign to shake off Ottoman rule. **DS**

Kaunas Historic City Walk
Kaunas, Lithuania

Start Freedom Avenue   End Vytautas Church
Distance 6 miles (10 km)   Time 4 hours
Grade Easy   Type Cobbled streets, sidewalks
Map goo.gl/EZFr7a

To say Kaunas has had a turbulent history is an understatement. Founded in 1030, it was raided by Teutonic knights, attacked by Russian and Swedish armies, destroyed twice by Napoleon, occupied by the Poles, attacked by the Nazis, and made part of the Soviet Union before independence came in 1991.

You could be forgiven for wondering if anything of historical importance could possibly be left. But the Old Town of Kaunas has managed better than most European cities to preserve and maintain its centuries-old legacy. A good place to start is its leafy Laisvės

> *"The remarkable Old Town is a collection of ancient architectural monuments."*

www.kaunas.it

Alėja, Freedom Avenue, the city's main thoroughfare with its monument to Vytautas the Great, with the fourteenth-century symbol of Lithuanian might standing over the bodies of a Russian, a German, a Pole, and a Tartar. Walk the length of the avenue to the lovely blue-colored, neo-Byzantine St. Michael Church, then up the nearby hill (or take the funicular) to the stunning Resurrection Church, started in the 1930s but only recently completed. The Town Hall Square, with its impressive sixteenth-century German merchant houses, is next, and no visit to Kaunas is complete without a walk through and around the glorious, Gothic, Vytautas Church. So much history, in a city that has fought hard to keep it. **BDS**

St. Petersburg Walking Tour St. Petersburg, Russia

Start Admiralty building   **End** Alexander Nevsky Lavra   **Distance** 3 miles (4.8 km)   **Time** 2 hours
Grade Easy   **Type** Sidewalks   **Map** goo.gl/VkcX2t

Created from nothing by Peter the Great in 1703, the city of St. Petersburg soon became one of the finest neoclassical cities in Europe. Thousands of conscripted peasants labored for years to build the city, joined by Swedish prisoners of war captured during the Great Northern War that brought Russia the land on which the city emerged. Tens of thousands of these workers died. Peter moved his capital from Moscow to St. Petersburg in 1712, where it remained, but for a short gap, until 1917. During this time, three Russian tsars were assassinated in or near the city. St. Petersburg saw the start of the Revolution against tsarist rule in 1905, and in 1917—by then renamed Petrograd—the city saw the storming of the Winter Palace on October 25, 1917, by Lenin and the Bolsheviks, which led to the Russian Revolution. The government soon moved back to Moscow while Petrograd was renamed Leningrad after the death of Lenin in 1924. Famously, the city resisted an 872-day siege by German forces that lasted from September 1941 to January 1944. With the end of Communist rule in 1991, the city reverted to its historic name.

St. Petersburg is designed around the Nevsky Prospect, a wide avenue running from the Admiralty building and the Winter Palace to the Moscow Railway Station and Vosstaniya Square, where it turns toward Alexander Nevsky Lavra, or monastery. Along its route lie the magnificent Stroganov Palace, the vast Kazan Cathedral—a monument to Catherine the Great—and a number of famous churches and other buildings. St. Petersburg is a city that encourages walking, so do so at your leisure. **SA**

⬆ **The Hermitage Museum is the city's gift to the world.**

Ephesus Walking Tour Izmir, Turkey

Start House of the Virgin Mary   **End** Harbor Road   **Distance** 3 miles (4.8 km)   **Time** 7 hours   **Grade** Easy
Type Archaeological site   **Map** goo.gl/fPKJzV

Ephesus was an ancient Greek and later a Roman city on the coast of Ionia, 2 miles (3.2km) south of Selçuk, Turkey, and the Ephesus Walking Tour is the best option if you have only a day to spend at this fabulous UNESCO World Heritage Site.

It starts in the middle of an olive grove at the House of the Virgin Mary, which is believed to have been the last dwelling place of Mary, mother of Jesus Christ, and from there enters the confines of the Hellenistic Wall and continues to the state agora, the town square, the city's political rallying point. In one corner are the stoa basilica and the odeon, a small theater built in around 150 CE. Advancing across the northeastern flank of the square, turn right into Via Curetes, past the Gate of Hercules, Trajan's Fountain, and the public baths, before reaching the Temple of Hadrian, which was built in the second century and

has been reconstructed from surviving fragments. Among the figures depicted on the reliefs here are Emperor Theodosius I and his wife and son.

Next come the Library of Celsus and, adjacent to it, a large arch leading into the lower agora, the ancient marketplace. To the left, on the northern side, are the remains of the Temple of Artemis, which was one of the Seven Wonders of the Ancient World until it was destroyed in 401 CE by St. John Chrysostom. Behind it, to the east, is the Great Theater, built to accommodate 25,000 people. It is the largest in the ancient world and was originally intended for drama, but it later became the site of gladiatorial contests. The tour ends at the top of Harbor Road, which leads down to Kusadasi Port on the Aegean Sea. **GL**

⬆ The facade of the Library of Celsus at Ephesus.

Gastronomy Route
Corum, Turkey

Start Iskilip   **End** Kargi   **Distance** 81 miles (130 km)   **Time** 7 days   **Grade** Easy to moderate   **Type** Hills, mountain trails   **Map** goo.gl/k1xE7n

The Kizilirmak River—at 847 miles (1,363 km) the longest waterway in Anatolia—was a trade route and a settlement magnet from the dawn of history. Today, the river is a source of hydroelectricity, and its basin area is promoted by the Turkish government as a holiday destination for ecotourists, especially those with an interest in the culinary traditions of a gastronomic crossroads, where the styles of Arabia fused with European traditions more than 3,000 years ago.

The route currently includes twenty-five marked hiking trails extending for 120 miles (193 km), together with numerous divergent alternative tracks that take the total to 190 miles (305 km). The recommended itinerary begins 100 miles (160 km) northeast of Ankara at Iskilip, a hilltop citadel and modern gastro-town. From here to the first suggested overnight stop at Ahmetçe it is only 4.5 miles (7 km), but the descent into the river valley is steep and the views worth taking time to savor.

Hikers walk twice as far on day two through part of the Aladağ (Crimson Mountains) to the village of Yalakyayla. The third night is spent in Sorkun at the end of a 7-mile (11-km) walk, and, after a typically Anatolian dinner there, the next day's path leads to Karayanik, a further 9 miles (14 km).

At the end of day five comes Kargi, and this holiday village will be the base for the next three days during which you can make circular tours of surrounding points of topographical interest and, above all—in view of the fact that this is a gastronomic excursion—sample the local cuisine, the highlights of which include rice; okra; and tulum peyniri, a crumbly goat's milk cheese. **GL**

"You can sample the delights of local traditional delicacies with strange-sounding names."

www.cultureroutesinturkey.com

⬆ The Gastronomy Route begins at the picturesque town of Iskilip in Turkey's Corum province.

Hittite Trail
Corum, Turkey

Start/End Various   **Distance** 241 miles (387 km)
Time 3–4 weeks   **Grade** Strenuous
Type Long-distance trail
Info goo.gl/OrbTXp

South of the city of Çorum, which is about 125 miles (200 km) northeast of Ankara in Turkey, is a network of connected trails that together make up the Hittite Trail, or Hittite Way. There is no particular start or end point, and you can do various combinations of the seventeen routes that together make up the trail. This is another fine example of the long-distance paths that have been created in recent years in Turkey, which combine the best of the country's wonderful landscapes and fascinating cultures, making them accessible to both hikers and cyclists.

The Hittites were an ancient people whose empire centered on Turkey, but spread throughout the Middle East and into North Africa. Their empire was at its peak in the mid-fourteenth century BCE, and their capital was at Hattuşa near modern-day Boğazkale, roughly 50 miles (80 km) southwest of Çorum. Many of the hiking trails explore both the Hittite and the Boğazkale national parks, as well as visiting significant Hittite archaeological sites. These naturally include Hattuşa, which, despite its historical importance and designation as a UNESCO World Heritage Site, is little visited in a part of Turkey that sees few foreigners.

Other sites that the trails take you to include Şapinuva and Alacahöyük, the burial site of Hittite kings and queens. The three main sites of Hattuşa, Şapinuva, and Alacahöyük form a triangle, and the hiking trails follow old trading routes that once connected these Hittite centers. The trails pass through woodland and agricultural landscapes in a quiet yet scenic part of the Turkish interior where you're likely to have only your own thoughts as company. **MG**

"The Anatolian Peninsula is a cultural mosaic, a synthesis of successive civilizations that left their mark on this land."

www.culureroutesinturkey.com

⤒ A long-distance trail that highlights the achievement of one of the world's lesser-known empires.

Geghard Monastery
Kotayk, Armenia

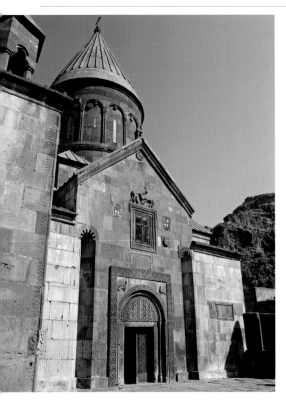

Start/End Garni   Distance 12 miles
(19.3 km)   Time 6 hours
Grade Easy   Type Stone paths
Map goo.gl/oBGYSV

Armenia holds a unique position in religious history as the first country in the world to become officially Christian, a feat it achieved in 301 CE, ten years before Emperor Galerius officially tolerated Christianity in the Roman Empire in 311. Armenia then occupied a very different and much extended territory to its current denuded size, squashed into the mountain ranges of the Lower Caucasus Mountains. The country has had a tumultuous, often violent history since, but it remains Christian to this day, a fact recalled by the inspiring Geghard Monastery in the center of the country.

St. Gregory the Illuminator—his title refers to his illuminating enlightenment, not his skills as an illustrator—is the patron saint and first official head of the Armenian church, as well as the man credited with converting Armenia to the new faith. At some time before his death in circa 331, he founded a monastery at the site of a scared spring inside a cave, hence its original name of Ayrivank, or "monastery of the cave." Its common name today, Geghardavank, "monastery of the spear," originates from the spear that wounded Christ at his crucifixion and was allegedly brought to Armenia by the Apostle Jude.

This extraordinary monastery sits among the towering cliffs of the Azat River gorge. The trail to the monastery, taking you 6 miles (9.3 km) out of the town of Garni, ends with a spectacular approach to the monastery along the gorge. The monastery buildings largely date to the 1200s, a series of churches, chapels, and rooms dug out of solid rock. And above the monastery are a series of ancient monastic caves—more lures for the compulsive hiker on a day of discovery in Ancient Armenia. **SA**

"A number of churches and tombs, most of them cut into the rock … illustrate the very peak of Armenian medieval architecture."

whc.unesco.org

⬆ Geghard Monastery is a monumental testament to faith in the world's first official Christian nation.

Painted Churches of Troodos

Nicosia, Cyprus

Start Kalopanagiotis   **End** Pedoulas
Distance 91 miles (146 km)   **Time** 6–7 days
Grade Moderate   **Type** Mountain trail
Map goo.gl/qLH7OY

In the simple stone and wooden churches of the Troodos Mountains, Byzantine Christs of the highest artistic order peer down from multidomed apses, their arms spread wide; below them, elongated saints with golden haloes and red and blue robes fill every inch of the walls. Such figures are the fruit of a cultural flowering in Cyprus that lasted from the eleventh century until the Italo-Byzantine period in the sixteenth century. The wall paintings are all the more exquisite for the buildings' rustic exteriors.

UNESCO has identified ten churches and monasteries of outstanding universal value in three areas of the Troodos—Solea, Marathasa, and Pitsillia. They can all be visited by road, sometimes with a short hike across a meadow, but the best way to see them is to follow one of three designated trails. Each area has its appeal, but for scenery and culture head for Marathasa in April when the cherry trees are in blossom. The trail begins at the Monastery of Agios Ioannis Lampadistis in Kalopanagiotis, which spans the palimpsest of Troodos art and then picks its way alongside streams and over little stone bridges to the chapel of Panagia (Our Lady) Moutoulla, a single-aisle basilica containing thirteenth-century frescoes in the Crusader style. The last stop is the fifteenth-century Church of Archangelos Michael in Pedoulas. Among the host of evangelists, virgins, and saints is a painting of the chapel's benefactor and his wife offering a model of the church to Archangel Michael.

Highlights on the other trails include the Agios Nikolaos tis Stegis in Kakopetria, in which the richly colored lining of New Testament characters represents 600 years of Byzantine art. **DS**

"The complex … all richly decorated with murals, provides an overview of Byzantine and post-Byzantine painting."

whc.unesco.org

⊡ The frescoes in the Troodos churches testify to an artistic renaissance in the eleventh century.

Marrakech Medina
Marrakech, Morocco

Start/End Jemaa el-Fna
Distance 3 miles (4.8 km)   **Time** 6 hours
Grade Easy   **Type** Roads and alleys
Map goo.gl/RcZZSu

The name alone is enough to conjure up the excitement of this ancient city, for a long time a stop-off on the 1960s hippie trail but today a destination for every serious traveler. Marrakech is, in one word, overwhelming: a visual and aural feast to be totally immersed in. The city was founded by the Almoravid rulers of Morocco in 1062 and was surrounded by the red sandstone walls that gave it the nickname of the "Red" or "Ochre City." The city has now spread well outside these walls, but the ancient medina, or town, that lies within contains enough sights for a lifetime.

"Koutoubia Mosque … is one of the important landmarks of the urban landscape."

whc.unesco.org

Quite where to start is debatable, but a good choice is the central Jemaa el-Fna square, said to be Africa's busiest. Here is the tumult of a city going about its daily business of buying and selling goods. In the evening, dancers, storytellers, magicians, musicians, and traditional healers take over. Food stalls appear to satisfy the massive crowd. North of the square are the souks, the traditional markets laid out in a honeycomb of narrow alleys that sell fresh fruit, foodstuffs, spices, rugs, lanterns, belts, bags, and bells. You can even buy an alligator skin if so inclined. Haggling here is essential, and if this city does get too overpowering, a walk around its perimeter wall provides a welcome perspective on the clamor below. **SA**

Berber Migration Route Tadla-Azilal/Souss-Massa-Draa, Morocco

Start Tamada, High Atlas   **End** Ait Youl,
Dadès Gorge   **Distance** 30 miles
(48 km)   **Time** 6 days   **Grade** Moderate
Type Mountain tracks   **Map** goo.gl/T2Y8IU

Twice a year, the nomadic Berber people of Morocco pack up their tents and other belongings; gather up their goats, sheep, donkeys, and camels; and move home. In spring, they head up the Atlas Mountains to feed their animals on the higher pastures, so as to avoid the summer heat. In fall, they head back down the mountains again to the lower slopes, which will be warmer during the coming winter months. These Berbers follow traditional routes that have been used for more than 4,000 years, a history of nomadic travel that is now under threat from reduced rainfall and an increasingly settled lifestyle. To make this biannual migration pay, some Berber families now take groups of tourists with them.

Each Berber family has its own route, but a popular route is the fall trek from the High Atlas village of Tamada down to Ait Youl in the Dadès Gorge to the southeast. The reverse trek in the spring is only for the strong-legged. The pace is leisurely, as one can only walk as fast as the slowest sheep, and the descent mainly gradual. All around is the most beautiful scenery, the majestic High Atlas towering up above to more than 13,120 feet (4,000 m).

The route snakes through mountain passes, over green meadows, and along winding paths that cling to the mountainside. Tucked into the valleys are ancient villages inhabited by more settled Berbers. Each night is spent in a rustic Berber tent, with some fine Berber cooking to enjoy as well. Fresh mint tea will fortify you as you hike during the day. The trek ends in the rocky Dadès Gorge, a green slit in the mountains covered with fig, almond, walnut, and poplar trees. **SA**

Leptis Magna
Al-Khums, Libya

Start/End Visitor center
Distance 2 miles (3.2 km)   **Time** 3 hours
Grade Easy   **Type** Stone and earthen paths
Map goo.gl/mrU92Z

One might suppose that the place to go to see well-preserved Roman remains would be in, well, Rome. But no, for some of the best remains are to be found across the Mediterranean Sea in Libya. There, in the modern-day town of Al-Khums, 81 miles (130 km) east of the Libyan capital, Tripoli, sits one of the most spectacular and unspoiled Roman cities of all.

Leptis Magna was founded by the local Berbers in around 1000 BCE, when it was known as Lpqy. It became part of the mighty Carthaginian Empire during the 300s BCE, until it fell to the Romans at the end of their Third Punic War with Carthage in 146 BCE. Under Roman rule it prospered as a trading center and port but sprung to prominence when, in 193 CE, a local Berber became emperor as Septimius Severus.

The ruins of this magical city are extensive, and absolutely deserve to be visited. A good place to start a walk here is beneath the Arch of Septimius Severus, built in 203 CE. Continue on along the paved road to the Plastra, a courtyard built alongside the Hadrian Baths, constructed in 126–27 CE. Make your way to the Old Forum (c. 300 BCE) and the Basilica, and from there to the Phoenician-built market area. Leaving the market, you then walk through an old residential area, under the arches of Trajan and Tiberius, and on into the Theater, built in the first century CE and restored under Emperor Augustus in the second century; it is large enough to seat 5,000 people.

A kilometer or so from the Theatre, and a nice walk away from the city's heart, lies the wonderful ampitheatre, built around 56 CE in a depression—or perhaps a quarry for the city's stones—alongside the deep, deep blue of the Mediterranean Sea. **SA**

"Leptis Magna is a unique artistic realization in the domain of urban planning."

whc.unesco.org

⤒ Leptis Magna was the second city of the Roman province of Africa, second only to Carthage.

Valley of the Kings
Luxor, Egypt

Start/End Ticket office, Valley of the Kings
Distance 2 miles (3.2 km)   Time 3 hours
Grade Easy to moderate   Type Earthen and
stone paths   Map goo.gl/XIhVlH

Egyptian royal protocol required that its pharaohs and powerful nobles be buried on the western side of the River Nile, nearer to the setting sun. As Thebes (now Luxor) was the most important Egyptian city of its time, and home to the eighteenth dynasty of pharaohs, the great and the good of ancient Egypt from the sixteenth to the eleventh centuries BCE were all buried across the river in two wadis or dry riverbeds, up in the hills that form the Valley of the Kings. Their wives and princesses were buried in the nearby Valley of the Queens. To date, sixty-five tombs and chambers have been discovered in the Valley of the Kings, ranging in size from simple pits to massive complexes containing more than 120 chambers.

Everyone will know of at least one dead pharaoh buried here, but in reality Tutankhamun was a minor pharaoh and his tomb dull in comparison to his illustrious relatives. However, his was the last, almost intact royal tomb, to be discovered, so do drop in if it is open. Most of the tombs in the valley are not open to the public, and although eighteen are accessible, they rarely open at the same time. Admission to the valley gives you access to three tombs, with more tickets to see Tutankhamun and Rameses VI. Mass tourism is hugely damaging to the tombs and their wall paintings, which is why photography in the tombs is forbidden, tour guides can no longer lecture in the tombs, and visitors must move along quickly in single file when passing through a tomb. But ignore the crowds, catch a quiet moment, and just wonder at the civilization that created this city of the dead. **SA**

◁ Some of the area's magnificent bare rockscapes.

Elephantine Island
Aswan, Egypt

Start/End On the island
Distance 2 miles (3.2 km)   Time 3 hours
Grade Easy   Type Tarmac roads, earth paths
Map goo.gl/qohOu9

If truth be told, this walk is one of the easiest. A doddle, once you have gotten yourself there. Elephantine Island is a 3,900-foot-long (1,200 m) and 1,300-foot-wide (400 m), largely flat island in the Nile by Aswan, the main city of southern Egypt. It was likely named because the rocks around its banks resemble elephants or because it was once a trading center for ivory. In any case, the island is now elephant-free, and you are strolling its easy length for its history not its wildlife.

Elephantine Island once contained a fort that marked the southern border of Egypt. Beyond it were

"Elephantine Island [has] wonderful gardens and some truly significant artifacts."

www.touregypt.net

the first impassable cataracts of the Nile, guarded by Khnum, the ram-headed god of the cataracts, who guarded and controlled the river waters from his cave below the island. The ancient Egyptians worshiped Khnum in an island trilogy alongside Satis, the war goddess, and their daughter, Anuket, who personified the annual flood. A temple to Khnum survives, along with other ancient temples and structures, as do two Nilometers standing in the river's flow, which measure the water level during the annual flood. In human terms, the island is home to a sizable Nubian population and once boasted a House of Yaweh, a temple built by the island's Jewish community during the sixth century BCE. **SA**

Djenné
Mopti, Mali

Start/End The Great Mosque
Distance 4 miles (6.4 km)   Time 3 hours
Grade Easy   Type Earthen roads
Map goo.gl/CpbfJo

From the 1300s until the 1600s, the city of Djenné was one of the most prosperous trading towns in Africa. Situated on the floodplain between the Niger and Bani rivers, at the southern end of the inland Niger Delta, the town prospered from the trans-Sahara trade in gold, salt, and slaves that passed north up to Timbuktu and then across the desert to North Africa and the Middle East. As Timbuktu flourished, so too did Djenné. The town became a center of Islamic learning and scholarship, only declining when the Portuguese started to steal its trade through their trading posts on the coast to the south.

What distinguishes Djenné is its architecture—2,000 buildings made out of that most humble of materials: mud. These adobe bricks are made from mud from the riverbank mixed with chopped straw; they are then packed into wooden molds and left out to dry in the sun. The walls of bricks are held together with mortar and then covered with a protective layer of mixed earth and rice husks. Bundles of palm sticks, known as *toron*, project from the walls and serve as scaffolding to help builders repair the walls after the annual summer rains. Most buildings are completely replastered every other year. The greatest of these mud-brick buildings, the Great Mosque, was built in 1907, and it remains one of the great achievements of Sudano-Sahelian architecture. Around it, clusters of mud-brick buildings are built on hillocks (*toguere*), and their irregular layout, following the contours of the land, make for plenty of serpentine trails. Finding a guide will enhance the experience, and the people are friendly as you walk through the town square and the bustling market of this compact city of mud. **SA**

"The property is characterized by the intensive and remarkable use of earth specifically in its architecture."

whc.unesco.org

⤴ Walk past historic architecture such as the mosque at Djenné—the largest mud structure in the world.

Royal Palaces of Abomey

Zou, Benin

Start/End RNIE4   Distance 2 miles
(3.2 km)   Time 3 hours
Grade Easy   Type Earth paths
Map goo.gl/pGTvJ3

Between around 1600 and 1894, when the region was colonized by France, the kingdom of Dahomey was one of the major trading states of West Africa. Its main export was slaves, supplying one-fifth of all the slaves sold to European traders for shipment across the Middle Passage to the Americas. It was also a military powerhouse, renowned for its core of female soldiers, known as the Dahomey Amazons. The nineteenth-century British explorer Richard Burton remarked on their "masculine physique … enabling them to compete with men in enduring toil, hardship, and privations." The modern state of Benin, successor to Dahomey, no longer trades slaves and is defended by men, but the royal palaces of its former rulers in Abomey form a UNESCO World Heritage Site of great interest.

King Houegbadja, who ruled from around 1645 to 1685, first settled his roving, tribal kingdom on the Abomey plateau, founded its capital city, and built himself a royal palace. Each of his eleven successors built their own palace, creating a vast compound that now spreads over 99 acres (40 ha) in the center of Abomey. The palaces at Abomey are among West Africa's most historically significant traditional sites, and a guided walking tour here will take around an hour. It includes a visit to two of the palaces, those of kings Glélé and Guézo (both palaces are part of the Historical Museum of Abomey), as well as various outbuildings, one of which was constructed using the blood and ground-up bones of enemies of the Abomey kingdom. Walking through the site is an evocative experience and offers a rare insight into a lost West African kingdom that lasted, ruled by twelve monarchs, for almost 300 years. **SA**

Fugitives' Trail

KwaZulu-Natal, South Africa

Start Isandlwana Hill   End Buffalo River
Distance 5 miles (8 km)   Time 3 hours
Grade Moderate   Type Grasslands
Map goo.gl/f4m6GA

In order to federate the independent African kingdoms, as well as the two Boer states and tribal areas, into a British-led South Africa, the British authorities in Cape Colony issued an ultimatum to the Zulu king, Cetshwayo, to disband his army and accept a British resident or controller in his kingdom. Knowing he could not comply with this threat to his independence, the British declared war and in January 1879 invaded his kingdom. A column of British troops made camp near Isandlwana Hill. Unbeknown to them, a 20,000-strong Zulu army tracked the force and swept down the hill toward its

"Beautiful scenery made poignant by the whitewashed rocks that mark the graves of those who died."

www.walkopedia.net

camp, catching the British unawares. Only 200 British soldiers out of around 1,700 survived what was one of the worst-ever disasters for the British army. Those who survived the carnage made their way across country to the Buffalo River and into British-controlled Natal. This trek to safety is commemorated in this trail.

The trail starts at the imposing rock of Isandlwana Hill and heads west through the grassy plain down a long slope. After crossing a stream, the trail climbs up a rough hillside and crosses a hilltop before coming to a halt at the edge of a cliff. Down below at the end of the trail is the drift or ford where the desperate survivors tried to swim the fast-flowing Buffalo River while they were picked off by the Zulus lining its eastern bank. **SA**

Beirut Heritage Trail
Beirut, Lebanon

Start Beirut Souks   **End** "Tell" archaeological area   **Distance** 1.5 miles (2.4 km)   **Time** 1 hour   **Grade** Easy   **Type** Sidewalk   **Map** goo.gl/1umnOK

Beirut is a city of many layers—layers of history built one after the other upon the crumbling remains of its predecessors stretching back more than 5,000 years. The Beirut Heritage Trail, a project by the Lebanese joint-stock company Solidere in partnership with the Ministry of Culture, is an attempt to link various archaeological sites, heritage buildings, and public spaces on a 1.5-mile (2.5-km) circuit through the historic heart of the city. With more than 300 buildings now restored and the chaos of the 1975–90 civil war an increasingly distant memory, the Beirut Heritage Trail makes use of historic maps, old photographs, bronze medallions set into its sidewalks, and more than fifty stone panels to guide visitors through the tumultuous history of this proud city.

The trail begins at the Beirut Souks, which still follows its 2,500-year-old street grid, and takes you through the heart of the Phoenico–Persian quarter and along the city wall and its moat, past the Emir Munzer mosque, 2,000-year-old Roman baths, and the Riad El Solh Square. You will be able to touch Crusader stones embedded in Ottoman fortifications and even the remains of an ancient Canaanite wall. When the French came here and transformed Beirut into the "Paris of the East," they placed ancient Roman columns on either side of their entry doors.

Whereas elsewhere the phrase "heritage trails" might conjure up little more than corny linguistics and docents in period dress, there is nothing of that here. Beirut has no need to create any artificial histories. What it has hidden in the layers beneath its pavements and in the restored buildings above them is history enough for a dozen docent-laden sites. **BDS**

"Reveals the story of 5,000 years of history and takes the visitor through a historic journey of the key sites and monuments."

www.solidere.com

⬆ A city in the midst of one of the world's largest urban renewal projects has not forgotten its roots.

Jerusalem Ramparts Walk

Jerusalem

Start/End Jaffa Gate
Distance 2.5 miles (4 km)
Time 2 hours **Grade** Easy
Type Stone ramparts **Map** goo.gl/c9zmbS

If you want to get a feel for walking the streets of the Old City of Jerusalem, but don't like the idea of becoming lost in its labyrinth of alleyways, the Jerusalem Ramparts Walk offers the best of both worlds. The city walls were restored by Suleiman the Magnificent in the sixteenth century and for hundreds of years after they served as the city's primary fortifications. For a small fee you can climb above the clamor and onto these ancient walls and not only see the city below, but also peek voyeuristically into places you'd never notice from the street, such as the cloistered Armenian compound, with the added thrill of gazing over the walls to the many beautiful areas that surround this timeless city.

It isn't possible to circumnavigate the entire Old City in one go, as access to the ramparts surrounding the Temple Mount is not possible and a road interrupts the wall at the Jaffa Gate. However, the Jaffa Gate is a great place to start; it leads to Zion Gate and from there to Dung Gate close by the Jewish quarter, with its views over the Sultan's Pool, Mount Zion, and the Mount of Olives. In the Muslim quarter, as you make your way toward the Temple Mount from Damascus Gate, you can peer inside the courtyards of Muslim homes.

From the Citadel that was built by the Crusaders in the Middle Ages, you can see what was once a moat that surrounded King Herod's palace. If you know where to look, you can also spot the City of David excavations and even the ruins of fourth- and fifth-century Byzantine cisterns on a fascinating walk that takes you through 2,000 years of tumultuous, world-changing events. **BDS**

Masada Snake Path

Southern, Israel

Start/End Snake Path trailhead
Distance 1.2 miles (1.9 km) **Time** 1–1.5 hours
Grade Moderate **Type** Rock, dirt path
Map goo.gl/eOXmB5

Few places in Israel have such a hold on the nation's consciousness and as glorious a place in its history as Masada, a rocky plateau near the western shores of the Dead Sea. Its Hebrew name means "fortress," and there in 73 CE a group of Jewish zealots called the Kanai finally fell after having held out on their fortress-like mountaintop against Roman occupation for seven years. The Romans were forced to build an earthen ramp to Masada's summit in order to breach its defenses, but when they broke through, however, they found only corpses. Rather than be captured and

---

"Masada is one of Israel's most popular, iconic, and impressive sites, and one which has a great story."

www.touristisrael.com

---

either killed or forced to live as slaves, the zealots had instead chosen to take their own lives. Their story endures today as one of defiance against all odds, despite no evidence of a mass suicide ever being uncovered by archaeologists.

Masada is a UNESCO World Heritage Site, you can get to the top via the famous Snake Path. The path weaves up Masada's slopes from its trailhead in a series of switchbacks, and once you scramble onto the plateau, the views across the Dead Sea and to the Moab Mountains in neighboring Jordan make it well worth the climb. You can explore the extensive ruins, including thermal baths, a synagogue, and the remains of King Herod's tiered palace. **BDS**

Petra Trails

Ma'an, Jordan

Start/End The Siq **Distance** Various
Time Various **Grade** Easy to moderate
Type Dirt, rock trails
Info goo.gl/CW9Hpe

One of the world's great archaeological and anthropological treasures, the ancient city of Petra on the slopes of Jebel al-Madhbah in southern Jordan is the country's most-visited tourist attraction. Unknown to the Western world until 1812, its remains are nestled among sandstone pinnacles and cliffs that glow orange in the afternoon sun. Established in the fourth century BCE by the Nabateans, a nomadic people from southern Arabia of which even now little is known, Petra lies in a valley that runs south from the Dead Sea to the Gulf of Aqaba and it has been a UNESCO World Heritage Site since 1985. For hundreds of years it flourished as a trading center, thanks largely to an ingenious system of cisterns and aqueducts that captured and funneled water throughout its vast assemblage of buildings and public spaces.

There are a multitude of walks you can do here, from one-hour strolls to multiday treks. Must-sees include the Siq and city center, and a tough slog to the "High Places" of Jebel umm al'Amr with its sequence of unforgettable views over the treasury and the royal tombs. Longer walks include the Al Deir Monastery Circuit, Little Petra to Petra via the Three Valleys, and the six to seven-hour walk to the top of 4,429-foot-tall (1,350-m) Jebel Haroun where, tradition says, Aaron the brother of Moses lies buried in its white mountaintop shrine. Walks farther afield include a two-day return trip through the beautiful Wadi Tibn siq to the Roman theater at Sabra, and a climb up to the remains of an Iron Age settlement on Umm al-Biyara, an energy-sapping three-hour ascent southwest of a city so vast that no single walk can begin to make sense of its astonishing complexities. **BDS**

"Petra, the world wonder, is without a doubt Jordan's most valuable treasure and greatest tourist attraction."

www.visitjordan.com

⬅ The siq is the evocative entrance to the age-old city.

⬆ Even in a desert, Petra's aqueducts carried 12 million gallons (54 million liters) of fresh water a day.

Ancient Samarra

Salah Al-Din, Iraq

Start/End Khatib Street, Samarra
Distance 5 miles (8 km)   Time 4 hours
Grade Easy   Type Beaten earth paths
Map goo.gl/u6O9Ni

The ancient city of Samarra lies 78 miles (125 km) north of the Iraqi capital of Baghdad, on the banks of the Tigris River. The city was founded in 836 CE, when the Sunni Abbasid Caliph al-Mu'tasim moved his capital here from Baghdad. He built lavish palaces surrounded by garrisons of guards to protect him, as did his successors. The most important building, the Great Mosque, with its spiral minaret, was erected in 847, but the city declined when Caliph al-Mu'tadid returned to Baghdad in 892. As the Abbasid Empire fell apart, the city was abandoned in 940, its ruins

> "The city's artistic, literary, and scientific splendors have remained a legend in Arab history."

www.atlastours.net

the only large city of late antiquity that are available for archaeological study.

The city is a major Shia shrine, famous for the al-Askari Mosque, which contains the mausoleums of the tenth and eleventh Shia imams, and its neighboring mosque built on the site where the twelfth, or hidden, imam underwent an occultation, or disappearance. Religious differences between Sunni and Shia Muslims have created tensions in Samarra; the Shia mosques remain closed after bomb attacks in 2006 and 2007. However, it is possible to wander around the ruined city in safety. What is visible is the only surviving Islamic capital city that retains its original street plan and architecture. **SA**

Ruins of Persepolis

Fars, Iran

Start/End Persepolis
Distance 3 miles (4.8 km), not including Naqsh-e Rostam
detour   Time 1 day   Grade Easy   Type Stone paths
Map goo.gl/JLjfU3

Their very names speak to us across the centuries: Cyrus the Great, founder of the Achaemenid, or Persian Empire, which straddled the Middle East during his reign from 559 to 530 BCE; and Darius I or the Great, in whose reign from 522 to 486 BCE, the empire was at its peak, stretching from the borders of India in the east to Egypt, Libya, and the Balkans in the west. It was Cyrus who chose the site of his new ceremonial capital at Persepolis in what is now southern Iran, and Darius who built the terrace and its great palaces, the ruins of which are still visible today.

A broad stairway approaches the terrace from the west, its 111 shallow steps allowing visiting dignitaries to maintain their composure while ascending. A number of vast stone buildings, all made of dark gray marble, stand on the terrace; they are in surprisingly good shape, considering that the city, sacked by Alexander the Great in 330 BCE, gradually fell into disuse. The city, a glorious symbol of the Achaemenid dynasty, radiates out in all directions from the Hall of 100 Columns atop the Persepolis Terrace, which is a good spot to get your bearings. From there you can see all of the primary sites: the Gate of All Nations; the Council Hall; the Apadana Palace, the site's most magnificent structure used for official audiences; and the remains of Tachara, Darius I's ceremonial palace. Everywhere you go, you will pass capitals, columns, and friezes depicting Persians, Medes, ordinary soldiers, and images of horses, bulls, and lions. A few kilometers away is Naqsh-e Rostam and the tomb of Darius I; the walk from Persepolis is both easy and essential. Anything less than a day spent here would be an absolute travesty of time management. **SA**

Frankincense Route
Dhofar, Oman

Start/End Al-Balid, Oman
Distance Various **Time** Various
Grade Easy **Type** Unmarked desert trails
Info goo.gl/eaG55G

Frankincense, once valued more highly than gold, was first traded more than 5,000 years ago along the historic Frankincense Trail—an ancient trading route of caravan oasis and trading points. The rather epic trade route—which caused entire civilizations to emerge from the desert—stretched from southern Oman, through Yemen, up to coastal ports and out to sea. The elusive and little written about tourist trail in southern Oman, however, covers only a few sites dotted around Dhofar's capital, Salalah.

Salalah was also founded on frankincense, and its modern-day markets are still alive with its heady scents, while its terrain remains covered in the valuable, but rather modest-looking, boswellia sacra tree from which the aromatic resin is gathered. To explore the camel train of sites in the region, head to the port of Khor Rori, which lies 25 miles (40 km) to the east of Salalah. The port, once used by traders, was reclaimed by the sea but, after significant excavations, the ruins are again visible today. Al-Balid is an elevated site that extends along the coast with a history of being attacked and partially destroyed by both Arab rulers and Persian traders. It's now a barren landscape dotted with ruins. Then along a flat wadi bed you find the Frankincense Park of Wadi Dawkah, a UNESCO World Heritage Site, which boasts a large area of mature frankincense trees. This concentrated trail is magical and really immerses you in the history of the region. Go in the summer monsoon season from June to September, when the countryside is green and you'll travel past lush papaya, banana, and coconut plantations, which give the region a delightfully tropical air. **NE**

"The frankincense trees ... vividly illustrate the trade in frankincense that flourished in this region for many centuries."

whc.unesco.org

⭱ The trail is a collection of isolated groves near wadis and plateaus that impart a sense of discovery.

Mohenjodaro Archaeological Ruins Sindh, Pakistan

Start/End Mohenjodaro   **Distance** 2 miles (3.2 km)   **Time** 3 hours   **Grade** Easy
Type Earthen paths   **Map** goo.gl/OX5P4w

Ancient documents from the kings of Ur that date to around 2110 BCE refer to a thriving trade between the region and Meluhah. It is likely that this is the vast civilization of the Indus Valley established around the twin cities of Mohenjodaro and Harrapa to its northeast. This flourishing civilization began in around 2600 BCE and soon developed a lively trade with Mesopotamia: one shipment contained 13,007 pounds (5,900 kg) of copper for export to the Middle East. The two main towns had populations of around 40,000 each, making them the largest cities in the world at that time. Their walls were built of mud bricks and included a citadel with public buildings, granaries, streets laid in a grid pattern, and an impressive underground drainage and sewage system. Its people were literate, but its pictographic script has yet to be deciphered.

Mohenjodaro is the modern name for the town and means "mound of the dead" in Sindhi. Its original name is unknown, but a seal discovered at the site suggests it might have been called "Kukkutarma" (city of the cockerel). The ruins lay undiscovered until an officer of the Archaeological Survey of India found them in 1922. There are no temples, palaces, or monuments here, and little evidence of a royal seat or even a bureaucracy. Nor was the 250-acre (100-ha) town heavily fortified. What you will see, however, as you walk over the mounds of the site is abundant evidence of a very ordered urban environment with stupas, public baths, and countless crumbling walls that, while eroded, provide a fascinating glimpse into the ancient civilizations of the Indus Valley. **SA**

⬆ One of the world's premier archaeological sites.

Ajanta Caves Maharashtra, India

Start Cave #1 **End** Cave #13 **Distance** 1 mile (0.6 km) **Time** 3–4 hours **Grade** Easy
Type Sealed pathways **Info** goo.gl/6InTkc

This UNESCO World Heritage Site consists of up to thirty caves (some are not completed) cut into a horseshoe bend of volcanic lava rock in the forest ravines of the Sahyadri Hills. Each of the caves offers cultural riches in the form of Buddhist architecture and features some of the finest surviving examples of Indian art.

The reclining Buddha in cave twenty-six is a tourist favorite, but, really, your eyes have plenty to take in from the start. The exclusively Buddhist-themed paintings are extraordinarily detailed and vibrant—the colors veer from red and yellow ocher to lime and bright blue. Even the ceilings didn't escape the attention of the monk's skilled hands and are covered with geometric and floral decorations. Now accessible by a modern path running alongside, connecting the caves, each cave was reached originally by its own stairs or ladders leading up from the Waghora River, 35 to 110 feet (10.5–33 m) below.

Depending on the time of year, the caves—made up of *chaitya grihas* (monument halls) and *viharas* (monastic halls of residence)—run through either heavy, lush, green vegetation or an arid, brown landscape. The benefits of each depend on where you rank picture-perfect holiday snaps versus coping with heavy rains. Visiting toward the end of the monsoon season, which runs from June to September, will reward with a full river, running waterfalls—do take the walk to view them—and plenty of greenery, plus, you'll be avoiding the oppressive heat of March to May. Locals offer rudimentary sedan chair rides, if you fancy avoiding the walk up to the caves. **NE**

⌂ Ajanta is a precious arc of caves and art.

Great Wall of China
Hebei, China

Start Jinshanling **End** Simatai
Distance 6.5 miles (10.5 km)
Time 5 hours **Grade** Easy
Type Stone paths **Map** goo.gl/yktQr6

It is a great mistake to talk about the Great Wall of China as if there is only one. In fact, the Great Wall consists of a series of stone walls, earthen ramparts, natural ditches, ridges, and cliffs that stretch across northern China, often running parallel or at right angles to each other. Historians disagree about their total length, but one recent survey has estimated them to stretch for 13,170 miles (21,196 km), which is about five times as long as the United States is wide. The walls might be long, but they are only as wide as a narrow country lane.

The first walls were built in northern China during the Zhou dynasty and Warring States period of 770 to 221 BCE to keep out hostile nomads living to the north. These walls were then linked and strengthened by the first emperor of China, Qin Shi Huangdi, between 221 and 210 BCE and then extended and added to in later years. During the Ming dynasty of 1368 to 1644, the eastern end of the wall was largely rebuilt in stone and brick, and it is this wall that we are familiar with today and along which you will be walking.

International tour companies offer different sections of the wall to walk along, but one of the most popular is the Jinshanling section in the mountainous Luanping County, 77 miles (125 km) northeast of Beijing, which was rebuilt in around 1570. Highlights along this stretch, which snakes along the top of the hills from east to west, include sixty-seven towers and two beacon towers. For those whose legs have failed them, a cable car is available for the final ascent to the highest point. **SA**

← The oldest sections date to the seventh century BCE.

Potala Palace
Tibet, China

Start/End Lhasa **Distance** 2 miles (3.2 km) **Time** 3 hours **Grade** Easy
Type Stone staircases and corridors
Map goo.gl/aSY1JI

According to Buddhist myth, the *bodhisattva* or enlightened being Avalokiteśvara lived on Mount Potalaka, which was somewhere in the seas south of India. The mountain is first mentioned in the Avatamsaka, or Flower Garland Sutra, of the late third century CE, in which the protagonist journeys to the mountain to seek advice from the *bodhisattva*. It is from this mountain that the Potala Palace in Lhasa, capital of Tibet, gets its name. The palace is one of the most recognizable buildings in the world, a whitewashed structure with rows of windows standing

> *"Potala Palace is composed of two parts, the Red Palace as the center and the White Palace as two wings."*
>
> www.travelchinaguide.com

on top of the Red Hill, 1,000 feet (305 m) above the valley. At its center is the Red Palace, which is completely devoted to Buddhist religious study and prayer. The entire palace is vast, measuring 750 feet (400 m) from east to west and 650 feet (350 m) from north to south. Its thirteen stories contain more than 1,000 rooms, 10,000 Buddhist shrines, and about 200,000 statues.

To book a guide for an exploration of the corridors of the Potala Palace, you must bring your passport to the southwest exit at least a day beforehand. The tours are free, but be sure to arrive half an hour before your tour starts. A circumnavigation of the great monastery will take about an hour. **SA**

Yungang Grottoes Shanxi, China

Start/End Yungang Grottoes ticket office   **Distance** 0.6 mile (1 km)   **Time** 4–5 hours   **Grade** Easy
Type Modern walkway   **Info** goo.gl/6q5jIu

"Not to be missed," "a must-see," and "out of this world" are just some of the words visitors to China's Yungang Grottoes use to describe the sight of these fifty-three breathtaking human-made grottoes—including around 1,000 niches—carved out of sandstone cliffs on the southern foot of the Wuzhou Mountains in the Shi Li River Valley. A fabulous example of rock-cut architecture and one of three major Buddhist cave clusters in China consisting of more than 51,000 stone statues, the Yungang Grottoes illustrate the power of Buddhist belief in China. Representing a fusion of religious symbolic art and Chinese cultural traditions, it became a UNESCO World Heritage Site in 2011.

A monk named Tan Yao is believed to have orchestrated the creation of the grottoes and, with the help of more than 40,000 Buddhists, it reportedly took only fifty years to complete. The caves are divided into three areas: east, middle, and west, and the grottoes are numbered from east to west. The eastern area predominantly consists of pagodas (Buddhist temples), the center section is made up of front and rear chambers containing Buddha statues—a colossal 55-foot-high (17 m) Buddha is located in grotto number 5—while the western section houses the majority of the grottoes.

Aside from the grottoes, the area includes the remains of a castle and a defense wall; the plain above the grottoes also features a beacon tower from the Ming dynasty. A short 10-mile (16-km) drive from downtown Datong, the grottoes afford tourists a trip back in time to around 453 CE, without a difficult trek, and the walkways are flat and well maintained. **NE**

⬆ The grottoes are the zenith of Chinese Buddhist art.

Hongcun and Xidi Ancient Villages Anhui, China

Start Hongcun   **End** Xidi   **Distance** 2 miles (3.2 km)   **Time** 3 hours   **Grade** Easy
Type Cobblestones   **Map** goo.gl/TxkML9

The pace of change in modern China is rapid beyond belief. Skyscrapers now dominate the old cities, new towns spring up almost overnight, traffic clogs up the roads, and pollution fills the skies. Everything is developing at full speed as China hurtles through the twenty-first century. It is thus a relief to know that one small corner of China has remained unaffected by this rapid change. The villages of Hongcun and Xidi in Anhui province in eastern China are both relics of an ancient way of life. Unsurprisingly, they have been made UNESCO World Heritage Sites. If you feel you are walking through familiar territory, it is because Hongcun features in the background of several scenes in the movie *Crouching Tiger, Hidden Dragon* (2000).

The two villages were founded in the 1000s and flourished during the Ming dynasty of 1368 to 1644 as centers of local trade. Wealthy merchants and government officials built houses here, establishing villages that have remained unchanged in their architecture and street plans to the present day. Xidi is surrounded by mountains and built along three streams, while Hongcun is located at the foot of a hill next to two pools, Yuezhaon Pond and South Lake. Their buildings are made of wood, painted in plain colors, and adorned with decorated gables. Elegant carvings of Chinese mythology and scenes from nature, some gilded in gold, decorate the wooden beams and wall panels. Canals bring water to the front of each house. Both villages are a delight to wander around, their narrow cobbled streets a maze in which it is a pleasure to get lost. A short bus ride will take you the 11 miles (16 km) between the two villages. **SA**

⬆ The ancient village of Xidi is defying modernization.

Neng Gao Historic Trail
Nantou/Hualien, Taiwan

Start/End Tunyuan trailhead
Distance 24 miles (38.6 km)   **Time** 2–3 days
Grade Moderate   **Type** Well-maintained forest paths
Map goo.gl/wi7Be4

"The Neng Gao Historic Trail is Taiwan's most internationally known historic trail."

www.taiwan-panorama.com

⬆ A high-altitude walk in Taiwan's rugged central mountain range is a sensory tour de force.

Cut through the mountains 200 years ago by the local Ata-yal and See-diq people as a way of traversing the country's Central Mountain Range between Puli and Hualien, the Neng Gao Historic Trail was expanded and garrisoned by the Japanese during their occupation of the island in World War II. It was later further improved by the Taipower Company in the 1950s, who used it as the preferred route for the construction of their main east–west transmission lines. Today, this trail gives access to the nation's "spine," the mountains that run in a north–south direction through the island's heart. Despite its course through the mountains, the hike is a relatively easy one, with a long, though gradual, ascent, and with information boards along the way, describing its history as well as the surrounding flora and fauna. There is some shale and slate to negotiate at the beginning of the trail, and a few wooden suspension bridges (a limit of five people at any one time applies) to cross, as well as boardwalks past stands of red pine and hemlock. Landslides are not uncommon here, nor are frequent mists and fogs.

This is a hike, though, where the views up close are spectacular, with three-tiered waterfalls and dramatic walks over shale-strewn mountain slopes guaranteed to keep the adrenaline flowing. A series of huts and campgrounds provides the option of bunk beds or tents, a welcome choice in a region where the weather can go from clear to miserable in the blink of an eye. The goal is a climb to the Qi-laili South Peak (10,849 feet/3,307 m) with its (hoped for) views over the Central Mountains, while keeping an eye out for the trail's famed giant earthworms. **BDS**

Basho Walk
Tokyo to Kyoto, Japan

Start Kokufu-Tagajo   End Kanazawa
Distance 46 miles (74 km), involves bus/train
connects   Time 10 days   Grade Easy   Type Forest
paths, mountain trails   Map goo.gl/6cqgU5

Born the son of a samurai in 1644 in Honshu's mountainous Iga Province, Matsuo Basho began writing poetry as a child, and in 1674, was accepted into the haiku profession. Haiku—short poems that use image-drenched words to convey an experience of nature—was still in its infancy in Japan, but Basho became its most accomplished proponent. The following is the last recorded haiku Basho ever wrote:

"Falling sick on a journey
my dream goes wandering
over a field of dried grass."
—Matsuo Basho

He became a hermit/poet, and in 1684—two years' after his hermit's hut burned to the ground—he set off on the first of a number of famous pilgrimages, an odyssey he called the "journey of a weather-beaten skeleton." In time, he became the epitome of the "wandering monk," and when he embarked on his most ambitious walk of all—a 1,550-mile (2,500-km) trek through the wilds of Honshu, accompanied by his apprentice, Sora—he kept a diary of his travels that is now considered one of the great poetic diaries in Japanese history: The Narrow Road to the Deep North. It was this monumental journey that is the inspiration for Walk Japan's Basho Walk.

The Basho Walk follows, as best it can, in the footsteps of the poet. You will cross the forest streams that Basho had to cross; traverse the Natagiri Pass where he feared he would be set upon by bandits,;and visit the Buddhist shrine on Mount Haguro-san, where Basho slept. You also walk the Hokurikudo, once an ancient highway, but now a series of hilly paths, also walked by the great poet, and now by you. **BDS**

Shogun Trail
Tokyo to Fukuoa, Japan

Start Tokyo   End Fukuoka
Distance 19 miles (30 km)   Time 10 days
Grade Easy   Type Sealed paths, sidewalk
Map goo.gl/dUYKQN

If only we could all have a life half as adventurous as that of William Adams. The English navigator arrived in Kyushu in April 1600 with twenty sick and dying crew on his ship, *Liefde*. Adams was taken in by shogun chief Tokugawa Ieyasu, who asked him to build Japan's first Western-style ships. Tokugawa bestowed upon Adams the status of samurai and made him his direct retainer, a position of great power and influence.

Walk Japan has created the Shogun Walk to celebrate Adams's life and achievements. It begins in the heart of Tokyo and ends where it all began, on the

"Adams [was] depicted as John Blackthorne in James Clavell's epic novel Shogun."

www.walkjapan.com

island of Kyushu. The actual walking distance is only 19 miles (32 km) over ten days, with much use being made of Japan's vaunted public transport system to help traverse the hundreds of kilometers that separate the tour's start and end points. The first stop is at Adams's townhouse in Edo (Tokyo) near the grounds of neighboring Edo Castle. A train then takes you to Miura Peninsula, the site of his country estate, followed by a walk along the beaches at Ito, where he constructed two galleons for the shogun's navy. Visits to Nagasaki and Kyoto are followed by a tour of Hirado in northwest Kyushu, the place where he eventually died, and arrival in Fukuoka ends a fascinating insight into one man's extraordinary life. **BDS**

Philosophers' Walk

Kyoto, Japan

Start Ginkakuji   End Nanzenji
Distance 1.2 miles (1.9 km)   Time 1 hour
Grade Easy   Type Stone sidewalk
Map goo.gl/K9ugh5

Some walks are best done in springtime, and nowhere is this more of an axiom than on Kyoto's Philosophers' Walk, a short but beautiful stone path that follows the old Shishigatani Canal. It is lovely at any time of year but is transformed into a positively serene experience in spring, when the hundreds of hand-planted cherry blossom trees that line the canal, every year from late March or early April, turn this tiny waterway into a veritable riot of pink and white.

The path was created in honor of Nishida Kitaro, founder of the Kyoto School of philosophy in 1913, a

> *"During the day you should be prepared for crowds … a night stroll will definitely be quieter."*

www.lonelyplanet.com

movement which blended Zen teachings with Western beliefs in an attempt to harmonize the two. Constructed during the Meiji period, the canal was designed to revive a moribund Kyoto economy and was the source of Japan's first hydroelectric power plant. Kitaro was often seen walking and meditating along the canal as he made his way to and from nearby Kyoto University.

The canal remains a popular gathering place, and the grounds of Honenin Temple, adjacent to the path, are the final resting place for a number of famous academics. There is also a memorial to Nishida Kitaro which reads: "Let others do as they will, I am who I am. And I will walk the way that I make my own". **BDS**

Nara Walk

Nara, Japan

Start/End Nara
Distance 4 miles (6.4 km)   Time 3 hours
Grade Easy   Type Sidewalk
Map goo.gl/sOCJkX

Uniquely, Japan has had not one but numerous capital cities, each one founded wherever the emperor lived. As the emperor moved around the country, so too did his capital. In 710 this peripatetic practice came to end when the empress Gemmel moved the capital from Fujiwara-kyo to Heijo-kyo, also known as Nara. Here the capital was established with a short gap until 784, giving its name to the Nara period of history, before resuming its travels until, in 1180, it finally came to rest in Kyoto. There it remained until Tokyo took over in 1868. Today, Nara is a major city and a UNESCO World Heritage Site, thanks to its eight ancient palaces, temples, shrines, and ruins.

Walking around its ancient core is a leisurely delight. The city was originally modeled on Chang'an, capital of Tang dynasty China, and takes the form of an irregular rectangle. Among the ancient buildings is the Todai-ji temple, which houses a tall, bronze statue of Buddha inside the largest wooden structure in the world. The nearby Kasuga Taisha shrine is one of the most famous Shinto shrines in the country. Worth a visit, too, is Nara Park. According to legend, the god Takemikazuchi arrived in the newly built capital on a white deer to guard the city. Ever since, deer have been regarded as heavenly animals and allowed to wander freely throughout the city.

Many of Nara's historic sites are within easy walking distance of Nara Park, including Shin-Yakushi-ji Temple (747), the Isuien Gardens, the Sagi-ike Pond, and the Kasuga Wakamiya Shrine. And when you're done with temples, make for nearby Wakakusayama Hill, at 1,122 feet (342 m) an ideal vantage point for surveying all that you have conquered—or still intend to. **SA**

Kumano Kodo Pilgrimage Trails
Wakayama, Japan

Start Takijiri-oji **End** Kumano Hongu Taisha
Distance 25 miles (40 km) **Time** 2 days
Grade Moderate **Type** Earthen paths
Map goo.gl/I2IjNU

The Kumano region of the Kii Hanto peninsular on Honshu in Japan has been a place of religious significance since prehistoric times. The area was, and still is, considered to be a place of physical healing, to which pilgrims would walk to heal their bodies and souls. The Kumano shrine consists of three separate shrines—Hongu Taisha, Hayatama Taisha, and Nachi Taisha—based on three mountains that lie between 12 and 24 miles (20–40 km) from each other. Each shrine originally had its own form of nature worship, but during the tenth century the three fell under the influence of Buddhism and were worshipped together as three linked deities. The first pilgrims were members of the imperial family or nobles, but by the fifteenth century, most were commoners. They gained the name "Kumano ants," because they wound through the valleys like columns of ants on the march.

The various pilgrimage routes have been registered as UNESCO Sacred Sites. Walkers can tackle any of these routes, but the most popular is the Kijii route, which runs along the west of the Kii Hanto peninsular to the city of Tanabe. Here it forks into two: the Nakahechi route heads east into the rugged mountains toward Hongu Taisha while the Ohechi continues along the coast. The Nakahechi route was the most popular with pilgrims from the imperial capital of Kyoto. Modern walkers often start on this route at Takijiri-oji and stop for the night at the halfway stage of Chikatsuyu-oji, where you can stay at the local family inn. Once at Hongu Taisha, pilgrims and walkers can undergo purification and healing inside a small, rocky bath at the Yunomine hot spring, the only World Heritage hot spring in the world. **SA**

"The Kodo (old ways) are a key part of the region's UNESCO designation, and have been in use for over 1,000 years."

www.japan-guide

⊡ Walk the pilgrims' route of the Kumano ants along sacred, tranquil trails.

88 Temple Pilgrimage Tokushima to Kagawa, Japan

Start/End Temple #1, Ryzenji   **Distance** 670 miles (1,078 km)   **Time** 45–60 days   **Grade** Moderate to strenuous
Type Forest paths, sidewalks, and beaches   **Info** goo.gl/FxBeiz

This popular Buddhist pilgrimage begins and ends on the southeast corner of Japan's Shikoku Island at temple #1 at Ryzenji. However, it's not necessary to start at the first temple, and although it's typical to move clockwise around the island, some even consider it lucky to actually traverse it in reverse.

The pilgrimage is a trail through ancient and modern Japan, through terraced rice fields, busy intersections, forests, and sandy beaches. At each temple a priest puts a red ink stamp in your book, called *nokyocho* or *shuincho*, which can be purchased at the first temple, and many temples are on mountaintops, which makes for plenty of climbs and descents.

The best time of year to make this pilgrimage is in spring, when the pink cherry blossom contrasts with yellow mustard seed blooms. The weather is favorable, too, with lovely spring breezes replacing the rainy season's high winds and monsoons. Finding accommodation along the way is easy, but winging it works, too. Camping is also a popular choice, with many walkers sleeping outside in the trail's myriad green spaces.

The pilgrimage can take between forty-five and sixty days to complete if you undertake it all in one go, but you don't have to complete the entire route to gain satisfaction from this trail—you can do as little or as much as you choose. Devout Japanese pilgrims aim to visit all eighty-eight temples, but for many it will take several visits. If you're set on seeing them all, but are short on time (or if walking it all is too daunting), parts or all of the pilgrimage can be done by bike, car, train, or bus. **NE**

⊡ The trail encircles Japan's most rural island.

Vine Bridges of the Iya Valley Tokushima, Japan

Start/End Iya-gawa River   **Distance** 450 feet (137 m)   **Time** 2 hours   **Grade** Easy
Type Rope bridges   **Info** goo.gl/ykjQ1F

The Iya Valley, on Japan's southern island of Shikoku, is a remote area, its dramatic mountains; steep, wooded valleys; and rock-strewn rivers a favored retreat over the centuries for warriors, refugees, and bandits. Defeated armies took refuge here, although now the area is a peaceful tourist destination. The west of the valley has good road access, but the eastern end, known as Oku-Iya, is difficult to enter and thus largely undisturbed. Historically, its rivers, of which the Iya-gawa is the main one, were difficult to cross except by vine bridges, three of which have survived to this day.

The bridges are made from wisteria vines, a tough and sturdy vine that grows to great lengths. One vine was grown on each side of the river. When each vine was long enough, the two were pulled together and woven to form a bridge. Short planks were set into the vine at 8 to 12 inches (3–4.7 cm) apart to form a walkway. Traditionally, the bridges had no sides, terrifying those who had to walk along their bouncing lengths, but a good deterrent to those intending to visit the reclusive valley residents. Iya-no-Kazura-bashi is located in the western valley, but two more—known as the Oku-Iya Niju Kazura-bashi, or the husband and wife bridges—are found an hour's drive away to the east. Their year of construction is thought to date to the 1100s. The bridges are rebuilt every three years and are reinforced with wire and provided with side rails, but at around 147 feet (45 m) long, and with a considerable drop to the river below, these bridges still have the ability to frighten the life out of anyone brave enough to attempt a crossing. **SA**

⤴ Traditions are still palpable in the Iya Valley.

Kunisaki Trek
Fukuoka/Oita, Japan

Start/End Yamaga   **Distance** 41 miles
(66 km)   **Time** 10 days   **Grade** Easy
Type Mountain and forest trails
Map goo.gl/CWdzDT

The Kunisaki Peninsula is tucked into the western shores of Japan's Seto Inland Sea on the island of Kyushu; its highest point, Mount Futago at 1,433 feet (437 m), surrounded by forests and small rural communities. It is a quiet corner of a bustling nation, a piece of "Old Japan" that few Japanese visit. For centuries, it was the epicenter of Japanese Shugendo, an early form of Buddhism, and it is here where Mine-iri, the habit of walking through mountains in a state of prayer—is still practiced. Kunisaki's once-influential religious institutions may no longer exist, but its

> *"Excellent walking through sleepy hamlets, verdant forests, along craggy ridges.…"*
>
> www.walkjapan.com

temples, shrines, Buddhist statuary, and religious folklore mean this overlooked corner of Japan has become one of its most tranquil and walkable regions.

A ten-day Kunisaki Trek—mostly on forest trails, but also involving a bit of rock scrambling and some short, steep ascents—takes you deep into a world of shrines and thermal spas following in the 1,000-year-old footsteps of monks, hermits, and recluses. Two-thirds of those ancient trails have been lost to time, but enough remain to ensure that over ten days you'll never walk the same trail twice as you grapple with chain- and rope-assisted climbs and cross over stone bridges, experiencing this tiny window into Japan as it was in the time of Shugendo. **BDS**

Angkor Wat
Siem Reap, Cambodia

Start/End Angkor Wat
Distance 2 miles (3.2 km)
Time 6 hours   **Grade** Easy
Type Stone paths   **Map** goo.gl/P12S8Y

Built by King Suryavarman II, who ruled the country from 1113 to 1150, Angkor Wat originally was built to honor the Hindu god Vishnu. But when the country converted to Buddhism in the late 1200s, the temple followed suit and it is now a Buddhist shrine.

Everything about Angkor Wat is vast. The temple is surrounded by a 625-foot-wide (190 m) moat and an outer wall that forms an oblong 3,360 feet (1,024 m) long and 2,632 feet (802 m) wide. A 1,150-foot-long (350 m) causeway leads up to the temple, which stands on a raised terrace. Five elaborately decorated towers dominate the temple, the center one of which is 213 feet (65 m) tall. The towers are thought to represent the five peaks of Mount Meru, home of the Hindu gods, while the surrounding walls and moats represent nearby mountains and oceans. Inside, the three main galleries represent Brahma the god of creation; Vishnu the Supreme Being; and the moon. Carvings and stone figures of *devata* (gods) and *apsaras* (female spirits of the clouds and water) decorate the temple, which is filled with statues of Vishnu and other Hindu gods.

Angkor Archaeological Park covers a mammoth 154 square miles (399 sq km) and includes scores of other temples, all of which can be accessed on foot via a network of well-maintained paths and rural roads. Hiring a bicycle will minimize your travel time between each temple, but, to immerse yourself in the grandeur of the ancient Khmers, walking is the only way to get through encroaching jungle and over and around the eroded walls once you arrive. **SA**

➡ **Angkor Wat is a captivating Buddhist shrine.**

Lurujarri Heritage Trail
Western Australia, Australia

Start Minarriny (Coulomb Point)   **End** Minyirr
(Gantheaume Point)   **Distance** 45 miles (72.4 km)
Time 6 days   **Grade** Easy   **Type** Aboriginal coastal
trails   **Map** goo.gl/7iZ3ti

The Lurujarri Trail is part of the Heritage Trail Network, inaugurated by the West Australian government in 1988 to commemorate the nation's 200th birthday and raise awareness of Australia's cultural roots. Lurujarri, which means "coastal dunes," is inextricably linked to the Dreamtime, that time long ago when great ancestral beings created everything that we see around us—every rock, every landscape, every living thing. When you walk the Lurujarri Trail, you share in this experience of the Dreamtime, a continuing state of being that draws together all things from the past,

"This is a loose, authentic, contemporary Aboriginal experience."

www.australiangeographic.com.au

the present, and the future. The trail follows an age-old song cycle that originated with these Dreamtime beings—a song that is still sung by Aborigines today.

The trail begins at Minarriny, 50 miles (80 km) north of Broome, and heads south for 45 miles (72.5 km) to Minyirr, along the "coast where the sun goes down." It is divided into six segments, all of which can be accessed by car, which means any one section can be done as a day walk. Each segment has a host of sacred Aboriginal sites that are still intact along a coastline that has not altered in 6,000 years. Significant points along the trail all have their place in the song cycle, and each has its own peculiar characteristics or feeling—what Aborigines call "Le-an." **BDS**

Railway Reserves Heritage Trail Western Australia, Australia

Start Bellevue   **End** Wooroloo Reserve
Distance 37 miles (59.5 km)   **Time** 3 days
Grade Easy   **Type** Loose, hard-packed rubble
Map goo.gl/7UVMbE

The Railway Reserves Heritage Trail was, in years gone by, the Eastern Railway that linked the seaside town of Fremantle to the inland pioneering town of York. Along the way, the trail splits in two and follows both sides of the Great Eastern Highway before joining up at Mount Helena, thus forming a convenient loop, before continuing southeast as a single track for another 14 miles (22.5 km) to its finishing point at Wooroloo Reserve. Now an important wildlife corridor through the picturesque Perth Hills, the Darling Range, and John Forrest National Park, the trail follows a route that first began to be laid out from Fremantle to Guildford in 1879. The line reached its country terminus at York in 1885, and the main line remained in use until 1966.

Much of the trail's associated history has been well preserved. There is the Mundaring Stationmaster's House, built in around 1903; the old railway platform at Darlington, one of the settlements that once thrived along this vital rail link; the wonderfully preserved Swan View Station; and the 1,115-foot-long (340 m) Swan Tunnel, completed in 1895. Comprising of more than 330,000 bricks, the tunnel proved a poor piece of engineering—a little too narrow and over a steep gradient that led to the near-asphyxiation of train crews. Remember to bring a flashlight, as the interior of the tunnel is not lit.

Western Australia was an isolated outpost on a continent that was still more than twenty years away from achieving nationhood when this rail line opened for business in the latter decades of the nineteenth century. This is a fact worth remembering as you walk or cycle this multiuse trail in the dry heat of the Western Australian sun. **BDS**

Uluru Circuit
Northern Territory, Australia

Start/End Mala parking lot
Distance 6.5 miles (10.5 km) **Time** 3.5 hours
Grade Easy **Type** Rock, dirt trails
Map goo.gl/s8brbl

Uluru-Kata Tjuta National Park, located 280 miles (450 km) west of Alice Springs in the center of Australia, is home to two of the nation's most iconic landforms: the thirty-six domed rocks of Kata Tjuta (The Olgas); and Uluru (Ayers Rock), the world's largest inselberg, an "island mountain" of coarse-grained sandstone, feldspar, and rounded fragments of sedimentary rock. Every Australian—and, indeed, most people in the world—whether they have visited Uluru or not, knows its shape, if not its mythology, through photographs and the media. For many Australians, to see it is a rite of passage, a pilgrimage to one of those very few places that make you feel Australian to the core just by virtue of looking at it.

A walk around the base of Uluru begins at the Mala parking lot and traces a meandering path through grassed claypans and acacia woodlands. It is worth doing the walk with an Aboriginal guide, so you can gain an understanding of the importance of the rock and to learn about the land the indigenous custodians refer to simply as "Country." The walk gets you up close and personal to flora you cannot see in Uluru's typical postcard images such as red gum groves, permanent water holes, and a virtual gallery of rock art, as well as kangaroos, button quails, and even feral camels. In addition to the circuit, there is also a variety of shorter walks for families and walking tracks specially designed for wheelchair and stroller access.

Ulura stands at 1,141 feet (348 m) high, but it is like an iceberg—what you see is only the tip of a rock thought to extend as far as 3.5 miles (5.6 km) below the surface. It is sacred, too, so a walk around it rather than on it is appreciated by those who live there. **BDS**

"UNESCO-listed Uluru has a mesmerizing, awe-inspiring quality—the thing has presence."

www.secretearth.com

⤒ The trails, through acacia woodland and grassed claypans, are designed to minimize environmental impact.

The Rocks Historic Walking Tour New South Wales, Australia

Start/End Pier One Sydney Harbour Hotel   **Distance** 4 miles (6.4 km)   **Time** 2 hours   **Grade** Easy
Type Sidewalk   **Map** goo.gl/g5YQGA

The Rocks precinct on Sydney's Circular Quay, with its twisted, crooked streets and alleyways, was the city's first neighborhood. The colony was a compact, intimate place. When the First Fleet landed at Sydney Cove in 1788, its cargo of convicts, some 700 of them, was sent to the Rocks side of the cove and told to make homes using whatever means they could find. Most of the cove was forested, but its eastern side was particularly rocky. Some of the men built primitive huts. Others lived for years in the hollows of trees. The bubonic plague broke out here in 1900, and when the approaches and pylons of the Sydney Harbour Bridge began to be constructed through the middle of the area in the 1920s, entire streets were obliterated.

Now, almost 240 years after that original settlement, the grittiness of this eclectic neighborhood can be felt on a walking tour that begins at Cadman's Cottage

(1816), one of the few sandstone cottages left from the colony's first thirty years. It continues westward up Argyle Street toward the four line houses of Susannah Place (built in the 1840s), and Garrison Church (1848), the nation's oldest church, which faces the village green of Argyle Place, modeled on English examples, where every Australian still has the legal right to graze sheep. The Lord Nelson Brewery Hotel (1841) and the Hero of Waterloo (1843) on Windmill Street, with its tunnel built to smuggle rum from its cellars to waiting ships, are highlights as you make your way north along Gloucester Walk to Dawes Point, site of the city's first cemetery. The walk concludes down by the waterside, shaded by the looming Sydney Harbour Bridge. **BDS**

⊡ The Rocks is Australia's most historic neighborhood.

Mungo National Park Fossil Trails New South Wales, Australia

Start/End Grasslands Nature Trail   **Distance** Various   **Time** 2–3 hours   **Grade** Easy
Type Rock, sand trails   **Info** goo.gl/QORrCI

Lake Mungo is a dry lake about 472 miles (760 km) west of Sydney in Mungo National Park, in the far southwest corner of New South Wales. Tens of thousands of years before the last Ice Age, it was a lake up to 12 miles (19.3 km) long, more than 6 miles (9.7 km) wide, and 30 feet (9 m) deep. Humans first set foot here 35,000 to 40,000 years ago, when the region was made up of a large series of deep, connecting lakes. Today, the area's most prominent features are its lunettes, a 16-mile (25.8-km) long series of archaeologically rich sand dunes along its eastern shore that have given up a wealth of artifacts, including stone tools and grinders for making flour. The partially cremated body of the 35,000-year-old Mungo Lady was found there, as were the 40,000-year-old remains of Mungo Man, the oldest human remains ever found on the Australian continent. But that's not all there is.

Within the park are a number of excellent trails, including the 164-foot (50-m) Red Top lookout and boardwalk, accessible to wheelchairs, that offers bird's-eye views over the deep ravines of the park, and the 0.6-mile (1-km) loop of the Grasslands Nature trail, which highlights elements of the park's flora, including copper bush, cypress pines, and mallee scrub. There is the Wall of China walk, a 1,640-ft (500-m) out-and-back trail past clay deposits sculpted by eons of wind and rain. Finally, there is a jewel not to be missed: 20,000-year-old fossilized footprints, frozen into a magnesite pavement. There are more than 450 of them, more of their type than at all other sites on Earth combined. Called "trackways" by the Aborigines, they are poignant echoes of our rambling ancestors. **BDS**

⊼ Walk trackways made by Australia's first inhabitants.

Lilydale to Warburton Rail Trail Victoria, Australia

Start Lilydale   End Warburton
Distance 25 miles (40 km)   Time 2 days
Grade Easy   Type Fine, compressed gravel
Map goo.gl/D6kHeS

The wine-growing region of the Yarra Valley, an hour's drive east of the Victorian capital of Melbourne, is renowned as one of the country's premier wine districts. The way in for most Melbournians has always been to drive the Maroondah Highway to towns such as Warburton or Healesville, but now there is an alternative: drive to Lilydale, on the northeastern perimeter of the city, and walk there instead, on the Lilydale to Warburton Rail Trail.

The trail begins at the rear of Lilydale railway station, and once you cross the Maroondah Highway

> *"Most regular "Warby Trail" users agree, that the trail really comes into its own from Killara Station."*
>
> www.dotheyarravalley.com.au

overpass, you are surrounded by typical Yarra Valley bushland, which accompanies you to the first stop, the historic township of Mount Evelyn. Follow fern-lined gullies and wildflower-rich bushland to Wandin, cross the first of seventeen restored railway bridges, and walk over wetlands inhabited by the elusive platypus.

Take a break in the Carriage Cafe in Seville and walk over open fields to Killara. There are views of the Central Highlands from the Woori Yallock Creek bridge, and of grazing lands along the Yarra River near Launching Place. The trail's final section bisects dense native forest and ends at Warburton, where you can refuel or have a sleepover at Oscar's on the Yarra, one of the region's finest hotels. **BDS**

Battery Point Historic Walking Tour Tasmania, Australia

Start Salamanca Place   End Kelly's Steps
Distance 4 miles (6.4 km)   Time 2 hours
Grade Easy   Type Sidewalk
Map goo.gl/PDkBoe

A self-guided walk through Hobart's historic precinct of Battery Point is a wonderfully relaxing way to spend a few hours as you amble down its quiet streets lined with period homes from quaint little cottages to imposing Georgian mansions, along with a wealth of cafés and galleries that give this suburb of "Old Hobart Town" a strong and recognizable connection to Australia's colonial past that few urban areas in the country can match. It is one of the country's most fashionable and expensive suburbs, filled with some of the nation's oldest houses.

You can start outside the old line of warehouses on the Hobart waterfront known as Salamanca Place, and from there walk along Hampton Road, past the houses named Mafeking and Pretoria, which were built just after the end of the Boer War in 1902. Continue to the corner of De Witt Street and soak in the graceful lines of the 1883 sandstone house Invercoe. The high point of the walk has to be the idyllic Arthur Circus, a very English-looking circle of cottages constructed around a central park, and one of Australia's first planned subdivisions. All the cottages in the Circus have been maintained meticulously and display an enviable level of originality.

After you've walked a circuit (or three) of this picture-perfect little enclave, continue to Colville Street and walk up the hill to the Shipwright Arms Hotel, then down Trumpeter Street toward the water and the line of mansions along Clark Avenue, Tasmania's most expensive street. Stroll through Princes Park, home to the gun batteries that gave the neighborhood its name, then back to the "real world" of the Hobart waterfront. **BDS**

Otago Central Rail Trail
Otago, New Zealand

Start Middlemarch   **End** Clyde
Distance 93 miles (150 km)   **Time** 8 days
Grade Moderate   **Type** Rails-to-trails conversion
Map goo.gl/GdSGME

The Otago Central Rail Trail, New Zealand's first rails-to-trails project, became a possibility in 1983 when the New Zealand government relaxed regulations designed to protect railway freight services. With road freight taking business away from railways, options were opening up to transfer the land occupied by rail lines over to more recreational uses. The line closed to freight in 1990, and the Clyde to Middlemarch corridor was purchased by the Department of Conservation in 1993. Over the next seven years, the trail was "re-decked," almost seventy bridges given handrails, and eleven replica "gangers'" sheds were built along its length. Cattle grates were added where farm boundaries were crossed, and after various other surface upgrades, interpretive signs and topographic maps were added and the trail officially opened to the public in 2000.

The results were phenomenal. This wonderful mixed-use trail built for walkers, cyclists, and horseback riders gets more than 15,000 visitors a year, not bad for an attraction located near the bottom of New Zealand's South Island. From Middlemarch it loops through the spectacular Strath Taieri, a glacial valley and site of an 1860s gold rush, and then heads into the Maniototo, a sparsely populated elevated region and part of the Canterbury Otago tussock grasslands. The journey will take you through three tunnels (bring a flashlight) and over numerous viaducts as it climbs to its maximum elevation of 2,028 feet (618 m). However, you don't have to worry about the incline: frequent snow on the old rail lines meant that the gradients had to be small ones—a necessity for the old steam locomotives and a blessing for today's hikers. **BDS**

"The Otago Central Rail Trail reveals truly breathtaking treasures ... unlike any others in New Zealand."

www.centralotagonz.com

⬆ A stunning rails-to-trail conversion now draws more than 15,000 people every year.

Don't underestimate the coastal walk—there is often a lot more to following a coastline than strolling on a beach. Coastal sand dunes can be as high as 500 feet (152 m), and cliffs and headlands often involve tackling a series of tiring ascents and descents. The coastal walks featured here have the power to both relax and exhaust the hardiest walker.

COASTAL & SHORELINE

← The Peaks Island Loop in Maine traces the island's graceful shoreline, and provides sweeping views of Casco Bay.

Umnak Island Aleutian Islands, Alaska, USA

Start/End Nikolski   **Distance** 4–70 miles (6.4 km–112 km)   **Time** 2 hours to 3 days   **Grade** Easy
Type Easy   **Info** goo.gl/xgNKRb

A remote and seldom visited island in the eastern Aleutians, Umnak Island is a wondrous land of mud pots, heated geysers, hot springs, deep green volcanic hills, and broad wildflower-filled valleys. The island rises steeply out of the waters of the Bering Sea, and is Alaska's most geothermally active region. Needless to say, it is a fabulous wilderness through which one can walk.

Part of the Alaska Maritime National Wildlife Refuge, Umnak Island is entirely uninhabited save for the tiny Aleut community of Nikolski (the population is less than 100) on the island's western coastline, and a small ranch at Fort Glen, the site of a U.S. Army base constructed in 1942 in the wake of the Japanese raid on Pearl Harbor. Umnak Island's topography is dominated by the 5.8-mile-wide (9.3 km) Okmok Caldera (3,519 feet/1,072 m), a shield volcano in the east of the island that last erupted in February 2010, its flanks pockmarked with satellite and lava domes.

The landscape on a sunny day resembles an outdoor wellness spa, with scattered hot springs to soak in and fresh, bubbling streams to cool off in when you're done. There are even hot springs on its beaches you can lounge in when the tide is out! The region's mild, maritime climate has given life to high grasses and fields of wild berries, and because there are no bears on the island, its population of reindeer has flourished. It can get extremely windy here, and fogs are common, but this only adds to Umnak's mystique. The Aleuts have had a presence here for 12,000 years, and when you see it all for yourself, it isn't hard to see why. **BDS**

⬆ Walk an Aleutian Island hot spring wonderland.

West Coast Trail British Columbia, Canada

Start Pachena Bay   **End** Gordon River   **Distance** 47 miles (75.6 km)   **Time** 5–7 days   **Grade** Strenuous
Type Coast trail   **Map** goo.gl/3PZ3xx

The West Coast Trail—along the southwestern coast of Vancouver Island, off the west coast of Canada—has been called one of the ten best hikes in the world and it offers a dual challenge even to the experienced hiker. The first part is the strenuous nature of the hike, along a rugged coast, through boggy land, across rivers, down to beaches, and then up and over cliffs. The other challenge is the logistical one. The trail is only open from May 1 to September 30 each year, and in addition, you need a permit if you're going to overnight on the trail. Only sixty of these are issued per day, thirty at each end of the trail, in order to help control the numbers, because the trail is part of the Pacific Rim National Park Reserve. In July and August the demand for permits is high, and you may have to wait a day or two to get one. No permit is required for the first and last two weeks that the trail is open, but at those times the weather can be harsh. Even when you have a permit, you are required to take part in an orientation session before the rangers will allow you onto the trail.

People are prepared to go through all this because the rewards for the serious hiker are well worth it. You will be walking through barely touched Canadian wilderness, where wildlife thrives. In the rain forests, bears, mountain lions, and wolves all live. Out to sea, at the right time of year you might spot whales and sea lions. The hike is incredibly varied, with beautiful deserted beaches, waterfalls, caves, creeks, and even shipwrecks. Hopefully, you won't be wrecked at the end of it, but you certainly will have enjoyed one of the finest hikes of your life. **MG**

⬆ Demand for permits is high on this great trail.

Stanley Park Seawall British Columbia, Canada

Start Coal Harbour **End** Kitsilano Beach **Distance** 14 miles (22.5 km) **Time** 5 hours
Grade Easy **Type** Paved walk, bikeway **Map** goo.gl/P3qOnZ

The battle to construct Vancouver's Stanley Park Seawall was a race against the very forces of nature. For decades the employees of Stanley Park had been battling the erosive effects of the wind, weather, and tides that wore away at the park's edges, and it was clear to all that the only way to put an end to its being chiseled away was to build a wall of beach rock to protect it. The first segments of the wall were built during World War I, and in the decades that followed, beginning on opposite sides of the park, further sections were added until at last they met at Third Beach in 1971.

From 1931 until his death in 1963, the project was the life's work of the great master stonecutter James Cunningham. To see the park now is to realize that the enormous human effort that went into the wall's creation remains largely concealed, as though it is and always has been a part of the natural environment. It is seamless; it is nature "improved."

Today, Vancouver's Stanley Park Seawall extends far beyond the boundaries of the park, but it is still a testament to Cunningham's original vision and ingenuity. Providing a great hike without the need to leave the city, the seawall passes Granville Island and Stamps Landing, past Rogers Arena Stadium and on to Yaletown, then encircling Stanley Park and heading off down the shoreline of Burrard Inlet and into English Bay. And if you start off determined to complete the route in out-and-back form but discover you have bitten off more than you can chew, the False Creek ferries and various aquabus services can bring you back in style. **BDS**

⬆ Stanley Park Seawall blends into its surroundings.

North Coast Trail British Columbia, Canada

Start Shushartie Bay   End Cape Scott trailhead   Distance 36 miles (57.9 km)   Time 4–7 days   Grade Moderate to strenuous   Type Sand, mud, fixed ropes, boardwalks, forest trails   Map goo.gl/TJX7gT

The North Coast Trail, which extends over the beaches and through the forests along the northern tip of Vancouver Island in the Canadian province of British Columbia, would not exist in the form it does today if it wasn't for the dedication and vision of the Northern Vancouver Island Trails Society. The trail runs through 55,100 acres (22,290 ha) of Cape Scott Provincial Park, a park renowned for its wealth of old-growth forests, marshlands, and long sandy beaches, as well as for a notoriously wet and stormy climate. It also possesses a history of human settlement that includes the remains of the former outpost of Cape Scott, initially settled by two First Nation tribes, and later by Danish-Canadian immigrants in the late 1800s.

The trail is an unabashed challenge, but also an intensely rewarding one that takes you deep into the raw beauty of the island's rugged north coast. The majority of hikers start the trail by catching a water taxi from Port Hardy, the "gateway" to Cape Scott, to Shushartie Bay, and then set out across its unkempt shoreline through a world of blowholes, sea caverns, lonely lighthouses, forests of Sitka spruce, hemlock and cedar, past the sites of old shipwrecks, and with the chance to see wildlife ranging from eagles and sea lions to cougars, black bears, and migrating whales.

The trail has much in common with the sort of wilderness experience that the nearby West Coast Trail had in abundance twenty or more years ago, before its secret got out. The secret will no doubt get out here, too, but for now it remains an unknown world that requires just enough effort to reach to ensure it stays wild for a long while yet. **BDS**

⬆ A challenging trail on Vancouver's north coast.

Bow Falls Trail
Alberta, Canada

Start/End Bow River Bridge
Distance 2 miles (3.2 km)   Time 1 hour
Grade Easy   Type Riverside trail
Map goo.gl/bOQuzE

Surrounded by the grandeur of the Banff National Park, the hike along the Bow River to see Bow Falls has rightly become one of the major attractions in the region and in the whole of the Canadian Rockies. The falls are hardly Niagara, being only 30 feet (9.1 m) high and 100 feet (30.4 m) across, but what is impressive is the sheer power of the water thundering through them. They are also a beautiful natural phenomenon, and the walk up to them through the splendors of the national park is exhilarating. The falls are appealing enough to have featured as a backdrop in several Hollywood movies, and they have co-starred with Marilyn Monroe and even Lassie.

There are two trails leading up to the falls along the south side of the Bow River, with separate paths for cyclists and for walkers. It's a very popular hike, and you're unlikely to have the trail to yourself, but there are also many other trails that interconnect in this area, and you can easily combine this simple walk with more challenging and longer hikes. Beyond the falls the path continues to the top of some cliffs, for views over the falls, though in winter this path is closed.

In winter, you're likely to see the falls frozen, which in itself is a startling sight, although the best time to visit is in the spring, when the snowmelt comes down off the Rockies and swells the rivers. The rapids that you walk alongside can be deafening then, and the falls are found close to where the Bow River swells as it joins the aptly named Spray River, for a double-dose of pounding Rocky Mountain water on its long journey to Hudson Bay. **MG**

◄ The hike to Bow Falls is a classic Rockies experience.

Crypt Lake Trail
Alberta, Canada

Start/End Crypt Landing, Waterton Lakes National Park
Distance 10.7 miles (17.2 km)   Time 8 hours
Grade Moderate to strenuous   Type Bare rock, forest trails   Map goo.gl/OtUOhs

Waterton Lakes National Park, on the southern edge of Alberta bordering Glacier National Park in Montana, United States, was formed in 1895 and named after Waterton Lake, a twin lake that lies on each side of the U.S./Canada border. Both were named for the Victorian conservationist Charles Waterton. An international Biosphere Reserve and World Heritage Site, the park has more than 120 miles (193 km) of hiking trails.

Crypt Lake, a past winner of the coveted "Canada's Best Hike" award, is a stunning alpine lake at the base of a lovely cirque that holds surface ice right through

---

"Crypt Lake Trail is an exciting hike to a stunning location—Rocky Mountain perfection!"

www.hikespeak.com

---

to August and is surrounded by scree and usually snow, and takes 45 minutes to circumnavigate. But the excitement doesn't begin at the lake. The entire trail is breathtaking, with the approach taking you through coniferous forests, past roaring waterfalls, and over some difficult but exhilarating fields of exposed rock, all the while getting closer to the hanging valley that awaits you. The trail ascends an open alpine mountain, there's a 20-inch-wide (50 cm) trail to tiptoe along, a steel ladder to climb, a 100-foot-long (30 m) tunnel, followed by a scramble over an inclined cliff hanging onto a well-placed cable that will leave you asking the only really relevant question: "Just how much fun is it possible to have in one day"? **MG**

Bruce Trail

Ontario, Canada

Start Queenston **End** Tobermory
Distance 553 miles (890 km) **Time** 6–7 weeks
Grade Strenuous **Type** Long-distance hiking trail
Info goo.gl/KDF3Oy

The Bruce Trail is the oldest and longest signposted hiking trail in Canada. It is a momentous walking experience, and some people devote many years to hiking the trail, section by section, although in October 2012, a twenty-three-year-old man managed to do the entire length in twelve days.

At its southern end, the trail passes through Niagara's vineyards, before reaching the 453-mile-long (729 km) Niagara Escarpment, the most famous stretch being the cliff over which the Niagara Falls plunges. Farther along, it takes you by the shores of Lake

> ## "Huge boulder beaches and massive caverns put you in the land of the giants."
>
> www.explorethebruce.com

Iroquois, an area also famous for its waterfalls, and on through the hardwood forests and wetlands of the Caledon Hills. This section attracts vast numbers of birds, and is best seen in its dazzling fall colors.

Farther on, the trail passes through the Blue Mountains, home to many ski resorts, while farther north still are high cliffs, deep valleys, more waterfalls, and finally the Bruce Peninsula National Park. Here black bears are found, along with porcupines, horseshoe hares, and Eastern massasauga rattlesnakes. Orchids are abundant, and rare ferns, too, as this outstanding trail continues to its conclusion between two mighty bodies of water—Georgian Bay on one side and Lake Huron on the other. **MG**

Bay Roberts East Shoreline

Newfoundland, Canada

Start/End Crane's Hill
Distance 3.7 miles (6 km) **Time** 1–2 hours
Grade Easy **Type** Shoreline trail
Map goo.gl/APBXFZ

The cries of the seabirds, the equally strong call of history, and the sounds of the winds and the waves are what you will experience on the Bay Roberts East Shoreline Heritage Walk in Newfoundland. Of course, on some days the winds will be gale force when the Atlantic Ocean chooses to batter the shoreline, but pick a fine day and there's no better outdoor experience in the whole of Newfoundland than this fairly short, easy walk.

The fishing here was so plentiful that from as long ago as the sixteenth century, fishermen would sail from as far away as Europe to enjoy the bounty of its waters. Inevitably, some of the fishermen settled, mainly those from England's West Country, and the fishing and shipping industries developed alongside each other. The close proximity of Bay Roberts to the Newfoundland capital of St. John's—only about 56 miles (90 km) away by road—also helped the area's prosperity. The Heritage Walk celebrates the area's history while leading you into the glorious natural world of Newfoundland. The path takes you along sheer cliffs, over headlands, down to wide beaches, and into sheltered coves. You might see whales in the bay, or bald eagles soaring high above in the skies, and you'll be treated to some wonderfully evocative landmarks, such as Whale's Back, Big Shag Rock, Salmon Island, and Mad Rock. The trail is also referred to as the Madrock Trail, the name deriving from the fact that the relentless pounding of the Atlantic waves at this point is enough to drive anyone mad. Today, you're far more likely to experience a feeling of joy and peace as you hike the trail, while you appreciate Newfoundland's abundant natural beauty. **MG**

Cape Breton Highlands National Park
Nova Scotia, Canada

Start/End Freshwater Lake
Distance Various **Time** Various
Grade Easy to strenuous **Type** Various
Info goo.gl/R5aHfC

There are so many magnificent hiking trails in Nova Scotia's Cape Breton Highlands National Park that it is impossible to single one out as being the absolute best. Located on the northern tip of Cape Breton Island, Cape Breton Highlands was established in 1936 as the first of Canada's National Parks on the Atlantic, and it covers an area of 366 square miles (948 sq km). It is renowned for its unrivaled views of both mountain highlands and the ocean, and there are few places that better capture the drama of Canada's coastal wildness.

The park's highland plateau is one of its most remarkable features, a lush forested area that reaches right to the Atlantic Ocean and then abruptly stops as steep cliffs plunge vertically down, broken by deep river canyons carving their way through to the sea. Most of the hiking trails are off the Cabot Trail, a 185-mile (298-km) scenic highway that loops around the northern end of Cape Breton Island and runs through the national park for one-third of its length. Trails range from short ten-minute strolls to more strenuous hikes lasting several hours. Due to the mountainous and rugged nature of the park's interior, and the sheer vastness of it, it is not possible to link all of these trails together, so if you are driving the Cabot Trail, you should plan in advance which hikes you wish to enjoy. Also bear in mind that winters here can be fierce, and the park authorities employ four snowplows, four salt trucks, and one snow blower to try to keep the roads in the park open. Late spring through to early fall is the best time to visit, and then you'll be treated to views of these forested mountains in all their spectacular glory. **MG**

"Boasting 26 hiking trails ... Cape Breton Highlands National Park is an ideal getaway for families, couples, or solo adventurers."

www.novascotia.com

⬆ Numerous trails of varying degrees of difficulty await you on the Cape Breton plateau.

Celtic Shores Coastal Trail
Nova Scotia, Canada

Start Port Hastings **End** Inverness
Distance 57 miles (91.7 km) **Time** 5 days **Grade** Easy
Type Coal-dust covered treadways, sealed paths
Map goo.gl/05SmNe

Tracing a north–south route down the beautiful west coast of Canada's Cape Breton Island, off the northern tip of Nova Scotia, the Celtic Shores Coastal Trail is a trail for everyone—from hikers to quad bikers. It will take you past fishing villages and warm-water beaches at Inverness, West Mabou, and Port Hood, and will introduce you to the west coast's renowned Celtic culture, including the rich musical heritage that has seen the ceilidh (traditional Gaelic folk music and dance gatherings) help preserve fiddle-playing styles that died out in Scotland more than 200 years ago and

"The easy, flat trail meanders along the coastline, through picturesque wilderness."

www.celticshores.ca

would now be likely lost if, in 1773, boatloads of impoverished Highlanders hadn't set their sights on a new life across the Atlantic.

The trail is organized into five segments, each with numerous access points and trailheads, and it begins at Port Hastings with its wonderful views out over St. George's Bay. A series of fishing villages follows, and don't miss the Celtic Music Center at Judique. The warm waters at Port Hood are next before heading inland to Mabou and the Red Shoe Pub. There's even a whiskey distillery, the Glenora Inn and Distillery, where a few glasses of its signature Glen Breton Rare Single Malt can seriously derail one's completion of this marvelous walk. **BDS**

Shipwreck Coast, Shi Shi Beach Washington, USA

Start Rialto Beach **End** Shi Shi Beach
Distance 35 miles (56 km)
Time 2–3 days **Grade** Easy
Type Coastal **Map** goo.gl/6EGXjM

The Shipwreck Coast that runs through Washington State and into Oregon is one of the most beautiful and dramatic stretches of coast in the United States, which is little compensation to the sailors who manned the many ships that have been shipwrecked along here. Some of the wrecks remain, as do the storms that caused the ships to founder. But on a good day this is an easy and awe-inspiring walk, mostly along beaches, with a bewildering variety of rocks, tide pools, and flotsam and jetsam to distract you along the way.

It is also a flexible walk—you can do as much or as little of it as you like, though doing this popular long stretch from Rialto Beach to Shi Shi Beach, just south of Cape Flattery, will give you a sense of achievement and delight. You don't need to be a seasoned hiker, and even families with young children can complete the walk if you go at a sensible pace and allow for the time that the children will want to spend exploring the beaches and the tide pools.

The Shipwreck Coast is at the northwestern tip of the Olympic Peninsula, where you'll also find the Olympic National Park. The park includes a long stretch of the Pacific Coast, although it isn't directly joined to the interior, where you'll find the only patch of rain forest in the United States. It's a heavily wooded region, with some of the tallest trees in the world, and because of the logging that has gone on here for centuries, as you walk you'll come across huge trees that have been washed up on the shoreline. Together with some enormous offshore rocks, this all contributes to make this a unique and very special coastal walk. **MG**

Oregon Coast Trail
Oregon, USA

Start South Jetty, Clatsop Spit, Columbia River   **End** Oregon/California border   **Distance** 425 miles (684 km)   **Time** 40–50 days   **Grade** Easy to moderate   **Type** Long-distance hiking trail   **Info** goo.gl/uodGnh

The Oregon State Trail, which runs the entire length of the Oregon coast, would not have been possible were it not for some fine examples of governmental common sense. In 1911, Oswald West was elected the state's governor on a pledge to reclaim Oregon's beaches as public land, and through a judicious use of the argument of public access saw the entire coastline from California to Washington purchased in 1913. When the state's claim to public land was challenged in 1966 by a Cannon Beach landowner, the local people revolted, cited their right to public access, and as a result, the landmark Oregon Beach Bill was passed in 1967. There would not be an unbroken Oregon Coast Trail today without it.

In its far-sighted history of proclamations, the Oregon state legislature has left us all a rare gift. For most of its length, the Oregon Coast Trail is a beach walk, leaving the sand only when landforms—typically the majestic headlands that characterize this rocky coast—force the trail inland through state parks, forest service trails, and other public lands. Points of interest include Cannon Beach, with its famous Haystack Rock, and Oregon Dunes National Recreation Area, the largest expanse of coastal sand dunes to be found in North America, some of which are as high as 500 feet (152 m). Portions of the trail are open to cyclists and equestrians, and camping is free.

Animals love it, too. Migratory birds follow the Oregon coast down from summer breeding grounds in the Arctic to warm wintering grounds in the south, while gray whales guide their young northward from calving grounds in Mexico to the Bering Sea in the waters alongside this glorious highway of life. **BDS**

"Offers varied recreational opportunities from day hikes to overnight treks."

www.coasttrails.org

⬆ The Oregon coast is hundreds of miles of public land, a rare legislative gift to the people.

Tillamook Head Trail Oregon, USA

Start Tillamook Head trailhead   **End** Indian Beach trailhead   **Distance** 6.3 miles (10.1 km)
Time 2 hours   **Grade** Moderate   **Type** Disused gravel road   **Map** goo.gl/SXTllm

It may have been at the mouth of Oregon's Columbia River in 1806 that explorers Meriwether Lewis and William Clark at last laid their eyes upon the blue waters of the Pacific Ocean, but that was not the view that left the deepest impression on them. That moment occurred 20 miles (32 km) to the south, at the top of a tilted remnant of a fifteen-million-year-old basalt flow that came out of the ground somewhere near Idaho and moved down the Columbia Gorge and then down the still-forming shoreline and came to rest, just as Lewis and Clark themselves had done—at Tillamook Head. From there they decided they would walk down to what is now Cannon Beach, to bargain with some Native Americans for the blubber of a stranded whale. Today, a segment of the Oregon Coast Trail follows the route they took to these towering 1,000-foot (305-m) cliffs, the westernmost point of their

journey, and to the precise vantage point—Clark's Point of View—that caused Clark to utter: "I behold the grandest and most pleasing prospect which my eyes never surveyed."

The same views that greeted Lewis and Clark can be yours today. The Tillamook Head Trail is a well-maintained, abandoned gravel road from which you can access free basic campsites, walk past World War II concrete bunkers, and experience the thrill of nudging your way toward the precipice of cliff-top overlooks with views to Tillamook Rock. It is a coastal walk with craggy cliffs; thundering waves; a lighthouse; fragrant dense stands of Sitka spruce, hemlock, and alder; and the sort of views that the tempestuous coastline of Oregon is so good at delivering. **BDS**

⬆ Tillamook Head's rocky cliffs give endless views.

The Lost Coast Trail California, USA

Start Mattole campground   **End** Shelter Cove   **Distance** 24 miles (38.6 km)   **Time** 2–3 days
Grade Strenuous   **Type** Beaches, forest trails   **Map** goo.gl/ghuZT1

When the builders of California's Highway 1, famous for relentlessly hugging the Californian coast on its journey north from Los Angeles, reached Humboldt County, the rugged coastline of the "Lost Coast" proved too intrusive to ignore, and the highway was forced, at last, to head inland at Rockport before coming back to the sea north of Ferndale. Highway 1 was beaten into submission by the massive uplift of sedimentary rocks of the North American Plate raised by the Mendocino Triple Junction, the meeting point for three tectonic plates and the reason why this region is one of the Pacific's most active seismic zones. Part of the King Range Conservation Area, the Lost Coast Trail owes its existence to this uplift.

Much of the trail is beach hiking, but where it leaves the beach, it loses no time in becoming a series of ascents and descents hundreds of feet high, through forests of coastal redwoods and firs, before emerging again through fields of Californian poppies and wild purple lilies, and then back onto lonely, windswept beaches. Just make sure you take a tidal chart with you, as high tides can make some low-lying sections practically impassable.

September and October are the best months for walking here. From June to early September, fog often blankets the coast, not only cooling the air but obscuring views, while October to April can see heavy storms that bring torrential rain. Nevertheless, it is these same fierce ocean breezes, fog banks, raging surf, and sea spray that help make this one of the all too few coastal wilderness hiking trails to be found in California. **BDS**

⬆ Stroll a stunning, rugged stretch of Californian coast.

Golden Gate Bridge
California, USA

Start Marina Green Park   **End** Fort Point
Distance 3 miles (4.8 km)   **Time** 1 hour
Grade Easy   **Type** Shoreline walk
Map goo.gl/9Jjr4Z

Although the Bay Area Ridge Trail is one dramatic way to approach the Golden Gate Bridge, another option, if you're staying in the city, is to start at Marina Green Park and make the classic approach to the bridge: from the shoreline. You cannot leave San Francisco without some memorable bridge views, and this short and easy walk certainly provides them. At the start of the walk, there are also good views toward Alcatraz Island.

The trail is well marked and easy to follow, being popular with joggers as well as walkers, and you

> *"One of the most famous and most beautiful bridges in the world."*
>
> www.nps.gov

certainly won't get lost as you head toward the magnificent sight of the bridge. You'll also be treated to unforgettable views across San Francisco Bay, but bear in mind that San Francisco is notoriously misty, and this usually occurs in the mornings. If it is misty in the morning of your hike, plan to set off in the afternoon instead. The walk takes you through Crissy Field, a one-time airfield and now a public park that's being reclaimed as wetland. Beyond here the trail sweeps around past Torpedo Wharf and heads to Fort Point, underneath the bridge. From Fort Point you can climb up to the bridge itself, if you retrace your steps a short way, for equally lovely views back the way you came. **MG**

Bay Area Ridge: Presidio
Trail California, USA

Start Arguello Gate   **End** Golden Gate Bridge
Distance 2.5 miles (4 km)   **Time** 1–3 hours
Grade Easy to moderate   **Type** Forest, shoreline
trails   **Map** goo.gl/b1QSjj

Mark Twain said that everybody loves two cities, their own and San Francisco. Few visitors to the city get to see it, or the Golden Gate Bridge, in the way that locals know about, on the Bay Area Ridge Trail. When it's finished, the entire trail will amount to more than 550 miles (885 km), mainly through the hills that surround San Francisco Bay. This section, the San Francisco Presidio, is both easily accessible from the city center and provides impressive views both near and far of the bay, the Pacific Ocean, and especially the Golden Gate Bridge. In addition to enjoying the walk, allow time to first explore the Presidio itself. This hilly district west of the city center was first fortified in 1776, and today it is a recreational park filled with pine, cypress, and eucalyptus forests, pathways, and views. The start of the trail passes through a grove of Monterey cypress trees, first planted in the 1890s.

Walking down the trail, there are breathtaking views of the whole of the bay, and Marin County beyond, and before long you'll have a distant and magnificent view of the Golden Gate Bridge. Farther on there's Pacific Overlook, followed by Golden Gate Overlook, and several other overlooks just off the trail and not to be missed, including Immigrant Point Overlook and Cemetery Overlook.

The trail leads you to the southern end of the bridge itself, for more impressive close-up views. There's no better way of approaching the bridge on foot than by picking your way down this trail and seeing it gradually get closer and closer. You'll soon know why Mark Twain said what he did. **MG**

→ Enjoy the Presidio's historic trails and overlooks.

California Coastal Trail
California, USA

Start Oregon border   **End** Mexico border
Distance 1,200 miles (1,931 km)   **Time** 4 months
Grade Easy to moderate   **Type** Beaches, boardwalks,
trails   **Info** goo.gl/LEZamW

The California Coastal Trail is a mammoth work in progress that was started in 1972 and follows, where possible, coastal trails that have been used for centuries. It currently has more than 550 signs and markers covering 198 miles (318 km) of trails from the Lost Coast of Humboldt County to the south of San Diego. When finished, this ambitious trail will stretch all the way from the Oregon border to Mexico, a total of 1,200 miles (1,931 km).

Rather than a single pathway, however, it will be a composite of various parallel trails that can be used by walkers, cyclists, and equestrians and will always, according to the Coastal Commission that is designing it, be "within the sight, sound, and scent of the sea," through redwood forests, cactus-covered hillsides, over bluffs and sand dunes, at all times separated from the din of motor traffic. Diversionary trails will skirt the beaches that are the home to breeding elephant seals, fragile tidal pools, and natural habitats of threatened species such as the California least tern.

A more or less continuous trail along this beautiful and often rugged coastline has long been a dream of Californians, and there are hopes that, when completed, it will succeed in helping to conserve the coastal environment and bring much-needed jobs, tourism, and investment to its local communities. The Pacific Crest Trail took more than thirty years to "almost" finish; the Appalachian Trail even longer. Good things come to those who wait, and when finished, the California Coastal Trail may well be in some very exclusive company. **BDS**

◁ The California Coastal Trail is an epic project.

Tanbark and Tin House Loop Trail
California, USA

Start/End Partington Creek   **Distance** 5.6 miles
(9 km)   **Time** 5–6 hours   **Grade** Strenuous
Type Forest, mountain trails
Map goo.gl/8gX3TU

This trail begins in a redwood forest on Partington Creek at Big Sur. Partington is a treat for any explorer of California's coastal forests, a promontory that is home to a myriad of animals, from sea otters to cougars. In 1874 a businessman named John Partington arrived here and cut a 100-foot-long (30.5 m) tunnel through a mountain (the tunnel is now part of the Partington Cove Trail), so he could haul tanbark—the natural tannins of which were used in the leather industry—down the adjacent canyon to a small landing that he built in the cove below and onto waiting ships.

"A strenuous loop into the hills above Big Sur with amazing views along the coast."

www.everytrail.com

From Partington Creek the trail ascends 1,600 feet (488 m) on a series of switchbacks through a forest of tan oak trees, some of which grow almost as tall as the redwoods. Continue along a final uphill stretch to a junction that will take you to a fascinating historical oddity, the Tin House, built in 1944 by Lathrop Brown, a former Congressman. Brown somehow procured the tin from an old gas station, at a time when tin was a sought-after wartime commodity, and laid wire around his giant conductor to divert lightning. Legend says Brown built it for his friend Franklin D. Roosevelt, but no one really knows. There is no record of the president ever coming here, which you will agree after seeing it, was to his misfortune. **BDS**

Tahoe Rim Trail California/Nevada, USA

Start/End Brockway Summit   **Distance** 165 miles (265 km)   **Time** 10–15 days   **Grade** Easy to strenuous
Type Long-distance hiking, mountain biking, and equestrian trails   **Info** goo.gl/9kZjyT

Tahoe Rim Trail encircles an enormous, deep-blue lake, the largest alpine lake in North America. It weaves through two states, through a landscape of lush, forested peaks; dark volcanic summits; outcrops of stark, glistening granite, and is within reach of hundreds of lakes sprinkled across the high alpine wilderness area that surrounds it. It has nine segments and accesses both the Sierra Nevada and the Carson Range Spur. It is astonishing to think that with all this natural beauty, it took until 2001 to complete the Tahoe Rim Trail. The lake itself, without which there would be no trail, is 22 miles (35 km) long and 12 miles (19 km) wide, the deepest subalpine lake in North America.

Glenn Hampton of Lake Tahoe Basin Management Unit proposed the idea of completing a mixed-use trail around the lake's rim. An association was formed, and the trail was begun in 1984 at Grass Lake. In 2001 the section between Rose Knob Peak, in the Mount Rose Wilderness, and Nevada's Mount Baldy, the last link in the chain, was finished.

There are bear, deer, mountain lions, bobcats, coyotes, marmots, squirrels, and porcupines, not to mention birdlife, including ospreys and bald eagles, and the fauna gives new meaning to the term "mixed-use trail." You will also encounter ranges in elevation from 6,240 feet (1,900 m) at the lake's outlet to 10,338 feet (3,151 m) at Nevada's Relay Peak. The hiking season is from June to September, depending on snowfall, and the trail will take you past extinct volcanoes and cinder cones, through meadows, and even on a detour through Desolation Wilderness, a vast expanse of granite swept clean by glaciers. **BDS**

⬆ Circumnavigate North America's most beautiful lake.

Pettit Lake–Hell Roaring Loop Idaho, USA

Start/End Pettit Lake campground   Distance 30 miles (48 km)   Time 3–4 days   Grade Strenuous
Type Loop trail through forests and by lakes   Map goo.gl/UfYLXr

Here in the Sawtooth Mountains of Idaho, where you'll also find the Sawtooth National Forest, is some of the finest hiking in the northwest United States. Idaho often gets overlooked as a state, even by many Americans who know it only as the place the best potatoes come from. With Washington and Oregon to the west, and Montana and Wyoming to the east, Idaho is more often a place to drive through to get to another destination. All the more reason to stop here and enjoy the overwhelming grandeur of the Sawtooth Mountains, which are part of the 217,000-acre (87,817-ha) Sawtooth Wilderness Area.

The jagged Sawtooth Range is part of the Rocky Mountains and rises to 10,751 feet (3,277 m) at Thompson Peak. To the south of the peak lies a string of glacial lakes with evocative names, such as Redfish Lake, Yellow Belly Lake, Hidden Lake, Hell Roaring Lake, and Pettit Lake. The last two form the focus of a lengthy loop trail that takes you up and down the mountain slopes; a part of a mosaic of trails that runs for hundreds of miles through the area.

Note that the harsh winter weather here in the mountains means that the trail is usually open only from July to October. From about mid-July to the end of August is the best time to tackle the hike—but remember to take plenty of mosquito repellent. Your rewards, however, will include the sight of meadows filled with colorful wildflowers making the most of the summer sunshine. You'll walk by mountain lakes, and hike up again to mountain passes giving views that will take your breath away, if the hike up there doesn't do it first. **MG**

↑ Traverse two memorable Sawtooth wilderness lakes.

Bonneville Shoreline Trail
Utah/Idaho, USA

Start Bridal Veil Falls, Utah
End Logan, Idaho   **Distance** 110 miles
(177 km)   **Time** 2 weeks   **Grade** Moderate
Type Mountain trail   **Info** goo.gl/NSRo6h

The Bonneville Shoreline Trail (BST) follows the eastern shoreline of Lake Bonneville, a prehistoric pluvial (landlocked) lake that once covered much of what is now the Great Basin region of the western United States. As the lake receded into the desert over thousands of years, it left behind a series of "benches," and the trail today follows the line of one of these benches (the Bonneville bench) as it follows the Wasatch Fault, the earthquake fault line that runs in a north–south direction along the western edge of the Wasatch Mountains, from central Utah 240 miles (386 km) to the Idaho border. The Idaho border also happens to be the eventual hoped-for terminus for the volunteer trailblazers who are still building this ambitious trail.

This is a lofty goal, and a potentially immensely popular one too, for when finished the trail will pass within 20 miles (32 km) of 80 percent of the entire population of the state. The views are quick in coming, with a steep ascent soon after leaving the trailhead at Bridal Veil Falls, giving panoramic views over the Utah Valley. The views are made all the wider because this is a trail with very little to no tree cover, a highly exposed path that means you need to come prepared with a cap, sunscreen, and plenty of water. However, its exposed nature means that it is also one of the first trails to dry out in the spring, bringing to it the first rush of new season hikers.

The residents of Salt Lake City love the BST, because it connects them to their beloved Wasatch Mountains, and because from its inception, it was a trail initiated by Utah citizens. And one day will be finished by them, too. **BDS**

"The unique urban-wildlife interface of the Bonneville Shoreline Trail offers many recreational activities."

www.slcgov.com

⌖ Bridal Veil Falls is on this popular Salt Lake City trail, which was built by locals to link the city to the mountains.

Superior Hiking Trail
Minnesota, USA

Start Jay Cooke State Park   **End** Pigeon River
Distance 275 miles (442 km)   **Time** 3 weeks
Grade Moderate   **Type** Ridge trail
Info goo.gl/tbwEOM

The Superior Hiking Trail is one of the great long-distance hikes in the United States, mostly following a ridgeway that provides great views over Lake Superior, the largest of the Great Lakes. Although it's long, it's a well-maintained and well-signposted trail that's easy to follow, and it presents a challenge to stamina and planning rather than orienteering. Up here in northeastern Minnesota, roughly between Duluth and the Canadian border, the Superior National Forest, alongside Lake Superior, provides some of the most beautiful wilderness in the United States. It's an area that's not too well known in other parts of the country, and the trail provides one of the simplest ways to see some of it, for those who are prepared to backpack and sleep a little rough.

One virtue of the trail is that it is purely a hiking trail—no horses, mountain bikes, or motor vehicles are allowed. Instead, you'll be sharing the trail with its abundant wildlife, such as eagles, moose, deer, and beavers, and you'll need to keep a watchful eye out for black bears. Another virtue of this epic hike is the abundance of campsites along the way. You'll find one about every 5 to 8 miles (8–13 km), making it easy to stop and rest, or push on. There are regular trailhead parking lots, too, meaning you can do what many people do and tackle the trail in sections. The greatest joy here is, of course, the landscape. For most of its way, it hugs Lake Superior, itself such a vast stretch of water that it's more like walking along an ocean than a lake. In places, you'll also get views of the Sawtooth Mountains, and you'll pass through several state parks. It's little wonder the trail is often included in lists of the best hikes in the United States. **MG**

"The Superior serves up every sensation of a great wilderness hike, but adds in all sorts of flexibility."

adventure.nationalgeographic.com

⬆ This is a walk that delivers stunning wilderness and Lake Superior views, and is often named a top U.S. trail.

Pow Wow Trail
Minnesota, USA

Start/End Isabella Lake parking area
Distance 30 miles (48 km)   **Time** 3–4 days
Grade Strenuous   **Type** Wilderness trail
Map goo.gl/PHNMMb

If you head for the Superior National Forest, tucked between Lake Superior and the Canadian border, you will feel you are stepping back in time to a true wilderness era. Hiking through an area of pine and cedar forests and picking your way past beaver dams, you'll find the biggest population of timber wolves in the continental United States. Just be ready to wade through a boggy landscape, which you'll also share with grouse and moose. There are black bear, and deer here too, the Canadian lynx, and more species of bird than in any other national forest in the United States.

The impression of going back to the times of the first explorers is reinforced by some of the names given to the lakes that the trail makes its way around, such as Superstition Lake, Pioneer Lake, Myth Lake, and Rock of Ages Lake. The lakes teem with fish: pike, bass, trout, and walleyes. It's a landscape of wetland and woodland, of fallen timbers, a land that the Native Americans hunted in and that the early fur traders and trappers trudged through going back and forth between what became the United States and Canada.

This is not a hike for the inexperienced walker. A lightning strike in 2011 caused the Pagami Creek fire, which badly affected much of the trail. Burned trees blocked the trail for miles, and though most of these were cleared by 2012, not all of the trail has yet been fully restored, and you'll need to be skilled with map and compass to pick your way through the sections that are still not fully waymarked again and are in places overgrown. It will make you feel even more like one of those early pioneers or trappers. **MG**

◁ The Pow Wow Trail still has a wilderness feel.

Sioux–Hustler Trail
Minnesota, USA

Start/End Trailhead parking lot, 17 miles from start of the Echo Trail   **Distance** 32 miles (51.4 km)   **Time** 3–4 days   **Grade** Strenuous
Type Tough wilderness trail   **Map** goo.gl/MsuAKK

The Sioux–Hustler Trail is a notoriously poorly maintained trail, best walked by experienced orienteers and hikers only. Those prepared to tackle it, however, will be rewarded with an experience they will never forget. The trail passes through a wilderness of grasslands, forests, hills, wetlands, rivers, and lakes. Your route will be blocked by fallen trees; and you will have to ford rapidly flowing streams and rivers.

This is a wild land, lying northwest of the Great Lakes, just south of the U.S.–Canadian border but farther north than Toronto, in the Boundary Waters

"You need a day-use permit to take the day trip and an overnight permit for camping."

www.bwca.net

Canoe Area Wilderness. Some hikers report that they even miss the trailhead, and you're advised to let someone know where you're going in case you get lost. It's probably best to tackle this trail in a small group. Others try to keep knowledge of this trail to themselves, to preserve its pristine, rugged nature. The first section of the hike can be done as a day trip, taking you to the deep granite gorge and waterfalls on the Little Indian Sioux River, known as the Devil's Cascade. This is near the start of the looped part of the Sioux–Hustler Trail. The Hustler part of the trail's name refers to Hustler Lake, one of the many lakes you'll see, most of which are inaccessible other than by canoe or on foot. **MG**

Bayfield Sea and Ice Caves Wisconsin, USA

Start/End Meyers Beach   **Distance** 2 miles (3.2 km)   **Time** 2–3 hours   **Grade** Easy
Type Ice, snow trails   **Map** goo.gl/JIqrPP

The sea and ice caves that line the foreshore of Wisconsin's Bayfield Peninsula on Lake Superior make a fine walk in spring, summer, and fall, and many a hiking trail will take you through the dense woodlands that line the lakeshore and down to the water's edge on the Lakeshore Trail.

However, this approach gets you much too close. Sometimes you need to step back to appreciate nature properly, and you can't do that with a choppy lake in the way; moreover, access to some of the caves can be difficult in stormy conditions. Also, while approaching them from the water may provide a far better view, this is not an ideal solution for anyone who ever felt uncomfortable in a kayak. Fortunately, if you don't feel comfortable paddling and rolling about on an icy lake, but at the same time hanker for the lake's perspective onto this interesting strip of

coast, you always have the option of waiting until the depths of winter and approaching it all on foot over frozen ice.

In winter, the Bayfield Sea and Ice Caves are transformed into majestic, sculpted ice caves, and a good cold winter sees conga lines of well-clad locals and well-informed outsiders making their way across the lake to view them immersed in a sea of white from vantage points usually denied. The thickness of the ice can vary, and wind and waves can break up even thick ice and make it very unstable. A Sea Caves Watch website and a telephone "Ice Line" should be checked before venturing out. Observing these ice-draped wonders while standing on a frozen lake is an experience not to be missed. **BDS**

⬆ Discover frozen caves on a thrilling sea of ice.

Finger Lakes Trail New York, USA

Start Allegheny State Park **End** Catskill Forest Preserve **Distance** 558 miles (897 km) **Time** 6–7 weeks
Grade Strenuous **Type** Long-distance trail **Info** goo.gl/KQ6iCw

The Finger Lakes Trail is the longest single network of trails to be found in New York state, with offshoots going in all directions. There are roughly 400 miles (644 km) that branch off and yet are still part of the Finger Lakes Trail, not to mention the other trails that Finger Lakes crosses, such as the 500-mile (800-km) Bruce Trail that heads up into Canada. The main Finger Lakes Trail on its own is a challenge for even experienced long-distance hikers, and it's estimated that only about twenty people a year complete the whole hike in one go. Many others tackle the trail a stretch at a time, sometimes over many years. Although it's not one of the most familiar U.S. trails, some people regard it as one of the best, partly due to its unfamiliarity. People hiking its full length report that they can walk for a week without seeing another person. It is a hike for the self-sufficient.

The scenery along the trail is not particularly dramatic, although the endless rolling hills are certainly attractive. What appeals here is the solitude, the feeling that you're doing something special, and the discovery that you don't have to have dramatic cliffs, mountains, or gorges to make for a beautiful walk and an exhilarating experience.

The trail is especially thrilling in the fall, when the autumn colors come to the trees, nowhere more so than at the western extremes of the Catskill Mountains. Spring, too, is a perfect time to hike, with the trees in blossom and the wildlife starting to get active again. Some people even hike the trail in winter, showing there's no bad time to hike New York state's longest, long-distance footpath. **MG**

⊤ Finger Lakes possess a labyrinth of great trails.

Bold Coast Trail
Maine, USA

Start/End Trailhead on ME Route 191
Distance 10 miles (16 km)   **Time** 4–5 hours
Grade Strenuous   **Type** Coastal cliffs, forest trails
Map goo.gl/iQPE8M

Maine's Bold Coast has been called an untouched treasure of the United States and has been compared to Ireland's west coast for its rugged, scenic beauty. Five miles (8 km) of the coast are open to hikers as part of a longer figure-eight, which is a tough challenge, but it can be halved by attempting only one loop of that figure-eight. The trail is less well known than most and is comparatively new. The 2,200 acres (890 ha) of land in which the trail sits was owned formerly by publishing magnate William Randolph Hearst, and was used originally for logging. In 1989 the state of Maine purchased the region's coastline, and five years later a group of enthusiasts built the trail with the aid of the National Guard, who helicoptered in cedar planks to help build the walkways that took the trail through its boggy stretches.

The result of that labor is a trail that can be strenuous in places, but the reward is the chance to hike along cliff tops and to feel a genuine sense of adventure. The cliffs tower above crashing waves, and some places are unfenced, providing a real sense of danger and drama.

To make the most of the adventure, use one of the several campsites and stay overnight. It provides a kinship with the Native American people who used to live along this coast in centuries past. Today, you'll meet birdwatchers coming to see some of the almost 200 bird species that have been recorded here, including peregrine falcons, several species of owl, and numerous seabirds. With meadows and forests, bogs and swamps, and the exhilaration of those cliff top hikes, the Bold Coast shows it is still possible to experience wilderness on the east coast of the United States. **MG**

"A pristine and at times solitary trek along rugged ocean cliffs and through forests of spruce."

www.yankeemagazine.com

⬆ A coastal walk so isolated that helicopters were needed to fly in materials to create its walkways.

Peaks Island Loop

Maine, USA

Start/End Jones Wharf
Distance 4 miles (6.4 km) **Time** 2 hours
Grade Easy **Type** Paved roads
Map goo.gl/j1RczJ

Peaks Island is the sort of place that, should you come here, you immediately begin thinking of retirement. Sitting in the middle of Casco Bay just 3 miles (4.8 km) and a twenty-minute ferry ride away from the center of downtown Portland, the lights of Maine's capital twinkle away every night as though in competition with the constellations above. The island's 720 acres (291 ha) has a population of a little more than 1,500, which can swell to more than 4,000 in the summer, many lured here by an ironic mix of proximity and isolation, and also of independence. The island's residents have made six attempts to secede from the city of Portland since 1883.

Once you are here, there is no better way to get a feel for the island and to meet the interesting mix of people who live here, from lobstermen to doctors, than by walking the Peaks Island Loop that follows graceful shoreline-hugging roads. It has always been an ideal walking island, with its interior crisscrossed by a labyrinth of narrow, winding streets that barely carry a car past the rows of cottages and modest-looking houses. The island's mass runs north to south, with its northern and eastern sides being the least developed. The eastern shoreline in particular has large expanses of open horizon and views across to some of the bay's other 211 islands, such as neighboring Little Diamond Island, and a variety of smaller islands are visible to the north. There are plenty of benches along the way as well, on which to relax and just gaze contentedly over the water and catch those refreshing Atlantic breezes in summer. And as Portland sizzles away, adjust your body clock to "Peaks Island" time and start winding down. **BDS**

"One of the best things is island hopping to one of the many islands in Casco Bay."

www.exploremainetoday.com

An island in Maine's Casco Bay has trails, tranquility, and sophisticated isolation.

The Bubbles
Maine, USA

Start/End Bubble Rock parking lot
Distance 2.6 miles (4.2 km)   **Time** 1–3 hours
Grade Easy   **Type** Mountain loop hike
Map goo.gl/RrXVnK

You may have seen The Bubbles walk without knowing it, since the teetering Bubble Rock is a popular feature and the subject of numerous photographs. Balanced near the summit of South Bubble (768 feet/234 m) in Acadia National Park in Maine, the rock gives the impression that it might go tumbling down the hill at any moment. It is what's known as a glacial erratic, a rock that originated about 40 miles (64 km) away and was deposited on South Bubble as a result of glacial action. It's one of the highlights of two short but highly enjoyable joined trails, taking you both to South Bubble and to North Bubble (872 feet/266 m).

The Bubbles may not seem very high, but the trail is popular because it gives you extensive views with comparatively little effort. From North Bubble you're high enough to have views out to the Atlantic Ocean, and of Jordan Pond, one of several large bodies of water in this part of the National Park. The Bubbles Trail is tucked between Jordan Pond which, despite its name, covers an area of 187 acres (76 ha), and Eagle Lake, which is twice the size. From South Bubble the views include Eagle Lake, Pemetic Mountain, Penobscot Mountain, and down to the pretty little town of Bar Harbor, on Frenchman Bay.

You start both hikes on the same trail, with the ascent to South Bubble an offshoot of the main trail, which you return to in order to continue on a looped trail to North Bubble and then back around to the parking area. If you have time you can explore other trails that intersect with the Bubble Trail and see a little more of Acadia National Park, which was established in 1919 and was the first National Park east of the Mississippi River. **MG**

"A carriage road on the western side of Jordan Pond provides spectacular views of the mountains."

ww.acadia.ws

⊡ The distinctive profile of The Bubbles as seen from the shore of Jordan Pond.

Cape Cod Rail Trail
Massachusetts, USA

Start South Dennis trailhead on Route 134
End Wellfleet trailhead   **Distance** 22 miles
(35 km)   **Time** 3 days   **Grade** Easy
Type Paved path   **Map** goo.gl/IhoC0e

Following the route of the former Old Colony Railroad, this is the perfect hike to experience Cape Cod at its best. With a few gentle hills, pretty ponds, and side trails taking you to some National Seashore beaches if you want a break or a picnic, the Cape Cod Rail Trail is hard to beat. It also leads you through some attractive Cape Cod villages as it heads between the two trailheads, and there are plenty of facilities and places to stop for food on the way.

The Old Colony Railroad completed its rail link between Boston and Provincetown, at the end of Cape Cod, in 1873. It made Cape Cod easily accessible for the first time, and turned it into a popular vacation destination for people from cities such as Boston and New York. The route was in operation until the mid-1960s, after which it was bought by the Massachusetts Department of Transportation and converted to recreational use. Although primarily a cycling route, a separate trail for hiking and horseback riding runs alongside it.

Not long after the start of the walk at the South Dennis trailhead you pass ponds and reservoirs, and there are plenty of opportunities to swim along the way, so go prepared. The route passes through the Nickerson State Park, alongside Cape Cod Bay, and soon after you're over on the other side of the Cape, able to enjoy the National Seashore along the Atlantic Ocean. This is one of the most beautiful seashores in the United States with miles of golden, sandy beaches and a feeling of peace and well-being. The Cape Cod Rail Trail is the kind of walk that, on a fine day, makes you feel you just want to turn around at the end and do it all over again. **MG**

"The trail has a wide unpaved shoulder on one side to accommodate horseback riding, walkers, and runners."

www.mass.gov

⬆ The Cape Cod Rail Trail is a rewarding walk on undemanding terrain.

Martha's Vineyard Trails Massachusetts, USA

Start/End Edgartown **Distance** Various **Time** Various **Grade** Easy **Type** Mostly grassy/sandy trails and meadows **Info** goo.gl/cDCEfK

There's a rock in the center, or thereabouts, of Martha's Vineyard, that island enclave off the southern coastline of Cape Cod. Known as Waskosim's Rock it marks the spot that locals refer to as the "middle line," the place where one of the island's earliest white settlers, Thomas Mayhew, brokered a deal with the leaders of the island's Wampanoag tribe for the division of the island's land. Everything to the southwest of the rock would, Mayhew promised, remain Wampanoag land, and everything else to the north and east would be his. The meeting is a turning point in the island's history, but there are no bronze plaques or signage telling you how to get here. And that is the way most local Vineyarders prefer their trails to be—understated and unmarked. A series of well-kept secrets.

The point is that not all of Martha's Vineyard trails need marking, when you are so frequently in sight of the Atlantic Ocean. This is the reason most visitors come here. They come to stroll the island's magnificent beaches, such as the 17 miles (27 km) along South Beach from Katama to Gay Head Lighthouse followed by watching a memorable sunset from the top of the Gay Head clay cliffs. Walking the beaches here, however, can be problematic—unlike most beaches in the United States the area between the high and low tide marks are not "held in trust for its citizens," so be on the lookout for over-zealous landholders. Fortunately, though, with typical Vineyard sanctuaries such as Peaked Hill, the banks of its inland streams, the scarlet oaks of Sepiessa Point, and the tranquillity of Tisbury Great Pond, there is plenty of peace here for everyone. **BDS**

⊞ The views from Gay Head Lighthouse are spectacular.

Terrace Pond Loop New Jersey, USA

Start/End Clinton Road trailhead parking lot   **Distance** 4.7 miles (7.5 km)   **Time** 3.5 hours   **Grade** Moderate
Type Wooded loop trail   **Map** goo.gl/qJooBx

Less than 50 miles (80.4 km) from the Empire State Building in Manhattan, the Wawayanda State Park in northern New Jersey is as far from big city life as you can get. In its 34,350 acres (13,900 ha) you'll find forests, mountains, abundant wildlife, camping, boating, and even a beach. You'll also find the delightful Terrace Pond Loop, just one of the many hiking trails in this tucked-away state park.

The Terrace Pond Loop is one of the most popular hikes, as it's easy to follow and gives you a varied walk in a short space of time. You start by climbing uphill through woods on the Terrace Pond North Trail, with a little bit of scrambling over rocks. The trail takes you to the Terrace Pond that gives the hike its name, a surprisingly large and hidden pond perched on top of Bearfort Mountain (1,380 feet/421 m), surrounded by woods and more rock formations. It's the perfect

place to cool off on a hot day. Look out for eagles, hawks, and herons, all of which live in the park, as do snakes and bears, so keep an eye and an ear out for those, although both tend to steer clear of humans and the trail is quite a busy one. The woods around here are varied and include beech, chestnut oak, maple, birch, and hemlock trees, and you'll also find rhododendrons in abundance.

Beyond the pond the path continues onto the Terrace Pond South Trail, through more thick and shady woods, and with some waterfalls hidden away just off the trail. It then loops back toward the starting point, going through some huge rhododendrons in a grove, dwarfing and covering the path in places. It's a lovely end to a wonderful walk. **MG**

⬆ Swampland on the Terrace Pond Loop.

Bear Cove Trail
South Carolina, USA

Start/End Devil's Fork State Park camping area
Distance 2 miles (3.2 km) **Time** 1 hour
Grade Easy **Type** Woodland trail with lake views
Map goo.gl/1FVoIw

Devil's Fork State Park is a man-made park on the shores of a man-made lake that is surrounded by the Appalachian Mountains, the Blue Ridge Mountains, and the Sumter National Forest. It's the kind of place where you take a deep breath of clean, fresh air and feel good to be alive. The park itself is a small one (622 acres/252 ha) and was only created in 1990, but since then it's become one of the most popular recreation spots in this part of South Carolina. About fifteen minutes' drive north of Salem, the park is on the shore of Lake Jocassee, which is fed by four mountain

---

"Scenic views of Lake Jocassee await you at the loop end of this hilly, mildly rugged, dirt trail."

www.sctrails.net

---

streams and several waterfalls. This not only keeps the water cool—a blessing in the hot summer here—but also means it's the perfect habitat for fish.

The main hiking trail in the park is the Bear Cove Trail, a partially looped trail that takes you through undulating woodland out onto a wooded headland jutting into the lake, and back again. There is a second trail within the State Park, the Oconee Bell Trail. This is named for the Oconee Bell, a plant with pretty white and pink flowers. It's a rare plant, once thought to have been extinct, but 90 percent of the world's population of it is found here in Devil's Fork State Park. They even have a Oconee Bell Festival in March, with an organized Oconee Bell Nature Walk. **MG**

Eastern Shore National Recreation Trail Alabama, USA

Start USS Alabama Memorial Park
End Weeks Bay **Distance** 36 miles (57.9 km)
Time 2 days **Grade** Easy **Type** Asphalt and elevated boardwalks **Map** goo.gl/weKLjc

Following the shoreline of Baldwin County along Mobile Bay in southern Alabama, the Eastern Shore National Recreation Trail owes its existence to the relentless efforts of the Baldwin County Trailblazers, a grassroots, non-profit organization dedicated to the development of a continuous multi-use pathway. The Trailblazers worked with local commissioners, newspapers, and the business community and proved once again that trails do not just happen—they are the product of communities who have something special to share.

Designated a National Recreation Trail in 2010, the trail begins at the USS Alabama Memorial Park and from there you pass over the Gator Alley Boardwalk where you can observe alligators from a safe distance, as well as seabirds and turtles. Although the trail skirts Mobile Bay it is essentially an urban pathway, mostly asphalt with elevated boardwalks, passing through the towns of Daphne, Montrose, and Fairhope before linking up with the Fairhope South Beach Trail and on to Point Clear. It was a lofty aspiration to want to connect the western and eastern shorelines of Mobile Bay. The trail takes you through the unsullied wetlands of Daphne and the oak-lined trails between Daphne and Montrose, through the ravines of Red Gully and Rock and Fly creeks that take you huffing and puffing up the bluffs to Montrose—the highest elevation of any spot on the eastern U.S. coast from Maine to Mexico—and the Confederate Rest Cemetery at Point Clear with its 500 unmarked Confederate graves. It is a grand achievement, and is testament to the determination and vision of the Baldwin County Trailblazers. **BDS**

Hana–Waianapanapa Coastal Trail
Maui, Hawaii, USA

Start/End Waianapanapa State Park
Distance 6 miles (9.6 km)   **Time** 2–3 hours
Grade Moderate   **Type** Coastal path
Map goo.gl/h1a8bH

To prove that not all of the Hawaiian islands are ringed with endless golden sandy beaches, this coastal hike near the eastern tip of Maui takes you over rugged black lava rock past blowholes showing that there is still volcanic activity here. Although the walk is easy to moderate, and certainly easy to follow, sturdy walking boots are recommended.

This scenic walk runs between the Waianapanapa State Park just north of Hana Bay, and can be done in either direction or as an out-and-back route if you want to get back to your starting point. Start and end it at the Waianapanapa end, where there is parking, a restroom, picnic facilities, some cabins to rent, fishing, swimming, and a beach park. Note also that the walk is sometimes referred to as the Ke Ala Loa O Maui, or Piilani Trail. Waianapanapa State Park covers 122 acres (49 ha) and, as well as people coming to enjoy the facilities, it attracts numerous seabirds, drawn by the "glistening fresh water," which is what Waianapanapa means in Hawaiian. The freshwater spring and pools create a delightful setting, so allow time to explore the park.

It's a very photogenic walk, with the black and craggy lava rock and cinders contrasting with the deep blue of the sea and the lush green vegetation. Inland are the slopes of the Haleakala Crater, part of another national park. The volcano still rumbles occasionally but hasn't erupted since the 1700s. About halfway along, look out for the *heiau* (Hawaiian temple site). When you get to Hana Bay, simply turn around and retrace your steps. Back in Waianapanapa, look for the unusual black sand beach, for a final photo stop on this exhilarating coastal walk. **MG**

"The hike follows the jagged windswept coastal cliffs, crossing lava flows above caves."

www.trails.com

⬆ The black lava rock, native vegetation, and crystal-clear water make for a striking coastline.

Diamond Head Hiking Trail O'ahu, Hawaii, USA

Start Diamond Head State Monument **End** Diamond Head **Distance** 1.6 miles (2.5 km) **Time** 2 hours
Grade Moderate **Type** Volcanic crater ascent **Map** goo.gl/EasnUJ

Many people go to Hawaii just to lie on the beach at Waikiki. However, a few minutes away is one of the most unusual walks—from the floor of the Diamond Head volcanic crater all the way up to the rim. It's one of the most popular and rewarding short hikes in Hawaii. Diamond Head is on O'ahu, the third largest of the islands, and was formed about 300,000 years ago during a single, spectacular explosion. It has, however, been dormant for about 150,000 years and is now a safe climb.

As a hike it looks worse from down below as a road takes you part of the way and into the Diamond Head State Monument, within the crater itself. It's still a bit of a challenge, however, mainly because of the combination of heat and lack of shade. You have to be prepared to hike in the full glare of the sun, so take plenty of water and sunscreen.

Diamond Head gets its name from the glittering calcite crystals in its rocks, which nineteenth-century British sailors thought were diamonds. The local name for it, though, is Le'ahi, because from a distance it resembles the shape of the dorsal fin of the Ahi tuna. In 1908 the U.S. Army, which had a base on Diamond Head, built the trail that visitors now enjoy from the crater to the rim. It starts on a paved path before switching to rather steep switchback stairways, with handrails. Although steep, there are plenty of opportunities to rest, including some viewpoints, and you don't have to be super fit to get to the top. There you will be rewarded with spectacular 360-degree views of the island and the ocean, as well as those surfers and sun-worshippers way down below. **MG**

⬆ The volcanic crater of Diamond Head State Monument.

Kalalau Trail Kauai, Hawaii, USA

Start Ke'e Beach   **End** Kalalau Beach   **Distance** 11 miles (17.7 km)   **Time** 1 day   **Grade** Strenuous
Type Forest and mountain trails   **Map** goo.gl/pFdpVZ

The Na Pali Coast on the north coast of the Hawaiian island of Kauai is a true wonderland: a landscape of towering sea cliffs and grand valleys that descend from the mountains and only end when they seemingly plunge into the ocean; a land of waterfalls and streams that flow in abundance and continue to gouge their way ever deeper into the island's fertile soils. The Kalalau Trail, the creation of which first began in the late 1800s, remains the only land access to the Na Pali coastline, and walking it, despite it being only 11 miles (17.7 km) long, will take you the better part of a day.

The first section begins at Ke'e Beach on an unmaintained trail that takes you into the Hanakapi'ai valley. The trail deteriorates at its halfway point and should be hiked only in good weather due to the ever-present threat of flash flooding. A series of steep switchbacks takes you 800 feet (244 m) up from the valley floor, through the hanging valley of Ho'olulu, and into the Hanakoa Valley past agricultural terraces that once used to grow taro and later coffee.

Be careful as you approach Hanakoa Falls as the trail may be badly eroded. Leaving Hanakoa Valley (there is the option of camping here) the canopy opens up and the trail becomes quite exposed, but the site of the Kalalau Valley's wonderfully fluted cliffs will urge you on. As you get closer to Kalalau Stream the trail narrows again and the drop-offs are significant, so be aware of your footing. Once over the stream, you arrive at Kalalau Beach where some shaded campsites can be found at trails' end, or continue 2 miles (3.2 km) to the Kalalau Valley. **BDS**

⬆ Your efforts will be rewarded with views such as this.

Beaches of Sayulita

Nayarit, Mexico

Start/End Sayulita   Distance Various
Time Various   Grade Easy
Type Beach walks and easy trails
Info goo.gl/JTFWsc

*"... the hikes between town
and outlaying beaches can be
full of adventure..."*

www.sayulitalife.com

⬆ From the Beach of the Dead to the Beach of the Caves,
the Sayulita coast has the beach for you.

The state of Nayarit on Mexico's Pacific Ocean coast is famed for having some of the most beautiful beaches in a country full of beautiful beaches. The best of these are in the little fishing village of Sayulita, 25 miles (40.2 km) north of the holiday playground of Puerto Vallarta. It is a world apart from the busy beach resort, but if you're based there, then it's well worth the drive to enjoy walking on and around these exceptional beaches.

There are no particular directions to take, and there are several different beaches in the area that are all worth seeing. One of the closest to Sayulita and also the most photographed is Playa Las Cuevas, Beach of Caves, just north of town. Here, the pounding of the waves that the surfers love so much has created a network of caves right on the beach, making for some dramatic photographs into and through the rocks. A little way farther on the path leads you to a good view over the Playa Malpasos, an even more remote beach. From here, if you want to explore some more, you can take a trail that leads into the jungle behind the beach.

To the south of the town is Playa de los Muertos, Beach of the Dead, which gets its name because it's close to the town cemetery. There's nothing sinister about this beach, though, which is sheltered by cliffs and is popular with families. Much farther south is Playa Patzcuaro, and if you have the energy, you can take a more challenging hike from here to the top of Monkey Mountain. This peak is sacred to the local Huichol Indians, and from the top you'll enjoy panoramic views of the beaches and the ocean for miles along the coast. **MG**

Cinnamon Bay Loop Trail
St. John, U.S. Virgin Islands

Start/End Cinnamon Bay campground
Distance 1.5 miles (2.4 km)
Time 1 hour **Grade** Easy **Type** Forest trail
Map goo.gl/v25poA

If you are visiting the Caribbean island of St. John, one of several islands that comprise the U.S. Virgin Islands (which the United States purchased from the Danish government in 1917 for US$25 million), and you only have time for one walk, then this should be it. The Cinnamon Bay Loop Trail offers a glimpse at the rugged terrain that is characteristic of the island's interior. It is fairly short, as well as being flat and well-shaded, and Virgin Islands National Parks have gone to a lot of trouble to locate some excellent information boards along this agreeable self-guided walk.

It begins by taking you through the remains of the island's old rum factory and sugar mill. The twelve remaining columns are all that remain of the warehouse that once stored hundreds of barrels of rum, molasses, and dried sugarcane stalks. Not far from the sugar mill are the extensive remains of the rum distillery, once owned and operated by the Danish West India Plantation Company, which owned Cinnamon Bay prior to the U.S. purchase. The trail into the forest begins here, past groves of bay rum trees that were grown for the production of bay leaf oil for use in colognes. A spur trail leads to the Cinnamon Bay Cemetery, which still contains the aboveground tomb of the plantation owner's wife, Anna Hjardemaal.

Keep your eye out for the mammee apple tree, the so-called South American or Saint Domingo apricot, and also for a stand of the Theobroma cacao, the chocolate tree, a native of the Americas, with brown seed pods from which chocolate is taken. The trail loops around and back to the plantation's estate house, rebuilt from galvanized steel after being demolished by a hurricane in the early 1900s. **BDS**

"A perfect choice for those who would like to experience a taste of the St. John interior."

www.stjohnbeachguide.com

⬆ The trail runs through the lush tropical forest of the island's interior.

Reef Bay Trail
St. John, U.S. Virgin Islands

Start Centreline Road, east of Cruz Bay
End Reef Bay **Distance** 2.4 miles (3.8 km)
Time 2 hours **Grade** Easy **Type** Forest trails
Map goo.gl/wZ65RT

" … the real reward for this hike is the final destination— Reef Bay."

www.naturalbornhikers.com

It might be the third smallest park in the entire U.S. National Parks network, but the Virgin Islands National Park still covers almost two-thirds of the island of St. John. And while the forest that fills it may seem at first glance to be typically aged, don't be fooled. The entire island was almost ripped free of trees during a frenetic period of logging in the 1800s, so everything you see here carries the mantle of a "recovering forest." Protected since 1956, it is estimated that it will take another hundred years for it to return to its original level of tropical complexity.

The Reef Bay Trail begins in the park headquarters in Cruz Bay and runs to Reef Bay, through dense tropical forests and rain forests at its higher elevations, following the course of an old Danish cart track. The forest, regenerating though it might be, is still full of treasures, including giant banyan trees, wild coffee, 200-year-old Kapok trees that the island's original inhabitants, the Tainos, in the past hollowed out and transformed into canoes, and terraced hillsides once used to grow sugar cane. On the ground you might see tree frogs and mongoose, as well as a range of diverse flora, from edible red limes and wild pineapples to the bizarrely named "stinky toe pod." The last is better known as the West Indian locust, a foul-smelling but delicious fibrous tan fruit that might look like a big brown toe but has plenty of iron and calcium and tastes a little like a mango.

After emerging from the forest and onto the pure white sands of Reef Bay, you can stay as long as you like in its warm sun-drenched waters. If you don't have the energy for the walk back, you can catch a boat to the park headquarters at Cruz Bay. **BDS**

⤒ The Reef Bay Trail runs through tropical forest that is still recovering from historical logging.

Antigua with the 5AM Hike Club Antigua

Start/End Various   Distance Various
Time Various   Grade Easy to moderate
Type Beaches, mountain, and forest trails
Info goo.gl/rBwqSS

It all began in 2009, when Connie Richmond and Oral Evanson, employees of the Antigua Public Utilities Authority, decided it was time to get serious about their health and so created the "5AM Hike." It started humbly enough, with just a few informal afternoon walks, and then one day a group of ten decided to do a walk from Falmouth, a coastal town on the south of the island, to Antigua's stunning Rendezvous Beach. Then they did another walk, and then another, and from nowhere the group had grown to more than seventy.

Now a "serious" organization with its very own executive, membership of 5AM Hike Club has grown to more than 140. "We are registering new members every day," says now-president Oral Evanson. The club is even looking beyond the shores of its 365-beach paradise—one for every day of the year—to other Caribbean hiking destinations. "We plan to visit other islands like Montserrat, Dominica, and St. Lucia," says vice president Craig Williams. For the 5AM Hike Club, the sky is the limit.

The 5AM Hike Club are a friendly bunch of people who like to welcome visitors and are easy to find thanks to their distinctive white T-shirts that boldly declare: "5AM Hikers discovering the world, one trail at a time." They have their work ahead of them: Pinching Bay, Soldier Point, Boggy Peak, Guana Island, Sugarloaf, Monk's Hill, Mount Obama, Cades Bay, Christian Valley—Antigua seems to have a trail to match every one of its beaches. Fortunately, the club also has a philosophy that suggests it will eventually do them all: "Take nothing but pictures; leave nothing but footprints; kill nothing but time . . . " **BDS**

Rio Zacate Trail Atlantida, Honduras

Start/End El Pino   Distance 3 miles (4.8 km)
Time 3–4 hours (or 90 mins one way)
Grade Moderate   Type River trail
Info goo.gl/VcvOXV

On the north coast of Honduras, overlooking the Caribbean, stands the triangular peak of Pico Bonito, 7,992 feet (2,436 m) high. It's part of a mountain range called the Cordillera Nombre de Dios and is at the core of the Pico Bonito National Park, the second largest national park in Honduras at 414 square miles (1,072 sq km). This is a tropical forest filled with lush vegetation, colorful birds and butterflies, and howling monkeys. It is also home to the Rio Zacate Trail, which provides breathtaking views of the Caribbean coast and, at the end, the beautiful sight of the Zacate Falls.

"The trail leads you up into the forest following the course of the crystal clear Zacate River."

www.tropicaldiscovery.com

It's a trail that's fairly easy to manage on your own, but there are some steep uphill stretches, especially at the start. For part of the way the path follows the Zacate River, with its crystal-clear waters and tempting pools in which you can swim. Eventually, you arrive at the waterfalls, a plunging double cascade surrounded by jungle. Listen for the sounds of howler monkeys and watch for the multicolored flash of flying macaws or toucans. The falls act as a magnet for wildlife, and you're sure to see the brightly colored blue morpho butterflies that live around them.

You can also bathe in the pools at the foot of the falls to cool off before the return journey, back the way you came through the steamy Honduras jungle. **MG**

Galápagos Islands Trails

Galápagos Islands, Ecuador

Start/End Various
Distance Various   Time Various
Grade Various   Type Various
Info goo.gl/pc8nbX

The majority of people visiting the Galápagos Islands to see their unique wildlife do so on day trips, mostly by boat. A more rewarding experience is to stay a few days on one of the inhabited islands (San Cristóbal, Santa Cruz, Floreana, and Isabela) and explore this fascinating place on foot. There are plenty of hikes that will get you up close to the best of the superb scenery and wildlife.

The islands are famous for inspiring Charles Darwin's theories on natural selection. They are home to a huge number of endemic species, many of which have evolved without any human contact and so exhibit little fear of mankind. This makes them very easy to get close to and photograph, although their natural lack of fear makes them easy pickings for predators that have been either deliberately or accidentally introduced to the islands.

It's easy to join organized hiking holidays to the Galápagos, but it isn't difficult to visit independently either. There are many marked trails, and plenty of information and maps available. You can also take boats trips to explore the uninhabited islands, such as Santa Fé, where you can see cacti that grow up to 33 feet (10 m) high as well as beautiful animals such as the Santa Fé iguana, found nowhere else in the world.

Elsewhere in this natural wonderland you'll see bright orange crabs, the blue-footed booby, sea lions, tortoises, hawks, and Galápagos penguins, the only penguins found in the northern hemisphere. The islands are a magical place that are quite rightly on most travelers' wish lists of places to visit. **MG**

◄ Marine iguanas are a common sight in the Galápagos.

Copacabana Beach

Rio de Janeiro, Brazil

Start Copacabana Beach (eastern end)
End The Promontory   Distance 2.5 miles (4 km)
Time 1 hour   Grade Easy   Type Street and
beach walk   Map goo.gl/uWUDpj

Copacabana is the world's most famous beach in one of the world's most pulsating cities and a simple walk along its promenades and sands is never less than memorable. Start at its eastern end where a wide pedestrian area stands between the beach and the beachfront hotels, a black-and-white design of a geometric wave that extends for the full 2.5-mile (4-km) length of the beach.

After twenty minutes or so, you'll see on your right the legendary Copacabana Palace Hotel, built in 1923, whose guests over the years have ranged from Albert

"In the morning, you can buy the fresh catch of the day [on the beach]."

www.lonelyplanet.com

Einstein to Princess Diana. It was here that the Rolling Stones played a free concert that drew more than a million people to the beach and surrounding streets.

On sunny days, you'll have a ringside seat at Copacabana life. The cries of vendors act as a backdrop to boys playing football while their big brothers flex their muscles and try to impress the beautiful girls walking around in next-to-nothing bikinis.

As the beach curves around farther on, you'll find the fish market, and at the far end of the headland are a few historical sites, including the Fort Copacabana, inside which is a military history museum, the Museu Histórico do Exército. From here you get a great view of the vibrant spectacle of Copacabana Beach. **MG**

Lagoinha do Leste Trails
Santa Catarina, Brazil

Start/End Matadeiro or Pantano do Sul
beaches Distance Various Time Various
Grade Moderate Type Hill and forest trails
Info goo.gl/HzUMJF

The beach at Lagoinha do Leste is one of the unspoiled marvels of the state of Santa Catarina in southern Brazil. This paradise can only be reached by boat or by hiking one of two enjoyable trails. This relative inaccessibility has meant that the beach has retained its pristine beauty, and you won't be sharing it with hundreds of other people.

The water here is crystal clear, and at the side of the beach is a pretty little lagoon fed by water from pure mountain springs. The whole area is protected—not only the land, but also the sea, because of the

"By either [trail, you] will have the chance to enjoy the biodiversity of the Atlantic forest."

www.braziltrails.com

southern right whales that pass through here. The freshwater lagoon is a natural draw for wildlife, and you'll see plenty of bird activity close to the beach.

To get there you need to go to one of two other nearby beaches, either Matadeiro Beach or Pântano do Sul. Both are appealing in their own right, and you may be reluctant to leave them, but you'll be glad you did, both for what you find at your journey's end and for what you see on the way. The trail from Matadeiro takes just under three hours and is a straightforward hike through the Atlantic forest and along the coast, with only a few mild ascents. From Pântano do Sul the walk is around an hour less, but it is a little more demanding, with steeper sections. **MG**

Isla del Sol
La Paz, Bolivia

Start/End Cha'llapampa Distance 5–10 miles
(8–16 km) Time 4–8 hours Grade Easy to
strenuous Type Open, sandy, and gravelly trails
Map goo.gl/zXexmJ

With no motor cars because there are simply no paved roads, the Isla del Sol (Island of the Sun) in Lake Titicaca is a natural magnet for hikers. In no time you will settle into the rhythms of island life, which here means two things: farming and fishing. Low-key tourism adds to the coffers of the 800 or so local families who live in several small villages scattered around the island. To get there, you need to take a boat from Copacabana, either one of the regular ferries or—more fun—hire a local boatman.

Although it measures only 6.25 miles (10 km) long and 2.5 miles (4 km) wide, there are some wonderful hiking opportunities. The landscape is gently hilly—while its highest peak is about 13,451 feet (4,127 m), Lake Titicaca itself is already 12,467 feet (3,800 m) above sea level. The dramatic views of the Andes Mountains surrounding the lake add greatly to the charms of walking here.

There are more than 180 ruins on the island dating from the Inca period, and you will see these wherever you go. Pre-Incan ruins have also been found under the lake. You are walking in the footsteps of the Incas as you roam this island, and little has changed since their time, with many of the trails used then still being used now. Inca remnants include slabs used for sacrificial purposes and the Rock of the Puma (Titi Kharka), from which the lake gets its name. Inca gold is also on display in the Gold Museum in Cha'llapampa, the main town at the northern end of the island. Spend a few days here and you might think that you, like the island, have been forgotten by time. **MG**

⮕ The island provides breathtaking views over the lake.

Longyearbyen Svalbard, Norway

Start/End Various   **Distance** Various   **Time** Various   **Grade** Moderate   **Type** Mountain, snow
Info goo.gl/MxaG1X

Here's a tip: if you go walking in Longyearbyen on the Norwegian island of Svalbard and wander outside of town, you must carry a shotgun capable of stopping a polar bear in its tracks. It's the law. Yes, this is an unusual place, the largest settlement on the Svalbard archipelago, but with only 2,500 inhabitants. High up in the Norwegian Arctic, it's one of the most northerly towns in the world. It even has a sundial that, during the summer, is in use twenty-four hours a day.

You can get to Svalbard by plane to Airport Longyear (named for the founder of the town, U.S. entrepreneur John Munro Longyear). During the summer, the town's port is open for business—after the pack ice melts. Once there, you can go on a prearranged guided hiking trip, walking out to the bird cliffs or to one of the many glaciers. You can also see evidence of the local coal industry: the area is dotted with machinery and other objects associated with mining activity. In Svalbard polar bears are prone to attack humans without warning, and there are regular warnings about bear safety. The polar bear population lives in unnerving proximity to the town, so you have to take precautions. There's a surprising amount to do in this small town, the population of which includes a heavy dose of tour guides and Arctic scientists. There is an art gallery, a museum, and a range of restaurants and bars. You can also go on snowmobile safaris and even dog sledding trips.

In late October, the town hosts its own blues festival, heralding in the winter season and the unbroken darkness. Just remember the gun rule, but maybe let someone else do the shooting. **JI**

⊡ **Longyearbyen, the largest town on Svalbard.**

Hoven Mountain Nordland, Norway

Start/End Hov golf course   **Distance** 2 miles (3.2 km)   **Time** 2 hours   **Grade** Easy
Type Dirt (often muddy) track   **Info** goo.gl/QhGsCB

Gimsøy forms part of Norway's magnificent Lofoten archipelago, which arcs its way west from the mainland into the Arctic waters of the Norwegian Sea. It is a small island, with an area of only 17.9 square miles (46.3 sq km). It has one school in Vinje, a golf course at Hov, a small fishing industry in the village of Barstrand, a tiny wooden church, and an abandoned fish factory, while its flat marshlands are a nature reserve for nesting birds. Gimsøy is connected to adjacent islands in the chain by two bridges, Sundklakkstraumen and Gimsøystraumen.

You can see almost all of these sights simply by walking to the top of Hoven Mountain, a graceful and wonderfully angled hill that rises out of the boggy flats in the north of the island. To call it a mountain is to be more than a little generous—only 1,207 feet (368 m) high, it was affectionately described by

Walkopedia founder William Mackesy as "a pimple of a summit." However, it is a decent option for a small hike, and a good choice if you're determined to be outdoors when the weather is not at its best. There is something alluring, almost magnetic, about Hoven Mountain's shape and scale—it draws you toward it. And when low clouds abound over Gimsøy, the top of Hoven is in all likelihood still below the clouds, so the mountain provides an unobstructed 360-degree view of the horizon most of the time, and is therefore a fantastic place to view the northern lights.

Ultimately, it is Hoven Mountain's geometric simplicity that contributes to such an uncomplicated and rewarding climb along a clearly visible, although occasionally muddy, track. **BDS**

⊼ The geometrical simplicity of Hoven Mountain.

Nusfjord to Nesland Nordland, Norway

Start Nusfjord **End** Nesland   **Distance** 2.9 miles (4.7 km)   **Time** 2 hours   **Grade** Easy
Type Exposed rock, grass paths   **Info** goo.gl/m8c37l

Nusfjord, on Norway's Flakstadoya Island, is one of the best-preserved fishing villages on the Lofoten archipelago. It was one of three rural communities chosen in the 1970s by the Norwegian government for preservation, to help raise and maintain awareness of the country's rich architectural heritage.

Nusfjord was first mentioned as a fishing community in the sixteenth century. Although it is now something of an outdoor museum, it remains a working port, with a wonderful old general store, waterfront cod-drying factories, and locals who are justly proud of their 500-year fish harvesting traditions and, latterly, of exporting their produce worldwide.

Dramatically situated at the base of the Lofot cliffs that plunge down into the surrounding ocean, a scene that is so emblematic of the entire Lofoten district, Nusfjord makes for the sort of starting point you really don't want to leave. But the walk will take you around a crenellated and dramatic coastline to the less populous, but equally traditional, fishing village at Nesland, home to Lofoten's only water mill.

The trail from Nusfjord south to Nesland—an old fisherman's path that is marked with cairns—begins a few hundred yards down the hill below the village schoolhouse. On some parts of the route, a certain amount of rock scrambling may be required, but in general the footing is good, and the views are constantly inspiring. There are few areas in the world as pleasing to the eye as Lofoten. A nice place to overnight on your arrival is the Lofoten Nesland Guesthouse, built in 1872 and now owned by descendants of the original owner. **BDS**

⬆ Nusfjord is a microcosm of the Norwegian fisheries.

Vaerøy Island Hike Nordland, Norway

Start/End Sørland **Distance** Various **Time** Various **Grade** Easy **Type** Grass paths, open fields
Info goo.gl/O6fs3M

Vaerøy Island is a tiny speck—almost the last speck—at the end of the crescent-shaped Lofoten archipelago. Its name is a combination of two ancient Norse words meaning "weather island," and most of its 750 hardy residents live in Sørland or in the only other community of note, Nordland.

Vaerøy was made for walking and fishing. And for nesting: Mount Mostadfjell in the southwest is home to more than one-and-a-half million seabirds, including sea eagles, arctic terns, puffins, guillemots, cormorants, petrels, kittiwakes, and gulls.

A number of well-trodden paths can take you to its many rookeries, but birds are not all that Vaerøy offers. One walk from the outskirts of Sørland leads over the Isthmus of Eidet to the all but abandoned east coast village of Mastad, whose inhabitants train their dogs to catch puffins.

There is also the option of ascending nearby Mahornet peak (1,427 feet/435 m), an arduous hour's walk up and a fun scramble back down. You can also take a walk to Lofoten's oldest church, the Vaerøy Kirke, which was moved here along with its fifteenth-century altarpiece from Kabelvag on Lofoten's Austvagoya Island, and reassembled in 1799.

Vaerøy has mountains as steep as any in Lofoten, but easier than many to climb, and sea caves with paintings that are 3,000 years old. The island is reached by boat from Moskenes, a route that crosses the world's most powerful maelstrom current, the Moskenesstraumen. But that is a small inconvenience when compared to the thrill of an Arctic stroll over the "bird mountains" of Weather Island. **BDS**

⬆ Approaching Vaerøy from an adjacent island.

Hoga Kusten Trail

Västernorrland, Sweden

> *"... affords outstanding opportunities for understanding the important processes that formed land uplift areas."*

UNESCO

⬆ Moon and cliff: both are rising inexorably on the Hoga Kusten Trail.

Start Harnosand **End** Ornskoldsvik
Distance 79 miles (127 km) **Time** 13 days **Grade** Easy
Type Rock, gravel trails, some rope-assisted climbs
Map goo.gl/dRjNrg

The Hoga Kusten (High Coast) of Sweden, between Harnosand and Ornskoldsvik on the Gulf of Bothnia, is a remarkable region of isostatic uplifted rock. When the ice sheets of the last Ice Age began to melt around 10,000 years ago—thus freeing the rock below from the massive ice sheets up to 2 miles (3.2 km) thick that had been suppressing the region's sedimentary rocks' natural urge to rise—the landscape of the Hoga Kusten was at last freed to resume its upward thrust. Since then, the rock strata have risen an astonishing 938 feet (286 m), and are continuing to rise at a rate of one-third of an inch (8 mm) every year. Nowhere else in the world has the disappearance of the great Ice Age ice sheets resulted in uplift of this magnitude. It is the most extreme example of the effect known by geologists as "rebound."

The Hoga Kusten is regarded by the hiking community as one of the best trekking regions in Sweden, and the 79-mile (128-km) Hoga Kustenleden has been rated as the finest Swedish walk by *Outdoor* magazine. But there is a lot more to discover than uplifted earth and the views it gives you over dozens of offshore islands. The valleys north of Harnosand are rolling and verdant, and the whole region is dotted with woodlands and various protected areas. The trail is well-marked, and the shelters and unlocked cabins that line the route cannot be pre-booked.

Inland, too, the scenery is stunning, but it's the craggy and crenellated cliffs that people come here to see. That they are the highest in the country is hardly surprising, considering they have been rising inexorably, with considerable tectonic assistance, for nearly ten millennia. **BDS**

Causeway Coast Way
Antrim, Northern Ireland

Start Ballycastle   **End** Portstewart
Distance 33 miles (53 km)   **Time** 2–3 days
Grade Easy   **Type** Coastal cliff paths
Map goo.gl/EoLRsN

It is Northern Ireland's most celebrated stretch of coastline and offers an easy, low-lying walk that should take someone of average fitness around two to three days to complete. It links the popular tourist towns of Portstewart and Ballycastle, and passes through some of the best-known tourist attractions in Northern Ireland, including the walk's centerpiece, the geologic wonder that is the Giant's Causeway. This UNESCO World Heritage Site is an area of mostly basalt columns, the result of molten rock that intruded through the surrounding chalk beds and then cooled to form hundreds of hexagonal columns up to 39 feet (11.8 m) high, columns you can now walk as though they are stepping-stones from the cliff base down into the waters of the Irish Sea.

The Causeway Coast Way traverses diverse terrain. In addition to cliff sections, there are beach walks, promenade strolls, and only occasional road walking. The trail mostly follows the line of the coast, so navigating your way along it is fairly straightforward.

Other highlights include a 66-foot (20-m) rope bridge that links the tiny island of Carrick-a-Rede to the mainland, and the medieval ruins of Dunluce Castle. Old Bushmills Irish whiskey distillery is also a short detour from the trail.

The highest point on the route is only 459 feet (140 m) above sea level and, with no sections being too remote, the Causeway Coast Way is a trail that can be enjoyed easily by the novice walker. The path is also a part of the Ulster Way trail, which traces a 620-mile (998-km) circuit of Northern Ireland, with the Moyle Way and the North Sperrins Way bookending the course. **BDS**

"An exhilarating route along the most celebrated stretch of coastline in Northern Ireland."

www.walkni.com

⬆ Part of the perfect coastal walk: elevated, spectacular, and diverse, with geology guaranteed to make you think.

Táin Way Louth, Ireland

Start/End Carlingford   **Distance** 25 miles (40 km)   **Time** 2 days   **Grade** Moderate
Type Quiet roads, forest tracks   **Map** goo.gl/vcaYdB

The Táin Way is a circular route around Carlingford Mountain (1,935 feet/590 m) that snakes all over the Cooley Peninsula, a finger of land in County Louth that juts into the Irish Sea. On the highest parts of the route, the views over Carlingford Lough and south down the east coast are superb. Walking it will take you along mountain paths, down forest tracks and quiet roads, and past portal tombs, passage graves, and the wonderfully preserved medieval town of Carlingford itself, where King John of England built a grand castle in 1210.

Don't let anyone tell you that the Táin Way is too isolated or too small to compete with the great trails of Ireland. On the contrary, this walk will take you into the spiritual heart of the nation. In order fully to appreciate its significance, it helps to know something about the Ulster cycle of heroic tales. One of the greatest of all of Ireland's epic legends concerns the Cattle Raid of Cooley, a mythical battle between Ulster and Connaught for the Brown Bull of Cooley, the owner of which was guaranteed invincibility. Ulster's young hero, Cú Chulainn, defeated Fer Diad of Connaught in a duel, but the Connaught army seized the prized Brown Bull, and so the Ulster army was forced to sue for peace.

These legends echo from many points along the Táin Way, particularly Trumpet Hill, where Cú prowled with his slingshot, and the tracks above Ballymakellet, where he beheaded his enemies. Then there is the Cronn River, which rose to the height of the surrounding trees when the Connaught forces came to cross it. **BDS**

⬆ Old stone dwellings line the route.

Burren Way Clare, Ireland

Start Lahinch **End** Corrofin **Distance** 71 miles (114 km) **Time** 5 days **Grade** Moderate to strenuous
Type Tarmac roads, green roads, droving roads, forest tracks **Map** goo.gl/rNUYVG

The Burren is a magical kingdom on Ireland's mid-west coast, a land of what geologists call "fertile rocks"—a living limestone pavement—that is host to more than 70 percent of Ireland's flora, twenty-two of its twenty-seven native orchids, pine martens, an array of butterflies, and even a mysterious snake-like worm that thrives in its sparse soil deposits. It is one of Europe's largest karst landscapes, a vast area of limestone pavement intersected by a network of grikes—vertical cracks up to 18 inches (0.5 m) wide caused by acidic water attacking lines of greatest weakness. Its human map is no less fascinating: 500 ring forts and almost 100 wedge-shaped Neolithic tombs, making it, in the words of cartographer Tim Robinson, "a vast memorial to bygone cultures." With all of this in an area less than 0.5 percent of the nation's total land mass, it seems outrageous that so much diversity should be bestowed upon so tiny a place. The Burren Way passes right through the heart of this ethereal environment of precious limestone grasslands.

Walking the Burren Way takes you inland from Lahinch on the Burren's western side to Doolin on the coast, then north on a gradual ascent to Ballinalacken Castle and into open fields around the shoulder of Slieve Elva. There are two north–south trails that are of particular archaeological significance, one from Bell Harbour to Killinaboy, and the other from Leamaneh Castle to Ballyvaughan. A descent to the Caher River crosses the Burren's interior through a gray, treeless world where there is nothing to punctuate the view as you head toward Carran and Corrofin. Also, don't miss the chance to walk along the Cliffs of Moher. **BDS**

⬆ Walk over the Burren Way's "fertile rocks."

Kerry Way
Kerry, Ireland

Start/End Killarney   **Distance** 133 miles (214 km)
Time 6–9 days   **Grade** Strenuous   **Type** Grassy paths,
boreens (unpaved rural roads), abandoned coach roads
Info goo.gl/ayA31x

First proposed in 1982 and later developed by members of the Laune Mountaineering Club, the Kerry Way begins in Killarney and passes through the gardens of nineteenth-century Muckross House. It passes along the shoreline of Lough Leane to the foaming, frothing beauty of Torc Waterfall, one of this walk's many landmarks.

From Torc Waterfall, you walk through the rugged and stark beauty of the Black Valley in the shadows of Ireland's mountainous MacGillycuddy's Reeks and the summit of its tallest mountain and one of the so-called Irish Munros, Carrauntoohil (3,406 feet/1,038 m). Seemingly endless glens and valleys follow until you reach the Caragh River Valley, cross Seefin Mountain, and from there on to some spectacular views over Dingle Bay.

Climbing the hills above Dingle Bay on a medieval coach road, you make your way toward Foilmore then along a 6.8-mile (11-km) spur that takes you along a series of ridges and the odd turf bog to Waterville, a favorite vacation haunt of actor Charlie Chaplin, who stayed there in the Butler Arms Hotel many times in the 1960s and 1970s. Here you have a choice: an inland trail over the mountains to Caherdaniel, or a coastal route around Farraniargh Mountain, with great views of the Skellig Islands. Both options take you to Sneem, a small town on the Iveragh Peninsula, followed by a coastal trail above the Kenmare River to Kenmare, nestled in an area gifted by Oliver Cromwell to William Petty for completing the mapping of Ireland in 1656. Finally, a mountain crossing over Windy Gap to Killarney completes the traverse of Ireland's longest hiking trail. **BDS**

"The landscape the route passes through is very varied, from the lakes of Killarney to high and remote mountain moorland."

www.irishtrails.ie

← Walk Ireland's oldest long-distance trail.

↑ The trail circles the Iveragh Peninsula.

Dingle Way
Kerry, Ireland

Start/End Tralee   **Distance** 101 miles (162 km)
Time 8–9 days   **Grade** Easy to moderate
Type Boreens (unpaved rural roads), grassy paths, meadows   **Map** goo.gl/O5BsHV

"The route is steeped in history and scattered with the ruins of ancient dwellings, forts, churches."

www.irishtrails.ie

⬆ The Dingle Peninsula is the northernmost peninsula in County Kerry and the westernmost landfall in Ireland.

When you walk the Dingle Way, its coastal paths will take you past standing and inscribed ogham stones, corbeled, drystone twelfth-century Fahan beehive huts on Mount Eagle, and the gloriously cut stonework of the Gallarus Oratory, the haunting little "House of Shelter," built without mortar in the shape of an upturned boat overlooking the harbor at Ard na Caithne (actually a small detour, but well worth it). You will pass through a diversity of landscapes that reveal themselves almost at every turn, from the Slieve Mish foothills and the shoulder of Mount Brandon (3,123 feet/952 m), the highest peak in the peninsula's central mountain range, to the golden sands of the beaches at Maharess. The interior is a sea of pastoral farmland surrounded by the unbridled power of the Atlantic that rolls into coastal communities, such as Inch, with its constant barrage of surf, and historic pubs, such as the South Pole Inn, the famous guesthouse opened in 1920 by Sir Ernest Shackleton's second officer Tom Cream, a Dingle native, and home to excellent memorabilia of early polar exploration.

The walk begins and ends in Tralee, and for most of its length, with the exception of Mount Brandon and a traverse of Masatiompan (2,076 feet/633 m), the walk is an easy to moderate one, with villages never farther than a few hours away. Most walk it in a clockwise direction from Tralee, which allows the legs to become accustomed to the ups and downs before tackling the higher peaks. The only negative is that almost half of the trail is made up of boreens—narrow, unpaved, rural roads. Fortunately, however, "traffic" remains a largely unfamiliar concept in Dingle's sparsely populated landscape. **BDS**

Papa Stour

Papa Stour, Shetland, Scotland

Start/End Housa Voe
Distance 10.5 miles (16.8 km)   **Time** 8 hours
Grade Moderate   **Type** Rocky, grassy paths
Map goo.gl/bnqknp

The island of Papa Stour has a population of about twenty people, who were lured here after a government appeal for residents during the 1970s. The landscape consists mostly of soft volcanic rock, with a coastline that has been eroded by the ocean for many millennia into a wondrous assortment of blowholes, sea caves, skerries, stacks, and arches. At its peak in the nineteenth century, when a fishing port was built in nearby West Voe, more than 350 people lived here. Now, apart from its handful of residents, the only other people who come here are walkers and nature lovers, who either get the only ferry from West Burrafirth or fly in from Tingwall airport. It may require a bit of effort, and there is no overnight accommodation, but the sights that await will soon have you forgetting all that.

Papa Stour is a Special Area of Conservation. Common and gray seals are here in abundance, and otters breed on the island. It has eighteen species of nesting birds and an impressive variety of lichens and wildflowers. You begin a circumference of this remote menagerie at Housa Voe and hug its impressive coastline with only minimal ascents and descents on a walk punctuated by a torrent of unexpected treasures, such as the subterranean passage and collapsed cave at Clingri Geo; the Mo Geo cliffs with their bright red rhyolitic lava; and the stunning variety of cave stacks, skerries, and arches on the cliff tops of Aesha Head. There are stunning views of St. Magnus Bay from the summit of Verda Field, and even ruins of Neolithic homesteads as you make your way back along a metaled track to Housa Voe. The best part is you will almost certainly have the track all to yourself. **BDS**

Steens of Stofast

Mainland, Shetland, Scotland

Start/End Trailhead south of Lunna Ness
Distance 6.2 miles (10 km)   **Time** 5 hours
Grade Moderate to strenuous   **Type** Rocky, grassy trails   **Map** goo.gl/dk5bV7

This circular walk offers the chance to walk by one of the Shetland Islands' most impressive inland glacial landscapes and one of the world's oddest geologic phenomena: its remarkable scattered "steens"—large fractured boulders carried over eons by glacial activity and dumped hundreds of feet from where they originated. For a good view of these rocks, follow a track that takes you past the Loch of Grutwick to where the North Sea's Ninian oil pipeline comes ashore. From the nearby quarry head northeast to the South Loch of Stofast, where the steens will greet you

---

"You could visit Lunna Kirk, one of Shetland's oldest and most beautiful tiny churches."

www.walkshetland.com

---

like silent sentinels. Then head north to the tiny inlets of Fugla Water and cross over to the slope's northern side, where you should find two planticrubs (small square plant shelters used for growing seeds).

The lochs of Winneries and Ward follow, set among small valleys and craggy peaks. In summer, you'll find the ground covered in blooming heather and wild roses. If you climb the Hill of State, you will be rewarded with magnificent views of the surrounding islands—Yell, Burravoe, Whalsay, Orfasay, Samphrey, Fish Holm, and Linga. Head down to the shore, turn south to the town of Outrabister (don't forget to pop into its antique shop), and follow the road back to the start point. **BDS**

Postman's Trail Isle of Harris, Outer Hebrides, Scotland

Start Rhenigidale **End** Tarbert
Distance 7 miles (11.2 km) **Time** 3 hours
Grade Moderate **Type** Rocky trails
Map goo.gl/ozhklu

The tiny hamlet of Rhenigidale on the Isle of Harris in the Outer Hebrides remained disconnected from the outside world by anything other than boat until 1990, when a road linking it to the rest of Britain was finally built. Before that the only access overland was along a 3-mile (4.8-km) hill path, one of many that trace gossamer lines over its rocky landscape. Parts of Harris are so lunar-like that it was used as the location for the planet Jupiter in the film *2001: A Space Odyssey* (1968). If you want isolation, then once you walk into the wilderness of this remote island along paths that have

---

"[The Postman's Trail] clings to the coastline and was used to take post to and from Achiltibuie."

www.scottishwildlifetrust.org

---

a tendency to peter out into nothingness, you will have attained solitude in abundance. The Isle of Harris is actually part of Long Island, a single landmass whose central mountains divide Harris (population 2,000) from Lewis (population 18,000), a land of peat bogs, lochs, and lochans. Both Harris and Lewis prefer to retain their titles of "isles." The Postman's Trail is an old, well-maintained path that links Rhenigidale to Tarbert. It takes you along the shore of Loch Trolamoraig, passes by waterfalls, and takes you up the flank of Beinn Tharsuinn (2,270 feet/692 m), with views to mighty peaks on Applecross peninsula and the walls of rock on neighboring Vatersay, before the descent into Tarbert. **BDS**

Skye Trail Isle of Skye, Scotland

Start Rubha Hunish **End** Broadford
Distance 79 miles (127 km) **Time** 10 days
Grade Moderate **Type** Open moorland and ridges
Map goo.gl/RsYLfq

Rubha Hunish is a wonderful spot to begin a long-distance walk. Tucked away on the northernmost part of the Isle of Skye, it even has its own trail, the Rubha Hunish Trail, which takes you along cliff tops and open moorlands to the ruins of remote, windswept Duntulm Castle and back. A three-and-a-half hour appetizer, perhaps, for the main event.

The Skye Trail begins at Rubha Hunish and passes over the astonishing geology of the Trotternish Ridge, which is a memorable experience in its own right. It then continues on down the coast to the scattered woodlands around Braes, the site of a mass protest by Skye crofters in 1882 and the last battle ever fought on British soil. A rough path along the shore of Loch Sligachan is next, as well as a visit to the Sligachan Inn, the cradle of Scottish mountaineering. You then descend to Loch Coruisk, most people's choice as Scotland's most atmospheric loch. With its shoreline of barren rocks at the base of the wonderfully jagged Black Cuillin, it was a sight that poet Lord Tennyson once described as "the wildest scene in the highlands." A farther descent to Torrin is followed by a coastal walk to the deserted villages of Suisnish and Boreraig, on the northern shore of Loch Eishort, before your final approach to Broadford along an old disused railway line.

This is a wild trail—it is not waymarked, and some of its segments do not even have a trail. It is strictly intended for the experienced hiker. There is accommodation at the end of every stage, and there are also opportunities to set up some once-in-a-lifetime campsites, particularly on the Trotternish Ridge. So don't forget to bring your backpack. **BDS**

Moray Coast Trail
Moray, Scotland

Start Forres **End** Cullen
Distance 44 miles (71 km) **Time** 2–3 days
Grade Easy **Type** Long-distance footpath
Map goo.gl/ZLLvKe

If you are looking for variety on a coastal walk, then the Moray Coast Trail in northeast Scotland delivers just that. It has pine and deciduous woodlands, sandy beaches, crescent-shaped bays, tidal mudflats, sea stacks, and coastal cliffs, not to mention the Moray Firth, a transition zone of salt and freshwater, with bottlenose dolphins leaping clear out of the water as ospreys soar high above. Talk to the locals here, and they will tell you there is no more stunning or varied coastline to be found anywhere in the United Kingdom. Macbeth was born in these parts, and Duncan was killed at the Battle of Burghead. Yet it remains one of Scotland's best-kept secrets.

Opened in 2004, the trail is a mix of paths, tracks, and small lanes that link its numerous villages, most of which wouldn't be out of place in Cornwall on a coast that is as old as it is spectacular. Between Hopeman and Covesea, 250-million-year-old sandstone cliffs rise more than 200 feet (60 m) above the shore, while down at sea level fields of marram grass-covered sand dunes take you past Covesea lighthouse and into the fishing village of Lossiemouth, which in prosperous times gone by was packed bow to stern with herring boats. Findhorn Bay, an almost landlocked tidal basin, was also once a notable shipbuilding center and remains an important habitat for migratory birds. Keep an eye out, too, for the carved stones and stone foundations of the ancient Picts, descendants of northeast Scotland's Iron Age tribes, who lived here from the first to ninth centuries. Today, the paths of the Moray Coast Trail offer real patches of wilderness while never being too far from coastal villages, quaint harbors, and the smell of roasted coffee. **BDS**

"The route . . . includes beaches, coastal paths, quiet roads, and old railways."

www.visitscotland.com

⊓ A perfect trail that links cliffs, caves, and coves on a coastline teeming with wildlife.

Kintyre Way Argyll & Bute, Scotland

Start Tarbert Harbor **End** Dunaverty Bay **Distance** 87 miles (140 km)
Time 6–7 days **Grade** Moderate **Type** Long-distance path **Map** goo.gl/aBUwkT

The Kintyre Peninsula in Western Scotland is roughly 30 miles (48 km) long and 11 miles (17.7 km) wide, but it seems more island than mainland. Prized by settlers for generations, even before the arrival of the Vikings, because of its rich, fertile coast and hinterland, the peninsula has the waters of the Kilbrannan Sound to its east and the wild seas of the Atlantic to its west beyond a spine of hilly moorlands. Since 2006 it has also provided the backdrop for the Kintyre Way.

The walk is a year-round destination, thanks to the warm waters of the North Atlantic and the temperate climate it bequeaths this hidden corner of Argyle. It begins in Tarbert at one of Scotland's most beautiful sheltered harbors, and from there heads south, crisscrossing the peninsula on its way to Dunaverty Bay, with its crescent-shaped beach. Leaving Tarbert, you cross a plateau with fabulous views back to Arran through forests of birch, elm, and willow before a descent into Skipness, with its thirteenth-century castle. Turn right and keep going till you reach Ronachan, where you follow the coast southward, walking over shingle beaches and past tern rookeries with views over the water to Gigha, the southernmost island of the Inner Hebrides and a destination in its own right, accessible by ferry. Cross the peninsula again, ascending as you head eastward before a winding descent on forest tracks to Carradale. From there it's on to Campbeltown, the peninsula's largest town and a center for whiskey production, and across the ditch again to one of Scotland's finest beaches at Machrihanish before the final tough, but most spectacular, segment to Dunaverty Bay. **BDS**

⬆ Discover a peninsula with an island feel.

John Muir Way Argyll & Bute to East Lothian, Scotland

Start Helensburgh   **End** Dunbar   **Distance** 134 miles (215 km)   **Time** 7–10 days   **Grade** Easy to moderate
Type Beaches, moorland, sidewalk   **Map** goo.gl/L8V2II

The original John Muir Trail through the Sierra Nevada in California was opened in 1938. It was named in honor of environmentalist and naturalist John Muir, who was born in Dunbar in East Lothian, near Edinburgh, in 1838, then immigrated in 1849 with his parents to the United States, where he devoted his adult life to wilderness preservation. In 2014, to mark the centenary of Muir's death, this commemorative trail was opened in his native Scotland.

The route was designed to echo John Muir's own life, linking Dunbar in East Lothian where he grew up, and Helensburgh in Argyll and Bute, his departure point for the United States. The trail was established in a remarkably short space of time—just three and a half years—and is designed to get people into the great outdoors, with around three million residents living close to the new walk/cycleway.

The coastal section of the trail offers mostly easy walking over East Lothian's varied and complex shores of white sand beaches, towering cliffs at St. Abbs Head with its views north over the Firth of Forth, weathered sandstone arches, and extensive dune systems, as well as woodlands, rivers, waterfalls, and the storm-battered remnants of a once-mighty castle above the port town of Dunbar, where you can also visit Muir's birthplace at 126 High Street.

The trail can be walked in either direction, in easy daily segments with plenty of access to public transport. Lagoons, museums, grand old country homes, and myriad interconnecting paths and circular routes make this trail a path of exploration of which Muir would no doubt have been proud. **BDS**

⊡ On the walk through bonny coastal Scotland.

Fife Coastal Path
Fife, Scotland

Start Kincardine Bridge **End** Newburgh
Distance 117 miles (188 km) **Time** 8 days
Grade Easy **Type** Sandy bays, rough foreshores, grassy paths **Info** goo.gl/yh3AOC

King James II of Scotland described the East Neuk (an old Scottish word for "corner") of Fife as a "fringe of gold on a beggar's mantle," and if you like the idea of walking in Scotland but are a little daunted at navigating your way through its remote highlands, the Fife Coastal Path could be just what you are looking for. Many of its towns are royal burghs, testifying to the historic importance of this tiny peninsula, which is why a walk here can still guarantee you that quintessential "Scottish" experience as you pass by its castles and historic buildings, many of which have witnessed great moments in the nation's history. There are also desolate beaches, sandflats, and idyllic fishing ports, each with its own distinctive characteristics and peculiarities. Just keep the ocean on your right or to your left, depending upon which end you begin, toss away your maps, and get walking.

The path stretches from Kincardine Bridge and ends at the small town of Newburgh, running through a myriad of simple coastal communities utterly lacking in pretense (perhaps with the exception of St. Andrews), over golden white sand beaches, nature reserves, and old industrial towns, such as Leven, giving you a taste of all the delights that the peninsula of Fife has to offer. Along the way be prepared for some expansive scenery: the view of Edinburgh across the Firth of Forth, the fine-grained basalt rock that is the Isle of May, and the northerly panoramas of the Angus coast and the Firth of Tay. This is a walk blessed with both beauty and heritage, everything from the eighteenth hole of the Old Course to the gorgeous crescent of houses on the water at Pittenweem, on James II's favorite little Neuk. **BDS**

> *"Links some of Scotland's most picturesque former fishing villages as well as the home of golf—St. Andrews."*

www.walkhighlands.co.uk

⊞ A center of royalty since the eleventh century, this region is still known as "the Kingdom of Fife."

Berwickshire Coastal Path
Scotland/England

Start Cockburnspath, Scotland **End** Berwick-upon-Tweed, England **Distance** 28 miles (45 km) **Time** 2–4 days **Grade** Easy to moderate **Type** Paths, trails, dirt roads **Map** goo.gl/k1rX9b

It's not often you pass a revolutionary milestone in the history of science, but that happens as you approach Siccar Point shortly after departing Cockburnspath on the Berwickshire Coastal Path. It was here in 1788 that geologists James Hutton and James Hall, and mathematician John Playfair, hired a boat and confirmed Hutton's Theory of the Earth. After observing horizontal layers of a segment of young, coastal red sandstone that overlaid older, steeply pitched, sedimentary rocks called Greywacke, they contradicted the creationists' "Young Earth" theory. Those same rocks are still there, and should not be missed as you walk this wonderful trail.

From the sedimentary wonders of Siccar Point, it's on to St. Helen's Church with its links to the Reformation, as you head south and slightly inland. A side trail takes you to the remains of fifteenth-century Fast Castle, four miles (6.4 km) northwest of Coldingham atop its lonely, rounded promontory that was visited by Mary Queen of Scots in 1566 and provided the inspiration for Sir Walter Scott's "Wolf's Crag" in his novel *The Bride of Lammermoor* (1819).

Then it's up over Tun Law—at 492 feet (150 m), the highest sea cliff in east Britain—and the site of two Iron Age forts, before visiting Gunsgreen House, designed by John Adams and built in the 1750s by smuggler John Nisbet. Make a short detour down Creel Path near St. Abbs, where fishermen once carried their gear to their boats. Continuing through the St. Abbs Head Nature Reserve, a series of easy descents lead from farmlands to beaches. Pause in Eyemouth's reinvigorated harbor, then cross the English border into Berwick-upon-Tweed. **BDS**

"The route takes in some dramatic cliff top scenery complete with arches, stacks, and crumbling castles."

www.walkhighlands.co.uk

⊼ Look out for this walk's famous slab of coastal sandstone that proved the Earth is anything but young.

Isle of Man Coastal Path (The Way of the Gull) Isle of Man

Start/End Douglas   **Distance** 95 miles (153 km)   **Time** 5–7 days   **Grade** Strenuous
Type Rocky paths, sealed rural roads   **Map** goo.gl/ZvrcDW

"Soon after passing Pigeon's Cove, where is some grand rock scenery, Douglas Head is reached, and the tourist finishes his circuit of the isle, in all probability better in health, mind, and spirit for the outing." This description of a walk around the Isle of Man is just as accurate today as it was when it was written in 1874 by visionary outdoorsman Henry Jenkinson.

The Isle of Man Coastal Path—in the local Manx language, Raad ny Foillan (Way of the Gull)—is a long-distance footpath around the circumference of this land in the middle of the Irish Sea. The Isle of Man extends 32 miles (51 km) from north to south and 14 miles (22 km) from east to west at its widest point. From the summit of its highest point, Snaefell (2,034 feet/620 m), it is claimed that on a clear day you can see six kingdoms—England, Ireland, Scotland, Wales, the Isle of Man, and Heaven.

On a clockwise circuit, the route leaves the modern capital, Douglas, along high cliff tops that gradually come down to a plain at Ronaldsway. Now the main airport, this was the site of the battle in 1275 in which the island lost its independence.

From there pass through Castletown, the ancient capital, and Port St. Mary before reaching the southern tip of the island, from which there are views across to the Calf of Man. Turning north past Port Erin and Peel, you arrive at the Point of Ayre, the northernmost tip of the island on a plain of shingle. The last leg of the journey goes through Ramsey, the cliffs at Maughold Head, Laxey (where there is a historic industrial waterwheel), and picturesque Groudle Glen. **BDS**

⬆ Part of the only land between England and Ireland.

Tarn Hows Cumbria, England

Start/End Rose Castle   **Distance** 1.8 miles (2.9 km)   **Time** 1 hour   **Grade** Easy
Type Path suitable for wheelchairs and strollers   **Map** goo.gl/XdcdsU

Until the early 1860s, Tarn Hows in England's Lake District National Park was for generations a small part of the open grazing land that belonged to the parish of Hawkshead. Then in 1862 the land was sold to a Liberal Party politician, James Garth Marshall, the member of parliament for Leeds, who insisted on "improving" upon what nature had bequeathed with the planting of spruce, larch, and pine, as well as the construction of the reservoir at Low Tarn, which still stands today.

Today, when you take a walk around the beauty spot of Tarn Hows, which was once described by the author H.S. Cowper as "beloved by skiers in winter and picnic parties in summer," you cannot fail to be overwhelmed by the legacy that Marshall left us, and hard, too, not to be grateful—and perhaps a little relieved—that he was a man with an obvious talent for taking what nature has provided and giving it a flattering makeover.

A tarn is a mountain pool or lake formed in a cirque carved by glacial activity. Fed at its northern end by a network of basin and valley mires, Tarn Hows, surrounded by thick woodlands and with a 1.5-mile (2.4-km) path around its serene shoreline, is one of the Lake District's most visited spots. It is loved by all who have been there, including the author and illustrator Beatrix Potter, who purchased it and its surrounds in 1929. Potter later sold the half of her new holdings that included the tarn to the National Trust, and then bequeathed the remainder to the trust in her will. The beneficiary of a series of safe, caring hands, Tarn Hows and its circular walk can now be enjoyed by all. **BDS**

↑ A mountain lake cared for by celebrity stewards.

Durham Heritage Coastal Path
Durham, England

Start Seaham Hall Beach **End** Crimdon Park
Distance 12.6 miles (20.2 km) **Time** 1 day
Grade Easy to moderate **Type** Path
Map goo.gl/oHpWk7

Durham has emerged from its industrial past to become an intriguing walking destination, with the northeastern county's cliffs offering a fascinating stretch of coastal path next to the North Sea. The distinctive geographical feature here is yellow magnesian limestone, which has formed cliffs around shallow sandy bays and rocky headlands. Above them, swathes of natural grasslands teem with wildflowers and butterflies in the spring. Clefts in the cliffs, called "denes" locally, are thickly wooded with oak trees. Yet a few decades ago, few would have thought of taking a stroll here. The coast was scarred by mining and industrial tipping, and beaches were black from dumped colliery waste. Now all the pits have closed. Environmentalists have been at work instead and, with the natural scouring effects of the sea, the remarkable transformation has occurred.

The area is now a National Nature Reserve, where experts find rare orchids and butterflies. Seals and basking sharks can be spotted in seawater that now passes strict environmental quality controls. The authorities have worked hard to promote this new attraction. Art installations have been placed at regular intervals along the path. There's a busy new yacht marina in the old coal port of Seaham, fossil hunters use the beach once dominated by Dawdon Colliery, and the polluted mine water at Horden has been cleared with the planting of reed beds.

The path ends at Crimdon—once the only clean spot along the coast, where miners' families came to enjoy vacations. Now it's an open space of sand and dunes, which ornithologists visit to watch migratory little terns, who come here to breed. **SH**

"A wonderful mosaic of great natural, historical, and geological interest with dramatic views."

www.durhamheritagecoast.org

⊼ The path takes you past Britain's finest display of magnesian limestone coastal grasslands.

Raven's View

North Yorkshire, England

Start/End Ravenscar Coastal Centre
Distance 1.3 miles (2.1 km)   **Time** 1 hour
Grade Easy   **Type** Coastal footpath
Map goo.gl/tvKtxv

The North Yorkshire coast is a favorite destination for walkers, an area where the wild hills of the North York Moors turn to rocky cliffs, jutting headlands, wooded valleys, and villages perched in deep clefts. It's rarely soft and pretty, but often inspiring and dramatic.

Ravenscar is a hamlet just north of the coastal town of Scarborough. It stands in Robin Hood's Bay, at the opposite end to where visitors head to visit cafés and art galleries in a winding lane down to the sea. At this southern end, there's less to attract the hordes, but plenty to interest the walker. The popularity of walks in this area is demonstrated by the number of paths you'll find. The Cleveland Way National Trail passes through on its 110-mile-(177-km) route between Helmsley and Filey, and the 40-mile (64-km)Lyke Wake Walk ends here. A local farmer devised the route to show you could walk across the Moors to the sea on heather all the way.

The Raven's View is a very short route, but there are optional loops to the old brick works inland and to the extensive ruins of the cliff-top alum works, where shale was turned into an important ingredient for tanning leather in the seventeenth century. The main path utilizes a disused rail track and passes through a deciduous wood that's filled with bluebells in spring. A stretch across open countryside is where you'll spot butterflies, flowers, and seabirds. Britain's only poisonous snake, the adder, is a summer visitor here—so tread carefully. A viewing platform overlooks a freshwater wildlife pond teeming with frogs and damselflies in summer. The main attraction, however, is the breathtaking view across the North Sea and along the shore of Robin Hood's Bay. **SH**

Doc Martin Walk

Cornwall, England

Start/End Port Isaac   **Distance** 7 miles (11.2 km)   **Time** 1 day   **Grade** Easy to moderate
Type Marked coast, country paths
Map goo.gl/tOfnDj

Doc Martin (2004–) is a popular British television series about a grumpy rural doctor. The show was filmed around the picturesque fishing village of Port Isaac on the north Cornish coast. For *Doc Martin* fans, the walk includes the farm where the stage sets were erected, and houses familiar locations such as the school, Bert's café, and the doctor's house itself. Commercial guides are also available to take paying customers on a tour of *Doc Martin* film locations. If you haven't seen the show, however, this is still a fine walking destination, whether exploring the circular route from Port Quin to

> *"A lovely seven-mile walk … past some of the memorable features of the popular [TV] series."*
>
> www.classicguides.co.uk

Port Isaac, or heading either west to Polzeath or east to Boscastle on the magnificent South West Coast Path. Any stretch of the coast path in north Cornwall features great views of a rocky shore that is notoriously dangerous and has been littered with shipwrecks over the centuries. The switchback of jagged cliffs and coves faces directly into the Atlantic and its prevailing winds. Villages such as Port Isaac are snuggled into the sheltered clefts of inlets along this crenellated coastline. Port Isaac is characterized by its narrow lanes and tightly packed fishermen's cottages. Parking is not easy, and that's why this route was designed to start at the National Trust parking lot in neighboring Port Quin. **SH**

Smugglers' Way Cornwall, England

Start Boscastle **End** Looe   **Distance** 36 miles (57.9 km)   **Time** 2–4 days   **Grade** Moderate to strenuous
Type Moorland, countryside   **Map** goo.gl/3IIuP7

Boscastle is a dramatic starting point for any walk. This bracing north coast spot seems a long way from the sandy beaches that make Cornwall such a popular destination. The tiny village huddles in wooded clefts amid a daunting rocky coastline. The only harbor for 20 miles (32 km) is here—a narrow, natural inlet that winds spectacularly between imposing black cliffs, protected by seawalls built by notorious Tudor seadog, Sir Richard Grenville, captain of HMS *Revenge*.

From there, this challenging walk heads straight for the rugged heart of the county. The Smugglers' Way climbs from the coast across the high and wild terrain of Bodmin Moor, then down through little-visited farmland and villages. Walkers find the picture-postcard version of Cornwall only right at the end point of Looe on the south coast. The route tackles the highest points in Cornwall as it crosses Bodmin

Moor. The rocky crown of Brown Willy stands at 1,378 feet (420 m), and nearby walkers can call in at the remote Jamaica Inn, a classic smugglers' pub featured in the writings of Daphne du Maurier. Beware, however, as the way is unmarked, and navigational skills are required to cross the open moor, especially during mists and severe weather.

After a sequence of quiet villages such as Herodsfoot, Dobwalls, and Sowdens Bridge, the trail meets a lush wooded valley that becomes the Looe Estuary. Pastel-painted fishermen's cottages stand on either side of the estuary where it meets the sea—a natural end to this path. Intrepid souls, however, may consider continuing along the epic, 630-mile (1,014-km) South West Coastal Path (opposite). **SH**

⊓ **Where excise-dodgers might repent along the way.**

South West Coastal Path Somerset to Dorset, England

Start Minehead   **End** Poole Harbour   **Distance** 630 miles (1,014 km)   **Time** 1–2 months
Grade Moderate to strenuous   **Type** Long-distance path   **Info** goo.gl/ic5Xhf

Originally laid down to help coastguards track and intercept smugglers, the South West Coastal Path is Britain's most popular walk and one of the world's great pathways. From its starting point at Minehead in Somerset, it weaves a path along the coast of North Devon, encircles the entire coast of Cornwall and passes along the South Devon coast, ending at South Haven Point in Poole. Along the way it passes through two World Heritage Sites, five Areas of Outstanding Natural Beauty, and one National Park.

Although a coastline walk, it drifts well inland at Exmoor after leaving Minehead to the point where you lose sight of the sea and you would be forgiven for thinking you were on a moorland hike. Farther south it's a roller-coaster ride up and down heavily incised coastal cliffs from Hartland Point to Bude, the walk's rawest section. The coastal landforms along the

length of this trail will leave truly lasting impressions: sights such as South Cornwall's Lizard Peninsula, the Granite Coast at Land's End, the perfect scoop that is Lulworth Cove, and the massive arched passageway of Durdle Door in Dorset, as well as the Jurassic Coast between Exmouth and the trail's end in Poole.

You can choose whether to backpack it with a tent and a sleeping bag, or end each day in lovely seaside hotels in the dozens of towns and villages nestled around its naturally sheltered harbors and deep-water channels. A guidebook with tide and ferry timetables is a must, as there are estuary crossings that require a ferry. The best time to walk is in late spring, when the wildflowers are in full bloom along a trail where no two days are ever the same. **BDS**

⊤   A coastal walk that loves to drift inland.

Saxon Shore Way

Kent/East Sussex, England

Start Gravesend   End Hastings
Distance 160 miles (257 km)   Time 1–2 weeks
Grade Easy   Type Long-distance trail
Info goo.gl/v1i8Pu

"Recognized as one of the most important estuarine habitats for birds in the UK."

www.visitkent.co.uk

⬆ The cliffs that inspired one of England's bynames, "Albion," from the Latin *albus*, meaning "white."

This may seem at first glance to be a straightforward coast walk, but remember that the route traces the shore as it was 1,500 years ago, which is certainly not the same as it is now. The Saxon Shore Way leads walkers inland, avoiding marshes that didn't exist at the end of the Roman occupation of Britain, and follows a line of cliffs that are now separated from the sea. All of this makes for a fascinating long-distance route, waymarked by a red Viking helmet symbol.

You'll still get a good sense of the sea as it is now, of course. There are several varieties of coast walking included: from the wide expanses of marshland bordering the mouths of the Thames and Medway estuaries to the famous chalky white cliffs of Dover and sandy beaches of the south coast. The theme is loosely set around the Roman coastal fortifications at Reculver, Richborough, Dover, and Lympne. These were built to keep the Saxon invaders from Denmark at bay, but there are other castles of varying ages along the 160 miles (257 km) of this trail, including some Iron Age hill forts, the nineteenth-century Martello Towers, and the great Norman castle at Dover. The path sticks to the cliffs between Folkestone and Rye, giving views over the miles of Romney Marshes that have appeared between the cliff and sea. Similarly, the North Kent marshes now separate the old shoreline from the sea. It's a route that passes through towns such as Gravesend, Folkestone, and Hastings, but there's plenty of wildlife in the countryside between them. In fact, the path crosses several nature reserves and Sites of Special Scientific Interest, while the North Kent marshes in particular are famed for attracting migrating birds. **SH**

Isle of Wight Coast Path

Isle of Wight, England

Start/End Various   Distance 69 miles (111 km)
Time 4–6 days   Grade Easy to moderate
Type Footpaths, some roads
Map goo.gl/xaokeF

Most people start this circular route around the coast of the Isle of Wight at one of the main ferry ports when they arrive—at either Yarmouth or Cowes—but it can really be started anywhere. Wherever you begin the trail guarantees an inspiring sequence of cliff-top views, sandy beaches, harbors, and estuaries. Any round-the-island walk includes an extra degree of satisfaction on completion, when you realize you have encircled the whole island.

The Isle of Wight is a popular spot for holidays, but generally is visited because it is unspoiled. With its quiet traffic, undeveloped countryside, and conservative lifestyle, the island often reminds British visitors of what the mainland used to be like in their childhoods. In practical terms, the walk avoids the steepest climbs and is well-marked and maintained, but can get busy in peak holiday times. The island is popular as a walkers' destination and holds walking festivals each May and October. The coast path isn't likely to become overcrowded, but it may not be deserted. The number of regular walkers means that there are lots of places to stay near the path and plenty of links to public transport.

The path features many highlights, such as the pretty fishing village of Yarmouth, the white rock seastacks known as the Needles, and the renowned homemade crab pasties on sale at Steephill Cove. The path goes right past Tennyson's Monument at Freshwater and the busy yacht harbor at Cowes. The island is full of tourist attractions, and from the path it is easy to visit the exotic gardens at St. Lawrence, the Roman villa at Brading, and Queen Victoria's favorite residence at Osborne House. **SH**

"Great views out to sea and many interesting places to visit, reflecting the island's heritage."

www.visitisleofwight.co.uk

⊞ Get up close to the island's striking chalk-cliff geology and walk barefoot in its multicolored sands.

Guernsey Coastal Walk
Guernsey, Channel Islands

Start/End Various Distance 38 miles (61 km) Time 2–7 days Grade Easy to moderate Type Coast path Map goo.gl/tBAp2d

"Walking is one of the best ways to explore the island's stunning coastline and countryside."

www.visitguernsey.com

The Channel Islands are British-administered territories lying off the northwest coast of France. Guernsey is one of the largest and most populated of the islands, but is still considered a genteel, unspoiled, and wealthy destination by British visitors. The climate is much milder than Britain, the environment more determinedly "green," and there are obvious French influences everywhere.

Circumnavigating the coastline of Guernsey can be done in a day, with an annual charity walk starting in the early hours and usually finishing in the early evening. A more leisurely approach is to start at the capital, St. Peter Port, and divide the walk into easy days. Commercial walking holiday companies allow up to a week for the round-the-island route. Whatever your pace, this is a charming path with pretty coves, long sandy beaches, and wild cliff tops. The seabirds, wildflowers, and inspiring sea views accompany you for most of the circuit, and impressive coastal fortifications of varying ages appear throughout. Generally, the south coast is more rugged. The constant sound of waves crashing against jagged shores will follow you along the paths here. Rocky headlands give way to sandy stretches backed by dunes along the west and north coast, then the gardens and buildings of St. Peter Port dominate the eastern shores. The capital town is built around an attractive harbor and castle, with a relaxed, affluent ambience and plenty of distracting shops, bars, and restaurants for walkers. At the most westerly point of Guernsey, the tiny island of Lihou used to be a retreat for monks. Include it in your round-the-island route, but be aware that it is accessible only at low tide. **SH**

⬆ Guernsey's villages, lanes, beaches and 30 miles (48 km) of cliff paths will have you walking for days.

Anglesey Coastal Path
Anglesey, Wales

Start/End St. Cybi's Church, Holyhead
Distance 124 miles (200 km)   Time 12 days
Grade Moderate   Type Long-distance footpath
Info goo.gl/ZkOxnT

Anglesey is a 276-square-mile (715-sq-km) island in the Irish Sea off the northwest coast of Wales. It is connected to the mainland by two bridges, the first of which, the Menai Suspension Bridge (1826), was the first of its type. Once you cross it, you enter a world where 95 percent of the coastline is a designated Area of Outstanding Natural Beauty (AONB), the largest of Wales's five such regions. This fabulous coastal walk takes you through twenty villages that lie on the path. These provide welcome respite after navigating farmland, dunes, salt marshes, coastal heaths, woodlands, cliffs (frequented by puffins, guillemots, razorbills, and terns), and Holyhead Mountain—the route's highest point, from the summit of which you can see Snowdonia on the mainland.

The official starting point for the walk is St. Cybi's Church, adjacent to an old Roman fort in the center of Holyhead. By the time you return here in around twelve days' time, you will have passed four working lighthouses, sunk your feet into the expansive sands of Newborough Beach, marveled at the carved sea arch at Rhoscolyn and the limestone escarpments along Anglesey's southern coast, and tramped your way through the sheer magnificence of moated Beaumaris Castle, built by Edward I in the thirteenth century as part of his conquest of North Wales and described by historian Arnold Taylor as the finest example in Britain of a symmetrical, concentric castle. There is much to like about walking this island, with its surprisingly mild climate, clear air, and linguistic challenges, such as pronouncing the name of Llanfairpwllgwyngyll—a village with the longest name in the U.K., customarily abbreviated to Llanfair PG. **BDS**

"Includes a mixture of farmland, coastal heath, dunes, salt-marsh, foreshore, cliffs, and . . . woodland."

www.visitinganglesey.co.uk

⊼ A mild climate and an abundance of history make Anglesey a walker's paradise.

Llyn Coastal Path

Gwynedd, Wales

Start Caernarfon   **End** Porthmadog
Distance 91 miles (146 km)   **Time** 7 days
Grade Moderate to strenuous   **Type** Long-distance
footpath   **Map** goo.gl/84eETO

Entire swathes of the Llyn Peninsula's coastline in northwest Wales is so stunning that it has been designated an Area of Outstanding Natural Beauty. Consequently, the peninsula's crenellated boundaries were regarded as an ideal backdrop for a long-distance footpath. The Llyn Coastal Path, established in 2006, takes advantage of an old pilgrimage route to Bardsey Island (a focal point for the Celtic Christian church), past the peninsula's many cliff-top crags and escarpments, and along a series of descents to hidden coves and quaint fishing villages.

Despite occasional inland detours that take you to heights in excess of 1,000 feet (305 m)—the highest is 1,345 feet (410 m)—the Irish Sea is nevertheless rarely out of sight on this trail. The route passes by a myriad of ancient stone churches, and also by the childhood home of former British prime minister David Lloyd George in the village of Llanystumdwy.

While you are in Caernarfon, make sure you take time to visit the well-preserved Roman fort at Segontium and its fabulous thirteenth-century church, built by King Edward I.

The Llyn Coastal Path may not be on the scale of, say, England's South West Coast Path, but that doesn't get in the way of it showcasing an impressive array of cliff walks, dunes, moorlands, mudflats, and mountains that contain some of the oldest rocks to be found anywhere in Britain—a combination of terrains that has led many to describe the path as being unsurpassed in its sheer variety. Unlike its longer and more famous cousins, it does not require a massive commitment of weeks or months to complete it. It can be undertaken in only seven days. **BDS**

"Partly based on an ancient pilgrimage route to Bardsey Island—a Christian shrine."

www.walkingnorthwales.co.uk

⬆ The walk along the plateau starts at the medieval bastion of Caernarfon Castle.

Great Orme Trails
Conwy, Wales

Start/End Llandudno   Distance Various
Time 1–3 hours   Grade Moderate
Type Sealed paths, grassy paths, tracks, small roads
Info goo.gl/OIdOqu

The Great Orme—a massive dolomite peninsula on the north coast of Wales, 1.8 miles (3 km) long and 1.2 miles (2 km) wide—is aptly named. Composed almost entirely of limestone formed more than 300 million years ago, this megalithic rock receives more than a half a million visitors every year, eager to experience its impressive geology, its heathlands, and its surrounding woodlands.

It has a vast array of flora and fauna, from coarse grasses such as Yorkshire fog, which thrives in its soil-depleted crevices, to breeding bird colonies of guillemots, kittiwakes, razorbills, and fulmars. More than 430 species of plant life have been cataloged here, and more than 33,000 bone tools and 2,400 stone hammers have been unearthed, detailing its long history of human habitation dating back to the Bronze Age. There's even a small herd of feral Kashmiri goats that were introduced to the headland in the early 1900s. Put simply, there isn't a more interesting or varied single rock in all of Great Britain.

You can walk around it or take a cable car to the summit, but you should allow ample time to do both. The Great Orme Nature Trail is a 4-mile (6.4-km) circular walk that starts on the summit and takes you around the headland, and there is also a choice of three equally scenic walks from Llandudno that go straight to the summit—the Haulfre Gardens Trail, the Happy Valley Trail, and the Zig Zag Trail.

The Great Orme is also home to a vast network of tunnels, hewn from the limestone by our ancestors more than 3,500 years ago in their search for copper. Its caves are now considered to be the world's largest network of prehistoric mines. **BDS**

Ceredigion Coast Path
Ceredigion, Wales

Start Aberystwyth   End Cardigan
Distance 60 miles (96.5 km)   Time 6–8 days
Grade Moderate   Type Meadows, cliff-top trails, sandy beaches   Map goo.gl/m5f8Pm

In terms of environmental credentials, Ceredigion Bay on the west coast of Wales has more to puff its chest out about than most, thanks to its four segments of designated Heritage Coast and two Marine Special Areas of Conservation.

Add to this the country's highest number of dolphin sightings; a treasure trove of Iron Age forts; a waterfall at Tresaith Beach, an unusual feature that is the result of past glacial activity; a dune system at Ynyslas; storm beaches; and sea caves galore. From Llangrannog to New Quay, there's a wonderfully

> *"Follows the spectacular and varied coastline of Cardigan Bay on the west coast of Wales."*
>
> www.ceredigioncoastpath.org.uk

precipitous trail cut into the side of a coastal slope, where one false step could be your last; from Cwn Tydu to New Quay there are spectacular examples of folded rocks, and forest trails that take you briefly inland from Cei Bach where poet Dylan Thomas lived and wrote, to the village of Aberaeron, where more than a quarter of all its buildings are heritage listed.

When you reach one of the trail's Heritage Coast sections between Llanrhystud and Aberystwyth, the dramatic coastline will lure you on through green cliff-hugging pastures to Constitution Hill, a vantage point that is guaranteed to give you pause as you gaze over twenty-six Welsh peaks spanning almost the entire length of the country. This walk is a real gem. **BDS**

Pembrokeshire Coast Path Pembrokeshire, Wales

Start St. Dogmaels **End** Amroth **Distance** 186 miles (299 km) **Time:** 9 days **Grade** Easy to moderate
Type Coastal pathway **Info** goo.gl/bs6lmL

If you're planning to walk all 186 miles (299 km) of the Pembrokeshire Coastal Path, from St. Dogmaels in the north to Amroth in the south, you might want to embark on a training regimen first, because more than 35,000 feet (10,668 m) of ascents and descents await you—the equivalent of climbing Mount Everest.

Thank goodness, then, for a sprinkling of coastal villages providing respite—although, oddly, the centuries-old presence of villages never resulted in the construction of so much as a pathway to link them: all communication between communities was effected by boat, not land. When it was time to map out a pathway along this rugged coastline, a series of logistical challenges had to be overcome: many of the proposed pathways were under private ownership, and cliff tops were difficult to access and were horribly overgrown. The coming-of-age of the path we have

now was the result of long and often complex negotiations with the people who for generations have called this place home. Fortunately for the rest of us, it was a home they were eager to share.

Most of the path lies within the boundaries of the Pembrokeshire Coast National Park, Britain's only coastal national park. Unceasing work by national park staff is required to keep it clear and navigable in the face of winter storms, the constant regeneration of the area's vegetation, and its trampling by countless soles. This particular path, though, can cope with a little trampling. Its constituent parts date back three billion years—volcanic pre-Cambrian granite and hard igneous rocks underlie everything on a pathway that isn't going anywhere in a hurry. **BDS**

⬆ This trail includes every type of maritime landscape.

Wales Coast Path Monmouthshire to Flintshire, Wales

Start Chepstow   **End** Queensferry   **Distance** 870 miles (1,400 km)   **Time** 3 months   **Grade** Moderate
Type Long-distance footpath   **Info** goo.gl/JOES3z

Officially opened on May 5, 2012, the Wales Coast Path takes you around the entire Welsh coast, but also, by linking up with the great Offa's Dyke Path, makes Wales the first country on Earth to be completely encircled by walking trails. The path proved instantly popular—its occasional diversions inland always bring you back to the coast to villages and hidden coves you'd miss if you were in a car. Lonely Planet liked it sufficiently to name it the world's number one destination to experience in 2012.

Created in part to capitalize on the popularity of the Pembrokeshire and Anglesey coastal paths, the route takes you through the Welsh landscape, as well as its history. Continual improvements and ongoing tweaking ensure it will always hug the Welsh coast as much as it can. Trails to nearby inland towns and circular loops will, over time, grow from the main path like the branches of a tree, providing walkers with a mind-boggling array of possible detours.

The path begins in Chepstow in the south and finishes on the north coast at Queensferry, with various segments available for cyclists, horseback riders, and those with impaired mobility. Although 20 percent of the trail is on roads, they are quiet and pleasantly rural. Welsh beaches receive more awards for clean water and environmental management than any others in Britain, so whether it's the Llyn Peninsula, the beautiful sweep of Cardigan Bay, the close to inaccessible bow-shaped and dream-like Tresaith Beach, or the pebble-strewn shorelines of Aberystwyth, the Wales Coast Path will give you one of the purest coastal walks you can undertake. **BDS**

⬆ At last, a single trail for all the Welsh coastline.

GR34 Customs Officers' Path Brittany, France

Start Bay of Mont Saint-Michel **End** Saint-Nazaire **Distance** 1,056 miles (1,700 km) **Time** 10–12 weeks
Grade Moderate **Type** Coastal trails, stairs, rural roads **Info** goo.gl/Ao6vmY

In the seventeenth and eighteenth centuries, when England had high import duties on wine, spirits, tea, and tobacco, enterprising French smugglers were busy filling the holds of their ships with the stuff in the coves and inlets of Brittany, rather than along the more heavily patrolled northern coastline, in an effort to avoid paying English taxes.

The French coastguard, of course, attempted to intercept these operations. Until the early decades of the twentieth century, hundreds of armed customs officers would be seen walking these paths day and night, regardless of whether they were being bathed in sunshine or battered by fierce Atlantic storms. This network of well-worn trails established along the cliff tops of Brittany formed the basis of the GR 34 coastal footpath, the Sentier des Douaniers (the Customs Officers' Path).

The route traces a line over almost the entire length of Brittany's rugged coastline and, at 1,242 miles (2,000 km), it is one of France's longest long-distance paths, meandering its way from the Bay of Mont Saint-Michel to the town of Saint-Nazaire. Marked by red and white trail markers, it is called by residents of Saint-Nazaire the "balcony above the sea"—a path, but also a sort of refuge infused with the scent of resin and pine as it takes you through forests of pine and evergreen oak—unexpected treats for a coastal path. It also passes great topographical landmarks, including the Pink Granite Rose Coast and Cap Frehel. The latter—an unpopulated peninsula with just two lighthouses above a rocky headland—is accessible only on foot. **BDS**

⬆ The jagged Breton coast has many inlets like this.

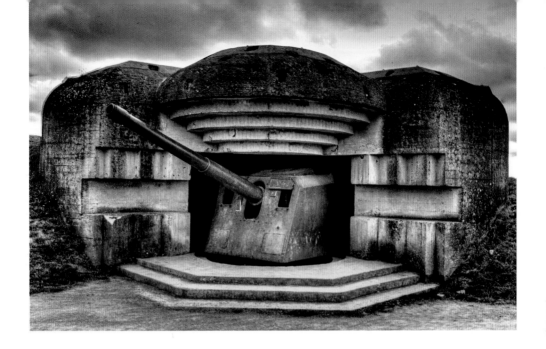

D–Day Beaches Basse-Normandie, France

Start/End Various **Distance** Various **Time** 3–10 days **Grade** Easy **Type** Dirt and grass paths, lanes, meadows
Info goo.gl/JHqQp7

Sword Beach is the easternmost of the five Normandy beaches where the liberation of Europe began in earnest on June 6, 1944. Above it, the Pegasus Bridge was captured by men of the Glider Pilot Regiment and the 6th British Airborne. Juno Beach bristled with pillboxes, gun emplacements, mines, and barbed wire. Gold Beach had the Longues-sur-Mer German gun emplacement—four antiaircraft guns with a range of more than 12 miles (19 km) that gave the Allied fleet a veritable pounding. Utah Beach, the most westerly of the beaches, was taken after the U.S. 4th Infantry Division came ashore at its poorly defended southern end. Omaha Beach was heavily defended from the top of its 150-foot (45-m) bluffs and left largely untouched by Allied bombing, a beach with no cover that became a killing zone for the men and boys of the U.S. 29th Infantry Division.

You can spend weeks walking here, and many of those who come to honor the sacrifice made by the thousands who took part in Operation Overlord do just that. At Sword, you can walk to the Hillman bunker complex captured by the Suffolk Regiment. At Juno, you can walk inland and trace the Canadian assault on the village of Tailleville. At Omaha, you can walk the Vierville Draw, depicted in the film *Saving Private Ryan* (1998), and from there over marshland to Timmes Orchard, where a small, mixed force of paratroopers fought without assistance until June 9, when they were able to link up with the 82nd Airborne. There are as many trails here as there were skirmishes, and to understand what happened, you need to retrace the steps of those who died here. **BDS**

⤒ German gun emplacements still line the coast.

GR21 Alabaster Coast Trail

Haute-Normandie/Picardie, France

Start Le Havre   End Le Tréport
Distance 111 miles (179 km)   Time 12 days
Grade Easy   Type Long-distance hiking path
Info goo.gl/NGHWU1

Normally when we think of white chalk cliffs battered by the waters of the English Channel, our thoughts turn to Dover. However, France has its own chalky coastline, an 80-mile (128-km) slash of white that runs from Dieppe to Étretat, northeast of Le Havre, and that shares the same geological origins as the Dover cliffs. The French call it La Côte d'Albâtre—the Alabaster Coast—and there isn't a stretch of coastline like it anywhere else in France.

The waymarked trail takes you to the very best vantage points while keeping a safe distance from the cliff's edge. It runs along the coast from Le Havre to Le Tréport, with occasional turns inland through woods and cultivated farmlands. At the edge of the Pays de Caux, a vast chalk plateau, the path is up to 393 feet (120 m) above the sea. This stretch has long been an inspiration for writers and painters, particularly the Impressionists, who were captivated by its interplay of light and shadow, its arches, and its famous rock needle, the Aiguille de Belval. It is also a coastline full of gorges—*valleuses*—which the GR21 long-distance hiking path does well to navigate, taking you past chapels and manor houses, and through the region's flora and fauna as side trails constantly branch off to take you down to the water and to fishing villages, such as Fécamp, the residence of the first dukes of Normandy until 1204, and many a beach that you think might be secluded but never is.

If you want to see the wonderfully sculpted landforms of the Alabaster Coast, hurry: it is eroding at the rate of more than 3 feet (1 m) a year. **BDS**

⬅ One of Normandy's natural limestone arches.

Côte Vermeille

France/Spain

Start Collioure, France   End Cadaqués,
Spain   Distance 50 miles (80 km)
Time 5 days   Grade Moderate   Type Coastal paths,
country lanes, mountain trails   Map goo.gl/AM9qzg

The Côte Vermeille (Vermillion Coast) was made for walking—straddling Spain and France at the end of the Pyrenees, it forms a series of coves and capes that could have been cut with pinking shears. The Chemin des Contrebandiers (Smugglers' Path) follows its course, dipping down to beaches and soaring along maquis-covered cliffs. Every so often the trail reaches a port, where hikers can stop or stay overnight.

The path can be accessed at many points, and there are spur trails for shorter walks, but it is well worth doing the five-day hike from Collioure to Cadaqués.

> *"Collioure … can rival anything the Riviera has to offer—at a fraction of the cost."*
>
> www.telegraph.co.uk

Both towns are associated with artists: Matisse, Picasso, Chagall, and Dufy and the Fauvists painted in Collioure; Salvador Dalí had a home in Port Lligat near Cadaqués. Between these end points are Banyuls-sur-Mer, Portbou, Port de la Selva, and the idyllic bays that make up the Cap de Creus nature reserve. From Collioure, the trail hugs the coast, rounding Cap Béar and its old lighthouse. Clipping the foothills of the Pyrenees, it continues south, with detours to Tour Madeloc and Col des Gascons (1,269 feet/387 m) before doubling up with the trans-Pyrenean GR10 trail to descend to Banyuls. Spain begins just before Portbou, the start of a string of bays and fishing villages ending at Cadaqués. **DS**

Promenade des Anglais to Castle Hill Provence, France

Start Hotel Negresco, Nice   End Castle Hill, Nice
Distance 2 miles (3.2 km)   Time 1 hour
Grade Easy   Type Promenade
Info goo.gl/sTuJlH

Imagine this: you are in Nice on the French Riviera and have just eaten a dinner you couldn't finish, and let's be honest, couldn't afford, at the Hotel Negresco's two Michelin-starred restaurant Le Chantecler. It occurs to you that it might be a good idea to "walk it off." You step outside onto the marbled Promenade des Anglais, built for English aristocrats in the nineteenth century so they could stroll along the beach without being bothered by panhandlers and locals. You look to your left and can see in the fading light the glow of Castle Hill, and you begin to walk.

"I love Nice. It is like being in a nest, surrounded on three sides by mountains. I grow here."

Marie Bashkirtseff, Russian painter

You pass the Belle Époque Westminster and West End hotels, as well as a mix of private and public beaches and beach bars, including the Plage Beau Rivage. There's the wonderful Art Nouveau façade of the defunct 1927 casino, the Palais de la Méditerranée, now a luxury hotel, before you turn down the Quai des États-Unis (Quay of the United States) and pass more beaches filled with imported sand and a rusted steel-girded sculpture, built to celebrate the 150th anniversary of Nice's decision to join France rather than remain as a protectorate of the Italian kingdom of Savoy-Piedmont. When you reach the Hotel Suisse, walk up to Colline du Chateau (Castle Hill), where you can savor the views over Baie des Anges. **BDS**

Calanques de Cassis Provence-Alpes-Côte d'Azur, France

Start Cassis   End Calanque de Saména
Distance 9 miles (14.5 km)   Time 6 hours
Grade Moderate   Type Well-maintained gravel trails, bare rock   Map goo.gl/VGNpUl

The Calanques de Cassis are twenty or so fish and snorkeler-filled inlets filled with saline algae (which gives the water its deep turquoise color) that cut their way inland into a range of beautiful limestone cliffs that plunge into the Mediterranean Sea between Marseilles and the town of Cassis on the French Riviera. A 9,880-acre (4,000-ha) expanse of protected hills and cliffs that draws millions of visitors every year, including walkers, cavers, and climbers, this dry, crenellated coast is a unique mix of the fjords of Norway (in miniature) and the white-baked coastlines of Greece. It's a karst-filled region of white- and orange-hued cliffs, where the mistral can blow so hard there are places where there are barely any trees of any height to speak of, while elsewhere pockets of endangered plants and shrubs endemic to the Mediterranean are found here and nowhere else.

Generally closed in the height of summer due to the risk of forest fires, the Calanques has more than 12 miles (19.3 km) of walking trails. The most visited, due to their ease of access from Cassis, are Port Miou, Port Pin, and Calanque d'En-Vau—all accessed via trails suitable for people of all ages. It is possible to continue past the third Calanque, but the trail becomes difficult and, to be honest, the first three are the most beautiful, although the golden sandy beaches of each Calanque are deserving of an energy-sapping hike just for the chance of having one all to yourself.

Designated a national park in 2012 (the first in France since 1979), this area of rugged wilderness and steep fjord-like inlets is a vehicle-free zone, and there are only a handful of trails that can get you to its turquoise and limestone wonders. **BDS**

Camargue Flamingo Trails
Provence-Alpes-Côte d'Azur, France

Start Saintes-Maries-de-la-Mer **End** Camargue sea dike **Distance** 13.5 miles (21.7 km) **Time** 1 day
Grade Easy **Type** Sealed paths, dirt trails
Map goo.gl/7Wv4Cc

The Camargue, a thirty-minute drive south of the Provence city of Arles on the Mediterranean Sea, is a land that has been cultivated since the Middle Ages. It is still so wild and untamed that walking here has been described as "walking the French Texas." It's a diverse environment populated by growers of the protected, healthy, and flavorsome Camargue red rice, sand (sables) winemakers, salt producers, and reed harvesters—a total of more than 7,000 people who call the Camargue their home.

Classified by UNESCO as a biosphere reserve, the Camargue is situated at the end of the Rhône River, the only river in France that has a delta. It is a world of salt plains, sand dunes, lagoons, farmlands, marshes, reed beds, and forest—a mix of environments that can't fail to guarantee a varied and fascinating walking experience. There are more than 1,000 varieties of flowering plants here, as well as the ubiquitous wild white horses and black bulls, and numerous bird species that either breed here or use it as a stopover on their north–south migration. Among these birds are the thousands of flamingoes, which have chosen the Camargue as their sole regular nesting ground on the European continent.

A full Camargue hiking holiday can take eight days if you begin at the walled town of Aigues-Mortes and take in the coastal plains. However, you can choose to view the flamingoes—one of the Camargue's most popular pursuits—over a day from Saintes-Maries-de-la-Mer, through the nature reserve and along the sea dike—a total distance of about 13.5 miles (22 km) that should have you feeling very much "in the pink" by the time you're done. **BDS**

"Home to unique breeds of Camargue horses and bulls, and to more than 400 species of birds including pink flamingoes."

www.midi-france.info

⊞ This precious UNESCO site at the end of France's only river delta has trails galore—and flamingoes!

Mala Beach Coastal Path
Monaco/France

Start Monaco   **End** Cap-d'Ail, France
Distance 2.2 miles (3.5 km)   **Time** 1 hour
Grade Easy   **Type** Dirt, gravel trails, sealed path
Map goo.gl/JMgFwk

One stop—and a world away—on the local train line from Monaco heading south along the coast in the direction of Nice is the town of Cap-d'Ail, a pleasant place that tumbles down to the Mediterranean along the rolling escarpments of the Tête de Chien Hills that rise up behind it.

It is home to all the familiar elements found in the south of France—Belle Epoque architecture, sumptuous villas, and swimming pools. However, it also has something a lot of towns don't have around here, and that is a reputation as a dormitory town for people who commute each day to work in the considerably more Belle Epoque–laden streets of their more fancied neighbor to the north. Of course, Cap-d'Ail has had its various claims to fame. Movie star Greta Garbo once lived here, as did Winston Churchill, Lord Beaverbrook, and pioneering filmmakers the Lumière brothers. Even if they hadn't lived there, a working-class population wouldn't be the only thing these two Riviera communities have in common. They are also linked by one quite lovely coastal footpath.

The Mala Beach Coastal Path, which lies so close to the ocean that you are warned not to walk along it when seas are rough, is easily accessed after a few minutes' walk from Monaco railway station. The walk is mostly flat, although the final approach up to Mala Beach requires a little effort. On the way you pass a series of rocky coves and bays, which provide lovely views. Local Cap-d'Ailans will tell you it is best started from Monaco—that way you are leaving the best till last. But of course they would say that, wouldn't they? **BDS**

"The high cliffs that reach from the sea to the sky add a dramatic backdrop to the beaches, especially on the western end."

www.riviera-beaches.com

⬆ The coastal path offers breathtaking views of the ocean, beaches, and cliffs.

Lake Zürich Shoreline Walk
Zürich, Switzerland

Start/End Hotel Baur au Lac   **Distance** 71 miles
(114 km)   **Time** 10 days   **Grade** Easy
Type Forest trails, sidewalk, beaches,
gravel paths   **Map** goo.gl/45tJFi

The exquisite Hotel Baur au Lac on the shores of Lake Zürich, which first opened its doors to guests in 1844, provides the perfect start to a ten-day circumnavigation of this 12,000-year-old lake, carved out during the last Ice Age by the retreating Linth Glacier and leaving a picturesque legacy of extensive woodlands, unspoiled shorelines, and even a couple of beaches—the Strandbad Mythenquai and the Strandbad Tiefenbrunnen, both of which are open from May through August.

The shoreline is dotted with historic towns and farmlands crisscrossed by clear, fast-flowing streams, and there are also tempting gourmet restaurants, generations-old vineyards, villas, castle grounds, and plenty of ascents away from the lakeside, such as a climb through the Sihl woods to Horgen on the Höhenweg Trail, or an ascent of Etzel-Kulm (3,602 feet/ 1,098 m), which provides stunning views over the lake to the Alps beyond.

The majority of time, however, is spent by or near the lake, walking through nature reserves full of waterfowl, gazing at the Glarner and Innerschweiz Alps, passing through the Pfannenstiel foothills, and visiting the "rose town" of Rapperswil, with its 15,000 rose bushes. Just don't leave Zürich without making your way to the Uetliberg, the city's own "private" mountain that towers 1,476 feet (450 m) above the city and provides wonderful views from the lookout on its summit. Take a number thirteen tram and get off at the last stop, and from there it's about an hour to the top through forest to the base of a long series of wooden steps that ends with a ladder and chain-assisted final ascent to its peak. **BDS**

"Shows the versatile region at its best; passing historical towns and villages, castle parks, settlements with noble villas."

www.myswitzerland.com

⬆ Lake Zürich is fed by the Linth River, which rises in the glaciers of central Switzerland's Glarus Alps.

Lake Geneva Shoreline Walk
Vaud/Geneva, Switzerland

Start Lausanne   **End** Geneva
Distance 21 miles (34 km)   **Time** 5 days
Grade Moderate   **Type** Sidewalk, gravel paths
Map goo.gl/Ye9mT5

"The 21-mile [33-km] Geneva Lake shore path allows hikers to walk through the backyards of striking century-old mansions."

www.tripadvisor.com

⬆ Walk a Swiss shoreline along one of Europe's largest lakes with some very French views.

At 43 miles (69 km) long and 8.7 miles (14 km) wide, on the border of France and Switzerland and surrounded by the majesty of the Alps, Lake Geneva is one of the largest lakes in Western Europe. While there's plenty of activity on the lake itself, it's also a great area to walk around, with numerous routes to choose from on both the northern and southern sides of the lake.

If you are walking on the north side of the lake, you would do well to start at the city of Lausanne toward the eastern end of the lake, then head west. The first town you'll come to is Morges, with its round turreted castle and port. Next is Aubonne—the birthplace of electrical engineer George de Mestral, the man who invented Velcro® (although there's much more to the town than that).

Other towns you'll pass through include the medieval cities of Nyon and Chavannes-de-Bogis, both picture-perfect. The route doesn't only take you along the lake shore, however, but also winds through woodlands and vineyards, and passes castles and villas. You'll cross alpine streams, and make your way through beautiful Swiss villages. In many aspects it's like an alpine walk without the climbing. The air is clear and fresh, and you are never out of sight of the majestic mountains.

As you near Geneva itself, you pass through the municipality of Versoix, home to the Swiss chocolate maker Favarger, and every year the town hosts its own chocolate festival. The walk eventually takes you into the heart of Geneva. A far cry from the rest of your walk, this is an affluent, cosmopolitan global center for banking and finance and one of the most expensive cities in the world to live in. **JI**

Defence Line of Amsterdam
Noord Holland, Netherlands

Start Muiden   **End** Volendam
Distance 84 miles (135 km)
Time 8–10 days   **Grade** Easy
Type Dirt walking paths   **Info** goo.gl/43GJ4u

Constructed between 1880 and 1920, but made redundant with the development of the tank and the airplane, the Defence Line of Amsterdam (Stelling van Amsterdam) is an 84-mile (135-km) line of forty-two fortifications surrounding the Dutch city, designed to flood the lowlands to a depth of about 12 inches (30 cm) in times of war. The hope was that this would prevent troops from advancing on the city and Amsterdam would thus become the country's last stronghold. Finally decommissioned in 1963 after never having seen combat, this remarkable engineering feat became a UNESCO World Heritage Site in 1996, and it's now possible to walk the Defence Line along a unique hiking route around its circumference that connects the towns of Muiden at the mouth of the Vecht with the port of Volendam. On the way you will pass dikes, sluices, old engineers' storehouses, and many forts and battlements.

Various segments include the Het Laarzenpad (Boot's Trail), which includes a walk to a lookout over the Naardermeer Reserve, and the Duin en Kruidberg, which goes through a wooded dune area where wealthy Amsterdam traders once lived and is now home to Shetland ponies, Highland cattle, and Konik horses. A separate hike is an 11.8-mile (19-km) walk around Lake Naardermeer through woods, swamps, and a cormorant colony that can be seen from a nearby observation hut. There are many points of interest along this historic route, and the largely untouched areas that surround it provide a perfect day's walk through a tranquil green belt that, despite the passage of time, still surrounds the suburbs of one of Europe's most beautiful cities. **BDS**

"Since the sixteenth century, the people of the Netherlands have used their expert knowledge of hydraulic engineering for defense."

whc.unesco.org

⊤ A nineteenth-century engineering feat, still wholly intact, forms the basis for a unique walking experience.

Mudflat Walking on the Wadden Sea Lower Saxony, Germany

Start/End The beach **Distance** Various
Time Various **Grade** Easy
Type Sand, tidal mudflats
Info goo.gl/fmwzp2

The Wadden Sea runs along the coasts of Germany, the Netherlands, and Denmark between continental Europe and the Wadden Island archipelago, which acts as a shield for one of the largest intertidal zones of mudflats and tidal trenches. Twice a day at low tide the waters recede, and it's possible to walk on the sea's sandy bed. Every year up to 45,000 hardy souls step into these frigid waters, often ending up waist deep by the time they're done, pushing their luck as the tide creeps back in. The Dutch call it *wadlopen*, and it is one of the most unusual walks on the planet.

> "An exciting and adventurous way of acquainting oneself with a unique nature reserve."

www.holland.com

Routes vary from short strolls to eight-hour explorations, and it's best to go with a tour guide who can help you navigate the deep mud trenches and stronger currents. The thrill is all in the timing, calculating that you have left yourself enough time to walk out to one of the islands and back before the tide comes in. Most start in the thick mud of the coastal salt marshes, which can be a hard slog for the unfit, but beyond them you can relax and appreciate the sea's movements and the channels that funnel its water. Which outer island you choose for your end point is up to you, but what is common to all who walk this is an eerie sense of calm and tranquillity at being surrounded by a serene, enveloping ocean. **BDS**

Tiefwarensee Ice Age Trail Mecklenburg-Vorpommern, Germany

Start/End Stude Ice House **Distance** 6.2 miles (10 km) **Time** 2–3 hours
Grade Easy **Type** Sealed path
Map goo.gl/mKNDKh

The lakes around the town of Waren in northern Germany, like so much of the landscape of the Mecklenburg Lake district, were formed by the processes of glaciation during the Weichselain glaciation 10,000 years ago. What was once a depression was filled by the Weichselain's glacial meltwaters to become a massive inland freshwater lake. When sea levels fell in the wake of the Ice Age, the lake broke up into a series of smaller lakes, and the Tiefwarensee Lake was born. Today, you can take a walk around the shoreline of this "young" lake on the Tiefwarensee Ice Age Trail, past seventeen "stations" with information boards that detail the various stages of the lake's formation.

Begin at the Stude Ice House, a warehouse where blocks of ice were once cut from the frozen lake in winter and stored in a nearby icehouse to be used by the region's fishing industry to keep its catches fresh. The site of a Roman Iron Age settlement and the remains of a sacrificial altar are passed before the geology lesson begins at the lake's ancient sandur, a small plain formed by glacial sediments, while, a little farther on, a glacial till and fine-grained silt can be seen. Then you come to Wolf Gorge, part of the ridge's terminal moraine with its rich stands of beech and where an observation tower gives a fine view over this ancient landscape. Farther around the lake there is another stand of beeches outside the town of Waren before you enter a Pomeranian meadow on the town's outer edge, filled with rare flora and orchids. The trail provides for a relaxing stroll, with insights into not only the lake's natural history, but also its patterns of human settlement. **BDS**

66 Lakes Trail
Berlin/Brandenburg, Germany

Start/End Potsdam **Distance** 258 miles
(415 km) **Time** 3–4 weeks **Grade** Easy
Type Unmade forest trails
Info goo.gl/8VXU56

Berlin is one of Europe's great "green" cities, blessed with an abundance of rivers and more bridges than Venice. It is also ringed by forests, and together with the surrounding state of Brandenburg contains Europe's largest network of inland waterways and dozens upon dozens of lakes, all interconnected by the undulating paths of the 66 Lakes Trail. "Really, there are seventy-one lakes," says Manfred Reschke, a long-time walker through the countryside surrounding Falkenberg to the north of the city and author of *The Lake Route 66 Trail.* "But the number sixty-six sounds much better." In fact, for the sake of accuracy, there are more than 3,000 natural bodies of water sprinkled throughout the Brandenburg region.

The 66 Lakes Trail is one of Germany's premier walks along a surprisingly untraveled route through a landscape of deciduous forests, tree-lined rural roads, and glacial moraines, valleys, and hillocks formed at the end of the last Ice Age. It takes the shape of a star that encircles the city and passes by Potsdam in the south, the trail's most popular starting point, and each of its pie-like sections can be done as a day hike. There are big surprises along this trail, including walking through the largest concentration of inland sand dunes to be found in northern Europe. There are bathing beaches and thermal baths set alongside dark, forbidding pine forests and the quiet streets of the spa town of Bad Saarow. You can walk along the banks of the Spree River and drop in and out of forests, and, there are lots of lakeside walks that will dispel any preconceived notions that the Brandenburg landscape might be a tad uniform. Nothing could be further from the truth. **BDS**

"A great way to discover Berlin's surrounding countryside of lakes and dense woodlands."

www.germany.travel

⌃ A diverse trail where coniferous forests turn deciduous, villages become castles, and heaths turn into rivers.

Eibsee Lake Circuit Bavaria, Germany

Start/End Eibsee cable car station   **Distance** 5 miles (8 km)   **Time** 2 hours   **Grade** Easy
Type Well-maintained shoreline path   **Info** goo.gl/mcxcl9

When it comes to location, few lakes in Germany are as alluring as the turquoise waters of Eibsee Lake, located 60 miles (96.5 km) southwest of Munich at the base of Germany's highest mountain, Zugspitze. Eibsee is a shallow lake, with an average depth of just 39 feet (12 m), and almost all of its surrounding hillsides are heavily forested with the peak of the Zugspitze and other peaks towering above it. Nor is it so big that an easy circumnavigation of it cannot be considered. With a length of 2 miles (3.2 km), an average width of around 900 feet (275 m), and a well-maintained path that takes you around its shoreline with only occasional easy ascents into the hills above, this is one lake that was made to be walked around.

The walk begins at the Eibsee cable car station, and once you reach the shoreline the lake can be walked in either direction. The vista of Zugspitze opens up once you get onto the lake's northern shoreline, but the views, including the raw beauty of the Waxenstein Ridge, are spectacular no matter where you are. The trail is shaded for much of its length, which guarantees a comfortable walk even in the height of summer, and there are several small waterfalls that defy you to walk by them and not to stop for either a refreshing splash or just to sit on the benches provided.

If you wish, you can start and finish your walk at the historic Eibsee Hotel, purchased when it was a ramshackle building by August Terne in 1884 when the lake was known affectionately as the "gypsy puddle" and frequented only by a handful of local fishermen. How times have changed. **BDS**

⬆ A stunning lakeside walk in the shadow of Zugspitze.

Green Lake Styria, Austria

Start/End Various   Distance 0.5 mile (0.8 km)   Time 1 hour   Grade Easy
Type Meadows, gravel trails   Info goo.gl/GFPVr9

Is it a lake or is it a meadow? Does it belong in the overland section of this book, or is it a coastal and shoreline walk? How do you categorize a place that can be walked on in sneakers in winter and scuba dived in summer? Austria's Green Lake, near Tragoess in Styria, is a conundrum. Used as parkland in winter when the area is dry, it slowly begins to fill with water when snows start to melt in the surrounding Hochschwab massif in the spring, and the rocks and grasses of the park combine with refracted light to give the icy waters a distinct greenish hue.

However, it is the arresting, unusual sight of scuba divers floating over the top of park benches and wooden bridges, above a hiking path, and past submerged trees and alpine flowers in full bloom, in waters of uncommon clarity in a "brand new" lake where the water depth can be as much as 30 feet (10 m) in late summer that provides the setting for the most surreal images and photographs the Alps have ever produced.

Every year beginning in May, the unconnected basins that make up the 16 acres (6.5 ha) of the Grüner See begin to merge as these flowering meadows are slowly covered by 39° F (4° C) waters. There are trout here, carried down from the mountains in the meltwaters, as well as water snails and crabs. The waters start to recede by the end of July, returning much of the trail to hikers. By late fall, the water level is down to 5 feet (1.5 m) or so, its western basin again an expanse of rocks and gravel, its eastern basin a mix of soft mud and mosses. And you wouldn't know there had been a lake here at all. **BDS**

⬆ A summer lake drains to become a winter meadow.

Lago de la Ercina Asturias, Spain

Start/End Lago de la Ercina   **Distance** 4.7 miles (7.5 km)   **Time** 2–3 hours   **Grade** Moderate
Type Mountain   **Map** goo.gl/6wDJpD

High up in the autonomous region of Asturias in northwestern Spain lies the village of Covadonga, the scene of battles between Iberian Christians and a Muslim army in the eighth century. Above the village lie two lakes—Enol and Ercina. Lago de la Ercina has a surface area of about 2 acres (0.8 ha) and is a shallow lake, only 6.5 feet (2 m) deep. It is also eutrophic, meaning the dense level of plant life in the lake steals oxygen from the water as it decomposes, which is bad news for fish and animals.

The Lago de la Ercina walk starts on the shores of the lake and takes you out past both stretches of water to the surrounding mountains. You walk through high pastures filled with wildflowers, and there are plenty of rocky outcrops and groves of beech trees. You will also quite possibly be walking through mists that can descend quickly in the afternoon and are so

thick they can obscure your trail, so you will need to keep your wits about you.

There are optional routes you can take to accommodate different levels of skills and experience. A shorter route lasts for less than three hours, while a longer option goes on for closer to six, with spots to stop for food and drink on both, such as the Refugio Vega de Ario—a stone building that looks down at the valley below and at the mountain peaks in the distance. There are two bedrooms here, with forty bunks on offer. You can drive right up to Lago de la Ercina, so getting to the start of your walk shouldn't be too difficult, but it can get busy up here at certain times of year. Remember, as gorgeous as the lakes look, you can't swim in them. **JI**

⭱ **A solitary trail through Spain's high alpine pastures.**

Barceloneta Beach Catalunya, Spain

Start/End Various **Distance** 0.7 mile (1.1 km) **Time** 1 hour **Grade** Easy
Type Beach **Info** goo.gl/8zrQL8

Barcelona has around 2.5 miles (4 km) of beaches, and the most popular is Platja de la Barceloneta, which is closest to the downtown district of the city and draws in locals and tourists. Barceloneta is the old fishermen's quarter, which has streets laid out in a distinctive grid system. In the later years of the twentieth century it became rundown, but then along came the Olympic Games in 1992, and the whole area was regenerated.

The beach is a colorful mix of Barcelona's human inhabitants. There are those who head there for a swim in the Mediterranean, others who go to strip off and bask in the Spanish sun. Then there are those who go there to walk and enjoy the many sights on offer. There's *L'Estel Ferit* (1992), a large twisted, cuboid monument by artist Rebecca Horn. Farther along toward the Port Olímpic, there is Frank Gehry's golden fish sculpture, *Peix d'Or* (1992). If you're feeling active, there are plenty of sports and other activities taking place on the sand and in the water. There are also numerous places to get a massage or a beer. The crowds are mixed, and there can be a lot of people here, thanks to the beach's proximity to the city. There are families, teenagers, tourists, itinerants, and office workers. During the summer, beach bars open up, and the sand plays host to alfresco parties. If you wander away from the beach, Barceloneta also has plenty of seafood restaurants, cafés, and interesting residential streets. It's easy enough to get to Barceloneta beach. Take the yellow Metro line, and get off at either the Barceloneta stop or Port Olímpic. It's also only a fifteen-minute stroll from the Old Town. **JI**

⬆ **Barceloneta Beach is a Barcelona favorite.**

Fisherman's Trail Setubal to Faro, Portugal

Start Porto Covo **End** Cerro da Fontinha **Distance** 74 miles (119 km) **Time** 8 days
Grade Moderate to strenuous **Type** Coastal paths, beaches **Map** goo.gl/1NIcF7

The Fisherman's Trail runs along some of the most undisturbed, best-preserved coastal cliffs in Europe, a complex interconnected world of ravines and bluffs in a continual state of erosion. The trail, which isn't a walk for anyone suffering from vertigo, has been eked out by generations of fishermen who made their way down from the cliff tops to the beaches below, where they would set out before dawn to bring home their catches, and it is still used by locals today.

Located entirely within the Southwest Alentejo and Vicentine Coast Natural Park in south central Portugal, a traditional region of native cork oaks and olive trees, the Fisherman's Trail is a single track designed only for walking, with excellent signage along its entire length. Its northern starting point is Porto Covo, a quaint coastal village with a history of human habitation dating back thousands of years to the Carthaginian Empire. Heading south from Porto Covo, you plunge your feet into the beach's ankle-deep sands with views of waves crashing into towering limestone cliffs.

The next leg, from Cercal do Alentejo to São Luís, is the trail's most physical as you scale the cliff tops and are rewarded with impressive views over the Atlantic Ocean and inland over the plains. A succession of alder forests, streams, and ponds follows, and the historic fishing village of Azenhas do Mar. The trail takes you through one of Europe's finest birding areas, while in spring the region is transformed into a deep green with wildflowers and rock rose blanketing its valleys as you stroll through one of Europe's best-kept coastal secrets. **BDS**

⬆ **Unspoiled beauty seen by very few tourists.**

Salema to Sagres Coastal Path Faro, Portugal

Start Salema beach parking lot **End** Sagres   **Distance** 10.5 miles (16.8 km)   **Time** 7 hours   **Grade** Moderate
Type Path   **Map** goo.gl/EbkUaC

Salema is a fishing village in the Algarve, 11 miles (17.7 km) west of Lagos and facing out onto the Atlantic Ocean. Home to a working fishing fleet, it also boasts a gorgeous white, sandy beach, and although it may be small, there are plenty of bars, cafés, and restaurants lining its quaint cobbled streets. Ten miles (16 km) along the coast is the town of Sagres, which at one time was believed to be the most westerly point in the world. It's also where, in the fifteenth century, the Portuguese prince Henry the Navigator brought together leading shipbuilders, mariners, and navigators at his naval school. It was the Age of Sail, and the prince wanted to see great ships sailing uncharted waters on great voyages of discovery.

You can walk between these two contrasting points in a single day. You leave Salema on the road heading out of town, before breaking off and taking a track through Cape St. Vincent Natural Park, created to preserve the outstanding beauty of this stretch of southern Portuguese coast. You'll enjoy walking weathered cliffs and along hidden beaches, all the while with the wild, roaring Atlantic beside you. However, you won't be entirely alone. This part of Portugal is popular with RV owners, and it's likely you'll stumble across a huddle of vans parked up together, with their inhabitants basking in the Portuguese sun. The walk is straightforward and requires no special preparation, but it does involve some scrambling up rocky inclines in places. Once you get to Sagres, you'll find another stunning Algarve beach, along with everything else the town has to offer on the edge of Henry the Navigator's Old World. **JI**

⤒ From here the Portuguese set sail around the world.

Mistérios do Sul do Pico

Azores, Portugal

Start Parque Florestal de São João End Capela do
Espírito Santo   Distance 5.4 miles (8.7 km)
Time 3 hours   Grade Easy   Type Coastal trail
Map goo.gl/VK2HhY

The island of Pico in the central Azores is, like the other islands that surround it, the product of volcanic activity. The highest mountain in Portugal, Mount Pico, is here, and its nickname—the Black Island—reflects its violent birth. The first inhabitants of Pico had no experience of volcanoes for almost a hundred years, until the eruption of 1562 burned down the island's forests and lit up the night sky with its lava flows for two years. Prior to 1562, however, the word that was often used to describe the strange black rock that always seemed to be such an odd and alien part of the

"This locale is well known for the unique characteristics of the spring water found here."

trails.visitazores.com

landscape of unending green, was *mistérios* (mystery). The Mistérios do Sul do Pico trail hugs the southern coastline of Pico for a little more than 5 miles (8 km) and is a quiet sort of amble along dirt paths that take you past tidal pools and down to various swimming spots, to a cheese museum (Pico is known for its soft, white cheeses), and to an old watermill—the Moinho da Ponta Rasa. You then come to the Mistério da Salveira, the lava formation deposited as a result of the eruption in 1720, which is typical of the broken, sharp, and difficult to negotiate lava fields that are found here. A further series of tidal pools and swimming spots follows, and the trail ends at the Capela do Espírito Santo chapel, erected in 1723. **BDS**

The Wayfarer's Trail

Lombardy, Italy

Start Abbadia Lariana   End Colico
Distance 28 miles (45 km)   Time 4 days
Grade Easy   Type Mountain trails
Map goo.gl/O7PVdE

First documented in the fourteenth-century municipal charters of Bellano, Dervio, and Lecco, the network of trails that stretches through the hills above the eastern shoreline of Italy's Lake Como was originally used by mules to transport produce and goods considered of insufficient value for the costlier option of taking them across the lake by boat.

The Sentiero del Viandante (Path of the Wayfarer) passes by smallholdings that have been farmed by the same families for generations in the hills high above Italy's most famous lake—but not so high that you need worry about the population of wild boars that still inhabits its uppermost reaches. This is an easy walk with modest ascents on a pathway that often intersects the Lecco–Colico rail line, which means you have the option of breaking off the walk at various stages and taking the train onward or back to your starting point.

Along the way on this quiet, largely tourist-free walk, you will encounter architectural gems, such as La Fabbrica, a 300-year-old home that has been a wayfarers' stop for as long as anyone can recall, and there are even rare cobblestone sections that take you through groves of fig, walnut, and cherry trees.

A worthwhile stop en route is the beautiful hamlet of Vezio and its increasingly overgrown eleventh-century castle, which is on the site of an ancient Roman fortress. The path also takes you across the Bellano Gorge north of Varenna, and over its narrow walkways and series of ladders before ending in Colico, which is dominated by Monte Legnone (8,559 feet/2,609 m) above—and the Ristorante Pizzeria Il Faro straight ahead. **BDS**

Santa Margherita to Portofino

Liguria, Italy

Start Santa Margherita   **End** Portofino
Distance 3.2 miles (5.1 km)
Time 45 minutes–1 hour   **Grade** Easy
Type Pavement   **Info** goo.gl/LHfaUv

Founded by the Romans and once renowned for the dolphins that played in its sheltered bay, Portofino today often tops the list of the most beautiful towns in Italy. Among its attractions are a perfect harbor opening out onto the Mediterranean, rows of pastel-colored buildings, the requisite number of expensive yachts and motor launches tied up along the seawalls and piers, and the exclusive villas and seriously expensive hotels that are sprinkled throughout the hills above.

One of the things, however, that Portofino is also well known for is that it is not a place that was designed to cater for the automobile. There is only one narrow road into town and it's the same road out. When Portofino's few parking lots are full, unless you're staying in a hotel or have a room with a car parking space, the only thing to do is turn around and return to the town of Santa Margherita, a few miles to the north back along the road you just came in on, and worthy of a walk in itself.

Leaving Santa Margherita (but not before visiting its sixteenth-century castle), you walk along its waterfront, past its fish market and marina, and then you have a choice—either continue on the promenade or take the steeper path through the trees. A pleasant option is to go one way and return by the other route. If you stay by the road, there is a footpath that separates you from the traffic, which you are in all likelihood getting ahead of, anyway. The magnificent views up the hill on the other side to the numerous private villas is just some of the eye candy you'll enjoy, denied to all those trapped in their cars on the crowded Strade Statale 227. **BDS**

"One of Italy's most romantic and colorful little towns. Portofino is truly beautiful and stunning."

www.virtualtourist.com

⤴ Wonderful Portofino: well worth a visit, but preferably not by automobile.

Cinque Terre Classic
Liguria, Italy

Start Riomaggiore **End** Monterosso
Distance 7.5 miles (12 km)
Time 3–4 hours **Grade** Easy
Type Village trails **Map** goo.gl/Ec3l52

If it were not for the existence of the five coastal villages of Monterosso, Vernazza, Corniglia, Manarola, and Riomaggiore—the first two of which can trace their origins back to the eleventh century—there would be no Cinque Terre Classic. The ancient paths that have linked these villages for almost 1,000 years take you so close to olive groves and vineyards you feel as if you are trespassing. They serendipitously dip into villages, each with its own distinct maritime history and distractions aplenty, which can turn a walk of a few hours into a much longer excursion.

It is not a difficult hike and can be completed easily by anyone with an average level of fitness. The usual route is east to west, starting at Riomaggiore and finishing at Monterosso, and it is a perfect fusion of Italy's natural and culinary heritage—dramatic coastal headlands mixed with pizzerias, cafés, and wine bars. It begins on the Via dell'Amore (Way of Love), a wide, level ocean-side promenade that takes you from Riomaggiore to Manarola, and spills down along its headland to the ocean below amid abundant cacti and prickly pears. The next village is Corniglia, with its labyrinthine alleyways and 1,000-year-old Romanesque church on a spur 300 feet (91 m) above the sea, along a trail that isn't much more than a goat path. After Corniglia the real ascent begins on the 3-mile (4.8-km) path to the cubist jumble that is Vernazza, through a perfumed undergrowth of wild thyme, rosemary, heather, and strawberries. Spend a night in Vernazza and wait for the day-trippers to leave, then on to Monterosso the next day. **BDS**

◄ The promenade from Riomaggiore to Manarola.

Old Walk of the Forts
Capri, Italy

Start Blue Grotto **End** Punta Carena
Distance 2 miles (3.2 km) **Time** 2–3 hours
Grade Easy **Type** Gravel path
Map goo.gl/DuJdv8

The ruins of a series of small coastal forts that once lined the cliffs of Capri—Orrico, Mesolo, and Pino—are set into the rocks and crevasses of the island's wonderfully crenellated, fjord-like western coastline. Built by the British as redoubts for short-range artillery during the Napoleonic Wars in the early nineteenth century, they were enlarged by the French in the wake of their retaking of the island in 1808 and raised over the foundations of ancient, existing watchtowers, built for protection against Saracen raiders who bedeviled the island's inhabitants from the ninth century.

"A dramatically beautiful coastal path, dotted with Capri's ancient block houses."

www.capri.com

Everywhere you look on this idyllic walk, your gaze is met with tranquil perfection. Hollows and depressions are filled with the tuffs of past volcanic eruptions as you pass through a forest of holm oak, alternating with maquis that live among the Passo della Capra, the island's limestone topography. In 1998 the Anacapri municipality, with help from the European Union, began to restore this line of ancient forts and the paths that link them. Orrico, still being lashed by the wind on its site atop the Punta del Miglio, retains its semicircular, white stone defenses and perimeter trench. The walk is best done one-way from the Blue Grotto to Punta Carena, where a bus will take you back to the town of Anacapri. **BDS**

Path of the Gods
Campania, Italy

Start Nocelle   End Agerola
Distance 4.5 miles (7.2 km)   Time 4 hours
Grade Easy   Type Old mountain paths
Map goo.gl/kcb7uL

Have you ever been to the Amalfi Coast and wondered how it might look with fewer people? The ribbon-like coastal road is always cluttered with traffic, and good luck trying to get an outside table at midday. Of course, this congestion is part of its allure. Everyone wants to live here, and if they can't live here, they will visit. You're always looking down to the azure blue of the wondrous ocean and its famously crowded beaches. That's what most people look at when they walk the streets of Praiano, Ravello, and Positano, but what would they see if they decided to look up instead?

"The views became more dramatic with every step; the sea fizzing over the craggy coast."

www.theguardian.com

The Path of the Gods—named for the Roman temples that once stood here—is an old pathway above Positano, and if you're staying in Positano then a bus up to the village of Nocelle will save you the trauma of climbing to its start point. Once up there, the path's name becomes self-evident. There are 1,000-foot (300-m) drops right by you, with no railings. Terraces growing fruit and vegetables cascade down sun-drenched hillsides. The bustling coastal towns below appear in miniature like postcard views, while around you Italians go about their business, farming their terraces as they have done for generations, and you will be enjoying views that those stuck on their sun loungers below can only dream of. **BDS**

Lake Bled Shoreline Walk
Gorenjska, Slovenia

Start/End Bled Castle   Distance Various
Time 6–8 hours   Grade Easy
Type Maintained forest trails
Info goo.gl/btrAap

Lake Bled, the "jewel of Slovenia," lies in the Julian Alps not far from Ljubljana. It is one of the most photographed lakes in the world with medieval Bled Castle, first mentioned by Emperor Henry II in 1011, dominating a bluff on its northern shoreline, and its waters encircling the fairy-tale–like Bled Island, the only real island in the entire country and home to the Church of the Assumption of Mary Pilgrimage. People have been coming here to walk the shoreline for thousands of years. Interconnected trails help you navigate it, and take you to the top of some wonderful peaks for views over the lake and the Julian Alps.

One of these paths, the Straža, is a lime-, oak-, and birch-covered walk on an established trail to the lake's southeast, which gives the quintessential view over the lake to Jelovica Plateau and Mount Stol. Another favorite viewpoint for photographers is Osojnica, a steep forty-five minute walk to Mala Osojnica (2,247 feet/685 m) followed by another short climb to the summit of Velika Osojnica (2,480 feet/756 m), which gives you the finest views over the lake all the way to the Karavanke Mountains, the Kamnik–Savinja Alps, and the Gorenjska Plain. After circumnavigating the lake, why not make the dramatic climb to magnificent Bled Castle. When the Bohinj Glacier retreated during the last Ice Age and carved out the valley that made Lake Bled possible, it left untouched the 456-foot (139-m) limestone bluff at the lake's northern end on which this striking castle sits, a doubly fortified structure with outer walls that housed servants and inner walls that protected its feudal lords. **BDS**

→ Bled Castle has it all: towers, drawbridge, and a moat.

Walking Trails of Naxos

Naxos, Greece

Start/End Various Distance Various
Time Various Grade Easy to moderate
Type Rocky trails
Info goo.gl/v8wmgq

The Cyclades have an austere, sun-bleached beauty—ancient ruins in silvery olive groves and solitary chapels on craggy points. Not, however, the island of Naxos. The largest of the Cyclades and well-watered by springs, Naxos is a bushy-topped Eden in which crops and orchards flourish, and sheep and cattle graze. Unlike other Cycladean islands, which import fresh produce, Naxos's trug overflows. Lorries laden with fat lemons, aubergines, potatoes, and cherries have season tickets on the Athens ferries. This natural bounty means Naxos also has the most varied hiking

> *"The interior of Naxos is a paradise for hikers. It is the largest, highest, most fertile island in the Cyclades."*
>
> www.gonaxos.com

in the Cyclades, from climbing peaks (Mount Zeus is the highest at 3,290 feet/1,003 m) and village-hopping in the lush interior to coastal walks. Hikers will not be alone on any of these trails, but Naxos is spacious and absorbs its many visitors well. Come in spring for fewer people, and also the best hiking weather. One of the best hikes runs from the village of Filoti to Apeiranthos via the chapel of Agia Marina and the fortified monastery of Fotodotis. Taking the best part of a day to complete, the trail along mule tracks leads through the foothills of Mount Zeus. For a hike that also takes in classical ruins and long white sands, the Ano Sagri to Plaka Beach trail via the Temple of Demeter comes top of the list. **DS**

Fira to Oia

Santorini, Greece

Start Fira End Oia
Distance 6 miles (9.6 km) Time 2 hours
Grade Easy Type Cinder, paved paths
Map goo.gl/gwYCGR

Even if you did not know Santorini's extraordinary geological history, you would guess it from the clues. There are 980-foot (300-m) cliffs plunging directly into the ocean along most of the west coast, cinder paths, and gritty black-sand beaches. Most telling of all are the chunks of polished lava and baskets of pumice stone in Fira's souvenir shops.

The whole island of Santorini is actually the rim of a caldera—the collapsed cone, or partial cone, of an exhausted volcano that last erupted in 1645 BCE. The sea on its western side is the water-filled sunken crater, which is effectively a deep lagoon.

To walk inside the lip of the caldera from Fira to Oia (pronounced "ee-ah"), its northernmost point, is thrilling and virtually a rite of passage for first-time visitors to the island. The trail—sometimes cinder, sometimes paved, with a short stretch on the road around Imerovigli—snakes along the inside of the rim. On the way are chapels and shrines, a mobile café (honey and yogurt rather than hot dogs and burgers), and lookouts for particularly good views, which become increasingly dramatic. Look forward over the tiered and narrowing headland and back to see the whitewashed cubes of Fira, which look like icing on a wedding cake. At Oia, you can see west to the island of Therasia, the exposed rim of the far side of the caldera, and also north to the islands of Ios and Sikinos. The time to visit is at sunset, except that everyone does the same, and from late afternoon in summer the trail is a crocodile of sunset seekers. Nonetheless, life on Santorini does not get better than watching a fiery-red sun slip below the horizon while sinking a glass of Assyrtiko, the island's fine volcanic wine. **DS**

Thera–Perissa Trail

Santorini, Greece

Start/End Perissa   **Distance** 2.7 miles (4.3 km)
Time 2 hours   **Grade** Moderate
Type Well-maintained rocky trails
Map goo.gl/5QRoqa

Lying on Santorini's Perissa beach has its limitations. Sooner rather than later, anyone with a grain of energy, curiosity, or ambition will want to put down their novel, pull on some sneakers, and climb up Mesa Vouno, the peak behind the resort, in search of Thera—the ancient city that gave the island of Santorini ("Thira" in Greek) its name. Eyed from beach level, the rocky mountain looks steep and barren, but a well-signposted trail leads up the side, with steps cut into the rock in some sections. As you climb, the chirp of crickets drowns out the sounds of the retreating town, and breathing in draws up the exhilarating scent of the herb-laden maquis. The higher you go, the more expansive the views. Thera lies on a ridge just under the summit, from where you can see over the southeastern tip of the island and far out to sea, a strategic advantage that must have attracted its founders.

Dorian sailors, led by Theras, a regent of Sparta, founded the city in the eighth century BCE, 1,000 years after a volcanic eruption destroyed Akrotiri in the north of the island. Habitation lasted until well into the Christian era. Ancient paved streets lead between Hellenistic and Roman remains, including an agora (marketplace), theater, temples to Apollo, baths, and a densely packed residential area delineated by walls and pillars. A couple of Byzantine churches are testament to the early Christian settlement.

You won't be alone at the top—a road brings coaches here from all corners of the island—but the site is extensive and it is easy to shake off company. Find a rocky perch on the periphery of the site and gaze out over the impossibly blue Aegean. **DS**

"It is an ancient path, its history hidden under the undergrowth and the rocks."

www.santorini-hotels.info

⬆ The unforgettable cliff-top view from Santorini's Mesa Vouno.

Moní Zoödóchou Pigís to Panagía Kalamiótissa
Anafi, Greece

Start Moní Zoödóchou Pigís   End Panagía Kalamiótissa
Distance 1 mile (1.6 km)   Time 1.5 hours
Grade Moderate   Type Rocky track
Map goo.gl/5yi3pC

Twelve miles (19.3 km) southeast of Santorini, its reclusive sister Anafi lies on the very edge of the Cyclades archipelago. Anafi is a hot, dry outpost—cacti thrive here—with just a few hundred inhabitants and a small number of visitors who come for the peace and quiet. Its thin trickle of boats almost dries up in winter. Nevertheless, Anafi has a monastery—Moní Zoödóchou Pigís, near the eastern end—and this has a church, Panagía Kalamiótissa, a Cycladean cluster of cubes and domes about an hour's hike up the slopes of Mount Kalamós. The walk between the monastery and the church (there is no road) gives a profound sense of the remoteness of the Cyclades before tourism took over.

Dating from the seventeenth century, Moní Zoödóchou Pigís sits atop a temple of Apollo built, legend says, by Jason and the Argonauts after Apollo raised Anafi from the seabed to save Jason and his men from a storm. In ancient times, worshippers of Apollo would walk to the temple from Kastelli, the first settlement on the island. Stones from the temple walls lie in the monastery courtyard, and there is original paving from the pilgrims' road. The trail to the church is picked up near the sea. It is unmarked and steep with dramatic switchbacks. As it climbs the scrubby slopes of Mount Kalamós, spectacular views open out below, with Crete visible to the south on a clear day. The church perches just below the summit. One or two days before September 8 each year, islanders carry the icon of the Virgin Mary from the monastery up the trail to the church. After an all-night vigil, they return the way they came, ready to celebrate the Madonna of Anafi's feast day. **DS**

"The view from [the monastery] or from the little pillar indicating the trigonometrical point . . . is absolutely unique."

www.cycladen.be

⊡ A walk to Panagía Kalamiótissa will immerse you in the Cyclades of generations past.

Hora Sfakion to Mouri
Crete, Greece

Start Hora Sfakion **End** Mouri **Distance** 5 miles
(8 km) **Time** 4 hours **Grade** Easy to moderate
Type Rock and dirt tracks, *kalderimi* (stone) paths
Map goo.gl/JN87Bp

Hora Sfakion, which lies on the southern coastline of Crete, was a renowned center of Cretan/Greek independence and resistance, first against the Venetians and later the Turks, thanks in part to the rocky beaches to its south and the forbidding-looking White Mountains to its north. In peacetime, the bald limestone summits of the White Mountains provided a different kind of refuge, cool respite from the scorching summer heat, to which the people of this small, isolated town would flock along an old mule track that took them well up into the cool Cretan air. One of the most popular of these mountain refuges was Mouri.

In order to get to Mouri you have to climb out of Hora Sfakion, and this is done via a nicely preserved *kalderimi*, an old cobblestone pathway built for the hooves of Hora Sfakion's mules out of flat, vertically laid stones. The path still zigzags its way up a nearby hillside before running in a straight line above an adjacent ravine. It then levels off and crosses a westerly lying ravine, and soon after this begins to peter out when it leaves the strong foundations of the crags behind.

You then take a footpath along a shepherds' road and an old mule track, which steepens considerably as you approach the tree line. After crossing a shallow north–south gully, you traverse a heavily grazed plain and then its up through cypress forests to Kavis Gorge and on to Anopolis, and from there to Mouri. The walk certainly takes some effort—and whatever you do, try and source a local map before setting out—but Mouri's evocative church and town ruins are definitely a sight worth struggling for. **BDS**

Aphrodite Nature Trail
Nicosia, Cyprus

Start/End Baths of Aphrodite, near Latsi
Distance 4.6 miles (7.4 km) **Time** 3–4 hours
Grade Moderate **Type** Rocky path
Map goo.gl/mOTw77

Aphrodite was the Greek goddess of love and the daughter of Zeus. She was also known as Cypris, or Lady of Cyprus, and has a strong connection with the island that lays claim to being the place of her birth. The Aphrodite Nature Trail takes you in a loop around the northern coast of Cyprus and is a great way to see the island away from the tourist destinations. The start (and end) point is at the Baths of Aphrodite on the Akamas Peninsula. If you take the trail clockwise, then you'll begin by heading northwest toward the ruins of the Pyrgos tis Rigainas, or Queen's Tower, thought to

> *"According to legend it was here the Goddess of Aphrodite … met her lover, Adonis."*
>
> www.paphospeople.com

be part of a medieval monastery. The ground underfoot may be rocky in places but the going is generally good, if a little tiring, and the gradient won't leave you breathless. Eventually, you reach Moutti tis Sotiras peak (1,213 feet/370 m), which gives outstanding views of the island's northwest coast. From Moutti tis Sotiras descend back down toward the sea, and on the last segment of the walk you'll be hugging the northern coastline of the island, with views down over deep blue lagoons of legendary beauty. The route is waymarked, and you'll soon reconnect with the section you first covered as you were heading up into the hills. Then it's a short stretch back to the Baths of Aphrodite. **JI**

Selous Game Reserve Walking Safari Morogoro, Tanzania

Start/End Northern Selous Game Reserve   **Distance** 25 miles (40 km)   **Time** 5 days   **Grade** Easy
Type Grass and earth tracks   **Map** goo.gl/APVfya

Ironically, the Selous Game Reserve in southern Tanzania is named after a British big-game hunter, Frederick Selous, who died in its territory while fighting the Germans in 1917. The park was first set up as a protected area by German colonists in 1896 and became a hunting reserve in 1905. It acquired its current name in 1922 and has since expanded to become one of the largest animal reserves in the world. UNESCO made it a World Heritage Site in 1982 because of its diverse wildlife and undisturbed nature. That said, about 90 percent of the park—the entire southern tract—remains a game reserve for trophy hunting to this day.

The walking safaris take place in a small section at the top of the park, north of the Rufiji River, in which hunting is prohibited. Over the course of five days, guides take you out in the bush, where you can see elephants, hippos, and many other animals, including all the big cats. The pace is slow, enabling you to stop, keep quiet, and watch animals wander slowly past. Expert guides will take you to the right locations to see such sights at surprisingly close range. A gentle drift on the Rufiji, almost 1 mile (1.6 km) wide at the first base camp, provides another fine view of the area's fauna. Each night is spent fly-camping in a new base camp, sleeping on bedrolls under the stars (and a mosquito net).

The best times to visit are in the dry season from July to October, or during January and February when the migrating game moves to fertile feeding grounds. Bird watching is particularly good at this time of year. **SA**

⊼ A rare bit of shade in a giant of a park.

Skeleton Coast Kunene, Namibia

Start Ugab River   **End** Hoanib River   **Distance** 124 miles (200 km)   **Time** 7 days   **Grade** Strenuous
Type Sandy tracks   **Info** goo.gl/pqqQLD

Not for nothing is the northern Atlantic coast of Namibia known as the Skeleton Coast. The shoreline is littered with whale and seal bones, leftovers from the old whaling and fishing industries. These have been joined by the wrecks of more than 1,000 vessels, lost in the dense oceans fogs that envelop the area, caused by the upwelling of the cold Benguela Current offshore. The ships were then driven ashore by the heavy surf and wrecked. Among them is the *Dunedin Star*, a Blue Star liner thrown ashore on November 29, 1942, while carrying munitions and supplies for the Allied war effort, as well as more than one hundred passengers and crew who were traveling from Liverpool around South Africa to Egypt. In 1944, John Henry Marsh wrote a book about the shipwreck titled *The Skeleton Coast*, a name that quickly stuck to the entire coast. The Bushmen of the Namib interior call the region "the land god made in anger," while Portuguese mariners heading south down the coast on their way to India during the 1400s referred to it as "the gates of hell."

Today, the entire Skeleton Coast from the Ugab River in the south up to the Angolan border in the north is a national park. With gravel plains inland in the south and high sand dunes in the north, the sandy coastline is a walkers' paradise. Most of the organized walks start at the Ugab River and then head north for up to seven days, stopping at any point up to the Hoanib River. North of that river, the national park has been designated a wilderness area, and tourists can enter only on exclusive fly-in safaris organized by commercial concessions. **SA**

⊺ Wander a coastline of shipwrecks and fog.

Selinda Walking Trail Ngamiland, Botswana

Start Selinda camp **End** Zarafa camp **Distance** 15 miles (24.1 km) **Time** 3 days **Grade** Easy
Type Earthen paths **Map** goo.gl/ahCYqn

The Selinda Reserve is a privately owned wildlife sanctuary in the far north of Botswana. In the Khoisan language of northern Botswana, *selinda* means "many small pools of water"—something this reserve has plenty of. Covering 300,000 acres (125,000 ha), the reserve surrounds the Selinda Spillway that weaves its way between the Linyanti Swamps to the east and the inland Okavango Delta to the west. The reserve is off the main tourist routes and is teeming with wildlife. Lions, cheetahs, and leopards roam around, as do packs of hyenas, jackals, and wild dogs. Elephants are common, particularly in the dry season from May to October, along with giraffes, roan and sable antelope, elands, zebras, buffaloes, and wildebeests. Hippos lurk in the rivers and water beds, while civets, servals, wild cats, honey badgers, aardvarks, and aardwolves come out at night.

The owners of this ecofriendly reservation are serious about conservation and have set aside a special area in the north of the reserve for walking safaris. The trails follow the time-honored paths of the elephants and antelope through the riverbank forests and open plains. The usual route starts in the shady Selinda camp at the eastern end of the Selinda Spillway and stops overnight first in the semipermanent Mokoba camp, which looks out on a large floodplain, and then second in the heavily wooded Tshwene camp before ending at the Zarafa camp on the edge of the Linyanti Swamps. The pace is not arduous, giving you plenty of time to enjoy the experience. Night walking and driving safaris can also be undertaken. **SA**

⬆ A water-laden, undeveloped jewel of a park.

Mana Pools Walking Safari Mashonaland West, Zimbabwe

Start/End Various   Distance 15 miles (24.1 km)   Time 3–4 days   Grade Easy
Type Grass and earthen paths   Map goo.gl/1EJrd9

Mana means "four" in Shona, a reference to the four, large, permanent pools formed by the meanderings of the Zambezi River. Around these four lakes is the Mana Pools National Park, based in a region of the Zambezi where each rainy season turns the floodplain into a mass of lakes. As the season ends and the waters elsewhere dry up, the park attracts large animals in search of water. Interestingly, water was almost the end of this park, as it was threatened in the 1980s by a hydroelectric scheme—a fate it was spared by its UNESCO Word Heritage Site listing. The park has Zimbabwe's largest number of hippopotamuses and crocodiles, joined in the dry season by elephant and buffalo. This 965-square-mile (2,500-sq-km) watery expanse is covered with forests of mahogany trees, wild figs, and baobabs, making it one of the least developed national parks in southern Africa.

Walking safaris are arranged by commercial companies. The tours make use of both permanent and temporary camps and offer experienced guides who will show you the wildlife. It is quite safe to walk along the lightly wooded river terraces, where you will see elands, impalas, zebras, warthogs, waterbucks, baboons, monkeys, and predators such as wild dogs and cheetahs. The bird life is magnificent, and the river full of fish for those who want to catch their supper.

The best time to visit is the dry season from June to October. The rainy season lasts from November to the end of April, during which time the animals move away from the river toward the northern escarpment. The park is closed to vehicles at this time, and many of the camps are also shut. **SA**

⬆ Big game in a big park.

Matobo Hills
Matabeleland South, Zimbabwe

Start/End Various **Distance** 6–18 miles
(9.6–29 km) **Time** 1–3 days **Grade** Easy
to moderate **Type** Grass and earthen paths
Map goo.gl/IEOy2s

The Matobo or Matopos Hills region of southern Zimbabwe is an area of isolated granite hills known as kopjes. They were formed two billion years ago and have since eroded into extraordinary shapes. These hills are surrounded by wooded valleys and thickets of vegetation through which swampy rivers flow. Mzilikazi, founder of the Ndebele nation, gave the area its name, which means "bald heads," during the late 1800s. Part of the area has been turned into a 163-square-mile (425-sq-km) national park, of which 39 square miles (100 sq km) is set aside for hunting.

> *"This small, easily accessible national park contains some of the region's most arresting scenery."*

www.expertafrica.com

The park is home to many species of wildlife, notably black and white rhinos and the world's densest population of both leopards and black eagles. There are also more than 200 different species of trees and one hundred species of grass. The park additionally contains more than 3,000 sites of rock art produced by the San Bushmen around 2,000 years ago, as well as a number of important archaeological sites. A variety of walking safaris are organized by commercial groups operating out of a range of permanent and temporary camps. Expert guides will take you to the best places to see the rhinos and other creatures. Routes are along the valley floors, but some will venture up into the nearby hills and outcrops. **SA**

Eve's Trail
Western Cape, South Africa

Start Duinepos **End** Seeberg
Distance 19 miles (30 km) **Time** 2 days
Grade Easy **Type** Sandy and rocky paths
Map goo.gl/WNIOYU

In 1995 a footprint was discovered in the rock at Kraalbaai in the Western Cape that was said to have belonged to a woman who lived around 117,000 years ago. Named Eve, it is in her honor that this trail has been developed through the West Coast National Park. For those who are interested, her original footprint is now housed at the South African Museum in Cape Town.

The trail follows existing paths within the national park and takes two days to accomplish, although some tours add an extra afternoon at the start to get to know the area. The first day is a 10-mile (16-km) walk from Duinepos in the interior of the park, west through the fynbos scrub to the Atlantic Ocean and then north along Sixteen Mile Beach before returning to Duinepos for the night. Those brave enough might like to swim in the icy Atlantic, but most others will no doubt prefer to gaze at it from a warmer distance. Alternatively, you can make a slight detour to Kraalbaai to see where Eve's footprints were first found.

The second day's walk is a 9-mile (14-km) hike along the eastern shore of Langebaan Lagoon up to Seeberg, the highest point in the park. The lagoon is a salt marsh wonderland for wading birds, both migrant and permanent. The shore has many fossilized oyster shells and other creatures embedded in the rocks that are exposed by the falling tide. The entire walk takes place within a designated Biosphere Reserve, dedicated to preserving the abundant flora and fauna, some of which is either endangered—notably the black harrier bird and the kelkiewyn plant—or vulnerable. For those less concerned by such issues, the spring flowers are just superb. **SA**

Cape of Good Hope Hiking Trail

Western Cape, South Africa

Start/End Entrance gate, Table Mountain National Park **Distance** 20.5 miles (33 km) **Time** 2 days **Grade** Easy to moderate **Type** Rocky paths, sand **Map** goo.gl/1TXePj

Hanging south from Cape Town is a fingertip of land that contains both the world-famous flat-topped Table Mountain and ends at the even more famous Cape of Good Hope. The area is a national park, containing three separate areas of mountain and ridge. The two-day hike around its southern tip is quite magnificent: a combination of history, scenery, and wildlife unsurpassed almost anywhere else.

The trail follows a circular route from the entrance gate to the Table Mountain National Park. Walkers must complete the Overnight Hiking Register to get keys for the overnight hut. The current tariff is R210 (US$20/£12) per person, with additional daily conservation and entry fees payable on arrival. You are advised to start before 9 a.m. to ensure you reach your hut by nightfall. Once you have paid and gathered your equipment, you can begin to experience the extraordinary wealth of vegetation: there are said to be more than 2,800 species of plant in the park, more than in the entire United Kingdom. This shrub vegetation, known in Afrikaans as *fynbos* (fine scrub), includes proteas, heathers, and reeds that can be startlingly vivid. Ostriches, baboons, lizards, and many other creatures will observe your progress. If you head clockwise, your first day's walk is 8 miles (13 km) alongside False Bay to the east, a bumpy path that skirts around rocky buttresses and then descends first to dry grasslands dotted with tiny wildflowers and then along the seafront. The overnight camp gives you stunning views over both False Bay and the Atlantic Ocean. The return 12-mile (20-km) journey follows the flat Atlantic coastline through *fynbos* and across sandy beaches. **SA**

"Hiking takes you off the tourist trail, giving you full access to the essence of the region."

www.hiketablemountain.co.za

⊼ The commanding view from the heights of Table Mountain National Park.

Otter Trail
Eastern Cape, South Africa

Start Storms River mouth   **End** Groot River mouth
Distance 26.4 miles (42.5 km)   **Time** 5 days
Grade Strenuous   **Type** Rugged shoreline walk
Map goo.gl/Na7FIy

The Otter Trail is one of the best coastal walks in South Africa. The trail follows the spectacular shoreline of the Eastern Cape between the mouths of Storms River and Groot River. It crosses other rivers along the way, but most of the route is along high cliff tops with impressive views along the coast, and there are several places where you can take a break and look out to the ocean in the hope of spotting dolphins and whales.

The fact that you average only about 5 miles (8 km) each day shows how slow the going is, and you will have to be fit enough to carry a full pack while ascending to those cliff tops and occasionally scrambling over boulders. The trail is divided up into specific sections, with overnight huts where you can rest up between hiking days and from where you can also get some impressive sunset views. The first day can be a challenge, but you always have the option of turning around and going back—many, in fact, hike only the first section for a glimpse of the trail and this fabulous stretch of coast.

On the first day's hike there's a cave to explore and a waterfall to cool off in. The second day sees some hiking in the coastal forests while the third day has some refreshing walking by the sea, with chances to swim in the sea or in rivers. The fourth day is the longest and hardest and needs to be timed carefully to cross a river at low tide, but once you are safely over there is the possibility of seeing or hearing monkeys and baboons, or watching otters and seals on the shoreline. The trail ends with a final easy stretch along the beach—perhaps rounded off with a final dip in the ocean. **MG**

"The Otter Trail's incredibly diverse natural beauty—taking in the best of forest and coast ... will make a huge impression on you."

www.southafrica.net

← This is a tough, cliff top to sea walk that will have you averaging just a few miles a day.

↑ A waterfall near the start of the trail at Storms River mouth.

Corniche Doha, Qatar

Start Four Seasons Hotel, West Bay district   **End** Museum of Islamic Art   **Distance** 4.5 miles (7.2 km)
Time 1.5 hours   **Grade** Easy   **Type** Pavement   **Info** goo.gl/kOuKXC

The modern metropolises of the Persian Gulf, places such as Sharjah and Dubai, have undergone exponential growth over the past thirty years with new developments coming at a cost. Human scale and a sense of belonging have become secondary to whatever grand schemes can be lifted off the drawing board and plonked on flat, open terrain and often fail to provide a heart to new neighborhoods, without which a city can lose its appeal. Give a city a harbor, however, and there is something to work with, a space capable of providing a city with an aesthetic focal point. Many coastal cities in the Middle East possess a corniche, a sweeping crescent-shaped waterfront, but few provide any sense of place. When you walk the Corniche in the Qatari capital of Doha, however, there is no sense of rampant expansion, no feeling that your needs are being neglected or that you are being forced to the water's edge for respite. In contrast to many of the Gulf's other tourism hot spots, this elegant, green, and thoroughly civilized promenade makes Doha's burgeoning skyline appear beautiful, restrained, inviting, and almost provincial.

The Corniche connects Doha's new West Bay district to the city's south, and you can see it all laid out before you in one glorious arc as you begin your walk. Modern and traditional dress mingle seamlessly here as children play on impossibly green grass, and locals and tourists alike come out to enjoy a coffee or just to look across the water at the sheer magnificence of the Museum of Islamic Art, an island at the end of the purpose-built causeway—the jewel in the crown of this perfect example of urban planning. **BDS**

⌷ The corniche is the focal point of this vibrant city.

Prashar Lake Himachal Pradesh, India

Start Baggi   End Prashar Lake   Distance 4.6 miles (7.4 km)   Time 6 hours   Grade Moderate
Type Grassy paths and mud tracks   Map goo.gl/dpgd9d

High in the foothills of the Himalayas in Himachal Pradesh state in northern India is one of the most astonishing lakes in the world. Prashar Lake is surrounded by grassy mountain slopes and sits 8,477 feet (2,584 m) above sea level. Its waters are deep blue, their exact depth unknown as apparently no diver has yet taken the plunge. A floating island of vegetation lazily moves around the lake, which freezes solid in the winter months. A three-story pagoda, dedicated to the Hindu sage Prashar and built in the thirteenth century, sits by its side. One legend has it that the lake was built by a baby from a single tree, while another from the Mahabharata states that one of the Pandava brothers formed the oval-shaped lake with his elbow. Whatever its origins, the lake today attracts people from all faiths, some of whom throw coins into its depths for luck.

The trail starts in Baggi village and heads first along a forested valley and then up forest ridges and grassy slopes, passing some villages and small rivers on the way. As you climb, you catch sight of the beautiful Dhaladhar range of mountains in the distance. The trail itself is not marked, so it is necessary to take directions with you. The same goes for water, since the only source of fresh water occurs five minutes after the start of the walk. The trail is quiet and contemplative, its breathtaking views getting better and better as the path nears the lake. If truth be told, the trek is at its most beautiful during the winter, when snow covers the ground and the surrounding peaks are capped in white. This is not an option that everyone will take up. **SA**

⬆ No one has ever got to the bottom of this lake.

Rara Lake

Karnali, Nepal

Start Jumla **End** Rara Lake
Distance 31 miles (49.8 km) **Time** 5 days
Grade Strenuous **Type** Earth and rock tracks
Map goo.gl/MlTqzo

*"It's a beautiful, calm place ...
with the snowy peaks reflected
in the still waters."*

www.themountaincompany.co.uk

⬆ Rara Lake is also known as Mahendra Daha, after the late king of Nepal.

Rara Lake is the biggest lake in Nepal, with an area of 3.9 square miles (10.1 sq km) and a maximum depth of 548 feet (167 m). For such a regal lake, it's not surprising that it is also known as Mahendra Daha, after the late king of Nepal. The lake sits in its own national park in the west of Nepal, some 9,810 feet (2,990 m) above sea level. At such an elevation, temperatures drop well below freezing during the winter months, making spring and fall the best times to visit this beautiful spot.

Rara Lake has long been a favorite destination for hardy walkers, attracted by the diverse flora and fauna of the national park. The alpine park is forested in spruce, pine, and juniper trees, and is also home to musk deer, Himalayan black bears, leopards, red pandas, and many other creatures. Views of the snow-capped Himalayan peaks can be seen in the distance to the north.

Its remoteness makes it a difficult lake to access, however. Most people who make the trek to the lake first fly into Jumla to the southeast of the park. The five-day trail then heads north through Chere and Kotta, crossing Danphe Lagna—at 12,210 feet (3,720 m) the highest point on the trail—on the way. At the Sinja River, the trail heads east and then north at Laha, and into the national park at Gorosingha before reaching the lake. The return route to Jumla follows a more eastern route, although it is possible to trek farther north on to Simikot. This is an adventurous trail, with few facilities along the way. Nonetheless, the effort is more than worthwhile, for this inaccessible lake is indeed what one walker described as the mountain kingdom's "shimmering blue jewel." **SA**

Changthang Lake Walk

India/China

Start/End Various, usually Kyamar or Rumtse
Distance 56 miles (90 km)   **Time** 7–14 days
Grade Moderate to strenuous   **Type** Mountain
Info goo.gl/6DfD4J

Changthang is a high plateau that runs from western Tibet into eastern Ladakh, a region of India that lies between the Kunlun and Great Himalayan mountain ranges. The area is home to nomadic tribes, or Chagpas, who tend to their herds of goats, yak, and sheep with help from their muscular mastiff dogs. A number of crystal-clear lakes lie in the Changthang, some of which are saltwater, such as Tso Kar and Karsok. The area is also a haven for wildlife, including kyang, the Tibetan wild ass. You may even see a snow leopard if you're lucky.

Getting to Changthang is an adventure in itself. Most organized treks involve flying into Delhi before taking a domestic flight over the mighty Himalayas to Leh. After taking time to acclimatize, there follows a road journey farther up into the mountains before the walking starts in earnest. All of this can last for up to a week, depending on whether or not you take an excursion to one or more of the local monasteries. Once you are out on the trail, you will be passing through high mountain meadows, negotiating narrow passes, walking along the shores of the saltwater lakes, and exploring villages and hamlets. This is generally done to a fixed itinerary, with set points to pitch camp.

It helps to be fit and experienced to undertake this trek—the altitude alone is enough to catch out the unwary, and you'll be carrying everything you need with you as you go, unless you travel with an organized group. However, the warmth of the welcome from the local people combined with the stunning backdrop of the all-conquering Himalayas make it a challenge many choose to accept. **JI**

Lake Manasarovar Kora

Tibet, China

Start/End Chiu Monastery
Distance 56 miles (90 km)   **Time** 4–5 days
Grade Moderate to strenuous
Type Mountain   **Map** goo.gl/uSfHJA

Manasarovar, a holy lake in Tibet, is one of the clearest, cleanest water stretches in the world. According to Hindu tradition the lake was created by Brahma, the god of creation, as a place of ritual and purification. Anyone who drinks from the waters of Manasarovar is cleansed of their sins, and every summer, pilgrims come from Tibet, India, and Nepal to bathe in the lake. To those of other faiths this is also a special place, drawing hikers from across the world who come to complete a circumnavigation of the lake. A good starting point is the Chiu Monastery.

> *"'Kora' in Tibetan means 'a pilgrimage route around a sacred temple, a holy mountain, or lake.'"*
>
> www.tibettour.org

This is not an easy walk, partly due to the altitude. You are at nearly 15,091 feet (4,600 m) above sea level, and this can cause health problems if you're not prepared. Even in summer the air is cold and damp and temperatures can vary greatly. You'll need to go at a slower pace than you may be used to. Navigation isn't much of an issue—just follow the edge of the lake, under the watchful gaze of Mount Lailas. The surface underfoot varies from shingle to boggy areas, and you can cut inland in places to avoid the marshes to the north. There are guesthouses, monasteries, and camping spots to stop at, but you'll need to be largely self-sufficient. You'll also need to make sure you have the proper travel documentation with you. **JI**

West Sayan to Ergaki Krasnoyark, Russia

Start/End West Sayan main road **Distance** 24 miles (38.6 km) **Time** 4 days
Grade Moderate **Type** Rocky paths **Map** goo.gl/52ANG5

The Western Sayan mountains, of which the Ergaki mountain range is a part, lie to the east of the Altai Mountains in southern Siberia, to the northwest of Mongolia. Stretching for more than 310 miles (498 km) and often towering over 9,840 feet (3,000 m), these mountain peaks and lakes produce the tributaries that come together to form the Yenisei River. Their landscape is alpine, with deep valleys, rocky ridges, torrential waterfalls, and clear lakes. The Ergaki range itself got its name from the Turkic word for "fingers." Look closely at the mountains and you can see that many of them resemble upward-pointing fingers spread widely apart.

The area is ideal for trekking, with many routes crisscrossing the area. A favorite trek is based on the town of Abakan, capital of Khakassia, a small autonomous republic of Russia. A car journey of around four hours takes you to the start of the trek, which leads up through the Ergaki nature park past Svetloe Lake and through Ptica Pass to Khudozhnik Lake and then returns via Karovoe Lake to the main road again. Side routes encompass day-long treks to the deep blue Zolotarnoye Lake, an ascent of Zub Dracona Mountain, and the Hanging Stone, a vast slab of rock precariously balanced on top of the mountain ridge. The scenery is idyllic, with clear blue skies, mirror-like lakes, and swathes of cedars and conifers among the alpine meadows and upland tundra. The meadows are often awash with beautiful flowers, such as blue and sapphire columbines, Altai violets, and yellow primroses. Thickets of rosebays and bergenias shelter chipmunks, which bound out in search of food. **SA**

⊞ **Experience the allure of the Sayan mountain lakes.**

Olkhon Island Trek Irkutskaya, Russia

Start Unshuy Cape   **End** Shunte Gulf   **Distance** 45 miles (72.4 km)   **Time** 4 days   **Grade** Easy
Type Earthen roads and tracks   **Map** goo.gl/Z8cWfX

Lake Baikal in southern Siberia is a natural wonder, a vast and deep expanse of water containing approximately 20 percent of the world's unfrozen freshwater. The lake is also the world's deepest (5,387 feet/1,642 m), clearest, and oldest, dating back twenty-five million years.

Lying off its west coast is the island of Olkhon, itself something of a wonder as the fourth-largest lake-bound island in the world, with an area of 270 square miles (730 sq km). There are two stories concerning the origin of its name, which comes from the local Buryat language. One states it comes from the word *oikhon* (wooded), the other from *olhan* (dry). Both suit Olkhon's character well, as this is a wooded and dry island of great beauty—there are taiga forests and even a small desert on the island.

For the Buryat shamans, the island is also a spiritual place, home to the "thirteen lords of Olkhon."

A modern cult figure, Burkhan is said to live in a cave below Shaman's Rock on the west coast. Covering an area of 270 square miles (700 sq km), Olkhon is long and thin. Around 1,500 people live on the island, in five main villages and other smaller settlements. Winters are mild, the climate is dry, but it is often windy. It is best to visit during the short spring and summer. Access to the island is by ferry from the mainland from May through to December. When the lake freezes over in the winter, the crossing is by ice bridge. Steep mountains line its eastern shore, with Mount Zhima towering 2,684 feet (818 m) above the waters of Lake Baikal. As a result, the trek along the island follows the west coast, an easy stroll along earthen roads and tracks from end to end. **SA**

⊡ Stroll around the world's fourth largest island lake.

Lake Kurilskoye Kamchatka, Russia

Start/End Grassy Point Lodge   **Distance** Various   **Time** Various   **Grade** Easy
Type Sand, pebbly shoreline   **Info** goo.gl/kh1S15

Determining your start and end points for a walk around Lake Kurilskoye in Russia's remote southern Kamchatka Peninsula isn't difficult, although getting there can be. The peninsula is the size of several European countries, and outside the capital of Petropavlovsk, there are few main roads. Access to the lake is via Soviet MI-8 helicopters, which take about an hour to fly you over some of the most inspiring mountain terrain on the planet until the lake appears below you. A crater lake with a surface area of 33 square miles (85 sq km) and an average depth of 577 feet (176 m), it is Eurasia's premier spawning ground for sockeye salmon, which explains the presence of hundreds of Kamchatkan brown bears and why a ranger and shotgun accompany you whenever you venture beyond the perimeter of the only accommodation, the eighteen-bunk Grassy Point Lodge.

The lodge sits on a tiny peninsula that juts into the lake and is surrounded by electrified wire to keep out hairy unwanted guests. The good news, though, is that the bears, which are plentiful, prefer salmon to humans and the thing to do once you get here and unpack your kit is to walk. Pass through grasses to nearby rivers and see bears catching salmon in their paws, or walk along the lake's shoreline with bears sometimes only scant feet away. Views extend over the lovely symmetry of Ilinsky and Kambalny volcanoes, which frame the lake as bear cubs chase each other across open meadows. The entire scene is almost too much to comprehend; a glimpse into how the world must have looked before human beings began to reproduce. You *must* come here. **BDS**

⛨ Grassy Point Lodge is not just shelter—it is sanctuary.

Ulleung-do Island Ulleung-do, South Korea

Start/End Dodong village   Distance Various   Time Various   Grade Easy to moderate
Type Well-maintained mountain trail   Info goo.gl/TyPb5C

They call it South Korea's "mystery island," a volcanic remnant 75 miles (120 km) off the Korean Peninsula's east coast crowned with crenellated peaks. The trails take you to the edge of extinct calderas, and along a coastline of gnarled, rocky slopes that plunge precipitously into the surrounding ocean in a land where level ground is hard to find.

Inhabited since the first millennium BCE, Ulleung-do Island is a three-hour ferry ride from the mainland—just enough separation to keep tourist numbers down. For those few who come here, it is a revelation. Skiers love it because it gets more snow than the mainland, a feat in itself, and without the expense. Hikers come here because of its fern-covered lowlands, many areas of which have never been touched and are as pristine as the day they began to evolve, and there are serpentine trails aplenty. There are two paths to Dodong Lighthouse, for example: one is the coastal path that begins at Dodonghang Port, or there is a slightly longer trail that immerses you in the emerald green slopes of Haengnam Mountain.

The island's highest point, Seonginbong peak (3,234 feet/986 m), is covered in fog for 300 days a year, but don't let that stop you from making the climb through forests of linden and beech up what Koreans call the "sacred man." The climb from Dodong via Gwanmobong should take you around three hours, and once there you can see the entire island, fog permitting, and be grateful that there are still some parts of hiking-mad South Korea where you can have a horizon all to yourself. **BDS**

⊞ An island that is more a climb than a walk.

Jeju Olle Trail
Jeju, South Korea

Start Siheung   **End** Jongdal
Distance 10 miles (16 km)   **Time** 4–5 hours
Grade Easy to moderate   **Type** Earth, rock, and sand
paths   **Map** goo.gl/QXoApf

In the local Jeju dialect of South Korea, *olle* was originally used to refer to the narrow path between the street and one's doorstep. Children would agree to "meet at the *olle*." The word is now in common use across the country and refers to the series of long-distance walking paths that run around the entire coastline—and two offshore islands—of the southern island of Jeju.

The trail was conceived by journalist Suh Myung-suk, and the first of the twenty-one main routes and five subroutes opened in 2007. All the routes are marked with blue arrows, or blue and orange ribbons that are set into stone walls, tied to nearby trees, or stand on poles. Each of the routes can be tackled by itself—an average of 10 miles (16 km) long—or combined into longer treks. The entire trail stretches for 260 miles (418 km), and since opening it has attracted 1.2 million people a year, coming not only from mainland South Korea, but also from further afield. The trail is best tackled during spring and fall, although it is perfectly accessible at all other times of the year.

Along the way, walkers will capture something of the ecosystem and lifestyle of this beautiful island. Route 8 gives glimpses of the stone pillars caused by the eruption of Mount Halla; Route 1 provides a chance to visit the odd-looking tuff cone or volcanic lump of Seongsan Ilchulbong. Women divers known as *haenyo*, searching for abalone and conch, can be seen at work on Route 4. Throughout the walk, the scenery regularly changes, with coral beaches and sandy tracks giving way to forested valleys and glades of pampas grass and wildflowers. **SA**

"For the global traveler looking for a unique destination, the olle walking paths on Jeju Island are highly appealing."

english.visitkorea.or.kr

← Jeju Island has more than 350 *oreums*—small volcanic mountains.

↑ Walk the *olle*, South Korea's "narrow path."

Cape to Cape Western Australia, Australia

Start Cape Naturaliste **End** Cape Leeuwin   **Distance** 83 miles (134 km)   **Time** 5–7 days
Grade Easy to moderate **Type** Graded tracks, stony paths, sandy beaches   **Map** goo.gl/ubEu2O

Situated in the far southwestern corner of Western Australia, the Cape to Cape track follows the north–south spine of the Leeuwin–Naturaliste Ridge between lighthouses at either end. It runs along a broad limestone ridge with a series of rounded hills up to 656 feet (200 m) high that lie parallel to a coastline of steep limestone cliffs dotted with some of the Southern Ocean's finest sandy bays, steep dune systems, and rocky promontories. The track also has several loop trails that lead inland into sheltered woodlands such as the Boranup Karri Forest.

The track passes through coastal heath, with buttercups, holly-leaved banksias, wattles, and blue fan-flowers on the ridge's exposed, windswept western slopes, while Rottnest tea trees and peppermint trees grow in its sheltered gullies. On its protected eastern side are jarrah and she-oak. The track's most abundant residents are wrens, robins, rosellas, ospreys, and black cockatoos. Multiple access points make it possible to do the track in segments.

The limestone ridge also contains a cave-riddled wonderland that is easily accessible from the track, including Lake Cave, with its underground lake; Jewel Cave, Western Australia's largest cave with its beautiful flowstones; Mammoth Cave, the "Dawn of Creation," with more than 10,000 recovered fossils; and Devil's Lair, one of Australia's earliest known sites of human occupation. The longest coastal walk in Australia remains one of Western Australia's premier trails and is a year-round destination, although it may be best in spring when the state's famous carpets of wildflowers are in full bloom. **BDS**

⬆ Sights like this clamor for attention on this route.

Whitsunday Great Walk Queensland, Australia

Start Brandy Creek   **End** Airlie beach   **Distance** 17 miles (27.3 km)   **Time** 3 days   **Grade** Easy
Type Rain forest trails   **Map** goo.gl/wAtGGv

The tropical refuge of Conway National Park is home to a lush rain forest with magnificent coastal views, and the Whitsunday Great Walk takes you on a 17-mile (27-km) journey through the midst of it all, over the Conway Range.

Starting at Brandy Creek, a ten-minute drive from the township of Airlie Beach, you will find everything that the Whitsundays are known for, from majestic tropical rain forests to seasonal creeks, all the while looking out from under the park's thick canopy with glimpses over coastal townships to the Whitsunday Islands beyond. Your senses are tantalized on this fine trail, whether by the electric blue flash of a Ulysses butterfly, the fragrance of lemon myrtle flowers, or the distinctive call of the Wompoo fruit dove.

The Whitsunday Great Walk is usually done in three days, and there are two excellent campgrounds along the way, first at Repulse Bay (reached on the first night) and then Bloodwood. Shorter walks are also possible, and all are linked to the main track and cover varying distances for different levels of difficulty, so anyone can explore the secondary trails that weave their way through this tropical park overlooking one of Australia's top holiday destinations, the seventy-four islands in the Whitsunday group, from a unique perspective. The trail is well-maintained and wide, and its high point is Mount Haywood at 1,446 feet (441 m).

If you want to really test your physical limits, why not time your arrival so you get there for the biannual "Run the Whitsunday Great Walk" event, and leave your appreciation of the vines and delicate creepers for the recovery walk the next day. **BDS**

⊤ **Views of the Whitsundays will be yours on this walk.**

Fraser Island Great Walk
Queensland, Australia

Start Happy Valley   End Dilli Village
Distance 41 miles (66 km) to 56 miles (90 km)
Time 4–8 days   Grade Easy to moderate
Type Coast, lake, and forest trail   Map goo.gl/gtAjYv

The world's largest sand island might sound like a rather dull place for a walk, but the Fraser Island Great Walk soon proves you wrong: the path leads through fabulous subtropical scenery with great views. Fraser Island is a UNESCO World Heritage Site, and the sand that forms this island on Australia's east coast supports a huge range of environments: eucalyptus woodland, rain forests, ancient dunes, freshwater lakes, mangroves, peat swamps, and coastal heaths. The variety of vegetation makes for a diverse range of wildlife, too: there are crocodiles, dingos, and 300 types of birds.

"The combination of shifting sand dunes, tropical rain forests, and lakes makes it an exceptional site."

whc.unesco.org

Fraser Island's pristine and diverse ecosystems have become an increasing attraction for tourists, and in 2004 a network of walking tracks was opened. The core part is the 41-mile (66-km) trail from the small beach resort of Happy Valley, which loops inland and ends at the Dilli Village campsite farther down the coast. Other walking trails branch off the main route and together form the 56-mile (90-km) Great Walk.

Highlights include the crystal-clear Wanggoolba Creek that runs through the rain forest and the sandy beaches of Lake McKenzie. It may be mostly at sea level, but this is a serious trek, and hikers have to be self-sufficient. Spring is the best time to tackle the walk to avoid rain and mosquitoes. **SH**

Thorsborne Trail
Queensland, Australia

Start Ramsay Bay, Hinchinbrook Island   End George Point   Distance 20 miles (32 km)   Time 3–4 days
Grade Moderate   Type Rough unhardened trail, beaches
Map goo.gl/5V35bz

The rugged, cloud-covered mountains of Hinchinbrook Island lie off Australia's northeast coast, and in the midst of this untouched tropical paradise of lush rain forest and mangroves, walkers can explore a trail leading through sweeping bays and rocky headlands. The route, named after the late naturalist Arthur Thorsborne, passes down the east coast through some of the most protected areas in the country.

Just how protected is it? The island is a national park, the surrounding seas are all marine parks, and the whole area is part of the Great Barrier Reef site. The path is strictly managed to reduce any environmental impact, and restricted permits mean no more than forty walkers are on the route at any one time. The path itself is rough and unhardened but well-marked. There are seven basic campsites, all with steel boxes to secure food from scavenging wildlife, but walkers need to be self-sufficient and equipped with water, food, cooking utensils, and camping gear.

First, you have to get to the Ramsay Bay trailhead, which usually involves a prebooked boat trip from Cardwell on the mainland. The island makes for a daunting sight, with mountains reaching 3,678 feet (1,121 m), but thankfully the path skirts the highest peaks, passing through jungle alive with butterflies and creeks with turtles and crocodiles. Occasionally, the trail opens onto pure white beaches that give you a chance to stop for a snorkel on the reefs or to spot some blue soldier crabs. There are waterfalls amid the dense vegetation and memorable views across the neighboring islands. At George Point, many walkers turn around and head back the same way, but you can take it easy and wait for a boat back to the mainland. **SH**

Coffin Bay Oyster Walk
South Australia, Australia

Start/End Coffin Bay **Distance** 7.5 miles (12 km)
Time 12 hours **Grade** Easy
Type Coast path and boardwalk
Map goo.gl/cXY4j2

The small town of Coffin Bay stands in its own national park on the Eyre Peninsula in South Australia. The park comprises a long finger of land, sheltering a bay, swathes of sand dunes, and a spectacular, convoluted coastline of islands and reefs.

This short walk near the foot of the peninsula is a good introduction to the national park. Be aware that it can get busy—this attractive area is invaded by visitors during the summer. The trail consists of several loops around the town and you can shorten or lengthen the total distance to suit all abilities.

The walk starts in the old town of Coffin Bay, originally known as Oyster Town, where the clean, clear waters are perfect for harvesting the naturally occurring shellfish. A small settlement of oyster fishermen was established in the mid-nineteenth century, and when the native oysters were fully harvested, oyster farming began. Today, chefs all over the continent prize Coffin Bay's Pacific oysters.

This gentle walk meanders around the foreshore of the inner bays, past wooden seaside shacks and picturesque yacht moorings. The path is well-defined and maintained, weaving between enviable holiday homes and patches of rare, protected coastal vegetation, with glimpses of the sea beyond. The route includes wooden boardwalks and barbecue points. Apart from the stunning scenery, the area is renowned for its wildlife. Visitors can spot seabirds, ranging from sea eagles and albatrosses to fairywrens and rock parrots. At one point the path makes a short climb up a small hill to the Kellidie Bay lookout point. It is worth the ascent, even on a hot day, for the panorama across the islands and waterways. **SH**

"The park conserves a representative sample of diverse coastal landscapes."

www.environment.sa.gov.au

⬆ Coffin Bay was named in 1802 by explorer Matthew Flinders, but remained uncharted until 1839.

Hanson Bay Hike South Australia, Australia

Start Kelly Hill Visitor Centre, Kangaroo Island **End** Hanson Bay **Distance** 11 miles (17.7 km)
Time 6 hours **Grade** Moderate **Type** Coastal path **Map** goo.gl/BxmLeB

Australia's third largest island is relatively little known, yet Kangaroo Island is a fertile expanse of beautiful, protected national parklands and nature reserves. It is 93 miles (150 km) long and 56 miles (90km) wide, only 70 miles (112 km) south of Adelaide, the capital of South Australia. Best of all, for hikers, it is crisscrossed with a multitude of walking trails that vary in length and difficulty, all showcasing the island's unspoiled scenery and wildlife.

One of the best trails is the Hanson Bay Hike in the Kelly Hill Conservation Park in the west of the island, an 11-mile (17-km) route from the Kelly Hill Visitor Centre to Hanson Bay and back that takes most walkers a day. You will see pink gum woodlands, eucalyptus shrubland, coastal heaths, ancient sand dunes, and freshwater lagoons. There are also spectacular sea views from designated viewing points and Hanson Bay

Wildlife Sanctuary provides an opportunity to spot koalas, wallabies, possums, kangaroos, and echidnas.

The Clifftop Hike at Cape Borda is a short detour that serves as a good introduction to the island's coastline, with a stone lookout point for spotting dolphins and whales—don't forget your binoculars. The Ironstone Hill Hike in Baudin Conservation Park follows an old bullock track to Cape Willoughby via relics of the area's farming heritage, and a trail along American River leads to an historic fish cannery. There are cliff-top hikes, walks leading to lighthouses, and paths around freshwater lagoons, past shipwrecks, Aboriginal sites, and rocky outcrops. Some even tackle an entire walk around the island—a hefty hike of more than 300 miles (483 km). **SH**

⬆ Kangaroo Island is one of Australia's wild places.

Royal National Park Coast Track New South Wales, Australia

Start Bundeena   **End** Otford   **Distance** 16 miles (25.7 km)   **Time** 1–2 days   **Grade** Moderate
Type Forest trail, coast path, and beach walking   **Map** goo.gl/jGJb2s

Established in 1879, the Royal National Park is Australia's oldest national park and was one of the first in the world, second only to Yellowstone. Although less than an hour's drive from Sydney, there is a wide range of unspoiled nature here, from empty sandy beaches to lush temperate rain forests.

The "Nasho," as locals call it, is crisscrossed by scores of walking routes, but one path stands out in particular. The Coast Track is one of the continent's best-known walks, offering a 16-mile (26-km) sequence of beautiful ocean views with highlights that include passing cliff-top waterfalls, crossing creeks on stepping stones, walking through a jungle of palms, and spotting sea eagles if you are lucky.

The path winds up and down towering sandstone cliffs and across pristine beaches, through eucalyptus forests and grassy heaths. There are a few steep bits, and some sections can become muddy, especially in winter. But it is all signposted and maintained so well that trail runners can complete the whole path in half a day. Mountain bikes, however, are not allowed.

In the summer, many walkers cool off with a dip on one of the beaches, and in winter it is possible to spot migrating humpback whales. Summer walkers need to carry more water, while winter brings the risk of rain and swollen rivers that may be difficult to cross. Fast walkers often tackle the whole route in a day, but most prefer to make an overnight stop at the basic North Era campground at Garie Beach, which is famous for its surfing waves—although most surfers are put off by the thought of having to carry their board all the way there and back. **SH**

⬆ Untouched wilderness less than an hour from Sydney.

Cape Byron Walking Track
New South Wales, Australia

"The loop leads you on a hike through rain forest and across cliff tops with stunning views of the ocean and the hinterland."

www.nationalparks.nsw.gov.au

⬆ Cape Byron is the most easterly point of Australia.

Start/End Lighthouse parking lot
Distance 2.3 miles (3.7 km)   **Time** 1–2 hours
Grade Easy   **Type** Paved walkway, forest track, and boardwalk   **Map** goo.gl/szyWM1

When Captain James Cook sailed past the most easterly point of the Australian mainland in 1770, he named it after another British explorer, John Byron. Today, walkers can follow in Cook's footsteps: the headland is a conservation zone that features several walking trails, the most popular being the charming Cape Byron Walking Track.

The route is well-used since many visitors take part of it to reach the well-known lighthouse on the beach. The benefit of this is that the path is mostly well-maintained with boarded and paved sections, good steps on inclines, and clear signage. Only occasional short stretches are genuinely steep, while graded sections can be shared with baby carriages, bicycles, and wheelchairs. The circular path can be joined at many points and there are four parking lots.

This is mostly an easy, convenient stroll through lush rain forest and across cliff tops with panoramic views of the ocean. The path runs under distinctive bangalow palms and ancient burrawang trees, crosses grasslands with grazing kangaroos, and dips down toward clean sandy beaches, finally reaching Cape Byron Lighthouse atop its 308-foot-high (94 m) cliff overlooking the headland. The lighthouse was built from concrete blocks more than a hundred years ago to warn passing ships and has been fully automated since 1989. Visitors can take a guided tour that also includes a small maritime museum.

The Cape Byron Marine Park extends out to sea for 3 miles (4.8 km) from the shore, which makes the headland a great spot to look for marine life such as turtles, stingrays, dolphins, and migrating humpback whales between May and November. **SH**

Bouddi Coastal Walk
New South Wales, Australia

Start Putty Beach   **End** MacMasters Beach
Distance 5 miles (8 km)   **Time** 2–5 hours
Grade Easy to moderate   **Type** Coastal path, boardwalks   **Map** goo.gl/iEtquQ

The Bouddi Coastal Walk winds through the Bouddi National Park, hugging a coastline that is rich in beaches, birdlife, and lookouts, and even has a shipwreck. It is a walk full of sweeping ocean views, stretches of lush and shady rain forest, and beguiling picnic spots amid wildflowers. The path is renowned as a particularly scenic route along this section of Australia's central coast, as suitable for families as it is for hikers. For those who need a regular rest, there are benches to sit on and admire the best panoramas. And for those who need a bit more adventure, there are plenty of hardcore side trails to explore.

The Bouddi Coastal Walk features steep cliffs, rocky platforms, sandy beaches, heathland, and eucalyptus forest. It is also popular with swimmers, surfers, and shore fishermen, who use it to get to remote and scenic spots away from the crowds, yet it is easily reached from Gosford and Sydney.

Along the way the path leads up wooden steps to the boardwalk toward the Gerrin Point Lookout, where you may spot migrating humpback whales. At the northern end of Maitland Bay lies the wreck of the *Maitland*, a paddle steamer that sank in 1898 and can be seen clearly from the rock platform at low tide.

There are some beachfront campsites at Putty Beach, at the start of the walk, and Little Beach, 1 mile (1.6 km) from MacMasters Beach. Little Beach sits in a cove backed by the Bouddi Grand Deep Rainforest, and the campsite here offers free gas barbecues. Multiple access points mean the trail can be easily tackled in smaller sections. In the summer, check before you leave, however—the path is sometimes closed in times of high fire risk. **SH**

Light to Light Walk
New South Wales, Australia

Start Boyds Tower, Ben Boyd National Park
End Cape Green   **Distance** 19 miles (30 km)
Time 1–3 days   **Grade** Easy   **Type** Coast path, seashore and creek crossings   **Map** goo.gl/IhV3El

The Light to Light Walk hugs the shoreline between two historic lighthouses in Ben Boyd National Park, and if you want a walk across giant pebbles along a beach backed by thick rain forest, with waves crashing into walls of red rock on the headland around you, then this is the walk for you.

Start at the northern end overlooking Twofold Bay, where in the 1840s entrepreneur Benjamin Boyd built a lighthouse to help establish Eden as a major commercial port. Despite his efforts, however, the tower never received official approval, and it was

> *". . . the track was so easy to follow and the views were out of this world."*
>
> Hiker feedback; www.nationalparks.nsw.gov.au

mainly used by whalers trying to spot lucrative catches from the shore. To the south, Green Cape Lighthouse opened in 1883 as part of former ship captain Francis Hixson's plan to "light the coast like a street with lamps." The light still works today, although it is now fully automated.

Between the two lights are 19 miles (31 km) of engrossing coastline, bordered by thick forest, open heathland, tea tree groves, and banksia woods, where you will find sheltered coves alternating with towering red-rock platforms. From special seafront vantage points you can spot seals, seabirds, and whales.

Some tackle the whole stretch in one day, others make it last; guided walks take up to four days. **SH**

Lake Burley Griffin Walk
ACT, Australia

Start/End Hyatt Hotel, Canberra
Distance 25 miles (40 km)   Time 8 hours
Grade Easy   Type Pavement
Map goo.gl/IQ8bAK

Walter Burley Griffin was born in 1876 in Maywood, a suburb of Chicago, Illinois, and studied to be an architect at the University of Illinois. A devotee of the Prairie School–style of architecture—characterized by overhanging eaves, horizontal lines, and flat roofs—he worked for a time in the famous Oak Park studio of Frank Lloyd Wright. In 1911 he won an international competition to create a design for Australia's new capital city of Canberra, to be built in the bush at a midway point between its two largest cities, Melbourne and Sydney.

"[The lake] consists of three formal water basins (Central, West, and East Basins)."

www.nationalcapital.gov.au

The design incorporated several geometric motifs that aligned it with the surrounding landscape, but government interference meant that Griffin left Australia before any substantial work started. It wasn't until 1960 that excavations began and the Scrivener Dam was built. The lake was officially opened in 1964.

This irregularly shaped, ornamental lake is 6.8 miles (11 km) long and 0.75 mile (1.2 km) at the widest point, with an average depth of 13 feet (4 m). The walking and cycling path that surrounds it runs for 25 miles (40 km) and showcases the many sides of the nation's capital, from its quiet western shoreline and the residence of the governor-general to the eastern loop past the city's great museums. **BDS**

Great Ocean Walk
Victoria, Australia

Start Apollo Bay   End The Twelve Apostles
Distance 65 miles (105 km)   Time 3–8 days
Grade Easy to moderate   Type Coastal path
Map goo.gl/hU1OAE

The Great Ocean Road has helped make the stretch of the southern Victoria coast to the west of Melbourne justly famous, and a new footpath takes you to places the road never reached: the Great Ocean Walk. It was devised at great expense by the state authorities to highlight the diverse landscapes of the coast. The environment seems to change with every hill as the route winds through national parks along the edge of some of Australia's highest cliffs, passes through rain forests across sandy beaches, and traverses spectacular open coastal heathland. Walkers find wind-sculpted sand dunes, high mountain ash woods, groves of gum trees, rocky slopes, and fertile farmland.

The trail gets more demanding as you head west. It starts off very gently in the pretty seaside town of Apollo Bay, but continues to a sensational finale at the renowned limestone stacks known as The Twelve Apostles. Walkers of the whole trail will see a lighthouse, shipwrecks; waterfalls; and wildlife, including koalas, kangaroos, wallabies, albatrosses, and a colony of little penguins. Looking out to sea, you can spot sea eagles, whales, and dolphins. The area is also rich in dinosaur fossils from millions of years ago.

In practical terms, the Great Ocean Walk is a flexible challenge. There are numerous trailheads to access the path and seven ecocampsites, so walkers can tackle as much or as little as they want. There are guided walks available, too, and pick-up services to drive you back to more luxurious accommodation. Whatever you choose, however, all walkers are required to register before departing. **SH**

➡ Victoria's majestic sea stacks of the Twelve Apostles.

Wilson's Promontory Lighthouse Walk Victoria, Australia

Start/End Telegraph Saddle parking lot   **Distance** 24 miles (38.6 km)   **Time** 2 days   **Grade** Easy to moderate
Type Vehicleway track, footpath   **Map** goo.gl/IdO2dw

The first sighting of Wilson's Promontory Lighthouse comes only after a long day's walking. The lighthouse has stood here on this slender finger of land that juts into the treacherous Bass Strait since 1859, and it is its wild remoteness that is its appeal. In the nineteenth century, supplies were delivered to the lighthouse keepers only once every six months by boat.

Today, you have to walk a 12-mile (19-km) route along the Telegraph Track, a gravel road, to get to the lighthouse and then hike back again. An optional, more scenic coastal route via Waterloo Bay adds 2 miles (3.2 km) to the return journey and other linked-up routes can add even more distance and variety.

The lighthouse is near the southernmost point of Australia's mainland. Two park rangers live here full-time, and walkers can stay in the comparative luxury of the three old adjacent cottages, complete with beds, hot showers, and a kitchen. Known locally as "the Prom," the lighthouse is a three-hour drive southeast of Melbourne.

The whole area is known for its temperate rain forests, unspoiled beaches, and abundant wildlife, and there is a wide range of walking trails, from short beach strolls to multiday hikes that require more stamina and navigation skills.

The Lighthouse Walk is a good midrange option. The maintained track tackles lush forest, muddy hills, white sand beaches, and blackened stumps of bushfire zones, but the gravel track makes for easy progress. The highest point comes after a gradual climb to the 950-foot-high (290-m) Martin's Hill, but there are a few steeper sections on the Waterloo Bay track. **SH**

⊞ Be energized by the wild Bass Strait.

French Island Trails Victoria, Australia

Start/End Tankerton Jetty or French Island Vineyards on Long Point Road (parking lot)   **Distance** Various
Time Various   **Grade** Easy   **Type** Beaches, coastal hinterland, gravel roads   **Info** goo.gl/Yz9pon

There are some curious facts that apply to French Island, the 39,500-acre (16,000-ha) island in Melbourne's Western Port Bay—both to the land and to the 115 or so people who live on it—that no other place in Australia can lay claim to.

Residents don't pay taxes or land rates because there is no water, electricity, or garbage collection, or, indeed, any other sign of government, local or otherwise. There are no sealed roads, and the only school building has fewer than twenty pupils, and a "mainlander" catches the tiny cork-like ferry every day to teach them. There is no police or medical service; the cars don't have number plates; and if you're not the sort of person who is good at fixing things when they break, well, you shouldn't be living there.

What French Island does have in abundance, however, is solitude. Most of the land is a national park

or open farmland. There are few streams and the island's highest point is Mount Wellington at 305 feet (93m), but there are vast mudflats, salt marshes, and mangroves that are home to a wealth of birdlife including shearwaters and sea eagles and as many as 10,000 black swans—in all, 240 of the 400 bird species found in Victoria are present here.

Some trails are still in the process of being developed, yet it is the undeveloped nature of these wetlands that makes walking here such a treat. Trails can take an hour to complete (the Pinnacles Track, for example), a half day, or several days—and everywhere around you all you will see is nature. Four hundred koalas live on the island too, so bring your binoculars and you may spot one or two. **BDS**

⬆ One of the world's 621 biosphere reserves.

South Coast Track

Tasmania, Australia

Start Melaleuca   **End** Cockle Creek
Distance 53 miles (85 km)   **Time** 5–9 days
Grade Strenuous   **Type** Wilderness trail, mountain
scramble, river crossings   **Map** goo.gl/JM3PzI

With its beautiful, empty sandy beaches, towering rain forests, and alpine mountain peaks, why is it that so few walkers tackle Tasmania's South Coast Track? Because it is a demanding route that requires stamina, experience, and resilience. Most walkers start from Melaleuca, flying or sailing in and walking out (flights are weather-dependent, so it is best to start with the flight rather than wait for a good moment to get back).

Originally, this trail through Tasmania's Southwest National Park was established as an escape route for shipwreck survivors along the notoriously remote

"This walk offers a spectrum of Tasmanian scenes, from empty beaches to towering rain forests."

www.tasmanianexpeditions.com.au

coastline, and to cross the New River Lagoon, you have to use one of the rowing boats that are tied to the banks at either side. A day is spent climbing from sea level over the Ironbound Range at 3,280 feet (1,000 m) and back down again, and perils include ocean waves suddenly crashing onto exposed sections of the trail during high seas; long stretches of knee-deep mud; snakes; and unexpected hail, sleet, or snow even in summer. And of course you have to carry a full pack with supplies for rough camping at night.

All of this attracts only the hardiest souls, but the rewards include the finest, unspoiled scenery and wildlife: you could spot wombats and even the orange-bellied parrot, one of the world's rarest birds. **SH**

Maria Island

Tasmania, Australia

Start/End Darlington
Distance 26 miles (42 km)
Time 3–4 days   **Grade** Easy   **Type** Sand
Map goo.gl/6dbDJf

For countless generations the land now known as Maria Island, off the east coast of Tasmania, was inhabited by the local Tyreddeme Aboriginal people who arrived in reed canoes and called it Toarra-marra-monah. After they were forcibly removed from their lands, the white settlers established sealing and whaling stations. A penal colony followed in 1825, but with the decline of whaling in the early decades of the twentieth century the settlement began to shrink until it was little more than a small-scale farming community, and it has remained so ever since—which is good news for the whales, and for visitors.

Twelve miles (20 km) long and 7.5 miles (12 km) wide, the island is, in fact, made up of two islands joined by a narrow isthmus, with Shoal Bay on one side and Riedle Bay on the other. There are just a handful of high points on the otherwise flat land, with Mount Bishop and Clerk at 1,995 feet (608 m) and Mount Maria at 2,326 feet (709 m), and the surrounding undulating terrain is ringed by miles of pure white sand beaches that, since 1972, have comprised Maria Island National Park, the backdrop for one of Australia's finest walks.

Native animals flourish here, including kangaroos, wombats, echidnas, wallabies, and brush-tailed and ring-tailed possums; if you're lucky, you may even see some rare Cape Barren geese. You can spend as long as you like in Darlington, the island's only real town, and stay overnight in bunk beds in the former penal colony. You can also go and see the Painted Cliffs and Fossil Cliffs near Darlington. And as for trails? Well, the one you come here for is the beach itself: sweeping swathes of sand and a silence broken only by the sounds of nature. **BDS**

Tasman Coastal Trail
Tasmania, Australia

Start Waterfall Bay **End** Cape Pillar
Distance 28 miles (45 km) **Time** 3–5 days
Grade Moderate **Type** Marked forest and cliff-top trail
Map goo.gl/M1mmMd

The Tasman Coastal Trail is a daunting but exciting one: a signposted gravel road leads to Waterfall Bay and soon the path opens onto a thickly wooded mountain landscape, eventually descending to Fortescue Beach, a wide sandy bay backed by thick rain forest. Most walkers camp here for the first night. The next day the route winds out to views of the sea stacks and jagged rock columns at Cape Hauy (pronounced "Hoy") before climbing through ferns and mosses over Mount Fortescue. The next day you march on to Cape Pillar, where towering buttresses of volcanic dolerite face the sheer cliffs of Tasman Island across the narrow Tasman Passage.

The views are spectacular along most of this stretch of the Tasman National Park, thanks to the imposing volcanic rock formations and Australia's highest sea cliffs, which top a dizzying 984 feet (300 m). With unfenced sheer drops like these and wild seas crashing onto the rocks below, this trail is not for the fainthearted, but the landscape is magnificent enough to make it worthwhile and the path is surprisingly easy for such rugged terrain. Apart from a strenuous, slippery stretch in damp forest conditions over 1,575-foot (480-m) Mount Fortescue, the trail is easily navigable.

The logistics, however, are more challenging: you'll need to carry your own water, food, tent, and wet weather clothing, and the weather on the southeastern coast can also change with alarming speed. Very cold, storm-force winds may blow in from the south at any time, and names such as Tornado Ridge and Hurricane Heath along the trail give a hint of the challenging conditions that may lay ahead. **SH**

"You can find some of Tasmania's most dramatically beautiful coastal scenery on the east coast."

www.twe.travel

⊼ A strange rock formation on a Tasman beach.

Freycinet Peninsula Circuit
Tasmania, Australia

Start/End Walking Tracks parking lot, near Coles Bay **Distance** 17 miles (27.3 km) **Time** 1–3 days **Grade** Easy to moderate **Type** Maintained track, beaches, mountain path **Map** goo.gl/i3TxVO

White sand frames the bright blue sea in a perfect semicircle with a backdrop of mountains rising behind—this is the breathtaking view of Wineglass Bay, the highlight of this walk around the tip of the beautiful and rugged Freycinet Peninsula, part of Freycinet National Park on Tasmania's east coast. The park is known for the peach-colored granite mountains surrounded by clear turquoise bays and pristine, squeaky sands.

The Freycinet Peninsula Circuit is considered a short walk among Tasmania's hardy trekkers, and most complete the route in a day. There are campsites at some of the beaches, however, and there's no reason why you shouldn't make the adventure last longer. Indeed, it seems negligent not to stop for a swim in the crystal-clear waters instead of just tramping along the fringe and back into the bush. This ridiculously pretty bay often gets included in collections of the world's top beaches, but the bay is probably best appreciated from the heights of the mountains around it. There is certainly plenty to explore among the bush-covered mountains and deserted forests of white gum trees. A trek to the top of Mount Freycinet is an optional extra, but it is rewarded by views across the entire peninsula.

There's no way around the clamber up Mount Amos, though, as that's where the main path leads, but again the views make it worthwhile, and the path on the south slopes is the best place to admire the symmetry of Wineglass Bay. Walkers need a permit for this route, and authorities request that they tackle the route in a counterclockwise direction to prevent the spread of the deadly plant disease "root rot." **SH**

"The side trip down to Bryans Beach from Cooks Hut (5 km return) is well worth the effort."

www.thehikinglife.com

⊡ The famous, gentle arc of Wineglass Bay is one of the highlights on this hike.

Yasawa Island

Fiji

Start/End Yasawa Island Resort and Spa
Distance Various   Time Various
Grade Easy   Type Sand
Info goo.gl/lOPkU1

It isn't easy to find a traditional Fijian island that is close to the main island of Viti Levu yet sufficiently separated from it to have escaped an uncomfortable degree of development and infrastructure, but Yasawa Island in the Yasawa group of islands to the northwest of Viti Levu is one tranquil exception. It has miles of unspoiled beaches, is the home of several communities that have lived there for countless generations, and has tourist numbers capped to preserve the environment and the peace. No matter when you go on the island, you can be assured of a tropical paradise that, once you leave the confines of the exceptional Yasawa Island Resort and Spa, you will have largely to yourself.

The first European to sight the Yasawa group was Captain William Bligh of HMS *Bounty* fame in 1789, but even then, they remained uncharted until 1840 and the arrival of the six U.S. sailing ships that comprised the Wilkes Expedition. Visitors were not allowed to set foot on the pristine beaches until the 1950s, and land-based tourism wasn't introduced until the late 1980s. The Yasawa group has a long tradition of taking things slowly.

This slow approach to—well, everything—is palpable from the moment you arrive. There are no designated walking trails, but that hardly matters as the entire 12.5 square miles (32 sq km) of the island is one giant trail, with numerous time-worn paths crisscrossing it and taking you to plentiful bays and beautiful headlands. There are eleven deserted beaches on this tiny island, but no telephones, no banks, and no shops. This is the way paradise was meant to be. **BDS**

Cross Island Track

Rarotonga, Cook Islands

Start Avarua Harbor   End Wigmore's Falls
Distance 4.5 miles (7.2 km)
Time 4 hours   Grade Easy
Type Mountain trails   Map goo.gl/M2jtJ1

The Cook Islands are sometimes called the "Secret Pacific," and it isn't hard to see why, tucked away as they are almost anonymously between Samoa and French Polynesia. An archipelago of fifteen islands, the landscape is pure Tahitian—volcanic peaks, palm-fringed lagoons, and endless white sand beaches.

Rarotonga is the island group's main island and it is home to the Cross Island Track, one of the Cook Islands' signature experiences. It begins on the north coast at Avarua Harbor and leads you through dense tropical forest and a mountainous interior to the

"Wear adequate shoes, take plenty of drinking water, and slather on the mosquito repellent."

www.lonelyplanet.com

pinnacle of rock called Te Rua Manga—the Needle. Climbing the Needle is possible, but it is best left to experienced climbers. From there the track continues south and comes to an end near Wigmore's Falls on the south coast, where there is a bus to take you back along the coast road to your starting point.

Some sections can be badly eroded and are often slippery, but the trail can easily be done in all types of weather. And if you walk with Pa, of "Pa's Treks," this colorful local character will ensure that you see everything this fabulous trail offers—exotic butterflies, endemic plants and ferns—and all the while listening to Pa's retelling of the island's litany of ancient myths and legends. **BDS**

Cape Brett Track
Northland, New Zealand

Start Oke Bay   End Lighthouse, seaward end, Cape Brett Peninsula   Distance 10 miles (16 km) Time 8 hours   Grade Moderate   Type Coastal trails   Map goo.gl/l8EqxW

The Bay of Islands is aptly named—144 islands strung out between Cape Brett and the Purerua Peninsula in the Northland region of New Zealand's North Island. Made famous in the 1930s by U.S. author and fishing enthusiast Zane Grey, who called it "the angler's El Dorado," this region features many walking trails—one of the best is the Cape Brett Track.

The walk begins at Oke Bay and continues along the peninsula's spine in a northeasterly direction, concluding at an old lighthouse at the peninsula's seaward end. You can reverse the walk by catching a

---

"You can take a side track down to Deep Water Cove, where you can enjoy a refreshing swim."

www.doc.govt.nz

---

boat to the lighthouse and walking back toward the mainland. The trail is well-marked and maintained, and can at times be decidedly steep, yet the track's high point is an easily scalable 1,131 feet (345 m). It passes through a wealth of native and regenerated coastal heathlands, but the real rewards are the many drop-offs and steep cliffs you pass on the way. You will also have (if you begin at Oke Bay) the welcoming sight of the Cape Brett Hut at the trail's end, with its cooking facilities and twenty-three comfortable bunks.

Be sure not to touch the electrified fence that was installed across the peninsula in 1995 to prevent encroachment of possums into the peninsula's fragile coastal flora. **BDS**

Abel Tasman Coast Track
Tasman, New Zealand

Start Marahau   End Totaranui Distance 25 miles (40 km)   Time 3–5 days Grade Moderate   Type Beaches, forest trails Map goo.gl/QIA9Nn

An officially designated "Great Walk," the Abel Tasman Coast Track runs through the Abel Tasman National Park—New Zealand's smallest national park, and named for the Dutch seafarer who was the first European to visit the country in 1642—in the northwest corner of New Zealand's South Island. It is a well-formed path that is easy to navigate, with a good number of benches, revealing glorious white sand beaches—probably the most lingering memory for those who walk it and one reason why it is now one of the nation's most popular walks with more than 200,000 visitors annually.

And it's all wonderfully civilized. As you walk the beaches along the western side of Tasman Bay, with views out to the Marlborough Sounds, water taxis are never far away to pick up your backpack and take it to your next accommodation. And when you are not on a beach with an intoxicating name like Apple Tree Bay or on the squeaky sands of Anchorage Bay, you will be walking through regenerating podocarp forests. The crossing of the inlet at Torrent Bay alone is enough to make you a fan of this trail, with its beach cabins so perfect that you'll want to put a deposit on them. Beyond the bay the trail climbs through forests of pine and across a swing bridge over Falls River, the park's largest river.

More stunning bays follow with Medlands Bay and Bark Bay and another inlet, if the tides allow, before walkers climb to the trail's highest point, a scant 442 feet (135 m) up a hill that doesn't even have a name, then down again to the historic granite mine of Tonga Quarry. Then it's still more beaches—Onetahuti, Awaroa, Waiharakeke Bay, and Goat Bay. So much sand; so little time. **BDS**

Queen Charlotte Track
Marlborough, New Zealand

Start Ship Cove **End** Anakiwa
Distance 44 miles (71 km)
Time 4 days **Grade** Easy to moderate
Type Forest trails **Map** goo.gl/uGOiA8

The Queen Charlotte Track starts in the very same harbor that gave shelter to Captain James Cook on five occasions in the 1770s, which even now can only be reached by boat. As you make your way to your first stop at Resolution Bay, you pass lookouts with views over Marlborough Sound, toward New Zealand's North Island. Then it's along an old bridle path, over another ridge, and down into Endeavour Inlet, descending through forests of kamahi and beech. Tracing the inlet's coastline past groves of tree ferns, you see tomtits, silvereyes, and warblers overhead, and go to sleep in Camp Bay. Two days have passed; you are almost halfway done.

Camp Bay to Portage is the longest and most rewarding day on the track. It begins with a steep ascent to 360-degree views of the Queen Charlotte and Kenepuru sounds that will make you want to linger and maybe even pitch a tent. There are many views like this as you make your way to Torea Saddle and descend to an old road once used by Maoris to haul their canoes between the Queen Charlotte and Kenepuru sounds (doing this meant a lot less paddling). You can then bed down for the night in a hotel around Portage Bay.

The next day you scale 1,312-foot-high (400 m) summits on a two-and-a-half-hour walk to Mistletoe Bay, and on the last day you chalk up more bridle paths and skirt some farmland and a regenerating forest inhabited by waxeyes, fantails, and wekas. Now by the ocean, it's more beech forest and one last bridle path as you enter the town of Anakiwa, with a population of around sixty, at the head of Queen Charlotte Sound. And already you want to come back. **BDS**

"The Queen Charlotte Track ... has rapidly become known as the finest and most diverse coastal track in New Zealand."

www.wildernessguidesnz.com

⊡ The Queen Charlotte Track is a fabulous walk around a drowned river valley.

Milford Track
Southland, New Zealand

Start Glade Wharf, Lake Te Anau **End** Sandfly Point, Milford Sound **Distance** 33 miles (53 km) **Time** 4 days **Grade** Moderate **Type** Forest trails (often muddy), boardwalks **Map** goo.gl/tsilX7

The poet and prison reformer Blanche Edith Baughan wrote an essay about Milford Track titled "Finest Walk in the World," in London's *Spectator* in 1908, and while it's easy to say that her experience of the world's walks must have been limited, her bold claim is one that can still be argued. Baughan described the environment as "truly the 'region of the perpendicular'—the mountains split right straight down from their summits to within a few hundred feet of sea level . . . the frowning white-tipped walls begin to draw together above the canyon, [and] you realize that you are walking at the bottom of a gigantic furrow of the earth."

Only walkable in one direction, the trail begins at Lake Te Anau and traverses suspension bridges, boardwalks, and a mountain pass, past New Zealand's tallest waterfall, Sutherland Falls at 1,902 feet (580 m), below the soaring mountain peaks and above V-shape valleys that descend into clouds of mist and spray. On a sunny day is scenery as fine as can be found anywhere, but only when it rains, and torrents of water tumble down the mountainsides, turning sections of the track into muddy ditches, do you really experience the true magic of it all.

And you are likely to experience that magic. The Clinton and Arthur valleys, separated by the Mackinnon Pass—at 3,740 feet (1,140 m) the highest point of the walk—receive a whopping 268 inches (6.8 m) of rainfall a year. Camping isn't permitted, but there is a shelter hut on Mackinnon Pass, a welcome sight if it is a bad (or beautiful?) wet Milford day. **BDS**

◄ A walk that gets better the wetter it gets.

North West Circuit
Stewart Island, New Zealand

Start/End Oban **Distance** 78 miles (125 km) **Time** 10–12 days **Grade** Strenuous **Type** Muddy **Map** goo.gl/dHvT74

An hour's ferry ride across Foveaux Strait from the town of Bluff, at the bottom tip of New Zealand's South Island, Stewart Island offers what few places can: a week's walk on a beautiful coastline without any civilization to ruin it all. The majority of the 380-something inhabitants live in the town of Oban, which is where this challenging trail begins and ends, and you quickly leave it behind. The beaches can be a bit bouldery, but feature golden sands, often with backdrops of impressive dunes and nestled between some genuinely impressive headlands. West-facing

"Stewart Island is a haven for native birdlife [and] enjoys the perfect environment for hiking ..."

www.tourism.net.nz

beaches are often being pounded by waves and wind and offer an impressive spectacle. Keep an eye out for yellow-eyed penguins riding in on the surf.

If you are keen to tramp the North West Circuit, there's one thing you probably already know: you need to be prepared for mud. Walking shoes have been known to give on day one. The mud is truly legendary, sometimes up to hip height and even in the wake of dry weather it can be so thick, clingy, and deep that it is best to wear leather boots and gaiters. The undulating walk takes you over headlands and down into gullies, and while it follows the coastline, much walking will be done through the island's podocarp forests. You might even see a kiwi. **BDS**

Index of Walks by Distance

65 miles (105 km)

High Sierra Trail	429
Great Ocean Walk	936
Langtang Valley Trail	597
Rhine Castle Trail	734
Speyside Way	180

67 miles (108 km)

Ausonius Way	736

68 miles (109 km)

Backbone Trail	429

69 miles (111 km)

Isle of Wight Coast Path	875

70 miles (112 km)

Apolo Trail, Pelechuco to Apolo	152
Laurel Highlands Hiking Trail	105
Matterhorn Circuit	518
Painters' Way	740
Tulum to Yaxuna	681
Upper Mustang	596

71 miles (114 km)

Burren Way	857
Lake Zürich Shoreline Walk	889
Saffron Trail	203

71.4 miles (115 km)

Hardangervidda Plateau Traverse	167

73 miles (117 km)

Grand Canal Way	179
Miner's Way and Historical Trail	694

74 miles (119 km)

Alta Via 1	546
Fisherman's Trail	898
Gorges Trail	224

75 miles (120 km)

Namib Naukluft Hiking Trail	266

76 miles (122 km)

Foothills Trail	128
Sarchu to Padum	593

77 miles (124 km)

Greenbrier River Trail	124

78 miles (125 km)

Everest Base Camp	598
Lechweg	230
North West Circuit	947
Yorkshire Wolds Way	196

79 miles (127 km)

Eselsweg	221
Great Glen Way	180
Hoga Kusten Trail	854
Rob Roy Way	185
Skye Trail	862

80 miles (129 km)

Accursed Mountains	564
Monte Rosa Circuit	519
Wicklow Way	176

81 miles (130 km)

Gastronomy Route	770

82 miles (132 km)

Essex Way	203

83 miles (134 km)

Cape to Cape	928

84 miles (135 km)

Dales Way	192
Defence Line of Amsterdam, The	891
Towpath Trail	664

85 miles (137 km)

Hadrian's Wall Path	698
Ridgeway, The	201
Susquehannock Trail System	106

87 miles (140 km)

Kintyre Way	864

90 miles (145 km)

White Horse Trail	200

91 miles (146 km)

Llyn Coastal Path	878
Painted Churches of Troodos	773

93 miles (150 km)

Otago Central Rail Trail	805
Wonderland Trail	427

95 miles (153 km)

Isle of Man Coastal Path (The Way of the Gull)	868
West Highland Way	187

97 miles (156 km)

Cheshire Ring Canal Walk	700

99 miles (160 km)

Padjelanta Trail	169

100 miles (160 km)

Berlin Wall Trail	733
Meket to Lalibela	576
South Downs Way	204

101 miles (162 km)

Dingle Way	860
E5, Oberstdorf to Merano	530
Huayhuash Circuit	476

102 miles (164 km)

Cotswold Way	199

103 miles (165 km)

Arctic Circle Trail, The	160
GR221 Drystone Route	542

104 miles (167 km)

Rennsteig Trail	223

105 miles (169 km)

Tour du Mont Blanc	507

106 miles (170 km)

Hermann's Walk	524

108 miles (174 km)

Baltoro Glacier	591
Greensand Way	204

110 miles (177 km)

Bonneville Shoreline Trail	856
Cleveland Way	193
George S. Mickelson Trail	79

111 miles (179 km)

GR21 Alabaster Coast Trail	885

112 miles (180 km)

GR20	545
Walkers Haute Route	505

113 miles (182 km)

Mera Peak Summit	600

114 miles (183 km)

Waitukubuli Trail	140

115 miles (186 km)

Bartram Trail	129

117 miles (188 km)

Fife Coastal Path	866

120 miles (193 km)

Flint Hills Nature Trail	81
GR70 Stevenson Trail	719

124 miles (200 km)

Anglesey Coastal Path	877
Cathar Trail	723
Skeleton Coast	911

124–240 miles (200–386 km)

Rideau Canal National Historic Site	653

128 miles (206 km)

Annapurna Circuit	595

133 miles (214 km)

Kerry Way	859

134 miles (215 km)

John Muir Way	865

135 miles (217 km)

Glyndwr's Way National Trail	211
Saar–Hunsrück Trail	219

136 miles (219 km)

Wye Valley Walk	209

138 miles (222 km)

Larapinta Trail	311

Contributors

Simon Adams: Simon Adams is a historian and writer living and working in London. He studied history and politics at universities in London and Bristol, and has written extensively for both adults and children. A lazy walker who should get out more, he enjoyed dreaming of the great outdoors when writing entries for this book.

Natalie Egling: Natalie Egling is a Johannesburg-born, London-based city girl with a soft spot for the countryside. She fantasizes about living in an Airstream trailer surrounded by fruit trees, and aims to take at least one good photo a day. A writer by day, she spends her nights hunting for bargains on eBay.

Mike Gerrard: Mike Gerrard writes about travel and spirits and contributes to websites, newspapers, and magazines. He has also written over thirty books and three radio plays. His accolades include two Awards for Excellence from the Outdoor Writers and Photographers Guild and being chosen as the AITO Online Travel Writer of the Year.

Simon Heptinstall: Simon Heptinstall has written about travel and adventure for books, magazines, newspapers, and websites all over the world. On his days off he has competed in epic trekking races across England's

Dartmoor, hired local guides to tackle mountains in Wales and Scotland, and completed Britain's notorious Three Peak Challenge . . . twice.

Jerry Ibbotson: Jerry Ibbotson is a writer, journalist, and broadcaster who has worked on and off for the BBC for more than twenty years, as well as freelancing for magazines and websites. He lives in North Yorkshire, which boasts of having some of the greatest walking in England, as well as the best beer.

George Lewis: George Lewis is an expatriate Manxman who's walked a lot and asserts a simple dogma: the finest foot trail in the world is the Isle of Man Coastal Path that circumnavigates his ancestral island.

Bruno MacDonald: Bruno MacDonald is a book and magazine subeditor, on titles ranging from *Marie Claire* to *Air Guitar: A User's Guide*. His favorite walks include climbing Lion's Head in Cape Town, striding from Midtown Manhattan to Greenwich Village, and strolling along the Seine. He lives in Hertfordshire, England, with a patient wife and high-maintenance cats.

Amy Scurr: Amy Scurr is a student at the University of Wollongong in Australia, currently working through

a Bachelor of Communications and Media Studies/Bachelor of Arts, majoring in Journalism and Professional Writing, Photography, and International Media and Communications. A prolific walker, she has tramped through rain forests in New Caledonia and Vanuatu, and throughout her native Australia.

Dorothy Stannard: Dorothy Stannard's career as a travel editor and writer has taken her to many parts of the world, from West Africa to Western Australia. "Almost any destination," she says, "is best explored on foot." When not traveling, she divides time between London and the Welsh border, where she puts in plenty of practice walking Offa's Dyke Path.

Barry Stone (general editor): Barry Stone is an internationally published author of twelve general history titles and has written for most of Australia's premier travel magazines. In 2013, he was a finalist at the National Travel Industry Awards in the category of Best Travel Writer. Wherever he travels, he loves nothing more than to dump his bags in his room, drop his keys at reception, and get walking.

Picture Credits

Images/Motion / Alamy **714** © Peter Titmuss / Alamy **716** © Cyrille Gibot / Alamy **717** © Jolli Village **718** © Martin Miles **719** jeanjoaquim **720** © Eithne Gallagher **722** © Brian Jannsen / Alamy **723** © irishphoto.com / Alamy **724** © amana images inc. / Alamy **725** © Vincent Toriel **726** © Miles Banbery **727** © Ines Saraiva **728** © Caro Sternberg **729** © George Carruthers / Alamy **730** © Nathanael Callon **731** © Morpheus **732** © German National Tourist Board **733** © FocusEurope / Alamy **734** © German National Tourist Board **735** © Wolfgang Staudt, **736** © Prisma Bildagentur AG / Alamy **737** © imageBROKER / Alamy **738** © German National Tourist Board **740–741** © blickwinkel / Alamy **743** © Julie Remizova **745** © Tour Spain **746** © Scott Goodno / Alamy **748** © Christian Zacke **751** © Eyebyte / Alamy **752** © Peter Oliver / Alamy **753** © Alex Segre / Alamy **754** © B Lawrence / Alamy **755** © Robert Harding Picture Library Ltd / Alamy **756** © Mattia Camellini **757** © Michael Tyler **758** © David Ball / Alamy **759** © Vekypula **760** © SuperStock / Alamy **763** © Pink Cigarette **764** © Dado **765** © nagelestock.com / Alamy **766** © Hercules Milas / Alamy **768** © Masha Che **769** © Esther Lee **770** © Images & Stories / Alamy **771** © Michael Jeddah **772** © Shaun Dunphy **773** © imageBROKER / Alamy **775** © Sebastia Girault **777** © Robert Harding World Imagery / Alamy **778** © Gavin Hellier / Alamy **780** © Graham Prentice / Alamy **782** © dbimages / Alamy **783** © Wilmar Photography / Alamy **785** © Jake **786** © Aflo Co. Ltd. / Alamy **787** © Ashok Prabakaram **788** © JLImages / Alamy **790** © Julian Chau **791** © Hemis / Alamy **792** © Stuart Dawson **795** © westward / Alamy **796** © Barry Stone **797** © Tourism Shikoku **799** © Arco Images GmbH / Alamy **801** © redbrickstock.com / Alamy **802** © The Rocks Sydney **803** © New South Wales Parks & Wildlife **805** © David Wall / Alamy **806–807** © James M. Hunt / Alamy **808** © Tom Doyle **809** © Paxon Walber **810** © Destination BC **811** © Joyce Perolta **812** © Jeff Wallace **815** © All Canada Photos / Alamy **817** © Jesse Estes **818** © Wil Clouser **819** © Aurora Photos / Alamy **821** © Manzurer Khan **822** © Kevin Eddy **824** © Beau Rogers **825** © Chris Boswell / Alamy **826** © Robert Harding World Imagery / Alamy **827** © Nina Nasunto **828** © Menique Koos **830** © Bayfield Chamber of Commerce **831** © Jun Yang **832** © Visit Maine **833** © James M. Hunt / Alamy **834** © Brian Jannsen / Alamy **835** © Just Me Robin **836** © Mira / Alamy **837** © Steven Reynolds **839** © David Olsen / Alamy **840** © David L. Moore - HIO / Alamy **841** © Mark A. Johnson / Alamy **842** © Kevin Ebi / Alamy **843** © JRS III **844** © David H **846** © blickwinkel / Alamy **849** © David Noton Photography / Alamy **850** © Robert Harding Picture Library Ltd / Alamy **851** © Elin Jakobsen **852** © Tobias Scandolara **853** © Stein Liland **854** © Ulf Bodin **855** © Paolo Trabattoni **856** © Conor McEneaney **857** © Bernard Golden / Alamy **858** © nagelestock.com / Alamy **859** © Paul Mogford / Alamy **860** © Rob & Monika **863** © Pleasure Principle **864** © Steve **865** © Visit Scotland **866** © Visit Scotland **868** © Keith Fergus / Alamy **868** © Trey Ratcliff **869** © David Noton Photography / Alamy **870** © Durham County Council **872** © Pauline Grimshaw **873** © Visit Britain **874** © Paul **875** © Kathleen Jowitt **876** © Pete **877** © Suggy Snaps **878** © Mel Garside **880** © Realimage / Alamy **881** © Mark Andrew **882** © Joel Douillet / Alamy **883** © Harold **884** © Radius Images / Alamy **887** © Andrea Schaffer **888** © Robert Harding World Imagery / Alamy **889** © Roberto Herrett / Alamy **890** © Roy LANGSTAFF / Alamy **891** © Defence Line Amsterdam **893** © LOOK Die Bildagentur der Fotografen GmbH / Alamy **894** © Marcela **895** © Westend61 GmbH / Alamy **896** © X Hunter **897** © Prisma Bildagentur AG / Alamy **898** © Tom Bulley **899** © Alan Harris **901** © Giovanni Marachioli **902** © Sebastian Wasek / Alamy **905** © funkyfood London - Paul Williams / Alamy **907** © Alamy **908** © Stein Lauritsen **910** © National Geographic Image Collection / Alamy **911** © NBay photos / Alamy **912** © Safari Partners **913** © Safari Partners **915** © John Mac **916** © Reinhard Dirscherl / Alamy **917** © blickwinkel / Alamy **918** © Boaz Rottem / Alamy **919** © Prasanth Jose **920** © Sangharsha **922** © Irina Andreeva **923** © Marco Fieber **924** © Ngaire Lawson **925** © Andre Seale / Alamy **926** © Michael Snell / Alamy **927** © Eric Hevesy **928** © Inspiration Outdoors **929** © Ball Miwako **931** © Sid Kid **932** © Danita Delimont / Alamy **933** © Tourism NSW **934** © David McKelvey **937** © Chad Ehlers / Alamy **938** © Mark Wassell **939** Ed Dunens **941** © Paul Vos **942** © Alistair Scott / Alamy **945** © age fotostock Spain, S.L. / Alamy **946** © David Wall / Alamy

Acknowledgments

I would like to thank Brad Atwal and all those at UTracks for organizing a walk along the historic Via Francigena in Tuscany. See www.utracks.com. I would also like to thank Llewelyn Thomas and all those at Walk Japan for making me aware of Japan's marvelous pilgrimage trail, the Nakasendo Way. See www.walkjapan.com.

I would also like to thank senior editor Ruth Patrick of Quintessence, without whose organizational skills and eye for detail this project would have a worrying degree of contradictions and omissions, and also to designer Damian Jaques for sourcing the images that I couldn't find myself. And last but certainly not least to the Quintessence editorial director Jane Laing, who entrusted me with this project, and without whose support over many years and enabling me to participate in a fistful of other 1001 titles as a contributor, I would have been singularly underprepared to tackle such a mammoth undertaking and assume the mantle of general editor. Thank you, Jane.